READINGS IN
Money,
National Income,
and Stabilization
Policy

THE IRWIN SERIES IN ECONOMICS

Consulting Editor
LLOYD G. REYNOLDS
Yale University

READINGS IN
Money,
National Income,
and Stabilization
Policy

Edited by

WARREN L. SMITH

Late Professor of Economics

and

RONALD L. TEIGEN

Professor of Economics

The University of Michigan

 Third Edition • 1974

RICHARD D. IRWIN, INC. Homewood, Illinois 60430
IRWIN-DORSEY INTERNATIONAL London, England WC2H 9NJ
IRWIN-DORSEY LIMITED Georgetown, Ontario L7G 4B3

Third Edition

First Printing, January 1974

ISBN 0-256-01513-9
Library of Congress Catalog Card No. 73–84297
Printed in the United States of America

PREFACE

This third edition of our book of readings in money, national income, and stabilization policy reflects the same approach and viewpoint and is organized in the same way as the revised edition which it supplants. There are, however, several significant changes. Many of the readings in the revised edition—particularly those dealing with inflation and unemployment, monetary policy, and international finance—have been replaced with new, up-to-date material. There is a more thorough treatment of the Keynesian-monetarist controversy, and new topics in the area of monetary policy theory and practice are represented, including the role of uncertainty, trade-offs between short- and long-run policy goals, and the new emphasis on monetary aggregates as intermediate policy targets.

This new edition, like its predecessors, has been designed for supplementary use in courses in monetary economics, national income analysis, business cycles, and stabilization policy. Its contents reflect our belief that in such courses a structural framework should be developed which enables the student to understand the mechanisms and linkages through which both monetary and fiscal policy produce their effects on income, employment, the price level, the rate of growth, and so on. To that end, these readings were selected to supplement the available textbooks on such topics as the relationship between monetary changes and changes in output, employment, and income; and the ways in which monetary and fiscal policy are related in their joint capacity as instruments of stabilization policy. Relatively few pages are devoted to material on the institutional details of the money and capital markets, the mechanics of treasury operations, and similar topics. Such subjects are well covered in most textbooks, and a good deal of supplementary reading material of this type can be obtained free of charge from the Federal Reserve System and other sources.

Thus, most of the book is devoted to aspects of monetary and fiscal policy in the context of the theory of income determination. Within these subjects, the selection of readings reflects the "view of the world" of the editors—a view which is accepted, by and large, by a great many economists, though not all. Alternative points of view on controversial issues are represented; however, most of the readings were selected to serve as "building blocks" for the development of the particular approach used, which is set forth in the rather extensive introductory material that precedes each of the chapters. These introductory sections also serve to relate the readings within each chapter to one another. The general viewpoint presented is consistent with the post-Keynesian posture of modern macroeconomics. In terms of stabilization policy, the readings are selected to show that the currently accepted primary goal of full employment with reasonable price stability can best be pursued through the active use of flexible fiscal policy, supplemented by the use of monetary policy to achieve the desired balance between consumption and investment within the constraint imposed by the balance of payments.

In addition to the criteria mentioned above, the readings are selected to be comprehensible to typical advanced undergraduate students, and to be interesting to such students. Readability at this level was a major criterion in the choice of material, and the introductions to each chapter should be a substantial help to the student in the development and integration of ideas.

The preparation of this edition has been possible through the help and cooperation of a number of people. Thanks are due to the authors and original publishers of the selections in this book for permission to use them, with special appreciation to Robert S. Holbrook and Saul H. Hymans for allowing the use of original material that has not been published elsewhere.

The preparation of the manuscript was greatly facilitated by the help of Iris Knapp and Phyllis Romo. Karen Lundgren provided valuable assistance in proofreading.

· ·

While this edition was still in the early stages of preparation, my co-editor, colleague, and friend Warren L. Smith passed away suddenly. The extent of his influence on this book from its earliest inception is inestimable. His wisdom and judgment were sorely missed as work on the present revision progressed. I wish to dedicate this edition to his memory.

December 1973   RONALD L. TEIGEN

CONTENTS

chapter 1

THE THEORY OF INCOME DETERMINATION

The readings in this chapter are divided into two parts. Those in the first part deal with the determination of aggregate income, employment, and prices and the propagation of income changes, with special reference to the way in which fiscal and monetary policies may influence aggregate demand. The readings in the second part deal with the question of the inflationary process, its measurement and costs, and its relationship to employment.

A. MONETARY AND FISCAL POLICIES AND AGGREGATE DEMAND

It is important for the student beginning the study of national income and money and banking to develop an integrated framework which he can use effectively to analyze the problems and issues that arise. It is best that he get this framework at the start so that the relevant institutional material can be fitted into it as he progresses. It is our hope that the material presented in this introduction, together with the readings contained in this section, will help the student to develop such a framework of analysis.

Economic reality is exceedingly complex, involving the outputs and prices of thousands of goods and services, the wages of thousands of different kinds of labor, and so on. If the economist tried to deal with all of the vast multitude of variables and relationships involved, he would soon become hopelessly bogged down. The only way to make headway, therefore, is to work with "models" which abstract from most of the detail and focus on the important variables related to the issue at hand. Of course, the model to be used depends on the kind of problem being dealt with. The models we shall develop have proved to be useful in analyzing the forces determining many of the major variables relating to the economy as a whole: the level of national income and employment, the general level of prices, and so forth. While we shall attempt to keep the models relatively simple, we feel that they represent the major economic relationships sufficiently well to enable the student who has a thorough grasp of them to comprehend and analyze many important issues of economic policy. It should be pointed out that there has been much statistical testing of models which, while more detailed and complex than those presented here, are of essentially the same character; and the statistical testing suggests that they explain the behavior of the economy quite well. Indeed, the results of some of the statistical studies are presented in readings included in this book.

We shall begin with the simplest kind of Keynesian static multiplier model of income determination with which the student is almost surely familiar from his other reading. Then we shall proceed to introduce fiscal and monetary elements in a way which, we hope, will help the student to understand questions of economic policy. We shall use an algebraic and arithmetic approach for the most part; however, the algebra does not extend beyond that covered in a course that would be taken in high school, or at the most in the first year of college. We shall also stick to linear relationships—that is, relationships that appear as straight lines when plotted graphically. Linear relationships are often reasonably good approximations to reality; moreover, the gain in simplicity of presentation is great.

Throughout the present discussion, no attention is paid to changes in the price level; in effect, we shall be assuming that prices (and wages) are unchanged and that changes in the money values of variables are paralleled by changes in their real values. However, the analysis is broadened in the first two readings in this section—the papers by Robert S. Holbrook and Warren L. Smith—which treat prices and wages as variables which are determined by the interplay of economic forces as are income, employment, and so on.

The presentation in this introduction is divided into two major parts. The first deals with static analysis—that is, it is merely designed to tell what will ultimately happen to the variables when some change is introduced into the model, without making any effort to describe the time paths followed by the variables in the process of adjustment. The second part introduces some quite elementary dynamics.

1. STATIC ANALYSIS

Model I: The Simple Keynesian Multiplier

This model is represented by the following three algebraic equations:

$$C = C_o + cY \qquad \text{(consumption function)} \qquad (1.1)$$
$$I = I_o \qquad \text{(investment relationship)} \qquad (1.2)$$
$$Y = C + I \qquad \text{(equilibrium condition)} \qquad (1.3)$$

Here C is consumption expenditure planned by households, I is investment expenditure planned by firms, and Y is gross national product (GNP). The subscript o indicates that the variable is not explained within the model but is determined by outside forces. In this model C_o stands for the amount of consumption which is unrelated to income, and c is the marginal propensity to consume (MPC), assumed to be a positive fraction between zero and unity in value. By substituting the expressions for C and I given by equations (1.1) and (1.2) into equation (1.3), we obtain the following:

$$Y = cY + C_o + I_o. \tag{1.4}$$

When this is solved for Y, the following result is obtained:

$$Y = \frac{1}{1-c}(C_o + I_o). \tag{1.5}$$

If there is a change in C_o or I_o, income and consumption will also change. Suppose that investment spending rises to a new level, $I_o + \Delta I_o$, and remains there. Then we will find that income will also change by some amount, ΔY, so that the new level of income may be expressed as follows:

$$Y + \Delta Y = \frac{1}{1-c}(C_o + I_o) + \frac{1}{1-c}\Delta I_o. \tag{1.6}$$

Subtraction of (1.5) from (1.6) results in the following expression for the change of income (from the former equilibrium position to the new equilibrium) due to the change in investment spending:

$$\Delta Y = \frac{1}{1-c}\Delta I_o. \tag{1.7}$$

Since ΔI_o is multiplied by the term $1/(1-c)$ to obtain the income change, ΔY, this term is called the "multiplier." This is the standard textbook "formula" expressed in the statement, "the multiplier equals $1/(1-MPC)$." The student should not, however, view it as a formula to be memorized but rather as a relationship which summarizes a complex pattern of economic behavior, a pattern to be thought through and understood. It is particularly important to realize that the multiplier expression changes as the details of the model change, and that in the real world the multiplier process cannot be summarized in as simple a formula as that shown above. We shall now make the model, and the multiplier expression, somewhat more realistic.

Model II: The Introduction of Fiscal Policy

One of the most serious shortcomings of the simple model just discussed is that no allowance is made for the activities of government. To correct this defect we shall introduce government expenditures and taxation. For simplicity, we shall assume that all taxes are levied on households and that consumption depends on *disposable* income—that is, income after taxes. The new model is expressed in the following equations:

$$
\begin{aligned}
C &= C_o + cY_d & 0 < c < 1 & \tag{2.1}\\
Y_d &= Y - T & & \tag{2.2}\\
T &= T^* + xY & 0 < x < 1 & \tag{2.3}\\
I &= I_o & & \tag{2.4}\\
G &= G^* & & \tag{2.5}\\
Y &= C + I + G & & \tag{2.6}
\end{aligned}
$$

In this and following models, as was the case above, the subscript o identifies variables which are determined by forces outside of the model and which cannot be controlled by the government for policy purposes. We now introduce a second category of variables determined outside of the model: those which are manipulable by the authorities. Such variables are sometimes called "policy instruments" and will be denoted by an asterisk (*) throughout the remainder of this discussion. In Model II, government spending for goods and services (G^*) and that part of tax collections which is unrelated to income (T^*) are policy instruments. The equation $G = G^*$ states that the entire amount of government spending is determined outside of the model, while the equation describing tax collections, equation (2.3), indicates that only a part of total collections is under the direct control of the fiscal authorities. T is total collections, and it is composed of T^*, the level set by the authorities, plus xY, the part related to the level of income. The coefficient x is the marginal propensity of the public to pay taxes out of GNP.[1] Finally, Y_d is disposable income (i.e., household income after taxes); and c is the marginal propensity to consume out of disposable income.

Upon substitution of equation (2.2) and (2.3) into (2.1), the following equation is obtained:

$$C = C_o - cT^* + c(1 - x)Y. \tag{2.7}$$

Then, equations (2.4), (2.5), and (2.7) can be substituted into equation (2.6) to obtain

$$Y = C_o - cT^* + c(1 - x)Y + I_o + G^*. \tag{2.8}$$

Solving this equation explicitly for Y, we obtain

$$Y = \frac{1}{1 - c(1 - x)} [C_o - cT^* + I_o + G^*]. \tag{2.9}$$

Suppose now that government purchases of goods and services are increased from G^* to $G^* + \Delta G^*$. The new equilibrium income will be given by

$$Y + \Delta Y = \frac{1}{1 - c(1 - x)} [C_o - cT^* + I_o + G^* + \Delta G^*]. \tag{2.10}$$

Subtracting (2.9) from (2.10) and dividing through by ΔG^*, we obtain the multiplier applicable to government purchases:

$$\frac{\Delta Y}{\Delta G^*} = \frac{1}{1 - c(1 - x)}. \tag{2.11}$$

Multipliers could also be computed for independent changes in investment (ΔI_o), in the level of consumption (ΔC_o), or in the level of taxes (ΔT^*). The first two of these multipliers would be the same as that for a change in government purchases while the multiplier for a change in taxes would be

$$\frac{\Delta Y}{\Delta T^*} = \frac{-c}{1 - c(1 - x)}.$$

This last multiplier is negative, because an increase in taxes would lower disposable income, reduce consumption, and lead to a decline in income.

There is a final technical point which should be noted. So far, all of the multipliers we have discussed have summarized the effects on GNP of a change

---

[1] Strictly speaking x as well as T^* should be regarded as a policy instrument, since changes in tax legislation could (and, in practice, usually would) change the slope as well as the level of the tax function. In the interest of simplicity, however, we are confining our analysis to changes in the level of taxes (T^*).

in one of the variables determined by forces outside the model. The multiplier concept is more general than this, however, and it is possible to derive a multiplier expression which summarizes the effect of a shift in any of these variables on any variable determined within the model. Thus, for example, the effects on total tax collections (ΔT) of a shift in the level of the consumption function (ΔC_o) can easily be derived. From the tax function (2.3) we note that

$$\frac{\Delta T}{\Delta C_o} = x\,\frac{\Delta Y}{\Delta C_o}.$$

Using the approach employed in deriving the multiplier $\dfrac{\Delta Y}{\Delta G^*}$ above, we find that

$$\frac{\Delta Y}{\Delta C_o} = \frac{1}{1 - c(1 - x)}.$$

It follows directly that

$$\frac{\Delta T}{\Delta C_o} = \frac{x}{1 - c(1 - x)}.$$

As a general rule, it is possible to derive multipliers showing the effects on any of the variables determined by the model (the variables Y, Y_d, T, C, I, and G in this case) of a change in any of the variables which are set by outside forces (C_o, I_o, T^*, and G^* here).

A numerical example may be helpful at this point. Suppose the marginal propensity to consume out of disposable income is 75 percent $(c = .75)$ while the tax system is such that taxes tend to increase by 20 percent of any rise in GNP $(x = .2)$. Suppose further that $C_o = 70$, $T^* = -40$, $I_o = 145$, and $G^* = 155$ (amounts expressed in billions of dollars). In this case the equations (2.1) to (2.6) become:

$$\begin{aligned}
C &= 70 + .75Y_d \\
Y_d &= Y - T \\
T &= -40 + .2Y \\
I &= 145 \\
G &= 155 \\
Y &= C + I + G
\end{aligned}$$

The multiplier relating changes in GNP to changes in government purchases (or investment, or autonomous changes in consumption) is

$$\frac{\Delta Y}{\Delta G^*} = \frac{1}{1 - c(1 - x)} = \frac{1}{1 - .75(1 - .2)} = 2.5,$$

and equilibrium income, calculated from (2.9), is

$$\begin{aligned}
Y &= 2.5\,[400],\ \text{or} \\
Y &= \$1{,}000\ \text{billion.}
\end{aligned}$$

The values of all the variables, which can easily be calculated from the above equations, are given in the first ("original equilibrium") column of Table I. Two additional variables, not referred to earlier, are shown in the table: private saving and government deficit. Private saving is simply the difference between disposable income and consumption and amounts to $140 billion. The government surplus (taxes minus expenditures) is $5 billion. It may be noted that private saving ($140 billion) plus the government surplus is equal to investment ($145 billion). This is the equivalent of the well-known proposition that "saving must equal investment" for an economy containing a government sector.

Now suppose government purchases of goods and services increase by $20 billion from the original level of $155 billion per year to a new annual level of $175 billion, and remain there. Since the multiplier for government purchases is 2.5, income will rise by $50 billion to a new equilibrium value of $1,050 billion. The new values of all variables are shown in the second ("new equilibrium") column of Table I, and the changes from the original position are shown in the last column.

TABLE I   NUMERICAL EXAMPLE OF MULTIPLIER FOR GOVERNMENT
EXPENDITURES IN MODEL II (amounts in billions)

	Original Equilibrium	New Equilibrium†	Change
Gross national product (Y).............	$1,000	$1,050	+$50
Consumption (C).....................	700	730	+ 30
Investment (I).......................	145	145	0
Government purchases (G)...........	155	175	+ 20
Taxes (T)............................	160	170	+ 10
Disposable income (Y_d).	840	880	+ 40
Private saving (Y_d − C)................	140	150	+ 10
Government deficit (G − T).............	−5	5	+ 10

† After an increase of $20 billion in the rate of government purchases.

The new equilibrium will not, of course, be reached immediately. The movement of GNP and its components to the new level involves a complex and time-consuming set of economic adjustments. The chain starts when the increased government purchases stimulate production and employment, which adds directly to GNP. Incomes are raised; a portion of the additional income, 20 percent in this case, is paid over the government in taxes; of the remaining 80 percent, 25 percent is saved, and the other 75 percent—which amounts to 60 percent (75 percent of 80 percent) of the rise in GNP—is spent on consumption, thereby stimulating further production and employment in industries producing consumer goods. The process continues through repeated "rounds" of spending and responding until GNP has been raised by $50 billion (the multiplier of 2.5 times the initial increase of $20 billion in government purchases). The time lags and the speed with which the adjustment to the new level of GNP can be expected to take place are discussed below.

A reduction in the level of taxation—that is, a change in T^*—would also raise GNP. In this case, if $c = .75$ and $x = .2$, we have, as indicated earlier,

$$\frac{\Delta Y}{\Delta T^*} = \frac{-c}{1 - c(1 - x)} = \frac{-.75}{1 - .75(1 - .2)} = -1.875.$$

Thus a cut in taxes of $20 billion ($\Delta T^* = -20$) would raise GNP by $37.5 billion. The multiplier applicable to a tax cut is smaller in absolute value (1.875) than that applicable to an increase in government purchases (2.5). The reason is that the entire increase in government purchases is a direct increase in GNP, while a portion of the tax cut is saved, and only the part that is spent on consumption (75 percent in this case) adds to GNP. It is suggested that the student work out a table similar to Table I above to illustrate the effects on income and the other variables determined within the model of a tax cut of $20 billion.[2]

Model II illustrates in a simple way the rationale for the use of fiscal policy—changes in government expenditures and taxes—to regulate aggregate demand for goods and services in the interest of full employment and price stability. This subject is taken up in considerable detail in Chapter 4. The model used in this illustration is substantially oversimplified. In practice, for example, not all taxes are levied on households—there are direct and indirect taxes on business as well—and some saving is done by businesses as well as by households. Despite the added complexities, however, the multiplier of 2.5 for government purchases that we used above is fairly realistic. Estimates obtained by sophisticated statistical techniques applied to much more complicated models have fairly consistently turned out to be in this neighborhood.

Model III: The Introduction of Money and Interest

The student will no doubt have noticed that we have not yet mentioned money or interest rates. It is now time to remedy this deficiency in our analysis. The essence of the problem can be handled quite well and without greatly complicating the presentation by adding additional variables and equations to Model II. The resulting Model III, which takes account of money and interest, includes the following equations, five of which (the first three and the fifth and sixth) are exactly the same as those of Model II.

$$C = C_o + cY_d \tag{3.1}$$
$$Y_d = Y - T \tag{3.2}$$
$$T = T^* + xY \tag{3.3}$$
$$I = I_o - vr \tag{3.4}$$
$$G = G^* \tag{3.5}$$
$$Y = C + I + G \tag{3.6}$$
$$M_d = M_o + kY - mr \tag{3.7}$$
$$M_s = M^* \tag{3.8}$$
$$M_d = M_s \tag{3.9}$$

Here, r is the interest rate (there is assumed to be only one interest rate). v is the slope of the investment function with respect to the interest rate, or, in Keynesian terminology, the slope of the marginal efficiency of capital (or investment) schedule. v is assumed to be greater than zero, but it carries a negative sign in the investment function—i.e., the lower the interest rate the more investment. M_d is the quantity (stock) of money (demand deposits and currency) demanded by the public and is assumed to be related positively to income and negatively to the interest rate. k is the number of dollars by which the public will desire to increase its money holdings per dollar increase in GNP (i.e., the slope of the money demand function with respect to income). k is, of course, positive—i.e., the higher the level of income the more money the public will want to hold (at a given interest rate). m is the slope of the demand for money function with respect to the interest rate. m is assumed greater than zero, but it carries a negative sign in the money demand func-

---

[2] For a detailed discussion of the way in which a tax cut can increase aggregate demand and employment, see the selections entitled "The Effects of Tax Reduction on Output and Employment," by the Council of Economic Advisers, and "Measuring the Impact of the 1964 Tax Reduction," by Arthur Okun, in Chapter 4 below.

tion—i.e., the lower the interest rate, the more money the public will want to hold (at a given income). M_o is the amount of money demanded without regard to income or the rate of interest; its level is determined by forces outside of the model. M_s is the supply of money; it is equal to a constant, M^*, which can be changed at will by the monetary authorities (e.g., the Federal Reserve System) through actions such as open market operations, changes in the discount rate, or changes in the reserve requirements of the banks.

Model III is changed from Model II by introducing the interest rate into the investment equation (3.4) and by introducing three new equations, (3.7), (3.8), and (3.9), to represent the "monetary sector" of the economy. Equation (3.9) is an equilibrium condition which says that the demand for money must be equal to the supply of money in order for an equilibrium to exist.

Substituting (3.2) and (3.3) into (3.1), we obtain

$$C_i = C_o - cT^* + c(1 - x)Y. \tag{3.10}$$

Then, substituting (3.4), (3.5), and (3.10) into (3.6), we obtain

$$Y = C_o - cT^* + c(1 - x)Y + I_o - vr + G^*, \tag{3.11}$$

or, solving explicitly for r in terms of Y,

$$r = \frac{C_o - cT^* + I_o + G^*}{v} - \frac{1 - c(1 - x)}{v} Y. \tag{3.12}$$

Next, substituting (3.7) and (3.8) into (3.9), we obtain

$$M^* = M_o + kY - mr, \tag{3.13}$$

or, solving explicitly for r in terms of Y,

$$r = \frac{M_o - M^*}{m} + \frac{k}{m} Y. \tag{3.14}$$

Equation (3.12) is the *IS* curve discussed in the Holbrook and Smith articles in this chapter. It is derived from equations (3.1) to (3.6) in the above model and represents the various combinations of income and the interest rate that will equilibrate the market for goods and services—that is, will result in aggregate demand $(C + I + G)$ being equal to total output (Y). The slope of the line $(\Delta r / \Delta Y)$ is $-[1 - c(1 - x)]/v$. Since c and x are both less than unity, $1 - c(1 - x)$ is necessarily positive, as is v. Consequently, the slope of the *IS* curve is negative—that is, it slopes downward to the right. The commonsense economic explanation is that a reduced rate of interest will lead to more investment, which, through the multiplier, will raise income; thus, a fall in the rate of interest will be associated with a higher level of income. The *IS* curve is shown as a downward-sloping line in Chart I.

Equation (3.14) is the *LM* curve, also discussed in the Holbrook and Smith articles. It is derived from equations (3.7) and (3.9) and represents the various combinations of Y and r that will result in equilibrium in the money market—i.e., equality of demand for and supply of money—with the given stock of money, M^*. The slope of the *LM* curve $(\Delta r / \Delta Y)$ is k/m. Since k and m are both positive numbers, the slope must be positive. It is useful to think of money holdings as consisting of two parts: transactions balances required for the conduct of current economic activity by households and firms and asset balances held as a part of wealth portfolios. The demand for transactions balances may then be regarded as related positively to income, and the demand for asset

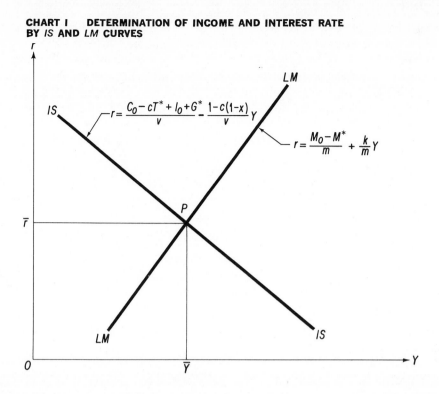

balances as being related negatively to the interest rate. (The demand for money is discussed at some length in Ronald L. Teigen's paper in this chapter.[3]) Then, moving along the *LM* curve, a rise in income will increase the transactions demand for money, thereby leaving a smaller portion of the fixed supply (*M**) of money available to satisfy the asset demand and causing the interest rate to rise as asset holders attempt to restore portfolio equilibrium by selling bonds. The *LM* curve is shown as an upward-sloping curve in Chart I.

Equilibrium for the entire economy—including both the market for goods and services and the money market—occurs at the point of intersection of the *IS* and *LM* curves. This is point *P* in Chart I, and the equilibrium values of GNP and the interest rate are $\bar{Y}$ and $\bar{r}$.

The equilibrium level of GNP can be derived explicitly by eliminating *r* between equations (3.12) and (3.14). When this is done, we have

$$\frac{C_o - cT^* + I_o + G^*}{v} - \frac{1 - c(1-x)}{v} Y = \frac{M_o - M^*}{m} + \frac{k}{m} Y,$$

or, solving explicitly for *Y*,

$$Y = \frac{1}{1 - c(1-x) + \dfrac{vk}{m}} \left[C_o - cT^* + I_o + G^* - \frac{v}{m}(M_o - M^*) \right]. \quad (3.15)$$

---

[3] It should be noted that, as explained in Teigen's paper, some economists believe that the demand for money is almost entirely a transactions demand but that the transactions demand is dependent on both income and the interest rate. This leads to essentially the same conclusions about the functioning of money in the economy that are reached if the demand consists of a transactions component dependent on income and an asset component dependent on the interest rate.

This model contains three policy instruments which the authorities can adjust in order to control aggregate demand: the fiscal authorities can change government expenditures (G^*) or the tax level (T^*), while the monetary authorities can adjust the stock of money (M^*). Multipliers which show the leverage of each of these instruments in changing GNP can be calculated quite easily. For example, the multiplier for government expenditures ($\Delta Y / \Delta G^*$) can be derived as follows: suppose the level of government purchases of goods and services is increased from G^* to $G^* + \Delta G^*$. The new level of GNP is given by

$$Y + \Delta Y = \frac{1}{1 - c(1 - x) + \dfrac{vk}{m}} \left[C_o - cT^* + I_o + G^* + \Delta G^* - \frac{v}{m}(M_o - M^*) \right]. \quad (3.16)$$

Subtracting (3.15) from (3.16) and dividing through by ΔG^*, we have

$$\frac{\Delta Y}{\Delta G^*} = \frac{1}{1 - c(1 - x) + \dfrac{vk}{m}}. \quad (3.17)$$

By a similar procedure, the multipliers for changes in taxes and in the stock of money can be derived:

$$\frac{\Delta Y}{\Delta T^*} = \frac{-c}{1 - c(1 - x) + \dfrac{vk}{m}} \quad (3.18)$$

$$\frac{\Delta Y}{\Delta M^*} = \frac{1}{[1 - c(1 - x)] \dfrac{m}{v} + k} \quad (3.19)$$

Comparing the multiplier for government purchases (3.17) with that developed in Model II above (2.11), we find that the difference consists in the presence of the additional term vk/m in the denominator of (3.17). Since v, m, and k are all positive, the term vk/m is positive. It increases the denominator of (3.17) and therefore reduces the size of the multiplier. This term arises from the existence of monetary forces in Model III which were not included in Model II. In deriving expression (3.17) for the multiplier effects of a change in government purchases in Model III, it was assumed that the stock of money, M^*, was held constant. An increase in government purchases increases GNP, and the rise in GNP increases the demand for money for transactions purposes. With a constant stock of money, the needed transactions balances must be obtained from asset balances, and this necessitates a rise in the interest rate. This rise in the interest rate, in turn, reduces investment expenditure, thereby canceling out a portion of the effect of the initial increase in government purchases and cutting down the size of the multiplier.

The relationships can perhaps best be understood by means of a numerical illustration. Suppose, as in the example used to illustrate Model II, that $c = .75$, $t = .2$, $C_o = 70$, $T^* = -40$, and $G^* = 155$. In addition, in this case let us suppose that the interest slope of the investment equation (3.4) is -4 (i.e., $v = 4$); the constant term of the investment equation, I_o, is 165; the income slope of the money demand equation (3.7), k, is .25; the interest slope of the money demand equation is -10 (i.e., $m = 10$); and the constant term of this equation, M_o, is 20. Finally, suppose the stock of money, M^*, is 220. In this case, the equations (3.1) to (3.9) become:

$$C = 70 + .75Y_d$$
$$Y_d = Y - T$$
$$T = -40 + .2Y$$
$$I = 165 - 4r$$
$$G = 155$$
$$Y = C + I + G$$
$$M_d = 20 + .25Y - 10r$$
$$M_s = 220$$
$$M_d = M_s$$

The multiplier for government purchases (or investment) is

$$\frac{\Delta Y}{\Delta G^*} = \frac{1}{1 - c(1 - x) + \dfrac{vk}{m}} = \frac{1}{1 - .75(1 - .2) + \dfrac{4(.25)}{10}} = 2,$$

and equilibrium income, calculated from (3.15), is:

$$Y = 2[500]$$
$$Y = \$1,000 \text{ billion.}$$

The values of all the variables are given in the first column of Table II.

TABLE II   NUMERICAL EXAMPLE OF MULTIPLIER FOR GOVERNMENT EXPENDITURES IN MODEL III (dollar amounts in billions)

	Original Equilibrium	New Equilibrium†	Change
Gross national product (Y)	$1,000	$1,040	+$40
Consumption (C)	700	724	+ 24
Investment (I)	145	141	− 4
Government purchases (G)	155	175	+ 20
Taxes (T)	160	168	+ 8
Disposable income ($Y - T$)	840	872	+ 32
Saving ($Y_d - C$)	140	148	+ 8
Government deficit ($G - T$)	−5	7	+ 12
Interest rate (r)	5%	6%	+1%

† After an increase of $20 billion in the rate of government purchases.

Now let us suppose that government expenditures increase by $20 billion from the original rate of $155 billion to $175 billion. Since, as we have seen, the multiplier is 2, this will raise GNP by $40 billion. The new values of all the variables are shown in the second column of Table II. The main difference between the results shown here and those produced by an increase of $20 billion in government expenditures in Model II (see Table I) is that in this case the rise in GNP increases the demand for money and drives up the interest rate from 5 to 6 percent, and this, in turn, reduces investment by $4 billion. That is why the multiplier is only 2 instead of 2.5 as in Model II.

Our illustration can also be presented in terms of *IS* and *LM* curves. In the original situation (before the increase in government expenditures), substitution into equation (3.12) yields the following numerical *IS* curve:

$$r = 105 - .1Y.$$

Similarly, the *LM* curve, obtained by substitution into (3.14), is

$$r = -20 + .025Y.$$

These two curves have been plotted in Chart II as the lines IS_1 and *LM*. Their

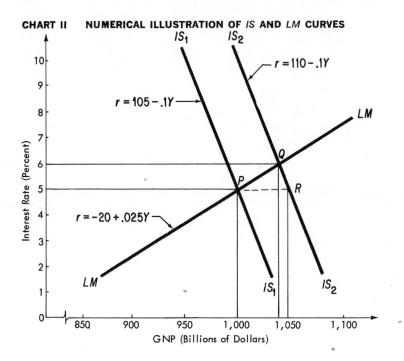

CHART II   NUMERICAL ILLUSTRATION OF *IS* AND *LM* CURVES

intersection (point *P*) yields equilibrium values of $1,000 billion for GNP and 5 percent for the interest rate.

An increase of $20 billion in government expenditures shifts the *IS* curve to the right, and its equation becomes

$$r = 110 - .1Y.$$

This is plotted as line IS_2 in Chart II. Its intersection with the *LM* curve (point *Q*) yields the equilibrium values of $1,040 billion for GNP and 6 percent for the interest rate.

As can be seen from Chart II, if the interest rate had not risen when government expenditures were increased, the equilibrium point would have moved from *P* to *R* and GNP would have risen by $50 billion for a multiplier of 2.5—the same as the multiplier in Model II. But due to the tightening of credit in the face of a fixed money supply, the equilibrium point moves to *Q* rather than *R*, GNP rises by $40 billion instead of $50 billion, and the interest rate rises from 5 to 6 percent. Thus, the operation of the "monetary effect" cuts the multiplier by 20 percent below what it would have been in the absence of the effect.

It will be useful to consider also the effects produced by an increase in the money stock. Suppose the stock is increased by $20 billion as a result, let us say, of open market purchases of U.S. government securities by the Federal Reserve System. The multiplier applicable to an increase in the money stock, according to (3.19) above, is

$$\frac{\Delta Y}{\Delta M^*} = \frac{1}{[1 - c(1 - x)]\dfrac{m}{v} + k}.$$

Using the values of our illustration, this becomes:

$$\frac{\Delta Y}{\Delta M^*} = \frac{1}{[1 - .75(1 - .2)]\dfrac{10}{4} + .25} = \frac{1}{1.25}$$

$$\frac{\Delta Y}{\Delta M^*} = .8$$

Thus, an increase of $20 billion in the money stock will increase GNP by $16 billion. The effects on all of the variables in the system are shown in the second column of Table III. For purposes of comparison, the original values

TABLE III   NUMERICAL EXAMPLE OF MULTIPLIER FOR AN INCREASE IN THE MONEY STOCK IN MODEL III (dollar amounts in billions)

	Original Equilibrium	New Equilibrium†	Change
Gross national product (Y).............	$1,000	$1,016.0	+$16.0
Consumption (C).....................	700	709.6	+ 9.6
Investment (I)........................	145	151.4	+ 6.4
Government purchases (G)..........	155	155.0	0
Taxes (T)............................	160	163.2	+ 3.2
Disposable income (Y − T)............	840	852.8	+ 12.8
Saving (Y₀ − C)......................	140	143.2	+ 3.2
Government deficit (G − T)...........	−5	−8.2	− 3.2
Money stock (M*)....................	220	240.0	+ 20.0
Interest rate (r)......................	5%	3.4%	− 1.6%

† After an increase of $20 billion in the money stock.

are again shown in the first column. The increase in the money stock produces its effects by lowering the interest rate from 5 percent to 3.4 percent, thereby stimulating investment; the rise in investment spending stimulates production and income, setting off a multiplier effect which raises consumption. It is interesting to note that the increase in income leads to a rise in tax collections which reduces the government deficit.

According to our analysis of Model III, it is possible to change aggregate demand and GNP by fiscal policy measures—changes in government expenditures or in taxes—or by monetary policy—changes in the monetary stock. (It is suggested that the student work out another table similar to Tables II and III summarizing the effects of a $20 billion tax cut and compare the results with those produced by the other measures.) And, of course, the three types of measures could be combined in various ways to produce a desired effect on GNP. (Another suggested exercise for the student: calculate the size of the increase in the money stock that would be needed to accompany an increase in government expenditures in order to hold the interest rate at 5 percent and achieve a multiplier effect of 2.5.) Choice of the proper combination in given circumstances would depend on various considerations—the relative speeds with which they produce their results, their effects on goals other than the level of GNP, such as the rate of long-term growth, the nation's balance-of-payments position, and so on. Many of these considerations are discussed in readings in this book, especially in Chapters 4, 5, and 7. In particular, the introduction to Chapter 7 contains an extensive discussion of the relationship between multiple policy goals and the instruments of policy. The discussion is based on a linear model which is almost identical to Model III; thus a thorough understanding of the material in the present section will be particularly useful to the student in studying the material in Chapter 7.

Model III provides a useful starting point for a discussion of some of the major doctrinal controversies that have plagued the subject of money, particularly those having to do with the relative efficacy of monetary policy and fiscal policy. This discussion is extended considerably in the two papers by Leonall C. Andersen and Ronald L. Teiger, respectively, which are found at the end of this part of Chapter 1. The policy controversies which we wish to examine here can conveniently be summarized as the opposing views of two schools of thought. The *Classical quantity theorists* (or "monetarists," as quantity theorists have come to be known) may be said to believe that fiscal policy can have no significant and lasting effect on real output or employment, while monetary policy is viewed by members of this school of thought as being very potent in terms of its effects on these variables. The terms "Classical" and "monetarist" will be used more or less interchangeably in what follows. At the other end of the spectrum are some of the *extreme versions of Keynesianism*, which view monetary policy as impotent and fiscal policy as being extremely effective. To see the basis for these views in terms of the analysis we have used so far, it will be useful to bring together once again the multipliers for changes in government expenditures and for changes in the money stock (assuming, as we have up to now, that the entire money stock is under the direct control of the monetary authorities—a qualification which we later will relax). These multipliers are:

$$\frac{\Delta Y}{\Delta G^*} = \frac{1}{1 - c(1 - x) + \dfrac{vk}{m}} \tag{3.17}$$

$$\frac{\Delta Y}{\Delta M^*} = \frac{1}{[1 - c(1 - x)]\dfrac{m}{v} + k} \tag{3.19}$$

At the beginning of this discussion, it should be emphasized that these multipliers describe very simple economies and in particular that, in these economies, prices and wages remain unchanged as income changes in response to policy or for any other reason. That is, these economies have significant amounts of unemployed resources, so that increasing demand is reflected in rising employment rather than price inflation. Such chronic underemployment is ascribable to a rigidity or inflexibility in the system—in this case, wage rates which are not free to respond to the relationship between the supply of and demand for labor. If the price of unemployed productive factors—i.e., the wage rate—were free to move as unemployed labor competed for work with those employed, presumably a wage could be found at which all of the workers who desired work could get it; however, if the wage rate is fixed by law or restricted in movement by some other arrangement, those out of work who want jobs may not be able to find them. Wage inflexibility and other rigidities which hinder the achievement of full employment undoubtedly are present in the real world, and it is therefore appropriate to conduct our analysis using a model which recognizes that they exist. The student should, however, be aware that theoretical analysis is sometimes also carried out using macroeconomic models which do not reflect these impediments to full employment; in effect, such models assert that full employment rather than underemployment is the normal state of affairs. If prices and wages are flexible and determined in competitive markets so that there exists more or less continuous full employment, it is apparent that the results of the application of monetary and fiscal policy will be different from the results in an economy which is chronically underemployed. One important dimension of the Keynesian-monetarist controversy over policy is the assumptions which each side makes about the functioning of labor markets, with Keynesians typically assuming money wage rigidity, and monetarists taking wage flexibility as the norm. This aspect is emphasized in the paper on monetarist economics by Ronald L. Teigen in this chapter; and the conclusions in Leonall C. Andersen's paper on the relative effectiveness of monetary versus fiscal impulses could be ascribed to monetarist assumptions about such markets.

It is also worth observing at the outset that conclusions regarding the effectiveness of policy based on models of the simple types presented here are likely to be somewhat sensitive to the degree of detail included. Innumerable marginal details about the world are, of course, omitted because they would greatly increase the algebraic complexity of the analysis without adding anything of substance to the conclusions. There is, however, an important detail which has been overlooked in most discussions about policy but which will have an important effect on the results of the analysis, especially when the models used include a demand-for-money function with zero interest sensitivity. This is the question of the interest sensitivity of the supply of money. Its implications for the controversy over policy which has been focused on the significance of the *demand* for money will be examined below.

With these thoughts in mind, let us turn to the Classical view as summarized earlier. In one version which we shall consider, the treatment of the demand for money differs substantially from the approach taken in Keynesian analysis. The Classical economists generally postulated that money balances were held only to finance the transactions of households and business and that the quantity of money demanded therefore depended only on transactions or income. Since money yielded no return, the possibility that the demand for money might also depend on the interest rate was not considered by most of them. This is the version of the Classical model mentioned in the preceding paragraph, in which the interest sensitivity of the demand for money balances, m, is assumed to be zero, and (3.7) reduces to:

$$M_d = kY. \tag{3.20}$$

This is the so-called "quantity theory of money" equation.[4] A model containing a demand-for-money function with an interest sensitivity of zero is generally viewed as belonging to the Classical approach, and the monetarist analysis by Andersen which is reprinted in this chapter is consistent with this assumption (in a world in which wages are inflexible, monetarist policy conclusions depend

---

[4] The quantity theory can be expressed in two ways. The form given above, $M = kY$, is often called the "Cambridge equation" because it reflected the thinking of a group of economists in Cambridge University. The other version is $MV = Py$, where V stands for the income velocity of money, P is the price level, and y is real income ($Y = Py$). This version is often called the "Fisher equation," after the late Professor Irving Fisher of Yale. The quantity theory assumption is that the demand for money is not related to the rate of interest; if it were, the behavioral assumption that velocity is constant, which is crucial to this theory, is lost. Given the assumption that the demand for money is a pure transactions demand, $MV = Y$ is equivalent to $M = kY$; i.e., $k = 1/V$.

on this assumption and exogenous control of the money supply by the monetary authority).[5] While assuming the interest elasticity of the demand for money to be zero may not seem to represent a major change in the model, this difference actually is crucial in terms of assessing the relative usefulness of monetary and fiscal policy in a chronically underemployed economy in which the supply of money is under the direct control of the central bank.[6]

It will be convenient to discuss monetary policy and fiscal policy in such an economy for the extreme cases in which the interest elasticity of the demand for money is zero in value, and in which it is infinitely large. In the version of the Classical case in which m, and hence this elasticity, is zero, it is seen from (3.17) that vk/m becomes infinitely large, and the fiscal policy or expenditure multiplier $\Delta Y/\Delta G^*$ becomes zero. In such a world, therefore, fiscal policy is ineffective; for example, an increase in government spending with no change in the money stock would necessarily raise the interest rate enough to depress private investment as much as government spending had increased, thereby merely reallocating resources from the private to the public sector but having no net effect on aggregate demand, output, or employment. From (3.19), however, it is apparent that the monetary policy multiplier, $\Delta Y/\Delta M^*$, reaches its maximum possible value, $1/k$, when m is zero. (Note: In the above numerical example, the money stock multiplier becomes 4 if $m = 0$—in contrast to the value of .8 that we calculated.) As m rises in value from zero, the term $[1 - c(1 - x)]m/v$ increases, reducing the value of this multiplier. The result that $\Delta Y/\Delta M^* = 1/k$, or that $\Delta M^* = k\Delta Y$, follows directly from the quantity theory equation, $M = kY$. On this basis, therefore, the typical Classical policy prescription for changing the level of money income is to use only monetary policy. While pamphleteers and popular writers had advocated government spending as a means of dealing with unemployment for many years, it is not surprising that this approach was not accepted by respectable professional economists until Keynes introduced the interest rate as a determinant of the demand for money in his *The General Theory of Employment, Interest and Money* in 1936. Nor is it surprising that modern monetarists, such as Milton Friedman, attach little or no importance to fiscal policy as a means of influencing aggregate demand (although, as we shall see below, members of this school of thought—particularly Friedman—have recently attempted to argue that fiscal

---

[5] This statement is subject to further qualifications. First, if prices and wages are assumed to be flexible, the Classical or monetarist conclusions about the effectiveness of monetary and fiscal policy hold even if the demand for money is interest sensitive—fiscal policy cannot change real income or employment, but merely shifts the mix between government and private spending, while changes in the money stock merely result in proportional changes in money wages and prices. This is the sort of model many monetarists now are using, as is shown in Teigen's paper on monetarism in this chapter. Second, the Keynesian conclusions—namely, that both monetary policy and fiscal policy can change income and employment—hold for an underemployed economy even if the interest sensitivity of the demand for money is zero, as long as the interest sensitivity of the *supply* of money is not zero. This point is discussed later in this introduction, as well as in Teigen's paper in this chapter on the demand for and supply of money.

[6] The coefficient m represents the change in the demand for money as an asset corresponding to a unit change in the interest rate; that is, $\Delta M = -m\Delta r$, or $\Delta M/\Delta r = -m$. The *elasticity* of demand for money with respect to the interest rate ($\eta_{M^D \cdot r}$) is the *percentage* change in the demand for money divided by the *percentage* change in the interest rate. Thus:

$$\eta_{M^D \cdot r} = \frac{\Delta M/M}{\Delta r/r} = \frac{\Delta M/\Delta r}{M/r} = -\frac{m}{M/r}.$$

Since m appears in the numerator of this expression, when m takes the extreme values of zero or infinity, the elasticity also is zero or infinity.

policy is impotent while recognizing that the demand for money is interest sensitive).

The conclusion that aggregate income changes in direct proportion to the money stock if m is zero (assuming also, as above, that the supply of money does not respond to interest rate changes) is based on the usual comparative static equilibrium analysis, and does not take the dynamics of the system into account. Friedman agrees with the spirit of the Classical approach, but goes further and argues that monetary policy is not only powerful but erratic: while changes in the money stock have a strong leverage on income, the behavioral lags are variable and undependable so that, in some cases, the effect on income may be rapid, while in others it may be very slow.[7] This leads to his recommendations that discretionary monetary policy be abandoned and a "rule" providing for a constant percentage growth in the money stock be substituted for it, a proposal which has been debated with increasing intensity recently.[8] Friedman's views concerning lags are hotly disputed by many monetary economists.

In other writings, Friedman has contended that his views regarding monetary and fiscal policy do not depend critically on the absence of a significant interest elasticity of demand for money. Indeed, he has expressed the view that the demand for money should, in principle, be responsive to interest rate changes. In his own empirical work, he does not find evidence in support of a significant degree of interest sensitivity.[9] But, in this respect, his results differ from those of most other investigators, as he has recognized.[10] Some of the evidence from studies which find significant interest sensitivity is summarized in Teigen's paper on the demand for and supply of money in this chapter. We have seen that if rigidity of money wage rates creates impediments to the automatic achievement of full employment, *both* monetary and fiscal policy will be capable of changing real income and employment unless the interest elasticity of demand for money is zero. However, as Friedman has pointed out, the situation is different if money wages are flexible.[11] Accordingly, it is useful to examine the effects of monetary and fiscal policy under these conditions.

As is shown in the papers by Holbrook and Smith in this chapter, if money wages are flexible—that is, if they decline readily when the number of persons willing to work at the going wage rate exceeds the number of jobs available—the economy will normally tend automatically toward full employment regardless of the monetary and fiscal policies being followed. That is, real output and employment will be determined by the volume of real resources available and their productivity. The Classical quantity theory of money will hold in its extreme form: an increase in the stock of money will cause an equal proportional change in prices and in money income but will leave real income and employment unchanged. This will be true without regard to the magnitude of the

---

[7] The empirical evidence on which this conclusion is based is presented in Milton Friedman, "The Supply of Money and Changes in Prices and Output," in *The Relationship of Prices to Economic Stability and Growth,* Compendium of Papers Submitted by Panelists Appearing before the Joint Economic Committee (Washington, D.C., 1958), pp. 249–50.

[8] Chapter 5 contains readings which are concerned with this debate.

[9] See Milton Friedman, "The Demand for Money: Some Theoretical and Empirical Results," *Journal of Political Economy,* Vol. LXVII (August 1959), pp. 327–51. In order to get this result, Friedman uses a special definition of income.

[10] See Milton Friedman, "Interest Rates and the Demand for Money," *Journal of Law and Economics,* Vol. IX (October 1966), pp. 71–85.

[11] Ibid. See also his paper, "A Theoretical Framework for Monetary Analysis," *Journal of Political Economy,* Vol. LXXVIII (March/April 1970), pp. 193–238.

interest elasticity of demand for money.[12] Fiscal policy will likewise not affect real income or employment. If government expenditures are increased without a corresponding increase in taxes, the government will have to borrow in the capital market to finance the resulting deficit. The additional government borrowing will necessarily raise interest rates enough to cause real private investment to decline as much as real government expenditures increase. The result will be a transfer of real resources from the private to the public sector of the economy, but total income and employment will be unaffected. Thus, as Friedman points out, fiscal policy will be incapable of affecting income and employment under a regime of flexible wages, whether or not the demand for money is sensitive to interest rates.

It should be noted, however, that even if wages are flexible, the effects of fiscal policy do depend to some degree on whether the demand for money is sensitive to interest rates. If the demand for real money balances depends only on real income and not on interest rates, the price level and therefore the level of money income is determined by the stock of money alone. In this case, a change in fiscal policy will leave the price level and money income unchanged. If, however, the demand for money is sensitive to interest rates, the outcome will be different. An increase in government expenditures not accompanied by an increase in taxes will, as explained earlier, cause interest rates to rise. If the demand for money is sensitive to interest rates, the rise in interest rates will cause a reduction in the amount of real money balances people want to hold (remember that real income is unchanged because it is determined by the amounts of real resources available and their productivity). With the nominal stock of money unchanged (by assumption), the price level will have to rise enough to bring the real value of cash balances into alignment with the reduced demand for such balances.[13] Thus, fiscal policy will, in this case, affect the price level and money income. To summarize: If wages are flexible, fiscal policy will be incapable of affecting real income and employment, whether or not the demand for money is elastic to interest rates; however, even with flexible wages, fiscal policy will have effects on the price level and money income unless the interest elasticity of demand for money is zero.

Assuming that the demand for money is sensitive to interest rates, as the bulk of the empirical evidence indicates, the above discussion raises an important

---

[12] Provided the interest elasticity is not infinitely large—if this is the case, as Smith's article shows, the Classical mechanism which makes the economy tend automatically toward full employment may break down. (In this discussion, we are neglecting the so-called "Pigou effect," which is discussed in Smith's article.)

[13] This can be seen by examining the LM curve for a model similar to those presented above except that prices are now assumed to be free to change. The equation of the LM curve is derived by equating the demand for real money balances (which is assumed to depend on real income (Y/P) and the rate of interest) with the real value of the nominal money stock (M^*/P). Thus we have

$$\frac{M^*}{P} = M_o + k\frac{Y}{P} - mr.$$

If real income (Y/P) is fixed at the full-employment level and M^* is given, an increase in government expenditures which causes the interest rate to rise will reduce the demand for real money balances (the right-hand side of the equation). In order to maintain equilibrium in the money market, the supply of real money balances will have to be reduced also, and with M^* fixed this reduction can only be brought about by a rise in P. If P rises, Y must rise in the same proportion if Y/P is to remain constant. Thus, fiscal policy affects money income and prices. However, if $m = 0$ so that the interest rate does not affect the demand for money, none of these adjustments is necessary, and fiscal policy leaves money income and prices unaffected.

question. Which of the following alternative assumptions is the more realistic: (*a*) wages are fully flexible so that monetary and fiscal policy are incapable of changing employment and real income, having effects only on the price level and money income; or (*b*) wages are rigid (or at least sticky), thereby giving monetary and fiscal policy an important leverage over employment and real income? It seems clear that in a world of imperfect markets, less than full mobility of resources, trade unions, minimum wage laws, and the like, the rigid-wage assumption is by far the more reasonable one to adopt. Accordingly, we shall continue to assume rigid wages during the remainder of this introduction, deferring the bulk of our discussion of wages and prices until the second part of this chapter.

There is still another dimension to the controversy over the role of interest rates in relation to monetary and fiscal policy—a dimension which has received less attention than it deserves. We refer here to the responsiveness of the money *supply* to changes in the interest rate through the operation of the banking system. Up to this point in our discussion, for simplicity, we have treated the stock of money, M^*, as a variable that is under the direct control of the monetary authorities. Strictly speaking, this is not correct. In the United States, the Federal Reserve System implements monetary policy primarily by buying and selling U.S. government securities in the open market, by changing the reserve requirements of member commercial banks, and by varying the discount rate at which member banks may borrow from the System. Thus, it is these variables rather than the money stock itself that are properly regarded as being under the control of the authorities. Since the amount of reserves obtained by borrowing from the Federal Reserve as well as the amount of reserves held in excess of legal requirements seem to be affected by interest rates available in the market relative to the discount rate charged by the Federal Reserve, the money supply is determined jointly by the actions taken by the authorities and the responses of the banks and the public. One of the results is that the supply of money as well as the demand for money is sensitive to interest rates. The implications for monetary and fiscal policy of this more sophisticated approach to the supply of money are discussed thoroughly in the first paper by Teigen. We can bring our introductory discussion to completion by examining the results of substituting a very simple money supply equation for equation (3.8). Let us suppose that the monetary authorities are able to vary only the reserve base (R^*) and that the commercial banks extend more loans and hence increase the amount of demand deposits in response to increases in the interest rate, and vice versa. Instead of (3.8), Model III now contains the following money supply equation:

$$M_s = aR^* + er, \qquad a > 0, e > 0. \tag{3.21}$$

We may now derive multiplier expressions summarizing the effects of fiscal policy and monetary policy in exactly the same way as before. Instead of the expressions given by (3.17) and (3.19), we now obtain:

$$\frac{\Delta Y}{\Delta G^*} = \frac{1}{1 - c(1 - x) + \dfrac{vk}{m + e}} \tag{3.22}$$

$$\frac{\Delta Y}{\Delta R^*} = \frac{a}{[1 - c(1 - x)]\dfrac{m + e}{v} + k} \tag{3.23}$$

In both of these expressions, we note that the interest sensitivity of the *supply* of money (e) is combined additively with the interest sensitivity of the demand for money (m). Thus even if the latter were zero, as most of the Classical economists have assumed, fiscal policy remains effective as long as the interest sensitivity of the supply of money is not zero. In the same way, the larger is the interest elasticity of the money supply, the less potent is monetary policy, given the value of the interest sensitivity of demand. It appears, then, that the crucial question relating to policy for an economy in which there are impediments to full employment is not whether the *demand* for money is interest sensitive, but whether either the demand *or* supply of money exhibit interest sensitivity. Only if *both* sensitivities are zero do the extreme Classical conclusions hold.

The Classical position represents one extreme view of the size of the interest elasticity of the demand for money (as we have noted, both the Classical and the Keynesian schools have disregarded the interest elasticity of the money supply). The other polar view is that the interest elasticity of demand is infinitely large; this is the "extreme Keynesian" assumption, and is sometimes referred to as the "liquidity trap" case. If m were infinitely large, the expenditure multiplier (3.17) becomes $1/[1 - c(1 - x)]$. The monetary sector has no inhibiting effect on the expenditure multiplier at all, and fiscal policy reaches maximum effectiveness. However, the monetary policy multiplier (3.19) becomes zero. Monetary policy is completely ineffective because changes in the money stock have no effect on the interest rate and hence on expenditures. The "liquidity trap" means that increases in the money stock are simply absorbed into idle balances, since it is universally expected that the interest rate will rise and bond prices fall. If the possibility of interest-induced changes in the money supply is recognized, a glance at equations (3.22) and (3.23) indicates that an infinitely large interest elasticity of supply will yield similar results—if e is infinitely large, (3.22) becomes $1/[1 - c(1 - x)]$, its largest possible value, while the multiplier summarizing the effects on income of changes in bank reserves, (3.23), becomes zero. Such a result might occur in a period of deep depression when interest rates were very low and seemed almost certain to rise in the near future. Under these conditions the banks, fearing a fall in security prices, might be very reluctant to buy securities, and they might be extremely fearful of making additional loans at the prevailing very low interest rates in view of the high risks of default. Under these conditions, any increase in bank reserves, resulting, let us say, from open market operations, might merely cause the banks to add a corresponding amount to their excess reserves without leading to any increase in the money supply.

It is almost certain that neither the Classical nor the extreme Keynesian assumptions accurately characterize our economy under normal conditions. The evidence appears overwhelming that both the demand for and the supply of money possess some degree of interest elasticity but that neither of these elasticities is infinitely great.[14] With one further qualification in the case of monetary policy—that the sensitivity of investment to the interest rate is not zero—it may be seen from (3.22) and (3.23) that in this case both fiscal policy and

---

[14] It should be noted that Keynes himself felt that this would be the normal situation and that both fiscal and monetary policy would therefore be capable of influencing aggregate demand. He regarded the "liquidity trap" situation as one that might occur only in times of deep depression, such as the 1930s. It is totally wrong to regard the liquidity trap case as the essence of Keynes' analysis.

monetary policy are capable of influencing income. Most recent studies have verified that investment (especially in new houses and in plant and equipment) responds to changes in the rate of interest. Some evidence on the interest elasticities of different categories of investment demand is presented in the article by Michael J. Hamburger in Chapter 5. In a system with nonzero but finite interest elasticities of demand for and/or supply of money, and a nonzero interest elasticity of demand for investment, the efficacy of monetary policy, as well as fiscal policy, depends on the structure of *both the real sector* (*i.e., the markets for goods and services*) *and the monetary sector.* In fact, both the expenditure multiplier and the monetary policy multiplier expressions contain the same terms: the marginal propensities to consume and to add to money balances with respect to income; the responsiveness of investment, the demand for money, and the supply of money to the rate of interest; and the marginal response of tax payments to income.[15] From (3.22) and (3.23) it is easy to determine the conditions that are conducive to the effectiveness of monetary policy and of fiscal policy, respectively. It should not be concluded from the discussion of the polar cases above that all of the conditions which are favorable to fiscal policy are unfavorable to monetary policy, or vice versa. In fact, there are a number of conditions that are conducive to the effectiveness of both kinds of policy. Both multipliers will be larger:

1. The larger the marginal propensity to consume with respect to disposable income (c), and the lower the marginal response of tax payments to income (x). This is true because these coefficients determine the size of induced expenditure and income changes set off by an initial change in government expenditures or tax collections produced by fiscal policy, or by an initial change in private investment resulting from a change in interest rates produced by monetary policy.

2. The smaller is the responsiveness of the demand for money to changes in income (k). For a given increase in income, for instance, the interest rate will rise less and induced investment spending will fall less, the less cash is drawn into transactions balances to accommodate the rising level of income.

The two multipliers are affected differently by variations in the interest sensitivity of investment and of the demand for and supply of money (v, m, and e). Fiscal policy is more effective, and monetary policy less effective:

1. The lower the interest sensitivity of investment expenditure (v). That is, the lower this sensitivity, the less will such expenditure be reduced by rising interest rates which accompany rising expenditure and income brought about by an increase in government expenditures or a reduction in taxes. On the other hand, the lower this sensitivity, the less effect will a given change in the money stock and the resulting interest rate change have on investment spending.

2. The greater the interest sensitivities of the demand for money (m) and the supply of money (e). The greater these sensitivities, the less will expenditure

---

[15] In addition, the monetary policy multiplier, (3.23), has in its numerator the sensitivity of the money supply to changes in the reserve base (a). If the money supply does not respond to changes in the reserve base, then monetary policy as expressed through open market operations can have no effect on the interest rate, investment, and income. As Teigen's article shows, the structure of the monetary system is such that this sensitivity is not zero. As a matter of fact the coefficient a turns out to be the standard credit expansion multiplier, as Teigen demonstrates.

be reduced by rising interest rates accompanying rising expenditure and income caused by expansionary fiscal measures; but, on the other hand, the less effect will a given monetary change have on the interest rates and hence on spending.

In summary, monetary policy is more effective when the interest sensitivities of the demand for and supply of money are low, so that changes in the money stock or reserve base have greater effects on the rate of interest, and when the interest sensitivity of investment expenditure is large, so that changes in the interest rate have larger effects on spending. Fiscal policy is more effective when the interest sensitivity of the demand for and supply of money is large, so that an increase in transactions requirements for money and the resulting reduction in money balances left to satisfy asset requirements does not affect the interest rate very much and also, to some extent, induces the banks to create new money balances, and when the interest sensitivity of investment expenditure is low, so that rising interest rates do not deter very much investment expenditure.

The conclusions of this discussion of the factors influencing the effectiveness of monetary and fiscal policy—as measured by the size of the multipliers $\Delta Y / \Delta G^*$ and $\Delta Y / \Delta R^*$—are summarized in Table IV.

TABLE IV

	Effect on:	
Increase in:	$\dfrac{\Delta Y}{\Delta R^*} = \dfrac{a}{[1 - c(1 - x)]\dfrac{m + e}{v} + k}$	$\dfrac{\Delta Y}{\Delta G^*} = \dfrac{1}{1 - c(1 - x) + \dfrac{vk}{m + e}}$
c............	increase	increase
x............	decrease	decrease
m............	decrease	increase
e............	decrease	increase
v............	increase	decrease
k............	decrease	decrease

The student will benefit, as he studies this book, from trying to see how the materials fit into the framework developed above, and how some of the readings suggest important extensions to this simple framework. As has already been noted, for example, some of the material in Chapter 5 is concerned with the size of v, the interest sensitivity of investment decisions. At the same time, other papers in Chapters 1 and 5 take the point of view that the "monetary transmission mechanism," or link between the monetary and real sectors of the economy, is much broader than the interest rate-investment relationship as expressed in the size of v. The monetarists have taken this position, and in fact, they claim it as one of the identifying characteristics of monetarism. But Warren L. Smith's article in Chapter 5, "A Neo-Keynesian View of Monetary Policy," identifies three broad channels through which monetary influences can affect real variables; his list includes the general portfolio-adjustment process named by the monetarists. Thus, it appears that both sides have in common a more general view of the transmission mechanism than is represented in the somewhat elementary models discussed here. To take another example, the discussion of the working of banks and financial intermediaries in Chapter 2 and of the "slippages" in the financial system in Chapter 5 are significant primarily because they bear on the size of m and e, the interest sensitivities of the demand for and supply of money.

2. SOME RUDIMENTARY DYNAMICS

(a) The Dynamics of the Multiplier

Changes in aggregate demand, whether produced by autonomous shifts in private spending or by changes in fiscal and monetary policy, are not reflected immediately in changes in production and income. There are three major lags in the process of income generation: (1) the lag between the receipt of income and the expenditure of that portion of it that the recipient decides to spend; (2) the lag between changes in expenditure and related changes in production and income; (3) the lag between the earning of income and its receipt. These lags have been called the *expenditure lag*, the *output lag*, and the *earnings lag*, respectively. While the lags are essentially additive, it appears that the expenditure and earnings lags are relatively short and that the output lag is by far the longest and most important.[16] It is this lag that receives most of the attention in the article by Gardner Ackley on the multiplier time period reprinted in this chapter. It arises because of the relationships between sales, inventories, and output. For example, an increase in sales of consumer goods will commonly lead to a reduction in retail inventories in the first instance. After a delay, which will depend on the practices of the industry, on marketing channels, and on the general business situation, retailers will increase their orders to restore depleted inventories, and these increased orders will in due course cause manufacturers to increase production and employment. Thus, significant changes in output usually occur only after a delay, which may be considerable.

Elementary expositions of the dynamics of income change commonly employ an expenditure lag, assuming, for example, that consumption adjusts to income with a lag of one period. However, in view of the fact that the output lag appears to be the most important and is the one stressed by Ackley, we shall build our exposition around that lag. This seems more realistic, although the algebraic results are very similar with an expenditure lag.

Model IIA: A Dynamic Version of Model II

To begin our discussion of the dynamic multiplier—that is, the process through which the system adjusts from one equilibrium position to another when some component of spending changes—we will use a version of Model II, modified by dating all of the variables in such a way that this period's output (and hence current income) depends only on spending during the previous period. After we have become familiar with the adjustment process using this simple model, we shall turn to a version of Model III, in which the monetary sector plays a role. The dynamic version of Model II is as follows:

$$C_t = C_o + cY_{d_t} \tag{2a.1}$$
$$Y_{d_t} = Y_t - T_t \tag{2a.2}$$
$$T_t = T^* + xY_t \tag{2a.3}$$
$$I_t = I_o \tag{2a.4}$$
$$G_t = G^* \tag{2a.5}$$
$$Y_t = C_{t-1} + I_{t-1} + G_{t-1} \tag{2a.6}$$

Here the subscript t designates the value of the indicated variable in the current

---

[16] Lloyd A. Metzler, "Three Lags in the Circular Flow of Income," in *Income, Employment, and Public Policy: Essays in Honor of Alvin H. Hansen* (New York: W. W. Norton & Co., Inc., 1948), pp. 11–32.

period, the subscript $t - 1$ refers to the previous period, and so on. In equilibrium, the value of each variable is unchanged from period to period. Accordingly, all time subscripts can be dropped, and the solution of this model is the same as the solution of Model II. However, the interpretation of equation (2a.6) is now different—it is no longer an "equilibrium condition" (although equilibrium values of the variables can be obtained by assuming that equilibrium exists [that is, that $C_t = C_{t-1}$; $I_t = I_{t-1}$; and $G_t = G_{t-1}$], and substituting these values into the equation). Rather, (2a.6) is a statement of the rule that firms are assumed to follow in deciding how much to produce. It says that they produce in a particular period an amount equal to their sales in the previous period; that is, output is adjusted to sales with a lag of one period. Thus, equation (2a.6) implies that an increase in spending in the current period has no effect on current production and national income; rather, inventories are drawn down to fill the new orders, and production responds during the following period. Other rules could have been specified, of course, but this one is simple and at the same time realistic enough to be useful.

In Model IIA, the length of each "period" need not correspond to any particular unit of calendar time, such as a month or year, but is determined by the behavioral lag between a change in spending and the change in production which it induces. In reality, it is a "distributed lag"; that is, the change in production does not occur entirely in one period but is spread out over a number of periods. For example, the production adjustment may begin slowly, rise to a peak, and then gradually taper off. Here we treat the production response to a given change in sales as occurring in one discrete unit time period. In tracing the path followed by income in response to a spending change, we will also assume that the marginal propensity to consume out of disposable income (c) and the marginal propensity to pay taxes out of GNP (x) do not change in value over time.

We will consider the effects of two types of spending changes, using changes in government purchases of goods and services as an example—although, of course, similar effects would be produced by shifts in consumer spending, investment spending, or tax collections. In Case 1, we will suppose that government purchases rise from G^* to $G^* + \Delta G^*$ *during one period only,* and then revert to the original level, G^*, and remain there. In Case 2, we start from the same equilibrium and suppose that government purchases rise to $G^* + \Delta G^*$ and *remain at the new level indefinitely.* In each case, we will trace the path of income from the original equilibrium level to the new equilibrium position. While we will consider the effects of an increase in spending, the same analysis will apply in reverse for a spending decrease.

Case 1: One-Shot Injection. Starting from an equilibrium position, suppose that, in the first period under consideration, government purchases of goods and services rise from the original level, G^*, to a new level, $G^* + \Delta G^*$—that is, government purchases change by ΔG^*. In the second period, government purchases revert to their former level, G^*, and remain there in all future periods. Because production is determined only by the previous period's spending, income—that is, the total value of current production—does not change in period 1; rather, inventories are drawn down so that the investment actually realized by firms for the period is $I_o - \Delta G^*$, not I_o as planned (that is, inventory investment falls by the same amount that spending by government increases). Since income does not change, there is no change in tax collections, disposable income, or consumption expenditure.

In period 2, firms continue to produce the (as yet unchanged) amounts of output corresponding to spending by households and by firms themselves for investment purposes, and also produce the total amount bought by government in period 1, $G^* + \Delta G$.[*17] Therefore income rises by ΔG^* in period 2, and corresponding to this income increase, current tax collections rise by $x\Delta G^*$. Disposable income in period 2 changes by the amount of the change in income, ΔG^*, less the change in tax collections, $x\Delta G^*$, or by $(1 - x)\Delta G^*$, and so consumption spending in the amount of $c(1 - x)\Delta G^*$ is induced in period 2, drawing down inventories by this amount.[18] In period 3, firms produce an amount equal to their sales in period 2, which exceed the level prevailing in the initial equilibrium by $c(1 - x)\Delta G^*$. Thus income in period 3 is greater than its initial equilibrium level by this amount; however, it is lower than income in period 2, due to an increase in household savings of $(1 - c)(1 - x)\Delta G^*$ in period 2. The increment of income $c(1 - x)\Delta G^*$ in period 3 induces consumption spending of $c(1 - x)[c(1 - x)\Delta G^*]$, or $c^2(1 - x)^2\Delta G^*$, etc. In general, the initial increase in spending produces an increment of induced production (and hence income) in each succeeding period, beginning with the period following the spending change; each increment is smaller than the one preceding it, since a part of each is drained off by the government in taxes and another part is saved by households, until finally these increments approach zero in value and equilibrium is restored *at the original level of income.*

It may help to illustrate the nature of this process if an example is employed, using the same numerical assumptions as in Model II. That is, suppose we have

$$C_t = 70 + .75Y_{d_t}$$
$$Y_{d_t} = Y_t - T_t$$
$$T_t = -40 + .2Y_t$$
$$I_t = 145$$
$$G_t = 155$$
$$Y_t = C_{t-1} + I_{t-1} + G_{t-1}$$

The equilibrium values of the variables in this model are shown in the column labeled "original equilibrium" of Table V below. In period 1, government pur-

TABLE V   THE DYNAMICS OF A "ONE-SHOT" SPENDING INJECTION

	Original Equilibrium	Time Period (t) 1	2	3	4		New Equilibrium
Y	1,000	1,000	1,020	1,012.0	1,007.20	...	1,000
C	700	700	712	707.2	704.32	...	700
I	145	145	145	145.0	145.00	...	145
G	155	175	155	155.0	155.00	...	155
T	160	160	164	162.4	161.44	...	160
Y_d	840	840	856	849.6	845.76	...	840
S	140	140	144	142.4	141.44	...	140
ΔY_t†	...	0	20	12.0	7.20	...	0

† ΔY_t refers to the difference between income in the tth period and the original equilibrium value.

---

[17] Note that in this model, production in each period is equal to *planned* spending by all sectors in the previous period. Thus the inventory change that occurred in period 1 is disregarded in period 2.

[18] Since firms are producing the incremental amount bought by government in period 1, there is actually a net inventory accumulation of $\Delta G^* - c(1 - x)\Delta G^*$, or $[1 - c(1 - x)]\Delta G^*$, during the period.

chases of goods and services rise by $20 billion to $175 billion from the initial level of $155 billion; they revert to $155 billion in period 2 and remain there in all succeeding periods. The paths followed by income and other variables are shown in columns numbered 1, 2, 3, and 4, where the column numbers correspond to the time periods. As can be seen, income rises to a peak of $1,020 billion during period 2, and then declines until it ultimately reaches the former equilibrium level of $1,000 billion as shown in the final ("new equilibrium") column. In the row labeled ΔY_t, the change in income in each period measured from the original equilibrium level is shown. The general expression for ΔY_t is shown in the following tabulation:

	\multicolumn{5}{c}{Time period (t)}	New Equilibrium
	1	2	3	4	n	
ΔY_t	0	ΔG^*	$c(1-x)\Delta G^*$	$[c(1-x)]^2\Delta G^* \ldots$	$[c(1-x)]^{n-2}\Delta G^* \ldots$	0

Since c and x are positive fractions between zero and unity in value, $c(1-x)$ is also such a fraction, and $[c(1-x)]^m$ declines steadily in value as m increases. Since the new equilibrium position is not reached until an infinite amount of time has passed, the term $[c(1-x)]^m$ goes to zero, and the new equilibrium is therefore the same as the original equilibrium that existed before the "one-shot" increase in government purchases. The explanation is that, since government spending fell back to its original level in the second period of our example, and remained there, the equilibrium solution of the system is unchanged. However, the one-period spurt in spending initiated a dynamic process of adjustment which takes an infinite number of periods to complete. In each of these periods, income will be greater than equilibrium income, although it will be approaching the equilibrium value as time passes.

Case 2: Continuing Injection. Now let us consider the dynamics of the case in which government purchases change and remain at the new level; that is, the case in which there is a change in the equilibrium level of government purchases. Let this change be represented by ΔG^* as previously (remember that shifts in consumption or private investment will have the same effect). As before, income will change by ΔG^* in period 2 as producers respond to the change in government spending in period 1. During period 2, there will be another injection of government spending greater than the old equilibrium by ΔG^*; at the same time, households will be induced to spend $c(1-x)\Delta G^*$, which in turn will induce that much production in period 3, and so on. In each period after the second, income will differ from the initial equilibrium level by the sum of a new component of production for the government sector equal to the previous period's increased spending (compared to the former equilibrium level of government spending) and one or more components which correspond to induced spending by the household sector in the previous period. The income changes for several such periods are written out in Table VI using the numerical version of Model IIA.

To find the amount by which income has changed at the end of any period as a result of the change of government spending, all of the increments of induced production (and hence income) in that period which arise from this spending change must be added to the production which corresponds to the previous period's "new" additional government spending. For example, in period

TABLE VI   THE DYNAMICS OF A CONTINUING SPENDING INJECTION

	Original Equilibrium	Time Period (t)					New Equilibrium
		1	2	3	4		
Y	1,000	1,000	1,020	1,032.0	1,039.20	...	1,050
C	700	700	712	719.2	723.52	...	730
I	145	145	145	145.0	145.00	...	145
G	155	175	175	175.0	175.00	...	175
T	160	160	164	166.4	167.84	...	170
Y_d	840	840	856	865.6	871.36	...	880
S	140	140	144	146.4	147.84	...	150
ΔY_t†	...	0	20	32.0	39.20	...	50
$\dfrac{\Delta Y_t}{\Delta G^*}$	...	0	1	1.6	1.96	...	2.50

† ΔY_t refers to the difference between income in the tth period and the original equilibrium value.

3, income is $32 billion higher than its initial equilibrium level. This is due to the fact that, in period 2, government spending on goods and services was $20 billion higher than its initial level, inducing that much new production for the government sector in period 3; in addition, $12 billion of goods was produced in period 3 in response to the induced rise in consumption spending of $12 billion in period 2.

Model IIIA: A Dynamic Version of Model III

Now let us examine the effects on the process of income change of a shift in spending in a model containing a monetary sector. For this purpose we shall use a dynamic version of Model III. Since the adjustment of a household's or firm's cash balance is a simple matter and presumably takes less time to accomplish than either changes in spending plans or production decisions, we shall assume that there are no lags in the monetary sector. As was the case in Model IIA, therefore, the only lag in the system will be an output lag. The dynamic version of Model IIIA is as follows:

$$C_t = C_o + cY_{d_t} \qquad (3a.1)$$
$$Y_{d_t} = Y_t - T_t \qquad (3a.2)$$
$$T_t = T^* + xY_t \qquad (3a.3)$$
$$I_t = I_o - vr_t \qquad (3a.4)$$
$$G_t = G^* \qquad (3a.5)$$
$$Y_t = C_{t-1} + I_{t-1} + G_{t-1} \qquad (3a.6)$$
$$M_{d_t} = M_o + kY_t - mr_t \qquad (3a.7)$$
$$M_{s_t} = M^* \qquad (3a.8)$$
$$M_{d_t} = M_{s_t} \qquad (3a.9)$$

In this discussion, we will consider only the "continuing injection" version of the process of income change, as it is the typical multiplier case. Starting from equilibrium, let there be an increase in government spending of ΔG^* in period 1. According to Model IIIA, in which income in any period responds only to spending in the previous period, this spending change will have no effect on income until period 2. In that period, producers will increase their output, and therefore income, by ΔG^*. As a consequence, changes in spending by both households and firms are induced in this period. The change in household spending can easily be deduced from the first three equations of our model. An income increase of ΔG^* causes an increase in disposable income of $(1 - x)\Delta G^*$, leading to a rise in consumption spending of $c(1 - x)\Delta G^*$ in the same period. To isolate the effects of a change in income on the spending decisions of firms, the investment equation (3a.4) must be examined together with the equations describing the monetary sector—(3a.7), (3a.8), and (3a.9). First, by differencing equation (3a.4), we note that

$$\Delta I_t = -v\Delta r_t, \qquad (3a.10)$$

or that rising interest rates cause business firms to reduce investment, and vice versa. The effects of rising income on the rate of interest can be found from the monetary equations. Combining (3a.7), (3a.8), and (3a.9) produces the following *LM* equation:

$$M^* = M_o + kY_t - mr_t. \qquad (3a.11)$$

If we write this equation in differenced form, remembering that the money supply, M^*, is assumed to remain constant, we get:

$$0 = k\Delta Y_t - m\Delta r_t; \qquad (3a.12)$$

or, solving this equation for Δr_t in terms of ΔY_t, we find

$$\Delta r_t = \frac{k}{m}\Delta Y_t. \qquad (3a.13)$$

Substituting this result into (3a.10) yields

$$\Delta I_t = -\frac{vk}{m}\Delta Y_t, \qquad (3a.14)$$

the general expression for the change in planned investment spending which is induced by a change in income, ΔY_t. Since the income change in period 2 is ΔG^*, the induced change in investment spending in that period is

$$-\frac{vk}{m}\Delta G^*.$$

Thus the *total* change in induced spending in period t will be

$$\left[c(1 - x) - \frac{vk}{m} \right] \Delta Y_t,$$

and in period 2 it will be

$$\left[c(1 - x) - \frac{vk}{m} \right] \Delta G^*.$$

In addition, the autonomous spending increase of ΔG^* is assumed to continue. Thus the total income change in period 3, which is the sum of induced and autonomous spending changes in period 2 in our model, is

$$\left[c(1 - x) - \frac{vk}{m} \right] \Delta G^* + \Delta G^*.$$

This in turn will induce further new spending in period 3, according to the rule given above, of

$$\left[c(1 - x) - \frac{vk}{m} \right]\left[c(1 - x) - \frac{vk}{m} \right] \Delta G^*,$$

or

$$\left[c(1-x) - \frac{vk}{m} \right]^2 \Delta G^*,$$

which, when added to the autonomous spending component ΔG^* will generate further income change in period 4, and so forth.

It may be useful to illustrate this process with a numerical example, using a model which yields the same equilibrium values for income and their other common endogenous variables as the numerical version of Model IIA, but which contains a monetary sector whose parameters have the same values as those of Model III, as follows:

$$C_t = 70 + .75Y_{d_t}$$
$$Y_{d_t} = Y_t - T_t$$
$$T_t = -40 + .2Y_t$$
$$I_t = 165 - 4r_t$$
$$G_t = 155$$
$$Y_t = C_{t-1} + I_{t-1} + G_{t-1}$$
$$M_{d_t} = 20 + .25Y_t - 10r_t$$
$$M_{s_t} = 220$$
$$M_{d_t} = M_{s_t}$$

Changes in income and several other variables which result from a continuing injection of $20 billion of new government spending initiated in period 1 are written out in Table VII.

TABLE VII   THE DYNAMICS OF A CONTINUING SPENDING INJECTION IN A MODEL WITH A MONETARY SECTOR

	Original Equilibrium	Time Period (t)					New Equilibrium
		1	2	3	4		
Y	1,000	1,000	1,020	1,030	1,035.0	...	1,040
C	700	700	712	718	721.0	...	724
I	145	145	143	142	141.5	...	141
G	155	175	175	175	175.0	...	175
T	160	160	164	166	167.0	...	168
Y_d	840	840	856	864	868.0	...	872
S	140	140	144	146	147.0	...	148
M	220	220	220	220	220.0	...	220
r	5%	5%	5.5%	5.75%	5.875%	...	6%
ΔY_t†	...	0	20	30	35.0	...	40
$\dfrac{\Delta Y_t}{\Delta G^*}$	...	0	1	1.5	1.75	...	2.0

† ΔY_t refers to the difference between income in the tth period and the original equilibrium value.

Again we find the total amount of income change for any period due to a change in government spending by adding all of the increments of induced production (or income) in that period to the production corresponding to the previous period's "new" government spending. In the present example, for instance, income in period 3 is $30 billion higher than its original equilibrium level. This change is due to three causes: First, government spending on goods and services in period 2 was $20 billion higher than its initial level, inducing that much new production for the government sector in period 3; second, $12 billion of goods was produced in period 3 in response to the induced rise in consumption spending of $12 billion in period 2; finally, $2 billion *less* of investment goods was produced in period 3 than initially because spending by firms declined by that amount in period 2 due to a rise in the rate of interest from 5 percent to 5.5 percent. It is possible to calculate multipliers for each successive time period. This is done by dividing the rise in income for that period by the increase in the level of government purchases that caused the rise. These multipliers are shown in the $\Delta Y_t / \Delta G^*$ rows of Tables VI and VII: thus, in Table VII, the multiplier is 1.00 after two periods, 1.50 after three periods, and so on. It should be noted that the multipliers shown in Table VII for each period are somewhat smaller than their counterparts in Table VI, except for the first two periods; this is due to restraining influence of the monetary sector on the expansion process in Model IIIA, a phenomenon which is not present in Model IIA. The multipliers calculated in this way, of course, eventually equal the static multipliers appropriate to the underlying model (2.00 in the case of Model IIIA, for example).

This concept of the multiplier differs from the *static equilibrium multipliers* expressed in equation (2.11) or equation (3.17). The multiplier expressions in those equations give the change in *equilibrium* income which would result from a sustained change in the level of government purchases in each case. The multiplier values shown in Tables VI and VII—and also in Table VIII below—on the other hand, represent a dynamic or disequilibrium view of the multiplier. Rather than allowing the system to reestablish equilibrium, we have chosen to relate the amount by which income differs from its original equilibrium value at the end of any arbitrarily selected number of periods to the original spending change. Each of the expressions in the row labeled $\Delta Y_t / \Delta G^*$ in Tables VI and VII—or Table VIII—is a multiplier. Since the multiplier process has not been allowed to work itself out completely, however, any such multiplier is sometimes called a "truncated" multiplier. When the dynamic process is fully worked out and equilibrium income is reestablished, the change in equilibrium income will be that predicted by the comparable static multiplier equation. (This would be equation (3.17). But notice that, if we assume $v = 0$, which is the essential difference between Model IIA and Model IIIA, then the comparable static multiplier equation will be (2.11).) Thus the truncated multiplier approaches the static equilibrium multiplier in value over time. Both of these versions of the multiplier are consistent with the general definition of the multiplier as being the ratio of the change in income to the spending change which induced it.

The general expressions for the induced increase in income above the initial equilibrium level in any period, ΔY_t, and for the truncated multiplier for any period, $\Delta Y_t / \Delta G^*$, are developed in Table VIII. In using this table, it is important to understand that the ΔY_t for any period is found by adding all of the items in the column corresponding to that period—that is, by adding *vertically* down a column. To find the value of the multiplier in the new equilibrium, we must evaluate a sum such as is found in the lower right-hand corner of Table VIII, except that we must allow an infinite amount of time to pass. That, is, we consider the value of the sum:

$$\frac{\Delta Y}{\Delta G^*} = \lim_{t \to \infty} \sum_{r=0}^{t-2} \left[c(1-x) - \frac{vk}{m} \right]^r.$$

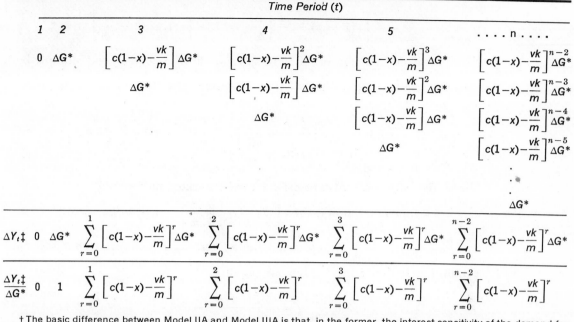

Let $b = c(1-x) - \dfrac{vk}{m}$.

Time Period (t)					
1 2		3	4	5	....n....
0 ΔG^*		$\left[c(1-x)-\frac{vk}{m}\right]\Delta G^*$	$\left[c(1-x)-\frac{vk}{m}\right]^2\Delta G^*$	$\left[c(1-x)-\frac{vk}{m}\right]^3\Delta G^*$	$\left[c(1-x)-\frac{vk}{m}\right]^{n-2}\Delta G^*$
		ΔG^*	$\left[c(1-x)-\frac{vk}{m}\right]\Delta G^*$	$\left[c(1-x)-\frac{vk}{m}\right]^2\Delta G^*$	$\left[c(1-x)-\frac{vk}{m}\right]^{n-3}\Delta G^*$
			ΔG^*	$\left[c(1-x)-\frac{vk}{m}\right]\Delta G^*$	$\left[c(1-x)-\frac{vk}{m}\right]^{n-4}\Delta G^*$
				ΔG^*	$\left[c(1-x)-\frac{vk}{m}\right]^{n-5}\Delta G^*$
					$\vdots$
					ΔG^*
ΔY_t‡ 0 ΔG^*		$\sum\limits_{r=0}^{1}\left[c(1-x)-\frac{vk}{m}\right]^r\Delta G^*$	$\sum\limits_{r=0}^{2}\left[c(1-x)-\frac{vk}{m}\right]^r\Delta G^*$	$\sum\limits_{r=0}^{3}\left[c(1-x)-\frac{vk}{m}\right]^r\Delta G^*$	$\sum\limits_{r=0}^{n-2}\left[c(1-x)-\frac{vk}{m}\right]^r\Delta G^*$
$\dfrac{\Delta Y_t‡}{\Delta G^*}$ 0 1		$\sum\limits_{r=0}^{1}\left[c(1-x)-\frac{vk}{m}\right]^r$	$\sum\limits_{r=0}^{2}\left[c(1-x)-\frac{vk}{m}\right]^r$	$\sum\limits_{r=0}^{3}\left[c(1-x)-\frac{vk}{m}\right]^r$	$\sum\limits_{r=0}^{n-2}\left[c(1-x)-\frac{vk}{m}\right]^r$

† The basic difference between Model IIA and Model IIIA is that, in the former, the interest sensitivity of the demand for investment, v, is zero; thus there is no link between the monetary sector and the rest of the model, and the monetary sector cannot affect expenditure decisions and hence is omitted. In this table, the expressions as written are based on Model IIIA, but if v, the interest sensitivity of investment demand, is set equal to zero, the expressions will reflect the properties of Model IIA.

‡ In this table, for convenience, we employ the standard notation for the sum of a series of terms having a variable in common. To take a simple example, suppose we wished to write the sum $Z_1 + Z_2 + Z_3 + Z_4 + Z_5$ in an abbreviated way. It is conventional to write this as $\sum\limits_{r=1}^{5} Z_r$. This is read: "The summation of Z_r, with r taking on values from one to five." The symbol Σ is the *summation sign* and is the Greek letter sigma. In this expression, the subscript r provides a convenient way of handling the "length" of this sum—i.e., the fact that it includes all Z's from Z_1 to Z_5. In the expression

$$\sum_{r=0}^{n-2}\left[c(1-x)-\frac{vk}{m}\right]^r,$$

r is used to represent a variable exponent; that is, this expression represents the sum

$$\left[c(1-x)-\frac{vk}{m}\right]^0 + \left[c(1-x)-\frac{vk}{m}\right] + \cdots + \left[c(1-x)-\frac{vk}{m}\right]^{n-3} + \left[c(1-x)-\frac{vk}{m}\right]^{n-2}$$

or, since any number raised to the zero power is unity,

$$1 + \left[c(1-x)-\frac{vk}{m}\right] + \cdots + \left[c(1-x)-\frac{vk}{m}\right]^{n-3} + \left[c(1-x)-\frac{vk}{m}\right]^{n-2}.$$

This sum is found in the following way:

a)   Consider the partial sum

$$\frac{\Delta Y_t}{\Delta G^*} = 1 + \left[c(1-x)-\frac{vk}{m}\right] + \left[c(1-x)-\frac{vk}{m}\right]^2 + \cdots + \left[c(1-x)-\frac{vk}{m}\right]^{t-2}.$$

b)   Multiply both sides of this expression by the term $-\left[c(1-x)-\frac{vk}{m}\right]$:

$$-\left[c(1-x)-\frac{vk}{m}\right]\frac{\Delta Y_t}{\Delta G^*} = -\left[c(1-x)-\frac{vk}{m}\right] - \left[c(1-x)-\frac{vk}{m}\right]^2 - \cdots$$
$$-\left[c(1-x)-\frac{vk}{m}\right]^{t-2} - \left[c(1-x)-\frac{vk}{m}\right]^{t-1}.$$

c) Add these two equations (note that all the terms on the right-hand side cancel out except the first term of (*a*) and the last term of (*b*)):

$$\frac{\Delta Y_t}{\Delta G^*} - \left[c(1 - x) - \frac{vk}{m} \right] \frac{\Delta Y_t}{\Delta G^*} = 1 - \left[c(1 - x) - \frac{vk}{m} \right]^{t-1}.$$

d) Factor $\Delta Y_t / \Delta G^*$ out of the left-hand side of this equation, and multiply both sides by $1/\left[1 - c(1 - x) + \dfrac{vk}{m} \right]$:

$$\frac{\Delta Y_t}{\Delta G^*} = \frac{1}{1 - c(1 - x) + \dfrac{vk}{m}} \left\{ 1 - \left[c(1 - x) - \frac{vk}{m} \right]^{t-1} \right\}.$$

(Note: this is the general expression for the truncated multiplier.)

e) Let *t* approach infinity; then $\left[c(1 - x) - \dfrac{vk}{m} \right]^{t-1}$ approaches zero,

$1 - \left[c(1 - x) - \dfrac{vk}{m} \right]^{t-1}$ approaches unity, and $\Delta Y_t / \Delta G^*$ approaches the static equilibrium value $\Delta Y / \Delta G^*$. Thus, we obtain:

$$\frac{\Delta Y}{\Delta G^*} = \frac{1}{1 - c(1 - x) + \dfrac{vk}{m}}.$$

We have shown that the truncated multiplier approaches the static equilibrium multiplier as the number of periods which have passed since the initial injection of spending becomes very large, just as was demonstrated for the specific numerical examples in Tables VI and VII. In the present case, also, the truncated multiplier is zero for the first period and unity in the second period; after that its value rises steadily until it approaches the limiting value represented by the static equilibrium multiplier.

If the potential impact of a change in government spending on income is being studied, interest is focused on the resulting income level within a year, or some other relatively short period of time; it is not very useful to know what the new equilibrium level of income will be, since that level will not occur until an infinite amount of time has passed. Thus, the speed with which the multiplier process works is a matter of great practical significance, and this speed, measured in terms of calendar time, can be said to depend on two factors:

1. The number of unit time periods required to achieve some specified portion of the total ultimate effect; and
2. The length of a unit time period expressed in weeks or months.

The first of these factors, the number of time periods required, depends upon all of the marginal propensities and sensitivities in the multiplier expression—the marginal propensity to consume out of disposable income (*c*), the marginal propensity to pay taxes out of GNP (*x*), the marginal sensitivity of investment spending to the rate of interest (*v*), the marginal sensitivity of the demand for money balances to income (*k*), and the marginal sensitivity of the demand for money balances to the rate of interest (*m*). (If the model contained a supply-of-money relationship, instead of treating the money supply as fixed by the government, the number of periods required would also depend on the marginal sensitivity of the supply of money balances to the interest rate (e).) The nature of this dependence is illustrated in Table IX by a number of numerical examples involving various values of the marginal propensity to consume and the marginal propensity to pay taxes. We are omitting the monetary sector in this illustration (assuming, in effect, that $v = 0$) as a means of keeping the presentation relatively simple, so that the calculations in Table IX are based on Model IIA. The table is divided into four main sections, one each for marginal propensities

TABLE IX   THE SPEED OF THE MULTIPLIER FOR VARIOUS COMBINATIONS OF THE MARGINAL PROPENSITY TO CONSUME OUT OF DISPOSABLE INCOME (c) AND THE MARGINAL PROPENSITY TO COLLECT TAXES OUT OF TOTAL INCOME (x), BASED ON MODEL IIA†

	1	2	3	4	5
	Marginal Propensity to Collect Taxes Out of Income (x)	Static Multiplier Value	Value of Truncated Multiplier at End of Fifth Period‡	Percent of Total Income Change Achieved by End of Fifth Period (3) ÷ (2) × 100	Number of Periods Needed to Achieve at Least 90% of Total Income Change§
$c = .9$					
	.2	3.57	2.61	73.1%	9
	.3	2.70	2.27	84.1	6
	.4	2.17	1.99	91.7	5
$c = .8$					
	.2	2.78	2.31	83.1	7
	.3	2.27	2.05	90.3	5
	.4	1.92	1.82	94.7	5
$c = .7$					
	.2	2.27	2.05	90.3	5
	.3	1.96	1.85	94.4	5
	.4	1.72	1.67	97.1	4
$c = .6$					
	.2	1.92	1.82	94.8	5
	.3	1.72	1.67	97.1	4
	.4	1.56	1.53	98.3	4

† In this table, the speed of the multiplier is measured in terms only of the number of periods needed to achieve 90 percent of the total change in income, and the change in income achieved by the end of the fifth period. The period referred to is the period required to adjust production to sales.

‡ This value is computed from the formula

$$\frac{\Delta Y}{\Delta G^*} = \frac{1}{1 - c(1 - x)} \{1 - [c(1 - x)]^{t-1}\}$$

when $t = 5$. This is the general expression for the truncated multiplier for model IIA.

§ This value is calculated through the use of an expression for the ratio $\frac{\Delta Y_t}{\Delta Y}$, which can be found from the general expressions for the truncated multiplier and the static multiplier given on p. 32 (assuming $v = 0$) as follows:

$$\frac{\Delta Y_t}{\Delta Y} = \frac{\Delta Y_t/\Delta G^*}{\Delta Y/\Delta G^*} = \frac{\{1 - [c(1 - x)]^{t-1}\}/[1 - c(1 - x)]}{1/[1 - c(1 - x)]}$$
$$= 1 - [c(1 - x)]^{t-1}.$$

To find the number of periods needed to achieve 90 percent of the total change in income, set $\frac{\Delta Y_t}{\Delta Y}$ equal to 0.9 and solve for t:

$$0.9 = 1 - [c(1 - x)]^{t-1},$$
so
$$[c(1 - x)]^{t-1} = 0.1.$$

Using logarithms, we have
$$(t - 1) \log[c(1 - x)] = \log 0.1;$$
$$t \log[c(1 - x)] = \log 0.1 + \log[c(1 - x)]$$
and
$$t = \frac{\log 0.1 + \log[c(1 - x)]}{\log[c(1 - x)]}.$$

to consume of 90 percent, 80 percent, 70 percent, and 60 percent. For each value of the marginal propensity to consume, multiplier calculations are presented for marginal propensities to pay taxes of 20 percent, 30 percent, and 40 percent. The values of the static equilibrium multiplier, as shown in column 2, decline as the marginal propensity to consume declines and as the marginal propensity to pay taxes increases. The same is true of the truncated multiplier calculated after five periods, as shown in column 3. It is interesting to note, however, that large multipliers work *relatively* more slowly than do smaller multipliers. Thus, while larger static multipliers (column 2) are associated with larger multipliers after five periods (column 3), the *percentage* of the total multiplier effect that is achieved at the end of five periods is smaller for large than for small multipliers, as is shown in column 4. Column 5 brings out this same tendency in a different way: it shows that the number of time periods needed to achieve 90 percent of the total static multiplier effect is larger for large than for small multipliers.

The second factor determining the speed of the multiplier, the length of a unit multiplier time period, is the subject of the Ackley article included in Part A of this chapter. The article shows that the effects produced in a given "round" of multiplier expansion are spread out over time rather than all occurring at once and that the lags differ according to the type of expenditure involved. Thus, the time period is best viewed as a kind of average. Moreover, the time period varies according to the reaction times of businessmen in adjusting inventories and production rates. The article is analytical rather than empirical—that is, it makes no real effort to estimate the actual length of the period. Indeed, there has been little or no significant empirical research on the multiplier time period.

It may be useful to indicate at least in a crude way the probable dimensions of the speed of the multiplier. If we take the time period to be one quarter of a year, an estimate that seems not unreasonable based on the Ackley article, and take the marginal propensity to consume (c) to be 90 percent and the marginal propensity to pay taxes (x) to be 40 percent, values which are fairly realistic, the static multiplier is 2.17, and the multiplier applicable after five periods, or 15 months, is 1.99. Thus, according to this estimate, a sustained increase of $10 billion in the annual rate of government purchases should raise GNP, expressed at annual rates, by about $20 billion after five quarters or 15 months.

Attention should perhaps be called explicitly to four important assumptions underlying this discussion. First, as we have already pointed out, no allowance is made in the model used to analyze the speed of the multiplier for the restraining effect of the monetary sector. We have assumed that this effect is inoperative; that is, we suppose that the real and monetary sectors of the model are unrelated, or, alternatively, that the Federal Reserve supplies enough bank reserves to enable the money supply to meet the rising demand for money associated with increasing GNP without any increase in interest rates. If these assumptions are erroneous, the expansion will produce a "feedback" effect which will push up interest rates. This will reduce the size of the static multiplier, as we already know. Using the analysis on which Table IX is based, we can also infer the effects on the speed of the multiplier of changes in the size of the various monetary sensitivities. The larger the interest sensitivities of the demand for money and the supply of money, the larger the static multiplier but the slower the multiplier process (in the sense represented by the calculations in Table IX). In other words, increases in m and e have the same effect on multiplier speed as increases in c. On the other hand, increases in the interest sensitivity of investment, v, or in the income sensitivity of the demand for money, k, have similar effects on the speed of the multiplier. The larger is either of these, the smaller the static multiplier value, but the more rapid the multiplier process.

The second assumption we have made is that there are sufficient unutilized resources to enable the expansion to take place without any appreciable effect on the price level. This assumption was emphasized earlier, in our comparison of Neoclassical and Keynesian views on monetary and fiscal policy, but it deserves repeating here. The situation will be different if the economy is operating close to full employment so that an increase in government spending will have its main effect on prices and only a moderate impact on output and employment. Third, no allowance is made for the possibility—indeed, probability—that businessmen will attempt to maintain or build up their inventories in the course of the expansion. If this were allowed for, it would undoubtedly raise the multipliers somewhat above the levels indicated.[19] Fourth, no consideration is given—either in this example or elsewhere in our discussion—to the possibility that an expansion of the multiplier type may induce an increase in private investment. This is, however, a likely possibility because the expanded sales will increase business profits and because the expanded production will increase the extent of utilization of existing plant and equipment. If such an increase in investment does occur, it is likely to add another important dimension to the expansion—in effect, raising the multiplier well above the levels we have been discussing. However, we have not attempted to include this possibility because, while the response of consumption to income changes is reasonably predictable, the investment response is a good deal less dependable, less well understood, and more likely to depend in a major way on the circumstances in which the expansion occurs.[20]

Some quantitative estimates of the size of the multiplier can be obtained from econometric models of the U.S. economy. One such model has been constructed and progressively refined by the Research Seminar in Quantitative Economics at the University of Michigan. This model is quite detailed, containing several dozen behavioral equations; however, it is basically similar to Model II, having equations to describe the behavior of households, firms, and the government sector. The coefficients are estimated statistically on the basis of past behavior of the variables. Some of the typical multiplier values yielded by this model, based on the latest available estimates of its coefficients, are as follows.[21]

---

[19] Actually the introduction of inventory investment complicates the analysis considerably. Since in full equilibrium inventories would presumably have reached the level in relation to sales that businessmen desired, there would, under these conditions, be no further additions to inventories. For this reason, inventory investment would have no effect on the static equilibrium multiplier. However, it would greatly affect the time path of movement from one equilibrium position to another; indeed, inventory investment may introduce a self-generating cycle in economic activity. In any case it would increase the effective truncated multipliers for the early stages of the expansion. See Lloyd A. Metzler, "The Nature and Stability of Inventory Cycles," *Review of Economic Statistics*, Vol. XXIII (August 1941), pp. 113–29.

[20] For a discussion of the multiplier effects of tax reduction, including probable effects on investment, see the selection entitled "The Effects of Tax Reduction on Output and Employment," from the *Annual Report of the Council of Economic Advisers*, January 1963, reprinted in Chapter 4 of this book.

[21] A discussion of the basic principles underlying the derivation of models such as this is found in Daniel B. Suits, "Forecasting and Analysis with an Econometric Model," *American Economic*

	Increase of $1 Billion in:		
	Government Purchases of Goods and Services	Private Investment in Plant and Equipment	Federal Income Tax Collections
Effect on GNP after one year...........	$1.7 billion	$1.8 billion	−$1.0 billion

This model, like all such econometric models of the economy, is dynamic in nature: that is, a change in (say) government purchases will set off a sequence of adjustments. However, it is important to note that the time unit used in such models is not an analytical multiplier time period but is rather some arbitrary unit of calendar time, usually a quarter or a year. The reason for this, of course, is that empirical observations on the variables are not available for such an essentially unmeasurable and irregular period as the multiplier time period. The model referred to above is based on quarterly observations on the variables, and the multipliers in the above table relate to the estimated effects in the first year.

(b) Lags Associated with Adjustments in Monetary and Fiscal Policy

In addition to the lags involved in the working of the multiplier discussed above, there are further lags related to adjustments in monetary and fiscal policy that need to be considered. These lags are presented schematically in the following diagram, which relates specifically to monetary policy.

The process is assumed to start with a change in the economic situation which calls for some adjustment in monetary policy. For example, there might be a slowdown in the expansion of GNP and a rise in unemployment which calls for a shift toward a more expansionary Federal Reserve policy. The time when this occurs is indicated by the caption "action needed," at the left-hand end of the time scale.

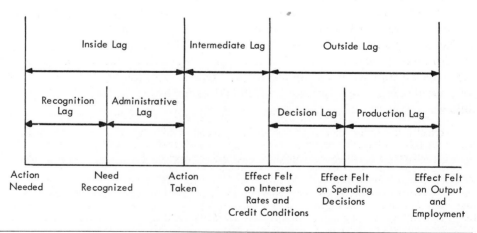

Review, Vol. LII (March 1962), pp. 104–32. The structure of the present model is described in Saul H. Hymans and Harold T. Shapiro, "The Michigan Quarterly Econometric Model of the U.S. Economy," in *The Economic Outlook for 1973: Papers and Proceedings of the Twentieth Annual Conference on the Economic Outlook* (Ann Arbor: Research Seminar in Quantitative Economics, University of Michigan, 1973), pp. 114–55. The multiplier values given in the text are based on the most recent (June 1973) revision of that model.

Three main elements in the lag in monetary policy adjustments can be distinguished:

1. The *inside lag*. This is the lag within the Federal Reserve System between the time action is needed and the time the action is actually taken. This lag can be broken into two subdivisions: (*a*) the *recognition lag* between the time action is needed and the time the need is recognized by the Federal Reserve authorities, and (*b*) the *administrative lag* between the time the need for action is recognized and the time the action (such as open market purchases of U.S. government securities) is actually taken. The length of the recognition lag presumably depends on the efficiency of the Federal Reserve in collecting and interpreting data relating to economic conditions. As a result of the organizational independence and flexibility of the Federal Reserve System, the administrative lag is presumably very short. These matters are discussed in several of the selections in Chapters 3 and 5.

2. The *intermediate lag*. This is the lag between the time the Federal Reserve takes action and the time the action produces a sufficient effect on interest rates (and other credit terms) to influence spending decisions significantly. The length of this lag depends on the behavior of commercial banks and other financial institutions and the functioning of financial markets—matters which are discussed in the selections in Chapters 2 and 5.

3. The *outside lag*. This is the lag between the change in interest rates (and credit conditions) and the initial impact on production and employment. This lag can be subdivided into two parts: (*a*) the *decision lag* between the change in interest rates and the change in spending decisions, and (*b*) the *production lag* between changes in spending decisions and the related initial changes in production and employment. It should be noted that the production lag referred to here is in principle the same lag between changes in sales and changes in production that formed the basis for our earlier discussion of the multiplier time period. However, in this case, we are not discussing the full cumulative multiplier effects but merely the "first round" effects of the change in policy. After the effects discussed here had occurred, the multiplier process would take over and produce further effects not here taken into account.

The selection by Hamburger in Chapter 5 discusses the lags in monetary policy, paying particular attention to the production lag. The analysis includes investment in new housing and other consumer durables as well as business investment in inventories and in plant and equipment, and addresses itself to the magnitude of the effects of changes in interest rates on investment decisions in these various categories as well as to the lags in the appearance of these effects. It should be pointed out that there has been some controversy concerning the lags in monetary policy. It is an area in which research is just beginning, and the findings summarized by Hamburger should be taken, in general, as preliminary and suggestive rather than as in any sense conclusive.

For fiscal policy, the recognition lag is likely to be about the same as for monetary policy, since there is no reason to suppose that the economic intelligence apparatus of the authorities responsible for fiscal policy is either more or less efficient than that of the monetary authorities. However, the administrative lag for fiscal policy is likely to be much longer than that for monetary policy. This is especially true for tax adjustments, which ordinarily require a long (and uncertain) process of executive recommendation and legislative action. Changes in government expenditures may also require legislative action; however, even if all that is involved is a speedup of expenditures on projects that have already been approved by Congress, substantial time is likely to be needed to prepare plans and activate projects. All in all, the inside lag is likely to be much longer for fiscal than for monetary policy. On the other hand, the intermediate lag—which, in the case of fiscal policy, is the lag between the time when action is taken and the time when income or spending is affected—is likely to be much shorter for fiscal than for monetary policy. The decision lag also may be short—indeed, there is no such lag for changes in government purchases of goods and services. Since the production lag is in principle no different for fiscal than for monetary policy—although it may depend on the kind of expenditures that are involved—the outside lag is likely to be shorter for fiscal policy. To summarize:

> Inside lag........................longer for fiscal policy
> Intermediate lag..................shorter for fiscal policy
> Outside lag......................shorter for fiscal policy

Because of the much greater length of the administrative component of the inside lag, the overall lag for fiscal policy may frequently be longer than for monetary policy. Note, however, that the long administrative lag is not inherent in fiscal policy, but is capable of being shortened greatly by changes in administrative arrangements. If this could be done—for example, by giving the President some authority to make countercyclical adjustments in tax rates, as recommended in the reading in Chapter 4 by the Council of Economic Advisers entitled "Formulating Fiscal Policy"—fiscal policy might become more quick-acting than monetary policy. An interesting study of the lags involved in a particular episode—the 1964 tax reduction—is presented by Arthur Okun in his paper in Chapter 4.

THE INTEREST RATE, THE PRICE LEVEL, AND AGGREGATE OUTPUT

Robert S. Holbrook*

I. INTRODUCTION

Discussions of short-run income determination usually make use of the well-known *IS–LM* curve analysis,[1] in which real income and the rate of interest occupy the center of the stage. The price level, if it is allowed to vary at all, seldom appears explicitly, and does most of its work behind the scenes. In the typical presentation the price level is unaffected by variations in aggregate demand, so long as some arbitrary "full-employment" level is not exceeded. Once this full-employment level has been attained, however, further increases

* Robert S. Holbrook is Associate Professor of Economics, University of Michigan.

The author wishes to express his appreciation to Professors W. L. Smith, R. L. Teigen, and B. Munk, and to Harvey Rosen, for their suggestions and encouragement. The author regretfully accepts full responsibility for those errors and ambiguities which remain.

[1] This analysis was first developed by J. R. Hicks, in "Mr. Keynes and the 'Classics': A Suggested Interpretation," *Econometrica*, Vol. V (April 1937), pp. 147–59. It is now very widely used as an expositional device in macroeconomic textbooks, e.g., M. J. Bailey, *National Income and the Price Level* (New York: McGraw-Hill, 1962), pp. 19–83; G. Ackley, *Macroeconomic Theory* (New York: Macmillan, 1961), pp. 369–87; and T. F. Dernburg and D. M. McDougall, *Macroeconomics* (New York: McGraw-Hill, 1968), pp. 161–75.

in demand result only in rising prices, without any increase in output. The price level is thus a sort of *deus ex machina* which is called upon when necessary, but does not play an active role throughout the analysis.

This paper uses a modified version of the usual technique and brings the price level directly into the analysis from the beginning. The relationships between the price level and aggregate demand and supply will be illustrated through the derivation of aggregate demand and supply curves. These curves will then be used to examine the implications of several alternative assumptions about the nature of the underlying economic relationships.

Section II presents a quick review of the standard model of aggregate demand without a supply constraint and with fixed prices. Its purpose is primarily to familiarize the reader with the notation and techniques which are used later in the more complex analysis. In Section III the price level is permitted to vary, and an aggregate demand curve is derived. Sections IV and V introduce aggregate supply curves under the assumptions of flexible and rigid money wages, respectively, and examine the policy implications of these alternatives. Section VI concludes the body of the paper, and is followed by an appendix which presents an exact solution for some multipliers which are only described in Section V.

II. DEMAND WHEN PRICES ARE CONSTANT

Since the emphasis here is on the development of an expositional method, the model will be kept as simple as possible and almost all equations will be linear. It is assumed that the reader is familiar with the theory underlying the typical model of aggregate demand, and each equation will not be discussed in detail here. For such a discussion the reader is referred to any good macro-economics text.[2]

The initial version of the model assumes a fixed price level, and can be written as follows:

$$C = C_o + cY_d \qquad \text{(consumption function)} \qquad (1)$$
$$I = I_o - vr \qquad \text{(investment function)} \qquad (2)$$
$$Y_d = Y - T \qquad \text{(definition of disposable income)} \qquad (3)$$
$$T = T^* + xY \qquad \text{(tax function)} \qquad (4)$$
$$G = G^* \qquad \text{(government expenditures)} \qquad (5)$$
$$Y = C + I + G \qquad \text{(equilibrium condition)} \qquad (6)$$
$$M_d = s + kY - ur \qquad \text{(demand for money)} \qquad (7)$$
$$M_s = M^* \qquad \text{(supply of money)} \qquad (8)$$
$$M_s = M_d \qquad \text{(equilibrium condition)} \qquad (9)$$

The symbols are defined as follows, all in real terms:

$$C = \text{consumption expenditures}$$
$$I = \text{investment expenditures}$$
$$Y_d = \text{disposable income}$$
$$Y = \text{national income (or GNP)}$$
$$T = \text{taxes}$$
$$G = \text{government expenditures on goods and services}$$
$$M_d = \text{the amount of money demanded}$$
$$M_s = \text{the amount of money supplied}$$
$$r = \text{the rate of interest.}$$

---

[2] See, for example, those cited in note 1.

An asterisk beside a variable (i.e., M^*, T^*, and G^*) implies that it is a policy tool whose value is exogenously determined.[3] The first six equations can be solved for Y in terms of r to obtain the equation for the IS curve:

$$Y = \frac{C_o + I_o + G^* - cT^*}{1 - c(1 - x)} - \frac{v}{1 - c(1 - x)} r, \tag{10}$$

while the solution to the final three equations yields the LM curve,

$$r = \frac{s - M^*}{u} + \frac{k}{u} Y. \tag{11}$$

These curves are plotted in Figure 1. Their point of intersection (r', Y') simulta-

FIGURE 1

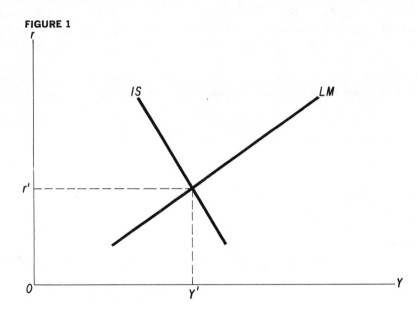

neously satisfies the equilibrium condition in each market, and thus represents a solution for the entire system of nine equations.

These equilibrium values can also be obtained by substituting the value for r in (11) into (10). This yields

$$Y' = \frac{C_o + I_o + G^* - cT^* + \dfrac{v}{u}(M^* - s)}{1 - c(1 - x) + \dfrac{vk}{u}} \tag{12}$$

and a value for r' could be obtained by substituting Y' from (12) in place of Y in (11).

Before introducing the price level explicitly, it is useful to examine the implications for this simple preliminary model of various restrictions on the equations. In this way the reader will become more familiar with the relationships between the equations and the diagrams and will gain facility in moving from one to the other. This facility will prove useful during discussions of the more complex

---

[3] To be perfectly correct, the coefficient of income in the tax function should also have an asterisk, since it is also policy-determined. This asterisk is omitted only to avoid unnecessary multiplication of symbols.

versions of the model later in the paper. Let the interest elasticity of investment be zero, by setting v in (2) equal to zero. This implies that the second term on the right-hand side of (10) is zero, and Y no longer depends on the rate of interest. Given the value for Y, the quantity of money then determines the rate of interest (in [11]), but has no effect on aggregate demand. In this case, the *IS* curve in Figure 1 becomes vertical, and (12) reduces to

$$Y' = \frac{C_o + I_o + G^* - cT^*}{1 - c(1 - x)}.$$

Another possibility is that the demand for money is not responsive to the interest rate, i.e., that $u = 0$ in (7). Multiply both numerator and denominator of (12) by u before setting it equal to zero; the result is

$$Y' = \frac{M^* - s}{k} \tag{13}$$

and Y is now determined by the money stock. The presence of s in the numerator of (13) allows for some desired minimum (or asset) balances which are unresponsive to the rate of interest. If s and u are both zero, (13) reduces to the pure quantity theory result. In either case, the *LM* curve in Figure 1 becomes vertical.

A third possibility is that the *LM* curve is horizontal, the liquidity trap situation. In this case (7), (8), and (9) can be replaced with the single equation,

$$r = r_o. \tag{14}$$

In this case, (10) determines Y', and the money stock plays no role.

A convenient way to characterize the results of these changes in the underlying assumptions is to examine the effect of each change on the various policy multipliers. Table 1 shows the multipliers for government expenditures and the

TABLE 1   INCOME MULTIPLIERS UNDER ALTERNATIVE ASSUMPTIONS
(fixed prices)

Restrictions on the Model	$\dfrac{\Delta Y}{\Delta G^*}$	$\dfrac{\Delta Y}{\Delta M^*}$
A. None	$\dfrac{1}{1 - c(1 - x) + \dfrac{vk}{u}}$	$\dfrac{1}{\dfrac{u}{v}[1 - c(1 - x)] + k}$
B. Interest elasticity of investment $= 0$ $(v = 0)$	$\dfrac{1}{1 - c(1 - x)}$	0
C. Interest elasticity of demand for money $= 0$ $(u = 0)$	0	$\dfrac{1}{k}$
D. Liquidity trap $(r = r_o)$	$\dfrac{1}{1 - c(1 - x)}$	0

money supply under the alternative assumptions just discussed. With the aid of the table, the policy implications of the assumptions should be quite clear. Fiscal policy (changes in G^* or T^*) has its greatest impact in cases B and D, while monetary policy is impotent. Precisely the opposite conclusion follows in case C.

Although s and u do not figure in the equation of the *LM* curve when it is horizontal, (14), it will be useful to examine what happens to them as the

curve becomes more nearly horizontal. The typical curvilinear liquidity preference curve is shown in Figure 2 as *GBH*, where M_a is the asset demand for

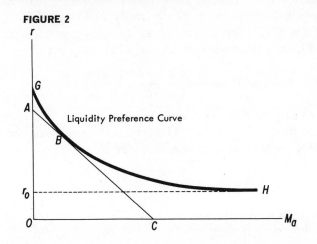

FIGURE 2

Liquidity Preference Curve

real money balances, as distinguished from the transactions demand (assumed
to equal kY).[4] The line *ABC* is tangent to *GBH* at *B*, and serves as an approximation to the true relationship between r and M_a in that neighborhood.

This tangent is the curve represented by the equation

$$M_a = s - ur. \tag{15}$$

Clearly, s is the value of M_a when r is zero, and is equal to the distance *OC*.
Similarly, $-u$ is the reciprocal of the slope of the curve in the vicinity of *B*, and
is equal to minus the ratio of *OC* to *OA*. As *B* moves farther to the right along
the liquidity preference curve, *OA* becomes progressively smaller and *OC* larger,
and both s and u become very large.[5]

Figure 3 depicts the values of s and u which obtain for each of several

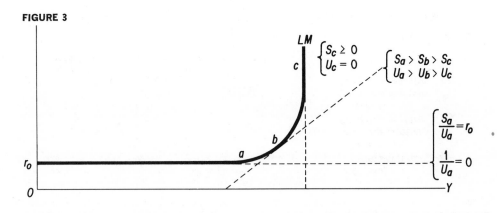

FIGURE 3

---

[4] For a discussion of the demand for money and its separation into asset and transactions
demands, see, for example, Dernburg and McDougall, *op. cit.*, pp. 136–47.

[5] As the curve approaches the horizontal, it can be shown that the ratio of s to u approaches
r_o, and making this substitution in (12) while letting u become very large will result in a return to (10), with r_o in place of r. The reader may already have noted that (15) is reversed
from the normal "slope-intercept" form, as are many other equations in this paper and the
economic literature, generally.

segments of the *LM* curve, on the assumption that there is some minimum interest rate, r_o (which may be zero), and that the liquidity preference curve becomes progressively steeper at higher rates of interest. These relationships will be useful in the next section, where the slope of the *LM* curve becomes of crucial importance.

III. DEMAND WHEN PRICES ARE VARIABLE

In this section a change in the price level is assumed to affect aggregate demand in two ways. The first is through an accompanying change in the real money stock. Let the monetary authorities control only the nominal stock of money and replace (8) with

$$M_s = \frac{m^*}{p}, \tag{16}$$

where p is the price level.[6] The second effect of the price level is in the tax equation, (4). Assume that the tax law is written in nominal terms, such that nominal tax revenue is a certain number of dollars (t^*) plus a fixed fraction of nominal income. This can be written as

$$pT = t^* + xpY \tag{17}$$

or

$$T = \frac{t^*}{p} + xY. \tag{18}$$

After making the substitutions of (16) for (8) and (18) for (4), the *IS* and *LM* curves can again be obtained. The solution for the *LM* curve is presented in a slightly different format than before, for the sake of convenience in the discussion of Figure 5, below.

$$Y = \frac{C_o + I_o + G^*}{1 - c(1 - x)} - \frac{ct^*}{1 - c(1 - x)}\left(\frac{1}{p}\right) - \frac{v}{1 - c(1 - x)} r \quad (IS \text{ curve}) \tag{19}$$

$$Y = \frac{m^*}{k}\left(\frac{1}{p}\right) - \frac{s}{k} + \frac{u}{k} r \quad (LM \text{ curve}) \tag{20}$$

A change in the price level can be seen to affect the positions of the two curves, but not their slopes. A rise in the price level shifts the *LM* curve to the left and is equivalent to a reduction in M^* as described in Section II. The effect of a price change on the *IS* curve depends on the sign of t^*. Assume that the average tax rate, $\frac{T}{Y}$, increases with income, which implies that t^* must be negative (for a linear tax function).[7] On this assumption, the *IS* curve also moves to the

---

[6] "Nominal" refers to the "current dollar" or "money" value, as opposed to the "constant dollar" or "real" value. The nominal value of a variable can be deflated to its real value by dividing by the price level.

[7] The average tax rate is

$$\frac{T}{Y} = \frac{\dfrac{t^*}{p} + xY}{Y} = \frac{t^*}{pY} + x.$$

Since x and p are both positive, if T/Y is to be an increasing function of Y, t^* must be negative.

left as prices rise, since tax revenue at a given real income level will be larger, with no offsetting expenditure increase.

These equations for the IS and LM curves can be combined as before to obtain solutions for Y and r, but this time they are each functions of the price level. The solution for Y is:

$$Y = \frac{C_o + I_o + G^* - \dfrac{vs}{u}}{1 - c(1 - x) + \dfrac{vk}{u}} + \frac{\dfrac{vm^*}{u} - ct^*}{1 - c(1 - x) + \dfrac{vk}{u}} \left(\frac{1}{p}\right). \qquad (21)$$

Inspection of (21) reveals that it is a rectangular hyperbola, which approaches the Y axis as p approaches zero, as shown in Figure 4. As p becomes larger the second term on the right-hand side of (21) approaches zero, and Y becomes equal to the first term alone. This curve is seriously deficient, however, in that it is applicable only for a fixed pair of values for s and u. As the price level varies, the LM curve shifts; as it shifts, its slope at the intersection with the IS curve changes; and as its slope changes, the values of s and u are changing. The effect of these changes on the shape of the curve in Figure 4 must be

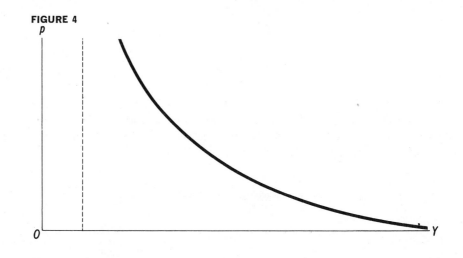

FIGURE 4

examined before it will be possible to construct a curve which accurately reflects the effect on aggregate demand of a change in the price level.[8]

The procedure to be used is a combination of an analytical and graphical approach. Figure 5 shows a series of IS and LM curves drawn for different price levels and based on (19) and (20). So that these curves will be evenly spaced, the interval chosen (say J) is fixed in terms of the reciprocal of the price level $\left(\text{i.e., } \dfrac{1}{p_1} - \dfrac{1}{p_2} = \dfrac{1}{p_2} - \dfrac{1}{p_3} = \dfrac{1}{p_i} - \dfrac{1}{p_{i+1}} = J \right)$. The IS curve for a price level equal to p_i is shifted to the right of the IS curve for p_{i+1} by an

---

[8] It is likely that most, if not all, of the relationships described in (1) through (9) are really nonlinear, and a full exposition would have to examine the implications of all these nonlinearities. This paper is concerned primarily with the implications of a nonlinear liquidity preference curve, as it is this issue which tends to dominate elementary discussions of the determinants of aggregate demand.

FIGURE 5

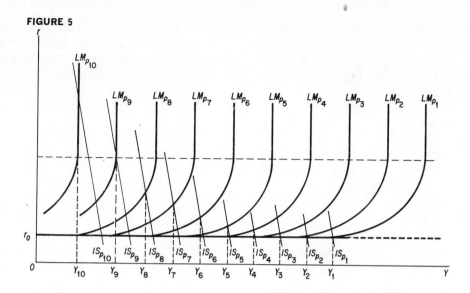

amount equal to $\dfrac{J\,ct^*}{1 - c(1 - x)}$. Similarly, the LM curve for price level p_i is shifted to the right of the LM curve for p_{i+1} by an amount equal to $\dfrac{Jm^{*}}{k}$.[9]

It is useful to examine the nature of the solution in the two limiting cases for the LM curve. When the LM curve is vertical (s and u both equal to zero), (21) can be reduced to[10]

$$Y = \frac{m^*}{k}\left(\frac{1}{p}\right). \tag{22}$$

For any price level above p_9, (22) describes the relation between output and the price level, and this is illustrated in Figure 6 by the hyperbola ABE (only the solid portion AB above p_9 is operative).[11]

At the other extreme, when the LM curve is horizontal at r_o, (21) becomes

$$Y = \frac{C_o + I_o + G^* - vr_o}{1 - c(1 - x)} - \frac{ct^*}{1 - c(1 - x)}\left(\frac{1}{p}\right). \tag{23}$$

This is another hyperbola, with its vertical asymptote offset to the right from the p axis by an amount equal to the first term. The important question which must be answered is whether this hyperbola is above or below ABE when the price level is such that the economy is in the liquidity trap. Figure 5 shows that the level of income actually realized when the economy first reaches the liquidity trap (Y_2) is considerably less than that which would have occurred

---

[9] The diagram is based on the assumption that

$$\frac{m_0}{k} > \frac{-ct^*}{1 - c(1 - x)}.$$

It seems reasonable to suppose that this would be true for an actual economy, but the reader may be interested in examining the implications of the alternative assumption.

[10] This solution can be obtained by multiplying both the numerator and denominator by u, before setting u equal to zero.

[11] The curves in Figure 6 are not drawn to the same scale as those in Figure 5, but are exaggerated in the interest of clarity.

if the *LM* curve had been vertical throughout.[12] Thus, the hyperbola generated by (23) will be below the one generated by (22) at any price level below that at which we enter the liquidity trap region of the *LM* curve.[13] This hyperbola is drawn in Figure 6 as *FCD*, and the relevant portion is the segment labeled *CD*.

FIGURE 6

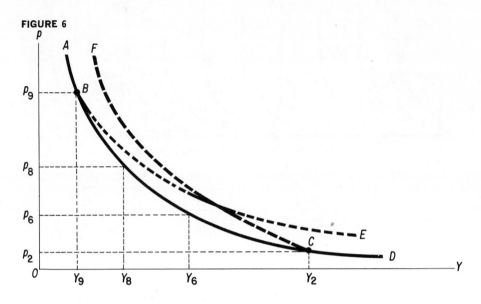

The two segments *AB* and *CD* have been constructed, and the only problem which remains is to construct the missing link (*BC*). This intermediate segment is composed of a continuous series of points, each of which lies on a hyperbola whose equation (21) depends on the values of *u* and *s* at that point. It is possible to work through the problem analytically, but the solution is more easily obtained through another examination of Figure 5.

Start at the right end of Figure 5, in the liquidity trap situation, and let prices rise. The *IS* and *LM* curves shift to the left, the interest rate begins to rise, and income will be less than it would have been had the interest rate remained at r_o.[14] Thus, as the price level rises, the economy traces out a path below and to the left of *FCD*.

Now start at the left end of Figure 5, where the intersection is in the vertical portion of the *LM* curve, and let prices fall. The *IS* and *LM* curves move to the right, the interest rate begins to fall, but the asset demand for money becomes greater than zero and prevents the rate from falling as far as it would in the absence of such an asset demand.[15] Thus, again, income will be less

---

[12] The relevant curve at this point is LM_{p2}. The argument is essentially that LM_{p2} becomes vertical at some point considerably to the right of Y_2. Thus, if the *LM* curves did not slope down and to the left, but were entirely vertical (as assumed in deriving *ABE*), the level of income would be greater than Y_2 when the price level was p_2.

[13] This will actually be true for somewhat higher price levels as well, and the point of intersection could easily be calculated.

[14] Figure 5 shows that when the price level rises from p_2 to p_3 the *LM* curve shifts far enough to the left so that the *IS* curve (which also shifts to the left) intersects it at an interest rate higher than r_o. If the *LM* curve had not begun to slope upward, the *IS* curve would have intersected it at r_o, and income would have been slightly larger than Y_3.

[15] For example, when the price level falls from p_9 to p_8, both curves shift to the right, but their intersection is to the left of the vertical portion of LM_{p8}.

than it would have been had the *LM* curve remained vertical, and the economy traces out a path below and to the left of *ABE* as prices fall below p_9. Eventually these paths meet, completing the segment *BC* which lies to the left of the two curves generated earlier. The entire curve *ABCD* will be called the "aggregate demand curve."[16]

It is useful to examine the effects of fiscal and monetary policy on the aggregate demand curve just derived. An increase in government expenditure shifts the *IS* curve to the right by an amount determined by the multiplier, and it could be expected that the aggregate demand curve will respond in a similar fashion. By examining (21) and (23), it can be seen that a larger value for G^* will indeed result in a larger value for Y (given a value for the price level). Above point *B*, however, where (22) is the controlling equation (and the *LM* curve in Figure 5 is vertical) a change in G^* has no impact on demand (which is determined entirely by the real money stock). The result is a shift only in the *BCD* portion of the curve, as illustrated in part A of Figure 7.

FIGURE 7

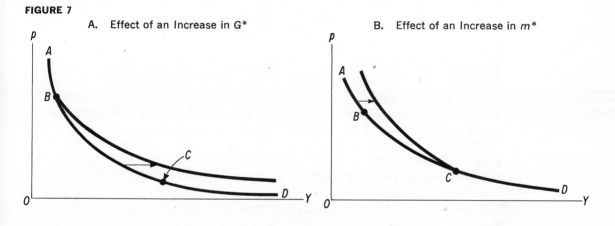

A. Effect of an Increase in G*

B. Effect of an Increase in *m**

The effect of an increase in the nominal money stock (m^*) with a fixed price level is to shift the *LM* curve to the right. Equations (21) and (22) imply that the *ABC* segment of the demand curve is also shifted to the right. In the liquidity trap case, however, when (23) holds, the nominal money stock is of no consequence. Thus the *CD* segment is unaffected by monetary policy, as is shown in part B of Figure 7. It seems highly probable that the economy is normally operating in the range *BC* of the aggregate demand curve—the range within which the interest elasticity of demand for money is neither zero nor infinitely large and both fiscal and monetary policy are therefore effective.

It is of no value to compute multipliers at this stage, because if the price level is assumed to be constant, the result is the same as that presented earlier in Table 1. But there is as yet no way to predict how the price level will react to policy changes, since the aggregate demand curve only provides us with a set of equally acceptable combinations of price and income. These pairs of values all satisfy the set of equations which are summarized in (21), when s and u are allowed to vary in accordance with the assumed curvature of the

---

[16] There are several macroeconomic texts which make use of versions of this aggregate demand curve in a somewhat different fashion from that used here (e.g., K. C. Kogiku, *An Introduction to Macroeconomic Models* (New York: McGraw-Hill, 1968), and J. Lindauer, *Macroeconomics* (New York: John Wiley, 1968)).

LM curve. By itself, however, the aggregate demand curve does not convey any information about the particular level of income at which the economy will achieve equilibrium.

IV. DEMAND AND SUPPLY WHEN WAGES ARE FLEXIBLE

The "aggregate supply curve" provides a second relationship between output (i.e., income) and the price level, and can be combined with the aggregate demand curve to establish a single pair of values which will satisfy both relationships simultaneously. Let the capital stock be fixed, while labor, the only variable factor of production, is subject to diminishing returns and is paid the value of its marginal product. This latter assumption insures that the demand function for labor is equal to the slope (or the first derivative) of the production function. These assumptions can be represented by the following two equations:

$$Y = eN - \tfrac{1}{2}fN^2 \qquad \text{(production function)} \qquad (24)$$

$$\frac{w}{p} = e - fN_d; \text{ or } N_d = \frac{e}{f} - \frac{1}{f}\left(\frac{w}{p}\right) \qquad \text{(demand for labor)} \qquad (25)$$

The new variables introduced here are N, the number of workers employed; N_d, the number of workers demanded (assumed to be equal to N); and w, the money wage. These curves are depicted in Figure 8 where the real wage which employers are willing to pay (w/p) at a given level of employment is equal to the slope of the production function at that level of employment.

The more interesting element of the labor market (at least in Keynesian income theory) is the supply function; this paper examines the implications of two assumptions about the nature of the supply of labor. One assumption, typically associated with the classical model, is that the supply of labor is an increasing function of the real wage.[17] This assumption is sometimes characterized as one of "flexible wages," since wages are assumed to rise or fall as necessary to bring about an equilibrium in the labor market. The labor supply function for this case is:

$$N_s = g + h\frac{w}{p} \qquad \text{(flexible wages).} \qquad (26)$$

and the equilibrium condition is represented by:

$$N_d = N_s \qquad \text{(equilibrium condition).} \qquad (27)$$

The more interesting assumption about the supply of labor is that workers will supply any amount of labor demanded up to some limit at the existing money wage, but will not offer any labor at a lower money wage. This situation will be characterized as one in which "money wages are rigid downward." This section presents the case of flexible wages and derives an aggregate supply curve under that assumption, leaving the rigid wage case to Section V.

By substituting (25) and (26) into (27), an equilibrium value of the real

---

[17] Most of the analysis does not require that it be an increasing function; it could be vertical or even "backward bending" so long as it is steeper than the labor demand curve at their intersection.

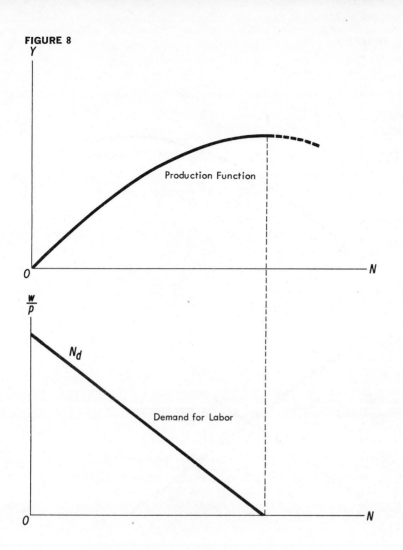

FIGURE 8

Y

Production Function

0   N

$\frac{w}{p}$

N_d

Demand for Labor

0   N

wage, $\left(\frac{w}{p}\right)$, can be obtained. In a similar fashion one can solve for equilibrium quantities of labor employed (N'), and of output (Y'). These relationships are shown graphically in Figure 9.[18]

Figure 10 depicts the aggregate supply curve for the case of flexible wages superimposed on the aggregate demand curve derived earlier. The supply curve is simply a vertical line at $Y = Y'$, since in this case output is entirely determined in Figure 9, and is independent of the price level. The intersection of the demand and supply curves determines the price level (p'), and given the price level, one can solve for the rate of interest (r'). Either the IS curve (19) or the LM curve (20) can be used for this purpose, since the method of constructing the demand curve from which the price level was determined will insure that the IS and LM curves intersect at r' and Y'.

One clear implication of Figure 10 is that neither fiscal nor monetary policy can have any impact on output, and the multipliers of the sort illustrated in

---

[18] It is possible to solve explicitly for these equilibrium values, but they are merely complicated functions of the coefficients of the model. The only interesting fact is that the equilibrium level of output is fixed so that the supply curve is vertical.

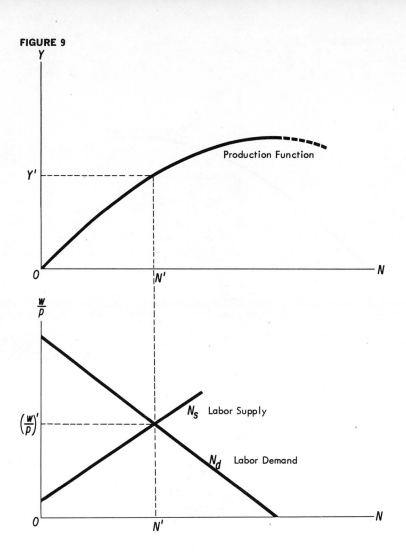

FIGURE 9

Table 1 are all zero. The effects of policy on the price level can be examined, however, with the aid of the earlier results and Figure 10.

Figure 7 showed that an increase in government expenditures will shift the aggregate demand curve to the right so long as the demand for money has an interest elasticity different from zero at that point. Thus, if the supply curve intersects the demand curve below *B*, expansionary fiscal policy will raise the price level, but if the intersection is above *B* there will be no effect on prices.[19]

An increase in the money supply will raise prices if the intersection is to the left of point *C* on the aggregate demand curve (i.e., if it is not in the liquidity trap region), and will have no effect if it is to the right of *C*. The rise in the price level will shift the *IS* curve to the left somewhat, and the new equilibrium will be reached with a slightly lower interest rate than before. It should be noted that the assumptions of this model give monetary policy

---

[19] Above point *B* the entire adjustment is made through a shift in the *IS* curve which raises the interest rate so as to reduce investment by precisely the amount of the increase in government spending. Below *B*, however, the *LM* curve also shifts, due to the rise in prices. This price rise increases tax revenue (through the nominal tax function), and both consumption and investment are reduced.

FIGURE 10

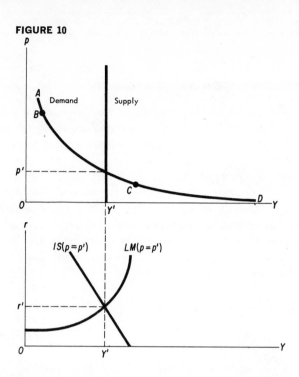

a role in the determination of the rate of interest even in the case where prices and wages are flexible. The source of this influence is the nominal tax function; if taxes were fixed in real terms (or were zero) the *IS* curve would be unaffected by price changes and would fix the interest rate once the level of output was determined.[20] On the assumptions of this paper, the rate of interest is neither a strictly real nor a strictly monetary phenomenon but is determined jointly by both real and monetary forces.[21]

Freeing the *IS* curve from monetary influence also yields the pure quantity theory result that changes in the money supply will bring about proportional changes in the price level. A simple means of observing this is to let t^* be zero in (21), and fix Y at its full-employment level. Clearly, to maintain the resulting relationship, changes in m^* would have to be accompanied by equal proportional changes in p. If t^* is less than zero, the required change in p is somewhat less than proportional to the change in m^*, since part of the effect is reflected in a change in r.

There are a number of other questions which could be explored with the use of the model as thus far presented, but the really interesting problems

---

[20] It is the independence of the *IS* curve from monetary influences that frees the interest rate from monetary influences; the interest elasticity of the demand for money (so long as it is not zero) has no effect on this result.

[21] W. L. Smith ("A Graphical Exposition of the Complete Keynesian System," *Southern Economic Journal*, Vol. XXIII (October 1956), pp. 115–25) has demonstrated the same result by assuming a "real balance" or "Pigou" effect on consumption. It is argued that as the price level falls, the value of consumers' cash balances (and certain other assets) will rise, resulting in an increase in their wealth. This is assumed to have an expansionary effect on consumption expenditures, and the net effect is essentially equivalent to the one obtained in this paper through the use of the nominal tax function. For an exhaustive discussion of the Pigou effect and its ramifications, see D. Patinkin, "Price Flexibility and Full Employment," *American Economic Review*, Vol. XXXVII (September 1948), pp. 543–64, reprinted with slight modifications in F. A. Lutz and L. W. Mints (eds.), *Readings in Monetary Theory* (Homewood, Ill.: Richard D. Irwin, Inc., 1951), pp. 252–83.

arise when wages are not flexible downward, and these are examined in the next section.

V. DEMAND AND SUPPLY WHEN WAGES ARE RIGID

In this section the initial assumptions about the demand for labor as expressed in (25) are retained, but the assumption about the supply of labor is modified. Assume that the maximum quantity of labor which will be supplied is an increasing function of the real wage, and that when demand exceeds the maximum supplied at a given real wage, real wages must be raised in order to obtain more labor. This is all entirely comparable to the case of flexible wages discussed in the previous section. The distinction arises when the demand for labor falls short of the maximum amount supplied. In that case it is assumed that the money wage (w) does not fall, although workers who are willing to work at the current money wage (w_o) cannot find employment. Equation (28) characterizes these relationships explicitly.

$$\left| \begin{array}{l} \text{A.} \quad w = w_o \quad \text{if} \quad \left[\frac{e}{f} - \frac{1}{f}\left(\frac{w_o}{p}\right) \right] < \left[g + h\left(\frac{w_o}{p}\right) \right] \\[2ex] \text{B.} \quad N_s = g + h\left(\frac{w}{p}\right) \text{ otherwise} \end{array} \right|$$

(money wages rigid downward)   (28)

Case A holds if there is unemployed labor (supply exceeds demand), while case B holds if demand is equal to or greater than supply.

These assumptions are depicted graphically in Figure 11. Part B relates

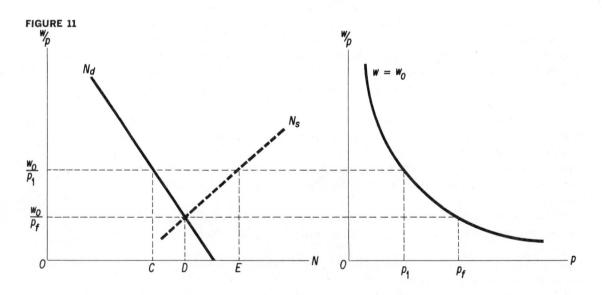

the real wage to the price level, given that the money wage is fixed at $w = w_o$,[22] while the curve labelled N_d in part A is the labor demand curve as before, and the dotted curve N_s indicates the maximum amount of labor which will be supplied at each real wage. If the price level is p_f, the level of employment would be OD, and this will be termed "full employment," since everyone

---

[22] The equation of this curve $(w/p)(p) = w_o$, is that of a rectangular hyperbola.

who wants to work at that real wage is employed. If the price level were to fall to p_1, however, this would raise the real wage to $\frac{w_o}{p_1}$, and only OC labor would be demanded, while amount supplied would rise to OE.[23] The crucial assumption here is that the existence of unemployed labor will not affect the money wage (in particular it will not lower it), so that unless the labor demand curve can be shifted or the price level lowered, there is no way to bring about full employment. The situation when the price level is p_1 is often called an under-employment equilibrium since, despite the existence of excess supply in the labor market, there are no apparent forces generated by this excess supply which would tend to eliminate it.

The effect of this assumption about the nature of the labor market on the shape of the aggregate supply curve can now be examined. Even under the new assumptions in (28), if the excess supply of labor is zero or negative, the classical results hold as in (26). Therefore at any price level above p_f the supply curve will be vertical as before. The new assumption only affects its shape below p_f, and that part of the curve will be examined more closely.

Substitute w_o for w in (25), solve for N and substitute that value into (24), to obtain

$$ Y = \frac{1}{2f}\left[e^2 - \left(\frac{w_o}{p}\right)^2 \right]. \tag{29} $$

This is an increasing function of the price level (p), with a positive intercept on the vertical axis and a vertical asymptote at $Y = \frac{e^2}{2f}$. The upward sloping part of the aggregate supply curve in Figure 12 corresponds to the situation when output is less than the full-employment level, and the vertical portion, described in the preceding paragraph, corresponds to the situation when the economy is at full employment. If demand is below Y_f, the sloping part of the curve is operative, but if demand equals Y_f it is the vertical part of the curve which is operative.[24]

An aggregate demand curve can now be superimposed on the new aggregate supply curve, to obtain a final solution for equilibrium price level and output, as in Figure 13. If $ABCD$ is the current demand curve then Y_1 is current output and p_1 the current price level. Either fiscal or monetary policy can be used

---

[23] A vertical labor supply curve could be used here, which would reduce the excess supply at the lower price level, but would not eliminate it. It could also be assumed that labor supply will respond to higher money wages irrespective of the price level. This latter assumption is much more difficult to justify than the one in the text, however. Given the nature of wage contracts and the usual inability of the unemployed worker to bargain for a lower wage, the assumption used here is probably the most reasonable at this level of abstraction.

[24] A simplification which is frequently made is to assume that the marginal product of labor is constant until capacity output is reached, at which point marginal productivity falls to zero or below. In this case, the labor demand curve is horizontal at less than capacity output, so that the real wage is fixed at that level, as shown in Figure A, below. If money wages are flexible, the shape of the labor demand curve has no effect on the aggregate supply curve, which will be vertical, as before. If money wages are rigid downward, however, both nominal and real wages are fixed, implying that the price level is also fully determined. The aggregate supply curve will thus be horizontal at that price level to the left of full-employment output and vertical at full-employment output, with a right angle at the junction, as in Figure B. In this case, monetary and fiscal policy can be used to move the economy to full employment output (Y_f) without any effect on the price level, while once full employment has been reached, no further expansion of output is possible,

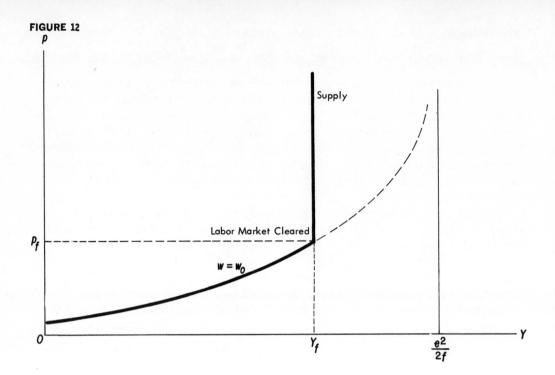

FIGURE 12

p

Supply

Labor Market Cleared

p_f

$w = w_0$

0

Y_f

$\dfrac{e^2}{2f}$

Y

to move the economy to full employment, Y_f, but either will be accompanied by a rise in the price level to p_2.

In the appendix the analytic solution is obtained, together with the multipliers for the several alternative cases. The advantage of the device illustrated in Figure 13, however, is that once it has been constructed, the answers to many theoretical questions as well as the results of most policy changes can be derived merely from observation, without working through the algebra and/or calculus necessary to produce an exact answer. An examination of some of these topics follows.

There is some confusion about the nature of the crucial assumption in a Keynesian model which leads to the possibility of an equilibrium at less than full employment. In particular, the question is raised as to whether it is the rigidity of money wages or the interest elasticity of the demand for money (or perhaps the liquidity trap) which makes this possible. In the version of the model used here, the culprit is clearly the behavior of labor supply, since the aggregate demand curve shows that demand can be increased without limit

---

and any increase in demand results only in a rise in prices. Under the assumptions in this paper, each increment in output comes at a higher and higher cost in terms of rising prices, and as demand expands the economy moves gradually from output expansion to price inflation.

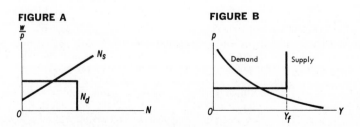

FIGURE A

$\dfrac{w}{p}$

N_s

N_d

0 — N

FIGURE B

p

Demand | Supply

0 — Y_f — *Y*

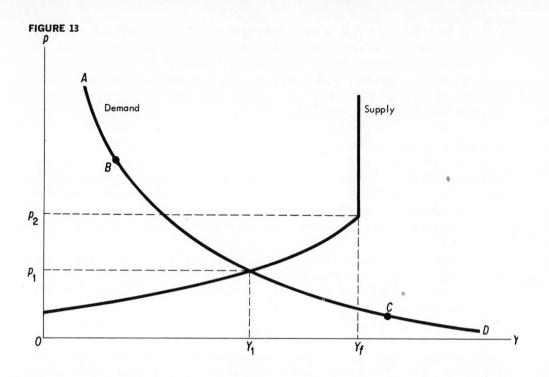

FIGURE 13

by a falling price level. As should be very evident by now, it is the assumption about the nominal tax function which insures this result. If this assumption had not been made, falling prices would not have had an impact on the *IS* curve, demand would have been at a maximum when the interest rate was at its minimum (liquidity trap) level, and further price declines would have had no impact on demand.[25] If the maximum level of aggregate demand were less than full-employment output and prices and wages were flexible, the economy would not achieve full employment, but neither would it achieve an equilibrium, since wages and prices would fall without limit, responding to the excess supply in the labor market. Thus, even when the position of the *IS* curve is unaffected by changes in the price level, the achievement of an unemployment *equilibrium* depends ultimately on the downward rigidity of wages.

Return now to the practical problem of monetary and fiscal policies designed to bring about full employment in the face of rigid wages. The effect of fiscal policy on the aggregate demand curve differs according to whether the economy is above or below point *B* in Figure 13, where points *A*, *B*, *C*, and *D* have the same meaning as in Figure 10. Thus if the supply curve intersects the demand curve in the *AB* region, fiscal policy will affect the level of investment through changes in the interest rate but will have no impact on aggregate output. Monetary policy would have to be used to move the economy toward full employment in that case, and it would accomplish this by increasing the money available for transactions purposes, lowering the interest rate, and increasing investment and consumption. As output rises, however, prices also rise, which

---

[25] In the absence of the tax effect, other mechanisms could have been assumed through which falling prices would act to shift the *IS* curve to the right. The Pigou effect is one such mechanism, and another would be some sort of money illusion. The nominal tax function has been relied upon here because it seems most realistic and is not subject to the many objections which are raised regarding the validity of the alternate mechanisms.

will act to reduce the real money stock and to increase taxes, and damp the expansion somewhat below what it would have been had prices been stable.

At the other extreme, if the supply curve intersects the demand curve in the *CD* region, monetary policy will have no impact, and only fiscal policy can be effective. Fiscal policy can increase the level of aggregate demand through the multiplier mechanism, but again the rising price level will act to increase tax revenue and keep the expansion below what it would have been if prices had remained constant.

If the curves intersect in the *BC* range of the demand curve, both fiscal and monetary policy can be effective in moving the economy toward full employment. In either case, however, the rising supply curve (reflecting the diminishing marginal product of labor) will cause the increase in output to be accompanied by an increase in the price level, and the expansive impact of either policy is somewhat dampened.

The rising price level which accompanies the rightward shift of the demand curve along the upward-sloping supply curve naturally brings to mind the problem of inflation. Within this framework, a price rise could be defined as resulting from "demand pull" if it is the result of a shift in the demand curve, and "cost push" if it is the result of a shift in the supply curve. A cost-push situation could arise, for example, as the result of an increase in the money wage to a higher level. This will not affect the vertical portion of the supply curve, but the sloping part will shift upward. Such cost-push inflation would be accompanied by a decline in total output and employment unless the demand curve were simultaneously shifted to the right through monetary or fiscal policy.

In this model, increasing output results in rising prices, but the process stops once the new equilibrium is reached. Inflation is usually defined as a continuing rise in the price level, however, and this would require a continuous movement in one curve or the other. One way in which continuing price increases could occur in this model would be if the policy makers are unwilling (or politically unable) to allow unemployment to rise above a certain level, U_1, while labor forces are strong enough to gain money wage increases as long as unemployment stays below U_2, and U_2 is above U_1. This can be represented in terms of aggregate demand and supply curves if the unemployment rates are translated into corresponding output levels, Y_1 and Y_2. The result is shown in Figure 14, where it is assumed that fiscal or monetary policy will be used in order to maintain demand at a level no lower than Y_1, while money wage increases will be sought and obtained as long as output is above Y_2. From an initial position at point *A*, wages increase, the supply curve rises, and the economy moves toward point *B*. This is politically untenable, by assumption, and the demand curve is shifted to the right toward point *C*. The process can continue indefinitely as long as Y_1 is to the right of Y_2, and the result is continuing inflation.[26]

The model assumes that price changes caused by shifts in the aggregate demand curve are reversible so long as the two curves intersect in the sloping portion of the supply curve (i.e., if the demand curve shifts and then returns to its former position the price level will also return to its former level). If the demand curve shifts so far to the right that it intersects the vertical part

---

[26] The inflation in this case is seen as resulting in part from market power on the supply side of the labor market. This is the only type of market power built into the system, since output is viewed as being produced under purely competitive conditions. If monopolistic elements in industry had been included, the cost-push forces could have arisen through administered price increases just as well as through wage increases.

FIGURE 14

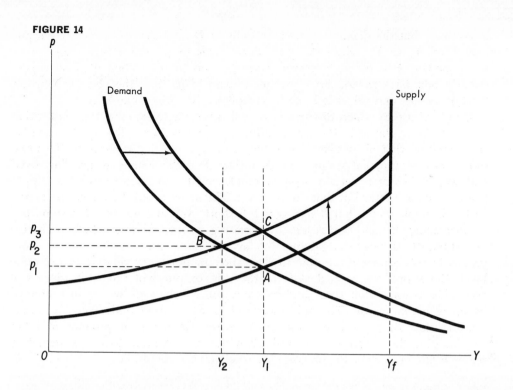

of the supply curve, however, the price level will no longer return to its earlier position as demand subsides. Travel upward along the vertical part of the supply curve implies that money wages are being bid up, so when demand begins to decline and the money wage remains at its new level, the economy moves to the left along a new sloping supply curve corresponding to the highest level of money wages attained. This process is illustrated in Figure 15, where it

FIGURE 15

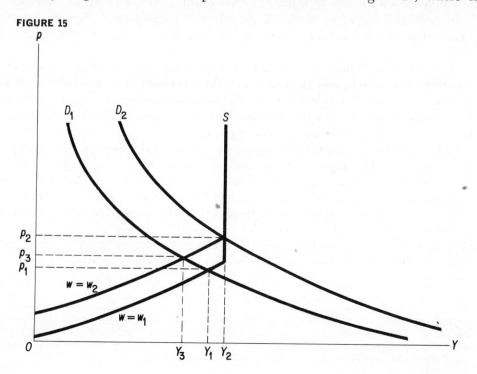

is assumed that the demand curve is initially at D_1 and then shifts to D_2. Output rises from Y_1 to Y_2, while the price level rises to p_2. Once full employment is reached at $w = w_1$, money wages are bid up to w_2. When demand subsequently falls back to D_1, money wages remain at w_2, and the new equilibrium level of income and prices is Y_3 and p_3 respectively, rather than Y_1 and p_1.[27]

One final use to which this structure will be put is to examine the implication of an escalator clause in the wage contract for all workers. Taking the extreme case, suppose that all workers have their money wage tied directly to the price index, so that the real wage is fixed, rather than the money wage. This fixed real wage dictates a certain level of employment and output, and the supply curve becomes vertical at that output level. This level could, by chance, coincide with full employment, but it may also fall short. Any attempt to increase output by increasing demand will result in increasing prices and wages but no change in output. If, through bargaining, by law, or some other device one or more groups in this economy are able to raise their money wage relative to the price level, the supply curve will shift to the left, output will fall and prices will rise. This assumes that these higher wages, once achieved, are again protected by an escalator clause. The only means of raising output under such a system (besides lowering the real wage) is to raise the marginal product of labor by changing the nature of the production function. Neither fiscal nor monetary policy is effective, since the problem lies solely on the supply side.

VI. CONCLUSION

This paper has developed a framework for the analysis of a complete Keynesian (or classical) model which can provide immediate answers to most questions about the effect on the system of various policy decisions or of changes in the underlying assumptions. Several problems of analysis have been examined, and this framework has been used in their solution. Other problems could have been analyzed, including those of growth and technological change and the implications of price and wage controls, but these have been left for the interested reader.

The model used here is an extremely elementary one, utilizing the simplest equations throughout, and including only the minimum of complications. Other assumptions could be introduced in the area of business saving, imports, an interest-elastic money supply, etc. One area in particular which could benefit from more elaboration is investment. Such additions or modifications, however, would in most cases have little impact on the general shape of the aggregate demand and supply curves that have been developed here. Introduction of major new nonlinearities could change the character of the curves somewhat, but again, their general shape and behavior would still be unlikely to be greatly affected.

It cannot be overemphasized, however, that this paper has only described a device which may make it easier for the student to come to grips with many problems in macroeconomic analysis. The ability to make successful use of this device requires an understanding of the basic model which lies hidden beneath

---

[27] It is assumed in this discussion that money wages do not rise until absolutely full employment is reached. This could be modified by letting money wages begin to rise before the economy reaches full employment (due to bottlenecks, improvement in the bargaining position of unions, etc.). Depending on the precise nature of these alternative assumptions, the supply curve may become much steeper as it approaches full-employment output, or may even shift upward continuously, requiring a constantly *increasing* level of demand (and *rising* prices) to maintain a given *level* of output and employment.

the supply and demand curves and depends ultimately on an understanding of the behavior of individuals, firms, and governments as they react to various economic stimuli.

APPENDIX

Derivation of Multipliers in the Complete System for the Case of Fixed Money Wages

The equations needed are reproduced below. Equation (21) is the demand curve, while (29) is the equation of that part of the supply curve which is relevant when the economy is at less than full employment.

$$Y = \frac{C_o + I_o + G^* - \dfrac{vs}{u}}{1 - c(1 - x) + \dfrac{vk}{u}} + \frac{\dfrac{vm^*}{u} - ct^*}{1 - c(1 - x) + \dfrac{vk}{u}} \left(\frac{1}{p}\right) \tag{21}$$

$$Y = \frac{1}{2f}\left[e^2 - \left(\frac{w_o}{p}\right)^2\right] \tag{29}$$

Solve (29) for $\dfrac{1}{p}$ as in (A.1), and insert that solution into (21), yielding (A.2).

$$\frac{1}{p} = \frac{1}{w_o}(e^2 - 2fY)^{1/2} \tag{A.1}$$

$$Y = \frac{C_o + I_o + G^* - \dfrac{vs}{u} + \left(\dfrac{vm^*}{u} - ct^*\right)(e^2 - 2fY)^{1/2}\left(\dfrac{1}{w_o}\right)}{1 - c(1 - x) + \dfrac{vk}{u}} \tag{A.2}$$

The simplest method for deriving multipliers from (A.2) is to differentiate Y with respect to the policy variables G^* and m^*. Those readers who are not familiar with this technique can proceed directly to Table A, where the multipliers are displayed. Since p is only an index of prices, it can be defined as equal to unity without loss of generality.

Differentiating Y with respect to G^* yields

$$\frac{dY}{dG^*} = \frac{1 + \left(\dfrac{vm^*}{u} - ct^*\right)\left(\dfrac{1}{w_o}\right)(e^2 - 2fY)^{-1/2}(-2fY)\left(\dfrac{1}{2}\right)\left(\dfrac{dY}{dG^*}\right)}{1 - c(1 - x) + \dfrac{vk}{u}}$$

$$= \frac{1}{\left[1 - c(1 - x) + \dfrac{vk}{u}\right] + \dfrac{f\left(\dfrac{vm^*}{u} - ct^*\right)}{w_o(e^2 - 2fY)^{1/2}}} \tag{A.3}$$

but from (29) one can obtain

$$(e^2 - 2fY)^{1/2} = \frac{w_o}{p} = w_o, \tag{A.4}$$

and substituting this in (A.3), the final result is:

$$\frac{dY}{dG^*} = \frac{1}{\left(1 - c(1 - x) + \dfrac{vk}{u}\right) + \dfrac{f}{w_o{}^2}\left(\dfrac{vm^*}{u} - ct^*\right)}. \qquad (A.5)$$

This is smaller than the multiplier illustrated in Table 1, since the second expression in the denominator of (A.5) is positive. The economic explanation, of course, is that increasing output lowers the marginal product of labor and raises the price of output. This rise in prices increases real taxes and decreases the real money supply, and both of these effects act to reduce demand below what it would have been had prices been stable.[28] This multiplier expression is presented in Table A, along with its value in various special circumstances.

TABLE A   INCOME MULTIPLIERS UNDER ALTERNATIVE ASSUMPTIONS (fixed nominal wages)

Restrictions on the Model	$\dfrac{dY}{dG^*}$	$\dfrac{dY}{dm^*}$
A. None	$\dfrac{1}{\left[1 - c(1 - x) + \dfrac{vk}{u}\right] + \dfrac{f}{w_o{}^2}\left(\dfrac{vm^*}{u} - ct^*\right)}$	$\dfrac{1}{\left[\dfrac{u}{v}(1 - c[1 - x]) + k\right] + \dfrac{f}{w_o{}^2}\left(m^* - \dfrac{uct^*}{v}\right)}$
B. Interest elasticity of investment $= 0$ $(v = 0)$	$\dfrac{1}{[1 - c(1 - x)] - \dfrac{fct^*}{w_o{}^2}}$	0
C. Interest elasticity of demand for money $= 0$ $(u = 0)$	0	$\dfrac{1}{k + \dfrac{fm^*}{w_o{}^2}}$
D. Liquidity trap $(r = r_o)$ $\left(\text{or } \dfrac{1}{u} = 0\right)$	$\dfrac{1}{1 - c(1 - x) - \dfrac{fct^*}{w_o{}^2}}$	0

The multiplier for monetary policy can be obtained in a similar fashion. Differentiating (A.2) and making substitution as before, one obtains:

$$\frac{dY}{dm^*} = \frac{\dfrac{v}{u}(e^2 - 2fY)^{1/2}\left(\dfrac{1}{w_o}\right) + \left(\dfrac{vm^*}{u} - ct^*\right)(e^2 - 2fY)^{-1/2}\left(\dfrac{1}{w_o}\right)(-2f)\left(\dfrac{1}{2}\right)\left(\dfrac{dY}{dm^*}\right)}{1 - c(1 - x) + \dfrac{vk}{u}}$$

$$= \frac{1}{\left[\dfrac{u}{v}(1 - c[1 - x] + k)\right] + \dfrac{f}{w_o{}^2}\left(m^* - \dfrac{uct^*}{v}\right)} \qquad (A.6)$$

It can be observed that this differs from the similar multiplier in Table 1 by the addition of a second term in the denominator, which plays essentially the same role it played in (A.5). This multiplier, as well as its value under special assumptions, is displayed in Table A. Similar multipliers for the price level, the interest rate, or any other endogenous variable can easily be obtained through the same general procedure.

---

[28] If the marginal product of labor had been constant, f would have been zero, and the second expression in the denominator would have been eliminated, the same result as before.

A GRAPHICAL EXPOSITION OF THE COMPLETE KEYNESIAN SYSTEM*

Warren L. Smith†

The purpose of this paper is chiefly expository. A simple graphical technique is employed to exhibit the working of several variants of the Keynesian model. Many of the issues discussed have been dealt with elsewhere,[1] but it is hoped that the analysis presented here will clarify some of the issues and be useful for pedagogical purposes.

I. THE KEYNESIAN SYSTEM WITH FLEXIBLE WAGES

This system can be represented symbolically by the following five equations:

$$y = c(y,r) + i(y,r) \tag{1}$$

$$\frac{M}{p} = L(y,r) \tag{2}$$

$$y = f(N) \tag{3}$$

$$\frac{w}{p} = f'(N) \tag{4}$$

$$N = \varphi\left(\frac{w}{p}\right) \tag{5}$$

Here y = real GNP (at constant prices), r = an index of interest rates, M = money supply (in

current dollars), p = index of the price level applicable to GNP, N = the volume of employment (in equivalent full-time workers), w = the money wage. The model represents a theory of short-run income determination with capital stock fixed and labor the only variable factor of production.

The working of this model is illustrated in Figure I. Figure I should be studied in clockwise fashion, beginning with Chart I(a) in the lower lefthand corner. In I(a), DD represents the demand for labor [equation (4)], and SS represents the supply of labor [equation (5)]. The level of employment and the real wage are determined at the full employment levels, N_f and $(w/p)_f$. Proceeding to I(b), the curve OP represents the aggregate production function [equation (3)], its shape reflecting diminishing returns.[2] With employment of N_f, y would be at the level y_f, indicated in I(b).

Chart I(c) is the type of diagram developed by Hicks and utilized by others to depict the condition of monetary equilibrium in the Keynesian system.[3] The IS curve in I(c) depicts equation (1) and indicates for each possible level of the interest rate (r) the equilibrium level of income (y) which would prevail after the multiplier had worked itself out fully.[4] We treat the

*From *Southern Economic Journal*, Vol. XXIII (October 1956), pp. 115–25. Reprinted by permission of the publisher.

† The development of the technique employed in this paper is a result of discussions with many persons, particularly Professor Daniel B. Suits of the University of Michigan, to whom the writer wishes to express his thanks.

[1] See particularly L. R. Klein, "Theories of Effective Demand and Employment," *Journal of Political Economy*, Vol. LV (April 1947), pp. 108–31, reprinted in R. V. Clemence (ed.), *Readings in Economic Analysis*, Vol. I (Cambridge, Mass.: Addison-Wesley Press, 1950), pp. 260–83, and *The Keynesian Revolution* (New York: Macmillan Co., 1950), Technical Appendix; F. Modigliani, "Liquidity Preference and the Theory of Interest and Money," *Econometrica*, Vol. XII (Jan. 1944), pp. 45–88, reprinted in F. A. Lutz and L. W. Mints (eds.), *Readings in Monetary Theory* (Homewood, Ill.: Richard D. Irwin, Inc., 1951), pp. 186–239; also V. Lutz, "Real and Monetary Factors in the Determination of Employment Levels," *Quarterly Journal of Economics*, Vol. LXVI (May 1952), pp. 251–72; L. Hough, "The Price Level in Macroeconomic Models," *American Economic Review*, Vol. LXIV (June 1954), pp. 269–86.

[2] According to the mathematical formulation of our model in equations (1)–(5), the curve DD in I(a) is the derivative of curve OP in I(b), the relation reflecting the operation of the marginal productivity law under competitive conditions. This precise condition is not important, however, and we shall make no attempt to draw the curves in such a way as to fulfill it. For one thing, the presence of monopoly in the economy or failure of entrepreneurs to seek maximum profits would destroy the precision of the equations, but relations of the type depicted in Figure I would in all probability continue to hold.

[3] For a detailed discussion of this diagram, see J. R. Hicks, "Mr. Keynes and the 'Classics': A Suggested Interpretation," *Econometrica*, Vol. V (April 1937), pp. 147–59; also A. H. Hansen, *Monetary Theory and Fiscal Policy* (New York: McGraw-Hill, 1949), chap. 5. The reader's attention is directed to the fact that we have reversed the axes of the Hicks diagram; we measure the interest rate on the horizontal axis and income on the vertical axis.

[4] It should be noted that the formal analysis in this paper falls entirely in the category of comparative statics, that is, it refers to conditions of equilibrium

FIGURE I

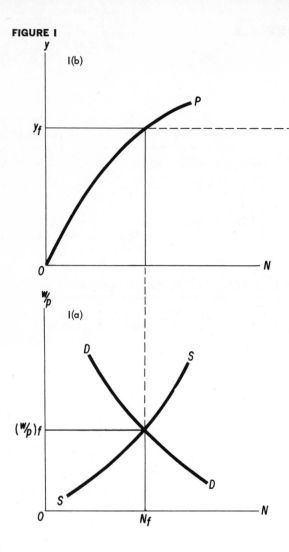

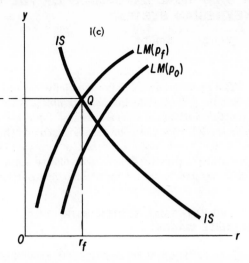

stock of money as an exogenous variable determined by the monetary authority. Given M, the LM curves in I(c), of which there would be one for each possible price level (p) which might prevail, represent equation (2) in our model. For example, if the price level were held constant at p_0, the curve $LM(p_0)$ depicts the different interest rates that would be required to preserve equilibrium in the money market at different income levels. The fact that rising income levels are associated with higher interest rates reflects the presumption that as income rises, transactions cash requirements are larger, leaving less of the

and changes in the equilibrium values of the variables brought about by changes in data or exogenous variables and does not pretend to describe the *paths* followed by the variables as they move from one equilibrium position to another.

fixed (in real terms) quantity of money to satisfy demands for idle balances, thus pushing up the interest rate.

If prices and wages are flexible and the situation is as depicted in Figure I, full employment will automatically be maintained, since the price level will adjust to the level p_f, establishing the LM curve in the position $LM(p_f)$ where it will intersect the IS curve at point Q which corresponds to the full employment level of income (y_f). If, for example, the real wage is initially above $(w/p)_f$, money wages will fall due to the excess supply of labor. This will reduce costs, resulting in increased output and employment and lower prices. Falling prices shift the LM curve upward by increasing the real value of cash balances (M/p), thus lowering the interest rates and expanding aggregate demand to the point where the market will absorb the output corresponding to full employment.[5]

Two important and related propositions can be set down concerning interest and money in the above model:

1. The rate of interest is determined solely by saving and investment and is independent of the quantity of money and liquidity preference.

2. The quantity theory of money holds for this model—that is, a change in the quantity of money will bring about an equal proportional change in the price level and will have no effect on real income or employment.

In other words the quantity of money and liquidity preference serve not to determine the interest rate, as alleged by Keynes, but the price level. As can readily be seen from Figure I, income is established at the full employment level [I(a) and I(b)], the interest rate adjusts to equate savings and investment [on the IS curve in I(c)] at this income level, and the price level adjusts so as to satisfy liquidity requirements at this interest rate [establishing the LM curve at the appropriate position in I(c)].

It is a comparatively simple matter to modify the analysis of Figure I to take account of the possible effect of changes in the real value of liquid assets on consumption (the Pigou effect).[6] The real value of the stock of liquid assets would be included in equation (1), and falling prices would then shift the IS curve to the right, thus strengthening the tendency toward full employment equilibrium. This suggests the question: Does the introduction of the Pigou effect give the quantity of money the power to change the rate of interest when prices and wages are flexible? The answer to this question cannot be deduced from the curves of Figure I, but it is not difficult to find the answer with the aid of the following simple model:

[5] We abstract from the possibility of dynamic instability which may arise due to falling prices if the public has elastic expectations. See D. Patinkin, "Price Flexibility and Full Employment," *American Economic Review,* Vol. XXXVII (September 1948), pp. 543–64, reprinted with slight modification in Lutz and Mints, *op. cit.,* pp. 252–83.

[6] On the Pigou effect, see A. C. Pigou, "Economic Progress in a Stable Environment," *Economica,* New Series, Vol. XIV (August, 1947), pp. 180–88, reprinted in Lutz and Mints, *op. cit.,* pp. 241–51; Patinkin, *op. cit.,* G. Ackley, "The Wealth-Saving Relationship," *Journal of Political Economy,* Vol. LIX (April 1951), pp. 154–61; M. Cohen, "Liquid Assets and the Consumption Function," *Review of Economics and Statistics,* Vol. XXXVI (May 1954), pp. 202–11; and bibliography in the latter two articles.

$$\bar{y} = c(\bar{y},r,a) + i(\bar{y},r)$$

$$\frac{M}{p} = L(\bar{y},r)$$

$$a = \frac{A}{p}$$

Here a = the real value of liquid assets which is included in the consumption function and A = their money value. The last three equations of our original model are assumed to determine the real wage, employment, and real income. These equations are dropped and y is treated as a constant (having value $\bar{y}$) determined by those equations. We can now treat M and A as parameters and r, a, and p as variables, differentiate these three equations with respect to M, and solve for dr/dM. This gives the following expression:

$$\frac{dr}{dM} = \frac{\dfrac{c_a}{i_r}\dfrac{A}{M}(1 - \eta_{AM})}{p\left(1 + \dfrac{c_r}{i_r} + \dfrac{A}{M}\dfrac{L_r c_a}{i_r}\right)}. \qquad (6)$$

In this expression, the subscripts refer to partial derivates, e.g., $c_a = \delta c/\delta a$. Normally, the following conditions would be satisfied: $c_a > 0$, $i_r < 0$, $L_r < 0$. We cannot be sure about the sign of c_r, but it is likely to be small in any case. The coefficient η_{AM} has the following meaning:

$$\eta_{AM} = \frac{M}{A}\frac{dA}{dM} = \frac{\dfrac{dA}{A}}{\dfrac{dM}{M}}$$

For example, if a change in M is brought about in such a way as to produce an exactly proportionate change in A, η_{AM} will be unity. Or if the change in M is not accompanied by any change in A, η_{AM} will be zero. It is apparent from the above expression that a change in the quantity of money will not affect the rate of interest if $\eta_{AM} = 1$, while an increase (decrease) in the quantity of money will lower (raise) the rate of interest if $\eta_{AM} < 1$.[7] Thus, the way in which changes in the quality of money affect the rate of interest depends upon what asset concept is included in the consumption function (i.e., what is included in A) and how the volume of these

[7] We assume that $c_r < 0$, or if $c_r > 0$,

$$1 + \frac{A}{M}\frac{L_r c_a}{i_r} > \frac{c_r}{i_r}$$

so that the denominator of (6) is positive.

FIGURE II

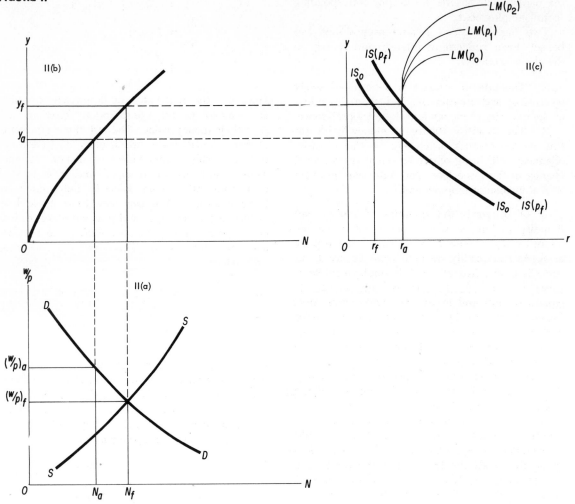

assets is affected by monetary change. If M itself is the appropriate asset concept to include in the consumption function (i.e., if $A = M$), changes in M will not affect the interest rate, since in this case η_{AM} is equal to unity. However, the consensus of opinion seems to be that some other aggregate, such as currency, deposits, and government securities held by the non-bank public minus the public's indebtedness to the banks, is more appropriate.[8] If this concept is employed, most of the usual methods of increasing the money supply will ordinarily either leave A unchanged ($\eta_{AM} = 0$) or cause it to increase less than in proportion to the increase in M ($0 <$

$\eta_{AM} < 1$).[9] We may conclude that the Pigou effect gives monetary changes power to influence the rate of interest, even if wages and prices are fully flexible. An increase (decrease) in the quantity of money will ordinarily lower (raise) the rate of interest and also increase (decrease) investment

[8] The question of what asset concept is appropriate is discussed in Patinkin, *op. cit.*, Cohen, *op. cit.*, and J. Tobin, "Asset Holdings and Spending Decisions," *American Economic Review Papers and Proceedings*, Vol. XLII (May 1952), pp. 109–23.

[9] Open market purchases of government securities by the central bank from the nonbank public will leave A unchanged, since the initial purchase transaction will result in a decline in the public's security holdings and an equal increase in M, while any induced expansion of loans and investments by the banks will result in an increase in M offset by an equal increase in the public's indebtedness to the banks. On the other hand if the Treasury prints currency and gives it to the public, A will be increased by the same absolute amount as M but the increase in A will be proportionately smaller than the increase in M (provided the public's holdings of government securities exceed its indebtedness to the banks so that $A > M$).

and decrease (increase) consumption, but will not change income and employment which are determined by real forces (the last three equations of our complete model).[10],[11]

II. POSSIBILITIES OF UNDEREMPLOYMENT DISEQUILIBRIUM

There are several possible circumstances arising from the shapes of the various schedules which might produce a situation in which, even though the relations in the above model held true, it might be impossible, at least temporarily, for equilibrium (full employment or otherwise) to be reached. The most widely discussed of these possibilities is depicted in Figure II.

II(a) and II(b) are similar to I(a) and I(b). However, the LM curves in II(c) are drawn to reflect the much-discussed possibility mentioned by Keynes[12] that the liquidity preference schedule might become infinitely elastic at some low level of interest rates [r_a in II(c)], due either to the unanimous expectations of investors that interest rates would rise when they reached this extremely low level relative to future expectations or to the cost of investments. In the case depicted, full employment (N_f) would involve a level of income of y_f. If the IS curve were at the level IS_0, the interest rate required to make investment equal to saving at income y_f would be r_f. But the infinite elasticity of the LM schedule prevents the interest rate from falling below r_a. The result would be that employment

and income would be prevented from rising above the level N_a and y_a by inadequate effective demand. The real wage would hold at the level $(w/p)_a$ which is above the full employment level $(w/p)_f$. Competition for employment would reduce money wages, costs, and prices. But the falling price level, although it would increase the quantity of money in real terms, would not affect the interest rate, hence would not increase investment. As prices fell, the LM curve would take successive positions, such as $LM(p_0)$, $LM(p_1)$, $LM(p_2)$, etc., leaving the interest rate unaffected.[13]

A special case of the situation depicted in Figure II may arise if a negative interest rate is required to equate investment to full employment savings. In this case, the IS curve would cut the y-axis and lie to the left of it at an income corresponding to full employment. Then, even if there were nothing to prevent the rate of interest from approaching zero, it could not go below zero,[14] and the LM curve would have a floor at a zero rate, thus preventing full employment from being attained.

It is interesting to note that if the Pigou effect is operative, a full employment equilibrium may be attainable even in the case illustrated in Figure II. As prices fall, the real value of liquid assets increases. If this increases consumption expenditures, the IS curve will shift to the right until it attains the position $IS(p_f)$, where a full employment equilibrium is reached.

Certain other conceivable situations which might lead to an underemployment disequilibrium are worthy of brief mention. One possibility is that the supply of labor might exceed the demand at all levels of real wages. Such a situation seems very improbable, however, since there is reason to believe that the short-run aggregate labor supply is quite inelastic over a considerable

[10] The fact that the existence of a wealth effect on savings may confer upon the quantity of money the power to affect the rate of interest even with flexible wages is demonstrated in L. A. Metzler, "Wealth, Saving, and the Rate of Interest," *Journal of Political Economy*, Vol. LIX (April 1951), pp. 93–116. Metzler's conclusions, which differ from those given here, can be attributed to assumptions that he makes, particularly the assumption that the only assets are money and common stock.

[11] If the supply of labor is affected by the real value of wealth held by workers, changes in the quantity of money may affect output and employment by shifting the SS curve in Figure I (a). Also, even though monetary change does not affect the *current* level of income and employment, if, due to the operation of the Pigou effect, it changes the interest rate and thereby investment, it may affect the *future* level of employment, since the change in capital stock will ordinarily shift the demand for labor [DD curve in Figure I (a)] at a future date. Both these points are mentioned in V. Lutz, *op. cit.*

[12] J. M. Keynes, *General Theory of Employment, Interest, and Money* (New York: Harcourt, Brace and Co., 1936), pp. 201–4.

[13] Equations (1)–(5) above apply to the situations covered in both Figure I and Figure II. In the latter case, however, the equations are mathematically inconsistent and do not possess a solution. Mathematics does not tell us what will happen in this case (although the additional conditions necessary to describe the results could be expressed mathematically). The statements made above concerning the results (i.e., that income will be y_a, prices and wages will fall together, etc.) are propositions in economics.

[14] Since the money rate of interest cannot be negative, as long as it costs nothing to hold money. In fact, a zero rate of interest would be impossible, since in this case property value would be infinite; however, the rate might *approach* zero. The *real* rate of interest, *ex post*, may be negative due to inflation, but this is not relevant to our problem. On this, see I. Fisher, *The Theory of Interest* (New York: Macmillan Co., 1930), chaps. ii, xix, and pp. 282–86.

range of wage rates and declines when wage rates become very low.[15]

Disequilibrium situations could also arise if (a) the demand curve for labor had a steeper slope than the supply curve at their point of intersection, or (b) the IS curve cut the LM curve in such a way that IS lay to the right of LM above their intersection and to the left of LM below their intersection in Figure I(c) or II(c). Actually, these are situations of unstable equilibrium rather than of disequilibrium. However, in these cases, a slight departure from equilibrium would produce a cumulative movement away from it, and the effect would be similar to a situation of disequilibrium.

III. UNDEREMPLOYMENT EQUILIBRIUM DUE TO WAGE RIGIDITY

Next we may consider the case in which the supply of and demand for labor are essentially the same as in Figures I and II, but for institutional or other reasons the money wage does not fall when there is an excess supply of labor.[16] This rigidity of money wages may be due to various factors, including (a) powerful trade unions which are able to prevent money wages from falling, at least temporarily, (b) statutory provisions, such as minimum wage laws, (c) failure of employers to reduce wages due to a desire to retain loyal and experienced employees and to maintain morale,[17] or (d) unwillingness of unemployed workers to accept reduced money wages even though they would be willing to work at lower real wages brought about by a rise in prices.[18]

A situation of this kind is depicted in Figure III. The fixed money wage is designated by $\bar{w}$. In order for full employment (N_f) to be attained, the price level must be at p_f (such as to make $\bar{w}/p_f$ equal to the real wage corresponding to full employment), income will be y_f, and the interest rate must reach r_f. However, in the case shown in Figure III, the quantity of money, M,

is such that when p is at the level p_f, the LM curve [$LM(p_f)$] intersects the IS curve at an income (y_0) below the full employment level and an interest rate (r_0) above the full employment level. Hence full employment cannot be sustained due to inadequate effective demand. On the other hand, if production and employment are at y_0 and N_0, with a price level such (at p_0) as to establish a real wage appropriate to this volume of employment, the LM curve will be at a level above $LM(p_f)$. This is because p_0 must be less than p_f in order to make $\bar{w}/p_0$ higher than $\bar{w}/p_f$. In this case production and employment will tend to rise because aggregate demand exceeds current output. Therefore, income must be between y_f and y_0, employment between N_f and N_0, the interest rate between r_f and r_0, the price level between p_f and p_0. An equilibrium will be reached somewhere between these limits, say at N_e, y_e, p_e, and r_e.[19]

This is a case of underemployment equilibrium. It should be noted that full employment can be attained by an increase in the quantity of money (M) sufficient to shift the $LM(p_f)$ curve to the position where it will intersect the IS curve at point Q. Two propositions can be set down here to be contrasted with the two stated in connection with Figure I:[20]

1. Changes in the quantity of money cause changes in both the price level and the level of output and employment, and the quantity theory of money does not hold true.[21]

2. An increase (decrease) in the quantity of money causes a decrease (increase) in the rate of interest. In this case, the interest rate is determined by the interaction of all the relations in the model. Saving, investment, liquidity preference, and the quantity of money all have a hand in its determination.

---

[15] On the probable shape of the short-run aggregative supply of labor, see G. F. Bloom and H. R. Northrup, *Economics of Labor Relations* (Homewood, Ill.: Richard D. Irwin, Inc., 1954), pp. 250–53.

[16] We will assume that this rigidity does not prevail in an upward direction—i.e., money wages will rise when there is an excess demand for labor.

[17] See A. Rees, "Wage Determination and Involuntary Unemployment," *Journal of Political Economy*, Vol. LIX (April 1951), pp. 143–53.

[18] Keynes, *op. cit.*, chap. 2; J. Tobin, "Money Wage Rates and Employment," in S. E. Harris (ed.), *The New Economics* (New York: Knopf, 1947), pp. 572–87.

[19] In the case depicted in Figure III, an additional equation $\bar{w} = w$ is added to equations (1)–(5) above. This gives six equations and only five unknowns (y, N, p, w, and r). Such a system of equations is *overdetermined* and does not, in general, possess a solution. If the quantity of money is treated as a variable which is adjusted so as to maintain full employment, we have six equations and six unknowns and there will be a solution (unless the equations are inconsistent).

[20] See p. 63, *supra*.

[21] In the limiting case in which the DD curve has a horizontal stage which includes the current level of employment, the entire effect of an increase in M is on y, with no change in p. A considerable part of Keynes' *General Theory* (prior to the discussion of wages and prices in Book V) has reference primarily to this situation.

FIGURE III

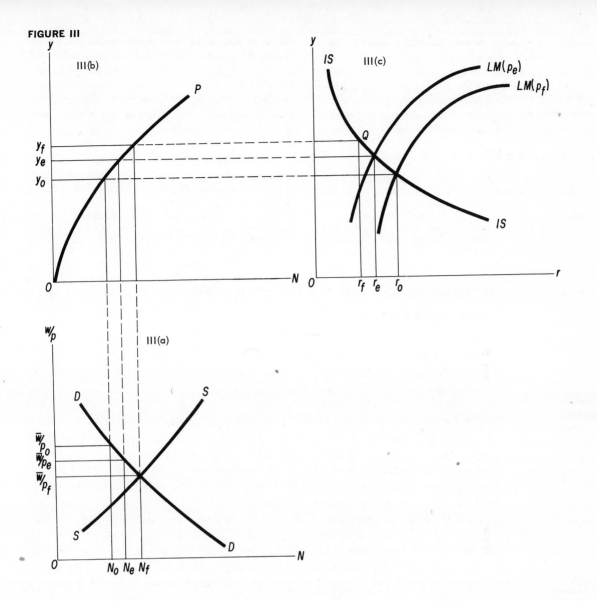

Introduction of the Pigou effect into Figure III would not prevent the occurrence of an under-employment equilibrium, although it would some-what complicate the process of adjustment since changes in p or M would cause changes in the IS curve as well as the LM curve.

To summarize, our analysis of Figures I and III indicates that rigidity of money wages is, in general, a necessary condition for (a) the oc-currence of an underemployment equilibrium, (b) the quantity of money to have an effect on the level of real income and employment. The rate of interest will not be affected by the quantity of money and liquidity preference unless (a) there is rigidity of money wages or (b) the Pigou effect is operative with $\eta_{AM} \neq 1$. Monetary

theories of the rate of interest, whether of the loanable funds or liquidity preference variety, ordinarily assume rigidity (or at least stickiness) in the structure of money wages.[22]

IV. CONCLUDING COMMENTS

In conclusion, we would like to call the reader's attention to further uses to which our graphical technique can be put. With appropriate modifications to suit the occasion, it can be used to analyze other variations of the Keynesian

---

[22] The relative merits of loanable funds and liquid-ity preference types of monetary interest theories we do not consider, except to say that when appropri-ately formulated, the two are equivalent.

model.[23] Additional factors affecting the income, employment, and price levels, such as those suggested by Hough[24] and by Lutz[25] can be quite easily introduced into the analysis through appropriate shifts in the schedules shown in our system of graphs. Fiscal policy and its relation to monetary policy can be dealt with, since fiscal policy influences the level and shape of the IS curve. Finally, it provides a useful starting point for the study of economic growth. Factors affecting the rate of growth, such as capital accumulation, population growth, technological change, etc., can be brought in by allowing for their effects on the various schedules.

[23] For example, the models with which Modigliani begins his analysis (*op. cit.*, pp. 46–48 in original, pp. 187–90 in *Readings in Monetary Theory*). Analysis of these models requires some alteration in the graphical technique, since he assumes that consumption, investment, and the demand for money, all in current dollars, depend upon money income and the rate of interest, thus introducing "money illusions" into his scheme at several points.

[24] L. Hough, "The Price Level in Macroeconomic Models," *American Economic Review*, Vol. LXIV (June 1954), pp. 269–86.

[25] V. Lutz, "Real and Monetary Factors in the Determination of Employment Levels," *Quarterly Journal of Economics*, Vol. LXVI (May 1952), pp. 251–72.

THE DEMAND FOR AND SUPPLY OF MONEY

*Ronald L. Teigen**

The monetary relationships found in current macroeconomic models, particularly the demand-for-money function, are the result of a long process of theoretical development and empirical investigation. To the extent that such models are used as a guide for policy decisions, accurate knowledge concerning the proper form and arguments of these functions, and their elasticities, is crucial for the correct choice of economic policy instruments. Yet there is substantial disagreement among monetary economists concerning such basic issues as whether or not interest rates play a role in determining the demand for money. This disagreement reflects the fact that substantially different theories concerning the role of money in the macroeconomic system have developed somewhat independently. It is the purpose of this paper to trace the development of these differing views, which may be categorized as Classical and Neoclassical on the one hand, and Keynesian and post-Keynesian on the other; to discuss briefly but critically the relevant empirical studies supporting them; and to demonstrate the implications for policy of a proper understanding of the behavioral relationships involved.

Section I summarizes the development of the theory of the demand for money from the Classics to the present; in Section II, the theory of the supply of money is discussed. Some empirical information on demand and supply elasticities is used to evaluate policy multipliers in Section III, and Section IV contains some concluding comments. A linear version of a macroeconomic model which includes a monetary sector is given in the Appendix. Fiscal and monetary policy multipliers are derived from this model and reference to the model and to these multiplier expressions will clarify many of the points discussed below.

I. THE DEMAND FOR MONEY

A. The Classical View

No attempt will be made to discuss the work of the many writers in the Classical tradition who considered the role of money and the reasons for holding

* The author is indebted to Professor Warren L. Smith for his valuable comments.

it, as the subject has received extensive coverage elsewhere.[1] The Classical approach is summed up in the famous "quantity theory of money." This venerable[2] hypothesis reflects the Classical view that, since money has no inherent utility, the only rational motive for holding cash balances is to facilitate transactions. According to the Classics, money not needed for transacting should be converted into income-yielding assets, such as bonds. The Classical view of the demand for money is conveniently summarized by Patinkin as follows:

> In its cash balance version . . . neoclassical theory assumed that, for their convenience, individuals wish to hold a certain proportion, K, of the real volume of their planned transactions, T, in the form of real money balances. The demand for these balances thus equals KT. Correspondingly, the demand for nominal money balances is KPT, where P is the price level of the commodities transacted. The equating of this demand to the supply of money, M, then produced the famous Cambridge equation, $M = KPT$. In the transactions version—associated primarily with the names of Newcomb and Fisher—the velocity of circulation, V, replaced its reciprocal, K, to produce the equally famous equation of exchange, $MV = PT$. These equations were the paradegrounds on which neoclassical economists then put the classical quantity theory of money through its paces.[3]

This view of the role of money implies that the economic process is not accurately represented by static-equilibrium analysis, but is essentially dynamic—that is, it occurs through time. Under the comparative static theory of exchange, all market transactions in effect occur instantaneously. No one who emerged from the market-clearing procedure holding cash balances could be considered to be in equilibrium, since money, which is only useful for transacting, could have been exchanged for goods in the market and a higher level of utility could have been reached. Another way of stating it is that no transactions balances would be required under static assumptions, which imply that receipts of income and requirements for payment are in effect perfectly synchronized. In fact, however, income receipts and payment obligations do not arise simultaneously; rather, they occur at different points in time.

Modern analysts point out that the time dimension—or disparity between receipts and payments—is a necessary condition for the holding of transactions balances, but that it is not sufficient to explain their existence. If the institutional structure is such that currently idle transactions balances can be converted into income-yielding assets with practically perfect liquidity (such as savings deposits), why will not all such balances be exchanged immediately upon receipt for these assets, to be held until needed; at which time they can be reconverted into money? Some of the later writers in the Classical tradition recognized that, under static assumptions, no one would wish to hold cash balances and therefore the velocity of circulation (defined as the ratio of the money value of income, Y, or the money value of transactions, T, to the stock of money) would tend to approach infinity; they ascribed the fact that velocity is finite to the existence of uncertainty with respect to future transactions needs. This motive for holding money is termed the "precautionary motive" and is based on the notion that

---

[1] See Don Patinkin, *Money, Interest, and Prices*, second edition (New York: Harper & Row, 1965), Chap. VIII and Notes A–J for an exhaustive discussion of the Classical position, as well as for references to the important Classical works. In addition, there is a useful discussion of the views of a number of late Classical and early Keynesian writers in J. S. Gilbert, "The Demand for Money: The Development of an Economic Concept," *Journal of Political Economy*, LXI (April 1953), pp. 144–59.

[2] The quantity theory in crude form is said to be found in writings as early as the sixteenth century. See A. C. L. Day and S. T. Beza, *Money and Income* (New York: Oxford University Press, 1960), p. 277.

[3] Patinkin, *op. cit.*, p. 163.

unforeseen contingencies—or opportunities—may arise which require immediate cash outlay and which may lead to further expense and inconvenience (in the case of a misfortune), or the loss of an unexpected purchasing opportunity, if adequate purchasing power is not available.[4] Like transactions demand, the demand for money to satisfy the precautionary motive was usually taken to be a function of the level of transactions.[5] Since perfectly liquid, income-yielding assets can satisfy the precautionary motive, if they are available, this motive does not furnish a satisfactory explanation for the existence of transactions balances. In an important modern approach to the demand for money, it has been shown that money balances will be held for transactions purposes if the cost of converting these balances into and out of income-yielding assets exceeds the return from holding these assets. This view will be discussed below.[6]

Summing up the general Classical view, the demand for money varies with the level of transactions. In the framework of a macroeconomic model, it is more convenient to refer to income than to transactions, and since the level of transactions is closely related to the level of income, the quantity theory may be expressed as

$$M = kY \qquad 0 < k < 1$$

or

$$M = kPQ$$

where M represents the nominal money stock, P is the price level, Q is a measure of the volume of physical output (GNP at constant prices, for example) and Y is the money value in current dollars of national income or product (such as GNP measured in current dollars).

The parameter k, the fraction of money income held as cash balances, is determined by institutional factors such as payment and transactions patterns and procedures (that is, k would tend to be larger the less often wage and salary payments are received; it would be smaller if most expenditures are made

---

[4] The precautionary motive has been discussed by a number of authors. See, for instance, Frank H. Knight, *Risk, Uncertainty and Profit* (London School of Economics and Political Science Reprints, 1948), pp. 76 ff., and Albert G. Hart and Peter B. Kenen, *Money, Debt, and Economic Activity*, third edition (Englewood Cliffs, N.J.: Prentice-Hall, Inc., 1961), pp. 237–39 and 257–59.

[5] This approach was taken by Keynes, who classified the motives for holding money balances as (1) the transactions motive; (2) the precautionary motive; (3) the speculative motive. See J. M. Keynes, *The General Theory of Employment, Interest, and Money* (New York: Harcourt, Brace and Company, 1936), pp. 170–72.

[6] Some hints at a more extensive view of the demand for money can be found in the Classical literature. Wicksell seemed to acknowledge that money may act as a store of value over time, but he is careful to say that ". . . the object in view is nearly always that of procuring something else for it at a future time. In other words, it is the exchange value which it is desired to preserve; it is money as a future medium of exchange which is hoarded." [Knut Wicksell, *Money* (Volume II of *Lectures in Political Economy*, ed. Lionel Robbins, 2 vols., London: Routledge and Kegan Paul, Ltd., 1935), p. 8]. Thus Wicksell apparently is referring to the precautionary motive for holding money. Alfred Marshall once wrote, ". . . let us suppose that the inhabitants of a country . . . find it just worth their while to keep by them on the average ready purchasing power to the extent of a tenth part of their annual income, together with a fiftieth part of their property; then the aggregate value of the currency of the country will tend to be equal to the sum of these amounts." [Alfred Marshall, *Money, Credit, and Commerce* (London: Macmillan and Company, Ltd., 1923), p. 33]. Rather than suggesting that there is a demand for money as a means of holding wealth as well as a transactions demand, Marshall appears to be extending the transactions concept to recognize that transactions may not only be related to income, but also may be affected by wealth (or property, to use his term). See Section I.D.3 below for a discussion of a modern version of this view.

immediately after the receipt of income, rather than being spread out over time; and it would also be smaller the greater the degree of vertical integration in business firms). It is assumed to be stable over time, implying that the income velocity of money, Y/M, is constant.[7] The Classics assumed that the interest elasticity of the demand for money is zero, but one of the major Keynesian contributions is the demonstration that there are circumstances, depending on the rate of interest, in which it is rational to hold money balances as part of asset portfolios as well as for transactions purposes. If the demand for money is related to the rate of interest, as well as to income, velocity is no longer constant. Suppose, for example, that an interest rate term is added to the quantity equation:[8]

$$M = kY - mr \qquad m > 0$$

where r is the rate of interest. From the definition of velocity, we have

$$V = \frac{Y}{M} = \frac{Y}{kY - mr}.$$

Since the demand for money must equal the given stock of money, the expression $(kY - mr)$ must be constant. Thus the interest rate and income must change in the same direction. If Y rises, r must rise sufficiently so that the value of $(kY - mr)$ does not change; when Y rises, however, velocity rises, so velocity varies directly with the rate of interest and with income.

As a result of the assumption that income velocity is constant, the quantity theory implies that the income elasticity of the demand for money is unity.[9] This is easily demonstrated using the definition of elasticity:

$$\eta_{M \cdot Y} = \frac{\Delta M}{\Delta Y} \cdot \frac{Y}{M}.$$

If $M = kY$, $\Delta M = k\Delta Y$ and $\Delta M/\Delta Y = k$. Therefore

$$\eta_{M \cdot Y} = k \frac{Y}{M} = k \frac{Y}{kY} = 1.$$

These properties—constant velocity (or unitary income elasticity) and zero interest elasticity—are hallmarks of the pure quantity theory of the demand for money. In addition, in the Classical model, real output and employment are determined independently of the monetary sector, and it was assumed for reasons not taken up in this paper that the system always tended to be at full employ-

---

[7] Without this requirement, the quantity equation becomes simply a definition of velocity, or its reciprocal. Only M, P, and Q can be observed: k (or V, in the "equation of exchange" version, $MV = PQ$) is measured, or defined, by substituting values for M, P, and Q into the equation. If we add the proposition that "velocity is a constant" or, equivalently, that "people desire to hold a constant fraction of their income in the form of money balances," the quantity equation becomes a testable hypothesis instead of a definition of velocity. Note that $k = 1/V$.

[8] The inverse relationship between the demand for money and the rate of interest is due to the assumption that higher-than-average observed values of r generate expectations that r will fall and that bond prices will rise; this leads to a smaller demand for money. See Section I.B. for a more extensive discussion.

[9] While the constant velocity assumption of the quantity theory implies a unitary income elasticity of money demand, a unitary income elasticity does not imply constant velocity. This can be seen by studying the work of Christ, Latané, and others discussed below.

ment.[10] Consequently, real income or output could not be affected by economic policy. Monetary policy—changes in the stock of money by the monetary authority—simply tended to change the level of prices and money wages proportionately, leaving real wages, employment, and output unchanged. That is, the monetary policy multiplier, $\Delta Y/\Delta M$, had the value $1/k$ in the Classical model and affected money income through changes in prices only; the allocation of resources was unaffected. Fiscal policy—changes in taxing and spending—had no effect on output or prices. The expenditure multiplier, $\Delta Y/\Delta G$, had a value of zero: government expenditure was simply a means of diverting resources from the private sector to the public sector or vice versa [see equation (A.14) in the appendix; this multiplier is zero when $\eta_{L \cdot r}$, the interest elasticity of demand for money, is zero as the Classics assumed].

During the days of Marshall and Wicksell, the lack of national income data made empirical testing of the quantity theory very difficult. As will be shown below, our present information indicates that income velocity is definitely not constant (although it may be more or less constant over short periods of time), the demand for money is responsive to changes in the interest rate, and the income elasticity of the demand for money is probably less than unity (although there is substantial disagreement on this point). Thus the quantity theory as stated above appears to be inadequate. Under the leadership of Milton Friedman, another modern school of thought has developed whose goal is to "restate" the quantity theory in such a way that it is consistent with our knowledge of the world. Friedman's work is discussed in Section I.D. 2 below.

B. The Early Keynesian View

Keynes found the Classical transactions approach to the demand for money to be incomplete because it overlooked the possibility that people may choose to hold money *as an asset* instead of other liquid assets—particularly bonds—when their prices are expected to fall. The price of money, by definition, is fixed; however, the price of bonds in terms of money is not fixed, and Keynes pointed out that the decline in capital value of a bond corresponding to even a rather small increase in the rate of interest could more than offset the coupon payment. If such a fall in the price of bonds were expected, it would not be irrational behavior to convert one's bonds into money, even though money is "sterile" in the sense that it pays no return or yields no utility. To account for such behavior, Keynes added an additional category—the speculative, or asset demand for money—to transactions demand and precautionary demand.[11] It should be emphasized that Keynes' theory of the demand for money was based on the assumption that liquid assets could be held in two, and only two, ways: riskless money and risky bonds (the risk arising only from the possibility of changes in capital value, since all bonds were assumed to be identical nonmaturing government bonds, called consols, which were free of risk of default). Under these circumstances, asset holders will rationally choose to hold their financial wealth as money when bond prices appear to be abnormally high, and therefore seem likely, on balance, to fall (i.e., wealth will be held as cash balances when interest rates appear to be unusually low), and as bonds in the opposite circumstances. Therefore, the demand for money as a means

---

[10] For a thorough discussion of the properties of the Classical model, see Gardner Ackley, *Macroeconomic Theory* (New York: The Macmillan Company, 1961), Part Two.

[11] Keynes, *op. cit.*, pp. 195–200.

of holding financial wealth—the asset demand for money—varies inversely with the rate of interest.[12] This conclusion, of course, depends on the hypothesis that a higher-than-average observed value of the interest rate leads to the conclusion that the rate is likely to fall in the future, and vice versa. Such expectations are said to be "inelastic."

For simplicity, Keynes expressed the demand for money of an individual as the sum of a transactions demand (which included a precautionary component) and an asset demand as follows:

$$M_i = M_1(Y_i) + M_2(r), \frac{\Delta M_i}{\Delta Y_i} > 0, \frac{\Delta M_i}{\Delta r} < 0.$$

Here M_i is the ith individual's total demand for money, M_1 is the transactions demand component, assumed to be a positive function of the individual's income, and M_2 is the relationship expressing the individual's choice between money and bonds (the asset demand function), with the demand for money as an asset supposed to be inversely related to the rate of interest. With respect to this component of demand, Keynes suggested that there may exist a floor below which the interest rate could not be driven. That is, there may exist some very low (but nonzero) value of the interest rate such that everyone would prefer to hold liquid wealth as cash balances whenever this rate of interest was reached, since it would unanimously be expected that the interest rate would rise in the future. The interest elasticity of the demand for money would be infinite at that level of interest rates. This situation has been labelled the "liquidity trap," since new injections of money would simply be absorbed into idle balances, without any effect on the rate of interest, rather than being converted into bonds and causing bond prices to rise (and the interest rate to fall). Graphically, the asset demand for money, as well as the total demand, increases as the interest rate falls and then becomes horizontal at the interest rate floor (if such a floor exists). The curves representing both the asset demand and total demand have sometimes been described as having an "inverse J" shape, and the derivation of the total demand for money balances is illustrated in Figure 1.

Although Keynes' formulation was intended only to approximate the behavior of an individual, it formed the basis for some early macroeconomic studies, chiefly those by Brown, Tobin, Khusro, and Kisselgoff.[13] Since these studies have been quite widely quoted as presenting substantial empirical evidence in support of the asset demand hypothesis, the methodology used and the validity of the results will be discussed briefly.

---

[12] This inverse relationship is of course due to the fact that the rate of interest varies inversely with the market value of bonds. In these discussions, all bonds are assumed to be government consols—bonds with no maturity date and no default risk. Their present discounted value or market price reduces to the simple expression $PDV = R/r$, where R is the coupon payment and r is the market interest rate.

[13] The studies to which reference is made are A. J. Brown, "The Liquidity-Preference Schedules of the London Clearing Banks," *Oxford Economic Papers*, No. 1 (October 1938), pp. 49–82; A. J. Brown, "Interest, Prices, and the Demand Schedule for Idle Money," *Oxford Economic Papers*, No. 2 (May 1939), pp. 46–69; James Tobin, "Liquidity Preference and Monetary Policy," *Review of Economic Statistics*, Vol. XXIX (February 1947), pp. 124–31, reprinted in American Economic Association, Arthur Smithies and J. Keith Butters, eds., *Readings in Fiscal Policy* (Homewood, Ill.: Richard D. Irwin, Inc., 1955), pp. 233–47; A. M. Khusro, "Investigation of Liquidity Preference," *Yorkshire Bulletin of Economic and Social Research*, Vol. IV (January 1952), pp. 1–20; Avram Kisselgoff, "Liquidity Preference of Large Manufacturing Corporations," *Econometrica*, Vol. XXIII (October 1945), pp. 334–44.

FIGURE 1   THE DEMAND FOR MONEY BALANCES

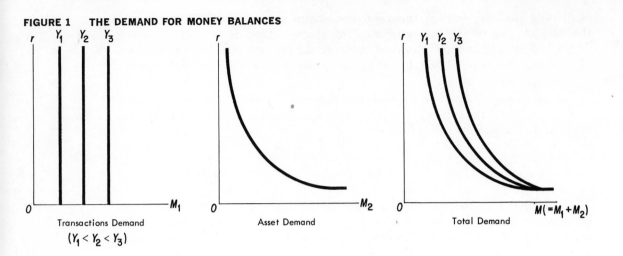

Transactions Demand

$(Y_1 < Y_2 < Y_3)$

Asset Demand

Total Demand

These writers attempted to demonstrate empirically that the "inverse J" asset demand function exists, and Keynes' additive demand function provided the basis for a simple approach to the problem. The studies are based on the common assumption that the asset demand for money was zero during some year in which the level of economic activity was extraordinarily high (usually 1929). The entire money stock for that year is assumed to have been needed to finance the flow of income, and the ratio of money stock to income for the year is used as an estimate of the proportion of income required for transactions balances for each year included in the study, on the assumption that this "transactions requirement factor" does not change from year to year. These estimates of transactions balances are then subtracted from the total money stock in each year, and the residuals are assumed to measure asset balances, which then are plotted against the interest rate. The studies generally covered the interwar period, and they appeared to show that idle balances, calculated as described, were not only inversely related to the interest rate but they followed the "inverse J" pattern which Keynes suggested.

It is doubtful whether these results constitute meaningful evidence on the nature of the asset demand for money. The assumptions on which the calculations of asset balances are based—that the ratio of transactions balances to income was constant over the entire period studied, and that asset balances were zero in years of high levels of economic activity—are open to serious question. Even if this procedure yielded accurate estimates of asset balances, however, there is a more basic problem.

The liquidity preference function is a demand curve, representing the demand for cash balances as a function of price, measured by the rate of interest. As in any market, the quantity observed at a given time, as well as the corresponding price, represents a point on the demand curve *and* supply curve—that is, a point of supply-demand *intersection,* or an equilibrium quantity and price. Both the demand and supply curves tend to *shift* over time, either systematically in response to variables other than price, or randomly. When such shifting occurs, the observed supply-demand intersections tell us very little directly about the nature of either the supply curve or the demand curve. This is illustrated in Figure 2, where three such observations are shown. In this case, both the supply curve and the demand curve are drawn to be relatively inelastic, and they

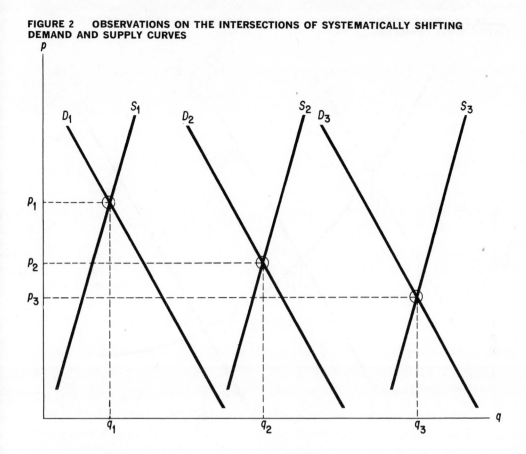

are both shifting steadily outward; the locus of points which is observed, however, appears rather elastic. Since supply is shifting relatively more extensively than demand, the curve traced by their intersections is downward sloping. It is tempting to interpret this curve to be a relatively elastic demand curve. As can be seen from an inspection of Figure 2, however, the curve itself tells us nothing about the properties of the true demand curve, which we cannot observe directly.

This general analysis is directly applicable to the analysis of the supply of and demand for asset balances, taking the rate of interest to be the price of holding these balances (since the supply of asset balances is a residual, it may be taken to be inelastic with respect to the rate of interest for purposes of discussion). It is clear from Figure 2 that the intersections will only "trace" the true demand curve if that curve is perfectly stable over time while supply is shifting. Such a situation is pictured in Figure 3. In the studies of Tobin and others, however, it seems almost certain that both the demand and supply curves were shifting in such a way as to generate a set of points somewhat similar to those in Figure 2. Over the interwar years—the period covered by most of these studies—the money stock increased considerably more rapidly than money income, so that the supply of asset balances probably increased. With respect to the demand for asset balances, these studies neglect the possibility that these balances may be related to wealth, and national wealth increased

FIGURE 3   OBSERVATIONS ON DEMAND-SUPPLY INTERSECTIONS WHEN ONLY THE SUPPLY CURVE IS SHIFTING

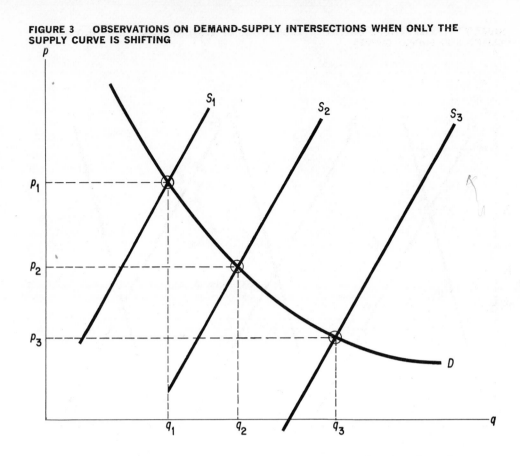

substantially during these years.[14] It appears, in conclusion, that the curves which Tobin and others believed to be aggregate asset-demand relationships actually provide no evidence as to the nature of the aggregate asset demand for money.[15]

---

[14] From June, 1922, until June, 1941, for example, the stock of money rose 127 percent (from $21.4 billion to $48.6 billion) while GNP in current dollars rose 47 percent (from $85.9 billion to $126.4 billion). National wealth, as measured by Goldsmith's data on net worth, rose from $328 billion in 1924 to $467 billion in 1929, a rise of 42 percent; fell to $302 billion by 1932; and then rose to $403 billion in 1941 for an overall increase of 23 percent. Source: Goldsmith et al., *A Study of Saving in the United States* (Princeton, N.J.: Princeton University Press, 1956), Table N-1 for the GNP data, and the *Federal Reserve Bulletin*, various issues, for the data on the money stock. See section I.D.3 below for a discussion of the role of wealth in the determination of the demand for money.

[15] This view is supported by our knowledge of monetary conditions during the interwar period. The curves derived by Tobin and Khusro exhibit a general downward movement during the 1920s and a flattening out at a low interest rate during the 1930s. The speculative pressures characteristic of the 1920s probably caused the demand for liquid balances to decline during that period (Tobin assumes it reached zero in 1929). At the same time, reserves and the money stock were increasing, largely through extensive member-bank borrowing from the Federal Reserve System. The combination of a rightward shift in the supply schedule and a shift of demand to the left could result in the approximately vertical locus of intersection points which are observed for the 1920s. During the 1930s, the high level of liquidity in the banking system in the form of excess reserves would suggest a disequilibrium situation in which commercial banks stood ready to lend to creditworthy applicants at an interest rate somewhat higher than that which would eliminate excess reserves. That is, the money supply function appears to have been perfectly elastic at an "institutional minimum" rate of interest (it might be mentioned that this situation can be termed a "liquidity trap" on the supply side of the market). As the demand for money increased, a fairly level locus of intersection points would be observed. This is the general pattern found by Tobin and Khusro.

C. Some Refinements

A number of economists have attempted to reformulate the simple Keynesian demand for money function in such a way as to make empirical testing more meaningful. Two somewhat different approaches have been followed. One group of investigators has introduced other variables besides income and the rate of interest into the demand relationship, and thereby has lessened the problem of secular shifting mentioned above. Among studies of this type are those by Stedry and by Bronfenbrenner and Mayer.[16] Both of these studies follow Tobin in separating the money stock into transaction and asset components (in addition, Bronfenbrenner and Mayer attempt to explain total balances) and both introduce wealth as an additional explanatory variable for asset balances (although Stedry takes the ratio of transactions to wealth to be constant—a questionable assumption—in his empirical work, and uses transactions to represent the influence of wealth on the demand for liquid balances). Another approach has been used by several investigators who avoid the problems associated with attempts to classify the money stock according to transactions and asset uses by attempting to explain the total demand for money. The procedure used is typically to relate income velocity (or its reciprocal) to some function of the rate of interest. Studies of this type are those by Kalecki, Behrman, Latané, and Christ.[17] While these studies are not as vulnerable to criticism as is the work of Tobin, Khusro, and others mentioned above, they contain a common, and serious, flaw: they treat either the interest rate or the money stock (usually the former) as given, and fail to recognize that causality runs both from the rate of interest to the stock of money, and vice versa; that is, that the rate of interest and the stock of money are determined jointly by the intersection of a demand schedule and a supply schedule for money. Due to the neglect of this "simultaneity," the estimates of the coefficients of the demand function which are reported in these studies are "biased" and result in biased estimates of the respective demand elasticities. (Loosely speaking, the statistical estimate of a coefficient or elasticity is said to be biased if, on the average, its estimated value differs from the true value.) It is important to be aware of such biases in elasticity estimates because, as will be seen, policy decisions may be based on such estimates. This particular type is called "simultaneous equations bias."[18]

---

[16] Andrew C. Stedry, "A Note on Interest Rates and the Demand for Money," *Review of Economics and Statistics*, Vol. XLI (August 1959), pp. 303–307; Martin Bronfenbrenner and Thomas Mayer, "Liquidity Functions in the American Economy," *Econometrica*, Vol. XXVIII (October 1960), pp. 810–34.

[17] M. Kalecki, "The Short Term Rate of Interest and the Velocity of Cash Circulation," *Review of Economic Statistics*, Vol. XXIII (May 1941), pp. 97–99; J. N. Behrman, "The Short-Term Interest Rate and the Velocity of Circulation," *Econometrica*, Vol. XVI (April 1948), pp. 185–90; Henry A. Latanté, "Cash Balances and the Interest Rate—A Pragmatic Approach," *Review of Economics and Statistics*, Vol. XXXVI (September 1954), pp. 456–60; Henry A. Latané, "Income Velocity and Interest Rates: A Pragmatic Approach," *Review of Economics and Statistics*, Vol. XLII (November 1960), pp. 445–49; Carl F. Christ, "Interest Rates and 'Portfolio Selection' Among Liquid Assets in the U.S.," in Christ et al., *Measurement in Economics* (Stanford, Calif.: Stanford University Press, 1963), pp. 201–18.

[18] As explained above, real-world observations on quantities and prices usually do not correspond either to a supply curve or a demand curve as such; rather, they are intersections of supply and demand curves, both of which are probably shifting systematically and/or randomly in response to outside forces. If this is the case, then single-equation statistical estimates of these curves, which essentially involve the fitting of a line to the observed data, actually result in curves which are neither true demand curves nor true supply curves. The usual estimation procedure (least squares linear regression) is to fit a line through the set of observations which minimizes the sum of the squared deviations of the observations on the dependent variable from the line. The illustration below demonstrates the source

In spite of their shortcomings, these studies are significant because of the uniform support which they give to the existence of a relationship between money balances, on the one hand, and income *and* the rate of interest, on the other. Some of the results are summarized in Table 1. While the studies represented in this table covered somewhat different periods of time and employed rather widely-differing formulations (as shown in Column 6), in each study the statistically-estimated coefficient carried the expected sign (except for the national wealth term in Bronfenbrenner and Mayer's total balances equation) and, although not shown, each coefficient (except for the same Bronfenbrenner-Mayer term) was highly significant statistically. That is, we may assume with a very high degree of confidence that the true value of each of these coefficients (with the exception mentioned) is not zero. In most of the studies, the income elasticity of the demand for money is constrained to be unity by the approach adopted—the same income elasticity as is displayed by the Classical model.[19] It is quite noteworthy that each study discloses a substantial interest elasticity of demand for money (Table 1, Column 3) under these circumstances. In other words, the studies show that there is strong evidence supporting an

and nature of "simultaneous equations bias." Here both demand and supply curves are shifting randomly between D and D' and between S and S' respectively; furthermore, the supply curve is shifting more extensively than the demand curve. Therefore all of the observed intersections tend to lie in the trapezoid $ABCE$. If a "least-squares" line is fitted through these observations, such that the sum of the squared deviations of observed quantities from the line (measured horizontally) is minimized, it will pass through points A and C, and its slope will not be the slope of the demand curve—that is, the estimate of the slope is biased.

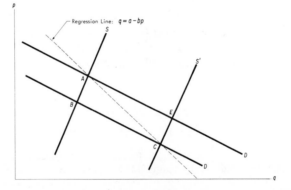

[19] In any of the studies attempting to explain velocity (Latané, Christ, and Stedry), an income elasticity of unity is implied. Consider a general expression for the reciprocal of velocity where we follow the investigators mentioned in using M/Y as the dependent variable (in this derivation, the elasticity $\eta_{M \cdot Y}$ is to be considered a partial elasticity; that is, in differencing the equaton $M = Y \cdot f(r)$, it is assumed that $\Delta f(r) = 0$):

$$M/Y = f(r) \qquad \text{or} \qquad M = Y \cdot f(r).$$

Since

$$\eta_{M \cdot Y} = \frac{\Delta M / \Delta Y}{M/Y},$$

we have

$$\Delta M = f(r) \Delta Y$$

or

$$\Delta M / \Delta Y = f(r),$$

and

$$\eta_{M \cdot Y} = \frac{f(r)}{f(r)} = 1.$$

TABLE 1   A COMPARISON OF SEVERAL DEMAND-FOR-MONEY STUDIES

(1)	(2)	(3)	(4)	(5) R^2 (Fraction of Variance of Dependent Variable Explained by Equation)	(6)
Study	Period Covered	Interest Elasticity of Demand for Money	Income Elasticity of Demand for Money		Regression Equation
Latané (1954)	1919–52	− .70	1.00	.76	$M = .8\dfrac{Y}{r_l} + .1Y$
Latane (1960)	1909–58	− .89	1.00	*	$M = \dfrac{Y}{.77r_l + .38}$
Stedry (data from non-financial transactions)	1919–55	− .62	1.00†	.72	$\log M = -1.44 - .62 \log r_s + \log T$
Bronfenbrenner-Mayer:					
Idle balances	1919–56	−1.16	3.67‡	.90	$\log M = 9.16 - 1.16 \log r_s + 3.67 \log NW$
Total balances	1919–56	− .33	1.23	.91	$\log M = .38 - .33 \log r_s - .42 \log NW + 1.23 \log Y$
Christ	1892–1959	− .58	1.00	.76	$M = \dfrac{.72Y}{r_l} + .13Y$

Here M is the money stock, Y is GNP (in the Bronfenbrenner-Mayer study, it is GNP less government purchases of goods and services), r is the interest rate (r_l is the long-term rate, and r_s is the short-term rate), T is debits to commercial bank demand deposits, and NW is real national wealth (Goldsmith series).
* Not available.
† Stedry substitutes transactions for income in his work, so this figure is a "transactions elasticity."
‡ This equation uses national wealth but omits income; hence, this elasticity refers to national wealth.
Source: Latané, op. cit.; Stedry, op. cit.; Bronfenbrenner and Mayer, op. cit.; Christ, op. cit.

interest-elastic demand function *given* the Classical assumption of a unitary income elasticity. However, the estimates are biased and suggest that further work must be done to obtain unbiased estimates for use as a basis for policy decisions.

D. Some Modern Approaches to the Demand for Money

1. Interest-Elastic Transactions Demand. Except for Friedman and some of his followers, most investigators have concluded that the available empirical evidence supports the hypothesis that the demand for money is related to income (or perhaps wealth) and the rate of interest. At the same time, the early Keynesian notion that this demand consists of a transactions component, based on income, and an asset component, based on the rate of interest, has lost favor as a testable empirical hypothesis. It is recognized that the assumptions which underlie it—that asset holders may choose only between money and bonds, all of which are assumed to be identical as to maturity and risk—are substantially at variance with the real world, even though the hypothesis is logically consistent, given those assumptions. Therefore an important aspect of modern work on the demand for money concerns the nature of this demand in an economy where liquid assets of many varieties, some almost identical with money, are readily available. In such a world, the type of choice which Keynes described as the demand for money as an asset really involves the choice between holding liquid assets whose yield is high but for which the risk of capital loss is great and liquid assets whose yield and risk are both low. If an asset or spectrum of assets not including money can be found which satisfies the asset holder's desires for yield and safety, the simple Keynesian asset-demand hypothesis is no longer relevant to the holding of money balances, but rather determines the prices of the liquid assets or the structure of interest rates.[20] Savings deposits constitute one such asset; they are in fact perfectly liquid (i.e. they can be converted into money without delay at their face value) and they yield a positive return. Treasury bills which are close to maturity, while not completely free of risk of capital loss, formally speaking, are riskless as a practical matter, and also yield a return. Such assets dominate money as a means of holding wealth (though not as a means of payment). If the Keynesian asset demand for money becomes a means of determining the structure of interest rates—that is, the relative prices of these nonmonetary liquid assets—then any interest elasticity of the demand for money which exists must be due to the interest-responsiveness of transactions demand.

The possibility that the demand for transactions balances might be interest elastic was mentioned by Hansen in 1949; however, a systematic theory of the relationship between transactions balances and the rate of interest was first worked out by William J. Baumol and by James Tobin.[21] Their hypotheses, which are quite similar, recognize that there is an opportunity cost for holding transactions balances idle: it is the rate of return on time deposits or securities. Assuming that the transactions for which balances are held are spread out evenly over the period between income receipts so that the average transactions balance which is held over the period is not trivially small, it may be profitable to invest part of the inflow of income until it is needed for transacting, at which time the asset purchased may be reconverted into cash. Whether or not such activity is profitable depends, of course, on the rate of interest available on liquid assets compared with the costs of buying and selling securities.[22] As the return rises relative to cost, the inducement to economize on transactions balances in this way becomes greater, and the average money balance corresponding to a given income level falls. Thus it is concluded that transactions balances

---

[20] An extensive body of theoretical and empirical literature on the term structure of interest rates has grown up during the past several years. For example, see F. A. Lutz, "The Structure of Interest Rates," *Quarterly Journal of Economics*, Vol. LV (November 1940), pp. 36–63, reprinted in American Economic Association, W. Fellner and B. Haley, eds., *Readings in the Theory of Income Distribution* (Philadelphia: The Blakiston Company, 1951), pp. 499–529; John M. Culbertson, "The Term Structure of Interest Rates," *Quarterly Journal of Economics*, Vol. LXXI (November 1957), pp. 485–517; David Meiselman, *The Term Structure of Interest Rates* (Englewood Cliffs, N.J.: Prentice-Hall, Inc., 1962); Arthur M. Okun, "Monetary Policy, Debt Management and Interest Rates: A Quantitative Reappraisal," in *Stabilization Policies: A Series of Research Studies Prepared for the Commission on Money and Credit* (Englewood Cliffs, N.J.: Prentice-Hall, Inc., 1963), pp. 331–80.

[21] Alvin H. Hansen, *Monetary Theory and Fiscal Policy* (New York: McGraw-Hill Book Company, 1949), pp. 66–67; William J. Baumol, "The Transactions Demand for Cash: An Inventory Theoretic Approach," *Quarterly Journal of Economics*, Vol. LXVI (November 1952), pp. 545–56; James Tobin, "The Interest-Elasticity of Transactions Demand for Cash," *Review of Economics and Statistics*, Vol. XXXVIII (August 1956), pp. 241–47.

[22] For example, suppose the recipient of $1,000 knew that this income would not be needed for transacting for a period of one month from receipt. If there were a fixed charge of $1.00 per transaction into and out of, say, Treasury bills, and in addition there were a variable charge of $.50 per $1,000 of securities transacted, then it will cost a total of $3.00 to buy a bill and sell it again at the end of the month. If the rate of return on the bill were 4 percent, the holder will earn $3.33 by holding for a month, for a net gain of $.33. At a rate of return of 3 percent, however, the holder will earn $2.50; this will not cover the cost of transacting, and he will prefer to hold money. At a rate of return of 3.6 percent per year, the return for holding the bill one month will be exactly $3.00, and the income recipient will be indifferent between holding the bill and holding money. (Note: for simplicity, this example assumes that bills are the only liquid asset available as an alternative to holding money.)

are directly related to income and inversely related to the rate of interest. However, the relationship between average money balances and income tends to be nonproportional (the implied income elasticity is less than unity). The demand for money under this hypothesis is said to exhibit "economies of scale" in that the higher is the initial level of income, the smaller is the increase in money balances needed to finance a given income increase.[23]

As yet, very little empirical work has been done using the Baumol-Tobin hypothesis directly. It is an important hypothesis, however, for it recognizes that the Keynesian liquidity-preference theory does not reflect the real world accurately, and at the same time, it provides an alternative rationale for the interest elasticity of the demand for money. And a nonzero interest elasticity of demand for money is an important condition for the effective operation of both fiscal and monetary policy.

2. The Neoclassical Approach. Although it is now generally accepted that the interest elasticity of the demand for money is not zero, the work of one group of investigators continues to be based upon the quantity theory. The chief spokesman for the "modern quantity theorists" is Milton Friedman. Friedman and his followers view the relationship between income and money balances as the most stable macroeconomic relationship, and thus the one on which policy decisions should be based.[24] While the reformulated quantity theory used by Friedman includes several rates of interest in principle, he concludes that no such interest elasticity of money demand can be shown to exist empirically. However, the demand for money is shown to be quite responsive to changes in income (income is defined in a special way, as explained below); the income elasticity is 1.8—substantially greater than unity, rather than being less than unity as the Baumol-Tobin hypothesis would suggest.[25]

Friedman achieves a high income elasticity, and concludes that the interest elasticity is zero, through the use of some statistical techniques and certain definitions which are not commonly used by other investigators. First he chooses

---

[23] An interesting aspect of this approach is that the management of money balances is analogous to the management of inventories of physical goods. Baumol's article demonstrates explicitly how inventory-management principles can be applied to transactions balances, and he derives an expression for the optimal level of transactions balances relative to the interest rate and income in which these balances are shown to vary proportionately with the square root of income and in inverse proportion to the square root of the rate of interest. This finding implies that the income elasticity of the demand for money balances should be 0.5, and that the interest elasticity should be −0.5. The "square root rule" for inventory management has been known and used for some time in the management of inventories of physical goods. The square root relationship as applied to the management of money balances depends on certain simplifying assumptions which are unlikely to be fulfilled in the real world, and thus empirical results which yield elasticities slightly different than those noted above should not necessarily be interpreted as providing strong evidence against the hypothesis. For example, findings of income elasticities between 0.5 and unity could be viewed as being consistent with it.

[24] Milton Friedman and David Meiselman, "The Relative Stability of Monetary Velocity and the Investment Multiplier in the United States, 1897–1958," in *Stabilization Policies: A Series of Research Studies Prepared for the Commission on Money and Credit* (Englewood Cliffs, N.J.: Prentice-Hall, Inc., 1963), pp. 165–268. For a general outline of the modern quantity theory, see Milton Friedman, "The Quantity Theory of Money—A Restatement," in M. Friedman, ed., *Studies in the Quantity Theory of Money* (Chicago: University of Chicago Press, 1956), pp. 3–21. Friedman's empirical conclusions concerning the interest elasticity of the demand for money are reported in Milton Friedman, "The Demand for Money: Some Theoretical and Empirical Results," *Journal of Political Economy*, Vol. LXVII (August 1959), pp. 327–51.

[25] These results, and the reasoning which is summarized in these paragraphs, are discussed in Friedman, "The Demand for Money . . . ," *op. cit.*

to define the money stock as consisting of currency outside banks plus *all* deposits—demand deposits and time deposits—in commercial banks, instead of employing the usual definition, based on money's unique function as a means of payment, of currency outside banks plus *demand* deposits in commercial banks.[26] Friedman justifies this usage by arguing that time deposits are such close substitutes for money that less error is introduced by including them as money than by omitting them. If this argument is followed to its logical conclusion, of course, savings in other financial intermediaries—savings and loan shares, mutual savings bank deposits, etc.—should also be included. In any case, including commercial bank time deposits "stacks the cards" against the possibility of finding any significant interest elasticity of demand for money (as defined). As was pointed out in the discussion of the Baumol-Tobin hypothesis, variations in the interest rate relative to the cost of shifting into and out of other liquid assets (such as time deposits or short-term securities) are felt by some to be the source of the interest elasticity of money demand. Lumping time deposits together with the money stock obscures movements between them based on changes in the interest rate. Therefore, it is not surprising that an interest rate response cannot be found.[27]

In addition to using an unorthodox definition of the money stock, Friedman's definition of income differs from that usually employed in these studies. Instead of relating money stocks to GNP or some similar national-accounts concept of income, he uses aggregate "permanent income," defined as the sum over all households of the amounts each could consume while keeping its wealth intact. Less rigorously, it stands for the sum over all households of their expected average earnings. In practice, since "permanent income" cannot be observed directly, it is approximated by using a weighted average of present and all past values of disposable income, with weights declining exponentially for incomes further and further into the past. Under this hypothesis, real per capita money balances, m, are related to per capita permanent income, y_p, as follows:

$$m_t = \beta y_{p_t}{}^\alpha,$$

or, in logarithmic form,

$$\log m_t = \log \beta + \alpha(\log y_{p_t}),$$

where α represents the elasticity of demand for real money balances with respect to permanent income. Based on annual data for the United States from 1869—1957, Friedman estimates the income elasticity, α, to be 1.8. He employs this formulation to explain what he considers to be an apparently contradictory set of "facts": that the observed income velocity of money (defined, for example,

---

[26] More precisely, the usual definition of the money stock is currency outside banks plus "demand deposits adjusted"—total demand deposits less U.S. government deposits, interbank deposits, and checks in process of collection. Friedman's definition includes currency outside banks plus demand deposits adjusted plus time deposits in commercial banks.

[27] The results are biased against interest rate effects in another way. Friedman first regresses money balances on income (both defined in his particular way, as described). Thus, all variations in his money stock which correspond to changes in income are "explained." Then the residual variance—that which is unexplained in this regression—is regressed on the interest rate, and no significant relationship is found. This conclusion is biased against the interest rate, however, because there is a rather close relationship between interest rates and income. The closer is the relationship, the greater the variation in money balances ascribable jointly to income and the rate of interest which is explained by income alone. Only if there were no relationship at all between income and the rate of interest would the Friedman approach constitute an unbiased test.

as the ratio of gross national product to the money stock) rises during relatively high levels of economic activity and falls during recessions—i.e., it exhibits procyclical movements—but over the very long run, income velocity appears to be falling. It should be stated here that these "facts" are not altogether clear—while income velocity did fall from 1929 until 1946, it has been rising quite steadily since then, and most observers fail to discern a secular downtrend in it. In any case, if Friedman's facts were accurate, his finding of a permanent income elasticity of money demand substantially greater than unity—a sign that money balances are considered to be a "luxury" by households—reconciles the apparent paradox which these facts disclose. Observed velocity, based on standard definitions of income, rises and falls cyclically because observed income rises and falls relative to measured permanent income (since permanent income is measured by an average of incomes in the recent past, it tends to fluctuate much less than observed income). In the long run, however, permanent income is the meaningful concept (according to Friedman) and money balances rise faster than income, thus causing a secular decline in velocity. His distinction between observed and permanent income also results in his relatively high income elasticity of demand for money. Since his operational definition of permanent income is a weighted average of past incomes and hence is relatively more stable over time than observed income (but related positively to it), movements of the money stock are greater relative to movements of permanent income than to movements of observed income.

Friedman's findings are important, not only because they are the result of ingenious work and are presented persuasively, but because of their implications for the relative importance of monetary and fiscal policy. If the interest elasticity of the demand for money is zero (assuming the money stock is given), fiscal policy can have no effect on the level of income. Increases in government spending merely divert resources from the private sector to the government sector, with total demand unchanged. On the other hand, monetary policy reaches maximum effectiveness. Other writings of Friedman reflect this view of the relative power of monetary and fiscal policy; on the basis of this conclusion and other evidence he has adduced, Friedman concludes that monetary policy affects income very strongly but with an undependable lag. Therefore he recommends that discretionary monetary policy should be abandoned because it results in considerable instability, and a "rule" should be substituted under which the money stock would be made to grow by a fixed percentage each year.[28]

3. The Role of Wealth. In the above discussion, reference has been made to the use by some investigators of wealth as a variable in the demand-for-money function. The precise way in which changes in wealth affect the demand for money and for other assets is a subject of considerable current discussion, and at least three viewpoints—not necessarily inconsistent with one another—can be distinguished.

First, Bronfenbrenner and Mayer, Stedry, and others have attempted to show empirically that there exists a relationship between wealth and the demand for *idle balances*. The theoretical rationale for this view has been developed

---

[28] Milton Friedman, "The Supply of Money and Changes in Prices and Output," in *The Relationship of Prices to Economic Stability and Growth*, Compendium of Papers Submitted by Panelists appearing before the Joint Economic Committee (Washington, D.C., 1958), pp. 249–50. For a critique of these findings, see John Kareken and Robert Solow, "Lags in Monetary Policy," in *Stabilization Policies: A Series of Research Studies Prepared for the Commission on Money and Credit* (Englewood Cliffs, N.J.: Prentice-Hall, Inc., 1963), pp. 14–25.

by Tobin in response to the particularly unsatisfactory early Keynesian theory of the asset demand for money. Under that theory, as noted above, wealthholders are governed by their expectations about future bond prices in deciding whether to hold their financial assets as money or as bonds (the only two financial assets assumed to be available). The theory is objectionable not only because such a two-asset world is completely unrealistic, but also because each wealthholder responds to his expectations (which are assumed to be held with certainty) by holding his entire portfolio either as bonds or as money—never as a mixture of the two. In the aggregate, under this theory, a smooth, downward-sloping function relating the demand for idle balances to the interest rate appears to exist only because different individual wealthholders presumably have different expectations about future bond prices (or interest rates).

By introducing risk into this analysis, Tobin was able to show that individual economic units, behaving rationally, might hold *both* money and securities in their portfolios simultaneously.[29] In this analysis, it is assumed that the possible return (including capital gain or loss) from holding a bond for a certain length of time can be represented by a frequency distribution whose characteristics can be summarized by the average or expected value of returns and the variance or dispersion of possible returns. For the typical investor, who prefers higher to lower yields but dislikes risk, indifference curves between yield and risk may be drawn such that, as risk increases by constant amounts, he must be compensated by greater and greater increments of yield in order to maintain the same utility level. At the same time, an "opportunity locus" can be constructed specifying all of the yield-risk combinations available to him as he varies the composition of his portfolio from all money, at the one extreme, to all bonds, at the other. As the proportion of bonds in the total portfolio increases, both the yield and the variance (risk) of the portfolio rise. In the usual case, the individual risk-averting investor will maximize utility by holding a diversified portfolio, rather than holding all money or all bonds as the early Keynesian analysis suggested.

In the Tobin analysis, changes in the yield on securities, other things equal, change the position of the opportunity locus and induce the wealthholder to vary the composition of his portfolio.[30] Changes in wealth, however, should have no effect on an individual's desired portfolio composition unless there is reason to believe that such changes alter the shape of the indifference curves or change the opportunity locus (as might happen, for example, if the wealthholder's portfolio were so large that his market transactions had a noticeable effect on the price of securities). If these possibilities are disregarded, the Tobin theory suggests that changes in wealth change the demand for money in the same direction, and that, at least at the microeconomic level, the elasticity of the demand for money with respect to wealth is unity.

Tobin's analysis is an obvious improvement over the early Keynesian theory of the asset demand, particularly in that it introduces risk into the problem

---

[29] James Tobin, "Liquidity Preference as Behavior Toward Risk," *Review of Economic Studies,* Vol. XXV (February 1958), pp. 65–86.

[30] At the microeconomic level, this theory is consistent with either a negative or positive interest elasticity of the asset demand for money. The direction of the relationship depends on the shape of the individual's indifference curves, and it is not difficult to construct a case in which the elasticity is positive. The reason for the ambiguity is of course that a yield change results in both an income effect and a substitution effect. A positive interest elasticity would indicate that the former is greater in absolute value than the latter (and of course opposite in sign).

and allows for the holding of diversified portfolios. However, it is based on the same two-asset world as the earlier theory, and therefore on the assumption that money is not dominated by other assets as a means of holding wealth. If such assets exist—and savings deposits and Treasury bills close to maturity are obvious possibilities—then the Tobin theory has nothing to do with the demand for money as usually defined, but rather explains choices between non-monetary financial assets of differing degrees of riskiness (including at least one such asset with zero risk but with non-zero yield).

Even if money as a means of holding wealth is inferior in every way to savings deposits or Treasury bills, it is possible to advance an alternative argument supporting wealth as an explanatory variable in the demand for money balances. The argument is that asset portfolios at any point in time would usually be observed to contain money balances, which are the temporary manifestation of uncompleted shifts between other assets. That is, they would constitute transactions balances in wealth portfolios, and the size of such balances would probably be related positively to total wealth.

If an asset demand for money exists, then, we would expect it to be determined by wealth and interest rates. If transactions demand were determined by income and interest rates (and perhaps also by wealth), the total demand for money would be a function of income, interest rates, and wealth. Because income and wealth are closely correlated, it is difficult to separate their influences in empirical studies, as is demonstrated by the work of Stedry and of Bronfenbrenner and Mayer. For this reason, the empirical evidence in support of this view is weak.

The third, and most general, view of the role of wealth stems from the notion that the demand for money is part of the overall problem of the demand for financial and physical assets; money is viewed as one of the very many ways of holding assets in general. The choice among these assets is presumably "constrained" by some measure of wealth in the same way that consumption choices are said to be constrained by income.[31] This approach is not necessarily antithetical to those discussed above; in fact, the Tobin approach can be thought of as a special case of the third view. It should be noted that the problem of dominance arises here as well as in the Tobin analysis. However, this third view, which is meant to encompass the transactions, precautionary, and speculative motives for money holding, leads to a demand-for-money function which omits income and includes only wealth and yields on the other assets as explanatory variables. Friedman's use of permanent income as a determinant of the demand for money balances identifies his work with this view. Brunner and Meltzer have reported the results of extensive tests of demand-for-money functions using wealth instead of income.[32] However, the role of wealth remains one of the major unsettled questions in monetary theory.

---

[31] The Tobin liquidity-preference analysis described previously is also based on utility maximization subject to a constraint. In Tobin's model, however, the constraint is the total size of the financial portfolio; in the most general view, the constraint is total wealth (financial and physical).

[32] Friedman, "The Demand for Money . . . ," op. cit.; Karl Brunner and Allan H. Meltzer, "Predicting Velocity: Implications for Theory and Policy," Journal of Finance, Vol. XVIII (May 1963), pp. 319–43; Allan H. Meltzer, "The Demand for Money: The Evidence from the Time Series," Journal of Political Economy, Vol. LXXI (June 1963), pp. 219–46; Allan H. Meltzer, "A Little More Evidence from the Time Series," Journal of Political Economy, Vol. LXXII (October 1964), pp. 504–8; Karl Brunner and Allan H. Meltzer, "Some Further Investigations of Demand and Supply Functions for Money," Journal of Finance, Vol. XIX (May 1964), pp. 240–83.

4. *Joint Estimation of Monetary Elasticities.* A recent development in the study of behavioral relationships in the monetary sector has been the estimation of elasticities which are relatively free of "simultaneous equations bias." As noted above, this bias arises when two or more variables are actually determined jointly by the interaction of a set of relationships (in the manner that the price and quantity traded of a good are jointly determined by the interaction of a supply function and a demand function, for example), but when the coefficients are estimated statistically using only one equation. In the demand-supply system mentioned, for example, the estimates would be biased if quantity were regressed on price in order to obtain a price elasticity of demand; such an estimate assumes that market price is not determined by the model and that causation runs from price to quantity rather than recognizing the two-way nature of causality.

A logical way to eliminate the simultaneous equations bias to which the demand coefficients (and elasticities) are subject in the studies noted is to demonstrate that a supply function for money exists, and then to estimate the coefficients of the demand-for-money function and the money supply function jointly, thus taking account of the interdependence of the functions.[33] Relatively little theoretical or empirical work has been done on the money supply relationship. However, there is good *a priori* reason to suspect that such a function exists due to the response of the commercial banking sector to changes in the profitability of making loans. One of the earliest pieces of empirical evidence on this point was reported in a study by Polak and White.[34] They found that the ratio of net free reserves of member banks (excess reserves less borrowings from the Federal Reserve banks) to demand deposits fell when the short-term interest rate rose, and vice versa. Net free reserves are sterile assets, but they provide a cushion of liquidity against unexpected reserve losses. The Polak-White assumption is that banks desire to hold net free reserves equal to some fraction of deposits in order to provide such a cushion, but that free reserves are "economized" when the return from loans rises, in order to supply more loans and deposits. Polak and White demonstrated empirically that the rate of interest was inversely related to the ratio of free reserves to demand deposits (that is, that banks respond to the interest rate in supplying deposits), but they did not use their supply hypothesis for the purpose of obtaining demand or supply elasticity estimates free of simultaneous equations bias.

Some work on demand and supply functions for money has also been done by Brunner and Meltzer, and they have reported joint estimates as well as single-equation estimates of the demand and supply coefficients, using various linear and nonlinear functional forms. Limitations of space preclude a discussion of their work here.[35] In general, the notion that the supply of money is determined by the economic system rather than being set by the monetary authority is relatively new, and work on determining the form of and variables in the supply function is only beginning.

---

[33] Space limitations prohibit a discussion of the techniques involved in the joint estimation of these coefficients. However, statistical procedures are available which make allowance for the interaction of the behavioral functions of a model and which yield joint estimates of the coefficients. It should be emphasized that estimates of coefficients may be biased even though the simultaneous equations problem is taken into account. If the model is incorrectly specified, it is subject to "specification bias."

[34] J. J. Polak and W. H. White, "The Effect of Income Expansion on the Quantity of Money," *International Monetary Fund Staff Papers*, Vol. IV (August 1955), pp. 398–433.

[35] See, for example, Karl Brunner, "A Schema for the Supply Theory of Money," *International Economic Review*, Vol. II (January 1962), pp. 79–109; Karl Brunner and Allan H. Meltzer, "Some Further Investigations . . . ," *op. cit.*

II. THE SUPPLY OF MONEY

In this section, a theory of the supply of money will be developed which is somewhat similar to the approach suggested by Polak and White. The hypothesis is based on the notion that commercial banks act in a profit-maximizing way in response to changes in the return from lending relative to the cost. Both the return and the cost are represented by short-term interest rates: in principle, the return is the yield on loans, and the cost is measured by the cost of acquiring the reserves necessary to support the new loans. When it becomes more profitable to make loans, banks are assumed to be willing to supply more deposits and to increase the money stock. However, member banks are constrained in supplying deposits by the reserve requirements imposed by the Federal Reserve System, and if excess reserves are scarce, member banks will tend to increase their borrowings. Therefore this hypothesis states that member banks will tend to increase their borrowings and decrease their excess reserves when the return from lending rises relative to the cost of making loans. This analysis is developed within the framework provided by a very simple version of a standard consolidation of Federal Reserve System and Treasury accounts, showing the sources and uses of member bank reserves.[36] The following table lists the most important factors which affect reserves:

Sources	Uses
$P =$ Federal Reserve portfolio of U.S. government securities	$R^{r(d)} =$ Required reserves for member bank demand deposits
$B =$ Borrowings from the Federal Reserve System by member banks	$R^{r(t)} =$ Required reserves for member bank time deposits
$A =$ All other sources less all other uses	$R^e =$ Member bank excess reserves
	$N =$ Currency held by the nonbank public

Since the left-hand side of this table must equal the right-hand side, we may write

$$P + B + A = R^{r(d)} + R^{r(t)} + R^e + N \tag{1}$$

and by rearranging terms. We find that

$$(P + A) = [R^{r(d)} + R^{r(t)} + (R^e - B)] + N. \tag{2}$$

The term $(P + A)$ includes the Federal Reserve System's holdings of U.S. government securities plus all of the other factors affecting reserves which are not explicitly mentioned.[37] These latter factors are watched carefully by the Federal

---

[36] The tabulation known as the "Sources and Uses of Member Bank Reserves," of which the above table is a very simple example, is a basic tool for the analysis of changes in the reserve base. A good discussion of its derivation and contents may be found in William J. Frazer, Jr., and William P. Yohe, *The Analytics and Institutions of Money and Banking* (Princeton, N.J.: D. Van Nostrand Company, Inc., 1966), chaps. 9–10. In brief, the "Sources and Uses" table as of a given date is derived by combining the consolidated balance sheet of the twelve Federal Reserve banks with the Treasury's statement of monetary assets and liabilities as of that date, canceling some offsetting items, consolidating other items, and rearranging the resulting entries. Sources and uses tables appear in several publications, most notably the *Federal Reserve Bulletin*, published monthly by the Board of Governors of the Federal Reserve System. It appears each month in that publication under the title "Member Bank Reserves, Federal Reserve Bank Credit, and Related Items."

[37] These factors include the monetary gold stock, Treasury currency (i.e., assets held by the Treasury to support its silver certificate and coin liabilities), Federal Reserve float, Treasury cash (the Treasury's monetary net worth, defined as the difference between its monetary assets and monetary liabilities), the U.S. Treasury general account, foreign and other deposits held at the Federal Reserve banks, and other Federal Reserve accounts.

Reserve System; in fact, the System makes daily forecasts of them. Unless the expected changes in these variables happen to coincide to some extent with planned changes in bank reserves desired for policy reasons, the Federal Reserve will use open market operations to offset them and they may be viewed as being under the close control of the System.[38] Thus it is clear that the sum of the portfolio plus all of the items in the "other sources and uses" category is under the System's control as long as a policy of offsetting these items is followed. Likewise, it is clear that any change in this sum represents a policy decision by the System. Therefore the sum $(P + A)$ may be viewed as representing the Federal Reserve System's discretionary open market operations instrument, and for convenience we will use the definition

$$R^* = P + A.$$

On the other side of equation (2) we find total reserves (consisting of required reserves plus excess reserves) less member bank borrowing from the Federal Reserve, plus the stock of currency held by the nonbank public. Assuming that changes in the items which comprise the "all other sources and uses" category are offset by defensive open market operations in the manner outlined above, it is clear that all member bank reserves arise either through borrowing or from open market operations. Thus the terms in parentheses on the right-hand side of equation (2) above sum up to total reserves less borrowed reserves, or unborrowed reserves (those originating in discretionary open market operations). It follows that the Federal Reserve System, through discretionary open market operations, is able to control the sum of unborrowed reserves plus currency but cannot exercise direct control over either one separately. In fact, a given open market transaction will usually result in a fairly substantial change in currency holdings by the public. By deriving our money supply hypothesis within the structure of the sources-and-uses identity, however, these currency flows will be taken into account.

As noted above, the money supply hypothesis will be based on the proposition that given the cost of borrowing, rising loan rates induce banks to increase their borrowings from the Federal Reserve and to reduce excess reserves; by the same token, increases in the cost of borrowing, other things equal, induce banks to reduce their borrowing and to increase their cushion of excess reserves. The difference between excess reserves and borrowing is known as "free reserves," and we will summarize the behavior described above by supposing that free reserves (R^f) fall when market rates of interest rise, but rise when the Federal Reserve discount rate rises, other things equal. Thus we can rewrite equation (2) as follows:

$$R^* = R^f(r, r_d) + R^{r(d)} + R^{r(t)} + N, \quad \frac{\Delta R^f}{\Delta r} < 0, \quad \frac{\Delta R^f}{\Delta r_d} > 0, \tag{3}$$

where r is a short-term market rate of interest and r_d is the Federal Reserve discount rate. In order to convert this into a full-fledged money supply equation, we must introduce another definition and further behavioral assumptions.

The money supply is defined as consisting of demand deposits at commercial

---

[38] Such open market operations are called "defensive" (as opposed to "dynamic" open market operations, which are those that are used in pursuit of policy goals). See Robert V. Roosa, *Federal Reserve Operations in the Money and Government Securities Markets* (New York: Federal Reserve Bank of New York, 1956), pp. 64–79.

banks (except U.S. government deposits) plus currency in circulation outside banks. Thus we may write

$$M = D' + D'' + N, \tag{4}$$

where D' are demand deposits in member banks, D'' are demand deposits in nonmember banks, and N is defined in the same way as above. For simplicity, we will assume that the currency stock, nonmember bank demand deposits, and time deposits are all proportional to the money stock:

$$D'' = hM \qquad 0 < h < 1 \tag{5}$$
$$N = nM \qquad 0 < n < 1 \tag{6}$$
$$T = sM \qquad 0 < s \tag{7}$$

From these assumptions and equation (4), it follows that $D' = (1 - h - n)M$. Next, we convert the required reserve terms in equation (3) into the corresponding deposit totals, where

g = reserve requirements on member bank demand deposits $\qquad 0 < g < 1$
t = reserve requirements on member bank time deposits[39] $\qquad 0 < t < 1$

so that $R^{r(d)} = gD'$ and $R^{r(t)} = tT$. It now follows that

$$R^* - R^f(r, r_d) - tsM - nM = g(1 - h - n)M \tag{8}$$

and therefore that

$$M = \frac{1}{g(1 - h - n) + n + ts} [R^* - R^f(r, r_d)].$$

In words, this equation states that the supply of money is a multiple of the difference between the policy-controlled reserve base, R^*, and free reserves. The factor of proportionality relating the money supply to this difference is determined by the reserve ratio for demand deposits in member banks and the reserve ratio for time deposits in member banks (both of which are controlled by the Federal Reserve System), the ratio of nonmember bank demand deposits to the money stock, the currency ratio, and the ratio of time deposits to the money stock. While R^* is determined entirely by monetary policy, under our assumptions, the level of free reserves depends both on market forces, as expressed in the market rate of interest, and on policy decisions of the Federal Reserve System, as expressed through movements in the discount rate. We expect the supply of money to vary positively with R^*. Since free reserves vary inversely with market interest rates but directly with the discount rate, the relationship of the supply of money to these variables is just the opposite: the supply increases with increases in market interest rates but falls when the discount rate is increased, other things equal. Finally, the supply of money will respond inversely to changes in reserve requirements (g and t); when these increase, the supply of money falls, and vice versa.

Having become familiar with the procedure for deriving a supply function for money, we may now broaden the analysis somewhat in the interest of greater realism. We have assumed above that the demand for currency and the demand for time deposits were both proportional to the demand for money balances; however, recent studies seem to indicate that demand behavior in both cases is somewhat more subtle than this. It is usually found that the demand for

---

[39] For simplicity, we are disregarding the fact that reserve requirements differ for different member bank categories and for different time deposit classes.

both of these assets (as well as for money balances) is a function of the short-term market rate of interest (i.e., the rate on Treasury bills) and the rate on time deposits as well as income.[40] Thus we may replace equations (6) and (7) with the following:

$$N = N(r,r_t,Y) \qquad \frac{\Delta N}{\Delta r} < 0, \qquad \frac{\Delta N}{\Delta r_t} < 0, \qquad \frac{\Delta N}{\Delta Y} > 0 \qquad (10)$$

$$T = T(r,r_t,Y) \qquad \frac{\Delta T}{\Delta r} < 0, \qquad \frac{\Delta T}{\Delta r_t} > 0, \qquad \frac{\Delta T}{\Delta Y} > 0 \qquad (11)$$

We would expect the demand for both currency and time deposits to fall as market rates rise. Time deposit demand would increase with an increase in the rate on these deposits, r_t, while the demand for currency would presumably decline in those circumstances. For purposes of this illustration, we will assume that both time deposits and currency are superior goods; that is, that the demand for each is positively related to income.

Now we may see how these changes affect our supply-of-money hypothesis. On the basis of equations (4), (5), and (10), the definition of the money stock can now be written as follows:

$$M = D' + hM + N(r,r_t,Y). \qquad (12)$$

As a consequence, D' may be expressed in the following way:

$$D' = M(1 - h) - N(r,r_t,Y). \qquad (13)$$

Now we again convert the reserve terms in equation (3) into the corresponding deposit totals on the basis of the respective reserve requirements, and then substitute equations (11) and (13) for time and demand deposits. This yields

$$R^* - R^f(r,r_d) - tT(r,r_t,Y) - N(r,r_t,Y) = g(1 - h)M - gN(r,r_t,Y). \qquad (14)$$

Solving equation (14), for M, the supply of money, we find:

$$M = \frac{1}{g(1 - h)} [R^* - R^f(r,r_d) - tT(r,r_t,Y)] - \frac{(1 - g)}{g(1 - h)} [N(r,r_t,Y)]. \qquad (15)$$

This formulation shows how changes in market yields, rates on time deposits, and income all affect the supply of money (it should be noted that these variables all have quite separate and simultaneous effects on the *demand* for money). Holding other things constant, increases in income will reduce the supply of money because holdings by the nonbank public of time deposits and currency will increase. In the first case, increases in time deposits absorb reserves which could be used to support an expansion of demand deposits. In the second, an increase in currency in itself constitutes an increase in the supply of money; however, it also represents an equivalent drain of reserves from the banking system and will therefore generate a multiple contraction of demand deposits. The net result will be a contraction of the money stock. Increases in market interest rates will decrease free reserve holdings of banks, the demand for time deposits, and the demand for currency; all of these effects will expand the money stock (in the case of currency, the argument is the reverse of that used

---

[40] Some investigators find that only one of these rates—the Treasury bill rate—affects the demand for currency, while others find that both yields are important. For the purpose of this demonstration, we shall include both.

above: currency will flow into the banking system, providing the base for a multiple expansion of deposits). Increases in the yield on time deposits will have a depressing effect on the supply of money through direct effects on time deposit demand; however, according to the hypothesis, there will be a simultaneous reduction in the demand for currency. The net effect depends on the relative size of the two elasticities of demand and the relative size of the terms $t/g(1-h)$ and $(1-g)/g(1-h)$.

In this section we have attempted to demonstrate that the supply of money is responsive both to market forces, as expressed in interest rates such as the yield on Treasury bills or similar market instruments or the rate on time deposits, and to policy instruments of the Federal Reserve System. This demonstration was based on certain behavioral assumptions having to do with the supposed response of free reserves, the demand for time deposits, and the demand for currency to various interest rates and income. It remains to demonstrate that these assumptions are supported by empirical evidence. A discussion of some recent evidence, and its implications for policy, is the subject of the next section.

III. JOINT ESTIMATION OF SUPPLY AND DEMAND ELASTICITIES

A. Empirical Results

Several empirical supply-of-money hypotheses have been developed along the lines described above and have been tested on postwar data. The coefficients of these supply functions were estimated within a structure in all of the studies to be discussed in this section. That is, other hypotheses describing behavior in both the financial and real sectors were developed, and the coefficients of all of these functions were estimated simultaneously in such a way that the problem of simultaneous equations bias, described in footnote 18 above, is overcome. The elasticity estimates for several of the monetary equations based on these coefficients are reported in Table 2.

These estimates are noteworthy in several respects. First, the interest elasticities of the demand for currency and demand deposits appear to be considerably smaller than was indicated by the single-equation studies summarized in Table 1. Most of those studies reported interest elasticities of demand of −0.6 to −0.9, whereas the values shown above are much smaller, generally lying below −0.2. De Leeuw finds slightly larger elasticities, but his formulation includes the yield on private securities rather than the bill rate; since the former is a longer-term rate than the latter, it fluctuates less and is bound to display a larger elasticity. However, it should be noted that several of the earlier studies used the short rate and obtained interest elasticities of the demand for money of from −0.6 to as high as −1.16 (Bronfenbrenner and Mayer). While part of this difference could be due to differences in the period covered, restriction of the income elasticity to be unity, etc., much of it must be due to disregard of the supply relationship. Second, these studies generally tended to find that elasticities which are based on coefficients estimated within a structure, both on the supply and demand sides, are somewhat larger than their biased counterparts. This is particularly true of the supply elasticities. Third, the estimates of the income elasticity of the demand for currency and demand deposits lie within a range between about 0.6 and 1.1. This may be interpreted as weak evidence in support of the Baumol-Tobin hypothesis, but it should be noted that the results really do not permit us to discriminate sharply between alterna-

| | Demand for | | | | | | | | | Supply of Money | |
| | Currency | | | Demand Deposits | | | Time Deposits | | | | |
Elasticity with Respect to →	r	r_t	Y	r	r_t	Y	r	r_t	Y	r	r_d
Study and Period Covered (all studies are quarterly)											
de Leeuw[1] (1948–62)	—.36*	—.14	n.a.	—.35*	—.17	n.a.	—.37	.68	n.a.	.25	—.35
Goldfeld[2] (1950III–1962II)	—.07	—.14	.64	—.11	—.18	.80	—1.62†	.37	.65	.22	—.08
Teigen[3] (1953–64)	n.a.	n.a.	n.a.	—.10	—.43	1.11	—2.82†	3.76	2.09	.14‡	—.10‡

n.a. = not available.
Note: In the above tabulation, the variables are defined as follows, unless otherwise noted:

r = rate on three-month Treasury bills.
r_t = rate on time deposits. (In the Goldfeld and de Leeuw studies, an annual series reported by the Federal Deposit Insurance Corporation is used; it is interpolated to yield quarterly data in a way described in the de Leeuw study. In the Teigen paper, this rate is a weighted average of commercial bank time deposit rates, the rate on savings and loan shares, and the rate on mutual savings bank deposits.)
Y = gross national product at current prices.

* Yield on private securities. It should be noted that at least part of the difference in results reported by de Leeuw compared to those in the other studies is based on this difference in specification.
† Yield on long-term U.S. government bonds. It should be noted that at least part of the difference in results reported by Goldfeld compared to those in the other studies is based on this difference in specification.
‡ Supply of demand deposits.
[1] Frank de Leeuw, "A Model of Financial Behavior," in James S. Duesenberry, Gary Fromm, Lawrence R. Klein, and Edwin Kuh (eds.), *The Brookings Quarterly Econometric Model of the United States* (Chicago: Rand McNally & Co., 1965), chap. 13.
[2] Stephen M. Goldfeld, *Commercial Bank Behavior and Economic Activity* (Amsterdam: North-Holland Publishing Company, 1966).
[3] Ronald L. Teigen, "An Aggregated Quarterly Model of the U.S. Monetary Sector, 1953–1964" in Karl Brunner (ed.), *Targets and Indicators of Monetary Policy* (San Francisco: Chandler Publishing Co., 1969), chap. IX.

tive hypotheses in this respect.[41] Finally, the rather low interest elasticities together with the high degrees of explanation achieved (as measured by R^2) suggest that the Keynesian "liquidity trap," the notion that the demand for money tends to become infinitely elastic at low rates of interest, does not exist. It might be mentioned in this context that some estimates of supply and demand functions have also been made using prewar data, and the interest elasticity of demand found in that study, —0.19, was of the same order of magnitude as those reported above.[42] This result provides no support for belief that a liquidity trap existed during that period. In fact, we have experienced low interest rates in both the prewar and postwar periods, and these studies should have disclosed liquidity traps had they existed.

B. Policy Implications

The treatment of the supply of money as a behavioral relationship and the joint estimation of the monetary elasticities are innovations which are of some significance for both monetary and fiscal policy decisions. With respect to fiscal policy, the expression for the static multiplier applicable to a change in govern-

[41] See footnote 23 on p. 81 above for a brief discussion of the elasticities implied by this hypothesis.

[42] See Ronald L. Teigen, "Demand and Supply Functions for Money in the United States: Some Structural Estimates," *Econometrica*, Vol. XXXII (October 1964), pp. 476–509, for a discussion of these results.

ment purchases of goods and services, $\Delta Y/\Delta G$, will be altered because the elasticity of the supply of money with respect to the rate of interest is now included. The way in which this term enters may be seen by comparing the expenditure multiplier expressions based on a model with a given money stock and a model including a money supply relationship, respectively. The derivation of these multipliers is given in the Appendix.[43]

1. Multiplier for government purchases with given money stock:

$$\frac{\Delta Y}{\Delta G} = \frac{1}{1 - c(1 - x) + \dfrac{\dfrac{I}{Y}\eta_{I\cdot r}\eta_{L\cdot Y}}{\eta_{L\cdot r}}} \tag{16}$$

2. Multiplier for government purchases with a money supply relationship:

$$\frac{\Delta Y}{\Delta G} = \frac{1}{1 - c(1 - x) + \dfrac{\dfrac{I}{Y}\eta_{I\cdot r}\eta_{L\cdot Y}}{\eta_{L\cdot r} - \eta_{M\cdot r}}} \tag{17}$$

From (16) and (17), it can be seen that the introduction of the money supply elasticity, $\eta_{M\cdot r}$, tends to increase the size of the multiplier for given values of the other terms in the expression—that is, for given values of the terms in (16), the introduction of $\eta_{M\cdot r}$ into (17) will make its value larger than the value of (16). As is true of the interest elasticity of demand, the larger the value of the supply elasticity, the larger the expenditure multiplier value. These two elasticities have different signs, and since they appear in (17) as a difference, increases in their respective absolute values increase the multiplier value, and decreases reduce it. It is easy to see why a positive supply elasticity with respect to the rate of interest increases the size of this multiplier. Increasing government expenditures raise the transactions demand for money, thereby increasing interest rates and deterring private investment spending to some extent; and interest rates will rise more the less money is available to finance the expansion in income. But if the supply of money responds positively to interest rate increases, the interest rate increase itself is restrained and total spending and income rise by larger amounts.

Introducing a supply function for money not only alters the multiplier for government purchases; it also permits the derivation of other interesting multipliers, particularly those related to monetary policy. If the money stock is taken as given, the only monetary policy multiplier which can be derived is $\Delta Y/\Delta M$. However, the evidence quoted above suggests that the Federal Reserve System does not determine the money stock unilaterally. On the basis of the simple supply function described in Section II of this paper (see equation (9) above),

---

[43] In these multiplier expressions, the terms are defined as follows:

$\eta_{I\cdot r}$ = the elasticity of investment expenditure with respect to the rate of interest
$\eta_{L\cdot Y}$ = the elasticity of demand for money with respect to income
$\eta_{I\cdot r}$ = the elasticity of demand for money with respect to the rate of interest
$\eta_{M\cdot r}$ = the elasticity of supply of money with respect to the rate of interest
c = the marginal propensity to consume out of disposable income
x = the marginal propensity to collect taxes out of total income
I = investment expenditures
Y = gross national product

multipliers related to the instruments of monetary control actually at the disposal of the System—open market operations and changes in the discount rate—can be derived instead of the multiplier $\Delta Y/\Delta M$. The derivation of the multiplier on income for open market operations—$\Delta Y/\Delta R^*$—and the multiplier on income for discount rate changes—$\Delta Y/\Delta r_d$—is given in the Appendix. The expressions that result are:

$$\frac{\Delta Y}{\Delta R^*} = \left[\frac{1}{g(1-h-n)+n+ts}\right] \frac{\dfrac{I}{M}\eta_{I\cdot r}}{[1-c(1-x)][\eta_{L\cdot r}-\eta_{M\cdot r}]+\dfrac{I}{Y}\eta_{I\cdot r}\eta_{L\cdot Y}} \tag{18}$$

$$\frac{\Delta Y}{\Delta r_d} = \frac{\dfrac{I}{r_d}\eta_{I\cdot r}\eta_{M\cdot r_d}}{[1-c(1-x)][\eta_{L\cdot r}-\eta_{M\cdot r}]+\dfrac{I}{Y}\eta_{I\cdot r}\eta_{L\cdot Y}} \tag{19}$$

Both the open market multiplier, $\Delta Y/\Delta R^*$, and the discount rate multiplier, $\Delta Y/\Delta r_d$, are smaller in value the larger the interest elasticity of supply. This follows from the fact that the rising interest rates which accompany attempts by the monetary authorities to restrict credit induce bankers to economize on reserves, increase borrowing, and expand loans and deposits, thus offsetting the attempt at restriction to some extent.

Finally, treatment of the money supply as a behavioral relationship enables us to derive an expression for the credit expansion multiplier, $\Delta M/\Delta R^*$. This expresses the degree to which the money stock will change for a given amount of open market operations. As shown in the Appendix, the following expression is obtained:

$$\frac{\Delta M}{\Delta R^*} = \frac{1}{g(1-h-n)+n+ts}\left[\frac{1}{1-\dfrac{\eta_{M\cdot r}}{\eta_{L\cdot r}}}\right]. \tag{20}$$

It should be noted that this expression represents the "impact multiplier" for open market operations—that is, it expresses the degree to which the money stock will change disregarding the effects on the stock of money of changes in income which are induced by open market operations. This multiplier concept is used because it is more similar in spirit to the usual textbook credit expansion multiplier with which it is compared below than is the full multiplier (including the effects of income feedbacks).

Numerical values for these multipliers may be obtained by substituting values for the various elasticities and propensities involved and by using values which approximate reality for the other variables. Following are the values that will be used to evaluate multiplier expressions derived from a model containing a money supply function:

$M = \$250$ billion	$\eta_{L\cdot Y} = 0.8$	$c = 0.75$
$Y = \$1,200$ billion	$\eta_{L\cdot r} = -0.15$	$x = 0.2$
$I = \$200$ billion	$\eta_{M\cdot r} = 0.20$	$h = 0.175$
$r = 6$ percent	$\eta_{M\cdot r_d} = -0.20$	$n = 0.215$
$r_d = 6$ percent	$\eta_{I\cdot r} = -0.15$	$g = 0.13$
		$t = 0.04$
		$s = 1.2$

The values used for h, n, g, t, s, the money stock, investment expenditures, income, the short-term rate of interest, and the discount rate are approximately equal to those observed as of April, 1973. The values of the elasticities of the demand for and supply of money are consistent with those given in Table 2 and are based on the short-term interest rate.[44] The value shown for the interest elasticity of investment expenditure is based on the recent work of Kareken and Solow.[45] They find that this elasticity, based on the long-term interest rate, is -0.4. Since the model from which the multipliers are derived contains only one rate of interest, it is necessary to convert this elasticity into an elasticity with respect to the short-term rate. The result is the value of -0.15 given above.[46]

Let us first consider the value of the government purchases multiplier. Using the expressions given in equations (16) and (17) we have:

$$\frac{\Delta Y}{\Delta G} = \frac{1}{1 - .75(1 - .2) + \dfrac{\dfrac{200}{1,200}(-.4)(1)}{(-.6)}} = 1.96,$$

based on a given money stock. [Note: Since equation (16) is derived from a model in which the stock of money is assumed to be determined by the monetary authorities, it is appropriate to substitute values for the monetary demand elasticities which were found in single-equation studies. This has been done above; the values used for $\eta_{L \cdot r}$ and $\eta_{L \cdot Y}$ are -0.6 and 1, respectively, and are from the Christ study cited in Table 1. Since Christ used the long-term interest rate in his demand-for-money function, the value of the interest elasticity of invest-

---

[44] The value used for the elasticity of the supply of money with respect to the interest rate, 0.2, is slightly smaller than those given in Table 2. This smaller value was chosen because the studies referred to in Table 2 were conducted on the basis of money supply relationships which responded to interest rate changes through time deposits and currency as well as free reserves—i.e., these studies used money supply functions similar to equation (15), while the multipliers derived in this paper are based on a simpler money supply relationship [equation (3)], in which only the interest sensitivity of free reserves influences the money supply; time deposits and currency holdings are assumed to be proportional to total money holdings. Such a function formed the basis for the results reported in Teigen, *op. cit.*, and the interest elasticity of the supply of money was found to be 0.2 in that study.

[45] John Kareken and Robert M. Solow, "Lags in Monetary Policy," in *Stabilization Policies: A Series of Research Studies Prepared for the Commission on Money and Credit* (Englewood Cliffs, N.J.: Prentice-Hall, Inc., 1963).

[46] This adjustment was made by noting that $\eta_{I \cdot r_s} = \eta_{I \cdot r_l} \eta_{r_l \cdot r_s}$. To determine the response of the short-term interest rate, r_s, to changes in the long-term rate, r_l, the expectations hypothesis concerning the relationship between short and long rates was employed. Under this hypothesis, the long rate is an average of short rates. Consequently, the long rate was regressed on the short rate, using quarterly data for the postwar period. The short rate used was the Treasury bill rate on new issues, and the long rate was the corporate Aaa bond yield; all of the data were smoothed using a four-quarter moving average. Based on a simple regression of the long rate on the short rate, the value of the elasticity $\eta_{r_l \cdot r_s}$ was found to be 0.44. When a time trend was added to the regression to attempt to account for other variables which might influence the relationship, a value of 0.17 was found for this elasticity. As a compromise, a value of 0.38 was used. Thus the value of -0.15 assigned to $\eta_{I \cdot r}$ above results from the multiplication of the elasticity based on the long rate of -0.4 found by Kareken and Solow by this factor of 0.38.

ment expenditure is also based on the long rate.] Alternatively, we have:

$$\frac{\Delta Y}{\Delta G} = \frac{1}{1 - .75(1 - .2) + \dfrac{\dfrac{200}{1,200}(-.15)(.8)}{-.15-.2}} = 2.19,$$

based on an interest-responsive money supply. The introduction of the interest elasticity of money supply, and the changes in the other elasticities, have increased the value of the expenditure multiplier from the previous estimate of 1.96 to 2.19 (for the sake of comparison, we note that if the other elasticity values had remained unchanged, the inclusion of an interest elasticity of money supply of 0.2 would have resulted in a multiplier value of 2.07). Thus an increase of government expenditure on goods and services of $1 billion is expected to increase equilibrium gross national product by $2.19 billion (note that a zero interest elasticity of investment demand or demand for money with respect to income, or an infinite demand or supply elasticity with respect to the interest rate, makes the second term in the denominator disappear, and the resulting "pure expenditure multiplier" reaches its maximum value of 2.5).

Using equation (18), the value of the multiplier relating open market operations to income changes can be calculated:

$$\frac{\Delta Y}{\Delta R^*} = \left[\frac{1}{.13(1 - .175 - .215) + .215 + (.04)(1.2)}\right] \left\{ \frac{\dfrac{200}{250}(-.15)}{[1 - .75(1 - .2)][-.15 - .2] + \dfrac{200}{1,200}(-.15)(.8)}\right\} = 1.96.$$

According to this estimate, open market purchases of $1 billion by the Federal Reserve System will increase equilibrium income by about $2 billion, and sales of $1 billion will decrease equilibrium income by the same amount.

The value of the discount rate multiplier is as follows:

$$\frac{\Delta Y}{\Delta r_d} = \frac{\dfrac{200}{6}(-.15)(-.2)}{[1 - .75(1 - .2)][-.15 - .2] + \dfrac{200}{1,200}(-.15)(.8)} = -6.25.$$

Thus an increase (decrease) of one point in the discount rate will reduce (increase) equilibrium gross national product by $6.25 billion, according to this estimate.

Finally, equation (20) enables us to calculate a value for the credit expansion multiplier:

$$\frac{\Delta M}{\Delta R^*} = \left[\frac{1}{.13(1 - .175 - .215) + .215 + (.04)(1.2)}\right]\left[\frac{1}{1 - \dfrac{.2}{-.15}}\right] = 1.25.$$

That is, the equilibrium money stock will increase by about $1.25 for each dollar of open market purchases of securities by the Federal Reserve System and will decrease by the same amount for each dollar of open market sales.

This value may seem unduly low on the basis of commonly held views concerning the size of this multiplier. A typical method of calculating its value is to assume that, at the outset, the commercial banking system is completely loaned up, with both excess reserves and borrowings equal to zero. Then, for every dollar of the money stock, there must exist $[g(1 - h - n) + n + ts]$ dollars of reserves in the private sector (including currency in circulation), and therefore:

$$\frac{M}{R^*} = \frac{1}{g(1 - h - n) + n + ts} \quad \text{or} \quad M = \frac{1}{g(1 - h - n) + n + ts} R^*. \quad (21)$$

If open market purchases of amount ΔR^* are carried out by the monetary authorities, banks are assumed to expand their loans and deposits until a new equilibrium is reached in which excess reserves and borrowings are both again zero. That is:

$$(M + \Delta M) = \left[\frac{1}{g(1 - h - n) + n + ts} \right] (R^* + \Delta R^*) \quad (22)$$

and

$$\Delta M = \left[\frac{1}{g(1 - h - n) + n + ts} \right] \Delta R^* \quad (23)$$

or

$$\frac{\Delta M}{\Delta R^*} = \left[\frac{1}{.13(1 - .175 - .215) + .215 + (.04)(1.2)} \right] = 2.92.$$

This approach overlooks the response of member bank borrowing to interest rate changes which result from open market operations; such a response is the basis for the money supply function derived above. If the interest elasticity of the supply of money is zero, as is assumed in the approach summarized by equation (23)—that is, if there is no supply response on the part of the commercial banks—the value of the credit expansion multiplier based on the model used in this paper [equation (20)] corresponds to the value shown for equation (23). This can be seen by examining equation (20), which for convenience is reproduced as equation (24):

$$\frac{\Delta M}{\Delta R^*} = \frac{1}{g(1 - h - n) + n + ts} \left[\frac{1}{1 - \dfrac{\eta_{M \cdot r}}{\eta_{L \cdot r}}} \right]. \quad (24)$$

If $\eta_{M \cdot r} = 0$, this expression is the same as equation (23). Therefore this equation (and the approach which it summarizes) is a special case of the general credit expansion multiplier given in equation (24).

IV. CONCLUSIONS

This paper has been an attempt to trace the main strands of the development of the theory of the demand for and supply of money from the Classical writers to the present and to summarize the available empirical evidence. The study of these behavioral relationships is important for decisions concerning the use of both fiscal and monetary policy. While some economists still hold to the view that the demand for money is determined only by income, and while it is quite common to assume the stock of money to be determined only by the monetary authorities without reference to the commercial banking system, it now appears that both of these views are incorrect. The weight of evidence supporting the hypothesis that the demand for money is interest responsive seems almost overwhelming. And recent work on the supply of money indicates strongly that the neglect of commercial banks' supply response to interest rate changes cannot be justified, although the exact nature of this response is not yet fully understood.

If either the demand for money or the supply of money is interest responsive, both fiscal and monetary policy are effective in stimulating income (assuming that some category of spending responds to interest rate changes). The relative effectiveness of monetary policy, compared to fiscal policy, depends on the size of the interest elasticity of demand for and supply of money, the income elasticity of the demand for money, and other elasticities and propensities. Accurate knowledge concerning the size of these elasticities and propensities is therefore necessary for the proper use of policy. While all of the estimates presented above are subject to various biases, a substantial amount of research effort is now being devoted to the relationships discussed, and it is to be hoped that eventually these biases will be minimal and our knowledge of policy processes correspondingly improved.

APPENDIX

Model 1

This is a linear version of a standard liquidity preference model with a given money stock. Since it is to be used for the derivation of various multipliers, it will be convenient to write it in first difference form:

$$
\begin{array}{lll}
\textit{Real Sector} & & \\
\Delta C = c\Delta Y_d & 0 < c < 1 & \text{(A.1)} \\
\Delta Y_d = \Delta Y - \Delta T & & \text{(A.2)} \\
\Delta T = x\Delta Y & 0 < x < 1 & \text{(A.3)} \\
\Delta I = -v\Delta r & v > 0 & \text{(A.4)} \\
\Delta Y = \Delta C + \Delta I + \Delta G & & \text{(A.5)}
\end{array}
$$

$$
\begin{array}{lll}
\textit{Monetary Sector} & & \\
\Delta M^D = k\Delta Y - m\Delta r & 0 < k < 1, \quad m > 0 & \text{(A.6)} \\
\Delta M^S = \Delta M^D = \Delta M & & \text{(A.7)}
\end{array}
$$

$$
\begin{aligned}
C &= \text{consumption expenditure} \\
Y_d &= \text{disposable income} \\
T &= \text{tax collections} \\
Y &= \text{gross national product} \\
I &= \text{investment expenditure} \\
G &= \text{government expenditures on goods and services} \\
M^D &= \text{demand for money balances} \\
M^S &= \text{supply of money}
\end{aligned}
$$

To derive the income multiplier applicable to a change in government expenditures, we solve the model by substituting into equations (A.5) and (A.7), and then solving the resulting pair of equations jointly. That is, from equations (A.1) through (A.5), we have

$$\begin{aligned}
\Delta Y &= c\Delta Y_d - v\Delta r + \Delta G \\
&= c(\Delta Y - x\Delta Y) - v\Delta r + \Delta G \\
&= c\Delta Y - cx\Delta Y - v\Delta r + \Delta G.
\end{aligned} \tag{A.8}$$

From (A.6) and (A.7):

$$\Delta M = k\Delta Y - m\Delta r; \tag{A.9}$$

$$\Delta r = \frac{k}{m}\Delta Y - \frac{1}{m}\Delta M. \tag{A.10}$$

Substituting (A.10) into (A.8) and solving for ΔY:

$$\Delta Y = c\Delta Y - cx\Delta Y - \frac{vk}{m}\Delta Y + \frac{v}{m}\Delta M + \Delta G; \tag{A.11}$$

$$\Delta Y = \frac{1}{1 - c(1-x) + \dfrac{vk}{m}}\Delta G + \frac{\dfrac{v}{m}}{1 - c(1-x) + \dfrac{vk}{m}}\Delta M. \tag{A.12}$$

The government expenditure multiplier, $\Delta Y/\Delta G$, is derived by assuming that government expenditures change by the amount ΔG while the money supply is held constant ($\Delta M = O$). Then:

$$\Delta Y = \frac{1}{1 - c(1-x) + \dfrac{vk}{m}}\Delta G \quad \text{or} \quad \frac{\Delta Y}{\Delta G} = \frac{1}{1 - c(1-x) + \dfrac{vk}{m}}. \tag{A.13}$$

[Note that the same procedure can be used to find the effects of a change of ΔM in the given money stock when government expenditures are held constant. Then

$$\Delta Y = \frac{\dfrac{v}{m}}{1 - c(1-x) + \dfrac{vk}{m}}\Delta M \quad \text{or} \quad \frac{\Delta Y}{\Delta M} = \frac{\dfrac{v}{m}}{1 - c(1-x) + \dfrac{vk}{m}}$$

so

$$\frac{\Delta Y}{\Delta M} = \frac{1}{\dfrac{m[1 - c(1-x)]}{v} + k}\Bigg].$$

In this expression for the government expenditure multiplier (as well as for the monetary policy multiplier), the "real" effects of changes in government spending (or changes in the money stock) are conveniently separated from the "monetary" effects. The denominator contains a sum consisting of a term containing the "real" parameters c (the marginal propensity to consume out of disposable income) and x (the marginal propensity to collect taxes out of total income). The "monetary" terms are the marginal propensity to hold money balances with respect to total income, k, and the interest rate coefficients of the demand-for-money and investment functions (m and v, respectively). It is common to express these monetary terms as elasticities; for example, in the case of the interest rate coefficient in the investment function, we know that the interest elasticity of the demand for investment is:

$$\eta_{I \cdot r} = \frac{\dfrac{\Delta I}{\Delta r}}{\dfrac{I}{r}}.$$

From (A.4), we have

$$\frac{\Delta I}{\Delta r} = -v.$$

Therefore

$$\eta_{I \cdot r} = \frac{-v}{\dfrac{I}{r}}, \qquad \text{or} \qquad v = -\eta_{I \cdot r} \frac{I}{r}.$$

Proceeding in this way for the terms k and m, and substituting the resulting expressions into (A.13), we get

$$\frac{\Delta Y}{\Delta G} = \frac{1}{1 - c(1 - x) + \dfrac{\dfrac{I}{Y} \eta_{I \cdot r} \eta_{L \cdot Y}}{\eta_{L \cdot r}}}. \qquad (A.14)$$

[Note: in (A.14), the elasticities $\eta_{L \cdot Y}$ and $\eta_{L \cdot r}$ are the elasticities of the demand-for-money relationship with respect to total income and the rate of interest, respectively. The "L" in these expressions refer to "liquidity preference" or the demand for money. In the next section we will amend the model to include a supply-of-money relationship; supply elasticities will use the symbol "M" to stand for the money supply function.]

Model 2

This model is identical to Model 1 except that it includes a supply-of-money function rather than assuming that the stock of money is determined unilaterally by the monetary authority. The supply function to be used is based on equation (9) in the text:

$$\Delta M^S = z \Delta R^* - z \Delta R^f(r, r_d), \qquad (A.15)$$

where r is the short-term interest rate, r_d is the Federal Reserve discount rate, and where

$$z = \frac{1}{g(1 - h - n) + n + ts}.$$

In order to use this equation in our model, we will assume for the sake of simplicity that free reserves are a linear function of the market rate of interest and the discount rate, and that they vary inversely with the former and directly with the latter. That is, we will assume

$$\Delta R^f = -b \Delta r + d \Delta r_d \qquad b, d > 0 \qquad (A.16)$$

so that

$$\Delta M^S = z \Delta R^* + z b \Delta r - z d \Delta r_d. \qquad (A.17)$$

To derive multiplier expressions for the model including this supply relationship, the expressions for ΔM^D and ΔM^S are equated and the resulting expression is solved jointly with (A.8) for ΔY as before:

$$k\Delta Y - m\Delta r = z\Delta R^* + zb\Delta r - zd\Delta r_d. \qquad (A.18)$$

This gives

$$\Delta r = \frac{k}{(m + zb)}\Delta Y - \frac{z}{(m + zb)}\Delta R^* + \frac{zd}{(m + zb)}\Delta r_d. \qquad (A.19)$$

Substituting (A.19) into (A.8):

$$\Delta Y = c(1 - x)\Delta Y - \frac{vk}{(m + zb)}\Delta Y + \frac{vz}{(m + zb)}\Delta R^* - \frac{vzd}{(m + zb)}\Delta r_d + \Delta G; \qquad (A.20)$$

$$\Delta Y = \frac{zv}{[1 - c(1 - x)](m + zb) + vk}\Delta R^* - \frac{zvd}{[1 - c(1 - x)](m + zb) + vk}\Delta r_d$$

$$+ \frac{1}{[1 - c(1 - x)] + \dfrac{vk}{m + zb}}\Delta G \qquad (A.21)$$

1. The Expenditure Multiplier

Now the government expenditure multiplier can be found by assuming that a change in expenditures occurs with no change either in unborrowed reserves or in the discount rate (i.e., $\Delta R^* = 0$ and $\Delta r_d = 0$) and we have

$$\frac{\Delta Y}{\Delta G} = \frac{1}{[1 - c(1 - x)] + \dfrac{vk}{m + zb}}, \qquad (A.22)$$

or, in terms of elasticities,

$$\frac{\Delta Y}{\Delta G} = \frac{1}{1 - c(1 - x) + \dfrac{\dfrac{I}{Y}\eta_{I \cdot r}\eta_{L \cdot Y}}{\eta_{L \cdot r} - \eta_{M \cdot r}}}. \qquad (A.23)$$

Thus the elasticity of the supply of money with respect to the interest rate enters additively in the denominator of the second denominator term. Since it is opposite in sign to the demand elasticity with respect to the interest rate, its inclusion tends to make the expenditure multiplier larger in value.

2. Monetary Multipliers on Income

Equation (A.21) contains two explicit terms which represent instruments of monetary policy— ΔR^* and Δr_d (the variable representing reserve requirement changes is hidden in the parameter z: reserve requirements are not treated as an important instrument of discretionary monetary policy in this analysis, although it would not be difficult to calculate multipliers with respect to reserve requirement changes). Open market operations are represented by ΔR^*, while Δr_d stands for changes in the discount rate.

A. Open Market Policy. To find the multiplier expressing the effects of open market operations on income, we assume $\Delta r_d = \Delta G = 0$ in equation (A.21), and find that:

$$\frac{\Delta Y}{\Delta R^*} = \left[\frac{1}{g(1-h-n)+n+ts}\right]\frac{v}{[1-c(1-x)](m+zb)+vk}, \quad (A.24)$$

or, in terms of elasticities,

$$\frac{\Delta Y}{\Delta R^*} = \left[\frac{1}{g(1-h-n)+n+ts}\right]\frac{\dfrac{I}{M}\eta_{I\cdot r}}{[1-c(1-x)][\eta_{L\cdot r}-\eta_{M\cdot r}]+\dfrac{I}{Y}\eta_{I\cdot r}\eta_{L\cdot Y}}.$$

$$(A.25)$$

B. Discount Rate Policy. The multiplier summarizing the effects on income of a change in the discount rate is derived by assuming $\Delta R^* = \Delta G = 0$ in equation (A.21), which yields:

$$\frac{\Delta Y}{\Delta r_d} = \left[\frac{1}{g(1-h-n)+n+ts}\right]\frac{-vd}{[1-c(1-x)](m+zb)+vk}. \quad (A.26)$$

Converting this expression to elasticities, we have:

$$\frac{\Delta Y}{\Delta r_d} = \frac{\dfrac{I}{r_d}\eta_{I\cdot r}\eta_{M\cdot r_d}}{[1-c(1-x)](\eta_{L\cdot r}-\eta_{M\cdot r})+\dfrac{I}{Y}\eta_{I\cdot r}\eta_{L\cdot Y}} \quad (A.27)$$

3. The Credit Expansion Multiplier

The credit expansion multiplier, $\Delta M/\Delta R^*$, expresses the relationship between open market operations and changes in the money stock. It can be derived by using equations (A.6) and (A.17). Dividing these two equations by ΔR^*, we have:

$$\frac{\Delta M^D}{\Delta R^*} = k\frac{\Delta Y}{\Delta R^*} - m\frac{\Delta r}{\Delta R^*} \quad (A.28)$$

$$\frac{\Delta M^S}{\Delta R^*} = z\frac{\Delta R^*}{\Delta R^*} + zb\frac{\Delta r}{\Delta R^*} - zd\frac{\Delta r_d}{\Delta R^*}. \quad (A.29)$$

Rearranging terms, and assuming that changes in R^* are unrelated to discount rate changes (i.e., $\Delta r_d/\Delta R^* = 0$), we have:

$$\frac{\Delta M^D}{\Delta R^*} + m\frac{\Delta r}{\Delta R^*} = k\frac{\Delta Y}{\Delta R^*} \quad (A.30)$$

$$\frac{\Delta M^S}{\Delta R^*} - zb\frac{\Delta r}{\Delta R^*} = z. \quad (A.31)$$

Now we assume that $\Delta M^D = \Delta M^S$; this yields two equations in the two unknowns

$$\frac{\Delta M}{\Delta R^*} \quad \text{and} \quad \frac{\Delta r}{\Delta R^*}.$$

Solving for $\dfrac{\Delta M}{\Delta R^*}$, we have:

$$\frac{\Delta M}{\Delta R^*} = z \, \frac{\left(m + kb \, \dfrac{\Delta Y}{\Delta R^*}\right)}{(m + zb)}. \tag{A.32}$$

This expression for the effects on the money stock of changes in the Federal Reserve System's portfolio includes the term $(kb)\,\Delta Y/\Delta R^*$, which reflects the "feedback" effects on the money stock of changes in income generated by the reserve change. It is generally acknowledged that the lag between a monetary change and the income change which it generates is quite long. Since the credit expansion multiplier derived here will be compared with textbook-type credit expansion multipliers (such as the reciprocal of the reserve requirement), which approach quite closely their equilibrium values after a relatively short period of time and do not take account of these income feedbacks, the "impact" version of equation (A.32) in which $\Delta Y/\Delta R^*$ is taken to be zero must be used in order to make a meaningful comparison. For $\Delta Y/\Delta R^* = 0$, we have

$$\frac{\Delta M}{\Delta R^*} = z \, \frac{m}{m + zb}. \tag{A.33}$$

This multiplier measures the effect on the money stock of changes in the Federal Reserve portfolio disregarding the effects of induced income changes. In terms of elasticities, it becomes:

$$\frac{\Delta M}{\Delta R^*} = \frac{1}{g(1 - h - n) + n + ts} \left[\frac{1}{1 - \dfrac{\eta_{M \cdot r}}{\eta_{L \cdot r}}}\right]. \tag{A.34}$$

Since discussions of the effects of open market operations on money and credit are often carried on in terms of free reserves, it may be useful to express this multiplier in terms of the response of free reserves to interest rate changes, rather than in terms of the interest elasticity of the supply of money as we have above. To do so, we first reproduce equation (A.16):

$$\Delta R^f = -b\Delta r + d\Delta r_d \tag{A.35}$$

and note that, holding $\Delta r_d = 0$, this equation implies that

$$\frac{\Delta R^f}{\Delta r} = -b,$$

which further implies that

$$b = -\frac{R^f}{r} \, \eta_{R^f \cdot r}.$$

Using this result and equation (A.33), we find that the credit expansion multiplier may be expressed in the following way [which is equivalent to equation (A.34)]:

$$\frac{\Delta M}{\Delta R^*} = \frac{1}{g(1 - h - n) + n + ts + \dfrac{R^f}{M}\left(\dfrac{\eta_{R^f \cdot r}}{\eta_{L \cdot r}}\right)}. \tag{A.36}$$

THE MULTIPLIER TIME PERIOD: MONEY, INVENTORIES, AND FLEXIBILITY*

Gardner Ackley

The multiplier concept was introduced into economics as a device in comparative statics, showing the extent to which equilibrium levels of less-than-full-employment income differ with different magnitudes of "injections"—i.e., expenditures whose size does not depend on the level of income. In this setting, the multiplier is, of course, merely a "fifth wheel," to use Professor A. G. Hart's phrase.[1] The analysis can be developed without using it at all. Nevertheless, it does constitute a convenient summary of some aspects of the behavior of the simpler model systems. And it cannot be denied that the multiplier has had a certain usefulness in *dramatizing* the importance of investment expenditures (and public expenditures or deficits) in policy discussions.

Used as a device in comparative statics, however, the multiplier concept is of little use to the policy maker, whose interest is not only in the *size* of the ultimate increase in income assumed to result from a given increment in, say, deficit-financed expenditure, but as much in *when* this will occur: what the results will be in one month, six months, one year. To answer the latter question, the multiplier must be recast in dynamic terms; the process of income change must be thought of in terms of successive "rounds" of partial respending of income, with the ultimate increase seen as the cumulant of successive increments of spending, each a fraction of the previous one. The question "how much increase when" depends on the length of these "rounds" of income. If, when the multiplier is two, nearly 97 percent of the ultimate effect is achieved within five "rounds," does this take five weeks, five months, or five years? This indeed is an important question, to which various answers have been given, none perhaps fully satisfactory.

I

One answer was that the time period depended on the speed with which money circu-
lates, or, more precisely, on the marginal circular velocity of active money. This was the position taken in Professor Fritz Machlup's well-known article "Period Analysis and Multiplier Theory."[2] The argument that attempts to identify the multiplier time period with the velocity concept usually runs in terms of a simple example.[3] Let us suppose that there is new expenditure, say by government, financed by "new money." This money is, let us say, paid out as income to leaf-rakers on Monday. On Tuesday, they spend a portion of this new money for consumer goods. This is not yet income, however. It will become additional income only as the added payment filters down through the economic system from retailers to wholesalers to manufacturers to raw material suppliers, and so on, with a fraction of it becoming income payment at each level (retailer, wholesaler, manufacturer, supplier, etc.) in the form of wages, profit, interest, or rent, and the rest moving along in intermediate transactions. There is, however, some *average* interval between initial income payment and the resulting secondary income payments. The length of this period can be seen to be both the length of the multiplier period, and, as well, the average time that it takes a dollar (or at least a marginal dollar of active money) to make the circuit from one income recipient to another.

Now the above argument is specifically based on the assumption that no "hoarding" or "dishoarding" occurs by business firms. Upon receipt of

* From *American Economic Review*, Vol. XLI (June 1951), pp. 350–68. Reprinted by permission of the publisher and the author. Gardner Ackley is Henry Carter Adams University Professor of Political Economy, University of Michigan.

[1] *Money, Debt, and Economic Activity* (Prentice-Hall, Inc., 1948), n., p. 190.

[2] Reprinted in *Readings in Business Cycle Theory*, G. Haberler (ed.) (Irwin, 1944), pp. 203–34. Not quite the same point of view is expressed in Professor Richard Goodwin's article in *The New Economics*, S. E. Harris (ed.) (Knopf, 1947), pp. 482–99. Professor Goodwin states that "It is obvious from the way the problem is stated, that the time from income creation to income creation implied in the velocity concept is the same as the over-all lag implied in the multiplier. . . . One should say, rather, that the two concepts agree if we mean the income velocity of active money" (p. 488). Goodwin, however, is careful to recognize that "velocity has no explanatory value" (p. 489), but rather merely that "multiplier analysis can make important use of the rich empirical evidence from monetary studies" (p. 488). See also n. 7, below.

[3] See, for example, Machlup's "primitive story" (*op. cit.*, p. 210).

an additional stream of money payments, business firms, after their customary payment intervals, make enlarged money payments to factors of production and suppliers. None of the new money stream is added to "idle" balances, nor is money withdrawn from "idle" balances to finance new production or purchases prior to the receipt of the enlarged money flow which originated with consumers.

On the basis of the above assumptions the argument is undoubtedly correct. The length of the multiplier "round" depends upon payment habits, degree of integration, and the other institutional and psychological factors which determine the velocity of active money. Our quarrel is only with the realism of the assumptions.

Note first that this argument implies that money flows *precede* the reverse flow of goods. The retailer sends the new money to the wholesaler, from whom it reaches manufacturer and suppliers, who use the new stream of money to finance added production (and income payments), following which the added goods move back up the stream to the retailer.

One very important fault with the assumption is that business is not ordinarily done this way. Rather, payment is made at each stage only *after* receipt of goods previously ordered. With his enlarged order, the retailer includes payment for his last, *normal-sized* shipment (assuming that he waits until payment time to enlarge his order, which, of course, he may not do). The wholesaler does the same. The manufacturer, like his suppliers *ad infinitum,* then receives an enlarged order, for which he will receive correspondingly enlarged money payment *after he ships the enlarged flow of goods.* With business done in this way the speed of the flow of the new money is seen to depend on the rate at which an added flow of goods is forthcoming, and there exists no logical reason for supposing that the rate at which production increases will bear any connection with any pre-existing speed of money flows. The sequence assumed in the money circulation argument seems to rest on the view that *money* is the limiting factor in determining the rate of production. Production cannot increase until the money arrives to finance the increase, and this added money will arrive on a schedule predetermined by customary payment habits, etc. But this makes for a logical impasse if money flows typically *follow* the reverse flow of goods; and, of course, it ignores the other *possible, necessary,* and *usual* means of financing added production through borrowing (either "new money" or someone else's idle balance), use of one's own idle

balance, or liquidation of security or inventory assets.

This apparently is realized by Machlup when he remarks: "Through the medium of induced dishoarding on the part of business firms the actual propagation of incomes may be much faster than that which is possible on the basis of the circuit flow of money. For the present, however, we shall rule out induced dishoarding, as it has been ruled out by most writers on the subject."[4] But why should we rule it out if that is a necessary feature of the way business is done? And having refused to rule it out, it is clear that the speed of money flows makes little difference in the timing of the multiplication of income.

If, to take an extreme case, the retailer recognized, on the second day after the newly received money had been spent by the workers, that his business was expanding, and telegraphed an enlarged order to the wholesaler, who in turn immediately telegraphed an enlarged order to the manufacturer, who, the next day, activated an idle production line, new income would be generated almost immediately. If, on the other hand, the retailer's and/or the wholesaler's expansion of the stream of new orders was delayed (inventories being drawn down at one or the other stage);[5] or, if the manufacturer chose to meet or was forced to meet the increased demand out of finished goods inventory for a considerable period, before increasing his rate of production and income payment, there might be a prolonged delay in the second increase in income, despite the fact that the new money spent by the initial workers had long since reached his hands.[6]

Presumably it is "induced dishoarding" that speeds up the process of income creation in the first of our two examples; "induced hoarding" that delays it, in the second. But what exactly is the "induced" hoarding or dishoarding?

The two cases clearly give different income velocities: the quantity of money is the same

---

[4] *Op. cit.,* p. 215.

[5] And if the manufacturer did not find out about the increased business by other means, and try to prepare for what he thought would be its impact on him.

[6] The irrelevance of money flows can be seen perhaps even more clearly in the reverse case—that of a decline in consumer demand. Does the manufacturer keep on making money payments to his workers at the old rate so long as money continues to flow to him at the old rate in payment for *previous* sales? Hardly. Once his orders decline, he is apt to reduce employment as rapidly as he can. To be sure, since the money flows continue, I suppose that he will be engaging in "induced hoarding" if he does this.

on both, the levels of income different. Machlup wants to explain this by saying that the quantity of *active* money (the velocity, or marginal velocity, of which remains constant) has been altered by some kind of an act of hoarding or dishoarding that we can appropriately "rule out." What is this "act"?

We suppose that both before and after the increase in income to, and increase in spending by, the first set of workers, all cash settlements are made, say, monthly, payment being made at that time for whatever goods were received during the previous month. Suppose further that there is no change in the degree of integration (there remain the same number of stages between which transactions must take place). The objective determinants of velocity have not changed. Nor, we suppose, has liquidity preference increased in the sense of a change in the attitude toward holding wealth in cash versus other forms. Yet in the one case we have dishoarding; in the other, hoarding. That is, money must have moved from "idle" to "active" balances, or *vice versa.*

One way in which we can *always* reach this conclusion is simply to define the quantity of "active" money as some stable percentage of income. Knowing income, we then know the necessary quantity of "active" money. The circuit velocity of "active" money is obviously constant, and we can always explain any deviation of the multiplier time period from the time period implied in our constant velocity by stating that "hoarding" or "dishoarding" has occurred. This obviously begs the question, and is of little help.

A second approach is to try to give to "active" money some definition which is independent of the level of income. For example, we could (with Machlup, *op. cit.*) define "active" money as the difference between average and recurring minimum balances. This gives the concept of active money an operational definition, permitting its measurement, and a testing of the assumption that the circuit velocity of active money so defined is constant. The author knows of no serious attempt to make such a test, however.[7] He has

constructed hypothetical sequences of income and cash balance change, one of which indeed shows the ratio of active money so defined to income remaining constant during periods of income change, others showing wide and unsystematic variation of the ratio.

The real difficulty arises from the fact that while the quantity of "active" money may be a precise concept under stationary conditions, it breaks down when we consider income change. The quantity of "money work" that has to be done, or the quantity of "active" money, in a stationary economy is a precisely measurable amount. We can measure this amount by the difference between average and minimum balances, or perhaps in other ways, and find that for each period it remains a constant fraction of a constant income. Another way of putting this is to say that under stationary conditions, new production is self-financing. Receipt of funds in payment for a previous period's production provides the means to finance this period's income payment.

But when income changes, this is no longer true. If there is to be an increase in income payments, it must be otherwise financed. A decrease in income payments will release some means of finance. The quantity of "active money" loses its precision of definition. As a result, when income changes, the speed of the change will depend not on any previous speed of money circulation, but upon non-monetary factors of the sort we have suggested above, and will discuss in more detail in the next section. If those factors result in a constancy of the circuit velocity of active money (under any particular definition) it will be mere coincidence. The speed of the process of income change depends primarily on these non-monetary factors.[8]

---

[7] Goodwin (*op. cit.*) follows the second sentence quoted above (n. 2) by the statement: "Keynes always accepted the hypothesis that the velocity of active money is substantially constant. The evidence for such a constancy is considerable. The average income velocity in the United States for 1909–18 was 3.11, and for 1919–28 it was 3.08 according to Professor Angell. This constancy was maintained in spite of large variations in both money and income. By taking long periods, we have some hope of eliminating the effects of idle money."

But what does this prove? If we *assume* the veloc-

ity of active money is constant, we can attribute the short-run changes in total velocity to changes in the proportions of active and idle money. But the long-run stability of total velocity tells us nothing about the short-run stability of the velocity of active money; or even about its long-run stability. There might as well have been a downward trend in the proportion of active money and an increase in its velocity. Unless we give active and idle money operational definitions and measure the concepts so defined, we prove nothing.

[8] Naturally, there are necessary mathematical relations between money turnover periods and the time period of the multiplier. Knowing the time rates of change of income and money supply we can compute the time rate of change of velocity, and vice versa. And if we define the quantity of active money as a constant fraction of income, there is a mathematical relationship between the time rates of change of income and of the shift from idle to active balances.

To summarize the argument of this part:

1. The velocity explanation of the multiplier time period seems to assume that availability of money to finance production (income creation) is the limiting factor in income change. Income payments cannot increase until the money arrives, and they will not decrease until the money flow decreases.

2. In the case of expansion, this involves a logical impasse, if, as is normally the case, changes in money flows *follow* changes in the reverse flow of goods.

3. In fact, other sources of financing must be, and normally are, available.

4. Dismissal of these other means of financing as "induced dishoarding" seems to involve the question-begging definition of active money that assumes its velocity constant in order to define it.

5. The actual factors which normally determine the time lag in the multiplier must be explained otherwise.

II

Professor Lloyd Metzler in a recent paper[9] approaches our question in a different way. He describes three lags in the process of income creation: first, the lag between a change in disposable income and a change in consumer expenditures (Professor Robertson's well-known "day"); second, the lag between a change in consumer expenditure and a change in production rates (during which time inventories absorb the change in spending); and, third, the lag between production, i.e., income creation, and income payment (disposable income). He further demonstrates that such evidence as exists shows the first lag to be small or nonexistent, the second to be substantial though irregular, and the third to be substantial (primarily in the case of dividends) but unimportant. Without dismissing the first and third lags, let us, however, direct our attention to some factors determining the length of the second lag—the period between an enlarged (or diminished) rate of consumer spending and an enlarged (or diminished) rate of production and income creation.

Let us assume, to begin with, that sellers at each level of production are initially satisfied with their inventory positions at the level of sales currently taking place, and proceed to consider the effects of an additional stream of expenditures on final goods, not anticipated by sellers. The

immediate effect will be a reduction of the inventories carried by sellers of final goods, making them now dissatisfied with their inventory positions, and leading them to take some action to increase their purchases or production. There are two questions here that we shall attempt, as best we can, to keep separate, for we are primarily concerned only with the second of them. The first has to do with the *magnitude* of their reaction, the second with its *timing*. Only under very special circumstances will the addition to their purchases or production be of the same magnitude as the increase in their sales. If, for example, they wish to keep inventories a constant percentage of sales, and they expect the new rate of sales to continue, purchases or production will increase by more than sales. Or, if they project the increase in sales to mean that further increases will follow, purchases or production will increase by more than sales. Although this difference in magnitudes will affect the value of the "truncated multiplier"—its size as of some specific date—it will not affect the ultimate size of the multiplier when the new equilibrium is achieved; nor do we see any reason to believe that it would materially affect the *length* of the multiplier "round."[10]

The increase in sales will lead sellers to take action which will, after some lag, result in enlarged income. How long will it take for the enlarged income to be realized, whatever the degree of enlargement may be? The problem is of course complicated by the fact that the enlarged income, when received, will normally lead to further enlargement of sales of final products, to further enlargement of income, etc. And since some of the income generated by the first stream of new expenditures will be received quickly, part of the "second round" (or even the third

---

[9] "Three Lags in the Circular Flow of Income," in *Income, Employment, and Public Policy: Essays in Honor of Alvin H. Hansen* (Norton, 1948), pp. 11–32.

[10] The result of this lack of balance in magnitudes may well create a cyclical pattern of adjustment. See L. A. Metzler, "The Nature and Stability of Inventory Cycles," *Review of Economics and Statistics*, Vol. 23 (August 1941), pp. 113–29. We have only this comment on Professor Metzler's results. His model sequences assume a single, uniform lag of income creation behind sales. This period's sales, together with the seller's idea of the inventory he wants to keep, determines next period's production and income creation. When it is recognized that part of the income will be created immediately, other fractions at varying intervals thereafter, the results are far less clear. We have, in fact, not a single lag but a distributed lag. This should certainly dampen severely the cycles shown to result from his model. Put otherwise, Metzler's model has only one level of production and of inventory holding instead of the many levels that in fact exist.

or fourth) may begin to be felt long before the first is completed. But what we want to know is how long *one* round takes. What will determine the average time period between a new expenditure and that income creation that results from *that* expenditure? It may not necessarily be true, however, that the average length of second, third, fourth, and subsequent rounds will be the same as the first, a complication difficult to deal with, but noted below.

We can, I think, isolate several factors determining the length of the time between a disinvestment in inventory, and the subsequent act of income creation. They include:

1. *The time that it takes for sellers to realize that their rate of sales has increased relative to their rate of purchases or production.* Even if a seller desires to maintain a fixed stock, or stocks as a fixed percentage of sales, he needs some time to assure himself that what has occurred was other than a random fluctuation in his sales volume. Presumably, the more erratic his normal daily or weekly or monthly sales, the longer it takes him to sort out the genuine increase from a mere random fluctuation. This lag occurs at each level involved in the production of the good—retailer, wholesaler, manufacturer, supplier, supplier's supplier, etc., and the lags are additive.

2. *The time interval between the giving (or acceptance) of orders.* If orders are given (or accepted) weekly, a realization of a changed sales rate can quickly make itself felt at the next level. If sellers open their books only quarterly, or even annually, then the lag is much greater. These lags are also additive.

3. *The time that it takes to transmit orders.* Unless used to include (1) and/or (2) this is probably short, although again additive.[11]

4. *The time that it takes to change the rate of production.* Assuming, still, that the seller at each stage desires to keep a constant or proportional inventory, and, whenever he realizes his rate of sales has increased, immediately takes steps to increase purchases or production, there are physical limitations to the speed with which he may do so. These limitations include, of course, the time necessary to activate idle machinery, and to hire and, if necessary, train or retrain workers. But there is also an important

limitation based on the existence or nonexistence of inventories at each stage of production. Assume an increased level of disposable income has increased retail sales of shoes; retailers have immediately increased their orders to wholesalers, who have immediately increased their orders to manufacturers. The shoe manufacturer cannot start increasing his rate of shoe production (and income creation at his level) *unless he has inventories of leather in excess of minimum working requirements.* If the manufacturer has no inventory of leather, he must get it from his tanner. His tanner in turn can supply him only if he has more than minimum inventory of leather. If not, the tanner must first increase his input of cured hides (and output will increase only some weeks later). But this he cannot do unless he or his supplier has excess inventory of cured hides. If there are no such inventories, hides must be cured at an increased rate (I hesitate to suggest that cows must be killed—even bred—at an increased rate, yet, unless there are inventories, this is the case); cured hides must be tanned; tanned hides made into shoes; and shoes wholesaled and retailed. The whole process may take many, many months.

On the other hand, if there are inventories of goods at each stage (raw materials for the next stage), *if* a realization that sales have increased occurs quickly at each stage, *if* orders increase immediately when sales increase, the whole process may take only a matter of days or weeks.[12]

It is interesting that an argument can be developed here which is almost the exact opposite of the money circulation argument. Assume that no seller carries any "excess" inventories. Then when the signal is given for increased production, the process has to start at the very bottom. Work cannot be done at an increased rate at stage 2 until goods arrive at an increased rate from stage 1, and so on. If this is the case, the lag in income creation (in addition to the other relevant ones) will amount to approximately one-half

---

[11] Lags (2) and (3) can be short-circuited if sellers attempt to predict orders rather than merely wait for them. If, for example, a shoe manufacturer receives current data on retail shoe sales, he may determine his production rate in advance of the receipt of actual orders.

[12] Although our attention has been concentrated on the problem of speed of income increase, it should be noted that all of the lags up to this point except this last one operate also in the reverse case—the shrinkage in income resulting from an initial decline in spending. Instead, however, of the existence or lack of existence of inventories, we have as the crucial factor the length of irrevocable commitments to suppliers and factors. Even here, however, inventories cannot be neglected. If, at any stage, a seller has inventories which exceed the necessary minimum, he can contract his production (income payments) and/or orders prior to the completion of his contract, and fill the balance of it from inventory.

the fabrication time.[13] In this view, it is not the arrival of *money,* coming *down* the line from consumers that delays the process, but arrival of *goods,* coming *up* the line from "ultimate" producers that is relevant.

Now both views are wrong, and for the same reason. The reason is that there are typically at hand, or readily obtainable, inventories both of money and of necessary materials. Hence production rates are normally more flexible than either view might suggest. The approach that makes *money* flows the limiting factor assumes (tacitly or otherwise) that sellers fail to carry idle balances—or that others fail to carry them available for lending or security purchase. Why is this assumption made? Because money is needed as a medium of exchange and for no other reason. Hence no one holds an "idle" balance. If he holds cash at all, it is only to bridge the gap between an in-payment and an out-payment. He lends out any excess. Idle balances are sterile, and gain-motivated firms and individuals will shun them. For the same reason no one holds "excess" inventories of goods. They are sterile, hence do not exist.[14]

Now neither view is carried to the extreme. Since in-payments and out-payments fail exactly to coincide, and because extremely short term lending and borrowing are obviously impracticable, balances are not "idle" if not larger than necessary to meet recurrent peaks in the need for cash. (Though whether a balance more than enough to meet, say, weekly or monthly peaks but not larger than necessary to meet, say, quarterly or annual peaks is "idle" is a moot question.) Likewise, since deliveries and shipments do not coincide exactly with production flows, and small deliveries or shipments are impracticable, inventories are not "excess" if no larger than necessary to meet recurrent peak needs. (Again, there may be ambiguity in precise definition, though this is unimportant.)

The question really is whether and why individuals and firms hold larger inventories of money or goods than are necessary for the above purposes, which can be described as "transactions demands" for money and inventories respectively. One reason is the speculative one. Money is held awaiting an expected rise in its "price"—i.e., an expected fall in the price of debt. (It is not held—theoretically—waiting a fall in the price of goods; for, unless the price of debt is likewise expected to fall, the money can be loaned out—at interest—while awaiting the fall in the price of goods.) There is a parallel "speculative" reason for holding goods—to await an expected rise in their price. Another reason for holding idle money—and excess inventories—is the precautionary one. They are held to be ready for some unexpected demand for their use on short notice—the failure of a debtor to make an expected payment, or the failure of a supplier to make an expected delivery.

What Professor A. G. Hart (and others) have increasingly emphasized in recent analyses of *money* holding is the importance of uncertainty in connection with all of these motives, although particularly in connection with the precautionary one. Hart argues that what is wrong with most previous analyses of the motives for holding money is the tacit assumption of certainty (or a "certainty equivalent") as to future needs. He points out that even the transactions demand depends on expectations with respect to the future (what are the peak requirements for which money will need to be held?), and hence, with uncertainty, merges into the precautionary one. His "linkage of risk" and "financial respectability" principles are further used to explain why uncertainty leads to the desire for liquidity.[15]

---

[13] See Goodwin, *op. cit.,* p. 488. Goodwin attributes the discovery of this principle to Frisch. However, the essence of this view appears in Taussig's *Wages and Capital* (Appleton, 1896, page references to 1915 edition). In Chapter IV, "The Elasticity of the Wages Fund," Professor Taussig argues that the real income of the community is rather inelastic in the short run, because the current flow of final output is largely predetermined by the nature of goods in process. "What is now available, and what will be available for a year or two to come, has been determined once for all. If all the active members of the community work harder or more effectively [or, what Taussig was precluded from saying, if there is fuller employment], they may secure more enjoyable things after a space; but present income depends on the manner and the extent to which the preparatory stages of production have been carried on" (pp. 88–89).

[14] Taussig (*op. cit.,* p. 89) recognizes the possibility that inventories might provide slight flexibility, but argues: "Every dealer keeps enough in stock to meet current demand, and tries to keep no more. It is to his advantage to diminish his holdings to the minimum consistent with satisfying his customers. For every business manager, whether merchant or manufacturer, a needlessly large stock similarly means a needlessly large commital of his funds. . . . The drift in all must be to accommodate the supplies to habitual and expected demands, and to keep no excess." It is interesting that in earlier passages, Professor Taussig emphasized the elasticity of the money supplies from which wages could be paid and materials purchased.

[15] *Money, Debt, and Economic Activity* (Prentice-Hall, 1948), pp. 198–208.

Our emphasis is a parallel one. Uncertainty as to the future leads not only to monetary liquidity, but as well to the holding of inventories larger than theoretically necessary simply to facilitate the *current* flow of production. Just as the transactions demand for money depends on expectations, which if uncertain, lead to the holding of balances larger than necessary to finance most probable needs, so uncertainty as to future sales leads to holding of inventories in excess of those necessary to meet most probable circumstances. A prudent businessman in an uncertain world ought to hold "idle" money (although it is sterile and may depreciate as against goods or debt); and he ought also to hold "excess" inventory (although it is sterile and may depreciate as against money or debt). Unless he is willing to speculate on a fall in interest rates or a rise in goods prices—and it takes more than mere uncertainty to make him want to speculate—he will hold money. Unless he is definitely expecting a fall in goods prices he will hold excess inventories. For not to have the money or the inventories when needed to meet an unexpected, but always possible, increase in demand or failure of supply would. mean missing an opportunity to profit.[16]

Again, this statement needs qualification. He need not hold idle money if he is sure he can borrow (or has reasonably liquid assets).[17] And he need not hold excess inventories of what are (to him) raw materials if he knows that his supplier holds excess inventories of what are (to the supplier) finished goods. All this means is that there must be knowledge that *someone else* has excess inventories of money or goods if a prudent businessman is not to hold them himself.[18]

It is interesting to note, however, that just as there may be monetary liquidity available to an individual but not to an economy (one firm can borrow or dispose of securities, but perhaps only if everyone else is not simultaneously trying

to), there may also be an illusive sort of inventory "liquidity." Each individual buyer of a good may know that his supplier carries sufficient excess stock to meet his unexpected peak demands; but if one firm supplies many purchasers, and if all purchasers try to obtain increased supplies at once, none may succeed in any measure in doing so. This is especially true the farther "back" we go toward common basic materials used in many industries.[19]

There is an interesting difference, however. The extra monetary liquidity can be created by commercial banks, or, if not, by central banks, almost at the stroke of a pen. This is particularly the case with respect to the kind of money needs we are talking about here—to finance current output—in a banking system, like ours, designed to provide a flexible money supply to facilitate just this kind of a process. The same is not true for stocks of goods. There is another important difference, of course. Money has no carrying charges; many kinds of goods do (storage, insurance, physical deterioration, risk of obsolescence). These factors operate to restrain inventory holdings—to induce firms to sacrifice flexibility, despite its advantages.

Both of these differences suggest that, as between inventories of money and goods, it may more frequently be lack of inventories of goods that constitutes a bottleneck factor in expansion of output. Clearly neither inventories of goods nor money could ever constitute a technical bottleneck to contraction. In general, however (and generalities here become not too useful) sufficient flexibility seems to exist in most lines of output to permit moderate expansion without serious bottlenecks or delays while production flows are expanded "from the bottom up." More detailed consideration of individual industries will doubtless lead both to illustrations of this as well as to the recognition of certain exceptions.[20]

We have argued, thus far, that firms have normally reason to hold inventories in excess of

---

[16] Hart, *op. cit.*, p. 523, makes a similar comparison of money and inventory holdings.

[17] Thus, to some extent, idle money and excess inventories are alternatives.

[18] See, for example, the interesting discussion by M. Abramovitz, *The Role of Inventories in Business Cycles,* Occasional Paper 26 (National Bureau of Economic Research, 1948), pp. 8–10, in which a contrast is made between the inventory behavior of manufacturers' stocks of raw rubber and raw silk. Stocks of the latter are held by dealers, and manufacturers' stocks adjust quickly to changes in output. Stocks of the former are held by tire manufacturers, and their movement is inverse to that of tire production. Presumably, *average* manufacturers' stocks relative to sales are much larger for rubber than for silk.

[19] But just as many firms, having painfully discovered the illusiveness of the liquidity of securities or goods or lines of credit, have learned to hold idle money, so, surely, many firms recognize the need to hold excess inventories themselves rather than to count on being able to acquire them rapidly.

[20] See Abramovitz (*op. cit.*) for emphasis on, and illustrations of the different inventory situations of manufacturers. It should be noted, however, that the frequent showing by Abramovitz of long lags of inventory changes behind output, or even of inverse movement of inventories and output, strongly reinforces our view that inventories are typically in excess of "transactions" needs. Otherwise, stocks and output would have to move together.

those needed for "transactions purposes" (analogous to the "transaction demand" for money). And, if they do, we have shown that the availability of excess inventories at each stage in a production process will permit the flow of income to be expanded much more rapidly than if such inventories did not exist. The contrasting case would be one in which (*a*) *no* excess inventories were held, or (*b*) *only* inventories of final products. In either case, an increase in demand for final products could lead only to a slow expansion of production and income, as goods moved up the line from the earliest stages of production. Cases (*a*) and (*b*) do present in themselves interesting contrasts. If there were no excess inventories even of finished products, an increase in demand could succeed only in bidding up prices, first at retail, and then successively "down the line" toward the earliest stages of production. Sufficient expansion of output "from the bottom up" would presumably ultimately bid prices back down again if contractual money rates of factor remuneration had not in the meantime been raised. But real spending on final goods could not increase until real income (production) increased. In the other case, inventories of final products could permit an increase in real spending to take place prior to an increase in real income, without the same pressure on prices, the increase in spending on final products being offset by disinvestment in inventories of final products during the period in which output and income were gradually rising. Our point has been that this period of disinvestment can be much shorter if there are inventories at each stage to be temporarily drawn down while income the more rapidly rises.[21]

However, and this is important, the existence of inventories at each stage may *permit* a more rapid expansion of income than would otherwise be possible, but it does not *guarantee* it. In fact, the existence of inventories at each stage may very well make the process of income expansion much slower than would be the case if they did not exist. Suppose, for example, that at each stage

of production there were substantial excess inventories both of finished products (for that stage) and of raw materials (for that stage). Suppose, further, that the behavior of each seller were as follows: when demand increases, meet the enlarged demand out of excess finished goods inventory as long as possible before increasing the rate of production. Then use up excess raw material inventories for as long as possible before buying more. The supplier of the added material in turn does the same, and so does his supplier, etc. Under these circumstances the expansion of income might be terribly slow. Since inventories are larger, the period during which real spending can increase at the expense of inventory disinvestment is likewise much greater. A full "round" of income payments might be very long.[22]

This leads us to consider the circumstances which might lead to inventory decisions of the sort described above. Why might a seller choose to disinvest in inventories rather than to increase his rate of production and/or purchases? Several sorts of reasons can be distinguished.

1. The first reason has already been accounted for in the first of our previous list of "lags." It is, namely, that sellers may have trouble distinguishing a genuine increase in sales from a mere random fluctuation. Since we have already counted this as a source of delay, we should not count it again. But this category can be made to expand more or less indefinitely, unless we draw a line that is indeed difficult to draw. The cases of "perverse expectations" can be fitted in here with only a slight stretch of the definition: sales increase, but *because they have increased*, the seller concludes that they will be lower later on, and avoids taking action to increase his supplies. While, if there is an inventory cushion, perverse expectations do not lead to the disturbing results that can be shown to exist in a model in which there is no such cushion, such expectations might indeed result in substantial delays in income change. What seems to be involved is the question of the length of the seller's horizon: what is the future period concerning which

<hr>

[21] After the preceding pages of Part II had been written and rewritten many times, the author discovered that much of their substance is included in the long paragraph on page 288 of Keynes' *General Theory*, a paragraph that he had read many times, without, apparently, full appreciation of its import. As Hansen remarks: "Time and again when I thought I had discovered this or that error in the Keynesian analysis, . . . I have been surprised to find how often, on examination, the point had already been anticipated and covered in the *General Theory*" (*The New Economics*, p. 136).

[22] One should suppose that this policy would lengthen only the first "round." For subsequent rounds, there would then be no excess inventories to delay the process of income expansion. But this very exhaustion of excess inventories would then prolong the second round as well, by forcing production to be expanded "from the bottom up." Here, however, our method begins to break down, for, since *some* of the income increment will have been paid out early, the second and third rounds will begin to be confused with the first, leading to numerous complexities.

he has formulated an expectation as to average sales, within which period he interprets a rise in demand merely as a chance fluctuation, to be followed by an offsetting decline which will restore the average to the level he has anticipated? Does he have any concept akin to the statistical concept of probable error, and react only when the change in sales is sufficiently great to be hardly explainable by random forces? My opinion is that we do not know enough about opinion-formation, planning, and the revision of plans in business firms to be able even to suggest realistic considerations with respect to this case.

2. A second reason for allowing inventories to be drawn down is like the first, although, I think, capable of distinction. A seller realizes, let us suppose, that sales have increased, and interprets it as a genuine increase, one that will require increased production and/or purchases to restore his inventories to their previous level (which, while in one sense "excessive," is nevertheless the level he desires to maintain). But one of the purposes of holding excess inventories (which we intentionally omitted from our previous discussion) is to allow the seller some leeway in adjusting his rate of production to every change in sales. If he had no inventory of finished goods other than enough to meet random fluctuations and delivery discontinuities, every rise in demand would require either an immediate change in production rate, or a rise in price or rationing of his customers. And, likewise, if he were to avoid greater inventories, he would need promptly to turn down his rate of production every time sales declined. Now such frequent changes are awkward and costly. Much better to use inventories as a cushion. When demand rises, he then has time to assess the probable extent and duration of the increase, and to adjust his production rate more deliberately and efficiently. But this may also be a source of lag. Inventories are held as a cushion, and they are allowed to do their cushioning.[23]

3. A third reason why sellers might deliberately allow inventories to be drawn down could be found in the situation in which sellers' inventories were initially larger than they desired to keep. Although we can dismiss this case, theoretically, as outside our domain (multiplier discussion usually assumes initial equilibrium), practically speaking, the importance of this case cannot lightly be dismissed. A fiscal planner considering the effect of increased spending ought to take account of excessive inventories ("excessive" now used to mean not merely in excess of transactions needs, but in excess of desired holdings). Such excessive inventories may seriously delay at least the first "round" of the propagation of income.[24]

But a policy of allowing inventories to decline has its counterpart in a policy of attempting to build up inventories. To the extent that such occurs, this can be interpreted as a case in which income is created prior to or concurrently with the expansion of sales, and can be described as a case in which the lag in the multiplier is negative or zero.[25]

---

[23] Abramovitz makes this point explicitly for manufacturers' stocks of finished staples (which, at least in short cycle phases, move inversely to output): "In view of the perennial uncertainty surrounding the business future, manufacturers wish to minimize the costs involved in changing their rate of operations, of which the chief is probably the cost of dispersing large numbers of workers who may have to be reassembled in the not distant future" (*op. cit.*, pp. 18–19).

[24] Reasons 1 and 2 in the above list presumably merely affect the timing of the multiplier, not its ultimate size. Ultimately, inventories will be restored to some "normal" level. Reason 3 could be described as a reduction in the size of the multiplier rather than a delay in its timing. It can be thought of both as a lag and as a reduction in the size of the multiplier if expansions typically turn into contractions before inventories are built up to "normal" and contractions turn into expansions before inventories are reduced to "normal." See J. R. Hicks, *The Trade Cycle* (Oxford University Press, 1950), Chapters 2 and 3, for demonstration of how consumption lags can reduce the effective size of the multiplier when investment fluctuates back and forth. The same is true of inventory lags.

[25] See the summary by Ruth P. Mack of preliminary findings of her study of the shoe and leather industries which appears in *The Cumulation of Economic Knowledge* (Twenty-Eighth Annual Report of the National Bureau of Economic Research, 1948), pp. 42–44. "We find that hide marketing, leather tanning, shoe production and retailing all seem to reach peaks or troughs more or less together. This is true, moreover, not only of movements associated with business cycles but also of minor movements clearly identifiable in the shoe, leather, and hide industry. . . . Orders placed by retailers or wholesalers with shoe manufacturers appear to be the gear connecting retail sales and production. Orders for shoes seem to reach peaks and troughs about two months ahead of sales, and since this is also approximately the period by which orders precede production of shoes, synchronous timings of retail sales and production results." This might be described as a zero multiplier time period (or even negative, since income payments must reach peaks and troughs somewhat before shoe production). The process by which the necessary forecasts are made, and corrected, is given highly condensed discussion in the reference.

The real question, into the very middle of which we have now plunged, is whether to treat inventory investment or disinvestment as exogenous or as endogenous. The declines (increases) in inventories experienced by sellers who have not expected an increase (decrease) in demand are clearly endogenous, and their attempts to restore the *status quo ante,* which lead to a subsequent change in income, can reasonably be described as part of a lag between demand and income changes. Indeed, the multiplier theory makes no sense at all in a dynamic setting unless we do go behind the initial act of disinvestment and consider the subsequent act of income creation. But any very realistic analysis of the process requires us to recognize that inventory policies are apparently not confined to the mere attempt to maintain stable inventories. Professor Abramovitz, as already noted, finds that inventories of staple manufactured goods in the hands of their producers typically vary inversely with output, i.e., there is inventory disinvestment while output expands and investment while it contracts. As he shows, this can hardly be accounted for merely as a lag of adjustment.[26] Yet for industry as a whole, investment in inventories fluctuates directly with business cycles, with the turning points of inventory investment apparently coinciding closely with turning points in general business activity. Inventories (as opposed to inventory investment) lag perhaps six months behind activity at turning points but thereafter move in the same direction.[27] Thus inventory investment accompanies income expansions, and inventory disinvestment accompanies income contractions.

If we could appropriately consider all inventory change as endogenous, we could, perhaps must, consider inventory policies as factors contributing to the determination of the size and timing of the effective multiplier. But, in the present state of our knowledge, it may be more appropriate to consider some part of inventory change as exogenous—i.e., to recognize that the forces which relate income change to inventory change are so complicated and variable that we cannot include them in our model. This latter choice, however, although probably forced upon us, almost requires that we abandon any attempt

at realistic analysis of the multiplier time period. For, if a rise in final demand is preceded, accompanied, or followed by a rise in inventory demand, we surely cannot distinguish the timing of that part of income creation which arises from the increase in final demand from that arising from the new inventory demand, and hence can say nothing very useful about the timing of income change.

Perhaps by this time we have sufficiently succeeded in demonstrating the difficulties of determining "the" time period for the multiplier. If changes in spending are foreseen, the effect may be extremely rapid; if sellers react "passively," by changing production and/or purchases as rapidly as feasible, the delays may be slight or extensive depending on numerous factors, the one of which we have emphasized being the existence or non-existence of inventories at each stage in production; yet the existence of such inventories, which *permits* expansion to be more rapid, also permits sellers who do not react passively to delay the speed of income propagation very substantially; and the "exogenous" changes in inventories which in fact accompany income changes prevent us from isolating the time period of the multiplier in the true sense.

In other words, what we are suggesting turns out to be not another theory of the multiplier time period, but rather that no neat theory can be appropriate. We reject the approach that makes a previously existing speed of money flow determine the time period; nor does the view that it depends on fabrication time seem much better. That there may be a substantial lapse of time in the operation of the multiplier is clear; empirical studies might even succeed in disclosing some regularity in its duration. But there appears to be no simple basis for the determination of its length on abstract grounds.

III

The theory of the multiplier is ordinarily developed in a setting of assumptions in which labor and fixed resources are assumed to be underutilized. That is, we assume that there is idle labor seeking employment and that there are either idle machines or at least that existing machines can be utilized more intensively with little or moderate loss of efficiency. For these reasons, we ordinarily assume that output and income are "flexible"—i.e., can be expanded readily in response to rising demand.

But in any considerable expansion of output,

---

[26] *Op. cit.*, pp. 17–18. The above statement is modified for unusually long expansions or contractions: inventories begin to turn down in the late stages of long contractions and to turn up in the late stages of long expansions.

[27] *Op. cit.*, pp. 3–5.

or in any expansion whose form is different from that of previous expansions, shortages of particular kinds of labor or fixed assets may also occur at various points in the economy. Or, if the expansion takes place after a plateau of low output long enough for idle fixed assets to have been worn out and not replaced, bottlenecks of fixed asset capacity may also frequently be encountered. What essential difference in treatment does this require?

Consider first a bottleneck of fixed asset capacity. In terms of *physical limitations* on speed of output and income expansion, it only adds the fact that such assets are often not carried in inventory, and frequently take long periods to construct. But a far more important difference is that these aids to production are durable. They will not be used up in producing added current output necessary to meet currently enlarged demand. This has two consequences for our analysis: (1) if the decision is made to acquire them, there is an additional primary increment in income (injection) equal to the difference between current depreciation of such assets and their total cost—to buy a current unit of asset service you must also buy now many future units of asset service; and hence (2) the decision to acquire them depends not only on current demand for the product for which the asset service is desired but also on the expectation of future demand. As a result of this fact, the asset may not be acquired even though there might be the possibility of present profitable use of the asset service, and, on the other hand, it may be acquired even if there is not immediate need for its service if such continuing need is expected to occur in sufficient volume in the near future.

Likewise, it is clear that bottlenecks of labor of particular kinds or at particular places may prevent the expansion of employment and output. A theory of income flexibility in a larger sense cannot therefore be constructed without extensive and careful analysis of these bottlenecks and how

they are broken. Detailed consideration here would lead us far afield. It should be clear, however, that even in a less-than-full employment economy, the multiplier theory, and particularly any dynamic discussion of multiplier time periods, is seriously incomplete and misleading if it ignores bottleneck problems.[28]

The theory of the multiplier is a bold and challenging piece of analysis. But it is true only as a first approximation, under ideal conditions. Not only does income change only by a process that takes time, but to determine the speed and extent of that process involves an analysis of business practices, attitudes, responses; of technical conditions of production and supply; of consumer behavior, income distribution, lay-off and hiring procedures; of indirect impacts on government budgets through effects on tax collections, transfer payments, social security contributions; of indirect impacts on the money market; indeed of every aspect of the economic process. To understand them we need a vast fund of institutional knowledge about the business system, and, perhaps even more important, an understanding of the psychological frames of reference of business firms and individuals, which determine the way in which and the speed with which they respond to changes in objective facts.

A War Production Board trying to estimate the speed with which a less-than-full employment economy could achieve full production for war would find the multiplier theory of little practical use in planning. I hasten to add, of course, that a War Production Board which ignored the multiplier effect—i.e., the induced consumption demand accompanying rising income—would do a very bad job of planning indeed.

---

[28] We should, however, note an asymmetry here. These bottlenecks operate only to restrain expansions, not to delay contractions. The same was true, it should be recalled, of possible shortages of money and inventories.

A MONETARIST VIEW OF DEMAND MANAGEMENT*

Leonall C. Andersen

THE GENERAL MONETARIST VIEW

In the United States, monetarists have stressed the importance of monetary actions in determining the course of economic activity. Monetary actions include such actions of the Federal Reserve System as changes in the discount rate, changes in commercial bank reserve requirements, and open-market purchases and sales of Government securities. They also include the Treasury's management of its cash position. These are the basic exogenous variables of monetary management, with the major emphasis given to open-market transactions.

The role assigned to the money stock in the monetarist analysis is not generally understood. The money stock is most frequently used as an indicator of the thrust or influence of monetary actions on the economy. In the United States, there is a close empirical relationship between current and lagged changes in money and changes in nominal GNP. Money is not necessarily considered a causal factor. It is used, instead, as a summary measure of the influence of exogenous monetary variables, primarily those controlled by the Federal Reserve, on aggregate demand. Actions of commercial banks regarding their holdings of excess reserves and actions of households and business firms regarding their holdings of currency, demand deposits, and time deposits are recognized as influencing movements in the money stock. Nevertheless, it is maintained that the usefulness of money as an indicator of central bank monetary influences is not seriously impaired by such actions, because there is considerable empirical evidence that Federal Reserve actions dominate movements in the money stock.

The role assigned to interest rates in the monetarist analysis has also been subject to misunderstanding. Contrary to general opinion, interest rates are an important aspect of the monetarist transmission mechanism linking monetary actions to economic activity; but interest rates are no more important than prices of goods and services. Monetary actions of the Federal Reserve are considered a disturbance which influences the acquisition of financial and real assets. Rates of return

on real and financial assets and market prices of goods and services adjust to create a new equilibrium position of the economy; therefore, these changes are considered the main channels of monetary influence on aggregate demand. This transmission mechanism is basically the same as that of the neo-Keynesian portfolio approach, except that it takes into consideration many more rates of return and market prices of goods and services than is customary in the portfolio analysis. There is one important difference, however: monetarists generally are concerned with the influence of monetary actions on aggregate demand measured in nominal terms, while the neo-Keynesian analysis focuses on aggregate demand measured in real terms.

The influence of monetary actions through market interactions is considered to be widely diffused across all of the markets for financial assets, real assets, and services. Consequently, it is contended that the influence of monetary actions on movements in total demand is more important for monetary analysis than their influence on demands of individual sectors. This is contrary to the more conventional view which first considers the response of individual sector demands to monetary actions. Such responses, in turn, are then summed to give aggregate demand. The monetarist position is that the allocative effects of monetary actions have little bearing, if any, on movements in aggregate demand.

A central monetarist proposition is that the economy is basically stable and is not necessarily subject to wide variations in output and employment. In other words, the economy will naturally move along a trend path of output determined by growth in its productive potential. Exogenous events such as wars, droughts, strikes, shifts in expectations, changes in preferences, and changes in foreign demand may cause variations in output around the trend path. Such variations, however, under most circumstances, will be mild and of relatively short duration. This basic stability is brought about by market forces which change rates of return and prices of goods and services in response to these exogenous events. It is admitted that markets are not perfectly competitive and are subject to many rigidities. Such market "imperfections," however, do not greatly impair the stabilizing function of markets; they mainly

---

* From Federal Reserve Bank of St. Louis *Review,* September 1971, pp. 3–11. Reprinted by permission of the Federal Reserve Bank of St. Louis and the author. Leonall C. Andersen is Senior Vice President, Federal Reserve Bank of St. Louis.

result in an inefficient allocation of resources. Market imperfections also influence the time pattern of the response of output and prices to monetary actions.

The basic source of short-run economic instability, which will be discussed in more detail later, is monetary actions which result in accelerations and decelerations in the rate of money growth. In the long run, however, the trend rate of monetary expansion does not influence output and employment, but only movements in the price level and other nominal variables.

MONETARIST VIEW OF DEMAND MANAGEMENT

The monetarist view of the role of monetary and fiscal actions in demand management makes a clear distinction between the influence of such actions on real and nominal economic magnitudes. It also differentiates between the short-run and the long-run aspects of monetary and fiscal actions.

Monetary Actions

The major impact of monetary actions is believed by monetarists to be on long-run movements in nominal economic variables such as nominal GNP, the general price level, and market interest rates. Long-run movements in real economic variables such as output and employment are considered to be little influenced, if at all, by monetary actions. Trend movements in real variables are essentially determined by growth in such factors as the labor force, natural resources, capital stock, and technology.

In the short run, however, actions of the central bank which change the trend rate of monetary expansion or produce pronounced variations around a given trend rate exert an impact on both real and nominal variables. The timing and the extent to which such real variables as output and employment are affected depends on initial conditions at the time of a change in the rate of monetary expansion. Two major initial conditions are the level of resource utilization and the expected rate of inflation. For example, an acceleration in the rate of monetary expansion at a time of a high level of resource utilization will have little short-run influence on output but a quick influence on the price level. On the other hand, a reduction in the rate of monetary expansion will result in slower growth in real output in the short run, with a faster and larger response if there is a high level of inflationary expectations than if there is a low level.

Fiscal Actions

The monetarist view of fiscal actions is that their main impact is on long-run movements of real output. Government spending and taxing programs can change the rate of growth of potential real output by altering the composition of actual output. An expenditure program which re-allocates resources from current consumption (for example, reduced low income subsidies) to investment (for example, education) will tend to increase the growth rate of potential output. Or, a tax program which encourages private investment will have a similar impact on potential output. Since actual output naturally grows at the same rate as potential output in the long run, these allocative fiscal actions do influence the rate of growth of actual output.

While a faster rate of growth of potential output will tend to reduce the inflationary aspect of a given rate of monetary expansion, this influence is believed to be relatively minor and slow to develop. The reason for this is that the allocative affects of the usual magnitude of such fiscal actions on potential output are not too large and take time to appear.

In the short run, fiscal actions are believed by monetarists to exert some but little lasting influence on nominal GNP expansion and, therefore, have little effect on short-run movements of output and employment. It is argued that Government expenditures financed by taxes or borrowing from the public tend to crowd out over a fairly short period of time an equal amount of private expenditures, either by interest rate and price changes or by credit rationing. There is some influence exerted over the first part of the adjustment period by a given change in Government expenditures financed in this manner; consequently, an acceleration or deceleration in the rate of Government spending will exert a short-lived influence on total demand. Changes in tax rates, according to some monetarists, can influence economic activity in the short run inasmuch as such changes alter rates of return on capital assets.

Summary of Views on Demand Management

The monetarist position on demand management may be summarized as follows:

1. Demand management is mainly the use of monetary actions to foster an acceptable trend rate of inflation.
2. Short-run instability of output and employment can be greatly reduced if monetary actions are

avoided which result in accelerations and decelerations in the rate of money growth.

3. Fiscal actions are not an important aspect of short-run demand management, but the allocative aspect of such actions can be important for such other purposes as promoting economic growth or redistributing wealth.

A MONETARIST VIEW OF TWO DECADES OF DEMAND MANAGEMENT IN THE UNITED STATES

In analyzing the demand management experience in the United States from the monetarist point of view, the last two decades will be divided into three episodes involving different trend rates of growth of the money stock. The experience of each episode will be presented, and then reasons for the recorded course of money supply growth will be developed.

Demand Management Experience

The last twenty years can be divided into three episodes according to trend rates of monetary expansion—1952 to 1962, when money grew at a 1.7 percent average annual rate; 1962 to 1966, when the trend rate of monetary growth was accelerated to a 3.7 percent annual rate; and 1966 to the present, when there was a further acceleration to a 6.1 percent annual rate of growth in the money stock (Chart I).

During the decade ending in 1962, demand management was primarily the Federal Reserve's responsibility. Only one major fiscal action, the income tax cut of 1954, was undertaken for the purpose of influencing aggregate demand. An examination of the published minutes of the Federal Open Market Committee indicates that several monetary actions were taken for the purpose of promoting economic stability. From 1952 to 1962, the United States' money stock increased at a 1.7 percent average annual rate. There was, however, considerable short-run variability around this trend rate, with periods of fairly rapid increase followed by absolute decrease.

The price level performance, except for a short burst of inflation in 1956 and 1957, was very good, and such performance continued into 1965. The GNP deflator rose at a trend rate of less than 2 percent from 1952 to 1965. Performance of the real sector of the American economy, however, was far from acceptable as the decade was marked by three recessions. Over this ten year period, the unemployment rate averaged 4.5 percent. Despite an average unemployment rate of this magnitude, however, real output grew only

slightly less rapidly than the 3.5 percent estimated growth rate of potential output.

The next episode—1962 to 1966—marked the emergence of attempts at "fine tuning" movements in aggregate demand. Fiscal actions became the main tool of such management of the economy, while monetary actions, in the Keynesian tradition, were assigned a purely accommodative role. Little consideration was given to the possibility that monetary actions could exert any independent influence.

Major fiscal actions undertaken during this period for purposes of stimulating aggregate demand were the investment tax credit and accelerated depreciation provisions of the Revenue Act of 1962, the Revenue Act of 1964 which reduced individual and corporate income tax rates, and the Excise Tax Reduction Act of 1965. Then as inflationary pressures began to mount late in the period, the Investment Credit Suspension Act of 1966 was adopted to reduce growth in aggregate demand.

Monetary actions, in their accommodative role, were expansive. The money stock rose at a 3.7 percent trend rate from mid-1962 to the end of 1966 (Chart I). The rate of monetary expansion was variable over this period. It accelerated to a 6 percent rate from April 1965 to April 1966, and then money did not grow to the end of 1966.

This episode marked the beginning of accelerating inflation in the United States. The GNP deflator rose at over a 3 percent annual rate during 1966, compared with a rate less than 2 percent during the 1952–1962 period.

Many have viewed the movements in output and employment from 1962 to 1966 as very satisfactory. Output rose rapidly, eliminating the gap between potential and actual output which had existed in the early 1960s. As a result, the unemployment rate fell from 5.5 percent in 1962 to less than 4 percent in 1966. These developments have been cited as evidence proving the success of the fiscal, "fine-tuning" view of demand management.

The last episode—1966 to the present—is one in which attempts were made to dampen growth in aggregate demand so as to curb an accelerating inflation. An overriding consideration, however, was to accomplish this objective without too great a loss of output and employment. First, fiscal actions were used, and then monetary actions.

The Revenue and Expenditure Control Act of 1968 imposed a temporary 10 percent surcharge on individual and corporate income taxes and restricted the rate of increase in Federal

CHART I

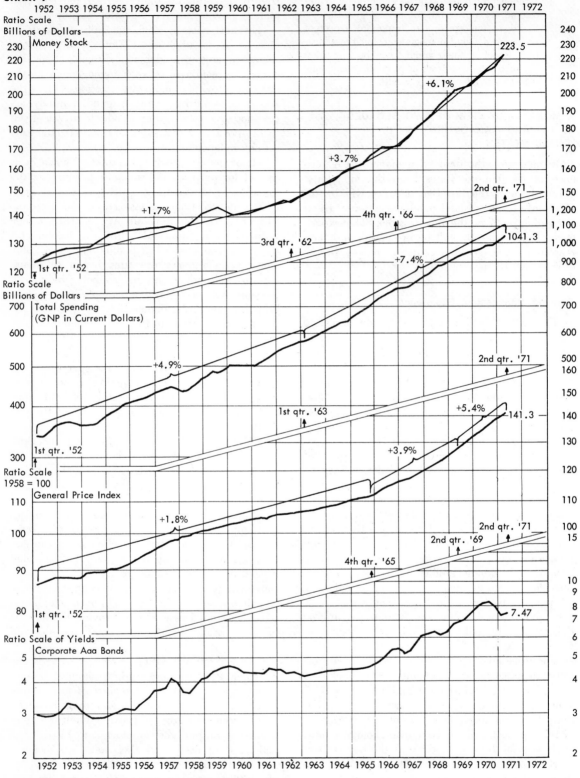

All data except bond yields are seasonally adjusted.
Percentages are annual rates of change for periods indicated.

Government expenditures. Next, the investment tax credit, which had been restored in early 1967, was repealed. Then as output grew more slowly later in the period and the unemployment rate rose, the income tax surcharge was allowed to phase out.

Monetary actions were of a stop-and-go nature similar to fiscal actions. At times during the period, monetary actions were assigned an independent role in demand management in contrast to the purely accommodative role during the 1962–66 episode. In addition, greater emphasis was placed on controlling movements in the money stock. Money grew at a 7 percent annual rate in 1967 and 1968. Then, steps were taken to curb inflation, and money grew at a markedly lower 3 percent rate in 1969. But when considerable economic slack appeared, the rate of monetary expansion was accelerated to a 5 percent rate in 1970 and to a 10 percent rate thus far in 1971. The over-all trend rate of monetary expansion over the whole four and one-half year period was about 6 percent, a marked acceleration from the 3.7 percent rate recorded from 1962 to 1966 (Chart I).

The performance of the American economy since 1966 has been considered highly unsatisfactory. The results of monetary and fiscal actions since 1966 have been a recession accompanied by a high rate of inflation. Inflation accelerated to over a 5 percent annual rate, and the unemployment rate rose to over 6 percent.

The experience of the last two decades demonstrates the great lack of success of demand management in the United States. This is particularly evident in the 1960's when very activist stabilization actions were undertaken. Some cite this experience as demonstrating the inability of traditional monetary and fiscal actions to promote economic stability. I do not accept such a view. Instead, I contend that the generally accepted economic foundation of demand management is faulty. Basing stabilization actions on this foundation is a sure formula for failure.

Reasons for Failure of Stabilization Policies

I attribute the very poor record of United States economic stabilization efforts to four main factors. First, and foremost, is lack of understanding of the independent impact of monetary actions, as measured by changes in the money stock, on the course of economic activity. Second, is the great emphasis given to guiding the course of real variables—output and employment—and the little emphasis, except for short intervals of time, given to controlling inflation. Third, is the great emphasis given to fiscal actions, especially in the 1960s. Fourth, is the use of market interest rates as an indicator of the influence of monetary actions on economic activity.

Role of Monetary Actions Ignored. According to the monetarist view, central bank actions which alter the trend growth rate of the money stock exert an important long-run influence on nominal GNP and the price level. Accelerations and decelerations of the money stock have only an important short-run influence on output and employment. Evidence supporting these two propositions is presented in Charts I and II.

The money stock panel (Chart I) indicates three trend growth rates of monetary expansion, which were set forth in the preceding section. Money grew at a 1.7 percent average annual rate from I/1952 to III/1962. Money growth then accelerated to a 3.7 percent trend rate to IV/1966 and to a 6.1 percent trend rate to II/1971. Total spending (nominal GNP) and the price level responded to the changes in the trend rate of monetary expansion as postulated by monetarists. Total spending rose at a 4.9 percent annual rate from I/1952 to I/1963 and then rose at a 7.4 percent trend rate. The price level (GNP deflator) rose first at a 1.8 percent rate, then at a 3.8 percent rate, and since II/1969 at a 5.4 percent rate. The corporate Aaa bond rate, another nominal magnitude, also moved in a manner similar to changes in the trend growth of money.

Chart II, top panel, presents deviations in the money stock from its trend growth. These deviations are expressed as the ratio of the money stock to its trend value for each quarter. The dashed line at the end of each episode is the ratio calculated on the basis of the previous episode's trend for a few quarters after a change in the trend. This overlap is used to allow for the fact that a change in the trend growth of money is not recognized immediately. The second panel presents the ratio of actual real GNP to potential real GNP. The trend growth of potential real GNP, as indicated on the second panel, has been estimated by the Council of Economic Advisers. The bottom panel presents the unemployment rate.

Regardless of the trend rate of monetary growth (1.7, 3.7, or 6.1 percent), whenever the ratio of money to its trend value rose (an acceleration in money growth), the ratio of actual real GNP to its potential value rose soon thereafter, and the unemployment rate fell. The opposite happened whenever the rate of money growth decelerated. Despite such short-run developments and despite different trend rates of money growth, the unemployment rate averaged about the same from 1952 to 1962, when money growth was relatively slow, as from 1962 to 1971, when the trend rate of money growth was much greater.

The developments summarized in Chart II are consistent with the monetarist view that accelerations and decelerations of monetary expansion exercise a short-run influence on output and employment, but there is little, if any, long-run influence. These influences were given little consideration in demand management, particularly during the activist period from 1962 to 1968.

Focus Placed on Output and Employment. Another factor accounting for the poor stabilization record in the United States is the fact that demand management has been primarily focused on producing desired movements in output and employment. This was true of monetary actions for the 1950s and early 1960s when some independent monetary actions were taken, the period in the mid-1960s of fine tuning using planned fiscal actions and accommodative monetary actions, and the active use of monetary actions after 1968.

If the economy responds to monetary actions, as indicated above, a focus of policy primarily on output and employment can explain the existence of both inflation and high unemployment. In attempting to promote rapid expansion of real output after mid-1962, active use of fiscal actions and accommodating monetary actions resulted in the money stock rising at an accelerated rate until early 1966. Inflation accelerated, and in response, monetary authorities reduced drastically the rate of money growth for two quarters. But then when economic slack appeared in early 1967, money growth was allowed to accelerate to a trend rate greater than the previous one. This sequence of events happened again in 1969 and 1970, producing a still higher rate of money growth. In these latter years, however, monetary actions were on more of a discretionary basis than earlier.

The end result, thus far, of guiding stabilization policy on real variables has been higher and higher trend rates of monetary expansion and greater inflation. Periodically, there have been temporary periods of monetary restraint to curb inflation, which in turn have produced slower output growth and rising unemployment. Such developments, in turn, induce stabilization authorities to initiate a still higher trend rate of money growth, which leads to further inflation.

Thus, the American economy may be faced with high rates of inflation without achieving economic stability, unless the main emphasis of policy is shifted to curbing inflation.

Main Emphasis Given to Fiscal Actions. A third reason for the poor record of economic stabilization in the United States is the emphasis given to fiscal actions, particularly from 1962 to 1968. Until recently, fiscal actions in the form of Government spending and taxing programs have been given the main emphasis in economic stabilization efforts to the virtual exclusion of monetary actions. Such a development was an outgrowth of conventional economics which for the past 25 years has taught that Federal Reserve actions exercise little independent influence on total demand for goods and services.

According to this widely accepted view, changes in the money stock bring about changes in market interest rates, but total demand is little influenced by interest rate movements. Consequently, monetary actions have been thought to be of little use in any program of economic stabilization. On the other hand, increased Government expenditures are viewed as adding directly to total demand and tax reductions as adding to disposable income which would be used to purchase goods and services. Consequently, this view has argued that fiscal actions have an immediate and powerful influence on total spending. This analysis has received wide acceptance as evidenced in discussions of economic stabilization by the general public, in the press, in the Congress, and in the Reports of the Council of Economic Advisers from 1962 to 1969.

It is my belief that the accelerating inflation of the last half of the 1960s can be attributed, in large part, to the great emphasis given to fiscal actions and the downgrading of monetary influence. Monetary authorities did not reduce the rapid rate of monetary expansion during a large part of that period because there was a desire to let fiscal actions curb inflation and a belief by some that only fiscal actions would be effective. Then, when restrictive fiscal actions were taken in mid-1968—the surtax and slower increases in Government spending—many economists, on the basis of conventional wisdom, predicted "fiscal over-kill" by early 1969. In response to such predictions, monetary authorities continued even more expansionary actions.

Faulty Method of Monetary Management Used. A fourth reason for the poor stabilization record of the last 20 years has been due to the fact that the usual method of carrying out United

CHART II

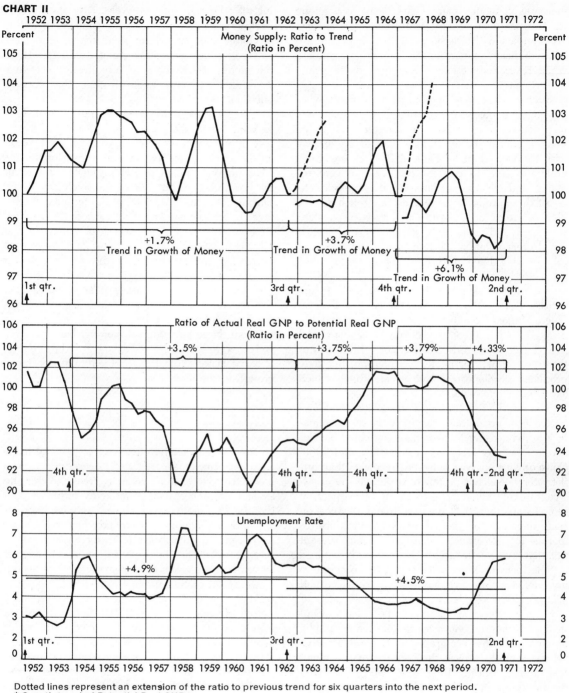

1952 1953 1954 1955 1956 1957 1958 1959 1960 1961 1962 1963 1964 1965 1966 1967 1968 1969 1970 1971 1972

Money Supply: Ratio to Trend
(Ratio in Percent)

+1.7%
Trend in Growth of Money

+3.7%
Trend in Growth of Money

+6.1%
Trend in Growth of Money

1st qtr.   3rd qtr.   4th qtr.   2nd qtr.

Ratio of Actual Real GNP to Potential Real GNP
(Ratio in Percent)

+3.5%   +3.75%   +3.79%   +4.33%

4th qtr.   4th qtr.   4th qtr.   4th qtr.-2nd qtr.

Unemployment Rate

+4.9%   +4.5%

1st qtr.   3rd qtr.   2nd qtr.

1952 1953 1954 1955 1956 1957 1958 1959 1960 1961 1962 1963 1964 1965 1966 1967 1968 1969 1970 1971 1972

Dotted lines represent an extension of the ratio to previous trend for six quarters into the next period.
* Growth trend of Potential Real GNP.
Growth trend from IV/70 to the present 4.4%.
All data are seasonally adjusted.

States monetary policy in the 1950s and 1960s was faulty. Discretionary monetary policy was reinstated in 1951 after its suspension during World War II and up through the early part of the Korean War. The purpose of the 1951 change was to permit monetary authorities to fight the inflation of the Korean War. In conducting its monetary policy responsibilities since then, the Federal Open Market Committee has relied almost exclusively, until just recently, on measures of money market conditions as a guide to its operations. I am sure that most of you are familiar with the view that falling interest rates indicate expansionary monetary actions, while restrictive actions are indicated by rising interest rates.

Such a view was in general agreement with the conventional wisdom, which holds that monetary actions work primarily through changes in market interest rates. It also was in agreement with the view that the Federal Reserve has great ability to "set" market interest rates. Recent research and experience, however, have tended to reject these propositions. For example, it has been demonstrated that rapid monetary expansion, such as in 1967 and 1968, stimulates total spending, fosters inflation, and thereby generates rapidly growing demand for credit and rising interest rates, not lower rates.

By using market interest rates to indicate the thrust of its actions in the 1950s, the Federal Open Market Committee frequently resisted the pace at which rates fell during recessions and rose during recoveries. Such actions did not alter the trend growth of money or inflation, but they produced accelerations and decelerations which led to economic instability.

Then in the fine tuning of the 1960s, the Committee concluded that, despite very rapid monetary growth, rising interest rates indicated considerable monetary restraint during 1967 and 1968. Consequently, it was believed by many that further steps need not be taken to reduce the excessive rate of monetary growth. In retrospect, it is now apparent that the traditional reliance on such measures of money market conditions as market interest rates contributed to our present inflation and to instability in the real sector.

The focus on market interest rates in conducting monetary management during the last half of the 1960s also led to higher trend rates of monetary expansion in two other ways. Constraints on interest movements imposed by public opinion and the Congress on Federal Reserve actions caused, in part, the very expansive monetary actions during 1967 and 1968. Following the rapid rise in market interest rates during the credit crunch of 1966, there was a belief that the extent of the increase was too great because of the dislocations which had occurred in the savings and housing industries. In order to forestall further dislocations, there was a desire to hold back the magnitude of interest rate increases; this led to passage of the Interest Rate Control Act of 1966. Presently there is a reluctance to allow rates to rise for fear of "choking-off" the economic recovery. Attempts to hold back interest rate increases at a time of expanding economic activity require great injections of bank reserves which contribute to a rapid growth in the money stock. This, in turn, fosters excessive total demand and feeds further the fires of inflation.

The focus on market interest rates also helped to bring about the extremely high rates of monetary growth during 1967 and 1968 as a result of the decision to finance the expansion of the Vietnam War and rapidly rising welfare programs by borrowing rather than exclusively by taxes. During 1967 and 1968, large Government financings in the security markets caused the Federal Reserve, because of an even-keel policy of stabilizing money markets at times of Government borrowing, to buy large quantities of Government securities. As mentioned earlier, there was great upward pressure on market interest rates from the private sector. Hence, with large demands for funds from both private sources and the Government, large injections of member bank reserves were required for even-keeling by the Federal Reserve. These injections helped to foster rapid growth in the money stock.

CONCLUSIONS

Now to answer the question, "Is demand management illusion or reality?" According to the monetarist view, the answer is "reality," but the essence of such reality is markedly different than that of the more conventional, activist view of demand management. Monetary actions should be directed primarily at fostering an acceptable rate of inflation; this requires the following of an appropriate trend rate of monetary expansion. With regard to output and employment, monetary actions should be conducted so as *not* to be a source of economic instability; this requires the avoidance of periods of marked accelerations and decelerations in the rate of money growth. Thus, I believe that there are strong economic reasons for the monetary growth rule and little room for discretionary, short-run monetary management.

The recent American experience demonstrates the potential of short-run monetary actions to produce both inflation and economic instability. For instance, the 6 percent trend growth of money since 1966, given the 1.5 percent trend increase in velocity that has occurred since then, is consistent with a 7 to 8 percent annual rate of increase in nominal GNP. If potential real output should continue to rise at its recent 4.3

percent annual rate, this rate of money growth implies a trend rate of inflation between 3 and 4 percent. If velocity, however, should resume its higher 3.5 percent average annual rate of increase recorded from 1952 to 1966, the recent trend rate of money growth implies a 5 to 6 percent rate of inflation. The monetary restraint of 1969, when money rose at only a 3 percent rate, produced the recent recession in the United States, but since this was only a relatively short-lived deceleration in money growth, the rate of inflation was little influenced.

Stabilization actions since 1966 have not been conducive to a marked reduction in the rate of inflation. The United States inflation will not be reduced substantially until a lower trend rate of money growth is established; a 3 to 4 percent rate probably would be optimal. Since the present high rate of inflation has been in existence for several years, however, expectations are for a continued high rate of price advance. In such a case, a move to less expansionary monetary actions will result in considerable adjustment costs in terms of slower expansion in output and employment. Such costs cannot be avoided if the United States inflation is ever to be contained, and attempts to avoid them will probably lead to higher rates of inflation.

A CRITICAL LOOK AT MONETARIST ECONOMICS*

Ronald L. Teigen

Until just a few years ago, the viewpoint which lately has come to be known as "monetarist" was not taken very seriously by anyone except a few dedicated disciples. Its central postulate—that changes in the level of aggregate money income were due essentially to prior money stock changes—was viewed as a totally inadequate oversimplification, especially since the proponents of this approach failed to provide an adequately detailed explanation of the theoretical structure upon which this tenet was based.[1] The empirical evidence presented in support of this "quantity theory" viewpoint was subjected to criticism so severe that the evidence has never been taken very seriously.[2]

However, recent years have witnessed something of a turnaround. The conventional wisdom as embodied in modern Keynesian theory has been cast into doubt, while monetarist thinking has increased greatly in popularity, to the point where its proponents, and even some of its critics, speak of a "monetarist revolution."[3] The reasons for this rather sudden change are no doubt related in part to the apparent inconsistency of the Keynesian analysis (or at least an elementary version of it) with economic events in the United

* From Federal Reserve Bank of St. Louis Review, January 1972, pp. 10–25. Reprinted by permission of the Federal Reserve Bank of St. Louis.

[1] In particular, Milton Friedman's well-known article, "The Quantity Theory of Money—A Restatement," in M. Friedman, ed., Studies in the Quantity Theory of Money (Chicago: University of Chicago Press, 1956), pp. 3–21, which has been cited as the basis for much monetarist work, has been shown by Don Patinkin to be a sophisticated version of Keynes' liquidity preference theory rather than the up-to-date statement of an alleged Chicago oral tradition that monetarists take it to be. See Don Patinkin, "The Chicago Tradition, the Quantity Theory, and Friedman," Journal of Money, Credit and Banking (February 1969), pp. 46–70.

[2] I am referring chiefly to the controversy triggered by the work of Milton Friedman and his associates in the late 1950s and early 1960s, especially Friedman's evidence on lags observed between changes in the rate of change of the money stock and changes in GNP, as presented in his paper, "The Supply of Money and Changes in Prices and Output," Joint Economic Committee, U.S. Congress, 1958, and elsewhere, and in the Milton Friedman and David Meiselman paper on, "The Relative Stability of Monetary Velocity and the Investment Multiplier in the United States, 1897–1958," in Commission on Money and Credit, Stabilization Policies (Englewood Cliffs, N.J.: Prentice-Hall, Inc., 1963). The regression results reported in the latter paper were severely criticized by Donald Hester in the November 1964 Review of Economics and Statistics and by Albert Ando-Franco Modigliani and Michael DePrano-Thomas Mayer in the September 1965 American Economic Review. The lead-lag observations discussed in the former paper were criticized by John M. Culbertson in the December 1960 Journal of Political Economy, and by James Tobin in the May 1970 Quarterly Journal of Economics.

[3] See Karl Brunner, "The 'Monetarist Revolution' in Monetary Theory," Weltwirtschaftliches Archiv (No. 1, 1970), pp. 1–30, and Harry G. Johnson, "The Keynesian Revolution and the Monetarist Counter-Revolution," American Economic Review, Papers and Proceedings (May 1971), pp. 1–14.

States during the late 1960s,[4] in some degree to monetarist criticism of Keynesian analysis (mostly directed at a *very* elementary version of it), and in part to other causes, including substantial development by the monetarists of their own theoretical position, as well as the appearance of new and more convincing empirical findings.[5]

While the increase in popularity of monetarism has been rapid, and the rate of growth of the monetarist literature impressive, a critical literature has also appeared, charging that monetarist theory has turned out largely to consist of old concepts clothed in new names, and that the empirical evidence purportedly supporting the monetarist position is biased and undependable.[6] The purpose of the present paper is to attempt to summarize in a general way the main features of the present monetarist theoretical stance, and to examine the monetarist view of modern Keynesianism. Since much of the debate bears directly on the stabilization policy process and the relative usefulness of different instruments of policy, particular attention will be given to the nature of the transmission mechanism under the two approaches. The empirical evidence will not be discussed in a systematic way in this paper, although reference will be made to it, where appropriate, in the discussion of the theories. In conducting this comparison, I shall attempt to identify issues between the two camps which are real, and those which seem to be false.

THE STRUCTURE OF MONETARIST THOUGHT

Although the roots of modern monetarist thought extend far back in time (the writings of classical economists are often cited, Irving Fisher being particularly popular), it is only lately that detailed expositions of this theory have begun to appear. In this paper, no systematic discussion of the entire literature will be undertaken. Instead, important summary statements which recently have become available in articles by Andersen, Brunner, Fand, Friedman, and others will be taken to be representative of present-day monetarist thought.[7]

[4] The apparent failure of the income tax surcharge of June 1968 to reduce aggregate demand rapidly has been interpreted by some to be evidence of the failure of the "new" economics. However, it is not at all clear that the surtax was ineffective. In a recently-published study by Arthur Okun, evidence is provided that, at least in some categories of spending (nondurable goods and services in particular), the surcharge seems to have reduced demand substantially. But in other categories (especially demand for new automobiles) no reduction is apparent. See Arthur M. Okun, "The Personal Tax Surcharge and Consumer Demand, 1968–70," *Brookings Papers on Economic Activity* (No. 1, 1971), pp. 167–204. More generally, the notion that demand should have been observed to fall after the surtax was imposed is based on simplistic and partial analysis. When the surtax is analyzed within the context of a complete model (in which government spending is taken into account), and one which incorporates the sophisticated theories of consumption behavior recently developed—the "permanent income" hypothesis of Milton Friedman or the "life-cycle" hypothesis of Albert Ando and Franco Modigliani—there appear a number of considerations which suggest that no substantial diminution of total demand could be anticipated. This point of view is argued persuasively by Robert Eisner in his paper, "Fiscal and Monetary Policy Reconsidered," *American Economic Review* (December 1969), pp. 897–905. Eisner reasons that rising Government expenditure had been expanding demand rapidly at the time when the surtax was enacted; furthermore, under the Friedman and Ando-Modigliani theories, which postulate that it is some long-run measure of income or wealth rather than current-period income which determines a household's living standard, a temporary tax change (such as the 1968 surcharge) would be expected to have only minor effects on spending because it does not change long-run expected income significantly. See Milton Friedman, *A Theory of the Consumption Function* (Princeton, N.J.: Princeton University Press, 1957), and Albert Ando and Franco Modigliani, "The 'Life-Cycle' Hypothesis of Saving: Aggregate Implications and Tests," *American Economic Review* (March 1963), pp. 55–84.

[5] Harry Johnson, "The Keynesian Revolution and the Monetarist Counter-Revolution," suggests that the successful monetarist upsurge may also be due to the factors related to the conversion of the "Keynesian revolution" of the 1930s into the economic orthodoxy of the 1960s.

[6] Ibid., for a general discussion of monetarist theory and its relationship to Keynesian orthodoxy. There have been published a large number of papers critical of the recent monetarist empirical studies; references to some are given in footnote 2, and a summary of the criticism of more recent monetarist empirical work is contained in Ronald L. Teigen, "The Keynesian-Monetarist Debate in the U.S.; A Summary and Evaluation," *Statsökonomisk Tidsskrift* (January 1970), pp. 1–27.

[7] Some of the important articles include Leonall C. Andersen, "A Monetarist View of Demand Management: The United States Experience," *Federal Reserve Bank of St. Louis Review* (September 1971), pp. 1–11; Leonall C. Andersen and Keith M. Carlson, "A Monetarist Model for Economic Stabilization," *Federal Reserve Bank of St. Louis Review* (April 1970), pp. 7–25; Leonall C. Andersen and Jerry L. Jordan, "Monetary and Fiscal Actions: A Test of Their Relative Importance in Economic Stabilization," *Federal Reserve Bank of St. Louis Review* (November 1968), pp. 11–24; Karl Brunner, "The Role of Money

Models, Assertions, and Themes

As a useful starting point in establishing a general framework for the discussion to follow, we may refer to recent articles by Brunner and Friedman containing inclusive statements of the monetarist position.[8] Friedman provides an explicit statement of the static-equilibrium structure which he views as being consistent with both the monetarist and Keynesian schools of thought. The theme he stresses—that it is the particular features of or assumptions about particular characteristics of the general analytic structure, rather than the fundamental nature of the structure itself, which differentiate monetarists and Keynesians—also appears in the writings of Brunner and others. In summary form, the model set out by Friedman is as follows:

$$\frac{Y}{p} = C\left(\frac{Y}{p}, r\right) + I(r) \qquad (1)$$

$$M_0 = p \cdot L\left(\frac{Y}{p}, r\right) \qquad (2)$$

$$Y = py \qquad (3)$$

where Y is money income, p is the general price level, r is the rate of interest, M_0 is the nominal exogenously-set money stock,[9] y is real income or output, and C, I, and L stand for the consumption, investment, and demand-for-money functions, respectively.

Equation (1) is of course the familiar *IS*

curve, from which can be obtained all combinations of real income and the interest rate which will make the flow of planned spending equal to available output, and hence will result in equilibrium in the market for goods and services. Equation (2) is the *LM* curve, which yields all combinations of real income, the interest rate, and the price level which will equate the demand for real balances with the real value of the nominal money stock. Equation (3) is a definition relating nominal income and real income or output through the price level. There are of course other markets which could be considered, but which are not explicitly accounted for in equations (1) or (2); in particular, the bond and labor markets are not made explicit. Friedman argues that the assumptions made by the two camps in order to accommodate these markets and simultaneously close the system of equations constitute a fundamental point of difference between monetarists and Keynesians. As written in equations (1)–(3), the model posited by Friedman contains four endogenous variables —Y, p, r, and y—and therefore is underdetermined. Monetarism is said by Friedman to include with the above equations a vast number of additional relationships; specifically, a whole Walrasian system of demand equations, supply equations, equilibrium conditions, etc., which in and of themselves determine y, the level of real output. The inclusion of a Walrasian system of course implies that the equilibrium position of the model is one of full employment. (There is no such implication for the short-run dynamics of the system, however.) With real output predetermined from the standpoint of equations (1)–(3), equation (1) can be solved for the equilibrium value of the interest rate, and (2) yields the equilibrium price level. Elementary manipulation of this system gives the result that only the price level (and the money wage rate, which is not made explicit in equations (1)–(3)) will change in response to a money stock change; the equilibrium value of the interest rate is not shifted, and therefore is said to be determined only by "real" variables.[10] In other words, this version of the model displays the well known "classical dichotomy."

According to Friedman, the Keynesian approach utilizes a much different and less satisfactory procedure by assuming that the *price level,*

and Monetary Policy," *Federal Reserve Bank of St. Louis Review* (July 1968), pp. 9–24; idem, "The 'Monetarist Revolution' in Monetary Theory;" idem, "A Survey of Selected Issues in Monetary Theory," *Schweizerische Zeitschrift für Volkswirtschaft und Statistik* (No. 1, 1971), pp. 1–146; idem, The "Monetarist View of Keynesian Ideas," *Lloyds Bank Review* (October 1971), pp. 35–49; David I. Fand, "Keynesian Monetary Theories, Stabilization Policy, and the Recent Inflation," *Journal of Money, Credit, and Banking* (August 1969), pp. 556–87; idem, "Monetarism and Fiscalism," *Banca Nazionale del Lavoro Quarterly Review* (September, 1970), pp. 275–89; idem, "A Monetarist Model of the Monetary Process," *Journal of Finance* (May 1970), pp. 275–89; Milton Friedman, "A Theoretical Framework for Monetary Analysis," *Journal of Political Economy* (March/April 1970), pp. 193–238; idem, "A Monetary Theory of National Income," *Journal of Political Economy* (March/April 1971), pp. 323–37.

[8] Friedman, "A Theoretical Framework," and Brunner, "The 'Monetarist Revolution'."

[9] In one version of Friedman's statement, the money supply is made a function of the interest rate rather than being assumed to be exogenous. However, this makes no essential difference to the present discussion, as Friedman points out.

[10] This statement is not accurate if the system contains a government sector which issues money-fixed claims against itself, and if real wealth is an argument in the expenditure functions, and/or if the government establishes a tax-expenditure system based on nominal variables.

rather than real income, is determined outside of the postulated structure (Friedman refers to ". . . a *deus ex machina* with no underpinning in economic theory.").[11] By taking the price level to be exogenous with respect to this structure, the number of variables again is reduced to three (Y, y, and r in this case). However, the system no longer is dichotomized, and all of the variables now are determined jointly rather than recursively. In particular, the static equilibrium levels of both real income and the interest rate can now be changed by both money stock and expenditure changes.[12]

It would be a mistake to conclude from the foregoing discussion that monetarists view themselves as differing from Keynesians only in terms of the assumptions utilized to provide a unique equilibrium solution to the static *IS-LM* model. There are several other typically monetarist assumptions about the static and dynamic dimensions of this system. Recently, Karl Brunner has introduced four propositions which he asserts are "defining characteristics of the monetarist position." These are: (1) the transmission mechanism for monetary impulses involves a very general kind of portfolio adjustment process ultimately

affecting the relationship between the market price of physical assets and their production cost, rather than only the relationship between borrowing costs and the internal rates of return on potential acquisitions of new physical capital, as is asserted to be the mechanism characteristic of modern Keynesian analysis; (2) most of the destabilizing shocks experienced by the system arise from decisions of the government with respect to tax, expenditure, and monetary policy, rather than from the instability of private investment or of some other aspect of private-sector behavior, as the Keynesian view is said to assume. A related belief is that the demand-for-money function is very stable, while the policy-determined supply of money balances is unstable; (3) monetary impulses are the dominant factor in explaining changes in the pace of economic activity, in contrast to the Keynesian position which assertedly takes real impulses as primary; (4) in analyzing the determinants of change in the level of aggregate activity, detailed knowledge of "allocative detail" about the working of financial markets and institutions is of secondary importance and can be disregarded. This implies that the relationship between policy instruments and economic activity can be captured in a very small-scale model—perhaps even in one equation—while the Keynesian position is that knowledge of allocative detail (e.g., substitution relationships between various financial assets) is necessary for the proper understanding of policy processes, implying a need for complex structural models.[13]

The statements by Brunner and Friedman are attempts to sketch the fundamental structure of monetarism. As such, they do not emphasize or even identify explicitly some of the specific characteristic themes which permeate monetarist writing, including their own. Several such themes can be identified.

(1) Great importance is attached to the demand-for-money function, and it is in fact the central behavioral relationship in the monetarist model.[14] Particular stress is laid on its stability,

---

[11] Friedman, "A Theoretical Framework," p. 222.

[12] In a more recent article, Friedman has proposed another means of closing this system of equations, which he labels a "third way" to distinguish it from the two procedures outlined in the body of the present paper. He views this approach as intermediate in respect to its theoretical position vis-à-vis the others. However, since it reduces to a relationship between income and the past history of the money stock, as Friedman demonstrates, it seems clearly to fit in with the monetarist point of view. In this approach, it is assumed that the current market rate of interest and the expected market rate are kept equal by the actions of asset holders. The expected market rate, in turn, is set by the expected real rate plus the expected rate of price change (which by definition is the difference between the expected rate of change of nominal income and of real output). By assuming the expected real rate of interest, the expected rate of growth of real output, and the expected rate of growth of nominal income all to be determined outside the system, the market rate of interest is made into a variable determined outside the system also. Assuming further that the income elasticity of demand for money is unity, Friedman establishes a direct link between nominal income and the money stock (because under his assumptions velocity becomes a predetermined variable); this, in turn, enables the "real" sector to be solved. One of the features of this procedure is that it provides an alternative to the assumption of full employment. However, it entails some disadvantages of its own, which are noted in the section of the present paper entitled "Stabilization Policy." See Friedman, "A Monetary Theory of Nominal Income."

[13] These "defining characteristics" are discussed at some length in Brunner, "The 'Monetarist Revolution'," Section II.

[14] Thus, for example, David Fand states, "The quantity theory, in its post-Keynesian reformulation, is a theory of the demand for money and a theory of money income," "Keynesian Monetary Theories," p. 561. Also, he writes, ". . . the modern quantity theory uses the money demand function to predict the level of money income and prices if output is given, or *changes* in money income if output varies with changes in [the money stock]," "Monetarism and Fiscalism," p. 228. Friedman has written, "The

by which is meant not only that the variance of its error term is small, but much more importantly, that it contains very few arguments. Friedman has written that:

The quantity theorist accepts the empirical hypothesis that the demand for money is highly stable—more stable than functions such as the consumption function that are offered as alternative key relations. . . . . [T]he stability he expects is in the functional relation between the quantity of money demanded and the variables that determine it . . . [and] he must sharply limit, and be prepared to specify explicitly, the variables that it is empirically important to include in the function. For to expand the number of variables regarded as significant is to empty the hypothesis of its empirical content; there is indeed little if any difference between asserting that the demand for money is highly unstable and asserting that it is a perfectly stable function of an indefinitely large number of variables.[15]

(2) A particular aspect of the demand for money emphasized by monetarists is that, in their analysis, the stable *demand* for money is concerned with real, not nominal, balances, while the authorities control the nominal *supply*, which tends to be quite variable relative to demand.[16] This state of affairs is usually contrasted with the Keynesian case, in which the demand for money is said to be a demand for nominal balances, either because it is (incorrectly) specified that way,[17] or because, as in Friedman's discussion

summarized above, the price level is fixed so that real and nominal balances are the same. Monetarists use this distinction as part of a rationalization for their contention that their analysis implies a much broader concept of the transmission mechanism for monetary impulses than does the Keynesian model, being based on a very general portfolio adjustment process working through changes in a broad spectrum of asset yields and price level changes, in contrast to the narrow cost of credit channel which is implied by the Keynesian demand-for-money function. This point is developed further in the section entitled "The Transmission Mechanism for Monetary Impulses" below.

(3) Further, monetarists believe the interest elasticity of demand for money balances to be quite low. Until recently, it was generally thought that they viewed this elasticity to be zero so that the demand for money was linked directly to income as implied by the naive quantity theory. However, such a view has been rejected outright by Friedman and others;[18] if it ever was held, the accumulation of empirical evidence to the contrary has made it untenable now.[19]

Presently, monetarists take the reputedly different views held by themselves and Keynesians on the size of this elasticity as a basis for contrasting inferences about the expected behavior of velocity in response to a monetary shift. A substantial interest elasticity of demand for money, said to be the Keynesian position, is viewed as implying unstable velocity; Keynesians are viewed by monetarists as not being able to "depend" on the stability of velocity, for as the money stock rises and falls, offsetting velocity changes insulate the rest of the system to a great extent. On the other hand, while not believing velocity to be perfectly constant, monetarists take the position that ". . . although marginal and average velocity differ, the velocity function is sufficiently stable to provide a relation between changes in money and changes in money income."[20] In other words, some, but not much, short-run variation in velocity may be expected.[21]

___

quantity theorist not only regards the demand function for money as stable; he also regards it as playing a vital role in determining variables that he regards as of great importance for the analysis of the economy as a whole, such as the level of money income or of prices. It is this that leads him to put greater emphasis on the demand for money than on, let us say, the demand for pins, even though the latter might be as stable as the former," "The Quantity Theory of Money—A Restatement," p. 16.

[15] Friedman, "The Quantity Theory of Money—A Restatement," p. 16.

[16] On this point Fand writes, "The sharp distinction drawn between the supply determined nominal money stock and the demand determined real stock—a key feature of monetarism—endows the authorities with effective control over the nominal money stock, while severely limiting the extent, and the circumstances, in which they may hope to influence the real value of this stock. If the former assumption extends their control over nominal variables, the latter assumption severely limits their influence and control on endogenous variables such as the real money stock." See "Monetarism and Fiscalism," pp. 280–81.

[17] This view is taken by David I. Fand in, "Some Issues in Monetary Economics," *Banca Nazionale del Lavoro Quarterly Review* (September 1969), pp. 228–9 and footnote 24, p. 229.

[18] Milton Friedman, "Interest Rates and the Demand for Money," *Journal of Law and Economics* (October 1966), pp. 71–86.

[19] Some of this evidence is summarized in David Laidler, *The Demand for Money: Theories and Evidence* (Scranton, Pa.: International Textbook Company, 1969).

[20] Fand, "Keynesian Monetary Theories," pp. 563–4.

[21] Monetarists do not necessarily expect velocity to change inversely with changes in the money stock. Friedman recently has written that ". . . the effect

To some monetarists, the essential difference between the two positions is summed up in the demand for money-velocity nexus. Fand writes:

The post-Keynesian quantity and income theories thus differ sharply in their analysis of the money demand function. In the modern quantity theory it serves as a velocity function relating either money and money income or marginal *changes* in money and money income . . .; in the income theory, it serves as a liquidity preference theory of interest rates, or of *changes* in interest rates (if the price level is given and determined independently of the monetary sector).[22]

Although it has become fairly common practice to discuss the behavior of velocity in terms of the properties of the demand-for-money function, it is improper to do so because observed velocity depends on all of the behavior—real and monetary—in the macroeconomic system. This point will be discussed in greater detail below.

(4)   The final monetarist theme which I shall mention is concerned with the nature of the response of interest rates to a monetary shift. Monetarists distinguished three components in the observed movement of interest rates: a "liquidity" effect, which is the immediate response before income or other variables have changed, and thus is expected to be in the opposite direction of the monetary shift; an "income" effect, which is the induced reaction of interest rates to the change in income brought about by the monetary impulse, and hence is expected to be in the same direction as the money stock change; and a "price expectations" effect, which comes about because monetary changes cause lenders and borrowers to anticipate a changing price level and lead lenders to protect themselves against the expected depreciation in the value of their funds by charging higher rates. This last effect would cause market interest rates to change in the same direction as the monetary change.[23]

In looking back over this summary of monetarist thought, it becomes quite apparent that there is a good deal of truth to Friedman's contention that the differences between Keynesians and monetarists are essentially empirical rather than theoretical, having to do with the assumptions made about specific aspects of the commonly-accepted structure, the relative stability and importance in the analysis of different functional relationships, the sizes of various elasticities, etc.[24] There appears to be little disagreement between the two camps over the specification of Friedman's basic model.[25] And of Brunner's four points, at least two are essentially empirical (points numbered (2) and (3) above), while one of the remaining two (point (1) above) makes a distinction between monetarist and Keynesian views of the transmission mechanism which I believe is false with respect to current post-Keynesian income-expenditure analysis. Only his last point—that it is appropriate to study the relationship between policy instruments and economic activity without depending on knowledge of "allocative detail"—appears to be one about which there are genuine differences at the theoretical (or perhaps more properly, the methodological) level. Finally, among the four monetarist themes mentioned above, the third one is clearly empirical in nature, and monetarists and Keynesians both in fact hold that this elasticity is nonzero but small in absolute value. In the next section, it is demonstrated that modern Keynesians take the price level to be endogenous, which suggests that the monetarist-Keynesian distinctions summarized above as the second theme

---

on [velocity] is empirically not to absorb the change in M, as Keynesian analysis implies, but often to reinforce it. . . .," "A Theoretical Framework," p. 217.

[22] See Fand, "Some Issues," p. 228.

[23] For a discussion of these distinctions, see e.g., William Gibson, "Interest Rates and Monetary Policy," *Journal of Political Economy* (May/June 1970), pp. 431–55.

[24] This position is expressed in several of Friedman's writings; for example, see Milton Friedman and David Meiselman, "The Relative Stability," p. 168, and Milton Friedman, "Post-War Trends in Monetary Theory and Policy," *National Banking Review* (September 1964), reprinted in M. Friedman, *The Optimum Quantity of Money and Other Essays* (London: Macmillan and Co., Ltd., 1969), p. 73.

[25] Not all monetarists view this particular model as an appropriate description on which to build an analysis, however. Brunner recently wrote, "It is useful to emphasize . . . that the logic of the monetarist analysis based on the relative price theory approach requires that attention be directed to the interaction between output market, credit market and Walrasian money market. This requirement cannot be satisfied by the general framework used by Friedman. This framework is the standard IS-LM analysis offered in an essentially Keynesian spirit. And this very choice of basic framework actually creates the analytical problems clearly recognized by Friedman in his subsequent discussion. . . . Our analysis . . . established however that the standard IS-LM diagram is not a very useful device for the analysis of monetary processes." Karl Brunner, "A Survey of Selected Issues in Monetary Theory," p. 82.

are not valid. I shall try to show below that monetarist emphasis on the importance of the demand-for-money relationship (the first theme) is unwarranted, at least in so far as this relationship is viewed as the basis for predicting velocity. I shall also show that the two components of interest rate change in response to a monetary impulse identified in theme four as monetarist are either clearly present in or at least consistent with Keynesian analysis and assumption.

Monetarism, Keynesianism, and the Price Level

As already noted above, monetarists see one of the essential differences between the two sides to be the question of the determinants of the price level in comparative static equilibrium analysis. Keynesians are said to take prices to be fixed so that monetary shifts are reflected in output changes, while quantity theorists believe that monetary changes affect only the price level in this sort of analysis, with real output being determined by a separate subsector of the system.

There is no doubt whatsoever that many practitioners of the Keynesian viewpoint have assumed that prices could conveniently be taken as given for some problems—especially those associated with substantial unemployment—and that it has often been convenient for simplicity of exposition in undergraduate classroom exercises or for other purposes to make the assumption of rigid prices. It is quite dubious, however, that this assumption, or the liquidity trap assumption which also has been an important element in the monetarist view of Keynesianism, reflects the thinking of most Keynesian economists today.[26] Rather, the standard static "complete Keynesian system" is widely recognized to be one in which the general price level is one of the variables determined by the interaction of the system, and hence is free to move, but to be one in which there are imperfections in the labor market—most typically, a money wage rate which is inflexible downwards. In other words, rather than assuming that prices are fixed as a means of making the simple static model determinate, modern Keynes-

ians introduce an aggregated labor market and production function into the analysis.[27] This could be viewed as the Keynesian equivalent of the "Walrasian system of equations" asserted by Friedman to be the hallmark of the adherents to the modern quantity theory approach. It is of course much less satisfactory in that all labor market activity and all kinds of production are aggregated into perhaps as few as two equations (i.e., a reduced-form labor market equation and an aggregate production function) rather than having each market and each activity represented by specific equations. It is more satisfactory on two counts: first, the equations at least are explicitly specified, and second, these equations do not yield the full employment outcome, as is typically the case when depending on a Walrasian system.[28]

The essential difference in this regard between monetarists and Keynesians therefore would appear to be that the former view *all* prices (including wages) as flexible, while the latter consider all prices *except* the money wage rate to be flexible (money wages are viewed as inflexible, at least in a downward direction, due to such structural phenomena as minimum wage laws, union contracts, and the like). This distinction has significant implications for the analysis.

In the first place, the Keynesian treatment

[26] The liquidity trap is rejected by most economists today because little support for it has been found in the many empirical studies of the demand for money which have recently been made. For a summary of some of this evidence, see Ronald L. Teigen, "The Demand for and Supply of Money," supra, Table 2, page 92, or "The Importance of Money," *Bank of England Quarterly Bulletin* (June 1970), pp. 159–198.

[27] As evidence for the assertion that modern post-Keynesian static analysis in its most general form typically assumes the price level to be an endogenous variable, and that the system of equations usually is made determinate by introducing a supply subsector consisting of a labor market and aggregate production function, the following standard works are cited: Gardner Ackley, *Macroeconomic Theory* (New York: Macmillan, 1961), Chap. IX; R. G. D. Allen, *Macro-Economic Theory* (London: Macmillan, 1967), Chap. 7, esp. sections 7.6–7.8; Martin J. Bailey, *National Income and the Price Level*, 2nd. ed. (New York: McGraw-Hill, 1971), Chap. 3, esp. section 2; Robert S. Holbrook, "The Interest Rate, the Price Level, and Aggregate Output," supra, pp. 38–60. Franco Modigliani, "The Monetary Mechanism and its Interaction with Real Phenomena," *Review of Economics and Statistics* (February 1963 Supplement); and Warren L. Smith, "A Graphical Exposition of the Complete Keynesian System," *Southern Economic Journal* (October 1956), reprinted in W. Smith and R. Teigen, eds., *Readings in Money, National Income, and Stabilization Policy*, 3d ed., as well as in several other standard collections of readings in macroeconomics.

[28] This discussion is not meant to imply that the simple static Keynesian system contains an adequate description of the processes which determine the price level. It states simply that the price level is an endogenous variable in the model.

now cannot be said to be fundamentally less satisfactory than the monetarist one in terms of methodology, except perhaps on grounds having to do with problems of aggregation (Friedman, it will be recalled, used the pejorative term "deus ex machina" to describe what he understood to be the Keynesian approach). Rather, the difference now lies in the analytic usefulness of the assumptions themselves. Is it more appropriate to assume that wages and prices are flexible, or that money wages are sticky while prices can adjust? The answer to this question depends on the nature of the problem being studied in any particular case, and this suggests that an important difference between the two schools of thought may be that Keynesians are more concerned with short-run analysis (for instance, that related to countercyclical stabilization) while monetarist assumptions are more consistent with long-run analysis.

Second, dropping the rigid-price assumption tends to reduce the basis for the heavy emphasis placed by monetarists on the demand-for-money function and its properties. One place where such emphasis is evident is in the discussion of velocity. We turn next to an inquiry into the factors affecting velocity, with particular emphasis on the relationship of velocity to the demand-for-money function.

The Demand-for-Money Function and Velocity

Monetarists, as we have already noted, tend to think of the demand-for-money function as a "stable velocity function" while holding that Keynesians view velocity as unstable, justifying this position by appeal to contrasting assumptions about the price level and the interest elasticity of demand for money (see e.g. the quotes from Fand and others above). The fact of the matter is that the behavior of velocity under the two approaches in response to a monetary shift depends basically on the assumptions made about the *labor market,* not about the demand for money or about prices, since, as we have seen, both approaches take prices as flexible and, if that is the case, the same general demand-for-money function $\left(\frac{M}{p} = L(y,r) \right)$ would be characteristic of both. This point can be demonstrated quite easily. First we note that the definition of velocity implies the following relationship:

$$E_{V \cdot M_0} = E_{y \cdot M_0} + E_{p \cdot M_0} - 1, \qquad (4)$$

where E stands for elasticities calculated on the basis of the interaction of the entire structure, so that (for instance) $E_{y \cdot M_0}$ represents the elasticity of real output with respect to changes in the nominal money stock when the response of the entire economic system to the money stock change is taken into account. To distinguish such "systemic" elasticities from "partial" elasticities—those calculated along one function only—the symbol η will be used to represent partial elasticities. Thus, for instance, $\eta_{L \cdot r}$ will stand for the interest elasticity of the demand for real balances, holding income and other variables constant.

Under the monetarist assumption of flexible wages and prices, real output is determined uniquely by Friedman's "Walrasian system" and, as he points out, is to be considered as predetermined from the standpoint of equations (1)–(3). This means that a monetary shift cannot change real output $\left(\text{i.e., the multiplier } \frac{dy}{dM_0} = 0 \right)$, so that $E_{y \cdot M_0}$, which is defined to be $\frac{M_0}{y} \frac{dy}{dM_0}$, is also zero. By differentiating equations (1)–(3) with respect to M_0 while holding y constant, it is easy to show that the elasticity $E_{p \cdot M_0}$, which is equal to $\frac{M_0}{p} \frac{dp}{dM_0}$, has a value of unity. Inserting these results into (4) gives the quantity theory result that $E_{V \cdot M_0} = 0$, the "stable velocity" result referred to previously. It is important to note that no particular assumptions unique to the monetarist position were made about the demand for money *per se;* the assumption which yielded this result was that the demand for labor and the supply of labor both were functions of the real wage rate, and that the market was always cleared.

On the other hand, let us consider the Keynesian case, which we now define as one in which *money wages* are sticky (i.e., there exists money illusion in the supply of labor), but in which the price level is an endogenous variable. To analyze this case, we must add three equations to the basic model: an aggregate production function (equation (5) below); a labor market summary equation which states that the supply of labor services per unit time (N) is infinitely elastic over a wide range of employment at whatever money wage rate prevails, and that the demand for labor (N^p) is determined by the real wage (w) (equation (6)); and a definition which states that the real wage is the ratio of the money wage rate (W) and the price level (equation (7)). The bar over the money wage rate indicates that it is being held constant here.[29] This gives:

$$y = y(N) \quad (5)$$
$$N = N^D(w) \quad (6)$$
$$w = \frac{\bar{W}}{p}. \quad (7)$$

By differentiating the system defined by equations (1)–(3) and (5)–(7) totally with respect to M_0, expressions for the systemic elasticities $E_{y \cdot M_0}$ and $E_{p \cdot M_0}$ can be found. They are as follows (see the appendix for their derivation):

$$E_{y \cdot M_0} = \cfrac{1}{\cfrac{\eta_{S \cdot y} \eta_{L \cdot r}}{\eta_{I \cdot r} - \eta_{S \cdot r}} + \eta_{L \cdot y} - \cfrac{1}{\eta_{y \cdot N} \eta_{N^D \cdot w}}} \quad (8)$$

$$E_{p \cdot M_0} = - \cfrac{1}{\eta_{y \cdot N} \eta_{N^D \cdot w} \left[\cfrac{\eta_{S \cdot y} \eta_{L \cdot r}}{\eta_{I \cdot r} - \eta_{S \cdot r}} + \eta_{L \cdot y} \right] - 1} \quad (9)$$

Here S stands for the savings function; otherwise all of the notation has already been defined. The usual slope assumptions are made, and on the basis of these assumptions, both of these systemic elasticities will be positive.[30] Whether velocity will rise, fall, or remain constant in the face of a monetary shift depends on the sizes of all of the partial elasticities and their relationships to one another as given by these expressions. The demand-for-money elasticities play a role, but are by no means the only relevant elasticities. In general, we would not expect the elasticity of velocity with respect to nominal money balances to be minus unity in value, as the "liquidity trap" assumption implies. It will approach that value if $\eta_{L \cdot r}$ or $\eta_{S \cdot y}$ are very large, or if the term $(\eta_{I \cdot r} - \eta_{S \cdot r})$ is very close to zero.[31]

---

[29] This is the simplest method of introducing a Keynesian-type assumption into the analysis; it is by no means the only possible way of doing so. The nature of and reasons for the existence of money illusion in the labor market is the subject of a considerable amount of literature. See, for example, Axel Leijonhufvud, *On Keynesian Economics and the Economics of Keynes* (London: Oxford University Press, 1968).

[30] It is assumed that $\eta_{S \cdot r}$ is either positive or, if negative, that it is smaller in size than the absolute value of $\eta_{I \cdot r}$. A listing of all the slope assumptions is given in the appendix.

[31] Since the numerator of the expression for $\eta_{S \cdot y}$ is one minus the MPC, $\eta_{S \cdot y}$ is not expected to be large. As noted in footnote 26, belief in a very large interest elasticity of demand for money ($\eta_{L \cdot r}$) is not

To summarize, the main point of this exercise was to show that, using a common model with no special assumptions about the properties of the demand for money, it has been possible to derive "monetarist" and "Keynesian" results for the response of velocity to a monetary shift. It is improper to speak of the demand for money as a "velocity function," *especially* in the monetarist case where it is assumed that money wages are flexible so that the system equilibrates at full employment. In that case, the velocity elasticity will be zero no matter what the sizes of the demand-for money elasticities.

Eliminating the rigid-price assumption as a basic point of difference between the two schools reduces the basis for monetarist emphasis on the demand for money for other reasons besides its implications for velocity. It also is important for monetarist views on differences in the nature of the transmission mechanism for monetary policy. It is to this subject that we turn next.

The Transmission Mechanism for Monetary Impulses

One of the most characteristic themes of monetarism is the heavy emphasis which is placed on differences between the quantities of money demanded and supplied as the prime factor motivating spending and, hence, changes in income and prices. Friedman and others have explained again and again how the authorities can change the nominal money stock, but how it is money holders who determine the velocity with which that stock is used, and ultimately who determine the stock of real balances through the effects of spending decisions on the price level. As Friedman puts it, "The key insight of the quantity-theory approach is that such a discrepancy [between the demand for and supply of money] will be manifested primarily in attempted spending, thence in the rate of change in nominal income."[32] In other words, when households and firms are holding more cash balances than are desired at current levels of income and interest rates, they convert these excess balances into other assets, both financial and physical; the mar-

---

a characteristic Keynesian stance. Reference to the summaries of available empirical evidence mentioned in that footnote will show that this elasticity actually appears to be rather small (almost certainly less than unity in absolute value, and in many studies smaller in absolute value than 0.2).

[32] Friedman, "A Theoretical Framework," p. 225.

ket value of physical assets ultimately changes, making the production of new assets more attractive. The change in the general price level which occurs as a result of this process, and the change in output, both work toward a re-equating of the real value of the nominal money stock and the demand for real balances. Thus the monetarists clearly embrace a very general kind of portfolio adjustment view of the transmission mechanism in which the relevant portfolio contains financial and physical assets of all kinds.[33] It will be recalled that this is the first of Brunner's four "defining characteristics." At the same time, monetarists have been taking Keynesian analysis to task for focusing almost exclusively on interest rates representing the "cost of finance" as the channel through which monetary impulses are felt. The following quotation makes these distinctions very clear:

The Income-Expenditure theory of the Fiscalists adopts a particular transmission mechanism to analyze the effects of a change in the money stock (or its growth rate) on the real economy. It assumes that money changes will affect output or prices only through its effect on a set of conventional yields—on the market interest rate of a small group of financial assets, such as government or corporate bonds. A given change in the money stock will have a calculable effect on these interest rates . . . given by the liquidity preference analysis, and the interest rate changes are then used to derive the change in investment spending, the induced effects on income and consumption, etc.

Monetarists, following the Quantity theory, do not accept this transmission mechanism and this liquidity preference theory of interest rates for several reasons: First, they suggest that an increase in money may directly affect expenditures, prices, and a wide variety of implicit yields on physical assets, and need not be restricted to a small set of conventional yields on financial assets. Second, they view the demand for money as determining the desired quantity of real balances, and not the level of interest rates. Third, and most fundamentally, they reject the notion that the authorities can change the stock of real balances—an endogenous variable—and thereby bring about a permanent change in interest rates. . . .

Monetarists reject the liquidity preference interest rate theory because it applies only as long as we can equate an increase in nominal money with a permanent increase in real balances. This suggests that the liquidity preference theory may be useful as a theory of the short run interest rate changes—the

liquidity effect—associated with the impact effects of nominal money changes.[34]

Statements like this, and the quotation from Friedman in footnote 14 indicate that monetarists believe their view of the transmission mechanism to differ from the position they impute to the Keynesian camp most essentially in differences in assumptions about characteristics of the demand-for-money function. The interpretation of the interest rate term in this function plays a role; so does the question of price flexibility. As the preceding discussion and quotation indicate, monetarists think of their own view as an extremely general one. The interest rate term in their model really stands for a vector of yields on many assets, some of them financial yields determined in the money and capital markets, and some of them implicit yields on real assets. A monetary impulse sooner or later affects all of these yields, and hence adjusts the demand for real balances directly as well as indirectly through the effects of yield changes on income. At the same time, changes in the price level which result will adjust the real value of the nominal money supply. Therefore the adjustment process is seen as being summarized in the characteristics of the demand-for-real balances function and its relationship to the nominal money supply. Keynesians are said to include only a few market-determined yields on financial assets in their liquidity-preference function; furthermore, the price level is exogenously determined. Therefore the process of adjustment to a monetary impulse is supposedly seen by them in much narrower terms—the entire process takes place through adjustment of the *demand* for money, and basically is said to focus on the cost of credit as reflected in market interest rates. Furthermore, the belief in a substantial interest elasticity of demand for money, often attributed to Keynesians, means that a monetary impulse will have a relatively small effect even on these rates.

These distinctions must be regarded as artificial. First, there is nothing inherent in the Keynesian system which is inconsistent with the introduction of a general portfolio adjustment transmission mechanism; and, indeed, there has been a substantial development in this direction in Keynesian thinking and practice during the last several years. On the theoretical side, the work of Tobin and others may be cited, while at the operational level, the developers of the Federal Reserve Board-MIT econometric model

---

[33] A description of the classes of assets involved and the nature of their yields is given in Milton Friedman, "The Quantity Theory of Money—A Restatement."

[34] Fand, "A Monetarist Model," pp. 280–81.

of the U.S. economy have attempted to incorporate such a mechanism into their model.[35] While all of the problems involved in this attempt have not yet been solved, work is continuing and improvements will be made. Second, as we have already shown, Keynesians take the price level to be endogenous, and thus recognize the same process of adjustment of the nominal money supply through price level changes as the monetarists.[36]

There remain certain problems with monetarist thought on two subjects related to the transmission mechanism. One is a misunderstanding, in my opinion, of the relationship between money and interest rates implied by Keynesian theory. The other has to do with the monetarist position on the money stock as a force driving income through the portfolio process mentioned above.

Liquidity Preference Theory, Money, and the Rate of Interest. Monetarists view themselves as holding a "monetary theory of the price level" under which monetary shifts are reflected (in the longer run, at least) primarily in price level changes. They take the stance that Keynesians hold a "monetary theory of the interest rate." Under this phrase, at least two positions are subsumed. Some monetarists seem to think that Keynesians see the money supply together with the demand-for-money function (specified in nominal terms) as determining the level of interest rates. Others recognize that the interest rate in Keynesian analysis is determined jointly as one of the outcomes of an interacting system of relationships rather than just by one behavioral relationship (i.e., by some version of an *IS-LM* system like Friedman's summary model). Whichever view is held, however, it is asserted that Keynesian analysis leads to the conclusion that monetary shifts result in interest rate changes in the *opposite* direction, while monetarist analy-

sis suggests that movements of M and r in the *same* direction will be observed.[37]

Neither version of the "monetary theory of the interest rate" is an accurate representation of Keynesian thought, for both imply that an expansionary monetary impulse (for example) can *only* result in a lower interest rate in the new equilibrium. In other words, it appears that of the two monetary effects on interest rates often mentioned by monetarists which are relevant for static analysis—the liquidity effect and the income effect—Keynesians are supposed to recognize only the liquidity effect, or more generally, are supposed to be basing their analysis on assumptions which can only result in an inverse relationship between monetary impulses and interest rate changes.

This is certainly not the case. When the entire structure is taken into account, rather than only the liquidity preference function, the level of interest rates in the new equilibrium relative to the initial position is determined by a number of elasticities, most importantly those which are the determinants of the slope of the *IS* curve. If its slope is positive—which is the case if all of the propensities to spend with respect to total income sum to more than unity—then both income and interest rates will be higher in the new equilibrium than in the old.[38] This is such

---

[35] For a non-monetarist example of the development of portfolio theory, see James Tobin, "An Essay on Principles of Debt Management," in Commission on Money and Credit, *Fiscal and Debt Management Policies* (Englewood Cliffs, N.J.: Prentice-Hall, Inc., 1963), pp. 143–218, esp. Part II. Features of the Federal Reserve Board-MIT model are discussed in Frank de Leeuw and Edward M. Gramlich, "The Channels of Monetary Policy," Federal Reserve *Bulletin* (June 1969), pp. 472–91.

[36] Semantic as well as real issues are involved in discussions of this subject. For example, Brunner labels anyone who subscribes to a portfolio adjustment view of the monetary transmission mechanism a "weak monetarist". See Karl Brunner, "The Role of Monetary Policy," Federal Reserve Bank of St. Louis *Review* (July 1968), pp. 9–24.

[37] As an example of the first of these positions, the following quotation from a recent article by Fand is offered: "In the Keynesian theory the exogenously given quantity of money, together with the liquidity preference function, determines the interest rate." Fand, "Keynesian Monetary Theories," p. 564. The second is illustrated by a quotation from Zwick: "The alternative concepts of Keynes and Fisher concerning the adjustment of the economy to monetary changes are mirrored in their different notions concerning interest rate determination and the response of interest rates to monetary changes. The IS-LM framework suggests that, so long as the IS and LM schedules represent independent relations, a monetary expansion causes interest rates to fall because of the outward shift of the LM schedule. In the Fisherian model, a monetary increase raises the level of expenditures; the upward response of loan demand due to the increased expenditures causes interest rates to rise." Burton Zwick, "The Adjustment of the Economy to Monetary Changes," *Journal of Political Economy* (January/February 1971), p. 78.

[38] An upward-sloping IS curve cannot be obtained from Friedman's summary model, because only consumption spending is related to income in that model, and the notion that the MPC is less than unity is a fundamental postulate of macroeconomic analysis. However, the level of income might well appear in other expenditure functions, such as the investment relationship (where the rationalization would be that investment depends on profits, which in turn are a function of the level of income).

a well-known case as to require no further comment.

Of course, equilibrium positions are not observed in the real world; instead, the economy is always in transition, moving toward resting points, which themselves are repeatedly being disturbed. It may be inferred from some monetarist writings that it is the *observed* tendency of interest rates and money to move in the same direction which is thought to be inconsistent with Keynesianism, rather than the possibility that money and interest rates can move together in terms of comparative equilibrium points. In other words, the discussion may refer to the dynamics of the system, rather than the comparative statics. In this area, the monetarists have done us all a service by stressing the possible importance of price-expectation effects on interest rates, a phenomenon which typically has not been incorporated into dynamic Keynesian models. I will argue that observed parallel movements between money and interest rates are quite consistent with the basic *IS-LM* structure (no matter which way the *IS* curve slopes), given the reasonable and widely-accepted premise that the monetary sector adjusts much more rapidly than the real sector to external shocks. Under this premise, observed values of income and the rate of interest may be supposed, at least approximately, to be such that the *LM* equation is always satisfied during the process of adjustment from one equilibrium to another, while the *IS* equation is not. I will argue further that price-expectation effects are readily accommodated by this analysis.

The implications of these differing speeds of adjustment are illustrated on the accompanying figure, which happens to be drawn with a downward-sloping *IS* curve. Assume the system to be initially in equilibrium at point *F*, so that the equilibrium values of the interest rate and income levels are *r* and *y*. Now let there occur an expansion of the money supply, so that the *LM* curve shifts outward to a new position, *LM'*. According to the assumption made above concerning the relative speeds of adjustment of the monetary and real sectors, this shift will result first in a fall in the interest rate from its initial equilibrium level to a new level, *r'*. It should be noted that this is the "liquidity effect" which is recognized by monetarists as being present both in their own and in Keynesian thinking. It represents a movement along the liquidity preference function in response to a change in the money supply, holding income constant. Next, income will begin to respond, and income and the rate of interest both will rise along the segment *GH* of *LM'* to point *H*, the final equilibrium position. This movement, of course, reflects the "income effect."

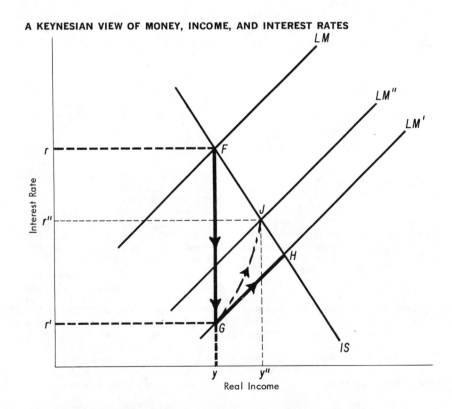

A KEYNESIAN VIEW OF MONEY, INCOME, AND INTEREST RATES

If rising income is accompanied by rising prices, there will also be an induced shift of the *LM* curve during the transition. For example, it might move to a position like *LM''* as shown. Alternatively, it could move to a position to the right of *LM'*.

Such *LM* shifts reflect the operation of two forces. First, rising prices reduce the real value of the new nominal money stock and "tighten the money market" after the initial expansionary pulse. This has the effect of moving the *LM* curve leftward. Second, rising prices may engender expectations of future price increases. If, as has been suggested, the demand for money depends on nominal interest rates while real expenditures are determined by real rates, then the "price expectations effect" mentioned previously would cause a rightward *LM* shift, resulting in a lesser leftward overall shift in the *LM* curve than that brought about due only to the drop in the real value of the nominal money stock, or perhaps even a net rightward movement (in this discussion, the vertical axis is interpreted as measuring the real rate of interest). If these effects are present, the adjustment path followed from point *G* might be the dotted one instead of the solidly-drawn one, and the system would end up at a point like *J* instead of *H*, so that the new equilibrium income level would be *y''*, and the equilibrium real interest rate *r''*. Incidentally, if price-expectation effects are present, a value of *r''* for the real rate is quite consistent with a market rate above *r*.

We may conclude from this discussion that there is no reason to be surprised by the fact that during much of the time following an increase in the money supply, interest rates are observed to rise. A standard assumption about relative speeds of adjustment, much used by Keynesians, directly reflects both the "liquidity effect" and the "income effect" often discussed by monetarists, and is perfectly consistent with the presence of price expectation effects. Second, it is appropriate to point out that this entire discussion has been carried out in the context of a pure multiplier model. If accelerator effects are present, they may accentuate the pure multiplier effects of a monetary shift on interest rates, at least during parts of the adjustment period. Finally, there is the likelihood that in many cases in which interest rates and the money stock move together, the monetary authorities are reacting to shifts in spending. For instance, if total spending rises, interest rates will go up and the monetary authorities will often try to moderate the interest rate increase by expansionary open market operations, resulting in a rise in the money stock.

The Monetarist View of Money as a Force Driving Income. It is self-evident that monetarists typically have assigned great importance to changes in the money stock as the prime moving force behind income changes. For instance, one of Brunner's "defining characteristics of monetarism" is that ". . . the monetarist analysis assigns the monetary forces a dominant position among all the impulses working on the economic process."[39] And, of course, Friedman's investigations into the lead-lag relationship between changes in the rate of change of the money stock and changes in income are too well-known to require further comment.[40] At the same time, monetarist writings often seem to suggest that Keynesians view monetary policy as ineffective.

Keynesians view monetary policy as effective and useful, and to suggest the opposite is to raise false issues. But this does not mean that they necessarily consider changes in the money stock to have particular causal significance. Monetary policy is carried out through the traditional instruments—open market operations, discount rate changes, and variations in reserve requirements—and not by direct manipulation of the money stock. It is true that in simplified versions of the Keynesian model, monetary policy is represented by the money stock, which is assumed to be controlled by the authorities and which replaces the instruments named above. It is also possible that the authorities could control the nominal money stock to almost any desired degree of precision. But in the real world, or in the more sophisticated models of it, the nominal money stock is not exogenous, nor has it been controlled as an objective of policy by the central bank in the United States; it, or its components, are determined jointly by the central bank, the commercial banks, and the public, and it is basically a passive outcome of the interaction of the economic system, not a driving force.

The doubt the Keynesians feel concerning monetarist assertions about the potency of money stock changes reflects the fact that monetarist descriptions of the adjustment process themselves seem to give no particular reason for regarding money stock changes as causal. These descriptions

---

[39] Brunner, "The 'Monetarist Revolution'," p. 7.

[40] Milton Friedman, "The Supply of Money and Changes in Prices and Output," in *The Relationship of Prices to Economic Stability and Growth*, Compendium of Papers Submitted by Panelists Appearing Before the Joint Economic Committee, 85th Congress, 2nd sess., 1958, pp. 241–56.

typically run as follows, using an open market purchase of Treasury bills as an example:[41] at the outset, there is an exchange of assets between the central bank and a Government securities dealer, with the central bank giving the dealer its check drawn on itself in exchange for bills. This exchange results in the following: (1) a reduction in the yield on bills, with consequent disequilibrium among holders of securities; (2) an increase of bank reserves of an equivalent amount (disregarding drains into currency holdings, etc.); (3) an initial increase in the money supply of the same amount as the transaction; and (4) a decrease in bill holdings by the private sector, with a concomitant increase in the central bank's portfolio. In a process described in some detail by Friedman and Schwartz, the next step will involve action to readjust portfolios in response to yield and wealth changes; meanwhile, banks will be interested in expanding loans on the basis of their newly-acquired reserves (and incidentally in creating new deposits). Eventually the adjustment affects the yield on equities and therefore the market value of the existing stock of physical capital. The existing capital stock will rise in value, stimulating the production of new capital and thus causing income to rise. There may also be other effects, such as direct effects on spending of changes in wealth.

The question would seem to be whether it is the initial increase in the money stock, the full increase (including the new deposits generated as a consequence of loan decisions), the increase in bank reserves, the reduction in private bill holdings, the fall in yields, the increase in the central bank's portfolio, or some other factor which is responsible for the income change. Rather than arbitrarily selecting some one factor from this list, it would seem preferable to take the more general view that the initiating force was the disturbance of a portfolio equilibrium, effected in this case through open market operations. (Such a disturbance, with similar effects, could arise for other reasons: e.g., if there were a change in wealthholders' preferences for holding a particular security category at existing yields.) The change in the money stock is properly viewed as one of the several results (along with changes in income, interest rates, prices, etc.) of this disturbance. Such a position of course implies that monetary policy is effective, but does not assign the starring role in the drama to changes in the money stock.

STABILIZATION POLICY

Modern Keynesian static analysis, based on the complete Keynesian system with flexible prices and inflexible money wages, yields the result that both monetary and fiscal policy are able to effect changes in income, interest rates, prices, employment, and other variables. Monetarist analysis, however, takes the position that only monetary policy has significant effects on the pace of economic activity, at least in the short run. This suggests that the two schools of thought disagree not in their views about monetary policy, but rather on the effectiveness of fiscal policy.

Until recently, monetarists were interpreted as basing their belief that fiscal policy is ineffective directly on the presumed existence of a stable demand-for-money function with zero interest elasticity, together with the assumption of an exogenously-set money stock. Such a demand-for-money function links money and income directly together, so that income cannot change unless the money stock changes. Shifts in government spending financed by bond issue, for instance, were said to result in interest rate changes of sufficient magnitude to reduce private spending to the degree required to keep total demand at a constant level.

However, given the many research studies which show otherwise, it has become impossible to maintain that the interest elasticity of the demand for money is zero. This development has had a considerable effect on the tone of monetarist discussions. Thus Fand, in discussing stabilization policy, refers to ". . . the *exceptional* case of a completely (interest) inelastic demand for money."[42] Furthermore, a relevant recent finding is that the *supply* of money is interest-elastic, and that this is sufficient to loosen the tight link between the money stock and income even if the interest elasticity of demand is zero.

Therefore monetarists have had to rationalize their dismissal of fiscal policy in other ways. Some have tried to find other means of solidifying the money-income link and of segregating the monetary sector from the remainder of the system by neutralizing the connection provided by the interest rate. One way of doing so is by considering the interest rate to be determined exogenously. This, in effect, is the procedure fol-

---

[41] See, for instance, Milton Friedman and David Meiselman, "The Relative Stability," Sec. VII, and Milton Friedman and Anna J. Schwartz, "Money and Business Cycles," *Review of Economics and Statistics* (February 1963 Supplement), esp. pp. 60–61.

[42] Fand, "Monetarism and Fiscalism," p. 289 (italics added).

lowed by Friedman in his paper entitled, "A Monetary Theory of National Income."[43] If interest rates do not respond to changes in real and financial variables, the rigid money-income connection is preserved. This may be considered the most extreme approach, because under it fiscal policy does not even affect the rate of interest and the division of output among the various sectors.

Another way is to make the standard quantity-theory assumption of flexible wages and prices, and hence full employment, while accepting the fact that the demand for and supply of money balances are interest-elastic. In such a world, fiscal policy cannot affect the levels of real variables like output or employment, which are entirely determined by the labor market and the production technology of the system—but then, neither can monetary policy.

Assumptions are not a matter of logic, assuming that they are internally consistent. In weighing these various approaches to the analysis of stabilization policy, the most important questions probably should be: Which of the alternative approaches is the most realistic and the most relevant for the real-world question of fiscal policy's effectiveness? Is it the case of flexible wages and prices, so that full employment is the rule and not the exception, and neither monetary policy nor fiscal policy can affect the level of real activity? Is it the case involving exogenously-determined interest rates, so that fiscal policy cannot even affect the division of output, let alone the level of activity? Or is it the case of flexible prices but a sticky wage level, in which case monetary and fiscal policy both are capable of affecting the level of real activity?

Brunner has taken a somewhat different approach to the analysis of fiscal policy than have most other monetarists. He asserts that fiscal policy is ineffective or perverse because the effects on asset values due to interest-rate changes of the cumulation or decumulation of claims against the Government held by the public, resulting from a fiscal policy deficit or surplus, outweigh the direct effects on the flow of output and income of new spending and taxing and of the changes in the stock of financial claims held by the private sector which result.[44] This position implies the view that the disturbance of portfolio equilibrium from *any* source (not only money stock changes) has powerful repercussions, and thus paradoxically tends to downgrade the importance of changes in the money stock. As far as is known, this position is not supported directly by empirical evidence.

SUMMARY

In this paper, I have attempted to sketch the main outlines of monetarist thought and to examine some aspects of the monetarist view of Keynesian analysis. In doing so, I have paid particular attention to the roles of the instruments of stabilization policy under the two views.

My examination of the monetarist-Keynesian debate has indicated that the version of Keynesianism which the monetarists use to establish a contrast for their own point of view is out of date and inadequate—a "vulgar" version of post-Keynesian thinking, to use Professor Johnson's term. When it is recognized that Keynesianism implies sticky wages and money illusion in the labor market rather than rigid prices, and that portfolio adjustment as the basis for the transmission of monetary impulses is not only consistent with the Keynesian approach but indeed is being built into Keynesian models, it is seen that there is very little if anything in monetarist theory which is new and different. Rather, the two approaches diverge in ways which basically are methodological and operational. The monetarists are willing to commit themselves to the use of very simple, very small (even one-equation) models for policy analysis; Keynesians typically are not. On this point, the monetarist stance seems to be a matter of faith rather than logic; the common theoretical basis on which both positions rest certainly implies the use of a structural approach.[45] There certainly are substantial differences in the kinds of operational assumptions that are made about particular dimensions of the theoretical structure, and these have implications of various kinds for policy. The typical Keynesian assumption of money wage inflexibility is consistent with a shorter-run analysis; it leads to the conclusion that both monetary policy and fiscal policy can affect the level of activity. The typical monetarist assumption of wage and price flexibility (i.e., of full employment) is more relevant for the analysis of secular changes. This assumption essentially bypasses the whole question of short-run policy effects. For the long

---

[43] See the discussion of this approach in footnote 12.

[44] Karl Brunner, "The 'Monetarist Revolution'."

[45] Karl Brunner has written, "The monetarist disregards . . . the allocative detail of credit markets when examining patterns of allocation behavior. . . . Such detail is simply asserted . . . to be irrelevant for aggregative explanation." Ibid., p. 15.

run, paradoxically, it suggests that fiscal policy is more important and interesting than monetary policy, for fiscal policy at least changes the rate of interest (unless the rate of interest is exogenously determined), and therefore the division of output, and presumably affects growth; whereas monetary policy affects only prices, money wages, and the like.[46] There appear to be some analytic confusions in many monetarist discussions. I have tried to show above that it is incorrect to view the demand-for-money function as a velocity relationship from either point of view. In the monetarist case, this is especially true because the stability of velocity in the face of monetary changes depends on assumptions about the labor market and is unrelated to the characteristics of the demand-for-money relationship. It also appears that monetarist fascination with the money stock is unwarranted by monetarist logic, which seems to me to place great emphasis on portfolio disequilibrium as a potent driving force in the economy. It does not follow from this view, as a matter of logic, that observed changes in the money stock have any particular significance as a causative force.

On the positive side, monetarists have contributed to the development of macroeconomic thought by stressing that the links relied upon for years by most Keynesians to connect the real and monetary sectors overlook entirely the important substitution and wealth effects which are the concomitants of portfolio adjustment. They also have called our attention to the distinction, apparently first made by Irving Fisher many years ago, between market and real interest rates, and therefore to the potentially important role of price expectations in dynamic macroeconomics. These phenomena are extraordinarily difficult to capture in empirical models, but work is proceeding along these lines. It is to be hoped that during the next few years, they will be made standard features of Keynesian (that is, structural) theoretical and empirical models, and that dependable evidence will be gathered so that the *real* questions which divide us—chiefly, in my opinion, the question raised by Brunner and others concerning the need for large-scale structural models for aggregative analysis—can be answered satisfactorily.

APPENDIX

Following are the derivations which underlie equations (4), (8), and (9) in the text. They

---

[46] The reservations expressed in footnote 10 apply to this statement also.

are based on equations (1)–(3) and (5)–(7), which are reproduced here for convenience:

$$y = C(y,r) + I(r) \qquad (1)$$

$$\frac{M_0}{p} = L(y,r) \qquad (2)$$

$$Y = py \qquad (3)$$

$$y = y(N) \qquad (5)$$

$$N = N^D(w) \qquad (6)$$

$$w = \frac{\bar{W}}{p} \qquad (7)$$

The following slope assumptions are used throughout: $O < C_y < 1$; $C_r < O$ or, if positive, $C_r < |I_r|$; $I_r < O$; $L_y > O$; $L_r < O$; $y_N > O$; $N^D_w < O$.

A. The Elasticity of Velocity

Equation (4) in the text is an expression for the elasticity of velocity with respect to a monetary shift, and is reproduced for convenience:

$$E_{V \cdot M_0} = E_{y \cdot M_0} + E_{p \cdot M_0} - 1. \qquad (4)$$

It is derived by differentiating the expression for velocity $\left(V = \frac{Y}{M_0} \right)$ with respect to the money stock, and converting the result into elasticity form.

Thus we have:

$$\frac{dV}{dM_0} = \frac{1}{M_0} \frac{dY}{dM_0} - \frac{Y}{M_0^2}. \qquad (A.1)$$

From (3), we have

$$\frac{dY}{dM_0} = p \frac{dy}{dM_0} + y \frac{dp}{dM_0}. \qquad (A.2)$$

Substituting (A.2) into (A.1) and multiplying the resulting equation by $\frac{M_0}{V}$ yields

$$E_{V \cdot M_0} = E_{y \cdot M_0} + E_{p \cdot M_0} - 1, \qquad (A.3)$$

which is equation (4).

This result is derived only from definitions. Next we investigate the values of $E_{y \cdot M_0}$ and $E_{p \cdot M_0}$, and therefore of $E_{V \cdot M_0}$, which are implied by monetarist and Keynesian assumptions respectively.

B. The Monetarist Case

Monetarists assume that wages and prices are flexible so that real output, y, may be considered exogenous for the purpose of static analysis, and only equations (1) and (2) are relevant. Differentiating (1), which is the IS curve, yields:

$$C_y \frac{dy}{dM_0} + (C_r + I_r) \frac{dr}{dM_0} = \frac{dy}{dM_0}. \quad \text{(B.1)}$$

However, if y is exogenous to this system, $\frac{dy}{dM_0} = 0$ so that we get:

$$(C_r + I_r) \frac{dr}{dM_0} = 0, \quad \text{(B.2)}$$

which implies that $\frac{dr}{dM_0} = 0$.

Differentiating the LM curve (2) yields:

$$L_y \frac{dy}{dM_0} + L_r \frac{dr}{dM_0} = \frac{1}{p} - \frac{M_0}{p^2} \frac{dp}{dM_0}. \quad \text{(B.3)}$$

Since we have found that, in this case,

$$\frac{dy}{dM_0} = \frac{dr}{dM_0} = 0,$$

(B.3) reduces to:

$$\frac{M_0}{p} \frac{dp}{dM_0} = E_{p \cdot M_0} = 1. \quad \text{(B.4)}$$

Substituting these findings into (A.3), we find that $E_{V \cdot M_0} = 0$ using static analysis under monetarist assumptions.

C. The Keynesian Case

Keynesians take money wages to be inflexible while prices are an endogenous variable. This means that real income or output may no longer be considered exogenous; instead, it becomes endogenous, and equations (5)–(7) are added to the IS-LM system as represented by (1) and (2) in order to close the set of equations.

To derive expressions for the elasticities $E_{y \cdot M_0}$ and $E_{p \cdot M_0}$, we must again differentiate the system totally with respect to M_0, now treating y as a variable. In addition to equations (B.1) and (B.3), this differentiation yields

$$\frac{dy}{dM_0} = -y_N N_w^D \frac{\bar{W}}{p^2} \frac{dp}{dM_0} \quad \text{(C.1)}$$

which is derived by differentiating equations (5)–(7) and substituting where possible.

It will be convenient to make some further substitutions. First, since the MPC with respect

to income is one minus the MPS with respect to income, and since the MPC with respect to the interest rate is the negative of the MPS with respect to the interest rate, we make the substitutions $(1 - C_y) = S_y$ and $C_r = -S_r$, where S stands for the saving function (the model implies $S = S(y,r)$). Second, (C.1) can be used to eliminate the term involving $\frac{dp}{dM_0}$ in (B.3). Making these substitutions and collecting terms yields the following pair of equations in the two variables $\frac{dy}{dM_0}$ and $\frac{dr}{dM_0}$:

$$S_y \frac{dy}{dM_0} - (I_r - S_r) \frac{dr}{dM_0} = 0 \quad \text{(C.2)}$$

$$\left(L_y - \frac{M_0}{\bar{W} y_N N_w^D} \right) \frac{dy}{dM_0} + L_r \frac{dr}{dM_0} = \frac{1}{p} \quad \text{(C.3)}$$

Solving these equations for $\frac{dy}{dM_0}$ gives:

$$\frac{dy}{dM_0} = \frac{\dfrac{1}{p}}{\dfrac{S_y L_r}{I_r - S_r} + L_y - \dfrac{M_0}{\bar{W} y_N N_w^D}}. \quad \text{(C.4)}$$

To convert this into elasticity form, two steps are needed:

(a) each of the propensities (or partial derivatives) shown in the denominator may be converted into a partial elasticity by using the relationship between any two variables x and z given by the definition of a partial elasticity; i.e., if $z = f(x)$, then $\eta_{z \cdot x} = f_x \cdot \dfrac{x}{z}$ and thus $f_x = \dfrac{z}{x} \eta_{z \cdot x}$;

(b) to find the systemic elasticity $E_{y \cdot M_0}$, both sides of (C.4) must be multiplied by $\dfrac{M_0}{y}$.

Carrying out these operations and cancelling terms where possible, we get

$$E_{y \cdot M_0} = \frac{1}{\dfrac{\eta_{S \cdot y} \eta_{L \cdot r}}{\eta_{I \cdot r} - \eta_{S \cdot r}} + \eta_{L \cdot y} - \dfrac{1}{\eta_{y \cdot N} \eta_{N^D \cdot w}}}. \quad \text{(C.5)}$$

To find an expression for the systemic elasticity $E_{p \cdot M_0}$, equation (C.4) is substituted into (C.1) and a systemic expression for $\dfrac{dp}{dM_0}$ is derived. When this expression is multiplied by $\dfrac{M_0}{p}$, the partial derivatives are converted to elasticities, and the necessary algebra is carried out, the following expression results:

$$E_{p \cdot M_0} = - \cfrac{1}{\eta_{y \cdot N} \eta_{ND \cdot w} \left[\cfrac{\eta_{S \cdot y} \eta_{L \cdot r}}{\eta_{I \cdot r} - \eta_{S \cdot r}} + \eta_{L \cdot y} \right] - 1} \cdot$$

$$\text{(C.6)}$$

From (C.5) and (C.6), it can be seen that the behavior of velocity now depends on all of the partial elasticities in the system. First, if either $\eta_{y \cdot N}$ or $\eta_{N^D \cdot w}$ are zero, output will not change in response to a real wage change brought about by a monetary shift, so that $E_{y \cdot M_0} = 0$ and $E_{p \cdot M_0} = 1$, resulting in stable velocity. Second, if either $\eta_{y \cdot N}$ or $\eta_{N^D \cdot w}$ are extremely large, $E_{p \cdot M_0}$ approaches

zero and the response of velocity to a monetary shift depends on a special case of equation (C.5) in which the last denominator term approaches zero. Whether $E_{V \cdot M_0}$ is positive or negative in this case depends on whether $E_{y \cdot M_0}$ is greater or smaller than unity. The condition for $E_{V \cdot M_0} < 0$ is that

$$|\eta_{I \cdot r} - \eta_{S \cdot r}| < \eta_{S \cdot y}(|\eta_{L \cdot r}|) + \eta_{L \cdot y}(|\eta_{I \cdot r} - \eta_{S \cdot r}|).$$

Thus the larger in value are $\eta_{S \cdot y}$, $\eta_{L \cdot y}$, and $|\eta_{L \cdot r}|$, the more likely it is that $E_{V \cdot M_0} < 0$. Finally, for nonzero but finite values of $\eta_{y \cdot N}$ and $\eta_{N^D \cdot w}$, $E_{y \cdot M_0}$ and $E_{p \cdot M_0}$ will tend toward zero (and $E_{V \cdot M_0}$ toward -1) if $\eta_{S \cdot y}$ or $|\eta_{L \cdot r}|$ are very large, or if $(\eta_{I \cdot r} - \eta_{S \cdot r})$ is very close to zero in value. A large value for $\eta_{L \cdot y}$ would also give this result.

B. INFLATION AND ITS RELATION TO UNEMPLOYMENT

During much of the period since the late 1940s, the United States has been experiencing "creeping inflation": a slow, general upward movement of prices, as measured by such price indexes as the Consumer Price Index (CPI), the Wholesale Price Index (WPI), and others. There have been periods, such as 1946–48, 1950–51, 1955–57, and the years since 1965, in which the rate of price increase has accelerated; on the other hand, there have also been periods, such as 1958–64, when prices have been relatively stable, especially as measured by the WPI. However, the "cost of living" as measured by the CPI has been particularly prone to slow but steady increase, even in periods of substantial unemployment. Since the indexes are widely and frequently reported, there is general public concern over the real and imagined causes and consequences of inflation. Economists and economic policy makers are also concerned with the causes of inflation and the nature of the inflationary process, because inflation may entail real social costs, particularly with respect to the distribution of income and wealth, and because it may make other goals of economic policy more difficult to achieve. For instance, under a system of fixed rates of exchange between national currencies, if a country's costs and prices rise more rapidly than those of its competitors, its exports of goods and services may decline and its imports may increase, leading to a balance-of-payments deficit which may add to the difficulties of achieving employment and growth targets. Some opponents of inflation stress its possible unfavorable effects on the long-term rate of growth, pointing out that inflation reduces incentives to save. However, it can be argued that mild inflation is favorable to growth. Indeed, the relation between inflation and growth is quite complex and not well understood. Of course, no one questions the undesirability and disruptive effects of extremely rapid rates of price increase, such as might be experienced during wartime. We refer here to the slow or "creeping" inflation which has been typical of much of our postwar experience.

According to the traditional view, inflation is attributable to excess money demand for output at a given set of initial prices: "too many dollars chasing too few goods." Such "demand-pull" inflation could be prevented or halted without significant cost in unemployment by the simple expedient of adopting a sufficiently restrictive monetary and fiscal policy. Excessive growth of the money stock, especially growth resulting from government spending financed by printing money or by selling securities to the central bank, was often thought to be the prime cause, and the proper remedies appeared to be responsible government budgeting, avoidance of large deficits, and the financing of such deficits as do occur by selling bonds to the public rather than the banks. Some of the fallacies in the normative application of these policy prescriptions are discussed in the readings in Chapter 5; our postwar experience has made them seem less than universally acceptable as ways of halting or avoiding inflation. While there have been times, especially during the periods of hostilities in Korea and Vietnam, when inflation has been caused by excessive growth of demand fueled by heavy federal spending and budget deficits, there have also been extended periods when aggregate demand has not been adequate to keep unemployment at an acceptable level. Yet the price indexes—especially the CPI—have continued to creep upward, with few interruptions. To some extent, this phenomenon may be due to upward biases in the indexes themselves; this is one of the subjects discussed in the paper by Harold M. Levinson. However, not all of the inflation can be explained away in this fashion, and since the simple demand-pull theory does not satisfactorily account for what remains, alternative explanations have been developed.

The most widely discussed alternative to the demand-pull theory of inflation discussed above is the "cost-push" or "market power" hypothesis. According to this hypothesis, there may be a continuing general rise in prices even though unemployment persists and aggregate demand is inadequate. This can happen because certain groups in the economy, particularly strong labor unions and big business enterprises, are able to exercise monopoly power and thereby exert more or less continuous upward pressure on wages and prices.

The cost-push inflation hypothesis has led to a good deal of discussion and research, which has improved our understanding of the inflationary process by focusing attention on industry structure, market power, and so on—institutional considerations which are not taken into account in the demand-pull analysis. However, it is now apparent that it is exceedingly difficult to determine whether any particular inflationary experience is demand-pull or cost-push in nature. Indeed, there are usually elements of both—increasing demand tightens particular labor markets, high profits and sales levels make producers reluctant to accept the interruptions of production that strikes would bring, and declining unemployment among union members strengthens the position of unions in collective bargaining negotiations. Most writers on the subject have concluded that the analytic distinction between demand and cost inflation is often not a useful device for categorizing inflationary experiences or for devising policies to deal with particular situations. The problem is that labor and product markets are not perfectly competitive; furthermore, there are frictions, rigidities, and bottlenecks which impede the adjustment of prices and quantities in response to external impulses.

Once it is recognized that markets contain imperfections so that wages and prices may begin to rise in response to an increase in aggregate demand or in response to an exercise of market power while substantial unemployment continues to exist, the concept of full employment becomes imprecise. Under the assumption of perfect markets, full employment was taken to mean the level of employment determined by the intersection of the demand for and supply of labor functions (see, for example, Warren L. Smith's discussion of the Keynesian system with flexible wages, contained in his article in the first part of this chapter). Instead, it is now natural to think of different levels of employment or unemployment, each associated with some level of demand for labor relative to its supply and thereby to some given rate of change of money wages and, ultimately, prices. The higher the level of employment, the more rapid the rate of wage and price increase over the usual range in which employment varies. In other words, there may be a range of price change-employment combinations among which society can choose, rather than there being one level of "full employment" determined by market forces.

Such a set of price change-employment combinations is known as a Phillips curve, named after A. W. Phillips, a British economist who first traced it out for the British economy. This curve shows that the rate of change of money wages (or prices) is inversely related to the level of employment and rising more and more rapidly as unemployment declines. Further studies have shown that other variables, such as labor productivity, also play a role in the Phillips curve.

The paper by James Tobin which begins this part of the chapter surveys the development of the theory concerning Phillips curve relationships, and deals extensively with a number of questions which bear on current controversies in this area. Much of this discussion is related to the fact that there exist today two opposing viewpoints concerning the Phillips curve and the underlying behavior and institutional structure which it represents. One side, which may be labeled post-Keynesian, holds that certain factors having to do with the adjustment of labor markets in response to external impulses, as well as the institutional rigidities and market imperfections already mentioned, result in the availability of lasting tradeoffs at the aggregate level between unemployment and the rate of change of prices. The precise tradeoff available may vary with, for example, the stage of the business cycle in which the economy finds itself; the systematic forces which cause the tradeoff to change over the cycle are made explicit in the wage-price model presented in the paper by Saul H. Hymans. The important consideration is that from the post-Keynesian viewpoint, there always is a tradeoff, both in the short and long run. The Neoclassical stance (which has also come to be known as the "accelerationist" position) holds that any such tradeoffs as may exist are only temporary, and in the longer run employment will return to the "natural" level determined by market forces. Under this view, stabilization policy manipulations can have no permanent effects on employment, although the rate of inflation may change in response to monetary impulses. In order to understand the arguments on each side, let us first set out the behavior summarized in the Phillips curve which both sides accept.

In general, the Phillips curve is the outcome at the aggregate level of the behavior of many labor markets, each adjusting toward equilibrium, but each being disturbed again and again by exogenous shocks. These shocks generate excess demands or supplies in the individual markets. The rate of change of money wages is taken to be proportional to the excess demand for labor across these markets, which in turn is viewed as being inversely related to the unemployment rate. Consequently, there is an inverse relationship between the rate of change of money wages and the unemployment rate. The relationship is nonlinear because there is an irreducible minimum below which the unemployment rate cannot be driven by increases in demand. (On the other hand, the unemployment rate can increase more or less continuously with increases in excess supply.) Obviously, the rate cannot go below zero; actually, the floor lies somewhat above zero because of the frictional unemployment involved in job changes, the rapid turnover of employees in low-paying, "dead-end" jobs, and other causes. In his paper in this chapter on strategies to reduce this floor, Martin S. Feldstein states that it probably is now about 4 percent or more of the labor force; however, the empirical estimates provided by Hymans of points on the steady-state Phillips curve indicate that it is somewhat lower than that.

An interesting implication of this nonlinearity in the wage change-unemployment relationship is that even if there exists overall "balance" in the demand for and supply of labor, there will be more upward pressure on wages (and eventually on prices) in the individual labor markets exhibiting excess demand than there will be downward pressure from labor surplus markets. Thus, a rising wage and price level is perfectly consistent with aggregate labor market balance, and the net upward pressure will be greater, the wider is the difference in unemployment rates among labor markets.

From this background, Tobin examines the two points of view mentioned earlier. In the papers by Smith and Holbrook in the first part of this chapter, as well as in the Teigen paper on monetarism, static models of the Keynesian system are used which include aggregated labor market subsectors. Obviously, a dynamic unemployment-wage change relationship does not fit comfortably into static models of this kind; rather, they produce the "Keynesian" result that monetary and fiscal policy are able to make permanent adjustments in employment, real wages, and output because money wages are taken to be inflexible downward. This assumption has often been criticized on the grounds that it attributes "money illusion" to workers, suggesting that they are concerned only with their money wage rate and would offer more labor services if, for example, it were doubled, even if the price level were doubled simultaneously. In other words, the analysis suggests that workers behave irrationally. According to Tobin, however, the rigid-wage assumption can be interpreted in a way consistent with rational behavior. A worker's immediate concern is with his wage relative to the whole wage structure; therefore an attempt to lower money wages in any given market will be resisted because it will be viewed as an attempt to reduce the position of workers in that market relative to other workers. On the other hand, given the demand for labor, real wages must somehow be reduced if employment is to be increased. Since there is no rapid and easy way of adjusting money wages downward, overall real wage reduction is achieved by a rising price level instead. The assumption of inflexible money wages found in static Keynesian models is a way of incorporating this dynamic labor market adjustment process.

While the Neoclassical economists would agree with much of this description, they contend that the conventional Phillips curve is merely a transitory relationship.[1] In their view, as we have noted above, both the demand for labor by employers and the supply of labor forthcoming from workers depend basically upon the real wage. There is a so-called "natural rate of unemployment" consistent with stable prices (or perhaps with any one of several constant rates of change of prices), corresponding to that real rate at which the demand for

---

[1] This view is expressed by Milton Friedman in "The Role of Monetary Policy," *American Economic Review,* Vol. LVIII (March 1968), pp. 1–17, reprinted in Chapter 5 below.

and supply of labor are equated. It is possible temporarily to reduce unemployment below the natural rate by expanding aggregate demand. By causing prices to rise, this lowers the real wage, inducing employers to expand production and employment. At first workers do not realize that the increase in prices has reduced their real wage. Once they do realize it, however, they demand and obtain higher money wages, and the reduction in real wages below the equilibrium level can only be maintained by a further rise in prices. As prices and wages continue to rise at a steady rate, workers eventually come to anticipate the price increases and to act on their anticipations. Thus, in the course of time real wages and employment fall back to their equilibrium levels—unemployment is restored to its natural rate—and all that is happening is that prices and wages are rising together, with real wages remaining constant. Under this view, a lasting reduction in unemployment could only be achieved by a continuously accelerating inflation, so that workers never learn to ask for a large enough wage increase to offset the current inflation fully (hence the term "accelerationist").

A variation on this approach referred to by Tobin is known as "search theory." Workers and firms have incomplete information about wages, employment opportunities, and so forth elsewhere. There is therefore an inducement to spend time and effort getting such information, and there will typically be some "search unemployment" of an amount such that at the margin, the gains to be obtained from further information gathering and its associated costs are just balanced by the value of leisure. Under this view, an increase in demand which causes money wages to rise in a particular market will result in the acceptance by searchers of jobs on the mistaken assumption that wage rates in other markets will remain constant, so that they have been fortunate enough to find jobs with higher relative real wages. Therefore employment will rise temporarily; but when it is noted that wages are also rising elsewhere, the searchers who accepted employment will realize their mistake, return to the pool of "search unemployment," and employment will fall again to its "natural" level.

According to the Neoclassical view of the inflation process, the long-run Phillips curve is simply a vertical line drawn at the natural rate of employment. The natural rate may vary from country to country and from time to time in the same country, depending upon the degree of labor mobility, the extent of unionization, and so on. It may be shifted to the left by measures which succeed in improving the economic performance of labor markets. Several such measures appropriate for the U.S. economy are suggested in Feldstein's paper.

This long-run view of the relation between inflation and unemployment is based largely on deductive reasoning from certain assumptions about the behavior of employers and workers. The Neoclassical model seems to imply that, given sufficient time, wages adjust fully to compensate for changes in prices and prices adjust fully to compensate for changes in unit labor costs. Rigorous empirical tests of relationships that are supposed to hold true only in the long run are especially difficult to carry out. For what it is worth, however, as Saul H. Hymans points out in his empirical paper on the Phillips curve, the various investigations that have been carried out have uncovered little evidence that complete adjustments of wages to prices and prices to unit labor costs actually do occur. Milton Friedman, who holds the Neoclassical view, has suggested that a full adjustment of expectations to a new and unexpected inflation rate may take as long as 20 years, and that the adjustment process may not even begin for 2 to 5 years.[2] Thus, there is good reason to view the Neoclassical hypothesis with some skepticism.

The paper by Hymans presents a compact summary model describing the interrelationships between the rates of wage and price change and the levels of productivity and unemployment. In this model, attention is centered on a version of the Phillips curve relationship between the rate of wage change, the unemployment rate, the rate of price change, and the "wage gap" or difference between the trend rate of productivity growth and the rate of change of wages; this relationship is supplemented by a markup equation relating price change to wage change, and the necessary definitions to complete the model. On the basis of this simple structure, Hymans is able to derive both short-run and steady-state tradeoff relationships between the rate of price change and the unemployment rate. Among other things, he shows how changes in the rate of productivity growth and in the "wage gap" over the business cycle shift the price change-unemployment rate tradeoff in a systematic way. The pattern of price change-unemployment combinations generated by his small conceptual model is displayed by simulations based on various unemployment rates, using a very large econometric model of the U.S. economy. From these simulations, Hymans estimates that the steady-state annual inflation rate corresponding to an aggregate unemployment rate of 3.5 percent is just under 5 percent per year (remember that in this calculation the cyclical forces affecting the tradeoff have been neutralized), suggesting that the unemployment rate "floor" mentioned earlier is less than 3.5 percent. The analytic model can also be manipulated to show that the accelerationist "no-tradeoff" result is based on the assumption of full adjustment of the rate of change of wages to the rate of change of prices. Interpreted from the Neoclassical point of view, the requirement is that there must be full adjustment of wages to the *expected* rate of change of prices. As Hymans points out, this result requires that society be given time to become accustomed to some particular actual inflation rate, and to adjust their expectations accordingly. However, it is very improbable that the system could ever settle down to one such growth path long enough for this to happen. Therefore, he concludes that, for all practical purposes, a meaningful tradeoff exists whether or not the economic system is structured in such a way that wage changes are in fact fully adjusted to price changes.

The analysis presented in these readings suggests some of the measures which may be helpful in combating inflation while maintaining high employment. At any given time, the Phillips curve specifies at least roughly the available choices between price stability and employment that can, in principle, be achieved by regulating aggregate demand through fiscal and monetary policy. However, structural changes which might alter the Phillips curve may make it possible to achieve a given level of unemployment with less inflation. Some of the measures which are fairly obvious include the promotion of competition through enforcement of the antitrust laws, programs to retrain and move labor away from declining industries and from pockets of unemployment, and, in general, the elimination of policies and practices which create or perpetuate bottlenecks, rigidities, and immobilities. Some further possibilities are explored in the paper by Feldstein, who suggests that the problem is not the existence of a chronic group of unemployed, but rather is related to a high rate of turnover among holders of unattractive, dead-end jobs. Among the measures he suggest to improve this situation are: better on-the-job training, including a program of

---

[2] Ibid.

scholarships to support young workers while they are being trained; wage subsidies for severely handicapped workers; reform of the unemployment compensation system to reduce its disincentive effects; and others.

Even with effectively managed aggregate demand and programs designed to achieve structural reforms, government intervention to restrain the undue exercise of market power may be desirable or necessary in a high-employment economy experiencing continuing upward pressure on prices. We have experienced two such interventions in the last several years. The "wage-price guideposts" of the Kennedy-Johnson Administration represented a very mild effort to influence the outcome of bargaining negotiations in an anti-inflationary direction without resort to coercion or direct controls.[3] Under the guideposts as promulgated in 1962, wage increases in particular industries were, in general, not supposed to exceed the economywide trend increase in labor productivity (output per worker). Adherence to the guideposts would keep labor costs per unit of output from rising and avoid the upward pressures on prices that have sometimes arisen from excessive wage increases. On the price side, the guideposts called for prices to be reduced in industries in which productivity increased by more than the national average and to be increased in industries in which productivity increased by less than the average.[4] The guideposts were abandoned in 1966. In August 1971, President Nixon imposed a 90-day freeze on most prices, wages, and rents. The freeze was followed by "Phase II," during which a Cost of Living Council was given the responsibility of establishing overall goals, determining coverage of the control program, and overseeing enforcement, while actual decisions on proposed changes in prices and wages were made by a Price Commission and a Pay Board. These mandatory wage and price controls were ended in mid-January 1973, reintroduced in June, and (with some exceptions) removed again in July.

The selection by Harold M. Levinson is on the deficiencies of our most widely used measures of price change—the CPI and WPI—and on the gains and losses from inflation. These are important aspects of the study of inflation. Since the price indexes discussed by Levinson are so widely reported and discussed (and in some cases are used as the basis for calculating cost-of-living wage increases), their intelligent interpretation and use rests upon a full comprehension of their biases and inadequacies. And intelligent policy choices concerning the level of unemployment and the rate of price increase which should be tolerated presuppose knowledge of the costs—and the benefits—which are associated with inflation.

The Levinson paper was written in 1959, and, consequently, some of the information contained in it is out of date. For example, at the time the article was written, the "market basket" used in calculating the CPI reflected consumer spending patterns in 1951–52. Since the article was written, a new study has been made, and the present market basket reflects these patterns in 1960–61. However, the fundamental character of the index has not been changed, and

---

[3] For a full explanation of the guideposts, including some qualifications not referred to in this brief discussion, see the January 1962 *Annual Report of the Council of Economic Advisers*, pp. 185–90.

[4] There is a good deal of misunderstanding about the relationships between price changes, productivity changes, and wage changes, and this misunderstanding is particularly apparent in some discussions of the "wage-price guideposts." In general, prices can remain stable if money wages rise at the same percentage rate as productivity increases. This will tend to preserve the existing distribution of income between labor and the other factors of production. It is *not* true, as some think, that if wages and productivity rise at the same rate, labor is appropriating all of the output gains resulting from the increase in productivity.

the validity of Levinson's evaluation of the CPI has not been appreciably affected by the updating of the weights.

If the economic, political, and social costs of continuing inflation are judged to be above the tolerance level in the future, it is likely that interventions like the guideposts or the recent price freezes may again occur. Gardner Ackley's paper evaluates the guidepost program and suggests one alternative mechanism for implementing an "incomes policy" to restrain wage and price increases in the future. Ackley advocates a "Stabilization Agency," created by law and possessing an adequate staff, which would monitor wage and price decisions involving only the largest firms and which would be empowered to intervene when necessary to prohibit price and wage changes inconsistent with its standards. The standards themselves, and the policy stance of the Agency, would be formulated in forums involving labor, management, and the public. This approach would be a "middle way" between voluntary compliance to guidepost standards, as in the early 1960s, and mandatory controls, as in 1971–73.

INFLATION AND UNEMPLOYMENT*

James Tobin

The world economy today is vastly different from the 1930s, when Seymour Harris, the chairman of this meeting, infected me with his boundless enthusiasm for economics and his steadfast confidence in its capacity for good works. Economics is very different, too. Both the science and its subject have changed, and for the better, since World War II. But there are some notable constants. Unemployment and inflation still preoccupy and perplex economists, statesmen, journalists, housewives, and everyone else. The connection between them is the principal domestic economic burden of presidents and prime ministers, and the major area of controversy and ignorance in macroeconomics. I have chosen to review economic thought on this topic on this occasion, partly because of its inevitable timeliness, partly because of a personal interest reaching back to my first published work in 1941.

I. THE MEANINGS OF FULL EMPLOYMENT

Today, as thirty and forty years ago, economists debate how much unemployment is volun-

* From *American Economic Review*, Vol. LXII (March 1972), pp. 1–18. Reprinted by permission of the publisher and the author. James Tobin is Sterling Professor of Economics, Yale University.

Presidential address delivered at the Eighty-Fourth Annual Meeting of the American Economic Association, New Orleans, Louisiana, December 28, 1971.

tary, how much involuntary; how much is a phenomenon of equilibrium, how much a symptom of disequilibrium; how much is compatible with competition, how much is to be blamed on monopolies, labor unions, and restrictive legislation; how much unemployment characterizes "full" employment.

Full employment—imagine macroeconomics deprived of the concept. But what is it? What is the proper employment goal of policies affecting aggregate demand? Zero unemployment in the monthly labor force survey? That outcome is so inconceivable outside of Switzerland that it is useless as a guide to policy. Any other numerical candidate, yes even 4 percent, is patently arbitrary without reference to basic criteria. Unemployment equal to vacancies? Measurement problems aside, this definition has the same straightforward appeal as zero unemployment, which it simply corrects for friction.[1]

A concept of full employment more congenial to economic theory is labor market equilibrium, a volume of employment which is simultaneously the amount employers want to offer and the amount workers want to accept at prevailing wage rates and prices. Forty years ago theorists with confidence in markets could believe that full employment is whatever volume of employ-

[1] This concept is commonly attributed to W. H. Beveridge, but he was actually more ambitious and required a surplus of vacancies.

ment the economy is moving toward, and that its achievement requires of the government nothing more than neutrality, and nothing less.

After Keynes challenged the classical notion of labor market equilibrium and the complacent view of policy to which it led, full employment came to mean maximum aggregate supply, the point at which expansion of aggregate demand could not further increase employment and output.

Full employment was also regarded as the economy's inflation threshold. With a deflationary gap, demand less than full employment supply, prices would be declining or at worst constant. Expansion of aggregate demand short of full employment would cause at most a one-shot increase of prices. For continuing inflation, the textbooks told us, a necessary and sufficient condition was an inflationary gap, real aggregate demand in excess of feasible supply. The model was tailor-made for wartime inflation.

Postwar experience destroyed the identification of full employment with the economy's inflation threshold. The profession, the press, and the public discovered the "new inflation" of the 1950s, inflation without benefit of gap, labelled but scarcely illuminated by the term "cost-push." Subsequently the view of the world suggested by the Phillips curve merged demand-pull and cost-push inflation and blurred the distinction between them. This view contained no concept of full employment. In its place came the tradeoff, along which society supposedly can choose the least undesirable feasible combination of the evils of unemployment and inflation.

Many economists deny the existence of a durable Phillips tradeoff. Their numbers and influence are increasing. Some of them contend that there is only one rate of unemployment compatible with steady inflation, a "natural rate" consistent with any steady rate of change of prices, positive, zero, or negative. The natural rate is another full employment candidate, a policy target at least in the passive sense that monetary and fiscal policy makers are advised to eschew any numerical unemployment goal and to let the economy gravitate to this equilibrium. So we have come full circle. Full employment is once again nothing but the equilibrium reached by labor markets unaided and undistorted by governmental fine tuning.

In discussing these issues, I shall make the following points. First, an observed amount of unemployment is not revealed to be voluntary simply by the fact that money wage rates are constant, or rising, or even accelerating. I shall recall and extend Keynes's definition of involuntary unemployment and his explanation why workers may accept price inflation as a method of reducing real wages while rejecting money wage cuts. The second point is related. Involuntary unemployment is a disequilibrium phenomenon; the behavior, the persistence, of excess supplies of labor depend on how and how fast markets adjust to shocks, and on how large and how frequent the shocks are. Higher prices or faster inflation can diminish involuntary, disequilibrium unemployment, even though voluntary, equilibrium labor supply is entirely free of money illusion.

Third, various criteria of full employment coincide in a theoretical full stationary equilibrium, but diverge in persistent disequilibrium. These are (1) the natural rate of unemployment, the rate compatible with zero or some other constant inflation rate, (2) zero involuntary unemployment, (3) the rate of unemployment needed for optimal job search and placement, and (4) unemployment equal to job vacancies. The first criterion dictates higher unemployment than any of the rest. Instead of commending the natural rate as a target of employment policy, the other three criteria suggest less unemployment and more inflation. Therefore, fourth, there are real gains from additional employment, which must be weighed in the social balance against the costs of inflation. I shall conclude with a few remarks on this choice, and on the possibilities of improving the terms of the tradeoff.

II. KEYNESIAN AND CLASSICAL INTERPRETATIONS OF UNEMPLOYMENT

To begin with the *General Theory* is not just the ritual piety economists of my generation owe the book that shaped their minds. Keynes's treatment of labor market equilibrium and disequilibrium in his first chapter is remarkably relevant today.

Keynes attacked what he called the classical presumption that persistent unemployment is voluntary unemployment. The presumption he challenged is that in competitive labor markets actual employment and unemployment reveal workers' true preferences between work and alternative uses of time, the presumption that no one is fully or partially unemployed whose real wage per hour exceeds his marginal valuation of an hour of free time. Orthodox economists found the observed stickiness of money wages to be persuasive evidence that unemployment, even in the Great Depression, was voluntary. Keynes found decisive evidence against this inference in the willingness of workers to accept a larger volume of employment at a lower real wage resulting from an increase of prices.

Whenever unemployment could be reduced by expansion of aggregate demand, Keynes regarded it as involuntary. He expected expansion to raise prices and lower real wages, but this expectation is not crucial to his argument. Indeed, if it is possible to raise employment without reduction in the real wage, his case for calling the unemployment involuntary is strengthened.

But why is the money wage so stubborn if more labor is willingly available at the same or lower real wage? Consider first some answers Keynes did not give. He did not appeal to trade union monopolies or minimum wage laws. He was anxious, perhaps over-anxious, to meet his putative classical opponents on their home field, the competitive economy. He did not rely on any failure of workers to perceive what a rise in prices does to real wages. The unemployed take new jobs, the employed hold old ones, with eyes open. Otherwise the new situation would be transient.

Instead, Keynes emphasized the institutional fact that wages are bargained and set in the monetary unit of account. Money wage rates are, to use an unKeynesian term, "administered prices." That is, they are not set and reset in daily auctions but posted and fixed for finite periods of time. This observation led Keynes to his central explanation: Workers, individually and in groups, are more concerned with relative than absolute real wages. They may withdraw labor if their wages fall relatively to wages elsewhere, even though they would not withdraw any if real wages fall uniformly everywhere. Labor markets are decentralized, and there is no way money wages can fall in any one market without impairing the relative status of the workers there. A general rise in prices is a neutral and universal method of reducing real wages, the only method in a decentralized and uncontrolled economy. Inflation would not be needed, we may infer, if by government compulsion, economy-wide bargaining, or social compact, all money wage rates could be scaled down together.

Keynes apparently meant that relative wages are the arguments in labor supply functions. But Alchian (pp. 27–52 in Phelps et al.) and other theorists of search activity have offered a somewhat different interpretation, namely that workers whose money wages are reduced will quit their jobs to seek employment in other markets where they think, perhaps mistakenly, that wages remain high.

Keynes's explanation of money wage stickiness is plausible and realistic. But two related analytical issues have obscured the message. Can there be involuntary unemployment in an equilibrium, a proper, full-fledged neoclassical equilibrium? Does the labor supply behavior described by Keynes betray "money illusion"? Keynes gave a loud yes in answer to the first question, and this seems at first glance to compel an affirmative answer to the second.

An economic theorist can, of course, commit no greater crime than to assume money illusion. Comparative statics is a nonhistorical exercise, in which different price levels are to be viewed as alternative rather than sequential. Compare two situations that differ only in the scale of exogenous monetary variables; imagine, for example, that all such magnitudes are ten times as high in one situation as in the other. All equilibrium prices, including money wage rates, should differ in the same proportion, while all real magnitudes, including employment, should be the same in the two equilibria. To assume instead that workers' supply decisions vary with the price level is to say that they would behave differently if the unit of account were, and always had been, dimes instead of dollars. Surely Keynes should not be interpreted to attribute to anyone money illusion in this sense. He was not talking about so strict and static an equilibrium.

Axel Leijonhufvud's illuminating and perceptive interpretation of Keynes argues convincingly that, in chapter 1 as throughout the *General Theory*, what Keynes calls equilibrium should be viewed as persistent disequilibrium, and what appears to be comparative statics is really shrewd and incisive, if awkward, dynamic analysis. Involuntary unemployment means that labor markets are not in equilibrium. The resistance of money wage rates to excess supply is a feature of the adjustment process rather than a symptom of irrationality.

The other side of Keynes's story is that in depressions money wage deflation, even if it occurred more speedily, or especially if it occurred more speedily, would be at best a weak equilibrator and quite possibly a source of more unemployment rather than less. In contemporary language, the perverse case would arise if a high and ever-increasing real rate of return on money inhibited real demand faster than the rising purchasing power of monetary stocks stimulated demand. To pursue this Keynesian theme further here would be a digression.

What relevance has this excursion into depression economics for contemporary problems of unemployment and wage inflation? The issues are remarkably similar, even though events and Phillips have shifted attention from levels to time rates of change of wages and prices. Phillips curve doctrine[2] is in an important sense the postwar analogue of Keynesian wage and employment theory, while natural rate doctrine is the contemporary version of the classical position Keynes was opposing.

Phillips curve doctrine implies that lower unemployment can be purchased at the cost of faster inflation. Let us adapt Keynes's test for involuntary unemployment to the dynamic terms of contemporary discussion of inflation, wages, and unemployment. Suppose that the current rate of unemployment continues. Associated with it is a path of real wages, rising at the rate of productivity growth. Consider an alternative future, with unemployment at first declining to a rate one percentage point lower and then remaining constant at the lower rate. Associated with the lower unemployment alternative will be a second path of real wages. Eventually this real wage path will show, at least to first approximation, the same rate of increase as the first one, the rate of productivity growth. But the paths may differ because of the transitional effects of increasing the rate of employment. The growth of real wages will be retarded in the short run if additional employment lowers labor's marginal productivity. In any case, the test question is whether with full information about the two alternatives labor would accept the second one—whether, in other words, the additional employment would be willingly supplied along the second real wage path. If the answer is affirmative, then that one percentage point of unemployment is involuntary.

For Keynes's reasons, a negative answer cannot necessarily be inferred from failure of money wage rates to fall or even decelerate. Actual unemployment and the real wage path associated with it are not necessarily an equilibrium. Rigidities in the path of money wage rates can be

explained by workers' preoccupation with relative wages and the absence of any central economy-wide mechanism for altering all money wages together.

According to the natural rate hypothesis, there is just one rate of unemployment compatible with steady wage and price inflation, and this is in the long run compatible with any constant rate of change of prices, positive, zero, or negative. Only at the natural rate of unemployment are workers content with current and prospective real wages, content to have their real wages rise at the rate of growth of productivity. Along the feasible path of real wages they would not wish to accept any larger volume of employment. Lower unemployment, therefore, can arise only from economy-wide excess demand for labor and must generate a gap between real wages desired and real wages earned. The gap evokes increases of money wages designed to raise real wages faster than productivity. But this intention is always frustrated, the gap is never closed, money wages and prices accelerate. By symmetrical argument, unemployment above the natural rate signifies excess supply in labor markets and ever accelerating deflation. Older classical economists regarded constancy of money wage rates as indicative of full employment equilibrium, at which the allocation of time between work and other pursuits is revealed as voluntary and optimal. Their successors make the same claims for the natural rate of unemployment, except that in the equilibrium money wages are not necessarily constant but growing at the rate of productivity gain plus the experienced and expected rate of inflation of prices.

III. IS ZERO-INFLATION UNEMPLOYMENT VOLUNTARY AND OPTIMAL?

There are, then, two conflicting interpretations of the welfare value of employment in excess of the level consistent with price stability. One is that additional employment does not produce enough to compensate workers for the value of other uses of their time. The fact that it generates inflation is taken as prima facie evidence of a welfare loss. The alternative view, which I shall argue, is that the responses of money wages and prices to changes in aggregate demand reflect mechanics of adjustment, institutional constraints, and relative wage patterns and reveal nothing in particular about individual or social valuations of unemployed time vis-à-vis the wages of employment.

---

[2] Phillips himself is not a prophet of the doctrine associated with his curve. His 1958 article was probably the most influential macroeconomic paper of the last quarter century. But Phillips simply presented some striking empirical findings, which others have replicated many times for many economies. He is not responsible for the theories and policy conclusions his findings stimulated.

On this rostrum four years ago, Milton Friedman identified the noninflationary natural rate of unemployment with "equilibrium in the structure of real wage rates" (p. 8). "The 'natural rate of unemployment,'" he said, ". . . is the level that would be ground out by the Walrasian system of general equilibrium equations, provided that there is embedded in them the actual structural characteristics of the labor and commodity markets, including market imperfections, stochastic variability in demands and supplies, the costs of getting information about job vacancies and labor availabilities, the costs of mobility, and so on." Presumably this Walrasian equilibrium also has the usual optimal properties; at any rate, Friedman advised the monetary authorities not to seek to improve upon it. But in fact we know little about the existence of a Walrasian equilibrium that allows for all the imperfections and frictions that explain why the natural rate is bigger than zero, and even less about the optimality of such an equilibrium if it exists.

In the new microeconomics of labor markets and inflation, the principal activity whose marginal value sets the reservation price of employment is job search. It is not pure leisure, for in principle persons who choose that option are not reported as unemployed; however, there may be a leisure component in job seeking.

A crucial assumption of the theory is that search is significantly more efficient when the searcher is unemployed, but almost no evidence has been advanced on this point. Members of our own profession are adept at seeking and finding new jobs without first leaving their old ones or abandoning not-in-labor-force status. We do not know how many quits and new hires in manufacturing are similar transfers, but some of them must be; if all reported accessions were hires of unemployed workers, the mean duration of unemployment would be only about half what it is in fact. In surveys of job mobility among blue collar workers in 1946–47 (see Lloyd Reynolds, pp. 214–15, and Herbert Parnes, pp. 158–59), 25 percent of workers who quit had new jobs lined up in advance. Reynolds found that the main obstacle to mobility without unemployment was not lack of information or time, but simply "anti-pirating" collusion by employers.

A considerable amount of search activity by unemployed workers appears to be an unproductive consequence of dissatisfaction and frustration rather than a rational quest for improvement. This was the conclusion of Reynolds' survey twenty-five years ago, p. 215, and it has been reemphasized for the contemporary scene by Robert Hall, and by Peter Doeringer and Michael Piore for what they term the secondary labor force. Reynolds found that quitting a job to look for a new one while unemployed actually yielded a better job in only a third of the cases. Lining up a new job in advance was a more successful strategy: two-thirds of such changes turned out to be improvements. Today, according to the dual labor market hypothesis, the basic reason for frequent and long spells of unemployment in the secondary labor force is the shortage of good jobs.

In any event, the contention of some natural rate theorists is that employment beyond the natural rate takes time that would be better spent in search activity. Why do workers accept such employment? An answer to this question is a key element in a theory that generally presumes that actual behavior reveals true preferences. The answer given is that workers accept the additional employment only because they are victims of inflation illusion. One form of inflation illusion is overestimation of the real wages of jobs they now hold, if they are employed, or of jobs they find, if they are unemployed and searching. If they did not under-estimate price inflation, employed workers would more often quit to search, and unemployed workers would search longer.

The force of this argument seems to me diluted by the fact that price inflation illusion affects equally both sides of the job seeker's equation. He over-estimates the real value of an immediate job, but he also over-estimates the real values of jobs he might wait for. It is in the spirit of this theorizing to assume that money interest rates respond to the same correct or incorrect inflationary expectations. As a first approximation, inflation illusion has no substitution effect on the margin between working and waiting.

It does have an income effect, causing workers to exaggerate their real wealth. In which direction the income effect would work is not transparent. Does greater wealth, or the illusion of greater wealth, make people more choosy about jobs, more inclined to quit and to wait? Or less choosy, more inclined to stay in the job they have or to take the first one that comes along? I should have thought more selective rather than less. But natural rate theory must take the opposite view if it is to explain why under-estimation of price inflation bamboozles workers into holding or taking jobs that they do not really want.

Another form of alleged inflation illusion refers to wages rather than prices. Workers are myopic and do not perceive that wages elsewhere are, or soon will be, rising as fast as the money wage of the job they now hold or have just found. Consequently they under-estimate the advantages of quitting and searching. This explanation is convincing only to the extent that the payoff to search activity is determined by wage differentials. The payoff also depends on the probabilities of getting jobs at quoted wages, therefore on the balance between vacancies and job seekers. Workers know that perfectly well. Quit rates are an index of voluntary search activity. They do not diminish when unemployment is low and wage rates are rapidly rising. They increase, quite understandably. This fact contradicts the inflation illusion story, both versions. I conclude that it is not possible to regard fluctuations of unemployment on either side of the zero-inflation rate as mainly voluntary, albeit mistaken, extensions and contractions of search activity.

The new microeconomics of job search (see Edmund Phelps et al.), is nevertheless a valuable contribution to understanding of frictional unemployment. It provides reasons why some unemployment is voluntary, and why some unemployment is socially efficient.

Does the market produce the *optimal* amount of search unemployment? Is the natural rate optimal? I do not believe the new microeconomics has yet answered these questions.

An omniscient and beneficent economic dictator would not place every new job seeker immediately in any job at hand. Such a policy would create many mismatches, sacrificing efficiency in production or necessitating costly job-to-job shifts later on. The hypothetical planner would prefer to keep a queue of workers unemployed, so that he would have a larger choice of jobs to which to assign them. But he would not make the queue too long, because workers in the queue are not producing anything.

Of course he could shorten the queue of unemployed if he could dispose of more jobs and lengthen the queue of vacancies. With enough jobs of various kinds, he would never lack a vacancy for which any worker who happens to come along has comparative advantage. But because of limited capital stocks and interdependence among skills, jobs cannot be indefinitely multiplied without lowering their marginal productivity. Our wise and benevolent planner would not place people in jobs yielding less than the marginal value of leisure. Given this constraint on the number of jobs, he would always have to keep some workers waiting, and some jobs vacant. But he certainly would be inefficient if he had fewer jobs, filled and vacant, than this constraint. This is the common sense of Beveridge's rule—that vacancies should not be less than unemployment.

Is the natural rate a market solution of the hypothetical planner's operations research problem? According to search theory, an unemployed worker considers the probabilities that he can get a better job by searching longer and balances the expected discounted value of waiting against the loss of earnings. The employed worker makes a similar calculation when he considers quitting, also taking into account the once and for all costs of movement. These calculations are like those of the planner, but with an important difference. An individual does not internalize all the considerations the planner takes into account. The external effects are the familiar ones of congestion theory. A worker deciding to join a queue or to stay in one considers the probabilities of getting a job, but not the effects of his decision on the probabilities that others face. He lowers those probabilities for people in the queue he joins and raises them for persons waiting for the kind of job he vacates or turns down. Too many persons are unemployed waiting for good jobs, while less desirable ones go begging. However, external effects also occur in the decisions of employers whether to fill a vacancy with the applicant at hand or to wait for someone more qualified. It is not obvious, at least to me, whether the market is biased toward excessive or inadequate search. But it is doubtful that it produces the optimal amount.

Empirically the proposition that in the United States the zero-inflation rate of unemployment reflects voluntary and efficient job-seeking activity strains credulity. If there were a natural rate of unemployment in the United States, what would it be? It is hard to say because virtually all econometric Phillips curves allow for a whole menu of steady inflation rates. But estimates constrained to produce a vertical long-run Phillips curve suggest a natural rate between 5 and 6 percent of the labor force.[3]

So let us consider some of the features of an overall unemployment rate of 5 to 6 percent. First, about 40 percent of accessions in manufacturing are rehires rather than new hires. Temporarily laid off by their employers, these workers had been awaiting recall and were scarcely engaged in voluntary search activity. Their unemployment is as much a deadweight loss as the disguised, unemployment of redundant workers on payrolls. This number declines to 25–30 per-

---

[3] See Lucas and Rapping, pp. 257–305, in Phelps et al.

cent when unemployment is 4 percent or below. Likewise, a 5–6 percent unemployment rate means that voluntary quits amount only to about a third of separations, layoffs to two-thirds. The proportions are reversed at low unemployment rates.

Second, the unemployment statistic is not an exhaustive count of those with time and incentive to search. An additional 3 percent of the labor force are involuntarily confined to part-time work, and another ¾ of 1 percent are out of the labor force because they "could not find job" or "think no work available"—discouraged by market conditions rather than personal incapacities.

Third, with unemployment of 5–6 percent the number of reported vacancies is less than ½ of 1 percent. Vacancies appear to be understated relative to unemployment, but they rise to 1½ percent when the unemployment rate is below 4 percent. At 5–6 percent unemployment, the economy is clearly capable of generating many more jobs with marginal productivity high enough so that people prefer them to leisure. The capital stock is no limitation, since 5–6 percent unemployment has been associated with more than 20 percent excess capacity. Moreover, when more jobs are created by expansion of demand, with or without inflation, labor force participation increases; this would hardly occur if the additional jobs were low in quality and productivity. As the parable of the central employment planner indicates, there will be excessive waiting for jobs if the roster of jobs and the menu of vacancies are suboptimal.

In summary, labor markets characterized by 5–6 percent unemployment do not display the symptoms one would expect if the unemployment were voluntary search activity. Even if it were voluntary, search activity on such a large scale would surely be socially wasteful. The only reason anyone might regard so high an unemployment rate as an equilibrium and social optimum is that lower rates cause accelerating inflation. But this is almost tautological. The inferences of equilibrium and optimality would be more convincing if they were corroborated by direct evidence.

IV. WHY IS THERE INFLATION WITHOUT AGGREGATE EXCESS DEMAND?

Zero-inflation unemployment is not wholly voluntary, not optimal, I might even say not natural. In other words, the economy has an inflationary bias: When labor markets provide as many jobs as there are willing workers, there is inflation, perhaps accelerating inflation. Why?

The Phillips curve has been an empirical finding in search of a theory, like Pirandello characters in search of an author. One rationalization might be termed a theory of stochastic macroequilibrium: stochastic, because random intersectoral shocks keep individual labor markets in diverse states of disequilibrium; macroequilibrium, because the perpetual flux of particular markets produces fairly definite aggregate outcomes of unemployment and wages. Stimulated by Phillips's 1958 findings, Richard Lipsey proposed a model of this kind in 1960, and it has since been elaborated by Archibald, pp. 212–23 and Holt, pp. 53–123 and 224–56 in Phelps et al., and others. I propose now to sketch a theory in the same spirit.

It is an essential feature of the theory that economy-wide relations among employment, wages, and prices are aggregations of diverse outcomes in heterogeneous markets. The myth of macroeconomics is that relations among aggregates are enlarged analogues of relations among corresponding variables for individual households, firms, industries, markets. The myth is a harmless and useful simplification in many contexts, but sometimes it misses the essence of the phenomenon.

Unemployment is, in this model as in Keynes reinterpreted, a disequilibrium phenomenon. Money wages do not adjust rapidly enough to clear all labor markets every day. Excess supplies in labor markets take the form of unemployment, and excess demands the form of unfilled vacancies. At any moment, markets vary widely in excess demand or supply, and the economy as a whole shows both vacancies and unemployment.

The overall balance of vacancies and unemployment is determined by aggregate demand, and is therefore in principle subject to control by overall monetary and fiscal policy. Higher aggregate demand means fewer excess supply markets and more excess demand markets, accordingly less unemployment and more vacancies.

In any particular labor market, the rate of increase of money wages is the sum of two components, an equilibrium component and a disequilibrium component. The first is the rate at which the wage would increase were the market in equilibrium, with neither vacancies nor unemployment. The other component is a function of excess demand and supply—a monotonic function, positive for positive excess demand, zero for zero excess demand, nonpositive for excess supply. I begin with the disequilibrium component.

Of course the disequilibrium components are

relevant only if disequilibria persist. Why aren't they eliminated by the very adjustments they set in motion? Workers will move from excess supply markets to excess demand markets, and from low wage to high wage markets. Unless they overshoot, these movements are equilibrating. The theory therefore requires that new disequilibria are always arising. Aggregate demand may be stable, but beneath its stability is never-ending flux: new products, new processes, new tastes and fashions, new developments of land and natural resources, obsolescent industries and declining areas.

The overlap of vacancies and unemployment—say, the sum of the two for any given difference between them—is a measure of the heterogeneity or dispersion of individual markets. The amount of dispersion depends directly on the size of those shocks of demand and technology that keep markets in perpetual disequilibrium, and inversely on the responsive mobility of labor. The one increases, the other diminishes the frictional component of unemployment, that is, the number of unfilled vacancies coexisting with any given unemployment rate.

A central assumption of the theory is that the functions relating wage change to excess demand or supply are nonlinear, specifically that unemployment retards money wages less than vacancies accelerate them. Nonlinearity in the response of wages to excess demand has several important implications. First, it helps to explain the characteristic observed curvature of the Phillips curve. Each successive increment of unemployment has less effect in reducing the rate of inflation. Linear wage response, on the other hand, would mean a linear Phillips relation.

Second, given the overall state of aggregate demand, economy-wide vacancies less unemployment, wage inflation will be greater the larger the variance among markets in excess demand and supply. As a number of recent empirical studies, have confirmed (see George Perry and Charles Schultze), dispersion is inflationary. Of course, the rate of wage inflation will depend not only on the overall dispersion of excess demands and supplies across markets but also on the particular markets where the excess supplies and demands happen to fall. An unlucky random drawing might put the excess demands in highly responsive markets and the excess supplies in especially unresponsive ones.

Third, the nonlinearity is an explanation of inflationary bias, in the following sense. Even when aggregate vacancies are at most equal to unemployment, the average disequilibrium component will be positive. Full employment in the sense of equality of vacancies and unemployment is not compatible with price stability. Zero inflation requires unemployment in excess of vacancies.

Criteria that coincide in full long-run equilibrium—zero inflation and zero aggregate excess demand—diverge in stochastic macroequilibrium. Full long-run equilibrium in all markets would show no unemployment, no vacancies, no unanticipated inflation. But with unending sectoral flux, zero excess demand spells inflation and zero inflation spells net excess supply, unemployment in excess of vacancies. In these circumstances neither criterion can be justified simply because it is a property of full long-run equilibrium. Both criteria automatically allow for frictional unemployment incident to the required movements of workers between markets; the no-inflation criterion requires enough additional unemployment to wipe out inflationary bias.

I turn now to the equilibrium component, the rate of wage increase in a market with neither excess demand nor excess supply. It is reasonable to suppose that the equilibrium component depends on the trend of wages of comparable labor elsewhere. A "competitive wage," one that reflects relevant trends fully, is what employers will offer if they wish to maintain their share of the volume of employment. This will happen where the rate of growth of marginal revenue product—the compound of productivity increase and price inflation—is the same as the trend in wages. But in some markets the equilibrium wage will be rising faster, and in others slower, than the economy-wide wage trend.

A "natural rate" result follows if actual wage increases feed fully into the equilibrium components of future wage increases. There will be acceleration whenever the nonlinear disequilibrium effects are on average positive, and steady inflation, that is stochastically steady inflation, only at unemployment rates high enough to make the disequilibrium effects wash out. Phillips tradeoffs exist in the short run, and the time it takes for them to evaporate depends on the lengths of the lags with which today's actual wage gains become tomorrow's standards.

A rather minor modification may preserve Phillips tradeoffs in the long run. Suppose there is a floor on wage change in excess supply markets, independent of the amount of excess supply and of the past history of wages and prices. Suppose, for example, that wage change is never negative; it is either zero or what the response function says, whichever is algebraically larger.

So long as there are markets where this floor is effective, there can be determinate rates of economy-wide wage inflation for various levels of aggregate demand. Markets at the floor do not increase their contributions to aggregate wage inflation when overall demand is raised. Nor is their contribution escalated to actual wage experience. But the frequency of such markets diminishes, it is true, both with overall demand and with inflation. The floor phenomenon can preserve a Phillips tradeoff within limits, but one that becomes ever more fragile and vanishes as greater demand pressure removes markets from contact with the zero floor. The model implies a long-run Phillips curve that is very flat for high unemployment and becomes vertical at a critically low rate of unemployment.

These implications seem plausible and even realistic. It will be objected, however, that any permanent floor independent of general wage and price history and expectation must indicate money illusion. The answer is that the floor need not be permanent in any single market. It could give way to wage reduction when enough unemployment has persisted long enough. But with stochastic intersectoral shifts of demand, markets are always exchanging roles, and there can always be some markets, not always the same ones, at the floor.

This model avoids the empirically questionable implication of the usual natural rate hypothesis that unemployment rates only slightly higher than the critical rate will trigger ever-accelerating deflation. Phillips curves seem to be pretty flat at high rates of unemployment. During the great contraction of 1930–33, wage rates were slow to give way even in the face of massive unemployment and substantial deflation in consumer prices. Finally in 1932 and 1933 money wage rates fell more sharply, in response to prolonged unemployment, layoffs, shutdowns, and to threats and fears of more of the same.

I have gone through this example to make the point that irrationality, in the sense that meaningless differences in money values *permanently* affect individual behavior, is not logically necessary for the existence of a long-run Phillips tradeoff. In full long-run equilibrium in all markets, employment and unemployment would be independent of the levels and rates of change of money wage rates and prices. But this is not an equilibrium that the system ever approaches. The economy is in perpetual sectoral disequilibrium even when it has settled into a stochastic macroequilibrium.

I suppose that one might maintain that asymmetry in wage adjustment and temporary resistance to money wage decline reflect money illusion in some sense. Such an assertion would have to be based on an extension of the domain of well-defined rational behavior to cover responses to change, adjustment speeds, costs of information, costs of organizing and operating markets, and a host of other problems in dynamic theory. These theoretical extensions are in their infancy, although much work of interest and promise is being done. Meanwhile, I doubt that significant restrictions on disequilibrium adjustment mechanisms can be deduced from first principles.

Why are the wage and salary rates of employed workers so insensitive to the availability of potential replacements? One reason is that the employer makes some explicit or implicit commitments in putting a worker on the payroll in the first place. The employee expects that his wages and terms of employment will steadily improve, certainly never retrogress. He expects that the employer will pay him the rate prevailing for persons of comparable skill, occupation, experience, and seniority. He expects such commitments in return for his own investments in the job; arrangements for residence, transportation, and personal life involve set-up costs which will be wasted if the job turns sour. The market for labor services is not like a market for fresh produce where the entire current supply is auctioned daily. It is more like a rental housing market, in which most existing tenancies are the continuations of long-term relationships governed by contracts or less formal understandings.

Employers and workers alike regard the wages of comparable labor elsewhere as a standard, but what determines those reference wages? There is not even an auction where workers and employers unbound by existing relationships and commitments meet and determine a market-clearing wage. If such markets existed, they would provide competitively determined guides for negotiated and administered wages, just as stock exchange prices are reference points for stock transactions elsewhere. In labor markets the reverse is closer to the truth. Wage rates for existing employees set the standards for new employees, too.

The equilibrium components of wage increases, it has been argued, depend on past wage increases throughout the economy. In those theoretical and econometric models of inflation where labor markets are aggregated into a single market, this relationship is expressed as an autoregressive equation of fixed structure: current wage increase depends on past wage increases. The same description applies when past wage increases enter indirectly, mediated by price inflation and productivity change. The process of mutual interdependence of market wages is a good deal more complex and less mechanical than these aggregated models suggest.

Reference standards for wages differ from market to market. The equilibrium wage increase in each market will be some function of past wages in all markets, and perhaps of past prices too. But the function need not be the same in every market. Wages of workers contiguous in geography, industry, and skill will be heavily weighted. Imagine a wage pattern matrix of coefficients describing the dependence of the percentage equilibrium wage increase in each market on the past increases in all other markets. The coefficients in each row are non-negative and sum to one, but their distribution across markets and time lags will differ from row to row.

Consider the properties of such a system in the absence of disequilibrium inputs. First, the system has the "natural rate" property that its steady state is indeterminate. Any rate of wage increase that has been occurring in all markets for a long enough time will continue. Second, from irregular initial conditions the system will move toward one of these steady states, but which one depends on the specifics of the wage pattern matrix and the initial conditions. Contrary to some pessimistic warnings, there is no arithmetic compulsion that makes the whole system gravitate in the direction of its most inflationary sectors. The ultimate steady state inflation will be at most that of the market with the highest initial inflation rate, and at least that of the market with the lowest initial inflation rate. It need not be equal to the average inflation rate at the beginning, but may be either greater or smaller. Third, the adjustment paths are likely to contain cyclical components, damped or at most of constant amplitude, and during adjustments both individual and average wage movements may diverge substantially in both directions from their ultimate steady state value. Fourth, since wage decisions and negotiations occur infrequently, relative wage adjustments involve a lot of catching up and leap-frogging, and probably take a long time. I have sketched the formal properties of a disaggregated wage pattern system of this kind simply to stress again the vast simplification of the one-market myth.

A system in which only relative magnitudes matter has only a neutral equilibrium, from which it can be permanently displaced by random shocks. Even when a market is in equilibrium, it may outdo the recent wage increases in related markets. A shock of this kind, even though it is not repeated, raises permanently the steady state inflation rate. This is true cost-push—inflation generated neither by previous inflation nor by current excess demand. Shocks, of course, may be negative as well as positive. For example, upward pushes arising from adjustments in relative wage *levels* will be reversed when those adjustments are completed.

To the extent that one man's reference wages are another man's wages, there is something arbitrary and conventional, indeterminate and unstable, in the process of wage setting. In the same current market circumstances, the reference pattern might be 8 percent per year or 3 percent per year or zero, depending on the historical prelude. Market conditions, unemployment and vacancies and their distributions, shape history and alter reference patterns. But accidental circumstances affecting strategic wage settlements also cast a long shadow.

Price inflation, as previously observed, is a neutral method of making arbitrary money wage paths conform to the realities of productivity growth, neutral in preserving the structure of relative wages. If expansion of aggregate demand brings both more inflation and more employment, there need be no mystery why unemployed workers accept the new jobs, or why employed workers do not vacate theirs. They need not be victims of ignorance or inflation illusion. They genuinely want more work at feasible real wages, and they also want to maintain the relative status they regard as proper and just.

Guideposts could be in principle the functional equivalent of inflation, a neutral method of reconciling wage and productivity paths. The trick is to find a formula for mutual deescalation which does not offend conceptions of relative equity. No one has devised a way of controlling average wage rates without intervening in the competitive struggle over relative wages. Inflation lets this struggle proceed and blindly, impartially, impersonally, and nonpolitically scales down all its outcomes. There are worse methods of resolving group rivalries and social conflict.

V. THE ROLE OF MONOPOLY POWER

Probably the most popular explanation of the inflationary bias of the economy is concentration of economic power in large corporations and unions. These powerful monopolies and oligopolies, it is argued, are immune from competition in setting wages and prices. The unions raise wages above competitive rates, with little regard for the unemployed and underemployed workers knocking at the gates. Perhaps the unions are seeking a bigger share of the revenues of the monopolies and oligopolies with whom they bargain. But they don't really succeed in that objective, because the corporations simply pass the increased labor costs, along with mark-ups, on to their helpless customers. The remedy, it is argued, is either atomization of big business and big labor or strict public control of their prices and wages.

So simple a diagnosis is vitiated by confusion between levels and rates of change. Monopoly power is no doubt responsible for the relatively high prices and wages of some sectors. But can the exercise of monopoly power generate ever-rising price and wages? Monopolists have no reason to hold reserves of unexploited power. But if they did, or if events awarded them new power, their exploitation of it would raise their real prices and wages only temporarily.

Particular episodes of inflation may be associated with accretions of monopoly power, or with changes in the strategies and preferences of those who possess it. Among the reasons that wages and prices rose in the face of mass unemployment after 1933 were *NRA* codes and other early New Deal measures to suppress competition, and the growth of trade union membership and power under the protection of new federal legislation. Recently we have witnessed substantial gains in the powers of organized public employees. Unions elsewhere may not have gained power, but some of them apparently have changed their objectives in favor of wages at the expense of employment.

One reason for the popularity of the monopoly power diagnosis of inflation is the identification of administered prices and wages with concentrations of economic power. When price and wage increases are the outcomes of visible negotiations and decisions, it seems obvious that identifiable firms and unions have the power to affect the course of inflation. But the fact that monopolies, oligopolies, and large unions have discretion does not mean it is invariably to their advantage to use it to raise prices and wages. Nor are administered prices and wages found only in high concentration sectors. Very few prices and wages in a modern economy, even in the more competitive sectors, are determined in Walrasian auction markets.

No doubt there has been a secular increase in the prevalence of administered wages and prices, connected with the relative decline of agriculture and other sectors of self-employment. This development probably has contributed to the inflationary bias of the economy, by enlarging the number of labor markets where the response of money wages to excess supply is slower than their response to excess demand. The decline of agriculture as a sector of flexible prices and wages and as an elastic source of industrial labor is probably an important reason why the Phillips trade off problem is worse now than in the 1920s. Sluggishness of response to excess supply is a feature of administered prices, whatever the market structure, but it may be accentuated by concentration of power per se. For example, powerful unions, not actually forced by competition to moderate their wage demands, may for reasons of internal politics be slow to respond to unemployment in their ranks.

VI. SOME REFLECTIONS ON POLICY

If the makers of macroeconomic policy could be sure that the zero-inflation rate of unemployment is natural, voluntary, and optimal, their lives would be easy. Friedman told us that all macroeconomic policy needs to do, all it should try to do, is to make nominal national income grow steadily at the natural rate of growth of aggregate supply. This would sooner or later result in price stability. Steady price deflation would be even better, he said, because it would eliminate the socially wasteful incentive to economize money holdings. In either case, unemployment will converge to its natural rate, and wages and prices will settle into steady trends. Under this policy, whatever unemployment the market produces is the correct result. No tradeoff, no choice, no agonizing decisions.

I have argued this evening that a substantial amount of the unemployment compatible with zero inflation is involuntary and nonoptimal. This is, in my opinion, true whether or not the inflations associated with lower rates of unemployment are steady or ever-accelerating. Neither macroeconomic policy makers, nor the elected officials and electorates to whom they are responsible, can avoid weighing the costs of unemployment against those of inflation. As Phelps has pointed out, this social choice has an intertemporal dimension. The social costs of involuntary unemployment are mostly obvious and immediate. The social costs of inflation come later.

What are they? Economists' answers have been remarkably vague, even though the prestige of the profession has reinforced the popular view that inflation leads ultimately to catastrophe. Here indeed is a case where abstract economic theory has a powerful hold on public opinion and policy. The prediction that at low unemployment rates inflation will accelerate toward ultimate disaster is a theoretical deduction with little empirical support. In fact the weight of econometric evidence has been against acceleration, let alone disaster. Yet the deduction has been convincing enough to persuade this country to give up billions of dollars of annual output and to impose sweeping legal controls on prices and wages. Seldom has a society made such large immediate and tangible sacrifices to avert an ill defined, uncertain, eventual evil.

According to economic theory, the ultimate social cost of anticipated inflation is the wasteful use of resources to economize holdings of currency and other noninterest-bearing means of payment. I suspect that intelligent laymen would be utterly astounded if they realized that *this* is the great evil economists are talking about. They have imagined a much more devastating cataclysm, with Vesuvius vengefully punishing the sinners below. Extra trips between savings banks and commercial banks? What an anti-climax!

With means of payment—currency plus demand deposits—equal currently to 20 percent of *GNP*, an extra percentage point of anticipated inflation embodied in nominal interest rates produces in principle a social cost of 2⁄10 of 1 percent of *GNP* per year. This is an outside estimate. An unknown, but substantial, share of the stock of money belongs to holders who are not trying to economize cash balances and are not near any margin where they would be induced to spend resources for this purpose. These include hoarders of large denomination currency, about one-third of the total currency in public hands, for reasons of privacy, tax evasion, or illegal activity. They include tradesmen and consumers whose working balances turn over too rapidly or are too small to justify any effort to invest them in interest-bearing assets. They include corporations who, once they have been induced to undertake the fixed costs of a sharp-pencil money management department, are already minimizing their cash holdings. They include businessmen who are in fact being paid interest on demand deposits, although it takes the form of preferential access to credit and other bank services. But, in case anyone still regards the waste of resources in unnecessary transactions between money and interest-bearing financial assets as one of the major economic problems of the day, there is

a simple and straightforward remedy, the payment of interest on demand deposits and possibly, with ingenuity, on currency too.

The ultimate disaster of inflation would be the breakdown of the monetary payments system, necessitating a currency reform. Such episodes have almost invariably resulted from real economic catastrophes—wars, defeats, revolutions, reparations—not from the mechanisms of wage-price push with which we are concerned. Acceleration is a scare word, conveying the image of a rush into hyperinflation as relentlessly deterministic and monotonic as the motion of falling bodies. Realistic attention to the disaggregated and stochastic nature of wage and price movements suggests that they will show diverse and irregular fluctuations around trends that are difficult to discern and extrapolate. The central trends, history suggests, can accelerate for a long, long time without generating hyper-inflations destructive of the payments mechanism.

Unanticipated inflation, it is contended, leads to mistaken estimates of relative prices and consequently to misallocations of resources. An example we have already discussed is the alleged misallocation of time by workers who over-estimate their real wages. The same error would lead to a general over-supply by sellers who contract for future deliveries without taking correct account of the increasing prices of the things they must buy in order to fulfill the contract. Unanticipated deflation would cause similar miscalculations and misallocations. Indeed, people can make these same mistakes about relative prices even when the price level is stable. The mistakes are more likely, or the more costly to avoid, the greater the inflationary trend. There are costs in setting and announcing new prices. In an inflationary environment price changes must be made more frequently—a new catalog twice a year instead of one, or some formula for automatic escalation of announced prices. Otherwise, with the interval between announcements unchanged, the average misalignment of relative prices will be larger the faster the inflation. The same problem would arise with rapid deflation.

Unanticipated inflation and deflation—and unanticipated changes in relative prices—are also sources of transfers of wealth. I will not review here the rich and growing empirical literature on this subject. Facile generalizations about the progressivity or equity of inflationary transfers are hazardous; certainly inflation does not merit the cliché that it is "the cruelest tax." Let us not forget that unemployment has distributional effects as well as dead-weight losses.

Some moralists take the view that the government has promised to maintain the purchasing power of its currency, but this promise is their inference rather than any pledge written on dollar bills or in the Constitution. Some believe so strongly in this implicit contract that they are willing to suspend actual contracts in the name of anti-inflation.

I have long contended that the government should make low-interest bonds of guaranteed purchasing power available for savers and pension funds who wish to avoid the risks of unforeseen inflation. The common objection to escalated bonds is that they would diminish the built-in stability of the system. The stability in question refers to the effects on aggregate real demand, *ceteris paribus,* of a change in the price level. The Pigou effect tells us that government bondholders whose wealth is diminished by inflation will spend less. This brake on old-fashioned gap inflation will be thrown away if the bonds are escalated. These considerations are only remotely related to the mechanisms of wage and price inflation we have been discussing. In the 1970s we know that the government can, if it wishes, control aggregate demand—at any rate, its ability to do so is only trivially affected by the presence or absence of Pigou effects on part of the government debt.

In considering the intertemporal tradeoff, we have no license to assume that the natural rate of unemployment is independent of the history of actual unemployment. Students of human capital have been arguing convincingly that earning capacity, indeed transferable earning capacity, depends on experience as well as formal education. Labor markets soggy enough to maintain price stability may increase the number of would-be workers who lack the experience to fit them for jobs that become vacant.

Macroeconomic policies, monetary and fiscal, are incapable of realizing society's unemployment and inflation goals simultaneously. This dismal fact has long stimulated a search for third instruments to do the job: guideposts and incomes policies, on the one hand, labor market and manpower policies, on the other. Ten to fifteen years ago great hopes were held for both. The Commission on Money and Credit in 1961, pp. 39–40, hailed manpower policies as the new instrument that would overcome the unemployment-inflation dilemma. Such advice was taken seriously in Washington, and an unprecedented spurt in manpower programs took place in the 1960s. The Council of Economic Advisers set forth wage and price guideposts in 1961–62 in the hope of "talk-ing down" the Phillips curve (pp. 185–90). It is discouraging to find that these efforts did not keep the problem of inflationary bias from becoming worse than ever.

So it is not with great confidence or optimism that one suggests measures to mitigate the trade-off. But some proposals follow naturally from the analysis, and some are desirable in themselves anyway.

First, guideposts do not wholly deserve the scorn that "toothless jawboning" often attracts. There is an arbitrary, imitative component in wage settlements, and maybe it can be influenced by national standards.

Second, it is important to create jobs for those unemployed and discouraged workers who have extremely low probability of meeting normal job specifications. Their unemployment does little to discipline wage increases, but reinforces their deprivation of human capital and their other disadvantages in job markets. The National Commission on Technology, Automation and Economic Progress pointed out in 1966 the need for public service jobs tailored to disadvantaged workers. They should not be "last resort" or make-work jobs, but regular permanent jobs capable of conveying useful experience and inducing reliable work habits. Assuming that the additional services produced by the employing institutions are of social utility, it may well be preferable to employ disadvantaged workers directly rather than to pump up aggregate demand until they reach the head of the queue.

Third, a number of measures could be taken to make markets more responsive to excess supplies. This is the kernel of truth in the market-power explanation of inflationary bias. In many cases, government regulations themselves support prices and wages against competition. Agricultural prices and construction wages are well-known examples. Some trade unions follow wage policies that take little or no account of the interests of less senior members and of potential members. Since unions operate with federal sanction and protection, perhaps some means can be found to insure that their memberships are open and that their policies are responsive to the unemployed as well as the employed.

As for macroeconomic policy, I have argued that it should aim for unemployment lower than the zero-inflation rate. How much lower? Low enough to equate unemployment and vacancies? We cannot say. In the nature of the case there is no simple formula—conceptual, much less statistical—for full employment. Society cannot escape very difficult political and intertemporal choices. We economists can illuminate these choices as we learn more about labor markets, mobility, and search, and more about the social and distributive costs of both unemployment and inflation. Thirty-five years after Keynes, welfare macroeconomics is still a relevant and challenging subject. I dare to believe it has a bright future.

REFERENCES

Beveridge, W. H. *Full Employment in a Free Society,* New York 1945.

Doeringer, P., and Piore, M. *Internal Labor Markets and Manpower Analysis,* Lexington, Mass. 1971.

Friedman, M. "The Role of Monetary Policy," *Amer. Econ. Rev.,* Mar. 1968, *58,* 1–17.

Hall, R. "Why is the Unemployment Rate so High at Full Employment?," *Brookings Papers on Economic Activity,* 3, 1970, 369–402.

Keynes, J. M. *The General Theory of Employment, Interest, and Money,* New York 1936.

Leijonhufvud, A. *On Keynesian Economics and the Economics of Keynes.* New York 1968.

Lipsey, R. G. "The Relation Between Unemployment and the Rate of Change of Money Wage Rates in the United Kingdom, 1862–1957: A Further Analysis," *Economica,* Feb. 1960, *27,* 1–31.

Parnes, H. S. *Research on Labor Mobility,* Social Science Research Council, Bull. 65, New York 1954.

Perry, G. L. "Changing Labor Markets and Inflation," *Brookings Papers on Economic Activity,* 3, 1970, 411–41.

Phelps, E. S. "Phillips Curves, Expectations of Inflation and Optimal Unemployment Over Time," *Economica,* Aug. 1967, *34,* 254–81.

Phelps, E. S. et al. *Micro-economic Foundations of Employment and Inflation Theory,* New York 1970.

Phillips, A. W. "The Relation Between Unemployment and the Rate of Change of Money Wage Rates in the United Kingdom, 1861–1957," *Economica,* Nov. 1958, *25,* 283–99.

Reynolds, L. G. *The Structure of Labor Markets,* New York 1951.

Schultze, C. L. "Has the Phillips Curve Shifted? Some Additional Evidence," *Brookings Papers on Economic Activity,* 2, 1971, 452–67.

Tobin, J. "A Note on the Money Wage Problem," *Quart. J. Econ.,* May 1941, *55,* 508–16.

Commission on Money and Credit, *Money and Credit: Their Influence on Jobs, Prices, and Growth,* Englewood Cliffs 1961.

Economic Report of the President 1962, Washington 1962.

U.S. National Commission on Technology, Automation, and Economic Progress, *Technology and the American Economy,* Washington 1966.

THE INFLATION-UNEMPLOYMENT TRADE-OFF: THEORY AND EXPERIENCE

*Saul H. Hymans**

I. INTRODUCTION

In the mid-1960s, as the American economy was approaching full employment—or at least the 4 percent interim target of that period—substantial public and professional debate grew up around the question: how much inflation would have to be tolerated at full employment. By the early 1970s, the American economy had turned from strong expansion to a mild recession, the unemployment rate had climbed to a peak about 3 percentage points above the low point in 1969, and the inflation rate was running between 4 and 5 percent despite the context of recession. The question of the day turned to: why had so much inflation been generated and why was it proving to be so stubborn.

The frame of reference for both aspects of this issue has been the celebrated "Phillips Curve." The seminal work on the Phillips Curve was done by A. W. Phillips [18] who first noticed a long empirical regularity between money wage

* Saul H. Hymans is Professor of Economics and Co-Director, Research Seminar in Quantitative Economics, The University of Michigan.

changes and the rate of unemployment in the United Kingdom. Subsequently, Lipsey [12] displayed a dynamic labor market adjustment mechanism which provided the theoretical underpinning for the observed relation. Since the early 1960s Perry [15], Eckstein and Wilson [2], Pierson [19], R. J. Gordon [5], and others have implemented more or less expanded versions of the Phillips-Lipsey mechanism to obtain empirical wage equations for the U.S. economy. In recent years, Perry [16], Holt and co-workers [9], Mortenson [13], Tobin [20] and others have made important analytical contributions which have improved our understanding of the wage adjustment mechanism.

In the Phillips-Lipsey approach it is posited that the rate of change of money wages depends positively on the rate of excess demand in the labor market. Further, the rate of excess demand for labor varies inversely with the unemployment rate. The result is the standard Phillips-Lipsey wage equation in which the rate of increase of money wages varies directly with the inverse of the unemployment rate. But, as Phillips and Lipsey clearly realized, this is only a part of the wage adjustment process. For in the presence of a variable price level, the rate of inflation is directly relevant to the real value of any wage settlement. Barring a situation of complete money illusion in the supplying of labor services, the rate of inflation must be assumed to be an integral part of any wage adjustment mechanism. The manner in which money wage rates adjust to the rate of inflation turns out, as will be seen below, to be of critical importance both for describing the interrelations between inflation and unemployment and for understanding the options available to policy makers who might wish to pursue policies which have an effect on the overall level of employment.

Underlying the whole process of wage-price-unemployment adjustment is the rate of growth of productivity in the economy; i.e., the rate of increase of output per employed man-hour. The real growth of the economy depends on productivity growth and the growth of available man-hours.[1] The progress of per capita output, or the growth of real income to be earned by an hour's work is therefore constrained in the long run by the growth of productivity. This is a fact which cannot be circumvented in the aggregate, is undoubtedly coming to be broadly understood by those who sit on either side of the labor bargaining process, and plays a strong role in the process of wage determination.

Since price changes are not independent of either wage or productivity changes, and since the path of aggregate demand affects unemployment and (short-term) productivity growth which then affect wage changes, the underlying inflation-unemployment trade-off function is actually the result of the dynamic interaction of a number of important relations of which the wage equation is only one. Further, it is not at all obvious that the rate of inflation which would accompany a steady state of full employment is the same as that which would accompany either fluctuation around full employment or a concerted effort to drive the economy from a position of high unemployment to a state of full employment.

The next section of this paper presents a theoretical model which is used to shed light on the question of the existence of a trade-off relation and to indicate the nature of the trade-off as it exists in the short run, particularly

---

[1] This is true no matter how we measure economic growth. The productivity which we generally measure is in units of real GNP per man-hour. If we changed our output notion, say by subtracting the production of effluents from the GNP, the productivity measure would change in definition, but the statement made in the text would still hold.

in the context of a cyclical movement of employment. In Section III we use the model to investigate the problem of a long-run or steady-state trade-off and consider the accelerationist position which specifically denies the possibility of a long-run trade-off. In the final section of the paper we compare the predictions of the theoretical model with the actual behavior of inflation and unemployment in the United States over the period 1960–1972. For this purpose we employ an econometric model of the U.S. economy to approximate empirically the relations derived from the theoretical model of Sections II and III.

II. THEORETICAL MODEL: SHORT-RUN BEHAVIOR

The basic theoretical model can be specified by the four equations numbered (II.1)–(II.4) below. For ease of exposition the equations are taken to be linear in parameters.[2] In all that follows the symbol $\dot{\Delta}$ is used to represent a percentage change.

$$T_g = \bar{T} - T \tag{II.1}$$
$$W_g = \bar{T} - (\dot{\Delta}W - \dot{\Delta}P)_{-1} \tag{II.2}$$
$$\dot{\Delta}W = \alpha_0 U^{-1} + \alpha_1 \dot{\Delta}P + \alpha_2 W_g \tag{II.3}$$
$$\dot{\Delta}P = \beta_0(\dot{\Delta}W - \bar{T}) + \beta_1 T_g. \tag{II.4}$$

The first equation defines the productivity-gap variable (T_g) as the difference between the normal or trend growth of productivity $(\bar{T})$ and the actual growth of productivity (T). In the private sector of the U.S. economy productivity growth has averaged about 3 percent per year in the post-World War II period, and the reader can think of $\bar{T}$ as being approximately 3 if measured on an annual basis. Actual productivity growth often differs from $\bar{T}$ due to short-term cyclical movements in the rate of growth of total output and the rate of utilization of labor and capital.

Equation (II.2) defines the wage-gap variable (W_g) as the difference between $\bar{T}$ and the (average) rate of growth of the real wage rate $(\dot{\Delta}W - \dot{\Delta}P)$ in the recent past.[3] A "positive wage-gap" is an indication that, in the recent past, the growth of the real wage rate has tended·to lag behind the trend growth of productivity.

The wage adjustment mechanism is given in equation (II.3). The percentage increase in the money wage rate depends, in Phillips-Lipsey fashion, on both the inverse of the unemployment rate (U) and the rate of inflation $(\dot{\Delta}P)$. The rate of wage increase depends inversely on the level of the unemployment rate, so that $\alpha_0 > 0$. The coefficient α_1 measures the short-run or instantaneous response of the wage rate to the rate of price inflation. If $\alpha_1 = 0$, wages do not respond at all to inflation in the short run, while $\alpha_1 = 1$ implies full short-run adjustment. All available empirical evidence denies the former possibility and we shall therefore consider α_1 to be strictly positive, and possibly as large as unity. The final term in the wage equation measures the positive $(\alpha_2 > 0)$ response of the wage rate to the wage-gap. This term measures a longer run

---

[2] Virtually the same results could be derived from a more general framework, but the added complications hardly seem to justify the increased generality.

[3] $\dot{\Delta}W$ is the percentage change in the money wage rate; $\dot{\Delta}P$ is the precentage change in the price level. Since the real wage rate is defined as the ratio $\dfrac{W}{P}$ the percentage change in the real wage rate is measured as $(\dot{\Delta}W - \dot{\Delta}P)$. The subscript "−1" on $(\dot{\Delta}W - \dot{\Delta}P)$ in equation (II.2) is meant to indicate that the change in the real wage rate is being measured as of one "period" ago.

response of the wage rate to the recent progress of the real wage. If the growth of the real wage has been lagging behind the normal growth of productivity, substantial labor demands build up for compensatory increases in the wage rate in order to maintain labor's normal share of real output. In the case of a negative wage-gap, wage rate increases are held down by employer attempts to avoid the continued erosion of profit margins.

The final equation (II.4) describes the rate of price increase as a direct function ($\beta_0 > 0$) of the rate of growth of normal unit labor cost—i.e., the rate of growth of the wage rate less the trend rate of growth of productivity. The productivity-gap is also assumed to affect the rate of change of prices, with abnormally low productivity growth contributing positively to the rate of inflation ($\beta_1 > 0$). Most empirical evidence—e.g., [1], [14]—suggests that β_1 is a good deal smaller than β_0; i.e., prices respond more strongly to current wage changes than to current productivity changes (of the same magnitude).

There are at least three major shortcomings of the model represented by equations (II.1)–(II.4). First, all time lags have been ignored except for that associated with the wage-gap variable. For purposes of empirical measurement, the equations would have to be specified more carefully with respect to a number of time lags in the behavior of wages and prices. The longest time lag, however, would likely be in the wage-gap variable and the theoretical model therefore displays the *essential* dynamic features of an empirically more realistic model. Secondly, the price equation (II.4) contains no variable measuring the direct effects of demand pressures on the rate of inflation. Demand pressures appear only indirectly as they affect output levels, hence the unemployment rate, and thus the rate of wage increase. Finally, the model contains no explanation of either the unemployment rate (U) or the actual growth of productivity (T). To explain U and T would require an aggregative model of output determination, complete with links to monetary and fiscal policy. Our interest here, however, is in determining the response of wage and price inflation to the state of the labor market. For this purpose we can take the level, or time path, of the unemployment rate as coming from outside of our model and concentrate on the wage-price interaction which results. We shall, of course, have to consider the behavior of productivity in the process.

In order to determine any kind of trade-off relation between price inflation and unemployment, it will be necessary to combine the separate wage and price equations since the model states that wage and price changes are jointly determined. By substituting equation (II.3) into equation (II.4), we can eliminate the current rate of wage change and display the short-term trade-off relation between $\dot{P}$ and U. Thus, by substitution,

$$\dot{P} = \beta_0(\alpha_0 U^{-1} + \alpha_1 \dot{P} + \alpha_2 W_g) - \beta_0 \bar{T} + \beta_1 T_g,$$

which can be solved for $\dot{P}$ to yield:

$$\dot{P} = \frac{-\beta_0 \bar{T}}{1 - \beta_0 \alpha_1} + \frac{\alpha_0 \beta_0}{1 - \beta_0 \alpha_1} U^{-1} + \frac{\alpha_2 \beta_0}{1 - \beta_0 \alpha_1} W_g + \frac{\beta_1}{1 - \beta_0 \alpha_1} T_g. \quad \text{(II.5)}$$

In order to understand the meaning of equation (II.5) let us begin by supposing that $W_g = T_g = 0$. This yields the special case

$$\dot{P} = \frac{-\beta_0 \bar{T}}{1 - \beta_0 \alpha_1} + \frac{\alpha_0 \beta_0}{1 - \beta_0 \alpha_1} U^{-1} \quad \text{(II.6)}$$

The Inflation-Unemployment Trade-Off   163

which describes the short-run inflation-unemployment trade-off when there is neither a wage-gap nor a productivity-gap. Figure 1 displays (II.6) graphically

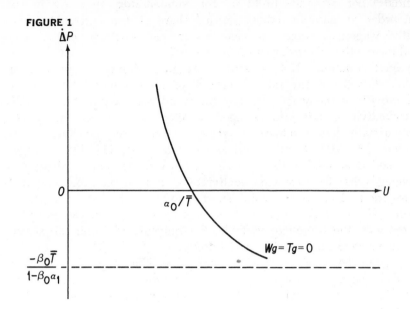

FIGURE 1

assuming $(1 - \beta_0\alpha_1) > 0$. An unemployment rate of $U = \frac{\alpha_0}{\bar{T}}$ implies $\dot{\Delta}P = 0$, i.e., a zero rate of inflation. If the unemployment rate is below $\alpha_0/\bar{T}$, the result is a positive rate of inflation, and the lower is the unemployment rate the higher is the corresponding inflation rate. There is also an asymmetry to be noted. The rate of price *increase* can become arbitrarily large as the unemployment rate declines (still assuming $W_g = T_g = 0$), but the rate of price *decrease* is limited to at most $\beta_0\bar{T}/(1 - \beta_0\alpha_1)$ as the unemployment rate increases. This familiar curvature property of the trade-off relation implies that if U cycles around the level $\alpha_0/\bar{T}$, with equal amplitude and duration on either side of $\alpha_0/\bar{T}$, the average rate of inflation over the cycle will be positive rather than zero. For a cyclical economy to maintain an average inflation rate of zero, it would have to "spend more time" on the high side of $\alpha_0/\bar{T}$ than on the low side.

In the absence of either a wage- or productivity-gap, the unemployment rate $U = \alpha_0/\bar{T}$ implies $\dot{\Delta}P = 0$ and, through equation (II.3), this is seen to require a rate of wage increase equal to the trend rate of growth of productivity—the well-known "guidepost" wage formula.

The steepness of the trade-off relation in Figure 1 depends on the product $\beta_0\alpha_1$. The closer is this product to unity, the steeper is the trade-off relation. In the limit, as the product approaches unity, the trade-off relation becomes vertical. This can only be interpreted as the absence of any meaningful trade-off relation. In other words, if $U = \alpha_0/\bar{T}$ the rate of inflation will be zero. But any attempt to push U below $\alpha_0/\bar{T}$ will lead to ever-accelerating inflation, and any attempt to push U above $\alpha_0/\bar{T}$ will lead to ever-accelerating deflation. The unemployment rate $U = \alpha_0/\bar{T}$ is termed the "natural" unemployment rate by those who adhere to such an accelerationist position. Few who take the "no trade-off" position, however,—e.g., Friedman [4], Phelps [17], Fellner [3]—would maintain that a meaningful trade-off fails to exist in the short run. It is only in the long run that the accelerationists argue that the product $\beta_0\alpha_1$ can be expected to approach unity, a consideration to which we shall return below.[4]

The trade-off relation between inflation and unemployment as shown in Figure 1 is relevant if $W_g = T_g = 0$ or, more generally, if $\alpha_2\beta_0 W_g = -\beta_1 T_g$ so that the gap terms cancel out in equation (II.5). It will be argued that this is not likely to be the case, so that the short-run trade-off must in fact be analyzed in the context of equation (II.5) rather than (II.6).

It is clear that since $\alpha_2\beta_0 > 0$, a positive wage-gap will result in a higher rate of inflation for any given unemployment rate than would occur with $W_g = 0$. The same effect occurs with a positive productivity-gap since $\beta_1 > 0$. Figure 2 compares the short-run trade-off curves for various gap situations, with the heavy curve merely repeating Figure. 1.[5]

It is unlikely that any particular trade-off curve will remain relevant for more than a short period of time. If, at a point in time, the economy has a zero wage-gap and a plus one percentage point productivity-gap, these are initial conditions defining its short-run trade-off relation between movements in inflation and unemployment; i.e., under such circumstances the economy would move along the dashed curve in Figure 2. But if this movement should change the

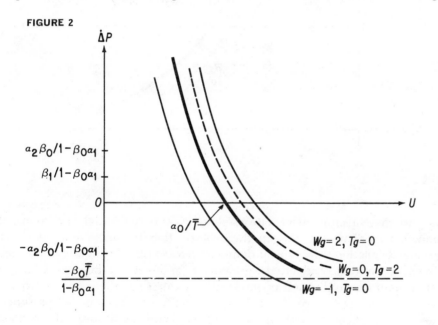

FIGURE 2

size of W_g or T_g, the initial conditions would change and further movement would take place along a different trade-off curve.

The position of the relevant short-run trade-off relation depends on the past progress of wages, prices and productivity, as well as the cyclical position of the economy. Suppose, for example, that the economy is as pictured at point no. 1 in Figure 3: a high unemployment rate, zero wage- and productivity-gaps, and prices declining slightly. From this point a cyclical upswing in production

---

[4] The accelerationist position is that monetary and fiscal policy can be used to drive U below the natural rate without an accelerating inflation in the short run. But an attempt to hold the unemployment rate below the natural rate permanently, must ultimately result in ever accelerating inflation as $\beta_0\alpha_1$ approaches unity. See Friedman [4].

[5] Figure 2 considers the empirically likely case in which $\alpha_2\beta_0 > \beta_1$.

FIGURE 3

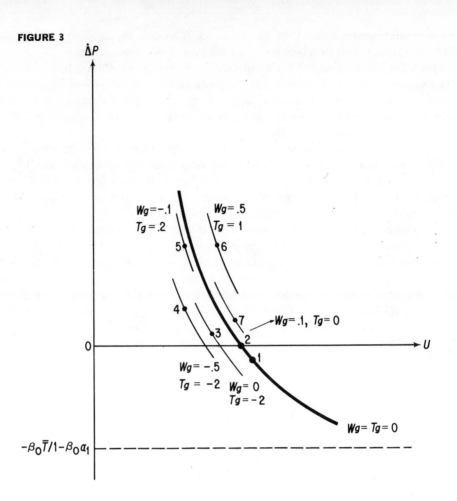

begins and the unemployment rate declines. Given the initial conditions, the economy moves along the no-gap trade-off relation to, say, point no. 2 with a zero rate of inflation. The typical dominant effect at the beginning of a cyclical upswing is a spurt in productivity growth—a "productivity bonus"—which derives from improved utilization of productive resources as the economy expands. This results in a negative productivity gap, usually sizeable, and let us suppose $T_g = -2$ (percentage points). If the wage-gap remains at zero, the economy moves to a lower trade-off curve and the further decline in the unemployment rate leads to a point such as no. 3 in Figure 3. Note that the decline in U, in going from point no. 2 to point no. 3, has produced substantially less inflation than would have been the case if movement had continued along the no-gap curve. The movement from point no. 2 to point no. 3 can be expected to have generated a negative wage-gap. The substantial decline in unemployment generates a rise in the nominal wage. Along with only a modest rate of price increase this permits the real wage to rise more rapidly than the trend productivity rate, leading to a negative wage-gap, say $W_g = -.5$. If the productivity bonus continues, the trade-off curve shifts down again, and the expansion carries the economy to a point like no. 4 in Figure 3. As the expansion progresses and fuller utilization of capacity and labor resources develop, the productivity bonus dwindles away. Indeed, as capacity becomes over-utilized and less efficient resources are called into use a positive productivity-gap generally results. This shifts the trade-off curve upward, leading to a much higher rate of inflation. With little further decline in the unemployment rate, and an initially negative wage-gap, wages fail to accelerate as rapidly as prices and the wage-gap closes. Suppose, then, that the economy moves to point no. 5: an unemployment rate little changed from point no. 4, with gaps near zero and a much higher rate of inflation. Suppose that from point no. 5 the economy begins a downswing with rising unemployment. The level of output is still high enough, relative to capacity, that productivity performance is poor and T_g increases. The weakening in the employment market will help to keep wages from accelerating and if the short run response of prices to wages (β_0) exceeds the short run response of wages to prices (α_1), the growth of real wages is certain to decelerate substantially and lead to a positive wage-gap. The result is very likely to be a movement like that shown from point no. 5 to point no. 6 in Figure 3: an increase in the unemployment rate with virtually no relief in inflation.[6] During the process of recession, rearrangement of productive resources (de-employment of inefficient resources) restores a more nearly normal productivity performance and T_g approaches zero which slows the rate of price increase and in and of itself thereby contributes to decreasing the positive wage-gap. The continued rise in the unemployment rate decreases ΔW, but the previously positive wage-gap offsets this in part, thereby contributing to a recovery in the real wage and the wage-gap is further decreased. This produces a point such as no. 7 in Figure 3 as the economic contraction approaches bottom: near-zero gaps, a high unemployment rate, and a much reduced rate of inflation. To summarize the process:

1. The early upswing (decline in U) is dominated by productivity bonuses and rapidly rising real wages (T_g and $W_g < 0$) which implies less inflation than would occur with zero gaps.
2. Ultimately the productivity-gap closes and even turns positive which speeds up the inflation and contributes to closing the negative wage-gap which further accelerates the inflation.
3. The early downswing (increase in U) is dominated by a positive productivity-gap and price increases outpacing wage increases which results in a positive wage-gap.
4. Ultimately the positive wage-gap produces a recovery in the real wage which reduces the wage-gap. In combination with improved productivity performance, this reduces the rate of inflation as the downswing progresses.[7]

III. THEORETICAL MODEL: STEADY-STATE BEHAVIOR

In the previous section, we used our model to investigate the short-run (cyclical) trade-off between inflation and unemployment. At this point, we want to abstract from cyclical aberrations and consider what the trade-off would be like if stabilization policy could be used to keep the economy growing smoothly

---

[6] In discussing the persistence of inflation in 1970 when unemployment was rising, R. J. Gordon referred to this phenomenon as a "horizontal Phillips Curve" [6]. The phenomenon, of course, is that of a horizontal movement *between* two short-run trade-off curves.

[7] Note that any substantial decline in the inflation rate requires both an increase in unemployment and the elimination of the positive wage- and productivity-gaps which dominate the early downswing phase. The inflation would "unwind" to a much smaller extent if the gaps remained positive; i.e., if productivity performance continued to be poor, and the real wage failed to recover.

so as to maintain some desired rate of unemployment.[8] This can be viewed as steady-state equilibrium growth. The resulting steady-state trade-off relation displays the inflation rate associated with alternative, permanently maintained rates of unemployment.

To investigate the steady-state trade-off two modifications of our model are required. First, in a situation of smooth equilibrium growth the productivity-gap, T_g, is by definition zero. Second, the time lag in the wage-gap variable is irrelevant since $\dot{W} = \dot{W}_{-1}$ and $\dot{P} = \dot{P}_{-1}$; i.e., the rate of wage and price increases are constant through time at any maintained level of U. Equation (II.3) can then be re-written as

$$\dot{W} = \alpha_0 U^{-1} + \alpha_1 \dot{P} + \alpha_2[\bar{T} - (\dot{W} - \dot{P})]$$
$$= \alpha_0 U^{-1} + (\alpha_1 + \alpha_2)\dot{P} + \alpha_2\bar{T} - \alpha_2\dot{W}.$$

Solving the latter for $\dot{W}$, we obtain the steady-state wage equation:

$$\dot{W} = \frac{\alpha_0}{1 + \alpha_2} U^{-1} + \frac{\alpha_1 + \alpha_2}{1 + \alpha_2} \dot{P} + \frac{\alpha_2}{1 + \alpha_2} \bar{T}. \tag{III.1}$$

The corresponding steady-state price equation simply drops the T_g variable:

$$\dot{P} = \beta_0(\dot{W} - \bar{T}). \tag{III.2}$$

The steady-state trade-off relation results from substituting (III.1) into (III.2) and solving for $\dot{P}$ to yield

$$\dot{P} = -\frac{\beta_0\bar{T}}{1 - \beta_0\alpha_1 + \alpha_2(1 - \beta_0)} + \frac{\alpha_0\beta_0}{1 - \beta_0\alpha_1 + \alpha_2(1 - \beta_0)} U^{-1}. \tag{III.3}$$

To find the non-inflationary unemployment rate, we set $\dot{P} = 0$ in (III.3) and solve to yield $U = \alpha_0/\bar{T}$, precisely as in the case of the no-gap short-run trade-off equation (II.6). Further, if $U = \alpha_0/\bar{T}$ and $\dot{P} = 0$ are substituted into (III.1) the result is $\dot{W} = \bar{T}$, again the guidepost rule for non-inflationary wage increases. Finally, note that $\dot{W} = \bar{T}$ and $\dot{P} = 0$ imply a zero wage-gap. Thus the zero inflation point on the short-run curve in Figure 1 is also a point on the steady-state trade-off relation. In fact, (III.3) differs from (II.6) only in the term $\alpha_2(1 - \beta_0)$ which appears in the denominator of each term on the right-hand side of (III.3). But $\alpha_2(1 - \beta_0)$ is positive (or at least non-negative), so that the steady-state trade-off is necessarily less steep than (or, at most, as steep as) the curve shown in Figure 1. But suppose that $\alpha_2(1 - \beta_0)$ is strictly positive so that the steady-state trade-off is flatter than the curve in Figure 1. Let us calculate the steady-state wage-gap implied by an unemployment rate maintained below $\alpha_0/\bar{T}$. We can represent $U < \alpha_0/\bar{T}$ by writing

$$U^{-1} = \frac{\bar{T}}{\alpha_0} + \epsilon, \qquad \text{with } \epsilon > 0. \tag{III.4}$$

Substitution of (III.4) into (III.3) yields

$$\dot{P} = \frac{\alpha_0\beta_0\epsilon}{1 - \beta_0\alpha_1 + \alpha_2(1 - \beta_0)} > 0. \tag{III.5}$$

---

[8] If the economy has a natural tendency to cycle—which is a view with a long history in economics—then a smooth, non-cyclical growth path requires active stabilization policy. Alternatively, recent econometric evidence seems to side with another old view that major cyclical swings have resulted primarily from destabilizing shocks—including those arising from unwise government policy. See [8].

Substitution of (III.4) and (III.5) into (III.1) yields

$$\dot{W} = \bar{T} + \frac{\alpha_0 \epsilon}{1 - \beta_0 \alpha_1 + \alpha_2(1 - \beta_0)},$$

or

$$\dot{W} = \bar{T} + \frac{\dot{P}}{\beta_0}. \tag{III.6}$$

Equations (III.5) and (III.6) imply a wage-gap, for U maintained below $\alpha_0/\bar{T}$, given by

$$W_g = \bar{T} - (\dot{W} - \dot{P}) = \bar{T} - \left(\bar{T} + \frac{\dot{P}}{\beta_0} - \dot{P}\right) = -\dot{P}\left(\frac{1 - \beta_0}{\beta_0}\right). \tag{III.7}$$

Thus, an unemployment rate permanently maintained below the non-inflationary value ($\alpha_0/\bar{T}$) implies a permanently negative wage-gap if $\beta_0 < 1$. This is clearly an untenable situation, since it implies an ever-increasing share of real output accruing to labor; i.e., a profit share going inexorably to zero. In the long run—in a steady-state growth equilibrium—the wage-gap cannot remain permanently negative. The wage-gap can vary around zero cyclically, but it cannot remain non-zero secularly.[9] This implies that in the long run β_0 must converge to unity which implies that prices change at a rate precisely equal to the trend rate of change of unit labor costs.

If we set $\beta_0 = 1$, equation (III.7) implies a wage-gap permanently equal to zero and the steady-state trade-off relation (III.3 with $\beta_0 = 1$) becomes

$$\dot{P} = \frac{-\bar{T}}{1 - \alpha_1} + \frac{\alpha_0}{1 - \alpha_1} U^{-1}. \tag{III.8}$$

This coincides with the zero-gap relation in Figure 1 if $\beta_0 = 1$ in the latter, otherwise it is steeper than the curve shown in Figure 1.

For the steady-state trade-off relation to be vertical, it is sufficient that $\alpha_1 = 1$. Thus with $\alpha_1 = 1$, there is a natural unemployment rate at $U = \alpha_0/T$; no other unemployment rate can be maintained in the long run without either accelerating inflation or accelerating deflation. Even if $\alpha_1 = 1$, however, the short-run trade-off can still exist if $\beta_0 < 1$ in the short run. There is much empirical evidence which supports this requirement.[10]

But let us return to the accelerationist requirement that $\alpha_1 = 1$. It is argued by Friedman and others that (a) the term $\dot{P}$ in the wage equation should really measure the *expected* rate of inflation, that (b) the expected rate of inflation should be exactly the inflation premium demanded by labor, and (c) in the long run the expected rate of inflation should converge to the actual rate under any rational expectations mechanism. This would imply that α_1, at least in the long run, should approach unity if a fixed positive rate of inflation persisted. In other words, equation (III.8) might be a relevant "semi long-run" trade-off relation with $\alpha_1 < 1$. But as society becomes accustomed to some specific inflation rate corresponding to an unemployment rate less than $\alpha_0/\bar{T}$, α_1 would creep up toward unity. In the "super long-run" the trade-off would cease to exist. This is an attractive and powerful theoretical argument. But no growth situation ever seems likely to persist, unchanged, for long enough to be able to test such an argument.

---

[9] A tenable secular change in the wage share would have to result from changes in relative prices, the structure of production, and so on.

[10] See [1], [10], [14].

A related argument, which probably has much greater empirical relevance, is the threshold argument.[11] This argument states that the price coefficient α_1 in the wage equation is less than unity if unemployment and inflation are variable in the short run. But a long period of steadily declining unemployment—such as occurred between 1961 and 1969—will inevitably lead to an upward trend in the rate of inflation even though $\alpha_1 < 1$ (as illustrated by our discussion surrounding Figure 3). For a time labor may be satisfied to make up for too low an inflation premium in wage changes via the wage-gap variable, or some other similar lagged adjustment process. As the upward trend in ΔP persists however, a point is reached—a threshold—at which the trend of rising inflation gets built into expectations about the future and it becomes clear that the inflation premium can be collected sooner rather than later. From the point of view of our model this means a rising value for α_1. This will, of course, drive the rate of inflation even higher, thus reinforcing the expectations mechanism and, eventually, pushing α_1 to unity. At such a point the trade-off curve becomes vertical and no further decline in the unemployment rate is possible without ever-accelerating inflation. The threshold argument, even if correct, still leaves monetary and fiscal policy a good deal of leeway in attempting to steer the unemployment rate below the natural rate level without quickly producing a galloping inflation.

IV. THE EMPIRICAL RELATION

Our theoretical analysis suggests that if a steady-state trade-off relation exists—at least for the semi long run—it should look very much like the curve in Figure 1, assuming β_0 at least close to unity. During a period in which the unemployment rate undergoes a cycle, the observed rate of inflation should be less than that predicted by the steady-state curve in the early upswing stage, and should converge toward the steady-state curve as the upswing "ages." The ensuing downswing should be characterized by inflation rates above those predicted by the steady-state curve, but should move closer to the curve as the downswing "ages."

We can investigate the empirical accuracy of this scenario by calculating the steady-state trade-off relation implied by the wage-price-productivity sector of an actual econometric model. For this purpose we shall use the *Michigan Quarterly Econometric Model of the U.S. Economy* [11], generally known as the Michigan Model.[12] The steady-state relation was calculated by means of a computer simulation technique which ran the model for enough time periods to observe the equilibrium inflation rate implied by a chosen and maintained unemployment rate. Such a long period simulation was repeated for each of

---

[11] This is related to the findings of R. J. Gordon [7] who determined that α_1 is a variable coefficient which rises with the observed rate of inflation. Tobin [20] has presented a similar argument in which he assumes the existence of a "floor" (perhaps zero) for the rate of decline of the money wage rate in markets with an excess supply of labor. In markets with an excess demand for labor $\alpha_1 = 1$, i.e., there is a full inflation premium. As long as there exist some markets with an excess supply, the "average" value of α_1 will be less than unity for the economy as a whole. As economic expansion proceeds and the number of excess supply labor markets diminishes, the economywide value of α_1 rises. At some "critically low rate of unemployment" [20; p. 11] the economywide value of α_1 reaches (virtual) unity and the tradeoff ceases to exist.

[12] The Appendix to this paper contains the principal wage and price equations of the Michigan Model. The reader will note that these are highly elaborated versions of equations (II.3) and (II.4).

FIGURE 4

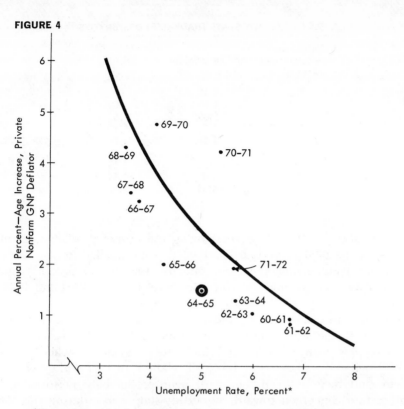

* Unemployment points plotted in the figure are unemployment rates for males 20 and over (*UM*) converted to aggregate unemployment rates (*U*) via the relation $UM = -1.129 + .935U$

a large number of unemployment rates to permit us to sketch the long-run trade-off relation. The result is shown in Figure 4.[13] According to this empirical trade-off relation, maintaining an unemployment rate of 4 percent leads eventually to an inflation rate of 4 percent as well. A 6 percent unemployment rate, if maintained, would be accompanied by an inflation rate of only 1.7 percent. Table 1 displays the steady-state trade-off possibilities implied by the Michigan Model. The last column of Table 1 displays the trade-off rate itself—the increase in the inflation rate per unit decline in the unemployment rate. The nonlinearity of the trade-off relation comes through most clearly. In the neighborhood of 6 percent unemployment, a drop of $1/10$ of one percentage point in the unemployment rate costs only about $7/100$ of a percentage point in the rate of inflation; in the neighborhood of 4 percent unemployment, a drop of $1/10$ of one percentage point in the unemployment rate costs $15/100$ of a percentage point in the rate of inflation.

---

[13] Each simulation forced the rate of growth of real GNP to a level which would maintain the desired unemployment rate; and the (annual) rate of growth of productivity was fixed at 3 percent throughout all simulations. For the purposes of the simulation it was assumed that consumer prices (the price variable in the wage equation) would rise at the same rate as the private non-farm GNP deflator (the variable explained by the main price equation of the model), which has in fact been the case, on the average, in the post-World War II period. Finally, the wage equation in the Michigan Model uses the unemployment rate for males 20 years of age and over. Figure 4 shows the relation between inflation and the aggregate unemployment rate by using an empirical regression equation to relate the aggregate unemployment rate to the male 20 and over rate.

TABLE 1   STEADY-STATE TRADE-OFF POSSIBILITIES

Aggregate Unemployment Rate (%), U	Annual Inflation Rate (%), ΔP	Trade-off Rate $\dfrac{\Delta(\Delta P)}{\Delta(U)}$
7.5	0.71	....
7.0	1.01	.60
6.5	1.35	.68
6.0	1.72	.74
5.5	2.13	.82
5.0	2.62	.98
4.5	3.21	1.18
4.0	3.95	1.48
3.5	4.93	1.97

Figure 4 is also a scatter diagram showing the observed inflation-unemployment points for the 1960–72 period. The circled point labelled "64–65," for example, shows the average unemployment rate for 1964–65 (5 percent) and the rate of increase of the private nonfarm price level between 1964 and 1965 (1½ percent).

In 1960–61, a recession period, the observed unemployment-inflation point was very close to the steady-state curve. From 1961 to 1966 the economy expanded, unemployment declined, and the rate of inflation—while rising—remained well below the steady-state trade-off relation. In 1967 real growth ceased very briefly and then resumed, but with poor productivity performance, and the inflation rate converged toward the steady-state curve during the 1966–69 period. When the economy weakened and unemployment rose after 1969, the inflation rate rose above that predicted by the steady-state curve, and indeed the 1969–70 inflation rate even exceeded that of 1968–69. By 1970–71 the inflation rate dropped a full percentage point as the unemployment rate rose sharply. But there was no evidence yet of a movement back toward the steady-state curve. The real wage rate and productivity growth were just beginning to improve in 1971 after the experience of large positive wage and productivity gaps in 1969 and 1970.[14] At that point, of course, in the closing months of 1971, Phases I and II of President Nixon's anti-inflation program came into being. In 1971–72 the economy's observed inflation-unemployment point was virtually back on the steady-state curve. It is difficult to imagine that the inflation situation would not have improved in 1971–72 in any case, given the direction in which the wage and productivity gaps had begun to move in 1971. But it would be equally difficult to deny the conjecture that the improvement in 1972 was substantially stronger than would have occurred without the change in Federal policy.

In summary, the results displayed in Figure 4 are strongly consistent with the theoretical analysis presented earlier. They suggest that the interactions between wages, prices and productivity as derived from the theoretical model of Section II provide a useful frame of reference for the analysis of the short-term trade-off between unemployment and inflation. Finally, the empirical evidence which we have just discussed lends support to the view that a meaningful trade-off between unemployment and inflation exists, at least for a period a good deal longer than any policy maker's short-run horizon.

---

[14] See for example, Appendix Table C-33 in *Economic Report of the President*, January 1973.

APPENDIX. WAGE AND PRICE EQUATIONS FROM THE MICHIGAN MODEL

Notation

CMH Compensation per man-hour, private nonfarm sector; index, 1967 = 100.
$CMHD$ Real compensation per man-hour; CMH deflated by PC.
GNP Gross national product; billions of 1958 dollars.
PC Personal consumption expenditures implicit deflator; index,
           1958 = 100.
$PPNF$ Private nonfarm GNP implicit deflator; 1958 = 100.
QMH Output per man-hour, private nonfarm sector; index, 1967 = 100.
u A regression residual used to correct for first order autocorrelation.
$UM\%$ Unemployment rate, males 20 and over; percent.

Compensation per Man Hour, Private Nonfarm Sector

$$\ln \frac{CMH}{CMH_{-2}} = \underset{(.002)}{.003} + \underset{(.160)}{.440} \ln \frac{PC_{-1}}{PC_{-3}} - \underset{(.091)}{.543} \left[\ln \left(\frac{CMHD_{-2}}{CMHD_{-6}} \right) - .032 \right]$$

$$+ \underset{(.010)}{.050} \left[\frac{2}{UM\%_{-1} + UM\%_{-2}} \right] - \underset{(.002)}{.005} \left[\frac{UM\%_{0-1} - UM\%_{0-3}}{2} \right] + \underset{(.123)}{.603} \; u_{-1}$$

$$\bar{R}^2 = .724 \qquad SEE = .0042 \qquad DW = 1.62$$

GNP Deflator, Private Nonfarm Sector

$$\Delta \ln PPNF = \underset{(.001)}{-.004} + \underset{(.100)}{.769} \sum_{i=1}^{4} \gamma_i \, \Delta \ln CMH_{-i}$$

$$- \underset{(.065)}{.077} \left[\sum_{i=1}^{4} \gamma_i \, \Delta \ln QMH_{-i} - .0079 \right]$$

$$+ \left[\underset{(.123)}{.222} - \underset{(.028)}{.055} \left(\frac{UM\%_{-1} + UM\%_{-2}}{2} \right) \right] \sum_{i=2}^{4} \beta_i \, \Delta \ln GNP_{-i}$$

Weights		
Lag	γ_i	β_i
1	0.4	0
2	0.3	0.25
3	0.2	0.30
4	0.1	0.45
sum	1.0	1.00

$$\bar{R}^2 = .645 \qquad SEE = .0024 \qquad DW = 1.79$$

REFERENCES

1. Eckstein, Otto and Fromm, Gary. "The Price Equation," *American Economic Review*, December 1968.
2. ———— and Wilson, Thomas A. "The Determinants of Money Wages in American Industry," *Quarterly Journal of Economics*, August 1962.
3. Fellner, William. "Phillips-Type Approach or Acceleration?," *Brookings Papers on Economic Activity*, 2:1971.

4. Friedman, Milton. "The Role of Monetary Policy," *American Economic Review*, March 1968.

5. Gordon, R. J. "The Recent Acceleration of Inflation and Its Lessons for the Future," *Brookings Papers on Economic Activity*, 1:1970.

6. _____. "Prices in 1970: The Horizontal Phillips Curve?," *Brookings Papers on Economic Activity*, 3:1970.

7. _____. "Wage-Price Controls and the Shifting Phillips Curve," *Brookings Papers on Economic Activity*, 2:1972.

8. Hickman, Bert G. (ed.). *Econometric Models of Cyclical Behavior*. Volumes 1 and 2, N.B.E.R., Columbia University Press, 1972.

9. Holt, Charles C., MacRae, C. D., Schweitzer, S. O., and Smith, R. E. "Manpower Proposals for Phase III," *Brookings Papers on Economic Activity*, 3:1971.

10. Hymans, Saul H. "Prices and Price Behavior in Three U.S. Econometric Models," in O. Eckstein (ed.), *The Econometrics of Price Determination*. Board of Governors of the Federal Reserve System, 1972.

11. _____, and Shapiro, Harold T. *The Michigan Quarterly Econometric Model of the U.S. Economy*, R.S.Q.E., The University of Michigan, 1973.

12. Lipsey, Richard G. "The Relation between Unemployment and the Rate of Change of Money Wage Rates in the United Kingdom, 1962–1957; A Further Analysis," *Economica*, February 1960.

13. Mortenson, Dale T. "A Theory of Wage and Employment Dynamics," in Phelps et al., *Microeconomic Foundations of Employment and Inflation Theory*. W. W. Norton, 1970.

14. Nordhaus, William D. "Recent Developments in Price Dynamics," in O. Eckstein (ed.), *The Econometrics of Price Determination*. Board of Governors of the Federal Reserve System, 1972.

15. Perry, George L. "The Determinants of Wage Rate Changes and the Inflation-Unemployment Trade-Off for the United States," *R. E. Studies*, August 1964.

16. _____. "Changing Labor Markets and Inflation," *Brookings Papers on Economic Activity*, 3:1970.

17. Phelps, Edmund S. "Phillips Curves, Expectations of Inflation and Optimal Unemployment over Time," *Economica*, August 1967.

18. Phillips, A. W. "The Relation between Unemployment and the Rate of Change of Money Wage Rates in the United Kingdom, 1962–1957," *Economica*, November 1958.

19. Pierson, S. Gail. "The Effect of Union Strength on the U.S. Phillips Curve," *American Economic Review*, June, 1968.

20. Tobin, James. "Inflation and Unemployment," *American Economic Review*, March 1972.

POLICIES TO LOWER THE PERMANENT RATE OF UNEMPLOYMENT*

Martin S. Feldstein

In its hearings on reducing unemployment, the Joint Economic Committee has emphasized the importance of lowering the permanent rate of unemployment from the high 4.5 percent average that has prevailed during the postwar period. At the committee's request, I have prepared a report that examines the sources of our current unemployment problem and the prospects for achieving a substantially lower rate of unemployment through specific public policies.[1] In the following remarks, I will concentrate on reviewing

* From *Reducing Unemployment to 2 Percent* (Hearings before the Joint Economic Committee, 92d Cong., 2d sess.) (Washington, D.C.: U.S. Government Printing Office, 1972), pp. 24–28. Reprinted by permission of the author. Martin S. Feldstein is Professor of Economics, Harvard University.

[1] *Lowering the Permanent Rate of Unemployment*, Joint Economic Committee, U.S. Congress, 1973.

the general conclusions and policy recommendations of that study. The specific details, the appropriate caveats and the technical analysis will
be found in the background report itself.

A BRIEF SUMMARY

My basic conclusions can be summarized
briefly:

First, I believe that we probably can lower
the permanent unemployment rate to a level substantially below the average of the postwar period
without inducing an unacceptable rate of inflation. An average unemployment rate significantly
less than three percent for those seeking permanent full-time employment, and possibly close
to two percent, is a realistic goal for the next
decade.

Second, the economy is not likely to achieve
such a goal, or indeed to perform any better
than it did in the past two decades, without
significant changes in employment policy.

Third, expansionary macroeconomic policy
cannot be relied upon to achieve the desired
reduction in unemployment. Any possible increase in aggregate demand that does not have
unacceptable effects on the rate of inflation would
leave a high residue of unemployment. I believe
that this is true even if one is very optimistic
about the possibility of increasing aggregate demand without accelerating the rate of inflation.
The structure of unemployment and the current
functioning of our labor markets imply a high
overall rate of unemployment even when the
labor market is extremely tight. Better management of aggregate demand has a role to play,
but it cannot do the entire job.

Fourth, lowering the overall rate of unemployment will require new types of policies aimed
at increasing the stability of employment among
young workers, at eliminating unnecessary seasonal and cyclical fluctuations in labor demand,
and at increasing the speed with which the unemployed return to work. Several such policies
are examined in the report and will be described
in this testimony. Let me stress again that lowering
the rate of unemployment in this way can be
achieved without creating inflationary pressures.

THE LIMITED EFFICACY OF INCREASING
DEMAND

Most macroeconomic analyses of unemployment are based on ideas about the causes and
structure of unemployment that are inappropriate

and out of date. The conventional view of postwar unemployment might be described as
follows: "the growth of demand for goods and
services does not always keep pace with the expansion of the labor force and the rise in output
per man. Firms therefore lay off employees and
fail to hire new members of the labor force at
a sufficient rate. The result is a pool of potential
workers who are unable to find jobs. Only policies
to increase the growth of demand can create
the jobs needed to absorb the unemployed."

This picture of a hard core of unemployed
workers who are not able to find jobs is an inaccurate description of our economy and a misleading basis for policy. A more accurate description
is an active labor market in which almost everyone who is out of work can find his usual type
of job in a relatively short time. The problem
is not that these jobs are unavailable but that
they are unattractive. Much of the unemployment
and even more of the lost manpower occurs
among individuals who find that the available
jobs are neither appealing in themselves nor re-
warding as pathways to better jobs in the future.
For such individuals, job attachment is weak,
quitting is common and periods without work
or active job seeking are frequent. The major
problem to be dealt with is not a chronic aggregate shortage of jobs but the instability of individual employment. Decreasing the overall rate of
unemployment requires not merely more jobs but
new incentives to encourage those who are out
of work to seek employment more actively and
those who are employed to remain at work. As
I shall explain below, an important part of these
incentives is a change in the kinds of jobs that
are available.

It is difficult to replace our old notions about
demand determined unemployment by this new
view. Let me therefore describe in more detail
some of the characteristics of American unemployment during the past decade. First, the typical duration of unemployment is quite short. Even
in a year like 1971 with a very high unemployment rate, 45 percent of those unemployed had
been out of work for less than five weeks. Second,
job losses account for less than half of total unemployment. In 1971, only 46 percent of the unemployed had lost their previous jobs. The remainder are those who voluntarily left their last jobs,
are reentering the labor force or never worked
before. Third, the turnover of jobs is extremely
high. Data collected from manufacturing estab-
lishments show that total accessions and separations have each exceeded 4 percent of the labor
force per month since 1960. Moreover, the num-

ber of quits has consistently exceeded layoffs during the past five years. Even with the high unemployment rate of 1971, more workers quit manufacturing jobs than were laid off.

This structure of unemployment implies that the long run unemployment rate probably cannot be reduced significantly below four percent by expansionary fiscal and monetary policies. A study of alternative policy simulations with an econometric model developed by Data Resources indicates that the overall rate of unemployment would remain high even in extremely tight labor markets that pushed the unemployment rate for mature men below historic lows. These conclusions are also supported by a detailed statistical examination of the relation between the unemployment rate for mature men and the unemployment rates in other demographic groups. For example, if increases in aggregate demand reduced the unemployment rate for men over 25 years old to only 1.5 percent—lower than we have ever seen in the postwar period—the rate for teenagers would probably remain over ten percent. More generally, the statistical analysis predicts that the overall unemployment rate would then be approximately 3.4 percent. In short, while there is currently a cyclical excess of unemployment, the long-run problem is not a lack of adequate demand.

UNEMPLOYMENT AMONG YOUNG WORKERS

Although the potential efficacy of macroeconomic policy in therefore very limited, the prospect for lowering unemployment without raising inflation by using specific employment policies is much more optimistic. In particular, substantial progress should be possible in dealing with the special problems of young workers. In 1971, male teenagers had an official unemployment rate of 16.7 percent, more than three times the rate for adults. In contrast, the teenage unemployment rate in Britain is absolutely very low and less than 50 percent higher than the adult rate.

Youth unemployment is not primarily due to inadequate demand. There are two main sources of the chronic high unemployment in this age range: (1) unnecessarily slow absorption of new entrants and (2) low job attachment among those at work. Because of the slow absorption, a very significant part of the unemployment of young workers is among new entrants to the labor force and others who are seeking their first full-time job. Among teenagers, new entrants contributed 6.7 percent to the unemployment rate; new en-

trants therefore accounted for 40 percent of total teenage unemployment. A special Youth Employment Service, firmly linked to the schools and primarily concerned with the transition from school to permanent employment, could have a major impact on unemployment in this group. I believe that the use of such a placement service has been of great value in Britain.

The problem of *unstable* employment among young workers is both more serious and more difficult to solve. Much of the unemployment among experienced young workers occurs not because jobs are unavailable but because they are unattractive. For many young workers, the available entry level jobs are also deadend jobs. They offer neither valuable training nor opportunities for significant advancement within the firm. Since employers have made no investment in these workers, they do not hesitate to lay them off whenever demand falls. Since comparable jobs are easy to find, these young workers do not hesitate to quit. The growth of our economy during the past few decades now permits relatively high wages even for those with entry level jobs. Among the young and single, these high wages encourage an increased demand for leisure. If the content of the job and the structure of the firm's employment policy do not outweigh this, job attachment will be weak and quit rates high.

The key to this problem is better on-the-job training and experience for young workers. Unfortunately, the current minimum wage law prevents many young people from accepting jobs with low pay but valuable experience. Those who come to the labor market with substantial skills and education need not be affected by the minimum wage. They are productive enough to permit employers to pay at least the minimum wage while also providing further training and opportunities for advancement. But for the disadvantaged young worker, with few skills and below average education, producing enough to earn the minimum wage is incompatible with the opportunity for adequate on-the-job learning. For this group, the minimum wage implies high short-run unemployment and the chronic poverty of a life of low wage jobs. Reducing the minimum wage for young workers might be useful but it would not be sufficient. A more effective policy would emphasize Youth Employment Scholarships that temporarily supplement earnings and allow young workers to "buy" better on-the-job training. The concept of Youth Employment Scholarships is developed further in the background report. An Employee Investment Tax Credit could provide specific incentives to employers to reduce turnover and to develop opportunities for internal advancement for these young workers.

SOURCES OF ADULT UNEMPLOYMENT

Better management of aggregate demand has a more important role to play in lowering adult unemployment than in improving the teenage employment situation. Nevertheless, even here macroeconomic policy can achieve only a small part of the total possible reduction in unemployment. The background study analyzes the implications of four different sources of adult unemployment: (1) the high cyclical and seasonal volatility of the demand for labor; (2) the weak labor force attachment of some groups of workers; (3) the particular problem of finding permanent employment for persons with very low skills and specific occupational handicaps; and (4) the unnecessarily long average duration of unemployment among job losers.

The American unemployment rate is not only higher than the rates observed in foreign countries but also much more cyclically volatile. A comparison with British postwar experience shows that most of the greater U.S. volatility reflects the more sensitive response of American unemployment to changes in aggregate demand. The seasonal variation in employment is also substantially greater in the United States than in Britain. This contrast in the cyclical and seasonal variation in labor demand is not well understood. It may reflect a number of institutional differences between the two countries. Within the American context, however, the current system of unemployment compensation is likely to increase substantially the extent of cyclical and seasonal unemployment.

Some of the adult unemployment that can be described as weak labor force attachment is actually desirable. The ability of married women and of older students to enter and leave the labor force is a positive feature of our economy. The really serious problems are associated with low skill workers. In this group, nonparticipation rates are much higher than unemployment rates. These non-participation rates have continued to increase during periods of rising wages and tightening labor markets. This indicates that expansionary macroeconomic policy is not likely to reduce the current high rates of voluntary unemployment. The solution lies instead in combining manpower policies that can improve the quality of available jobs with changes in our system of incentives to encourage workers to accept full-time employment in the jobs that are available.

There are more severe problems for some workers with major physical, psychological or mental handicaps. Because of their very low productivity, these workers cannot obtain permanent employment at the minimum wage that is currently established by law and custom. Two forms of job creation for these permanently disadvantaged workers have been suggested: subsidies to firms and direct permanent public employment. Both of these are examined in detail in the background paper. On the basis of this analysis I have concluded that if earnings in the subsidized employment are limited to the prevailing minimum wage and if the wage subsidy is attached to the individual rather than to the specific job, the system of wage subsidies would be a more effective and efficient method of dealing with the problem of the very low skilled worker. There is also a third possible option: integrating the minimum wage law with income maintenance policy. By including both the market wage and an appropriate fraction of the annual public income maintenance payment in the definition of the minimum wage, the administrative problems of direct wage subsidies to employers could be avoided while still permitting those with very low skills to find permanent employment. Such an integration of the minimum wage and income maintenance would reinforce the desirable features of a negative income tax.

The final source of our high adult unemployment rate is the unnecessarily long average duration of unemployment. An individual's delay in returning to work generally does not reflect an inability to find employment. Instead, the period of unemployment may involve searching for a better job, waiting to be recalled to a previous position without taking alternative temporary employment, or merely using the time for activities in the home.

IMPROVING THE INCENTIVE EFFECTS OF UNEMPLOYMENT COMPENSATION

Unfortunately, the current system of unemployment compensation encourages excessive delays in returning to work. For many lower and middle income families, the combined effect of unemployment compensation and personal taxes is to reduce greatly, and often almost eliminate completely, the cost of remaining unemployed for an additional one or two months. The background study shows that for most of the insured unemployed in Massachusetts the effective marginal tax rate on the wages earned by returning to work is probably over 80 percent. Moreover, the analysis developed there also demonstrates that it is not difficult to have a marginal rate over 100 percent; i.e., to receive a higher net income by remaining unemployed than by returning to work, especially in a family with two earners.

Our current unemployment compensation system also provides both employers and employees with the incentive to organize production in a way that increases the level of unemployment. It makes the seasonal and cyclical variation of employment too large and makes temporary jobs too common. These important adverse incentives arise because, for all types of unstable work, the unemployment compensation system raises the net wage to the employee relative to the net cost to the employer.

Statistical evidence supports the common observation that these disincentives have an important economic effect. Moreover, when the British introduced earnings related unemployment benefits in 1966, their unemployment increased substantially and the previous relation between unemployment and vacancies broke down.

The exact magnitude of the disincentive effect of our unemployment compensation system is unknown. It is clear, however, that even rather small changes in the duration of unemployment, the cyclical and seasonal fluctuation in labor demand, and the frequency of temporary jobs can have a very important cumulative effect on total unemployment. For example, a decrease of only two weeks in the current average duration of unemployment of three months would lower the overall unemployment rate by 0.75 percent. Estimates of the potential reductions in cyclical and seasonal unemployment suggest that the current unemployment compensation disincentives may increase the overall permanent unemployment rate by at least 1.25 percent.

The current system of unemployment compensation should be reformed in a way that strengthens its good features while reducing the harmful disincentive effects. Eliminating the maximum and minimum limits on the rate of employer contribution and taxing unemployment compensation

benefits in the same way as other earnings would substantially improve the incentive effects of the current system. A much more important reform could be achieved by shifting the basis of experience rating from the firm to the individual. This would have the advantage of making the individual consider properly the costs of a longer duration of unemployment and of a job with a greater risk of unemployment. The higher wages that would result for jobs with unstable employment would encourage employers to limit the seasonal and cyclical variations in labor demand. Because the switch to individual experience rating would significantly reduce the tendency to draw excessive benefits, it would be possible to strengthen the protection provided by unemployment compensation through raising the benefit rate and increasing the maximum level of benefits.

All of the analysis of the current study supports the conclusion that our permanent rate of unemployment can be lowered substantially without inducing an unacceptable rate of inflation. It is important to recognize, however, that macroeconomic policy is unlikely to lower the permanent rate of unemployment much below the 4.5 percent that has prevailed during the postwar period. Nevertheless, a series of specific policies could reduce the unemployment rate for those seeking permanent full-time employment to a level significantly below 3 percent and perhaps closer to 2 percent. Speeding the absorption of young workers into employment and stabilizing their employment through better on-the-job training could lower the overall unemployment rate by at least 0.5 percent. A restructuring of the unemployment compensation system could reduce the unemployment resulting from cyclical and seasonal instability and from unnecessarily long durations by an additional 1.25 percent or more. Further desirable reductions in unemployment could be achieved by subsidizing wages or incomes for handicapped workers and others with very low skills. There is, in short, no reason to allow the high average rate of unemployment that has prevailed in the postwar period to continue in the future.

SOME PROBLEMS OF PRICE INDEXES AND THE GAINS AND LOSSES FROM INFLATION*

Harold M. Levinson

Changes in the level of prices, as measured by the three major indexes, have now become an important basis upon which vital Government and private policy decisions are made. Monetary policy aimed at price stabilization may be considerably affected by monthly movements in the CPI or WPI;† similarly, wages affecting millions of employees are adjusted regularly on the basis of changes in the "cost of living," as reflected in the CPI, and many business purchase contracts, particularly for fixed capital assets, include provisions for escalation in line with the WPI or one of its segments. Society in general, as consumers, savers, or producers, makes decisions based upon past and anticipated movements in the price level. The nature of these decisions themselves, based upon past changes in price indexes, may have a profound effect on the future movements in prices.

A brief evaluation of the nature and limitations of these indexes is therefore necessary. The Consumer Price Index measures changes in the prices of a particular "market basket" of goods and services bought at retail by city wage earners and clerical workers, with the composition of that market basket determined by consumer spending patterns in 1951–52. By definition, therefore, it does not presume to represent all consuming units, though there is no obvious reason to believe it understates or overstates the movement of consumer prices to other persons in the economy—self-employed, nonurban, or extreme income groups.

The CPI, however, suffers from several important deficiencies, most of which are extremely difficult to deal with by precise statistical techniques. Perhaps the most serious problem is that of dealing with changes in quality, particularly in the services sector, which represents almost one-third of the total CPI. Since the basic unit of measurement is a fixed transaction—e.g., the price of a hospital room per day—no recognition is given to the fact that the quality of the good or service may be changed. Thus, for example,

the far greater effectiveness of modern diagnosis and treatment may effect a cure with many fewer hospital days. In the case of goods, changes in styling, improvements in design and durability, greater ease of operation, etc., may all occur with no change in price. On the presumption that over time, the quality of most goods and services will improve, an upward bias is introduced into the index—that is, it tends to overstate the actual cost to the consumer of (say) recovering from a sickness. Other examples come readily to mind. A particular tire at a constant price may yield a lower price per mile because of improvements in the quality of rubber; a man's suit at a constant price may yield longer wear because of improvements in the fabric; etc.

A similar problem arises from the use of fixed weights and the failure to take account of the introduction of new products which may be close substitutes for older and higher priced goods.[1] On both counts, current changes in the prices of a given "market basket" of goods tend to overstate current changes in the cost of living, or in the costs to the consumer of acquiring an equivalent level of satisfaction. Perhaps the most widely known situation of this type has occurred within the past year with the introduction of the smaller car by American automobile producers. For many uses, the new car represents an adequate and cheaper mode of transportation; its very introduction, in fact, was a reflection of consumer preferences for a more economical vehicle. Yet this important deflationary development finds no reflection in the current Consumer Price Index, even after the prices of these vehicles are introduced into the index under present techniques.

The Wholesale Price Index is subject to the same general qualifications, though it is designed to measure price changes for commodities as they enter markets at various levels in the productive process. Thus, for example, the price of steel enters into the index as a primary metal; it may affect the index again as part of the price of a fabricated metal part; and yet again as part of the price of a refrigerator. In addition, very difficult issues of quality enter into an evaluation

---

* From *Staff Report on Employment, Growth, and Price Levels* (Joint Economic Committee, 86th Cong., 1st sess., 1959), pp. 106–14. Reprinted by permission of the author. Harold M. Levinson is Professor of Economics, University of Michigan.

† Editor's Note: The CPI is the Consumer Price Index, while the WPI is the Wholesale Price Index.

[1] At the time of this writing, the base period used in the CPI was 7 years out of date; a revision is in process, however.

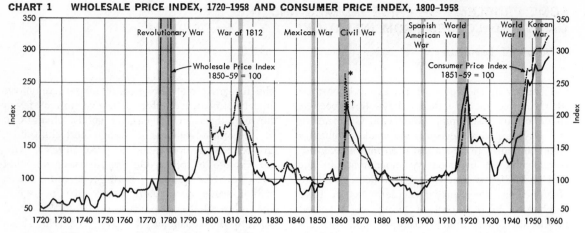

Source: Joint Economic Committee, *Study of Employment, Growth, and Price Levels* (Hearings, Part 2—Historical and Comparative Rates of Production, Productivity, and Prices, April, 1959), p. 394.
* Higher Index Cotton at prewar importance.
† Lower Index Cotton reduced in importance.

of improvements in metals, industrial machinery, and other goods. The index is also based upon constant weights which are revised about every 5 years. On balance, therefore, some degree of upward bias is probably involved.

It will be noted that one important segment of economic activity—Government—is not included in either the CPI or the WPI. Also, the direct costs of all types of construction—residential, commercial, and industrial—are not measured in either index. It is largely for this reason that the GNP deflator, which includes a measure of these sectors as well as those in the CPI and WPI, is considered to be the most widely representative price index available for the economy as a whole. Furthermore, its construction gives some greater recognition to current spending patterns. Nevertheless, most of the individual prices which go to make up the GNP deflator are taken from other sources, including the components of the CPI and WPI, and hence are subject to the qualifications regarding quality, new products, etc., already noted.

Two additional deficiencies, however, both of which result in an upward bias in the GNP deflator, relate to the Government and the construction components. The price index which is applied to the Government sector in constructing the GNP deflator is essentially a measure of changes in the cost of *inputs*—i.e., in the level of wages and salaries of Government employees—rather than a measure of changes in the price of Government *services rendered*. In other words, the Government price index does not take into account any rise in productivity of Government

employees. While the general nature of Government work may be such that increases in productivity are relatively low, there can be no doubt that improvements in data-handling equipment, accounting and office machinery, and others have resulted in very considerable reductions in the price of many services rendered by Government.

The index of "new construction" is also based largely on data provided by private trade organizations whose methods and reliability are not completely known. In an industry like construction, which is characterized by a high degree of specialization among subcontractors and in which many structures are unique, it is extremely difficult to obtain even a proximate measure of changes in productivity. Under these conditions, it is probable that private trade sources rely heavily on changes in wage rates and in building materials costs as a measure of "construction costs." If so, improvements in productivity will not be fully reflected in the construction price index and the GNP deflator is biased upward thereby.

Because of these deficiencies in the data, some observers have suggested that the apparent inflation since 1955 is more statistical than real. It is certainly very probable that the amount of inflation reflected in the indexes is overstated; it seems most unlikely, however, that the increase of 2 to 2½ percent per year since 1955 can be accounted for solely by this means. Furthermore, it must be recognized that at least some counterbalancing biases are probably present in the data; changes in quality are not always in an upward direction, nor are changes in styling always a net benefit to consumers. The problems of inflation, therefore, do not seem to be so easily assumed away.

What is strongly indicated, nevertheless, is that a considerably greater effort should be made by the BLS or other agencies to study and improve the design of these price indexes so that they would more accurately reflect quality and productivity changes and the introduction of new products. This is vitally important in the case of the CPI, which is widely publicized as reflecting changes in the cost of living and which is widely used as a basis for wage adjustments in collective bargaining and elsewhere. For this reason, a relatively small upward bias in the CPI can have secondary effects which in turn create further upward movements in costs and prices. Both the BLS and the Department of Commerce are, of course, fully cognizant of the problems discussed here and have done a great deal to overcome them. Many of the deficiencies still remaining, however, could certainly be reduced if funds and personnel were made available. The potential gains would be well worth the added costs.

THE GAINS AND LOSSES FROM INFLATION

To most individuals and families in society, inflation is much more than a distant and impersonal phenomenon. Its effects can be seen daily in the prices they must pay for the goods and services they buy. The severest effects of inflation, however, are found in the great burden it imposes on those persons whose incomes, for various reasons, do not rise in step with the increasing prices of the things they need. Among the groups who are most hurt are the aged, the sick, and those who must live on fixed incomes or on past savings. In effect, inflation robs these groups of their share in the distribution of income and reduces the real value of their wealth. In the following discussion, therefore, we will be concerned with the effects of the postwar inflation (1) on the distribution of income and (2) on the ownership of wealth.[2]

[2] This discussion draws heavily on several papers written in conjunction with the present study, particularly S. E. Harris, *The Incidence of Inflation: or Who Gets Hurt,* Study Paper No. 7; A. H. Conrad, *The Share of Wages and Salaries in Manufacturing Incomes,* 1947–56. Study Paper No. 9; and G. L. Bach, "How Important Is Price Stability in Stable Economic Growth," in *The Relationship of Prices to Economic Stability and Growth,* a compendium of papers submitted to the Joint Economic Committee, Mar. 31, 1958.

The Distribution of Income

As a payment for productive services rendered by their labor or their capital, people in society receive incomes in the form of wages, salaries, profits, interest, or rent. These people are then able in turn to utilize these incomes to purchase the goods they need or want from others. In this way, goods and services are continually being exchanged for money, and vice versa, in a never-ending flow.

Clearly, the ability of any individual to command a share of the goods produced will depend upon the price of his productive service (including the quantity of it he can sell) relative to the prices of the goods he wishes to buy. If inflation develops, so that all prices rise, the effects of that inflation on each individual's share of the income produced—i.e., on the distribution of income—will depend upon whether his income (price) rises more or less rapidly than prices he pays. And this, in turn, will depend upon a number of other considerations, including the presence or absence of long-term contractual commitments, the mobility of the suppliers of services, the degree to which custom plays a role in price setting, etc.

On this basis, it had usually been presumed that the major group which benefits from inflation is the profit recipient, since costs tend to lag behind prices during an upswing. Wage earners may also often gain since their payments are more flexible upward than those of fixed-income recipients. At the other extreme are those who earn interest and rent, whose payments are often fixed at contractual levels for long periods of time. Finally, there is a broad group of salaried workers, many of whose incomes are quite "sticky"—teachers, nurses, white-collar groups, etc.—and begin to move upward only with a considerable lag. If the inflation continues for long, however, even the fixed and sticky incomes are renegotiated and the continuing redistribution effects of the inflation tend to become considerably less.

These expectations have been only partially supported by the actual distribution of income trends during the postwar inflation. These trends, of course, may have been affected by other factors than the inflation. The major shifts in income shares since 1946 have been the following:

1. The share of national income going to all employees—a heterogeneous category which includes all types of wage and salaried workers, from a corporation's president to its janitor and from a schoolteacher to a lathe operator—rose

from about 65 to 69 percent. It is very probable that a portion of this increase was due to a change in the "product-mix," particularly the shift away from agriculture into services (which would shift many people out of the category of unincorporated businessmen into employees). This possibility is given support by the fact that within the manufacturing sector only, the wage and salary share remained quite stable throughout the period. A further portion is explained by the shift in the relative importance of Government employment, since income originating in this sector is 100 percent labor income.

2. By far the greatest loss has been suffered by unincorporated business, whose share was cut by almost 50 percent from 1947 to 1957. Here again, however, a large portion of this decline was a reflection of the drastic reduction in total farm income, due in part to the declining level of agricultural prices and in part to a sharp decline in the number of persons in agriculture.

3. For the entire period, the share of corporate profits before taxes declined very slightly. During the period, however, this share rose at the beginning of each inflationary upswing in 1947–48 and 1950–51. After the initial upsurge, the share again declined. Within the manufacturing sector alone, the corporate share remained quite stable.

In evaluating these trends in corporate profits, it must be noted that they are net of depreciation. If depreciation charges are included in the returns to corporations, their share shows no decline. To the extent that depreciation charges are based on historical rather than replacement costs, however, this share will be overstated.

4. The interest share rose slightly, while the rent share remained about the same. However, both of these shares had already declined very markedly during the war years and even in the late 1930s, largely as a result of Government monetary policies and wartime controls. The minor recovery of the postwar decade, therefore, is not surprising, and does not indicate that these shares did not suffer markedly. In fact, it is largely as a result of the declining share going to interest that the older people in society have suffered the most, since they are no longer in a position to provide a labor service and are dependent primarily on fixed incomes from savings accumulated in the past.

5. Within the broad employee group mentioned under item 1, above, various subgroups were affected very diversely. The most important lagging income groups were employees of governments, educational institutions, and religious and charitable organizations. In some instances, salaries of these groups lagged so greatly that their real incomes have actually declined over the past two decades.

Of greater importance as a measure of the unequal burden of inflation on individuals is the fact that it is primarily the incomes of older retired persons which have been most unresponsive to a rising price level. This arises, of course, from the fact that it is this group more than any other which must depend upon interest income, pensions, life insurance annuities, or other types of fixed income payments. Furthermore, older persons have little or no capacity or opportunity to supplement their incomes by active employment. By the same token, older persons who depend upon social security payments for their major source of support have been able to avoid serious reductions in their real standard of living only because of numerous upward revisions in the tax and benefit programs. *Continuing revisions of this type are essential if the burden of inflation on these groups is not to become severe.* The same is true, of course, for other recipients of social security benefits through unemployment insurance, workmen's compensation, etc.

Nor does the available evidence indicate that the period of inflation has seen any improvement in the share of income going to those families at the bottom end of the income scale. According to Lampman[3] "the lowest fifth of income receivers now get 5 percent of all income. It received 5 percent of income in 1947. It apparently received about 5 percent of income in the 1930s." Lampman also points out, however, that the income share of the top 5 percent of income receivers has been lowered considerably at the expense of a gain in the share of the upper middle income group. It is not clear, however, whether this redistribution is attributable solely, or even primarily, to the inflation. Data on the distribution of income by families are given in Table I.

The Distribution of Wealth

In addition to its effects on the distribution of current income, inflation brings about a redistribution in the ownership of wealth, measured by the net worth (the market value of assets less liabilities) of different households, business enterprises, or governments. As in the case of income, this redistribution is due to differences in price movements of various assets during and

[3] Robert J. Lampman, *The Low Income Population and Economic Growth,* Study Paper No. 12.

Quintile	Before Tax			1957		
	1935–36	1944	1954	Before Tax	After Tax	Average Income After Tax*
Lowest.....................	4.1	4.9	4.8	4.8	5.1	$1,428
2d.........................	9.2	10.9	11.1	11.3	11.8	3,290
3d.........................	14.1	16.2	16.4	16.3	16.8	4,690
4th........................	20.9	22.2	22.5	22.3	22.7	6,326
Highest...................	51.7	45.8	45.2	45.3	43.6	12,154
Total...................	100.0	100.0	100.0	100.0	100.0	......
Top 5 percent.............	26.5	20.7	20.3	20.2	18.2	20,279

* Federal individual income tax.
Source: *Survey of Current Business,* June 1956 and April 1959, and earlier studies of the staff of the National Income Division of the U.S. Department of Commerce.

under the influence of inflation. While the dollar value of monetary assets such as bank deposits, saving and loan shares, mortgages, Government and corporate bonds, life insurance contracts and claims under most pension and social insurance contracts remains unchanged, inflation commonly increases the price of equities and tangible assets such as common stock, real estate, producer and consumer durables and inventories. Obviously individual economic units or groups of them will profit to the extent that they hold price-sensitive rather than monetary assets; that the price-sensitive assets they hold increase in price; and that the assets they hold have been financed by borrowing which is payable in dollars. Because the share of price-sensitive assets in total assets held by different groups, the extent to which their price-sensitive assets increase in value, and their debt-to-asset ratios vary, they are differently affected by inflation.

From the end of 1939 to the end of 1959, the price of common stock has increased by about 350 percent. That of real estate, for which our information is much more deficient, has advanced by 200 to 250 percent. On the other hand, the cost of living has advanced during the same period only by approximately 110 percent. A household without debt holding all its assets in monetary form would therefore have suffered a decline of a little more than 50 percent in the purchasing power of its net worth, as the result of inflation. On the other hand, a household that had divided all its assets between real estate and common stock and had at the beginning of the period financed one-half of its total assets by borrowing, would at the end of the 20-year period not only have preserved intact the purchasing power of its net worth, but would actually have increased it by 60 percent.

The available statistics, defective as they are,

indicate that for most of the major sectors in the economy, monetary assets were either less than debt or not much in excess of debt, so that the purchasing power of their net worth has been little if at all damaged by inflation. This is the case, for instance, for nonfarm households, farmers, unincorporated business enterprises, corporate business, and State and local governments. All these sectors have owned enough assets that have advanced in price and have been sufficiently in debt to offset the losses in purchasing power suffered on their monetary assets. The Federal Government has on balance profited from the inflation since the purchasing power of its debt has been substantially reduced by the rise in prices.

While the inflation of the last two decades thus has not impaired the net worth of the major sectors of the economy or sharply changed the distribution of national wealth among them, there undoubtedly have been substantial groups of households, and also some groups of businesses, that have suffered an impairment in net worth as a result of inflation, though there are others who have benefited. On the basis of our information about the character of assets held by different groups of households, business, and governmental units, and about their debt-to-asset ratios, it is known, or at least it is very likely, that the main groups of households whose net worth has been impaired by inflation have been people in the older age groups and of modest income and wealth, particularly those that did not own their home. On the other hand, households with heads in their twenties or thirties, who often acquire homes and consumer durables on credit, and individuals in the upper wealth groups concentrating their assets in common stock, have actually seen the purchasing power of their net worth increased by the differential price movements accompanying the inflation of the last 20 years. Such increases have been particularly marked during the last 6 years during which the level of stock prices more than doubled while the cost of living increased by less than 10 percent.

The statistics available now are not sufficient to show in detail the effect that inflation has had on the purchasing power of the net worth of different groups of households, business enterprises, and governmental units, and on the distribution of total national wealth among them. They do suffice to show, however, that at least among individuals, the postwar inflation has increased the inequality in the distribution of wealth. It is estimated[4] that the share of the top percentile of wealthholders, that is, the one percent of individuals ranking highest if measured by total assets, which had fallen from 32 percent to 21 percent between 1922 and 1949, increased to 24 percent in 1953 and to 26 percent in 1956, the latest date for which such estimates can be

[4] R. J. Lampman, *Review of Economics and Statistics,* Vol. XLI (1959).

made. Because of the further sharp advance in stock prices in the last few years, it is likely that the share of the top 1 percent of wealth-holders has increased and by the end of 1959 may not be far from its level of 1922, if the calculation is made on the basis not of individuals but of families. Thus the postwar inflation appears to have reversed, at least for the time being, the trend toward a more equal distribution of personal wealth and to have restored inequality to approximately the level of the early 1920s.

The Volume of Real Output and Its Rate of Growth

Inflation may affect not only the distribution of output, but also the total available to be distributed. Inflation may lead to waste, to less saving, to a poor allocation of resources, etc. Conversely, a rising price level can raise investment and facilitate readjustments within the economy. In the United States there has been no clear relationshp between output and prices; we have experienced rising output in periods of both rising prices and declining prices; the precise relationship between them, therefore, is far from clear.

AN INCOMES POLICY FOR THE 1970s*

Gardner Ackley

I believe it a safe guess that wage-price policy will assume, in the 1970s, a position of coordinate importance with employment policy, both in the United States and in most other industrialized countries which rely on reasonably free markets. Committed, as they are, to the maintenance of "full employment," these economies will remain prone to a degree of intermittent and creeping inflation which, although modest by comparison with celebrated inflations of the past, will nevertheless be exceedingly visible. Even if the costs in economic terms of such inflation may be judged tolerable, I doubt that its costs in social and political terms will permit any government simply to ignore it, or to rely on policies that appear ineffective.

Today's endemic inflationary problem is obviously no simple phenomenon. Its "causes" surely

* From *Review of Economics and Statistics,* Vol. LIV (August 1972), pp. 218–23. (Cambridge, Mass.: Harvard University Press, copyright 1972 by the President and Fellows of Harvard College.) Gardner Ackley is Henry Carter Adams University Professor of Political Economy, The University of Michigan.

relate to fairly stable "structural" aspects of labor and product markets (of the sort analyzed by Phelps, Mortenson, Holt, Tobin et al.), the effects of which depend on the degree of resource utilization—which we can assume will usually be "high." Another important element is the dynamic mechanism through which current perceptions of price and income changes are generated from past events.[1] But in addition to these basically economic elements, the process involves major sociopsychological and political aspects.

My vision of the type of inflationary process which now concerns us sees it as essentially the

[1] I use the word "perceptions" rather than "expectations." There has been debate whether the inflationary process basically involves efforts to "catch up" with past changes, to "keep up" with other current changes, or to anticipate future changes. Since any systematic explanation of "expectations" derives only from past and present events, the argument makes no operational difference. But, in fact, what influences current decisions is a complex "perception" of an on-going process, involving past, present, and future values. The perception-generating mechanism may not only be nonlinear, but also quite unstable.

by-product of a struggle over income distribution, occurring in a society in which most sellers of goods and services possess some degree of market power over their own wages or prices (in money terms). The extent of each firm's or union's power at any given time is affected by structural and market factors; the manner in which that power is used is affected by perceptions of what is happening, and by political attitudes and social norms. Market power is used both in an attempt to increase real incomes, and, defensively, in an effort to protect real incomes from past and expected increases in production or purchase costs. An inflationary process can be tripped off in any of a number of ways. And, once it begins, most increases in wages and prices are basically defensive—made in an effort not to fall behind. Yet every defensive wage or price increase threatens the real incomes of other sectors, and prompts an endless chain of further defensive moves. Although some groups achieve relative gains and others experience loss of position during such a price-wage spiral, the main effect is simply to raise the entire level of prices and money incomes.

In my view, this model of an inflation-generating struggle to increase or protect income shares—although here grossly oversimplified—provides a substantially meaningful description of wage and price behavior in a modern industrial economy. But what is most significant is that the problem it describes appears to have become aggravated in recent years, as the social norms regulating group behavior have for various reasons become more tolerant of—or even now encourage—an increasingly aggressive use of market power. Moreover, there is an increasing sophistication of business and union leadership, along with better and prompter measurements of relative position—i.e., the perception-generating mechanism is altering. And recent experience with inflation has substantially heightened the sensitivity of most groups to actual or potential losses of relative position. For these reasons, there is a tendency to react more quickly, more fully, and frequently preemptively. The more prompt and complete are the defensive reactions to inflation, the faster is its rate—that is, the more there is to defend against.

Few would deny, I think, that society is becoming more sensitive to the existence of "inequities" or "injustices" in the distribution of income, and is therefore more supportive—or at least more tolerant—of efforts by "under-privileged" groups to improve their relative incomes, through political or economic action or both. But

when the market prices of products and productive services become weapons in a struggle over income shares, the underprivileged—who often possess little market power—are likely to lose out to the already favored groups. In the absence of new social instruments for resolving these problems, I am convinced that our society and economy remain subject to substantial inflationary pressures—particularly when at the same time we remain determined to maintain full employment,—i.e., labor markets and product markets strong enough that almost every group has some considerable degree of market power.

I conclude that the inflationary consequences of a struggle over income shares can only be controlled through the institution of an "incomes policy"—a system of direct restraints (i.e., more explicit and forceful social norms) limiting efforts to advance incomes through raising wages and prices. The pattern of these direct restraints can and should be systematically integrated with tax and other measures, so as together to guide the evolution of income shares in a manner which society judges to be fair and equitable.

Belief that an incomes policy is needed of course does not mean that *other* methods for the control of inflation can or should be neglected. Perhaps the single most important thing we can do to improve our control of inflation is to make more vigorous and timely use of fiscal and monetary policies to combat surges of aggregate demand that occur when the economy is already at or close to full employment. But inflation will not disappear merely by avoiding future mistakes of demand-management policy, of the kind we made in 1966–1968. Moreover, some policy mistakes are nearly unavoidable, and we should have other means to assure that mistakes will not be disastrous.

There are many structural changes which could reduce the inflationary bias in our economy. Many of the most important would be improvements of manpower policy, designed to make the labor supply more easily shiftable from one employer, one industry, one occupation, one region, to another. We should also work to eliminate a host of private practices and government policies which grew up or were adopted in an effort to protect one or another private interest in an era when full employment was neither a policy nor a reality. Today these create strong downward rigidities of particular wages and prices and unnecessary bottlenecks and immobilities at high employment. Some provide artificial support for the market power of particular groups. Others directly and unnecessarily raise costs. Unfortunately, it is a slow and politically difficult job to achieve each of these many changes. It is important to get ahead with this job, whatever else we do. But it will not solve the immediate problem.

Beyond this, there are, of course, possibilities for major changes in basic labor legislation and institutions, which would effectively reduce the market power of labor unions, and for direct limits on the size and/or market shares of giant corporations. Even if, on balance, desirable, these changes are not going to occur in the near future. In any case, I believe that the more practicable approach is not a head-on attack on the basic sources of market power, but is rather a limitation on the exercise of that power where it specifically contributes to inflation—and, for that matter, where its use collides with other important social objectives.

Elsewhere, I have considered at some length the possibility of a permanent system of compulsory wage and price controls, and have concluded that it would inevitably create distortions and inefficiencies of resource use so serious as to make the system undesirable and probably unworkable.[2] There is not space to repeat that argument. But there are other options for the design of a system of direct restraints. One would be to return essentially to the system of wage-price "guideposts" used by the Kennedy and Johnson Administrations. As is well known, the guideposts constituted a set of definitions of patterns of wage and price behavior which, if generally followed, would be consistent with efficient resource allocation, reasonable equity, and approximate stability of the overall price level. Adherence to the guideposts was voluntary; but the Government was prepared to—and frequently did—publicly criticize behavior which appeared to be inconsistent with the guideposts, and commend behavior which appeared consistent. It also propagandized generally about the importance and desirability of adherence to the guideposts, and frequently held private discussions with firms and unions in which it urged their specific adherence.[3]

Many critics—economists and others—asked how a system of purely voluntary standards and government appeals could cause *any* wage or price setter to accept a wage or price below that which would maximize net income. Is not the answer that, in collective bargaining and most industrial pricing, wage rates and prices are set not by impersonal market forces but rather by human (usually collective) decisions? The decision makers have room for judgment (or there would be no real decision). Over the relevant time horizon, they usually do not know even approximately what wage or price would maximize net income. They must and do settle questions by rule of thumb, comparison, or compromise; by considerations of equity, policy, or public appearance.

To the extent that the Government's arguments for restraint made sense to any of the participants in a decision; to the extent that some of the participants preferred to avoid or minimize public criticism; and to the extent that they believed the Government's appeals—*and their own decisions*—would affect *other* wage and price decisions, the guideposts clearly could and would have made some difference for their own decision.

To be sure, many professional mediators reported that the guideposts never appeared consciously to have entered anyone's thinking during wage bargaining which they observed in the 1960s. Interestingly, however, many unions professed to believe that the guideposts were influencing collective bargaining, and frequently and bitterly attacked the Government's policy. Moreover, 3.2 percent settlements came up much more frequently than they would have by chance alone. I believe that the guideposts did have some impact on wage decisions, primarily through influencing employers' bargaining positions, rather than by directly affecting union attitudes or aggressiveness, although I do not rule that out.

So far as prices are concerned I personally know that many significant price increases were either avoided or postponed, their size or their coverage reduced, or, in a fair number of cases that came to public attention, rolled back in full or in part. When, after 1965, the rate of unemployment fell progressively below 4 percent, it was not surprising that a voluntary system was unable to prevent an acceleration of wage and price increases. But, even then, I am convinced that it made an appreciable difference. The real question, of course, is whether the guideposts made *enough* difference. Could voluntary guideposts have survived as a viable system even if there had been a less serious mistake of fiscal

[2] See "The Future of Wage and Price Controls," *Atlanta Economic Review*, 22 (April 1972), pp. 24–33, and my "Statement" before the Joint Economic Committee, August 31, 1971, in *Hearings on the President's New Economic Program.* (Part 2, pp. 242–256).

[3] For a good review, see J. Sheahan, *The Wage-Price Guideposts* (Brookings, 1967). See also G. P. Shultz and R. Z. Aliber (eds.), *Guidelines: Informal Controls and the Market Place* (Chicago: Chicago University Press, 1966).

policy than the one actually made in 1966–1968? Before attempting to answer this question, let me first indicate some specific and, I believe remediable, weaknesses of the guidepost system of the 1960s.

(1) It seems to me undeniable that any successful stabilization system—whether described as "compulsory" or "voluntary"—demands the consent or at least the tolerance of those whose wages and prices are to be stabilized. For this consent to be forthcoming, those regulated—and the general public as well—must see the system as one that is basically fair and equitable, or, at least, that embodies sacrifices by "our side" roughly equivalent to those imposed on the "other side." Moreover, members of each group must believe that the restrictions its members accept on their freedom to do as they please will achieve something important—that slowing the rise in prices is a highly desirable objective, and that this system will be effective in achieving it.

In my view, this consent can only be secured through an active participation by the major groups in society—and particularly by the organizations of labor and business—in the process of recognizing the problem to which the policy is addressed, in planning the strategy to be used, and in formulating the basic standards. This was not the case for the guideposts. Rather, the guideposts were unilaterally promulgated by the Government, with no serious effort to involve the leadership of labor, business, and public opinion in the process. I know that many individual business and labor leaders did recognize the problem, and had sympathy for the approach used. Their active participation, even in an advisory role, could have made them assume some responsibility for the success of the guideposts, and surely would have given the policy somewhat greater "legitimacy" in the eyes of others. Moreover, Congress was never asked to consider the matter, so that the guideposts drew no legitimacy from the legislative branch of our political system.

(2) Administration of the policy in the Council of Economic Advisers, with the occasional involvement of the White House, had advantages. The prestige of the Presidency—whether exerted directly by the President or reflected through an agent known to have the President's confidence—was an important asset in securing adherence by business and labor. But the President's support for the steps needed to make the policy work had to be affected by broader political considerations. For example, a time when labor support was vitally needed for passage of a crucial element in the President's legislative program was not a good time for him or his personal representative to be exerting pressures for wage restraint against a strong union.

(3) The Government never made an adequate commitment of resources to the administration of the guidepost program. There were, at most, one to three staff members at the Council of Economic Advisers devoting some fraction of their time to guidepost activities, with occasional research assignments to others. It was thus impossible to anticipate more than the most obvious problems, or to provide the kinds of information and analysis needed to deal effectively with potential or actual cases of guidepost violation.

Moreover, the policy never had Government-wide support. Although Presidents Kennedy and Johnson gave it their clear backing, the Secretaries or other high officials of the Departments of Labor, Commerce, Interior, and others were often indifferent or hostile, as were relevant independent agencies, such as the Conciliation and Mediation Service, and the regulatory commissions.

(4) One basic problem was that although everyone knew when important wage questions were coming up for decision, there was no way fully to anticipate major price increase decisions and to bring to bear the relevant information, persuasion, and considerations of the public interest which the Government might wish the price setters to be exposed to at the time when it would do the most good. Clearly, it is far easier to prevent or delay or modify an inappropriate price increase before rather than after it has been publicly announced. At one point businesses were requested to notify the Council in advance of major price changes. Some did, and were willing to discuss them before their announcement, but most did not. Indeed, some price changes which previously would have been publicly announced now began to be heard about only second hand.

Even if the foregoing weaknesses of the guidepost policy had been avoided (as they perhaps are in the proposals made below), and even if there had been no serious mistake of fiscal policy in 1966–1968, the question remains whether a purely voluntary policy could have succeeded during a prolonged period of high employment, or whether a chain reaction of increasingly serious violations of the policy would not ultimately have destroyed it.

I do not think that the answer is clear-cut. Yet, as I review the experience and the current problem, I conclude that it might be unwise to take a chance on a purely voluntary system. Even if the policy can enlist the support of a substantial majority of the public and of the leaders of labor, business, and other interests, will there not always be a number of smaller firms and unions, and at least a few reasonably important ones, whose publicized and flagrant noncooperation may progressively erode the adherence of others? I wonder if—rather than overfull employment—it was not the clear desire of the leadership of the airline mechanics in 1966 to prove that they could successfully defy the Government—thereby encouraging other unions to do the same—that caused the wage guidepost to crumble. Indeed, the attempt to obtain adherence mainly through giving widespread publicity to violations may be a potentially self-destructive policy. The airline mechanics' case was inherently unimportant. It was only the union's rejection of repeated highly publicized efforts by President Johnson to secure their approximate cooperation that made the case important—and its outcome so destructive of cooperation by other unions.

Doubts about the validity of a system which lacks any means of effective enforcement against the occasional flagrant noncooperator lead me to conclude that the existence of a "big stick in the back of the closet"—seldom used, and the use of which is not entirely predictable—could mightily enhance the force of public opinion in deterring clear and deliberate violations of the standards, thereby making it easier for all others to give at least approximate adherence to the standards.

I come, thus, to my suggestions for a future system of longer-run wage and price restraints for the United States.[4] For want of a better name I will call this system the "Stabilization Agency." It would be created by legislation and responsible directly to the Congress.

1. The authority of the Stabilization Agency would be limited to the wages, fringe benefits, salaries, and executive compensation paid by employers who engage in significant collective bargaining, and to the prices of listed basic materials and of goods and services sold by the 1,500–2,000 largest corporations. However, all retail prices, rents, personal services, and farm prices would be excluded. On the price side, this means covering essentially the firms which make up "Tier I" in the present price control system, with a few exclusions and additions.

2. The Agency's legitimacy would derive, first, from its creation through legislation, and, second, from some formal arrangement for labor-management-public participation in the formulation and review of its basic principles and policies. A relatively small tripartite Board would have the basic "legislative" responsibility for formulating the Agency's wage and price standards and its procedures for intervention in particular cases. But a much larger body representing the principal interest groups and segments of public opinion would meet regularly to debate major policy statements and periodic reports on the Agency's activities, and might participate in the selection of the nonpublic members of the Board.

3. The executive functions would be performed by a full-time staff of several hundred professionals, headed by a single Administrator (appointed by the President), rather than by the tripartite Board.[5] He would be authorized to intervene, formally or informally, publicly or privately, in the determination of all wages and prices subject to the restraints. The Administrator would have legal authority to require that significant price and wage changes be reported in advance, to delay for limited periods the putting into effect of proposed changes while the Agency studied them, and to require submission of relevant information from firms, unions, and Government agencies. Based on its analysis of any case in which it chose to intervene, the Agency would have the authority to recommend specific changes of wages or prices privately to the parties or publicly to the country. It could also make appropriate recommendations on related matters to Federal, State, or local government agencies.

4. The Agency's standards would be widely publicized, explained, and adherence to them promoted. However, the standards would not need to be so simple or numerical that they could in all cases be easily self-applied either by those making decisions or by the public in judging the propriety of those decisions.

5. As a last resort, in particularly flagrant

---

[4] My own proposals resemble in many respects those recently made for Britain by E. H. Phelps Brown, a long-time student of British incomes policies, in "A Workable Incomes Policy for Great Britain," National Institute for Economic and Social Research (NIESR/SSRC Conference: Incomes Policy in Britain), January 3/4, 1972 (mimeo). Many of our similar proposals developed independently; but several of mine have been definitely influenced by his.

[5] My belief is that tripartite bodies will set and adhere to sounder principles and policies if they do not have the responsibility also for applying those principles and standards in specific and always difficult individual cases. However, others may argue that the only way to keep principles and standards realistically viable is through letting them evolve in the process of reviewing the tough cases, in a forum where the emotions, perceptions, and values of the interest-group representatives are directly represented.

or crucial cases, authority would be available to prohibit specific wage or price changes substantially inconsistent with the Agency's standards. The Administrator could apply to a special court set up for this purpose for an injunction, running for a specific period of time, up to (say) one year, against the charging by named firms of specific listed or described prices, or against the payment by named employers of specific wage rates. The request for injunction would have to demonstrate that the specific changes in prices or wages to be enjoined were clearly inconsistent with the Agency's standards for wages or prices, and that other workers or employers were, in general, voluntarily observing these standards. There would be no direct compulsory arbitration; but, in effect, the Agency (and the special court) could in crucial cases determine the highest wage level it would permit to be paid.

I believe that a system set up along these general lines could be reasonably effective in exercising an appropriate restraint on wage and price increases, and, assuming adequate support from fiscal and monetary, farm, import, and manpower policies, in keeping inflation under reasonable control. Since the basic adherence would be voluntary, the system could not insure absolute price stability, nor should it attempt to. But, in part for the same reason, I believe that it offers enough flexibility to permit the relative wage and price changes that are essential for efficient resource allocation. Of course, it may be expected that, sooner or later, there would be a breakdown of consensus and hence of the system. After an appropriate interval, and with new names, faces, and slogans, it will then have to be renegotiated.

Incomes policies attempt to assure that the income claims within their purview—along with the income claims left to other determination—

add up to roughly 100 percent of the total national income generated by current aggregate production, valued in current prices. But in this process, it is almost impossible to escape questions as to the *appropriate distribution* of aggregate income: as among wages, profits, farm and professional and interest incomes, and managerial compensation—and, within wage income—the appropriate differentials among various skills, occupations, industries, and regions. This distribution is only in part affected by the standards set in a wage and price policy; but it is also significantly affected by the Government's tax, regulatory, tariff, agricultural, minimum wage, social security, manpower, and other policies.

Many believe that the "consent" of the great economic interest groups—which, in the long run, is the only possible basis for a successful system of inflation control—can only be secured and maintained if the system of wage-price restraints is coordinated with the other tools of government policy in order quite consciously to promote a progressive *redistribution* of income in specific directions which society approves. Indeed, to the extent that the source of existing inflationary pressure lies in a fundamental dissatisfaction with the existing income-distribution on the part of one or more powerful groups, while other groups resist any significant change in that distribution, there can probably be no real "consent" to an incomes policy unless that policy is directed not only toward the total of incomes but as well to their relative size.

Others fear that mixing up such questions with the control of inflation simply guarantees the failure of an incomes policy. An explicit policy on income shares might be avoided at the beginning of an incomes policy. But I suspect that sooner or later it cannot be escaped.

chapter 2

COMMERCIAL BANKING AND FINANCIAL INTERMEDIARIES

The financial system of the United States is complex and highly developed. There are about 13,950 commercial banks—that is, banks which accept deposits subject to check. These banks range in size from the Bank of America in California, which has total deposits of some $30 billion, down to nearly 3,000 banks having less than $5 million of deposits. Somewhat less than half of the banks are members of the Federal Reserve System, but member banks hold a little over 75 percent of total deposits. Payment of interest on demand (checking) deposits is prohibited, but commercial banks also accept interest-bearing time and savings deposits. Thus, in addition to serving as administrators of the nation's payments system and the primary channel through which money—defined as demand deposits and currency—is injected into or withdrawn from the economy, commercial banks also form part of an elaborate system of savings institutions. In addition to commercial banks, these institutions include a network of savings and loan associations which provide savings facilities on a nationwide basis, mutual savings banks which operate in a few of the 50 states, and life insurance companies. Private pension and retirement systems, which invest funds set aside for employee retirement benefits by business concerns and state and local government units, have become an increasingly important element in the capital market in recent years.

Major borrowers include households which borrow on installment credit contracts for the purchase of automobiles and other consumer durable goods and on longer term mortgages for the purchase of houses; state and local government units which finance the construction of schools, highways, and streets, water and sewer facilities, and the like through the issuance of bonds; and the federal government, which at times borrows substantial sums to cover budget deficits. Private business enterprises commonly use internally generated funds—retained profits and depreciation allowances—to finance much of their investment in inventories and plant and equipment, but they are also heavy borrowers through loans and bond issues, particularly at times when economic activity is brisk.

There is a considerable amount of specialization on the part of financial institutions. The investment activity of savings and loan associations is largely confined to the acquisition of mortgages for the financing of housing construction. Mutual savings banks are also heavy participants in the mortgage market in the states in which they are located, although not quite to the same degree as savings and loan associations. Life insurance companies are important both as mortgage lenders and as suppliers of long-term financing for business enterprises. While commercial banks also play an important role in the mortgage market, they, together with individual investors, provide the most important market for the securities of state and local government units. In addition, commercial banks are the chief source of consumer installment credit, lending directly to households and also supplying funds to a large number of sales finance companies of widely varying size which specialize in consumer financing. Finally, commercial banks serve as the main source of loans to business firms, particularly the vast multitude of smaller enterprises.

The extent of competition in financial markets in the United States varies considerably, depending upon the type of borrower and his geographic location. For large business enterprises whose reputations are known throughout the country or throughout a major region, the alternative sources of funds available are numerous and the degree of competition is high. For the household desiring to borrow on an installment loan or a mortgage, the situation varies from one city or community to another, but there is frequently a considerable amount of competition involving commercial banks, savings and loan associations, local agents of life insurance companies, and sales finance companies. The smaller business enterprise, on the other hand, is frequently limited in its source of loan funds to commercial banks located in its immediate vicinity, and these local banking markets are frequently rather concentrated. The geographical area within which a particular commercial bank is permitted to operate varies greatly from one part of the country to another. In some states, notably California, commercial banks are allowed to establish branches throughout the state. In a few states, branch banking is completely prohibited, while, in the majority of states, branches are permitted but on less than a statewide basis.

Since Federal Reserve policy works, in the first instance, primarily by controlling the supply of cash reserves available to the commercial banks, the responses of the banks to changes in the amount of reserves available to them are clearly a very important part of the mechanism by which the effects of monetary policy are transmitted to the economy. The paper by G. Walter Woodworth discusses the ways in which banks make the adjustments required by changes in reserve availability. Suppose, for example, that customers' loan demands are increasing at a time when the Federal Reserve, desiring to restrain inflationary pressure, is supplying no additional reserves to the banking system through open market operations. There are two kinds of adjustments banks can make to accommodate their customers' requirements for funds in such a situation: they can reduce other types of assets to obtain funds to lend, or they can attract additional funds by increasing their liabilities. Asset adjustments would include reduction of excess cash reserves and sales of U.S. government or other securities out of existing portfolios. Liability adjustments would include borrowing excess reserves from other banks through the federal funds market, borrowing from the Federal Reserve banks, selling new securities in the capital markets, taking measures to attract more deposits, and borrowing from abroad through the so-called "Euro-dollar market." During the 1950s, banks usually made such adjustments primarily by selling U.S. government securities from their portfolios. More recently, however, as Woodworth explains, the emphasis, especially in the case of the large money-market banks in New York and other major cities, has shifted rather dramatically toward "liability management." When such banks need to obtain additional funds for lending, they now commonly attempt to attract them by offering higher interest rates on negotiable time certificates of deposits (C/D's). Alternatively, if the interest rate ceilings on such deposits under the Federal Reserve's Regulation Q prevent the banks from raising rates sufficiently to obtain C/D funds, they may attempt to meet their needs by borrowing in the Euro-dollar market. The role of each of these adjustments is assessed by Woodworth.

Most of the adjustments referred to above will serve to transmit the effects of monetary policy beyond the commercial banks to the capital markets and other financial institutions. For example, bank sales of U.S. government securities will depress the prices of these securities and raise their yields. Since C/D's compete against short-term securities, increases in the interest rates offered on C/D's will exert upward pressure on other short-term interest rates. As banks have to incur higher costs to obtain funds for lending, they will raise interest rates charged on loans and, in some instances, also tighten lending standards, thereby making funds less readily available to borrowers.

The paper by Daniel H. Brill with Ann P. Ulrey surveys the development of financial institutions in the United States in recent years. The article makes a useful distinction between "contractual intermediaries"—so-called because their inflows of funds are mainly governed by contractual arrangements that are infrequently changed—and "depository intermediaries." Contractual intermediaries include mainly life insurance companies, corporate pension funds, and the retirement systems of state and local governments. The chief types of depository intermediaries are commercial banks, savings and loan associations, and mutual savings banks. The article discusses the operations of these various types of financial institutions, including their investment policies, and assesses the costs and benefits to the economy of the kinds of intermediation they provide.

According to the traditional view which was almost universally accepted until recently, commercial banks possess the power to create money on the basis of cash reserves and in the process to expand credit in the form of loans and investments, while other financial institutions—so-called intermediaries such as savings banks and savings and loan associations—serve only to collect the savings of the public and channel them into investment. This view of the financial system was first challenged by John G. Gurley and Edward S. Shaw. A portion of one of their papers on financial intermediaries is reprinted here. In their view banks are unique among financial institutions in their ability to create demand deposits, which are used as means of payment and therefore constitute the major portion of the money supply. But other institutions likewise have the unique ability to create the particular kinds of financial claims that are their specialty—such as savings and loan shares in the case of savings and loan associations—and they all share with banks the ability to expand credit in the form of loans and investments. A similar view is expressed in the article by James Tobin.

Those who hold this view that so-called financial intermediaries other than commercial banks share with banks the ability to create credit are generally of the opinion that these institutions should be subjected to controls—such as reserve requirements—similar to those that are applied to banks. If they are not controlled, it is said that their credit expansion will tend to accelerate when the banks are being restrained by Federal Reserve policies, with the result that the effectiveness of monetary policy in controlling credit will be weakened.

In trying to decide which point of view to accept, the student should be aware of a number of important considerations. First, while it is true that financial intermediaries can create credit, the nature of the process is different from that of commercial banks. Aside from their ability to attract deposits from banks, which will be discussed below, intermediaries depend heavily on flows of savings for new funds. Income is created by production; some of it is saved, and part of the saving takes the form of deposits at intermediaries, making new loanable funds available (on the assumption that the saver's alternative is to hoard the funds as idle cash balances). The spending generated by this round of income creation (partly financed by intermediary loans) induces new production, income, and saving, some of which flows into intermediaries, and so on. The time period associated with a round of income generation and the associated expansion of loanable funds through intermediaries is at least several months in length. By contrast, when new funds flow into the commercial banking system, new loans are created, and the associated deposits typically are checked away, only to reappear in a few days at another bank which then is able to expand credit, and so on. The two cases are different because the commercial banks manage the payments system and can expand loans essentially as fast as funds can be transferred from bank to bank by check, whereas the financial intermediaries depend on the income-generation process and conscious acts of saving for their flows of funds.

When financial intermediaries are viewed strictly as collectors and processors of savings, the above implies that their credit-creating effects may be more of a long-run than a short-run phenomenon. In terms of trend effects, there is indeed no question but what the growth of financial intermediaries has resulted in more credit being available at better terms than would be the case if there were no intermediaries. The reasons for this are explained in detail in the readings by Gurley and Shaw and by Tobin.

In the shorter run, however, intermediaries may be able to increase the total amount of credit available in another way; namely, by collecting idle cash balances and putting them to work. In a period of accelerating economic activity accompanied by monetary restraint, for instance, the yields on market securities will begin to rise, enabling financial intermediaries to increase the interest rates they pay to depositors. This may induce some holders of idle checking deposits at commercial banks to exchange them for deposits in intermediaries. Financial intermediaries typically are not subject to legal reserve requirements, and usually hold only a small amount of reserves relative to deposits. Because of the difference in reserve requirements, the intermediary is able to make a new loan of an amount depending on the reserve ratio it customarily observes (if the intermediary holds no reserves, and if there are no cash drains, and so on, then the loan can be of an amount equal to the deposits it has attracted). What has happened, in effect, is that the intermediary has mobilized an idle cash balance and converted it into an active balance by raising the rate it pays on its deposits. The student may wonder whether the idle balance would not have been mobilized if the intermediary did not exist, or did not raise its rates, through purchase by the owner of the balance of one of the market securities whose yields have risen. The answer is: very likely not; the cashholder was induced to exchange his funds for the intermediary deposit partly because he considered that deposit to be a very close substitute for money, whereas securities he could have bought in the market, such as government or industrial bonds, are much less moneylike.

While there is no question that intermediaries are capable of causing such cyclical deposit shifts and increasing the supply of credit in the face of monetary restraint, there is not much evidence that they do so. The exception seems to have been commercial banks themselves, whose time and savings deposit operations essentially function as financial intermediaries. By aggressive sales of certificates of deposit in times of restraint, for example, commercial banks have been able to attract considerable amounts of funds from other intermediaries as well as mobilizing idle balances in the banking system itself. Because reserve requirements for commercial bank time deposits are of the same order of magnitude as the cash ratios observed by intermediaries, the effects of shifts from intermediary to bank time deposits will mainly be on the allocation rather than the total volume of credit. In particular, intermediaries channel large quantities of funds into new housing construction, while banks devote much of their resources to commercial loans. Largely as a consequence of such changes in credit allocation, the housing industry has often been starved for funds while the rest of the economy is expanding. Several innovations designed to remedy this situation are discussed in Warren L. Smith's paper on government intermediaries and residential mortgage markets in Chapter 5. At other times, commercial banks have sold off government security holdings when demands for credit were high. The resulting increases in market yields have at times been adequate to cause idle balance holders to exchange these balances for bonds; these deposits then in effect were channeled (through the medium of new loans) to those anxious to borrow in order to purchase goods and services.

One of the questions raised by Tobin is whether banks can create money, an interesting parallel to the question discussed above of whether intermediaries can supply new loanable funds. In considering Tobin's arguments, it should be noted that his analysis, as well as that of Gurley and Shaw, is essentially static in character, describing the ultimate equilibrium that will be reached after all adjustments have been completed. He points out that while an injection of reserves into the banking system may generate a deposit-expansion process of the kind described in money and banking texts, ultimately the new deposits will disappear unless assetholders can be persuaded to hold them. In other words, they are like any other asset (such as claims against financial intermediaries, for example) in that they will be held if their yield is attractive relative to other asset yields. Since banks are prohibited by law from paying interest on demand deposits, the yields on other assets must be lowered if there is to be a permanent increase in the money stock. In contrast to Tobin's focus on initial and final equilibrium positions, the typical discussion of bank deposit expansion attempts to explain, at least in a rough-and-ready way, the dynamic sequence of adjustments which will occur during the process of equilibration. If some of the time lags are relatively long, as seems likely, the dynamic sequence of events may be quite important, even though the ultimate equilibrium reached may be that described by Gurley and Shaw and by Tobin.

It should also be noted that in the last several years, interest rates on time deposits and savings and loan shares have risen substantially, and the investing public has become more sensitive and sophisticated in shifting funds among deposits, shares, and open-market securities in response to changes in the relative returns on these alternative forms of financial assets. As a consequence, shifts of funds among these uses have become more significant, and management of interest rate ceilings of the Regulation Q type, which may either encourage or impede such shifts, has taken on greater importance as an instrument of monetary policy. The significance of these matters for the impact of monetary policy on homebuilding activity is especially great since, as we have mentioned, homebuilding relies heavily on savings and loan associations and mutual savings banks for its financing through mortgage loans. Smith's paper in Chapter 5 on residential mortgage markets discusses in some detail the effects on home-building of these institutional arrangements.

COMMERCIAL BANK LIQUIDITY MANAGEMENT*

G. Walter Woodworth

I. OVER-ALL LIQUIDITY MANAGEMENT

Basically, commercial bank management involves administration of a continuous flow of funds into and out of the bank. The predominant source of funds is deposits, but funds are also obtained by borrowing and by the increase of capital accounts. Deposits and reserve money flow to a bank from many sources, including repayment of loans, sale or maturity of investments, inflow of currency, gains of deposits from other banks, and purchases of securities by the Federal Reserve Banks. After providing for proper physical facilities, management of the outflow of funds involves: (1) holding cash assets to meet legal requirements and working cash liquidity needs; (2) holding enough short-term U.S. securities and other liquidity reserves to meet the excess of fund outflows over inflows that is probable from month-to-month and during the cyclical swings of economic activity; (3) making credit-worthy loans to businesses, consumers and governments in the area served; and (4) investing the remaining funds in appropriate open-market obligations. Net profits accrue to the extent that gross income from loans, investments, and other services exceed the cost of acquiring funds (mostly deposits) and of providing the services.

The problem of holding the proper amount of cash assets—currency, balances with other banks, and legal reserves—is an important one.

* From G. Walter Woodworth, *The Management of Cyclical Liquidity of Commercial Banks* (Boston: The Bankers Publishing Co., 1967), pp. 1–7 and 20–48 (with minor revisions). Reprinted by permission of the publisher and the author. G. Walter Woodworth is Professor Emeritus of Finance and Banking, The Amos Tuck School of Business Administration, Dartmouth College.

Since these are non-earning assets, they should obviously be kept at the minimum from day-to-day consistent with smooth and efficient operations. Similarly, short-term liquidity reserves should be systematically adapted to meet regularly recurring seasonal variations in deposits and loans. These problems of short-term liquidity have many facets, including the management of vault cash, balances with correspondent banks, check clearings and collections, operations in the Federal funds market, and borrowings at the Federal Reserve Bank. They require alert and systematic administration, but in general they are largely mechanical and readily manageable.

In contrast with the administration of short-term liquidity requirements, the problem of managing cyclical liquidity is an exceedingly complex and difficult one. Faulty judgment and wrong decisions in this area have major consequences over several years. How large should holdings of liquidity reserves be at a given point in time to meet the possible drain on reserves during the next cyclical downturn, or during the next phase of cyclical expansion? If unnecessarily large reserves are maintained, the bank sacrifices earning power and competitive growth. On the other hand, if liquidity (secondary) reserves are well below a reasonable level because of investment in intermediate- and long-term securities, the penalties may be heavy, even disastrous. That is, the larger current earnings realized may be exceeded severalfold by the subsequent capital losses sustained if the securities must be sold to meet customer loan requirements during a period of economic expansion. The present study is concerned with these problems of cyclical liquidity management, and only incidentally with shorter-term liquidity.

	Dec. 31, 1960	Dec. 31, 1965
U.S. Treasury bills..	6,402	9,441
U.S. Certificates of Indebtedness................................	2,296	
U.S. notes maturing in 1 yr. or less.............................	7,943*	5,325
U.S. bonds maturing in 1 yr. or less.............................	2,094†	1,713
Federal agency securities maturing in 1 yr. or less.............		2,128
Obligations of States and subdivisions (⅕ of total).............	2,828	6,518
Corporate bonds and notes (⅕ of total)........................	381	243
Bankers' acceptances (⅔ of total)...............................	1,352	2,262
Commercial paper, dealer-placed (⅓ of total outstanding).......	448	634
Finance company paper, directly placed (⅓ of total outstanding)..	1,036	2,369
Loans to security brokers and dealers (½ of total).............	1,562	2,458
Total maturing in 1 yr. or less............................	26,342	33,091
U.S. securities maturing in 1 to 5 yrs...........................	22,922	17,720
Total maturing in 5 yrs. or less..........................	49,264	50,811
Proportion maturing in 1 yr. or less to total assets (%).........	12.2	10.6
Proportion maturing in 5 yrs. or less to total assets............	22.7	16.2

    * Estimated at 52.7 per cent of total notes (1965 proportion).
    † Estimated at 11.7 per cent of bonds maturing in 5 years or less (1965 proportion).
    Sources: *Member Bank Call Report*, Dec. 31, 1960, p. 6; *Summary Report of Member Banks*, Dec. 31, 1965, p. 4; *Federal Reserve Bulletin*, July, 1966, p. 1012.

II. LIQUIDITY RESERVE ASSETS

Liquidity reserves may be defined as those earning assets which may be readily converted to money during a reserve deficiency period without appreciable capital loss. Assets which meet these qualifications include the following:

U.S. Treasury marketable obligations maturing preferably within one year but in not over five years

U.S. Government agency obligations maturing within one year

Prime bankers' acceptances

Prime open market commercial paper

Prime finance company paper placed directly

Call loans to large U.S. security dealers

High-grade marketable obligations of State and local governments, and of corporations, maturing within one year

A more concrete view of liquidity reserves is given by Table 1 which presents the estimated amounts of these items of member banks at the end of 1960 and 1965. Obligations maturing in one year or less totalled $26.3 billion, or 12.2 percent of total assets at the end of 1960 and $33.1 billion, or 10.6 percent at the end of 1965. If marketable U.S. securities maturing in 1 to 5 years are included, the amounts become $49.3 billion and $50.8 billion, respectively, and the proportions become 22.7 percent and 16.2 percent.[1] Table 1 also shows the preponderance of

U.S. securities in the secondary reserve category—71.1 percent of such assets maturing in one year or less in 1960, and 56.2 percent in 1965. Obligations of States and political subdivisions notably increased in importance. In addition, there was a significant decline in over-all asset liquidity between the two years as measured by these ratios.

Where the maturity line should be drawn for inclusion of U.S. securities in the liquidity reserve category is a controversial question and a matter of judgment. If depression conditions are contemplated a good case can be made for including all maturities of U.S. securities, since their prices typically rise along with the decline of interest rates and they can be sold at a profit if reserve money is needed. But if conditions of economic expansion are in mind the line should be drawn somewhere between three and five years. The average length of the three recovery periods in the 1949–1960 span was 34 months. The shortest, 1958–1960, was 25 months, and the longest 1949–1953, was 43 months. But the present expansion, 1961–1966, has already lasted 69 months as of November and appears to be destined to proceed at least several more months. Hence, perhaps a workable maturity line may be drawn at about five years. Then after the passage of three years the five-year issues have moved to

---

[1] Since member banks accounted for 82.2 percent of the earning assets of all commercial banks at the

end of 1965, the totals for the banking system may be estimated, as follows: maturing in 1 year or less—in 1960, $32 billion; in 1965, $40.3 billion; maturing in 5 years or less—in 1960, $59.9 billion; in 1965, $61.8 billion.

two years and the four-year issues to one year. In the event of forced sale at the end of three years, the capital losses on one-year and two-year obligations would not be serious.

Liquidity reserves may be converted to reserve money either by redemption at maturity or by sale in the money market. Bankers usually prefer to rely most heavily on the former method by arranging the flow of maturities to correspond with variations in reserve needs. Efficient bankers also strive to hold no more liquidity reserves than are needed since yields are usually higher on other earning assets, and since growth of their bank is closely associated with the expansion of customer loans.

III. BANK LOAN LIQUIDITY

When a bank increases the amount of loans, it is usually taking a step toward a less liquid position, since it shortly parts with reserve money and holds instead the largely non-marketable promissory notes of customers. This fact has led many bankers and other observers to the erroneous conclusion that there is little usable liquidity in the loan account. Actually, the typical bank can count on a continuous inflow of funds from loan repayments in the normal course of business. The size and stability of this inflow depends on the quality of borrowers, types of loans, and the extent to which repayments are on an installment basis. When the flow of repayments exceeds the flow of new loans, reserve money accumulates. When repayments just equal new loans, the reserve position is not affected. But if repayments are less than new loans, the reserve position deteriorates. From this it follows that the loan account provides substantial liquidity to meet deposit withdrawals during periods of business decline when the rate of loan repayment rises and customer loan requirements subside. But the point should be underscored that the loan account uses up liquidity, instead of providing it, during periods of business expansion when loan demands are strong. In aggregate, gross extensions of loans exceed gross repayments.

IV. INVESTMENT LIQUIDITY

A considerable degree of liquidity also attaches to the typical bank investment portfolio which may be defined for the present purpose to include securities with maturities exceeding five years. Since most of these securities are high-grade, marketable issues, the question arises: Why is it not reasonable for a bank to depend on them to meet liquidity needs? The answer is that price changes of these securities are considerably wider than those of short-term issues. Also, in the case of municipal and corporate issues, the credit risk is greater. Hence, the sale of intermediate- and long-term securities may involve a substantial capital loss, especially if most banks are selling at the same time. However, at times it may be advantageous to sell securities from the investment account instead of from secondary reserves. This may be the case, for example, during a period of low interest rates when bond prices are high—a condition usually present during recessions. In addition to realization of a profit, there is often an income tax motive for such sales. But most banks then have no need to sell for liquidity reasons since normal loan liquidation usually provides funds to meet a possible reduction of deposits. Nevertheless, the banker can reasonably count on his bond account for substantial liquidity protection against the contingency of deposit withdrawals during recessions.

But while the investment account provides substantial liquidity protection against the contingency of deposit withdrawals during recessions it should not be depended on at all to meet expanding loan demands during periods of business expansion. Interest rates are likely to be rising and high, and bond prices to be declining and low at such times. Hence, conversion of bonds to reserve money involves a considerable capital loss. Despite this fact, under some circumstances it may be advantageous to reduce longer-term holdings rather than liquidity reserves during the expansion phase of the cycle. If a material rise of interest rates is expected, longer-term issues may be sold, even at a capital loss, to avoid pressure sales later or to meet growing loan demands. But this circumstance arises only when inadequate liquidity reserves were provided in the first place. That is, such action would be taken only as a means of minimizing capital losses that loom on the horizon because of a previous error in liquidity policy.

V. LIABILITIES MANAGEMENT

During the 1960s a new theory of cyclical bank liquidity emerged, which may be labelled the "liabilities management theory." While asset management to achieve liquidity was not discarded, the emphasis shifted markedly toward liability management, especially in the large city banks.

According to this new doctrine, it is unnecessary to observe traditional standards in regard to self-liquidating loans and liquidity reserves, since reserve money can be borrowed or "bought" in the money market whenever a bank experiences a reserve deficiency. There are seven possible sources from which the individual bank may acquire reserves by the creation of additional liabilities: (1) acquisition of demand deposits; (2) issuance of time certificates of deposit; (3) purchase (borrowing) of Federal funds; (4) borrowing at the Federal Reserve Bank; (5) issuance of short-term notes; (6) raising capital funds from the sale of capital notes, preferred stock, or common stock, or from retained earnings; and (7) the Eurodollar market. Each of these sources requires additional comment.

1. Acquisition of Demand Deposits

The acquisition of demand deposits as a means of meeting liquidity needs during the last phase of cyclical expansion periods may be summarily dismissed. It might have been included before 1933 when banks were free to pay whatever rates they wished in bidding for demand deposits. But the Banking Act of 1933 prohibited such interest payments, and removal of this restriction does not seem probable in the near future, if ever. Moreover, even if banks were free to pay interest, there has been a definite tendency for total demand deposits to decline during the last half of cyclical expansion periods, largely in response to the tight rein of Federal Reserve policy. In this setting the average individual bank must, of course, lose deposits rather than gain them. A bank that increases demand deposits must draw them competitively from a smaller total reservoir by aggressive promotion and by effective enforcement of balance requirements. The competitive redistribution of existing demand deposits among banks is a continuous process, with some gaining and others losing. Management cannot count on opening this valve when funds are needed to meet cyclical loan demands.

2. Issuance of Time Certificates of Deposit

The predominant liability source of reserve money for the individual bank since the early 1960s has been issuance of time certificates of deposit, mainly in the form of negotiable certificates (CD's). The negotiable certificate market was launched in early 1961 by the large money-market banks of New York City, mainly as a means of attracting deposits of large corporations. Prior to this time New York City banks paid no interest on corporate time deposits as a matter of policy. But during the first quarter of 1961 they began to offer negotiable certificates with original maturities ranging between 90 days and one year at rates competitive with Treasury bills, commercial paper, bankers' acceptances, Federal agency securities, and other money market instruments. At the same time the large bond dealers began to develop a secondary market in CD's which materially enhanced their liquidity features. Growth in the amount of CD's was meteoric, rising steadily from zero in early 1961 to $18.6 billion in August, 1966—$7.4 billion in New York City and $11.2 billion in other cities.[2] With some time lag, the practice spread—first to the large banks outside New York, and later to intermediate-size banks throughout the country, although certificates of the latter were not ordinarily negotiable and did not reach the secondary market. A better idea of overall growth is conveyed by the fact that "other time deposits of individuals and businesses" (largely certificates) of all member banks increased from $7.1 billion in April, 1961 to nearly $28.7 billion at the end of 1965.[3] Thus, a vigorous new segment of the money market, second only to short-term Treasury securities, grew to maturity in an incredibly short time.

The financial environment of those years provided fertile soil for growth of this new market. The period was one of rapid expansion in the economy accompanied by robust credit demands from businesses, consumers, and governments. These demands furnished the banks with unusual lending opportunities which supplied the incentive to compete strongly for deposits. At the same time Federal Reserve policies were friendly toward the market's development. An easy monetary policy with relatively abundant bank reserves prevailed until the first quarter of 1965 after which the reins were gradually tightened, but not to the point of reducing the rate of expansion of member bank legal reserves until the second quarter of 1966. Also, the Federal Reserve Board raised the maximum rates which banks could pay on time deposits (Regulation Q) from time to time, so that the banks were not handicapped in bidding up rates to compete for funds. Thus, the stage was perfectly set for this spectacular new development.

Disregarding details, the growth process of

---

[2] *Federal Reserve Bulletin*, September, 1966, p. 1369.

[3] Board of Governors of the Federal Reserve System, *Summary Reports of Assets and Liabilities of Member Banks*, April 12, 1961, p. 3; December 31, 1965, p. 3.

Items	February, 1961	September, 1966	Amount of Increase
Demand deposits*......................	112.1	132.6	20.5
Time deposits†...........................	60.6	157.1	96.5
Total member bank reserves............	18.9	23.5	4.6
Total loans and investments‡...........	199.3	313.8	114.5

* "Demand deposits adjusted" as a component of the money supply (seasonally adjusted).
† At all commercial banks.
‡ All commercial banks.
Source: *Federal Reserve Bulletin*, June, 1961, pp. 673 and 675; Oct., 1966, pp. 1478 and 1480.

the CD market may be explained in the following manner. Whenever a commercial bank needed additional reserve money to take advantage of profitable lending opportunities, it could raise its offering rate on CD's enough to draw more deposits and reserves in its direction. When a corporation bought CD's from Bank A with a check drawn on Bank B, the latter lost both demand deposits and reserves to Bank A, and Bank A was then in position to make the desired loans or to purchase the desired municipals. Bank B, in turn, could then repair its reserve deficiency by offering CD's at favorable rates, thereby transferring the reserve deficiency to bank C which could repeat the procedure. Thus, a chain reaction was set in motion which spread to Bank D and other banks throughout the system, each one meeting its reserve deficiency by issuing more CD's. Now for the entire banking system this process involved a shift from demand deposits to time deposits with a resultant release of required legal reserves. More specifically, a shift of $1 billion of demand deposits with a reserve requirement of 16.5 percent to time deposits with a reserve requirement of 4 percent comprised a reduction in required reserves of $125 million. This new increment of released reserves then became available to support a multiple expansion of bank loans and investments—and therefore of demand deposits—of $600 million, assuming an expansion coefficient of 4. Thus, the net effect of the process would be an increase of time deposits of $1 billion, a reduction of $400 million in demand deposits, and an increase in total deposits of $600 million. Assuming no net free legal reserves at the outset, the banking system would again return to the same reserve position. Theoretically, the process could be repeated *ad infinitum* until all demand deposits were shifted to time deposits with an increase of $1 billion in time deposits for each $400 million reduction in demand deposits. But in reality it would not continue beyond a certain point because of the demand for money to hold in the form of checking accounts, and because of intervention of Federal Reserve authorities to prevent such a deflationary decline in the active money supply.

With the background of the foregoing example, it is of interest to see what actually happened during the period, 1961–1966, as indicated in Table 2. It is evident that over four-fifths of the demand deposits created by the expansion of bank loans and investments were shifted to time deposits. The expansion of bank loans and investments was made possible by (1) the release of required reserves associated with the process of shifting demand deposits to time deposits, (2) the additional reserve money provided by the Federal Reserve Banks, and (3) a reduction in the legal reserve requirement against time deposits from 5 to 4 percent in the last quarter of 1962.

The relative ease with which the large city banks could buy reserve money by issuance of CD's during the period, 1961 to 1965, masked some of the limitations of this source under tight credit conditions. Lulled by this comfortable five-year experience, many bankers overlooked these limitations and placed too much reliance on CD's as the answer to cyclical liquidity needs. Tight credit conditions almost invariably develop sometime during the last stage of a cyclical expansion, and in the current expansion they began to appear in the last half of 1965. Demands for bank credit continued their upsurge, and on the supply side the Federal Reserve tightened the credit reins another notch. Net free reserves of member banks,[4] which had shown a substantial surplus since the last quarter of 1960, moved to a deficit position in the first quarter of 1965 which averaged about $150 million during the remainder of the year. Further restraint was applied in 1966, and by July net borrowed reserves exceeded $400

---

[4] Excess legal reserves less borrowings at Federal Reserve Banks.

million. Meanwhile, in December, 1965 the discount rate of the Federal Reserve Banks was raised from 4 to 4½ percent. In this setting open-market rates moved up sharply. The 3-month Treasury bill rate rose from 3.99 percent in August, 1965 to 5.66 percent in September, 1966, and the 4- to 6-month prime commercial paper rate increased in the same period from 4.58 percent to 6.26 percent.[5] In order to compete for money the leading banks were forced to make corresponding increases in the rates offered on CD's—from 4.50 percent in August, 1965 to 5.50 percent by midyear 1966 on certificates of 30 days and more.

The foregoing situation points up the first limitation on CD's as a dependable source of reserve money during boom conditions, namely, Federal Reserve control of maximum rates payable. If the structure of rates on competing money-market instruments—principally Treasury bills, Federal agency securities, commercial paper, and repurchase agreements for Federal funds—rises above the ceilings on CD's set by the Federal Reserve, the banks can no longer sell them. And if this situation should persist, the amount of outstanding CD's would shrink as maturities occur. Since maturities of outstandings range from one day to one year or a little more, the drain on reserves of the individual bank would begin immediately and would continue until all interest-sensitive CD's were liquidated. For the banking system as a whole there would be a substantial increase in legal reserve requirements arising from the shift from time deposits back to demand deposits. In fact, the banks would be taking the return voyage from the preceding illustration, although in fact it is likely that the Federal Reserve would soften the blow. That is, assuming reserve requirements of 16½ percent against demand deposits and of 4 percent against time deposits, a shift of $1 billion would raise legal requirements by $125 million. Moreover, the typical individual bank would share in this pinch on reserves.

Thus, it becomes clear that domestic CD's are no more dependable as a source of reserve money than the disposition of the Federal Reserve Board to lift the rate ceiling a notch as it is approached by competing money rates. They did so in December, 1965 after some discomfort when maximum rates payable were raised from 4½ percent to 5½ percent. But market rates soon closed the gap and rose above the ceiling, with the result that the amount of outstanding CD's

declined almost $3 billion between August and November, 1966. These examples call attention to the uncertainties and possible embarrassments which face the bank which relies excessively on CD's as a source of reserve money.

Another limitation on CD's as a dependable source of reserves is the fact that the banks must compete strongly among themselves for existing reserve money in boom periods when it is scarce. This point has already been mentioned but it deserves more emphasis in view of the prevalent disposition of bankers to disregard this reality. If Bank A issues more CD's it draws deposits and reserves from other banks. The large money-market banks, it is true, hold an advantage in this regard over the smaller banks because of the wider acceptability of prime, large-denomination certificates, and of the lower rates at which they may be sold. This means that the penalty of excessive dependence on CD's is definitely heavier on intermediate- and small-size banks, since they reach the rate ceiling first. But the money-market banks also compete among themselves for reserves to a large extent, and so are not immune to difficulty. One aspect of the problem somewhat modifies the sharpness of competition for existing reserves. This is the fact, already mentioned, that the shift from demand deposits to time deposits in the banking system reduces legal reserve requirements. But this is not enough to shield the individual bank from reserve deficiencies when competition for reserves is active.

A final limitation on CD's as a dependable source of reserves is the fact that the Federal Reserve authorities are almost certain to implement a monetary policy of restraint, thereby changing adversely the whole environment of the money market with respect to availability of reserves. In contrast with conditions of business recession when the Federal Reserve is typically on the side of the banks in providing abundant reserves at low rates, it shifts to the opposing side sometime during the last stage of cyclical expansion. Witness 1952–1953, 1956–1957, 1959, and 1966—all periods of rising net borrowed reserves, and of sharply increasing money rates. In large part these conditions were created, or at least validated, by Federal Reserve policies and actions—whether by sales of U.S. securities, by raising legal reserve requirements, by rationing advances and increasing the discount rate, or by some combination of these methods. In other words, the banker who would place heavy reliance on CD's as a source of reserves must face up to the fact that during boom times he will be competing with other banks for a stock of

---

[5] Rates adjusted to comparable basis—actual yield on 360-day year.

	(1) July 7, 1965	(2) Dec. 29, 1965‡	(3) Change between (1) & (2)	(4) June 29, 1966	Change between (2) & (4)
Savings deposits..............	48,313	48,084	− 229	48,413	+ 329
CD's*.........................	15,587	17,063	+1,476	18,268	+1,205
Other time deposits†.........	5,234	5,471	+ 237	10,419	+4,948

* Negotiable CD's issued in denominations over $100,000.
† Time deposits of individuals, partnerships, and corporations.
‡ Estimated by raising old "Leading Cities" series by 6 percent.
Source: *Federal Reserve Bulletin*, January, 1966, p. 70; July, 1966, p. 1008.

reserves that will be restricted, or even reduced, by the Federal Reserve authorities.

In addition to the issuance of negotiable CD's to large corporations a significant new development took place at the retail level in non-negotiable CD's and other time deposits beginning in December, 1965. On December 6, 1965 the Federal Reserve Board raised the maximum rates payable on time deposits with maturities of 30 days and over from 4½ to 5½ percent. This opened a new door through which commercial banks could compete for savings. Previously this door had been nearly closed by the rate ceilings which were below rates paid by savings and loan associations and mutual savings banks, and below yields obtainable on open-market securities.

As indicated in Table 3, the banks aggressively entered this field with a variety of time deposit plans. Rates offered were soon bid up to the 5½ percent maximum which exceeded those paid by competitive institutions, and the 4% ceiling on passbook savings. "Other time deposits" increased $4,948 million during the first half of 1966 compared with only $237 million in the last half of 1965. The gain represented largely the diversion of a greater proportion of savings to the banks. The savings and loan associations, which had enjoyed phenomenal growth since the Second World War, suffered heavily. During the first seven months of 1966 their savings capital increased only $577 million compared with $3,758 million in the same period of 1965. Mutual savings banks were also hit hard, the respective gains in deposits during the same periods being $1,080 million and $1,995 million.[6]

The plight of these institutions and the associated threat to residential construction was so acute that the situation became one of considerable national concern. After extensive hearings,

the House Banking Committee in late July, 1966 approved a bill that would impose a 4½ percent maximum until August 1, 1967 on all commercial bank time deposits of $100,000 and less, thus removing the present discretionary authority of the Federal Reserve Board over maximum rates in this area.[7]

However, the bill which became law September 21, 1966 (Public Law 89–597) did not in the end set maximum rate ceilings but granted more flexible authority to the Federal Reserve Board over maximum rates payable by member banks. Similar authority was given the Federal Deposit Insurance Corporation over non-member banks, and the Federal Home Loan Bank Board over savings and loan associations.[8]

The foregoing developments have been summarized because of their relevance in regard to consumer-type time deposits as a source of bank liquidity. Owing to the almost certain regulation of maximum rates, such deposits should not be counted on by the individual bank, except to a limited extent, as a dependable source to meet liquidity needs during the last phase of cyclical expansion.

3. Purchase of Federal Funds

The third source from which the individual bank may acquire reserve money by the creation of additional liabilities is the purchase (borrowing) of Federal funds. This is the market in which banks with deficient legal reserves borrow from other banks having excess reserves. Lenders and borrowers are brought together by two or three broker-dealers in New York City who receive reports by wire from banks all over the country in regard to bids and offers of funds, and by a few large money-market banks that act in part

---

[6] *Federal Reserve Bulletin*, October, 1966, pp. 1493–94.

[7] *Wall Street Journal*, July 26, 1966, p. 3.

[8] *Federal Reserve Bulletin*, October, 1966, p. 1451.

as dealers and in part as brokers and clearing centers of information. There are two principal methods of dealing in this market: (1) straight one-day loans; and (2) repurchase agreements. The great bulk of Federal funds is loaned on a one-day, unsecured basis, although a significant part is secured by U.S. securities. Banks also utilize repurchase agreements under which the borrowing bank actually sells U.S. securities under contract to buy them back in one or more days at a predetermined rate and price. Rates are very sensitive in response to changing currents of supply and demand. They are closely related competitively to other rates in the money market, and particularly to those on Treasury bills. Also, in ordinary times the Reserve Bank discount rate marks the upper limit of their fluctuations since banks seldom choose to pay more when they can borrow at the discount rate. But in periods of strong loan demand and tight money, the Federal funds rate may rise well above the discount rate. This situation, which existed during the last half of 1965 and the first three quarters of 1966, developed from a combination of credit rationing by the Reserve Banks, a relatively low discount rate, and exceptionally inviting loan and investment opportunities.

A more specific idea of the market's background is conveyed by the fact that in September, 1966 total member bank legal reserves were $23,239 million while required reserves were $22,847 million, so that excess reserves were $392 million. The greater part of the excess reserves—$291 million—was held by the smaller country banks, with only $101 million in the large reserve city banks, including New York City and Chicago.[9] It should be noted that the average size of excess reserves in the banking system materially understates the availability of Federal funds. This is true since the reserve position of each individual bank varies widely from day-to-day and within each day during the reserve computation periods—one week in reserve city banks and two weeks in country banks. The lightning-like turnover of available Federal funds is indicated by the fact that combined purchases and sales of 46 major reserve city banks during the first four weeks of September, 1966 amounted to $19.7 billion—an annual rate of $1,022 billion.[10] More relevant to the present purpose, average borrowings of Federal funds by weekly reporting large banks during September, 1966

amounted to $5.8 billion—over two-fifths of their total legal reserve balances.[11]

The limitations of the Federal funds market as a dependable source of cyclical reserve money for the individual bank are similar in important respects to those just discussed in regard to CD's, but there are also significant points of difference. A summary of the similarities will suffice since there is no need for repetition. The first is that the banks must compete actively among themselves for existing reserve money when it is scarce during the last phase of business expansions. This may lead to a very high cost of funds, as illustrated between August and November, 1966 when Federal funds typically traded at 6 percent when the Reserve Bank discount rate was 4½ percent—a differential of 1½ percentage points. The other similar limitation is the fact that a bank must face the high probability of a restrictive Federal Reserve policy in boom periods whether it expects to acquire reserves through CD's or Federal funds. This magnifies the degree of reserve scarcity which would exist in the absence of such a policy. That is, Federal Reserve operations are likely to reduce member bank reserves in relation to the need for them, and may go so far as to reduce them absolutely. In addition, the cost of borrowing reserves will be raised.

There are three significant differences between Federal funds and CD's as dependable cyclical sources of reserve money. First, the Federal fund rate is not subject to Federal Reserve regulation, nor is such a regulation likely. On this count, Federal funds have a distinct advantage over CD's which are subject to maximum rates under Regulation Q. This feature of CD's, it will be recalled, seriously limits their dependability as a source of reserves during the last phase of cyclical expansions. In contrast, a bank can count on the freedom to bid as high as it wishes to draw reserve money from other banks through the Federal funds market. However, the price may be too high to contemplate in practice when other alternatives to provide liquidity are considered, and under extreme conditions of restraint this source may nearly dry up at any price.

Second, there is no legal reserve requirement against the borrowing of Federal funds, whereas a reserve requirement of between 3 and 10 percent applies to time deposits. This difference has both a positive and negative aspect with respect to the use of Federal funds. On the positive side, the net cost of borrowing Federal funds is somewhat lower than the net cost

[9] *Federal Reserve Bulletin*, October, 1966, p. 1468; preliminary figures.

[10] *Ibid.*, p. 1470.

[11] *Ibid.*, pp. 1486–89.

of CD's when market rates are the same—the difference depending on the reserve requirement against time deposits. But on the other side there is no release of required legal reserves in the banking system when borrowings of Federal funds are increased. In contrast, although not visible to the individual bank, required reserves are released when CD's are expanded in view of the associated shift from demand deposits to time deposits. This aspect of the situation gives CD's a somewhat greater expansion potential than borrowings of Federal funds on the assumption of a given amount of legal reserves in the banking system. However, this point loses practical significance if one assumes that the Federal Reserve will make offsetting reserve adjustments.

Last, Federal funds are bought and sold by banks on a very short-term basis—predominantly for one day only, and seldom for more than one week while original issues of CD's are for considerably longer periods. Most of them have maturities in the range of 3 to 12 months, although a significant part has maturities after one year and beyond 2 years.[12] The exceedingly short-term nature of Federal funds borrowing makes this source inconvenient and undependable for cyclical purposes, even though it may be most appropriate for day-to-day, and week-to-week adjustments of reserve position. Re-borrowing large amounts every day or so to meet longer-term cyclical needs is a time-consuming task pervaded with uncertainty concerning the availability and cost of funds.

In conclusion, the Federal funds market does not qualify except in a minor way as a source of cyclical liquidity for the individual bank. This follows from its very short-term features, and from the probable unavailability of funds at reasonable rates during boom periods when they are most needed. Its contribution, which is a major one, lies principally in facilitating short-term liquidity adjustments, including day-to-day, week-to-week, and seasonal variations in needs.

Closely related to Federal funds is the borrowing of reserves by smaller banks from their large city correspondent banks. A part of such loans is made according to the prevailing practices in the Federal funds market and may therefore be included in the funds market proper. But another part is made on a customer basis under prearranged lines of credit, and with maturities and other terms usually arranged to meet the needs of the smaller bank. It is not wise, however, for the smaller banks to count too heavily on

this source to meet cyclical liquidity needs. Liquidity pressures focus on the large city banks. Consequently, they are likely to be least able to provide such loans when smaller banks face cyclical reserve deficiencies.

4. Borrowing at Federal Reserve Banks

The fourth source of reserves by creation of liabilities is borrowing from the Federal Reserve Bank. In fact, the founders of the Federal Reserve System visualized the discount window as the principal pipeline through which high-powered reserve money would be released and withdrawn from commercial banks. The use of the term, "high-powered," calls attention to the profound difference between this source and those just discussed—CD's and Federal funds. When a member bank borrows $10 million from the Reserve Bank it constitutes, other things being equal, an addition to total bank reserves. While this increment will augment Bank A's lending or investing ability by only about the same amount, it forms the reserve base for an increase of some $40 million of loans and investments (and therefore of deposits) in the banking system as a whole—assuming an expansion coefficient of 4. This multiple expansion feature does not apply to either CD's or Federal funds since these markets deal only with existing bank reserves and do not in themselves bring forth newly-created reserves. However, both markets do have a multiple-expansion effect insofar as they bring about a more complete utilization of existing legal reserves—that is, insofar as dealings through them reduce the amount of "excess legal reserves" in the banking system, or activate shifts of demand deposits to time deposits. This effect is a significant one during boom conditions when bank reserves become relatively scarce and money rates rise sharply. For example, excess reserves exceeded $700 million during the recession of 1960–1961, but as the economy recovered and interest rates rose they gradually declined, and during the first half of 1966 they were in the vicinity of $350 million.[13]

In practice, member bank borrowing at the Reserve Bank predominantly takes the form of a renewable promissory note for 15 days or less secured by U.S. securities. Seldom utilized are other possible form of borrowing, namely, (1) discounting of eligible paper consisting of customer notes with remaining maturities not in excess of 90 days and the proceeds of which were

---

[12] *Federal Reserve Bulletin*, April, 1963, p. 465.

[13] *Federal Reserve Bulletin*, July, 1966, p. 988.

TABLE 4   MEMBER BANK BORROWINGS AND REQUIRED LEGAL RESERVES ON SELECTED DATES, 1920–1966* (in millions of dollars)

Dates	(1) Member Bank Borrowings at F. R. Banks	(2) Required Legal Reserves	(3) Percentage, (1) to (2)
October, 1920.............	2,780	1,815†	153.2
July, 1929.................	1,096	2,292	47.8
December, 1952...........	1,593	20,457	7.8
April, 1957................	1,011	18,580	5.4
August, 1959..............	1,007	18,141	5.6
September, 1966...........	766	22,842	3.4

* Monthly averages of daily figures.
† Total legal reserves.
Sources: Board of Governors of the Federal Reserve System, *Banking and Monetary Statistics; Federal Reserve Bulletin,* various issues.

used for working capital purposes,[14] and (2) a promissory note with a maximum maturity of 4 months and secured by any satisfactory bank assets. However, in the last case a penalty rate of ½ percent above the regular Reserve Bank discount rate applies.

Regardless of the method of borrowing, the Reserve Banks observe certain guiding principles in the administration of discounts and advances. Federal Reserve credit is generally granted as a privilege, rather than a right, to meet day-to-day and seasonal liquidity needs of member banks. Under ordinary conditions dependence on borrowing for longer-term purposes, including cyclical loan expansion, is not regarded as appropriate. Also, advances are not to be used in support of speculative activities in securities, commodities, or real estate. Only in unusual situations arising from national or local difficulties can a member bank count on borrowing continuously for longer periods.[15] In practice, a Reserve Bank seldom refuses the first application for an advance to meet a purpose in line with the foregoing principles, but a large member bank which has borrowed continuously for three or four reserve computation periods is likely to be called on the carpet.

Some idea of the extent to which member banks have depended on borrowings from the Reserve Banks to meet liquidity needs at cyclical peaks may be gained from Table 4. It will be noted that this dependence was very heavy in the 1920s. The record amount of borrowings occurred in October, 1920 when they reached $2,780 million, or 153 percent of total legal reserves. At that time total member bank deposits

were $25.1 billion as compared with $271.2 billion in September, 1966, so that a corresponding amount of borrowings in September, 1966 would be $30 billion! A similar comparison with July, 1929 would correspond with borrowings in September, 1966 of $8.3 billion, in contrast with actual borrowings of $766 million. Since the Second World War Reserve Bank borrowings have been modest even at cyclical peaks—never exceeding 8 percent of required legal reserves.

This marked decline in the relative importance of borrowings at the Reserve Banks is largely attributable to (1) the profound change in the entire banking and financial environment, and (2) a change in Federal Reserve policy with respect to the release of reserve money through the discount window. In the 1920s the financial environment did not provide liquidity alternatives to Reserve Bank borrowing to anything like the degree that existed after the Second World War. The short-term U.S. security market was relatively small, the Federal funds market had not yet developed, the negotiable CD market did not exist, the bankers' acceptance market was small and was dominated by the Reserve Banks, the commercial paper market was likewise small, and there was not an active market in short-term obligations of states and political subdivisions, Federal agencies, and corporations. The large banks depended heavily on call loans to security brokers and dealers for asset liquidity. Such loans ordinarily served the purpose quite well when loans called by one bank could readily be shifted to other banks. But they became almost frozen in cyclical booms and financial crises when all banks needed additional reserves at the same time. The peak of borrowings in 1920 also reflected highly inflationary conditions superimposed upon the financing of the First World War when Treasury policy was to sell bonds directly

---

[14] Nine months in the case of agricultural paper.

[15] Board of Governors of the Federal Reserve System, *Regulation A,* 1955 Revision, Foreword—General Principles.

to the public rather than to commercial banks. To support this program banks were urged to lend to the public with U.S. securities as collateral, and the Reserve Banks were encouraged to advance adequate amounts of reserve money to the banks.

In contrast with the 1920s, the short-term money markets developed enormously after the Second World War. The U.S. securities market was, of course, predominant. At midyear 1947 marketable U.S. securities with maturities under 1 year totalled $51.2 billion, and those with maturities of 1 to 5 years amounted to $21.9 billion. By the end of August, 1966 these categories were, respectively $92.2 billion and $62.9 billion.[16] Also, significant growth took place in the bankers' acceptance market and the commercial paper market, and several new divisions of the money market developed, *viz.*, Federal funds, Federal agency securities, short-term municipal securities, and negotiable certificates of deposit. Thus, it is evident that commercial banks enjoyed materially wider alternatives in liquidity management after the Second World War than during the 1920s. They were not so dependent for liquidity on borrowings from the Reserve Banks.

The other main reason for the decline in relative importance of borrowings at the Reserve Banks since the 1920s is a change in Federal Reserve policy in regard to discounts and advances to member banks. The Reserve Banks have applied the rule of short-term borrowing rather assiduously, and they have apparently developed greater member bank reluctance to borrow and to stay in debt. They have administered "discounts and advances" with a firm hand during cyclical booms when the banks most needed reserves. They have preferred to release reserve money on their own initiative by purchasing U.S. securities in the open market and by reducing percentage reserve requirements from time to time. The best evidence of a firm policy of rationing reserve credit is the fact that Treasury bill yields have risen well above the Federal Reserve discount rate during the last phase of every cyclical expansion since the Second World War, thus making it profitable to borrow. But despite the greater profit incentive borrowings have remained at modest levels. Also, in 1965–1966 the Federal funds rate has typically exceeded the discount rate by from ½ to 1 percentage point. In fact, Federal funds often traded at 6 percent during the period August–November, 1966 when the dis-

count rate was 4½ percent—a differential of 1½ percent at a time when member bank borrowings averaged only about $750 million.

In conclusion, borrowing at the Federal Reserve Bank does not appear to be a dependable source, except within narrow limits, to meet the liquidity needs of the individual bank during the last phase of cyclical expansion. This source of liquidity should be utilized principally for short-term requirements, including emergency and seasonal needs. Of course, the validity of this conclusion rests on the assumption that historic Federal Reserve policy in regard to discounts and advances to member banks will not be materially liberalized. But until this expressly takes place, bank management has no solid reason to shape a cyclical liquidity program on the assumption that Federal Reserve policy will be more liberal in the future.[17]

5. Issuance of Short-Term Notes

A fifth source from which the individual bank may acquire reserve money by the creation of additional liabilities is the issuance of unsubordinated, short-term, promissory notes. This new member of the money-market family was launched by the First National Bank of Boston in September, 1964. The unsecured notes were offered in negotiable form with maturities to suit corporate and other large short-term investors. Shortly afterward, First Boston Corporation announced that it would make a market in the notes. Other large banks and security dealers followed suit, and with the blessing of the Comptroller

---

[16] *Economic Report of the President*, January, 1966, p. 275; *Federal Reserve Bulletin*, October, 1966, p. 1499.

[17] In its 1963 and 1964 Annual Reports the Federal Reserve Board recommended legislation which would enable a member bank to borrow from the Federal Reserve Bank on the security of any sound asset without the existing penalty rate of ½ percent when the security consists of non-eligible assets. This recommendation is embodied in a bill (S. 1559) which passed the Senate in August, 1965. Despite the fact that the "Board urges enactment of S. 1559 in order to repeal the restrictive provisions of present law and thus to facilitate rather than to penalize efforts by banks to meet the changing credit needs of the economy,"[a] the House has taken no action up to the present time (November, 1966).

If this legislation should pass, the expectation might readily arise that henceforth member banks will have greater access to reserves through the discount window under boom conditions. But this conclusion is not warranted, since it is unlikely that the Board will relax the rationing of Reserve Bank credit at such times even though the banks have larger potential borrowing power.

[a] Board of Governors of the Federal Reserve System, Annual Report, 1965, p. 235.

of the Currency and the Federal Reserve Board the new market seemed to be off to a promising start.

There were significant advantages of such notes over CD's. Since they were not classified as deposits they were not subject to maximum rate regulation (Regulation Q). For this reason a bank could regard them as a more dependable reserve source because there was no obstacle in bidding up rates to attract or to retain funds. This constituted a special advantage for banks outside the circle of leading money-market banks. The smaller institutions had to offer somewhat higher rates of CD's to compete, and whenever market rates approached the rate ceiling they tended to lose CD's to leading banks. Another advantage of the notes was that they were officially classified as borrowed funds and not as deposits. Consequently, they were not subject to either legal reserve requirements or to deposit insurance assessments. This represented an annual cost saving at the time of about 0.2 percent.

The only apparent disadvantage of the notes were certain legal restrictions on borrowing. A national bank was prohibited from borrowing in excess of capital stock and 50 percent of surplus, and state-chartered banks were also restricted in this regard. In addition, the banking law of New York was interpreted to bar the issuance of such notes, whether negotiable or non-negotiable. Without a legal change, this would of course seriously limit growth of the market, since the great money-market banks in New York City were excluded. In August, 1965 partial relief came to New York banks when the State Banking Department ruled that *non-negotiable* short-term notes, issued for specified periods in units of $1 million or more, were permissible. With this assurance, several large New York banks sold significant amounts of non-negotiable short-term notes to corporations and others.[18] However, the prohibition of negotiable notes in New York remained a major obstacle to development of an active secondary market, and to the potential growth of the new market. Pending a permissive change in the New York banking law, it seemed improbable that a major national market could be established in view of the predominance of New York City as a financial center.

Even if the New York banking law should be amended to permit issuance of negotiable notes, their future growth is called to question by restrictive measures taken in June, 1966 by the Federal Reserve Board. Effective September 1, 1966, short-term promissory notes of banks became subject to the regulations governing reserve requirements and payment of interest on deposits. The Board's purpose was, "to prevent future use of these instruments as a means of circumventing statutory and regulatory requirements applicable to bank deposits."[19] This action erased the advantages of such notes over CD's, except perhaps for use in individual situations. Moreover, in view of the limits on bank borrowings, the legal barrier to negotiable notes in New York, and the great head-start of the CD market, it now appears unlikely that a comparable new market in notes will develop.

Now that short-term promissory notes of banks have become subject to legal reserve requirements, the analysis of their effects on the money market becomes identical with that pertaining to CD's. That is, the individual bank may acquire liquidity through their issuance only by drawing existing reserves and deposits from *other* banks. The only difference is that the process involves a shift in the banking system from demand deposits or time deposits to note liabilities; whereas in the case of issuance of CD's there is a shift only from demand deposits to time deposits. In both cases there is a reduction in the amount of required legal reserves when the shift is from demand deposits to a liability against which a materially lower percentage reserve requirement applies. The general conclusion is also the same as that with respect to CD's: Short-term notes are not a dependable source, except to a limited extent, to meet the liquidity needs of the individual bank during the last phase of cyclical periods of expansion.

6. Raising Capital Funds

The sixth source from which the individual bank may acquire reserve money by the creation of liabilities is by raising capital funds in any one of several forms—sale of common stock, preferred stock, or capital notes, and retention of earnings. While these forms differ in character, the effect of their increase on the asset liquidity position of the individual bank and the banking system is the same. When Bank A, having a legal reserve deficiency of $10 million, increases its capital funds by this amount, say by sale of common stock, its cash reserve is increased and so is its common stock account. Assuming that the stock is paid for by checks on other banks, total demand deposits of the banking system are im-

---

[18] *The Wall Street Journal,* September 3, 1965, p. 8.

[19] *Federal Reserve Bulletin,* July, 1966, p. 979.

TABLE 5   CAPITAL ACCOUNTS OF ALL MEMBER BANKS, 1961 AND 1965 (in millions of dollars)

	Dec. 30, 1961	Dec. 31, 1965	Increase	Percentage Distribution
Common stock*	5,512	7,002	1,489	23.7
Capital notes and debentures	16	1,553	1,537	24.4
Preferred stock	7	32	25	0.4
Surplus and other capital accounts	13,102	16,341	3,238	51.4
Total†	18,638	24,926	6,288	100.0

* An unknown part of the increase in common stock took place as a result of stock dividends which capitalize surplus or undivided profits. Hence, the table overstates to that extent the raising of new capital funds in this manner, and understates retained earnings as a source of new funds.

† Discrepancies are a result of rounding figures.

Source: Board of Governors of the Federal Reserve System, *Summary Report*, Dec. 30, 1961, p. 3; Dec. 31, 1965, p. 3.

mediately reduced by $10 million. At the same time required legal reserves are reduced by $1.5 million when the percentage requirement is 15 percent. Given time, the released reserve provides the basis for loan and investment expansion (and therefore deposit expansion) of $10 million, so that the demand deposits initially extinguished may be re-created. Thus, the end result, assuming net free reserves of zero at the outset and full utilization of the released reserves, is no change in total demand deposits, an increase of $10 million in total capital accounts, and an equal increase in total loans and investments. It should also be noted that these transactions have made no change in total legal reserves of the banking system. Hence, the cash reserves that Bank A gained were drawn away from other banks which, collectively, are assumed to have excess reserves of $10 million—just enough to provide for Bank A's reserve deficiency. Thus as a generalization, deposits are the immediate source of additional capital funds in the banking system, and an increase of capital funds of the individual bank causes a redistribution of existing cash reserves rather than an increase in total reserves.

We now come to the question: To what extent should the individual bank include raising capital funds in its plans to meet liquidity needs in boom periods? As the basis for an answer attention is called to Table 5 which shows the changes in capital accounts of all member banks between 1961 and 1965. While over half the total increase of $6.3 billion came from retained earnings, much dependence on this source does not seem at all practicable. In periods of increased earnings stockholders expect higher dividends instead of a sharp and sudden reduction. Issuance of preferred stock may also be dismissed in view of its insignificance in the banking field, and also because of the depressed level of preferred stock prices during periods of high interest rates.

The sale of common stock likewise has a very small potential for this purpose. Bank stock prices

are likely to be depressed by the high interest rates associated with boom conditions. For example, the index of bank stock prices reached a peak in the third quarter of 1964 and had declined one-fourth by June, 1966, while Standard and Poor's index of industrial stock prices rose 8 percent during the same period.[20] In addition, banks are often reluctant to issue more common stock because of dilution of per share equity, and because of control considerations.

One possibility for use of common stock in this connection would be issuance at an earlier stage of the business expansion cycle when the price is favorable, as in 1964. A rather large offering could be made with both long-term growth and the coming cycle peak in view. Proceeds could be held in short-term U.S. securities and other liquidity reserves which then offer attractive yields. But the practicability of such a program is open to serious question. Success would depend on a higher degree of accuracy in business forecasting than past experience demonstrates, and also on timely action in accordance with the forecast. While bank officers may wish to sell common stock as part of an overall liquidity program, the uncertainties and limitations commit it to a minor role.

Capital notes have become a major source of capital funds since December, 1962 when the Comptroller of the Currency approved their issuance if they were subordinated to deposits. As shown by Table 6, between 1963 and 1965 they represented 47 percent of the increase in total capital funds and over three-fourths of total capital raised in the investment market by reserve city banks.[21]

In New York City the proportion of the increase in total capital funds represented by capi-

[20] M. A. Schapiro & Co., Inc., *Bank Stock Quarterly*, June, 1966, p. 5.

[21] Allowing for the fact that an appreciable part of the increase in capital stock occurred by transfer from surplus and undivided profits.

TABLE 6   CAPITAL ACCOUNTS OF RESERVE CITY MEMBER BANKS, 1963 AND 1965*
(in millions of dollars)

	Dec. 20, 1963	Dec. 31, 1965	Increase	Percentage Distribution
Common stock........................	3,640.2	4,237.8	597.6	23.2
Capital notes and debentures..................	78.4	1,294.5	1,216.2	47.2
Surplus and other capital accounts..................	8,959.1	9,721.4	762.3	29.6
Total capital accounts...........	12,677.7	15,253.7	2,576.0	100.0

* Includes New York City and Chicago member banks.
   Source: Board of Governors of the Federal Reserve System, *Summary Report*, Dec. 20, 1963, p. 3; Dec. 31, 1965, p. 3.

tal notes was appreciably higher during the same period—58 percent. Thus it is evident that the banks eagerly grasped the opportunity to acquire liquid funds by this method during this phase of business expansion. It afforded the advantage of tax-free capital at a relatively low interest cost when customer loan demands were strong.

Additional information on the sale of capital notes by banks was recently reported by M. A. Schapiro & Co., Inc.[22] Over 200 banks sold nearly $1.8 billion of capital notes between mid-1963 and mid-1966. The average interest rate was 4.56 percent, and the average maturity was 24.3 years. Most of the issues (194) were non-convertible but a few were convertible into common stock.

One aspect of the compilation has special significance for this study. During the first half of 1966 only 12 capital note issues totalling $43.7 million were sold. This compares with 100 issues in 1965 amounting to $863.9 million, and with 82 issues in 1964 totalling $642.9 million. The principal explanation lies in the sharp tightening of the investment market in 1966—when the average rate on the issues was 5.31 percent compared with 4.60 percent in 1965. Understandably, the banks were reluctant to commit themselves to a high fixed interest charge for periods ranging from 15 to 30 years. This situation illustrates a serious limitation on capital notes as a method of acquiring liquidity during the last phase of cyclical expansions. However, the period, 1963–1965, illustrates that capital notes may be utilized during earlier stages of an economic expansion as part of an overall cyclical liquidity program. Capital funds may then be raised on a favorable basis in larger amounts than currently needed, looking forward both to growth and the next cycle peak. Proceeds labelled for liquidity needs should be invested in liquidity reserves.

7.   The Eurodollar Market

A final source of reserves for the large money-market banks is the Eurodollar market. In the simplest terms this market deals in interest-bearing time deposits, denominated in dollars, on the books of large foreign banks—largely in London, but also in other European financial centers. Eurodollars originate when the holder (usually a foreign bank or firm) of a demand deposit in a U.S. bank transfers funds to a foreign bank with instructions to open a Eurodollar account. This transaction leaves the foreign bank with a new dollar liability in the form of a time deposit, and a counterpart demand deposit on the books of the U.S. bank. Thus, the foreign bank has become an intermediary between the original owner of the demand deposit and the U.S. bank. Having a claim on dollars, the foreign bank is then in position to make loans to others who wish to borrow dollars—whether they be foreign business firms and financial institutions, or U.S. banks and other interests.

While European banks accepted and transferred deposits in dollars (and other foreign moneys) as far back as the post-World War I years, this market had its real beginnings in the mid-1950s and most of its development took place after 1958. According to estimates of the Bank for International Settlements the gross Eurodollar deposit liabilities of the eight principal European countries[23] at mid-1966 were $11.5 billion and the net amount was $10 billion. The rest of the world, mainly Canada and Japan, accounted for another $1 billion.[24]

The reasons for the growth of this market, its complex features, functions, and outlook repre-

---

[22] M. A. Schapiro & Co., Inc., *Bank Stock Quarterly*, June, 1966, pp. 8–12.

[23] United Kingdom, Switzerland, Sweden and the five Common Market countries—Belgium, Netherlands, France, Italy, and West Germany.

[24] Milton Gilbert, "The Euro-Currency Market," Bank for International Settlements, H.S. 383, p. 4.

sent a long story which cannot be told here. Suffice it to say that one of its principal functions is to provide an international money market for the leading banks of all major nations—a market where they can place excess funds and where they can usually obtain needed liquid funds. This is the aspect which is relevant for the present purpose.

During 1965 and 1966 U.S. banks experienced growing liquidity pressures, largely from the up-surge in loan demands, outflows of currency and gold, and increasing restraint by the Federal Reserve. Individual banks met these pressures by tapping the various liquidity sources already discussed. In addition according to official estimates,[25] the large banks turned to the Eurodollar market for funds—in the net amount of $2 billion during 1965 and the first quarter of 1966. Such borrowings apparently continued to grow rapidly during the remainder of 1966, as indicated by the fact that short-term liabilities of U.S. banks to Europe increased by $3.2 billion between March and November, 1966.[26]

In conclusion, the Eurodollar market is not an appropriate source of cyclical liquidity for any bank below the tier of large money market institutions. Dealings are in wholesale lots with a minimum of $1 million, and with most single transactions in tens of millions. Direct access to this market is beyond the reach of small- and intermediate-size banks, and indirect access through correspondents involves uncertainties. But the Eurodollar market is, within limits, an appropriate source of cyclical liquidity for a large money-market bank. This does not mean, however, that it should place undue reliance on this source. International monetary conditions are subject to unpredictable changes in larger measure than domestic conditions. The supply of Eurodollars may shrink when needs are most imperative, and even if available their cost may become prohibitively high. During 1965 and the first half of 1966 the three-month rate in London on Eurodollars averaged about ½ percentage point higher than that on CD's in New York and on occasion the spread became as much as 1 percent.[27] We may conclude, therefore, that the Eurodollar market merits a place in the cyclical liquidity program of a large money-market bank, but that the main bulwark of such a program should be composed of relatively short-term liquid assets.[28]

8. Summary and Conclusions

The management of bank liabilities deserves a rather limited role in the overall program designed to meet liquidity needs during the last phase of a cyclical expansion. The timely issuance of capital notes is the best candidate for this purpose. The management of liabilities is best adapted to short-term liquidity needs where it can make a major contribution.

At this point the question arises: If the management of bank liabilities can make only a limited contribution to cyclical liquidity, by what methods can a bank provide for this essential need? In brief, the answer lies in the management of asset liquidity. In fact, on the assumption of fixed total legal reserves in the banking system, there is no way in which the individual bank can acquire legal reserves except at the expense of other banks.[29] Also, aside from changing the deposit mix there is no way in which total loans and investments can be expanded in the system as a whole beyond the point of complete reserve utilization. But there is a way in which the individual bank can meet its expanding customer loan demands without suffering heavy capital losses from the sale of depreciated intermediate- and long-term bonds. This is by holding an adequate amount of liquidity reserves—a method which may involve some loss of current income during the greater part of a cyclical expansion, but which is likely to avoid a far greater capital loss during the last phase of expansion. The essence of this liquidity management problem is to equate the probable earlier loss of income with the subsequent probable capital loss, taxes considered.

[25] Bank for International Settlements, *Thirty-Sixth Annual Report,* June, 1966, p. 149.

[26] *Federal Reserve Bulletin,* April, 1967, p. 668.

[27] Bank for International Settlements, *Thirty-Sixth Annual Report,* June, 1966, p. 150.

[28] For more comprehensive treatments of the Eurodollar market, see: G. Carroll Martenson, *The Euro-Dollar Market* (Boston: Bankers Publishing Co., 1964) 117 pp.; Norris O. Johnson, *Eurodollars in the New International Money Market* (New York: First National City Bank, 1964) 21 pp.; Bankers Trust Company, *The Euro-Dollar Market,* 1964) 28 pp.; Ernest Bloch, *Eurodollars: An Emerging International Money Market,* New York University, The Bulletin, No. 39, April, 1966, 31 pp.; Paul Einzig, *The Euro-Dollar System* (New York: St. Martin's Press, 1964).

[29] Note the rather minor qualification to the statement on page 199.

THE ROLE OF FINANCIAL INTERMEDIARIES IN U.S. CAPITAL MARKETS*

Daniel H. Brill with Ann P. Ulrey

In 1965, financial institutions in the United States supplied borrowers with more than $62 billion—or 85 percent of all money raised through the credit markets. In the period from 1961–64 these institutions supplied 83 percent of the credit market's funds. In the mid-1950s, financial intermediaries accounted, on average, for 78 percent of all funds flowing into credit markets.

I cite these figures to emphasize that the transformation of savings in the United States is, and for some time has been, accomplished primarily through the intermediation of financial institutions. The direct flow of funds from savers to borrowers is usually a minor element in the U.S. financial scene.

There have been periods of deviation from the usual pattern of financial flow, however. One such deviation occurred in 1955, another in 1959, and another has been occurring in 1966. The course of the deviation in all cases has been the same: strong credit demands and strong monetary restraint. When these two strong economic forces conjoin, interest rates in financial markets move up rapidly, more rapidly than financial institutions can accommodate by adjusting their portfolios and the returns they can offer to savers. In such periods, more sophisticated savers tend to move their funds out of institutions and directly into financial instruments, purchasing securities principally of the Federal Government and of State and local governments. Thus, in 1966, a year of strong credit demands and monetary restraint, the proportion of credit flows that have been intermediated by institutions has fallen to about 66 percent, from the proportion of about 85 percent in 1965.

While the adjustments made by intermediaries

to such fluctuations in the volume of savings flowing through them is a fascinating story, with repercussions not only throughout the structure of finance, but also throughout the structure of production, our emphasis today is on the longer-term configuration of U.S. financial flows. And the longer-term picture, abstracting from these cyclical episodes of shifts in savings channels, is one dominated by financial intermediaries. This paper attempts to explore some of the causes and consequences of the high proportion of intermediation in the U.S. saving-investment process.

I shall not bore you with a detailed catalog of all types of financial institutions that have emerged in this country, nor shall I recite to you volumes of statistics on financial flows and stocks so dear to the hearts of experts. Rather, the focus of my remarks will be on the factors that have given rise to this emphasis on intermediation, and on the consequences this has had for the shape of the U.S. financing mechanism. Nor shall I limit my role to that of a mere reporter; I would be remiss in my obligations if I were to avoid pointing out the pitfalls and shortcomings in, as well as the advantages conferred by, a financial system in which institutions play so large a role.

INSTITUTIONS AND CONSUMER SAVING FLOWS

The classic concept of a market as a meeting place for buyers and sellers visualizes the middlemen of that market in the role of matchmakers—simply bringing together the actual participants among whom mutually acceptable matches can then be made. But the instruments offered by those seeking long-term credit are not, in general, the assets that the bulk of the nonfinancial public is willing and able to hold. These instruments—notes, bonds, equity shares—lack one or more of the qualities sought by most savers, such as safety of principal, liquidity, convenience, or accessibility in readily divisible denominations. It is precisely these qualities that financial intermediaries are in business to offer. In recent years they not only have offered these qualities to the nonfinancial public but have offered them in increasingly diversified forms and at increasingly attractive rates of return.

* From *Federal Reserve Bulletin*, January 1967, pp. 18–31. Reprinted by permission of the Board of Governors of the Federal Reserve System and the authors. Daniel H. Brill, Senior Vice President, Commercial Credit Company, was Senior Adviser to the Board of Governors of the Federal Reserve System at the time this article was written. Ann P. Ulrey was formerly Staff Economist, Board of Governors of the Federal Reserve System.

This article is based on a paper submitted for the International Symposium on Savings and the Financing of Local Facilities, sponsored by the Caisse des Depots et Consignations, in October 1966 at Paris, France, to mark its 150th anniversary.

The success of intermediaries in capturing a larger share of a rising volume of saving can be illustrated by a comparison of the change in their role over the past four decades. In the 1920s, somewhat over half of the net increase in household financial assets was composed of securities purchased directly in the credit markets; by the mid-1950s this share had fallen below 20 percent; and in the last 3 years, 1962–65, market acquisitions averaged only about 2.5 percent of household financial savings. The remainder—except for net additions to currency holdings—flowed through financial intermediaries.

This massive shift from direct market acquisitions of securities to intermediation of savings flows has occurred even without much rise in the proportion of incomes saved by consumers, or in the proportion saved in financial form. Data for earlier periods are not strictly comparable, but the evidence available suggests that consumer acquisition of financial assets in the 1922–29 period amounted to about 10 percent of disposable income, not much below the 11 percent average in the 1962–65 period.

Perhaps the most important reason for the very marked change in the structure of consumer financial saving flows has been the rise in and diffusion of income, which has created a large class of small savers. Traditionally this type of saver has emphasized liquidity and safety of principal over immediate return or growth potential. And traditionally, these needs have been more easily and conveniently satisfied—particularly for small savers—through financial institutions than through financial market instruments. The difficulty of access to markets where financial instruments are traded, the relatively large size at which individual transactions are possible, and the relatively high cost involved in effecting small transactions have all contributed to small savers' preference for institutional saving. Moreover, the development of an elaborate apparatus of governmental insurance, guarantee, and supervision has made institutional saving even more desirable to the small saver seeking the attributes of liquidity and safety.

Traditionally, too, the small saver has sought the protection of the insurance principle. For savers whose predominant requirement is assurance that future needs can be met, individual accumulations of assets—however safe and easily converted into cash—often are not the most efficient way of providing for those needs. The future magnitude and cost of many contingencies are unpredictable on an individual basis but can be measured accurately for large groups. By applying insurance principles, a much smaller aggregate accumulation can assure all participants a given level of benefits than would be needed individually. Here, too, governmental assistance (mainly through favorable tax treatment) has facilitated the growth of institutional saving in the form of insurance and pension plan reserves.

In seeking liquidity for their savings, consumers have turned to such institutions as commercial banks (particularly into bank savings and time accounts), mutual savings banks, savings and loan associations, and credit unions. The flow of funds into such "depository institutions" has accounted for more than half of all consumer financial saving in recent years. In seeking protection against longer-term contingencies—for retirement, or for protection of a family's economic status after death of the principal earner—savers have relied principally on the contractual institutions, life insurance companies, and pension plans. The flow of saving into these institutions has represented between one-third and two-fifths of total consumer financial saving.

In terms of dollar magnitudes, consumer savings accounts at what I have called "depository institutions" amount to more than $300 billion, and the reserves of "contractual institutions" to more than $250 billion. Together, the depository and contractual institutions accommodate the vast bulk of the long-term credit demands in U.S. financial markets.

Before concluding this brief review of how consumers in the United States allocate their financial savings, it would be desirable to note two aspects of the saving structure. First, the liabilities issued by the depository and contractual institutions so favored by consumers are almost all of a fixed face value, that is, they are redeemable or payable only for the contracted amount and do not fluctuate with changes in the level of prices. The continued strong preference of consumers for such financial assets is an indication of the value consumers place on liquidity and security of principal in choosing repositories for saving. Perhaps because the United States has been spared the ravages of severe inflation, there is no evident strong disposition on the part of the bulk of consumers to seek savings outlets that tend to provide protection against price increases at the risk of fluctuation in nominal value.

The second aspect of the financial saving structure worth noting is the multitude of choices among institutions and savings instruments available to the small saver. The U.S. financial scene is marked by aggressive competition between institutions for small blocks of saving, competition among institutions of the same type and between different types. This competition has led to the offering of a wide variety of services and conveniences to attract savers as well as to a high rate of return on small savings. The small saver is assiduously courted and handsomely rewarded, and financial institutions have in consequence flourished even though the "spread" between the rates paid savers and those charged borrowers is quite narrow.

CONTRACTUAL INTERMEDIARIES

As was noted above, recent savings patterns contrast strongly with those of the 1920s.

Inflows

Since the 1920s the savings flowing from consumers have shifted from direct market participation to financial intermediaries. And there have been shifts in flows among intermediaries. Contractual flows of all kinds made up about 16 percent of consumer saving in the 1920s. In the mid-1950s, such flows accounted for a far larger proportion—about 40 percent—of a greatly increased total. Since 1960, however, although absolute amounts have continued to climb rapidly, the share in consumer saving of contractual flows has fallen to about 33 percent, reflecting the even more explosive growth of savings in depositary form.

The principal recipients of contractual savings flows are life insurance companies, corporate pension funds, and the retirement systems operated by State and local government units. All of these have experienced major growth throughout the postwar period, although for life insurance companies the long-term growth trend has slowed somewhat; more recently the strongest growth has been in reserves to provide pension and retirement benefits.

The increased emphasis in recent decades on financial provision for old age reflects a number of different facets of American economic life. Life expectancy has risen as also has population mobility, thus reducing the prevalence of established multigeneration consumers able to accommodate the retired at little marginal cost. Federal programs for providing retirement income through social security have probably stimulated private saving rather than reducing it since benefits are minimal in relation to pre-retirement income and the incentive to supplement them is strong. Furthermore, at least until recently, social security coverage has had many important gaps.

The rise of pension plans covering workers as part of their employment contracts is largely a wartime and post-war development. During World War II, the growth of corporate pension plans received a major impetus from wage control policies that severely limited the normal range of collective bargaining. Union emphasis shifted to demands for fringe benefits, and the establishment of pension funds—more clearly than most such benefits—represented a measurable economic value to covered employees. At the same time, tax advantages make it possible for employers to grant the union a larger economic package, as measured by eventual benefit to covered workers, at lower cost in this fashion than most others.[1]

Since 1954, the assets of private pension plans have increased fivefold, from $13 billion to $70 billion. Pension plans administered by insurance companies—usually those involving smaller groups of employees and smaller asset accumulations—have grown from $10 billion to nearly $28 billion in the past dozen years. And retirement systems operated by State and local governmental units have built their reserves from less than $10 billion to about $35 billion. Current estimates suggest that by 1980 nearly 50 million jobs will be included in pension plans supplementary to social security coverage.

These magnitudes, plus the continuing growth of life insurance reserves, all represent long-term inflows associated with contractually fixed obligations that will call for a predictable schedule of outlays. With such closely comparable obligations, it might be supposed that the investment objectives and policies of the three major contractual intermediaries would also be similar. In fact, however, widely differing regulatory and traditional constraints upon the investment latitude enjoyed by life insurance companies, private pen-

---

[1] To qualify for tax benefits, almost all private pension plans are funded; that is, provision is made for meeting future obligations at the time credits are earned. Employer contributions for this purpose (including, in the case of plans that are not mature, a reasonable provision for funding past service obligations) are current expenses and tax deductible as such to the corporation. But they are not taxable to the employee until years later as benefits are paid, and then at the lower rates associated with reduced retirement income. Meanwhile, investment income received by the fund during its period of accumulation is not subject to income tax and is fully available for compounding.

sion funds, and State and local retirement systems have led to very different patterns of asset accumulation.

Investment Patterns

Broadly speaking, life insurance companies divide their large and comparatively stable inflows in varying proportions among corporate debt securities and mortgages—both those secured by one- to four-family residences and those on income-producing property. Payments into insured pension funds are not ordinarily differentiated from insurance reserves (and until very recently could not legally have been invested differently in any case). The uninsured pension funds—those managed by trustees appointed by employer and employee representatives—have also become a major market for corporate securities, but with a high and rising proportion of their expanding inflows directed toward acquisitions of common stock. As for State and local retirement systems, the largest share of their funds reaching the capital markets is now channeled into corporate bonds—usually high quality, publicly offered issues. But a substantial amount still goes into Government securities which, until a dozen years ago, made up the bulk of the total. For all of these institutions, both regulatory constraints and investment policies have been changing over time, and in recent years the changes have occurred at an accelerating rate.

Investment standards for life insurance companies are set by each State and apply to all companies doing business within the State. Since the major companies seek nationwide business and particularly wish to sell policies in the largest and wealthiest States, the standards of these States tend to be controlling, and for most purposes the critical limitations have been those set by New York State. Among these, the most significant has been the limit on equity share holdings by insurance companies to a minor fraction of their total assets. It is questionable, however, whether legal restrictions are the major constraint on investment policies, since most insurance companies have not made use of the allowed proportion of equity investment.

It is in competing for a share of the pension fund business that the life insurance industry has found restrictions on equity purchases to be a distinct disadvantage. By acquiring equities during a decade of advancing market prices, many of the uninsured funds have enjoyed investment experience superior to the contracts life insurance carriers could offer. This competitive disadvantage was modified in 1962 when New York State law was changed to allow insurance companies to segregate pension fund reserves and invest them more liberally. The change did not apply retroactively to existing funds, however, and has had little impact as yet.

Thus life insurance companies remain predominantly investors in debt instruments—principally corporate securities and mortgages. Because they are more lightly taxed than either most corporations or individuals in the upper income brackets, they usually find yields on State and local government securities (the income from which is exempt from Federal income tax) less attractive. These instruments are ordinarily priced to reflect the value of their tax-exempt income to highly taxed owners. Holdings of U.S. Government securities, which traditionally constitute a liquidity reserve, have been declining on balance for many years—thus releasing funds for the acquisition of higher yielding assets. This long downtrend reflects, in part, the abnormally high level of Government securities in insurance company portfolios at the end of World War II.

Many State regulatory agencies apply earnings tests and other more or less mechanical standards to the quality of the debt securities insurance companies are free to count as assets for regulatory purposes. While such inhibitions may deny eligibility to some potential borrowers, they have not prevented insurance companies from playing a major role as suppliers of long-term corporate financing. Traditionally, indeed, they have been the dominant suppliers of funds to the corporate bond market. A dozen years ago, their holdings made up more than 60 percent of the outstanding total of corporate bonds, and even now—despite the increasing activity of pension and retirement funds—they account for about half of the corporate long-term debt outstanding.

Nor have restrictions on investment policy prevented the insurance companies from pioneering in the private placement of debt securities—an important financing technique that has broadened the availability of funds to borrowers who might find the public offering of a bond issue difficult and expensive. This is particularly the case for smaller companies, since the costs of offering small debt issues to the public through underwriters are high (as a practical matter, the designation of "small" may be applied to most issues below about $10 million). Lack of a widely known name may also preclude public flotation. Still other corporations in need of long-term financing may want indenture terms more flexible than those possible in a publicly held issue.

Private placements, in which an institutional investor or more generally a group of participating institutions arrange to make a loan in security form, do not require registration with the Securities and Exchange Commission so long as the unregistered securities are not later offered for resale to the general public. Terms that are agreed on in direct bargaining between borrower and lender can be more flexible than those associated with public issues. There is also a saving in registration fees and underwriter's compensation, though borrowers and lenders are frequently brought together—in return for a finder's fee—by the same investment banking fraternity that underwrites and markets public issues.

Since the mid-1950s, insurance companies have moved steadily into private placements, and they are rarely in the market for public offerings. This trend reflects several factors, including some liberalization of investment standards in quest of higher yields. A relatively large proportion of public offerings consists of premium priced bonds of top-rated issuers (especially electric, gas, and communication utilities) on which yields are lower than the rates that can be obtained from borrowers with a somewhat lower credit rating. But the increased emphasis on private placements reflects also the growing competition of other institutional investors (first the private pension funds and more recently those administered by local governments) for available investment outlets. In recent years, private placements have generally made up more than half of all corporate bond offerings and have come to include many corporations which are of a size and credit rating that would permit the sale of their securities to the general public on average or better-than-average terms. Nevertheless, they have chosen the convenience of private borrowing arrangements with institutional investors.

An additional factor contributing to reliance on the private placement technique has been the growing emphasis insurance investors have placed on matching investment outlays with the expected timing of their inflows. By arranging future loans—often with a staggered schedule of "takedowns" to match the precise times when borrowers expect to use the funds—the life insurance companies have been increasingly able to commit their predictable inflows in advance, avoiding loss of income through idle funds or low-yielding temporary investments. At the same time this lending technique appeals to borrowers by allowing them to make firm plans with assured financing, while saving the cost of incurring long-term debts before the funds are actually needed.

Life insurance companies have long been major mortgage lenders, but their investment patterns in this area also have shifted notably in recent years. Mortgages on single-family homes, which in the mid-1950s absorbed 40 percent of all funds available for market acquisitions (the same volume as outlays on corporate bonds), have declined in absolute and relative importance. In the past 4 years they made up, on average, only 15 percent of total insurance company acquisitions. Funds diverted from this outlet have been used to expand very sharply the financing of income-producing properties—primarily multifamily residential and commercial developments. Annual acquisitions of such mortgages, which averaged less than $1 billion in the mid-1950s, approached the $3 billion level throughout the past 4 years.

This shift, like that from publicly offered bonds to private acquisitions, can be traced to two distinct sets of forces. One has been the increasing competition for home mortgages offered by such specialized mortgage lenders as the savings and loan associations. The other has been the insurance industry's own desire to acquire higher-yielding assets through broader and more flexible lending policies. As nationwide lenders, insurance company mortgage departments often lack special familiarity with local real estate markets, and their acquisitions of home mortgages have traditionally been concentrated on those whose solvency is underwritten by agencies of the Federal Government—the Federal Housing Authority and (in earlier postwar years) the Veterans Administration. Safer and more uniform than the so-called "conventional" mortgage loan that local lenders are better equipped to appraise and service, federally underwritten mortgages also offer lower returns. In contrast, the more recent preference for higher yielding loans on income-producing properties has contributed strongly to the high level of multifamily and commercial construction.

Although the investment patterns of other contractual intermediaries differ greatly from those of life insurance companies, the general direction of change in their investment policies over recent years can be explained in almost identical terms. The managers of pension fund and retirement plan assets, like their counterparts in insurance companies, have moved in the direction of more flexible lending techniques and wider choices among investment alternatives. For them also, these longer-run trends were accelerated in recent years by two forces. First, the long period of high and rising inflows at all intermediaries led to vigorous competition for investment outlets, and, second, all managers have felt varying degrees of pressure to increase portfolio yields.

These pressures may be less obvious for institutions whose obligations are fixed by contract than they are at depositary intermediaries, where the cost of funds has climbed steeply as savers have been offered increasingly high rates of return. But there is vigorous intra-industry competition among life insurance companies and between insurance companies and banks for industrial group insurance contracts where cost estimates are based on expected investment return.

In their attempt to improve investment results, managers of private pension funds operate under few legal constraints other than the requirement for prudence and responsibility that applies to anyone serving in a fiduciary capacity. Definitions of prudence, of course, change over time, and the shift in asset structure of pension funds is striking in the aggregate.

In the early 1950s, Government securities made up 19 percent of all assets, and corporate bonds—almost entirely high-grade, publicly marketed issues—constituted more than half. Common stock accounted for slightly less than 25 percent of the total. By the end of 1965, stocks comprised well over half—56 percent—of the composite portfolio's $70 billion valuation, Government securities only 5 percent (about the same as mortgage investments), and corporate bonds only 33 percent. In selecting these bonds, moreover, the larger and more aggressive funds have increasingly turned from reliance on the public market to participation in private placements.

Over the same period, managers of State and local pension funds have been making comparable shifts, but starting from a very different base and under a very different set of constraints. Severely circumscribed by specified lists of legal investments, which often limit holdings to governmental securities and a narrow selection of high-quality corporate bonds, major steps have nevertheless been taken to achieve higher yields. Acquisitions of State and local securities by these governmental pension funds, which had constituted more than 25 percent of all fund assets, have all but ceased and some existing holdings have been sold on the secondary market. Strong market demand for municipal issues in the early 1960s, particularly from commercial banks, facilitated this shift in investment policy. Governmental units had often looked to their own pension funds as convenient "captive" markets for sizable fractions of their own bond issues, which offer lower yields than other types of debt instruments because the income is exempt from Federal income tax, although the pension funds received no benefit from the tax exemption features.

Holdings of U.S. Government securities, which in 1954 made up about half of the total portfolio of these government pension funds, had been worked down to 24 percent a decade later. Corporate bonds had risen to nearly half of the composite, and since most State and local funds are still barred from taking part in private placements they have become a principal market for public offerings. For many funds, mortgages have become a significant asset.

To sum up the trend for all contractual intermediaries, investment managers have used wider investment latitude and rapidly increasing inflows to give their institutions a broader and more variegated role in U.S. capital markets.

DEPOSITARY INTERMEDIARIES

The same factors affecting contractual intermediaries have influenced investment patterns of institutions receiving depositary-type savings: pressures arising from expanding inflows and the need to obtain higher yields, resulting in a trend toward more aggressive and flexible investment policies.

Inflows

The most dynamic factor for depositary intermediaries has clearly been the dramatic expansion of depositary savings (up from an average flow of about $10 billion annually in the mid-1950s to about $30 billion in the last 4 years) and the increasingly costly terms on which this growth was achieved.

The growth of depositary-type savings during the 1960s, and particularly the greatly expanded role of commercial banks in attracting time and savings deposits—with inflows of this type rising from $3 billion in the mid-1950s to recent levels in excess of $15 billion—are now a familiar chapter in recent U.S. financial history. I shall recapitulate only those aspects that bear directly on capital market participation.

Depositary savings flows have been on an uptrend throughout the entire postwar period. During the decade of the 1950s, the strongest growth element was provided by the rapid expansion of savings shares at savings and loan associations. These specialized mortgage lenders traditionally offered higher returns than other institutions could offer to savers seeking depositary-type assets, and record demands for home financing encouraged them actively to seek expansion. Not only were their rates relatively attractive, but many associations engaged in widespread promotion and also offered consumer savers an increasingly wide network of convenient locations, convenient hours, arrangements for deposit-by-mail, grace periods during which late deposits would earn interest from the first of the month, and other features of this kind. By the mid-1950s, their annual savings inflows of nearly $5 billion made up half of the total flow into depositary institutions, and the average effective return of about 3 percent on savings shares was a full 1.5 percentage points higher than the average return paid on time and savings accounts at commercial banks.

Deposits at mutual savings banks—which in the United States are geographically more limited than savings and loan associations, offered rates more modestly in excess of those available at commercial banks and also grew, but at a much slower pace. Together the specialized savings institutions attracted about 70 percent of depositary savings, drawing them exclusively from the household sector. Commercial banks accounted for the remainder.

The maximum rate on the interest banks were permitted to pay on savings deposits (2.5 percent prior to 1957 and 3 percent thereafter) precluded active competition for the deposits of those household savers who were rate conscious. Time deposits by corporate and other institutional investors increased during periods of business recession when short-term market outlets were unattractive or unavailable, but rising yields on market instruments quickly reversed this flow as economic recovery got underway.

For most of the postwar period, in fact, this cyclical character was stamped even on the total volume of depositary-type savings. Typically, the relative share of such funds in total savings flows turned downward during phases of strong economic growth and high market rates. This indicates that a significant, if marginal, portion of depositary flows has always come from yield-conscious savers who were in a position to consider direct market investment as an eligible alternative. Reduction in the growth of depositary savings has occurred, in 1955 and 1959, and again in 1966.

It should be noted that this cyclical pattern did not develop properly during the expansion that began early in 1961, because depositary intermediaries—and particularly commercial banks—were willing and able to compete for funds. Regulatory liberalization permitted banks to raise the returns they offered on time and savings deposits, and sharp increases in bank inflows were followed in turn by upward rate adjustments at competing institutions. While the relative strength of inflows to the various intermediaries (depositary types) reflected leads and lags in these rate adjustments, the specialized savings institutions were generally able to maintain and even increase their own growth rates through about 1964. In 1965, increasing inflows to commercial banks were partly offset by declining growth elsewhere, and in 1966 all institutions have lost ground to the market; that is, the flow into intermediaries has declined whereas the flow of savings directly into market instruments has risen sharply.

Investment Patterns

Over the past decade, the increase in savings inflows to depositary institutions, as well as the changes in competitive relationships among them, has given rise to significant changes in investment policy at most institutions. Broadly speaking, the changes fit the general description we have already given of investment shifts among contractual institutions. But differing legal and traditional backgrounds of different institutions have shaped the ways in which institutions have sought wider outlets and higher yields.

Savings and loan associations have been, and remain, predominantly mortgage lenders, both by law and by tradition. In recent years they have sought and acquired increased freedom to engage in a limited range of other lending (certain types of educational loans, for example), but the years of their peak inflows coincided with record demands for mortgage financing, and the trend toward more diversified and more liberal lending was exhibited mainly within the housing market. There, savings and loan associations have achieved greater geographic scope, freedom to offer borrowers more liberal terms and to make larger loans, and—most importantly—greater opportunity to participate in financing construction of commercial and multifamily developments. Loans of the latter type came to account for about 25 percent of total mortgage lending by savings and loan associations in the past 4-year period.

Savings and loan associations are subject to a variety of regulatory provisions, depending on whether they operate under Federal or State charters, but the effective limit on liberalization of lending policies for most associations in recent years has probably been the need to maintain their own borrowing privileges at regional Federal home loan banks, of which all federally chartered and most State associations are members. This is an important resource to associations in evening out flows and also has served, on balance, as a significant supplement to the industry's lending capacity. Aggregate indebtedness to the home loan banks has increased each year, reaching a total of $6 billion by the end of 1965. The ability to cut off or curtail access to these funds gives the Home Loan Bank Board a degree of regulatory control over associations whose lending patterns fail to meet prescribed standards.

Mutual savings banks, unlike savings and loan associations, are authorized to acquire a variety of financial instruments, but in practice they too have specialized in mortgage lending. In fact, their mortgage lending (net) has been in excess of their annual net savings inflows during most years of the past decade. This has been possible through reductions in their holdings of other assets—principally U.S. Government securities, which made up 30 percent of mutual savings banks' composite portfolio in 1954 and only 11 percent by the end of 1965. Holdings of other securities have also been allowed to decline, reflecting both the widespread preference for mortgages as higher yielding instruments, the fact that investments in securities are often circumscribed by State quality regulations, and by prohibitions in certain key States against broadening investment areas. Thus, for mutual savings banks the pursuit of higher yields has led to greater concentration on mortgage lending, with increased takings of mortgages on both single-family and income-producing properties.

Changes in asset composition by commercial banks since 1960 have been more striking than those at other depositary-type intermediaries, in part because they reflect much greater shifts in the size and composition of inflows. Beginning in 1962 and early 1963, banks greatly increased their acquisitions of capital market instruments—especially State and local government securities and mortgages of all types. Bank participation in these markets was not itself a break with tradition, but the extent and duration of that participation were.

The annual increase in mortgage loan portfolios, which had averaged less than $2 billion in the mid-1950s, more than doubled to $4.5 billion in the early 1960s. And over the same period, net acquisitions of State and local government securities climbed from $0.8 billion to $4.6 billion. At the same time, the need for higher yields to match the higher cost of inflows was reflected in greater acceptance of longer maturities and somewhat lower quality ratings. Holdings of U.S. Government securities declined on balance during both periods, but the recent liquidation was sharper and was accompanied by some shift toward longer maturities.

In cyclical periods of slack loan demand, portfolio-type investments—including capital market instruments as well as shorter-term Government securities—have traditionally served as a sort of balancing and residual use of funds for commercial banks. The recent massive swing by banks to broader participation in capital markets has had more of a longer-term investment character than did earlier, primarily cyclical, shifts. But it also began at a time when loan demands, particularly those by business corporations, were relatively moderate, and its continuation at exceptionally high levels through last year, concurrent with sharply expanded loan demands, was possible only because general economic conditions at that time did not necessitate severe restraints on credit expansion. In 1966, the pattern changed sharply as, with bank credit expansion restrained, banks have met their business customer loan demands by curtailing their intervention in capital markets.

COSTS AND BENEFITS OF INTERMEDIATION

The most distinctive feature of post-war developments in financial intermediation has been the dynamic competition among the intermediaries themselves, both for savings flows and for investment outlets. Over time, this process has increased the efficiency of intermediation, both by cutting its cost—that is, narrowing the spread between the cost of funds to ultimate borrowers and the returns to nonfinancial savers—and by widening the alternatives available to both savers and borrowers. The high and rising savings by the nonfinancial sectors of the economy have stimulated competition among the various types of intermediaries for a share in this flow. This has been evidenced by rising rates of return and a variety of fringe benefits (such as more frequent crediting and compounding of interest). It has also produced a proliferation of savings instruments (negotiable certificates of deposit for larger holders or its more recent equivalent for individual depositors called savings certificates) and benefit contracts (such as variable annuities that permit beneficiaries to participate in equity share developments as well as guaranteeing a fixed sum benefit).

Third, competition has resulted in a tendency to broaden areas of investment, or at least to press for changes in laws that limit investment powers of intermediaries. Many economists, and I number myself among them, applaud this trend. Institutions with overly specialized portfolios are vulnerable to the fate of all overly specialized animals. Recall that many prehistoric animals, such as the dinosaur, were unable to survive changes in their environment because of their high degree of specialization. This, too, can be the fate of contemporary financial institutions unable or unwilling to adapt to changes in their economic environment.

At the same time, competition for investment outlets has tended to hold down the spread between the cost of funds to the intermediaries and the costs of long-term financing to ultimate borrowers. These direct costs of intermediation—which are at least roughly measurable for savings flowing through depositary intermediaries—have been brought down to a range of about 1 to 1½ percentage points.

Having noted this benefit accruing from the trend to funneling savings through institutions, let me point out some problems that arise. For one, individual investors—and to some extent, even the smaller institutions—have increasingly found primary markets less hospitable to their needs while secondary markets in most debt instruments are thin or nonexistent. Dealers in Government securities are wholesalers to whom individuals have access usually only through banks or brokers; institutional buyers enjoy first claim on new corporate and municipal offerings, if in fact they are offered to the public at all; only if institutional demand fails to absorb an entire issue is the underwriter likely to engage in a retail sales effort. There is even some longer-run question whether increased institutional trading in common stocks will not ultimately erode the traditionally retail character of auction markets in that instrument. Thus, the widening of options available to savers among institutional outlets has been accompanied by some narrowing of their options among market acquisitions. The impact of these changes, at least up to the present, should not be exaggerated but, as with so many economies of scale, the price of increasing efficiency in the marketing process appears to include some diminution of initiative for the individual.

Second, the recent trends in investment policy of intermediaries raises questions about the possible mismatching of the time-profile of assets and liabilities. Consumers acquire the liabilities of institutions because they regard them as liquid instruments. In the competitive drive to seek higher returns to afford offering higher returns to savers, depositary institutions have increasingly turned to longer-term investments and, to some extent, to investments of less than premium quality. In conventionally defined terms, the liquidity of intermediaries has declined as they have competed in offering liquid havens for consumer savers. This tends to pose a problem not during recessions, when market rates tend to fall faster than those paid by institutions, but rather during periods of economic boom, strong credit demands, and a public policy of credit restraint. It is in such periods when market rates of interest rise rapidly, but rates offered by institutions lag. The lag is only in part the result of regulations limiting rate increases by depositary institutions. It is also a function of the fact that the portfolios of these are "locked-in" to the lower rates prevailing earlier. To increase returns offered to savers may mean a rise in rates paid on a large share of institutional liabilities, but a rise in rates charged borrowers can be made effective only for the net additions to portfolios, which will generally be a small share of the total stock of investments.

Since portfolio composition differs among the various types of depositary institutions, the impact of boom conditions in the U.S. economy is not evenly distributed among intermediaries. In 1966, for example, while all depositary institutions have shown lagging growth in their inflows, the sharpest reductions have been among savings and loan associations and mutual savings banks. Commercial banks, with stronger demand for the types of credit they customarily extend, with a quicker turn-around in the portfolios, and with newly achieved latitude in competing for savings, have not been affected so much by the rise in market rates. The change in competitive relationships among intermediaries has presented serious problems for the agencies of Government charged with supervising and regulating these matters and has brought forth legislation temporarily restricting competition among depositary-type intermediaries.

The trend toward institutions' acceptance of investments of lower-quality standing has also given rise to some expressions of concern over the soundness of institutional assets generally. It must first be recognized that we are not concerned here with individual mistakes in judgment by investment managers. Indeed, a "perfect" record might suggest a lack of initiative and daring with unfortunate consequences for a dynamic economy. The broad considerations must deal with the general pattern and level of the quality of investments of financial institutions. What data are available do not give ground for alarm, at least at this time. Liberalization of lending terms cannot automatically be identified as decline in quality. Given the size and diversity of most institutional portfolios and the size of savings inflows, it is not inappropriate for institutional managers to feel safe in including among their assets some proportion of a somewhat less than premium quality. This is not to say that supervisory authorities should not be on guard to insure that the proportion does not grow so much that the institution becomes vulnerable to moderate fluctuations in economic conditions and to repayment ability of those to whom they have loaned funds. But it does imply that diversity of investments and size and cash flows from loan repayments

are worthy of consideration along with traditional quality measures of individual investments in assessing the probable solvency of an institution.

And this observation brings us back full circle to our starting point. It is just this ability of financial intermediaries to accept and hold assets that do not possess directly all the characteristics needed by individual savers that gives intermediation its essential role in making financial savings available to long-term borrowers. The efficiency with which intermediaries perform this role may be measured by their ability to make savings available—at rates reasonably related to their own cost of funds—to borrowers who cannot offer liquid instruments of guaranteed security in convenient forms but who *are* able to furnish obligations good enough for the normal purposes of large-scale portfolios. On balance, that ability has increased over time, and by this test of resource allocation, financial intermediaries are playing a broader and more efficient role in U.S. capital markets.

FINANCIAL INTERMEDIARIES AND THE SAVING-INVESTMENT PROCESS*

John G. Gurley and Edward S. Shaw

It is fashionable these days to speak of the growing institutionalization of saving and investment. Rapid advances in recent years by pension funds, open-end investment companies, credit unions, and savings and loan associations, among others, have caught our eye. But the advance has been going on at least since the Civil War, and as Raymond Goldsmith has recently shown, it was quite pronounced during the first three decades of this century. It is with these three decades that our paper is primarily concerned. Our method of analyzing financial data, however, requires explanation since it is based on unconventional theory. Accordingly, the first portions of the paper are largely theoretical. After that, we get down to brass tacks.

DEFICITS, SECURITY ISSUES, AND GNP

It is easy to imagine a world in which there is a high level of saving and investment, but

in which there is an unfavorable climate for financial intermediaries. At the extreme, each of the economy's spending units—whether of the household, business, or government variety—would have a balanced budget on income and product account. For each spending unit, current income would equal the sum of current and capital expenditures. There could still be saving and investment, but each spending unit's saving would be precisely matched by its investment in tangible assets. In a world of balanced budgets, security issues by spending units would be zero, or very close to zero.[1] The same would be true of the accumulation of financial assets. Consequently, this world would be a highly uncongenial one for financial intermediaries; the saving-investment process would grind away without them.

Financial intermediaries are likely to thrive best in a world of deficits and surpluses, in a world in which there is a significant division of labor between savers and investors. In the ideal

* From the article of the same title, *Journal of Finance*, Vol. XI (May 1956), pp. 257–66. Reprinted by permission of the publisher and the authors. John G. Gurley and Edward S. Shaw are Professors of Economics, Stanford University.

[1] Securities might be issued by spending units to build up their financial assets or their holdings of existing real assets. However, in a world of balanced budgets, no spending unit would have a *net* accumulation of these assets, positive or negative.

world for financial intermediaries, all current and capital expenditures would be made by spending units that received no current income, and all current income would be received by spending units that spent nothing. One group of spending units would have a deficit equal to its expenditures, and the other group would have a surplus equal to its income. And, of course, the *ex post* deficit would necessarily be equal to the *ex post* surplus. In this setting, the deficit group would tend to issue securities equal to its deficit, and the other group would tend to accumulate financial assets equal to its surplus. Security issues and financial-asset accumulations, therefore, would tend to approximate GNP or the aggregate of expenditures. No more congenial world than this could exist for financial intermediaries.

Unfortunately for these intermediaries, our own economy has been much closer to the first than to the second world. With some exceptions during the past half-century, the annual security issues of spending units over complete cycles have averaged somewhat below 10 percent of GNP in current prices. These issues include government securities, corporate and foreign bonds, common and preferred stock, farm and non-farm mortgages, and consumer and other short-term debt. We shall call these primary security issues. Thus, at the turn of the century when GNP was around $20 billion, primary security issues ran a bit less than $2 billion per annum. In the late 1940s, with a GNP of approximately $250 billion, primary issues hovered around $20 billion per annum. Dividing the half-century into thirteen complete cycles, we find that the average annual ratio of primary issues to GNP was between 7 and 10 percent in nine of the cycles. The exceptional cases include World War I, when the ratio reached 20 percent, the 1930s, when the ratio fell to 3 or 4 percent, and World War II, when it climbed to 25 percent. However, if we consider longer phases, 1897–1914, 1915–32, and 1933–49, the ratio was between 9 and 10 percent in each phase. There is sufficient strength, then, in the link between borrowing and GNP to make the relationship useful for financial analysis. And while the ratio lies closer to zero than to 100 percent, still it is high enough to permit financial intermediation to be a substantial business.

THE ROLE OF FINANCIAL INTERMEDIARIES

What is the business of financial intermediaries? They lend at one stratum of interest rates and borrow at a lower stratum. They relieve the market of some primary securities and substi-

tute others—indirect securities or financial assets—whose qualities command a higher price. This margin between yields on primary and indirect securities is the intermediaries' compensation for the special services they supply.

The financial institutions that fit these specifications are savings and loan associations, insurance companies, mutual savings banks, Postal Savings banks, investment companies, common trust funds, pension funds, government lending agencies, and others. In addition, we count the monetary system, including commercial banks, as one among many intermediaries. It is a vitally important intermediary, in view of its functions and its size. But its elevated rank among intermediaries does not alter the principle that the monetary system, like other intermediaries, transmits loanable funds by issues of indirect financial assets to surplus units and purchases of primary securities from deficit units. The indirect financial assets, deposits and currency that it issues or creates, are, like the indirect financial assets issued or created by other intermediaries, substitutes for primary securities in the portfolios of spending units. We shall return to this point in a few moments.

INTERNAL AND EXTERNAL FINANCE OF EXPENDITURES

In a world of balanced budgets, each spending unit's current and capital expenditures would be financed entirely from its current income. Thus, aggregate expenditures in the economy would be self-financed or internally financed. Internal finance would be equal to GNP.

In a world of deficits and surpluses, some expenditures would be financed externally. The extent of such financing is measured by the sum of the deficits (or surpluses) run by spending units. If at a GNP of $400 billion, the sum of all spending units' deficits is $40 billion, then 10 percent of GNP is financed externally and 90 percent is financed internally.

External finance may take two forms: direct finance and indirect finance. The distinction is based on the changes that occur in the financial accounts of surplus units' balance sheets. The finance is indirect if the surplus units acquire claims on financial intermediaries.[2] It is direct

---

[2] In our empirical work, we exclude from indirect finance some kinds of claims on intermediaries, such as accrued expenses or even stockholder equities, that are essentially like debt issues of non-financial spending units.

if surplus units acquire claims on debtors that are not financial intermediaries.[3]

While the proportion of GNP that is externally financed has not changed much over the past half-century, the proportion that is indirectly financed has risen and, of course, the proportion that is directly financed has fallen. In short, a growing share of primary issues has been sold to financial intermediaries.[4] But the relative gainers have been the non-monetary intermediaries and the relative loser has been the monetary system. Now, if we look at these trends from the standpoint of surplus spenders, we have the following picture: the surplus units have accumulated financial assets in annual amounts that, over long periods, have been a fairly steady percentage of GNP. However, these accumulations have been relatively more and more in the form of indirect financial assets, and relatively less and less in the form of primary securities. Moreover, the accumulations of indirect financial assets have swung toward the non-monetary types and away from bank deposits and currency. Commercial banks and the monetary system have retrogressed relative to financial intermediaries generally.

A RECONSIDERATION OF BANKING THEORY

A traditional view of the monetary system is that it determines the supply of money: it determines its own size in terms of monetary debt and of the assets that are counterparts of this

---

[3] It may help to illustrate these financing arrangements. Suppose that at a GNP of $400 billion the sum of all spending units' deficits is $40 billion. Suppose further that $40 billion of primary securities, such as corporate bonds and mortgages, are issued to cover the deficits. The primary securities may be sold directly to surplus spending units whose aggregate surplus will also be equal to $40 billion, looking at it *ex post*. In this case direct finance will take place, with surplus spenders acquiring various types of primary securities. Alternatively, if the primary securities are sold to financial intermediaries, surplus spenders will accumulate claims on these intermediaries, indirect financial assets instead of primary securities. In this event we say that the expenditures represented by the primary securities have been indirectly financed. If indirect finance occurs through commercial banks, surplus spenders accumulate bank deposits; if through savings and loan associations, they acquire savings and loan shares; if through life insurance companies, policyholder equities; and so on.

[4] This growth has not been steady. Indeed, it is shown later that there was retrogression in intermediation from 1898 to 1921. The share of issues going to intermediaries rose in the 1920s, rose further in the 1930s, and remained high in the 1940s.

debt on the system's balance sheet. Other financial intermediaries transfer to investors any part of this money supply that may be deposited with them by savers. Their size is determined by the public's choice of saving media.

As we see it, on the contrary, the monetary system is in some significant degree competitive with other financial intermediaries. The growth of these intermediaries in terms of indirect debt and of primary security portfolios is alternative to monetary growth and inhibits it. Their issues of indirect debt displace money, and the primary securities that they hold are in some large degree a loss of assets to the banks.

Bank deposits and currency are unique in one respect: they are means of payment, and holders of money balances have immediate access to the payments mechanism of the banking system. If money were in demand only for immediate spending or for holding in transactions balances, and if no other financial asset could be substituted as a means of payment or displace money in transactions balances, the monetary system would be a monopolistic supplier exempt from competition by other financial intermediaries.

But money is not in demand exclusively as a means of payment. It is in demand as a financial asset to hold. As a component of balances, money does encounter competition. Other financial assets can be accumulated preparatory to money payments, as a precaution against contingencies, or as an alternative to primary securities. For any level of money payments, various levels of money balances will do and, hence, various sizes of money supply and monetary system.

The more adequate the non-monetary financial assets are as substitutes for money in transactions, precautionary, speculative, and—as we shall see—diversification balances, the smaller may be the money supply for any designated level of national income. For any level of income, the money supply is indeterminate until one knows the degree of substitutability between money created by banks and financial assets created by other intermediaries. How big the monetary system is depends in part on the intensity of competition from savings banks, life insurance companies, pension funds, and other intermediaries.

Financial competition may inhibit the growth of the monetary system in a number of ways. Given the level of national income, a gain in attractiveness of, say, savings and loan shares vis-à-vis money balances must result in an excess supply of money. The monetary authority may choose to remove this excess. Then bank reserves, earning assets, money issues, and profits are contracted. This implies that, at any level of income, the competition of non-monetary intermediaries may displace money balances, shift primary securities from banks to their competitors, and reduce the monetary system's requirement for reserves. In a trend context, bank reserves cannot be permitted to grow as rapidly as otherwise they might, if non-monetary intermediaries become more attractive channels for transmission of loanable funds.

Suppose that excess money balances, resulting from a shift in spending units' demand away from money balances to alternative forms of indirect financial assets, are not destroyed by central bank action. They may be used to repay bank loans or to buy other securities from banks, the result being excess bank reserves. At the prevailing level of security prices, spending units have rejected money balances. But cannot banks force these balances out again, resuming control of the money supply? They can do so by accepting a reduced margin between the yield of primary securities they buy and the cost to them of deposits and currency they create. But this option is not peculiar to banks: other intermediaries can stimulate demand for their debt if they stand ready to accept a reduced markup on the securities they create and sell relative to the securities they buy. The banks can restore the money supply, but the cost is both a decline in their status relative to other financial intermediaries and a reduction in earnings.

The banks may choose to live with excess reserves rather than pay higher prices on primary securities or higher yields on their own debt issues. In this case, as in the previous two, a lower volume of reserves is needed to sustain a given level of national income. With their competitive situation improved, non-monetary intermediaries have stolen away from the banking system a share of responsibility for sustaining the flow of money payments. They hold a larger share of outstanding primary securities; they owe a larger share of indirect financial assets. They have reduced the size of the banking system at the given income level, both absolutely and relatively to their own size, and their gain is at the expense of bank profits.[5]

---

[5] We may mention a few additional issues in banking theory. As intermediaries, banks buy primary securities and issue, in payment for them, deposits and currency. As the payments mechanism, banks transfer title to means of payment on demand by customers. It has been pointed out before, especially by Henry Simons, that these two banking functions are at least incompatible. As managers of the payments mechanism, the banks cannot afford a shadow of insolvency. As intermediaries in a growing economy, the banks may rightly be tempted to wildcat. They must be solvent or the community will suffer; they must dare insolvency or the community will fail to realize its potentialities for growth.

All too often in American history energetic intermediation by banks has culminated in collapse of the payments mechanism. During some periods, especially cautious regard for solvency has resulted in collapse of bank intermediation. Each occasion that has demonstrated the incompatibility of the two principal banking functions has touched off a flood of financial reform. These reforms on balance have tended to emphasize bank solvency and the viability of the payments mechanism at the expense of bank participation in financial growth. They have by no means gone to the extreme that Simons proposed, of divorcing the two functions altogether, but they have tended in that direction rather than toward indorsement of wildcat banking. This bias in financial reform has improved the opportunities for non-monetary intermediaries. The relative retrogression in banking seems to have resulted in part from regulatory suppression of the intermediary function.

Turning to another matter, it has seemed to be a distinctive, even magic, characteristic of the monetary system that it can create money, erecting a "multiple expansion" of debt in the form of deposits and currency on a limited base of reserves. Other financial institutions, conventional doctrine tells us, are denied this creative or multiplicative faculty. They are merely middlemen or brokers, not manufacturers of credit. Our own view is different. There is no denying, of course, that the monetary system creates debt in the special form of money: the monetary system can borrow by issue of instruments that are means of payment. There is no denying, either, that non-monetary intermediaries cannot create this same form of debt. They would be monetary institutions if they could do so. It is granted, too, that non-monetary intermediaries receive money and pay it out, precisely as all of us do: they use the payments mechanism.

However, each kind of non-monetary intermediary can borrow, go into debt, issue its own characteristic obligations—in short, it can create credit, though not in monetary form. Moreover, the non-monetary intermediaries are less inhibited in their own style of credit creation than are the banks in creating money. Credit creation by non-monetary intermediaries is restricted by various qualitative rules. Aside from these, the main factor that limits credit creation is the profit calculus. Credit creation by banks also is subject to the profit condition. But the monetary system is subject not only to this restraint and to a complex of qualitative rules. It is committed to a policy restraint, of avoiding excessive expansion or contraction of credit for the community's welfare, that is not imposed explicitly on non-monetary intermediaries. It is also held in check by a system of reserve requirements. The legal reserve requirement on commercial banks is a "sharing ratio"; it apportions assets within the monetary system. The share of assets allocated to the commercial banks varies inversely with the reserve requirement. The propor-

A RECONSIDERATION OF INTEREST THEORY

It is clear from the foregoing remarks that this way of looking at financial intermediaries leads to a reconsideration of interest theory. Yields on primary securities, the terms of borrowing available to deficit spenders, are influenced not only by the amount of primary securities in the monetary system—that is, by the supply of money—but also by the amount of these securities in non-monetary intermediaries—that is, by the supply of indirect financial assets created by these intermediaries. Suppose that savings and loan shares become more attractive relative to bank deposits, resulting in an excess supply of money. Now, if we suppose that the monetary system chooses and manages to keep the money supply constant under these circumstances, the excess supply of money will cause yields on primary securities to fall. The activities of non-monetary financial intermediaries, then, can affect primary yields. The same money supply and national income are compatible with various interest rate levels, depending upon the size of non-monetary intermediaries and upon the degree to which their issues are competitive with money.[6]

The analysis is only a bit more complicated when we allow for issues of primary securities and the growth of income. Let us take these one at a time. At any income level, some spending units will have deficits and others surpluses. During the income period, the deficit spenders will tend to issue primary securities in an amount equal to their aggregate deficits. Now, if the surplus spenders are willing to absorb all of the issues at current yields on these securities, there will be no tightening effect on security markets. Surplus spenders will accumulate financial assets, all in the form of primary securities, and financial intermediaries will purchase none of the issues.

But this is an unlikely outcome. Ordinarily, surplus spenders can be expected to reject some portion of the primary securities emerging at any level of income and demand indirect financial assets instead, unless their preference for the latter is suppressed by a fall in prices of primary securities and a corresponding rise in interest rates charged to deficit spenders. This incremental demand for indirect financial assets is in part a demand for portfolio diversification. The diversification demand exists because there is generally no feasible mixture of primary securities that provides adequately such distinctive qualities of indirect securities as stability of price and yield or divisibility. The incremental demand for indirect assets, however, reflects not only a negative response, a partial rejection of primary securities, but also a positive response, an attraction to the many services attached to indirect assets, such as insurance and pension services and convenience of accumulation. Part of the demand is linked to the flow of primary security issues, but another part is linked more closely to the level of income.

For these reasons, then, ordinarily some portion of the primary issues must be sold to financial intermediaries if present yields on these securities are to be defended. Assuming for the moment that the monetary system is the only financial intermediary, the increase in the money supply must be equal to the portion of primary issues that spending units choose not to accumulate at current yields. If the monetary system purchases less than this, spending units will accumulate the residual supply at rising interest rates to deficit spenders. The emergence of security issues and a diversification demand for money based on these issues means that the money supply must rise at a given income level to maintain current yields on primary securities.

Still retaining the assumption that the monetary system is the only financial intermediary, we now permit income to grow. As money income gains, spending units demand additions to their active or transactions balances of means of payment. An upward trend in money payments calls

---

tion of the commercial banks' share to the share of the central bank and Treasury is the "multiple of expansion" for the commercial banking system. The "multiple of expansion" is a remarkable phenomenon not because of its inflationary implications but because it means that bank expansion is anchored, as other financial expansion is not, to a regulated base. If credit creation by banks is miraculous, creation of credit by other financial institutions is still more a cause for exclamation.

[6] We can reach the same conclusion by looking at the supply of and the demand for primary securities. The shift in demand to savings and loan shares reduces spending units' demand for bank deposits by, say, an equivalent amount. Consequently, the demand by spending units for primary securities is unchanged at current yields. Also, there is no change in this demand by the monetary system, since we have assumed the money supply constant. However, there is an increase in demand for primary securities by savings and loan associations. So, for the economy as a whole, there is an excess demand for primary securities at current yields, which is the counterpart of the excess supply of money.

Downward pressure on primary yields is exerted as long as the indirect debt of non-monetary intermediaries is to some degree competitive with money and as long as the additional demand for primary securities by these intermediaries is roughly equivalent to their creation of indirect debt.

for an upward trend in balances too. The income effect also applies to contingency or precautionary balances. If spending units are increasingly prosperous in the present, they feel able to afford stronger defenses against the hazards of the future.[7]

The combination of the income and diversification effects simply means that, when income is rising, a larger share of the issues must be purchased by the monetary system to prevent a rise in primary yields. The system must supply money for both diversification and transactions, including contingency, balances.

We may now introduce non-monetary intermediaries. The growth of these intermediaries will ordinarily, to some extent, reduce the required growth of the monetary system. We have already presented the reasons for this, so it

suffices to say that primary yields may be held steady under growth conditions even with a monetary system that is barely growing, provided other intermediaries take up the slack.

In summary, primary security issues depend on aggregate deficits, and the latter in turn are related to the income level. At any income level, the diversification effect of these issues means that financial intermediaries must grow to hold primary yields steady. If income is rising, too, there is an incremental demand for money and perhaps for other indirect assets for transactions and contingency balances, requiring additional intermediary growth. To the extent that the issues of non-monetary intermediaries are competitive with money balances of whatever type, the required growth of the monetary system is reduced by the expansion of other intermediaries.

---

[7] For periods longer than the Keynesian short run, it is hardly safe to assume that transactions and contingency demands for additional money balances are proportional to increments in the level of money income. They may be elastic to interest rates on such primary securities as Treasury bills and brokers' loans. For any increment in money income, they may rise with real income. As a larger share of national income involves market transactions, as population moves from farms to cities, as a dollar of income is generated with more or fewer dollars

of intermediate payments, as credit practices change, as checks are collected more efficiently or as deposits cease to bear interest and bear service charges instead, one expects the marginal ratio of active balances to income to vary. And incremental demand for contingency balances must be sensitive not only to income, and perhaps to interest rates, but to the evolution of emergency credit facilities, to job security and social security, to an array of circumstances that is largely irrelevant in short-period analysis.

COMMERCIAL BANKS AS CREATORS OF "MONEY"*

James Tobin

I. THE OLD VIEW

Perhaps the greatest moment of triumph for the elementary economics teacher is his exposition of the multiple creation of bank credit and bank deposits. Before the admiring eyes of freshmen he puts to rout the practical banker who is so sure that he "lends only the money depositors entrust to him." The banker is shown to have a worm's-eye view, and his error stands as an introductory object lesson in the fallacy of composition. From the Olympian vantage of the teacher and the textbook it appears that the banker's dictum must be reversed: depositors entrust to bankers whatever amounts the bankers lend. To be sure, this is not true of a single bank; one bank's loan may wind up as another bank's de-

posit. But it is, as the arithmetic of successive rounds of deposit creation makes clear, true of the banking system as a whole. Whatever their other errors, a long line of financial heretics have been right in speaking of "fountain pen money"—money created by the stroke of the bank president's pen when he approves a loan and credits the proceeds to the borrower's checking account.

In this time-honored exposition two characteristics of commercial banks—both of which are alleged to differentiate them sharply from other financial intermediaries—are intertwined. One is that their liabilities—well, at least their demand deposit liabilities—serve as widely acceptable means of payment. Thus, they count, along with coin and currency in public circulation, as "money." The other is that the preferences of the public normally play no role in determining the total volume of deposits or the total quantity of money. For it is the beginning of wisdom

---

* From Deane Carson (ed.), *Banking and Monetary Studies* (Homewood, Ill.: Richard D. Irwin, Inc., 1963), pp. 408–19. Reprinted by permission of the publisher and the author. James Tobin is Sterling Professor of Economics, Yale University.

in monetary economics to observe that money is like the "hot potato" of a children's game: one individual may pass it to another, but the group as a whole cannot get rid of it. If the economy and the supply of money are out of adjustment, it is the economy that must do the adjusting. This is as true, evidently, of money created by bankers' fountain pens as of money created by public printing presses. On the other hand, financial intermediaries other than banks do not create money, and the scale of their assets is limited by their liabilities, i.e., by the savings the public entrusts to them. They cannot count on receiving "deposits" to match every extension of their lending.

The commercial banks and only the commercial banks, in other words, possess the widow's cruse. And because they possess this key to unlimited expansion, they have to be restrained by reserve requirements. Once this is done, determination of the aggregate volume of bank deposits is just a matter of accounting and arithmetic: simply divide the available supply of bank reserves by the required reserve ratio.

The foregoing is admittedly a caricature, but I believe it is not a great exaggeration of the impressions conveyed by economics teaching concerning the roles of commercial banks and other financial institutions in the monetary system. In conveying this mélange of propositions, economics has replaced the naïve fallacy of composition of the banker with other half-truths perhaps equally misleading. These have their root in the mystique of "money"—the tradition of distinguishing sharply between those assets which are and those which are not "money," and accordingly between those institutions which emit "money" and those whose liabilities are not "money." The persistent strength of this tradition is remarkable given the uncertainty and controversy over where to draw the dividing line between money and other assets. Time was when only currency was regarded as money, and the use of bank deposits was regarded as a way of economizing currency and increasing the velocity of money. Today scholars and statisticians wonder and argue whether to count commercial bank time and savings deposits in the money supply. And if so, why not similar accounts in other institutions? Nevertheless, once the arbitrary line is drawn, assets on the money side of the line are assumed to possess to the full properties which assets on the other side completely lack. For example, an eminent monetary economist, more candid than many of his colleagues, admits that we don't really know what money is, but proceeds

to argue that, whatever it is, its supply should grow regularly at a rate of the order of 3 to 4 percent per year.[1]

II. THE "NEW VIEW"

A more recent development in monetary economics tends to blur the sharp traditional distinctions between money and other assets and between commercial banks and other financial intermediaries; to focus on demands for and supplies of the whole spectrum of assets rather than on the quantity and velocity of "money"; and to regard the structure of interest rates, asset yields, and credit availabilities rather than the quantity of money as the linkage between monetary and financial institutions and policies on the one hand and the real economy on the other.[2] In this essay I propose to look briefly at the implications of this "new view" for the theory of deposit creation, of which I have above described or caricatured the traditional version. One of the incidental advantages of this theoretical development is to effect something of a reconciliation between the economics teacher and the practical banker.

According to the "new view," the essential function of financial intermediaries, including commercial banks, is to satisfy simultaneously the portfolio preferences of two types of individuals or firms.[3] On one side are borrowers, who wish to expand their holdings of real assets—inventories, residential real estate, productive plant and equipment, etc.—beyond the limits of their own net worth. On the other side are lenders, who wish to hold part or all of their net worth in assets of stable money value with negligible risk of default. The assets of financial intermediaries are obligations of the borrowers—promissory notes, bonds, mortgages. The liabili-

[1] E. S. Shaw, "Money Supply and Stable Economic Growth," in *United States Monetary Policy* (New York: American Assembly, 1958), pp. 49–71.

[2] For a review of this development and for references to its protagonists, see Harry Johnson's survey article, "Monetary Theory and Policy," *American Economic Review*, Vol. LII (June, 1962), pp. 335–84. I will confine myself to mentioning the importance, in originating and contributing to the "new view," of John Gurley and E. S. Shaw (yes, the very same Shaw cited in the previous footnote, but presumably in a different incarnation). Their viewpoint is summarized in *Money in a Theory of Finance* (Washington, D.C.: The Brookings Institution, 1960).

[3] This paragraph and the three following are adapted with minor changes from the author's paper with William Brainard, "Financial Intermediaries and the Effectiveness of Monetary Controls," *American Economic Review*, Vol. LIII (May, 1963), pp. 384–86.

ties of financial intermediaries are the assets of the lenders—bank deposits, insurance policies, pension rights.

Financial intermediaries typically assume liabilities of smaller default risk and greater predictability of value than their assets. The principal kinds of institutions take on liabilities of greater liquidity too; thus, bank depositors can require payment on demand, while bank loans become due only on specified dates. The reasons that the intermediation of financial institutions can accomplish these transformations between the nature of the obligation of the borrower and the nature of the asset of the ultimate lender are these: (1) administrative economy and expertise in negotiating, accounting, appraising, and collecting; (2) reduction of risk per dollar of lending by the pooling of independent risks, with respect both to loan default and to deposit withdrawal; (3) governmental guarantees of the liabilities of the institutions and other provisions (bank examination, investment regulations, supervision of insurance companies, last-resort lending) designed to assure the solvency and liquidity of the institutions.

For these reasons, intermediation permits borrowers who wish to expand their investments in real assets to be accommodated at lower rates and easier terms than if they had to borrow directly from the lenders. If the creditors of financial intermediaries had to hold instead the kinds of obligations that private borrowers are capable of providing, they would certainly insist on higher rates and stricter terms. Therefore, any autonomous increase—for example, improvements in the efficiency of financial institutions or the creation of new types of intermediaries—in the amount of financial intermediation in the economy can be expected to be, *ceteris paribus,* an expansionary influence. This is true whether the growth occurs in intermediaries with monetary liabilities—i.e., commercial banks—or in other intermediaries.

Financial institutions fall fairly easily into distinct categories, each industry or "intermediary" offering a differentiated product to its customers, both lenders and borrowers. From the point of view of lenders, the obligations of the various intermediaries are more or less close, but not perfect, substitutes. For example, savings deposits share most of the attributes of demand deposits; but they are not means of payment, and the institution has the right, seldom exercised, to require notice of withdrawal. Similarly there is differentiation in the kinds of credit offered borrowers. Each intermediary has its specialty—e.g.,

the commercial loan for banks, the real-estate mortgage for the savings and loan association. But the borrowers' market is not completely compartmentalized. The same credit instruments are handled by more than one intermediary, and many borrowers have flexibility in the type of debt they incur. Thus, there is some substitutability, in the demand for credit by borrowers, between the assets of the various intermediaries.[4]

The special attentions given commercial banks in economic analysis is usually justified by the observation that, alone among intermediaries, banks "create" means of payment. This rationale is on its face far from convincing. The means-of-payment characteristic of demand deposits is indeed a feature differentiating bank liabilities from those of other intermediaries. Insurance against death is equally a feature differentiating life insurance policies from the obligations of other intermediaries, including banks. It is not obvious that one kind of differentiation should be singled out for special analytical treatment. Like other differentia, the means-of-payment attribute has its price. Savings deposits, for example, are perfect substitutes for demand deposits in every respect except as a medium of exchange. This advantage of checking accounts does not give banks absolute immunity from the competition of savings banks; it is a limited advantage that can be, at least in some part for many depositors, overcome by differences in yield. It follows that the community's demand for bank deposits is not indefinite, even though demand deposits do serve as means of payment.

III. THE WIDOW'S CRUSE

Neither individually nor collectively do commercial banks possess a widow's cruse. Quite apart from legal reserve requirements, commercial banks are limited in scale by the same kinds of economic processes that determine the aggregate size of other intermediaries.

One often cited difference between commercial banks and other intermediaries must be quickly dismissed as superficial and irrelevant. This is the fact that a bank can make a loan by "writing up" its deposit liabilities, while a savings and loan association, for example, cannot satisfy a

---

[4] These features of the market structure of intermediaries, and their implications for the supposed uniqueness of banks, have been emphasized by Gurley and Shaw, *op. cit.* An example of substitutability on the deposit side is analyzed by David and Charlotte Alhadeff, "The Struggle for Commercial Bank Savings," *Quarterly Journal of Economics,* Vol. LXXII (February, 1958), pp. 1–22.

mortgage borrower by crediting him with a share account. The association must transfer means of payment to the borrower; its total liabilities do not rise along with its assets. True enough, but neither do the bank's, for more than a fleeting moment. Borrowers do not incur debt in order to hold idle deposits, any more than savings and loan shares. The borrower pays out the money, and there is of course no guarantee that any of it stays in the lending bank. Whether or not it stays in the banking system as a whole is another question, about to be discussed. But the answer clearly does not depend on the way the loan was initially made. It depends on whether somewhere in the chain of transactions initiated by the borrower's outlays are found depositors who wish to hold new deposits equal in amount to the new loan. Similarly, the outcome for the savings and loan industry depends on whether in the chain of transactions initiated by the mortgage are found individuals who wish to acquire additional savings and loan shares.

The banking system can expand its assets either (a) by purchasing, or lending against existing assets; or (b) by lending to finance new private investment in inventories or capital goods, or buying government securities financing new public deficits. In case (a) no increase in private wealth occurs in conjunction with the banks' expansion. There is no new private saving and investment. In case (b), new private saving occurs, matching dollar for dollar the private investments or government deficits financed by the banking system. In neither case will there automatically be an increase in savers' demand for bank deposits equal to the expansion in bank assets.

In the second case, it is true, there is an increase in private wealth. But even if we assume a closed economy in order to abstract from leakages of capital abroad, the community will not ordinarily wish to put 100 percent of its new saving into bank deposits. Bank deposits are, after all, only about 15 percent of total private wealth in the United States; other things equal, savers cannot be expected greatly to exceed this proportion in allocating new saving. So, if *all* new saving is to take the form of bank deposits, other things cannot stay equal. Specifically, the yields and other advantages of the competing assets into which new saving would otherwise flow will have to fall enough so that savers prefer bank deposits.

This is *a fortiori* true in case (a) where there is no new saving and the generation of bank liabilities to match the assumed expansion of bank assets entails a reshuffling of existing portfolios in favor of bank deposits. In effect the banking

system has to induce the public to swap loans and securities for bank deposits. This can happen only if the price is right.

Clearly, then, there is at any moment a natural economic limit to the scale of the commercial banking industry. Given the wealth and the asset preferences of the community, the demand for bank deposits can increase only if the yields of other assets fall. The fall in these yields is bound to restrict the profitable lending and investment opportunities available to the banks themselves. Eventually the marginal returns on lending and investing, account taken of the risks and administrative costs involved, will not exceed the marginal cost to the banks of attracting and holding additional deposits. At this point the widow's cruse has run dry.

IV. BANKS AND OTHER INTERMEDIARIES COMPARED

In this respect the commercial banking industry is not qualitatively different from any other financial intermediary system. The same process limits the collective expansion of savings and loan associations, or savings banks, or life insurance companies. At some point the returns from additional loans or security holdings are not worth the cost of obtaining the funds from the public.

There are of course some differences. First, it may well be true that commercial banks benefit from a larger share of additions to private savings than other intermediaries. Second, according to modern American legal practice, commercial banks are subject to ceilings on the rates payable to their depositors—zero in the case of demand deposits. Unlike competing financial industries, commercial banks cannot seek funds by raising rates. They can and do offer other inducements to depositors, but these substitutes for interest are imperfect and uneven in their incidence. In these circumstances the major readjustment of the interest rate structure necessary to increase the relative demand for bank deposits is a decline in other rates. Note that neither of these differences has to do with the quality of bank deposits as "money."

In a world without reserve requirements the preferences of depositors, as well as those of borrowers, would be very relevant in determining the volume of bank deposits. The volume of assets and liabilities of every intermediary, both nonbanks and banks, would be determined in a competitive equilibrium, where the rate of interest charged borrowers by each kind of institution just balances at the margin the rate of interest paid its creditors. Suppose that such an equilibrium is disturbed by a shift in savers' preferences. At prevailing rates they decide to hold more savings accounts and other nonbank liabilities and less demand deposits. They transfer demand deposits to the credit of nonbank financial institutions, providing these intermediaries with the means to seek additional earning assets. These institutions, finding themselves able attract more funds from the public even with some reduction in the rates they pay, offer better terms to borrowers and bid up the prices of existing earning assets. Consequently commercial banks release some earning assets—they no longer yield enough to pay the going rate on the banks' deposit liabilities. Bank deposits decline with bank assets. In effect, the nonbank intermediaries favored by the shift in public preferences simply swap the deposits transferred to them for a corresponding quantity of bank assets.

V. FOUNTAIN PENS AND PRINTING PRESSES

Evidently the fountain pens of commercial bankers are essentially different from the printing presses of governments. Confusion results from concluding that because bank deposits are like currency in one respect—both serve as media of exchange—they are like currency in every respect. Unlike governments, bankers cannot create means of payment to finance their own purchases of goods and services. Bank-created "money" is a liability, which must be matched on the other side of the balance sheet. And banks, as businesses, must earn money from their middleman's role. Once created, printing press money cannot be extinguished, except by reversal of the budget policies which led to its birth. The community cannot get rid of its currency supply; the economy must adjust until it is willingly absorbed. The "hot potato" analogy truly applies. For bank-created money, however, there is an economic mechanism of extinction as well as creation, contraction as well as expansion. If bank deposits are excessive relative to public preferences, they will tend to decline; otherwise banks will lose income. The burden of adaptation is not placed entirely on the rest of the economy.

VI. THE ROLE OF RESERVE REQUIREMENTS

Without reserve requirements, expansion of credit and deposits by the commercial banking system would be limited by the availability of assets at yields sufficient to compensate banks for the costs of attracting and holding the corresponding deposits. In a régime of reserve requirements, the limit which they impose normally cuts the expansion short of this competitive equilibrium. When reserve requirements and deposit interest rate ceilings are effective, the marginal yield of bank loans and investments exceeds the marginal cost of deposits to the banking system. In these circumstances additional reserves make it possible and profitable for banks to acquire additional earning assets. The expansion process lowers interest rates generally—enough to induce the public to hold additional deposits but ordinarily not enough to wipe out the banks' margin between the value and cost of additional deposits.

It is the existence of this margin—not the monetary nature of bank liabilities—which makes it possible for the economics teacher to say that additional loans permitted by new reserves will generate their own deposits. The same proposition would be true of any other system of financial institutions subject to similar reserve constraints and similar interest rate ceilings. In this sense it is more accurate to attribute the special place of banks among intermediaries to the legal restrictions to which banks alone are subjected than to attribute these restrictions to the special character of bank liabilities.

But the textbook description of multiple expansion of credit and deposits on a given reserve base is misleading even for a régime of reserve requirements. There is more to the determination of the volume of bank deposits than the arithmetic of reserve supplies and reserve ratios. The redundant reserves of the thirties are a dramatic reminder that economic opportunities sometimes prevail over reserve calculations. But the significance of that experience is not correctly appreciated if it is regarded simply as an aberration from a normal state of affairs in which banks are fully "loaned up" and total deposits are tightly linked to the volume of reserves. The thirties exemplify in extreme form a phenomenon which is always in some degree present: the use to which commercial banks put the reserves made available to the system is an economic variable depending on lending opportunities and interest rates.

An individual bank is not constrained by any fixed quantum of reserves. It can obtain additional reserves to meet requirements by borrowing from the Federal Reserve, by buying "Federal Funds" from other banks, by selling or "running off" short-term securities. In short, reserves are available at the discount window and in the money market, at a price. This cost the bank must compare with available yields on loans and investments. If those yields are low relative to the cost of reserves, the bank will seek to avoid borrowing reserves and perhaps hold excess reserves instead. If those yields are high relative to the cost of borrowing reserves, the bank will shun excess reserves and borrow reserves occasionally or even regularly. For the banking system as a whole the Federal Reserve's quantitative controls determine the supply of unborrowed reserves. But the extent to which this supply is left unused, or supplemented by borrowing at the discount window, depends on the economic circumstances confronting the banks—on available lending opportunities and on the whole structure of interest rates from the Fed's discount rate through the rates on mortgages and long-term securities.

The range of variation in net free reserves in recent years has been from −5 percent to +5 percent of required reserves. This indicates a much looser linkage between reserves and deposits than is suggested by the textbook exposition of multiple expansion for a system which is always precisely and fully "loaned up." (It does not mean, however, that actual monetary authorities have any less control than textbook monetary authorities. Indeed the net free reserve position is one of their more useful instruments and barometers. Anyway, they are after bigger game than the quantity of "money"!)

Two consequences of this analysis deserve special notice because of their relation to the issues raised earlier in this paper. First, an increase—of, say, a billion dollars—in the supply of unborrowed reserves will, in general, result in less than a billion-dollar increase in required reserves. Net free reserves will rise (algebraically) by some fraction of the billion dollars—a very large fraction in periods like the thirties, a much smaller one in tight money periods like those of the fifties. Loans and deposits will expand by less than their textbook multiples. The reason is simple. The open-market operations which bring about the increased supply of reserves tend to lower interest rates. So do the operations of the commercial banks in trying to invest their new reserves. The result is to diminish the incentives of banks to keep fully loaned up or to borrow reserves, and to make banks content to hold on the average higher excess reserves.

Second, depositor preferences do matter, even in a régime of fractional reserve banking. Suppose, for example, that the public decides to switch new or old savings from other assets and institutions into commercial banks. This switch makes earning assets available to banks at attractive yields—assets that otherwise would have been lodged either directly with the public or with the competing financial institutions previously favored with the public's savings. These improved opportunities for profitable lending and investing will make the banks content to hold smaller net free reserves. Both their deposits and their assets will rise as a result of this shift in public preferences, even though the base of unborrowed reserves remains unchanged. Something of this kind has occurred in recent years when commercial banks have been permitted to raise the interest rates they offer for time and savings deposits.

VII. CONCLUDING REMARKS

The implications of the "new view" may be summarized as follows:

1. The distinction between commercial banks and other financial intermediaries has been too sharply drawn. The differences are of degree, not of kind.

2. In particular, the differences which do exist have little intrinsically to do with the monetary nature of bank liabilities.

3. The differences are more importantly related to the special reserve requirements and interest rate ceilings to which banks are subject. Any other financial industry subject to the same kind of regulations would behave in much the same way.

4. Commercial banks do not possess, either individually or collectively, a widow's cruse which guarantees that any expansion of assets will generate a corresponding expansion of deposit liabilities. Certainly this happy state of affairs would not exist in an unregulated competitive financial world. Marshall's scissors of supply and demand apply to the "output" of the banking industry, no less than to other financial and nonfinancial industries.

5. Reserve requirements and interest ceilings give the widow's cruse myth somewhat greater plausibility. But even in these circumstances, the scale of bank deposits and assets is affected by depositor preferences and by the lending and investing opportunities available to banks.

I draw no policy morals from these observations. That is quite another story, to which analysis of the type presented here is only the preface. The reader will misunderstand my purpose if he jumps to attribute to me the conclusion that existing differences in the regulatory treatment of banks and competing intermediaries should be diminished, either by relaxing constraints on the one or by tightening controls on the other.

chapter 3

THE FEDERAL RESERVE SYSTEM

The readings contained in this chapter are primarily concerned with the tools, mechanisms, and administration of monetary policy, as opposed to its effects. The separation between the material included here and that included in Chapter 5 is somewhat artificial. However, the purpose of the present chapter is to explain the major instruments available to the Federal Reserve for the conduct of monetary policy; to appraise the relative usefulness of these instruments; to explore certain issues pertaining to the guides to be used in carrying out monetary policy; and to consider the relation of the monetary authority to the rest of the government—the question of Federal Reserve "independence." In Chapter 5 we will examine the channels through which monetary forces affect economic activity and discuss the conduct of monetary policy in a somewhat broader perspective.

The three chief instruments of monetary policy in the United States are open market purchases and sales of U.S. government securities, changes in the discount rates charged to member banks when they borrow from the Federal Reserve banks, and changes in the legal reserve requirements applicable to deposits at member banks. In the first paper included in this chapter, by Warren L. Smith, each of these instruments is discussed and appraised. The conclusion reached by the author is that the open market instrument is the most flexible, effective, and useful tool available to the Federal Reserve. The paper considers the appropriate ways of coordinating the use of other instruments—especially the discount rate—with open market operations.

In order to produce desired effects on aggregate demand for goods and services and thereby affect output, employment, and prices—its "ultimate" goals— the Federal Reserve appears to select certain "proximate" goals of a more directly monetary character as the immediate objects of its actions. It appears to consider a number of such proximate goals, including interest rates, total reserves, the stock of money, and so on; and just how much importance it attaches to each in given circumstances is not easy to say. A proximate goal that often commands a good deal of attention is the level of "free reserves"—the difference between the excess reserves of member banks and their outstanding borrowings from the Federal Reserve. The volume of free reserves has at times been given a good deal of weight by the Federal Reserve itself as an indicator of monetary conditions—although probably not as much as the System's critics sometimes imply. However, in many outside commentaries—in the newspapers, for example—it is certainly true that excessive attention has been paid to free reserves in judging the posture of monetary policy.

Measures of the reserve position of member banks have long occupied a prominent position as indicators of credit conditions and as guides to policy in the thinking of Federal Reserve officials. Originally, in the 1920s, primary emphasis was placed on member bank borrowing; the argument was that since member banks were reluctant to be in debt to the Federal Reserve, open market sales of securities, by reducing the volume of unborrowed reserves, would force the banks to borrow, and as their borrowing increased they would tighten lending standards and raise interest rates on loans. According to this view, causation ran from borrowings to market interest rates. Later on, primarily as a result of the vast increase in excess reserves in the 1930s, the doctrine was reformulated, using free reserves instead of borrowings as a measure of the reserve position of member banks. Nevertheless, essentially the same reasoning continued to be applied: a decline in free reserves (stemming mainly from an increase in borrowings such as might be induced by open market sales) would cause interest rates to rise and credit to tighten. Thus a decline in free reserves was unambiguously a sign of tighter credit; and, conversely, an increase in free reserves was an indication of easier credit.

Recent theoretical and empirical work has cast serious doubt on this simplistic view of the role of free reserves. It now appears that instead of causation running from free reserves to interest rates, it is primarily the other way around. That is, as market interest rates rise, with the Federal Reserve discount rate remaining constant, banks have an incentive to borrow more from the Federal Reserve to take advantage of the favorable climate for lending and investing, thereby causing free reserves to decline. Although the response of the banks may be constrained by their reluctance to be in debt and by the Federal Reserve's opposition to excessive or continuous borrowing by member banks, it is nevertheless present. On the other hand, if the discount rate is raised, the increase in the cost of borrowing in relation to the returns available on loans and investments will cause the banks to reduce their borrowings, causing free reserves to increase.

It may be noted that it is this tendency for free reserves to decline as market interest rates rise and to increase as interest rates fall that underlies the interest-elasticity of the money supply, as explained in the paper by Ronald Teigen on the demand for and supply of money in Chapter 1 of this book. This in turn makes the change in the money supply occurring in response to an open market purchase or sale of securities by the Federal Reserve smaller than it would otherwise be. The "money multiplier" presented in Teigen's paper (equation (20) on page 94 (above) is

$$\frac{\Delta M}{\Delta R^*} = \frac{1}{g(1 - h - n) + n + ts} \left[\frac{1}{1 - \dfrac{\eta_{M \cdot r}}{\eta_{L \cdot r}}} \right].$$

Here ΔM is the change in the stock of money (demand deposits and currency), ΔR^* is the change in the Federal Reserve's portfolio of U.S. government securities, g is the reserve requirement for member bank demand deposits, h is the marginal ratio of nonmember bank demand deposits to the money stock, n is the marginal ratio of currency to the money stock, t is the reserve requirement for time deposits, s is the marginal ratio of time deposits to the money stock, $\eta_{M \cdot r}$ is the interest elasticity of the supply of money, and $\eta_{L \cdot r}$ is the interest elasticity of the demand for money. As shown in the appendix to Teigen's paper (equation (A.36), page 103), this can be converted to

$$\frac{\Delta M}{\Delta R^*} = \frac{1}{g(1 - h - n) + n + ts + \dfrac{R^f}{M}\left(\dfrac{\eta_{R^f \cdot r}}{\eta_{L \cdot r}}\right)},$$

where R^f is free reserves, and $\eta_{R^f \cdot r}$ is the interest elasticity of the banks' demand for free reserves. It is clear that an increase in the value of $\eta_{R^f \cdot r}$ will increase the denominator of this expression, thereby reducing $\Delta M / \Delta R^*$. If $\eta_{R^f \cdot r}$ is zero, the expression reduces to a multiplier of the standard type appearing in orthodox textbook discussions of credit expansion.

With free reserves sensitive to interest rates in the manner indicated, it is not correct to view changes in the level of free reserves as a dependable indicator of changes in monetary policy. For example, as pointed out in Smith's paper on the instruments of credit control, credit tightening brought about by open market sales will generally be associated with a fall in free reserves, but credit tightening caused by a rise in the discount rate will be associated with an increase in free reserves.[1]

Furthermore, free reserves may be a seriously misleading indicator of monetary policy, especially in recession periods. If a decline in private demand for goods and services causes a decline in production, employment, and income, there is almost certain to be a fall in credit demand, which will cause interest rates to drop even if the Federal Reserve takes no positive action to expand credit. Such a fall in interest rates is a species of automatic monetary stabilizer,

---

[1] It should be noted that since the publication of the paper by Smith in 1963, the Federal Reserve Board of Governors has changed the definitions and procedures to be followed in the computation of required reserves in several significant respects. Effective September 18, 1968, the following procedural changes were made: (1) Required reserves were to be calculated by applying the reserve requirement percentages to average deposits over a coincident one-week period for both reserve city and country banks (formerly the period for country banks was two weeks). (2) The reserve requirement for a given weekly period was to be based on average deposits two weeks earlier (formerly the current period's deposits were used in calculating required reserves). (3) In calculating weekly average reserves held in satisfaction of reserve requirements, average vault cash held two weeks earlier was to be counted (formerly current holdings of vault cash were counted). (4) Either an excess or a deficiency in reserve requirements averaging up to 2 percent of required reserves was to be carried forward to the next reserve period (formerly deficiencies were carried forward but not excesses). Effective November 9, 1972, the system of reserve requirements was changed so that reserve requirements on member bank demand deposits would be uniform for all banks of a given size, regardless of a bank's location (formerly the reserve requirement applicable to a given bank was in general dependent on its location rather than its size). Under the new system, the first $2 million of net demand deposits at a member bank are subject to a reserve requirement of 8 percent; over $2 million to $10 million, 10 percent; over $10 million to $100 million, 12 percent; over $100 million to $400 million, 13 percent; and over $400 million, 17½ percent. While these ratios are in effect at the time of this writing, they can be changed within limits by the Board of Governors. The possible range of variation for reserve requirements on demand deposits is from 10 percent to 22 percent for reserve city banks, and from 7 to 14 percent for other banks. Any bank with more than $400 million of net demand deposits is considered a reserve city bank for this purpose.

which will help somewhat in checking the decline in income and employment, although it can hardly reverse the decline and start the economy moving upward again. When market interest rates fall relative to the discount rate—which is usually not adjusted downward nearly as rapidly as market rates decline—banks will reduce their borrowings from the Federal Reserve, thus causing free reserves to increase. If observers take the rise in free reserves to be a sign that an actively easier monetary policy is being followed, they will be seriously misled. Indeed, since reduced borrowings cause total reserves and therefore the supply of money and credit to decline, monetary conditions will not ease as much as they would have if the decline in interest rates had not produced an increase in free reserves.

It may be noted that the same problem exists in connection with the use of interest rates as a guide to policy, since, as pointed out above, a decline in private demand will cause interest rates to fall. Unless they are careful, the authorities may take the decline in interest rates as an indication that monetary policy has actively become easier when all that has in fact occurred is a passive response of interest rates to a decline in private demand. This does not mean that interest rates are of no value as a guide to policy. Indeed, since as is shown in Chapter 5, there is considerable evidence that changes in interest rates and associated changes in credit availability are one of the important linkages through which the effects of monetary policy are transmitted to the all-important real sector of the economy, it is appropriate for the authorities to place considerable emphasis on interest rates as a guide to the conduct of policy.

At the same time, however, it is certainly desirable to pay some attention to the money supply, for several reasons. For one thing, the tendency of the banks to repay borrowings at the Federal Reserve as interest rates decline causes total reserves and the money supply to fall in the absence of Federal Reserve action when private demand decreases. Thus, if the Federal Reserve makes sure that the rate of growth of the money supply increases when a recession sets in, it has some assurance that it is acting positively to induce recovery. The fact that the money supply has fairly commonly declined—or at least its rate of growth has decelerated—during recession periods makes one wonder whether the Federal Reserve may not at times have been misled by excessive emphasis on free reserves or interest rates into believing it was following an actively easy monetary policy when it was not in fact doing so. Another reason for using the money stock as an intermediate target, which is particularly relevant for periods of significant price change, is that in such periods market interest rates have built into them an expected price change component. For example, if it is expected that prices will rise at a 4 percent rate per year, then the "real" equivalent of a 7 percent market yield on a security with a year to maturity is 3 percent. The logical interest rate target for the monetary authorities would be the "real" rate, since that is likely to be the one which affects spending decisions. However, expectations vary among individuals and firms, and it is difficult for the authorities to know what the "real" rate is.

Considerations such as these, as well as the influence of monetarism with its insistence on the importance of variations in the money stock, have led the Federal Reserve System to shift its emphasis over the past few years from almost exclusive reliance on indicators of money market conditions, such as free reserves and interest rates, to a method of operation which gives considerable importance to the growth rate of monetary aggregates, particularly over periods longer than a few weeks or months. The first shift in this direction occurred in 1966, when a "proviso clause" was inserted into the instructions to the open-market trading desk, permitting deviation from the desired money-market conditions if bank credit appeared to be growing too fast or too slowly. Beginning in March 1970, explicit growth rate targets for aggregates such as the money stock were set, and the Federal Reserve now attempts to achieve such targets (within acceptable ranges) over longer periods while continuing to be concerned with interest rates, free reserves, and so on in the shorter run.

The selection by Henry C. Wallich in this chapter provides a discussion of the kinds of problems and choices faced by the Federal Reserve System in determining what the intermediate targets of monetary policy should be. In the article by Paul Meek and Rudolf Thunberg, the emphasis is on the considerations and problems involved in implementing an operational policy system involving both shorter and longer range targets.

It is a way of life with policy makers to be operating with uncertainties of all kinds. Some of these are discussed in the paper by Meek and Thunberg: for example, they describe the difficulties for monetary growth rate targets caused by periodic data revisions. There are also uncertainties of a much more fundamental type facing the policy maker, such as those relating to the true structure of the economic system. If this structure were known, policy making would be easy. Intermediate targets could be dispensed with, and policy could be brought directly to bear on target levels of income, employment, and so on. But since there is uncertainty about the exact linkages between the instruments of policy and the ultimate targets, intermediate targets are selected. In the paper by William Poole in Chapter 5, it is shown that the choice of an intermediate target should be influenced by the relative degree of uncertainty about the structures of the monetary and real sectors of the economy.

The findings of recent research to the effect that free reserve levels are sensitive to interest rates also suggests that perhaps monetary policy could be made more effective if a different approach to discount administration were employed.[2] Relying on the reluctance theory of member bank borrowing, the System has not attempted to make the discount rate a "penalty rate"—that is, has not kept it consistently higher than the interest rates the banks could earn by investing borrowed funds. If the profit motive governs member bank borrowing at least partially, however, the discount window as presently managed may constitute a serious offset to open market policy. This question is discussed in Smith's article on the instruments of monetary control, which also contains a comparison of open market operations, the discount rate, and reserve-requirement variation in terms of their relative usefulness in achieving policy goals and a discussion of their proper coordination.

Two brief readings on the issue of Federal Reserve "independence" conclude the chapter. At the present time, the Federal Reserve System is formally responsi-

---

[2] The Federal Reserve has recently advanced proposals for changing the operation and administration of the discount mechanism. As this is being written, these proposals are being discussed but have not yet been put into effect. It appears, however, that if effectuated, they would result in a substantial increase in the volume of member bank borrowing and make such borrowing even more responsive to cyclical fluctuations than is presently the case. For an explanation of the proposals, see "Reappraisal of the Federal Reserve Discount Mechanism," *Federal Reserve Bulletin*, July 1968, pp. 545–51. For some discussion of the proposals, see *Federal Reserve Discount Mechanism*, Hearings before the Joint Economic Committee, 90th Cong., 2d sess., September 11 and 17, 1968.

ble only to the Congress for the manner in which it conducts monetary policy. Appointment to the Board of Governors is for a 14-year term; as a result, that body is about as safe from the danger of deliberate political manipulation as one can imagine. Although the appointment of the Chairman—who is ordinarily by far the most influential figure in the System—is for a four-year term, his term is not coterminous with that of the President of the United States. Consequently there is no assurance that a new President will have an early opportunity to appoint a Chairman who is in sympathy with his economic policies. Formally speaking, therefore, the President and his administration have no dependable means of assuring that monetary policy will be conducted in a manner consistent with the overall objectives of the administration. The danger of outright conflict between the Federal Reserve and the administration is not great, however; considering the relative power inherent in their respective offices, it is difficult to imagine a Chairman defying a President with impunity for very long. Nevertheless, there is an important difference between wholehearted cooperation between the Federal Reserve and the administration in the conduct of economic policy on the one hand and a reluctant and foot-dragging Federal Reserve attitude on the other, and that difference may mean a good deal in terms of the achievement of the administration's economic objectives.

The rationale supporting an "independent" central bank is that the power to create the means of payment should not be given to those who have the responsibility of planning and financing government expenditures lest they be tempted to finance such expenditures, directly or indirectly, through money creation rather than by taxation, thus corrupting the monetary system and inducing inflation. While some weight is lent to this argument by the experience of other countries, it may be noted that there are few cases in modern history in which serious inflation has been caused in advanced industrial countries by using central bank credit—which is the sophisticated modern equivalent of the "printing press"—to finance government deficits except in time of war itself or during periods of immediate postwar disorganization.

It is sometimes said that the central bank needs to be independent in order to be able to carry out in a flexible manner the complicated day-to-day operations necessary for efficient monetary management. However, no sensible opponent of independence would want to interfere with this technical flexibility, which is indeed one of the great advantages of monetary policy as an instrument of stabilization. What bothers some students of the problem is that independence leaves the central bank free not only to use its tools in a flexible manner to achieve a specified set of objectives but also to choose the objectives themselves, at least to a certain extent.

Difficulties may arise when objectives that are each desirable in themselves are in conflict—that is, when fuller achievement of one objective requires the acceptance of less satisfactory results with respect to another. An example may be the relation between unemployment and inflation that was discussed in the articles by Tobin and by Hymans included in Chapter 1 of this book. Beyond some point, further reduction of unemployment through expansion of aggregate demand may be possible only if the nation is willing to accept more inflation. An independent Federal Reserve might in such a situation attach a greater weight to the prevention of inflation relative to the reduction of unemployment than is acceptable to the President and his administration. This might lead to a situation in which monetary and fiscal policy are working at cross-purposes, and the Federal Reserve is seeking to thwart the achievement of the objectives of a popularly elected executive—objectives which are presumably accepted by a majority of the people. The result might be frustration and inadequate economic performance with no clear delineation of responsibility.

The two papers on the subject present contrasting views regarding the relationship between the Federal Reserve System, the administration, and the Congress. George L. Bach's discussion is based upon the recommendations made by the Commission on Money and Credit designed to simplify the System's organizational structure by reducing the membership of the Board of Governors from seven to five and centering all monetary powers in the Board, and to provide somewhat greater assurance of harmony between the System and the administration by making the terms of the Board Chairman and Vice-Chairman coterminous with that of the President. Bach takes a moderate view: while agreeing with the recommendations, he feels they may not be worth the cost in "bitter argument and in deep wounds within the System."

Harry G. Johnson, on the other hand, argues strongly for integrating the monetary authority into the regular machinery of policy decision making, on the grounds that independence does not assure freedom from political pressure and that it tends to bias monetary policy toward stable prices as a goal at the expense of other objectives; furthermore, such independence is not consistent with democratic principles of responsibility to the electorate.

THE INSTRUMENTS OF GENERAL MONETARY CONTROL*

Warren L. Smith

I. INTRODUCTION

At the present, the Federal Reserve System possesses three major instruments of general monetary control: the power to buy and sell securities in the open market; the power to fix discount rates and regulate other conditions of member bank borrowing; and the power to change within specified limits the reserve requirements of member banks. This paper deals with the relative usefulness of these three credit-control instruments and with problems of their proper co-ordination.[1]

---

* From *National Banking Review*, Vol. I (September 1963), pp. 47–76. Reprinted by permission of the publisher.

[1] In addition to the three general credit-control instruments, the System has from time to time employed selective controls, including the regulation of consumer and real estate credit. At the present time, however, the only important selective control power that the System has is the authority to regulate margin requirements applicable to loans for purchasing and carrying securities. This paper makes no effort to deal with the uses of selective controls or their co-ordination with general controls.

II. THE PRIMACY OF OPEN MARKET OPERATIONS

Nearly all students of American monetary affairs would probably agree that open market operations constitute the primary weapon of monetary policy. The initiative with respect to such operations lies firmly in the hands of the Federal Reserve System, and the weapon possesses great flexibility with respect to both timing and magnitude. That is, operations can be used to produce large or small changes in credit conditions, and the direction of operations can be changed almost instantaneously.

In addition to their use to control credit in the interest of economic stability and growth, open market operations are carried on continuously for the purpose of offsetting the short-run effects on member bank reserves resulting from factors outside the control of the Federal Reserve—changes in float, currency in circulation, gold stock, Treasury and foreign deposits at the Reserve banks, and so on. These operations, which have been increasingly perfected in recent years, serve the important function of maintaining an even keel in the central money market. They also act as a kind of camouflage which frequently makes it rather difficult to discern and interpret the longer-run objectives of System policy as reflected in open market operations. Thus, since open market operations are generally going on continuously and are directed at the accomplishment of a rather complex variety of objectives, they are relatively free from the psychological overtones (sometimes called "announcement effects") that frequently accompany changes in discount rates or in reserve requirements. For reasons that will be explained below, I believe this absence of psychological implications is a rather important advantage of open market operations.

To the extent of its net purchases or sales of Government securities, the Federal Reserve changes not only the supply of bank reserves but the amount of interest-bearing Federal debt held by the public. In addition, by varying its purchases and sales in various maturity sectors of the market, it can influence the maturity composition of the publicly-held debt and, to some extent at least, the term-structure of interest rates. Thus, open market operations are a form of debt management. They should be closely co-ordinated with the Treasury's debt management decisions concerning the maturities of securities to issue or retire in its cash borrowing, refunding, and debt retirement operations.

For a period of about eight years beginning in March 1953, the Federal Open Market Committee, which is responsible for the conduct of System open market operations, adhered to the so-called "bills-only" policy, the key feature of which was that open market operations for the purpose of effectuating stabilizing monetary policy were confined to short-term securities, chiefly Treasury bills. Early in 1961, this policy was altered to a more flexible one which permitted operations in all maturity ranges of the U.S. Government securities market.[2] The primary reason for the 1961 change in policy was the emergence of a serious balance of payments deficit partly caused by substantial outflows of short-term capital to foreign money centers at a time when the domestic economy was suffering from substantial unemployment and underutilization of productive capacity.

Although System open market purchases of longer-term securities have actually been quite modest since early 1961, the greater flexibility of open market policy, together with associated shifts in the conduct of Treasury debt management activities, has undoubtedly helped to make it possible to maintain and even increase U.S. short-term interest rates in line with those abroad, thus preventing excessive outflows of short-term funds, while at the same time preventing increases in the long-term bond yields and mortgage interest rates which influence plant and equipment expenditures, capital outlays of State and local governments, and housing construction.[3]

Open market operations are firmly established as the fundamental weapon of monetary policy in the United States. Accordingly, the important questions concerning the proper co-ordination of monetary control instruments really have to do with the extent to which the other weapons—discount policy and reserve requirements policy—should be used to supplement (and perhaps in certain special circumstances to replace) open market operations. Let us begin by considering discount policy.

III. THE ROLE OF DISCOUNT POLICY

For many years prior to the Treasury–Federal Reserve Accord of March 1951, the amount of member bank borrowing from the Reserve banks was negligible. Throughout the later 1930s, the volume of excess reserves was continuously so large that it was seldom necessary for member banks to borrow. And during World War II, the Federal Reserve kept the banks amply supplied with reserves through open market operations so that there was little occasion for borrowing. The atrophied state of the discount mechanism

---

[2] The changes were made at the meetings of the Federal Open Market Committee on February 7 and March 28, 1961. See the Record of Policy Actions of the Federal Open Market Committee in the *Annual Report* of the Board of Governors of the Federal Reserve System covering the year 1961, pp. 39–43 and 54–55.

[3] In addition to open market operations and debt management, other policy actions have helped to "twist" the interest-rate structure; i.e., to raise short-term rates while exerting as much downward pressure as possible on long-term rates. The increase in interest-rate ceilings applicable to time deposits by the Federal Reserve and the FDIC at the beginning of 1962 enabled U.S. commercial banks to compete more effectively with foreign banks for deposits and also attracted an enlarged supply of funds into time deposits—funds which were largely channelled into mortgages and State and local government securities, thus bringing down yields on such securities. And the reduction of reserve requirements on time deposits from 5 to 4 percent in October and November 1962, combined with action to sustain Treasury bill yields, undoubtedly also helped to some extent.

is indicated by the fact that, for the entire period 1934 to 1943, member bank borrowing averaged less than one-tenth of 1 percent of total member bank reserves.

Since the Accord, the volume of borrowing has increased, especially during periods of credit restraint when the reserves of member banks have been under pressure. The Federal Reserve has encouraged this revival of the discount mechanism and has attempted to restore the discount rate to the important role it is supposed to have played in monetary policy prior to the 1930s.[4] But while member bank borrowing has increased in magnitude since the Accord, it is still very much less important as a source of reserves than it was in the 1920s. From 1951 to 1959, borrowing averaged 3.2 percent of total member bank reserves with average borrowings reaching peak levels of approximately 4½ percent of total reserves in the years 1957 and 1959, when monetary policy was relatively tight. In contrast, during the period 1922 to 1929, borrowing averaged 30.0 percent of total reserves, with the ratio rising as high as 40 percent in 1923 and 1929.

A. The Discount Rate as a Cost Factor

It is possible to distinguish two main facets of Federal Reserve discount policy. In the first place, the discount rate represents the cost of borrowed reserves, and the rate is changed from time to time for the purpose of regulating member bank borrowing. Changes in the rate for this purpose should be co-ordinated as closely as possible with open market operations. In addition, however, the discount rate at times plays an independent role in monetary policy, serving as a signal to the economy of changes in Federal Reserve policy. Let us first consider the discount rate as a regulator of member bank borrowing.

1. Cost versus "Reluctance" as a Regulator of Borrowing. Due to the organization of the banking and financial system in the United States,

it has not been feasible to establish the discount rate as a "penalty rate" in the sense in which this has been the case in Britain. There a penalty rate has been possible because the discount houses rather than the banks have customarily done the borrowing from the Bank of England. Since the discount houses have made a practice of carrying quite homogeneous portfolios of commercial bills and, in recent years, Treasury bills, it has been feasible to keep the Bank rate above the yield on such bills, so that when the discount houses are "forced into the bank" (as the phrase goes), they lose money on their borrowings. Traditionally, this penalty rate has served to keep borrowing from the Bank of England to a minimum and to make the interest rate structure highly sensitive to monetary action carried out through the co-ordinated use of open market operations and the discount rate.[5]

In the United States, member banks borrow directly from the Reserve banks, and since there are very many member banks operating in numerous local and regional, as well as national, credit markets and investing in a great variety of earning assets bearing a wide range of yields, it is not feasible to maintain a true penalty rate.[6]

Since the 1920s, it has come to be widely accepted doctrine that use of the System's discount facilities is restrained by a tradition against borrowing on the part of member banks.[7] As evidence in support of this view, which has come

---

[4] In connection with the Accord itself, the Treasury and the Federal Reserve agreed upon the desirability of reviving the discount mechanism as a means for making adjustments in bank reserve positions. See the identical statements concerning the Accord by the Secretary of the Treasury and the Chairman of the Board of Governors in *Monetary Policy and Management of the Public Dept–Replies to Questions and Other Materials for the Use of the Subcommittee on General Credit Control and Debt Management* (Joint Committee on the Economic Report, 82nd Cong., 2nd sess.) (Washington, D.C.: U.S. Government Printing Office, 1952), Part I, pp. 74–76 and 349–51.

[5] For a good recent discussion, see R. S. Sayers, *Modern Banking* (4th ed.; Oxford: Clarendon Press, 1958), pp. 104–14. As indicated by Sayers, both the indirect nature of the relation between the commercial banks and the Bank of England and the penal Bank rate have become somewhat attenuated in recent years, as the Bank has developed the alternative practice of supplying funds to the discount houses and in some cases to the commercial banks themselves by purchasing Treasury bills at the market rate.

[6] In order to be a penalty rate with respect to a particular bank, the rate does not need to be higher than the expected return on all of the bank's earning assets. In fact, in a sense, it is a penalty rate if it is higher than the expected return on the lowest yielding assets in the bank's portfolio. However, the discount rate can be a penalty rate in this sense in relation to some banks and not others, due to differences in the composition of the banks' portfolios.

[7] This argument was advanced in W. W. Riefler, *Money Rates and Money Markets in the United States* (New York: Harper & Bros., 1930), esp. chap. ii. According to Riefler, the tradition against borrowing existed among commercial banks prior to the formation of the Federal Reserve System and was strengthened during the 1920s by the System's discouragement of borrowing for other than temporary purposes.

to be known as the "reluctance theory," it was pointed out that in the 1920s open market interest rates were more closely related to the amount of outstanding member bank borrowing than they were to the discount rate, suggesting that member banks did not like to be in debt and, when they were, tended to liquidate secondary reserve assets in order to repay their borrowings, thus forcing up open market interest rates.[8]

Although the purposes for which banks borrow—to maintain their reserve positions in the face of customer withdrawals or clearing drains and to meet temporary (e.g., seasonal) increases in their customers' demands for loans—are commonly so pressing as probably to be quite cost-inelastic, it does not follow that member bank borrowing is insensitive to the discount rate. Banks have a choice of obtaining additional funds by borrowing at the Federal Reserve or by liquidating secondary reserves or other investment securities. Given a certain "reluctance to borrow," the major factor influencing the choice will presumably be the relevant cost of funds obtained by the various methods, and this depends chiefly on the relation between the discount rate and the yield on assets that the bank might liquidate. In principle, the relevant comparison is between the discount rate and the expected yield on the asset whose liquidation is being considered over the period of time for which the funds will be needed, taking account of any capital gains or losses that may be involved. For instance, if interest rates are expected to fall during the period, the relevant interest rate for comparison with the discount rate may be higher than the current interest rate on the asset. This factor will be more important the longer the maturity of the asset.[9]

Thus, there is little doubt that commercial banks are "reluctant" to borrow in the sense that borrowing is felt to involve a form of disutility. However, the banks' reluctance can be overcome provided that the profits to be obtained from borrowing (as compared with other means of obtaining reserves) are sufficiently attractive—that is, banks balance the disutility of borrowing

against the utility of further profits.[10] Moreover, not all banks are equally reluctant to borrow:[11] this is evidenced by the fact that the Federal Reserve has found it necessary to discourage "continuous borrowing" and to bolster the banks' reluctance in its regulations covering discounts and advances.[12] In addition, the System keeps the borrowing practices of individual member banks under constant surveillance and in this way attempts to reinforce the banks' reluctance to borrow. At the same time, the System apparently does not unequivocally refuse to lend to member banks, despite the fact that it has authority to do so under the Federal Reserve Act.[13]

2. Co-ordination of Open Market Operations and Discount Policy. It used to be said with reference to monetary policy in the 1920s that open market operations served the function of making the discount rate effective.[14] In order to implement a restrictive monetary policy, the Federal Reserve would sell Government securities in the open market; this would put pressure on member bank reserve positions and cause them to increase their borrowings. At this point the discount rate would be raised, and the increase in borrowings was supposed to help to insure that the discount rate increase would be transmitted through into an increase in other interest rates.[15]

---

[8] *Ibid.*, pp. 25–28; also W. R. Burgess, *The Reserve Banks and the Money Market* (rev. ed.; New York: Harper & Bros., 1946), pp. 219–21.

[9] See W. L. Smith, "The Discount Rate as a Credit-Control Weapon," *Journal of Political Economy*, Vol. LXVI (April 1958), pp. 171–77; Ralph Young, "Tools and Processes of Monetary Policy," in N. H. Jacoby, *United States Monetary Policy* (New York: The American Assembly, Columbia University, 1958), pp. 13–48, esp. pp. 26–27.

[10] For a systematic development of this point of view, together with some evidence to support it, see the interesting article by M. E. Polakoff, "Reluctance Elasticity, Least Cost, and Member-Bank Borrowing: A Suggested Integration," *Journal of Finance*, Vol. XV (March 1960), pp. 1–18.

[11] On this, see Lauchlin Currie, *The Supply and Control of Money in the United States* (Cambridge: Harvard University Press, 1935), chap. viii.

[12] See Regulation A of the Board of Governors regulating member bank borrowing as revised effective February 15, 1955, (*Federal Reserve Bulletin*, January 1955, pp. 8–14). The Foreword to the revised Regulation contains a statement of "General Principles" (pp. 8–9) which attempts to delineate in a general way the purposes for which member banks should and should not use the System's discount facilities.

[13] On the subtleties of non-price rationing in the administration of the discount window, see C. R. Whittlesey, "Credit Policy at the Discount Window"; R. V. Roosa, "Credit Policy at the Discount Window: Comment"; and Whittlesey, "Reply," *Quarterly Journal of Economics*, Vol. LXXIII (May 1959), pp. 207–16, and 333–38.

[14] Burgess, *op. cit.*, p. 239.

[15] This is rather similar to the classical British practice of selling in the open market to reduce the cash reserves of the commercial banks. To replenish their cash reserves, the banks would call some of

In view of the primary role of open market operations under present conditions, it is better to look at the matter the other way around and to say that the discount rate can be used to support and strengthen the effectiveness of open market operations. Thus, when the System, for example, wishes to implement a restrictive policy during a period of inflation, it uses open market operations to keep down the supply of reserves in relation to the swelling demands for credit. As a result, interest rates rise and member banks, finding their reserve positions under increased pressure, tend to increase their borrowings from the Reserve banks. In order to discourage the creation of additional reserves through borrowing, the System can raise the discount rate in pace with the increase of other interest rates. Thus the discount rate can be used to supplement and strengthen open market operations. Conversely, when the System desires to ease credit conditions, it provides additional reserves through open market operations, and in order to discourage member banks from using a portion of the new reserves to repay indebtedness at the Reserve banks, the discount rate can be lowered.[16]

A variant of this reasoning which stresses the reluctance of member banks rather than the discount rate has also been expressed by persons connected with the Federal Reserve System. According to this view, most member bank borrowing arises out of the fact that in a unit banking system such as ours with a very large number of banks, individual banks often find their reserve positions unexpectedly depleted as a result of unfavorable clearing balances associated with redistribution of reserves among the banks. Borrowing is a handy means of making temporary adjustments in reserve positions; if the depletion of a bank's reserve position lasts very long, the bank

may later adjust by liquidating secondary reserves, using the proceeds to repay its borrowing at the Reserve bank.[17] The pressure on banks to make prompt adjustments in portfolios in order to repay borrowing depends on the level of the discount rate in relation to other interest rates.

At times when monetary policy is tight and the Federal Reserve is maintaining pressure on bank reserve positions in the interest of limiting excessive growth of bank credit, more banks will be managing their reserve positions closely, reserve deficiencies will occur more frequently, and member bank borrowing will increase.[18] Due to the fact that the banks are reluctant to borrow, the increase in borrowing causes them to adopt more cautious lending policies and to reduce the availability of credit. However, since banks balance the disutility of borrowing against the utility of increased profits, it is necessary to make successive upward adjustments in the discount rate as interest rates rise due to the effects of the restrictive policy, in order to stiffen the banks' reluctance to remain in debt and to encourage them to contract their loans and investments.

It may be noted, however, that short-term open market interest rates are subject to a considerable amount of random variation in the short run and that, under present arrangements, the discount rate is only changed at irregular and rather infrequent intervals. For this reason, the differential between the discount rate and other interest rates varies rather erratically. This is apparent from Chart 1, which shows the movements of the discount rate and the yield on outstanding Treasury bills since 1953. As a result of the continuously shifting relation between the discount rate and other interest rates, the willingness of banks to borrow presumably undergoes considerable erratic variation.

3. *Does Borrowing Reinforce or Offset Open Market Operations?* There has been some dis-

---

their loans to the discount houses. The discount houses, in turn, would be forced to borrow from the Bank of England at the (penalty) Bank rate, and as a result of the ensuing adjustments bill rates would be forced up. Thus, open market operations were said to have the function of "forcing the market into the Bank."

[16] See the statement of the Chairman of the Board of Governors concerning the relation between the discount rate and open market operations in *United States Monetary Policy: Recent Thinking and Experience* (Hearings before the Subcommittee on Economic Stabilization of the Joint Committee on the Economic Report, 83rd Cong., 2d sess.) (Washington, D.C.: U.S. Government Printing Office, 1954), p. 11. A similar view is suggested in C. E. Walker, "Discount Policy in the Light of Recent Experience," *Journal of Finance*, Vol. XII (May 1957), pp. 223–37, esp. pp. 232–34.

[17] Roosa, *op. cit.*, p. 335.

[18] Ibid., p. 336. A similar argument is presented by Young, *op. cit.*, who says (p. 34): "As a policy of monetary restraint continues or is accentuated, there will be more frequent and more widespread reserve drains among member banks. This will lead an increasing number of banks to borrow temporarily at the discount window of the Reserve Banks in order to maintain their legal reserve positions. For each bank, the borrowing will be temporary, but the repayment by one bank draws reserves from other banks, which in turn will have need to borrow at a Reserve Bank. Thus, restrictive monetary action leads to a larger volume of member bank borrowings, as more banks find their reserve positions under pressure more often."

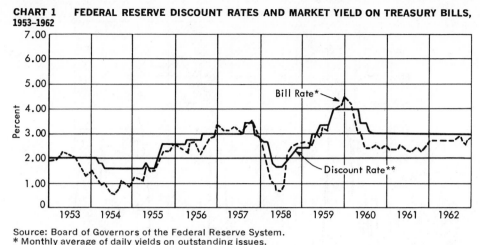

CHART 1   FEDERAL RESERVE DISCOUNT RATES AND MARKET YIELD ON TREASURY BILLS, 1953–1962

Source: Board of Governors of the Federal Reserve System.
* Monthly average of daily yields on outstanding issues.
** Average of discount rates at all Federal Reserve banks.

cussion as to whether the increase in member bank borrowing that occurs during a period of credit restriction is a factor which intensifies the restrictive effects or a loophole which weakens the effectiveness of monetary policy.[19] It is almost certainly true that, as a result of the reluctance of member banks to borrow, banks tend to follow somewhat more restrictive and cautious policies as far as loans are concerned when they are in debt to the Reserve banks than when they are not in debt. However, the important thing to bear in mind is that if banks were constrained not to borrow when their reserve positions were impaired by a restrictive policy, they would have to adjust their reserve positions in some other way. This would ordinarily mean contraction of loans or investments.[20] Thus, in the absence of

borrowing, the adjustment would itself *consist in* restricting credit. On the other hand, to the extent that borrowing occurs, restrictive effects are postponed and banks are merely put in such a position that they are somewhat more likely to restrict credit at some future time. Moreover, it should be noted that borrowing by one member bank for the purpose of adjusting its reserve position adds to the *aggregate* reserves of all member banks and thus indirectly takes some of the pressure off other banks. Adjustment of reserve position adds to the *aggregate* reserves of all member banks and thus indirectly takes some of the pressure off other banks. Adjustment of reserve positions through liquidations of securities, on the other hand, does not add to the reserves of the system of banks.[21]

Thus, it seems clear that the effect of increased member bank borrowing at a time when a restrictive policy is being applied is to offset rather than to reinforce the restrictive policy. The effect may not be very important in itself, since the induced increase in borrowing is not likely to be large enough to pose a serious problem for the authorities; it merely means that a somewhat more restrictive open market policy is required than would otherwise be necessary. However, there are a number of other offsetting reactions in the banking and financial system—such as shifts in the composition of bank portfolios from Government securities to loans, adjustments by financial intermediaries, and so on—and the addition of one more such reaction, even though not

---

[19] Roosa seems to imply that it has an intensifying effect ("Credit Policy at the Discount Window," *op. cit.*). Whittlesey ("Credit Policy at the Discount Window," and "Reply" [to Roosa's comment], *op. cit.*) contends that it is an offset, although not, under present conditions, a very important one.

[20] Another possibility is that banks might make greater use of the Federal funds market to adjust their reserves. Although use of this market has increased in recent years, the number of participating banks is still rather small, and there are technical impediments to a substantial increase. (See *The Federal Funds Market* [Washington, D.C.: Board of Governors of the Federal Reserve System, 1959]). Increased use of the Federal funds market during periods when credit is being restricted economizes the use of existing reserves, reduces excess reserves, and thereby constitutes an offset to the initial restrictive action (see H. P. Minsky, "Central Banking and Money Market Changes," *Quarterly Journal of Economics*, Vol. LXXI [May 1957], pp. 171–87). Thus, resort to the Federal funds market has effects similar to member bank borrowing (as explained below).

[21] Smith, "The Discount Rate as a Credit-Control Weapon," *op. cit.*, pp. 172–73; also P. A. Samuelson, "Recent American Monetary Controversy," *Three Banks Review*, March 1956, pp. 10–11.

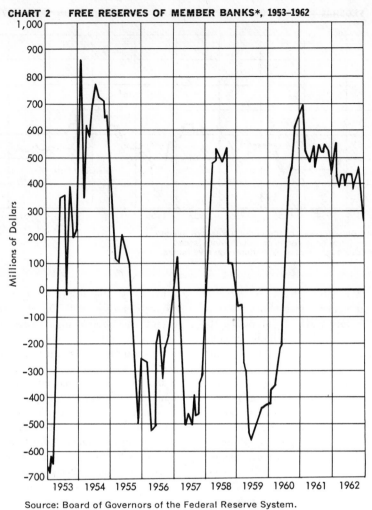

CHART 2   FREE RESERVES OF MEMBER BANKS*, 1953–1962

Source: Board of Governors of the Federal Reserve System.
* Monthly averages of daily figures.

quantitatively very large, may not be wholly without significance.

Another point of view that has been expressed concerning the discount mechanism is that, while it has an offsetting effect, this effect is actually helpful to the monetary authorities, because it can be likened to a brake on an automobile. It is said that brakes, by making it possible to control the car more effectively, permit one to drive at a higher rate of speed than would otherwise be possible.[22] Similarly, the discount mechanism, although seeming to weaken monetary controls, actually strengthens them by making it possible to use other controls (chiefly open market operations) more vigorously. However, this is not a proper analogy. If the automobile simile is retained, the discount mechanism is more like a

defective clutch than a brake, and few would argue that a slipping clutch makes it possible to drive at a higher rate of speed.[23] A brake is a discretionary weapon and not a device that automatically operates more intensively, the harder one pushes on the accelerator.

4. A Critique of the Concept of "Free Reserves." A by-product of the revival of the discount mechanism since the Accord is the emphasis that has been placed on the level of "free reserves" as an immediate guide to System policy. "Free reserves," of course, are simply the difference between aggregate member bank excess re-

---

[22] P. A. Samuelson, "Reflections on Monetary Policy," *Review of Economics and Statistics*, Vol. XLII (August 1960), p. 266.

[23] If the motor were too powerful for the car—e.g., if a Cadillac motor were mounted in a Volkswagen—I suppose a clutch that slipped might be helpful. But the proper analogy for the relation between monetary policy and the stability of the economy may well be just the reverse; i.e., monetary policy can be likened to a Volkswagen motor which has been assigned the task of operating a heavy Cadillac.

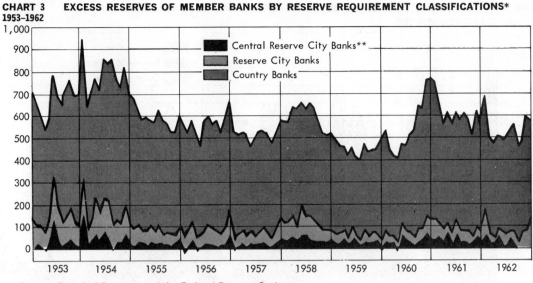

CHART 3   EXCESS RESERVES OF MEMBER BANKS BY RESERVE REQUIREMENT CLASSIFICATIONS*
1953–1962

Legend:
- Central Reserve City Banks**
- Reserve City Banks
- Country Banks

Source: Board of Governors of the Federal Reserve System.
* Monthly averages of daily figures.
** Central Reserve City Classification terminated July 28, 1962.

serves and aggregate member bank borrowings. It appears that, increasingly in the last few years, the System has been setting its proximate goals of monetary policy in terms of "target" levels of free reserves. As can be seen from Chart 2, free reserves have been positive (excess reserves greater than borrowings) during periods of credit ease, as in 1953–54, 1958, and 1960–63, while during periods of credit restriction, free reserves have been negative (i.e., borrowings have been greater than excess reserves, or there have been "net borrowed reserves"). It has become commonplace to judge the objective and direction of monetary policy to a considerable extent by the changes that take place in free reserves.[24]

The first thing to notice about free reserves is that the two components that compose them—excess reserves and borrowings—are distributed quite differently among member banks. Excess reserves tend to be heavily concentrated in the hands of country banks, while most of the borrowing is ordinarily done by reserve city banks. (See Charts 3 and 4.) Country banks tend to hold fairly substantial amounts of excess reserves most of the time, and are able to absorb pressure by drawing down such excess reserves. Reserve city banks, on the other hand, manage their reserve

positions more closely, hold relatively small amounts of excess reserves, and borrow more frequently from the Federal Reserve when they are placed under pressure. Of course, these behavior patterns do not coincide exactly with the arbitrary classifications of banks for reserve requirement purposes—some reserve city banks, for example, undoubtedly hold large excess reserves, while some country banks manage their reserve positions closely. Nevertheless, it is quite clear that there are substantial differences among banks with respect to holdings of excess reserves and reliance on borrowing from the Federal Reserve. And there is no reason to suppose that an increase in borrowings on the part of one group of banks would be exactly offset, insofar as effects on credit conditions are concerned, by an equal increase in holdings of excess reserves by another group of banks. That is to say, for example, that $500 million of net borrowed reserves might have quite different implications depending upon whether it was the resultant of $1.5 billion of borrowings and $1 billion of excess reserves or the resultant of $700 million of borrowings and $200 million of excess reserves.

It should be noted, however, that in practice a very large proportion of the variation in free reserves is attributable to variation in borrowings.[25] The amount of excess reserves is negatively correlated with member bank borrowing; consequently, an increase (decrease) in free reserves

---

[24] No matter what the shortcomings of free reserves as a guide to monetary policy, it is appropriate for those who are attempting to judge the character of System policy to pay close attention to this magnitude simply because the System does seem to use it as a guide.

[25] Young, *op. cit.*, p. 35.

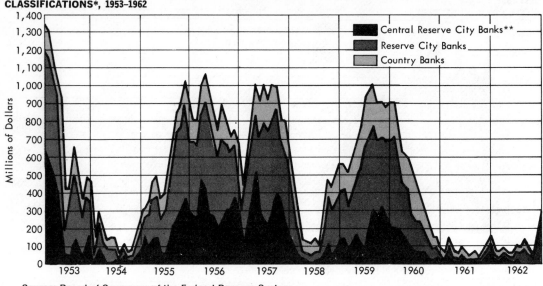

CHART 4   DISCOUNTS AND ADVANCES OF MEMBER BANKS BY RESERVE REQUIREMENT CLASSIFICATIONS*, 1953–1962

Legend:
Central Reserve City Banks**
Reserve City Banks
Country Banks

Source: Board of Governors of the Federal Reserve System.
* Monthly averages of daily figures.
** Central Reserve City Classification terminated July 28, 1962.

is likely to be attributable partly to a decrease (increase) in borrowings and partly to an increase (decrease) in excess reserves. However, as a comparison of Charts 3 and 4 indicates, the variation in borrowings is much greater than the variation in excess reserves; in fact, the variance of borrowings accounts for about 62 percent of the variance of free reserves, whereas the variance of excess reserves accounts for only 7.7 percent, the remainder being attributable to the effects of the negative correlation that exists between borrowings and excess reserves.[26] This suggests that the behavior of free reserves is largely explained by the behavior of borrowings and that

---

[26] Free reserves (R) is given by

$$R = X - B,$$

where X = excess reserves and B = borrowings from Federal Reserve banks. The variance of R is given by

$$\sigma_r^2 = \sigma_x^2 + \sigma_b^2 - 2r_{xb}\sigma_x\sigma_b, \qquad (1)$$

where σ_x^2 = variance of excess reserves, σ_b^2 = variance of borrowings, and r_{xb} is the coefficient of correlation between excess reserves and borrowings. Based on monthly data (averages of daily figures) for the period January 1953, through March 1960, r_{xb} is $-.697$. Using expression (1) the variance of excess reserves accounts for 7.7 percent of the variance of free reserves, the variance of borrowings accounts for 61.8 percent, and the remaining 30.5 percent is accounted for by the tendency for borrowings to vary inversely with excess reserves (as reflected in the term $-2r_{xb}\sigma_x\sigma_b$).

excess reserves are not ordinarily a very important factor.

It was pointed out earlier that the amount of borrowing that member banks will want to do can be expected to depend, among other things, on the relation between the discount rate and other interest rates, which can for our present purposes be represented by the Treasury bill rate. Since borrowing is the main element in free reserves, this suggests that the amount of free reserves member banks will desire to hold will vary inversely with the difference between the bill rate and the discount rate. As the bill rate rises relative to the discount rate, banks will tend to increase their borrowings and desired free reserves will fall; conversely, as the bill rate falls in relation to the discount rate, they will tend to repay existing indebtedness to the System, and desired free reserves will rise.[27]

Thus, during a period of credit restriction, as market interest rates rise with the discount rate lagging behind, desired free reserves will decline, and the banks will attempt to reduce actual free reserves. If the Federal Reserve attempts to hold free reserves constant, it will have to adjust its open market policy to increase total

---

[27] This is pointed out by Milton Friedman in *A Program for Monetary Stability* (New York: Fordham University Press, 1959), pp. 41–43. See also the excellent study by R. J. Meigs, *Free Reserves and the Money Supply* (Chicago: University of Chicago Press, 1962).

reserves, thereby weakening the over-all restrictive effect of its policy. Conversely, when economic activity begins to level off in the late stages of an expansion, market interest rates may begin to fall. Under these circumstances, with a given or lagging discount rate, desired free reserves will increase, and if the Federal Reserve attempts to hold free reserves constant, it will have to tighten its open market policy, and the over-all restrictive effect of monetary policy is likely to become stronger.[28]

This suggests that it is wrong to believe that a constant level of free reserves means a constant degree of credit tightness or ease. At the very least, it would be necessary to adjust the discount rate continuously to the changing level of market rates. Even if this were done, changes in other factors would mean that the effective degree of credit restriction could vary substantially while the level of free reserves was held constant.

Nor is an increase (decrease) in free reserves an unambiguous indication that credit has become easier (tighter). For example, if credit is tightened by raising the discount rate, the rise in the cost of borrowed reserves will cause the banks to reduce their borrowings, making offsetting adjustments in their reserve positions perhaps by selling Treasury bills. Total reserves will decline and interest rates will rise. But this tightening of credit will be accompanied by an increase in free reserves—indeed the increase in free reserves will be the means through which credit-tightening comes about.

On the other hand, if credit is tightened by open market sales of securities while the discount rate remains constant, the resulting rise in the bill rate (and other short-term open market interest rates) will make borrowing relatively more attractive as a means of obtaining reserves. The resulting increase in borrowing will reduce free reserves—thus, a tightening of credit will be associated with a decline in free reserves. But even in this case, the increased borrowing that is reflected in declining free reserves tends to increase total reserves and thereby to offset a portion of the restrictive effect of the initial open market sales.

"Free reserves" is an artificial construct, which has had the unfortunate effect of providing a spuriously exact guide to the monetary authorities—or at least has been so interpreted by persons outside the Federal Reserve System.[29] If the

discount rate were regulated in such a way as to maintain a constant differential between it and the Treasury bill rate (a possibility that is discussed below), the amount of free reserves might perhaps become a somewhat better index of credit conditions than it is at present. Even in that case, however, it would commonly be a mistake to assume that a constant level of free reserves would necessarily mean a constant degree of credit tightness or ease. It would be better under most circumstances for the System to set its proximate goals in terms of interest rate behavior and growth of total reserves and to allow free reserves to seek the levels required to achieve these goals.

B. The Discount Rate as a Signal

Thus far, we have been considering changes in the discount rate as an adjunct to open market operations, the purpose of which is to serve as a partial governor of member bank indebtedness by regulating the cost of obtaining reserves by borrowing as compared with sales of secondary reserves.

To some extent, the discount rate also plays an independent role in monetary policy by serving as a signal of the intentions of the monetary authorities. Particularly at turning points in business conditions, a change in the discount rate is often the first clear indication of a basic alteration in monetary policy. Discount rate changes of this kind are said to have psychological effects or "announcement effects," which may influence business conditions by altering the expectations of businessmen and financial institutions.[30]

1. Difficulties of Interpreting Discount Rate Adjustments. It is commonly taken for granted that the announcement effects of discount rate changes are normally such as to strengthen the impact of monetary policy. However, those who advance the expectations argument have not explained in any detail the way in which the expectational effects are supposed to work. Actually, there are several different possible expectational effects, and in the case of each of them there is some uncertainty concerning even the direction (let alone the magnitude) of the effects.

---

[28] Friedman, *op. cit.*, p. 42.

[29] The fact that the System officials are aware of the shortcomings of the free reserves concept is

apparent from the criticisms directed at it by Ralph Young (*op. cit.*, pp. 35–36). Young points out one defect not referred to above—the fact that the amount of free reserves is subject to considerable day-to-day and week-to-week variations, due to unpredictable changes in factors outside the control of the Federal Reserve authorities.

[30] See, for example, Burgess, *op. cit.*, pp. 221–230.

One of the difficulties is that many changes in the discount rate are merely technical adjustments designed to restore or maintain an appropriate relationship between the discount rate and other rates of interest, as indicated above. Most of the periodic adjustments that are made during periods when interest rates are gradually rising or falling are of this nature. However, the interpretation placed on even these rather routine changes is sometimes unpredictable, because their timing may be affected by various considerations not directly related to stabilization policy. Sometimes, for example, discount rate adjustments may be accelerated in order to get the possible accompanying disruptive effects on the securities markets out of the way before an important Treasury debt management operation is scheduled. Or, on the other hand, action may be postponed until the repercussions of a forthcoming debt management operation are out of the way. Furthermore, the very fact that technical adjustments are sometimes interpreted by the public as having policy implications may affect System decisions concerning the timing of such adjustments. Such factors as these not only tend to make the interpretation of discount rate changes difficult, but are also partly responsible for the System's difficulties, referred to earlier, in adjusting the discount rate frequently enough to maintain a reasonably stable relation between that rate and other interest rates.[31]

Partly as a result of erratic timing and partly due to the fact that the business situation is usually fraught with some uncertainty, discount rate changes that are in fact meant to be merely routine adjustments are sometimes endowed with importance as "straws in the wind" regarding System policy by the press and by students of financial and economic affairs. And sometimes even a *failure* to change the discount rate so as to maintain "normal" interest rate relationships is taken as a sign of a change of System policy. Moreover, it is quite common for different commentators to place different interpretations on System action—or even lack of action—with respect to the discount rate.

The truth is that changes in the discount rate constitute the crudest kind of sign language.[32] Why this Stone Age form of communication should be regarded as superior to ordinary English is really quite difficult to understand. And, in this particular case, the use of such crude signals is subject to a special disadvantage arising from the fact that the signal itself has an objective effect on the situation in addition to serving as a means of communication. That is, changes in the discount rate combine action and communication, and there may be times when it is proper to act and not speak and other times when it is proper to speak and not act.

It is possible that some of the disadvantages of discretionary discount rate changes could be overcome, if the changes that were made were accompanied, at least under some circumstances, by statements explaining the reasons underlying the action. However, a change in the discount rate requires action by the boards of directors of the Federal Reserve banks and approval by the Board of Governors.[33] As a result, a very large number of persons are involved and the reasons for the action may vary among the different participants—some of whom may not thoroughly approve of the action—thus making it difficult to agree upon a generally acceptable accompanying statement.[34] This raises an interesting ques-

---

[31] As Friedman puts it (*op. cit.*, p. 40): "The discount rate is something that the Federal Reserve must continually change in order to keep the effect of its monetary policy unchanged. But changes in the rate are interpreted as if they meant changes in policy. Consequently, both the System and outsiders are led to misinterpret the System's actions and the System is led to follow policies different from those it intends to follow."

[32] Some writers seem to show no realization of the difficulties involved in this peculiar form of communication For example, Walker (*op. cit.*, pp. 229–30) says: "Discount policy—particularly with respect to changes in the rate—is a simple and easily understandable technique for informing the market of the monetary authorities' views on the economic and credit situation. Open-market operations, which are used to cushion the effects of seasonal influences as well as for cyclical and growth purposes, may at times be confusing to some observers because the System may be supplying funds to the market . . . when cyclical developments clearly dictate a restrictive monetary policy, or vice versa. The time-honored device of raising or lowering discount rates, however, can hardly be susceptible to misinterpretation by even the most uninformed observers."

[33] In this connection, see the interesting paper by H. C. Carr, "A Note on Regional Differences in Discount Rates," *Journal of Finance*, Vol. XV (March 1960), pp. 62–68, which uses differences in the timing of discount rate changes on the part of different Reserve banks as a means of classifying the banks as "leaders," "follow-the-leaders," "middle-of-the-roaders," and "dissenters." By studying rate increases and rate decreases separately, he also tries to discern differences in the banks' attitudes toward inflation and deflation.

[34] This is pointed out by Burgess (*op. cit.*), who says: "No reasons for the action are ordinarily given out at the time, partly because the decision represents the views of many people, who have perhaps acted

tion: how can the general public and the business community help but be confused in their interpretations of a change in the discount rate when the persons who are responsible for making the change are not themselves entirely clear about the reasons for it?

2. Announcement Effects of Discount Rate Adjustments. In addition to the confusion resulting from the fact that some discount rate adjustments are meant to be signals of a change in monetary policy while others are not, there is a further question whether the resulting announcement effects, even when they are intended, will help to stabilize the economy. Announcement effects work through expectations, and the relationships involved are quite complex. It is possible to break down expectational reactions into reactions of lenders, reactions of borrowers, and reactions of spenders.[35]

a) Expectational Effects on Lenders and Borrowers. A discount rate change may cause shifts in lenders' supply curves of funds and/or in borrowers' demand curves, the nature of these shifts depending upon the kind of expectations prevailing among lenders and borrowers. If interest rate expectations are elastic, a rise (fall) in present interest rates creates expectations of an even larger proportionate rise (fall) in future interest rates, whereas, with inelastic expectations, a rise (fall) in present interest rates induces the expectation of a smaller proportionate rise (fall) in future interest rates.[36]

for somewhat diverse reasons, so that it would be an extremely difficult task to phrase a statement which would fairly represent the views of all the directors of the Reserve Bank concerned and the Washington Board; and partly because it would be equally difficult to make any statement which did not either exaggerate or minimize the importance of the change. Such a statement is always subject to misinterpretation, as has been repeatedly illustrated." This statement was written a number of years ago, but it probably still reflects rather accurately the problem involved and the attitudes of those responsible for the administration of the discount rate.

[35] Our approach follows that adopted in dealing with the expectational effects of monetary policy in general by Assar Lindbeck in his study entitled *The "New" Theory of Credit Control in the United States,* Stockholm Economics Studies, Pamphlet Series, No. 1 (Stockholm: Almquist & Wiksell, 1959), pp. 25–29, and 38–39. To a considerable extent, borrowers and spenders are the same people, of course, but it is useful to consider the two activities separately.

[36] We are using the Hicksian concept of the elasticity of expectations, defined as

$$N = \frac{r_2^e - r_1^e}{r_1^e} \bigg/ \frac{r_2 - r_1}{r_1},$$

Let us take the case of a discount rate increase and suppose that initially it causes a rise in market interest rates. If lenders have elastic expectations, they may reduce their present commitments of funds in order to have more funds available to invest later on, when interest rates are expected to be relatively more favorable. Conversely, if lenders have inelastic expectations, they may increase the amounts of funds they are willing to supply at the present time. Borrowers, on the other hand, may postpone their borrowing if they have inelastic expectations and accelerate it if they have elastic expectations. For a reduction in the discount rate, all of these reactions are reversed.

According to this view, the announcement effects of a discount rate adjustment will be clearly of a stabilizing nature if lenders have elastic expectations and borrowers have inelastic expectations, since in this case an increase in the discount rate will reduce both the demand for and the supply of funds, while a reduction in the discount rate will increase both demand and supply. On the other hand, if lenders have inelastic and borrowers elastic expectations, the effects will be clearly destabilizing, while if both groups have elastic or both have inelastic expectations, the outcome is uncertain and will depend on the relative strengths of the two reactions.[37]

Thus, in order to get favorable reactions on both sides of the market, it is necessary for lenders and borrowers to have the opposite kinds of expectations—a phenomenon that does not seem very likely. However, the significance of all of these considerations is considerably reduced due to the fact that, in practice, their main effects may be confined to producing changes in the interest rate structure. That is, a lender who has elastic interest rate expectations is not very likely to reduce the total supply of funds offered in the market; rather, he is likely to reduce his

where r_1 and r_2 stand for the present interest rate before and after the change, r_1^e and r_2^e stand for the expected future interest rate before and after the change. Elastic expectations, as the term is used above, means $N > 1$, while inelastic expectations means $N < 1$. See J. R. Hicks, *Value and Capital* (2d ed.; Oxford: Clarendon Press, 1946), chap. xvi.

[37] In the case of an increase in the discount rate, if both lenders and borrowers have elastic expectations, lenders will reduce their offerings of funds while borrowers will increase their demands. If both have inelastic expectations, lenders will increase their supplies and borrowers will reduce their demands. In each of these cases, the outcome will depend upon the relative magnitudes of the respective shifts of demand and supply, as well as on the interest elasticities of demand and of supply.

supply of funds in the longer-term sectors of the market, putting the funds into the short-term sector, while he awaits the expected rise in yields. Or, if he has inelastic expectations, he may shift funds from the short- to the long-term sector. Conversely, a borrower who has elastic expectations may not accelerate his total borrowings, but instead merely increase the proportion of his borrowing in the long-term market. Or, if he has inelastic expectations, he may shift a portion of his borrowings from the long- to the short-term market.[38] With our present limited knowledge concerning the effects of changes in the structure of interest rates on the level of expenditures, it is impossible to judge the effects of such shifts in the supply and demand for funds between the long- and short-term markets. It does seem safe to conclude, however, that the effects would not be very important.

b) Expectational Effects on Spenders. A discount rate adjustment may affect not only interest rate expectations of lenders and borrowers but also the sales and price expectations of businessmen on which spending plans are based. However, it is not entirely clear what the nature of these effects would be or how they would affect economic stability. Taking the case of an increase in the discount rate, two situations (doubtless there are many variants of these) may be distinguished to illustrate the possibilities.

First, if inflationary expectations were already widespread and quite firmly established, if the

possibility of restrictive anti-inflationary action by the Federal Reserve had not adequately been taken into account in the formation of these expectations, and if there was widespread confidence that monetary policy was capable of bringing inflation promptly and firmly under control, then a rise in the discount rate heralding the onset of a vigorously anti-inflationary monetary policy might have a bearish effect on sales and price expectations and thereby cause cutbacks and cancellations of expenditure plans. In this case, the announcement effects would be helpful to the authorities.

Second, if the outlook was somewhat uncertain but shifting in an inflationary direction, if observers were unaware of the Federal Reserve's concern about the situation and were waiting to see whether the System would act, and if—perhaps on the basis of past experience—it was felt that monetary policy (even though potentially effective) would take considerable time to be brought to bear effectively enough to check the inflation, then a rise in the discount rate might have a bullish effect by confirming the emerging view that the near-term outlook was inflationary. In this case the announcement effects would be destabilizing.

Similar alternative expectational reactions could be postulated in the case of a reduction in the discount rate for the purpose of stimulating business activity. Although it is difficult to generalize concerning such matters and the effects might differ considerably from one situation to another, the second of the possible patterns of reaction outlined above seems, in general, considerably more plausible than the first. That is, it seems likely that the announcement effects of discount rate changes on the expectations of businessmen may frequently be of such a nature as to weaken rather than strengthen the effectiveness of monetary policy. At the same time the actions of the Federal Reserve are only one of the factors—and ordinarily not a major one—on which business expectations are based, and it is therefore doubtful whether the announcement effects of discount rate changes are really very important one way or the other.

We may conclude that the "psychological" effects of discount rate changes on the domestic economy—like all expectational phenomena in economics—are highly uncertain and that the discount rate as a weapon of "psychological warfare" is of very dubious value to the Federal Reserve.

A change in the discount rate has traditionally been used as a "signal" by some countries in

---

[38] If lenders have elastic and borrowers inelastic expectations, both demand and supply will tend to shift from the long- to the short-term market following a rise in the discount rate, and the shifts will tend to cancel each other out as far as their effects on the interest rate structure are concerned. It may be noted that the typical behavior of the interest rate structure is consistent with the hypothesis that both borrowers and lenders have inelastic expectations, since in this case (with a rise in the discount rate), demand would shift from the long- to the short-term market while supply would shift from the short- to the long-term market and these reactions would cause a rise in short-term interest rates relative to long-term rates. When rates are generally high, short-term rates actually do often tend to be higher than long-term rates. This is also consistent with the behavior postulated by the general expectational theory of the interest rate structure when expectations are inelastic, as set forth in Tibor Scitovsky, "A Study of Interest and Capital," *Economica*, Vol. VII, n.s. (August 1940), pp. 293–317; see also F. A. Lutz, "The Structure of Interest Rates," *Quarterly Journal of Economics*, Vol. LV (November 1940), pp. 36–63, reprinted in W. Fellner and B. F. Haley (eds.), *Readings in the Theory of Income Distribution*, (Homewood, Ill.: Richard D. Irwin, Inc., 1946), pp. 499–529.

an entirely different connection. In time of balance of payments crisis, a sharp increase in the discount rate may be used to communicate to the rest of the world a country's determination to defend by whatever means may be necessary the external value of its currency. Britain has used discount rate changes for this purpose on occasion since World War II, and this was a major reason why Canada abandoned the "floating discount rate" system (discussed below) and raised the rate to 6 percent at the time of the Canadian balance of payments crisis in June 1962. While a long tradition has perhaps made discount rate increases a reasonably effective means of international communication in some situations of this kind, there are surely other equally satisfactory means available; e.g., English, French, Latin, or Zulu.

C. Conclusions Concerning Present Discount Policy

The above analysis suggests that the discount rate as presently handled is not a very effective element in Federal Reserve policy. At times when a restrictive policy is applied, the induced increase in member bank borrowing constitutes a minor "leakage" in the controls, since it permits member banks to postpone contraction of their loans and investments and also adds to the total supply of member bank reserves. For the purpose of controlling the amount of borrowing, the Federal Reserve relies on adjustments in the discount rate, together with a tradition against borrowing that prevails among member banks and System surveillance of the borrowing practices of the banks. Due to the fact that open market interest rates fluctuate continuously while the discount rate is changed only at somewhat unpredictable discrete intervals, the relation between the discount rate and open market rates (which largely determines the incentive to borrow) behaves in a very erratic fashion. The System relies on "free reserves" as an immediate short-run guide for monetary policy; however, the restrictive effect of a given amount of free reserves varies with (among other things) the relation between the discount rate and the yields on assets—especially Treasury bills—that banks might alternatively liquidate to adjust their reserve positions.

Discretionary changes in the discount rate may at times have rather unpredictable effects on the business and financial situation, partly because it is often uncertain whether such changes are meant to be passive adjustments to keep the discount rate in line with other interest rates or

whether they represent independent moves to tighten or ease credit. To the extent that changes in the discount rate do influence business conditions directly, they do so chiefly through psychological or "announcement" effects, the nature of which depends upon the kinds of expectations held by lenders, borrowers, and spenders. Although these announcement effects are quite complex and probably not of great importance in most cases, it seems likely that on occasion they may tend to increase economic instability.

D. Possible Reforms in Discount Policy

A number of students of monetary affairs have expressed discontent with the present discount policy of the Federal Reserve, although some of them have not made specific suggestions for a change.[39] However, at least three fairly specific proposals for reform have been suggested. Two of these would de-emphasize discount policy—one by getting rid of the discount mechanism entirely and the other by tying the discount rate to market interest rates and thereby eliminating discretionary changes in it. The third would move in the opposite direction by trying to reform the discount mechanism in such a way as to make the discount rate a much more powerful weapon of credit control. We shall discuss each of these proposals in turn.

1. Abolition of the Discount Mechanism. The proposal has been advanced quite forcefully by Professor Milton Friedman that the discount mechanism should be abolished altogether.[40] Friedman argues that the legitimate function of the central bank is to control the stock of money and that the discount rate is an ineffective instrument for this purpose. Many of his arguments are similar to the ones set forth above, and his analysis was cited at several points in our discussion.

[39] See, for example, E. C. Simmons, "A Note on the Revival of Federal Reserve Discount Policy," *Journal of Finance*, Vol. XI (December 1956), pp. 413–31.

[40] Friedman, A *Program for Monetary Stability, op. cit.*, pp. 35–45; see also his testimony in *Employment, Growth and Price Levels* (Hearings before the Joint Economic Committee, Part 9A) (Washington, D.C.: U.S. Government Printing Office, 1959), pp. 3019–28. A. G. Hart also suggested the possibility of abolishing discounting a quarter of a century ago in connection with a discussion of the 100 percent reserve plan; see his "The 'Chicago' Plan of Banking Reform," *Review of Economic Studies*, Vol. II (February 1935), pp. 104–16, reprinted in F. A. Lutz and L. W. Mints (eds.), *Readings in Monetary Theory* (Homewood, Ill.: Richard D. Irwin, Inc., 1951), pp. 437–56.

One difficulty with the complete elimination of discounting is that the discount mechanism serves a useful function as a "safety valve" by which banks are able to make adjustments in their reserve positions and the Federal Reserve is able to come to the aid of the banking system—or individual banks—in case of a liquidity crisis. In order to provide a means for individual banks to make short-run adjustments in their reserve positions, Friedman proposes the establishment of a fixed "fine" to be assessed on reserve deficiencies; the fine to be set high enough to be above likely levels of market interest rates, in order to prevent the device from becoming an indirect form of borrowing from the Federal Reserve.[41] As far as liquidity crises are concerned, he contends that, due to the success of deposit insurance in practically eliminating bank failures, such crises are now scarcely conceivable and that the "lender of last resort" function of the Federal Reserve is now obsolete, so that we need not worry about its elimination. It may be noted that if the discount mechanism were eliminated, it would be possible to use the repurchase agreement technique as a means of providing emergency assistance to the banking system in times of crisis.[42]

2. Tying the Discount Rate to the Treasury Bill Rate. An alternative to the complete abolition of borrowing would be to change the discount rate at frequent intervals in such a way as to maintain an approximately constant relation between it and some open market interest rate, such as the Treasury bill rate. For example, each week as soon as the average rate of interest on Treasury bills at the Monday auction became known, the discount rate could be adjusted so as to preserve a constant differential between the two rates.[43]

Under this arrangement, the discount rate would no longer be a discretionary credit control weapon, and the unpredictable and often perverse announcement effects on the expectations of businessmen and financial institutions would be done away with. To the extent that the Federal Reserve wanted to influence expectations and felt that it could manage such effects so as to contribute to economic stability, it could implement these effects through the issuance of statements concerning its intentions, the economic outlook, and so on. While the present writer is rather dubious about the value of such activities, it is surely true that to the extent that they can contribute anything useful they can be handled better by verbal means than through reliance on such a crude signal as the discount rate.

The major question involved in the adoption of an arrangement for tying the discount rate to the bill rate would be the choice of the proper differential between the two. Obviously, the discount rate should be above the bill rate; beyond this the establishment of the differential is a matter of judgment. The larger the differential, the smaller would be (a) the average amount of borrowing and (b) the swings in borrowing that would occur as credit conditions changed. In view of the wide variations among individual banks with respect to both portfolio composition and expectations, the present writer feels that a fairly large differential of perhaps 1 percent would be desirable, in order to keep down the amount of borrowing, which, for reasons discussed earlier, represents a minor leakage in monetary controls. But there does not seem to be any analytical principle that provides a basis for selecting the proper differential. Doubtless the best procedure would be to experiment with various differentials, retaining each one long enough to observe its effectiveness.

Under this arrangement, in contrast to the complete elimination of discounting, the discount mechanism would continue to be available to serve as a means of making temporary adjustments in bank reserve positions and as a "safety valve" that could be used in times of crises. If this approach were adopted, it would probably be desirable to give up the efforts to rely on such an intangible and unreliable means of controlling discounting as the traditional "reluctance" of member banks and the so-called "surveillance" of the Federal Reserve, recognizing borrowing

---

[41] Friedman, *A Program for Monetary Stability, op. cit.,* pp. 44–45.

[42] This possibility was mentioned by Hart in connection with his suggestion for the elimination of the discount mechanism (*op. cit.,* p. 110 in original, p. 447 in *Readings in Monetary Theory*).

[43] See Smith, "The Discount Rate as a Credit-Control Weapon," *op. cit.* Friedman (*A Program for Monetary Stability, op. cit.,* p. 45) refers to such an arrangement as an alternative (albeit a less desirable one in his opinion) to complete abolition of discounting. He points out, quite correctly, that if the differential between the discount rate and the bill rate were made large enough, the plan would be equivalent to abolishing discounting. Professor J. M. Culbertson ("Timing Changes in Monetary Policy," *Journal of Finance,* Vol. XIV [May 1959], pp. 145–60, esp. 157–158) concludes with respect to discount policy that the Federal Reserve "should subordinate

the discount rate by making adjustments in it routinely in response to changes in market rates and should seek a less ambiguous vehicle for such communication with the public as may be useful."

as a "right" rather than a "privilege" of member banks, and relying entirely on the discount rate (in relation to the bill rate) as a means of controlling it.[44]

A procedure of the kind discussed above was employed in Canada from November 1956, to June 1962. During this period, the Bank of Canada adjusted its lending rate each week so as to keep it ¼ of 1 percent above the average rate on Treasury bills at the most recent weekly auction. The reasons given for adopting such an arrangement in 1956 were similar to those set forth above.[45] The policy was abandoned at the time of the Canadian balance of payment crisis in June 1962, when, as part of a program for dealing with the crisis, the discount rate was raised to 6 percent as a signal to the rest of the world of Canada's determination to defend the external value of the Canadian dollar.[46] The traditional discretionary discount rate policy has been employed in Canada since that time.

3. Increasing the Effectiveness of the Discount Rate.

A proposal for reform of the discount mechanism very different from the two discussed above has recently been advanced by Professor James Tobin.[47] Instead of dismantling the discount mechanism entirely or abolishing discretionary changes in the discount rate, Tobin would greatly increase the importance of the rate and turn it into a major weapon of credit control.

The Tobin proposal calls for two changes in present procedures:

1. The Federal Reserve would pay interest at the discount rate on member bank reserve balances in excess of requirements.

2. The prohibitions against payments of interest on demand deposits and the ceilings on the payment of interest on time and savings deposits would be repealed.

These changes would greatly increase the leverage of the discount rate by making it an important consideration for banks that are not in debt to the Federal Reserve as well as for those that are. The opportunity cost to a bank of increasing its loans and investments would be the return it could earn by holding excess reserves, and this cost would be firmly under the control of the Federal Reserve. Moreover, the interest rate offered by the banks to holders of idle deposits would presumably be linked rather closely to the rate paid on excess reserves, since the bank could always earn a return on its deposits at least equal to one minus its reserve requirement times the discount rate. Thus, if the Federal Reserve wished to tighten credit, it could raise the discount rate, and this would increase the opportunity cost of lending for all of the member banks (whether they were in debt or not) and would, therefore, make them willing to lend only at higher interest rates than previously, while at the same time causing the banks to raise interest rates on deposits, thereby increasing the attractiveness of bank deposits relative to other assets on the part of the public.[48] The

---

[44] In this connection, Friedman (*A Program for Monetary Stability, op. cit.*) says: "If rediscounting is retained, it should be a right, not a privilege, freely available to all member banks on specified terms." It appears that Friedman exaggerates the amount of discretion exercised by the System with respect to lending to individual banks, although the views expressed by System officials, concerning the "administration of the discount window"—such as Roosa's attempt ("Credit Policy at the Discount Window: Comment," *op. cit.,* pp. 333–34) to draw a distinction between saying "No," and refusing to say "Yes"—are so ambiguous that it is very difficult to judge the amount of discretion employed.

[45] See Bank of Canada, *Annual Report of the Governor to the Minister of Finance,* 1956, pp. 45–46.

[46] See Bank of Canada, *Annual Report of the Governor to the Minister of Finance,* 1962, pp. 3–4 and 72–73.

[47] James Tobin, "Towards Improving the Efficiency of the Monetary Mechanism," *Review of Economics and Statistics,* Vol. XLII (August 1960), pp. 276–79.

[48] Allowing the banks to pay interest on deposits would have two related advantages. One is that it would probably reduce the propensity for the velocity of deposits to increase when a restrictive policy was applied, since the banks would be able to raise interest rates on deposits making them more attractive and weakening the tendency for rising interest rates on other claims to induce shifts of deposits into the hands of persons having a high propensity to spend. The other advantage is that it should reduce the amount of real resources devoted to the task of economizing the use of cash balances. Since the revival of flexible monetary policy, many large corporations, as well as state and local governments, have developed extensive facilities for handling short-term investments in order to minimize their holdings of sterile cash balances, and the amount of skilled personnel devoting its time to this kind of activity at present is certainly not trivial (see C. E. Silberman, "The Big Corporate Lenders," *Fortune,* August 1956, pp. 111–114, 162–70). Resources devoted to this purpose represent a form of economic waste, since the real cost of creating deposits is virtually zero so that there is no economic gain from exercising economy in their use. This is pointed out by Tobin and is emphasized even more strongly by Friedman (*A Program for Monetary Stability, op. cit.,* pp. 71–75). The two advantages (reducing destabilizing velocity changes and discouraging efforts to economize in the use of costless deposits) are related in the sense that the propensity to waste resources in economizing

discount rate could be used independently to control credit, or it could be combined with open market operations. It is not clear, however, what principle should govern the division of responsibility between the two weapons.

The proposal is ingenious and would certainly be practical and capable of being put in operation without causing disruption. And it might have the incidental advantage that the payment of interest on excess reserves might encourage more banks to become members of the Federal Reserve System. What is not clear, however, is why a flexible monetary policy could be implemented more effectively by means of the discount rate under this proposal than is now possible by means of open market operations. It is true that the proposal would presumably permit the Federal Reserve to control the cost of bank credit very effectively, but this can already be done—in principle at least—by open market operations. In part, the problems of monetary policy seem to stem from the fact that the demand for bank credit is not very sensitive to changes in interest rates and other monetary variables, so that it has proved to be difficult to operate forcefully enough to produce prompt changes of the degree necessary for effective stabilization. Perhaps it would be possible to bring the forces of monetary policy to bear more rapidly by means of the Tobin proposal but this is by no means obvious. If the proposal merely provides another way of doing what is already possible, it hardly seems worthwhile.

The repeal of the existing restrictions relating to payment of interest on deposits is in no way dependent upon provision for the payment of interest on excess reserves, and there is much to be said for the repeal of these restrictions, even if the remainder of the Tobin proposal is not adopted.

4. *Conclusions.* Of the three proposals for reforming the discount mechanism, the present writer feels that the strongest case can be made for the procedure of changing the discount rate each week in such a way as to maintain a constant spread between the discount rate and the Treasury bill rate. This would be a less drastic reform than the complete elimination of discounting, would eliminate the unpredictable effects of discretionary changes in the discount rate, would preserve the discount mechanism as a

safety valve, and would eliminate the effects on credit conditions that now result from erratic variations in the relation between the discount rate and open market rates. The Tobin proposal for increasing the potency of the discount rate as a credit-control weapon is worthy of careful study, but it is not yet clear that the proposal would greatly strengthen the hand of the Federal Reserve.

If the present system of making discretionary adjustments in the discount rate at irregular intervals is retained, it would be desirable to reform the administration of the discount mechanism, perhaps by shifting the authority for making changes in the rate from the individual Reserve banks to the Federal Open Market Committee. The purpose of such a change would be to reduce the number of persons involved in decisions regarding the discount rate so that it would be easier to agree on the reasons for making changes. This would facilitate the issuance of explanatory statements at the time changes are made, in order to eliminate the confusion that often results due to the varying interpretations that are frequently placed on rate changes in the absence of explanations. It should then be feasible to make more frequent technical adjustments in the rate with less need to worry about the danger of disruptive effects on the credit situation, thereby permitting closer co-ordination of the discount rate with open market operations.

IV. THE ROLE OF VARIABLE RESERVE REQUIREMENTS[49]

Since the accord with the Treasury in March 1951, the Federal Reserve has made no systematic anti-cyclical use of changes in member bank reserve requirements. Reductions in the reserve requirement percentages applicable to demand deposits were made in the recessions of 1953–54 (reductions in July 1953, and June-August 1954) and 1957–58 (reductions in February-April 1958). In the recession of 1960–61, reserves were released by permitting member banks to count vault cash as reserves—to a limited extent beginning in December 1959, and without limitation beginning in November 1960. And, finally, reserve requirements applicable to time

cash balances tends to increase during periods of credit restriction and rising interest rates, and this increased application of resources helps to permit a destabilizing rise in velocity.

[49] Much of the discussion in this section is based upon the author's study entitled "Reserve Requirements in the American Monetary System," in *Monetary Management,* prepared for the Commission on Money and Credit (Englewood Cliffs, N.J.: Prentice-Hall, Inc., 1963), pp. 175–315.

deposits were reduced from 5 to 4 percent in October-November 1962, at a time when output was expanding but unemployment remained high.

Under present provisions, the Board of Governors can change requirements on demand deposits between 10 and 22 percent for reserve city banks and between 7 and 14 percent for country banks, while it can change requirements on time deposits between 3 and 6 percent; as this is written (July 1963) the requirements are 16½ percent and 12 percent for demand deposits at reserve city and country banks, respectively, and 4 percent for time deposits.[50] The Board may permit member banks to count all or part of their vault cash as required reserves; at the present time vault cash may be counted in full.

A. Variable Reserve Requirements as a Credit Control Weapon

A change in reserve requirements alters both the amount of excess reserves available and the credit expansion multiplier, which determines the amount of potential credit expansion per dollar of excess reserves. For relatively small changes in reserve requirements, the first of these effects is much more important than the second—with net demand deposits amounting to roughly $100 billion, a reduction of one percentage point in requirements releases approximately $1 billion of excess reserves.

However, changes in reserve requirements have harsh and rather indiscriminate effects, at least when the changes made amount to as much as ½ or 1 percentage point, as has been customary in recent years. This does not cause serious problems in the case of reductions in requirements, because, as explained below, excessive bank liquidity generated by such reductions can be—and in practice has been—sopped up by open market sales of securities. Increases in requirements, however, have troublesome side effects which are not quite so easily dealt with.

Increases in requirements affect all banks—or at least all the banks in a particular reserve requirement classification—including some banks that are plentifully supplied with liquid assets which permit them to make easy adjustments in their reserve positions, as well as banks whose liquidity positions are less comfortable. To the extent that banks are forced to carry out troublesome portfolio readjustments, they are able to see

clearly that these adjustments were forced upon them by Federal Reserve action; whereas the adjustments resulting from open market operations are either voluntary or, to the extent that they are involuntary, appear to be the result of impersonal market forces. Thus, frequent reserve requirement increases are likely to cause resentment among member banks and, under present conditions, might even be a significant deterrent to membership in the Federal Reserve System. Moreover, while the initial effect of reserve requirement increases is felt by all the banks, it is likely that there will be substantial secondary effects which will be concentrated on banks in the larger money centers as interior banks draw down correspondent balances and sell Government securities in the central money market in order to restore their reserve positions.

B. Co-ordination of Reserve Requirement Changes and Open Market Operations

To some extent, it is possible to soften the unduly harsh impact of changes in reserve requirements by proper co-ordination with open market operations. The open market operations associated with the mid-1954 reductions in reserve requirements, which were designed to encourage continuing recovery from the recession of 1953–54, provide a good example of this co-ordination. The reserve requirement reductions that were made resulted in the injection of what the Federal Reserve authorities felt was an unduly large amount of excess reserves within a short period of time.[51] Accordingly the Federal Reserve sold securities in the open market at about the same time the reserve requirement reductions were made, in order to absorb a portion of the released reserves: then, over a period of several months, it purchased securities in order to feed reserves back into the economy at times when additional reserves appeared to be needed in the interest of orderly recovery.[52] Thus, a skill-

---

[50] Under legislation passed in July, 1959, the "central reserve city" classification of member banks was eliminated effective July 28, 1962.

[51] In a succession of changes in June, July, and August 1954, demand deposit reserve requirements were reduced by 2 percentage points at central reserve city banks and 1 percentage point at reserve city and country banks, while time deposit reserve requirements were reduced by 1 percentage point at all classes of banks. These adjustments released about $1.5 billion of reserves.

[52] Between June and August 1954, the Federal Reserve reduced its holdings of Government securities (average of daily figures) by $1.0 billion, while the net effect of factors outside the control of the Federal Reserve was to reduce member bank reserves by

ful blending of reserve requirement changes and open market operations produced a smooth and gradual adjustment.

Similar recent examples of the use of open market operations to soften the impact of reserve requirement increases during periods of inflation are not available, since the Federal Reserve has not made use of reserve requirement increases since the Accord.[53] The blending of open market operations with reserve requirement adjustments would probably not result in quite such a smooth adjustment in this case, because the problem here is not only to prevent an unduly sharp impact on the total supply of money and credit, but to alleviate harsh impacts on individual banks. Since some banks which were squeezed especially hard might not possess securities of the maturities being purchased by the System, these banks might not be helped directly by open market operations.

If reserve requirement changes have important advantages as a means of controlling credit, the technical difficulties in making two-way adjustments could be greatly reduced by making smaller changes in the requirements than have been customary in the past and by smoothing the impact by means of open market operations. It has been suggested that more frequent and smaller changes be made, and there is no techni-

cal reason why this could not be done.[54] And if more frequent use of reserve requirement changes would clearly permit the Federal Reserve to conduct monetary policy more efficiently than would otherwise be possible, the fact that such adjustments might be somewhat unpopular with commercial bankers should not be taken too seriously. The real question is: What advantages do reserve requirement adjustments have in comparison with other credit-control weapons, especially open market operations? To this question we now turn.

C. Possible Usefulness of Reserve Requirement Changes

Under most circumstances, the effects of (for example) expanding credit by lowering reserve requirements will almost surely be different in detail from those produced by the same amount of expansion (measured in terms of the increase in income-generating expenditures) produced by open market purchases. That is, the spending units which will be induced to increase their expenditures will be different in the two cases, as will the types of expenditures affected. Unfortunately, however, our knowledge of relative "incidence" of the two weapons is very poor, so that, while we may be sure that there are differences, there is very little that can be said about them. For this reason, we can scarcely even discuss intelligently the "mix" of the two that should be used to accomplish particular objectives. The best we can do is to indicate some rather general considerations which differentiate reserve requirement adjustments from open market operations and some special situations in which the reserve requirements weapon may be especially appropriate.

1. Neutrality. The Federal Reserve authorities in recent years have shown a strong antipathy toward selective credit controls and have taken the position that the central bank should confine its efforts to the control of the total supply of money and credit, leaving the task of allocating credit to market forces. This attitude has been reflected, for example, in the System's opposition to the establishment of consumer credit controls even on a stand-by basis. Although there are other considerations involved also, this philosophy seems to be one of the bases for the Federal Reserve's adherence to the "bills-only" policy be-

---

another $200 million. Thus, total reserves declined by $1.2 billion, and required reserves fell by the same amount, leaving excess reserves unchanged. From August to December 1954, the Federal Reserve increased its portfolio of Government securities by $0.9 billion as it fed reserves back to the banking system to meet seasonal demands. (Calculations based on data from *Federal Reserve Bulletin,* February 1955, p. 149).

[53] During the immediate postwar inflation in 1948 while the Federal Reserve was "pegging" the market for Government securities, reserve requirement increases were used on several occasions in an effort to implement a policy of credit restraint. In this situation, however, member banks were plentifully supplied with Government securities, which were saleable at virtually fixed prices. Consequently, the banks tended merely to sell more securities than they otherwise would have sold, and these securities had to be purchased by the System to prevent securities prices from falling. Thus, banks were able to replenish their reserves readily, and there was little effect on the cost or availability of credit. In this situation, open market purchases were, in effect, used to offset more or less permanently the effects of reserve requirement increases. Such operations did tend to reduce bank liquidity somewhat, since the banks were giving up liquid securities for less liquid required reserves; however, the operations were not on a sufficiently large scale to make this a significant factor.

[54] See C. R. Whittlesey, "Reserve Requirements and the Integration of Credit Policies," *Quarterly Journal of Economics,* Vol. LVIII (August 1944), pp. 553–70.

tween 1953 and 1961. During this period, the System carefully eschewed efforts to control the maturity structure of interest rates, leaving this to the determination of market forces.

If such a philosophy of "neutrality" were to be pushed to its logical conclusion, it would lead to reliance on reserve requirement adjustments as a means of monetary control. Even bills-only is not entirely neutral in its effects on the interest rate structure, since changes in the money stock produced by this method involve, as a by-product, changes in the stock of securities of a particular maturity (namely, Treasury bills) and have a special impact on short-term interest rates. Reserve requirement changes, on the other hand, have no direct effects on interest rates or on stocks of securities—all such effects are produced by the decisions and activities of borrowers and lenders (including commercial banks).

The "neutrality" argument for reliance on reserve requirement changes would carry weight only with those who accept the "neutrality" philosophy. Moreover, its implementation would require that all monetary adjustments be accomplished by reserve requirement changes. This would include the day-to-day operations of the Federal Reserve designed to counteract the effects of uncontrollable factors (float, currency in circulation, etc.) affecting member bank reserves. These operations seem clearly to serve a useful, if not indispensable, function in keeping the money market on an even keel and are now quite efficiently carried out by means of open market operations. While it would undoubtedly be possible to make smaller and more frequent adjustments in reserve requirements than have been employed in the past, it would surely be wholly impracticable to employ reserve requirement changes on a day-to-day basis. For this, as well as other reasons, the "neutrality" argument for the use of reserve requirement adjustments appears to be purely academic and of no practical importance.

2. *Announcement Effects.* Like discount rate adjustments and unlike open market operations, changes in reserve requirements are overt actions of the Federal Reserve which are widely reported and commented upon in the press. As such, they are likely to have "announcement effects" through their influence on the expectations of businessmen and financial institutions. In fact, it seems quite likely that the reductions in reserve requirements that were made in 1953 and 1958 were motivated partly by a desire to convince the public that the System intended to take vigorous anti-recession action.

The question of announcement effects was discussed at some length in connection with discount rate changes, and the conclusion of that discussion was that such effects are uncertain and unpredictable. This conclusion seems to apply also to reserve requirement changes. For example, it seems at least as plausible to suppose that a dramatic reduction in reserve requirements in the early stages of a recession will strengthen the feeling that business conditions are worsening, as to suppose that it will make people optimistic by showing that the Federal Reserve is actively on the job trying to maintain stability.

I believe the fact that reserve requirement changes tend to have announcement effects is a disadvantage rather than an advantage. The best way to produce announcement effects—if and when such effects seem likely to be desirable—is by means of carefully-worded public statements explaining the views or intentions of the authorities. Action and communication should, in general, be carefully separated rather than rigidly linked together.

3. *Speed of Reactions.* It has been argued that reserve requirements changes have more widely diffused effects than open market operations and therefore may affect economic conditions more promptly. The reasoning behind this argument is that open market operations are consummated in the central money market of the country in New York and therefore have their initial impact chiefly on the reserve positions of the money market banks. Effects are gradually diffused throughout the country, primarily by means of interregional flows of funds set in motion by the adjustments of these banks to the initial changes in their reserve positions—a process which takes some time to carry through. Reserve requirement changes, on the other hand, instantaneously affect the reserve positions of all banks and therefore produce more rapid effects on credit conditions outside the central money markets. Federal Reserve officials apparently accept this argument and think it is especially relevant with respect to anti-recession policies, since Chairman Martin of the Board of Governors has used it to explain why the System used reserve requirement reductions as a means of attacking the recessions of 1953–54 and 1957–58.[55]

One study covering the period from mid-1951 to mid-1953, when the Federal Reserve relied

---

[55] See Martin's testimony in January 1960 *Economic Report of the President* (Hearings before the Joint Economic Committee, 86th Cong., 2d sess.) (Washington, D.C.: U.S. Government Printing Office, 1960), pp. 163–212.

on open market operations to tighten credit rather gently at first and then with increasing intensity, suggests that the effects were felt first in New York and that there were noticeable lags in their transmission to the rest of the country.[56] The free reserve position of central reserve city banks appears to have been affected earlier and more strongly than that of other banks, and New York City banks showed an earlier and more pronounced tendency to shift the composition of their portfolios from investments to loans than did banks outside New York City. The author of this study suggests more frequent use of changes in reserve requirements, in order to shorten the lags in the regional transmission of monetary policy.

While this study is somewhat suggestive, it is not clearly convincing, since the statistical series involved are so ragged in their behavior as to be difficult to interpret, and because one cannot be sure that such differences in regional reactions as were present were not due to factors unrelated to monetary policy. There are several reasons for doubting whether the difference in the reaction speeds of the two weapons is great enough to be an important consideration. In the first place, as noted above, while the initial impact of reserve requirement changes is widely diffused, adjustments of interior banks via changes in correspondent balances and security transactions are likely to pass a disproportionate share of it back to the central money markets. Furthermore, to the extent that the initial effects of open market operations are more concentrated, the fact that central money market banks are very sensitive to changes in their reserve positions and prompt in reacting thereto would suggest that the transmission of effects to other parts of the economy is likely to get under way quickly and proceed rapidly. And finally, the other lags in monetary policy appear to be so long that it is doubtful whether such differences as do exist between the two weapons are of appreciable importance in the overall picture. In fact, one cannot even be sure that there is not frequently some advantage in open market operations, because commercial banks all over the country adjust their reserves through sales of securities (which largely clear through the central money market) so that purchases (for example) of securities may have some tendency to direct the flow of new reserves to the points where they are most needed, instead of scattering them indiscriminately over the map.[57]

4. National Emergencies. One circumstance in which the power to raise reserve requirements might be used to good purpose is in times of a war or major national defense emergency, which requires the expenditure of large amounts of borrowed funds by the Government during a period of full employment. Under such conditions, there is much to be said for the Treasury's obtaining such funds as it needs but cannot raise through taxation or through borrowing from the nonbank public by selling securities directly to the Federal Reserve, with the System raising reserve requirements to immobilize the excess reserves that are created when the Treasury spends the money. This process would avoid the accumulation of excessive liquidity in the hands of the commercial banks and the accompanying threat of post-emergency inflation and would save the Treasury some interest costs. It would, of course, require that the Federal Reserve be given virtually unlimited power to raise reserve requirements.

5. Conclusions. The upshot of the above discussion is that there appear to be few if any circumstances in normal times when reserve requirement changes are clearly superior to open market operations as a means of controlling credit. Reserve requirement changes have "announcement effects" while open market operations do not, but these may frequently turn out to be a nuisance rather than an aid to the Federal Reserve and, to the extent that they are desirable, can be produced more effectively by other methods. Conceivably, reserve requirement changes may affect business conditions more promptly than open market operations; however, this is not certain, and in any case the advantage is

---

[56] I. O. Scott, Jr., "The Regional Impact of Monetary Policy," *Quarterly Journal of Economics,* Vol. LXIX (May 1955), pp. 269–84.

[57] Chairman Martin of the Board of Governors has stated his belief that an increase in reserve requirements would be the best way to offset the effects on member bank reserves of a substantial gold inflow, if circumstances required such offsetting (see his testimony in January 1960 *Economic Report of the President,* [Hearings before the Joint Economic Committee, *op. cit.*], p. 187). Perhaps this would be true in some circumstances, but the present writer is inclined to believe that open market sales of securities might often be the more appropriate weapon for this purpose, since the funds resulting from the sale of gold to the Treasury by foreign governments are often likely to find their way to the central money market, so that the way to offset the effects of these flows with the minimum impact on domestic business activity might be through the sale of Treasury bills, which would, in the main, withdraw funds from the central money market.

unlikely to be great enough to be of much significance. In view of the superior administrative efficiency of the open market operations, together with the unpopularity among commercial bankers of frequent two-way adjustments of reserve requirements, there is much to be said for relying exclusively on open market operations under normal circumstances.[58]

V. CONCLUDING COMMENTS

As they are used at the present time, open market policy, discount policy, and reserve requirements policy are three instruments of monetary control with essentially a single purpose—the regulation of the total supply of money and bank credit. Open market policy is powerful, effective, and administratively flexible; it is unquestionably the key weapon of general monetary control. Discount policy, as reflected in changes in the discount rate, has a weak and to some extent even perverse effect on the total supply of money and credit and is, at the same time, a rather inept and confusing device for waging "psychological warfare" against economic instability via the public's expectations. Reserve requirements policy is a powerful weapon but too cumbersome for frequent use and not clearly capable of accomplishing anything under ordinary circumstances that cannot be done at least as well by means of open market operations.

Doubtless the three weapons have somewhat different economic effects; however, detailed knowledge of the impact of monetary changes is inadequate to permit a meaningful differentiation. Consequently, it is not possible to specify the circumstances in which one of these weapons rather than the others should be used. They are

all designed to serve the same purposes—one effectively and the other two rather ineptly.

Accordingly, I would favor placing complete reliance on open market operations, under ordinary circumstances, as the means of conducting general monetary policy. The best way of handling the discount rate would probably be to tie it to the Treasury bill rate as explained earlier in this paper. Reserve requirements should probably be fixed at an appropriate level and kept there.[59] I would also favor the elimination of the present threefold classification of banks for reserve requirement purposes and the establishment of uniform reserve requirements for demand deposits at all banks, including non-member banks. There does not appear to be any logical basis for differentiating among banks as far as reserve requirements are concerned, and uniform requirements would increase somewhat the precision of open market policy as a means of controlling the total supply of money and bank credit.[60]

There may be circumstances under which the Federal Reserve should try to affect economic activity by influencing the public's expectations, although this is clearly a tricky and possibly even dangerous form of activity. To the extent that it is employed, it should be divorced from actions designed to control bank reserves and should take advantage of the subtleties of everyday language. One of the advantages of open market operations is that they are necessarily being carried out continuously and are largely devoid of so-called "announcement effects."

One final question should perhaps be raised: Does not the situation of the last three years or so when monetary policy has had to be directed simultaneously at stimulation of the domestic economy and protection of the balance of payments against excessive outflows of short-term capital argue for the retention of all of the traditional credit control weapons, in order to maximize the flexibility of the monetary authorities? I do not believe so. It is true that, for example, by lowering reserve requirements and simultaneously selling enough Treasury bills to keep the bill rate from falling, the authorities could presumably stimulate the domestic econ-

---

[58] Another issue that has come up recently relating to the choice between open market operations and reserve requirement changes is the differing effects that these two weapons have on the Treasury's interest costs and on the profits of commercial banks. For example, the creation of a given amount of additional money by open market purchases will result in lower costs to the Treasury and lower profits to the banking system than would the creation of the same amount of money by lowering reserve requirements. (For an extensive discussion, see Smith, "Reserve Requirements in the American Monetary System," *op. cit.*, pp. 216–49.) However, this matter is relevant chiefly in connection with long-term developments related to the choice between open market purchases and reserve requirement reductions as alternative means of providing reserves to support the secular growth of the money supply. It has little bearing on the relative merits of the two weapons as alternative means of producing two-way anti-cyclical changes in credit conditions.

[59] The question of what is the "appropriate" level of reserve requirements is beyond the scope of this paper and, in any case, is a matter of judgment. It is in connection with this question that the effects of reserve requirements on bank profits and Treasury interest costs referred to in footnote 58 become relevant.

[60] Smith, "Reserve Requirements in the American Monetary System," *op. cit.*, pp. 175–99.

omy to some extent without increasing outflows of short-term capital. But such a result could equally well be brought about by requisite purchases of longer-term securities combined with sales of bills. It is difficult to see that adjustments in reserve requirements and the discount rate give the authorities any ability to change the structure of interest rates and the total credit supply that could not equally well be accomplished by sufficiently flexible use of Federal Reserve open market and Treasury debt management operations.

THE FED AT THE CROSSROADS*

Henry C. Wallich

During the last few years, the Federal Reserve has been confronted with an unprecedented number of difficult choices. It has had to choose among conflicting objectives in domestic and foreign economic policy, among conflicting theories of how monetary policy works, and among mutually exclusive operating targets. These choices have been forced upon the Fed by inflation and by the rise of monetarism. The Fed's difficulties, moreover, have been enormously compounded by the fact that fiscal policy has often failed to engage in the division of labor with monetary policy that conditions have demanded.

A well-worn dictum of standard economics says that when the needs of the balance of payments and the domestic situation are at odds, monetary policy should devote itself to preserving external stability and fiscal policy to internal stability. The reason is simple: both monetary and fiscal policy influence the economy by influencing income, but monetary policy in addition influences capital movements. It thus has a comparative advantage in the balance-of-payments field.

The U.S. repeatedly has faced a dilemma when the balance of payments called for restraint while the domestic situation demanded expansion—during the early part of the 1960s, and again in 1971. On the first occasion, the division of labor was implemented reasonably well. One would have to stretch a point to say the same of the latter case. Lately, in part at least because fiscal policy has not been sufficiently flexible, the Fed has been oriented almost entirely toward domestic concerns. That decision probably was inevitable. But the international monetary crisis during the early part of 1971—characterized by

* From *The Morgan Guaranty Survey,* October 1971, pp. 4–10. Reprinted by permission of the Morgan Guaranty Trust Company and the author. Henry C. Wallich is Seymour H. Knox Professor of Economics, Yale University.

a huge outflow of U.S. short-term capital to Europe, at first in response to higher interest rates abroad and later in anticipation of changes in exchange rates—was in large part the result of this ordering of priorities.

THE TWO-FRONT WAR

In its domestic endeavors, the Fed has had to choose repeatedly between fighting inflation and fighting recession. Inflation is the child of excess demand. So long as it walks hand in hand with its parent, the Fed's domestic choice is simple. But what if the parent disappears while the offspring is still around? When does the central bank stop fighting inflation and start fighting recession? In such a situation it becomes painfully obvious that one cannot pursue two objectives with a single instrument. That may be one reason why the Fed has developed an admiration for incomes policy, the other reason being that when one's own techniques are not producing very well one naturally develops a higher opinion of instruments wielded by others. The Congress' enthusiasm for monetary policy, at times of reckless fiscal overexpansion, is another instance of this.

In noninflationary periods, shifting from restraint to expansion and back is mainly a matter of catching the turning points of the cycle. Critics have assessed the Fed's performance over the years very differently. Two of the most severe critics of its over-all performance—Karl Brunner and Allan Meltzer—have nevertheless given it high marks for good timing.

In inflationary times, however, such as at the cyclical peaks of 1957 and 1969, it has been a matter of deciding when to break off the unfinished engagement with inflation and turn against the new and more serious enemy, recession. Toward the end of 1957, when the Fed reversed the discount-rate increase of August, Chairman William McChesney Martin gave the reason for the action: "The economy. It changed." Indeed it had, but some time previously, as the Fed undoubtedly knew. There is no law of economics to tell a central bank when to make such a choice.

In early 1970, after a period of extreme tightness, a similar decision had to be made. Once more—months after the cyclical peak—the battle against inflation was called off, mission not fully accomplished, and a more imminent or more serious danger faced. If the criterion had been to restrain the economy to the maximum extent possible without provoking a recession, the Fed narrowly failed. But I find wholly admirable the way in which a large organization with all the earmarks of unwieldiness managed to turn itself around.

THE MONETARIST CRITIQUE

In making such turns, the Fed has experienced one of its many brushes with monetarism. The monetarist reaction to these gyrations (in the Milton Friedman version) is simple: "Stop trying to zig and zag. Just keep increasing the money supply steadily, through inflation and recession, and there will be no inflation and recession." The basis for this rejection of anti-cyclical policy is Dr. Friedman's empirical finding that the lags of monetary policy are long and variable, and the conclusion that the lagged effects are more likely to be cyclically harmful than helpful. In the light of this monetarist doctrine, shifts of monetary policy are worse than useless.

Acceptance of this doctrine has been surprisingly wide. In 1968, the Joint Economic Committee requested the Fed to appear before it and explain whenever the growth rate of the money supply moved outside the 2%–6% range. The Fed promised to comply. Economists, bankers, and the press have evaluated Federal Reserve policy in terms of how closely it was hewing to some stable money-growth target. All this manifests the great strides monetarism has made in displacing its dominant rival, the Keynesian approach.

The innocent intellectual bystander is tempted to interpret the gains of monetarism in the light of the changing economic environment, instead of in terms of competing creeds. Keynesianism is chiefly the economics of underemployment. Monetarism is the economics of full employment and inflation. In times of slack, the relation between the money supply and the economy becomes loose. It tightens as interest rates rise, idle money is absorbed, and particularly as excessive growth of money pushes the economy into inflation. In broadest terms, one can view the movement from the 1920s to the 1930s and from there to the 1970s as a move first from the quantity-theory world of monetarism to the underemployment world of Keynes and back to a new quantity-theory world. Such a relativistic view of a doctrinal matter of course is anathema to the true faithful on either side.

The alignment of inflation with monetarism and of Keynesianism with stable prices is pure irony. Keynesians on the whole are tolerant of inflation. In fact they often welcome it as a means of reducing unemployment. Yet inflation has wrecked their models, made nonsense of their analysis of interest rates, and generally helped their monetarist opponents. Monetarists are in general anti-inflationary, fundamentally because they believe that inflation accomplishes nothing. Milton Friedman reminded the convention of the American Economic Association that he was hardly suspect of wanting to downgrade the importance of money. But, he added, monetary policy "cannot peg interest rates for more than very limited periods" and it "cannot peg the rate of unemployment for more than very limited periods." Yet one thing that inflation undoubtedly has accomplished is to put monetarism in the driver's seat.

The Fed is predominantly of a moderately Keynesian persuasion, although there are enough economists in the System with other views (including the monetarist one) to make this generalization vulnerable. On inflation, however, it parts company with the standard Keynesian approach. As befits a central bank, it has always treated inflation as a major evil requiring correction even at some cost in terms of other objectives.

INTEREST RATES AND INFLATION

Like other Keynesians, the Fed has had trouble with the interpretation of interest rates in conditions of inflation. In a well behaved Keynesian world, an increase in the money supply reduces interest rates. When the monetarists, with unnecessary fanfare, announced that an increase in money raised interest rates, and then explained that they meant that an increase in money after a while raised income and the increase in income after a while raised interest rates, most people found the paradox obvious and not very interesting. But when on some occasions in 1970 and 1971, as the Fed accelerated the growth of money, long-term interest rates began to rise immediately, the monetarist sequential analysis seemed to have become telescoped into instantaneity. The central bank seemed in danger of losing control of interest rates.

One explanation of this phenomenon is that the economy really behaves as the monetarists think, and that the market has become so convinced of this that it discounts the effect of faster money growth upon interest rates almost instantly. Another is that the market remains Keynesian but thinks the Fed has gone monetarist, and that it is determined to stick to a rigid money-supply target. In that case, any temporary acceleration of money growth presages an effort of the Fed to get back on track, with resulting stringency, which the market may also decide to discount instantaneously.

The Fed so far has thrown in its lot with the orthodox view that more money means lower interest rates, at least for a while. That seems the only possible explanation of the very rapid rate of increase in the money supply during the first half of 1971. And in making this choice among theories, the central bank can argue at least that the Keynesian belief in the inverse relation between money and interest rates rests upon a clearly perceived economic mechanism. The monetarist view that the relation is positive has a faint "black-box" connotation: in goes money, out—with long and variable lags—come unexplained effects.

The "black-box" image, to be sure, is no longer quite fair, because much work has been done to explain these effects. But the quick adaptation of interest rates to inflation remains puzzling. That "lenders demand compensation for the inflation loss" is a truism, but how do they make their demands effective? Stop saving during inflation? We have seen that they save more. Shift into common stocks? This would not have been a good ploy in recent years and does not seem to have happened. The best one can say is that in inflation some savers may shift from the bond market, where one can lose both in terms of purchasing power and of market value, to the short-term market, where savers face only one type of loss. Meanwhile borrowers may respond to inflation by offering higher rates provided they are making a high return on the use of the funds—which certainly was not true of most corporate borrowers in recent years. In any event, the relation between money and interest is far from clearly understood, and the Fed must make its decisions in partial darkness.

Monetarism, needless to say, has a prescription for this predicament also: "We cannot specify very exactly how interest rates are determined?

Very simple—ignore them. What matters is the volume of money, not its price. The Fed can't do that? Its entire philosophy is based on the control of interest rates, not of money? That is just what is wrong with it. The Fed has controlled interest rates, and to do this it has often overexpanded the money supply, or underexpanded it. That has landed us in whatever messes we have been or are in." Such has been the most forceful of the monetarist challenges, and here is where the Fed has made its main concessions to monetarism. Once more it is inflation that has made monetarism plausible—in fact irrefutable.

MISLEADING TARGETS

Inflation has distorted both interest rates and the money supply, but interest rates far worse than money. With inflation, at 5%, nobody can tell what the "real" interest rate is. To be sure, it is easy to figure out what the rate on one year bills was last year. Six percent interest minus 5% leaves 1% real interest to the nontaxable holder. But what is the real rate hereafter on a bond with twenty years to run? This depends on individual expectations of future inflation. There is no simplistic relation between expected inflation and interest rates. That was demonstrated in the fall of 1970 when long rates came down dramatically. It is unlikely that in November 1970 holders suddenly revised their expectations of future inflation.

Thus, it is very difficult for the Fed to know what an interest target of 6% or 8% means. The chances are that in an inflation, the central bank will underestimate the degree of distortion of rates and will set the nominal and therefore also the real rate too low. The economy will tell the central bank of its error, by demanding a rapidly growing volume of money which in turn fuels the inflation. This seems to have been the history of monetary policy in early 1967 and again in late 1968.

After the second of these monetary explosions, the Fed made the momentous shift from an interest-rate to a money-supply target. The matter may not have presented itself to the Federal Open Market Committee in quite those terms. The Fed spoke of giving greater weight to the monetary aggregates relative to money-market conditions. Later it became apparent that the Open Market desk, rejecting monetarist advice to use the monetary base (currency and member-bank reserves) as an intermediate target and aiming instead at the money supply directly, was still doing this via money-market conditions. But the market and the press began to publicize the money growth-rate target and to watch it like hawks.

At this point monetarists could claim victory. But it also was the moment of truth. For a host of questions descended upon the Fed now that monetarism had really been put on trial.

There was the question of the proper definition of the money supply. The Fed could side-step this by referring to monetary aggregates. But when the aggregates diverge as widely as M_1 and M_2 often do the matter ceases to be one of semantics.[1] The exclusion of government deposits from the money supply became troublesome precisely because of the shift to a money-supply target. The theory is that government is not guided in its expenditures by its cash balance, since it can borrow whatever it needs. Therefore government-held money does not count. But this typically Keynesian glorification of government loses its logic under a money-supply target because, although the government can borrow whatever it needs, in doing so it raises interest rates and squeezes out some alternative borrower. The traditional method of adding up the money supply, therefore, is probably wrong.

HOW FAST?

There was the question of the right rate of money growth. Even before the Great Depression, Carl Snyder, a statistician for the Federal Reserve Bank of New York, suggested that the business cycle and the price level could be stabilized by increasing the money supply at a 4% annual rate. But Snyder was nevertheless aware that velocity fluctuated with the cycle— that is, with interest rates. Unless the stable growth rate of money really succeeds in stabilizing the cycle, it will be expansionary in booms and contractionary in recessions.

Velocity had in fact been increasing throughout the postwar period, a phenomenon analyzed very carefully by Milton Friedman and Anna Schwartz in their classic work, *A Monetary History of the United States*. But velocity was not the Fed's main problem with a money-supply target. The real difficulty, which the monetarists ignored, was that inflation chewed up most of the additions to the money supply. The same

phenomenon which bedevils interest rates—the inflation-created gap between the nominal and the real rate—also affects the growth rate of the money supply. The principal difference is that the real rate of growth of the money supply can readily be computed, while the real long-term rate of interest depends on subjective expectations of inflation. Moreover, the consequences of error are less serious on the money-supply side. Fixing too low a nominal rate of interest during inflation would create an explosive situation as the inflation accelerated and the real rate became lower and lower. Fixing too low a rate of growth of the money supply might cause a temporary dip in the economy. The error is not explosive, however, but stabilizing. The worst that could happen to the central bank is that it might find itself stopping the inflation more quickly than intended.

To argue that the central bank should think in terms of the real rate of money growth does not mean, of course, that it should fix a rate equal to the desired real growth rate plus the rate of inflation. That would simply validate the inflation. In fact, since velocity rises with inflation, a rate of money growth equal to real GNP growth plus inflation would probably accelerate inflation. But the central bank should be aware that, when it has a money-supply growth target of zero, as the Fed seems to have had in the second half of 1969, a rate of inflation of 5% makes this a negative money-growth rate of 5%. Probably this was a little tougher than the Fed had intended, since it produced a mild recession. It is all the more impressive that the inflation did not yield to so powerful a dose of restraint. That the succeeding year brought so little expansion may not be unrelated to the fact that the M_1 growth rate of 5.4% which prevailed in 1970 was close to zero in real terms.

BACKING AWAY FROM MONEY

The "bug" in the monetarist prescription, however, that eventually caused the Fed to back away from a money-supply target was the destabilizing impact of this target upon interest rates. This impact had been predicted by various observers. In the spring of 1971 it began to be felt on a large scale. The reasons for the sudden spurt in the demand for money are obscure. Certainly it was not a rapid expansion of business. But this demand might have pushed interest rates through the roof if the Fed had stuck to a money-growth target of 6%–7%. A monthly model of the financial sector used by the Board's staff

---

[1] M_1 is the narrowly defined money supply, consisting of currency and demand deposits. M_2 is M_1 plus time deposits at commercial banks other than those represented by large-denomination certificates of deposit.

suggested that adhering to the money-growth target would produce a bill rate of well over 10%. Whether money-growth rates of 12.5% really were necessary to hold down interest rates I do not know. But once again I find impressive the ability of the Fed to change its mind when common sense suggests it.

Departure from a predetermined money-growth path need not mean abandonment of the money supply as a principal target. It means flexibility in reaching the target. There is too much evidence favoring a money-supply target, particularly in times of inflation, to warrant abandoning money, or the monetary aggregates, for the long term. For the short term, however, interest rates have something to recommend them.

The Fed, like other central banks, probably has often tended to give excessive weight to stability of interest rates. The money and capital markets are not the economy. Unstable rates, and widely fluctuating bond prices, are more easily borne—by the nonbanker part of the population anyway—than fluctuating employment. Nevertheless, financial instability is not without cost, quite aside from sleepless nights spent by portfolio managers. The cost takes the form of a risk premium that the lender adds to the required interest rate after he discovers that he can lose one third or more of his money in sound long-term bonds. There is merit, therefore, in following a short-term interest-rate target provided it is compatible with a long-term money-supply target.

The Fed must face a special case of this choice between a money-supply and an interest-rate target every time the Treasury undertakes a financing. Even-keeling can push the money supply well off its desired path. Once more Professor Friedman has an answer: Give up trying to place issues at a fixed price, and instead auction all government securities like Treasury bills. If it is argued that auctions for long-term bonds pose impossible bidding problems even for very sophisticated investors, there is another answer: Let the Treasury give up its present "discriminatory" auction system, in which everybody pays the price he bids. Use the "competitive" or "Dutch" system instead, in which everybody pays the same price—that is, the lowest price that must be accepted to cover the issue. Opinions naturally differ as to what this method would do to the Treasury's interest costs and to the willingness of dealers to participate in Treasury financings. What becomes clear from the discussion is that even-keeling may be more seriously at odds with monetary policy under a money-supply than under an interest-rate target.

The choices which the Fed has been making as it found itself confronted with the dilemmas or opportunities recounted thus far have been operating decisions. A more subtle choice is that among different philosophies about how monetary policy works. This is the problem of the transmission mechanism. Opting for one hypothesis or another may not call for immediate changes in anything the Fed may find itself doing. But over time, the Fed's view of the monetary process is bound importantly to color policy and execution.

IT WORKS—BUT WHY?

Monetary policy is still an effect in search of a cause. Almost everybody believes it works. But there is no agreement on how the effect is transmitted from the financial sector to the real sector. Some years ago, the dividing lines were drawn rather simply. Keynesians believed that the world and therefore the transmission mechanism was very complex, but that in the end every real problem could be solved very simply by printing a little more money. Monetarists thought the world and the transmission mechanism were simple—more money means more spending—but that the solution of real problems required complex market processes to which monetary or any other government policy could contribute little.

Meanwhile the transmission mechanism has been studied to the point where the division of views into Keynesians and monetarists quite fails to do justice to the subtlety of the analysis. To cite just the most puzzling of recent findings, the architects of the Keynesian-oriented Federal Reserve-MIT model now believe that in large part monetary policy works on consumption and not, as widely assumed, almost entirely upon investment. The channel of transmission, moreover, is not consumer credit, but the stockmarket. A finding of this sort suggests that the Fed cannot just take a pragmatic view of policy and assume that whatever works is true. The Fed must try to arrive at a theoretical understanding as well. Else some day, it may find that instead of controlling the heat it had merely been diddling the thermometer.

MONETARY AGGREGATES AND FEDERAL RESERVE OPEN MARKET OPERATIONS*

Paul Meek and Rudolf Thunberg

In 1970 the Federal Open Market Committee (FOMC) began to establish longer term objectives for the growth of selected monetary and credit aggregates as an integral part of its instructions for the conduct of open market operations in Government securities and other short-term credit instruments. This move was a natural extension of the Committee's greater emphasis on such quantities in recent years, but it did not imply any lack of concern with interest rates and financial flows in the credit markets generally. Indeed, the Committee gave precedence to calming financial markets in May through July, and beginning in August underscored its expansive monetary policy by calling for an easing in credit markets over the months ahead. The FOMC also continued to eschew significant policy changes during large Treasury financings.

The greater emphasis on aggregates involving the banking system did bring about changes in the Committee's formulation and tracking of its policy strategy. It also required some modification in the conduct of open market operations by the Manager of the System Open Market Account and his staff at the Trading Desk of the Federal Reserve Bank of New York. The present paper describes the nature of these changes.

THE CHANGE IN THE FOMC'S INSTRUCTIONS

The focal point of change was the second paragraph of the directive to the Federal Reserve Bank of New York, which is voted at each FOMC meeting.[1] For several years prior to 1970, the Committee's operating instruction usually called for the maintenance of specified money market conditions until the next FOMC meeting, subject to a proviso clause that called for modifying operations if bank credit appeared to be deviating significantly from current projections.[2] This instruction meant that the Manager would begin by seeking to hold mainly the following within ranges designated by the Committee: the Federal funds rate, member bank borrowings from the Reserve Banks, and free or net borrowed reserves (excess reserves less such member bank borrowings). With discount window administration within the framework provided by Regulation A and the discount rate in force, the Committee, in effect, established the terms and conditions on which reserves were to be made available to member banks through open market operations.[3] The Federal Reserve chose the opportunity cost of reserves to commercial banks as its instrumental variable for affecting the monetary and credit aggregates and interest rates in the credit markets.

The proviso clause, which originated in 1966, introduced a conditional element into the instructions to the Manager. It rested on a quantitative staff estimate of the growth in a selected aggregate over the weeks ahead that would result from maintenance of the specified money market conditions. When the FOMC was concerned about overly rapid growth in the aggregate, usually the bank credit proxy,[4] it expected the Manager

* From Federal Reserve Bank of New York *Monthly Review* (April 1971) pp. 80–84 and 87–89 (a section describing the events of 1970 in detail is omitted). Reprinted by permission of the Federal Reserve Bank of New York and the authors. Paul Meek is Assistant Vice President, Open Market Operations and Treasury Issues Function, Federal Reserve Bank of New York. Rudolf Thunberg is Manager, Domestic Research Department, Federal Reserve Bank of New York.

[1] "Monetary Aggregates and Money Market Conditions in Open Market Policy," *Federal Reserve Bulletin* (February 1971), pages 79–104, gives a detailed account of the evolution of the directive and the role of the aggregates in 1970. System policy makers have, of course, used data on the monetary aggregates in their analysis for many years.

[2] The directive issued on December 16, 1969, for example, had the following second paragraph: "To implement this policy, System open market operations until the next meeting of the Committee shall be conducted with a view to maintaining the prevailing firm conditions in the money market; provided, however, that operations shall be modified if bank credit appears to be deviating significantly from current projections or if unusual liquidity pressures should develop."

[3] Paul Meek, *Discount Policy and Open Market Operations (Fundamental Reappraisal of the Discount Mechanism)*, pages 4–8.

[4] Originally, the bank credit proxy was total member bank deposits subject to reserve requirements. As nondeposit liabilities became important sources of funds for money market banks, such liabilities were added to deposits to comprise an adjusted bank credit proxy. They include Euro-dollar borrowings and commercial paper issued by bank holding companies or other affiliates.

to move toward a higher Federal funds rate and higher member bank borrowings at the discount window whenever the aggregate persistently expanded more rapidly than expected. Conversely, if the FOMC were concerned with shortfalls, it would expect the Manager to relax the pressures on bank reserve positions when the aggregate was weak. The Committee's discussion gave the Manager guidance as to what constituted a significant deviation.

The FOMC's new approach to the directive in 1970 is exemplified by the second paragraph of the directive adopted at its March 10 meeting:

To implement this policy, the Committee desires to see moderate growth in money and bank credit over the months ahead. System open market operations until the next meeting of the Committee shall be conducted with a view to maintaining money market conditions consistent with that objective.

The policy record for that meeting indicates that the Committee was setting as its objectives a growth rate of 3 percent for the money supply (currency outside banks and private demand deposits) and 5 percent for the adjusted bank credit proxy over the second quarter. The Manager was told to adjust money market conditions as might be needed to achieve these longer run objectives. The Committee's discussion provided guidance as to the trade-off between the two quantitative objectives should one or both diverge from the growth rate desired.

Beginning in its August meeting, the Committee added "some easing of conditions in credit markets . . . over the months ahead" as an objective of open market operations. The coupling of this objective with the quantitative objectives represented an amplification of the Committee's policy intent, emphasizing its commitment to a moderately expansionary policy. It was recognized that the capital markets, in particular, were subject to supply, demand, and expectational factors as well as to the influence exerted by System open market operations. Within the context of the quantitative objectives, the Manager was expected to foster conditions at the short-term end of the credit markets that would tend to work in time toward an easing of long-term interest rates.

THE APPROACH TO POLICY STRATEGY

The 1970 directives embody a shift of emphasis in policy making, rather than a basic change in Committee members' analytical views of how the economy works. To be sure, the Committee

made the rates of growth to be achieved in the money supply and/or the adjusted bank credit proxy over a longer run period, often a calendar quarter, the focal point of its policy discussion. But the framework thus provided left each participant in the policy process free to assess the relative importance of fiscal policy, interest rates, the total flow of funds, or the monetary and credit aggregates themselves. Since the economic and financial analysis reviewed at each meeting looks four to six quarters into the future, the calendar quarter or somewhat longer provided a useful time horizon for policy implementation.

The directive helped make clearer the distinction between the intermediate financial objectives of policy and the instrumental variables for realizing them. The intermediate objectives are desired rates of growth in the monetary and credit aggregates over a specified time period, supplemented or even supplanted on several occasions in 1970 by special attention to credit market conditions. One would expect the quarterly objectives to change only infrequently, as the Committee changes its evaluation of the economic outlook or its estimate of the relation between the intermediate policy objectives and ultimate economic goals. In 1970, the Committee did, in fact, change its objectives only gradually over the year.

The form of the directive has fostered a willingness on the part of the FOMC to change money market conditions as this seemed necessary to the achievement of its objectives, whether couched in terms of growth rates of aggregates or credit market conditions. The directive itself incorporates a conditional instruction to the Manager to make such changes if necessary. And the FOMC has also changed the settings of the instrumental variables at its regular meetings.

The Committee pursued its quantitative objectives quite flexibly in 1970, fully mindful of its responsibility for fostering a smoothly functioning financial system and for protecting it from unusual strains. As will be discussed more completely below, open market operations continued to strive for reasonably steady money market conditions from day to day in the face of large short-run fluctuations in the factors affecting the demand for, and supply of, bank reserves. Beyond this, the Committee directed that operations moderate, first, the pressures that developed in the bond markets in May and, then, the liquidity pressures that grew out of the insolvency of the Penn Central Transportation Company in June. The addition of easier credit market conditions to its objectives in August added a further dimension to the stimulative thrust of the Committee's policy.

The policy process did not change a great deal under the 1970 directives, but the aggregates did provide a focus for policy discussions.[5] The directive that emerged from the FOMC meeting carried with it the emphases of the meeting itself—for example, the trade-offs between the various aggregates or the degree of concern with financial markets.[6] There was also a specification of both the intermediate objectives and the instrumental money market variables to be pursued in the short run. For each aggregate there was a path of monthly values that the staff projected as consistent with the target for the quarter or other time period. From April on, this was supplemented by a path of weekly values spanning the period until the next Committee meeting. It is perhaps appropriate to call these values tracking paths rather than target paths. The staff was aware that a tracking path could not be derived with great precision, and the Committee was well aware that the Manager could not hit these values. But it did expect him to respond to significant deviations of the aggregates from the path unless the validity of the path appeared dubious because of unforeseen Treasury operations or other developments.

THE STRATEGY OF OPEN MARKET OPERATIONS

In implementing the Committee's decisions, the Manager of the System Open Market Account pursues an operational strategy whose targets depend upon the length of the time period involved.[7] For each statement week, money market conditions provide a target that the Manager can usually approximate, although large errors in trying to predict the factors affecting nonborrowed reserves sometimes make it difficult to achieve the desired conditions. For each quarter, the aggregates provide a target to be approached through successive changes in money market conditions. This strategy thus aims at control of quantities over a longer time period—a procedure which many students of monetary policy have concluded is desirable. But it does so without trying to iron out week-to-week fluctuations in the aggregates. Indeed, no evidence has been presented that these short-run changes in money and credit interfere with, rather than facilitate, economic stability.

During the first statement week after the FOMC meeting, the Manager seeks to maintain money market conditions within the ranges specified by the Committee. Essentially, this strategy involves using open market operations to accommodate week-to-week changes in required reserves by varying nonborrowed reserves so that member bank borrowings at the discount window and/or the Federal funds rate remain within the desired range. A key part of the Manager's operational problem is the practical difficulty of forecasting the behavior of the market factors affecting the nonborrowed reserves of member banks.[8] Given the variability from year to year of patterns in the behavior of Federal Reserve float, currency in circulation, the Treasury's balances at the Reserve Banks, and other factors affecting reserves, the confidence limits that surround the statistician's best estimates are wide. The daily average deviation of the actual reserve effect of the market factors each week from the projections made by the New York Bank staff at the beginning of the statement week was about $250 million during 1970. (See Chart I for an illustration for the fourth quarter.) The choice of an accommodative weekly strategy rests to a considerable degree on the fact that this margin of uncertainty is large relative to the increments to the reserve base called for by a policy of achieving specified growth rates for the aggregates. (The average weekly addition to total member bank reserves in 1970 was less than $25 million.)

In this environment the Manager finds the Federal funds market an invaluable source of information concerning the current impact of market factors on non-borrowed reserves. The Manager begins each statement week with full knowledge of the required reserves of member banks since these depend upon deposits in a prior

[5] For a detailed description of the procedures at FOMC meetings, see "Monetary Aggregates and Money Market Conditions in Open Market Policy," *op. cit.*

[6] See Alan R. Holmes, "A Day at the Trading Desk" Federal Reserve Bank of New York *Monthly Review* (October 1970), pages 234–38.

[7] Jack M. Guttentag argued persuasively in "The Strategy of Open Market Operations," *The Quarterly Journal of Economics* (February 1966), pages 20–26, that a complete strategy should involve different targets for control periods of different lengths.

[8] The term, market factors, is used to designate sources and uses of nonborrowed reserves other than System open market operations. By definition, week-to-week changes in nonborrowed reserves are the sum of changes in market factors and the System's portfolio.

CHART I CHANGES IN UNCONTROLLED FACTORS AFFECTING NONBORROWED RESERVES PROJECTED AND ACTUAL (calculated from weekly averages of daily figures, not seasonally adjusted)

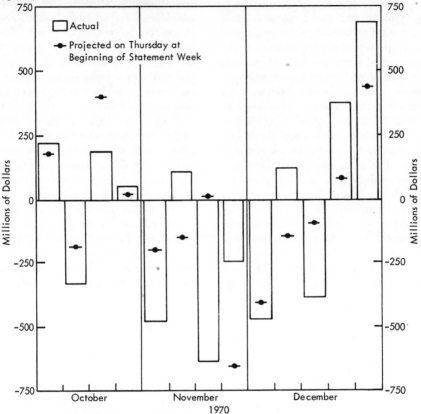

Note: Uncontrolled factors include Federal Reserve float, currency in circulation, Treasury currency outstanding, Treasury cash holdings, Treasury deposits at Federal Reserve Banks, foreign and other nonmember bank deposits at the Federal Reserve Banks, other Federal Reserve assets and liabilities, and cash held in the vaults of member banks two weeks earlier, but exclude Federal Reserve holdings of securities.

Source: Board of Governors of the Federal Reserve System and Federal Reserve Bank of New York.

period. Given some idea of the frictional volume of excess reserves likely to be needed in the banking system, the Manager knows approximately what total member bank reserve needs for the week will be. Accordingly, a burgeoning demand for Federal funds in relation to supply strongly suggests a shortfall in nonborrowed reserves below the level needed to keep member bank borrowings at the discount window in the FOMC's range. Failure to supply nonborrowed reserves through open market operations in this instance will tend to result in a rise in the Federal funds rate and in member bank borrowings at the Federal Reserve Banks, since excess reserves are already near a frictional minimum. Conversely, an abundance of reserves in the Federal funds market suggests that market factors are supplying a greater volume of nonborrowed re-

serves than is needed to stabilize the Federal funds rate or to maintain borrowing at the discount window within a given range. Failure to absorb nonborrowed reserves will lead to a decline in the Federal funds rate and in borrowing at the discount window unless, it is already at a frictional minimum. If borrowing is at such a minimum, a rise in excess reserves is bound to result.

The System's weekly strategy insulates the banking system reasonably well from swings in nonborrowed reserves due to market factors, but it accommodates week-to-week changes in required reserves at the same time. This approach enables the banking system to respond very flexibly to the volatile short-run demands of its customers for money and credit, since the System supplies and absorbs reserves on demand in an effort to keep the Federal funds rate within its prescribed range.[9] Under this accommodative posture, the week-to-week changes in the money supply clearly stem from shifts in demand rather than from reserve injection. These shifts do, in fact, produce large variations in the money supply. The absolute change in the narrowly defined money supply, before seasonal adjustment, averaged $2 billion from week to week in 1970. This compares with long-term growth that averaged about $200 million per week for the year as a whole.

Keeping a close tab on the aggregates provides a procedure for trying to assure that an open market strategy designed to accommodate short-run shifts in demand does not lead to a significant departure of the aggregates from their desired growth rate over the span of several months. Operationally, one is left with the problem of deciding whether the aggregates are departing significantly from their desired path. Then, there is the question of how much money market conditions are to be changed in an effort to nudge the aggregates back in the desired direction. As both 1969 and 1970 demonstrated, one must also be alert to the possibility that changes in banking practices lead to distortions of the underlying data.

Taking the money supply as an example, the basic point of departure is the weekly tracking path, covering the period between FOMC meetings. This path is presented by the Board staff as likely to be consistent with attaining the level desired by the Committee for the terminal month of its time horizon, often the calendar quarter. It is essentially a judgmental path, subject to a wide margin of error, which combines the desired growth and the staff's best estimate of the likely impact on the money supply of such factors as Treasury cash receipts, expenditures, and financings as projected at the time of the meeting. The weekly values may jump around considerably, and the possibility of poor specification exists.

Each Friday morning the Manager of the Account receives new data on the past behavior of the money supply and new projections of its future behavior. The Board staff reports preliminary daily average data for the statement week ended on the latest Wednesday and also revised data for the previous statement week. In addition, both the Board staff and the New

York Bank staff prepare revised projections of the behavior that they expect over the weeks through the next FOMC meeting on the assumption of no change in the money market conditions recently prevailing. Similarly, they give their projections of how the aggregates will behave for each month of the calendar quarter, assuming the continuation of those conditions.

These projections are subject to large revisions from week to week, as new data become available and as past data are revised. In addition, sometimes wide differences open up between the projections of the two staffs. Given the considerable uncertainty over the accuracy of the projections and the validity of the tracking path, the Manager does not change money market objectives between Committee meetings unless a pattern of deviations seems to be emerging. In practice, such changes typically involve shifting the target for the Federal funds rate range by ¼ to ½ percentage point. A further shift in the same direction would depend on the extent to which the deviation that prompted the shift persisted or grew.

. . . . .

SOME LESSONS OF THE 1970 EXPERIENCE

With a full year's operations as a background, it is possible to make a few observations on the actual workings of open market operations under the directives adopted by the FOMC in 1970. The quantitative approach facilitated the development of a policy strategy directed at a longer time horizon than the period between meetings. The experience of the past year lends some encouragement to the view, moreover, that targets of quarterly growth rates of the aggregates can be pursued by means of a money market conditions strategy of open market operations that is accommodative in the very short run. The narrowly defined money supply, for example, expanded at rates of 5.9 percent, 5.8 percent, and 6.1 percent in the first three quarters of the year, before registering 3.4 percent in the final quarter.[10]

[9] See Paul Meek and Jack W. Cox, "The Banking System—Its Behavior in the Short-Run," Federal Reserve Bank of New York *Monthly Review* (April 1966), pages 84–91.

[10] These represent the growth rates after the annual revision announced on November 27 (which was also intended to eliminate an understatement of the money supply stemming from the effects of certain international transfers on cash items in the process of collection). See "Revision of the Money Stock," *Federal Reserve Bulletin* (December 1970), pages 887–909. Before this revision the narrowly defined money supply was reported to have grown at annual rates of 3.8 percent, 4.2 percent, and 5.1 percent in the first three quarters of the year.

The 1970 experience also made clear a number of problems. There was the problem of measurement that led to the upward revision of money supply growth from 3.8 percent to 5.5 percent for the first ten months of the year. Whereas the money supply moved roughly in line with the Committee's desires in terms of the data available at the time, the *ex post* growth rate of the money supply (as revised) exceeded during the first three quarters the Committee's intentions at the time. And in the final quarter the growth rate fell short of the Committee's target of a 5 percent annual rate despite a progressive relaxation of money market conditions over the quarter. One should not claim too much precision—even

over a period of several months—for the influence exerted by the central bank over the narrowly defined money supply.

Somewhat greater emphasis on the aggregates did not involve attempts to stabilize the growth rate of the money supply or bank credit aggregates on a weekly or even a monthly basis. Indeed, the weekly and monthly variability of the aggregates continued to be quite wide in 1970 (see Chart II). The experience of 1970 suggests strongly that tight short-run control over the aggregates—even if it were possible—is not necessary to achieve a reasonable degree of control over periods of a quarter or longer.

Attempts at tighter short-run control over the

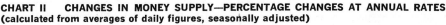

CHART II   CHANGES IN MONEY SUPPLY—PERCENTAGE CHANGES AT ANNUAL RATES
(calculated from averages of daily figures, seasonally adjusted)

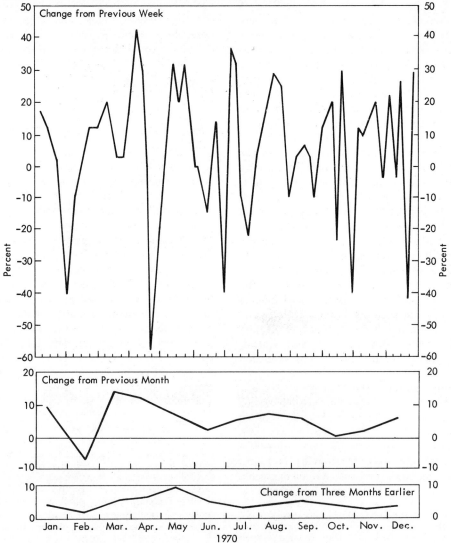

Source: Board of Governors of the Federal Reserve System.

aggregates would probably entail unacceptable side effects and would almost certainly be doomed to failure. Even if one assumed away the major operational problem of coping with the variability of float and other market factors, a strategy of weekly control would require that information on the targeted aggregates were up to date and accurate, that weekly noise could be screened out effectively in judging the significance of deviations from targeted paths, and that there were a highly predictable and extremely rapid linkage between System action and the particular quantity targeted. None of these conditions seem likely to be fulfilled unless the time period for control of the aggregates is extended to several months.

The first problem encountered in seeking to control the narrowly defined money supply or bank credit in the short run is that the current levels of these aggregates are unknown. Quite apart from the major revision in the money supply series mentioned above, there are often large differences between projections of the aggregates made at the beginning of a statement week, the preliminary estimates of the actual figures available at the end of the statement week, and the revised figures available several weeks thereafter. The difference between the projected and estimated, or between the estimated and final, levels frequently far exceeds the incremental amount by which the money supply or bank credit proxy would have to be increased weekly to keep it on a path of constant week-to-week growth.[11]

Aside from the confidence limits attached to weekly preliminary data, week-to-week shifts in the demand for money generate considerable statistical noise that renders it difficult to make a sensible judgment of the trend on the basis of a single week's preliminary data. To respond to each week's numbers would only foster sharp short-run variation in the Federal funds rate and increase the uncertainties within which commercial banks have to manage their individual reserve positions. It is difficult to see what gain would accrue from such a *modus operandi*, which would force the banking system to accumulate a larger buffer of excess reserves as insulation from the variability of central bank action.

Even if control of the aggregates in the short run were attempted, the present state of the art does not provide any means of hitting short-run targets. Stated differently, at present the precise

linkage between day-to-day open market operations and short-run changes in the money supply is not known. Research conducted at this Bank has indicated that weekly movements in private demand deposits (the principal component of the money supply) are strongly influenced by variables relating to Treasury receipts and disbursements and seasonal factors. Changes in nonborrowed reserves—the variable most immediately affected by open market operations—have little direct measurable effect on weekly changes in demand deposits, although they assume greater significance over monthly or quarterly periods.

The attention paid to the aggregates has underscored strongly the System's need to find operational answers in quantitative terms to some of the most basic questions of monetary policy. For example, what rates of growth in which of the monetary and credit aggregates seem most likely to help achieve the desired performance in the real economy, and what lags are involved? How much should the behavior of the credit markets and long-term interest rates condition the specification of the target growth rates of the aggregates? How does one translate quarterly target rates into monthly and weekly tracking paths to be used to help determine the significance of weekly developments? What rules of response should the Manager of the Open Market Account follow to avoid either under- or over-reacting to weekly deviations in the aggregates? A great deal of further research and further practical experience is needed to find satisfactory answers to fundamental questions such as these.

Despite greater emphasis on the aggregates, the FOMC continues to be concerned with money market conditions. The Committee has been somewhat more willing to allow changes in such conditions than before, and it has fostered changes in a sustained and purposeful manner that reinforced its basic policy thrust. The Committee has eschewed sharp changes in money market conditions late in a quarter, even when the quarter's goal for the aggregates seemed unlikely to be achieved. Instead, it has tended to fold this information into the formulation of its targets for the subsequent quarter. On the whole, this approach has made for continuity in money market conditions and has helped avoid fluctuations that might well have whipsawed market expectations and added to the problem of achieving target rates of change in the aggregates.

The greater steadiness in the growth of the narrowly defined money supply in 1970 does not seem to have been at the cost of larger week-to-week movements in interest rates than in the

---

[11] Subsequent revisions of seasonals, of course, change weekly data still further from that known to the FOMC and its staff at the time.

past. To be sure, interest rates—especially short-term rates—moved down significantly during the past year, but this reflected the shift to an expansionary monetary policy gradually interacting with the lessening of demand pressures on the credit markets. The accommodative strategy of open market operations in the short run—even while aiming at targeted growth rates of aggregates over longer periods—meant that operations were not a source of week-to-week variability in interest rates.

There were occasions, to be sure, when shifts in the thrust of open market operations were reflected in sharp movements in interest rates. The most notable example occurred in April, when open market operations shifted toward greater restraint as it appeared that the aggregates were growing significantly faster than desired by the Committee. The sharp reaction in market rates was, of course, only partly the result of the System's shift in emphasis. Market participants were just beginning to become aware of the System's greater concern with the aggregates, and some feared that the new emphasis in open market operations might foreshadow a wrenching of short-term rates back and forth in an effort to keep the aggregates on a straight and narrow path. Thus, the problems of April were partly transitional in nature. With greater market awareness and understanding of the new approach to open market operations, market reactions to the shading of money market conditions might reasonably be expected to be less exaggerated in the future.

There were times when market participants interpreted the data as suggesting a possible future need for System action. For example, the sluggishness of the money supply in October and November tended to confirm expectations that monetary policy would remain stimulative, leading to portfolio accumulation by banks and others. At other times, concern over the rapid growth of the money supply in late August-early September may well have resulted in some liquidation of short-term holdings. In any case, market participants seem to have become less sensitive to moderate changes in money market conditions, considering them as only one component of the broader analysis needed of the economic determinants of policy objectives.

The experience of April through June suggests that one must always bear in mind the shifts in demand for reserves that can occur within a period of a few months. At the time, the Desk was providing reserves much more aggressively than it would have had it been guided solely by an aggregates target. In retrospect, it appears that (abstracting from the subsequent revision in the figures) the System's action was necessary to maintain the desired growth in the face of a significant increase in liquidity demand arising out of the Cambodian and Penn Central crises. One should not exaggerate the ability of the Account Manager and the staff to discern the underlying thrust of these forces on a week-to-week basis.

CONCLUDING COMMENT

In summation, the Committee's increased attention to the monetary aggregates in 1970 should be viewed more as part of a continuing effort to improve policy making and its implementation than as the end product of that effort. The year's experience offered hope that judicious use of the aggregates might improve policy response to changing circumstances, although financial markets must remain an important concern. There remained a number of problems involved in defining and measuring different variants of the money supply and bank credit. The short-run volatility of the aggregates often made for considerable operational uncertainty in open market operations. Important analytical problems continued in assessing the behavior of the aggregates in relation to the FOMC's long-range economic objectives. The Committee used the monetary aggregates flexibly, not rigidly, in pursuit of its policy aims in 1970. A flexible approach may well lead to further shifts in operational emphasis from time to time, as perceptions of economic relationships and conditions change.

FEDERAL RESERVE ORGANIZATION AND POLICYMAKING*

George L. Bach

The Commission on Money and Credit, in a temperate analysis of governmental operations and Federal Reserve responsibilities, drew these conclusions concerning Federal Reserve independence:

1. The President must bear the central responsibility for governmental economic policy recommendations and execution.
2. Federal Reserve responsibilities for national economic policy are closely intertwined with those of other Government agencies, especially the Executive Office of the President and the Treasury.
3. Federal Reserve independence is now adequately protected, and Federal Reserve influence could be increased by closer participation in governmental policy determination.
4. To the end of closer and more informal working relationships between the Federal Reserve and the White House, the Federal Reserve Board Chairman and Vice Chairman should be designated by the President from among the Board's membership, with 4-year terms coterminous with the President's.
5. To improve efficiency and attract more able members, the Federal Reserve Board should be reduced from seven to five members, and all major Federal Reserve monetary powers should be centered in the Board.
6. To improve national economic policy formulation and coordination, the President should establish a cabinet-level "Advisory Board on Economic Growth and Stability," including the Chairman of the Federal Reserve Board.

These proposals have been widely criticized by conservatives on the ground that they would undermine the independence of the Federal Reserve. The critics suggest that the "liberals" on the Commission somehow outflanked the "conservatives" in bringing about this stab in the back for financial soundness (a neat trick if indeed it occurred, since two-thirds of the 20 Commission members were highly successful businessmen

and bankers, only 2 were labor leaders, and the other 5 were independent professional men). On such a vital issue of monetary arrangements as this, it is well to take a closer look.

CASE FOR INDEPENDENCE

Stated bluntly, the traditional argument for Federal Reserve independence is that, if independent, the Fed will stand against inflation and financial irresponsibility in the Government. History tells of many treasuries which have turned to money issue to pay their bills when taxes were inadequate. The modern world's major inflations have all come with large governmental deficits, covered by the issue of new money (currency or bank deposits). While legislatures vote the expenditures, treasuries must pay the bills. Thus, it is argued that treasuries have a predictable inflationary bias, however well intentioned their secretaries may be. Against this bias, central bankers are alleged to be basically conservative; they can be counted on to look out for the stability of the monetary unit.

Another variant is based on the presumption that the entire political process is inherently inflationary. It is always easier for Congress to spend money than to raise taxes; "politicians" are inherently financially irresponsible. Thus, an independent Federal Reserve is needed to call a halt to the over-spending tendencies of the politicians, and to the tendency of the politicians to plump too readily for good times for the economy as a whole, even though these good times may generate some inflation.

Lastly, there is an argument that the President, the politician par excellence, is not to be trusted on financial matters, and that an independent Federal Reserve is needed to see that he does not go too far with expansionary, inflationary economic policies.

MEANING OF INDEPENDENCE

These arguments suggest that we need to examine the meaning of the term "independence." Independence from whom? A Federal Reserve independent of the U.S. Treasury rests squarely on the realistic assessment of history. Treasuries have been inflationary in their biases, and we

* From "Economics, Politics, and the Fed," *Harvard Business Review,* January-February 1962, as reprinted (with minor changes) in *The Federal Reserve System after Fifty Years* (Hearings before the Subcommittee on Domestic Finance, Committee on Banking and Currency, House of Representatives, 88th Cong., 2d sess.) (Washington, D.C.; U.S. Government Printing Office, 1964), pp. 1393–98. George Leland Bach is Frank E. Buck Professor of Economics and Public Policy, Graduate School of Business, Stanford University.

therefore need a powerful agency in governmental economic circles to stand against these inflationary biases when they threaten the soundness of our economic structure.

But Federal Reserve independence from the Congress is hardly meaningful in our governmental system. Congress established the Federal Reserve. It can change it any time it wishes, or call it to account for any of its actions. Federal Reserve officials readily acknowledge their responsibility to Congress—though the Fed need not go to Congress for appropriations to conduct its affairs and though, in practice, Congress, happily, is reluctant to intervene directly in Federal Reserve policymaking.

The really difficult question is this: Should, or can, the Federal Reserve be independent from the President? The Constitution clearly allots to the Federal Government the power to create money and regulate the value thereof. In our society, where bank deposits comprise some 80 percent of our total money supply and currency only 20 percent, control over the supply of bank deposits is control over the volume of money. Federal Reserve officials have consistently recognized the basically governmental nature of their function, though they value the close relationships they have with private bankers.

Furthermore, control over the money supply of the Nation is a vital operating responsibility. Monetary policy is inextricably intermingled with fiscal policy and debt management policy, if the Nation's economic goals are to be achieved effectively. The President must ultimately be responsible for recommendation and execution of the Nation's basic economic policy. This logic leads clearly to the conclusion that the Federal Reserve must work closely with other agencies under the general responsibility of the President for executing national economic policy.

To give an independent Federal Reserve the power to negate the basic policies arrived at by the executive and legislative branches of the Federal Government would be intolerable for any administration, Republican or Democratic. But independence, looked at practically, is a matter of degree, not of black and white. The real question, thus, is the terms on which the Federal Reserve participates in governmental policymaking and execution.

NEED FOR COOPERATION

To be most effective, the Federal Reserve needs to be in a position to work closely with the other major Government agencies responsible for national economic policy—especially the Treasury, the Budget Bureau, and the Council of Economic Advisers. No Federal Reserve Chairman has ever claimed that the Board should disregard the debt management problems of the Treasury, or that the Government's financial needs should be given no weight.

On the contrary, all major Federal Reserve officials have agreed on the need for close working relationships with the Treasury on monetary, fiscal and debt policy. The times when the Federal Reserve has been least effective have been the times when it has been most isolated from the President and from effective, coequal working relationships from the Secretary of the Treasury and other high-level Government officials. This was substantially the case throughout the much-discussed decade of the 1940s when the Federal Reserve was most subservient to the Treasury debt-management needs. Secretaries Morgenthau and Snyder were close personal confidants of Presidents Roosevelt and Truman; but Federal Reserve officials seldom saw either President.

An effective Federal Reserve voice for the stable-money point of view can best be assured if the Fed is an active, continuous participant in the day-to-day process of governmental economic policy formation. Seldom indeed does a central bank undertake a major war with the Congress and the administration in a showdown on economic policy. Federal Reserve participation in policymaking will generally be a more effective device for presenting the sound-money point of view than will spectacular defiance of the Government's policies. Extreme independence is, unfortunately, likely to mean splendid isolation from the decisions that matter.

ON BALANCE

The need is for recognized Federal Reserve independence from the Treasury and for coequal voice with other major agencies in the economic policy councils of the Government. In other words, the need is to maintain a strong and substantially independent voice for a stable-money point of view without placing Federal Reserve officials in an untenably isolated position, where to use their independence involves major intragovernmental conflict and divided national economic policy. Budgetary and monetary matters call for the best efforts of wise men. But we must not fall into the trap of supposing that all wisdom will reside in appointed Federal Reserve officials, rather than in other Government officials appointed by the same President and approved by the same Senate. The President, the Secretary of the Treasury, and other high governmental officials also seek to advance the national welfare, as they see it. How best to mesh the judgments and responsibilities of these various public officials is the problem, not simply to set up an independent non-governmental board with a legal (but seldom practical) power to say no to the U.S. Government.

RECOMMENDED CHANGES

To improve the coordination of overall economic policy and to increase the influence of the Federal Reserve while maintaining its special quasi-independent status, the Commission recommended, primarily two modest changes:

1. The President should establish a Cabinet-level Advisory Board on Economic Growth and Stability which would include the Chairman of the Federal Reserve Board.
2. The term of office of the Chairman (and Vice Chairman) of the Federal Reserve Board should be made coterminous with that of the President, to eliminate the possibility that a Federal Reserve Chairman would be personally unacceptable to a President.

A new President could (as now) immediately appoint one new Board member, and could name him Chairman; or he could name a new Chairman from among existing Board members. The staggered-term membership of the Board would remain unchanged, except that it would be reduced from seven to five members. While further centralization of System authority in the Board would increase somewhat the President's power over the Fed, overlapping 10-year terms would go far to protect the stability and independence of the Board members from short-run political pressures.

These two recommendations might help substantially to assure effective working relationships between the Fed, the Presidency, and the rest of the administrative branch of the Government. To insist that a new President accept a Federal Reserve Chairman to whom he objected strongly would probably serve little purpose, and would be more likely to decrease the effectiveness of the Fed than to increase it. As a practical matter, the Chairman must represent the System in its most important contacts with the President, as well as with the Treasury and in most cases with Congress. Making the chairmanship coterminous with the President's term, though it might have little importance in most instances, makes practical administrative sense. It is significant that both

William M. Martin, the present Chairman of the Fed, and Marriner S. Eccles, Chairman for longer than any other man and the individual who was most responsible for the restored independence of the Fed in 1951, concur in the recommendation to make the chairmanship coterminous with the President's term.

Appointment by the President of an Advisory Board on Economic Growth and Stability would be one device for assuring closer coordination among the governmental agencies (including the Fed) responsibile for national economic policy. Whether such a special advisory board would be effective would depend heavily on whether the President wanted to use it. Some such device is obviously necessary. The Commission wisely avoided a recommendation to make such an advisory board mandatory by legislation, while stressing the importance of coordinated national policy formation in which the Federal Reserve has a strong voice.

Critics have labeled these recommendations a stab in the back for Federal Reserve independence. This appears to be a serious exaggeration. They reflect operating realities, and are modest proposals indeed when viewed in the light of the experience of most other nations, where central banks have been completely subordinated to treasuries or to governments.

ORGANIZATION AND OPERATIONS

Since the Commission apparently felt that the Federal Reserve has done a good job on monetary policy, we might expect few recommendations for change in Federal Reserve organization and operation. The Commission believed, however, that the Federal Reserve could do its job more effectively if its organization were modernized and if its controls were extended to all insured banks. It did not suggest that structural changes are of overriding importance, but that they would be useful and in keeping with modern needs and mores.

In essence, beyond the recommendations concerning the chairmanship of the Board, the Commission recommended that:

1. The Federal Reserve Board should, as noted, be reduced in size from seven to five members, with staggered 10-year terms.
2. Special occupational and geographical qualifications for Board members should be eliminated, and replaced by statutory stipulation that members be positively qualified by experience or education, competence, independence, and objectivity.

3. All major policy powers (over open market operations, Reserve requirements, and discount rates) should be vested in the Federal Reserve Board. The separate Federal Open Market Committee would be abolished, but the Board would be required to consult regularly with the 12 Reserve bank Presidents in determining its policies. Discount rate changes would no longer be inaugurated separately at the 12 regional Reserve banks.

4. Technical ownership of the Federal Reserve banks by member banks should be eliminated through retirement of the present capital stock; instead, membership should be evidenced by a special nonearning certificate for each member.

5. All insured banks should be required to become members of the Federal Reserve System, or at least be made subject to Federal Reserve established reserve requirements.

The basic purpose of these recommendations is to centralize the policymaking functions of the Federal Reserve System in one governmental body (the Federal Reserve Board), unmistakably responsible to the public rather than to the commercial banks; to increase the efficiency of Federal Reserve operations by streamlining the present complex organizational structure; and to extend the direct impact of monetary controls to substantially all commercial banks in the country.

The present complex Federal Reserve organization reflects the regional needs of a half century ago, modified here and expanded there as the focus shifted to national monetary policy and as new instruments developed. It looks terrible on paper. But, most observers agree, it works well on the whole. Given these facts, was the Commission right that some changes ought to be made? To answer this question thoroughly would take a small book. Only a few major issues can be noted here.

FOCUS OF RESPONSIBILITY

Few businessmen would tolerate in their own firms the complex organization and overlapping responsibilities for major policy that exist in the Fed. Open market operations, reserve requirements, and discount rates—all have identical general policy goals and need to be completely coordinated. To have a different group responsible for each invites delay and confusion. The day when discount rates needed to be set separately to meet differing regional needs is long past. Monetary policy is national policy, and is recognized as such by all concerned. Information on regional developments is indeed valuable in forming monetary policy, but this could be arranged readily without diluting and diffusing responsibility for monetary policy. So runs the argument for modernization.

But there are counterarguments. The main one is that, while this may well be true in principle, the present arrangement works well. Why change it? In fact, all 19 major Federal Reserve officials (7 Board members plus the 12 Reserve bank Presidents) consult together on all major policy issues, and, in effect, make policy together. Policy responsibility is thus not scattered. Instead, Federal Reserve policy is made in the best tradition of wide representation and careful consideration by a large group of responsible men. While monetary policy should not, of course, be regional in nature, the present system of regional banks draws presidents and board members of high ability into the System, where they could not be pulled without the attraction of policy responsibility. In policy deliberations, it is thus argued, Reserve bank Presidents both reflect regional interests and bring monetary judgments and insights which add significantly to those found in the Washington Board.

Conclusions? Much depends on this last argument. Over much of Reserve bank history, there is little evidence that Reserve bank Presidents (with the exception of the New York President) have added much to policymaking. The last decade has seen the appointment of a number of Reserve bank Presidents of especially high ability, men whose competence in monetary economics and in practical banking compares favorable with the best of the Washington Board. It is argued that such men could not be drawn to membership on the Washington Board, with the lower salaries there. The facts are not clear, either on this or on the contribution now made by the Reserve bank Presidents to policy formation. A priori, the case for a simpler organization is strong. And most argue that the national Board is more attractive to top-quality men. The Commission has a strong point, but not all the evidence is in to permit an unequivocal conclusion.

A SMALLER BOARD

Suppose we agree that policymaking responsibility should be centered in one group, be it the Federal Reserve Board or the Federal Open Market Committee. How big should this group be? The Commission believes that it should be smaller than the present 12-man Open Market Committee, and much smaller than the de facto

19-man group which now makes Federal Reserve policy. The Commission plumps for a five-man board because it feels this would be more efficient, less cumbersome, and less given to delay and indecision.

Few businessmen or students of organization believe that a 19-man, or even a 12-man, committee is small enough to do an effective job of running an organization and making day-to-day decisions on intricate major policy issues. A large decision-making group is needed when many separate interests must be represented. But sound monetary policy formation does not rest on a compromise of conflicting regional or occupational group interests represented on the Board. Excellent regional information is needed, but the information providers do not have to be policymakers. Except for regional differences, it is not clear that the 12 Reserve bank Presidents represent very different interests.

Or a large group is justified if additional members add significantly to the decision process. Both widespread experience and a priori reasoning cast doubt on the marginal gain from additional members after a committee totals a half dozen or so, unless the additional man is of especially high ability or holds quite different views from the others. In the Federal Reserve case, there seems little reason to suppose that going beyond the half dozen or so ablest men in the System is justified on either count.

We Americans traditionally distrust concentration of power in government; we value the combined judgement of a number of men. But the case for 19 decision-makers is hard to defend. The Commission's figure of five appears reasonable, and the smaller the group the better will be the chance of getting first-class men to serve on it. If a mixture of Reserve bank Presidents and Washington officials is desired, a small decision-making group could still be obtained by combining, say, three Board members with two Reserve bank Presidents on a rotating basis.

History suggests that, as a practical matter, System leadership has usually been highly concentrated in a few hands, notably Marriner S. Eccles' for many years and before that in those of Benjamin Strong (longtime President of the New York Fed). Realistically, the Chairman must represent the System in its most important contacts with the President, the Treasury, and Congress. The Federal Reserve is, in fact, a policymaking and operating agency, and it inescapably will have one or a very few men who carry most of the burden. The old judicial parallel, with the Reserve Board termed the "supreme court of finance," is not a realistic analogy. Courts apply common and statute law under an elaborate set of judicial precedents and safeguards.

As was noted above, the Fed sails on seas virtually uncharted by Congress and with heavy day-to-day operating responsibilities for our monetary mechanism. Hence, the Board is more like the Secretary of the Treasury than like the Supreme Court in its basic role (though it does have some commission-type regulatory duties). This fact further weakens the case for a large policymaking board. Chairman Martin plays the role of cooperative leader superbly, but even today there is some question whether System policy would be much different if he were a single governor, or if policymaking power were centered in a small board as the Commission recommends.

RESERVE BANK OWNERSHIP

Technical ownership of the Federal Reserve banks by the commercial banks flies in the face of the basic constitutional provision that the Federal Government shall "coin money [and] regulate the value thereof." Surely the Federal Reserve authorities in regulating our money must be responsible, not to the bankers, but to the people of the United States, just as are the Secretary of the Treasury and other governmental officials. Perceptive bankers are the first to agree.

It is clear that both Board members in Washington and the Presidents of the Reserve banks, in fact, view themselves as public officials, sworn to advance the welfare of the people, rather than as representatives of the bankers. Why, then, bother to change the situation, even though the present arrangement is admittedly a vestige of the thinking of a half century ago? The main answer is that our national monetary authorities must, like Caesar's wife, be above suspicion and reproach. Even though commercial bank ownership of Reserve bank stock clearly does not now mean control by the banks over national monetary policy, it opens a suspicion that such improper influence might be exerted.

BALANCING THE ARGUMENTS

The logical case for the Commission's recommendations of Federal Reserve Structure is a good one. But as a practical matter, history throws doubt on their importance. Moreover, the cost of these changes would be great—in bitter argument and in deep wounds within the System. It seems unlikely today that the gains would be worth the price. My guess is that before another decade goes by, Congress will want to take a hard look at Federal Reserve organization, possibly under the pressure of new financial needs generated by changing international or national conditions. If so, the Commission's recommendations will deserve a careful look, as part of a more thorough study of both alternative organizational arrangements and the lessons of monetary history.

SHOULD THERE BE AN INDEPENDENT MONETARY AUTHORITY?*

Harry G. Johnson

The argument for an independent monetary authority has two facets to it. One is the political argument that an independent monetary authority is desirable to prevent Government from being able to indulge in its natural propensity to resort to inflation. The other, which is less explicitly political, is that a stable monetary environment is essential to the proper functioning of a predominantly free enterprise society, and that an independent monetary authority is essential to maintain such a monetary environment.

The first argument seems to me utterly unacceptable in a democratic country. Indirectly, it is an argument for establishing the monetary authority as a fourth branch of the Constitution, charged with the function of forcing the Legislature and the Executive to follow conservative economic policies involving the balancing of the budget and restraint on Government expenditures. In other words, it involves the establishment of a special position in Government for the owners of one form of property—owners of money and of assets fixed in terms of money—a position which is inconsistent with the principles of democratic equality and the presumption of democracy that the purpose of government is to serve the social good.

Turning to the second argument, granted that a stable monetary environment is desirable, the question arises whether an independent monetary authority as presently understood is sufficient to provide such stability. The argument that it is assumes that, if free of control by the Executive and Legislature, the monetary authority will govern monetary policy in the light of the long-run best interests of the economy, and will conduct its policy flexibly and efficiently in the short run. This assumption is not consistent with the historical evidence of the behavior of monetary authorities; the evidence is rather that central banks have done little if anything to restrain inflationary policies in wartime—and war and its aftermath have been the almost exclusive source of serious inflation in the major countries in the 20th century—while in peacetime they have displayed a pronounced tendency to allow deflationary policies on the average. Moreover—I refer here particularly to the behavior of the United States and Canadian central banks in the past decade—in the short-run conduct of policy they have tended to overreact to changes in the economy and to reverse their policy with a substantial delay, thereby contributing to the economic instability that their policies are intended to combat.

These defects are in my judgment inherent in the conception, constitution, and operating responsibilities and methods of an independent monetary authority, and are unlikely to be modified greatly by gradual improvement of the techniques of central banking on the basis of accumulated experience and research. For one thing, freedom of a central bank from direct political control does not suffice to render it insensitive to contemporary political opinion. On the contrary, its position as the one agency of economic policy formation outside the normal political structure both exposes it to subtle and sustained political pressures and forces it to become a political animal on its own behalf, devoting considerable effort either to justifying its policies by reference to popularly-esteemed objectives or to denying responsibility for economic conditions and passing the buck on to the Executive or the Legislature, the result being to obfuscate the policy choices that have to be made. Secondly, the posi-

* From *The Federal Reserve System After Fifty Years* (Hearings before the Subcommittees on Domestic Finance, Committee on Banking and Currency, House of Representatives, 88th Cong., 2d sess.) (Washington, D.C.: U.S. Government Printing Office, 1964), pp. 970–73. Reprinted by permission of the author. Harry G. Johnson is Professor of Economics, University of Chicago, and Professor of Economics, London School of Economics and Political Science.

tion of the central bank as controller of the money supply inevitably must bias the monetary authority—except in times of national emergency such as war—toward emphasizing the pursuit of objectives connected with the value of money—resistance to domestic inflation, and preservation of the international value of the currency—to the underemphasis or neglect of other objectives such as high employment and economic growth. Thirdly, the methods of monetary management, which involve the central bank concentrating its attention on money market conditions and interest rates, and on member bank reserve positions and lending, rather than on the performance of the economy in general, are extremely conducive to the behavior pattern of overreaction and delayed correction of error already mentioned.

Because it concentrates on money market and banking phenomena, rather than the effects of its policies on the quantity of money and economic activity, and because the effect of monetary policy on the economy operates with a substantial lag, the central bank is extremely likely to push its policy too far and too fast before it realizes that the policy has taken effect and begins to consider moderating it; and because the realization of effectiveness comes late, it is likely to reverse its policy too sharply. In addition, the fact that the central bank stands in a special relation to its Government and domestic economy fosters the existence of an international fellow club member relationship among central banks, a relationship congenial to the formation and propagation of policy fads in central banking. It is only on the basis of fads in central banking opinion, I believe, that one can understand the emergence of the fear of runaway inflation as a dominant motif in central bank policy statements in 1957–58 and the belief at that time in the need to reduce bank liquidity by debt-funding, or the widespread belief that the dollar would soon be devalued that emerged in 1958–59 and persisted thereafter in spite of reiterated statement of the U.S. determination not to devalue.

Recognition of the undemocratic nature of the political argument for an independent monetary authority—together with scholarly documentation of the inadequacies of the historical performance of the Federal Reserve System, has led a number of economists—including my distinguished colleague, Milton Friedman, who will appear before this committee at a later date—to recommend that the goal of providing a stable monetary environment should be implemented, not by entrusting discretionary monetary management to an independent monetary authority, but by legislating that the monetary agency be required to increase the quantity of money at a fixed rate determined from historical experience. I have a certain sympathy with this recommendation, as an alternative to discretionary management as it has been conducted in the past, but there are, in my opinion, some overriding objections to it. In the first place, the proposal is essentially a component of a much broader program for transforming the country into a working model of an ideal competitive system, which system it is assumed would require no deliberate economic management; since the majority of public opinion seems in fact committed to the belief that economic management can improve on unfettered competition, adoption of the proposal would entail accepting a self-denying ordinance in a crucial area of policy, an inconsistency which I doubt would prove acceptable for long. In the second place, the proposal depends on the empirical assumption that the demand for money depends primarily on income and is relatively insensitive to changes in interest rates, an assumed fact concerning which the results of empirical research are in substantial conflict; if the demand for money is not a stable function of income only, the proposal might lead to more instability than discretionary management. Thirdly, the proposal abstracts from the complications of international competition. To be feasible, the proposal would have to be accompanied by the adoption of floating exchange rates, and even in that case might aggravate instability associated with international movements of capital in response to interest-rate differentials between countries; alternatively, it would have to be accompanied by policies of direct intervention in international trade and payments inconsistent with the efficient operation of a competitive economy.

My own view is that the pursuit of monetary stability through the separation of monetary management from other economic policy, and its placement under either an independent authority or a strict rule of increase, is an illusory solution to the problem. Instead, I believe that monetary policy should be brought under the control of the Executive and Legislature in the same way as other aspects of economic policy, with the administration bearing the ultimate responsibility for monetary policy as part of economic policy in general. In making this recommendation, I must admit that there is a danger of monetary mismanagement in the pursuit of political objectives; but I consider it preferable for such mismanagement to be a clear responsibility of the administration, and accountable to the electorate.

I would also point to a danger emphasized by the British economist, Sir Roy Harrod, at the time of the nationalization of the Bank of England, and confirmed, in my judgment, to some extent by subsequent British experience; namely, that bringing the monetary authority within the fold of Government may give more rather than less weight in policymaking to its definitions of, and opinions on, policy problems. In this connection, though, I would like to point out that the monetary authority can only too easily be cast as a scapegoat to conceal the unwillingness of public opinion and the administration to recognize and resolve genuine policy conflicts. In particular, in this country in recent years the fundamental policy problem has been the conflict between equilibrium in the balance of payments and a satisfactory level of domestic activity, imposed by the overvaluation of the dollar relative to the major European currencies; and I do not believe that an administration armed with complete control of monetary policy, but committed to preserving the international value of the dollar, would have conducted a monetary policy very different from what the Federal Reserve has in fact conducted. It might, of course, have taken the bold step of raising foreign loans on the order of $15 to $25 billion to tide over the years of waiting for European prices to inflate up to the American level, but there is no evidence that the administration has been prepared to contemplate such a policy. Given the commitment to a fixed exchange rate, domestic monetary policy must necessarily be subordinated to the balance-of-payments position; the burden of achieving a satisfactory level of employment and activity must be borne by fiscal policy rather than monetary policy, which, in recent circumstances, has meant a substantial tax cut; and it is the reluctance of public opinion, the Congress, and the administration to resort to a tax cut, rather than the policy of the Federal Reserve System, that is ultimately responsible for the unsatisfactory levels of employment and activity that have characterized the economy during the recent years.

While I believe that the monetary authority should be made part of the regular machinery of governmental economic policy making and policy execution, I am not too hopeful about the possibility that this change would result in a significant improvement in the efficiency of monetary policy as an instrument of short-run economic stabilization. My reasons for skepticism stem from the analysis of the influence of the monetary authority's position and responsibilities in the economy on its methods of conducting monetary policy that I have already sketched. This analysis leads me to a conclusion basically similar to that of the proponents of a fixed rule of monetary expansion: that the monetary policy instrument is not well adapted to the pursuit of short-run stabilization policy, and that it should instead be devoted, so far as possible, to the goal of providing a stable long-run monetary environment. I differ from the advocates of an expansion rule, however, in recommending that this goal should be established as a priority objective of discretionary monetary policy, operating as one of a group of instruments of economic policy rather than legislated as a rigid obligation on the monetary authority.

chapter 4

FISCAL POLICY

The selections in the remainder of this book deal with the use of fiscal policy, monetary policy, and debt management policy to regulate aggregate demand in the interest of economic stability and growth. The context for the discussion in this and the next chapter is a closed economy—that is, although there are occasional references to balance-of-payments problems, the discussion of fiscal and monetary policy in these two chapters will not make systematic allowance for the possibility that the country may experience a balance-of-payments deficit which may limit the freedom of its policy makers to use these policy instruments in the interest of achieving domestic goals. During almost the entire period since World War I up until about 1960, the U.S. balance-of-payments situation was such that we were able to use monetary and fiscal policy quite freely to control internal demand in the interest of domestic employment and price stability. At times—notably in the 1930s—we were strikingly unsuccessful in achieving satisfactory levels of employment, but our failure in this regard cannot in any sense be attributed to problems related to the balance of payments. However, during the past 15 years or so, the situation has changed rather markedly, and the balance of payments has acted as a significant constraint on our freedom to use fiscal and monetary policy—especially the latter—to regulate internal demand. The balance of payments and its relationship to fiscal and monetary policy are discussed in some detail in the selections included in Chapters 6 and 7. We feel, however, that before introducing that very relevant consideration, it is useful to discuss the functioning of the instruments of stabilization policy in a setting that abstracts from balance-of-payments problems.

This chapter is concerned with the proper use of fiscal policy. We take up fiscal policy before dealing with monetary policy and debt management (which are treated in the next chapter) because, in the United States at least, the major decisions about government expenditures and taxation are made in connection with the proposals concerning the annual budget made by the President each January and the succeeding decisions by the Congress, which ratify or alter the President's budget proposals. Thus, the decisions concerning the budget establish the overall economic framework within which Federal Reserve monetary policy must function. Furthermore, these decisions also determine the size of the publicly held Federal debt which the Treasury—and to some extent the Federal Reserve—must take the responsibility for managing.

It has increasingly come to be acknowledged that the potential of the economy for producing goods and services increases from year to year as a result of (1) growth of the labor force available for employment, (2) improvement in workers' skills as a result of improved education and training, (3) the accumulation of additional capital through investment and (4) invention and technological improvement which lead to the introduction of superior products and more efficient methods of production. At the same time, there is now quite general agreement that the federal government is able to influence the level of economic activity through the use of both its monetary policy and fiscal policy instruments, as explained in the introduction to Chapter 1. Prior to the 1930s, the main instrument used for this purpose was monetary policy, which, in the United States after the passage of the Federal Reserve Act in 1914, was the responsibility of the Federal Reserve System. Primarily as a result of the impact of Keynes' *General Theory,* which appeared in 1936, together with the work of a generation of scholars who followed up his insights, it is now recognized that by changing its expenditures in relation to its tax receipts, the federal government can exert a powerful effect on the flow of purchasing power, aggregate demand, and economic activity.

The prime responsibility of the stabilization authorities over any given time period is to ensure that aggregate demand grows at a rate which utilizes the available productive capacity at the desired level. We have already learned from the readings on the Phillips curve in the section on prices and inflation in Chapter 1 that this desired utilization level is not one in which literally every man and machine is employed. As a practical matter, such a level would be impossible to achieve in a dynamic economy; more importantly, any serious effort to drive the unemployment rate near to zero would result in an intolerable rate of inflation, given the institutional structure. Rather, the choice of an acceptable utilization rate represents a compromise between the costs of unemployment of a certain fraction of our resources, on the one hand, and of a certain rate of price change, on the other. Once such a target utilization rate has been chosen, it is possible to prepare estimates of "potential GNP" for each period under consideration, corresponding to the selected unemployment rate. That is, this level of potential output represents the amount of output the economy is capable of supplying within a given period at the highest level of capacity utilization consistent with reasonably stable prices: it is thus a concept of aggregate potential *supply.* This level of potential output, which, of course, grows over time for the reasons mentioned above, becomes the aggregate demand target, and the task of stabilization policy is to ensure that aggregate demand is equal to potential output at all times; that is, that it grows at the same rate.

In the article which begins the chapter, Arthur M. Okun discusses some of the assumptions and calculations which form the basis for "potential GNP" as it has been calculated by the Council of Economic Advisers for the past several years, and he also examines the factors which are responsible for the striking result, reflected in this calculation, that a change of 1 percentage point in the unemployment rate results in the short run in approximately a 3 percent change in real GNP in the opposite direction. As Okun is careful to emphasize, the estimates that are made are subject to error and the particular figures should not, in any case, be given too exact an interpretation. Nevertheless, the general approach employed is useful—indeed, almost indispensable—in establishing an appropriate working framework for policy decisions, as explained above. The way in which the potential GNP concept fits into such a framework is considered in the second selection, taken from the January 1969 *Annual Report of the Council of Economic Advisers.*

In analyzing the economic effects of fiscal policy, one of the difficulties is that there is a two-way relation between the budget and GNP. To illustrate, if Congress passes legislation which results in increased expenditures on public works, this action taken by itself will stimulate production and employment and increase GNP while pushing the budget toward a deficit—thus, in this case, an *increase* in GNP is associated with an *increase* in the deficit. On the other hand, a decline in private spending brought about by some independent cause—such as a drop in private investment resulting from a deterioration of business expectations—will cause a decline in production, employment, and GNP. The fall in incomes will cause a drop in tax collections (with no change in tax legislation) and push the budget toward a deficit—that is, in this case, a *decrease* in GNP is associated with an *increase* in the deficit.

The first of these cases is an example of what is sometimes called *active* fiscal policy—involving legislative or administrative changes in government expenditure programs (or, alternatively, changes in tax *rates*) which may be employed for the deliberate purpose of influencing economic activity. The second case is an illustration of so-called *passive* fiscal policy—the government takes no deliberate action but taxes fall as a *result* of the decline in income (and some expenditures, such as those for unemployment compensation, may also rise), thus moving the budget toward a deficit. Such a passive change in fiscal policy will, of course, help to sustain the after-tax incomes of households and businesses whose pretax incomes have dropped, thus helping to limit the decline in business activity and employment. For this reason, passive fiscal policy is another name for the so-called *automatic fiscal stabilizers.* These stabilizers are discussed in a brief reading which is also taken from the 1969 *Annual Report of the Council of Economic Advisers.*

The existence of this two-way relationship between the deficit and GNP creates difficulties in understanding fiscal policy and in interpreting the significance of changes in the deficit. The problem is similar to that which arises in demand and supply analysis, where an increase in demand (i.e., a shift to the right in the demand schedule) is normally associated with both an increase in the quantity bought (and sold) and an *increase* in the price, whereas an independent shift to the right in the supply schedule is associated with an increase in the quantity demanded (and supplied) and a *decrease* in the price. The full-employment surplus (FES) concept, which is explained in the reading taken from the January 1962 *Annual Report of the Council of Economic Advisers,* is a useful device for separating active from passive fiscal policy and straightening out the confusion that has resulted from the existence of a two-way interaction between the budget and GNP. Under this approach, different fiscal programs are "standardized" by calculating the surplus or deficit they would yield if the economy were operating at full employment, thereby correcting for the "passive" influence of varying income levels.

While the FES concept has been a very useful pedagogic and expository device for demonstrating that active and passive fiscal policy can yield quite different results, there remain a number of problems with its use as a analytic measure of active or discretionary policy. It is difficult to construct, and it rests on admittedly tenuous estimates of full-employment GNP, income shares at full employment, and so on. Because the multiplier effects of a given increase of government expenditures on goods and services is greater than that of a tax reduction of the same magnitude, the effects of a given change in the FES will differ somewhat depending on whether the change is produced by an expenditure adjustment or a tax adjustment. Most seriously, perhaps, the FES will increase over time as full-employment income grows, without any change in either tax rates or government spending, thereby signaling (incorrectly) a discretionary change toward restraint.

These defects have led economists to search for other simpler and less ambiguous indicators of the thrust of active fiscal policy. One approach which has been suggested is the "reduced form method" described in the paper by Saul H. Hymans and J. Philip Wernette. In this method, the budget surplus or deficit corresponding to a discretionary fiscal policy change is calculated at current income levels. Unlike the FES, which will change as capacity output rises, the budget indicator under the reduced form approach will change only if (a) discretionary government spending changes, or (b) the tax rate structure is changed.

While the reduced form method overcomes the most serious shortcoming of the FES approach, the two techniques have other problems in common: e.g., the treatment of equivalent expenditure and tax changes as having the same effects. Actually, too much attention to any concept of the budget surplus or deficit is likely to lead to misplaced emphasis and misunderstanding, somewhat as in the case of the national debt—it is really expenditures and taxes and their consequences rather than the deficit or debt that are the prime movers of fiscal policy.

Almost all professionally trained economists would now reject the idea that the budget should be balanced each year. However, an alternative balanced budget rule has sometimes been suggested; namely, that the budget *as it would be if the economy were at full employment* should be kept in balance—that is, that the full-employment surplus should be kept equal to zero. In practice this would mean, for example, that any increase in government expenditures should be accompanied by a tax increase which would bring in enough revenue *under conditions of full employment* to cover the increased expenditures. This would permit the automatic fiscal stabilizers to do their work. Accompanied by a vigorous and effective use of countercyclical monetary policy, it might be capable of producing a reasonably satisfactory degree of economic stability. However, rigid application of even such an attenuated balanced budget rule would create difficulties. First, it would greatly reduce the government's flexibility in seeking to achieve simultaneously a number of important goals—including not only full employment but a satisfactory rate of long-term growth, allocation of the necessary quantity of national resources to defense and other government programs, and so on. Second, if monetary policy is ineffective or if—as has been true in the last several years—freedom to use it is limited by the nation's balance-of-payments position, there is no assurance that even the goal of full employment (properly defined to take account of behavior of the price level) can be achieved "on the average" simultaneously with a balanced federal budget.

When active or discretionary fiscal policy is to be employed to speed up the growth of aggregate demand and reduce unemployment or to slow down the pace of demand expansion in order to check inflation, the question arises as to whether expenditures or taxes should be adjusted. In particular, changes in public works expenditures have often been viewed as a suitable means of implementing fiscal policy. Ronald L. Teigen's paper sets out some of the considerations, both theoretical and practical, bearing on the desirability of employing expenditures for public works as an instrument of fiscal policy.

At the beginning of 1963, President Kennedy recommended to the Congress a program of tax reduction and revision which would when fully in effect reduce the tax liabilities of households and businesses by roughly $11 billion. It is interesting to note that GNP was rising and the economy was not in recession or even in immediate danger of recession at the time the proposal was made. However, actual output was rising less rapidly than productive capacity or potential output, and the major purpose of the proposal was to increase output, reduce unemployment, and approach more closely the full-employment potential of the economy. With unemployment well above the immediate goal of 4 percent and with no signs of an increase in private demand that could be depended upon to reduce it, therefore, the Kennedy administration decided that a major economic stimulus was needed and that the stimulus should take the form of tax reduction to increase private demand for goods and services. While the Kennedy tax proposal was not passed in 1963, tax reduction was pressed vigorously by President Johnson after President Kennedy's assassination and a cut of approximately the magnitude originally proposed was enacted early in the following year in the Revenue Act of 1964. The selection entitled "The Effects of Tax Reduction on Output and Employment," taken from the January 1963 *Annual Report of the Council of Economic Advisers,* was written at the time the original Kennedy proposal was being prepared for submission to Congress, and it explains in some detail the process by which a reduction in personal and corporate income tax rates can be expected to stimulate the economy, including both the multiplier effects on consumption and the stimulus to private investment. The same analysis applies in the opposite direction, of course, to a tax increase such as the one which went into effect during 1968. At the time of this writing, only a limited amount of empirical work on the effect of the 1968 tax increase has been done. However, Arthur M. Okun's paper, "Measuring the Impact of the 1964 Tax Reduction," is a careful study of the results of the 1964 case. It is especially interesting and useful to read the analysis by the Council of Economic Advisers referred to above and the Okun paper in parallel, for, in looking back at the 1964 experience, Okun is able to quantify and trace through time many of the influences which the Council analysis, written before the fact, tells us to expect. Therefore, although that experience took place a decade ago, it is still of relevance from a methodological point of view.

It appears to many that the 1968 tax surcharge, in contrast to the 1964 tax reduction, was ineffective. Inflation and aggregate demand continued at a high level for some time after its enactment. However, there are differences of substance in the two cases; the most important probably being that the tax surcharge was to be temporary, while the tax reduction in 1964 was a permanent change. Since consumption decisions are now viewed as depending fundamentally on households' assessments of their long-run discretionary income prospects, a temporary tax surcharge ought not to affect such decisions greatly, while a permanent tax reduction will change those prospects considerably and therefore should affect consumption.[1]

When federal expenditures exceed tax revenues, it is necessary to raise the money in some fashion to cover the resulting deficit. This subject of "financing the deficit" has had considerable discussion from time to time, and a number of fallacies exist with respect to it. For instance, some discussions have implied that a deficit is all right if it is needed to increase employment but that inflation will result if the deficit is financed by borrowing from commercial banks, since this will increase the money supply. A corollary to this proposition is that "sound finance" requires that the deficit be financed out of "real saving." Alternatively, it is sometimes said that a tax reduction will have no effect on income if it is financed by borrowing from the public, because the government will then be handing out money with one hand and taking it away with the other. The Council of Economic Advisers staff memorandum on "Financing a Federal Deficit" discusses the problem in its several aspects; a careful reading of it should enable the student to see the fallacies in the propositions referred to above. The conclusion that should be drawn from the Council memorandum is that the question is not how the deficit should be financed but rather what kind of monetary policy should accompany a given fiscal policy. The answer, as might be expected, is that it depends on the circumstances under which the deficit is incurred and the several objectives that the government is seeking to achieve.

During the past several years, it has become apparent that fiscal policy, as it is presently constituted, does not possess the flexibility necessary for its role as the basic policy instrument for adjusting demand to the level of potential output. Diffusion of responsibility for budget matters among congressional committees and lack of any discretionary control over tax rates by the Executive branch are among the basic causes. The result has been that monetary policy has often been burdened with a much heavier share of the stabilization task than it has been able to bear; moreover, the fact that tax rates are much more difficult to change than expenditures has made it practically impossible to maintain a desirable balance, in terms of social needs, between private and public expenditures. These matters are discussed, and suggestions for improvement presented, in the reading entitled "Formulating Fiscal Policy" from the 1969 *Annual Report of the Council of Economic Advisers.*

Questions relating to the national debt—how fast it should grow (if at all), whether a debt such as we presently have in the United States is a threat to national solvency, who bears the "burden" of the public debt, and the nature of that burden—have received a great deal of attention in the press, in congressional addresses, and elsewhere. An unusual amount of irrationality and misunderstanding exists concerning these issues. A straightforward analysis of them is presented by David J. and Attiat F. Ott in their reading entitled "Fiscal Policy and the National Debt." A careful study of this paper should lead the

---

[1] For a careful study of the quantitative impact on spending of the 1968 tax surcharge, see Arthur M. Okun, "The Personal Tax Surcharge and Consumer Demand, 1968–70," *Brookings Papers on Economic Activity,* No. 1 (1971), pp. 167–211. Okun finds that at least in some spending categories (nondurable goods and services in particular), the surcharge apparently reduced demand considerably. But in other categories (e.g., new automobiles), no reduction was apparent.

reader to conclude that the important questions in this connection relate to such matters as the level of unemployment and the social productivity of government expenditures compared to private expenditures being displaced, not the size of the debt per se.

POTENTIAL GNP: ITS MEASUREMENT AND SIGNIFICANCE*

Arthur M. Okun†

POTENTIAL GNP AND POLICY

"How much output can the economy produce under conditions of full employment?" The concept and measurement of potential GNP are addressed to this question. It is a question with policy significance because the pursuit of full employment (or "maximum employment" in the language of the Employment Act) is a goal of policy. And a target of full employment of labor needs to be linked to a corresponding target of full employment output, since policy measures designed to influence employment operate by affecting aggregate demand and production. How far we stand from the target of full employment output is important information in formulating fiscal and monetary policy. Thus, quantification of potential output offers one of the guides to stabilization policy and one indicator of its success.

The quantification of potential output—and the accompanying measure of the "gap" between actual and potential—is at best an uncertain estimate and not a firm, precise measure. While there are more precise measures of economic performance, they are not fully substitutable for the concept of potential output. To appraise the vigor of an expanding economy, it is important and enlightening to study customary cyclical measures, such as advance over previous peak levels or advance over recession trough levels. But these measures do not tell us how far we have to go

* From *Proceedings of the Business and Economic Statistics Section of the American Statistical Association,* 1962. Reprinted by permission of the publisher and the author. Arthur M. Okun is a Senior Fellow, Brookings Institution.

† My research in this area was done principally while I served on the Staff on the Council of Economic Advisers, and I had the benefit of many helpful comments and suggestions from members of the Council and the Staff. But the views reported here are my own and do not necessarily reflect those of the Council.

to meet our targets, unless we are prepared to assume that each peak is like any other one and all troughs are likewise uniform. The record of the past decade testifies to the dramatic differences among cyclical peaks in levels of resource utilization.

The evaluation of potential output can also help to point up the enormous social cost of idle resources. If programs to lower unemployment from 5½ to 4 percent of the labor force are viewed as attempts to raise the economy's grade" from 94½ to 96, the case for them may not seem compelling. Focus on the "gap" helps to remind policymakers of the large reward associated with such an improvement.

THE 4 PERCENT UNEMPLOYMENT RATE

Potential GNP is a supply concept, a measure of productive capacity. But it is not a measure of how much output could be generated by unlimited amounts of aggregate demand. The nation would probably be most productive in the short run with inflationary pressure pushing the economy. But the social target of maximum production and employment is constrained by a social desire for price stability and free markets. The full employment goal must be understood as striving for maximum production without inflationary pressure; or, more precisely, as aiming for a point of balance between more output and greater stability, with appropriate regard for the social valuation of these two objectives.

It is interesting and perhaps surprising that there seems to be more agreement that a 4 percent unemployment rate is a reasonable target under existing labor market conditions than on any of the analytical steps needed to justify such a conclusion. Economists have never developed a clear criterion of tolerable price behavior or any quantitative balancing of conflicting objectives which could be invoked either to support or attack the target of a 4 percent rate. Indeed, I should expect that many economists who agree on the 4 percent target would disagree in estimating how prices and wages would behave if we were on target. Nor can the 4 percent rate be said to meet Beveridge's criterion for full employment—that job vacancies should be equal to the number of unemployed. We simply have no count of job vacancies and could not possibly translate Beveridge's goal into any available measure of unemployment.

Having said what the 4 percent unemployment rate is not, I shall now state that it is the target rate of labor utilization underlying the calculation of potential GNP in this paper. The statistical and methodological problems would not be altered if a different rate were selected; only the numbers would be changed.

POTENTIAL GNP AS A SHORT-RUN CONCEPT

In estimating potential GNP, most of the facts about the economy are taken as they exist: technological knowledge, the capital stock, natural resources, the skill and education of the labor force are all data, rather than variables. Potential differs from actual only because the potential concept depends on the assumption—normally contrary to fact—that aggregate demand is exactly at the level that yields a rate of unemployment equal to 4 percent of the civilian labor force. If, in fact, aggregate demand is lower, part of potential GNP is not produced; there is unrealized potential or a "gap" between actual and potential output.

The failure to use one year's potential fully can influence future potential GNP: to the extent that low utilization rates and accompanying low profits and personal incomes hold down investment in plant, equipment, research, housing, and education, the growth of potential GNP will be retarded. Because today's actual output influences tomorrow's productive capacity, success in the stabilization objective promotes more rapid economic growth.

THE MEASUREMENT PROBLEM

As it has been defined above, potential output is observed only when the unemployment rate is 4 percent, and even then must be viewed as subject to stochastic variation. At any other time, it must be regarded as a hypothetical magnitude. The observed actual measures of labor utilization tell us by a simple arithmetic calculation how

much employment would have to increase, given the labor force, to make the unemployment rate 4 percent. But they do not offer similar direct information on other matters that might make labor input at full employment different from its observed level:

a) how average hours worked per man would be altered if the level of aggregate demand were consistent with full employment;

b) how participation rates in the labor force—and hence the size of the labor force—would be affected under conditions of full employment.

Nor do the actual data reveal directly what aggregate labor productivity would be under full employment conditions. There are many reasons why productivity might be altered in the aggregate: the added workers, changed average hours, possible alterations in the sectoral distribution of employment, higher utilization rate of capital, and altered efficiency in the use of employees all could make a difference in productivity at full employment.

THE LEAP FROM UNEMPLOYMENT TO OUTPUT

Ideally, the measurement of potential output would appraise the various possible influences of high employment on labor input and productivity and evaluate the influences step-by-step, developing quantitative estimates for each adjustment to produce the desired measure of potential. While I shall discuss the steps individually below, the basic technique I am reporting consists of a leap from the unemployment rate to potential output rather than a series of steps involving the several underlying factors. Strictly speaking, the leap requires the assumption that, whatever the influence of slack economic activity on average hours, labor force participation, and man-hour productivity, the magnitudes of all these effects are related to the unemployment rate. With this assumption, the unemployment rate can be viewed as a proxy variable for all the ways in which output is affected by idle resources. The measurement of potential output then is simplified into an estimate of how much output is depressed by unemployment in excess of 4 percent.

Statistical Estimates

The answer I have to offer is simple and direct. In the postwar period, on the average, each extra percentage point in the unemployment rate above

4 percent has been associated with about a 3 percent decrement in real GNP. This result emerged from three methods of relating output to the unemployment rate.

1. First Differences. In one technique, quarterly changes in the unemployment rate (Y), expressed in percentage points, are related to quarterly percentage changes in real GNP (X). This regression equation, fitted to 55 quarterly observations from 1947–II to 1960–IV, yields:

$$Y = .30 - .30X \qquad (r = .79)$$

According to this estimate, the unemployment rate will rise by 0.3 points from one quarter to the next if real GNP is unchanged, as secular gains in productivity and growth in the labor force push up the unemployment rate. For each extra 1 percent of GNP, unemployment is 0.3 points lower. At any point in time, taking previous quarters as given, 1 percentage point more in the unemployment rate means 3.3 percent less GNP.

2. Trial Gaps. A second method consists of selecting and testing certain exponential paths of potential output, using alternative assumed growth rates and benchmark levels. The percentage "gaps" implied by these paths are then related to the unemployment rate (U) using a regression equation: $U = a + b(gap)$. The criteria for judging the validity of the assumed potential paths are: (1) goodness of fit, (2) absence of any trend in the residuals, and (3) agreement with the principle that potential GNP should equal actual GNP when $U = 4$.

The slope terms in this equation fitted to various paths and different periods consistently ran from .28 up to .38. One such equation was reported in the March 1961 statement of the Council of Economic Advisers to the Joint Economic Committee. It was:

$$U = 3.72 + .36 \, gap \qquad (r = .93)$$

where the gap was derived from a 3½ percent trend line through actual real GNP in mid-1955. The equation was fitted to quarterly data for 1953–60. It implies that an increment of unemployment of 1 percent is associated with an output loss equal to 2.8 percent of potential output—or a somewhat larger percentage of *actual* output when actual is below potential. The estimated unemployment rate associated with a zero gap is 3.72 percent, not too far from the 4.0 percent ideal.

3. Fitted Trend and Elasticity. The first method described above relied on the use of changes in GNP and in unemployment. The second method used *levels* but assumed the trend of output-growth at constant unemployment rates. It is also possible to derive the output-unemployment coefficient from data on levels without assuming a trend. The following model permits such a calculation:

a) There is a constant elasticity relationship in the relevant range between the ratio of actual (A) to potential (P) output, on the one hand, and the "employment rate" $(N = 100 - U)$ as a fraction of its potential level (N_F):

$$\frac{N}{N_F} = \left(\frac{A}{P}\right)^a$$

b) There is a constant growth rate (r) of potential output starting from some level P_o such that at any time t:

$$P_t = P_o e^{rt}$$

By substitution and rearrangement:

$$N_t = \frac{A_t{}^a \cdot N_F}{P_o{}^a \cdot e^{art}}$$

Logarithmically:

$$\log N_t = \log \frac{N_F}{P_o{}^a} + a \log A_t - (ar)t$$

The log of the employment rate is here related to a time-trend and to the log of actual real GNP. When a regression equation is fitted to $\log N$ as the dependent variable and $\log A$ and t as independent variables: (1) The coefficient of log A is the "output elasticity of the employment rate"; (2) the coefficient of time is the product of that elasticity and the potential growth rate; it therefore yields an estimate of the potential growth rate; and (3) the intercept yields the benchmark (P_o) for any given N_F, here taken as 96.

Fitted to varying sample periods, the estimated elasticity coefficient ran .35 to .40, suggesting that each one percentage point reduction in unemployment means slightly less than a 3 percent increment in output (near the potential level). The trend growth rate, fitted to 1947–60 quarterly data was 3.9 percent, but it was clear that this was not uniform throughout the period. For the post-Korean period, the estimated trend growth in potential was near 3½ percent, while, for the 1947–53 period, it was near 4½ percent.

The uniformity that emerged from these various techniques was the approximate 3 to 1 link between output and the unemployment rate. My own subjectively weighted average of the relevant coefficients is 3.2, yielding the following estimate of potential:

$$P = A[1 + .032(U - 4)]$$

When the unemployment rate is 4 percent, potential GNP is estimated as equal to actual; at a 5 percent rate of unemployment, the estimated "gap" is 3.2 percent of GNP. In the periods from which this relationship was obtained the unemployment rate varied from about 3 to 7½ percent; the relation is not meant to be extrapolated outside this range. I have no reason to expect the 3.2 coefficient to apply if unemployment were either 1 or 15 percent of the labor force.

SMOOTHING THE POTENTIAL PATH

The dashed line in the accompanying figure shows the implied time-series of potential GNP derived by applying the 3.2 coefficient to excess unemployment for the period 1954 to date. The result is a curve that wiggles from quarter to quarter, even dipping at times. The dips and small increases in estimated potential are concentrated in advanced stages of expansions— 1956–57, 1959, and early 1962. Quarters of rapid rise in estimated potential output occur in early expansion—1955, 1958, 1961.

The question that arises is whether (1) these wiggles and jiggles should be taken seriously, as indications of irregular or cyclical patterns in the growth of productive capacity or (2) whether they should be attributed to an imperfect correlation of the unemployment rate with unused potential output. In the former case, the irregular path upward shown by the dashed line would be the estimated series of potential GNP. In the latter case, some smoothing of that irregular path would be in order.

One way of smoothing which eliminates all the ripples is to substitute a simple exponential curve that corresponds with the trend and level of the wiggly series. Such a line is obtained by a trend that goes through actual output in mid-1955 as a benchmark and moves upward at a 3½ percent annual rate. The trend measure of potential is shown as the solid line in the figure.

POTENTIAL AND ACTUAL GNP, 1954–62

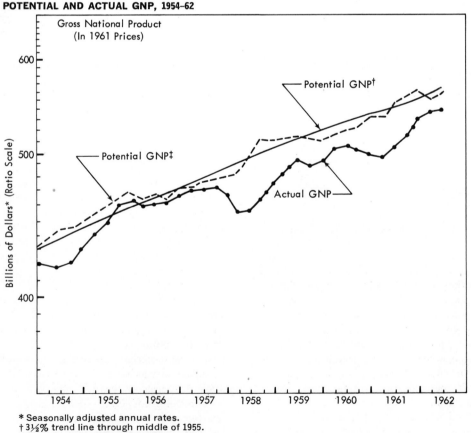

* Seasonally adjusted annual rates.
† 3½% trend line through middle of 1955.
‡ Based on unemployment rate.

It presents an opposite extreme alternative—the view that the upward path of potential GNP has been perfectly smooth in the post-Korean period. On the whole, the two measures agree quite well. A trend line with either a 3 or a 4 percent growth rate—or with a markedly different "benchmark" level—would clearly not fit the dashed line equally well. In general, periods of early expansion—like 1955; 1958–II to 1959–I; and 1961–II to 1961–IV—show larger gaps by the unemployment measure than by the trend technique. The reverse is true for late expansion and recession periods, like 1956–II to 1958–I and 1959–III to 1961–I.

My own inclination is to select the smooth trend measure of potential output for the post-Korean period. I find it difficult to accept the verdict that potential output has actually contracted at times, as the unsmoothed unemployment measure implies. Nor can I believe that the economy's *productive capacity* rises most rapidly in early expansion, even though actual production may be increasing briskly. This is not the period when investment expenditures—much less completed investment projects—are at a peak; nor is it a time of heavy innovations, by any external evidence I know.

The spurts shown in early expansion periods can be accounted for by the hypothesis that unemployment lags somewhat behind the movement of output, and therefore is slow to decline in early recovery. Indeed, in statistical tests of some of the regression equations reported above, it was found that unemployment in the current quarter depends on past as well as current levels of GNP, with a higher level of past output meaning less current unemployment. This implies that decisions on hiring labor for next quarter are strengthened by a high level of current output.

The cyclical ripples in the unemployment measure may also reflect, in part, a lead of the workweek in advance of employment. Total man-hours worked rise more rapidly than employment in early expansion and less rapidly in late expansion. The initial impact of a change in the pace of economic activity is particularly strong on the workweek and is later shifted more fully onto employment. Presumably, this lagged effect might be incorporated into the estimate of potential based on the unemployment rate, in such a way as to smooth that potential curve and bring it closer to the trend estimate of potential. But, for the post-Korean period, there is no obvious shift in the trend of potential; and the 3½ percent trend line, while obviously too smooth a time path, fills the assignment rather well.

The trend estimate of potential for the 1954–62 period still rests on the unemployment-output relationship reviewed above, that an excess of 1 point in the unemployment rate means, on the average, a loss of about 3 percent in output. The trend line, however, suggests that the output loss per point of the unemployment rate exceeds 3 percent in late expansion and in recession and is somewhat less than 3 percent in early expansion.

It should be noted that this trend does not fit the earlier postwar years. If one projected the 3½ percent trend back to 1947, the trend-technique would clearly overestimate potential output. The indicated potential growth of the 1947–53 period is nearer to 4½ percent. The lower potential growth rate of the post-Korean period is associated, in part, with less success in making full use of our potential. The "gaps" between potential and actual have held down the size and held up the average age of our capital stock, thereby lowering the growth of potential.

THE STEPS

The findings above assert that a reduction in unemployment, measured as a percentage of the labor force, has a much larger than proportionate effect on output. To appraise and evaluate this finding, it is necessary to inspect the steps which were leaped over in the statistical relationships between output and unemployment. Clearly, the simple addition of 1 percent of a given labor force to the ranks of the employed would increase employment by only slightly more than 1 percent: $100/100-U$ percent to be exact. If the workweek and productivity were unchanged, the increment to output would be only that 1+ percent. The 3 percent result implies that considerable output gains in a period of rising utilization rates must stem from some or all of the following: induced increases in the size of the labor force; longer average weekly hours; and greater productivity.

Labor Force

Participation in the labor force as we measure it consists of either having a job or seeking actively to work. The resulting measures of labor force are not pure reflections of supply; they are affected by job availability. In a slack labor market, people without a job may give up when they are convinced that job-hunting is a hopeless pursuit. They then may be viewed as having left the labor force though they stand ready and eager to work. Furthermore, there are secondary or passive members of the labor force who will not actively seek employment but would accept gainful employment if a job came looking for them. This latter group suffers little or no personal hardship in not having work, but the output they would contribute in a fully employed economy is a relevant part of the nation's potential GNP.

There may be induced changes in the labor force in the opposite direction: e.g., the loss of a job by the breadwinner of a family might increase the measured labor force by leading his wife and teen-age children to seek work. The prewar literature debated the probable net effects of these opposing influences on participation rates. However, the postwar record has convincingly delivered the verdict that a weak labor market depresses the size of the labor force. But the magnitude and timing of the effect are not clear.

Even the conceptual problems of defining a potential labor force is difficult—we should not wish to count only the secondary labor force members who would appear for work tomorrow morning; on the other hand, we would not want to include all those who might be attracted by many years of continued job availability. The response of participation rates is likely to be a complicated lagged phenomenon which will not be closely tied to the current unemployment rate. While this aspect of the difference between potential and actual output is hard to quantify, zero is certainly not a satisfactory estimate. At the end of 1960, the Bureau of Labor Statistics estimated the difference between actual and "normal" labor force at 561,000. If this figure is taken as the induced effect of poor opportunities for jobs, it implies that, in those recession conditions, for every 10 people listed as unemployed over and above the 4 percent rate, there were three additional potential workers who were not actively seeking work.

Hours

Taking into account the normal secular decline in output. When output has been rising rapidly, ship between movements in average hours and in output. When output has been rising rapidly, average hours have expanded—or, at least, have not contracted. On the other hand, periods of low growth or decline in GNP mean more rapid declines in average hours per man. The data point toward the concept of a full employment path of average annual hours. But the concept of full

employment hours is hard to quantify: e.g., in a rapid rise of output toward full employment, the amount of overtime might well push the workweek above the level consistent with steady full employment. Furthermore, economy-wide data on average hours are notoriously poor. However, using what evidence is available, we find that each 1 percent difference in output is associated with a difference of 0.14 percent in hours per man, including both overtime and part-time work.

The figure of 0.14 is obtained by fitting a least-squares regression line to annual data for 1947–59. The data are found in the Bureau of Labor Statistics Release (USDL–4155) of June 28, 1960. The variables are percent change in man-hours of work per person employed (Y) and percent change in private nonagricultural output (X), restricted to private nonagricultural output and employment; establishment figures are the source of the man-hour estimates. The fitted line is:

$$Y = 0.843 + .142X \quad (r = .85)$$

When this equation is used to compare average hours for different possible outputs at the same point in time, the 0.142 coefficient reflects the percentage difference in hours per man that accompanies a 1 percent difference in output.

Returning to the finding that a 1 percentage point reduction in the unemployment rate means 3.2 percent more GNP, the hours-output estimate above indicates that it will also be accompanied by an increase of nearly one half of 1 percent in hours per man, or an addition of about 0.2 of an hour to the workweek. With an allowance for induced gains in labor force, based illustratively on the 1960 estimate cited above, the reduction of one point in the unemployment rate means perhaps a 1.8 percent increase in total labor input measured in man-hours. Then, to get the 3.2 percent increment in output, man-hour productivity must rise by about 1.4 percent.

Productivity

The direct checks that could be made on productivity data were consistent with this implication of the output-unemployment relationship. The record clearly shows that man-hour productivity is depressed by low levels of utilization, and that periods of movement toward full employment yield considerably above-average productivity gains.

The implications and explanations of this phenomenon are intriguing. Indeed, many *a priori* arguments have been made for the reverse view—that depressed levels of activity will stimulate productivity through pressure on management to cut costs, through a weeding out of inefficient firms and low quality workers, and through availability of more and higher quality capital per worker for those employees who retain their jobs. If such effects exist, the empirical record demonstrates that they are swamped by other forces working in the opposite direction.

I have little direct evidence to offer on the mechanism by which low levels of utilization depress productivity. I can offer some speculation and try to encourage other researchers to pursue this problem with concrete evidence at a microeconomic level. The positive relationship between output and labor productivity suggests that much of labor input is essentially a fixed cost for fairly substantial periods. Thus high output levels permit the spreading of labor overheads, and low production levels raise unit fixed costs of labor. At times, we may take too seriously our textbook examples which view labor as a variable factor, with only capital costs as fixed. Even the most casual empiricism points to an overhead component in labor costs. There are many reasons why employment may not be easily variable:

1. *Contractual commitments* may tie the hand of management in a downward direction—employees may have guaranteed annual wages, supplementary unemployment compensation, rights to severance pay, etc., as well as actual contracts for a term of employment.

2. *Technological factors,* in a broad sense, may also be important. A firm plans on a division of labor and degree of specialization attuned to "normal" operations. If operations fall below normal, there may be marked indivisibilities which prevent the firm from curtailing its employment of specialists, clerical and sales personnel, and supervisors in parallel with its cutback in output.

3. *Transactions costs* associated with laying off labor and then, in the future, doing new hiring may be another influence retarding the adjustment of labor input to fluctuations in sales and output.

4. *Acquired skills* that existing employees have learned on the job may make them particularly valuable to the firm so that it pays to stockpile underemployed labor rather than run the risk of having to hire untrained men when business conditions improve.

5. *Morale factors* may also make layoffs undesirable.

All of these factors could help explain why slack economic activity is accompanied by "on-the-job underemployment," reflected in depressed levels of man-hour productivity. Firms obviously do lay off labor in recession but they do so reluctantly. Their problems may be mitigated, in part, by the presence of voluntary quits which permit a downward adjustment of employment without layoffs. In part, the impact of slack on man-hour productivity may be reduced by shortening average hours to spread the work and the wage-bill without a cut in employment. But these appear to be only partial offsets.

To the extent that the productivity losses of recessions are associated with fixity of labor costs, they would not be maintained indefinitely. If the recession was of long duration—or merely was expected to last a long time—firms would adjust their employment more drastically. On this reasoning, in an era when business cycle dips are continually short and mild, one might expect productivity to bear more of the brunt of recession and labor input to be less affected, even relative to the decline in output.

Changes in the level of economic activity are associated with shifts in the composition of employment and output by industry. A slack economy is accompanied by particularly depressed output in durable-goods manufacturing industries, where output per man-hour is especially high. My own intuition suggested that this might be an important explanation of the relationship between productivity and the unemployment rate. But calculations on the change in composition from recession to recovery years indicate that, while shifts in industrial composition do influence aggregate productivity in the expected direction, the magnitude of the effect is trivial. There is some significance to the compositional shift between agriculture and nonagricultural industries. Man-hour input in agriculture seems to be independent of overall economic activity in the short run, so all variations in labor input can be regarded as occurring in the nonagricultural sector. I assumed illustratively above that a point reduction in the unemployment rate means an increase in total man-hours of 1.8 percent. If all of that 1.8 percent goes into nonagriculture, this would add 0.1 percent to economy-wide productivity (for given levels of productivity in each sector). This is still only a minor part of the total productivity gain that accompanies reduced unemployment.

Thus far, I have ignored the dependence of labor productivity on plant and equipment capacity. The entire discussion of potential output in this paper has, in effect, assumed that idle labor is a satisfactory measure of all idle resources.

In fact, measures of excess capacity in industrial plant and equipment do show a close relationship to unemployment—idle men are accompanied by idle machines. But the correlation is not perfect and operating rates in industry should be considered along with employment data as an indicator of the gap between potential and actual output. Obviously, if capital were fully employed while there was much unemployed labor, this would hold down the productivity gains that could be obtained through full employment of labor. Robert Solow did use capital stock data together with unemployment data in fitting a production function for 1929 to date (see the *American Economic Review* of May 1962). His estimates of potential output for the post-Korean period agreed remarkably well with those I am reporting.

Still, I shall feel much more satisfied with the estimation of potential output when our data and our analysis have advanced to the point where the estimation can proceed step-by-step and where the capital factor can be explicitly taken into account. Meanwhile, the measure of potential must be used with care. The trend line yields a point-estimate of the "gap," e.g., $31.3 billion for 1962–II. But that specific figure must be understood as the center of a range of plausible estimates. By my personal evaluation of its degree of accuracy, I find potential output useful—and superior to substitute concepts—for many analytical purposes.

REALIZING THE ECONOMY'S POTENTIAL*

Council of Economic Advisers

How much the Nation's economy can produce—its supply capability—depends on the quantity and quality of its productive resources, including manpower, plant and equipment, and natural resources. The economy's aggregate demand is the total of spending for final output by all groups—consumers, businesses, government, and foreign buyers. When aggregate demand matches supply capability, resources are fully utilized and production equals the economy's potential. If aggregate demand should fall short of supply capability, part of the output that the economy is capable of turning out would not be produced, and some resources would be wasted in idleness. On the other hand, excessive demand—too much spending in relation to potential output—would generate inflationary pressures on prices and costs.

The basic task of fiscal and monetary policies is to help ensure a match between demand and productive potential. These measures operate primarily by affecting the demand side of the balance. Government purchases of goods and services are directly a part of total demand; increases or decreases in such purchases change total spending in the same direction. In addition, other government expenditures indirectly influence total demand through their impact on private incomes. Social security benefits, for example, are "transfer payments" which add to the purchasing power of individuals, and thus encourage additional private spending, especially for consumer goods and services.

Taxes, on the other hand, reduce the ability and willingness of families and business firms to spend, by drawing purchasing power out of private hands. By raising (or lowering) tax rates, the Federal Government can hold down (or add to) the flow of private spending.

Monetary policies affect private spending primarily by changing the cost and availability of funds required to finance certain types of expenditures. If borrowing becomes expensive and difficult, expenditures for new homes, business machinery, and other things may be discouraged or postponed.

The economy's potential output is continually expanding as a result of the growth of the labor force and increases in productivity. Economic policy must therefore aim at a moving target—helping demand to grow in pace so that an appropriate balance with potential is maintained. If demand does not expand or if it grows only sluggishly, men and machines become unemployed.

* From *The Annual Report of the Council of Economic Advisers,* January 1969, pp. 61–67. Reprinted by permission of the Council of Economic Advisers.

THE CHOICE OF A TARGET

Economic potential or capacity is not an absolute technical ceiling on output. It allows for some margin of unused human and physical resources. Even in most extreme boom, there are always some people unemployed, some who could be attracted into the labor force, some who would be willing to "moonlight" or work overtime. Similarly, there are always some plants that could be operated more intensively or for longer hours. To operate the economy at its utmost technical capacity would require demands far in excess of supply in most markets, with resulting rampant inflation.

The relevant concept of capacity, therefore, must allow for some margin of idle resources. The choice of a specific margin involves an appraisal of the behavior of prices and costs in a high-employment economy. But this appraisal involves more than a technical evaluation. If potential output is to be viewed as a target for policy, the choice of the ideal level of utilization is a social judgment that requires a balancing of national goals of high employment and reasonable price stability.

Balances of this sort are never simple. Both unemployment and inflation involve social and individual costs. The severe economic burden borne by those who have no jobs is obvious. At the bottom of the 1957–58 recession, there were more than five million workers out of jobs; and during 1958 more than 14 million workers experienced one or more spells of unemployment. Still others were forced to accept part-time employment or were relegated to jobs beneath their capacity. Some, in resignation, abandoned the search for jobs. The loss of income was tremendous. The costs in frustration, despair, and bitterness cannot be measured.

Some of the costs of unemployment linger on because skills and supplies of labor are impaired. When over-all unemployment is excessive, employers have little incentive to provide job training programs for the unskilled or to upgrade workers to better paying jobs. Labor unions become increasingly concerned about job security of existing members and often take measures that limit the supply of available labor for the longer run.

Although the burden of a slack economy falls most heavily on the unemployed, the loss of production associated with underutilized resources imposes serious costs on nearly all groups. The incomes lost by the unemployed represent far less than half of the total shortfall of output and income. A slack economy sharply reduces the profits of large and small businesses and cuts government tax revenues. Moreover, part of the burden falls on future generations, because under-

utilization of capacity weakens investment incentives, slowing the rate of capital accumulation and limiting future productivity gains.

It is difficult to balance the costs of inflation against those of an absolute loss of output and employment, because they are quantitatively and qualitatively different. Inflation has highly arbitrary and inequitable effects on the distribution of income and wealth. It benefits debtors at the expense of creditors; it hurts persons, such as some pensioners, whose incomes and asset values are fixed in money terms, and benefits those whose incomes and asset values increase more than in proportion to the over-all rise in prices. Since the impact of inflation on the welfare of an individual depends on the way in which both his income and the value of his wealth respond to the change in prices, its effects on broad classes of the population cannot be easily characterized. But there are many persons, in nearly all walks of life, who experience significant losses as a result of inflation. In general, financially sophisticated persons, who foresee the consequences of rising prices, can take steps to protect themselves, while the less sophisticated may lose.

There is also a danger that inflation can set in motion speculative behavior that will cause further acceleration of price increases, with serious consequences for economic and social stability. There are even extreme examples in history of the breakdown of financial and economic systems as a result of galloping inflation.

Finally, inflation may have adverse consequences for our balance of payments. If prices rise more rapidly in the United States than in other countries, our competitive position in world markets can be seriously undermined.

As a collective social decision, the choice of an employment objective can and should be the subject of continuous reexamination. Chapter 3 [of the Report] suggests a number of structural measures that can help to lessen the conflict between high employment and price stability. When combined with an improved performance of fiscal and monetary policy along lines discussed in this chapter, these measures may make it possible to achieve progressively lower rates of unemployment with reasonable price stability.

POTENTIAL OUTPUT

In light of the considerations discussed above, a 4-percent unemployment rate was established as an "interim" target for national policy early in the Kennedy Administration. In each of its last seven Annual Reports, the Council of Economic Advisers has based its estimates of potential output on a 4 percent rate of unemployment. This Report continues to make use of this definition.

The resulting estimated path of potential output for the period 1955 to 1968, together with the path of actual gross national product (GNP), is shown in Chart 1. Actual GNP was approximately equal to potential in 1955, but fell gradually below potential in the following years. The gap widened sharply in the 1957–58 recession, it failed to close fully in the ensuing expansion, and it widened again in the recession of 1960–61.

In the first quarter of 1961, the gap amounted to about $60 billion (in 1968 prices), and the unemployment rate was 6.8 percent.

From the first quarter of 1961 until the end of 1965, when the unemployment rate reached 4 percent, actual output was consistently below potential. But actual output grew more rapidly than potential, catching up and finally closing the gap. Since then, actual output has exceeded the calculated potential most of the time, as the unemployment rate has been below 4 percent.

It is estimated that potential output grew about 3½ percent a year from the mid-1950s to the early 1960s. After that, its growth appears

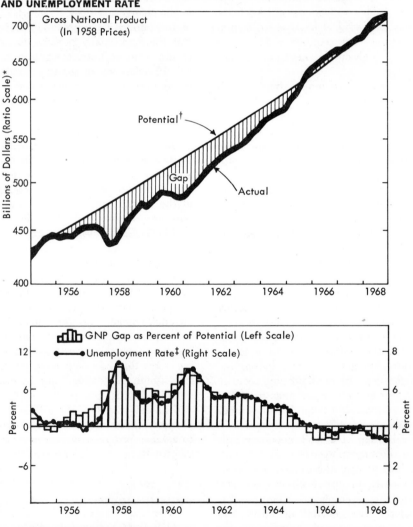

CHART 1   GROSS NATIONAL PRODUCT, ACTUAL AND POTENTIAL, AND UNEMPLOYMENT RATE

*Seasonally Adjusted Annual Rates.
†Trend Line of 3½% through Middle of 1955 to 1962–IV, 3¼% from 1962–IV to 1965–IV, and 4% from 1965–IV to 1968–IV.
‡Unemployment as Percent of Civilian Labor Force; Seasonally Adjusted.
Sources: Department of Commerce, Department of Labor, and Council of Economic Advisers.

to have speeded up gradually; for the last few years, it is estimated at 4 percent a year.

Growth of potential output reflects the combined effects of expansion of available man-hours of labor and rising output per man-hour.

Available Man-Hours

Sustained growth of the labor force has resulted in a substantial rise in potentially available man-hours despite a gradually declining trend in average hours of work. Over the long run, the labor force has increased roughly in line with the working-age population (16 years old and over). This tendency has continued in the 1960s. The rising participation of women in the labor force has been roughly offset by the effects of a shift in the composition of the working-age population toward teenagers and older people, who have relatively low participation rates.

Average hours worked per employed person have declined slowly over the long run, reflecting the secular trend toward more holidays, longer vacations, shortening of the workweek, and increasing participation of people who want to work only part time.

Growth of the potential labor force has accelerated from 1¼ percent a year in the early 1960's to a present rate of about 1¾ percent—reflecting the upsurge in births immediately after World War II. This has been partially offset by the secular decline in hours worked of about ¼ of 1 percent a year. The net result has been an acceleration of the growth of available man-hours from 1 to 1½ percent a year over the period.

Productivity

Many factors contribute to growth in output per man-hour—the productivity of labor. These include increases in the stock of productive capital and improvements in its quality; better educated, better trained, and more experienced labor; and advances in technology, production methods, and management techniques.

Since 1950, output per man-hour in the private economy has expanded at an average annual rate a little above 3 percent. For the entire economy, the calculated trend is somewhat lower, because improvements in the efficiency of Government workers are not measured statistically and are arbitrarily taken at zero. Thus the trend rate of increase in aggregate productivity—private and public—has been about 2½ percent a year. When added to the growth of available man-

hours, this results in the 3½ percent annual growth of potential output for the late 1950s and the 4 percent current growth rate.

Actual and Potential GNP

Over the entire period from the recession trough in the first quarter of 1961 to the fourth quarter of 1968, actual GNP rose by $288 billion (in 1968 prices), reflecting the combined result of keeping up with the growth of potential GNP and of closing the gap. Potential GNP rose by $216 billion, an increase of 33 percent. Thus the Nation is presently earning a huge additional bonus of $72 billion a year in output as a result of having eliminated a great waste of idle resources.

The unemployment rate in the first quarter of 1961 stood at 6.8 percent. At current levels of the labor force, the reduction of this rate to the 3.4 percent that prevailed in the fourth quarter of 1968—below the 4 percent rate that is used to define potential output—represents a gain in employment of 2.7 million. On the basis of current average productivity, this number of workers can be credited with a $31 billion contribution to output (annual rate).

However, the reduction of 3.4 percentage points in the unemployment rate accounts directly for only a portion of the gain in output associated with the closing of the gap. There were four other important factors involved:

1. In a slack economy, firms are often reluctant to lay off certain types of workers, particularly foremen, semi-professionals, and the highly skilled. The result is considerable on-the-job underemployment which depresses measured labor productivity. As the economy moves back toward potential, productivity increases more rapidly than the long-term trend. Since early 1961, output per man-hour has risen at an average annual rate of 3 percent, ½ of a percentage point more than trend.

2. Labor force participation has risen since 1961 as people who had not been looking for work responded to the greater availability of job opportunities.

3. The increased pace of economic activity slowed the secular decline in the length of the workweek.

4. The proportion of the labor force reporting involuntary part-time employment for economic reasons declined from 4.4 percent in early 1961 to 2.1 percent in the fourth quarter of 1968.

Together, these four factors contributed an

additional $41 billion to the output gain associated with the reduction of the unemployment rate.

The $72 billion of extra GNP resulting from reducing the unemployment rate amounts to about 11 percent of potential output at the start of the period—that is, there was about a 3 percentage point bonus of annual production for each 1 percentage point reduction in the unemployment rate.

AUTOMATIC STABILIZERS AND FISCAL DRAG*

Council of Economic Advisers

The potential sources of instability discussed above produced four recessions between 1948 and 1961. By prewar standards, these recessions were all relatively short and mild, though nevertheless costly. They were limited in intensity and duration by several elements built into the fiscal system which serve to moderate economic instability in an automatic and passive fashion. These so-called "automatic fiscal stabilizers" operate to bolster income flows to households and business firms in periods of declining output and, conversely, to slow down the growth in income in periods of expansion.

Almost every tax—including State and local taxes—responds in some degree to changes in economic activity. Federal personal income tax collections are particularly responsive to such changes. They are the most important automatic fiscal stabilizer, cushioning take-home pay against fluctuations in the before-tax incomes of individuals. Another important stabilizer is the automatic expansion of unemployment compensation benefits when unemployment increases. The corporate income tax serves to reduce fluctuations in after-tax profits and hence in business investment outlays and dividend payments.

By reducing the size of secondary effects on consumer and business outlays, these stabilizers reduce the severity of economic fluctuations. With the present tax system and schedules of unemployment compensation benefits, a decline in GNP automatically produces a reduction in government receipts and an increase in transfer payments. This limits the decline in private after-tax income—disposable personal income and retained corporate profits—to about 65 cents for each $1 of reduction in GNP.

During the postwar period, the automatic fiscal stabilizers have been a major factor in reducing

* From *The Annual Report of the Council of Economic Advisers,* January 1969, pp. 72–73. Reprinted by permission of the Council of Economic Advisers.

economic instability. They go to work at once and avoid the delays inherent in discretionary action. But valuable as these automatic stabilizers are, they work only to limit—not prevent—swings in economic activity. For example, they become operative in a recession only after the decline has begun and cannot, by themselves, generate a recovery. If the factors causing a downturn are strong and persistent, automatic stabilizers may not be powerful enough to prevent a long and severe recession.

The automatic stabilizers also operate without regard to the over-all level of economic activity. If the economy has fallen substantially below the path of potential output, the return to that path is made more difficult by the retarding effects of automatic fiscal stabilizers. The existence of the automatic stabilizers in such a situation means that a larger amount of fiscal or monetary stimulus—increased expenditures, reduced tax rates, or easing of credit conditions—will be required to achieve the needed increase in aggregate demand.

In addition, automatic stabilizers work in a fashion that may inhibit the long-run expansion of demand. As the economy moves along the potential output path with reasonably stable prices, the Federal tax system generates an increase in revenues of about 6 percent a year. Unless this revenue growth is offset by reductions in taxes or by increases in expenditures, it acts as a "fiscal drag" by siphoning off income. Actions by the private sector can conceivably offset this effect if businesses increase investment expenditures faster than the growth of internal funds, or if households reduce their rate of saving. But under normal conditions, needed expansion may be prevented.

In interpreting the economic impact of fiscal policy, it is essential to distinguish between the automatic changes in revenues and expenditures resulting from the operation of the automatic stabilizers, on the one hand, and discretionary changes brought about by changes in tax rates and expenditure programs, on the other. In order to measure the impact of discretionary fiscal policy, it is useful to prepare estimates of revenues and expenditures at a given—or "standardized"—level of income. When the difference between revenues and expenditures is estimated at the level of potential output, the result is sometimes referred to as the "full employment surplus."

The full employment surplus was a particularly enlightening measure of fiscal policy in the early 1960s when the economy was far below its potential. Actual Federal budgets were then in deficit. But after taking account of the large shortfall in tax revenues associated with the gap between potential and actual output, there was a large full employment surplus. It meant that the economy could realize its potential only if private investment far exceeded private saving. By that standard, discretionary fiscal policy was highly restrictive.

THE FULL EMPLOYMENT SURPLUS CONCEPT*

Council of Economic Advisers

The magnitude of the surplus or deficit in the budget depends both on the budget program and on the state of the economy. The budget program fixes both tax rates and expenditure programs. The revenues actually yielded by most taxes, and the actual expenditures under certain programs like unemployment compensation, vary automatically with economic activity. To interpret the economic significance of a given budget it is, therefore, essential to distinguish the *automatic* changes in revenues and expenditures from the *discretionary* changes which occur when the government varies tax rates or changes expenditure programs. The discussion that follows runs in terms of the national income accounts budget.

In Chart 1, this twofold aspect of fiscal policy is portrayed for the fiscal years 1960 and 1962. Since tax revenues and some expenditures depend on the level of economic activity, there is a whole range of possible surpluses and deficits associated with a given budget program. The particular surplus or deficit in fact realized will depend on the level of economic activity. On the horizontal scale, Chart 1 shows the ratio of actual GNP to the economy's potential, labeled the "utilization rate." On the vertical scale, the chart shows the Federal budget surplus or deficit as a percentage of potential GNP.

The line labeled "fiscal 1960 program" represents a calculation of the budget surplus or deficit which would have occurred at various levels of economic activity, given the Federal expenditure programs and the tax rates of that year. For

the reasons explained earlier, the same budget program may yield a high surplus at full employment and a low surplus or a deficit at low levels of economic activity. The actual budget position in fiscal year 1960, a surplus of $2.2 billion or 0.4 percent of potential GNP, is shown at point A; this accompanied a level of GNP 5 percent below potential. Had full employment been achieved that year, however, the same basic budget program would have yielded a surplus of about $10 billion, or nearly 2 percent of gross national product (point F in the chart). The line labeled "1962 program" similarly shows the relationship between economic activity and the surplus or deficit, for the budget program of 1962; the expected deficit is shown at point B, and the full employment surplus at point G.

It is the height of the line in Chart 1 which reflects the basic budget program; the actual surplus or deficit depends both on the height of the program line and the level of economic activity. In other words, discretionary fiscal policy, by changing the level of Government expenditures or tax rates, shifts the whole program line up or down. The automatic stabilizing effects of a given budget program are reflected in the chart by movements along a given line, accompanying changes in economic activity. One convenient method of comparing alternative budget programs, which separates automatic from discretionary changes in surplus and deficits, is to calculate the surplus or deficit of each alternative program at a fixed level of economic activity. As a convention, this calculation is made on the assumption of full employment. In Chart 1, the points F and G mark the full employment surplus in the budget programs of fiscal years 1960 and

* From *The Annual Report of the Council of Economic Advisers*, January 1962, pp. 78–81. Reprinted by permission of the Council of Economic Advisers.

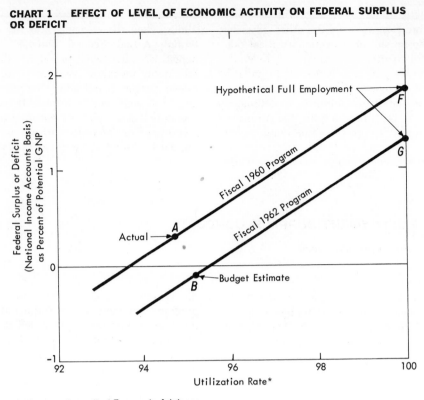

Source: Council of Economic Advisers.
* Actual GNP as percent of potential GNP.

1962, respectively. The statement, "the fiscal 1960 budget had a larger full employment surplus, as a fraction of potential GNP, than the 1962 budget" is a convenient shorthand summary of the fact that the 1962 budget line was below the 1960 line, yielding smaller surpluses or larger deficits at any comparable level of activity.

The full employment surplus rises through time if tax rates and expenditure programs remain unchanged. Because potential GNP grows, the volume of tax revenues yielded by a fully employed economy rises, when tax rates remain unchanged. Full employment revenues under existing tax laws are growing by about $6 billion a year. With unchanged discretionary expenditures, a budget line drawn on Chart 1 would shift upward each year by about 1 percent of potential GNP.

The full employment surplus is a measure of the restrictive or expansionary impact of a budget program on over-all demand. Generally speaking, one budget program is more expansionary than another if it has a smaller full employment surplus. One budget program might have the smaller

full employment surplus because it embodies greater Federal purchases of goods and services, in relation to potential GNP. By the same token, it leaves a smaller share of full employment output for private purchase. This means that full employment is easier to maintain under the budget program with the smaller surplus, because less private demand is required. It also means that inflation is more difficult to avoid, because there are fewer goods and services to meet private demand should it prove strong. Alternatively, one budget program might have a smaller full employment surplus than a second because it involves either lower tax rates or larger transfer payment programs. In that event, private after-tax incomes are larger at full employment for the first budget program than for the second. As a result, private demand would be stronger under the first program.

If the full employment surplus is too large, relative to the strength of private demand, economic activity falls short of potential. Correspondingly, the budget surplus actually realized falls short of the full employment surplus; indeed, a deficit may occur. If the full employment surplus is too small, total demand exceeds the capacity of the economy and causes inflation.

But whether a given full employment surplus is too large or too small depends on other government policies, as well as on economic circumstances affecting the general strength of private demand. If the full employment surplus is too large, more expansionary monetary and credit policies may strengthen private demand sufficiently to permit full employment to be realized. Changes in tax structure, stimulating demand while leaving the yield of the tax system unchanged, might have the same effect. Similarly, restrictive changes in other government policies can offset the expansionary influence of a low full employment surplus.

A mixture of policies involving (1) a budget program with a relatively high full employment surplus and (2) monetary ease and tax incentives stimulating enough private investment to maintain full employment has favorable consequences for economic growth.

THE IMPACT OF THE FEDERAL BUDGET ON TOTAL SPENDING*

Saul H. Hymans and J. Philip Wernette

One aspect of fiscal policy that is important both in the formulation of policy and in attempts to measure its effectiveness is that of determining the direction and magnitude of the initial impact of the Federal Government's budget on total spending. The budget is properly considered "expansionary" ("contractionary") when it leads to an increase (decrease) in total spending. An expansionary budget, of course, is not unambiguously a good thing. By all odds the federal budget was expansionary in fiscal 1968 when the economy was already at a point of high employment and in the midst of a worsening inflationary spiral. The tendency to impute normative significance to the state of the budget according only to whether it is contractionary or expansionary has led to great confusion, especially in the public press, and has undoubtedly frustrated attempts to improve the state of the policymaking art. In this paper, we are not concerned with whether a given state of the budget is "too expansionary" or "insufficiently expansionary." Indeed, such concepts have no objective meaning and competent analysts may well disagree on the appropriateness of the state of the budget, even in the case of complete agreement about "how the economy works."

The focus on total spending, or gross national expenditure, is a key starting point in the analysis of the impact of the budget. The path of economic activity is jointly determined by productive capacity, including physical capital and human effort, and the money demand for goods and services. The latter is the desired gross national expenditure. Because expenditure desires are frequently frustrated[1] by miscalculations, unfounded expectations, market imperfections, and so on, the desired gross national expenditure is not a measured quantity. The published measure which comes closest in concept is the gross national product (GNP) in current dollars which is the total of *actual* gross national expenditure on final goods and services.[2] In combination with the path of productive capacity—say, as measured by the economy's *potential output level*—the path of GNP determines the state of output, employment and inflation in the aggregate economy.

Our focus on GNP clearly leaves a number of important problems unanswered. In the concluding section of the paper, we shall have suggestions for further research.

There are several ways of calculating the influence of the budget on the gross national product, and thereby on the national economy. The three on which we shall focus are:

1. *The Surplus-Deficit methods:*
   A. A surplus is contractionary; a deficit is expansionary;

* From *Business Economics,* Vol. V (September 1970), pp. 29–34. Reprinted by permission of the publisher and the authors. Saul H. Hymans is Professor of Economics and Co-Director, Research Seminar in Quantitative Economics, University of Michigan. J. Philip Wernette is Professor of Business Administration, University of Michigan.

[1] The obvious example is the textbook case of the difference between desired and actual investment in inventories.

[2] The reader who is interested in a more detailed discussion of the distinctions between national product and national expenditure is referred to [4].

TABLE 1   METHODS OF MEASURING THE INITIAL IMPACT OF THE BUDGET ON THE GROSS NATIONAL EXPENDITURE (billions of current dollars)

Fiscal Year	Surplus-Deficit Methods (National Income Accounts Budget)		Full Employment Surplus Methods		Reduced Form Method (Expansionary +) (Contractionary −)
	A*	B	A*	B	
1962	− 2.1		+11.0		+ 8.7
1963	− 1.2	+ 0.9	+10.4	− 0.6	+ 5.2
1964	− 1.4	− 0.2	+ 9.9	− 0.5	+ 8.6
1965	+ 2.0	+ 3.4	+ 6.3	− 3.6	+ 4.4
1966	+ 0.9	− 1.1	− 1.0	− 7.3	+17.9
1967	− 7.2	− 8.1	− 8.3	− 7.3	+16.9
1968	−11.5	− 4.3	−12.6	− 4.3	+24.9
1969	+ 6.0	+17.5	+ 4.1	+16.7	− 8.1
1970 estimate	+ 3.6	− 2.4	+ 9.1	+ 5.0	+11.4
1971 projection	+ 1.6	− 2.0	+17.9	+ 8.8	+11.7

* Source of the figures in the A columns: Federal Reserve Bank of St. Louis, "Federal Budget Trends, 4th Quarter 1969" p. 2. The figures in the B columns are the first-differences of those in the A columns. The Reduced Form effects were calculated according to the method described in this article.

B. An "improvement" in the budget position (rising surplus or declining deficit) is contractionary; a "worsening" is expansionary.

2. *The full employment surplus[3] (FES) methods,* which appraise fiscal policy by what the state of the budget would be at full employment:

A. A calculated surplus at full employment is restraining; a calculated deficit is stimulative.

B. An "improvement" in the calculated budget position (rising surplus or declining deficit) is restraining; a "worsening" is stimulative.

3. *The Reduced Form[4] method,* which calculates the budget impact from changes in governmental expenditures and changes in the structure of tax rates, evaluated at current income levels, regardless of the surplus-deficit position and without regard to the induced changes in tax receipts that occur without any changes in the tax laws as the economy grows or contracts.

In Table 1 and the accompanying chart, the results of the five methods are presented for recent fiscal years. For this purpose we employ the national income accounts version of the federal budget, primarily in order to avoid the financial transactions which are contained in the new "unified budget" and which are more properly considered to be in the realm of monetary policy. In the case of the Surplus-Deficit and FES methods, the alleged directional impact of the budget on total spending is obtained by reversing the

[3] The best single reference on the full employment surplus is [1].

[4] In the literature on econometric models the term "reduced form" refers to an equation which displays the impact of an exogenous or "outside" change on a variable being explained in the model. In our context, we are interested in the impact of a change in the federal budget (the "outside" change) on GNP, and have therefore adopted this convenient terminology.

signs shown in Table 1, as has been done in the accompanying chart.

As the table and the chart indicate, there are many instances of similar results for all the methods, but the Reduced Form method clearly shows a larger expansionary impact than any of the other methods in all years except fiscal year 1969.

Possibly more significant are the deviations among the results of the methods in fiscal years 1970 and 1971. The Surplus-Deficit method A and both of the FES methods show the budget exerting a downward influence on total spending in both years. The Surplus-Deficit method B shows a small upward push in both years and the Reduced Form method indicates a substantial expansionary influence in both years. These differences are especially important and we shall return to them subsequently.

In what follows, we shall attempt to show that the objective impact of the budget is best measured by the Reduced Form method.

AN ESSENTIAL DISTINCTION

It is essential, in order to understand the impact of fiscal policy, to distinguish clearly between (1) the effect of the budget on the economy and (2) the effect of the economy on the budget.[5] The first effect includes changes in budget receipts and expenditures which result from deliberate discretionary action and tend to change

[5] The full employment surplus method was developed to make this distinction, but the proponents of the FES method insist on including induced changes in tax receipts in the calculation; see [3]. We shall argue that this yields a measure with few substantive uses.

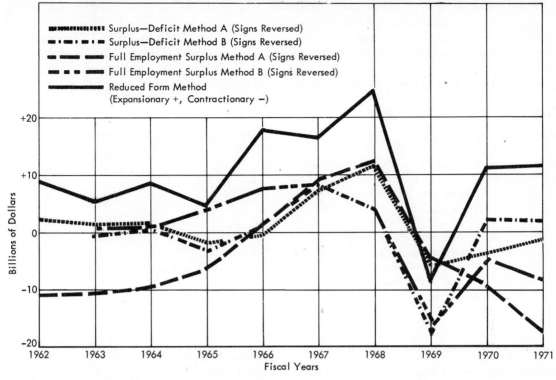

the gross national expenditure. The second effect includes changes in the receipts of the government which occur, without any change in the tax laws, when the gross national expenditure and national income change.

Financial flows of the first type may be described as "active," as "pushing" the gross national expenditure. The second type may be described as "passive" or "induced" changes. The former tend to move the gross national expenditure up or down. The latter merely *reduce* or *inhibit* the multiplier effects of any changes—public or private—in any of the streams of spending that make up the gross national expenditure. They have no *pushing* power. The induced changes in tax revenues are sometimes described as "automatic stabilizers," a term not wholly appropriate to their actual effects.

THE REDUCED FORM METHOD

We propose the following as an appropriate *single number* to be used to measure the impact of the federal budget on the economy:

> the current increase in government expenditures (net of induced changes in stabilizer elements such as unemployment insurance payments)

less

> the increase in tax revenues (measured at current income levels) resulting from any changes in the structure of the tax system, including both tax rates and tax base.

We shall motivate this suggestion, as well as compare it with the Surplus-Deficit and FES methods, by means of a simple illustrative model of the aggregate economy. The following notation will be used:

C: Consumer spending
Y: GNP
T: Tax revenues
G: Government spending (on goods and services)
r: The income-retention rate; i.e., one minus the tax rate
A: Autonomous spending
S: The government surplus

The model contains the following four equations.

$$C = b(Y - T) \qquad (1)$$
$$T = (1 - r)Y \qquad (2)$$
$$S = T - G \qquad (3)$$
$$Y = C + A + G \qquad (4)$$

Equation (1) states that consumer spending is proportional to after-tax income. Equations (2) and (3) define tax receipts and the government surplus respectively. Equation (4) defines GNP as the sum of consumer and government spending plus all other (autonomous) spending. The latter is taken to be determined outside of the system of four equations, i.e., independently of GNP. This is not a critical assumption for our purposes.

By substituting the first two equations into the fourth, we arrive at equation (5):

$$Y = rbY + A + G. \qquad (5)$$

If we solved equation (5) for the GNP (Y), we would have an equation explaining GNP by means of government and autonomous spending, the retention rate r, and the consumer spending parameter b (the marginal propensity to consume). Such an equation would be part of the reduced form of the original system. Our interest, however, is centered on changes in GNP, and we therefore calculate the total differential of (5) before solving. Thus:

$$dY = rbdY + bYdr + dA + dG.$$

Now solving for the change in GNP (dY):

$$dY = \frac{1}{1 - rb} dA + \frac{1}{1 - rb} dG$$
$$+ \frac{b}{1 - rb} (Ydr). \qquad (6)$$

The interpretation of equation (6)—the differential reduced form equation—is as follows. With b and r known,[6] the elements of fiscal policy which lead to a change in GNP are (1) a change in government spending (dG) and (2) the product of the change in the retention rate and the current level of GNP, which, in this simple model, is the equivalent of income. Now, by definition, the change in the retention rate is the negative of the change in the tax rate, say t. Thus

$$dr = -dt,$$

and equation (6) can be rewritten as

$$dY = \frac{1}{1 - rb} dA + \frac{1}{1 - rb} dG$$
$$+ \frac{b}{1 - rb} [(-dt)(Y)]. \qquad (7)$$

---

[6] The expression $\frac{1}{1 - rb}$ is, of course, recognized to be the Keynesian expenditure multiplier while $\frac{b}{1 - rb}$ is the so-called tax multiplier.

Now the product $[(-dt)(Y)]$ is the negative of the increase in tax revenues (measured at current income levels) resulting from a change in the structure of tax rates. The expression $[(dG) - (dt)(Y)]$ is precisely, for this model, the single number previously suggested as the appropriate measure of the impact of the budget on the economy.[7]

COMPARISON OF THE METHODS

The Surplus-Deficit method B amounts to looking at the change in the government surplus (dS). By substituting equation (2) into equation (3) we obtain

$$S = (1 - r)Y - G,$$

so that dS is given by

$$dS = dY - rdY - Ydr - dG. \qquad (8)$$

Substituting the expression for dY given by equation (7) into equation (8) and rearranging terms, we arrive at:

$$dS = (1 - r) \frac{1}{1 - rb} dA - \frac{r(1 - b)}{1 - rb} dG$$
$$+ \frac{1 - b}{1 - rb} [(dt)(Y)]. \qquad (9)$$

While the terms (dG) and $[(dt)(Y)]$ are contained in equation (9), so too is the term $dA/1 - rb$ which is the GNP change resulting from non-governmental spending increases. To include this term—as the Surplus-Deficit method clearly does—is tantamount to giving the federal budget credit for an income change which has nothing to do with changes either in federal spending or the structure of tax rates. The term $(1 - r) \frac{1}{1 - rb} dA$ is the *induced* revenue change resulting from the natural growth tendencies of the economy.[8] It is surely an important component of the federal surplus, but it contains absolutely no information about the impact of the budget on the economy. Indeed, the direction of causation is quite the reverse.

---

[7] One might argue, with good cause, that the expression $[(dG) - b(dt)Y]$ would be preferable. Such a "weighted" sum requires the use of a parameter, b, which would have to be estimated statistically. At this point we prefer to avoid such problems in order to arrive at an "objective" measure. This and other "weighting" problems will be referred to in the concluding section of the paper.

[8] This is related to the concept of "fiscal drag" which was popular in the mid-1960's.

TABLE 2   INITIAL IMPACT OF THE BUDGET ON THE GROSS NATIONAL PRODUCT IN FISCAL YEAR 1970

	Fiscal Years (National Income Accounts Budget)	
	1969 Billion	1970 Billion
Receipts..	$192.7	$201.8
Expenditures...	$186.7	$198.1
Surplus...	$ 6.0	$ 3.6
Calculation of Reduced Form Impact in fiscal year 1970:		
Increase in expenditures................................		+$ 11.4
Changes in tax receipts in FY 1970 due to tax rate changes:		
Personal tax and nontax payments..................	—$ 2.2	
Corporate profits tax accruals.......................	+ .2	
Indirect business tax and nontax accruals...........	0	
Contributions for social insurance...................	+ 2.0	
Net change...	0	0
Total Reduced Form Impact...........................		+$ 11.4

Source of the figures: U.S. Department of Commerce, Survey of Current Business, February 1970, p. 14. The calculation of the Reduced Form Impact is ours.

Finally, the FES method B is easily calculated from equation (8). If S^* represents the budget surplus at full employment, and Y^* represents full employment GNP, and dY^* is the change in full employment GNP, then

$$dS^* = (1 - r)(dY^*) - (dG) + (dt)Y^*. \quad (10)$$

Thus the change in the full employment surplus differs from the change in the actual surplus to the extent that either the level or the change in current income differ from those along the full employment path. In the FES method the revenue change resulting from a change in the tax structure is evaluated at the level of full employment income rather than the level of current income. As is clear from equation (7), the latter is the relevant evaluation. If the economy is over-inflated so that actual GNP (Y) exceeds full employment GNP (Y^*), FES method B will, other things equal, underestimate the restraining impact of a given increase in tax rates. Likewise, in a recessionary situation FES method B will overestimate the expansionary impact of a given reduction in tax rates.[9] Finally, of course, the FES method and the Surplus-Deficit method both

commit the error of including the revenue change induced by changes in income, and thus build in a factor which is possibly misleading and surely irrelevant to the directional impact of the budget.

THE BUDGET IMPACTS IN FISCAL 1970 AND 1971

In discussing his budget proposal for fiscal 1971, the President has expressed a desire to keep the budget tight in order to continue the fight against inflation, and has concluded that "Keeping the Federal budget in balance, as I have recommended, . . . will help achieve this result." [2, p. 8]. This statement refers, of course, to the actual budget. Okun and Teeters [3] have recently employed a modified FES technique to conclude that the fiscal 1971 budget actually imposes substantial restraint on the economy. In their words, "for the first half of calendar 1971, the fiscal program is markedly more restrictive than in 1969–70 and also considerably more restrictive than average historical experience."

Tables 2 and 3 present the impact calculation for fiscal 1970 and 1971 by means of the Reduced Form method.[10] In fiscal year 1970, the fact that, according to the January 1970 Budget Message,

---

[9] Note that FES method B indicates less restraint than the Surplus-Deficit method B in fiscal 1969 (Table 1) when the tax surcharge was put into effect. In fiscal 1965, when the economy was below full employment and the 1964 tax cut became effective, FES method B indicated a greater expansionary effect than the Surplus-Deficit method B by evaluating the revenue reduction at too high an income level.

[10] The calculation makes no allowance for induced changes in unemployment benefits. These are quite small, however, and should impart little bias to the calculation. Okun and Teeters [3] estimate that for fiscal 1971 the induced change in unemployment benefits will amount to only $0.3 billion.

TABLE 3   INITIAL IMPACT OF THE BUDGET ON THE GROSS NATIONAL PRODUCT IN FISCAL YEAR 1971

	Fiscal Years (National Income Accounts Budget)	
	1970 Billion	1971 Billion
Receipts...	$201.8	$205.4
Expenditures..	$198.1	$203.8
Surplus..	$ 3.6	$ 1.6
Calculation of Reduced Form Impact in fiscal year 1971:		
Increase in expenditures..............................		+$ 5.7
Changes in tax receipts in FY 1971 due to actual and proposed tax rate changes:		
Personal tax and nontax payments.................	−$ 8.9	
Corporate profits tax accruals......................	− .5	
Indirect business tax and nontax accruals..........	+ .7	
Contributions for social insurance.................	+ 2.6	
Net change...	−$ 6.0	+$ 6.0*
Total Reduced Form Impact...........................		+$ 11.7

*Sign reversed.
Source of the figures: U.S. Department of Commerce, Survey of Current Business, February 1970, p. 14. The calculation of the Reduced Form Impact is ours.

a surplus was projected did not accurately indicate the impact of the budget. As Table 2 indicates, the budget was in fact expansionary.

The budget proposal for fiscal year 1971 (Table 3) shows receipts up $3.6 billion, despite the end of the income tax surcharge and other tax changes. Trend revenue growth (an induced change) accounts for the gain, but it is merely a response to the rise in the economy; it doesn't push it down. The Reduced Form method shows that the budget will be substantially expansionary, though clearly by a good deal less than was true of fiscal years 1966–68 (see Table 1).

The mere fact that the budget is expansionary is not enough information on which to base any normative conclusion about the appropriateness of fiscal policy. Given the weakness of the economy in fiscal 1970, it is not obvious that the expansionary budget proposed for fiscal 1971 is at all inappropriate. The net result of private demand and budget stimulus in fiscal 1971 may well be a sufficiently mild increase in total demand as to be wholly consistent with unwinding the inflationary pressures in the economy.

CONCLUSIONS AND CONCERNS

In this paper we have used a simple illustrative model to distinguish between several methods for measuring the federal budget's impact on the economy. We conclude that neither the actual surplus position nor the full employment surplus position adequately measures this impact. Indeed,

these methods are misleading indicators of the effect of the budget on the economy. The Reduced Form method is theoretically attractive and avoids the pitfalls of the other two methods in common use. In addition, the calculations involved in the Reduced Form method are relatively easy to make.

The analysis of this paper, however, is far from complete. The analysis relates only to the initial impact of the budget and does not take account of the subsequent multiple effect of fiscal changes, which, over a period of time, may rise to two or three times the original change. The question as to whether a $1 billion increase in defense purchases and a $1 billion rise in transfer payments and a $1 billion tax cut are all equally stimulative has not been treated at all. In theory they are not, and a sum with different weights for different categories of expenditure and revenue change would be more appropriate.

Nor does the analysis take account of the influence of surpluses or deficits on the capital markets and Federal Reserve policy.

Furthermore, the analysis deals with *mechanical* links between the budget and the economy, not with *psychological* ones. If our people—consumers and businessmen—generally and genuinely believe that current fiscal policy is anti-inflationary (because of projected budget surpluses), the resultant break in the supposed inflationary psychology could be an effective element in slowing the inflationary spiral *despite an expansionary budget.*

Other aspects of budget impact that are not considered here are lags in both initial impact and subsequent reactions. Econometric studies indicate that the full impact of a change in government outlays is not felt at once. Similarly, the complete impact of a change in tax rates is delayed.

If, however, changes in either expenditures or tax rates are *generally anticipated,* some of the impact may occur *before* the passage of the legislation or its effective date—a *negative* lag. If so, the subsequent impact is reduced. For example, the personal saving rate rose and consumer expenditures were restrained *before* the income tax surcharge was enacted in 1968; its subsequent impact was smaller than expected.

The lags are so great, so little understood—and possibly even are changing gradually as a result of wider study and awareness—that they raise the question of the usefulness of counter-cyclical fiscal actions, especially in the case of modest departures from the potential or full employment path. Actions to "fine tune" the economy might turn out to be destabilizing or even cycle-intensifying.

The Reduced Form method does not relate the fiscal impact to any level of resource utilization or potential output, nor does it attempt to distribute the effects of fiscal actions between output and the price level.

All of these shortcomings are acknowledged and they deserve careful analysis. A necessary first step, however, is to put forth a correct understanding of the initial impact of budget actions on total spending. And that has been the sole aim of this paper.

REFERENCES

1. *The Annual Report of the Council of Economic Advisers,* January 1962, pp. 77–81.
2. *Economic Report of the President,* February 1970.
3. Okun, A. M. and Teeters, N. H. "The Full Employment Surplus Revisited," paper prepared for the first Conference of the Brookings Panel on Economic Activity, April 1970.
4. Wernette, J. P. "Gross National Product Versus Gross National Expenditure," *Business Economics,* Summer 1968.

THE EFFECTIVENESS OF PUBLIC WORKS AS A STABILIZATION DEVICE

Ronald L. Teigen

The advent of the Keynesian revolution during the depression of the 1930s rekindled interest in public works expenditures as a recession remedy. The logic seemed clear: if the cure involved the injection of spending power by government, a logical channel for such injection appeared to be new public works projects, leading to additions to the stock of useful social capital at the same time that full employment was regained. But the experience of the past 30 years and four recessions has shown that the solution to the business cycle problem is not that obvious.

Of course, there is no question about the desirability of stabilization, because of the economic waste resulting from unemployed resources in recessions, and from capricious income redistribution and other distortions during inflations. The object of this paper is to evaluate public works as a stabilization tool in terms of the requirements of an ideally efficient stabilization program. There are at least three such economic criteria which should be satisfied in order to consider any stabi-

lization program to be "ideally efficient": (1) the effects on income and employment must be felt with a minimal time lag; (2) the stabilization program must be efficient in the sense that marginal social cost must equal marginal social benefit; (3) the stabilization program must be of adequate size to meet countercyclical needs. The relative usefulness of public works projects as a stabilization device will be evaluated in terms of each of these criteria, and some other considerations will also be discussed.

TIME LAGS

First, an ideal program would be one which could be put into effect with a minimal delay and which would make itself felt (in terms of changes in real variables such as employment and output) in the shortest possible time. This requirement is related to several aspects of public works programs.

Such programs require a great deal of planning, advance preparation, and, often, intergovernmental coordination, due to their size, complexity, and public nature. In principle, much of the required planning and coordination could be accomplished in advance; in fact, the federal government maintains a "shelf" of public works projects for several years ahead. This does not necessarily mean, however, that it is possible to step up spending very rapidly. For example, in studying the 1957–58 recession experience, Ando and Brown found that an attempt by the federal government to accelerate expenditures on water resource projects which were already under construction had essentially no effect in stimulating income, at least within the time horizon necessary for effective countercyclical stabilization. While a decision was made in March 1958 to accelerate such construction wherever possible for countercyclical reasons, actual obligations of the Corps of Engineers and the Bureau of Reclamation (the agencies which undertake most of such work) for the fiscal year 1958 were only $30 million greater than the January 1958 estimate of such obligations.[1] It is noteworthy that approximately three fifths of direct federal construction consists of water resources projects.[2] In an earlier study, Maisel found a delay of approximately one year between the authorization of certain federal public works projects and the awarding of contracts.[3]

It is difficult to accelerate projects which are under construction, or which have been approved for construction, but much longer time lags are involved in getting new projects started because of the several additional steps involved. Preliminary studies must be made to assure that the project is feasible and is needed, and these studies can take as much as two to five years to complete. Then congressional authorization is required, after which work is begun on the design of the project. This in itself may require a great deal of time, depending on the size and complexity of the project. Only then can the contract-award procedure be initiated, and this process also involves lags due to mandatory waiting periods before the opening of bids, coordination between

various levels of governments, and so on.[4] Thus the very nature of these projects inevitably results in a period of at least several months, and more probably years, between initiation of the project and the beginning of construction, even at the federal level.

Effective use could be made of these projects if the cyclical swings could be forecast far enough in advance so that planning and other administrative aspects could be finished by the time new spending was needed to stimulate the economy. Unfortunately, forecasting techniques, while improving, are not refined to this degree. At present, forecasts are most useful for the immediate future; beyond one or two quarters the probability of error is substantial. Therefore spending which can be started and stopped very rapidly, and thus be guided by presently available forecasting procedures, is most useful for countercyclical purposes. Public construction is slow to start and difficult to stop and therefore is unsuitable from this standpoint.

The existence of lags in the flow of income heightens the need for speed of program reaction to economic stimuli, especially in view of the short inventory-type cycles which have been characteristic of the postwar period. Even after the public works program is operating, lags between income receipt, expenditure, inventory depletion, and increased industrial activity will prevent its effects from being felt for several months.[5] These lags are common to all stabilization programs, but if they are combined with the delays mentioned above, the effect might not be felt until well after the upswing had begun, or even considerably later; the result would be increased inflationary pressure, and reinforcement rather than damping of the cycle.

EFFICIENCY

A second requirement of an ideal stabilization program is that it be efficient; that is, that marginal social cost equal marginal social benefit. It is often argued that the marginal cost of unem-

[1] Albert Ando and E. Cary Brown, "Lags in Fiscal Policy," Part II of Albert Ando, E. Cary Brown, Robert M. Solow, and John Kareken, "Lags in Fiscal and Monetary Policy," in *Stabilization Policies: A Series of Research Studies Prepared for the Commission on Money and Credit* (Englewood Cliffs, N.J.: Prentice-Hall, Inc., 1963), p. 147.

[2] Ibid., p. 145.

[3] Sherman J. Maisel, "Timing and Flexibility of a Public Works Program," *Review of Economics and Statistics,* Vol. XXXI (May 1949), p. 149.

[4] Ando and Brown, "Lags in Fiscal Policy," pp. 146–47.

[5] Gardner Ackley, "The Multiplier Time Period," *American Economic Review,* Vol. XLI (June 1951), pp. 350–68. See also Lloyd A. Metzler, "Three Lags in the Circular Flow of Income," *Income, Employment, and Public Policy: Essays in Honor of Alvin H. Hansen* (New York: W. W. Norton & Co., Inc., 1948), pp. 11–32. For some quantitative estimates of the length of these lags, see Ando and Brown, "Lags in Fiscal Policy."

ployed resources is zero, and therefore public works projects during depressions are costless. In reality, however, this is rarely if ever true; for example, public works projects may require substantial amounts of labor relocation. Therefore it is a *non sequitur* to argue that public works are better than other public programs which could have equivalent stabilization impact, since the resulting distortions in the use of resources may more than offset the social benefit from the new capital stock which results from the project. An alternative program which increases demand through transfers or tax cuts could have an equivalent impact on employment and income, and could make large-scale movements of resources unnecessary.

The problem of distortions with respect to resource use may be particularly serious for the private construction industry and its suppliers if a serious effort is made to use public works countercyclically. The residential construction industry, particularly, often has experienced high levels of activity when the remainder of the economy has been depressed. Thus public spending may compete for scarce resources still fully employed by the private sector, while other resources released by declining private activity may be left unemployed. In general, to meet the efficiency test the public works program would have to hire those resources being released by the private sector and avoid those which are fully employed. This implies that such programs should use homogeneous, transferable resources. Unfortunately, different construction categories use widely differing and rather specialized resources. It is unlikely that a typical public works program could be tailored to a specific unemployment situation so as to use the unemployed resources and avoid these distortions, while merely taking a prepackaged program off the shelf is likely to result in even more serious distortions.

While the above discussion argues against the use of public works programs purely for countercyclical reasons, it does not follow on efficiency grounds that the level of public expenditure should be determined without reference to the level of economic activity. It is often argued that government expenditure should be decided by "social welfare considerations," and that the tax rate should be adjusted in the appropriate way to achieve full employment. The argument as stated is sound, but it typically leads to the false inference that, for a given institutional setting, there is a fixed optimal level of public expenditure. Samuelson has shown, however, that if choices between public and private expenditures

are made, as they should be, by comparing the relationships between social benefit and social cost for each alternative, then public expenditure should expand during periods of unemployment, simply because the relationships between benefits and costs change over the cycle for both public and private expenditure.[6] For example, in a downswing business spending on private investment is reduced because the present discounted value of the stream of anticipated net returns from new investment falls relative to cost, and resources become unemployed. While the social cost of utilizing these resources in the public sector is generally not zero, this cost tends to fall relative to benefits when unemployment arises. As Samuelson states,

> Public services at all times must be regarded as competing with each other for the use of our limited resources and they must be thought of as competing with all other uses as well—with current desires for private consumption goods, with current private capital-formation programs for resource use, etc. . . . All decisions must be made in terms of alternatives: when these change, the optimal decision must change.[7]

ADEQUACY OF SIZE

A third criterion for the evaluation of public works as a countercyclical policy tool is that the program must be of adequate size for the cyclical problem. Total spending must be great enough to restore full employment (given the level of use of other anticyclical tools); at the same time, individual projects must be of a size appropriate to the timing needs of the cycle. That is, if the downswing is short, projects must be small enough or divisible enough to be begun rapidly and ended easily. In practice, it has proven difficult to put together a program that is large enough in the aggregate to produce a major impact on GNP while at the same time being composed of individual projects that are sufficiently small and flexible to be capable of being activated rapidly. In terms of impact on income, the attempt noted above to increase the rate of expenditure on federal water resource projects in 1958 must have had only a negligible effect on current income. In 1954, Newcomb estimated that total government spending (federal, state, and local) on public works could expand at an

---

[6] Paul A. Samuelson, "Principles and Rules in Modern Fiscal Policy: A Neo-classical Reformulation," in *Money, Trade, and Economic Growth: Essays in Honor of John Henry Williams* (New York: Macmillan Co., 1951), pp. 157–76.

[7] Ibid., p. 158.

annual rate of only about $4 billion in the first year.[8] Newcomb's data, though out of date, lend some support to the conclusion that public works can play only a very limited role in combating the short cycles that have been typical of most of the period since World War II.

PUBLIC WORKS AS AN ANTI-INFLATION TOOL

In addition to being a rather unsatisfactory device for countering recessions, public works policy does not score well as an anti-inflationary tool. There may be some possibilities for postponing projects already planned but not undertaken as a means of reducing inflationary pressure. But if public works spending was accelerated to deal with the previous recession, projects which were initiated during that earlier phase may carry over into the inflationary upswing due to the planning, administrative, and construction lags; and such projects are difficult to stop before completion. As noted, however, this problem is less serious the smaller and more flexible are the projects involved.

PERIOD OF PROLONGED UNEMPLOYMENT

Up to now, we have been considering the usefulness of public works expenditures as a means of dealing with mild cyclical fluctuations when the economy is generally operating in the neighborhood of full employment. The situation is quite different in periods when unemployment is chronic and GNP is many billions of dollars below the productive capacity of the economy. Such was the case during the Great Depression of the 1930s and—although on a much smaller scale—from 1958 to 1964 when unemployment was persistently in excess of 5½ percent and often considerably greater than that and the "gap" between actual GNP and productive capacity ranged between $30 billion and $50 billion most of the time. Under such circumstances, the danger that demand will become excessive and threaten to generate inflation within a reasonable period of time is minimal, and public works expenditures, even though they are somewhat slow in producing their full effects, may be able to make a useful contribution to the restoration of full employment. Policies that act more quickly might be desirable, but if there are political or

[8] Robinson Newcomb, "Public Works and Economic Stabilization," in *Problems in Anti-Recession Policy,* a Supplementary Paper of the Committee for Economic Development (New York: September, 1954), p. 132.

other difficulties in adopting such policies, public works programs may be the best available alternative.

REGIONAL ASPECTS

When there are serious pockets of distress and unemployment in particular regions, as has been the case in the last few years, public works expenditures may be an especially useful component of an overall program to reduce unemployment, because the expenditures can be channeled directly into communities where unemployment is especially heavy. In this respect they are superior to tax reduction which is more general in its impact and less capable of being aimed deliberately at the problems of particular regions. Thus, while public works expenditures are of very limited usefulness in ironing out mild and relatively short-lived cyclical fluctuations, there are some situations in which they may be of considerable value in dealing with problems of serious and chronic unemployment, especially when the unemployment is somewhat concentrated in particular localities.

EXPENDITURES VERSUS TAXES: MULTIPLIER EFFECTS

In concluding, perhaps we should draw attention to a matter to which importance has sometimes been attached: that fact that the multiplier applicable to changes in government expenditures on goods and services is likely to be somewhat larger than that applicable to changes in tax collections. This point can be illustrated by the following rather simple model of a close economy:

$$\Delta Y = \Delta C + \Delta I + \Delta G \qquad (1)$$
$$\Delta C = c\Delta Y_d \qquad (2)$$
$$\Delta Y_d = \Delta Y - \Delta T \qquad (3)$$
$$\Delta T = t\Delta Y + \Delta T_o \qquad (4)$$

Here ΔY = the change in GNP, ΔC = the change in consumption, ΔI = the change in private investment, ΔG = the change in government expenditures on goods and services, ΔY_d = the change in disposable (after-tax) income, ΔT = the change in total tax collections, and ΔT_o = the change in that portion of tax collections that can be altered by governmental fiscal policy measures.

Substituting from equations (2), (3), and (4) into equation (1), the following result is rather easily obtained:

$$\Delta Y = c\Delta Y - ct\Delta Y - c\Delta T_o + \Delta I + \Delta G.$$

or

$$\Delta Y(1 - c + ct) = -c\Delta T_o + \Delta I + \Delta G$$

or

$$\Delta Y = \frac{1}{1 - c(1 - t)} [-c\Delta T_o + \Delta I + \Delta G].$$

Setting $\Delta I = 0$ (since no allowance is being made for a change in private investment) and $\Delta T_o = 0$, the following multiplier for government expenditures is obtained:

$$\frac{\Delta Y}{\Delta G} = \frac{1}{1 - c(1 - t)}.$$

Alternatively, setting $\Delta I = 0$ and $\Delta G = 0$, the following multiplier for a change in tax collections is derived:

$$\frac{\Delta Y}{\Delta T} = \frac{-c}{1 - c(1 - t)}.$$

The tax multiplier is negative (i.e., a reduction in taxes will increase income); moreover, since the marginal propensity to consume, c, can be taken to be less than unity, the tax multiplier is smaller in absolute value than the government expenditures multiplier.

To illustrate, suppose that the marginal propensity to consume out of disposable income is 80 percent (i.e., $c = .8$) and tax collections change by 37.5 percent of any change in GNP (i.e., $t = .375$). The reader can easily calculate that in this case the government expenditures multiplier ($\Delta Y/\Delta G$) will be 2, while the tax multiplier ($\Delta Y/\Delta T_o$) will be -1.6.[9]

---

[9] Incidentally, while it is tempting to conclude on the basis of casual reasoning that a change in government spending matched by an equivalent change in tax collections will have no net effect on equilibrium income, a comparison of the above government expenditure and tax multipliers will show that this is not the case. In the model employed above, an increase in spending of ΔG will raise equilibrium income by the multiplier $1/[1 - c(1 - t)]$. The deflationary effect of an increase in taxes of ΔT_o is given by the multiplier $-c/[1 - c(1 - t)]$. If $\Delta G = \Delta T_o$, so that the change in spending is matched initially by an equivalent change in tax collections, the net effect on equilibrium income is given by the sum of the two multipliers:

$$\frac{\Delta Y}{\Delta G} + \frac{\Delta Y}{\Delta T_o} = \frac{1}{1 - c(1 - t)} - \frac{c}{1 - c(1 - t)}$$

$$= \frac{1 - c}{1 - c(1 - t)}.$$

Since the terms c and $c(1 - t)$ are fractions with values between zero and unity, the expression

The reason for this difference in the multipliers is simple: by definition, the entire increase in government expenditures represents increased aggregate demand for goods and services, whereas a portion of a tax cut will be saved and only the portion spent on consumption will represent an increase in aggregate demand.

While the model used above is somewhat oversimplified, the principle illustrated is almost certainly correct. Its implication is that a given increase in the budget deficit will have a larger effect on GNP if the deficit is produced by increasing expenditures than if it is generated by cutting taxes. Or, alternatively, if GNP needs to be raised by a given amount, the "cost" in terms of budget deficit will be less if expenditures are increased than if taxes are cut. To put it simply, expenditure increases produce a "bigger bang per buck" (of deficit) than do tax cuts.[10]

If there are political constraints on the size of the deficit that is acceptable—as has sometimes been the case in recent years—the fact that expenditure increases have greater potency per dollar of deficit than tax cuts may possibly be a matter of some importance. But from the standpoint of economic analysis, the size of the deficit

---

$(1 - c)/[1 - c(1 - t)]$ is positive but smaller than unity in value. This means that a "balanced budget" increase in government spending has a net expansionary effect on income. In the numerical example used above (when $c = .8$ and $t = .375$), this multiplier has a value of 0.4, so that every $1 billion of new spending, matched initially by increased tax collections of $1 billion, will increase equilibrium income by $400 million. The multiplier $(1 - c)/[1 - c(1 - t)]$ is called the "balanced budget multiplier" and its value depends on the size of the marginal propensity to consume out of disposable income and the marginal tax rate. Its maximum value occurs when $t = 0$ (i.e., when there are no taxes related to income); in that case, its value is unity, and balanced budget spending increases result in dollar-for-dollar income increases.

[10] It should be noted that the rise in income produced by either an increase in expenditures or a reduction in taxes produces a "feedback" effect on tax revenues. Thus, in either case the deficit is ultimately cut back somewhat from the level initially reached immediately after expenditures were increased or taxes cut. In the above case, the "feedback" effect is 37.5 percent of the rise in GNP. Thus, if expenditures are increased by $1 billion, GNP rises by $2 billion (multiplier of 2). Tax receipts rise by $750 million ($2 billion $\times$ .375), and the net increment to the deficit after all adjustments are completed is $250 million. On the other hand, if taxes are cut by $1 billion, GNP rises by $1.6 billion (multiplier of -1.6), (induced) tax receipts rise by $600 million ($1.6 billion $\times$ .375), and the net increment to the deficit is $400 million.

is a matter of very little significance and should not govern the decision. The important economic questions are: (1) whether the available resources can more usefully be employed in the public sector through expenditure increases or in the private sector through tax reduction, and (2) the practical issues of timing and flexibility that were discussed earlier in this paper.

THE EFFECTS OF TAX REDUCTION ON OUTPUT AND EMPLOYMENT*

Council of Economic Advisers

Tax reduction will directly increase the disposable income and purchasing power of consumers and business, strengthen incentives and expectations, and raise the net returns on new capital investment. This will lead to initial increases in private consumption and investment expenditures. These increases in spending will set off a cumulative expansion, generating further increases in consumption and investment spending and a general rise in production, income, and employment. This process is discussed in some detail below.

INITIAL EFFECTS: CONSUMPTION

Effects on Disposable Income. The proposed reduction in personal income tax rates will directly add to the disposable income of households. In addition, the reduction in corporate tax rates will increase the after-tax profits of corporations as a result of which corporations may be expected to increase their dividend payments. The initial direct effect on the disposable income of households resulting from the entire program of tax reductions should be approximately $8½ billion, at current levels of income.

Consumer Response to Increase in Disposable Income. The ratio of total consumption expenditures to total personal disposable income has in each recent calendar year fallen within the range of 92 to 94 percent. Although there are lags and irregularities from quarter to quarter or even year to year, the change in personal consumption expenditures has in the past, after a few quarters, averaged roughly 93 percent of any change in personal disposable income. On this basis, the initial addition to consumer expenditures asso-

ciated with tax reductions would be on the order of $8 billion, although all would not be spent at once.

Additions to after-tax incomes resulting from tax reduction are likely to be spent in the same way as other additions to income. The largest part of the proposed tax reduction will be reflected in reduced withholding of taxes from wages and salaries, and therefore in larger wage and salary checks; thus, it will be indistinguishable from additional income arising from wage or salary increases, greater employment, or longer hours of work. Similarly, part of the reduced corporate taxes will be passed along to stockholders in increased dividend checks. Stockholders will not be able to identify the source of their additional dividends. Tax reduction dollars carry no identifying label, and there is no reason to expect recipients to treat them differently from other dollars.

Recent experience with tax reduction demonstrates clearly that additions to disposable income from this source are spent as completely as any other additions. Taxes were reduced by about $4.7 billion on May 1, 1948, retroactive to January 1, with resulting large refunds in mid-1949. Again taxes were cut, net, by about $6 billion, effective January 1, 1954, with further cuts later that year. Table 1 shows that the percentage of disposable income spent by consumers remained within the normal range of quarterly fluctuation during the periods following the enactment of each of these tax reductions.

It is sometimes suggested that tax reductions which add only a few dollars to the weekly pay check of the typical worker would do little good even if the money was spent, since the amounts involved would not be large enough to permit major expenditures—say on washing machines or automobiles. Instead, the money would be "frittered away" on minor expenditures and would do little good for the economy. But all purchases lead to production which generates in-

* From *The Annual Report of the Council of Economic Advisers,* January 1963, pp. 45–51. Reprinted by permission of the Council of Economic Advisers.

TABLE 1 PERSONAL CONSUMPTION EXPENDITURES AS PERCENT OF DISPOSABLE PERSONAL INCOME DURING TWO POSTWAR PERIODS OF TAX REDUCTION

1948–49		1953–55	
Quarter	Percent	Quarter	Percent
1948: I	97.3	1953: IV	91.5
II	94.0	1954: I	91.8
III	92.6	II	92.8
IV	93.2	III	93.0
1949: I	93.9	IV	93.2
II	95.2	1955: I	94.5
III	95.7	II	93.5

Source: Department of Commerce.
Note.—Based on seasonally adjusted data.

come and provides employment. Therefore, the purpose of tax reduction is achieved when the proceeds are spent on any kind of goods or services.

Actually, of course, tax reduction which expands take-home pay even by a relatively small amount each week or month may induce recipients to purchase durable goods or houses of higher quality, since the increased income would permit them to handle larger monthly installment payments. It may even induce a rearrangement of expenditure patterns and thus bring about purchases of durable goods that would not otherwise be made.

INITIAL EFFECTS: INVESTMENT

Investment is a more volatile element than consumption in national expenditure. The timing and magnitude of its response to tax changes is less predictable. But a cut in tax rates on business income will stimulate spending on new plants and new machinery in two ways. First, it will strengthen investment incentives by increasing the after-tax profits that businessmen can expect to earn on new productive facilities. Second, it will add to the supply of internal funds, a large part of which is normally reinvested in the business.

Since the largest part of business investment is made by corporations, the proposed cuts in the corporate income tax are especially significant. But investments of unincorporated businesses will also be encouraged by cuts in personal income tax rates, especially in the upper brackets.

Two important reforms affecting the taxation of business income designed to stimulate investment in plant and equipment were put into effect during 1962: the new depreciation guidelines and the investment tax credit.

Evidence to date clearly indicates that these measures are already stimulating some capital spending that would not otherwise have taken place. The impact of the 1962 actions and the 1963 proposals to reduce taxes on business will, of course, differ from company to company and industry to industry, depending in part on the adequacy of their internal funds and their levels of capacity utilization. Though the speed of response may vary, industry after industry will begin to feel pressure on its capital facilities and funds as markets for its products are expanded by the 1963 tax program.

Furthermore, there are many individual companies for which the supply of internal funds is a constraint on investment, and many others that do not have excess capacity. Moreover, it is estimated that some 70 percent of the investment in plant and equipment is for modernization and replacement rather than expansion, that is, it is designed to produce new or better products, or to reduce production costs rather than primarily to expand productive capacity. For this large segment of capital spending, the stronger inducement to invest provided by the business tax changes already adopted and those now proposed will translate much more readily into actual purchases of plant and equipment.

As production expands and existing capacity is more fully utilized, the depreciation guidelines and the investment tax credit and the new business tax reductions will provide an even stronger stimulus to investment.

CUMULATIVE EXPANSION: THE CONSUMPTION MULTIPLIER

Tax reduction will start a process of cumulative expansion throughout the economy. If the economy is already undergoing slow expansion, this cumulative process will be superimposed upon it. The initial increases in spending will stimulate production and employment, generating additional incomes. The details and timing of this process will vary from industry to industry. The first impact may be to draw down inventories rather than to expand production. But as inventories are depleted, retailers will quickly expand orders. As manufacturers' sales rise in response and their own inventories of finished goods decline, they will activate idle production lines, hire additional workers, place orders for materials and components. Thus the expansion will spread to other industries, leading to further expansion of production, employment, and orders.

Expanded sales mean increased profits. Increased employment means greater wage and salary income. Each additional dollar's worth of gross production necessarily generates a dollar of additional gross income.

But expansion does not proceed without limit. A considerable fraction of the value of gross production is shared with governments or becomes part of corporate retained earnings and does not become part of consumers' after-tax income. Some of the increase goes to pay additional excise and other indirect business taxes. Typically, when GNP is rising toward potential, corporate profits increase by about one-fourth of the rise in GNP. But a substantial part of this increase in profits is absorbed by Federal and State corporate income taxes, and another part is ordinarily retained by the corporations. Only the remainder is passed on to the households in dividend payments. Part of the additional wage and salary incomes associated with added production is absorbed by higher social security contributions. At the same time, increased employment means a drop in payments for unemployment insurance benefits.

When all of these "leakages" are taken into account, a little less than two-thirds of an additional dollar of GNP finds its way into the before-tax incomes of consumers in the form of wages, dividends, and other incomes. Part is absorbed by personal taxes, Federal, State, and local. The increase in personal disposable income is 50 to 55 percent. Of this amount a small fraction—about 7 percent—is set aside in personal saving, and the remainder—about 93 percent—is spent on consumption, as indicated earlier. Thus, out of each additional dollar of GNP, initially generated by the tax cut, roughly half ends up as added consumption expenditure. But the process does not stop here.

The additional expenditure on consumption that is brought about by the rise in GNP generates, in its turn, further production, which generates additional incomes and consumption, and so on, in a continuous sequence of expansion which economists call the "multiplier process." The "multiplier" applicable to the initial increase in spending resulting from tax reduction, with account taken of the various leakages discussed above, works out to roughly 2. If we apply this multiplier only to the initial increase in consumption (about $8 billion), the total ultimate effect will be an increase in annual consumption—and in production (and GNP)—of roughly $16 billion. Lags in the process of expansion will spread

this increase in GNP over time, but studies of the relationships between changes in disposable income, consumption, and production of consumer goods suggest that at least half of the total stimulus of an initial increase in disposable income is realized within 6 months of that increase.

CUMULATIVE EXPANSION: THE INVESTMENT RESPONSE

Tax reduction will also have important cumulative indirect effects on investment in inventories and in fixed productive facilities. These effects are much more difficult to predict than the induced effects on consumption.

Inventory Investment. The stocks of goods that businessmen wish to hold depend upon current and expected rates of sales and production and the volume of new and unfilled orders, as well as on price expectations and other factors. An expansion of aggregate demand can be expected to raise business inventory targets. Production for inventory will generate further increases in demand and income over and above the multiplier effects discussed above, and will in turn induce further increases in consumption spending.

Inventory investment is volatile, and induced inventory accumulation can add significantly to the expansionary effects of tax reduction within a few months. At the same time, it should be recognized that inventory investment is exceedingly difficult to forecast. As the increase in production and sales tapers off, stocks and the rate of inventory investment will be correspondingly adjusted.

Business Investment in Plant and Equipment. A tax reduction large enough to move the economy toward full employment will also stimulate business investment in plant and equipment. General economic expansion will reinforce the initial stimulus to investment of cuts in business taxes. In the first place, narrowing the gap between actual and potential output—now estimated at $30–40 billion—will increase the utilization of existing plant and equipment. As excess capacity declines, more and more businesses will feel increasing pressure to expand capacity. At the same time, increases in the volume of sales and in productivity will raise corporate profits—in absolute terms, relative to GNP, and as a rate of return on investment. Internal funds available for investment will rise, while at the same time higher rates of return on existing capital will cause businessmen to raise their estimates of returns on new investment. When investment incentives are strengthened by rising demand, internal funds are more consistently translated into increased investment than when markets are slack.

Residential Construction. The demand for housing depends on growth in the number of families, on the existing stock of houses, and on the cost and availability of mortgage credit. But housing demand also responds, to some extent, to changes in disposable income. Thus, tax reduction will have some direct effect on residential construction. And as production, employment, and income generally expand, the demand for new homes can be expected to increase further. This increase will, in turn, reinforce the other expansionary effects of tax reduction.

STATE AND LOCAL GOVERNMENT EXPENDITURES

State and local government units have found it difficult to finance the needed expansion of their activities. Given the present importance of income and sales taxes in State and local tax systems, government revenues at the State and local level expand automatically as GNP rises. The additional State-local revenues generated by economic expansion will assist these governments to meet their pressing needs. Moreover, since Federal tax liabilities are deductible under many State income tax laws, reduction in Federal tax rates will automatically generate some further addition to State-local tax revenues. Finally, a reduction in Federal taxes will enlarge the tax base available to State and local government units and may make it easier for them to raise rates or impose new taxes.

Undoubtedly, some of the added State-local tax revenues will be used either to retire existing debt or to reduce current borrowing rather than to increase expenditures. Whether the net result will be expansionary will depend upon whether the proportion of additional tax revenues spent on goods and services by State and local government units is greater or smaller than the proportion which would have been spent by the taxpayers from whom they collect the additional taxes. But whether or not the response of State and local government units is such as to strengthen the aggregate impact of Federal tax reduction on income and employment, the Federal tax program will ease, to some extent, the problems of these units in obtaining revenues needed to finance urgent public activities, such as education, transportation facilities, and urban development.

SUMMARY OF EFFECTS ON GNP

Tax reductions for consumers will have initial direct effects on the demand for goods and services, as consumers raise their spending level to reflect their higher after-tax incomes. Corporate tax reductions and the lower tax rates applicable to the highest personal income brackets will stimulate investment directly, through raising the rate of return on new investments and providing additional funds for their financing.

These direct or initial effects on spending would occur even if total output, employment, and incomes remained unchanged. But the increased spending cannot fail to increase total output, employment, and incomes. And as activity responds to the initially increased level of spending, cumulative impacts begin to develop in which the several elements interact to carry the expansion far beyond its initial point.

The higher incomes which consumers receive from the added production of both consumer and capital goods will lead to a further step-up in the rate of spending, creating further increases in incomes and spending. The same expansion process raises rates of capacity utilization, thereby interacting with the initial impact of tax reduction on business incomes to make investment both for modernization and expansion more profitable. This in turn generates higher consumer incomes and more spending, helping to provide the added demand which justifies the higher investment.

If there were no investment stimulus—either initially, or as a result of the cumulative process of expansion—we could expect that GNP would ultimately expand by about $16 billion. If the result were no more than this, the tax reduction would still be abundantly rewarding in terms of greater production, employment, purchasing power, and profits. What will really be given up to produce added output will be only unwanted idleness of workers (whose families have reduced neither their needs nor aspirations) and incomplete utilization of plant and machinery (which have continued to depreciate).

But the pay-off is much more than this purely consumption impact. There is also an investment impact, and each extra dollar of investment that is stimulated should bring roughly another dollar of added consumption and encourage still further investment.

No one can pretend to estimate with precision

the ultimate impact of a program so far-reaching as that which the President will propose: it would come into operation in stages extending from July 1, 1963 to January 1, 1965, and its effects would cumulate and spread into 1966 and beyond.

Our study of the program, and our tentative projections based upon it do, however, convince us that the program measures up to the challenge that the 1960s present to our economy; that it will surely set us on a path toward our interim employment target; and that it will lay the foundation for more rapid long-run growth.

MEASURING THE IMPACT OF THE 1964 TAX REDUCTION*

Arthur M. Okun

AUTHOR'S NOTE–JUNE 1967[1]

This paper was written during the summer of 1965. It reported on the way the Revenue Act of 1964 had served as a major stimulus to economic activity in the preceding year and a half. Just about the time that this paper was completed, we entered a new chapter in our economic history in which the key fiscal impact on the economy came from the extra defense expenditures required to fulfill our commitments in Southeast Asia. Any analysis of fiscal impact that covered the more recent period could no longer treat monetary policy as a passive supporting force, nor could it continue to ignore the influence of higher levels of aggregate demand on prices. Moreover, an updated version of this paper would revise the quantitative estimates associated with the tax reduction. Both revisions in earlier data and more recent experience would influence the point estimates. But neither the consideration of the most recent period nor the statistical refinement would change the basic conclusion that the tax cut of 1964 carried us a giant step toward full employment.

In the process of doing so, it also had important consequences for economic growth, which justify the inclusion of this topic in a volume of essays dealing with the subject of growth. To be sure, the Revenue Act of 1964 was aimed at the demand, rather than the supply, side of the nation's economy. Its objective and achievement was primarily to put productive capacity to work by raising private demand. Effects on the productive capability of the nation were largely incidental but nonetheless important.

By promoting fuller use of capacity, the tax cut created powerful incentives for growth-oriented activity by business. This was most apparent in the subsequent investment boom with its important widening, deepening, and updating of our capital stock. Fuller employment of labor, meanwhile, encouraged greater efforts in the private training of manpower and improved the mobility and upgrading of our human resources.

Finally, the tax cut set the stage for a heightened interest in public policy to stimulate growth. When the nation was failing to make full use of its existing productive capacity, there were good reasons for policy-makers to be unenthusiastic about measures that promised an accelerated growth of supply capabilities. Indeed, there was even a powerful attraction to proposals that sought deliberately to curtail growth, such as by enforcing artificially a marked shortening of the workweek or earlier retirement of senior workers. The realization of full employment was a prerequisite for the serious consideration of policies to stimulate economic growth. Once we can enjoy an environment of peacetime prosperity, growth policy will come to the fore. And it will owe much to the demonstration through the 1964 Revenue Act that we can make full use of rapidly growing productive capacity.

INTRODUCTION

The best-known fact about the Revenue Act of 1964 is that, in the year and a half since it took effect, economic activity has expanded briskly. But such *post hoc, propter hoc* reasoning will never do. Many things happened early in 1964, and, by reference only to the course of events, one could attribute the buoyant performance of the economy to Illinois' victory in the Rose Bowl or to Goldwater's decision to stand in the New Hampshire primary. *Post hoc, propter hoc* somehow always seems to be on the other

* From *Perspectives on Economic Growth,* edited by Walter W. Heller. Copyright © 1968 by Walter W. Heller. Reprinted by permission of Random House, Inc. Arthur M. Okun is a Senior Fellow, Brookings Institution.

[1] This paper was made possible by the able assistance of Allen Lerman.

guy's side. If the economy had slipped into recession in 1964, it would have been viewed as a refutation of the efficacy of the tax cut. It would have been awfully difficult to get a serious discussion of whether an even worse setback might have occurred if not for the tax cut. At least now one can attract an audience to consider more analytical types of reasoning.

The analytical principles of macroeconomics argue that rises in the incomes of individuals stimulate their consumer spending, while some combination of profit rates, cash flow, and sales is important as a determinant of business investment. The Revenue Act of 1964 affected these variables directly by adding to personal disposable income and to corporate profits after taxes. To the extent that the tax cut raised spending by consumers and businessmen through this direct route, it should also be credited with additional effects through the familiar multiplier process, whereby the spending of one individual or firm adds to the incomes and hence to the spending of others.

In the area of consumer spending, just a casual observation of the recent aggregative data suggests that there must be some validity to this story. By the second quarter of 1965, consumption expenditures had registerd a remarkable rise of $45 billion from their rate in the last quarter of 1963—the quarter immediately preceding the tax cut. Such an increase over six quarters is unmatched in our peace-time history. If one ignores the tax cut, that surge is an insoluble mystery. On the other hand, the expansion of consumer purchases is easily accounted for by the income gains associated with the tax cut and the hypothesis that consumers have treated the increase in take-home pay from the tax reduction in the same way they treat increases in take-home pay from other sources.

By definition, individuals do something with income gains—they cannot ignore them and, according to the principles of utility maximization, they will not throw income away. Hence, the issue is how they allocate the proceeds between consumption and saving.[2] Both on the average and on the margin, the bulk of disposable income

is consumed. If tax-cut gains are treated like other increases in income, most will be consumed and only a little will be added to saving.

The premise that tax-cut dollars are treated like other dollars of additional income is the foundation of the analysis. It is only fair to give warning that once this premise is accepted, the rest of the story follows readily. For our historical time-series data yield consumption-income relationships in which the marginal propensity to consume is very close to the average. Similarly, the quantitative record on investment tells us statistically that profits and sales have substantial effects on capital outlays. Indeed, this fundamental premise is the reason that so many economists expected so much from the 1964 Revenue Act. This premise can be subjected to some empirical check, although it cannot be supported by any refined verification from aggregative time-series data. If relationships established in the past hold up reasonably well after the tax cut, when tax-cut gains are added to other dollars of income, that supports the premise. But the real appeal is analytical: It is hard to see why people should want to segregate tax-cut dollars and treat them or think of them differently from other gains in their pay-checks or their corporate tills.

Given the fundamental premise, the analysis of the effects of the tax cut is an exercise in the dynamics of income-expenditure relationships. But that does not mean it is a simple exercise. Virtually every issue in aggregative econometrics bears on the result. The answer ought to be based on a fully articulated set of economic relationships that takes proper account of all the ways that everything depends on everything else in the economy. You will not be surprised to learn that the estimates developed below do not rest on such a complete analysis of the economy. Instead, they depend on a few key estimated functions and a liberal sprinkling of assumptions (which I note along the way) that other possible effects can be ignored.

In fact, I will temporarily assume that the only effects that need to be considered are those on consumption and personal disposable income. This gives us the familiar case of the pure consumption multiplier, where any and all effects on investment are ignored, and where the increment in Gross National Product is taken to consist entirely of consumption. The consumption gain can be divided into two parts. One reflects the direct result of tax reduction in raising personal disposable income, and the second stems from the extra incomes generated by additions to con-

---

[2] The Department of Commerce's recently amended conceptual framework introduces a new third option for consumers. They are now free to engage in personal transfers to businesses or to foreigners by paying interest on personal debt or making gifts to persons overseas. All empirical work in this paper is based on the revised national accounts data shown in the *Survey of Current Business*, August 1965.

sumer spending. The first of these is logically prior to the second. Nevertheless, because consumers do not adjust spending fully and immediately to the increases in their incomes, the two parts will overlap chronologically, and both will contribute to the growing increment in GNP over time.

The pure consumption case is interesting and instructive, and its dynamics are challenging. But it is certainly misleading. Nobody can really believe that a surge in consumer spending and a major rise in corporate profits and sales would have no impact on outlays for plant, equipment, and additional inventory. We must move on into the world of the accelerator or super-multiplier, as difficult as it is to quantify that world. Hence, I will emphasize quantitative estimates of the effects of tax reduction when both consumption and investment outlays are taken into account. But first I must back up and start at the beginning.

THE SIZE OF THE TAX CUT

The first question in evaluating the impact of the 1964 tax cut is how big was it? And the answer is not as easy as one would wish. We can estimate that the tax reduction for individuals lowered liabilities on Federal individual income taxes by $6.7 billion for 1964 and by $11.5 billion for 1965. But the reduced liability is not the way the tax cut shows up in personal disposable income.

Our national income accounting takes the view that the spending of individuals (unlike that of corporations) is influenced by income taxes when these are paid rather than when the liabilities accrue. Actual payments were affected when the withholding rate declined from 18 percent to 14 percent in March 1964. The corresponding reduction in withheld taxes during 1964 amounted to a good deal more than $6.7 billion; indeed, it was above $8 billion. During the year, people were getting increases in take-home pay that exceeded the reductions in their tax liabilities. In part, this was associated with a reduced claim on the Federal Government for tax refunds early in 1965—any nontaxable dollar to which withholding had been applied generated a 14-cent refund rather than the 18-cent refund associated with the old withholding rate. Moreover, it was no secret that the 14 percent rate applied to ten months of the year would leave many people on less of a pay-as-you-go basis than they had been under the previous regime. In principle, anyone who changed his withholding voluntarily

to maintain his degree of "pay-as-you-go" should have his adjustment subtracted from the dollar value of the tax cut for 1964.

There obviously were some such adjustments of withholding on a voluntary basis. Quantitatively, however, the best guess today is that they did not amount to much. Similarly, some of the self-employed reduced their estimated tax payments in June and September of 1964 in light of the lower tax rates. But, again, the adjustment does not seem to have been quantitatively significant and it would have operated in the other direction. Hence, we get a good approximation to the effect of the tax cut on disposable income through 1964 if we take actual withheld taxes after March, collected at a 14 percent rate, and apply a 2/7 ratio to them, so as to allow for the decline of four percentage points. For the first half of 1965, we must allow for the reduced refunds and the somewhat larger "clean-up payments" on the 1964 liabilities, which reduce the magnitude of the tax cut.

In principle, we should calculate the dollar value of the tax cut by applying the lower rates to incomes as they would have been in the absence of the tax cut and not to incomes as they actually turned out. But this difference is minor, and there are enough big problems to justify compromises on the little ones. I have rounded down the dollar estimates to make a rough allowance for this difference. The resulting estimates in billions of dollars (seasonally adjusted at annual rates) run as follows:

1964-I	3.2
-II	10.0
-III	10.0
-IV	10.0
1965-I	9.0
-II	9.5
-III	10.0
-IV	10.0

For corporations, the calculation is easier, simply because we treat taxes on a liability basis. The two-point reduction in the corporate tax rate for 1964, augmented by a switch between normal and surtax rates and by a liberalization of the investment credit, added up to $1.8 billion for the year. Another rate cut of two points took effect in 1965, and brought the 1965 total to $3 billion. The really important question about the corporate tax cut is whether it was shifted (either forward to consumers or backward to workers) or whether its benefits remained in the corporate sector. Without great conviction, I assume that there was no shifting in the short-run period covered by this paper.

THE PURE CONSUMPTION MULTIPLIER

The case of the pure consumption multiplier assumes away many of the difficult issues. To deal with it, all we need to know is (a) how much the tax cut adds directly to disposable income, (b) how much each dollar increase in disposable income adds to consumption, and (c) how much a dollar of additional consumption, in turn, adds further to disposable income.

The basic ingredient is the consumption-disposable income relationship. This is the most famous of all quantitative economic relationships, and it has appeared in all shapes, sizes, degrees of disaggregation, and other variations on the Keynesian theme. I shall use a simple form which treats consumer spending as a single total. It makes aggregate consumption in the current quarter depend only on aggregate consumption of the preceding quarter and on the personal disposable income of the current quarter. The presence of lagged consumption does, however, introduce a cumulative influence of the whole history of consumption and income on current consumption. The lagged consumption variable implies the presence of habit persistence or inertia in living standards. The equation has a respectable genealogy, going back (at least) to an article by T. M. Brown in *Econometrica* of July 1952.

The equation is spelled out in Table 1, as are its implications. According to it, an additional dollar of disposable income in the current quarter raises current consumption by 37.1 cents. If the income gain is maintained, consumption in the next period will be above its base level by 59.7 cents—the sum of 37.1 cents and .609 of 37.1 cents. Ultimately, the effect on consumption reaches 94.9 cents, as can be seen by solving the equation for $C_t = C_{t-1}$.

The intercept of this equation is a small negative number, surprisingly suggesting that the marginal propensity to consume is larger than the average propensity. But the difference is very small and has no economic significance despite the statistical significance of the intercept. If the consumption function is forced through the origin and fitted homogeneously, one obtains a very similar equation which yields essentially the same results over time. These equations were also fitted with lagged income as well as lagged consumption, but the results were not improved. Asset variables deserve an opportunity to help explain consumption, but they did not get their chance in this analysis. Nor was there any attempt to disaggregate consumption, such as by separating out expenditures for durable goods.

The consumption function alone would enable us to estimate the consumption gains associated with the direct income gains of the tax cut. But those direct income gains do not account for the full increase in personal disposable income. Part of the gain in disposable income results from the addition to consumption. Hence, we need to know how much each extra dollar of consumption (or, equivalently, of GNP) adds to disposable income. The best way I know to deal with the marginal share of disposable income in GNP is to subtract the other leakages that do not go into disposable income. It turns out that the marginal share of disposable income in GNP is considerably less than the average ratio of disposable income to GNP.[3] One major reason for this is that, in the short run, when GNP increases, Government transfer payments do not keep pace; in fact they are actually reduced through a decline in unemployment insurance benefits. The other and even more important reason is that corporate profits get a very large marginal share of GNP, particularly when the increase is sudden. Since dividends adjust very slowly through time, the bulk of the marginal share of profits is a withdrawal from disposable income.

As noted in Table 2, I have explained the sum of profits and corporate capital consumption

TABLE 1 INCREMENTAL CONSUMPTION ASSOCIATED WITH A MAINTAINED $1 INCREASE IN DISPOSABLE INCOME

Quarter	Incremental Consumption
0	0
1	.371
2	.597
3	.735
4	.819
5	.870
6	.901
.	.
.	.
.	.
∞	.949

$$C_t = 1.40 + .371Y_t + .609C_{t-1}$$

(billions of current dollars; fitted to period from 1954–I to 1964–IV)*

$\bar{R}^2 = .999$ $\quad \bar{S}_E = 1.71$

* A homogeneous form $C_t/Y_t = .343 + .635 C_{t-1}/Y_t$ gives virtually identical results.

[3] I have discussed this elsewhere. See "Short-Term Forecasting by the President's Council of Economic Advisers" in O.E.C.D., *Techniques of Economic Forecasting*, Paris, 1965, pp. 163–65.

	Quarter				
	0	1	2	3 · · ·	6
1. Gross National Product	0	1.000	1.000	1.000	1.000
2. Corporate Profits before Taxes	0	.667	.340	.340	.340
3. Corporate Taxes	0	.264	.134	.134	.134
3a. Federal	0	.248	.127	.127	.127
3b. State and Local	0	.015	.008	.008	.008
4. Corporate Profits after Taxes	0	.404	.206	.206	.206
5. Corporate Dividend Payments	0	.020	.029	.037	.058
6. Undistributed Corporate Profits	0	.384	.177	.169	.148
7. Indirect Business Taxes	0	.056	.056	.056	.056
7a. Federal	0	.023	.023	.023	.023
7b. State and Local	0	.033	.033	.033	.033
8. Social Insurance Taxes	0	.011	.025	.025	.026
8a. Federal	0	.009	.021	.021	.022
8b. State and Local	0	.002	.004	.004	.004
9. Transfer Payments	0	−.035	−.035	−.035	−.035
9a. Federal	0	−.035	−.035	−.035	−.035
9b. State and Local	0	0	0	0	0
10. Personal Income	0	.251	.572	.580	.600
11. Personal Taxes	0	.036	.082	.083	.086
11a. Federal	0	.030	.068	.068	.071
11b. State and Local	0	.006	.015	.015	.015
12. Disposable Personal Income	0	.215	.490	.497	.514
Addendum: Net Government					
Receipts	0	.402	.333	.334	.338
Federal	0	.345	.273	.274	.277
State and Local	0	.057	.060	.060	.061

$(10) = (1) − (3) − (6) − (7) − (8) + (9)$
$(12) = (10) − (11)$

Details may not add to totals due to rounding.
Corporate profits were estimated marginally from:

$(P + CCA)_t = −6.4229 + .1686 Y_t + .3267 \Delta Y_t − .5502 X_t$
$\bar{R}^2 = .961$ $\bar{S}_E = 1.403$ d.w. = .846

where $(P + CCA)$ is Corporate Profits before Taxes including Inventory Valuation Adjustment plus Corporate Capital Consumption Allowances
      Y is Gross National Product
and X is a measure of excess capacity associated with unemployment;

$$X = 3.2 (U − .0400) \times GNP,\text{ where } U \text{ is the unemployment rate.}$$

The equation was fitted to quarterly data (seasonally adjusted at annual rates) for the period 1954–I to 1964–IV, and variables were measured in billions of current dollars.
The incremental calculation estimates that the unemployment rate is reduced by one percentage point by a 3.2 percent increment in GNP.
Throughout, capital consumption allowances are taken to be unaffected by changes in GNP.
Dividend payments were determined quarterly on the margin from:

$$D_t = .92 D_{t−1} + .05 AP_t$$

where *AP* is Corporate Profits after Taxes.
Corporate profits taxes were estimated at 39.5 percent of corporate profits.
Other taxes were estimated by taking the actual 1964 ratio to either GNP (Y) or Personal Income (Y_p), as appropriate, and using the following elasticities:

Federal Indirect Taxes	0.9 on Y
State and Local Indirect Taxes	0.5 on Y
Federal Social Insurance Taxes	0.75 on Y_p
State and Local Insurance Taxes	0.75 on Y_p
Federal Personal Taxes	1.2 on Y_p
State and Local Personal Taxes	1.2 on Y_p

allowances, using as independent variables the level of GNP, the change in GNP from the preceding quarter, and a utilization variable which multiplies GNP by the excess of the unemployment rate over 4 percent. On the basis of this equation, the marginal corporate share is a strikingly large 67 percent when GNP rises in a quarter, and it remains at 34 percent in succeeding quarters if the gain in GNP is maintained. The importance of fixed costs supplies good analytical reasons for a large marginal corporate share. Still, the quantitative estimates of the marginal share derived from equations are always surprisingly large to me. After investigating the effect of alternative variables on the magnitude of the corporate marginal share, I bow to the persistence of the empirical results.

The other leakages in Table 2 are based on elasticity estimates which have a variety of underpinnings. They are nowhere nearly so troublesome as profits in the probable error they introduce in the marginal disposable income calculation. Taking account of the various leakages, we conclude that a dollar increase in GNP raises disposable income in the current quarter by 21.5 cents; if the GNP gain is maintained, the disposable income gain reaches about 50 cents in the second quarter. It keeps creeping up slightly because dividends keep rising very gradually in response to the increase in corporate profits. The whole process can be simplified and summarized adequately by assuming that, in the second and succeeding quarters, the marginal share of disposable income in GNP levels off at .505. In the pure consumption case, there is one further influence to take into account: The corporate tax reduction generates extra dividends through time. Quantitatively, this does not amount to much; but it is registered in the results shown in Table 3.

Now we have, in effect, a two-equation system. The marginal consumption tells us how much added consumption is generated by extra disposable incomes; while the marginal disposable income-GNP relationship tells us what further gains in disposal income are produced by added consumption. Tables 3 and 4 show the numerical solutions of this system. By the fourth quarter of 1964, through the pure consumption route, disposable income is estimated to have been $15.1 billion higher as a result of the tax cut and consumption to have been $10.5 billion higher. These gains continue to expand in the first half of 1965 but at a slower rate. In part, the leveling off reflects the downward bump in the size of the tax cut for the first half of 1965; in part, it suggests that the process was, by that time, beginning to approach its full effect.

But the ultimate full effect is considerably larger than the $13.4 billion gain in consumption shown for the second quarter of 1965. Holding the personal tax cut at $10 billion and the corporate reduction at $3 billion, we would ultimately reach a consumption gain of more than $21.2 billion.

The corporate tax reduction would be credited with a $3 billion contribution to consumption after the very long wait required for dividends to be fully adjusted. This is not a great performance as a consumption stimulus, but corporate tax cuts have never been expected to star in that respect.

The bulk of the ultimate consumption gain— $18.2 billion—would be attributable to the personal tax reduction. Based on a .949 marginal propensity to consume and a .505 marginal share

TABLE 3   SOURCES OF GAINS IN DISPOSABLE INCOME (PURE CONSUMPTION MULTIPLIER)
(in billions of current dollars)

	1964				1965	
	I	II	III	IV	I	II
Direct gain from personal tax reduction	3.2	10.0	10.0	10.0	9.0	9.5
Dividends attributable to corporate tax reduction..................................	0.1	0.2	0.3	0.3	0.4	0.6
Induced gains:						
a) Due to GNP gain of preceding quarter..	—	0.8	2.6	4.1	5.3	6.0
b) Due to additional GNP gain in current quarter...........................	0.3	0.7	0.6	0.5	0.3	0.3
Total increment in personal disposable income..	3.6	11.7	13.5	14.9	15.1	16.4

Details may not add to total because of rounding.
The results of Table 2 are used here in a simplified form, which assumes that the marginal share of disposable income is constant at .505 after a lag of one quarter. The simultaneous share is taken at .215 as shown in Table 2. Accordingly, the *induced* gain in disposable income consists of:

a) .505 of the preceding quarter's gain for GNP plus
b) .215 of the *increase* in the GNP gain in the current quarter.

The induced gains in disposable income shown here are calculated from the bottom line of Table 4. "Gain" or "increment" for a given quarter refers to the amount over and above the hypothetical no-tax-cut situation; it does not denote the quarter-to-quarter change.

TABLE 4   CONSUMPTION AND GNP GAINS RELATED TO DISPOSABLE INCOME GAINS (PURE CONSUMPTION MULTIPLIER)

Quarter	Gain in Disposable Income	Resulting Gain in Consumption in:					
		1964-I	1964-II	1964-III	1964-IV	1965-I	1965-II
1964:							
I........................	3.6	1.3	0.8	0.5	0.3	0.2	0.1
II.......................	11.7		4.3	2.6	1.6	1.0	0.6
III......................	13.5			5.0	3.0	1.9	1.1
IV......................	14.9				5.6	3.4	2.1
1965							
I........................	15.1					5.6	3.4
II.......................	16.4	—	—	—	—	—	6.1
Total consumption (or GNP) gain in given quarter............		1.3	5.1	8.1	10.5	12.0	13.4

Details may not add to totals because of rounding.
The cells above show the "phasing-out" of income gains into consumption gains in accordance with the consumption equation set forth in Table 1. That consumption equation and the disposable income relationship summarized in the note to Table 3 form a two-equation system in consumption and disposable income.
In the "pure consumption multiplier" case, the GNP gain is set equal to the consumption gain.

of disposable income, the steady-state multiplier is 1.82. Given the nature of this calculation, "close to two" remains a good familiar approximation to the pure consumption multiplier for a tax cut.

INDUCED INVESTMENT

Now I move to the more difficult but more realistic situation in which induced investment is recognized. We will continue to assume that neither net exports nor residential construction is affected by the tax cut or by the subsequent increases in incomes. These simplifying assumptions are not likely to be quantitatively important and at least they are offsetting in direction: Net exports would be lowered by higher GNP, while residential construction would be favorably affected, given the state of credit conditions. The induced effects we deal with are those on business fixed investment and inventory investment.

The choice of an equation for explaining business fixed investment is exceedingly difficult. Here, we cannot take advantage of the survey data and other barometric indicators that are so helpful in forecasting plant and equipment. Sales, utilization measures, and cash flow variables all have excellent claims for appearing in the equation. But when all of these are allowed to compete in equations fitted from time-series data, chaos results. The coefficients are highly unstable with respect to the choice of lags and the specification of variables. I trust that the econometric conflict between cash flow and accelerator models will be settled some day, but I am convinced that the decisive battle will not be fought with aggregative time-series data.

Many time-series equations with a few lags and a few variables perform about equally well. A cash flow equation with four quarterly lags in that single variable gave good results and reasonable coefficients. That is what I am using, as shown in Table 5. To the extent that cash

TABLE 5   INCREMENTS IN BUSINESS FIXED AND INVENTORY INVESTMENT FROM A MAINTAINED $1 INCREASE IN FINAL SALES OF GNP

Quarter	Business fixed Investment	Inventory Investment
0....................	0	0
1....................	0	.041
2....................	.118	.163
3....................	.134	.207
4....................	.163	.197
5....................	.276	.157
6....................	.154	.105

Business fixed investment was calculated marginally from:

$$I_t = 9.02 + .293F_{t-1} + .182F_{t-2} + .162F_{t-3} + .110F_{t-4}$$
$$\bar{R}^2 = .968 \qquad \bar{S}_E = 1.30 \qquad d.w. = .609$$

F is corporate cash flow (corporate profits after tax, including inventory valuation adjustment, plus corporate capital consumption allowances).
The equation is fitted to quarterly data for 1954-I through 1964-IV and all variables are quarterly totals at seasonally adjusted annual rates expressed in billions of current dollars.
F was estimated marginally using the profits function set forth in Table 2 and an estimated profits tax share of 39.5 percent, as noted in Table 2.
Inventory investment was calculated from:

$$V_t = -45.56 - .1715H_{t-1} + .5842V_{t-1} + .0428S_t + .1099S_{t-1}$$
$$\bar{R}^2 = .733 \qquad \bar{S}_E = 1.908 \qquad d.w. = 1.886$$

where *V* is the change in Business Inventories;
  H is *V* cumulated from 1947–I;
and *S* is GNP Final Sales.
Variables are quarterly totals, seasonally adjusted at annual rates in billions of 1958 dollars. The equation was fitted to 1954–I to 1964–IV but omitting the period from 1959–II to 1960–I.

flow really serves here as a proxy for other influences, such as sales and utilization, this should not be disturbing. The reliance on cash flow does credit the corporate tax cut with direct influence, but the omission of after-tax profits in the investment equation would assume that it had no direct effect. According to this equation, a dollar of extra after-tax corporate profits ultimately raises investment by 75 cents, working out its effects over the succeeding four quarters, as shown in Table 5.

The results of the inventory equation are also shown in Table 5. Inventory investment is explained using lagged stocks, lagged inventory investment, and current and last quarter's final sales of GNP. This equation and other inventory equations was a terrible estimator for the period from the second quarter of 1959 to the first quarter of 1960, when inventory investment was dominated by first the expectation, then the realization, and finally the recovery from the steel strike. Nevertheless, other periods of steel-dominated inventory activity did not show unreasonable results. Hence, the four misbehaving quarters were thrown out of the sample from which the equation was calculated. Because of the presence of the stock variable, there is no ultimate maintained level of inventory investment. As Table 5 shows, the induced inventory investment associated with a $1 maintained increase in GNP begins to decline after three quarters. It would eventually turn negative and oscillate, ultimately converging to zero.

The fixed investment and inventory equations do not include any monetary variables. In principle, they belong here. I would certainly expect a significant change in the costs or availability of credit to have an important influence on business investment. In practice, dealing with the period from early 1964 through mid-1965, I cannot believe that the omission of monetary variables can make a serious difference. By any measure of interest rates or credit conditions I know, there were no significant monetary changes that would have either stimulated or restrained investment to a major degree. Obviously, the rising incomes and investment of this period generated increased demands for financial assets and for loans. In this environment, the maintenance of stable interest rates and stable credit conditions required action by the monetary authorities to expand the reserve base more rapidly so as to accommodate expansion.

In this sense, monetary policies made a major contribution to the advance, but that contribution can be appropriately viewed as permissive rather than causal. The monetary authorities supplied a good sound set of tires for the economy to roll on, but they did not contribute the engine. That came from fiscal policies. If monetary policy had been the driving force, that would have shown up—at least initially—in a decline of interest rates and a relaxation of credit conditions.

It is reasonable to ask how much slower the overall economic advance might have been and how much less expansionary the tax cut would have been if monetary policy had not been accommodating. One could hypothesize an alternative monetary policy which held down the growth of bank reserves or the money supply (or other liquidity variables) to some stated degree. And one could then try to assess what difference this tighter monetary policy would have made in the pace of economic advance. That would be an interesting statistical exercise. It just does not happen to be the particular statistical exercise which this paper attempts to perform.

We can now put the whole process in motion, using the inventory and the investment equations along with the disposable income relationship and the consumption function discussed earlier. The results are shown in Table 6. The gains in GNP are, of course, larger than those estimated in the pure consumption case. Indeed, consumption itself rises more strongly because of the greater induced gains in disposable income. And, after a slow start, the investment components are contributing about one-third of the estimated total gain in GNP after the fourth quarter of 1964. The total gain in GNP reaches $17.1 billion in the final quarter of 1964 and goes on to $24.4 billion in the second quarter of 1965. If we continue the process for another two quarters, the GNP increase would exceed $30 billion in the fourth quarter of 1965.

And it will be rising. With a $10 billion personal tax cut and a $3 billion corporate reduction, the GNP gain would ultimately be $36.2 billion, $7.8 billion in business fixed investment and $28.4 billion in consumption. In this final situation, inventory investment would no longer contribute to the gain.

Of this "final" $36.2 billion gain in GNP, $25.9 billion results from the personal tax reduction and $10.3 billion from the corporate tax cut. The "steady state" multiplier for personal taxes is 2.59. The ultimate multiplier for the corporate tax cut is estimated at 3.4. But the corporate cut takes a much longer time to approach its full effects, because dividends creep up so slowly and gradually. Throughout the first two years following a tax cut, the estimated impact per dollar of

TABLE 6   GNP GAINS BY COMPONENTS ALLOWING FOR INDUCED INVESTMENT (in billions of current dollars)

	1964				1965	
	I	II	III	IV	I	II
Gains in:						
Corporate Cash Flow.........................	2.4	4.1	5.2	6.1	8.0	8.8
Direct from profits tax reduction..............	1.8	1.8	1.8	1.8	3.0	3.0
Induced profits before tax....................	1.0	3.8	5.6	7.2	8.3	9.6
Less: Induced profits taxes..................	−0.4	−1.5	−2.2	−2.8	−3.3	−3.8
Disposable Income...........................	3.6	11.9	14.5	17.1	18.5	21.2
Direct from personal tax reduction............	3.2	10.0	10.0	10.0	9.0	9.5
Dividends attributed to corporate						
tax reduction..............................	0.1	0.1	0.2	0.3	0.4	0.5
Induced......................................	0.3	1.8	4.2	6.8	9.1	11.2
Consumption................................	1.3	5.2	8.6	11.6	13.9	16.3
Business Fixed Investment...................	—	0.7	1.6	2.6	3.7	4.8
Inventory Investment........................	0.1	0.4	1.2	2.1	2.8	3.2
Total GNP....................................	1.4	6.3	11.4	16.3	20.5	24.4

the personal tax reduction is substantially greater than that of the cut for corporations. Moreover, we should recognize the possibility that the cash flow character of the investment equation may be too generous to the corporate tax cut.

According to these results, the Federal Government received $7 billion of extra net receipts in the second quarter of 1965 (on a national income accounts basis) as a result of the gains attributable to the tax cut. By this Federal budgetary criterion, the tax cut had paid for more than half of itself by then, and the fraction was rising. In addition, state and local governments were the beneficiaries of an estimated $1.5 billion increase in net receipts in the second quarter. In the ultimate situation, the induced gain in Federal net receipts would be $10 billion, and the state and local gain $2.2 billion, adding to a total that nearly matches the $13 billion of tax reduction.

CONCLUSION

This is not the first quantitative estimate that has been made for the Revenue Act of 1964; and it will not be the last. I trust also that it will not be the best. At the Council of Economic Advisers, we hope to improve the tools needed in this analysis and to remedy some of the limitations I have noted above.

Nevertheless, the results, shown in Table 6 look sensible and plausible to me. One way of viewing the conclusions is to consider what they imply about the hypothetical world in which no tax reduction had taken place. The hypothetical no-tax-cut world is constructed by subtracting from actual national accounts variables the esti-

mated gains from the tax cut over the six quarters from the beginning of 1964 to mid-1965. Instead of a rapid growth in GNP of more than $10 billion a quarter in that period, the world without a tax cut has an average quarterly increase of $6.3 billion, as shown in the accompanying chart. When the same thing is done for the other key variables, the results form a consistent pattern—

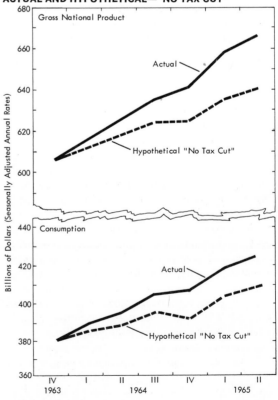

GROSS NATIONAL PRODUCT AND CONSUMPTION—ACTUAL AND HYPOTHETICAL—"NO TAX CUT"

slow growth in disposable income, small advances in consumption, and a leveling off in fixed investment in the first half of 1965 following some slippage in corporate profits during 1964. This no-tax-cut world would have shown rising unemployment and sagging operating rates.

I suggested at the outset one possible check on the fundamental premise that tax cut dollars are treated like other dollars: It consists of looking at empirical relationships established in the past to see whether they went haywire in the period following the tax cut. I can report that the equations held up quite well. Of course, they do not fit perfectly during the last year and a half, but neither did they fit perfectly in the years prior to the tax cut.

In the consumption function, there were sizable errors for two quarters, a $4.5 billion overestimate in the fourth quarter of 1964 and an offsetting $3.5 billion underestimate in the first quarter of 1965. In view of the slow deliveries of new cars during the auto strikes of the autumn of 1964 and the subsequent extraordinary catch-up, this pattern seems perfectly sensible. The profits equation fits unusually well during 1964 and the first half of 1965. Its largest error is in the second quarter of 1965, when it under-

states the level of profits by $1.7 billion; during the sample period, its standard error of estimate was $1.4 billion. The root-mean-square error in the inventory equation for the six quarters was identical to its $1.9 billion standard error of estimate over the sample period. Fixed investment is exceedingly well estimated for the first half of 1964; but it is underestimated consistently thereafter by amounts ranging from $1.2 to $3.5 billion and averaging $2 billion per quarter. There are grounds for suspicion that the investment equation we have used may have been conservative in its estimate of the induced effects stemming from personal tax reduction.

According to the estimates cited above, the tax cuts of 1964 are credited with a $25 billion contribution to our GNP by mid-1965, a $30 billion effect by the end of 1965, and an ultimate $36 billion increment. I have mentioned many reasons why these point estimates should be viewed as the center of a sizable range. Even with all the appropriate qualifications, these results provide important analytical confirmation that the Revenue Act of 1964 lived up to the intentions and expectations of its advocates, and that it has delivered a powerful stimulus to economic expansion.

FINANCING A FEDERAL DEFICIT*

Council of Economic Advisers Staff Memorandum

Discussions of deficit financing have long made a distinction between the inflationary impact of financing through credit expansion—i.e., selling securities to commercial banks—and the non-inflationary impact of financing through "real savings"—i.e., selling securities to the non-bank public. It seems appropriate to review this distinction.

A Federal deficit can be financed: (1) by drawing down Treasury cash balances; (2) by selling securities to non-bank investors; (3) by selling securities to the commercial banks; or (4) by selling securities to the central monetary authority. Regardless of which of these methods is employed, a Federal deficit is accompanied by an equivalent dollar-for-dollar increase in the net financial assets of non-bank investors—an increase which would necessarily show up as saving in our statistical records.

* Reprinted by permission of the Council of Economic Advisers.

If the deficit is financed by drawing down Treasury cash (deposit) balances, the result is to increase the public's money holdings by the amount of the deficit. (If the Treasury draws down its balances at Federal Reserve—as distinct from commercial—banks, member bank reserves are also increased, permitting a multiple expansion of private credit. However, since this secondary credit expansion increases the assets—in the form of deposits—and liabilities of the non-bank public by equal amounts, it does not affect the *net* financial assets of the non-bank public.)

If the deficit is financed by selling bonds to non-bank investors, the result, when the Treasury has spent the money collected from the sale of bonds, is that the public ends up with the same amount of money as originally but with more financial assets in the form of Government bonds. It is this method of deficit financing which has been traditionally labeled as good, sound, non-inflationary debt management.

The third and fourth methods—selling securities to commercial banks and to the central monetary authority—tend to be lumped together and considered inflationary. It is these two methods which need to be more closely considered.

If the deficit is financed by selling securities to the commercial banks, the banks pay for the securities by creating demand deposits for the Treasury, which, when spent, add to the public's money holdings. But this tells us little until we know where the commercial banks obtain the reserves needed to be held against these deposits.

If we suppose that the total amount of bank reserves is fixed, then the commercial banks can buy additional government securities in either of two ways. They might sell to the public an equivalent volume of other financial assets which they hold, reducing the public's money balances. In this case the results are exactly the same as the results of the second method: that is, the public holds the same amount of money but more of other financial assets than it did before by the exact amount of the deficit. Alternatively banks could reduce their lending to the non-bank sector, in which case the public's liabilities to the banks are reduced, which means an increase in the public's *net* financial assets.

On the other hand, the central bank might supply additional reserves in an amount exactly equal to the commercial bank purchases of new Federal debt. If it did this by open market purchases, it is clear that the effect would be virtually the same as if the new Federal securities had been purchased directly by the central bank, which is the fourth method listed above.

In this fourth case, it is clear that there could and would be a multiple expansion of credit. Private deposits would rise initially by the amount of the deficit itself. However, only a fraction of the added reserves would be needed to support the new deposits created in payment for the securities, and the remainder could finance an expansion of private credit. There would be a further rise of deposits resulting from the private credit expansion, but this would be matched by an equal expansion of private liabilities to the banks, with no added effect on *net* private assets.

Naturally there is a wide range of intermediate possibilities between the two extremes of providing no additional reserves and providing extra reserves in the amount of the deficit. For example, the central bank could create only enough additional reserves to support the new deposits created by the purchase of the securities. Or, the central bank could provide a somewhat larger or smaller amount of extra reserves.

Those who automatically look with disfavor on financing a deficit by sales of securities to commercial banks make no distinction among these various alternatives. They simply assume that all bank purchases of government securities are "inflationary." But the crucial question is not whether banks buy the bonds. It is rather what policy the central bank follows.

Each of the methods we have considered involves an increase in the public's total net holding of financial assets by an amount exactly equal to the amount of the deficit. In this sense they all involve financing a deficit through private "saving." But this is a purely definitional matter and is not very helpful in economic analysis. What we need to know is what the effect of the various methods is on the economy.

If the deficit is financed by selling bonds directly to the non-bank public, or if they are sold to the banks but no additional reserves are created, interest rates will rise, and this will have a restraining effect on private spending, which will partly offset the expansionary effect of the deficit itself. If, on the other hand, additional bank reserves are created which permit the bonds to be absorbed without any increase in interest rates, there will be no offset against the expansionary effect of the deficit. And, if more than this amount of reserves is created (as for example, by selling the bonds to the central bank or its equivalent), there will be an expansionary *monetary* effect to be added to the expansionary fiscal effect.

Thus we always have *two* effects to consider: the effect of the *fiscal* action (a reduction in taxes or an increase in expenditures) which produced the deficit—and which is always expansionary—and the effect of the method used to *finance* the deficit, which depends in significant measure on central bank policy, and which might be counter-expansionary (if no new reserves are created), neutral, or an addition to the expansionary effect of the deficit.

In determining which course the central bank should take with respect to commercial bank reserves, one must consider the economic setting in which the deficit occurs. If a Federal deficit occurs because total income, and thus Federal revenue, falls away in a recession, interest rates will tend to decline even if the quantity of reserves is held constant. But in these circumstances, it will usually be both appropriate and desirable that the central monetary authority pursue an actively expansionary policy—that is, providing additional reserves to the commercial banks so that interest rates fall even more than they would have with constant reserves. On the other hand, if the Federal deficit occurs because a national emergency requires large increases in expenditures at a time when the economy is already at full employment, it is appropriate and desirable to counter the expansionary effect of the deficit itself by a tightening of monetary policy, which would mean no increase—or even a contraction—of reserves. In fact, the deficit should have been avoided in the first place.

On the other hand, a deficit arising from fiscal action to stimulate the economy to move from a position of under-utilization to full employment does not readily fit either of the above two cases. The increased expenditures or reduced tax rates—which produced the deficit—will cause incomes and business activity to rise. The rise in activity will produce a general increase in the demand for money and credit, which—unless bank reserves are increased—will tend to raise interest rates and restrict credit. Thus, if the deficit is financed under conditions of monetary restraint, its stimulating impact will be partly offset. Another way of putting this is that a larger tax cut or increase in expenditures will be needed to achieve a given target level of income and employment if the stimulative fiscal action is accompanied by restrictive monetary policy. Any rise in interest rates or reduction in credit availability that accompanies a tax cut, for example, will reduce private demands for houses, automobiles, plant and equipment and so on, thereby diluting the effect of the expansionary fiscal policy.

It is important to note, however, that even if the central bank supplied no extra reserves, so that the bonds (or an equivalent volume of bank-held securities) had to be sold to the non-bank public, the rise in interest rates that would occur could, at most, provide only a partial offset to the expansionary effect of the deficit. If a deficit is brought about, for example, by reducing taxes, the effect is to increase *disposable income* and (as pointed out earlier) the *net liquid assets* of consumers; these effects are present no matter how the deficit is financed—although, of course, the *composition* (as distinct from the size) of the increase in the stock of net liquid assets depends on the method of financing. It is not correct to argue that the expansionary effect of the tax

reduction financed with no increase in bank reserves would be fully offset by the equal amount of security sales to the public. The idea that "the extra money you give consumers by tax reduction would be taken away by security sales" incorrectly identifies the effects of increases in *disposable income* and in *net liquid assets,* which clearly make consumers better off, with a *voluntary asset exchange,* in which security-buyers swap one form of asset (cash) for another (securities).

In the foregoing analysis, balance-of-payments effects have been ignored. In fact, in recent years, these effects have had an important influence on policy.

To the extent that international differences in short-term interest rates may influence the outflow of short-term funds, it may be necessary or desirable (depending on the state of the other items in the balance of payments) to hold domestic interest rates higher than would otherwise be desirable for reasons of domestic policy. A balance has to be struck between the stimulating domestic effects of an easier monetary policy and the necessity or desirability of stemming a loss of international reserves.

It should be noted, however, that it is primarily short-term interest rates that influence international capital flows, while long-term rates are more important as far as the domestic economy is concerned. Consequently, when a deficit is needed to stimulate the domestic economy and the balance of payments situation calls for financing of the deficit in such a way as to raise interest rates, it is appropriate for the Treasury to emphasize short-term borrowing in order to maximize the benefits to the balance of payment and minimize the harm to the domestic economy.

In conclusion it should be recognized that the question of how to finance the deficit is really subordinate to the more general questions of (*a*) how expansionary should monetary and fiscal policy be in a given situation, and (*b*) what should be the appropriate "mix" of monetary and fiscal elements? Concentrating on deficits (or surpluses) *per se* is not the most useful approach to the problems of fiscal policy, nor is concentrating on the financing of deficits *per se* the most useful approach to the problems of monetary policy.

FORMULATING FISCAL POLICY*

Council of Economic Advisers

The focus of fiscal policy in the United States is the annual Federal budget, which is presented in the Budget Message of the President in January. This budget covers the fiscal year starting 6 months later, on July 1. Any analysis of fiscal policy must begin with a consideration of the way in which this budget is formulated in the Executive Branch and the procedures by which the Congress acts on the President's recommendations.

The requirements of economic stabilization are not always fully met, however, by the fiscal program incorporated in the annual budget, no matter how carefully this program is formulated. Conditions may change during the course of the year in such a way as to call for a significant policy response after the annual budget has been planned. Some degree of continuing flexibility is therefore necessary.

One important forward step in budgetary practice was taken when the Federal budget for the fiscal year 1969 was presented. In accord with recommendations contained in the October 1967 Report of the President's Commission on Budget Concepts, a single unified budget was adopted, which covers in a comprehensive way all of the financial activities of the Federal Government. This unified budget provides a much improved statistical basis for formulating fiscal policy and evaluating its economic impact.

THE ROLE OF ECONOMIC FORECASTING

A certain amount of time is required for the economy to respond fully to changes in fiscal—and monetary—policies, and the actions taken at one point in time have effects that are felt over a considerable subsequent period. Whether a policy action will help or impair economic performance depends on the state of the economy in the period following the action. It cannot be judged adequately just by the facts of the economic situation at the time the decision is taken. It must be assessed in light of a forecast.

The responsibility within the Administration for projections of Federal revenues, expenditures, and economic activity rests jointly with the Department of the Treasury, the Bureau of the Budget, and the Council of Economic Advisers. Liaison is maintained with the Federal Reserve Board, which must also forecast economic activity as a basis for its decisions concerning monetary policy.

These projections are particularly important in formulating the annual budget, and they are set forth regularly in the Council's Annual Report. But the evaluation of the economic situation and outlook must be kept up to date during the year. Thus the forecasts are revised for internal use as new information becomes available—indeed, the process of assessing the economic outlook is essentially a continuous one. The projections are frequently supplemented by quantitative estimates of the probable effects of alternative policy actions which might be taken. Quantitative evaluations of the outlook have been prepared for the President essentially on a quarterly schedule ever since 1961. This procedure assures a regular review by the President, with his chief economic and fiscal advisers, of the suitability of the budget program for the needs of the economy.

The techniques used in preparing the Administration's economic projections have changed considerably over the years; but in general they depend on a set of quantitative relationships among economic magnitudes over time. The relationships that are relied upon may be based on formal statistical procedures, subjective expert judgment, or survey data.

To a considerable extent, forecasting relies upon the timely availability of data relating to the economy's past performance which can be used as a basis for projecting its future behavior. Although there are still gaps in economic statistics, considerable progress has been made in recent years by the Department of Commerce, the Department of Labor, and other Federal Government agencies in increasing the quantity and improving the quality of statistical data available for assessing the performance of the economy.

Government agencies also collect valuable information on the anticipated future behavior of some categories of expenditures. For example, the quarterly survey of investment anticipations provides a useful indication of the probable behavior of this highly volatile element of private demand. The Bureau of the Budget prepares up-to-date estimates of future Federal expenditures.

---

* From *The Annual Report of the Council of Economic Advisers,* January 1969, pp. 78–85. Reprinted by permission of the Council of Economic Advisers.

Estimates of Federal tax revenues are prepared and kept current by the Treasury Department.

Forecasting was notably successful in gauging in advance the rapid expansion of 1964 and the upsurge from late 1967 into 1968. On some occasions, however, difficulties have been encountered. The strength of the 1965–66 boom was not fully foreseen. Unexpected increases in the personal saving rate intensified the slowdown in economic activity that occurred in the first half of 1967. In the second half of 1968, private demand was stronger than had been anticipated, as noted in Chapter 1 [of the Report]. Nevertheless, the whole record makes clear that explicit quantitative projections are superior to extrapolations or hunches, which are the only alternative ways of guiding policy decisions that affect the future.

The need for greater precision in both forecasting and policy formulation has increased greatly in recent years. Between 1961 and 1965, when actual output was consistently below potential, there was little threat of a serious rise in prices, and the risks of excessive expansion were small. Thus emphasis could be placed upon achieving a growth of actual output in excess of that of potential in order to close the gap. Since 1965, however, as actual output has remained relatively close to potential, the need to anticipate and to offset fluctuations in demand has correspondingly increased.

PREPARING THE ANNUAL BUDGET

The Federal budget should be formulated with two objectives in view. One is to provide the amount of fiscal stimulus or restraint needed to keep the economy moving along the potential output path—or to move it back toward that path if a departure has occurred. The other is to choose a level of Federal expenditures that provides the appropriate allocation of national resources between private and public uses. In principle, these two objectives can be pursued independently, since fiscal stimulus or restraint can be provided either by adjusting public expenditures or by adjusting tax rates to influence private spending.

Determining the Extent of Expansionary Action

In developing a budget that is appropriate in terms of fiscal impact, it is necessary at the outset to prepare an economic forecast for a period extending a year and a half beyond the time of budget presentation. The forecast covering the first 6 months of this period—for which the budget outlook has already been fairly well determined—provides the point of departure for viewing economic prospects in the ensuing fiscal year. From that point on, forecasts of private demand are used to determine the appropriate degree of fiscal stimulus or restraint to be provided by the budget.

This determination takes account of the growth of Federal revenues when GNP grows in line with potential in a noninflationary environment at unchanged tax rates. When the economy is in reasonable balance on the path of potential output and private demand is expected neither to weaken nor to accelerate, the forecast will point to the need for expansionary fiscal action sufficient to offset the fiscal drag exerted by normal revenue growth.

If the projection suggests that private demand will weaken or if the economy is operating below potential at the beginning of the year, expansionary fiscal action will be called for in an amount more than sufficient to counteract the restraining effects of normal revenue growth. Conversely, if private demand is expected to strengthen or if the economy is operating above potential at the beginning of the year, an amount of expansionary fiscal action less than sufficient to offset the restraining effects of normal revenue growth will be required—or, in an extreme case, some additional restraint, beyond that provided by normal revenue growth, may be necessary.

The desired amount of expansionary (or restrictive) fiscal action, as indicated by the forecast, can be provided either by increasing (reducing) Government expenditures, by reducing (increasing) tax rates, or by some combination of the two. A decision therefore has to be made whether to adjust taxes, or expenditures, or both. This decision involves difficult choices about the allocation of resources between public sector programs and the private sector.

Public Expenditures and Tax Changes

In order to make these choices intelligently, it is necessary to examine carefully the proposed Federal expenditures having the highest priorities—whether they be for the expansion of existing programs or for new initiatives—and judge whether the public needs that would be met by these programs are more or less urgent than the demands of the private sector that would be satisfied by tax reduction.

Allowance ordinarily has to be made for a virtually unavoidable increase in expenditures sufficient to keep pace with rising costs and rising workloads under existing Federal programs. The decision would, however, still have to be made whether any needed restraint or additional stimulus over and above that provided by this built-in expenditure growth should come from changes in tax rates or in expenditures.

All of this suggests that there is no reason to suppose that the proper allocation of resources between public sector and private sector activities would be achieved by keeping tax rates constant and adjusting Federal expenditures to meet the requirements of fiscal policy. It should be perfectly normal for the President to recommend a change in tax rates in his annual Budget Message. Such proposed changes have in fact been a feature of the last seven annual budgets. Indeed, consideration of the appropriateness of tax rates should be a normal part of the budget program—if no change is being proposed, the President should explain why existing tax rates are regarded as appropriate. If Government expenditures move ahead year by year at a rate about equal to the growth of tax revenues, changes in tax rates may not need to be made very often. However, it would be a remarkable coincidence if a steady growth in Government expenditures at that rate simultaneously satisfied the needs of economic stabilization and the Nation's wishes over the long run with respect to the proper allocation of resources between the public and private sectors of the economy.

Sharp increases in defense spending pose special issues relating to the allocation of resources between Federal nondefense programs and the private sector. A sharp increase in defense expenditures normally requires a compensating fiscal adjustment to prevent the budget from becoming undesirably stimulative. In principle, any needed adjustment can be accomplished either by increases in tax rates or reductions in Federal nondefense outlays. For a number of reasons, however, increases in tax rates should normally be the main instrument. First, sharp slashes in Federal nondefense programs are simply not administratively feasible in the short run. Second, social priorities for the nonmilitary public sector would be violated if these programs carried the major burden of fiscal adjustment. The overhead cost on society of increased defense requirements should be expected to be borne primarily by the 80 percent of GNP that represents private uses of output. It seems evident that the roughly 10 percent of GNP which Federal nondefense spend-

ing represents should not be expected to carry the major part of the load. This seems particularly compelling in a Nation which is affluent in general and yet beset by serious social problems. While it is entirely appropriate for some types of nondefense spending to be cut and stretched out in order to ease the fiscal problem, there are strong grounds for avoiding reductions in social programs that deal with the urgent problems of poverty and urban blight.

CONGRESSIONAL PROCEDURES

If fiscal policy, as embodied in the annual budget, is to make its maximum contribution to economic stabilization, some changes in Congressional procedures for reviewing and determining the budget would be desirable.

General Budget Review

One important problem lies in existing Congressional procedures for determining budget authority and hence Federal expenditures. In both the House and Senate, budget authority is essentially controlled by 13 separate appropriations subcommittees which determine budget authority for individual agencies and programs. Their individual decisions can lead to a total of budget authority and outlays that is not controlled nor determined in a coordinated way. The Legislative Reorganization Act of 1946 called for a concurrent resolution on an expenditure total in advance of appropriations, but this limitation was not integrated into the appropriations procedures.

Congress needs new machinery which ensures that the actions taken on authorizations and outlays for particular programs will add up to a total that achieves an appropriate allocation of resources between Federal programs and the private sector of the economy. This machinery should focus specific attention on the level of taxes required in conjunction with any given total of outlays in order to achieve an appropriate fiscal policy. In making its judgments on these matters, the Congress would presumably begin with the Administration's expenditure and tax recommendations as contained in the January Budget. Then, assuming no major disagreement with, or change in, the basic economic outlook, any proposals to change the expenditure total substantially from that recommended in the Budget should be accompanied by a corresponding proposal for adjusting taxes. If such machinery could be satisfactorily introduced, it would help produce a more coordinated Congressional decision on both expenditures and taxes.

Procedures for Tax Changes

Procedures for a general review of the economy's fiscal needs along lines suggested above should expedite whatever specific action on taxes might be needed for fiscal policy purposes. In most circumstances, normal Congressional procedures for enacting the needed tax legislation would probably be satisfactory—especially if the Congress were to agree in advance on a form of tax adjustment that would be judged appropriate for this purpose. A proportional change in individual and corporate income taxes—like the current surcharge—might be a suitable form of adjustment.

However, the experience of the 1960's, including the costly delays in the passage of the 1964 tax cut and the 1968 tax surcharge, suggests the desirability of some other standby arrangement for obtaining prompt adjustments in tax rates to achieve fiscal policy objectives in case of a delay in reaching a decision through normal Congressional procedures. . . . the Administration has requested that the Congress consider giving the President discretionary authority, subject to Congressional veto, to remove the current surcharge entirely or partially if warranted by developments. A more permanent arrangement to provide the desirable flexibility could take various forms, including:

1. Presidential discretion to propose temporary changes in personal income tax rates within certain specified limits—such as 5 percent in either direction—subject to veto by the Congress within (say) 30 days. This year's Budget Message contains such a proposal.

2. A streamlined Congressional procedure for ensuring a prompt vote on Presidential proposals for changes in tax rates within certain specified limits. This would not shift any of the traditional powers of Congress to the President; the Congress would simply change its own rules.

Since changes in tax rates required for fiscal policy objectives would probably take the form of simple modifications of the basic schedule of rates, it would be necessary also to ensure opportunities for a thoroughgoing review of the over-all structure of the revenue system, including the tax base and rates. A structural review of rates would be especially appropriate if rates should drift downward (or upward) consistently for a period of several years as a result of fiscal adjust-

ments. It is important, however, that the issues of tax reform be treated and considered separately from the annual tax decisions related to fiscal policy.

Under the procedures outlined above, it would surely take several months for full legislative response to the President's January Budget. During that period, both the Congress and the Administration would be alert to any major unanticipated developments in the strength of private demand, in Federal defense needs, and in the desired mix of fiscal and monetary policy. Any such developments could and should be reflected in the implementation of the budget program.

If the annual budget is carefully formulated and implemented, the need for a significant subsequent revision of the budget program later in the year should be the exception rather than the rule. Stabilization requirements could largely be met by reliance on automatic stabilizers and monetary policy.

Much of the success of these stabilization efforts would depend upon the Federal Reserve's flexibility in adjusting monetary policy to circumstances as they unfold. In the development of the annual budget, there should be close consultation and coordination with the monetary authorities. A tentative projection of monetary and credit conditions should be prepared as part of the forecast underlying annual budget decisions. The fiscal program should minimize the risk of putting an excessive share of the burden of economic stabilization on monetary policy, as happened in 1966. But monetary policy should not be bound by the projections made at budget time—if conditions change, it should be adjusted accordingly. Indeed, given a reasonably appropriate fiscal policy, the further adjustments needed to keep the economy reasonably close to potential output should normally be within the capability of the Federal Reserve.

It should be recognized, however, that major unforeseen developments may significantly modify the path of demand anticipated in the annual budget. As mentioned earlier, private demand has on occasion exhibited substantial unexpected strength or weakness.

A major problem in recent years has stemmed from the uncertain path of increases in defense spending during the Vietnam buildup. While it is to be hoped that such a military buildup will not again be necessary, there can be no assurance in an insecure world that this will be the case. Accordingly, it is essential to be prepared to deal with such contingencies. Moreover, there could be similar and equally challenging problems of gauging the magnitude and timing of a demobilization—when peace is established. A special report to the President discussing the challenges and opportunities that will confront policymakers when peace comes in Vietnam is included in this volume.

The path of defense orders and outlays is inherently difficult to predict in a period of military flux. Through intensified efforts of the Department of Defense, considerable progress has never-theless been made in providing an improved flow of information relating to both the current and prospective economic impact of defense spending. Some of this information is now being made public by the Bureau of the Census in a monthly digest entitled *Defense Indicators*. Further efforts are needed, together with a full awareness of the importance of accurate information, especially at critical turning points in the trend of defense spending.

FISCAL POLICY AND THE NATIONAL DEBT*

David J. Ott and Attiat F. Ott

The federal government may have to run sizable deficits in times of weak private demand in order to raise planned spending to a high enough level to achieve full employment and balance-of-payments equilibrium. This means that there may be prolonged periods of increasing national debt, with no assurance that better times will produce the surplus required to offset the deficits.

It is precisely this possibility that disturbs many critics of discretionary fiscal policy. In their view, increases in the national debt impose a burden on "future generations," aggravate inflationary tendencies, and threaten the nation's solvency. Their concern is voiced in statements such as the following by Senator John L. McClellan of Arkansas:

One of the greatest crimes of all . . . is one that is rarely considered by many Americans to be an offense at all. . . .
The full effects of this crime will not likely fall upon the generation that is committing it, but may call for reckoning far in the future, and, unless the present trend is reversed, each succeeding generation will pay more heavily for it. The offense is being compounded annually, and its long-range effects are cause for serious alarm. This is the crime: the generation that controls the economy of this nation today and those who have important government responsibility are callously and mercilessly burdening the livelihood and earnings of the generation that will follow us with a tremendous oppressive national debt. . . .

We are saddling our grandchildren . . . with the bills for our luxurious living. We have no moral right to do this. . . .[1]

In contrast, consider this statement of the Council of Economic Advisers in connection with the 1963 tax cut proposal:

. . . Under the present circumstances there is no reason to fear such increases in the public debt as tax reduction may entail. The ratio of interest payments on the debt to national income is small and is likely to fall, not rise. Nor is there any danger that the increase in the federal debt will be a burden on future generations. Tax reduction will increase investment, and hence the wealth we will bequeath, not decrease it. The danger is the opposite one. By failing to take expansionary fiscal action, we will keep both consumption and investment depressed, thus hurting not only ourselves, but future generations as well.[2]

Concern over the size and growth of the national debt is frequently reflected in actual or proposed congressional legislation. In 1961 Texas Congressmen James C. Wright and Frank Ikard, Jr., introduced a bill that would require that no less than 1 percent of the present debt be paid off annually until the entire debt was retired. Congress has long imposed a ceiling on the national debt and has shown considerable reluctance at times to raise it (although it has not hesitated to legislate the spending authority that makes the debt increase necessary).

Who is right? Is there or is there not a burden imposed by a national debt? Does the national

* From David J. Ott and Attiat F. Ott, *Federal Budget Policy*, rev. ed. (© 1965, 1969 The Brookings Institution, Washington, D.C.), Chap. VII. Reprinted by permission of the authors and the Brookings Institution. David J. Ott and Attiat F. Ott are Professors of Economics, Clark University.

[1] "The Crime of National Insolvency," *Tax Review*, January 1964, pp. 2–3.
[2] *Economic Report of the President* (1963), p. 83.

TABLE 1   FEDERAL DEBT, JUNE 30, 1967 (in billions of dollars)

Item		Amount
Public debt (issued by Treasury)....................		322.9
Bills, certificates, and notes (marketable).........	113.2	
Treasury bonds (marketable).....................	97.4	
U.S. savings bonds (nonmarketable)..............	51.2	
Other bonds (nonmarketable)*....................	1.5	
Special Issues†..................................	56.2	
Other.........................	3.1	
Agency debt (Issued by agencies)...................		18.5
Total gross federal debt‡......................		341.3

Sources: *Federal Reserve Bulletin*, Vol. 54 (January 1968), p. A-36, and U.S. Bureau of the Budget, *The Budget of the United States Government, Fiscal Year 1969 (1968)*, p. 61. Details may not add to totals because of rounding.

* Deposition bonds, retirement plan bonds, foreign currency series, foreign series, and Rural Electrification Administration bonds.

† Issued to U.S. government investment accounts.

‡ Total includes noninterest-bearing debt, fully guaranteed securities, postal savings bonds, prewar bonds, adjusted service bonds, depository bonds, and armed forces leave bonds.

debt lead to inflation and government bankruptcy? These questions are obviously crucial to the design of a fiscal program.

To simplify our discussion of the issue, we will assume that all federal debt is held by residents of the United States. This is not far from the actual situation, since currently more than 95 percent of federal debt is held domestically.

First, a definition of "national debt" is called for, a more controversial exercise than one might think. Next will follow a brief summary of data relating the growth of the national debt to other economic magnitudes. The remainder of the chapter will deal with the issues surrounding the national debt: (1) the burden of the debt in a deficit setting that has resulted from attempts to alleviate unemployment by use of increased expenditures or reduced taxes; (2) the burden of the debt in a full employment setting; and (3) miscellaneous issues connected with the debt, such as inflation and national solvency.

DEFINITION OF THE NATIONAL DEBT

The federal debt consists of direct obligations or debts of the U.S. Treasury and obligations of federal government enterprises or agencies. It is shown, as of June 30, 1967, in Table 1, broken down into "public debt"—that part issued by the Treasury—and "agency debt"—that part issued by federal agencies. The public debt consists of issues (that is, bonds, notes, and bills), which are generally sold to the public (some are held by federal agencies and trust funds), and "special issues," which are held only by government agencies and trust funds. Of the issues sold to the public, some are "marketable," that is, they are traded on securities markets, and

some are "nonmarketable" and cannot be traded (for example, U.S. savings bonds). The latter may, however, be redeemed in cash or converted into another issue.

As is shown in Table 1, what is usually referred to as the "national debt," or "public debt," was $322.9 billion in 1967. However, some writers, following Maurice Stans, would give a much larger figure—some $1 trillion—as the "true" national debt of the government of the United States.[3] Stans obtained the $1 trillion total by adding $700–800 billion to the national debt as usually estimated to cover what he considered to be reasonably firm commitments of the federal government to *future* expenditures under existing federal plans, broken down as follows (rounded figures in billions of dollars):

Past services		
Civil Service retirement...................	$	30
Military retirement........................		40
Veterans' program.......................		300
Future services		
Unspent balances of prior year authorizations.....................		40
Public assistance.........................		50
Interstate highway system...............		30
Other (housing, public works, and so on)......................		30
Social security benefits....................		250–300
Total.................................		$770–820

There are several misconceptions and errors in this tabulation. The most basic is considering planned future expenditures as a debt without matching them against planned future taxes. The

---

[3] Maurice Stans, director of the Bureau of the Budget under President Eisenhower, in a syndicated column headed "Uncle Sam Faces $1 Trillion Debt," in the *Washington Post*, Feb. 19, 1962. This column has been widely quoted in newspaper editorials and columns.

result might indeed be a planned future increase in the debt, but it could just as well be a planned reduction. Even if it were assumed that Congress would not raise the necessary revenue to cover all of the government's spending commitments, only the uncovered amount would truly represent additional planned indebtedness. In any case, future congressional action on taxes or on spending commitments is impossible to predict, and any planned debt increase implied by such projections is at best a guess. This is not to say that awareness of such commitments for future spending is not 'important. It will have implications for tax rate changes if for nothing else. But it is misleading to call all future expenditures under existing programs a "debt" of the federal government.

Furthermore, the compilation contains other errors. In the case of the social security trust funds, no account is taken of future tax increases written into the current law, which would substantially reduce the debt figure. The highway expenditures figure also makes no allowance for receipts from the special taxes earmarked for the highway trust fund. Mr. Stans uses different concepts for different items; for example, the figure for veterans' benefits is an estimate of total future expenditures under existing laws, while the figure for the retirement systems represents net future liability discounted to present value.

The principal causes of the growth of our federal debt have been wars and depressions. During World War I the federal debt rose sharply by about $22 billion to a level of $25.5 billion in 1919. From there it decreased some $9 billion to $16.2 billion in 1930. The economic depression of the thirties led to government deficit spending, and the federal debt increased by approximately $27 billion between June 1930 and June 1940. During World War II it grew tremendously, reaching $269.4 billion in June 1946. Since 1946 the debt has continued to grow, especially during years of recession, and it stood at $341.3 billion in June 1967.

A substantial amount of this debt is held by the Federal Reserve System ($46.7 billion) and by government investment accounts ($72.2 billion). For purposes of economic analysis, the net federal debt that is held by the public—gross federal debt minus the holdings of the Federal Reserve System and government accounts—rather than the gross debt is the relevant figure. The net public debt stood at $222.4 billion in June 1967.[4]

[4] For more discussion and detail on the growth of the public debt, see Marshall A. Robinson, *The National Debt Ceiling: An Experiment in Fiscal Policy* (Brookings Institution, 1959), pp. 20–25.

The fact that most of the growth of the debt occurred during major wars does not in itself mean that debt inevitably accompanies war. In World War II, in particular, taxes were set too low relative to expenditures to prevent serious price pressures from developing. Rather than raise taxes sufficiently to reduce planned spending to a level consistent with stable prices, the government used price controls and rationing to suppress inflation. The rationale for this was that to raise taxes sufficiently to finance the war without inflation would have seriously impaired work incentives. Whether this rationale was in fact correct is now difficult to assess. If correct, it points to a serious limitation of the use of fiscal policy in periods of large defense outlays. There is evidence, however, that income taxes do not have a very important effect on work incentives.[5] Furthermore, it is hard to see why the same patriotic fervor used to sell savings bonds could not have been channeled into exhortations to work, if indeed work incentives were affected.

DATA ON THE FEDERAL DEBT

Merely looking at the growth of the net federal debt in isolation reveals little except that it has grown tremendously over the years the U.S. government has been in existence, from $75 million in 1791 to about $222.4 billion as of June 1967 (or about 3,000 times over). But so have other economic measures, in particular the volume of output and private debt. Likewise, federal net interest payments have grown immensely over the years, but so has our ability to carry them.

To get some perspective on the growth of the national debt, it is useful to make the comparisons shown in Figures 1 to 3. Figure 1 shows for five-year intervals from 1900 to 1930 and annually thereafter, the net federal debt and ratio of the net federal debt to GNP (in current dollars). The debt-GNP ratio was very low up to 1916, rose sharply during World War I, and then declined through the 1920's. In the 1930s it began another rise, which continued through World War II. It has fallen since and is currently back almost to the levels that prevailed in the middle

[5] See J. Keith Butters, Lawrence E. Thompson, and Lynn L. Bollinger, *The Effect of Taxation on Investments by Individuals* (Harvard University, Graduate School of Business Administration, 1953); George F. Break, "Income Taxes and Incentives to Work: An Empirical Study," *American Economic Review*, Vol. 47 (September 1957), pp. 529–49; and James N. Morgan, Robin Barlow, and Harvey E. Brazer, *Economic Behavior of the Affluent* (Brookings Institution, 1966).

FIGURE 1   NET FEDERAL DEBT AT FIVE-YEAR INTERVALS. 1900–30. AND ANNUALLY, 1931–67*

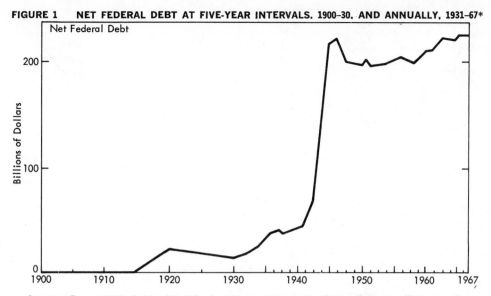

Sources: Raymond W. Goldsmith, *A Study of Saving in the United States* (Princeton University Press, 1955), Vol. 1, p. 985; Board of Governors of the Federal Reserve System, *Banking and Monetary Statistics* (FRS, 1943), pp. 509, 510, 512, and *Federal Reserve Bulletin*, Vol. 36 (December 1950), p. 1658; Executive Office of the President/U.S. Bureau of the Budget, *The Budget in Brief, 1969* (1968), p. 71; and U.S. Treasury Department, *Treasury Bulletin*, December 1967, p. 68.

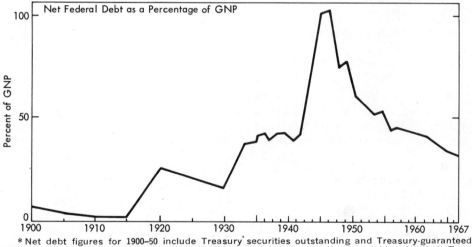

* Net debt figures for 1900–50 include Treasury securities outstanding and Treasury-guaranteed issues of government agencies. Data for 1951–67 include nonguaranteed agency debt and exclude Treasury debt issued to international lending organizations. Thus the data for 1951–67 are consistent with the new, unified budget, but the series has not been extended back to cover the earlier period.
   Sources: GNP data are from Goldsmith, *A Study in Saving* . . . , Vol. 3, p. 427; U.S. Department of Commerce, *The National Income and Product Accounts* . . . , pp. 2–3; and *Economic Report of the President* (1968), p. 209.

and late 1930s. In Figure 2 the growth of federal debt is compared with the growth of nonfederal debt since 1900. The figure shows clearly that federal debt grew faster than nonfederal debt during the periods 1917–19 and 1930–45 but that in the other 48 years of the 67-year period nonfederal debt grew faster.[6]

   [6] Because the vertical axes in Figure 2 are a ratio scale, the slopes, or "steepness," of the lines show the rates of growth of public and private debt.

   Finally, Figure 3 shows net interest paid on the federal debt, both in dollars and as a percentage of GNP. Since 1900, interest paid on the federal debt has not exceeded 2.0 percent of GNP—a level reached just after World War II. The percentage fell to 1.4 in 1951 and was 1.2 percent in 1955. The growth of federal debt, then, though large in absolute terms, appears less awesome when related to the growth of output or of private debt.

FIGURE 2   FEDERAL AND NONFEDERAL DEBT, 1920–66

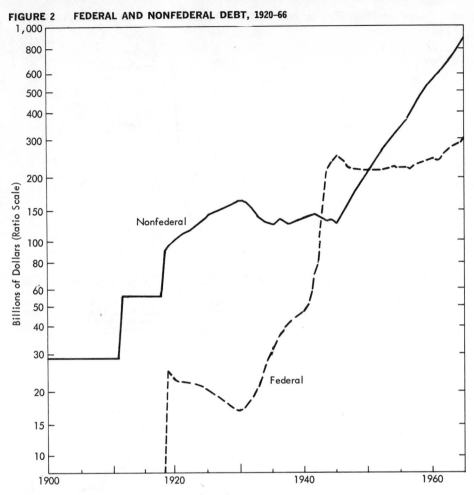

Source: Board of Governors of the Federal Reserve System.

THE BURDEN OF THE DEBT IN AN UNEMPLOYMENT SETTING

As was noted at the outset, hostility to the size of the national debt as well as to its continued growth generally arises from the view that the debt will impose a burden on future generations. To decide whether this view is justified, we will first consider, a society where there is unemployment and where the government plans to run a deficit to finance additional expenditures or to cut taxes in order to restore output to a full employment level. The issue then is, Does government borrowing to finance a planned deficit create a burden for future generations?

In one sense at least, there is clearly no burden on later generations. *A closed society cannot dispose of more goods and services than it currently produces; it cannot borrow tomorrow's output today.* In a period of unemployment there is essentially no competition between the government

and the private sector for resources. Goods and services acquired by the government at the time of the expenditure do not reduce the output available to consumers or private investors. In fact, increases in government spending or cuts in taxes tend to have a "multiplier effect," that is, tend to stimulate increases both in private spending and consumption. In short, deficit financing to restore full employment leaves future generations better off to the extent that private investment is stimulated, for, in the absence of an expenditure increase or tax cut, the added investment would probably not take place and future generations would have a smaller stock of private capital and lower output. A further gain in future output results from government spending of an investment type, for example, for schools, bridges, and roads.

What about the interest payments on the debt and possibly the repayment of the principal that

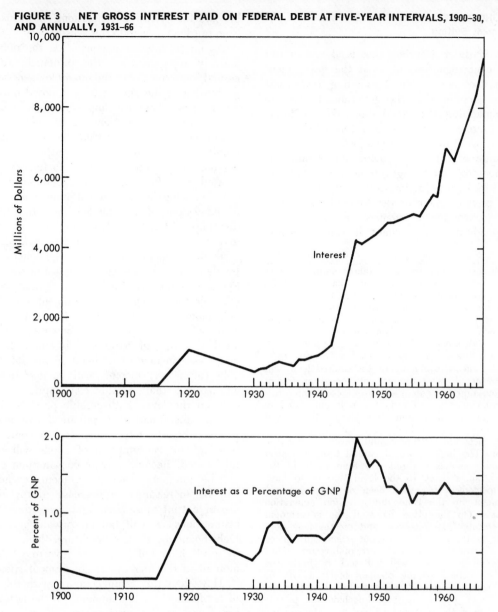

FIGURE 3   NET GROSS INTEREST PAID ON FEDERAL DEBT AT FIVE-YEAR INTERVALS, 1900–30, AND ANNUALLY, 1931–66

Interest

Interest as a Percentage of GNP

Sources: Data for 1900–25 are from Goldsmith, *A Study of Saving . . .* , Vol. 3, p. 445; and for 1930–66, from U.S. Department of Commerce.

fall to the lot of future generations? Are these not a burden? The answer is no. There is no aggregate burden on future generations who have to make interest payments on the debt and perhaps repay the principal, for these are simply *transfers* of income (or wealth) among members of society. There may indeed be "distributional effects"—wealth may be redistributed from taxpayers to bondholders to the extent that these are not the same individuals—but these do not necessarily leave the community in worse circumstances in the aggregate. In summary, deficit

financing and increases in the national debt do not impose a burden on future generations in an unemployment setting. In fact, running deficits to promote full employment leaves future generations better off in terms of increased real output and investment. In this setting at least, intergeneration equity is not violated.[7]

<hr>

[7] Franco Modigliani has come to a somewhat different conclusion on this question. He reasons that under certain conditions a deficit created to boost the economy from a depression or recession can leave future generations in worse circumstances than if

THE BURDEN OF THE DEBT IN A FULL
Employment Setting

Now consider a society that is always at full employment regardless of what the government does or does not do about spending, taxes, and the like. Assume that the government plans to spend an additional $100. Will it make any difference, in terms of a burden on future generations, if that expenditure is debt-financed?

Because of full employment, goods and services acquired by the government must always be paid for by a reduction in the output available to the private sector at the time of the expenditure. So, whether tax-financed or debt-financed, the expenditure is immediate; it cannot possibly

---

no government action had been taken. Suppose recessions or depressions are temporary, that is, that the economy will recover eventually even if no government action is taken. Suppose further that consumers and firms together have a plan of desired capital accumulation. A recession, then, will reduce the present generation's capital below the desired level, since saving and investment are reduced as income falls. The reduction in capital below the desired level will force the members of the present generation to cut their consumption over their lifetimes (even after full employment is restored) to an extent equal to the loss in capital accumulation during the period of unemployment. In short, they will have to save more to accumulate the capital "lost" during the recession. The higher rate of capital formation after full employment is restored will tend to build the stock of capital back to the level that could have been expected if there had been no temporary unemployment by the time the recession generation disappears. On the other hand, if the government acts to combat the recession and creates new debt in doing so, the new debt to some extent will replace the "lost" capital in the net worth of investors. Thus the present generation will not seek to build the capital stock back to the planned level; it will be content with government bonds rather than physical capital. Later generations may thus have less private capital than if the government had not attacked the recession by running a deficit.

Of course, the crux of Modigliani's argument is his assumption that recessions are in fact temporary and that government debt is unproductive. If, however, budget deficits are financed by issuing money, and if asset holders receive a stream of real returns from holding money or if money is a "factor of production," then even in Modigliani's argument, debt financing need not impose a burden, whether it occurs in a full employment or unemployment setting. See his article "Long-Run Implications of Alternative Fiscal Policies and the Burden of the National Debt," *Economic Journal*, December 1961, p. 731. For additional discussion of the burden of the debt from the point of view stressing the supply of capital, see Peter A. Diamond, "National Debt in a Neoclassical Growth Model," *American Economic Review*, December 1965, esp. p. 1141.

---

be paid for by future generations, and thus there is no burden on them in this sense.

As far as interest payments on the debt and possibly repayment of the principal are concerned, here, too, as in the unemployment setting, no burden in the aggregate is imposed on future generations. These are simply transfers of income (or wealth) among members of society.

However, while it is true that a closed community cannot increase today's output by borrowing tomorrow's, the way in which today's output is used can affect the output of tomorrow, and debt-financing has a different impact on the use of today's output from tax-financing. It is through this impact that debt-financing of expenditures may impose a burden on future generations.

If the economy is at full employment, then, by definition, the increase in government spending cannot increase total output. Prices will rise whether the increase in government spending is debt-financed or tax-financed.[8] But how is investment affected? Suppose an increase in government spending of $100 is debt-financed. Taxes on private income, and therefore private disposable (after tax) income, will be unchanged. If we assume that private consumption depends only on the level of disposable personal income of consumers and that private investment depends only on interest rates (credit conditions), then private consumption of goods will remain unchanged. Because private consumption outlays will be unaffected (and government expenditures will be increasing), a decrease in the private use of output must come and (according to our assumptions) it will fall on private investment. Debt-financing of an expenditure, then, will tend to result in a fall in private investment by the amount of the increase in government spending.[9]

How does this result compare with the result of tax-financing a like amount? In the latter case, some part of the tax increase will come out of private personal income. Private consumption will decline by some fraction of this reduction in disposable personal income, but not all since, as was noted earlier, consumers in the aggregate do not reduce consumption by the total amount

---

[8] An increase in government spending has a larger multiplier effect than an equal increase in taxes, and thus when taxes are raised to finance government spending, the net effect is expansionary and prices will rise.

[9] Under different assumptions, debt-financing need not lead to a fall in private investment by an amount equal to the increase in government spending. To some extent it may reduce consumer credit rather than investment credit.

of a decrease in disposable personal income. The balance of the impact will fall then on private investment. This means that both private consumption and investment will fall, with the total decline in both being just equal to the total increase in government spending.

A comparison of the two cases reveals that, although investment falls in both the debt-financed and tax-financed cases, it falls farther in the former. Here lies the burden on future generations. The burden can be measured in terms of the loss of potential output that will result from the loss of potential private capital. That is, debt-financing will reduce private investment more than tax-financing the same amount, thereby leaving future generations with less capital equipment for production and thus restricting them to a lower level of private output. Although both debt-financing and tax-financing leave future generations with less private capital and thus less output, debt-financing leaves them relatively worse off.[10]

Nothing has been said thus far about the effect of the use of government expenditures, and government outlays have implicitly been assumed to be unproductive. But government expenditures are not unproductive. They may be less, or more, productive than private investment. If government expenditures are less productive than, or equally as productive as, private investment, our conclusions about the relative burden still hold. If, however, government expenditures are more productive, future generations will be better off with the expenditures than without them, whether debt-financed or tax-financed. But they will be relatively less well off with debt-financing than with tax-financing. There will still be a greater burden in a full employment setting imposed by debt-financing than by tax-financing, in the sense that the gain to future generations will be smaller.[11]

---

[10] Note again that if money is "productive," and if the debt-financing consists of money issues, then even here there may be no burden from debt-financing.

[11] Some economists, notably E. J. Mishan, dispute the validity of the argument that a greater burden is imposed on future generations by borrowing than by taxing, even in a full employment setting. Mishan argues that since taxes reduce present consumption and borrowing reduces private capital for future generations, if one talks about a burden being imposed on future generations by borrowing, there is an equal obligation to consider the burden imposed on the present generation by taxing. Every decision society undertakes today affects future generations. Thus decisions to debt-finance government expendi-

In summary, deficit financing and increases in the national debt in a full employment setting do not necessarily impose an absolute burden on future generations. If government expenditures are more productive than private investment, future generations will be better off with debt-financed expenditures than without such expenditures. However, it is also clear that, in this setting, future generations will benefit relatively more from such expenditures if they are financed by increasing taxes rather than by increasing the federal debt.

DEFICITS AND OTHER ISSUES

Some newspaper and magazine writers and pamphleteers make categorical statements to the effect that "the increasing debt (deficit) is inflationary," linking together hostility to deficits and an increasing national debt and the general desire to avoid inflation. But the deficit (or "full employment deficit") is not a reliable measure of fiscal policy. A large deficit can result from a severe anti-inflationary fiscal policy if the government tightens up too much and induces a recession—or if expenditures drop in the private sector and the economy goes into a recession—and federal tax receipts fall as GNP declines. Large deficits occurred in the 1940s during a period of high employment and upward price pressure (which was suppressed by price and wage controls). During an earlier period, 1931–34, however, large deficits occurred during a period of severe unemployment and falling prices. Thus there is no basis for using the actual deficit or surplus to measure the inflationary or deflationary impact of federal fiscal action.

It is often implied that all inflation is due to increasing federal outlays, or that private and state-local outlays are not inflationary but that federal government outlays are. It is said, too, that private or state and local government outlays are productive whereas federal government outlays are unproductive. GNP is said to be an inaccurate measure of a nation's output, primarily because it includes in total output these unpro-

---

tures are no more of a burden on future generations than are decisions by individuals to consume rather than to invest. "After all, we could enormously increase provision for the future if we performed heroic feats of austerity during our lifetimes. Are we then not imposing a heavy burden on these future generations to the extent that we eschew these heroic feats of austerity and instead follow the path of our wonted self-indulgence?" ("How To Make a Burden of the Public Debt," *Journal of Political Economy*, December 1963, p. 540.)

ductive government purchases of goods and services.

Such arguments show a faulty understanding of what determines a nation's output, the nature of output, and the causes of inflation or depression. If government purchases of goods and services are unproductive, society might just as well discontinue such outlays and use the resources thus freed in the private sector. It could eliminate expenditures on missiles, planes, courts, police, highways, and education and use the resources to produce more cars, electric shavers, houses, and private planes. It should be obvious that federal (as well as state and local) government expenditures *are* productive in the sense that they satisfy certain social needs that are not met by the private market. These social needs are determined by elected representatives, who are responsible to the electorate.

It should be clear also that increases in private outlays for consumption and investment can at times be responsible for inflationary pressures, as they were in the period 1946–48. Whether private or government spending is at the root of inflation, the important thing is to bring about a reduction in aggregate spending.

The Public Debt and National Bankruptcy

There is a great deal of emotion in people's attitudes toward the public debt. For example, statements are frequently made to the effect that, if the national debt reaches some particular level, the government's credit standing will be impaired and disaster will follow in the form of something casually referred to as "national bankruptcy." While it is difficult to evaluate these statements, the idea is not a new one that there is a definite limit to the size of the national debt that can be carried without disaster. Individuals have long predicted that a debt of one-tenth, one-fifth, or one-half of the amount we now have would result in national bankruptcy, and they have had to revise the limit upward when it was indeed passed and ruin failed to follow.

How much can the federal government borrow? Is there a point beyond which borrowing would have to cease because people would refuse to lend? To answer these questions, one must understand the basis for credit standing of governments, whether federal, state, or local. Governments have a power not shared by other borrowers—they can impose taxes with which to pay interest on their debt and repay the principal. As long as a government does not abuse its taxing power, it will have the ability to borrow. It may have to pay higher interest charges if its debt becomes quite large, but it can borrow as long as it is willing to do so. And this is not all; central governments also have the power to coin and print money. They can always do this, instead of imposing taxes, to meet interest costs on their debts, and as long as they choose to do so, they can continue to borrow.

As a matter of fact, the securities of the U.S. Treasury are looked on by investors as a nearly riskless investment (from the standpoint of defaulting on interest payments), despite the enormous increase in the debt in the last half-century.

This does not mean that we should not worry about deficits and the growth of the debt. If the debt is growing because private demand is weak and the government is pursuing a policy of stimulating the economy with tax reduction (or expenditure increases), the deficit is not only harmless but a benefit to the health of the economy. If private spending is strong, however, and prices are rising, then low tax rates and a deficit are poor policy indeed. In short, there are good deficits and bad deficits. Good deficits occur when fiscal policy is used to stimulate the economy or to cushion it against economic declines. Bad deficits occur when, in the face of strong private spending, government refuses to raise taxes (given a planned level of government expenditures) to eliminate inflationary pressures.

The Psychological Effects

It has been held that, even though there may be no danger of burdening future generations, the stimulative effect of increasing the public debt to counteract recessions may be negated or partially offset by public hostility to debt increases. That is, irrational, unwarranted fear of such increases may reduce private spending (particularly investment), which will offset the stimulative effect of the fiscal action producing the deficit. Businessmen may say, "With such fiscal irresponsibility in the White House, I will not commit my company to new capital outlays."

On the other hand, the announcement itself of stimulative federal fiscal actions may have quite the opposite effect. The stock market's reaction to tax cut suggestions in 1963 and comments in the business press suggest that such positive fiscal action actually encourages business optimism and stimulates investment.

There is no clear answer as to which effect is likely to be dominant. It is hard to single out the effect on businessmen's expectations of a single action of an administration, such as incurring a planned deficit. It is probably true that the overall image of an administration has an important psychological influence on business investment decisions. It is not clear what influence a deficit by itself has or how strong that influence may be.

SUMMARY AND CONCLUSIONS

From the above discussion, it is clear that deficits may be economically defensible and even desirable under a great many conditions. They are unjustified, of course, when the economy is at full employment and there are inflationary pressures. If deficits are incurred as part of a rounded program to restore full employment, however, they are all to the good. They tend to increase output and employment and impose no easily identifiable real burden on future generations. Future interest payments and the repayment of principal are essentially financial transfers involving no aggregate real burden. Arguments to the effect that increasing the federal debt will somehow lead to national ruin or bankruptcy have little foundation in fact. And while there may be adverse psychological effects from deficits, there may just as well be salutary ones.

chapter 5

MONETARY POLICY

Monetary policy has been the subject of a good deal of controversy over the years, and views concerning its effectiveness have vacillated considerably, partly in response to changes in the economic environment and circumstances. Prior to the establishment of the Federal Reserve System in 1913, the United States could hardly be said to have had a monetary policy in the modern sense, because there was little in the way of machinery by which the federal government could deliberately influence monetary and credit conditions. The money supply was primarily determined by the gold stock, which, in turn, was determined by gold production and the flows of international trade and payments.

In the 1920s fiscal policy was not yet recognized as a means of regulating aggregate demand, and the monetary policy of the Federal Reserve was the sole instrument of economic stabilization. Fluctuations in economic activity were mild, and Federal Reserve policy was emphasized and given considerable credit for the satisfactory performance of the economy.

With the onset of the Great Depression, which began in 1929 and lasted for over a decade, ending only when the economy received a massive fiscal stimulus from heavy military spending associated with World War II, the reputation of monetary policy as an instrument of stabilization policy declined drastically. Huge gold inflows from politically unstable Europe caused a rapid expansion of bank reserves in the early 1930s. However, the depression weakened the financial structure, leading to a wave of bank failures culminating in the temporary closing of the entire banking system in March 1933. As a result of this experience, bankers were cautious; at the same time borrowers with credit standing high enough to satisfy them were few and far between. Excess reserves therefore piled up and money and credit did not expand, leading many to the conclusion that monetary policy was almost totally ineffective. Recent research on the period of the 1930s, however, has caused some students of monetary policy to conclude that its ineffectiveness during that period was somewhat exaggerated. In the first place, it seems plain that a sharply contractionary monetary policy at the start of the decade was one of the factors responsible for the seriousness of the depression. Moreover, careful statistical studies of the behavior of money suggest that if a more expansionary policy had been followed later on, it might have paid some dividends in alleviating the depression.

During World War II, the Federal Reserve gave up entirely its normal goal of economic stabilization and used all of its powers to support the market for U.S. government securities in order to assure the Treasury's ability to borrow at low and stable interest rates the huge quantities of funds needed to finance the war effort. The policy of supporting the market for U.S. government securities was continued during the early postwar period; however, the Federal Reserve became increasingly restive at the continued restrictions on its freedom to resume its normal role in the task of economic stabilization. The bond-support policy was finally ended with the famous "Treasury—Federal Reserve Accord" of March 1951.

Since the Accord, monetary policy has been used with increasing vigor. Credit was tightened moderately in late 1952 and early 1953 as a means of checking incipient inflationary tendencies. A vigorously expansionary monetary policy, which caused interest rates to fall sharply, was undoubtedly a factor in inducing a relatively prompt recovery from the recession of 1953–54. The expansion which resulted, lasting from the summer of 1954 to the summer of 1957, generated serious inflationary tendencies in its later stages; and from early 1955 onward monetary policy became progressively more restrictive. The ensuing recession of 1957–58 was sharp but short-lived, and a marked easing of monetary policy which reduced interest rates sharply was an important factor in inducing prompt recovery. However, the expansion that followed, which lasted from the spring of 1958 to the spring of 1960, proved somewhat abortive, as the unemployment rate did not decline significantly below 5 percent.

It was not possible to use expansionary monetary policy in the recession of 1960–61 with the same degree of vigor as in the recessions of 1953–54 and 1957–58. As a result of the increased degree of currency convertibility in Europe that developed during the late 1950s, by 1960 the sensitivity of international capital movements to differentials in national interest rates had increased greatly. Accordingly, in the face of a large and worrisome U.S. balance-of-payments deficit, it was felt that a sharp decline in short-term interest rates such as occurred in 1953–54 or in 1957–58 would induce such a large outflow of interest-sensitive capital as to threaten a serious international financial crisis. Under these conditions, the Federal Reserve attempted to contribute as much as it could to the recovery without allowing U.S. interest rates to decline below those prevailing in foreign financial centers.

A long period of economic expansion, lasting into 1969, began in early 1961. For nearly the first five years of this period—until late 1965—unemployment declined gradually and unused resources were put to use with little tendency for prices to rise. Fiscal policy played the major role in keeping the expansion going during this period, with an especially important contribution being made by the reduction in personal and corporate income tax rates provided for in the Revenue Act of 1964. Monetary policy accommodated the forces of expansion by allowing a sufficient growth of money and credit to meet the needs of expanding economic activity at interest rates competitive with those prevailing in foreign money centers.

In late 1965, the smooth and healthy expansion of the economy was disrupted by a sharp rise in defense spending associated with the escalation of the conflict in Vietnam. In the absence of an increase in tax rates, this rapid increase in military spending generated severe inflationary pressures. Accordingly, beginning at the end of 1965 monetary policy moved sharply toward restriction. Credit tightening, with the help of certain fiscal measures, most notably a temporary suspension of the 7 percent investment tax credit, did succeed in slowing the pace of the expansion sharply by early 1967. However, the impact of monetary restriction in 1966—sometimes referred to as a "credit crunch"—fell with special severity on residential construction and created severe strains in financial markets. After the economy slowed down in early 1967, monetary policy again became vigorously expansionary. In the fall of 1967, President Johnson recommended a 10 percent surcharge applicable to personal and corporate income taxes as a means of preventing a resurgence of inflationary pressures. However, the tax surcharge was not enacted by Congress until nearly a year later, taking effect in July 1968. The Federal Reserve tightened monetary policy somewhat as a means of tempering inflationary pressures while the tax proposal was being debated in Congress, relaxed its policy of restraint when the tax bill passed in the expectation that inflationary tendencies would begin to moderate, and then began to move back to a restrictive posture in late 1968 when it appeared that the tax increase by itself might not be sufficient to check inflation.

The restraint imposed by monetary and fiscal policy in 1968–69 eventually took its toll, resulting in a marked decline in real output and an increase in unemployment during 1970, although the price indexes continued to climb. The slowdown in activity was accompanied by a certain amount of turmoil in financial markets, creating additional complications for the monetary authorities. The period was one of innovation and change in some aspects of monetary policy. While credit had been restricted sharply in early 1969, the impact on residential construction was noticeable but was somewhat softened by substantial support from various federal credit agencies to the mortgage market. These new arrangements are reviewed by Warren L. Smith in his paper, "The Role of Government Intermediaries in the Residential Mortgage Market." In early 1970, the Open Market Committee of the Federal Reserve System shifted its attention from a fairly narrow range of intermediate targets—chiefly money market variables such as free reserves and the federal funds rate—to a broader spectrum which includes the money stock and other aggregates. This change was discussed in the paper by Paul Meek and Rudolf Thunberg in Chapter 3.

In 1971, the economy responded to the stimulative monetary and fiscal policy climate which had characterized 1970 and began to recover from the 1969–70 recession. While both instruments of stabilization policy remained expansionary, the recovery was very slow, while unemployment and the rate of inflation remained at high levels. In addition to these domestic difficulties, the country's balance-of-payments position deteriorated badly. On August 15, the President imposed a 90-day wage and price freeze which was to be followed by more flexible controls, in an attempt to break the inflationary mechanism; at the same time, dollar convertibility into gold was suspended, and in December the Smithsonian Agreement was signed, providing for exchange-rate realignment among the major trading countries.

The recovery accelerated in 1972, with some apparent progress in reducing inflation and unemployment, although this progress appears to have been reversed in 1973. In pursuing the targets established for monetary aggregates, the Federal Open Market Committee experienced considerable difficulty in achieving satisfactorily steady growth rates. As a consequence, the Committee moved to a more flexible target system under which target *ranges* for aggregate growth rates were pursued.

Much has been learned about monetary policy in the past 20 years or so as a result of the accumulation of experience in using it, together with extensive research and study. Nevertheless, monetary policy continues to be the subject of considerable controversy. In the late 1950s, there was much criticism of Federal Reserve monetary policy—and of federal fiscal policy as well—for placing undue emphasis on price stability as a goal of policy when this goal could be achieved only at a high cost in terms of unemployment. In recent years, this criticism has greatly abated. However, some students have been critical of the Federal Reserve for the frequent and sharp changes that have occurred in monetary policy in the past few years, contending that such a "stop and go" policy, far from helping to stabilize the economy, has actually added to its instability. Others contend that these frequent changes in monetary policy have been necessitated by failure to take needed fiscal policy actions to restrain the economy—or, as in the case of the tax surcharge of 1968, by excessive delay in taking such action. Because fiscal policy has not carried its share of the burden of economic stabilization, monetary policy has had to carry an undue share, thereby necessitating frequent gyrations in monetary policy. In the shorter run, the frequent accelerations and decelerations in the rates of growth of bank reserves, the money supply, and so on have reflected the Federal Reserve System's continuing concern with the need to accommodate shifts in the demand for liquidity and with orderly financial markets as well as with the steady growth of the monetary aggregates which is desired by those who oppose discretionary monetary policy and favor the adoption of some kind of "monetary rule."

The first selection in this chapter, by Warren L. Smith, is concerned with the mechanisms through which monetary policy and fiscal policy affect income, employment, and prices from the point of view of neo-Keynesian analysis. Most of the ideas developed here are extensions of the analysis set forth earlier in this book—notably in the Introduction to the first part of Chapter 1 and the papers by Smith, Holbrook, and Teigen (on monetarism) which appear there. It was shown in these readings that if, as the Classical economists commonly assumed, wages and prices are flexible, an increase in the stock of money will cause an equal proportional increase in prices but will leave the equilibrium interest rate unchanged, and employment and output will remain at their full-employment levels. On the other hand, if money wages are inflexible downward, deficient aggregate demand can cause unemployment, and if interest rates fall to such a low level that opinion is virtually unanimous that they will rise in the near future—as was the case in the Great Depression of the 1930s—the demand for money may become almost infinitely elastic at current interest rates. Under such conditions, monetary policy may lose nearly all of its power to stimulate economic activity, and fiscal policy may have to be relied upon almost entirely to induce a return to high-employment conditions.

Under most circumstances in modern industrial economies, neither the extreme Classical nor the extreme Keynesian conditions are likely to prevail. Wages do not decline readily in response to moderate amounts of unemployment—this rigidity of wages gives monetary policy a significant amount of influence over real income and employment. Indeed, expansion stimulated by monetary policy is normally divided between an increase in employment and real output and an increase in the price level in proportions that depend on the existing volume of unutilized resources; the closer the economy is to full employment, the greater will be the increase in prices and the smaller will be the increase in output for a given expansionary impulse. Moreover, the demand for money is responsive to interest rates but not infinitely elastic, as the ultra-Keynesian position implies. The conditions just described constitute the environment of the neo-Keynesian approach described by Smith in his article, "A Neo-Keynesian View of Monetary Policy," in which both monetary and fiscal policy can affect aggregate demand, and changes in aggregate demand can affect both real output and the price level. The Smith paper is devoted largely to a detailed exposition of the various channels and mechanisms through which both kinds of policy affect output, employment, and so on, and the discussion is carried on with an eye toward the Keynesian-monetarist debate discussed by Teigen in Chapter 1. Smith points out that neo-Keynesians think of monetary policy as working through several different channels; in fact, the channels are the same ones as those seen by the monetarists. It is on the efficacy of fiscal policy that the two sides diverge. Smith examines carefully the effects of pure fiscal policy changes on both flows of income and stocks of wealth, and the further implications of these effects for spending decisions. He concludes that most of the available evidence indicates that fiscal policy is capable of having substantial effects on economic activity.

Up to this point, most of the discussion of stabilization policy has taken place within the framework of a static, deterministic model—that is, one in which the intertemporal aspects of decisions play no role, and in which there are no random elements nor any lack of knowledge concerning the structure of the system. Unfortunately, this is not the framework in which the policy maker operates. He must make decisions concerning targets to be pursued and the amount of policy action needed, even though these decisions must be made in a context of considerable uncertainty about the exact structure of the economic system. In his paper, "The Theory of Monetary Policy under Uncertainty," William Poole examines the implications of the presence of uncertainty for the choice of a monetary policy target. Poole's analysis is, of course, based on a number of simplifying assumptions—he takes income stabilization as the only ultimate policy goal, and assumes that the uncertainty concerns only the intercepts of the behavioral relationships in the structure, and not their slopes. Nonetheless, he demonstrates quite convincingly that the choice of policy targets should be influenced by the relative degree of uncertainty present concerning the structure of different subsectors of the economy, and not merely by opinions or evidence on the sizes of various elasticities in the structure.

Another important operational consideration is the short- and long-run effects of particular policy actions. It is widely agreed that the effects of a monetary impulse on real variables such as income and employment are spread out over time. Therefore an all-out attempt to achieve a desired target for income (for example) in the current period through the use of monetary policy will have repercussions on income and other variables in many following periods, possibly causing more serious instability later on. Furthermore, such an attempt might result in unacceptable effects on financial variables now or later. James L. Pierce discusses these problems in his paper "The Trade-Off between Short- and Long-Term Policy Goals" in this chapter, and illustrates some of them with simulations using a large econometric model of the U.S. economy.

In recent years, a good deal of research effort has been directed at the estimation of the responses of different kinds of spending to changes in monetary policy. The expenditures that are most likely to be affected by monetary policy are those financed to a substantial extent by the use of credit. These include business investment in new plant and equipment; inventory investment; residential construction; consumer purchases of durable goods such as automobiles, electrical appliances, and furniture; and capital outlays by state and local governments. The paper by Michael J. Hamburger surveys a number of econometric studies that have been made of each of these categories of expenditures. These studies have uncovered considerable evidence that residential construction and business investment in plant and equipment are significantly affected by monetary policy. There are also indications of significant effects on consumer purchases of durable goods and on state and local government expenditures, although less research has been directed at the responses of these sectors. There is more uncertainty about the effects of monetary policy on inventory investment. A few studies suggest significant effects, but a number of investigators have been unsuccessful in isolating any monetary influences.

Two generalizations can be made concerning these studies. First, to the extent that monetary influences affect the various types of expenditures, the effects appear to work primarily through interest rates. Second, as was mentioned above, there are substantial time lags between changes in interest rates and the resulting changes in expenditures, although the lags seem to vary somewhat from one category of expenditures to another.

The results of this kind of investigation thus far can hardly be characterized as conclusive. In some cases, such as business investment in plant and equipment, in which a number of independent investigations have been carried out, the different investigators have used somewhat different models. While all of the recent studies indicate that monetary policy has significant effects on investment which operate with substantial lags, both the magnitude of the effect and the length of the lag vary considerably from one study to another. Clearly, much further study will be needed before we can predict the effects of monetary policy with very much confidence.

According to a Keynesian view, monetary policy has an initial impact on investment spending resulting from changes in interest rates. These changes in investment then have secondary effects on consumption through the multiplier process, and, in more sophisticated versions of the Keynesian model, on investment through accelerator-type responses. The survey in the Hamburger paper, discussed above, relates to the *initial impacts* on investment—defined broadly to include not only business investment but investment by households in new homes and durable goods and capital outlays by state and local governments. In a concluding section, Hamburger discusses briefly some results obtained by computer simulations using two large econometric models of the U.S. economy. These simulations provide estimates of the *total effects* on the economy of certain changes in monetary policy, including not only the initial impacts but also the secondary multiplier and accelerator effects. These simulations suggest that monetary policy has important effects but that the bulk of these effects are felt only after a considerable amount of time has elapsed following the initiation of a change in policy. One of the models referred to was constructed by a group of economists working under the auspices of the Brookings Institution and the other was assembled by two teams of economists, one from the Board of Governors of the Federal Reserve System and the other associated with the Massachusetts Institute of Technology. The reader will note that some of the results produced by the Brookings model are rather peculiar. This suggests that when a number of equations, each of which seems reasonable when taken separately, are assembled to form a large multiequation model, the interactions among the equations may produce rather unexpected results.

Econometric studies of the kind reviewed in the Hamburger paper do not always take full account of special institutional factors affecting the *availability* of financing for particular kinds of spending. This is especially true in the case of residential construction, as Hamburger points out. No doubt the demand for houses is affected by the cost of mortgage credit as reflected in mortgage interest rates. But as postwar experience has repeatedly demonstrated, most dramatically in the so-called "credit crunch" of 1966, changes in mortgage credit availability may greatly strengthen the impact of restrictive monetary policy on homebuilding and cause this impact to occur more rapidly than would be the case in the absence of these effects. There are three major ways in which mortgage credit availability may be affected by restrictive montary policy:

1. Commercial banks may raise interest rates on consumer-type time deposits to attract funds in order to be able to accommodate the loan demands of their business customers. If savings and loan associations do not raise the rates paid to their depositors or raise them less than the banks raise their rates, households may rechannel their saving flows away from savings and loan associations and toward the banks—or may even withdraw existing savings from savings and loan associations and shift them to banks. Even if banks do not raise interest rates on time deposits (because, for example, the Federal Reserve uses its power to establish ceilings on such interest rates under its so-called Regulation Q), a rise in interest rates on short- and intermediate-term open-market securities may set in motion a process of "disintermediation," with savers channeling their funds away from fixed-value redeemable claims generally (including deposits in both commercial banks and savings and loan associations) and directly into the securities markets. Either of the processes which drain funds away from savings and loan associations into commercial bank time deposits or into open-market securities can have a powerful effect on housing activity, because the associations are the most important source of funds for home financing. And with frozen portfolios of older mortgages, many of which may have been made at lower interest rates than currently prevail, these institutions may find it very difficult to pay substantially higher interest rates to attract and hold funds even if the regulatory authorities will permit them to do so.

2. When commercial banks feel the effects of credit restraint, they normally reduce their mortgage lending in order to be able to accommodate the needs of their business borrowers.

3. As interest rates rise, yields on corporate bonds typically rise relative to mortgage interest rates, and some institutional investors such as life insurance companies shift the composition of their investment flows away from mortgages and toward corporate bonds, which in any case have investment properties that make them more attractive than mortgages at equivalent yields. This tendency may be exacerbated by unrealistically low interest rate ceilings on FHA-insured and VA-guaranteed mortgages and by state usury laws applicable to conventional mortgages.

The paper by Warren L. Smith on government intermediaries in the residential mortgage market discusses the several institutional and behavioral changes which have recently been made by federal government agencies involved in this market. These changes are designed to strengthen the ties between the mortgage market and the capital market and to neutralize the role of changes in credit availability working through the channels described above in causing severe cyclical fluctuations in homebuilding in recent years. They were made in response particularly to the destructive effects of the "credit crunch" of 1966 on housing construction, as well as to the housing goals recently set in the Housing and Urban Development Act of 1968.

It has sometimes been alleged that capital outlays by state and local governments are also exceptionally vulnerable to the effects of restrictive monetary policy. The paper by John E. Petersen, which summarizes the results of a survey carried out by the Federal Reserve System and the Bureau of the Census, attempts to assess the effects of restricted credit availability in fiscal year 1970 on the borrowing and spending of state and local government units. The general conclusion is that the high interest rates of that year, combined with legal ceilings on maximum interest rates these governments could pay, caused a very substantial cutback in bond issues by these units but that the actual reductions in their capital spending were much smaller, since they turned to other sources—such as bank loans and liquidations of cash and security holdings—to maintain their spending.

In the next paper, Milton Friedman presents an analysis of the objectives which, in his judgment, monetary policy can and cannot accomplish. He concludes with a recommendation that efforts to conduct a discretionary monetary policy to counteract fluctuations be abandoned. In his view, our knowledge of the magnitude and the speed of the responses of economic activity to changes in monetary policy is so poor that efforts to conduct a discretionary countercyclical policy are likely to add to instability rather than subtract from it. In place of efforts to carry out a discretionary policy, he proposes that the monetary authorities adopt a "monetary rule"—that is, a publicly stated policy of allowing the supply of money to grow at a steady rate year after year. He does not specify what exact growth rate he would prefer but indicates that a rate between 3 and 5 percent per year would probably be appropriate.[1] In his opinion, the adoption of such a rule would reduce uncertainty and would represent the greatest contribution the monetary authorities could make to economic stability given the present state of knowledge about the working of monetary forces.

Friedman states his opinions vigorously and authoritatively, but the student should be warned that several of the propositions he advances either have little relevance to recent discussions concerning monetary policy or would not be accepted by many other close students of monetary phenomena. As Friedman points out, there can be little doubt that the Federal Reserve would encounter great difficulties if it attempted to "peg" interest rates at very low levels which would create severe inflationary tendencies. But while there may be some political figures who would favor such a policy, it would command almost no support among economists. Some economists would favor the use of interest rates as guides in the conduct of monetary policy, but the interest rate targets would be based on forecasts of future economic conditions and would change frequently as the economic outlook changed. Such an approach would not involve the "pegging" of rates for extended periods of time. There can be little doubt that the Federal Reserve can control interest rates with sufficient precision to make such an approach feasible.

---

[1] It may be noted that Friedman commonly employs a definition of money (sometimes referred to as M_2) that includes time deposits in commercial banks as well as demand deposits and currency. It is this broader total that he suggests should grow at a rate of 3 to 5 percent per year. This would imply a somewhat slower growth of the more conventional definition of the money supply (often called M_1), which includes only demand deposits and currency.

Friedman also expresses the view that there is a so-called "natural rate of unemployment" and that it is possible to reduce unemployment below this rate in the long run only at the cost of an accelerating rate of inflation. The natural rate of unemployment can be achieved in conjunction with stable prices or alternatively with prices rising or falling at a variety of steady rates—that is, in Friedman's view, in the long run the Phillips curve is simply a vertical line drawn at the natural rate of unemployment. The reader will recall that this possibility was discussed in the introduction to Chapter 1 in conjunction with the papers by James Tobin and Saul Hymans that are included in that chapter. The issue involved here is a very complex one, but Friedman's conclusion is certainly viewed with great skepticism by many students of economic policy.

Another controversial aspect of Friedman's paper is his interpretation of recent monetary policy. He blames the spotty performance of the economy during 1965–68 and the inflationary pressures that developed during that period on an excessively unstable Federal Reserve monetary policy. Many other observers would, however, place the chief blame on the rapid increase in defense spending associated with the escalation of hostilities in Vietnam combined with the excessive delay in the enactment of a needed increase in taxes—that is, on the poor performance of fiscal policy. Indeed, some would contend that the Federal Reserve's adjustments in monetary policy helped significantly to moderate the destabilizing forces generated by sharp fluctuations in the federal budget.

The paper by Lyle E. Gramley presents the case against the adoption of a simple monetary rule of the kind proposed by Friedman and for continued efforts to conduct a discretionary monetary policy. As Gramley points out, it is not proper to conclude that merely because the economy's responses to monetary policy are not fully understood, a rule is necessarily preferable to a discretionary policy conducted on the basis of the best knowledge available. Gramley argues that discretion is better than a rule, and the editors of this volume are disposed to agree with him. But we would point out that the issue is a complicated one which it is very difficult to settle conclusively, because we cannot replay history to see whether the economy would perform better or worse with a policy different from the one that was actually followed.

The selection from the 1969 *Annual Report of the Council of Economic Advisers* defends the use of discretionary monetary policy, arguing that it has made and can continue to make an important contribution to economic stability. It also expresses opposition to single-minded concentration on the stock of money or any other monetary aggregate as the sole guide in the conduct of discretionary policy. Indeed, it contends that considerable emphasis should be placed on interest rates and credit availability, since the available empirical evidence indicates that it is primarily through these variables that the effects of monetary policy are transmitted to the economy.

One point which is brought out in this selection—and which was also discussed in the introduction to Chapter 3—is worth emphasizing. Monetary policy, like fiscal policy, has both automatic and discretionary elements. When a weakening of private demand causes economic activity to recede, for example, interest rates automatically decline as credit demands are reduced, even with no action by the Federal Reserve. This automatic fall in interest rates should help to moderate the decline in economic activity, although the effect is unlikely to be great enough to induce recovery. In its conduct of discretionary policy the Federal Reserve should be sure that it reinforces that automatic tendency for interest rates to fall rather than inadvertently offsetting some part of the automatic effect, as it has sometimes done in the past. This argues for paying some attention to the money supply and credit flows even under a policy that is focused primarily on interest rates and credit availability. By making sure that the growth of the money supply and related monetary aggregates speeds up during recessions (and, of course, slows down during periods of inflationary boom), the Federal Reserve has some check to ensure that its discretionary actions are reinforcing the automatic element in monetary policy. As we know from the paper by Meek and Thunberg in Chapter 3, the Federal Reserve System now is giving a considerable amount of attention to the growth rates of monetary aggregates.

The last two papers included in the chapter deal with debt management and its relation to monetary policy. Debt management is a complex subject. Treasury cash borrowing and refunding operations—as well as the maturity composition of the Federal Reserve's purchases and sales of government securities in the course of its conduct of open market operations—affect the liquidity mix of the public's holdings of financial assets, as well as the maturity structure of interest rates. However, there is little solid evidence concerning the economic effects of such changes. We do not know, for example, how changes in liquidity or in the term structure of interest rates affect business investment decisions. Nor do we even have clear scientific knowledge concerning the effects of debt management operations on the rate structure itself. As the selection on the interest rate structure by Warren L. Smith points out, it seems likely that interest rate expectations are an important factor in determining the rate structure. If expectations are the predominant determinant—as a good deal of recent research seems to indicate—changes in the composition of outstanding debt may not have much effect, although they undoubtedly have at least some transient influence.

Given the unsatisfactory state of knowledge, it is not surprising that there are seriously conflicting views concerning debt management policy. The main competing theories and approaches to policy are sketched out in the article by William E. Laird. It will be plain to the reader that the whole subject is in a highly unsatisfactory state and that almost nothing that is really definitive can be concluded concerning it. Perhaps the reader will feel somewhat less upset if the editors of this volume express their judgment that debt management is a much less important matter for economic stabilization than either monetary or fiscal policy and that there are probably many alternative ways of managing the federal debt that are entirely consistent with effective use of the other policy instruments.

A NEO-KEYNESIAN VIEW OF MONETARY POLICY*

Warren L. Smith

Those of us who take an essentially Keynesian view in macroeconomics are often accused, some-

* From Federal Reserve Bank of Boston, *Controlling Monetary Aggregates*, Proceedings of the Monetary Conference held on Nantucket Island, June 8–10, 1969 (Boston, 1969), pp. 105–26. Reprinted by permission of the Federal Reserve Bank of Boston.

what unjustly, I believe, of minimizing the importance of monetary forces. That contention was probably true 20 years ago for a variety of historical and institutional reasons. But much water has passed over the dam since that time, and I believe it would now be difficult to find an example of the popular stereotype of the Keynesian economist who thinks fiscal policy is all-important and monetary policy is of no consequence. After all, in Keynesian analysis the power of monetary policy depends on the values of certain parameters, and if one is open-minded, he must be prepared to alter his views as empirical evidence accumulates. In some respects, this process has already proceeded quite far—some of the simulations performed with the FRB-MIT model, which is decidedly Keynesian in spirit, show monetary policy having very powerful effects indeed, albeit operating with somewhat disconcerting lags.

Thus, there is nothing inherent in the Keynesian view of the world that commits its adherents to the belief that monetary policy is weak. What is, it seems to me, distinctive about Keynesianism is the view that fiscal policy is capable of exerting very significant independent effects—that there are, broadly speaking, two instruments of stabilization policy, fiscal policy and monetary policy, and that the mix of the two is important. Indeed, I suppose most Keynesians would assign primacy to fiscal policy, although even this need not inevitably be the case. But in a certain fundamental sense, I believe the issue separating the Keynesians and the so-called Monetarist School relates more to fiscal than to monetary policy, since some Monetarists seem to deny that fiscal policy is capable of exerting any significant independent effects. In addition, the neo-Keynesian view seems to differ significantly from that of the Monetarists with respect to the role played by the stock of money in the process by which monetary policy affects the economy.

In this paper, I shall attempt to sketch what I would describe as a neo-Keynesian view of the process by which monetary and fiscal policy produce their effects on the economy and to evaluate some aspects of the recent controversy regarding stabilization policy in the context of this view. I shall then advance some suggestions concerning the conduct of monetary policy.

I. THE TRANSMISSION MECHANISM OF MONETARY POLICY

There appear to be several elements involved in the mechanism by which the effects of changes in monetary policy are transmitted to income, employment, and prices.

Portfolio Adjustments

The major advance in monetary theory in recent years has been the development of a sys-

tematic theory of portfolio adjustments involving financial and physical assets. This theory of portfolio adjustments fits very comfortably within a Keynesian framework and indeed greatly enriches Keynesian analysis and increases its explanatory power. The *General Theory,* itself, embodied a rudimentary theory of portfolio adjustments: the way in which the public divided its financial wealth between bonds and speculative cash balances depended on "the" rate of interest. The interest rate then affected investment expenditure, but Keynes failed to incorporate the stock of real capital into his analysis and relate it to the flow of investment spending. Indeed, many of the undoubted shortcomings of the *General Theory* stem from the failure to take account of capital accumulation.

The way in which monetary policy induces portfolio adjustments which will, in due course, affect income and employment may be described briefly as follows: A purchase of, say, Treasury bills by the Federal Reserve will directly lower the yield on bills and, by a process of arbitrage involving a chain of portfolio substitutions, will exert downward pressure on interest rates on financial assets generally. Moreover—and more important—the expansion of bank reserves will enable the banking system to expand its assets. If the discount rate is unchanged, the banks can be expected to use some portion of the addition to their reserves to strengthen their free reserve position by repaying borrowings at the Federal Reserve and perhaps by adding to their excess reserves. But the bulk of the addition to reserves will ordinarily be used to make loan accommodation available on more favorable terms, and to buy securities, thereby exerting a further downward effect on security yields.

With the expected yield on a unit of real capital initially unchanged, the decline in the yields on financial assets, and on the more favorable terms on which new debt can be issued, the balance sheets of households and businesses will be thrown out of equilibrium. The adjustment toward a new equilibrium will take the form of a sale of existing financial assets and the issuance of new debt to acquire real capital and claims thereto. This will raise the price of existing units of real capital—or equity claims against these units—relative to the (initially unchanged) cost of producing new units, thereby opening up a gap between desired and actual stocks of capital, a gap that will gradually be closed by the production of new capital goods. This stock adjustment approach is readily applicable, with some variations to suit the circumstances, to the demands for a wide variety of both business and consumer capital—including plant and equipment, inventories, residential construction, and consumer durable goods.

Wealth Effects

Since monetary policy operates entirely through voluntary transactions involving swaps of one financial asset for another, it does not add to wealth by creating assets to which there are no corresponding liabilities. Nevertheless, monetary policy does have wealth effects, which may be of considerable importance. An expansionary monetary policy lowers the capitalization rates employed in valuing expected income streams, thereby raising the market value of outstanding bonds as well as real wealth and equity claims thereto. In part, this strengthens the impact on economic activity of the portfolio adjustments, already referred to, by increasing the size of the net portfolios available for allocation. In addition, the increase in household wealth may significantly stimulate consumption. Indeed, in a recent version of the FRB-MIT model, the effect on consumption resulting from the induced change in the value of common stock equities held by households accounts for 35 to 45 percent of the initial impact of monetary policy in some simulations.

Credit Availability Effects

The portfolio and wealth effects appear to constitute the basic channels through which monetary policy has its initial impact on economic activity. In addition, however, the institutional arrangements for providing financing to certain sectors of the economy may be such as to give monetary policy a special leverage over the availability of credit to these sectors, thereby affecting their ability to spend. It is perhaps most illuminating to discuss changes in credit availability in the context of a restrictive monetary policy.

No doubt changes in credit availability affect many categories of expenditures to some degree. But the sector in which they are most clearly of major importance is homebuilding. Even in the absence of the rather unique institutional arrangements for its financing, housing demand might be significantly affected by monetary policy as changes in mortgage interest rates altered the desired housing stock. But as postwar experience has repeatedly shown, most dramatically in the "credit crunch" of 1966, changes in mortgage

credit availability may greatly strengthen the impact of restrictive monetary policy on homebuilding and cause the effects to occur much more rapidly than the stock-adjustment mechanism would imply. There are three different ways in which mortgage credit availability may be affected by a restrictive monetary policy.

First, commercial banks may raise interest rates on consumer-type time deposits to attract funds to meet the demands of their customers. If savings and loan associations do not raise the rates paid to their depositors or raise them less than the banks raise their rates, households may rechannel their saving flows away from the savings and loan associations and toward the banks—or may even withdraw existing savings from savings and loan associations and shift them to banks. Even if, as has recently been the case, the Regulation Q ceilings are used to prevent the banks from attracting household saving away from savings and loan associations, a rise in short- and intermediate-term open-market interest rates may set in motion a process of "disintermediation," with savers channelling their funds away from fixed-value redeemable claims generally and directly into the securities markets. Either of these processes which cut down the flows of funds to savings and loan associations can have, of course, a powerful effect on housing activity. With frozen portfolios of older mortgages made at lower interest rates than currently prevail, these institutions may find it difficult to pay substantially higher interest rates to attract or hold funds even if the Home Loan Bank Board will allow them to.

Second, when commercial banks feel the effects of credit restraint, they normally reduce their mortgage lending in order to be able to accommodate the needs of their business borrowers.

Third, as interest rates rise, yields on corporate bonds typically rise relative to mortgage interest rates, and some institutional investors, such as life insurance companies, shift the composition of their investment flows away from mortgages and toward corporate bonds, which, in any case, have investment properties which make them more attractive than mortgages at equivalent yields. This tendency may be exacerbated by unrealistically low interest rate ceilings on FHA and VA mortgages and by State usury laws applicable to conventional mortgages.

The way in which mortgage credit availability impinges on homebuilding has changed with the passage of time. In the 1950s, when FHA and VA financing was more important than it has been recently and when the FHA and VA interest rate ceilings were more rigid than they are now, restrictive monetary policy affected housing mainly by diverting the flows of funds coming from investors having diversified portfolios away from mortgages and toward corporate securities. That is, the third effect listed above was the most important. In 1966, when homebuilding was drastically curtailed by monetary restraint, all of the effects were operating, but the first— the drain of funds away from savings and loan associations—was by far the most important. In 1968 and 1969, interest rates have risen suffi- ciently to arouse concern about a repetition of the 1966 experience. But while housing seems currently to be feeling the effects of tight money, it has proved to be much less vulnerable than was generally expected. There are several reasons for this, but the one most worthy of mention is the adoption by the Federal Reserve and the various Federal housing agencies of a number of measures designed to cushion or offset the effects of high interest rates on housing activity.

Secondary Effects

Working through portfolio effects, wealth effects, and credit availability effects, the initial impacts of monetary policy will generate addi- tional income, and this will further increase the demand for consumer nondurable goods and ser- vices. It will also expand the demand for the services of durable goods, thereby giving a fur- ther boost to the desired stocks of these goods. Thus, the familiar magnification of demand through multiplier and accelerator effects comes into play. It is often overlooked that the sharp reduction in the multiplier since the 1930s as a result of the greatly increased income-sensitivity of the tax-transfer system has presumably had important effects on the working of monetary as well as fiscal policy. Indeed, I would judge this increase in "built-in stability" through the fiscal system to be a major factor making mone- tary policy less potent today than in earlier times.

A further chain of secondary effects is set in motion as the rise in income increases demands for demand deposits and currency for transactions purposes, thereby reversing the initial decline in interest rates. This induced rise in interest rates will exert a dampening effect on the expansion by a partial reversal of the forces that initially triggered the rise in income. Whether or not this secondary effect will carry interest rates all the way back to their initial level (or higher) is an open question, concerning which I shall have some comments later on in this paper.

Effects on Real Output vs. Prices

I think almost all economists of a Keynesian persuasion would accept the proposition that the way in which the effect of an increase in demand is divided between output response and price- level response depends on the way it impinges on productive capacity. Thus, expansion caused by monetary policy is generally no more or no less inflationary than expansion caused by fiscal policy (or, for that matter, by an autonomous increase in private demand). This statement needs to be qualified in a couple of minor re- spects. First, monetary expansion might be less inflationary than an equivalent amount of fiscal expansion over the longer run if it resulted in more investment, thereby causing labor produc- tivity to increase more rapidly. Second, the im- pacts of monetary policy are distributed among sectors in a different way from those of fiscal policy; and, with less than perfect mobility of resources, the inflationary effect might depend to some degree on this distribution.

II. SOME CONTROVERSIAL ISSUES

I would now like to discuss several of the issues that seem to be at the heart of the recent controversy regarding monetary and fiscal policy.

The Effectiveness of Fiscal Policy

For the purpose of isolating the effects of fiscal policy from those of monetary policy, I believe a "pure" fiscal policy action should be defined as a change in government expenditures or a change in tax rates without any accompanying change in the instruments of monetary policy. Under our present institutional set-up, the instru- ments of monetary policy are open-market opera- tions, changes in reserve requirements, and changes in the Federal Reserve discount rate. Open-market operations may be viewed as gov- erning unborrowed reserves plus currency, with defensive operations offsetting undesired changes in this total that would result from erratic varia- tions in float, gold stock, etc.

An increase in government purchases of goods and services, with tax rates constant, would affect the economy by three different routes. First, there would be a direct expansionary *income effect* resulting from the purchase of output by the government. Second, there would be an expan- sionary *wealth effect* as the private sector, experi- encing an increment to its wealth entirely in the form of net claims against the government, increased its demand for real capital in an effort to diversify its portfolios.[1] These income and wealth effects would set off a multiplier-accelerator process of economic expansion. This expansion, in turn, would activate a partially offsetting monetary effect as the rise in income increased the demand for money. If the dial settings of the monetary instruments remained unchanged, this would drive 'up interest rates. The rise in interest rates would cause some reductions in those types of expenditures that were sensitive to interest rates through portfolio, wealth, and availability effects.

The wealth effect of fiscal policy may be quite powerful, particularly because it is cumulative—that is, it continues to operate until the budget has been brought back into balance, thereby shutting off the increase in net claims against the government. But, unfortunately, no effort that I know of has been made to incorporate it in an empirical model; consequently there is no way to formulate even a crude estimate of its importance.

If we neglect the wealth effect simply because we do not know how much weight to give it, we are left with the income effect and the offsetting monetary effect. The monetary effect will be greater (a) the greater the proportion of expenditures in GNP that are affected by interest rates, (b) the greater (in absolute value) is the average interest elasticity of these expenditures, (c) the greater is the income elasticity of demand for money, (d) the smaller (in absolute value) is the interest elasticity of demand for money and (e) the smaller is the interest elasticity of the supply of money.[2]

Only if the interest elasticities of both the demand for and supply of money are zero will the monetary effect completely cancel out the income effect.[3] That is, there will be some leeway for fiscal policy to increase income if a rise in interest rates either induces economization in the use of demand deposits and currency or causes the supply of such monetary assets to expand (for example, by inducing banks to increase their borrowings at the Federal Reserve). Since the empirical evidence is overwhelming that both money demand and money supply possess some degree of interest elasticity, it seems clear that fiscal policy is capable of exerting an independent effect on income. This conclusion is heavily supported by evidence derived from large structural models of the U.S. economy. For example, while there is no unique multiplier for fiscal policy in the FRB-MIT model, a number of simulations with that model show fiscal policy to have very substantial independent effects on economic activity.

It is often pointed out, especially by those who emphasize the role of money in the economy, that the effect produced by a stimulative fiscal action is dependent on the way in which the resulting deficit is financed. This is in a sense true, but this way of putting it is somewhat misleading. For example, it is sometimes stated that, in order to achieve the full Keynesian multiplier effect, the entire deficit must be financed by creating money—some statements even say high-powered money. What is necessary to achieve this result is to create enough money to satisfy the demand for money at the new higher level of income and the initial level of interest rates.

Ordinarily, the required increase in the supply of money will be only a fraction of the deficit, and the required increase in high-powered money will be an even smaller fraction. Moreover, there

---

[1] For an extensive theoretical treatment of the wealth effect, see James Tobin, "An Essay on the Principles of Debt Management," in *Fiscal and Debt Management Policies* (Englewood Cliffs, N.J.: Prentice-Hall, Inc., 1963), pp. 142–218.

[2] It is possible to derive a more elaborate version of the static Keynesian multiplier incorporating the monetary effect. The following is such a multiplier equation.

$$\frac{dY}{dG} = \frac{1}{1 - e + \dfrac{\dfrac{I}{Y}\eta_{Ir}\eta_{LY}}{\eta_{Lr} - \eta_{Mr}}}$$

Here Y is GNP; G is government purchases; e is the marginal propensity to spend out of GNP; I/Y is the proportion of GNP that is sensitive to interest rates; η_{Ir} (< 0) is the average interest elasticity of interest-sensitive expenditures; η_{Lr} (< 0) is the interest elasticity of demand for money; η_{Mr} (> 0) is the interest elasticity of supply of money; and η_{LY} (> 0) is the income elasticity of demand for money. The usual

simple Keynesian multiplier without allowance for monetary effect is $1/(1 - e)$. The monetary effect is incorporated in the third term (taking the form of a fraction) in the denominator of the equation above. Since this term is positive, its presence reduces the size of the multiplier. The statement in the text above regarding the factors determining the size of the monetary effect is based on this expression.

[3] In this case, the supply of money may be regarded as exogenously determined. If the demand for money depends only on income, income will have to change sufficiently to eliminate any discrepancies that arise between the demand for and supply of money. Thus, money controls income, and fiscal policy is incapable of affecting it. The reader will note that if both η_{Mr} and η_{Lr} are zero, the multiplier for fiscal policy given in footnote 2 above becomes zero.

is a serious stock-flow problem. When income reaches its new equilibrium in a stable economy, the increased deficit (a flow) will be financed out of the excess of saving over investment generated by the rise in income. Additional demand deposits and currency are needed to meet the increased transaction demand at the higher income level, but this requires only a single increase in the money stock. In reality, there may be further complexities that require a modification of this principle—for example, if the demand for money depends on wealth as well as income or if the price level is determined by a Phillips Curve mechanism so that prices are not merely higher but are increasing more rapidly at higher levels of income.

Nevertheless, the principle is, I believe, basically correct. Rather than saying that the multiplier depends on how the deficit is financed, I think it is more accurate to say that it depends on the kind of monetary policy that accompanies the fiscal action. If monetary policy is such as to hold interest rates approximately constant, something analogous to the full Keynesian multiplier (with no monetary feedback) will be realized; if it allows interest rates to rise, the multiplier will be somewhat smaller; if it causes interest rates to fall, the multiplier will be somewhat greater.[4]

The Role of Money

Although I have used the term "money" in my discussion above, I am not sure the term is a very useful or meaningful one. Money (in the sense of means of payment) has two components, demand deposits and currency. Those two components are not, however, perfect substi-

tutes—they are held, by and large, by different kinds of spending units; demand for them responds in different ways to different stimuli; and, because they are subject to markedly different reserve requirements, shifts between them alter the total amount of credit that can be supplied by the financial system. They are best regarded as two different financial assets and treated as such.

Moreover, there is no apparent reason why "money"—whether in the form of currency or demand deposits—is more or less important than any of the myriad other financial assets that exist. It is now generally agreed that the demands for demand deposits and currency depend on the yields available on alternative assets and on income or related measures (and possibly, but by no means certainly, on wealth). Thus, the quantities of currency and demand deposits held by the public are generally agreed to be endogenous variables determined in a general equilibrium setting along with the prices and quantities of other financial and real assets.

Nor is there any appreciable evidence that money—whether in the form of demand deposits or currency—affects peoples' spending on goods and services directly. Such empirical evidence as there is suggests that people change their expenditures on goods and services because (a) their income changes; (b) their wealth changes; (c) their portfolios are thrown out of equilibrium by changes in relative yields on real and financial assets by actions taken by the monetary or fiscal authorities; (d) credit availability changes for institutional reasons altering in one direction or the other their ability to finance expenditures they want to make; or (e) their propensities to spend or their preferences for different kinds of assets change for essentially exogenous reasons, such as changes in tastes, changes in technology, and so on. That changes in the stock of money *per se* would affect spending seems to me highly improbable.

Of course, if changes in stocks of demand deposits and currency—or the combination of the two—were tightly linked to those changes in yields, in wealth, and in credit availability through which monetary policy operates, changes in the stocks of these monetary assets might be highly useful measures of the thrust of policy even though they played no part in the causal nexus. But this, too, I think is unlikely. In a highly sophisticated financial system such as ours, in which new financial instruments and practices are constantly being introduced, it seems highly improbable that the demands for monetary assets

---

[4] If fiscal policy has a wealth effect working through changes in the public's holdings of net claims against the government, it seems quite likely that the magnitude of this effect will depend on the form taken by the change in net claims. For example, a change in public holdings of short-term debt may have a larger effect on aggregate demand than an equal change in holdings of long-term debt. To the extent that this is the case, debt management policies which change the maturity composition of the public's holdings of government debt may have important economic effects. But there is no reason to focus special attention on the composition of increments to the debt resulting from deficits, since the increment to the debt in any year is only a tiny fraction of the total debt to be managed. In any case, as indicated earlier, we are entirely neglecting the wealth effect because in the present state of knowledge there is no way of forming a judgment concerning its importance.

are simple and stable functions of a few unchanging variables.

The many empirical studies of the demand for money that have been made in recent years have generally proved incapable of differentiating among alternative hypotheses. Consequently, one is free to choose among a variety of possible theories of the demand for money. The one that appeals to me is the hypothesis that money (i.e., demand deposits and currency) is dominated by time deposits and very short-dated securities, with the result that it is not a significant portion of permanent portfolios. This leaves the demand for monetary assets as an interest-elastic transactions demand along the lines postulated by Baumol and by Tobin.[5]

Such an explanation, however, makes sense only for relatively large business firms and wealthy individuals. It does not seem applicable to smaller units. Among such units, I suspect that the general rise in interest rates that has been going on for the past two decades has pushed these rates successively above the thresholds of awareness of different groups of people, causing them to abandon their careless habit of foregoing income by holding excessive cash balances. If I am right, this behavior is probably not readily reversible if interest rates should fall. It seems to me that there is still a substantial element of mystery about the demand for monetary assets—mystery that will probably be resolved, if at all, only on the basis of extensive study of the behavior of the cash-holdings of micro-units.

Relationship between Changes in Money and Changes in Income

None of the above should be taken to mean that there is no relation between changes in demand deposits and currency and changes in income. Indeed, I believe there are three such relationships, which are very difficult to disentangle.

First, an expansionary monetary policy that stimulated increased spending and income through portfolio effects, wealth effects, and credit availability effects would bring in its wake an increase in supplies of demand deposits and currency. This would be a sideshow rather than the main event, but it would nevertheless occur. But the size of the increase associated with a given stimulus might vary considerably from one situation to another.

Second, a rise in income caused by fiscal policy or by an autonomous shift of private demand, with the monetary dials unchanged, would react back on the money supply in three different ways.[6] (1) The rise in interest rates caused by the rise in income would cause the banks to increase their borrowings from the Federal Reserve and perhaps to economize on excess reserves. (2) The rise in market interest rates would cause investors to shift funds from time deposits and similar claims into securities if, as is likely, the interest rates on these claims did not rise fully in pace with market rates. This would cause the quantity of demand deposits to increase as investors withdrew funds from time accounts and paid them over to sellers of securities for deposit in demand accounts. (3) If banks and related institutions raised rates on time-deposit type claims, some holders of noninterest-bearing demand deposits would be induced to shift funds to time accounts. To the extent that issuers of these claims held cash reserves against them, the amount of reserves available to support demand deposits would be reduced, requiring a contraction in these deposits. Effects (1) and (2) would cause the money supply to increase, while effect (3) would cause it to fall. It seems likely that (1) and (2) would outweigh (3), leading to an increase in the supply of monetary assets. The probability of this outcome would be increased if the Federal Reserve was laggard in adjusting Regulation Q ceilings. Indeed, a rigid Regulation Q ceiling would completely immobilize effect (3) while maximizing the size of effect (2).

Third, under the rubric of "meeting the needs of trade" or "leaning against the wind," the Federal Reserve has, at times, adjusted the supply of reserves to accommodate, or partially accommodate, changes in the demand for money brought about by changes in income, thereby creating a third chain of causation running from income to money supply.

With perhaps three relations between money and income present at the same time—one running from money to income and two running

---

[5] See W. J. Baumol, "The Transactions Demand for Cash: An Inventory Theoretic Approach," *Quarterly Journal of Economics,* LXVI, November 1952, pp. 545–56; James Tobin, "The Interest Elasticity of the Transactions Demand for Cash," *Review of Economics and Statistics,* XXXVIII, August 1956, pp. 241–47.

[6] This discussion is based on an analysis developed in W. L. Smith, "Time Deposits, Free Reserves, and Monetary Policy," in Giulio Pontecorvo, R. P. Shay, and A. G. Hart (eds.), *Issues in Banking and Monetary Analysis* (New York: Holt, Rinehart and Winston, Inc., 1967), pp. 79–113.

from income to money—it is likely to be almost impossible to tell what is going on by direct observation. And, as Tobin has shown, in such a complex dynamic situation, it is almost impossible to infer anything conclusive about causation by studying the lags.[7]

Does Easy Money Cause Interest Rates to Rise?

One of the supposedly startling propositions that has been advanced recently is the notion that an easing of monetary policy—commonly measured in terms of the rate of increase in the money stock—will cause interest rates to rise and, conversely, that a tightening of monetary policy will cause interest rates to fall. To be sure, if the rate of growth of the money stock is accelerated, interest rates will decline at first. But before long, money income will begin to grow so rapidly that the resulting increase in the demand for money will, it is contended, pull interest rates back up above the level from which they originally started.

In the first place, this possibility has long been recognized in Keynesian economics. In a static Keynesian model it is possible for the IS curve to have a positive slope, with stability conditions requiring only that this slope be less than that of the LM curve. This could happen, for example, if income had a strong effect on investment.[8] In such a situation, a shift to the right of the LM curve, which might be caused by an increase in the money stock, would cause the equilibrium interest rate to rise. A more realistic possibility is that the economy contains endogenous cycle-generators of the accelerator or stock-adjustment type, which cause income to respond so vigorously to a stimulative monetary policy that interest rates rise above their original level at an ensuing cyclical peak.

---

[7] James Tobin, "Money and Income: Post Hoc Ergo Propter Hoc?" (mimeographed); also W. C. Brainard and James Tobin, "Pitfalls in Financial Model Building," *American Economic Review*, LVIII, May 1968, pp. 99–122.

[8] The actual condition required is that the sum of the marginal propensities to consume and invest must exceed one, but (as a condition for stability) be less than one plus a term measuring the size of the monetary feedback. (Even if the two propensities totaled less than unity, the IS curve could slope upward if a rise in interest rates caused total spending to rise. But this could occur only on the remote chance that the income effect dominated the substitution effect in saving behavior so powerfully that a rise in interest rates caused consumption to increase by more than it caused investment to decline.)

There is another chain of causation, working through the effects of inflation on nominal interest rates, which might cause a decline in real interest rates to be associated with a rise in nominal interest rates. This possibility has generally been neglected by Keynesians, but it is in no way inconsistent with Keynesian analysis. An expansionary monetary policy, which lowers nominal interest rates (and real interest rates) initially, will push the economy up the Phillips Curve, thus causing prices to rise more rapidly. As the increase in the actual rate of inflation generates a rise in the anticipated future rate of inflation, an inflation premium may get built into interest rates, causing nominal interest rates to rise. It seems possible that nominal interest rates could be pushed above their original level even though real interest rates remain below this level. This outcome would be more likely (a) the greater the expansionary effect of a given fall in the real rate of interest on real income, (b) the greater the decline in unemployment caused by a given increase in real income, (c) the greater the increase in the rate of inflation caused by a given decline in unemployment, and (d) the more sensitive the response of the anticipated rate of inflation to a change in the actual rate of inflation.[9] The probability that nominal interest rates would be pushed above their initial level by this mechanism is very difficult to evaluate, however, primarily because we know very little about the extent to which, and the speed with which, an increase in the actual rate of inflation gets translated into an increase in the anticipated rate of inflation.

Thus, the notion that an expansionary mone-

---

[9] Beginning with the equation $r = r' + p_e$, which expresses the relation between the nominal interest rate (r), the real interest rate (r') and the anticipated rate of inflation (p_e), the following expression can be rather easily derived.

$$\frac{dr}{dr'} = 1 + m \frac{dI}{dr'} \frac{du}{dY} \frac{dp}{du} \frac{dp_e}{dp}$$

Here m is the multiplier; dI/dr' is the response of interest-sensitive expenditures to a change in the real rate of interest; du/dY is the response of the unemployment rate to a change in real GNP; dp/du is the response of the rate of inflation to a change in the unemployment rate (i.e., the slope of the Phillips Curve); and dp_e/dp is the response of the anticipated rate of inflation to a change in the actual rate of inflation. Since three of the components of the second term on the right-hand side of the equation (dI/dr', du/dY, and dp/du) take on negative values, the second term as a whole is negative. Whether a fall in the real rate of interest will cause the nominal rate of interest to rise or fall depends on whether the second term on the right is larger or smaller than unity.

tary policy would ultimately cause nominal interest rates to rise above their initial level is in no way inconsistent with Keynesian views. Whether such a phenomenon actually occurs is a different matter. With fiscal policy changing and with the strength of private demand changing, it is not safe to conclude that, because an easing of monetary policy was followed at some later time by a rise of interest rates above their initial level, the easing of monetary policy *caused* the rise in interest rates. The best evidence I have seen is from simulations with the FRB-MIT model which show that an injection of bank reserves causes interest rates to fall sharply at first and then rise gradually but only part of the way back to their original level. But, of course, simulations starting from a different initial position might show different results. In all probability, the phenomenon in question occurs under some conditions but not under others.

III. SUGGESTIONS REGARDING POLICY

At the very beginning of this discussion of the conduct of monetary policy, let me make clear that I am not talking about the issue of rules versus discretion. That is a different subject, which I will discuss briefly at the conclusion of my paper. Assuming that the Federal Reserve will continue to conduct a discretionary policy, let us consider what is the best way to proceed with that task.

It seems to me that much of the recent literature on monetary policy has been obsessed with a search for a magic touchstone—some measure of the impact of monetary forces that can be used as the sole guide in the conduct of policy. Unfortunately, I don't believe there is such a touchstone—the world is too complicated and we know too little about it for that. There is a second related obsession with the problem of characterizing monetary policy. Is it "tight" or "easy"? Is it "tighter" or "easier" today than it was, say, six months ago?

The first of these questions is clearly a matter of judgment and opinion. The second, comparative form of the question sounds more capable of a scientific answer, but in fact I think it is equally unanswerable. Does it mean, "Is monetary policy contributing more to aggregate demand today than it was six months ago?" If it does mean that—and I can think of no other interpretation—I wouldn't have the faintest idea how to go about answering it. The problem facing the Federal Reserve, however, is not how to characterize monetary policy but how to carry

it out, and this puts things in a somewhat different light.

Since monetary policy affects economic activity with substantial lags, policy must clearly be based on forecasts of future economic conditions. While our knowledge has improved considerably, we still cannot be very sure about the lags, which undoubtedly depend upon underlying conditions. Moreover, the lags vary from sector to sector. It seems quite clear that monetary policy can affect homebuilding quite rapidly, at least under some conditions, if the dials of policy are adjusted in the right way. The lags in the effects on the other sectors appear to be considerably longer. Forecasting is also a difficult task, but there is no way to escape the need for it. Not the least of the difficulties of monetary policy, as has been demonstrated several times in the last three years or so, is the forecasting of fiscal policy.

While the ultimate goals of policy are high employment, price stability, the rate of growth of output, and so on, these cannot be used as immediate guides to policy, because it takes so long for policy measures to affect them. The authorities must choose as guides to policy some more immediate and more specifically monetary variables that appear to be related to the goals they are trying to achieve.

There are a number of monetary aggregates that the Federal Reserve can control with varying degrees of precision if it chooses to do so. It can obviously control its portfolio of securities exactly, and it can control unborrowed reserves plus currency outside member banks quite closely by employing defensive open-market operations to offset changes in uncontrollable factors affecting reserves, such as float, gold stock, Treasury deposits at Federal Reserve banks, etc. It can probably control total reserves plus currency (the monetary base) fairly accurately either by using open-market operations to offset changes in member bank borrowing or by changing the administration of discount policy to reduce the fluctuations in borrowing. The stock of demand deposits and currency would be more difficult to control, but I suspect that its average value over a quarter's time could be controlled fairly satisfactorily.

Alternatively, policy could be directed at regulating interest rates, although some interest rates would be easier to control than others. The Treasury bill rate could be controlled with any desired degree of accuracy under present operating procedures, because the Federal Reserve deals directly in the Treasury bill market. By a shift in its operating procedures, the Federal Reserve could control the yield on some other maturity of Federal debt. I believe it could, instead, maintain fairly close control of a variety of alternative interest rates on private debt—such as the Aaa corporate bond yield—although it would have to influence such rates indirectly unless it were to deal in private debt.

The basic issue of monetary policy is: Should the Federal Reserve focus primarily on controlling some monetary aggregate or should it focus on controlling interest rates? I believe there is a very strong *prima' facie* case for a policy that is oriented toward interest rates. The reason is that the portfolio effects, wealth effects, and credit availability effects through which the impacts of monetary policy are transmitted to the economy are better measured by changes in interest rates than by changes in monetary aggregates. The vast bulk of the empirical evidence supports this view, indicating that it is through interest rates that monetary policy affects expenditures on goods and services. Indeed, I know of no evidence that any monetary aggregate that the Federal Reserve could control an effect on expenditures.

Of course, if there were tight and well understood linkages between some monetary aggregate—say, the stock of demand deposits and currency—and interest rates, it would matter little which the Federal Reserve attempted to control, because a money target would imply an interest rate target. There are indeed linkages between monetary aggregates and interest rates—these linkages are, in my judgment, sufficient to prevent the Federal Reserve from controlling both monetary aggregates and interest rates except to a very limited extent. But the linkages are not well understood and are subject to change as a result of financial innovations and changes in patterns of financial behavior. Consequently, it does make a difference whether the Federal Reserve selects a monetary aggregate or an interest rate as a guide to policy.

Advantages of Treasury Bill Rate as a Guide to Policy

My specific suggestion is that the Federal Reserve focus on the Treasury bill rate as its basic guide for monetary policy. There are several advantages in this approach. First, the Federal Reserve can, without any basic change in its operating procedures, control the Treasury bill rate with virtually any degree of accuracy it desires. Second, there are many occasions on which the bill rate must be a focus of attention anyway, because it is the key short-term rate affecting international capital flows. Third, the bill rate is closely related to market interest rates on those forms of short- and intermediate-term debt that compete with fixed-value redeemable claims and are therefore of critical importance for the availability of mortgage funds. Fourth, there is considerable evidence that the bill rate works through an expectational mechanism to affect those long-term rates that are important in determining the cost of capital to business firms, State and local governments, and home buyers. Moreover, the wealth effect of monetary policy works through capitalization rates that would be indirectly affected by a policy aimed in the first instance at the Treasury bill rate.

Of course, the bill rate target would have to be selected on the basis of a forecast of economic activity several quarters ahead, including a forecast of fiscal policy. One could, for example, use a model such as the FRB-MIT model to estimate a pattern of behavior of the bill rate that could be expected to achieve the desired performance of the economy over the next three or four quarters, given the anticipated fiscal policy. This target could then be adjusted on the basis of special factors or judgmental considerations. I would not propose to peg the bill rate exactly but to establish a range of, say, 20 basis points within which it would be permitted to fluctuate. The bill rate target would, of course, be reexamined at each meeting of the FOMC on the basis of the latest forecast of the economic outlook.

I would not, however, adhere dogmatically to such a "bills-only" policy. If long-term interest rates should fail to respond in the anticipated way to a change in the bill rate target, I would not hesitate to nudge them along by open-market operations in long-term Treasury securities. Nor would I entirely neglect monetary aggregates. I would want to supplement the bill rate target with some kind of quantitative guideline to prevent gross mistakes in policy. In the case of a non-growing economy, using the stock of demand deposits and currency as the quantitative guideline, the matter is relatively simple—one should be sure that this stock increases when the economy is below full employment and declines when it is above full employment. The problem here is one of distinguishing between automatic and discretionary elements of policy—similar to the problem in fiscal policy that gave rise to the full-employment surplus concept. When the economy is weak, for example, interest rates decline automatically even if the monetary authorities do nothing, and it is desirable to be sure that the authorities are reinforcing this tendency by discretionary measures rather than offsetting it as they sometimes appear to have done in the past.

The problem of developing a suitable monetary guideline is considerably more complicated in the case of a growing economy. My procedure would be to begin by estimating a "normal" rate of monetary growth. For example, if the target point on the Phillips Curve is 4 percent unemployment which is judged to be associated with 2 percent inflation, if the rate of growth of productive capacity under full employment conditions is estimated to be 4 percent per year, and if the income elasticity of demand for monetary assets is judged to be unity, the "normal" rate of monetary growth would be estimated at 6 percent per year. At any particular time, if the objective of policy was to restrain the economy, growth should be less than 6 percent; if the objective was to stimulate the economy, growth should be more than 6 percent.

There is a problem of deciding what aggregate to use as an index of monetary growth. Should it be the monetary base as calculated by the Federal Reserve Bank of St. Louis, the money supply, total bank credit, or some other aggregate? Unfortunately, the significance of a change in the rate of growth of any of the commonly used aggregates depends upon the public's preferences for different categories of financial assets, including currency, demand deposits, time deposits, and securities. Since these preferences appear to change for reasons that we do not yet fully understand, problems of interpretation are bound to arise. My quite tentative suggestion would be to use the monetary base as the index of monetary growth. But I would also monitor the behavior of the other aggregates closely. If the selected bill rate target resulted in growth of the base inconsistent with the guideline for several weeks and if the behavior of the other aggregates seemed to support the conclusion that monetary growth was too slow or too fast, the whole situation, including the bill rate target, should be carefully reexamined.

Other Dimensions to Be Considered

I think an approach along the lines developed above would make sense in providing an overall rationale for monetary policy. But there are important dimensions that are omitted in the above discussion. It has long been my contention that those responsible for the conduct of monetary policy must pay close attention to its impacts on particular sectors of the economy, especially when a restrictive policy is being followed. An example of this dimension of monetary policy is the variety of measures that have been taken by the Federal Reserve and a number of other Federal Government agencies during the past year to cushion the impact of high interest rates on homebuilding.

The Federal Reserve has attempted to shield the savings and loan associations from bank competition by maintaining low ceiling rates on savings deposits and those forms of time deposits that compete most directly with savings and loan shares. The Federal Home Loan Bank Board has acted to encourage continued mortgage lending by savings and loan associations by reducing the liquidity requirement applicable to the associations and by making advances available to them. In addition, the Home Loan Banks have attempted to manage their own borrowings in the capital market in such a way as to minimize the possible impact on deposit flows. The Federal National Mortgage Association increased its mortgage holdings by $1.6 billion in 1968, and increased the scope and flexibility of its stabilizing activities in the mortgage market by introducing a new program of weekly auctions of mortgage commitments, beginning in May 1968. The ceiling rate applicable to FHA and VA mortgages was raised from 6 percent to 6¾ percent in May and was raised further to 7½ percent in January 1969. Finally, in its general conduct of monetary policy, the Federal Reserve has kept its eye on the flows of funds to savings and loan associations with a view to avoiding, if possible, a rise in short- and intermediate-term interest rates sufficient to set off a "disintermediation crises" of the type that occurred in 1966.

The impact of monetary policy on the economy would, I believe, have been substantially different in 1968, and thus far in 1969, in the absence of these precautionary actions by the Federal Reserve and by the various agencies with responsibilities in the housing field. In all probability, we would long since have experienced a sharp decline in housing starts and residential construction expenditures similar to that which occurred in 1966. There are a number of reforms which might be adopted to increase the efficiency and flexibility of the mortgage market and to reduce the excessive impact that monetary policy now tends to have on homebuilding. Unless and until such reforms are implemented, however, I believe it is appropriate for the monetary authorities to concern themselves specifically with the effects of their policies on the housing sector. Indeed, I believe structural measures of the kind employed in 1968–69 should be thought of as part of monetary policy and should be applied as the situation seems to warrant on the basis of close cooperation between the Federal Reserve and the other agencies involved.

No matter how skillfully monetary policy is conducted, things are bound to go wrong from time to time. The underlying strength of private demand will sometimes prove to be stronger or weaker than was anticipated; fiscal policy will depart from its expected path; and the timing and magnitude of the economy's response to monetary actions will seldom be exactly as anticipated. I do not count myself among the group of economists who believe the business cycle is dead. If we seriously attempt to keep the economy moving along a selected high-employment growth path, resisting departures from that path in either direction, I believe we can still expect some economic fluctuations. The hope is that we can keep these fluctuations mild. But our success in that respect is much more critically dependent on improving the performance of fiscal policy than it is on changing the techniques of monetary management. Improved fiscal policy would relieve the Federal Reserve of its recent impossible task of offsetting the effects of profoundly destabilizing movements of the Federal budget. Even operating within the framework established by a reasonably well-designed fiscal policy, the Federal Reserve is bound to make occasional mistakes, but it should be able to make an effective contribution to economic stabilization and do so without the sharp gyrations in monetary variables that we have witnessed recently.

IV. RULES VERSUS AUTHORITIES

There is no reason, in principle, why one holding Keynesian views must necessarily favor discretion over a monetary rule. One could believe that our knowledge of the responses and the lags in the system is so poor that efforts to conduct a discretionary policy add to instability rather than subtract from it. I think discretion conducted on the basis of the best information available can do a better job than a rule, but I find the question a very complex one, and I do not see how anyone can be sure of the answer.

Before a rule involving steady growth of some aggregate such as the monetary base could be seriously considered, however, it seems to me there would have to be procedural or institutional changes in three areas.

First, there would have to be some assurance of better fiscal policy than we have had recently. Our problems of the last three years are primarily the result of inaction and inordinate delay in fiscal policy, and discretionary monetary policy has helped by either taking the place of needed fiscal restraint or supplementing it when it was too-long delayed.

Second, if monetary policy is to disregard interest rates entirely, I believe we need an overhaul of the arrangement for financing housing.

And, third, interest rates cannot be disregarded until the international monetary system has been reformed in some way to remove the balance-of-payments constraint on domestic interest rates.

Having said all of this, let me add that I believe the discussion of monetary rules is largely academic anyway. Even assuming that a rule were adopted, I feel certain that there would be overwhelming pressure to abandon it the first time it appeared that discretion would enable us to achieve a better performance—and that, I believe, would occur quite soon after the rule was adopted.

THE THEORY OF MONETARY POLICY UNDER UNCERTAINTY*

William Poole

INTRODUCTION

This study has been motivated by the recognition that the key to understanding policy problems is the analysis of uncertainty. Indeed, in the absence of uncertainty it might be said that

* From William Poole, "Rules-of-Thumb for Guiding Monetary Policy," in *Open Market Policies and Operating Procedures—Staff Studies* (Washington, D.C.: Board of Governors of the Federal Reserve System, 1971), pp. 135–89. Reprinted by permission of the Board of Governors of the Federal Reserve System and the author. William Poole is Senior Economist, Special Studies Section, Division of Research and Statistics, Board of Governors of the Federal Reserve System.

there can be no *policy* problems, only *administrative* problems. It is surprising, therefore, that there has been so little systematic attention paid to uncertainty in the policy literature in spite of the fact that policy-makers have repeatedly emphasized the importance of the unknown.

In the past, the formal models used in the analysis of monetary policy problems have almost invariably assumed complete knowledge of the economic relationships in the model. Uncertainty is introduced into the analysis, if at all, only through informal consideration of how much difference it makes if the true relationships differ from those assumed by the policy-makers. In this study, on the other hand, uncertainty plays a key role in the formal model.

BASIC CONCEPTS

The theory of optimal policy under uncertainty has provided many insights into actual policy problems [1, 2, 3, 6]. While much of this theory is not accessible to the nonmathematical economist, it is possible to explain the basic ideas without resort to mathematics.

The obvious starting point is the observation that with our incomplete understanding of the economy and our inability to predict accurately the occurrence of disturbing factors such as strikes, wars, and foreign exchange crises, we cannot expect to hit policy goals exactly. Some periods of inflation or unemployment are unavoidable. The inevitable lack of precision in reaching policy goals is sometimes recognized by saying that the goals are "reasonably" stable prices and "reasonably" full employment.

While the observation above is trite, its implications are not. Two points are especially important. First, policy should aim at minimizing the average size of errors. Second, policy can be judged only by the average size of errors over a period of time and *not* by individual episodes. Because this second point is particularly subject to misunderstanding, it needs further amplification.

Since policy-makers operate in a world that is inherently uncertain, they must be judged by criteria appropriate to such a world. Consider the analogy of betting on the draw of a ball from an urn with nine black balls and one red ball. Anyone offered a $2 payoff for a $1 bet would surely bet on a black ball being drawn. If the draw produced the red ball, no one would accuse the bettor of a stupid bet. Similarly, the policy-maker must play the economic odds. The

policy-maker should not be accused of failure if an inflation occurs as the result of an improbable and unforeseeable event.

Now consider the reverse situation from that considered in the previous paragraph. Suppose the bettor with the same odds as above bets on the red ball and wins. Some would claim that the bet was brilliant, but assuming that the draw was not rigged in any way, the bet, even though a winning one, must be judged foolish. It is foolish because, on the average, such a betting strategy will lead to substantially worse results than the opposite strategy. Betting on red will prove brilliant only one time out of 10, on the average. Similarly, a particular policy action may be a bad bet even though it works in a particular episode.

There is a well-known tendency for gamblers to try systems that according to the laws of probability cannot be successful over any length of time. Frequently, a gambler will adopt a foolish system as the result of an initial chance success such as betting on red in the above example. The same danger exists in economic policy. In fact, the danger is more acute because there appears to be a greater chance to "beat the system" by applying economic knowledge and intuition. There can be no doubt that it will become increasingly possible to improve on simple, naive policies through sophisticated analysis and forecasting and so in a sense "beat the system." But even with improved knowledge some uncertainty will always exist, and therefore so will the tendency to attempt to perform better than the state of knowledge really permits.

Whatever the state of knowledge, there must be a clear understanding of how to cope with uncertainty, even though the degree of uncertainty may have been drastically reduced through the use of modern methods of analysis. The principal purpose of this section is to improve understanding of the importance of uncertainty for policy by examining a simple model in which the policy problem is treated as one of minimizing errors on the average. Particular emphasis is placed on whether controlling policy by adjusting the interest rate or by adjusting the money stock will lead to smaller errors on the average. The basic argument is designed to show that the answer to which policy variable—the interest rate or the money stock—minimizes average errors depends primarily on the relative stability of the expenditures and money demand functions rather than on the values of the parameters that determine whether monetary policy is in some sense more or less "powerful" than fiscal policy.

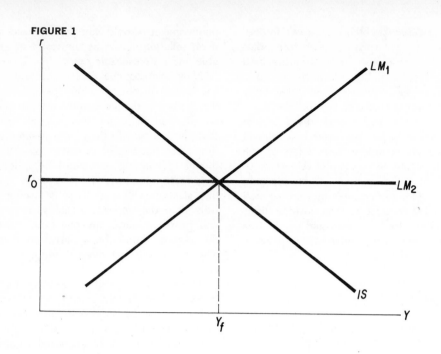

FIGURE 1

MONETARY POLICY UNDER UNCERTAINTY IN A KEYNESIAN MODEL[1]

The basic issues concerning the importance of uncertainty for monetary policy may be examined within the Hicksian *IS-LM* version 'of the Keynesian system. This elementary model has two sectors, an expenditure sector and a monetary sector, and it assumes that the price level is fixed in the short run.[2] Consumption, investment, and government expenditures functions are combined to produce the *IS* function in Figure 1, while the demand and supply of money functions are combined to produce the *LM* function. If monetary policy fixes the stock of money, then the resulting *LM* function is LM_1, while if policy fixes the interest rate at r_0 the resulting *LM* function is LM_2. It is assumed that incomes above "full employment income" are undesirable due to inflationary pressures while incomes below full employment income are undesirable due to unemployment.

If the positions of all the functions could be predicted with no errors, then to reach full employment income, Y_f, it would make no difference whether policy fixed the money stock or the interest rate. All that is necessary in either case is to set the money stock or the interest

rate so that the resulting *LM* function will cut the *IS* function at the full employment level of income.

Significance of Disturbances. The positions of the functions are, unfortunately, never precisely known. Consider first uncertainty over the position of the *IS* function—which, of course, results from instability in the underlying consumption and investment functions—while retaining the unrealistic assumption that the position of the *LM* function is known. What is known about the *IS* function is that it will lie between the extremes of IS_1 and IS_2 in Figure 2. If the money stock is set at some fixed level, then it is known that the *LM* function will be LM_1, and accordingly income will be somewhere between the extremes of Y_1 and Y_2. On the other hand, suppose policy-makers follow an interest rate policy and set the interest rate at r_0. In this case income will be somewhere between Y_1', and Y_2', a wider range than Y_1 to Y_2, and so the money stock policy is superior to the interest rate policy.[3] The money stock policy is superior because an unpredictable disturbance in the *IS* function will affect the interest rate, which in turn will produce spending changes that partly offset the initial disturbance.

The opposite polar case is illustrated in Figure

---

[1] For the most part this section represents a verbal and graphical version of the mathematical argument in [3].

[2] Simple presentations of this model may be found in [4, pp. 275–82] and [5, pp. 327–32].

[3] In Figure 2 and the following diagrams, the outcomes from a money stock policy will be represented by unprimed *Y*'s, while the outcomes from an interest rate policy will be represented by primed *Y*'s.

FIGURE 2

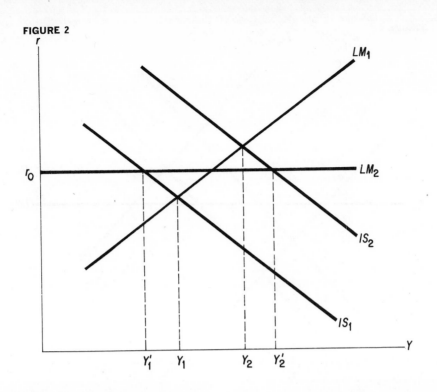

3. Here it is assumed that the position of the *IS* function is known with certainty, while unpredictable shifts in the demand for money cause unpredictable shifts in the *LM* function if a money stock policy is followed. With a money stock policy, income may end up anywhere between Y_1 and Y_2. But an interest rate policy can fix the *LM* function at LM_3 so that it cuts the *IS* function at the full employment level of income, Y_f. With an interest rate policy, unpre-

FIGURE 3

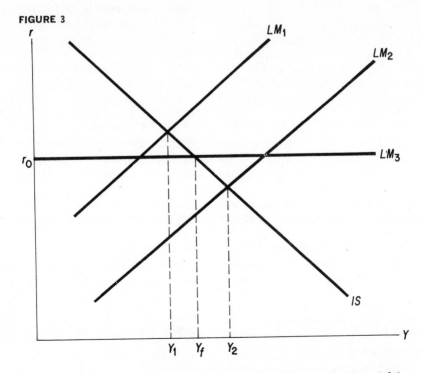

FIGURE 4

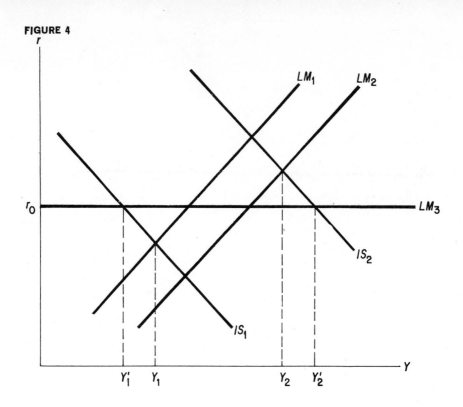

dictable shifts in the demand for money are not permitted to affect the interest rate; instead, in the process of fixing the interest rate the policy-makers adjust the stock of money in response to the unpredictable shifts in the demand for money.

In practice, of course, it is necessary to cope with uncertainty in both the expenditure and monetary sectors. This situation is depicted in Figure 4, where the unpredictable disturbances are larger in the expenditure sector, and in Figure 5 where the unpredictable disturbances are larger in the monetary sector.

The situation is even more complicated than shown in Figures 4 and 5 by virtue of the fact that the disturbances in the two sectors may not be independent. To illustrate this case, consider Figure 5 in which the interest rate policy is superior to the money stock policy if the disturbances are independent. Suppose that the disturbances were connected in such a way that disturbances on the LM_1 side of the average LM function were always accompanied by disturbances on the IS_2 side of the average IS function. This would mean that income would never go as low as Y_1, but rather only as low as the intersection of LM_1 and IS_2, an income not as low as Y_1' under the interest rate policy. Similarly, the highest income would be given by the inter-

section of LM_2 and IS_1, an income not so high as Y_2'.[4]

Importance of Interest Elasticities and Other Parameters. So far the argument has concentrated entirely on the importance of the relative sizes of expenditure and monetary disturbances. But is it also important to consider the slopes of the functions as determined by the interest elasticities of investment and of the demand for money, and by other parameters? Consider the pair of IS functions, IS_1 and IS_2, as opposed to the pair, IS_3 and IS_4, in Figure 6. Each pair represents the maximum and minimum positions of the IS function as a result of disturbances, but the pairs have different slopes. Each pair assumes the same maximum and minimum disturbances, as shown by the fact that the horizontal distance between IS_1 and IS_2 is the same as between IS_3 and IS_4. For convenience, but without loss of generality, the functions have

---

[4] The diagram could obviously have been drawn so that an interest rate policy would be superior to a money stock policy even though there were an inverse relationship between the shifts in the IS and LM functions. However, inverse shifts always reduce the margin of superiority of an interest rate policy, possibly to the point of making a money stock policy superior. Conversely, positively related shifts favor an interest rate policy.

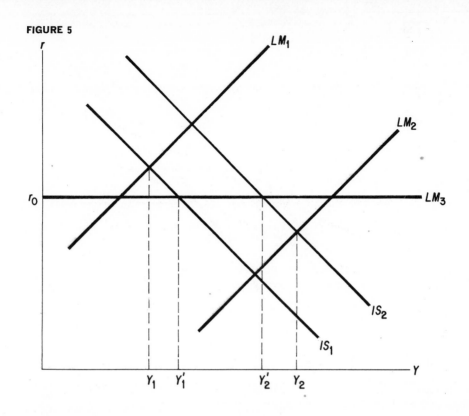

FIGURE 5

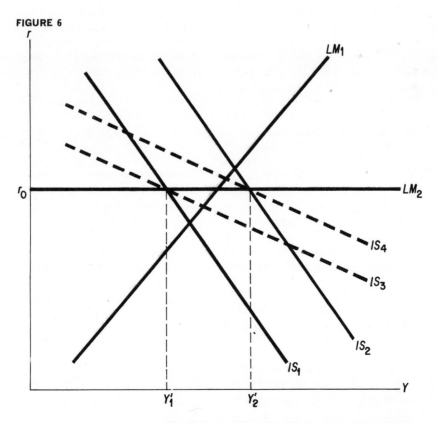

FIGURE 6

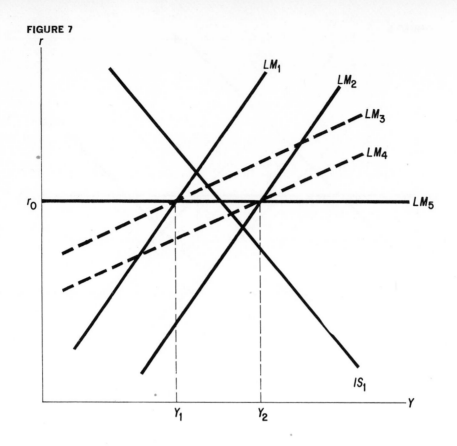

FIGURE 7

been drawn so that under an interest rate policy represented by LM_2 both pairs of IS functions produce the same range of incomes. To keep the diagram from becoming too messy, only one LM function, LM_1, under a money stock policy has been drawn. Now consider disturbances that would shift LM_1 back and forth. From Figure 6 it is easy to see that if shifts in LM_1 would lead to income fluctuations greater than from Y_1' to Y_2'—which fluctuations would occur under an interest rate policy—then a money stock policy would be preferred *regardless* of whether we have the pair IS_1 and IS_2, or the pair IS_3 and IS_4.

The importance of the slope of the LM function is investigated in Figure 7 for the two LM pairs, LM_1 and LM_2, and LM_3 and LM_4. The functions have been drawn so that each pair represents different slopes but an identical range of disturbances. It is clear that if shifts in IS_1 are large enough, then a money stock policy will be preferred regardless of which pair of LM functions prevails.

The argument of the preceding two paragraphs can be made more precise by saying that if variability of the LM function is small enough relative to the IS function, then a money stock

policy will be preferred to an interest rate policy regardless of the interest elasticities of the expenditures and money demand functions. How small is "small enough" depends on the income elasticity of the demand for money.[5] When the variability of LM relative to IS is not "small enough," then a money stock policy will be preferred for relatively high values of the ratio of the interest elasticity of the demand for money to the interest elasticity of expenditures; an interest rate policy will be preferred for relatively low values of this ratio.[6] The intuitive reason for this result is that monetary disturbances will have a larger impact on income the lower is the interest elasticity of money demand and the higher is the interest elasticity of expenditures.

The upshot of this analysis is that the crucial issue for deciding upon whether an interest rate or a money stock policy should be followed is the relative size of the disturbances in the expenditure and monetary sectors. Contrary to

[5] For the mathematical argument, see equation (14) in [3].

[6] Even this statement is subject to a qualification. The preferences for the money stock and interest rate policies may be reversed if the correlation between IS and LM disturbances is highly negative.

FIGURE 8

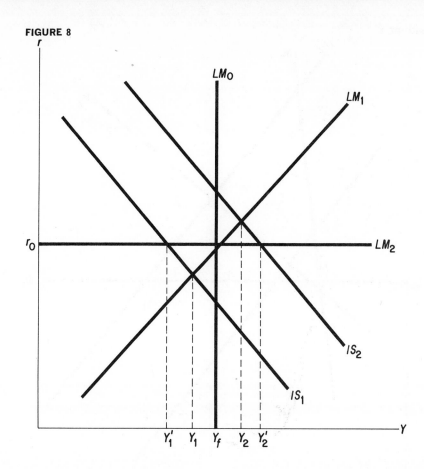

much recent discussion, the issue is not whether the interest elasticity of the demand for money is relatively low or whether fiscal policy is more or less "powerful" than monetary policy.

To avoid possible confusion, it should be emphasized that the above argument is in terms of the choice between a money stock policy and an interest rate policy. However, if a money stock policy is superior, then the steeper is the *LM* function, up to a point, the lower is the range of income fluctuation, as can be seen from Figure 7. It is also clear from Figure 6 that under an interest rate policy an error in setting the interest rate will lead to a larger error in hitting the income target if the *IS* function is relatively flat than if it is relatively steep. But these facts do not affect the choice between interest rate and money stock policies.

The "Combination" Monetary Policy. Up to this point the analysis has concentrated on the choice of either the interest rate or the money stock as the policy variable. But it is also possible to consider a "combination" policy that works through the money stock and the interest rate simultaneously. An understanding of the combi-

nation policy may be obtained by further consideration of the cases depicted in Figures 2 and 7.

In Figure 8 the disturbances, as in Figure 2, are entirely in the expenditure sector. As was seen in Figure 2, the result obtained by fixing the money stock so that LM_1 prevailed was superior to that obtained by fixing the interest rate so that LM_2 prevailed. But now suppose that instead of fixing the money stock, the money stock were reduced every time the interest rate went up and increased every time the interest rate went down. This procedure would, of course, increase the amplitude of interest rate fluctuations.[7] But if the proper relationship between the

---

[7] The increased fluctuations in interest rates must be carefully interpreted. In this model the *IS* function is assumed to fluctuate around a fixed-average position. However, in more complicated models involving changes in the average position of the *IS* function, perhaps through the operation of the investment accelerator, interest rate fluctuations may not be increased by the policy being discussed in the text. By increasing the stability of income over a period of time, the policy would increase the stability of the *IS* function in Figure 8 and thereby reduce interest rate fluctuations.

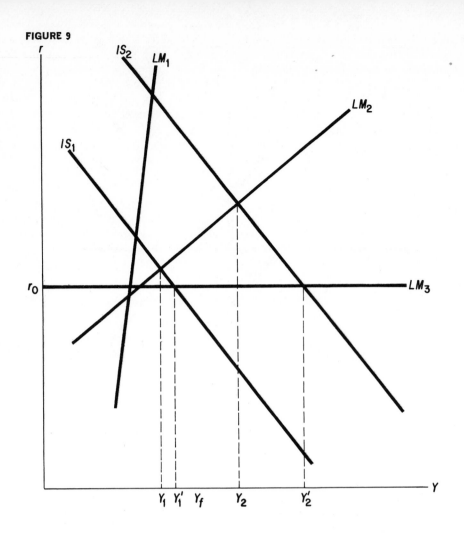

FIGURE 9

money stock and the interest rate could be discovered, then the *LM* function could be made to look like *LM₀* in Figure 8. The result would be that income would be pegged at *Yf*. Disturbances in the *IS* function would produce changes in the interest rate, which in turn would produce spending changes sufficient to completely offset the effect on income of the initial disturbance.

The most complicated case of all to explain graphically is that in which it is desirable to increase the money stock as the interest rate rises and decrease it as the interest rate falls. In Figure 9 the leftmost position of the *LM* function as a result of disturbances is *LM₁* when the money stock is fixed and is *LM₂* when the combination policy of introducing a positive money–interest relationship is followed. The rightmost positions of the *LM* functions under these conditions are not shown in the diagram. When the interest rate is pegged, the *LM* function is *LM₃*. If either

LM₁ or *LM₂* prevails, the intersection with *IS₁* produces the lowest income, which is below the *Y₁'* level obtained with *LM₃*. But in the case of *LM₂*, income at *Y₁* is only a little lower than at *Y₁'*, whereas when *IS₂* prevails, *LM₂* is better than *LM₃* by the difference between *Y₂* and *Y₂'*. Since the gap between *Y₂* and *Y₂'* is larger than that between *Y₁* and *Y₁'*, it is on the average better to adopt *LM₂* than *LM₃* even though the extremes under *LM₂* are a bit larger than under *LM₃*.

Extensions of Model. At this point a natural question is that of the extent to which the above analysis would hold in more complex models. Until more complicated models are constructed and analyzed mathematically, there is no way of being certain. But it is possible to make educated guesses on the effects of adding more goals and more policy instruments, and of relaxing the rigid price assumption.

Additional goals may be added to the model if they are specified in terms of "closer is better" rather than in terms of a fixed target that must be met. For example, it would not be mathematically difficult to add an interest rate goal to the model analyzed above, if deviations from a target interest rate were permitted but were treated as being increasingly harmful. On the other hand, it is clear that if there were a fixed-interest target, then the only possible policy would be to peg the interest rate, and income stabilization would not be possible with monetary policy alone.

The addition of fiscal policy instruments affects the results in two major ways. First, the existence of income taxes and of government expenditures inversely related to income (for example, unemployment benefits) provides automatic stabilization. In terms of the model, automatic stabilizers make the IS function steeper than it otherwise would be, thus reducing the impact of monetary disturbances, and reduce the variance of expenditures disturbances in the reduced-form equation for income. This effect would be shown in Figure 6 by drawing IS_1 so that it cuts LM_2 to the right of Y_1' and drawing IS_2 so that it cuts LM_2 to the left of Y_2'.

The second major impact of adding fiscal policy instruments occurs if both income and the interest rate are goals. Horizontal shifts in the IS function that are induced by fiscal policy adjustments, when accompanied by a coordinated monetary policy, make it possible to come closer to a desired interest rate without any sacrifice in income stability. An obvious illustration is provided by the case in which the optimal monetary policy from the point of view of stabilizing income is to set the interest rate as in Figure 5. Fiscal policy can then shift the pair of IS functions, IS_1 and IS_2, to the right or left so that the expected value of income is at the full employment level.

If the interest rate is not a goal variable, then fiscal policy actions that shift the IS function without changing its slope do not improve income stabilization over what can be accomplished with monetary policy alone, provided the lags in the effects of monetary policy are no longer than those in the effects of fiscal policy. An exception would be a situation in which reaching full employment with monetary policy alone would require an unattainable interest rate, such as a negative one.

These comments on fiscal policy have been presented in order to clarify the relationship between fiscal and monetary policy. While monetary policy-makers may urge fiscal action, for the most part monetary policy must take the fiscal setting as given and adapt monetary policy to this setting. It must then be recognized that an interest rate goal can be pursued only at the cost of sacrificing somewhat the income goal.[8]

All of the analysis so far has taken place within a model in which the price level is fixed in the short run. This assumption may be relaxed by recognizing that increases in money income above the full employment level involve a mixture of real income gains and price inflation. Similarly, reductions in money income below the full employment level involve real income reductions and price deflation (or a slower rate of price inflation). The model used above can be reinterpreted entirely in terms of money income so that departures from what was called above the "full employment" level of income involve a mixture of real income and price changes. Stabilizing money income, then, involves a mixture of the two goals of stabilizing real output and of stabilizing the price level.

However, interpreted in this way the structure of the model is deficient because it fails to distinguish between real and nominal interest rates. Price level increases generate inflationary expectations, which in turn generate an outward shift in the IS function. The model may be patched up to some extent by assuming that price changes make up a constant fraction of the deviation of income from its full employment level and assuming further that the expected rate of inflation is a constant multiplied by the actual rate of inflation. Expenditures are then made to depend on the real rate of interest, the difference between the nominal rate of interest and the expected rate of inflation. The result is to make the IS function, when drawn against the nominal interest rate, flatter and to increase the variance of disturbances to the IS function. These effects are more pronounced: (a) the larger is the interest sensitivity of expenditures; (b) the larger is the fraction of price changes in money income changes; and (c) the larger is the effect of price changes on price expectations. The conclusion is that since price flexibility in effect increases

---

[8] An interest rate goal must be sharply distinguished from the use of the interest rate as a monetary policy instrument. By a goal variable is meant a variable that enters the policy utility function. Income and interest rate goals might be simultaneously pursued by setting the money stock as the policy instrument or by setting the interest rate as the policy instrument.

the variance of disturbances in the *IS* function, a money stock policy tends to be favored over an interest rate policy.

REFERENCES

1. Brainard, William. "Uncertainty and the Effectiveness of Policy," *American Economic Review: Papers and Proceedings of the 79th Annual Meeting of the American Economic Association,* Vol. 57 (May 1967), pp. 411–25.
2. Holt, Charles C. "Linear Decision Rules for Economic Stabilization and Growth," *Quarterly Journal of Economics,* Vol. 76 (February 1962), pp. 20–45.
3. Poole, William. "Optimal Choice of Monetary Policy Instruments in a Simple Stochastic Macro Model," *Quarterly Journal of Economics,* Vol. 84 (May 1970), pp. 197–216.
4. Reynolds, Lloyd G. *Economics.* 3d ed. Homewood, Ill.: Richard D. Irwin, Inc., 1969.
5. Samuelson, Paul A. *Economics.* 7th ed. New York: McGraw-Hill, 1967.
6. Theil, Henri. *Optimal Decision Rules for Government and Industry.* Amsterdam, Neth.: North-Holland Publishing Company, 1964.

THE TRADE-OFF BETWEEN SHORT- AND LONG-TERM POLICY GOALS*

James L. Pierce

INTRODUCTION

The existence of long lags in the response of the real sectors of the economy to changes in monetary policy is well documented. These lags may require an horizon for monetary policy strategies that spans many calendar quarters. Even if long planning horizons are desirable, specific operating strategies still must be adopted for the actual short-run conduct of monetary policy. These, however, should be consistent with the long-term goals. If short-run considerations—such as stabilization of money market interest rate movements—cause modification of the operating strategy, the long-run goals in terms of income, employment, and the price level may suffer. This paper discusses some of the areas in which short- and long-term goals may conflict and attempts to evaluate the costs to the long-term targets of imposing short-run side conditions on policy actions.

SHORT-RUN VS. LONG-RUN GOALS

Available econometric evidence indicates that variations in monetary policy instruments can ex-

* From *Open Market Policies and Operating Procedures—Staff Studies* (Washington, D.C.: Board of Governors of the Federal Reserve System, 1971), pp. 97–105. Reprinted by permission of the Board of Governors of the Federal Reserve System and the author. James L. Pierce is Adviser, Division of Research and Statistics, Board of Governors of the Federal Reserve System.

Note: The author would like to thank William Poole for his constructive comments on an earlier version of this paper.

ert little influence on the nonfinancial sectors of the economy in the short run. Experiments with a recent version of the Federal Reserve–MIT model indicate that, other things equal, a $1 billion increase in the money stock in a given quarter will produce only a $0.3 billion increase in nominal gross national product in that quarter. Further, inspection of the coefficients for the relevant equations in the model suggests that even this small response is probably overstated. It is interesting to note that the long-run multiplier relation between money and nominal GNP is substantial. Other things equal, a $1 billion permanent rise in the money stock leads to a permanent increase in nominal GNP of approximately $3.2 billion.

Given the short-run multiplier, attempts to establish short-run (quarter by quarter) control over the economy may require variations in policy instruments that are unacceptably large. An example may clarify the issue. Assume that during a generally inflationary period, the decision is made to attempt to stop the inflation within a single quarter. To accomplish this end, a sharp rise in interest rates, and probably a substantial reduction in the levels of the monetary aggregates, would be required during the quarter. Even if this strategy were successful, a new problem would immediately develop. With the passage of time beyond the quarter, the economy would continue its deflationary adjustment— probably at an increased rate—in response to the monetary restriction. If an overresponse of the economy to the original policy restriction is to be avoided, policy must reverse itself immediately by sharply reducing interest rates and expanding the monetary aggregates. This easing of policy would require in turn a restrictive policy the next quarter. Thus, by never looking more than one quarter ahead, large short-term reversals of policy would be required to stabilize the economy.

Whether this myopic strategy of trying to hit targets in the real sector on a quarter-by-quarter basis can be successful over the long run depends, among other things, upon the existing parameters of the system.[1] It is quite possible that pursuit of such a strategy would have no long-run future because ever larger changes in monetary policy instruments would be required to achieve stability in the real sector. Even if the strategy produced permanent economic stability, it could create extreme fluctuations in financial markets.

It is quite possible, however, that large fluctuations in financial variables would alter interest rate expectations enough to weaken greatly the efficacy of the myopic policy strategy. Rapid reversals of monetary policy may encourage investors to expect wide fluctuations in short-term interest rates. In this situation, efforts to reduce long-term rates would be thwarted by investor expectations of a rise in rates in the near future. Thus, the pursuit of the myopic policy strategy could be self-defeating.

There are two obvious ways to approach the problem posed by the small amount of short-term control over the economy. First, monetary policy could pursue the myopic rule of attempting to hit a target quarter by quarter but could subject the strategy to constraints imposed by financial conditions. Thus, a specific target value for employment or for the price level would be pursued provided the act of attempting to hit the target did not cause excessive fluctuations in interest rates. If interest rates moved more than was deemed desirable, policy instruments would be changed sufficiently to bring interest rates within the allowable range. The imposition of such constraints could greatly reduce the ability of monetary policy to achieve short-term goals.

The second approach would involve a lengthening of the policy-planning horizon. In this situation, policy would take a view longer than one quarter into the future. The aim would be to achieve the best path of, say, employment over

[1] For a simple treatment of this problem, see E. Gramlich, "The Usefulness of Monetary and Fiscal Policy as Discretionary Stabilization Tools," presented at the Conference of University Professors sponsored by the American Bankers Association, Sept. 1969.

some interval of time consistent with acceptable performance of financial markets. Extension of the horizon would allow problems of the real sector and of the financial sector to coexist on a more equal basis. No immutable constraints would be placed on the system by money market conditions if the planning horizon could be extended. However, by giving up some short-term control over variables in the real sector, it should be possible to reduce fluctuations in financial variables to more manageable proportions.

Conceptually, it should be possible to determine the trade-off between (1) short-term control over employment and prices and (2) stability of the financial sector. In general, a lengthening of the policy-planning horizon to promote short-run stability in financial markets will come at the cost of reduced control over nonfinancial variables. Alternatively, a shortening of the planning horizon will come at the cost of increased short-run fluctuations in financial variables.

Lengthening the horizon for major policy goals raises some obvious problems. Because the long-term goals of employment and prices are relatively far in the future, it is easy to give them a back seat to the short-run stabilization problems often encountered in financial markets. The problem with this approach is that overattention to short-run problems may have important implications for the paths required to hit desired long-run targets. Further, if short-run constraints are continually imposed, it may be impossible to hit the long-run goals in the time specified. Under those circumstances it may be necessary to lengthen the horizon and to accept the ensuing costs of less desirable performance of the real sector.

The previous paragraph suggests that over the longer run the goals of price and output stability may not conflict with the goal of money market stability. Overzealous attempts to stabilize the money market in the short run may distort output and prices to the point that large changes in interest rates are required in the longer run to bring the economy under control. By allowing wider short-run fluctuations in money market conditions, it might be possible to avoid large swings in interest rates over the longer run.

The discussion suggests that, given a set of initial conditions in the economy, there is an optimal policy strategy available. The strategy determines simultaneously the length of the planning horizon, the paths of target variables such as employment and prices over the period, and the expected stability of financial markets. The determination of specific strategies is a problem in optimal control theory and is beyond the scope of this paper. Instead, the paper attempts to assess the trade-offs involved and illustrates problems that may arise from pursuing particular policy strategies.

SOME SIMULATION EXPERIMENTS

This section describes some simulation experiments that were conducted to illustrate the problems encountered when short-term and long-term goals conflict. The structure of a recent version of the FR–MIT model was used for the simulation exercises.[2]

The first experiment assumes a monetary policy that focuses on the rate of growth of the money stock provided the change in the Treasury bill rate over any quarter does not exceed some arbitrary value. An unconstrained growth in money is assumed to promote desired long-run behavior of the real sector. However, if the policy-determined money stock for a quarter led to a projected change in the bill rate over that quarter that exceeded the constraint value, then the money supply was changed sufficiently to bring the change in the bill rate back to its allowable range. In those situations in which monetary policy is attempting to offset either boom or recession, this constrained policy would lead to a performance of the economy that is inferior to one which is unconstrained.

If shifts in the demand for money are the source of wide interest rate fluctuations when policy is attempting to hit a money stock target, the situation is changed. Here, it would be appropriate to introduce interest rate constraints. Such constraints would automatically satisfy the demand for money after some point. Limiting interest rate movements in this case would promote long-run stability.[3] The results of the simulation experiments suggest, however, that one should have strong reasons for believing that shifts in money demand are causing wide quarter-to-quarter fluctuations in interest rates. If unexpected shifts in aggregate demand are the cause, long-run goals may suffer greatly.

To illustrate the problems that arise during periods of excess aggregate demand, various simulations of the FR–MIT model were run for the 1963–68 period. First, a control simulation was run that took all exogenous variables at their historical values but assumed that the money stock grew at a constant annual rate of 4.25 percent. This was the constant rate at which the initial money stock in 1962-IV had to grow to achieve its actual value in 1968-IV. Then additional simulation experiments were conducted by applying the same exogenous variables and the same 4.25 percent money growth rate to the model provided that the Treasury bill rate did not change during the quarter by more than a specified absolute amount. If the bill rate fell outside the allowable range, bank reserves and the money supply were changed sufficiently to bring the bill rate back to the nearest boundary of the range. All other exogenous variables were assumed to remain unchanged. Several absolute change values were attempted; results for absolute changes of 30 basis points and 10 basis points are reported.

The results indicate that the placement of sufficiently narrow bounds on the change in the bill rate can have a large impact on the simulated value of GNP. Figure 1 shows the differences between the simulated values of GNP for the steady rate of growth of money and those subject to maximum absolute changes in the bill rate of 30 and 10 basis points, respectively. In both cases, because interest rates could not rise in the later periods, there was a tendency to add to the existing excess demand conditions.

As indicated earlier, if interest rate fluctuations are caused by erratic shifts in the demand for money, then stabilization of interest rates may be a reasonable course of action. The simulation results suggest, however, that interest rate stabilization can be costly during periods of strong excess demand.

It is interesting to note that if stabilization of financial markets takes the form of constraining the rate of growth of the money stock, the problems encountered during periods of shifting aggregate demand are diminished. Assume that monetary policy attempts to hit an employment target by setting market interest rates at appropriate levels. Introducing a constraint on the allowable range of growth rates of the money stock in this situation can under some circumstances lead to improved performance of the economy. If it happens that the interest rate selected is not the correct one because aggregate demand is either stronger or weaker than expected, varia-

---

[2] Some of the simulation results reported here are drawn from an earlier paper on a related topic. See J. Pierce, "Some Rules for the Conduct of Monetary Policy," in *Controlling Monetary Aggregates* (Federal Reserve Bank of Boston, 1969).

[3] For a theoretical discussion of the desirability of interest rate versus money stock stabilization in a stochastic world, see W. Poole, "Optimal Choice of Monetary Policy Instruments in a Simple Stochastic Macro Model," *Quarterly Journal of Economics*, Vol. 84 (May 1970), pp. 197–216.

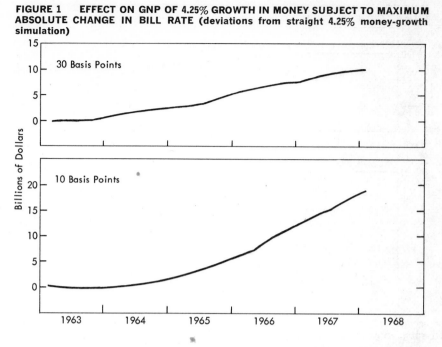

FIGURE 1   EFFECT ON GNP OF 4.25% GROWTH IN MONEY SUBJECT TO MAXIMUM ABSOLUTE CHANGE IN BILL RATE (deviations from straight 4.25% money-growth simulation)

tions in the rate of growth of the money stock can provide important evidence of this condition. For example, if aggregate demand is stronger than expected, given the interest rate and the demand for money, the growth in the money stock will be greater than expected. If the acceleration in the growth rate of money is taken as a signal to raise the interest rate, the growth rate of money will fall and the excessive growth in aggregate demand will be reduced.

If the unexpected growth in the money stock is the result of a shift in the demand for money, then the monetary expansion should be accommodated. In this situation, interest rates should not rise. There is really no way to avoid making judgments concerning the causes of fluctuations in the money stock and in interest rates. If the source is unexpected strength or weakness in aggregate demand, one course of action is called for. If the source is erratic shifts in the demand for money, quite a different policy reaction is required. The purpose of the simulation experiments was not to "prove" that aggregate demand is always the cause of money market fluctuations. Rather, the purpose of the exercises was to illustrate the potential costs of pursuing a policy strategy that implicitly assumes that money market fluctuations are caused primarily by an erratic, unpredictable demand for money.

Simulation experiments with the model were conducted to measure the impact of constraints on the growth rate of money. The control simula-

tion was one in which the interest rate was made to rise at a constant annual rate from a base period of 1963-I to achieve its actual value in 1968-I. In this simulation, the money stock is endogenous. Additional policy simulations were then conducted in which constraints on the growth rate of money were imposed on this interest rate policy. If the rate of growth of the endogenous money stock fell outside the allowable range, the interest rate was changed sufficiently to bring the growth in money back to the nearest boundary of its allowable range.

Figure 2 shows the difference between the values of GNP from the control simulations and those for maximum ranges of 3 to 5 percent and of 3.5 to 4.5 percent in the annual growth rate of money. The results indicate that this combination of interest rate and money supply policies would have been beneficial over the period of simulation.

Further simulation experiments were conducted taking the conditions of the 1960–61 recession as the starting point for the policy exercises. The results were similar to those described above for periods of excess demand. Control simulations were conducted for the period 1960-III to 1968-I under the assumption of a constant rate of growth of the money stock. Given the actual history of the exogenous variables in the system and given the initial conditions, the time required to get initially to full employment was a decreasing function of the money growth rate. Particularly

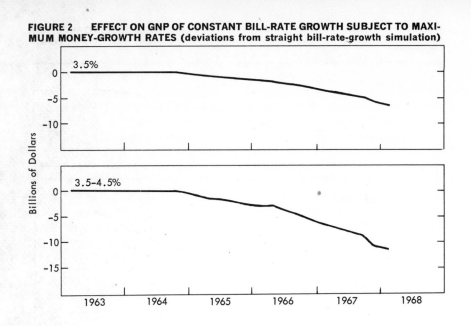

FIGURE 2   EFFECT ON GNP OF CONSTANT BILL-RATE GROWTH SUBJECT TO MAXI-
MUM MONEY-GROWTH RATES (deviations from straight bill-rate-growth simulation)

rapid growth rates, however, lead to substantial overshooting and can create chronic excess demand. Quite predictably, imposition of a constraint on policy in the form of maximum allowable quarterly changes in the Treasury bill rate made it more difficult to hit the full employment target. The interest rate constraint produced a slowing of the rate of expansion of output and employment from the recession base and lengthened the time necessary to hit a full employment target. The results also indicate that the degree of the slowdown of economic expansion resulting from the constraint depends upon how quickly the target level of employment is to be reached and how narrow is the allowable range of the quarterly change in interest rates.

It should be emphasized that a restriction on changes in interest rates is potentially less disruptive to the economy than is a restriction on the level of rates. Constraints on the maximum short-term change in interest rates can retard but not arrest desired adjustments of the economy. The existence of ceilings or floors on the level of interest rates may prevent the adjustments from ever occurring. Pegging the level of interest rates can lead to a total loss of control by policy over output, employment, and prices.

The recession results for a money supply constraint are also similar to those obtained for the excess demand case. A monetary policy that attempts to achieve its objectives through influencing money market conditions—interest rates—can be enhanced in the recession case by imposing a constraint on the rate of growth of money.

If the course of aggregate demand proves to be other than expected, variations in the interest rate promoted by the constraint imposed by an allowable range of growth in money rates will serve to push the rate of expansion in the desired direction.

CONCLUSIONS

The brief discussion in the preceding section suggests that high priority should be placed on coordinating short-run operating procedures with the longer-run goals of monetary policy. Failure to achieve such coordination can lead to a serious reduction in the ultimate effectiveness of monetary policy. Stabilizing short-term interest rate fluctuations can lead to destabilizing shocks to the real sectors of the economy.

Better information on the stability of the demand functions in the economy is sorely needed. The focus of policy on money market conditions may be badly misplaced if the money demand function is relatively stable and predictable through time. Certainly the hypothesis that the demand for money is erratic and unpredictable is not well documented. It is curious, therefore, that policy decisions should depend so strongly on money market conditions.

It might be argued that the central bank is obligated to stabilize the markets for debt instruments. An unfortunate paradox can result here. An overly zealous attempt to stabilize interest rates can so disturb the real sectors of the economy as to lead ultimately to extreme variations in market interest rates. The experience of the last few years appears to bear out this contention. It would appear that a monetary policy based almost exclusively on stabilizing short-run money market conditions is a luxury we can ill afford.

On a conceptual basis the appropriate course of action for policymaking appears to be clear. Given staff projections of the course of the economy over the coming year or so, the instruments of monetary policy should be set to promote the desired time paths of variables such as employment and prices over the period. In order to make such decisions meaningful, several policy alternatives should be presented showing alternative time paths for the target values in the real sector.

The policy alternatives should be compared both in terms of the expected values of such variables as output, employment, and prices, and in terms of the dispersion of these projections around their expected values. In assessing the variability of the projections, it is necessary to provide evidence as to the possible impacts on the projections of various shocks to the system. How sensitive are the projections to shifts in the demand for money or in the demand for investment goods? An analysis of the impact on the projections of alternative assumptions concerning the values of certain key exogenous variables such as Government spending is also crucial. Furthermore, it is quite likely that the sensitivity of the projections to shocks and alternative values of exogenous variables is not independent of the existing state of the economy. At times projections are quite insensitive to fairly large changes in the underlying specifications of the system, but at other times they are extremely sensitive to these specifications. It is essential, therefore, that evidence be provided concerning the likely dispersion of relevant variables around their projected values.

The fluctuations in interest rates and monetary aggregates implied by the various policy alternatives should also be projected. On the basis of all of this information, trade-offs between expected money market stability and the behavior of variables in the real sector can be assessed. The need for reliable econometric models and for seasoned judgment in these exercises is obvious. At this point, our ability to generate the required set of projections is quite limited. These limitations suggest that policy strategies should be fairly simple and straightforward. Elaborate policy strategies do not seem consistent with our ability to assess and trace through time the impact of policy acts on the economy.

Given a policy strategy over the coming year or so, how can the strategy be reduced to day-by-day operating procedures? Here, there is need for a document that presents projections of financial conditions to be expected over the near term. A blending of projections obtained from quarterly and monthly econometric models is sorely needed. Conceptually, such blends are difficult but possible. On the basis of these short-term projections and the basic policy strategy mentioned above, specific operating instructions can be formulated. Here, limitations on the ability to make short-term projections suggest that the operating procedures adopted should be fairly simple.

We now come to the central problem. How can we continue to link the basic policy strategy with operating procedures as the economic forecasts are modified and as monetary policy strays off course? As policy is currently conducted, there is no effective means of varying the basic strategy as new information comes in, and there is no way to relate changing conditions to actual operating procedures.

Ideally, we would like to generate new long-term forecasts each quarter and to map out new alternative policy strategies each quarter. Often, however, the new information that comes in leads to conflicting conclusions about changes in the future course of the economy. Further, econometric models and other procedures often do not predict with sufficient accuracy to allow useful quarter-by-quarter changes in implied operating strategy. The discussion of the original projections also suggests that the initial strategies may at times be very much in doubt.

A possible strategy under these conditions is to set quarterly operating instructions in terms of some combination of interest rates and money stock. A policy that sets an interest rate subject to constraints on the rate of growth of money is a very appealing candidate. By setting a range to the allowable growth of money, shifts in the money demand function are automatically accommodated up to the extreme points of the range. The width of the range should depend in part on estimates of likely quarterly fluctuations in the demand for money. In setting the range, however, it must be recalled that the wider the allowable range, the greater the potential loss in output and employment when variations in aggregate demand are the cause of money growth fluctuations. For this reason, a relatively narrow band, for example, 4 to 6 percent, seems desirable as a working principle.

Certainly, if there are persuasive arguments explaining why an unusual shift in money demand occurred in a particular quarter, then a growth rate of the money stock outside the range should be allowed. The point is, however, that relaxation of the constraints should be a rare event. In every case when such an action is being considered, the burden of proof should rest squarely on those who believe that an unexpected movement of money outside the range is caused by money demand and not by aggregate demand. Further, the longer the condition of unusually high or low money growth persists at existing interest rates the greater should be the presumption that the interest rate is inappropriate and should be changed.

These recommendations do not call for a drastic departure from current procedures; they call primarily for greater attention to be paid to the long-run objectives of economic stabilization policy. Such objectives are designed to put short-run stabilization of money market conditions in the context of possible costs to the economy in terms of income, employment, and prices.

Truly effective implementation of policy requires that operating strategies intended to achieve desired long-term goals be set forth explicitly. Such strategies must be followed under conditions of great uncertainty about the course of the exogenous variables in the system and about the performance of our models. In such a situation it would appear to be a mistake to focus attention primarily on the uncertainties of the money market. Monetary policy decisions must come to grips with the uncertainties we face with respect to aggregate demand. A policy strategy that relies as much as possible on projections but that also combines a setting of interest rates with allowable ranges on the money growth rate appears to be most appropriate for the near future.

THE IMPACT OF MONETARY VARIABLES: A SURVEY OF RECENT ECONOMETRIC LITERATURE*

Michael J. Hamburger

This article discusses the role attributed to monetary variables in a number of recent econometric studies of the components of aggregate demand. Specifically it considers (*a*) the types of monetary variables that have been used, (*b*) the statistical significance of the variables, and (*c*) the estimated lags between changes in monetary factors and the resulting effects on the level of economic activity. In concentrating on econometric analyses, the article does not consider two other important types of empirical research on the relationship between monetary and real variables, namely, studies by economists associated with the "money-supply" school (as discussed . . . by Richard Davis [17])[1] and surveys of the effects of interest rates and other financial measures on businessmen's investment decisions.[2]

The major conclusions with respect to the issues raised above are the following. First, the monetary variables which have been used most frequently are interest rates and some rather *ad hoc* measures of liquidity. The recent trend has been toward interest rates. Second, the frequency with which interest rates have been found to be statistically significant seems to increase with time. Several years ago it was thought that

* From *Essays in Domestic and International Finance* (New York: Federal Reserve Bank of New York, 1969), pp. 37–49. Reprinted with permission of the Federal Reserve Bank of New York and the author. Michael J. Hamburger is Senior Economist, Federal Reserve Bank of New York, and Adjunct Associate Professor of Economics, City University of New York.

This article is reprinted—with certain revisions—from a staff paper prepared at the Federal Reserve Bank of New York. A summary of the earlier version of the paper appeared in the *Federal Reserve Bulletin* (July 1967), pages 1094–95.

[1] Other references include Andersen and Jordan [3], Brunner [9], Brunner and Meltzer [10, 11], Friedman and Meiselman [28], and Friedman and Schwartz [29]. (The numbers in brackets refer to the bibliography.)

[2] For a review of this literature, see White [89, 90, 91]. The last article by White is particularly interesting since it attempts to reconcile the results of several noneconometric studies with those of the Federal Reserve–Massachusetts Institute of Technology econometric model [21, 79], discussed later in this article. The results of a recent Federal Reserve survey of the effects of monetary restraint in 1966 on state and local governments are discussed by McGouldrick and Petersen [65, 75].

changes in interest rates affected only residential construction and the expenditures of state and local governments. Now, however, evidence has been offered that fluctuations in interest rates also have a significant impact on investment in plant and equipment. In addition, current research suggests that interest rates may play a role in determining inventory investment and consumer expenditures on durable goods.

Finally, the estimated lags between changes in monetary variables and the resulting effects on economic activity reported in most of the studies appear to be quite long. For example, the results of a number of studies suggest that it may take more than a year before changes in interest rates have their first noticeable effect on business fixed investment. These findings have led some writers to conclude that monetary policy may be poorly suited for offsetting short-run fluctuations in economic activity.[3] However, such conclusions do not seem to give proper weight to two important considerations. First, the consistency with which long lags have been found, even in areas where they might be expected to be rather short, suggests that the empirical results may be biased by the statistical procedures which have been employed.[4] Second, the techniques which have generally been used do not permit the isolation of separate lags for monetary and nonmonetary variables. Consequently, the lags that have been reported in the literature may not provide a very good indication of the lag in effect of monetary policy.

The following five sections review briefly the regression equations that have been used to explain the movements in such variables as business fixed investment, investment in inventories, residential construction, consumption, and the expenditures of state and local governments. In view of the interest in the timing of the effect of monetary policy, attention is focused almost entirely on studies using quarterly observations. The concluding section in this article reports some numerical estimates of the effects of changes in monetary policy on the overall economy.

Business Fixed Investment

An examination of recent studies suggests that there is substantial agreement among econometricians on the role of monetary variables in the investment function. The models considered here are those of de Leeuw [19], Jorgenson [44], Fromm and Klein [31], Liu [56], and Bischoff (as summarized in [21]). One of the principal characteristics which these and most other recent analyses [33, 40, 43, 67] have in common and which distinguishes them from earlier work on the investment function is the importance attributed to the rate of interest and the estimated lags.[5] Bischoff, however, is the only investigator who considers the possibility of differences in the lags associated with monetary and nonmonetary variables. Table 1 indicates the industry classification or the type of investment used in each study and the nature of the lag structure.

In de Leeuw's analysis, attention is restricted to investment by manufacturers. The independent variables included in the study are the rate of interest (Moody's series for industrial bonds), the flow of internal funds (retained earnings plus depreciation allowances), and capital requirements (defined as the constant-dollar volume of capital projects which will bring productive capacity into an optimum relationship to output). The results indicate that all variables are statistically significant and have the anticipated signs. With respect to the timing relationships it appears that the effect on investment of changes in the explanatory variables builds slowly to a peak during the second year and then declines.

Jorgenson's study was conducted as part of the work on the Brookings Model [22]. It differs from de Leeuw's in two important respects. First, investment expenditures are disaggregated into four industrial classifications: durables manufacturers, nondurables manufacturers, total regulated, and all other industries included in the quarterly investment survey of the Department of Commerce and the Securities and Exchange Commission. Second, only two independent variables are considered: the lagged stock of capital

---

[3] See, for example, Mayer [63] and de Leeuw and Gramlich [21].

[4] Particularly disturbing is the finding of long lags in the adjustment of such variables as commercial bank holdings of free reserves (see Davis [18]) and inventories (see the section in this article on investment in inventories). Evidence presented by Bryan [12] suggests that such a bias may arise as a result of aggregation over both time and individuals. For a discussion of these and other problems associated with distributed lag models, see Griliches [37, 38], Mundlak [72], and White [91].

[5] Earlier studies found that the regression coefficients for interest rate variables were usually not only statistically insignificant, but of the wrong sign (positive) as well. See, for example, the works by Tinbergen [86], Klein [50], Klein and Goldberger [53], Meyer and Kuh [68], and Kisselgoff and Modigliani [49]. Comprehensive reviews of this literature have been compiled by Eisner and Strotz [25], especially pages 137–92, and Hammer [43], Chapter 2. A thorough tabular summary of the statistical findings obtained in many previous investigations is given by Meyer and Kuh [68], pages 23–25.

TABLE 1   SELECTED INVESTMENT FUNCTIONS

Study	Industry Classification or Type of Investment	Time in Quarters between the Change in	
		Interest Rates and the First Noticeable Effects on Investment	Interest Rates and the Peak Effect on Investment
De Leeuw [19]	Total manufacturers	*	6
Jorgenson [44]	Durables manufacturers	3	5
	Nondurables manufacturers	6	7
	Total regulated	5	7
	All others	3	4
Fromm and Klein [31]	Durables manufacturers	1	5
	Nondurables manufacturers	*	1
	Total regulated	1	5
	All others	*	1
Liu [56]	Plant (i.e., business construction)	0†	2†
	Equipment	0†	2†
Bischoff [21]	Plant	2	*
	Equipment	1	*

Note: The numbers in the brackets refer to the bibliography.
* Not specified.
† Lag assumed rather than estimated statistically.

and the ratio of the value of output to the implicit rental price of capital services (expressed as a function of the interest rate, the price of capital goods, the rate of depreciation on capital, and the tax structure).[6] Despite these differences, Jorgenson's results are similar to de Leeuw's. He finds that for all four industrial groups the explanatory variables are significant and the lags are quite long. Durables manufacturers and the "all others" category exhibit the fastest adjustment. For them, the first noticeable effects on investment occur three quarters after there is a change in one of the explanatory variables and the peak response occurs one or two quarters later. For the other two groups, the first noticeable response does not occur until after a year (see Table 1).[7]

Combining all four industrial classifications, the Jorgenson model suggests that the quantitative impact of interest rates on business fixed investment is quite large, particularly in the intermediate run. The elasticity of investment with

respect to interest rates one year after there has been a change in rates is approximately −0.50. The long-run elasticity is about −0.15 ([44], pages 78–89).[8]

The work by Fromm and Klein [31] was also done in conjunction with the Brookings model. It was conducted in an apparent attempt to bring the investment equation into closer agreement with the other relationships included in the model. The equation proposed by these writers differs from Jorgenson's in three respects: (a) the cost of capital is expressed solely as a function of the interest rate, (b) the ratio of output to the cost of capital is separated into two independent variables, and (c) an alternative method is used for estimating lags. Considering the apparently minor nature of the modifications, the results of this study differ markedly from those reported by Jorgenson. As Table 1 indicates, it now appears that of the four industry classifications the ones which adjust most quickly are nondurables manufacturers and "all others." For the other two groups—durables manufacturers and

[6] For optimal allocation of capital, a firm should charge itself an implicit rental equal to the user cost of capital services at each point of time. The user cost is an accounting (or shadow) price that arises from the fact that firms own capital stock from which they derive capital services.

[7] Evidence confirming the general nature of these results has been presented by Griliches and Wallace [39], Hall and Jorgenson [41], and Jorgenson and Stephenson [46, 47]. Conflicting evidence is presented by Eisner and Nadiri [24].

[8] Estimates of interest rate elasticities for other sectors of the Brookings model are not readily available. However, the numbers in Table 3 (discussed later) make it possible to compute the gross effects of interest rates on the various components of GNP implied by the model. These effects include both the direct impact of changes in interest rates on each expenditure item taken individually and the indirect or "accelerator" effect which occurs as a result of the impact of interest rates on other items.

total regulated—the peak response lags behind the change in interest rates by five quarters. The initial adjustment (i.e., the response which occurs one quarter after the change in interest rates) appears to be in the wrong direction. Unfortunately, Fromm and Klein make no attempt to explain the latter finding.

In Liu's model [56], disaggregation is based on the type of expenditure. Thus separate equations are used for investment in plant (business construction) and investment in equipment. The explanatory variables included in the former are gross national product (GNP), the ratio of Federal Government expenditures on goods and services to GNP, the yield on long-term corporate bonds, the lagged stock of capital, and the lagged value of the dependent variable. Once again the interest rate is statistically significant. In this study, no attempt is made to estimate the nature of the lag structure. Instead, it is *assumed* that the initial effect occurs during the period in which there is a change in the interest rate and that the peak response occurs two quarters later. The equation to explain producers' expenditures on durable equipment does not contain an explicit monetary variable. However, since business construction expenditures are used as an explanatory variable, interest rates enter the equation indirectly.

The last investment function to be considered is the one developed by Bischoff and incorporated in the Federal Reserve-MIT econometric model [21].[9] Disaggregation in this model is also by type of expenditure (structures versus equipment) rather than by industrial classification. The theoretical framework underlying the analysis is an extension of Jorgenson's neoclassical model of investment behavior [44, 45]. Among the more important modifications introduced by Bischoff are: the separation of the ratio of output to the implicit rental price of capital into two independent variables and the estimation of different lags for each variable. Another interesting feature of the model is that, for producers' equipment, the central demand variable is not final expenditures but new orders. Orders are then translated into expenditures through a variable weight distributed lag. A technique developed by Tinsley [87] is used to estimate the way in which the lag lengthens in periods of supply bottlenecks and shortens when the bottlenecks disappear. These modifications yield estimates of the lag between changes in the cost of capital and

the resulting effects on investment that are considerably longer than those reported in other studies. A change in the long-term corporate bond rate, for example, will not begin to affect expenditures on structures for two quarters and will not have its maximum effect until after *three years*. The lag in the producers' durables equation is very similar. The only noticeable difference is that the initial effect occurs one quarter sooner.

The quantitative impact of a change in interest rates implied by Bischoff's equations is fairly large. The results of a simulation experiment ([21], pages 19–20) suggest that, if the corporate bond rate increased by 1 percentage point above its actual value, beginning in the first quarter of 1963 (i.e., a 23 percent increase over its 1962 base), then at the end of twelve quarters expenditures on plant and equipment would be about $4 billion (or 5.4 percent) less than they otherwise would have been. This yields a three-year elasticity of investment with respect to interest rates of slightly less than −0.24, which is similar to the estimates obtained by Jorgenson [44] and other investigators.[10]

One limitation of most of the studies cited in this and later sections is that they do not allow the lag between changes in the factors affecting expenditure decisions and actual expenditures to vary over time. Moreover, even when variable lags are considered [2, 7], it is assumed that the variability may be attributed solely to technological considerations, i.e., supply bottlenecks. Virtually no attention is given to the possibility that the speed with which expenditure decisions are made and altered may also be a function of economic variables, such as the level of interest rates and the rate of change of income and prices. For a discussion of these considerations see Allais [1], Friedman [27], and White [91].

INVESTMENT IN INVENTORIES

Despite the substantial amount of attention that has been devoted to the explanation of investment in inventories (see Table 2), there remain several unresolved questions. The seriousness of these questions makes an evaluation of the role of monetary variables in the inventory

---

[9] The function is discussed in greater detail in [6, 7].

[10] Goldfeld [33], page 166, and Grunfeld [40], page 240, find long-run interest rate elasticities of business fixed investment of −0.5 or −0.6. Hammer [43], page 112, reports a short-run interest elasticity of −0.3 and a long-run elasticity of −0.5. On the other hand, Resek [80] found an interest elasticity for total manufacturing that varied from −1.0 to −1.4 in different models.

TABLE 2 INVENTORY STUDIES

Study	Industry Classification	Monetary Variables
Brown, et al. [8]...................	Total manufacturers	Short-term interest rate and maximum earning assets of commercial banks*
Darling and Lovell [16]............	Durables manufacturers Nondurables manufacturers Trade	Short-term interest rate Short-term interest rate Short-term interest rate
Duesenberry, et al. [23]...........	Total manufacturers	None
Fromm and Klein [31].............	Durables manufacturers Nondurables manufacturers Trade	Change in short-term interest rate Change in short-term interest rate Change in short-term interest rate
Goldfeld [33].....................	Total manufacturers	Short-term interest rate† and flow of commercial loans†
Klein [52]........................	Total inventories‡	None
Kuznets [54].....................	Total manufacturers	Short-term interest rate,† internal finance,† and external finance†
Liebenberg, et al. [55].............	Total inventories‡	None
Liu [56].........................	Nonfarm business	Short-term interest rate† and liquid assets of business
Lovell [57].......................	Nondurables manufacturers Durables manufacturers	Short-term interest rate Short-term interest rate
McGouldrick [64]..................	Durables manufacturers Trade	Short-term interest rate Loan-deposit ratio of commercial banks and liquid assets of business as a ratio to current liabilities
Rasche and Shapiro [79]...........	Nonfarm business	Short-term interest rate
Terleckyj [85].....................	Total manufacturers and trade	Short-term interest rate

Note: The numbers in the brackets refer to the bibliography.
* A measure of availability.
† Variable has proper sign and is statistically significant.
‡ As measured in the national income accounts.

equation difficult at the present time. Conse-quently, our discussion will concentrate on the issues that have been raised in the literature.

First, there is the question of the relevance of monetary variables. Several writers, among them Klein [52], Duesenberry, Eckstein, and Fromm [23], and the authors of the OBE (Office of Business Economics) model [55], do not even mention monetary variables as possible determi-nants of inventory investment.

Assuming that monetary variables are relevant, the next problem is to determine which variable (or variables) provide the best measure of changes in credit market conditions. As Table 2 indicates, the most commonly used component has been the short-term interest rate (e.g., the interest rate on four- to six-month prime commer-cial paper and the bank rate on short-term busi-ness loans). Other variables which have been considered are the availability of credit (the loan-deposit ratio of commercial banks and the flow of commercial loans) and liquidity (e.g., business liquid assets and internal finance—the sum of retained earnings and depreciation flows).

A third source of dispute has centered on the importance of the monetary variables that have

been used in the inventory equation. Recent studies (namely, those of Goldfeld [33], Kuznets [54], and Liu [56]) have found that monetary variables, particularly interest rates, have the proper signs and are statistically significant. Nevertheless, a number of investigators have re-ported either that monetary variables have the wrong signs or that they are not statistically significant.[11]

A fourth question complicating the assessment of the role of monetary variables in the inventory equation has been raised by Ruth Mack [59]. It concerns the estimates of the speed with which the actual levels of inventories are adjusted to their equilibrium values. Most of the studies listed in Table 2 are based on a flexible accelerator or stock adjustment model. This model assumes that the cost involved in changing the level of stocks leads only to a partial adjustment of inven-tories toward their long-run equilibrium level in each quarter. The estimates of the adjustment coefficient reported in the literature suggest that,

---

[11] Among others, see Brown, *et al.* [8], Darling and Lovell [16], Lovell [57], McGouldrick [64], Rasche and Shapiro [79], Terleckyj [85], and the discussion in Lovell [58].

on the average, about 20 percent of the adjustment in inventories is made during any given quarter and about 60 percent during a year. The question which Miss Mack poses concerns "the significance of an intention about so volatile a matter as stocks [of inventories] if a business moves only halfway toward its validation in the course of three months?"[12]

Finally, there is the problem of the *ad hoc* way in which many variables are introduced into the equation—for example, unfilled orders. This variable has been used as one of the principal determinants of both total inventories and inventories of work in process. Although numerous rationalizations have been offered for the influence of unfilled orders on inventories,[13] it seems appropriate to investigate whether these variables represent anything more than different ways of measuring the tightness or looseness in the production schedule. Thus, it seems likely that one of the consequences of an increase in the ratio of work-in-process inventory to sales would be an increase in the backlog of unfilled orders.

Consideration of these problems suggests that, despite the respectable correlation coefficients that have been obtained, our *understanding* of inventory investment and the role of both monetary and nonmonetary variables in its determination is quite limited.

RESIDENTIAL CONSTRUCTION

A considerable amount of research has also been done in an effort to develop an explanation of the expenditures for residential construction. Four studies—those by Liu [56], Maisel [61], Muth [73], and Sparks (as presented in [21])—are of particular interest, for although they differ in many respects they each attribute an important role to interest rates.[14]

Muth's paper is the most straightforward from a theoretical point of view. He assumes that expenditures on residential construction are positively related to income and negatively related to the existing stock of houses, the yield on ten-year corporate bonds, and Boeckh's index of residential construction costs. The empirical analysis which is based on annual observations for the period 1915–41 (excluding war years), supports Muth's approach: all the variables are statistically

significant. In addition, the estimate of the adjustment coefficient suggests that individuals make about one third of the ultimate adjustment in their housing stock during the year in which there are changes in the explanatory variables.

Liu's approach is more difficult to follow. To explain quarterly gross private investment in residential housing, he uses consumer holdings of liquid assets, Moody's long-term yield on corporate bonds, two lagged values of expenditures on residential construction, time, and the *per capita* stock of residential housing. No explanation is given as to why the latter variable is the only one measured on a *per capita* basis. Despite this peculiarity, Liu finds that both the liquid asset variable and the long-term interest rate are statistically significant and that changes in these variables have a noticeable impact on residential construction within a year.

Maisel arrives at essentially the same result. However, in his analysis, a great deal more attention is given to the institutional and technical characteristics of the construction industry. To begin with, residential construction is separated into two components, namely, expenditures on new dwelling units and additions and alterations to existing units. Expenditures on new dwellings are broken down into two additional components: the number of housing starts and the average value per start. The results show that both these variables are significantly influenced by changes in the short-term interest rate (the average yield on three-month Treasury bills) and that the effect should become apparent within six months. The relevance of the short-term interest rate, as opposed to mortgage rates, for example, is open to question, but what is more puzzling is the relationship which Maisel uses to explain additions and alterations. The latter equation contains no monetary variables. In fact, the only variables that it includes are the stock of houses and the price of new construction relative to the price of other GNP components. Thus, in Maisel's model, expenditures on additions and alterations are unaffected by income, the cost of credit, and the various demographic variables which are used to explain housing starts.[15]

To estimate the quantitative impact of monetary factors on housing expenditures, Maisel [60] has reestimated his equation for housing starts and used it to explain the movements in this variable during 1966. In its present form the model contains two monetary variables, one mea-

---

[12] Ruth Mack [59], page 226.

[13] See Darling and Lovell [16], pages 135–36, and Goldfeld [33], Chapter IV.

[14] For a review of the earlier literature, see Grebler and Maisel [35].

[15] See Maisel [62].

suring interest rates and the other the availability of financing. Other variables include the number of vacant housing units which are available and fit for use, disposable income per household, rents relative to construction costs, and the inventory of housing units under construction.

Between the last half of 1965 and that of 1966, the number of housing starts dropped by 480,000 (or 32 percent). Maisel's model estimated a decline in this period of only 326,000. It failed to account for 32 percent of the drop in this extremely dynamic period. Of the decrease estimated by the model, the two monetary variables accounted for 76 percent. The remainder was accounted for by an increase in the number of vacancies and a decrease in relative rents, offset to some extent by an increase in disposable income. Thus, the estimated impact of the monetary variables amounted to over one half of the actual reported change—the difference, of course, being the amount unexplained by the model.

The most recent treatment of residential construction activity is the analysis by Sparks, which is included as part of the Federal Reserve–MIT model [21].[16] Sparks' approach focuses on the determination of three basic variables: the rental cost of housing services, the price per unit of the stock of houses, and the change in the inventory of housing under construction. The rental cost of housing services is determined by the demand variables, income and the number of households, together with the predetermined stock of existing houses. The price per unit of the stock of houses is then determined by the return on investment in housing as reflected in the relationship between rent and the yield on new conventional mortgages. Finally, the change in the inventory of housing under construction (i.e., residential construction expenditures) is taken as a function of the rate of return on houses (the rental cost of housing services relative to the price of houses) and the mortgage rate.

Although certain aspects of Sparks' model are not supported by the evidence (see Goldfeld [32]), there is a clear indication that (a) mortgage rates are one of the more important determinants of residential construction expenditures and (b) the effects of a general increase in interest rates will be transmitted to the housing sector quite rapidly. Some of the effect will take place during the quarter in which the change in interest rates occurs, while approximately 30 percent of

the ultimate adjustment in the stock of housing will be completed within a year. The latter estimate, it should be noted, is practically the same as the one obtained by Muth. The one-year elasticity of housing expenditures with respect to interest rates implied by Sparks' model is approximately −0.45.

One possible limitation of the studies reviewed in this section is that interest rates may not capture all relevant dimensions of the ease or tightness of mortgage credit, especially in periods such as 1966 when nonbank financial institutions experienced a marked reduction in deposit inflows. Further work is under way on the Federal Reserve–MIT model to develop a more elaborate treatment of nonbank financial intermediaries and the credit side of the housing market.

CONSUMPTION

Since the publication of Keynes' *General Theory* [48], it has generally been assumed that consumers are insensitive to changes in interest rates.[17] Consequently, the only monetary variable that has been included in the consumption function with any regularity has been the stock of liquid assets held by households.[18] The reasons for including this component have varied. Sometimes it is used as a measure of liquidity, that is, the ability of consumers to make large purchases or downpayments (Klein [51]). At other times, it has been used as a proxy for total wealth (Klein [52]). On either account, we would expect the variable to be most important in explaining the demand for automobiles and other durable goods, but this has not been the case. Liquid assets are rarely significant in equations that have been used to explain the purchase of automobiles. On the other hand, they have been consistently helpful in explaining the consumption of services. For nondurable goods and for durable goods other than automobiles, the results are mixed.[19]

The monetary variable that Suits [82] has used to explain the demand for new automobiles is average credit terms, i.e., the average number of months to maturity for new automobile install-

---

[16] Slightly different formulation of the equations are presented in Sparks [81] and Rasche and Shapiro [79].

[17] See, for example, the discussion in Suits [83].

[18] Interest rates do enter indirectly into the consumption function when net worth or wealth variables (see [5] and [69]) are included because these change with fluctuations in interest rates.

[19] See Suits and Sparks [84], and Klein [52], Liebenberg, Hirsch, and Popkin [55], and Fromm and Klein [31].

ment contracts.[20] The major problem encountered with this variable is the assumption either that consumers make their credit decisions before their consumption decisions or that the value of the variable is imposed upon them. Both possibilities appear to be unlikely. Maximum credit terms may be imposed upon consumers, but not average terms. The latter arise as a result of consumers' simultaneous decisions to purchase goods and acquire credit.

Recently, Hamburger [42] has taken the view that consumer expenditures on durable goods should be treated like business investment expenditures. The results of this study suggest that the market rate of interest (measured either as the rate on long-term corporate bonds or as the yield on directly placed finance company paper) is one of the major determinants of the demand for automobiles and other durable goods. However, as in the case with business investment expenditures, the lags appearing in the estimated equations prove to be rather long. It takes more than four quarters for changes in interest rates to have their first noticeable effect on the purchases of these items.

Interest rates also appear in the consumption block of the Federal Reserve–MIT model [21].[21] In this analysis, a distinction is drawn between the services yielded by stocks of durable goods and expenditures on durable goods, the latter appearing as part of consumer spending in the national income accounts. The sum of the services of durable goods and expenditures on nondurables and services is the basic consumption variable related to current and lagged disposable income. The allocation of this sum among its components depends on relative prices, existing stocks of durable goods, recent income changes, and to a minor extent on interest rates. These forces are constrained so that, if they increase one component of consumption, they decrease one or more others by an *exactly* offsetting amount. Although this approach recognizes the possible effect of interest rates on the composition of consumption (as defined in the model) during any time period, it rules out the effect of interest rates on the substitution of current consumption for future consumption (saving). Moreover, it is difficult to determine what, if any, effect interest rates have on the measure

of consumer expenditures included in the national income accounts.

EXPENDITURES OF STATE AND LOCAL GOVERNMENTS

In contrast to consumption, the expenditures of state and local governments have traditionally been thought to be sensitive to changes in monetary variables. Nevertheless, there have been relatively few econometric studies of this sector of the economy. Most model builders have preferred to treat the receipts and expenditures of this sector as exogenous.

One of the most comprehensive econometric studies is by Ando, Brown, and Adams [4].[22] These writers identify five major expenditures of state and local governments for which fluctuations in interest rates might be important: expenditures on highways, sewer and water systems, educational facilities, hospitals, and administrative and service facilities. The only relationship in which the rate of interest (Moody's long-term municipal bond yield) is significant is the one used to explain expenditures on educational facilities. In this equation the interest rate enters twice, once by itself and once as a product with another variable. As far as the timing relationships are concerned, it appears to take approximately two quarters before interest rates have their first noticeable effect.

The other four equations contain no monetary variables. However, the model implied by three of the equations (those for hospitals, administrative and service facilities, and sewer and water systems) is open to considerable doubt. According to these equations, the desired stock of the asset in question is influenced by only one variable, the amount of service which is to be provided. Thus, it would appear that expenditures on these items are unaffected by the cost of credit, tax revenues, and commitments to other projects—three assumptions which are highly suspicious.

From this summary it can be seen that, although Ando, Brown, and Adams have contributed to our understanding of the expenditures of state and local governments, we still know very little about the reaction of these variables to changes in credit market conditions.

To rectify some of the shortcomings of the Ando, Brown, and Adams model, Gramlich [34]

[20] A similar variable is used by Evans and Kisselgoff [26].

[21] For an earlier version of these equations, see de Leeuw [20]. For a somewhat different formulation, see Rasche and Shapiro [79].

[22] Other (noneconometric) studies include those by Morris [70, 71] and Pickering [77, 78].

has formulated a set of equations, explaining the behavior of state and local governments, which has as its basis the constraint against borrowing on current account faced by these institutions.[23] This constraint introduces strong interdependence of spending and tax decisions for states and localities. For statistical reasons it is assumed that causality runs entirely from expenditures to taxes. The results reveal an important interest rate effect on state and local construction expenditures and a smaller, but still noticeable, effect on the proportion of current expenditures financed by taxes. Other variables that seem to have a significant effect on expenditures are Federal grants-in-aid, income, population, the proportion of the population of school age, and prices. The results of a simulation experiment ([21], pages 19–20) indicate that an increase in interest rates will cause a fairly sharp initial reduction in expenditures due to a postponement effect for wages and salaries, and a slightly larger long-run effect due to the delayed response of construction expenditures. The three-year elasticity of state and local expenditures with respect to interest rates is approximately −0.05.

Questions are raised by two of Gramlich's assumptions: (a) the one concerning the flow of causality from expenditures to taxes and (b) the ability of state and local governments to postpone wages and salaries. The former implies a very flexible and frequent adjustment of state and local tax rates so that the rates may be treated merely as details which are set to bring in the required amount of revenue.

SIMULATIONS OF CHANGES IN MONETARY POLICY IN COMPLETE ECONOMETRIC MODELS

Some numerical estimates of the effects on the aggregate economy of changes in monetary policy should also be considered. These estimates are derived from simulations of the two recent models: the Brookings model, simulated by Fromm [30], and the Federal Reserve–MIT model, simulated by de Leeuw and Gramlich [21].[24]

The time period simulated by Fromm is the eight quarters from 1961 through 1962. The ex-

ogenous variables are set equal to their actual values with the following exceptions: in one experiment, the discount rate is raised by 0.5 percentage point; in the other, the discount rate is raised by the same amount and the maximum rate payable on time deposits is increased by 1.0 percentage point. A control solution without either of these changes in the exogenous variables was also run.

The results are shown in Table 3, which is reproduced from Fromm's paper. Two sets of values are given for each variable. These represent the differences between the experimental values and the control solution. Hence, they indicate the impact of altering monetary variables. For example, at the end of eight quarters, real GNP (measured in 1954 dollars) is $4.9 billion lower than it would have been if the discount rate had not been increased. This figure is equivalent to a drop in real GNP of about 1 percent. Thus, according to the model, changes in the discount rate have a significant impact on the level of economic activity independent of any announcement or psychological effects.

Three other results also warrant comment. First, the fall in real GNP coincides with an increase in prices. Fromm suggests that the price change should really be treated as if it were zero. But even this seems surprising. The problem is that the Brookings model places too much emphasis on the effects of costs on prices and too little emphasis on the effects of demand.

Second, a restrictive monetary move is associated with an increase in free reserves. This somewhat unusual occurrence is due to the fact that the simulation assumes a situation where there is a change in the discount rate but no change in nonborrowed reserves. Hence, the rise in the discount rate forces borrowing down, thereby increasing free reserves.

Finally, and most important for our purposes, the initial effect of the increase in the discount rate is an increase in real GNP. The reason for this is that the interest rate coefficients in the Brookings inventory equations have the wrong signs. Corrections for this misspecification may not alter the estimate of the ultimate effect of monetary policy on GNP, but it will almost certainly reduce what otherwise appears to be a rather long lag in the effect.

The simulation conducted by de Leeuw and Gramlich [21] considers the case in which the Federal Reserve uses open market operations to increase the stock of nonborrowed bank reserves by $1 billion. The chart shows the differences between (a) solution values for the Federal Re-

---

[23] The discussion in the text is based on the revision of Gramlich's model, which is discussed in [21].

[24] For a thorough review of the Brookings model, see Griliches [36]. A general analytical treatment of the lag between changes in the money supply and the effect on aggregate demand is presented by Tucker [88].

TABLE 3   EFFECT OF MONETARY POLICY CHANGES: INCREASE IN DISCOUNT RATE OF 0.5 PERCENT AND INCREASE IN MAXIMUM ALLOWABLE RATE PAYABLE ON TIME DEPOSITS OF 1.0 PERCENT* (billions of dollars at annual rates, seasonally adjusted)†

Effects on	1961				1962			
	I	II	III	IV	I	II	III	IV
National income and product accounts:								
Gross national product	+0.2	−0.2	−0.6	−1.1	−1.4	−2.8	−3.5	−3.8
	+0.2	−0.2	−0.5	−1.0	−1.2	−2.6	−3.1	−3.2
Real gross national product	+0.4	−0.4	−0.9	−1.6	−2.2	−4.0	−4.5	−4.9
	+0.4	−0.3	−0.8	−1.3	−1.7	−3.6	−3.5	−3.5
Total real consumption	+0.1	−0.2	−0.4	−0.7	−1.0	−1.7	−2.1	−2.3
	+0.1	−0.1	−0.2	−0.3	−0.4	−0.9	−0.9	−0.9
Total real investment (excluding inventory investment)	+0.0	−0.2	−0.4	−0.6	−0.9	−1.8	−1.8	−1.9
	+0.0	−0.2	−0.4	−0.7	−0.9	−1.9	−1.9	−1.9
Business plant and equipment	+0.0	−0.1	−0.1	−0.2	−0.2	−1.1	−1.1	−1.2
	+0.0	−0.1	−0.1	−0.2	−0.2	−1.1	−1.1	−1.2
Nonfarm residential construction	+0.0	−0.1	−0.2	−0.4	−0.6	−0.7	−0.7	−0.6
	+0.0	−0.1	−0.3	−0.5	−0.7	−0.8	−0.8	−0.6
Real inventory investment	+0.23	−0.08	−0.16	−0.33	−0.40	−0.66	−0.84	−0.88
	+0.26	−0.07	−0.18	−0.36	−0.42	−0.69	−0.86	−0.92
Real disposable income	+0.2	−0.2	−0.4	−0.8	−1.2	−2.2	−2.5	−2.7
	+0.2	−0.2	−0.4	−0.7	−0.9	−1.8	−1.9	−1.9
Prices and unemployment:								
GNP implicit price deflator (Index: 1954 = 100.0)	+0.0	+0.1	+0.1	+0.2	+0.3	+0.5	+0.4	+0.4
	+0.0	+0.1	+0.1	+0.2	+0.2	+0.3	+0.2	+0.2
Unemployment rate (percent)	+0.0	+0.0	+0.0	+0.1	+0.1	+0.1	+0.3	+0.3
	+0.0	+0.0	+0.0	+0.1	+0.1	+0.1	+0.1	+0.2
Financial sector:								
Total bank deposits	−0.68	−1.21	−1.36	−1.99	−2.37	−2.59	−2.79	−2.98
	−0.06	−0.86	+0.66	+1.28	+1.96	+2.69	+3.42	+4.26
Government bill rate (percent)	+0.31	+0.31	+0.30	+0.28	+0.26	+0.27	+0.26	+0.26
	+0.35	+0.37	+0.36	+0.32	+0.29	+0.29	+0.27	+0.17
Government bond rate (percent)	+0.15	+0.12	+0.11	+0.12	+0.13	+0.15	+0.16	+0.17
	+0.17	+0.14	+0.13	+0.14	+0.15	+0.17	+0.17	+0.14
Free reserves (billions of dollars)	+0.058	+0.100	+0.139	+0.177	+0.211	+0.233	+0.256	+0.270
	+0.072	+0.132	+0.190	+0.245	+0.298	+0.334	+0.367	+0.444

* The first line for each variable is the effect when the discount rate is raised by 0.5 percent; the second line shows the effect of simultaneously raising the discount rate by 0.5 percent and the maximum allowable rate on time deposits by 1.0 percent.

† Unless otherwise indicated. Real variables are in 1954 dollars.

Source: *National Banking Review* (March 1966).

serve–MIT model beginning in the first quarter of 1963 with nonborrowed reserves $1 billion above actual values in each quarter and (b) solution values for the model beginning in the first quarter of 1963 with actual nonborrowed reserves. All other exogenous variables are held at actual values for both sets of solution values but, in both sets, lagged values of the endogenous variables are generated by the model as the solutions progress from quarter to quarter.

As indicated in the chart, the effects on fixed investment (partly due to lower interest rates and partly due to higher income) build up gradually to a little more than $3 billion after twelve quarters. The effects on GNP are small in the first few quarters; they accelerate as the increase in fixed investment has its multiplier influence and then decelerate as fixed investment reaches a peak. At the end of three years GNP has increased by more than $11 billion, which implies a higher multiplier for nonborrowed reserves than is shown by the Brookings model,[25] but approximately one half of the increase occurs during the last one and one-half years. This simulation says then that, while monetary policy is ultimately quite powerful, the lags are long. Most of the impact of a change in policy does not take place until after a year, when it is more difficult to predict the needs of stabilization policy. Thus,

[25] The three-year multiplier in the Brookings model is 8.2.

EFFECTS OF A STEP INCREASE OF $1 BILLION IN NONBORROWED RESERVES: FEDERAL RESERVE-MIT ECONOMETRIC MODEL

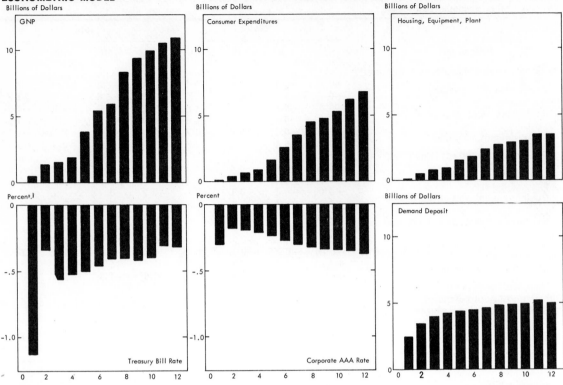

Note: Dynamic simulation, initial conditions of first quarter of 1963.
Source: *Federal Reserve Bulletin* (Washington, D.C.: Board of Governors of the Federal Reserve System, January 1968) page 27.

in its current formulation, the Federal Reserve-MIT model, like the Brookings model, suggests that monetary policy is difficult to use as a stabilization device.

These results must, however, be accepted with caution for, as Christ [13], Meltzer [66], and White [91] have argued, there may be reason to question the model's specification of the effects of monetary policy on the economy. Moreover, the consistency with which long lags have been found in econometric studies covering a wide variety of financial and nonfinancial markets raises questions regarding the adequacy of the estimating procedures that have generally been employed by econometricians to date.

BIBLIOGRAPHY

1. Allais, M. "A Restatement of the Quantity Theory of Money." *American Economic Review* (December 1966), pp. 1123–58.

2. Almon, S. "Lags between Investment Decisions and Their Causes." *Review of Economics and Statistics* (May 1968), pp. 193–206.

3. Andersen, L. C., and Jordan, J. L. "Monetary and Fiscal Actions: A Test of Their Relative Importance in Economic Stabilization." *Review* (Federal Reserve Bank of St. Louis, November 1968), pp. 11–24.

4. Ando, A., Brown, E. C., and Adams, E. W., Jr. "Government Revenues and Expenditures." In Duesenberry, J. S., Fromm, G., Klein, L. R., and Kuh, E. (eds.), *The Brookings Quarterly Econometric Model of the United States* (Chicago and Amsterdam: Rand McNally and Company and North-Holland Publishing Company, 1965), pp. 465–532.

5. Ando, A., and Modigliani, F. "The 'Life Cycle' Hypothesis of Savings." *American Economic Review* (March 1963), pp. 65–84.

6. Bischoff, C. W. "Elasticities of Substitution, Capital Malleability and Distributed Lag Investment Functions." Paper presented at the meeting of the Econometric Society, San Francisco, December 1966.

7. Bischoff, C. W. "Lags in the Fiscal and Monetary Impacts on Investment in Producers Durable Equipment." Unpublished paper, Brookings Institution, Washington, D.C., 1967.

8. Brown, E. C., Solow, R. M., Ando, A., and Kareken, J. H. "Lags in Fiscal and Monetary Policy." In Commission on Money and Credit, *Stabilization Policies* (Englewood Cliffs, N.J.: Prentice-Hall, Inc., 1963), pp. 1–165.

9. Brunner, K. "The Role of Money and Monetary Policy." *Review* (Federal Reserve Bank of St. Louis, July 1968), pp. 9–24.

10. Brunner, K., and Meltzer, A. H. "Predicting Velocity: Implications for Theory and Policy." *Journal of Finance* (May 1963), pp. 319–54.

11. Brunner, K., and Meltzer, A. H. "Some Further Investigations of Demand and Supply Functions." *Journal of Finance* (May 1964), pp. 240–83.

12. Bryan, W. R. "Bank Adjustment to Monetary Policy." *American Economic Review* (September 1967), pp. 855–64.

13. Christ, C. F. "Monetary and Fiscal Policy in Macroeconomic Models." In *The Economic Outlook for 1969* (Ann Arbor: University of Michigan, 1969).

14. Commission on Money and Credit. *Impacts of Monetary Policy* (Englewood Cliffs, N.J.: Prentice-Hall, Inc., 1963).

15. Commission on Money and Credit. *Stabilization Policies* (Englewood Cliffs, N.J.: Prentice-Hall, Inc., 1963).

16. Darling, P. G., and Lovell, M. C. "Factors Influencing Investment in Inventories." In Duesenberry, J. S., Fromm, G., Klein, L. R., and Kuh, E. (eds.), *The Brookings Quarterly Econometric Model of the United States* (Chicago and Amsterdam: Rand McNally and Company and North-Holland Publishing Company, 1965), pp. 131–62.

17. Davis, R. G. "The Role of the Money Supply in Business Cycles." Reprinted with certain revisions from the *Monthly Review* (Federal Reserve Bank of New York, April 1968).

18. Davis, R. G. "Testing Some Variants of the Free Reserves Hypothesis." Unpublished paper, Federal Reserve Bank of New York, 1966.

19. De Leeuw, F. "The Demand for Capital Goods by Manufacturers: A Study of Quarterly Time Series." *Econometrica* (July 1962), pp. 407–23.

20. De Leeuw, F. "A Portfolio Model of Household Saving and Investment." Unpublished paper, Board of Governors of the Federal Reserve System, Washington, D.C., June 1966.

21. De Leeuw, F., and Gramlich, E. M. "The Federal Reserve-MIT Econometric Model." *Federal Reserve Bulletin* (January 1968), pp. 11–40.

22. Duesenberry, J. S., Fromm, G., Klein, L. R., and Kuh, E. (eds.) *The Brookings Quarterly Econometric Model of the United States* (Chicago and Amsterdam: Rand McNally and Com-

pany and North-Holland Publishing Company, 1965).

23. Duesenberry, J. S., Eckstein, O., and Fromm, G. "A Simulation of the United States Economy in Recession." *Econometrica* (October 1960), pp. 749–809.

24. Eisner, R., and Nadiri, M. I. "Investment Behavior and Neoclassical Theory." *Review of Economics and Statistics* (August 1968), pp. 369–82.

25. Eisner, R., and Strotz, R. H. "Determinants of Business Investment." In Commission on Money and Credit, *Impacts of Monetary Policy* (Englewood Cliffs, N.J.: Prentice-Hall, Inc., 1963), pp. 60–338.

26. Evans, M. K., and Kisselgoff, A. "Demand for Consumer Installment Credit and Its Effects on Consumption." In Duesenberry, J. S., Fromm, G., Klein, L. R., and Kuh, E. (eds.), *The Brookings Model: Some Further Results* (Chicago: Rand McNally and Company, 1969), forthcoming.

27. Friedman, M. "Factors Affecting the Level of Interest Rates." In Jacobs, D. P., and Pratt, R. T. (eds.), *Savings and Residential Financing, 1968 Conference Proceedings* (Chicago: United States Savings and Loan League, 1968), pp. 10–27.

28. Friedman, M., and Meiselman, D. "The Relative Stability of Monetary Velocity and the Investment Multiplier in the United States, 1897–1958." Commission on Money and Credit, *Stabilization Policies* (Englewood Cliffs, N.J.: Prentice-Hall, Inc., 1963), pp. 165–268.

29. Friedman, M., and Schwartz, A. J. *A Monetary History of The United States* (Princeton, N.J.: Princeton University Press, 1963).

30. Fromm, G. "Recent Monetary Policy: An Econometric View." *National Banking Review* (March 1966), pp. 299–306.

31. Fromm, G., and Klein, L. R. "The Complete Model: A First Approximation." In Duesenberry, J. S., Fromm, G., Klein, L. R., and Kuh, E. (eds.), *The Brookings Quarterly Econometric Model of the United States* (Chicago and Amsterdam: Rand McNally and Company and North-Holland Publishing Company, 1965), pp. 681–738.

32. Goldfeld, S. M. "Discussion." In *1967 Proceedings of the Business and Economic Statistics Section* (Washington, D.C.: American Statistical Association, 1968), p. 85.

33. Goldfeld, S. M. *Commercial Bank Behavior and Economic Activity* (Amsterdam: North-Holland Publishing Company, 1966).

34. Gramlich, E. M. "State and Local Governments and Their Budget Constraint." *International Economic Review,* June 1969.

35. Grebler, L., and Maisel, S. J. "Determinants of Residential Construction: A Review of Present Knowledge." In Commission on Money and Credit, *Impacts of Monetary Policy* (Englewood Cliffs, N.J.: Prentice-Hall, Inc., 1963), pp. 475–620.

36. Griliches, Z. "The Brookings Model Volume: A Review Article." *The Review of Economics and Statistics* (May 1968), pp. 215–34.

37. Griliches, Z. "Distributed Lags: A Survey." *Econometrica* (January 1967), pp. 16–49.

38. Griliches, Z. "Serial Correlation Bias in Distributed Lag Models." *Econometrica* (January 1961), pp. 65–73.

39. Griliches, Z., and Wallace, N. "The Determinants of Investment Revisited." *International Economic Review* (September 1965), pp. 311–29.

40. Grunfeld, Y. "The Determinants of Corporate Investment." In Harberger, A. C. (ed.), *The Demand for Durable Goods* (Chicago: University of Chicago Press, 1960), pp. 211–266.

41. Hall, R. E., and Jorgenson, D. W. "Tax Policy and Investment Behavior." *American Economic Review* (June 1967), pp. 391–414.

42. Hamburger, M. J. "Interest Rates and the Demand for Consumer Durable Goods." *American Economic Review* (December 1967), pp. 1131–53.

43. Hammer, F. *The Demand for Physical Capital: Application of a Wealth Model* (Englewood Cliffs, N.J.: Prentice-Hall, Inc., 1964).

44. Jorgenson, D. W. "Anticipations and Investment Behavior." In Duesenberry, J. S., Fromm, G., Klein, L. R., and Kuh, E. (eds.), *The Brookings Quarterly Econometric Model of the United States* (Chicago and Amsterdam: Rand McNally and Company and North-Holland Publishing Company, 1965), pp. 35–94.

45. Jorgenson, D. W. "The Theory of Investment Behavior." In Ferber, R. (ed.) *Determinants of Investment Behavior*, Universities–National Bureau Conference Series No. 18 (New York: Columbia University Press, 1967), pp. 129–55.

46. Jorgenson, D. W., and Stephenson, J. A. "Investment Behavior in U.S. Manufacturing 1947–60." *Econometrica* (April 1967), pp. 169–220.

47. Jorgenson, D. W., and Stephenson, J. A. "The Time Structure of Investment Behavior in United States Manufacturing, 1947–1960." *Review of Economics and Statistics* (February 1967), pp. 16–27.

48. Keynes, J. M. *The General Theory of Employment, Interest and Money* (New York: Harcourt, Brace and World, Inc., 1936).

49. Kisselgoff, A., and Modigliani, F. "Private Investment in the Electric Power Industry and the Acceleration Principle." *Review of Economics and Statistics* (November 1957), pp. 363–79.

50. Klein, L. R. *Economic Fluctuations in the United States, 1921–1941* (New York: John Wiley and Sons, Inc., 1950).

51. Klein, L. R. "Major Consumer Expenditures and Ownership of Durable Goods." *Bulletin of the Oxford University Institute of Statistics* (November 1955), pp. 387–414.

52. Klein, L. R. "A Postwar Quarterly Model: Description and Applications." In National Bureau of Economic Research, *Models of Income Determination*, Vol. 28, Studies in Income and Wealth (Princeton, N.J.: Princeton University Press, 1964), pp. 129–55.

53. Klein, L. R., and Goldberger, A. S. *An Econometric Model of the United States, 1929–1952* (Amsterdam: North-Holland Publishing Company, 1954).

54. Kuznets, P. W. "Financial Determinants of Manufacturing Inventory Behavior." *Yale Economic Essays* (Vol. 4, No. 2, 1964), pp. 331–69.

55. Liebenberg, M., Hirsch, A. A., and Popkin, J. "A Quarterly Econometric Model of the United States: A Progress Report." *Survey of Current Business* (May 1966), pp. 13–39.

56. Liu, T. C. "An Exploratory Quarterly Econometric Model of Effective Demand in the Postwar U.S. Economy." *Econometrica* (July 1963), pp. 301–48.

57. Lovell, M. C. "Determinants of Inventory Investment." In National Bureau of Economic Research, *Models of Income Determination*, Vol. 28, Studies in Income and Wealth (Princeton, N.J.: Princeton University Press, 1964), pp. 129–55.

58. Lovell, M. C. "Forecasts of Inventory Investment." In *The Economic Outlook for 1969* (Ann Arbor: University of Michigan, 1969).

59. Mack, R. P. "Comment." In National Bureau of Economic Research, *Models of Income Determination*, Vol. 28, Studies in Income and Wealth (Princeton, N.J.: Princeton University Press, 1964), pp. 224–31.

60. Maisel, S. J. "The Effects of Monetary Policy on Expenditures in Specific Sectors of the Economy." *Journal of Political Economy*, Part II (July–August 1968), pp. 796–814.

61. Maisel, S. J. "Nonbusiness Construction." In Duesenberry, J. S., Fromm, G., Klein, L. R., and Kuh, E. (eds.), *The Brookings Quarterly Econometric Model of the United States* (Chicago and Amsterdam: Rand McNally and Company and North-Holland Publishing Company, 1965), pp. 179–203.

62. Maisel, S. J. "A Theory of Fluctuations in Resi-

dential Construction Starts." *American Economic Review* (June 1963), pp. 359–83.

63. Mayer, T. "The Inflexibility of Monetary Policy." *Review of Economics and Statistics* (November 1958), pp. 358–74.

64. McGouldrick, P. F. "The Impact of Credit Cost and Availability on Inventory Investment." In Joint Economic Committee, 87th Congress, 1st Session, *Inventory Fluctuations and Economic Stabilization, Part II* (Washington, D.C.: U.S. Government Printing Office, 1961), pp. 91–120.

65. McGouldrick, P. F., and Petersen, J. E. "Monetary Restraint and Borrowing and Spending by Large State and Local Governments in 1966." *Federal Reserve Bulletin* (July 1968), pp. 552–81.

66. Meltzer, A. "Comments on the Federal Reserve-MIT Econometric Model." Paper presented at a meeting of the Subcommittee on Monetary Research, Social Science Research Council, Washington, D.C., May 1967.

67. Meyer, J. R., and Glauber, R. *Investment Decisions, Economic Forecasting, and Public Policy* (Boston: Graduate School of Business Administration, Division of Research, Harvard University, 1964).

68. Meyer, J. R., and Kuh, E. *The Investment Decision* (Cambridge, Mass.: Harvard University Press, 1957).

69. Modigliani, F., and Brumberg, R. "Utility Analysis and the Consumption Function: An Interpretation of Cross-Section Data." In Kurihara, K. K. (ed.), *Post-Keynesian Economics* (New Brunswick, N.J.: Rutgers University Press, 1954), pp. 388–436.

70. Morris, F. E. "A Measure of the Impact of Tight Money on the Volume of Long-Term Municipal Issues during the Third Quarter." *IBA Statistical Bulletin,* No. 1, October 1956 (Washington, D.C.: Investment Bankers Association of America).

71. Morris, F. E. "The Impact of Monetary Policy on State and Local Governments: An Empirical Study." *Journal of Finance* (May 1960), pp. 232–49.

72. Mundlak, Y. "Aggregation over Time in Distributed Lag Models." *International Economic Review* (May 1961), pp. 154–63.

73. Muth, R. F. "The Demand for Nonfarm Housing." In Harberger, A. C. (ed.), *The Demand for Durable Goods* (Chicago: University of Chicago Press, 1960), pp. 29–96.

74. National Bureau of Economic Research. *Models of Income Determination,* Vol. 28, Studies in Income and Wealth (Princeton, N.J.: Princeton University Press, 1964).

75. Petersen, J. E., and McGouldrick, P. F. "Monetary Restraint, Borrowing and Capital Spending by Small Local Governments and State Colleges in 1966." *Federal Reserve Bulletin* (December 1968), pp. 953–82.

76. Phelps, C. "Real and Monetary Determinants of State Government Capital Outlays—A Progress Report." Paper presented at a meeting of the Subcommittee on Monetary Research, Social Science Research Council, Washington, D.C., May 1967.

77. Pickering, R. C. "Effects of Credit and Monetary Policy since Mid-1952 on State and Local Government Financing and Construction Activity." Unpublished paper, Board of Governors of the Federal Reserve System, Washington, D.C., April 1955.

78. Pickering, R. C. "State and Local Government Bond Financing during the First Half of 1958." Unpublished paper, Board of Governors of the Federal Reserve System, Washington, D.C., May 1959.

79. Rasche, R. H., and Shapiro, H. T. "The F.R.B.–MIT Econometric Model: Its Special Features." *American Economic Review* (May 1968), pp. 123–54.

80. Resek, R. W. "Investment by Manufacturing Firms: A Quarterly Time Series Analyses of Industry Data." *Review of Economics and Statistics* (August 1966), pp. 322–33.

81. Sparks, G. R. "A Model of the Mortgage Market and Residential Construction Activity." In *1967 Proceedings of the Business and Economic Statistics Section* (Washington, D.C.: American Statistical Association, 1968), pp. 77–83.

82. Suits, D. B. "The Demand for New Automobiles in the United States, 1929–1956." *Review of Economics and Statistics* (August 1958), pp. 273–80.

83. Suits, D. B. "The Determinants of Consumer Expenditures: A Review of Present Knowledge." In Commission on Money and Credit, *Impacts of Monetary Policy* (Englewood Cliffs, N.J.: Prentice-Hall, Inc., 1963), pp. 1–57.

84. Suits, D. B., and Sparks, G. R. "Consumption Regressions with Quarterly Data." In Duesenberry, J. S., Fromm, G., Klein, L. R., and Kuh, E. (eds.), *The Brookings Quarterly Econometric Model of the United States* (Chicago and Amsterdam: Rand McNally and Company and North-Holland Publishing Company, 1965), pp. 465–532.

85. Terleckyj, N. E. *Measures of Inventory Conditions.* National Industrial Conference Board Technical Paper No. 8, 1960. Reprinted in Joint Economic Committee, 87th Congress, 1st Session, *Inventory Fluctuations and Economic Stabilization, Part II* (Washington, D.C.: U.S. Government Printing Office, 1961), pp. 159–94.

86. Tinbergen, J. *Statistical Testing of Business Cycle Theories* (Geneva: League of Nations, 1938).

87. Tinsley, Peter A. "An Application of Variable Weight Distributed Lags." *Journal of the American Statistical Association* (December 1967), pp. 1277–89.

88. Tucker, D. P. "Dynamic Income Adjustment to Money Supply Changes." *American Economic Review* (June 1966), pp. 433–49.

89. White, W. H. "Interest Inelasticity of Invest-

ment Demand—the Case from Business Attitude Surveys Reexamined." *American Economic Review* (September 1956), pp. 565–87.

90. White, W. H. "Inventory Investment and the Rate of Interest." *Banca Nazionale del Lavoro Quarterly Review* (June 1961), pp. 141–83.

91. White, W. H. "The Timeliness of the Effects of Monetary Policy: The New Evidence from Econometric Models." *Banca Nazionale del Lavoro Quarterly Review* (September 1968), pp. 276–303.

THE ROLE OF GOVERNMENT INTERMEDIARIES IN THE RESIDENTIAL MORTGAGE MARKET*

Warren L. Smith

The most striking development in the residential mortgage market in recent years has been the massive support provided directly or indirectly by governmental or quasi-governmental agencies. Table I shows the net increases in residential mortgage debt and the portion accounted for by (*a*) net acquisitions of residential mortgages by the Federal Government (largely GNMA and its predecessor, the special assistance and management and liquidating functions of old

FNMA) and by FNMA, and (*b*) the change in advances by the Federal Home Loan Banks to savings and loan associations. Over the four and one half year period from the beginning of 1966 to mid-1970, Federal support, defined as the increase in mortgage holdings of the Federal Government and FNMA plus the increase in FHLB advances, amounted to 26.1 percent of the total increase in residential mortgage debt. In the latest year and a half—from the beginning of 1969 through the first half of 1970—Federal support amounted to 47.1 percent of the increase in mortgage debt. The recent volume of Federal support is much greater than was forthcoming in earlier years; from 1954 through 1965, Federal support averaged only 5.5 percent of the total

* From *Housing and Monetary Policy,* Proceedings of the Monetary Conference at Melvin Village, New Hampshire, October, 1970 (Boston, 1970), pp. 86–101. Reprinted by permission of the Federal Reserve Bank of Boston.

TABLE 1 NET INCREASE IN RESIDENTIAL MORTGAGE DEBT AND PORTION ACCOUNTED FOR BY FEDERAL SUPPORT ACTIVITIES, 1966–1970 (amounts in billions of dollars)

	(1)	(2)	(3)	(4)	(5)	(6)
		Net Acquisitions by		Change in		Ratio of Federal Support to Total
	Total Increase in Residential Mortgage	U.S.		FHLB Advances to Savings and Loan	Total Federal	Increase in Mortgage Debt [(5) ÷ (1)]
Year	Debt[a]	Government[c]	FNMA[c]	Associations	Support	percent
1966	$13.5	$0.9	$1.9	$0.9	$3.7	27.4
1967	16.1	0.9	1.1	−2.5	−0.5	—
1968	18.8	1.1	1.6	0.9	3.6	19.1
1969	20.0	0.8	3.9	4.0	8.7	43.5
1970[b]	15.5	0.7	5.5	2.6	8.7	56.1

[a] Includes the categories, "home mortgages" and "multifamily residential mortgages" as shown in the Federal Reserve flow of funds accounts.

[b] First six months, at seasonally adjusted annual rate.

[c] Prior to September 1968, data relating to the special assistance and management and liquidating functions of former FNMA are included under U.S. Government while secondary market operations are included under FNMA. Beginning with the division of former FNMA into GNMA and new FNMA in September 1968, GNMA is included under U.S. Government.

Source: *Flow of Funds Accounts, 1945–1968: Annual Total Flows and Year-End Assets and Liabilities,* March 1970; and *Flow of Funds, Seasonally Adjusted, 2nd Quarter, 1970* (preliminary, August 13, 1970).

increase in residential mortgage debt and in only two years did it exceed 10 percent.[1]

There can be no doubt that a portion of this exceptionally high level of Federal support for the mortgage market in the last few years can be attributed to a desire to offset a part of the disproportionate impact of restrictive monetary policy on the housing sector. At the same time, however, I believe a substantial part of it can be attributed to a change in the importance attached to housing among our national goals and to changes in the structure and functioning of the mortgage market, the full implications of which we have not yet seen. In this paper, I shall first attempt to sketch the structural changes in the mortgage market as they relate to the establishment of a greater role for governmental or quasi-governmental intermediaries, and, second, to speculate on the functioning of the new system of housing finance toward which these developments are rapidly leading us.

STRUCTURAL CHANGES IN THE MORTGAGE MARKET

Perhaps the most basic change in our attitudes toward housing and the mortgage market can be attributed to the establishment of a quantitative 10-year housing goal, calling for the production of 26 million new or substantially rehabilitated housing units in the Housing and Urban Development Act of 1968. Since 1949, the United States has had a statutory national goal of "a decent home and a suitable living environment for every American family." However, it was not until the passage of the 1968 Act that this objective was translated into a definite quantitative target. While the 1968 Act did not establish a set of policy instruments to be used to achieve the target, it did require the preparation by the Secretary of Housing and Urban Development of annual reports on national housing goals, and two such reports have thus far been prepared. The existence of a statutory quantitative national goal and the requirement of annual reports indicating the actions being taken to achieve that goal have, I believe, served to energize the activities of the Federal Government relating to housing and have led to innovations that would probably not otherwise have taken place. Whether it is desirable to have a specific national target for homebuilding alone among the many desirable activities that compete for our limited national resources is an issue on which I shall not comment.

In the wake of the Housing Act of 1968, a number of institutional and behavioral changes relating to the Federal Government's role in the mortgage market have already occurred, and a number of further innovations are in prospect.

First, the 1968 Act itself provided for an important reorganization of FNMA. FNMA was divided into two parts: A reorganized FNMA, which was constituted as a Government-sponsored private corporation to take over the responsibility for secondary market operations; and GNMA, which was established as an institution to be operated and financed by the Federal Government to continue the special assistance and management and liquidating functions of old FNMA. In May 1968, prior to the reorganization and in anticipation of it, FNMA changed its method of conducting secondary market operations by substituting the so-called "free-market" system of making commitments to buy mortgages on the basis of weekly auctions for the previous system based primarily on outright purchases at posted prices.

These changes in the structure and operations of FNMA have permitted a substantial increase in the scope and effectiveness of FNMA's operations. The "free-market" system has enabled the organization to focus its support at the important commitment stage where it does the most good in sustaining residential construction. It has also permitted FNMA to determine the volume of the support it will provide while letting the market determine prices. The shift of FNMA to private auspices has taken its operations out of the Federal budget, thereby removing the budget constraint and enabling it to expand the scale of its operations substantially. FNMA's portfolio of mortgages has increased from $6.5 billion in May, 1968, when the free-market system went into operation to $14.1 billion in July, 1970; and its outstanding commitments have increased from $0.5 billion to $4.7 billion over the same period.

GNMA has played an important role in the financing of the various Federal programs for providing housing to low- and moderate-income families, receiving important assistance from FNMA in carrying out this task.[2] In addition,

---

[1] These two years were 1957 (13.2 percent) and 1959 (18.0 percent).

[2] Since GNMA's operations fall within the Federal Budget, its lending activities add to the Federal deficit. In order to minimize the budgetary impact of the financing of Federal housing programs, a cooperative arrangement (referred to as the "Tandem Plan") has been worked out between GNMA and

the 1968 Act authorized GNMA, acting as an agent of the Federal Government, to guarantee principal and interest payments on securities issued by private institutions and backed by pools of FHA-insured or VA-guaranteed mortgages. Operations under this program have already begun and give promise of becoming more important in the years ahead.

No doubt as a result in large part of the commitment to a numerical national housing goal contained in the Housing and Urban Development Act of 1968, the Federal Home Loan Bank System has recently come to be much less dominated by its regulatory responsibilities and more concerned about supporting homebuilding through the medium of expanding its advances to member savings and loan associates. During the 10 months from March 1969 through January 1970, when restrictive monetary policy was imposing a severe constraint on net inflows of deposits to savings and loan associations, the Home Loan Bank System increased its outstanding advances by $4.5 billion. This expansion of advances, together with a reduction of $2.4 billion in holdings of liquid assets in part permitted by liberalization of FHLB requirements, enabled savings and loan associations to increase their holdings of mortgages by $7.3 billion despite an increase of only $0.6 billion in their deposit liabilities. When deposit inflows to associations began to pick up in the spring of 1970, the Federal Home Loan Bank System undertook a new program involving preferentially low interest rates on advances designed to encourage associations to postpone repayment of advances and instead to use the renewed inflows of deposits to expand mortgage loans. This program was undertaken in anticipation of the passage of the Emergency Home Finance Act of 1970, Title I of which authorized the appropriation of funds to subsidize a program of low-cost advances by the Home Loan Bank

FNMA. The procedure works as follows: In the financing of multi-family projects of nonprofit sponsors which provide either rent supplements or interest subsidies for lower-income families, GNMA issues commitments to buy mortgages at par, while FNMA undertakes to buy them at a special price which is equal to the market price plus an adjustment for the fact that the costs of servicing these mortgages are lower than for single-family home mortgages. When the time comes for the financing to be carried out, if FNMA's special price has reached par, FNMA purchases the mortgages. If, however, FNMA's special price is below par, GNMA buys the mortgages at par and resells them to FNMA at the special price. Thus, GNMA's net cash outlay, which is a charge against the Federal budget, is limited to the difference between par and FNMA's special price.

System. The Act was signed into law by President Nixon on July 24 of this year.

NEW SYSTEM OF HOUSING FINANCE

The Emergency Home Finance Act of 1970 contains two additional provisions, either or both of which may prove to be of major importance in the future development of the mortgage market. First, Title II authorizes FNMA for the first time to conduct secondary market operations in conventional mortgages. Second, Title III establishes a Federal Home Loan Mortgage Corporation (FHLMC), which is, in effect, a subsidiary of the Federal Home Loan Bank System; this new Corporation is also authorized to conduct secondary market operations in conventional mortgages, financing its operations by the sale of its own securities. The Corporation is also empowered to buy and sell FHA-insured and VA-guaranteed mortgages.

The developments I have been describing constitute the building blocks of a new—and, I believe, substantially improved—system of housing finance in the United States which can be expected to come to maturity in the next decade or so. The essence of the new system lies in the development of a number of bridges connecting the mortgage market with the open securities markets. It is possible to sort out eight links of this kind which already exist or may develop under the new system.

1. The Home Loan Banks may make advances to savings and loan associations, enabling these institutions to expand their holdings of mortgages in excess of their inflows of deposits. These advances are financed by sales of securities in the open market by the Federal Home Loan Bank System. This link has existed and has been used to a limited extent for many years; its use has been expanded substantially in the last two or three years as a result of the aggressive attitude of the Federal Home Loan Bank Board. However, it seems likely that its use in the future as in the past will be largely confined to the offsetting of the effects of declines in inflows of deposits during periods of restrictive monetary policy. Any effort to expand the volume of advances secularly as a means of channeling additional funds into housing is likely to be unsuccessful, because of the traditional tendency of many savings and loan associations to eschew continuous indebtedness to the Home Loan Banks.

2. FNMA has the power to purchase FHA-insured and VA-guaranteed mortgages, financing these purchases by selling its own securities in

the open market. As indicated above, it currently chooses to exercise this power largely through the "free-market" system of auctioning mortgage commitments, although it also purchases a much smaller quantity of mortgages to finance federally assisted housing, either directly or through GNMA. This link between the bond and mortgage markets has, also existed for many years, but the scale on which it can be used has been vastly expanded since the Housing and Urban Development Act of 1968 changed the status of FNMA to a private corporation, thereby freeing it from a severe Federal budget constraint.

3. Instead of selling its own securities to finance its acquisitions of FHA-insured and VA-guaranteed mortgages, FNMA may issue mortgage-backed securities against pools of these mortgages, obtaining from GNMA guarantees of payment of principal and interest on the securities. This method of financing has already been used by FNMA, which currently has $1 billion of such mortgage-backed bonds outstanding. As yet, it is too early to tell whether it will prove to be less expensive for FNMA to finance its operations by issuing its own debt or by issuing mortgage-backed securities. FNMA securities are not guaranteed by the United States but are general obligations of, and are guaranteed only by, FNMA. However, FNMA has a high financial rating and has the power, in emergencies, to borrow directly from the U.S. Treasury to the extent of $2.25 billion. Thus, it is not clear that the GNMA guarantee is capable of making mortgage-backed securities more attractive to investors than FNMA's own securities. Under some circumstances, however, there may be an advantage in the use of mortgage-backed securities, since these securities do not count against the debt limit of FNMA, which has currently been set by the Secretary of Housing and Urban Development at 20 times the sum of FNMA's capital and surplus.

4. GNMA may acquire mortgages in pursuance of its special assistance function, financing these purchases by selling its own notes to the U.S. Treasury, which obtains the necessary funds by borrowing from the public through the issuance of direct Treasury debt.

5. GNMA is prepared to guarantee mortgage-backed securities of the "pass-through" type—i.e., on which principal and interest are transmitted to the investor as collected—to be issued by mortgage lenders on the basis of pools of FHA-insured and VA-guaranteed mortgages. Indeed, an amount somewhat in excess of $50 million of these securities has already been issued.

The securities are sold on a negotiated basis to private investors in a manner somewhat similar to the private placement of corporate securities. Pass-through securities can be issued by, for example, mortgage companies on the basis of relatively small pools of mortgages (minimum $2 million) and are intended to tap new sources of mortgage funds, such as private pension and trust funds and state-and-local government pension funds.

6. Under Title II of the Emergency Home Finance Act of 1970, FNMA may purchase conventional mortgages from private holders, financing its purchases by sale of its own securities in the market. The legislation includes safeguards designed to insure the maintenance of the quality of conventional mortgages included in FNMA's portfolio and to assure that the funds disbursed by FNMA in purchasing conventional mortgages will go to lenders who are currently participating in mortgage lending activities.

7. The FHLMC created under Title III of the Emergency Home Finance Act of 1970 is specifically authorized to purchase, or make commitments to purchase, conventional mortgages from savings and loan associations or from other financial institutions (e.g., commercial banks) whose deposits or accounts are insured by an agency of the United States. It seems clear that the main activity envisaged for the Corporation is the purchase of conventional mortgages from savings and loan associations with these purchases being financed by issues of the Corporation's own debt. The Corporation provides, in effect, an alternative channel, in addition to the traditional advances mechanism, by which the Federal Home Loan Bank System can provide additional funds to savings and loan associations for mortgage lending, tapping the open securities markets to finance the operation. This new channel has an important advantage over advances by the Home Loan Banks as a means of adding permanently to the funds available for mortgage lending, because advances add to the liabilities of the savings and loan associations, which must, in principle at least, ultimately be repaid, whereas sales of mortgages to FHLMC do not increase such liabilities. The distinction here is somewhat akin to that between "owned reserves" and "borrowed reserves" in international finance.

8. FHLMC is also authorized to purchase FHA-insured and VA-guaranteed mortgages and to use these mortgages as a basis for issues of mortgage-backed securities with a GNMA guarantee. This provides an additional channel by which FHLMC can tap the bond market to ob-

tain funds to be injected into the mortgage market, presumably in the main through savings and loan associations.

There are other possible channels through which the bond market might be tapped to obtain funds for mortgage lending. For example, under the provisions of the Housing and Urban development Act of 1968 which established the mortgage-backed securities program, it would be possible, say, for a group of savings and loan associations to establish a pool of FHA-insured and VA-guaranteed mortgages, against which it would issue mortgage-backed bonds (as distinct from the pass-through type of mortgage-backed securities) with a GNMA guarantee. However, all issues of mortgage-backed securities must have the approval of the Treasury, and it seems likely that the Treasury will want to avoid a great proliferation of small issues of these securities which would not be conducive to the development of an effective market for them. Thus, for the moment, it appears that the issuance of mortgage-backed bonds is likely to be carried out largely by FNMA as one means of financing its portfolio of mortgages. Whether it will even be important here depends upon whether experience demonstrates that FNMA can raise funds more cheaply by issuing mortgage-backed bonds than by issuing its own securities. FHLMC may also issue mortgage-backed bonds with a GNMA guarantee; indeed, as this is being written the Corporation is in the process of accumulating a pool of FHA-insured and VA-guaranteed mortgages in preparation for its first issue of such bonds. However, it seems likely that the Corporation will ultimately focus mainly on what appears to be its primary function, namely, providing support for the conventional mortgage market, financing itself chiefly by issuing its own securities.

Although thus far its extent has been quite limited, it is possible that the pass-through type of mortgage-backed security with a GNMA guarantee has the greatest promise for attracting new sources of funds, such as pension and trust funds, into the mortgage market on a significant scale. The reason is that it permits securities to be designed individually on a negotiated basis to meet to the maximum possible extent the preferences of these institutions.

Assuming that the secondary market facility for conventional mortgages under the auspices of FHLMC proves workable and develops on a substantial scale, I would expect the use of Federal Home Loan Bank advances to recede to its old function of meeting temporary liquidity needs of savings and loan associations resulting primarily from deposit withdrawals. Indeed, it might be desirable to "fund" a portion of the advances now outstanding through purchases of mortgages by FHLMC with the associations using the proceeds to repay advances. This approach seems preferable to the cumbersome procedure provided for in Title I of the Emergency Home Finance Act of 1970 of giving a Federal subsidy to the Federal Home Loan Bank Board to enable the Home Loan Banks to lower the interest rates on these advances as a means of persuading the savings and loan associations not to repay them.

IMPLICATIONS OF THE EMERGING SYSTEM OF MORTGAGE FINANCE

By exploiting the linkages between the bond market and the mortgage market that are described above, I believe the financing of housing in the United States can be improved in some very important ways. The most far-reaching changes are likely to occur in the response of housing and the mortgage market to changes in credit conditions brought about by monetary policy.

There can be little doubt that restrictive monetary policy has a disproportionate—indeed, discriminatory—effect on homebuilding under the present institutional set-up. In part, the response of residential construction to changes in monetary conditions reflects the fact that the desired stock of housing depends upon mortgage interest rates. To the extent that housing demand responds disproportionately to changes in monetary policy on this account, there is nothing about the result that can be described as "discriminatory" toward housing. But it seems quite clear that during the postwar period, only a part—and at times probably a relatively small part—of the response of homebuilding to restrictive monetary policy can be attributed to the demand-restraining effects of high mortgage interest rates. Two other major sets of forces appear to be involved.

1. When credit tightens and market interest rates rise, commercial banks have an incentive to raise interest rates on savings deposits to attract or hold funds which they need to meet the burgeoning credit demands of their customers. If banks are permitted to raise savings deposit rates, they will pull funds away from savings and loan associations. Even if Regulation Q ceilings are used to hold down rates on bank savings deposits, as has recently been the case, the rise in open-market interest rates may induce savers to channel their savings flows away from savings and loan associations and toward direct investment

in securities. Since savings and loan associations are heavily specialized in mortagage financing, such a process of "disintermediation" may drastically reduce the availability of mortgage funds. And since savings and loan associations engage heavily in the practice of "borrowing short and lending long," they often have such a large portfolio of old mortgages made at an earlier time when interest rates were lower, that they are slow to benefit from rising interest rates, making it difficult for them to raise rates on their deposits to keep them in line with market rates, even if the regulatory authorities will permit them to do so.

2. The existence of ceilings on mortgage interest rates under state usury laws—and, on occasion, of unrealistically low ceiling interest rates applicable to FHA-insured and VA-guaranteed mortgages—has at times kept mortgage interest rates from rising fully in pace with yields on competitive investments, such as corporate bonds, thereby causing investors who hold diversified portfolios, such as life insurance companies and mutual savings banks, to shift the direction of their investments away from mortgages and toward the bond market.

It seems clear that as a result of these forces, mortgage interest rates have not served to clear the mortgage market during periods of monetary restraint. Credit rationing has played an important part in matching demand and supply, with the result that some potential home buyers who would have been willing to pay the current interest rate for mortgages have been unable to obtain credit.

A great improvement in the functioning of our financial system would be accomplished if we could find a way to move from the present cumbersome and inefficient system of mortgage finance to a system in which mortgage interest rates moved in such a way as to clear the market. Under such a system all potential mortgage borrowers who were willing to pay the going interest rate would be able to find accommodation, and the elements of arbitrary rationing of mortgage funds that now exist would be eliminated.

A MARKET CLEARING ARRANGEMENT FOR THE MORTGAGE MARKET

The development of links between the bond market and the mortgage market of the kind described earlier in this paper provides, I believe, a mechanism which will make it possible to move toward a market clearing arrangement in the mortgage market. However, so many new institu-

tional devices have been introduced into the mortgage market that it seems necessary to develop some kind of plan according to which they can be combined into a coherent system. Let me suggest one way of fitting together the pieces of the jigsaw puzzle.

First, every effort should be made to move toward a system in which mortgage interest rates are fully flexible. Title VI of the Emergency Home Finance Act extends through January 1, 1972, the provisions enacted in May 1968, which give the Secretary of Housing and Urban Development the power to set the maximum interest rates on government-supported mortgages at any level he deems necessary to meet market conditions. As I understand it, the intention is to use the authority provided under this legislation to put into effect on a trial basis the dual market system for FHA and VA mortgages that was recommended by the Commission on Mortgage Interest Rates.[3] This system should provide sufficient flexibility to enable the market to work effectively, and hopefully it may prove to be a transitory arrangement in the process of moving toward complete elimination of the rate ceilings. It is also necessary to continue the efforts to achieve liberalization of the usury laws applicable to mortgage interest rates in many states.

Second, I would like to see a vigorous development of secondary market operations in conventional mortgages by the new FHLMC. There are many problems involved in getting such a program under way—problems that arise mainly because conventional mortgages are not homogeneous with respect to risk and other investment properties. Assuming these problems can be solved, I would like to see the operations of the Corporation develop along the following lines. FHLMC would establish a schedule of purchase prices for mortgages having different maturities and bearing different interest rates. The yields corresponding to these purchase prices would bear a stable and consistent relationship to the current borrowing costs of the Corporation. The schedule of purchase prices would be changed frequently—perhaps once a month—as borrowing costs changed. The Corporation would stand ready to buy such mortgages as were offered to it by savings and loan associations at this schedule of prices.

Under such a system, potential mortgage borrowers should always be able to obtain accommo-

---

[3] *Report of the Commission on Mortgage Interest Rates to the President of the United States and to the Congress* (Washington: U.S. Government Printing Office, August 1969), pp. 63–73.

dation, provided they were willing to pay the prevailing interest rate. Suppose restrictive monetary policy caused "disintermediation" with the result that inflows of funds to savings and loan associations were curtailed. In such circumstances, savings and loan associations could set interest rates on new mortgage loans which were above the interest rates at which FHLMC would buy existing mortgages by an amount sufficient to cover the costs associated with sales of such mortgages to FHLMC. The associations could then make new loans at these rates, selling mortgages out of their existing portfolios to obtain the funds.[4] If there was excess demand at the existing schedule of rates, FHLMC would experience an increase in its holdings of mortgages which it would have to finance by selling more of its own securities. As the volume of its outstanding debt increased, its cost of borrowing would rise, pushing up interest rates on mortgages until the excess demand for mortgages was eliminated and the market was in equilibrium. The adjustments to a marked increase in the demand for living space and an associated increase in the demand for mortgage credit with no change in the underlying credit situation would bring a similar set of adjustments into operation.

It would be possible to make the operations of the system symmetrical by having FHLMC sell mortgages out of its portfolio when market conditions warranted, using the proceeds to repay a portion of its debt. This could be accomplished by having it post a schedule of selling prices for mortgages that was somewhat higher than its schedule of buying prices. The yields corresponding to the selling prices might be somewhat lower than the current borrowing costs of the Corporation. Under such an arrangement, if housing demand should slacken at a time when inflows of deposits to savings and loan associations were large, instead of mortgage interest rates falling enough to insure that the entire inflow of funds to savings institutions found lodgment in the mortgage market, a different sequence of events would occur. As soon as mortgage interest rates fell enough relative to other capital market rates to be slightly below the yields corresponding to the posted selling prices

---

[4] It might appear that a problem could arise due to the reluctance of savings and loan associations to take capital losses on sales of old mortgages. However, this could easily be avoided by selling only recent originated mortgages to FHLMC. Indeed, the Emergency Home Finance Act of 1970 imposes strict limitations on the authority of FHLMC to purchase conventional mortgages which were originated more than one year prior to the date of purchase.

of the Corporation, savings and loan associations would begin to buy old mortgages from the Corporation rather than new ones in the market. This would put FHLMC in possession of funds which it could use to retire a portion of its debt. This would serve to inject funds into the capital market generally, bringing down the general level of interest rates, rather than concentrating the downward pressure entirely on the mortgage market.

It should be recognized, however, that there are asymmetries in the system that make it less important to have FHLMC sell mortgages when interest rates decline than to buy them when interest rates rise. During periods of relatively low interest rates, the mortgage market clears under the present system. Moreover, if mortgage demand declines and interest rates fall, there is presumably some incentive for savings and loan associations to lower the interest rates on their deposits. Such a decline in deposit rates might divert funds away from savings and loan associations and help to cause a general decline in interest rates throughout the capital market. However, interest rates on deposits are notoriously sticky in a downward direction; consequently, there might be some benefit to housing over a full cycle of rising and falling interest rates if FHLMC operated asymmetrically, buying mortgages during periods of rising interest rates but not selling them during periods of falling rates. Under such a method of operation, the portfolio of FHLMC would (a) grow during periods when the private market experienced excess demand for mortgage funds because housing demand was strong relative to the volume of funds becoming available through private channels, and (b) remain constant under conditions in which the private market would clear without assistance.

Third, I would favor a continuation of the present FNMA system of weekly auctions of commitments to buy FHA and VA mortgages. This program has proved to be helpful not only in providing builders with a dependable basis for forward planning but also as a means of pumping a great deal of money into the mortgage market. I would expect, however, that the FNMA auctions would become a less important source of mortgage funds under a system in which interest rates moved consistently to clear the market. Under the FNMA auctions up to now, a very high proportion of the commitments have actually been taken up before the commitment period expired. To a considerable extent this is undoubtedly related to the fact that in periods when market interest rates are relatively high—as has been the case throughout the period since the auction technique was put into operation—the mortgage market has not cleared. That is, mortgage credit has not been available to many borrowers even if they were willing to pay the going interest rate. Under such conditions, many of the participants have undoubtedly used the auctions as a way of protecting themselves against lack of availability of mortgage funds, and auctions have helped to fill the credit availability gap.

Under a market clearing system in which borrowers could be assured of being able to obtain mortgage credit at a price, I would expect participation in the auctions to decline because borrowers would need to protect themselves only against the possibility of adverse movements of interest rates and not against the prospect of lack of availability of funds. Moreover, I would not expect as high a proportion of the commitments to be taken up as has been the case up to now. In some cases, interest rates would prove to be higher than the borrower anticipated and he would take up the commitment, but quite frequently rates should prove to be lower than he expected and it would be advantageous for him to borrow elsewhere.

I must confess that the FNMA auctions have some rather arbitrary aspects that do not really appeal to me. FNMA must decide each week the quantity of funds it is to make available. This involves an essentially subjective judgment about the amount of funds the market "needs." Second, not infrequently FNMA apparently finds that if it were to allot the full amount of commitments it initially announced as being available, it would be forced to accept offers it judges to involve "unreasonably" high prices. In such cases, the amount of funds actually allotted is cut back below that initially announced as being available. I would be happier if some way of conducting FNMA operations could be devised that was determined to a greater extent by objective market criteria and involved fewer subjective and, to my mind, essentially arbitrary decisions. It may be that in an environment in which interest rates moved to clear the mortgage market a different mode of operation involving less emphasis on quantities of funds supplied and more emphasis on mortgage interest rates as a guide to FNMA operations would be desirable.

Fourth, I believe it would be desirable to try to extend the use of the "pass-through" type of mortgage-backed securities with a GNMA guarantee. This program has not amounted to much yet in terms of volume, but it strikes me as the one element among the new instruments of mortgage finance that might be capable of attracting a significant amount of pension and trust fund money.

I view the arrangements I am suggesting primarily as a means of enabling housing to compete more effectively for its fair share of the funds available for investment in the face of the changing vicissitudes of the capital market. I do not think of these arrangements as a way of contributing—except possibly to a minor extent—to the process of mobilizing the vast increase in mortgage credit that will be needed over the next decade to meet the housing goals set forth in the Housing and Urban Development Act of 1968. The necessary funds to meet these goals will only be forthcoming if we rearrange our fiscal and monetary policies in such a way as to achieve the necessary flows of funds through the capital market. The establishment of an arrangement under which interest rates would move to clear the mortgage market would merely mean that homebuilding would be able to obtain the share of total credit flows to which it was entitled. To the extent that it might be necessary to use restrictive monetary policy from time to time to curtail aggregate demand, the impact on homebuilding would reflect, as it should, the response of home buyers to high costs of financing. It would no longer be either appropriate or desirable to engage in frantic actions designed to cushion the impact of credit conditions on housing.

It should be noted, however, that it would be quite proper for the Federal Government to act to offset the effects of restrictive credit conditions on subsidized housing programs designed to assist low- and moderate-income families. The way to accomplish this would be to increase the subsidy payments to the extent necessary to offset the higher interest costs involved in financing such programs.

Finally, it should be recognized that the establishment of an arrangement under which interest rates moved to clear the mortgage market would almost certainly reduce the potency of monetary policy as an instrument of economic stabilization. Under the present system, the largest and fastest impact of monetary policy is on residential construction, and this impact is to a considerable extent attributable to changes in mortgage credit availability. If the availability effects on housing were eliminated, monetary policy would, I am convinced, be significantly weakened. It would take larger monetary policy actions and larger swings in interest rates to produce a given effect, and the lags of response would become longer.

RESPONSE OF STATE AND LOCAL GOVERNMENTS TO VARYING CREDIT CONDITIONS*

John E. Petersen

In June 1969, the Board of Governors of the Federal Reserve System in conjunction with the U.S. Bureau of the Census began a series of experimental surveys of State and local government borrowing and capital spending. Because of the importance of the State and local sector to both the capital markets and the economy, the Federal Reserve has had a sustained interest in the size and structure of the credit demands of these governments and the impact of monetary policy upon their borrowing and spending decisions, And, to be of greatest usefulness, information about these demands and impacts is needed on a continuing basis, suitable for estimating national conditions.

In view of these requirements, the series of experimental surveys was designed to provide the following types of information: first, to gather advance, or *ex ante*, evidence about the planned long-term borrowing of State and local governments; second, to ascertain quickly the extent to which such borrowing plans were realized under differing credit market conditions; third, to provide additional knowledge about the linkage between borrowing and spending decisions; and fourth, to permit comparisons of behavior among units of different types. This article reports and analyzes the results of these surveys, which are based on the experiences of a sample of ap-

proximately 4,600 State and local governments, for fiscal year 1970.[1]

The principal findings of the surveys are summarized first. Then the objectives and design of the surveys are discussed briefly. The major portion of the article presents a detailed examination of the survey results. Particular emphasis is given to the relationship between borrowing and capital spending decisions and the effects of interest rates on these decisions, both over time and by type of government. The Appendix contains an analysis of the influence of legal interest rate ceilings on the market for State and local securities.

SUMMARY

Based on surveys of State and local government borrowing plans and realizations, it is estimated that the unsettled and restrictive credit conditions of fiscal 1970 led to setbacks (delays and decreases) in planned long-term borrowing by these governments amounting to nearly $7.4 billion. Throughout much of this period, the difficulties related to historically high interest rates were compounded by legal limitations on maximum interest rates that State and local governments might pay. Such ceilings made borrowing, even when desired, legally impossible.

Of the $7.4 billion in long-term borrowing setbacks experienced by State and local governments, $2.2 billion—though postponed—was still completed before the end of the fiscal year. The remaining $5.2 billion was effectively canceled for the fiscal year and therefore represented a net shortfall below planned levels for fiscal 1970. Thus, it is estimated, had interest rate factors not intervened, that State and local governments might have accomplished $18.5 billion in long-

* Reprinted with minor omissions from *Federal Reserve Bulletin,* March 1971, pp. 209–32. John E. Petersen is Director of Public Finance, Securities Industry Association.

Note: This article is a product of the author's research at the Federal Reserve and while on assignment with the Urban Institute, Washington, D.C. The article has benefited from the contributions of many. At the Federal Reserve, Edward Ettin, Chief of the Capital Markets Section, was responsible for the inception and supervision of the survey project. Much assistance was given by Paul Schneiderman and Eleanor Pruitt of that section and by Carol Siegler of the Division of Data Processing, who did the bulk of the computer programming. Special thanks are due to David McNelis, Chief of the Governments Division, U.S. Bureau of the Census, and to Maurice Criz and Sherman Landau of that division for their invaluable help in the collection and processing of the survey data. Finally, Robert King and the research staff of the investment Bankers Association generously aided in correcting and verifying the borrowing data against their own records.

[1] Throughout this article "governmental" and "governments" refer to State and local government units, including special districts and authorities, except when specified otherwise. "Long-term borrowing" refers to borrowing with original maturity of over 1 year. The surveys asked respondents to give borrowings by the date of sale (the date when the bid was accepted or when the underwriting agreement or other borrowing agreement was signed), not by the date of issue. "Fiscal 1970" refers to the period July 1, 1969, through June 30, 1970. Unless preceded by the word "fiscal," years are calendar years.

term borrowing rather than the $13.3 billion they actually borrowed during that period.

Borrowing difficulties induced by restrictive monetary conditions and interest rate ceilings led to an estimated $2.85 billion in setbacks of planned capital outlays. While a combination of lower interest rates and revisions in interest rate ceilings evidently permitted $1.25 billion of these capital projects to be reinstated, an estimated $1.60 billion remained suspended at the end of fiscal year 1970. This equals 5.6 percent of total capital expenditures by State and local governments in the preceding fiscal year. However, because of lags involved in the capital outlays process, the cutback in spending is stretched out over time.

The surveys were not explicitly designed to measure the impact of interest rate ceilings as a separate factor in borrowing and spending decisions. Nevertheless, comparison of the behavior of units in States with and without such ceilings suggests that ceilings did contribute to disproportionate amounts of borrowing and capital spending shortfalls. In fact, interest rate ceilings may have caused net spending cutbacks by State and local units in fiscal 1970 roughly double what they otherwise would have been.

State and local governments with approximately $4.5 billion in long-term borrowing shortfalls associated with high interest rates evidently were still able to proceed with their original spending plans by changing their financing arrangements. Thus, they raised 60 percent of the funds needed to finance these projects by short-term borrowing not subject to interest rate ceilings. Reductions in actual or planned liquid asset holdings were of secondary importance, and the use of current revenues to substitute capital for current expenditures were inconsequential.

BACKGROUND

High and rising interest rates may have a negative influence on the long-term borrowing and spending of State and local governments for a variety of reasons. First, in the short run, an increase in the interest rates raises the current cost of debt service. This higher cost may make borrowing impossible when current period expenditures cannot be increased because of inflexible revenues. Or, such increases in the cost of borrowing may lead governments to await periods of lower interest rates, in the hope that the burden of future debt service may be lessened. Second, over the longer term, an increase in the cost of borrowing means that the facilities themselves

have gone up in price, perhaps beyond a point where the government believes it worthwhile to make the expenditure.

Of special importance recently has been a third reason for the negative response of State and local governments' borrowing and spending to high interest rates. Most jurisdictions have a legal limit on the interest rate they are allowed to pay. For many governments these pre-set rate ceilings were exceeded by municipal bond yields through much of fiscal 1970. In such areas, the ceilings prevented long-term borrowing and thereby limited expenditures where alternative sources of funds were not available.[2]

Several recent studies have documented the responsiveness of State and local governments to varying credit conditions. Findings have uniformly shown the long-term borrowing of these units to be quite sensitive to fluctuations in municipal bond yields. In addition, past studies have found that the capital expenditures of these governments—which typically rely on long-term borrowing for about one-half of their capital funds—are also significantly influenced by the cost of borrowing.[3]

DESIGN OF SURVEYS

Because of the large number of State and local governments (about 80,000), it was not feasible to conduct a canvass of the borrowing plans and

---

[2] An extensive discussion of the possible reactions of governmental units to the levels of and changes in interest rates will be found in P. F. McGouldrick and J. E. Petersen, "Monetary Restraint and Borrowing and Capital Spending by Large State and Local Governments in 1966," Federal Reserve *Bulletin* (July 1968), p. 552. Appendix A of that article discusses the special institutional structure of State and local governments and the market in which they borrow, both of which are important in explaining their fiscal behavior and influence on the design of the surveys.

[3] The findings of an extensive Federal Reserve System survey of State and local experience during the credit stringency of 1966 are summarized in J. E. Petersen and P. F. McGouldrick, "Monetary Restraint, Borrowing, and Capital Spending by Small Local Governments and State Colleges in 1966," Federal Reserve *Bulletin* (Dec. 1968). Recent studies that focus on the impact of interest rates on State and local spending include E. M. Gramlich, "State and Local Governments and Their Budget Constraint," *International Economic Review* (June 1969); C. D. Phelps, "Real and Monetary Determinants of State and Local Highway Investment, 1951–1961," *American Economic Review* (Sept. 1969); H. Galper and J. E. Petersen, "Forecasting State and Local Government Capital Outlays and Their Financing," Urban Institute Working Paper (Feb. 1970).

realizations of all units. Rather, it was decided to employ a sampling technique similar to that used by the U.S. Bureau of the Census for its annual survey of local government finances. In particular, all State and larger local governmental units were canvassed and a stratified sample of smaller local governments was taken to create a sample frame that could be used as the basis for national estimates after the application of expansion factors.

To achieve a high rate of rapid response, the survey was conducted in two stages. The first stage (annual anticipation survey) consisted of a one-page questionnaire that was sent to all the units in the sample frame in June 1969. Units were asked to indicate their planned long-term borrowing, if any, for the four quarters of fiscal 1970. On the basis of this survey of borrowing anticipations, units that had indicated a plan to borrow were followed up with second-stage questionnaires (quarterly realizations surveys) to determine whether the anticipated borrowing had, in fact, been realized. If there were deviations from the expected levels of long-term borrowing, units were asked to explain why the discrepancies had occurred and to estimate the consequences for expenditures. Units were also asked to give their borrowing plans for the remainder of the fiscal year.

Of the 4,590 State and local governments in the original sample frame, 4,152 responded to the first questionnaire dealing with borrowing plans for fiscal 1970, for a response rate of 90.5 percent. (See Table 1.) Of the 1,351 first-stage respondents that indicated they planned to borrow in one or more quarters of fiscal 1970, 1,320 returned the quarterly questionnaires regarding the outcome of these plans, for a response rate of 96.7 percent.

In examining the results, it should be borne in mind that they are national estimates based on sample survey results. Although the estimates of aggregate borrowing generated by the sample compare favorably with those obtained by other sources, this is but one benchmark of their accuracy. Moreover, because of the limitations of the questionnaires and the survey procedure, it has been necessary to make many assumptions about unit behavior. The surveys present a dynamic record of the outcome of a set of borrowing plans formed at the beginning of fiscal 1970. Since the focus is on deviations from these original anticipations rather than on their original formulation, the analysis is more useful in explaining short-run impacts than in measuring long-term influences on borrowing and spending decisions.

BORROWING ANTICIPATIONS AND REALIZATIONS IN FISCAL 1970

Based on the annual anticipations survey of long-term borrowing, State and local governments indicated that they planned long-term borrowing of an estimated $23 billion during fiscal 1970. These plans included approximately $15 billion in borrowing that had already been authorized for sale by the electorate or by the governing body. The remainder of approximately $8 billion represented bond issues that had not yet been authorized and would not be ready to market until such authorization was obtained.

The planned levels of bond sales were exceedingly high in terms of the prevailing market conditions as of July 1969, since bond sales for the second quarter of 1969 had declined to roughly a $10 billion annual rate. However, the high level of anticipations was explainable for the following reasons: First, the anticipations contained approximately $8 billion in borrowing that had not yet been authorized and would need to secure approval of the voters or the governing bodies. Bond referendum results at that time indicated that perhaps one-half of these scheduled issues would not secure approval. Second, many re-

TABLE 1   STATE AND LOCAL GOVERNMENTAL UNITS INTENDING TO BORROW LONG TERM IN FISCAL YEAR 1970

Type of Unit	Respondents, Total	Respondents Intending to Borrow	
		Number	Percent
States and State agencies.............	240	71	29.6
State higher education.................	222	93	41.9
Counties............................	396	120	30.3
Cities and towns.....................	1,344	539	40.1
Special districts......................	683	138	20.2
School districts......................	1,267	390	30.8
Total.............................	4,152	1,351	32.5

| | | State Govern-ment | Local Government | | | | |
Experience	All Types		Total	County	City or Town	Special District	School District
(1) Anticipated borrowing[1]	23.13	7.00	16.12	1.97	6.63	2.47	5.05
(2) Net shortfall in borrowing	9.88	2.17	7.70	.72	3.18	1.26	2.54
(3) Actual borrowing[2]	13.25	4.83	8.42	1.25	3.45	1.21	2.51
(4) Ratio of actual to planned (percent)	.57	.69	.53	.63	.52	.49	.50

[1] Based on annual anticipation survey with adjustment for nonresponse.
[2] Based on realization surveys with adjustment for nonresponse and Federal Reserve State and local borrowing totals.
Note: Details may not add to totals due to rounding.

spondents, particularly those in larger units, volunteered that their plans were contingent upon either an easing of bond market conditions or a lifting of legal ceilings on interest rates. In the latter regard, it was estimated that approximately $2 billion of the authorized debt planned for sale in fiscal 1970 represented previously deferred bond issues. It was felt that were municipal bond market conditions to become accommodative—yields dropping substantially and, especially, below legal interest rate ceilings—units would be able to market approximately $19 billion in fiscal year 1970. This was after allowance for the attrition in expected borrowings caused by election defeats and routine administrative and technical delays.

As events unfolded, market conditions remained extremely tight through most of fiscal 1970, and State and local governments actually borrowed long-term $13.2 billion. This left a net discrepancy of nearly $10 billion between initially anticipated borrowing (as of July 1969) and that which was ultimately realized. Somewhat over one-half of this estimated shortfall could be attributed to high interest rates, which often rose beyond the levels that communities were permitted to pay legally. The remainder of this shortage was accounted for by delays in construction plans, failure to receive required approval, and various technical and administrative delays.

As Table 2 indicates, net shortfalls in actual borrowing below what was planned were heaviest for school and special districts, based on the quarterly surveys of realizations. All told, State and local governments were able to accomplish only 62 percent of the long-term borrowing that they had originally planned. However, it must be stressed that these plans contained a large amount of debt for which final approval was required. Moreover, earlier studies of borrowing realizations have indicated much planned borrowing must overcome various administrative and legal obstacles before it can be marketed.

Restrictive credit conditions proved to be the largest single factor accounting for the deviation of actual borrowings from the level originally anticipated by State and local units. According to the results of the quarterly realizations surveys, high interest rates kept a net volume of $5.2 billion from being successfully marketed in fiscal 1970. An additional $2.2 billion in borrowing represented bond sales that were postponed for interest rate reasons earlier in the fiscal year but that were subsequently sold before the end of that period. The remainder of this report investigates the nature and consequences of those long-term borrowing shortfalls that were related to interest rate difficulties.

BORROWING SHORTFALLS INDUCED BY HIGH INTEREST RATES

Survey results indicate that during fiscal 1970 State and local governments experienced $7.4 billion in delays and shortfalls in anticipated long-term borrowing because of high interest rates and generally restrictive credit market conditions.[4] Hereinafter, these interest rate-induced

[4] The terms "high interest rates" and "restrictive credit market conditions" are used synonymously throughout this article. The quarterly questionnaire on borrowing realizations simply asked respondents, in the event that they experienced a significant reduction in their borrowing below the planned level, if it was because interest rates were too high. In many cases, respondents volunteered alternative answers or additional information that was judged to pertain primarily to the high cost of borrowing. For example, responses explaining shortfalls in borrowing such as "money too tight," "poor market conditions," or "no buyers" were regarded as relating to either the high cost of borrowing or the limited availability of credit. Of particular importance during 1969 were the congressional discussions concerning the alteration of the tax laws in order to subject certain forms of tax-exempt income to the Federal income tax. Several respondents indicated that they refrained from borrowing during this period, presumably because they felt the general uncertainty over the taxation of interest income on State and local obligations

TABLE 3   LONG-TERM BORROWING SHORTFALLS INDUCED BY HIGH INTEREST RATES, FISCAL YEAR 1970 (in billions of dollars)

	1969		1970		
Borrowing Experience	Q3	Q4	Q1	Q2	Fiscal
(1) Shortfall in borrowing initiated by interest rate reasons............................	2.26	2.91	1.12	1.08	7.37
(2) Sale of offerings previously postponed for interest rate reasons............................	....	.29	1.37	.55	2.21
(3) Net shortfall in borrowing[1].........	2.26	2.62	—.25	.53	5.16
Item : actual borrowing[2]..............	2.46	2.98	4.10	3.71	13.25

[1] Shortfalls calculated as of the beginning of the survey period.
[2] Federal Reserve estimates.

delays and reductions in borrowing shall be referred to as *gross shortfalls* since they represent the amount of borrowing displaced from the quarter in which it was originally planned. Approximately 30 percent, or $2.2 billion, of these gross shortfalls represented borrowing that ultimately was accomplished within fiscal 1970 but that was delayed at least one quarter beyond the quarter for which it had been originally scheduled. These intrayear postponements of long-term borrowings shall be referred to as *temporary shortfalls*. The 70 percent of gross shortfalls, amounting to $5.2 billion, that remained at the end of fiscal 1970 shall be referred to as *net shortfalls*.[5]

---

had unduly depressed the municipal bond market. Wherever it was determined that long-term bond sales were forestalled for reasons related to the cost or availability of credit, they are hereafter classified as instances where high interest rates caused the borrowing shortfall.

In those instances where respondents attributed borrowing or spending shortfalls to more than one reason, dollar volumes were allocated equiproportionately among the reasons. Since multiple reasons were not common, such allocations were of little importance. If the dollar volumes of all shortfalls where high interest rates were at least a contributing factor were used, the totals would be only about 5 percent higher.

[5] This terminology is used to stress both the mechanics of the survey technique and the analytical uses of the shortfall information. When units reported delays or decreases in borrowing, they could not foresee whether they would be successful in remarketing their bonds, much less when this might be accomplished. Only by hindsight was it possible to determine those long-term borrowing shortfalls that proved to be temporary and those that proved to be longer term or complete cancellations.

The total gross shortfall in actual borrowing for a given quarter consists of new postponements or cancellations of borrowing originally planned for that quarter. These constitute a contribution to a pool of unsatisfied borrowing demands. By the same token, there are those issues that were previously postponed that are successfully sold during that quarter. These

Table 3 gives the quarterly pattern of borrowing shortfalls over fiscal 1970. It shows that gross borrowing shortfalls attributable to high interest rates were highest in the second half of 1969, peaking at $2.9 billion in the fourth quarter. From May through December municipal bond rates, shown in Figure 1, rose by 150 basis points. However, borrowing shortfalls quickly tapered off during the first half of 1970, when bond yields dipped by approximately 100 basis points in the first quarter. Although yields rebounded during the second quarter of 1970, the governments continued to sell bonds, primarily because the removal or revision of interest rate ceilings permitted the sale of many issues that had previously been postponed.

It should be noted that the amounts of borrowing shortfalls shown in Table 3 refer only to offerings initially postponed during a particular quarter; bond issues that were unsuccessfully reoffered in more than one quarter during fiscal 1970 are only counted once and only at the time of their originally scheduled offering. Line 2 of Table 3 gives the identifiable sales of bond issues that, after having been postponed earlier in the year, were successfully reoffered later in the fiscal year.[6]

---

represent a subtraction from this pool. Thus, the net contribution of the quarter to the pool of unsatisfied borrowing demands is equal to newly initiated, or gross, shortfalls minus those previous shortfalls that are successfully made up in that quarter.

This pool of shortfalls in long-term borrowing plans represents an overhang on the market of borrowers that would like to sell bonds. Their presence constitutes a demand for funds in addition to those needed for new project financing. The latter may themselves be displaced as previous postponements are made up, setting off new rounds of borrowing and spending effects.

[6] The figures given in line 2 of Table 3 must be viewed as highly judgmental because the governmental units were not directly asked to identify issues

TABLE 4 LONG-TERM BORROWING SHORTFALLS INDUCED BY HIGH INTEREST RATES, BY TYPE OF UNIT, FISCAL YEAR 1970 (in billions of dollars)

Borrowing Shortfalls Induced by High Interest Rates[1]	All Types	State Government	Local Government				
			Total	County	City or Town	Special District	School District
Gross shortfalls[2].............................	7.37	2.14	5.23	.64	1.70	.88	2.01
Postponed borrowing sold later in year (minus)[3].................................	2.21	.36	1.85	.24	.52	.10	.99
Net shortfall..................................	5.16	1.78	3.38	.40	1.18	.78	1.02
Item:[4]							
Gross shortfall ratio.........................	.40	.32	.44	.38	.37	.44	.57
Net shortfall ratio..........................	.28	.27	.29	.24	.26	.39	.29

[1] In cases where multiple reasons were given for shortfalls, the total amounts of shortfalls were prorated equiproportionally among the number of reasons.
[2] Includes long-term borrowings postponed beyond June 1970 and those temporarily postponed during fiscal year 1970.
[3] Borrowings judged to represent the subsequent sale of bond issues previously postponed for interest rate reasons.
[4] The ratio of shortfalls in long-term borrowing over estimated long-term borrowing (shown in Table 2) plus net shortfalls induced by high interest rates.

Approximately $2.2 billion of postponed bond issues were successfully remarketed in the last three quarters of fiscal 1970, with the largest volume occurring in the first quarter of 1970 when bond yields declined. Line 3 of Table 3 shows by quarters the indicated net reduction in borrowing associated with high interest rates. These amounts were derived by subtracting the comebacks of the earlier postponements from the gross shortfall figure.[7] In the last two quarters

that were remarketed after earlier postponement. The data were constructed by reviewing the borrowing plans of units, their shortfalls, and subsequent successful sales of bond issues. In those instances where the bond sale had not been anticipated at the outset of the survey and followed an earlier postponement of a borrowing, the amount of the earlier shortfall was credited as a "comeback" or return to market of a previously displaced bond issue. Had the bond issue been originally postponed because of high interest rates, it was assumed that the return to market of the bond issue "resulted from": an ability or willingness of the community to sell the bond at the rate prevailing at the time it was subsequently sold. Therefore, net shortfalls reflect only bond issues that were unable to be sold throughout the year because of high interest rates.

[7] Information on previous postponements (those arising from the period before fiscal 1970) is not available. Therefore, the amount of the net shortfalls in the first quarter of the survey is identical to the gross shortfalls, there being no allowance for previously setback issues that were brought back to market in 1969 Q3. It should be pointed out that some portion of borrowing shortfalls reported in the surveys represented long-term postponements that were carried forward from 1968 and the first half of 1969. That is, the anticipations survey—entering midstream of old and new borrowing plans—measured the existing pool of unsatisfied borrowing demand that had accumulated over the past. Therefore, the addition of new unsatisfied borrowing demands arising during

of 1969, shortfalls induced by high interest rates accumulated to nearly $5 billion. But the easing of credit market conditions in early 1970 and the extensive lifting of interest rate ceilings held the net increase in borrowing shortfalls to about a quarter of a billion dollars for the remainder of the fiscal year. Nonetheless, State and local governments concluded that year with an estimated net shortfall of $5.16 billion in long-term debt that was not sold because of high interest rates and restrictive credit market conditions.

Table 4 depicts the fiscal 1970 long-term borrowing shortfalls associated with high interest rates, classified by type of government. Again, the distinction is drawn between those setbacks that proved to be intrayear or temporary shortfalls and those net shortfalls that continued beyond June 1970. Gross shortfalls were heaviest for State governments and school districts (about $2 billion each), with those of cities and towns nearly as large. However, almost half of the shortfalls for school districts proved to be temporary. Hence State governments, which were evidently less inclined or less able to remarket deferred issues, experienced the largest net reduction—$1.8 billion—below planned borrowing.

A useful measure of the compositional effects of setbacks associated with high interest rates is the severity of these shortfalls relative to the borrowing that might have been accomplished except for adverse credit conditions. Two simple indices of the relative significance of these shortfalls may be formed by taking the ratios of gross

fiscal 1970 was undoubtedly less than $5.2 billion, although the restrictive conditions of that fiscal year were responsible for that amount of desired borrowing not being accomplished.

and net shortfalls, respectively, to the sum of borrowing accomplished and net shortfalls. In both these ratios, which are shown as items in Table 4, the denominator may be interpreted as an approximation of the total amount of long-term borrowing that units would have liked to accomplish had high interest rates not been a factor.[8]

The gross shortfall ratio shows that school districts far exceeded other types of units in the proportion of borrowing setbacks, with nearly 60 percent of their intended borrowing having been delayed or canceled because of interest rate difficulties. But, as already noted, many of these shortfalls proved to be temporary. By year-end almost half of the delayed borrowing had been made up; hence the net shortfall ratio fell into line with those experienced by other units. An exception to the generalization was the special districts, which failed to realize nearly 40 percent of the long-term borrowing that would otherwise have been accomplished.

For the State and local sector as a whole, the net shortfalls resulting from high interest rates were 28 percent of planned borrowing. The equivalent ratio for the tight-money period of 1966 was only 12 percent.[9]

CAPITAL OUTLAY CUTBACKS AND DELAYS

Almost all long-term borrowing by State and local governments is undertaken to finance capital outlay projects, and approximately one-half of total funds used to finance their capital spending are raised in the long-term bond market.[10] Unless other sources of financing are found, shortfalls in long-term borrowing below planned levels will also result in cancellation or delays of planned capital spending.

In the quarterly realizations questionnaires, those units that reported a significant shortfall in borrowings below planned levels were asked if the shortfall had led, or would lead, to an associated shortfall in capital spending. If the unit responded in the affirmative, it was further asked to estimate the amount of such capital spending impacts. As with the borrowing shortfalls discussed above, this report concentrates on the delays and reductions in capital spending that were associated with borrowing shortfalls related to high interest rates.

A distinction is made between capital outlays associated with gross and net borrowing shortfalls. In particular, it is explicitly assumed that capital spending setbacks that occurred in conjunction with postponed long-term borrowings were also reinstituted if and when the borrowings were later accomplished. It should be borne in mind that the capital spending shortfalls reported here refer to changes in plans that either occurred or were foreseen at the time of the associated borrowing setback. Because of the long lags inherent in the capital outlay process, the impacts on spending that evolve from delays or cancellations take several quarters to be felt in their entirety.

Table 5 gives the quarterly time pattern of estimated capital spending reductions that occurred in conjunction with borrowing shortfalls induced by high interest rates in fiscal 1970. The response of capital spending setbacks to rapidly rising interest rates is clearly evident in the third and fourth quarters of 1969. Planned capital projects amounting to about $2.5 billion were either delayed temporarily or canceled during that period. However, the easing of credit market conditions and the lifting of ceilings on interest rates in the first two quarters of 1970 evidently permitted the successful sale of bonds that had been postponed earlier. This, in turn, allowed the reinstitution of many projects that had been delayed.[11] In fact, it is estimated that the dollar

---

[8] The amount of temporary shortfalls is already included in the estimate of borrowing accomplished. These indices assume symmetrical behavior in terms of interest rate response; that is, shortfalls that reportedly occurred because of high interest rates would have been replaced by actual borrowings at some unspecified lower level of interest rates. Moreover, it is assumed that other reasons for borrowing delays and decreases were not systematically related to high interest rates nor would they have cropped up to further thwart the intended borrowing. While the measures are admittedly simple, they nonetheless are appropriate for making comparisons among units, there being no compelling reason to suspect that one type of unit is more given to asymmetrical behavior than another.

[9] The 1966 Federal Reserve System survey estimated net long-term borrowing shortfalls for that year of $1.7 billion, which is equivalent to 12 percent of $13.9 billion that might have been accomplished that year had not credit conditions been restrictive. See Petersen and McGouldrick, op. cit., p. 968.

[10] Over the last 4 years of the 1960s, new capital constituted approximately 99 percent of the gross

proceeds from bond sales and amounts raised for noncapital outlay purposes had been nil. See "New Issues of State and Local Government Securities," p. A-45, Federal Reserve Bulletin (Jan. 1970). For the sources of funds for State and local capital expenditure, see Galper and Petersen, op. cit., pp. 2–5.

[11] The quarterly realizations questionnaire did not ask if a particular borrowing represented a comeback of a previously postponed borrowing, nor did it ask

TABLE 5   CAPITAL SPENDING REDUCTIONS INDUCED BY HIGH INTEREST RATES, FISCAL YEAR 1970
(in billions of dollars)

	1969		1970		
Item	Q3	Q4	Q1	Q2	Fiscal
(1) Capital spending shortfalls initiated by high interest rates..............	.95	1.45	.21	.25	2.35
(2) Capital spending reinstituted by sale of previously postponed borrowings..........................	...	.14	.84	.27	.75
(3) Net shortfalls in capital spending[1]..........	.95	1.31	−.64	−.02	1.60

[1] Net shortfalls in capital spending calculated as of the beginning of the survey period.

volume involved in catching up on those projects exceeded the amounts involved in newly initiated delays. As a result, the pool of cutbacks in planned capital spending was reduced on balance by approximately $550 million in the last two quarters of the fiscal year. Accordingly, the net reduction in planned capital spending by the end of the fiscal year was trimmed to $1.6 billion.

It should be stressed that the figures in Table 5 are classified by the quarter in which the decision was made to delay or cut back capital projects. The actual expenditures arising from these decisions would have been strung out over several later quarters.

Table 6 classifies the impacts on capital spending by type of unit. Both the gross and net shortfalls in such expenditures are greatest for school districts. An estimated $1.2 billion of capital expenditure setbacks due to high interest rates occurred during fiscal 1970; $0.5 billion of these

if the proceeds were used to fund a postponed capital project. It is assumed that when a long-term borrowing did take place that was judged to be a remarketing of a previously deferred issue, then there was a symmetrical reinstatement of the deferred project.

constituted net shortfalls. Gross and net shortfalls were next most significant for State governments and their agencies.

In a manner analogous to that used in the preceding discussion of long-term borrowing shortfalls, the relative severity of capital spending setbacks induced by high interest rates can be measured by comparing the estimated amounts of setbacks to the levels of capital spending. As shown in Table 6, State and local governments in fiscal 1969 spent an estimated $28 billion on capital projects.[12] Therefore, capital spending de-

[12] Fiscal 1969 is the latest for which information on State and local capital spending is available. However, data on State and local construction (which represents about 80 percent of State and local capital expenditures) are available. These figures tend to indicate that the new construction component for fiscal 1970 was about $800 million, or 3 percent, less than in fiscal 1969. Therefore, total capital expenditures probably did not change markedly between the 2 years, in large part because of the impacts of credit market conditions. For 5 years prior to fiscal 1970, capital outlays had grown at an average annual rate of 9 percent. See U.S. Bureau of the Census, *Quarterly Public Construction Reports* (Sept. 1970).

TABLE 6   CAPITAL SPENDING REDUCTIONS INDUCED BY HIGH INTEREST RATES, BY TYPE OF UNIT, FISCAL YEAR 1970 (in billions of dollars)

	Type of Unit						
		State Govern- ment	Local Government				
Spending Shortfalls Induced by High Interest Rates[1]	All Types		Total	County	City or Town	Special District	School District
(1) Gross shortfall in capital spending.........	2.85	.74	2.11	.24	.50	.16	1.21
(2) Capital spending reinstituted by sale of previously postponed borrowings.......	1.25	.22	1.03	.13	.18	.02	.69
(3) Net shortfall in capital spending..........	1.60	.52	1.08	.11	.32	.14	.52
Item:							
Capital outlays							
Fiscal year 1969[1].........................	28.23	12.70	15.53	2.45	6.86	2.34	3.88
Gross shortfall ratio[2]........................	.101	.058	.136	.098	.073	.068	.312
Net shortfall ratio[3].........................	.056	.041	.069	.045	.047	.060	.134

[1] Calculated on the basis of U.S. Bureau of Census *Government Finances in 1968–69* (Sept. 1970).
[2] Ratio of Line (1) to capital outlays shown as item.
[3] Ratio of Line (3) to capital outlays shown as item.

lays and reductions of $2.85 billion represented 10.1 percent of the capital outlays accomplished by State and local governments. The estimated $1.60 billion in net shortfalls in capital expenditures amounted to approximately 5.6 percent of capital expenditures made in the preceding fiscal year. Among the types of units, capital spending delays and reductions induced by high interest rates were by far most severe for school districts. Their gross spending shortfalls equaled 31.2 percent of the capital outlays of school districts in fiscal 1969. On a net shortfall basis, the decrease in planned capital spending by school districts came to 13.4 percent for their fiscal year 1969 expenditures.[13] For State governmental units of all types, the ratio of spending setbacks induced by high interest rates to capital outlays of the preceding fiscal year was 5.8 percent on a gross shortfall basis, and 4.1 percent on a net shortfall basis for fiscal 1970.

The relative severity of capital spending cutbacks to total capital spending by type of unit is a function of the magnitude of the borrowing setbacks, the importance of borrowing as a source of funds, and the availability of alternative sources of finance. For example, the approximately $1 billion in net long-term borrowing shortfalls experienced by school districts resulted in $0.5 billion in capital spending shortfalls. Conversely, for State governments, the ratio of spending cutbacks to borrowing reductions was much smaller, with $1.6 billion in net borrowing shortfalls leading to about $0.45 billion in planned spending reductions. Generally, local governments are in a more exposed position because of their greater dependency on borrowed funds.

IMPACT OF INTEREST RATE LIMITATIONS

A major factor in the high level of borrowing setbacks experienced by State and local governments in fiscal 1970 was the prevalence of ceilings on the maximum rates of interest that units were legally allowed to pay. These statutory or, in some cases, constitutional limitations are found in most States and apply to most units. But, as in the case of other laws governing the issuance of municipal bonds, interest rate ceilings vary greatly among the States and are often not uni-

[13] Data on capital spending by type of unit of local government are not available annually. An estimate of these amounts was derived by applying the proportion of such spending done by types of government in 1967 (the latest year for which it is available from the Census of Governments) to the estimated amount of capital outlays for fiscal 1969.

form even within a given State: ceilings are different for different types of units, purposes, and types of debt instrument. Nonetheless, it is possible to generalize about the levels of ceilings applicable to the basic debt instrument issued by most governmental units—the full faith and credit general obligation bond. General obligation bonds typically represent 70 percent of the combined borrowing of State and local governments. Table 7 gives those interest rate ceilings that were in effect for State general obligations at the beginning and at the end of fiscal 1970. Table 8 gives the same information for local government general obligation issues at the same two points in time.

The interest rate ceilings in many States at the outset of the surveys (the first columns of Tables 7 and 8) were below the heights reached by municipal bond yields in the fall and winter of 1969 (see Figure 1) and caused a large blockage of bond issues that could not legally be sold. However, as may be seen in the second columns of both tables, by the end of fiscal 1970 the majority of States had revised upward, temporarily suspended, or completely lifted their ceilings. By that time, 39 States had ceilings at 8 percent or higher or had completely removed

TABLE 7   INTEREST RATE LIMITATIONS ON STATE GOVERNMENT GENERAL OBLIGATION BONDS (number of states)

Interest Rate Limit (Percent)	Mid-1969	Mid-1970
6 or below	14	5
Above 6 and below 8	6	8
8 or above	3	6
None[1]	17	21
No general obligation bonds[2]	10	10
Total	50	50

[1] Includes States that have suspended limitations for a specified period of time.
[2] State governments that are effectively prohibited from general obligation borrowing are Alabama, Arizona, Colorado, Florida, Georgia, Indiana, Michigan, Nebraska, North Dakota, and South Dakota.
Note: Based on *Daily Bond Buyer* reports for August 1969 and October 1970 and unpublished information supplied by First National City Bank of New York. Minor exceptions may exist to the ceilings on general obligation bonds for various types of governments or purposes of proceeds.

TABLE 8   INTEREST RATE LIMITATIONS ON LOCAL GOVERNMENT GENERAL OBLIGATION BONDS (number of states)

Interest Rate Limit (Percent)	Mid-1969	Mid-1970
6 or below	29	6
Above 6 and below 8	6	8
8 or above	4	14
None	11	22
Total	50	50

FIGURE 1   MUNICIPAL BOND YIELDS: BOND BUYER 20-BOND INDEX

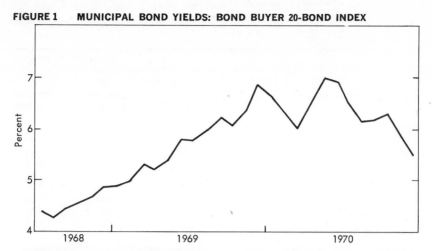

Monthly averages of *Bond Buyer* 20-Bond Index (composite index for 20-year, good-grade municipal bonds).

such limitations from State general obligation bonds and 42 similarly had high or no interest rate ceilings on local government general obligation bonds.[14]

The quarterly questionnaires did not ask units specifically if legal interest rate ceilings were responsible for borrowing shortfalls. Rather, this particular reason was subsumed under the general response of "high interest rates" as a cause for borrowing less than was originally intended. Nevertheless, respondents and the reports of the financial press made it clear that a good share, if not the bulk, of borrowing setbacks was related to legal limitations on interest rates. Thus it is possible to make some rough estimation of the over-all impact of ceilings on borrowing and spending shortfalls by comparing the experience of units in States where ceilings were in effect with that of units in States with no ceilings.[15]

[14] The ceiling of 8 percent was chosen as the cutoff point for effective interest rate ceilings because on numerous occasions during fiscal 1970 municipal bond yields reached or surpassed 7 percent for longer-term general obligation bonds. Hence, ceilings below 8 percent would have been effective in thwarting bond sales on several occasions, especially those contemplated by smaller communities with unrated or lower-rated credits. For example, *median* reoffering yields on BAA-rated, 20-year bonds reached 7.15 percent in December 1969 and averaged 7.04 percent for the first 6 months of 1970, reaching 7.40 in May of that year.

[15] It would be clearly mistaken to attribute all interest rate difficulties to legal ceilings in these States where the latter were in force during the survey period. However, to the extent that units in States with ceilings did experience greater shortfalls than those where ceilings were not in effect, much of that additional shortfall can probably be attributed

At the outset of the survey, 16 States did not have general interest rate ceilings in effect on either their local units, their State units, or both. In these States, therefore, it may be assumed that interest rate ceilings were of no importance in causing stoppages of intended borrowing or consequent cutbacks in capital spending. The remaining 34 States, however, did have many, if not general, limitations (at 8 percent or below). In Table 9 interest rate-induced shortfalls in borrowing and capital outlays experienced by units with effective ceilings are compared with similar shortfalls where there were no ceilings or where they were too high to have been effective. Although units in States with ceilings did experience much greater gross shortfalls, comparison of the net amount of borrowing shortfalls and the estimated borrowing actually accomplished shows that units with ceilings actually were no more disposed to experience abandonments of long-term borrowing plans than those in States where ceilings were not in effect (Table 9). That is, units in States with or without ceilings demonstrated almost the same proclivity to end fiscal 1970 with an interest rate-induced borrowing shortfall equal to approximately 38 percent of the actual borrowing accomplished. Thus it appears that had other things been equal, ceilings, while causing interruptions in borrowing plans, may not have contributed to high shortfalls over the entire fiscal year. Units that commenced the period with ceilings but later removed them

to the presence of ceilings. Implicit in this reasoning is a *ceteris paribus* condition that may or may not be fulfilled; that is, the units may differ in respect other than the existence of the ceilings.

**TABLE 9   REDUCTIONS IN LONG-TERM BORROWING AND CAPITAL SPENDING
INDUCED BY HIGH INTEREST RATES, BY INTEREST RATE LIMITATION**
(in billions of dollars)

| | | Interest Rate Limitation | |
| | | None or above 8 Percent | 8 Percent or Below |
Shortfalls Induced by High Interest Rates	Total		
Long-term borrowing:			
Gross shortfalls......................	6.87	2.55	4.32
Temporary postponements..........	1.71	.39	1.42
Net shortfall........................	5.16	2.16	2.90
Capital spending:			
Gross shortfalls......................	2.85	.41	2.45
Temporary postponements..........	1.25	.15	1.10
Net shortfall........................	1.60	.26	1.35
Item: Actual borrowing...............	13.25	5.45	7.75

Note: Includes those units in States, that as of mid-1969 had no or a high (above 8 percent) ceiling on interest rates paid by State and local units: Connecticut, Maine, Massachusetts, New Hampshire, Ohio, Tennessee, Washington, Wisconsin, Wyoming, New York (excluding certain State authorities), and New Jersey; and local units only in Maryland and Alaska. Various exceptions exist and corrections were made where possible. Based on the sources given in Table 7.

accounted for the bulk of units returning previous bond issues to market.

Nevertheless, as Table 9 shows, the similarity in borrowing experiences evidently did not reflect itself in spending. Fully 85 percent of the total net spending cutbacks occurred in those States where interest rate ceilings were in effect during the year. Altogether, the net cutbacks in spending attributed to high interest rates were five times larger in those States where ceilings were in effect, and net spending cutbacks as a proportion of net borrowing shortfalls were 47 percent as opposed to 17 percent for States where ceilings were not in effect.

The results indicate that units in States with interest rate ceilings were making borrowing postponements and cancellations that involved expenditure cutbacks to a much greater extent than those in States without ceilings. Units in States without effective ceilings had more decision flexibility and evidently would delay or reduce long-term borrowing only if this would not affect capital expenditures. Those in States with ceilings evidently had less flexibility in devising alternative means of financing projects in the face of long-term borrowing shortfalls. Several reasons probably account for the greater sensitivity of expenditure plans in those States with ceilings. First, the existence of these limitations undoubtedly created uncertainty as to when long-term bonds might ever be sold to finance projects. In such circumstances, few public officials wished to commence projects whose ultimate funding was uncertain. Second, the revision or removal

of interest rate ceilings was by no means a simple affair. For example, some State courts have held that bond issues approved at the time a particular ceiling was in effect must be resubmitted to the electorate for a new vote. Third, with construction prices rising rapidly throughout the year, a few months' delay might have seen the cost of the project rise beyond a point where it was feasible or where the original borrowing authorization was sufficient. Fourth, many States with legal ceilings on long-term interest rates likewise carried limits on short-term borrowing rates, thus potentially blocking off this major alternative source of temporary funds.[16]

A final factor is found in the regional composition of those States with and without ceilings. Those States without ceilings tend to be clustered in the northeastern part of the United States. Units in those States, with their traditional use of short-term borrowing, generally less restrictive laws governing borrowing, and proximity to the major money markets, were probably in a better position to buffer expenditure plans against restrictive credit conditions.[17]

---

[16] At the beginning of fiscal 1970, 24 States either did not authorize or issue local government short-term notes or had interest rate ceilings of 6 percent or less on such notes. Yields on short-term notes of the highest quality, federally guaranteed, hovered between 5 and 6 percent for much of the latter part of 1969.

[17] Units in the northeastern States of Maine, New Hampshire, Vermont, Massachusetts, Rhode Island, Connecticut, New York, and New Jersey were unencumbered by effective interest rate ceilings during

TABLE 10   BORROWING SHORTFALLS INDUCED BY HIGH INTEREST RATES: ALTERNATIVE MEANS OF FINANCING (fiscal year 1970)

Alternative Means	Billions of Dollars	Percentage Distribution
Short-term borrowing	2.68	59.8
Reductions in liquid assets	.65	14.5
Reductions in current expenditures	.03	.7
No immediate need	.80	17.9
Governmental loans	.11	2.4
Other	.21	4.7
Total	4.48	100.0

One can only speculate on possible impacts of high interest rates in the absence of interest rate ceilings. Nevertheless, had ceilings been removed, net aggregative spending impacts might have been considerably less, say on the order of 17 percent of $5.16 billion of the borrowing shortfalls, or $900 million. Such a figure would have been much closer to the behavior detected in earlier surveys of State and local responsiveness to high interest rates.[18] Thus, as a rough approximation, it is reasonable to estimate that the existence of ceilings may have accounted for $700 million, or just under one-half of the $1.60 billion, in net capital spending shortfalls that were reported in fiscal 1970.

ALTERNATIVE MEANS OF FINANCING

Of the nearly $7.4 billion in State and local long-term borrowing either postponed or abandoned in fiscal 1970 because of high interest rates, approximately $4.5 billion had no impact on capital expenditure plans because alternative means were used to finance projects. Table 10 gives the various alternatives employed. It is assumed that the amount of capital spending maintained by these alternative means is equal to the amount of the long-term borrowing shortfall. Among the alternatives, short-term borrowing clearly stands out as the principal source of funds. Short-term borrowing that was done as a direct consequence of long-term borrowing delays and shortfalls amounted to about $2.7 billion, or 60 percent, of the total of alternative means. Far behind as a source of funds was the use of liquid

fiscal 1970. Altogether they accounted for an estimated 31 percent of the long-term borrowing done that year ($4.3 billion of $13.2 billion). While they likewise experienced 31 percent of the total of net long-term borrowing shortfalls ($1.6 billion of $5.2 billion), they had net capital spending shortfalls equal to only about 10 percent of the national total ($.16 billion of $1.61 billion).

[18] Petersen and McGouldrick, *op. cit.*, pp. 967–71. See Appendix, pp. 231–32.

assets on hand, which represented less than 15 percent of the maintained expenditure.[19]

Nearly 18 percent of the dollar volume of projects to be financed by long-term borrowings were not affected because units planned to borrow well in advance of actual cash needs. The other alternative means were of minimal importance in maintaining expenditure plans. Although reductions in current expenditures proved to be of some importance in an earlier survey, the fiscal 1970 surveys showed it to be insignificant as a source of funds, evidently contributing only $30 million, or less than 1 percent, of the funds used to maintain expenditures.[20] However, it is quite possible that some of the alternative sources used—such as intragovernmental loans and the depletion of liquid asset positions—entailed some small expenditure impacts.

The estimated $2.7 billion in short-term net financing undertaken by State and local governments to maintain capital expenditures in the face of long-term borrowing shortfalls evidently accounted for a substantial share of the increase in short-term indebtedness of these units in fiscal 1970. During that period, State and local govern-

[19] There was a continuing shrinkage of State and local liquidity throughout 1969. While both current receipts and total expenditures rose by $12 billion between December 1968 and December 1969, total bank deposits and currency held by these governments dropped by nearly $5 billion during this period. Part of the decline reflected disintermediation, a shifting from time deposits to higher-yielding U.S. Government and U.S. agency securities, holdings of which rose by $3.5 billion over the year. On the other hand, part of the small rise in State and local government demand deposits (which partially offset nearly a $6 billion decline in their time deposits) reflected the greater use of short-term bank loans by these units, as is discussed in the Appendix. The easing of credit markets and increased sales of debt permitted a replenishing of $3 billion in time and savings deposits during the first half of 1970.

[20] According to the 1966 survey, reductions in current other expenditures sustained about $80 million in capital spending shortfalls induced by high interest rates. Peterson and McGouldrick, *op. cit.*, p. 969.

ments issued $14.4 billion in short-term securities and increased their outstanding short-term debt by $5.0 billion. On the basis of the survey, it would appear that approximately half of the increase in short-term indebtedness was accounted for by the substitution of such financing for long-term debt that was not sold because of high interest rates.[21]

CONCLUSION

Borrowing and capital spending decisions of State and local governments displayed a convincing sensitivity to fluctuations of interest rates and credit market conditions throughout fiscal 1970. The climb of interest rates through the last quarters of 1969, augmented by the widespread presence of low legal interest rate ceilings, resulted in a large volume of borrowing and spending postponements and cancellations. Conversely, the general easing of conditions in early 1970, aided by the lifting of ceilings, allowed many units to reinstate their original borrowing and spending plans. Although short-term borrowing was used extensively, such temporary buffers to insulate capital outlay spending plans from borrowing shortfalls were generally less used in fiscal 1970 than they had been during the credit restraint period of 1966. While many factors might account for this, a very important one was doubtlessly the chariness—or inability—of borrowers to use short-term financing when there was uncertainty over their ultimate ability to issue long-term debt to fund projects. While the survey data remain to be analyzed on the basis of size of unit, the experience of many school districts seems to underscore the earlier finding that smaller units of government must persevere with long-term borrowing plans if they wish to make capital expenditures. They generally lack temporizing alternative means of finance.

Interest rate ceilings represented a complicating feature and reduced the limits of discretionary behavior by State and local borrowers. It would appear that the presence of ceilings substantially increased the volume of interest rate-associated capital spending shortfalls for fiscal 1970, perhaps even doubling them. Upward revision and removal of these ceilings probably will reduce the sensitivity of State and local borrowers to interest rate changes in the future. On the other hand, as is discussed in the Appendix, such alterations very well may lead to higher rates of interest on municipal bonds and more discretionary delays in borrowing and spending for a given set of market conditions. But removing ceilings and allowing State and local units to make borrowing decisions at their own volition will return the allocation of credit to the bond market and will allow such decisions to be based on current values and priorities.

APPENDIX

DIAGRAMMATIC ANALYSIS OF THE INFLUENCE OF INTEREST RATE LIMITATIONS

The consequences of legal limitations on interest rates on the functioning of the municipal bond market can be illustrated by use of the familiar demand- and supply-curve diagram. In Figure 2 below, the rate of interest on municipal bonds, r, is plotted on the vertical axis and the dollar volume of bonds, v, is plotted on the horizontal axis.

The two demand curves DD and $D'D'$ represent the demand for municipal bonds on the part of investors. They are positively sloped indicating that the demand for bonds increases as the interest rates increase, other things being constant. The supply-of-bonds curves SS^n and SS^e are negatively sloped, reflecting that as interest rates rise the supply of municipal bonds offered by State and local governments decreases.[22]

---

[21] Based on Federal Reserve flow of funds figures. In fiscal 1969, short-term debt had increased by $3.4 billion and by the end of that fiscal year stood at approximately $14.2 billion. The short-term borrowing undertaken in fiscal 1970 to cover long-term borrowing shortfalls is not completely comparable with the increase in short-term indebtedness because (1) some of the earlier borrowing may have represented continuations of short-term loans from previous periods, and (2) borrowing done in conjunction with temporary delays perhaps was terminated when the bonds were ultimately sold before the end of fiscal 1970.

[22] The shapes of the demand and supply curves for municipal bonds in Figure 2 are for illustrative purposes and are not based upon specific estimates. Nonetheless, empirical studies do indicate that the demand and supply of municipal bonds do conform to the relationships implicit in that figure. Econometric studies have estimated the elasticity of supply of municipal bonds with respect to interest rates to be in the range of -1.0 to -2.0, by using quarterly data, although it may be considerably higher than this in the short run. The elasticity of the demand for municipal bonds is more difficult to estimate because of the extreme volatility of commercial bank acquisitions.

Bank investments in municipals seem to be largely insensitive to the yields on municipal bonds and are determined more by the availability of residual in-

FIGURE 2   MUNICIPAL BONDS: DEMAND AND SUPPLY CURVES UNDER VARIOUS CONDITIONS

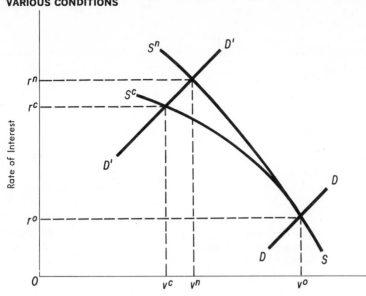

Dollar Volume of Bonds

In Figure 2, the supply-of-municipal-bonds curve branches along two segments, SS^c and SS^n. The lower segment, SS^c, illustrates the supply curve for all units where interest rate ceilings are in effect for many. The higher segment, SS^n, illustrates the supply curve where the rate limitations have been lifted. For expositional purposes, it is assumed that all other determinants of the supply of bonds remain the same in both cases.

In times of relatively easy monetary conditions when lower interest rates prevail, the demand and supply curves are brought into equilibrium at rates of interest below those where ceilings are encountered and they have no effect. This situation is depicted in the case where v^o bonds are sold at an interest rate of r^o. However, when monetary conditions tighten, investors' demand for municipal bonds shifts rapidly left to a position of $D'D'$ as the supply of credit dwindles and the yields on competing investments rise.

As drawn in Figure 2, the supply-of-municipal-bonds curve, SS^c, is bent sharply leftward illustrat-

vestable funds after prior claims for funds have been met. This would be illustrated by shifts in the demand curve rather than movements along it, because the supply (and cost) of investable funds is subsumed in the construction of the demand curves for any given period. The household sector, on the other hand, which absorbs the bulk of municipal bonds in times of restrictive credit conditions, evidently has a very high elasticity of demand for these securities. See Harvey Galper and John Petersen, "Strengthening the Municipal Bond Market," *Investment Dealers' Digest* (Oct. 20, 1970).

ing the effect on the legal ceilings of interest rates above which units are not allowed to pay on their bonds. In the case of individual States (and of particular types of units within a State), the supply-of-bonds curve is, of course, sharply kinked to the left. As the individual supply relationships are summed together to form a market supply, the total supply curve is progressively bent to the left, reflecting that more and more ceilings take effect, the higher the rate of interest. Given the existence of ceilings as implicit in curve SS^c, the supply-of-bonds curve will intersect the demand-for-bonds curve $D'D'$ at that point giving an interest rate of r^c and a volume of bonds sold of V^c.

The upper leg of the supply-of-bonds curve, (SS^n), indicates the supply of bonds forthcoming in the absence of ceilings. That is, were it not for the constraint imposed by the limitations of interest rates, many more bonds could have been offered for sale at the higher rates of interest.[23]

It is evident that in the absence of interest rate ceilings, the supply of and demand for municipal bonds would have equilibrated at higher yields and a greater volume of bonds would have been sold. This is shown by curve SS^n intersecting DD at yields r^n and volume V^n. Hence, those units that were precluded from bringing bonds

[23] Evidence of this is found in the rapidity with which ceilings were lifted during the year they became effective and is buttressed by the much larger volume of sales in the second quarter of 1970 when yields equaled and surpassed those of the third and fourth quarters of 1969.

to market helped to keep the interest rate from rising as high as it would have otherwise. For example, the limitations on units that restricted them from borrowing at 5 or 6 percent helped to lower the yields on bonds sold by units that could borrow at higher yields.

Several refinements could be added to the above analysis. First, it was evident from reports that credit rationing was practiced on the part of many lenders who bought municipal bonds at lower than market yields in order that State and local governments could sell bonds at interest rates at or just below the legal ceiling.[24] In the aggregate, this behavior could be interpreted as a selective flattening of the demand-for-bonds curve in the vicinity of the various ceilings. To the extent, however, that these rationed funds would have been available at somewhat higher yields to other borrowers, the latter may have experienced somewhat higher interest rates on their borrowings because of the diminished supply of funds in the remainder of the market. Hence, the over-all impact of this form of credit rationing on yields and on the dollar volume of bonds sold is by no means certain. Another complication arises from the fact that an unknown quantity of borrowers, who sold at rates of interest nominally below that prevailing in the market, had to make adjustments in the lending terms, which actually raised the effective rate of interest to competitive levels. For example, there were reported instances of bank loans to communities at the ceiling rate where the borrower was required to keep part of the loan proceeds on deposit for a specified interval of time. In this manner, the interest paid on the entire amount of the loan compensated the lender for the smaller amount of funds actually available to the borrower and, hence, drove the effective rate of return above that implied by the nominal interest rate on the loan.[25]

[24] See H. W. Kurtz, "Impact of Interest Rate Limitations," *Municipal Finance* (Aug. 1970).

[25] For example, were a community to agree to borrow $2 million for 2 years repayable at the end of the term with $60,000 in interest payments payable annually, the nominal and effective rate of interest on the loan would be 6 percent. However, where the community agrees to withdraw only $1 million the first year and does not withdraw the second $1 million until the second year, then the same annual interest payment of $60,000 with a term payment of $2 million at the end of the second year would produce for the lender an effective rate of interest of 9 percent on the transaction.

THE ROLE OF MONETARY POLICY*

Milton Friedman†

There is wide agreement about the major goals of economic policy: high employment, stable prices, and rapid growth. There is less agreement that these goals are mutually compatible or, among those who regard them as incompatible, about the terms at which they can and should be substituted for one another. There is least agreement about the role that various instruments of policy can and should play in achieving the several goals.

My topic for tonight is the role of one such instrument—monetary policy. What can it contribute? And how should it be conducted to contribute the most? Opinion on these questions has fluctuated widely. In the first flush of enthusiasm about the newly created Federal Reserve System, many observers attributed the relative stability of the 1920s to the System's capacity for fine tuning—to apply an apt modern term. It came to be widely believed that a new era had arrived in which business cycles had been rendered obsolete by advances in monetary technology. This opinion was shared by economist and layman alike, though, of course, there were some dissonant voices. The Great Contraction destroyed this naive attitude. Opinion swung to the other extreme. Monetary policy was a string. You could pull on it to stop inflation but you could not push on it to halt recession. You could lead a

* From *American Economic Review*, Vol. LVIII (March 1968), pp. 1–17. Reprinted by permission of the publisher and the author. Milton Friedman is Paul Snowden Russell Distinguished Service Professor of Economics, University of Chicago.

Presidential address delivered at the Eightieth Annual Meeting of the American Economic Association, Washington, D.C., December 29, 1967.

† I am indebted for helpful criticisms of earlier drafts to Armen Alchian, Gary Becker, Martin Bronfenbrenner, Arthur F. Burns, Phillip Cagan, David D. Friedman, Lawrence Harris, Harry G. Johnson, Homer Jones, Jerry Jordan, David Meiselman, Allan H. Meltzer, Theodore W. Schultz, Anna J. Schwartz, Herbert Stein, George J. Stigler, and James Tobin.

horse to water but you could not make him drink. Such theory by aphorism was soon replaced by Keynes' rigorous and sophisticated analysis.

Keynes offered simultaneously an explanation for the presumed impotence of monetary policy to stem the depression, a nonmonetary interpretation of the depression, and an alternative to monetary policy for meeting the depression and his offering was avidly accepted. If liquidity preference is absolute or nearly so—as Keynes believed likely in times of heavy unemployment—interest rates cannot be lowered by monetary measures. If investment and consumption are little affected by interest rates—as Hansen and many of Keynes' other American disciples came to believe—lower interest rates, even if they could be achieved, would do little good. Monetary policy is twice damned. The contraction, set in train, on this view, by a collapse of investment or by a shortage of investment opportunities or by stubborn thriftiness, could not, it was argued, have been stopped by monetary measures. But there was available an alternative—fiscal policy. Government spending could make up for insufficient private investment. Tax reductions could undermine stubborn thriftiness.

The wide acceptance of these views in the economics profession meant that for some two decades monetary policy was believed by all but a few reactionary souls to have been rendered obsolete by new economic knowledge. Money did not matter. Its only role was the minor one of keeping interest rates low, in order to hold down interest payments in the government budget, contribute to the "euthanasia of the rentier," and maybe, stimulate investment a bit to assist government spending in maintaining a high level of aggregate demand.

These views produced a widespread adoption of cheap money policies after the war. And they received a rude shock when these policies failed in country after country, when central bank after central bank was forced to give up the pretense that it could indefinitely keep "the" rate of interest at a low level. In this country, the public denouement came with the Federal Reserve-Treasury Accord in 1951, although the policy of pegging government bond prices was not formally abandoned until 1953. Inflation, stimulated by cheap money policies, not the widely heralded postwar depression, turned out to be the order of the day. The result was the beginning of a revival of belief in the potency of monetary policy.

This revival was strongly fostered among economists by the theoretical developments initiated by Haberler but named for Pigou that pointed out a channel—namely, changes in wealth—whereby changes in the real quantity of money can affect aggregate demand even if they do not alter interest rates. These theoretical developments did not undermine Keynes' argument against the potency of orthodox monetary measures when liquidity preference is absolute since under such circumstances the usual monetary operations involve simply substituting money for other assets without changing total wealth. But they did show how changes in the quantity of money produced in other ways could affect total spending even under such circumstances. And, more fundamentally, they did undermine Keynes' key theoretical proposition, namely, that even in a world of flexible prices, a position of equilibrium at full employment might not exist. Henceforth, unemployment had again to be explained by rigidities or imperfections, not as the natural outcome of a fully operative market process.

The revival of belief in the potency of monetary policy was fostered also by a re-evaluation of the role money played from 1929 to 1933. Keynes and most other economists of the time believed that the Great Contraction in the United States occurred despite aggressive expansionary policies by the monetary authorities—that they did their best but their best was not good enough.[1] Recent studies have demonstrated that the facts are precisely the reverse: the U.S. monetary authorities followed highly deflationary policies. The quantity of money in the United States fell by one-third in the course of the contraction. And it fell not because there were no willing borrowers—not because the horse would not drink. It fell because the Federal Reserve System forced or permitted a sharp reduction in the monetary base, because it failed to exercise the responsibilities assigned to it in the Federal Reserve Act to provide liquidity to the banking system. The Great Contraction is tragic testimony to the power of monetary policy—not, as Keynes and so many of his contemporaries believed, evidence of its impotence.

In the United States the revival of belief in the potency of monetary policy was strengthened also by increasing disillusionment with fiscal policy, not so much with its potential to affect aggregate demand as with the practical and political feasibility of so using it. Expenditures turned out to respond sluggishly and with long lags to at-

[1] In [2], I have argued that Henry Simons shared this view with Keynes, and that it accounts for the policy changes that he recommended.

tempts to adjust them to the course of economic activity, so emphasis shifted to taxes. But here political factors entered with a vengeance to prevent prompt adjustment to presumed need, as has been so graphically illustrated in the months since I wrote the first draft of this talk. "Fine tuning" is a marvelously evocative phrase in this electronic age, but it has little resemblance to what is possible in practice—not, I might add, an unmixed evil.

It is hard to realize how radical has been the change in professional opinion on the role of money. Hardly an economist today accepts views that were the common coin some two decades ago. Let me cite a few examples.

In a talk published in 1945, E. A. Goldenweiser, then Director of the Research Division of the Federal Reserve Board, described the primary objective of monetary policy as being to "maintain the value of Government bonds. . . . This country" he wrote, "will have to adjust to a 2½ percent interest rate as the return on safe, long-time money, because the time has come when returns on pioneering capital can no longer be unlimited as they were in the past" [4, p. 117].

In a book on *Financing American Prosperity*, edited by Paul Homan and Fritz Machlup and published in 1945, Alvin Hansen devotes nine pages of text to the "savings-investment problem" without finding any need to use the words "interest rate" or any close facsimile thereto [5, pp. 218–27]. In his contribution to this volume, Fritz Machlup wrote, "Questions regarding the rate of interest, in particular regarding its variation or its stability, may not be among the most vital problems of the postwar economy, but they are certainly among the perplexing ones" [5, p. 466]. In his contribution, John H. Williams—not only professor at Harvard but also a long-time adviser to the New York Federal Reserve Bank—wrote, "I can see no prospect of revival of a general monetary control in the postwar period" [5, p. 383].

Another of the volumes dealing with postwar policy that appeared at this time, *Planning and Paying for Full Employment*, was edited by Abba P. Lerner and Frank D. Graham [6] and had contributors of all shades of professional opinion—from Henry Simons and Frank Graham to Abba Lerner and Hans Neisser. Yet Albert Halasi, in his excellent summary of the papers, was able to say, "Our contributors do not discuss the question of money supply. . . . The contributors make no special mention of credit policy to remedy actual depressions. . . . Inflation . . . might

be fought more effectively by raising interest rates. . . . But . . . other anti-inflationary measures . . . are preferable" [6, pp. 23–24]. A *Survey of Contemporary Economics*, edited by Howard Ellis and published in 1948, was an "official" attempt to codify the state of economic thought of the time. In his contribution, Arthur Smithies wrote, "In the field of compensatory action, I believe fiscal policy must shoulder most of the load. Its chief rival, monetary policy, seems to be disqualified on institutional grounds. This country appears to be committed to something like the present low level of interest rates on a long-term basis" [1, p. 208].

These quotations suggest the flavor of professional thought some two decades ago. If you wish to go further in this humbling inquiry, I recommend that you compare the sections on money—when you can find them—in the Principles texts of the early postwar years with the lengthy sections in the current crop even, or especially, when the early and recent Principles are different editions of the same work.

The pendulum has swung far since then, if not all the way to the position of the late 1920s, at least much closer to that position than to the position of 1945. There are of course many differences between then and now, less in the potency attributed to monetary policy than in the roles assigned to it and the criteria by which the profession believes monetary policy should be guided. Then, the chief roles assigned monetary policy were to promote price stability and to preserve the gold standard; the chief criteria of monetary policy were the state of the "money market," the extent of "speculation" and the movement of gold. Today, primacy is assigned to the promotion of full employment, with the prevention of inflation a continuing but definitely secondary objective. And there is major disagreement about criteria of policy, varying from emphasis on money market conditions, interest rates, and the quantity of money to the belief that the state of employment itself should be the proximate criterion of policy.

I stress nonetheless the similarity between the views that prevailed in the late 'twenties and those that prevail today because I fear that, now as then, the pendulum may well have swung too far, that, now as then, we are in danger of assigning to monetary policy a larger role than it can perform, in danger of asking it to accomplish tasks that it cannot achieve, and, as a result, in danger of preventing it from making the contribution that it is capable of making.

Unaccustomed as I am to denigrating the importance of money, I therefore shall, as my first task, stress what monetary policy cannot do. I shall then try to outline what it can do and how it can best make its contribution, in the present state of our knowledge—or ignorance.

1. WHAT MONETARY POLICY CANNOT DO

From the infinite world of negation, I have selected two limitations of monetary policy to discuss: (1) It cannot peg interest rates for more than very limited periods; (2) It cannot peg the rate of unemployment for more than very limited periods. I select these because the contrary has been or is widely believed, because they correspond to the two main unattainable tasks that are at all likely to be assigned to monetary policy, and because essentially the same theoretical analysis covers both.

Pegging of Interest Rates

History has already persuaded many of you about the first limitation. As noted earlier, the failure of cheap money policies was a major source of the reaction against simple-minded Keynesianism. In the United States, this reaction involved widespread recognition that the wartime and postwar pegging of bond prices was a mistake, that the abandonment of this policy was a desirable and inevitable step, and that it had none of the disturbing and disastrous consequences that were so freely predicted at the time.

The limitation derives from a much misunderstood feature of the relation between money and interest rates. Let the Fed set out to keep interest rates down. How will it try to do so? By buying securities. This raises their prices and lowers their yields. In the process, it also increases the quantity of reserves available to banks, hence the amount of bank credit, and, ultimately the total quantity of money. That is why central bankers in particular, and the financial community more broadly, generally believe that an increase in the quantity of money tends to lower interest rates. Academic economists accept the same conclusion, but for different reasons. They see, in their mind's eye, a negatively sloping liquidity preference schedule. How can people be induced to hold a larger quantity of money? Only by bidding down interest rates.

Both are right, up to a point. The *initial* impact of increasing the quantity of money at a faster rate than it has been increasing is to make interest rates lower for a time than they would otherwise have been. But this is only the beginning of the process, not the end. The more rapid rate of monetary growth will stimulate spending, both through the impact on investment of lower market interest rates and through the impact on other spending and thereby relative prices of higher cash balances than are desired. But one man's spending is another man's income. Rising income will raise the liquidity preference schedule and the demand for loans; it may also raise prices, which would reduce the real quantity of money. These three effects will reverse the initial downward pressure on interest rates fairly promptly, say, in something less than a year. Together they will tend, after a somewhat longer interval, say, a year or two, to return interest rates to the level they would otherwise have had. Indeed, given the tendency for the economy to overreact, they are highly likely to raise interest rates temporarily beyond that level, setting in motion a cyclical adjustment process.

A fourth effect, when and if it becomes operative, will go even farther, and definitely mean that a higher rate of monetary expansion will correspond to a higher, not lower, level of interest rates than would otherwise have prevailed. Let the higher rate of monetary growth produce rising prices, and let the public come to expect that prices will continue to rise. Borrowers will then be willing to pay and lenders will then demand higher interest rates—as Irving Fisher pointed out decades ago. This price expectation effect is slow to develop and also slow to disappear. Fisher estimated that it took several decades for a full adjustment and more recent work is consistent with his estimates.

These subsequent effects explain why every attempt to keep interest rates at a low level has forced the monetary authority to engage in successively larger and larger open market purchases. They explain why, historically, high and rising nominal interest rates have been associated with rapid growth in the quantity of money, as in Brazil or Chile or in the United States in recent years, and why low and falling interest rates have been associated with slow growth in the quantity of money, as in Switzerland now or in the United States from 1929 to 1933. As an empirical matter, low interest rates are a sign that monetary policy *has been* tight—in the sense that the quantity of money has grown slowly; high interest rates are a sign that monetary policy *has been* easy—in the sense that the quantity of money has grown rapidly. The broadest facts of experience run in precisely the opposite direction from that which the financial community and academic economists have all generally taken for granted.

Paradoxically, the monetary authority could assure low nominal rates of interest—but to do so it would have to start out in what seems like the opposite direction, by engaging in a deflationary monetary policy. Similarly, it could assure high nominal interest rates by engaging in an inflationary policy and accepting a temporary movement in interest rates in the opposite direction.

These considerations not only explain why monetary policy cannot peg interest rates; they also explain why interest rates are such a misleading indicator of whether monetary policy is "tight" or "easy." For that, it is far better to look at the rate of change of the quantity of money.[2]

Employment as a Criterion of Policy

The second limitation I wish to discuss goes more against the grain of current thinking. Monetary growth, it is widely held, will tend to stimulate employment; monetary contraction, to retard employment. Why, then, cannot the monetary authority adopt a target for employment or unemployment—say, 3 percent unemployment; be tight when unemployment is less than the target; be easy when unemployment is higher than the target; and in this way peg unemployment at, say, 3 percent? The reason it cannot is precisely the same as for interest rates—the difference between the immediate and the delayed consequences of such a policy.

Thanks to Wicksell, we are all acquainted with a concept of a "natural" rate of interest and the possibility of a discrepancy between the "natural" and the "market" rate. The preceding analysis of interest rates can be translated fairly directly into Wicksellian terms. The monetary authority can make the market rate less than the natural rate only by inflation. It can make the market rate higher than the natural rate only by deflation. We have added only one wrinkle to Wicksell—the Irving Fisher distinction between the nominal and the real rate of interest. Let the monetary authority keep the nominal market rate for a time below the natural rate by inflation. That in turn will raise the nominal natural rate itself,

once anticipations of inflation become widespread, thus requiring still more rapid inflation to hold down the market rate. Similarly, because of the Fisher effect, it will require not merely deflation but more and more rapid deflation to hold the market rate above the initial "natural" rate.

This analysis has its close counterpart in the employment market. At any moment of time, there is some level of unemployment which has the property that it is consistent with equilibrium in the structure of *real* wage rates. At that level of unemployment, real wage rates are tending on the average to rise at a "normal" secular rate, i.e., at a rate that can be indefinitely maintained so long as capital formation, technological improvements, etc., remain on their long-run trends. A lower level of unemployment is an indication that there is an excess demand for labor that will produce upward pressure on real wage rates. A higher level of unemployment is an indication that there is an excess supply of labor that will produce downward pressure on real wage rates. The "natural rate of unemployment," in other words, is the level that would be ground out by the Walrasian system of general equilibrium equations, provided there is imbedded in them the actual structural characteristics of the labor and commodity markets, including market imperfections, stochastic variability in demands and supplies, the cost of gathering information about job vacancies and labor availabilities, the costs of mobility, and so on.[3]

You will recognize the close similarity between this statement and the celebrated Phillips Curve. The similarity is not coincidental. Phillips' analysis of the relation between unemployment and wage change is deservedly celebrated as an important and original contribution. But, unfortunately, it contains a basic defect—the failure to distinguish between *nominal* wages and *real* wages—just as Wicksell's analysis failed to distinguish between *nominal* interest rates and *real* interest rates. Implicitly, Phillips wrote his article for a world in which everyone anticipated that nominal prices would be stable and in which that anticipation remained unshaken and immutable whatever happened to actual prices and wages. Suppose, by contrast, that everyone antici-

---

[2] This is partly an empirical not theoretical judgment. In principle, "tightness" or "ease" depends on the rate of change of the quantity of money supplied compared to the rate of change of the quantity demanded excluding effects on demand from monetary policy itself. However, empirically demand is highly stable, if we exclude the effect of monetary policy, so it is generally sufficient to look at supply alone.

[3] It is perhaps worth noting that this "natural" rate need not correspond to equality between the number unemployed and the number of job vacancies. For any given structure of the labor market, there will be some equilibrium relation between these two magnitudes, but there is no reason why it should be one of equality.

pates that prices will rise at a rate of more than 75 percent a year—as, for example, Brazilians did a few years ago. Then wages must rise at that rate simply to keep real wages unchanged. An excess supply of labor will be reflected in a less rapid rise in nominal wages than in anticipated prices,[4] not in an absolute decline in wages. When Brazil embarked on a policy to bring down the rate of price rise, and succeeded in bringing the price rise down to about 45 percent a year, there was a sharp initial rise in unemployment because under the influence of earlier anticipations, wages kept rising at a pace that was higher than the new rate of price rise, though lower than earlier. This is the result experienced, and to be expected, of all attempts to reduce the rate of inflation below that widely anticipated.[5]

To avoid misunderstanding, let me emphasize that by using the term "natural" rate of unemployment, I do not mean to suggest that it is immutable and unchangeable. On the contrary, many of the market characteristics that determine its level are man-made and policy-made. In the United States, for example, legal minimum wage rates, the Walsh-Healy and Davis-Bacon Acts, and the strength of labor unions all make the natural rate of unemployment higher than it would otherwise be. Improvements in employment exchanges, in availability of information about job vacancies and labor supply, and so on, would tend to lower the natural rate of unemployment. I use the term "natural" for the same

<hr>

[4] Strictly speaking, the rise in nominal wages will be less rapid than the rise in anticipated nominal wages to make allowance for any secular changes in real wages.

[5] Stated in terms of the rate of change of nominal wages, the Phillips Curve can be expected to be reasonably stable and well defined for any period for which the *average* rate of change of prices, and hence the anticipated rate, has been relatively stable. For such periods, nominal wages and "real" wages move together. Curves computed for different periods or different countries for each of which this condition has been satisfied will differ in level, the level of the curve depending on what the average rate of price change was. The higher the average rate of price change, the higher will tend to be the level of the curve. For periods or countries for which the rate of change of prices varies considerably, the Phillips Curve will not be well defined. My impression is that these statements accord reasonably well with the experience of the economists who have explored empirical Phillips Curves.

Restate Phillips' analysis in terms of the rate of change of real wages—and even more precisely, anticipated real wages—and it all falls into place. That is why students of empirical Phillips Curves have found that it helps to include the rate of change of the price level as an independent variable.

reason Wicksell did—to try to separate the real forces from monetary forces.

Let us assume that the monetary authority tries to peg the "market" rate of unemployment at a level below the "natural" rate. For definiteness, suppose that it takes 3 percent as the target rate and that the "natural" rate is higher than 3 percent. Suppose also that we start out at a time when prices have been stable and when unemployment is higher than 3 percent. Accordingly, the authority increases the rate of monetary growth. This will be expansionary. By making nominal cash balances higher than people desire, it will tend initially to lower interest rates and in this and other ways to stimulate spending. Income and spending will start to rise.

To begin with, much or most of the rise in income will take the form of an increase in output and employment rather than in prices. People have been expecting prices to be stable, and prices and wages have been set for some time in the future on that basis. It takes time for people to adjust to a new state of demand. Producers will tend to react to the initial expansion in aggregate demand by increasing output, employees by working longer hours, and the unemployed, by taking jobs now offered at former nominal wages. This much is pretty standard doctrine.

But it describes only the initial effects. Because selling prices of products typically respond to an unanticipated rise in nominal demand faster than prices of factors of production, real wages received have gone down—though real wages anticipated by employees went up, since employees implicitly evaluated the wages offered at the earlier price level. Indeed, the simultaneous fall *ex post* in real wages to employers and rise *ex ante* in real wages to employees is what enabled employment to increase. But the decline *ex post* in real wages will soon come to affect anticipations. Employees will start to reckon on rising prices of the things they buy and to demand higher nominal wages for the future. "Market" unemployment is below the "natural" level. There is an excess demand for labor so real wages will tend to rise toward their initial level.

Even though the higher rate of monetary growth continues, the rise in real wages will reverse the decline in unemployment, and then lead to a rise, which will tend to return unemployment to its former level. In order to keep unemployment at its target level of 3 percent, the monetary authority would have to raise monetary growth still more. As in the interest rate case, the "market" rate can be kept below the "natural" rate only by inflation. And, as in the interest rate case, too, only by accelerating inflation. Conversely, let the monetary authority choose a target rate of unemployment that is above the natural rate, and they will be led to produce a deflation, and an accelerating deflation at that.

What if the monetary authority chose the "natural" rate—either of interest or unemployment—as its target? One problem is that it cannot know what the "natural" rate is. Unfortunately, we have as yet devised no method to estimate accurately and readily the natural rate of either interest or unemployment. And the "natural" rate will itself change from time to time. But the basic problem is that even if the monetary authority knew the "natural" rate, and attempted to peg the market rate at that level, it would not be led to a determinate policy. The "market" rate will vary from the natural rate for all sorts of reasons other than monetary policy. If the monetary authority responds to these variations, it will set in train longer term effects that will make any monetary growth path it follows ultimately consistent with the rule of policy. The actual course of monetary growth will be analogous to a random walk, buffeted this way and that by the forces that produce temporary departures of the market rate from the natural rate.

To state this conclusion differently, there is always a temporary trade-off between inflation and unemployment; there is no permanent trade-off. The temporary trade-off comes not from inflation per se, but from unanticipated inflation, which generally means, from a rising rate of inflation. The widespread belief that there is a permanent trade-off is a sophisticated version of the confusion between "high" and "rising" that we all recognize in simpler forms. A rising rate of inflation may reduce unemployment, a high rate will not.

But how long, you will say, is "temporary"? For interest rates, we have some systematic evidence on how long each of the several effects takes to work itself out. For unemployment, we do not. I can at most venture a personal judgment, based on some examination of the historical evidence, that the initial effects of a higher and unanticipated rate of inflation last for something like two to five years; that this initial effect then begins to be reversed; and that a full adjustment to the new rate of inflation takes about as long for employment as for interest rates, say, a couple of decades. For both interest rates and employment, let me add a qualification. These estimates are for changes in the rate of inflation of the

order of magnitude that has been experienced in the United States. For much more sizable changes, such as those experienced in South American countries, the whole adjustment process is greatly speeded up.

To state the general conclusion still differently, the monetary authority controls nominal quantities—directly, the quantity of its own liabilities. In principle, it can use this control to peg a nominal quantity—an exchange rate, the price level, the nominal level of national income, the quantity of money by one or another definition—or to peg the rate of change in a nominal quantity—the rate of inflation or deflation, the rate of growth or decline in nominal national income, the rate of growth of the quantity of money. It cannot use its control over nominal quantities to peg a real quantity—the real rate of interest, the rate of unemployment, the level of real national income, the real quantity of money, the rate of growth of real national income, or the rate of growth of the real quantity of money.

II. WHAT MONETARY POLICY CAN DO

Monetary policy cannot peg these real magnitudes at predetermined levels. But monetary policy can and does have important effects on these real magnitudes. The one is in no way inconsistent with the other.

My own studies of monetary history have made me extremely sympathetic to the oft-quoted, much reviled, and as widely misunderstood, comment by John Stuart Mill. "There cannot . . . ," he wrote, "be intrinsically a more insignificant thing, in the economy of society, than money; except in the character of a contrivance for sparing time and labour. It is a machine for doing quickly and commodiously, what would be done, though less quickly and commodiously, without it: and like many other kinds of machinery, it only exerts a distinct and independent influence of its own when it gets out of order" [7, p. 488].

True, money is only a machine, but it is an extraordinarily efficient machine. Without it, we could not have begun to attain the astounding growth in output and level of living we have experienced in the past two centuries—any more than we could have done so without those other marvelous machines that dot our countryside and enable us, for the most part, simply to do more efficiently what could be done without them at much greater cost in labor.

But money has one feature that these other machines do not share. Because it is so pervasive, when it gets out of order, it throws a monkey wrench into the operation of all the other machines. The Great Contraction is the most dramatic example but not the only one. Every other major contraction in this country has been either produced by monetary disorder or greatly exacerbated by monetary disorder. Every major inflation has been produced by monetary expansion—mostly to meet the overriding demands of war which have forced the creation of money to supplement explicit taxation.

The first and most important lesson that history teaches about what monetary policy can do—and it is a lesson of the most profound importance—is that monetary policy can prevent money itself from being a major source of economic disturbance. This sounds like a negative proposition: avoid major mistakes. In part it is. The Great Contraction might not have occurred at all, and if it had, it would have been far less severe, if the monetary authority had avoided mistakes, or if the monetary arrangements had been those of an earlier time when there was no central authority with the power to make the kinds of mistakes that the Federal Reserve System made. The past few years, to come closer to home, would have been steadier and more productive of economic well-being if the Federal Reserve had avoided drastic and erratic changes of direction, first expanding the money supply at an unduly rapid pace, then, in early 1966, stepping on the brake too hard, then, at the end of 1966, reversing itself and resuming expansion until at least November, 1967, at a more rapid pace than can be maintained without appreciable inflation.

Even if the proposition that monetary policy can prevent money itself from being a major source of economic disturbance were a wholly negative proposition, it would be none the less important for that. As it happens, however, it is not a wholly negative proposition. The monetary machine has gotten out of order even when there has been no central authority with anything like the power now possessed by the Fed. In the United States, the 1907 episode and earlier banking panics are examples of how the monetary machine can get out of order largely on its own. There is therefore a positive and important task for the monetary authority—to suggest improvements in the machine that will reduce the chances that it will get out of order, and to use its own powers so as to keep the machine in good working order.

A second thing monetary policy can do is provide a stable background for the economy—keep the machine well oiled, to continue Mill's analogy. Accomplishing the first task will contribute to this objective, but there is more to it than that. Our economic system will work best when producers and consumers, employers and employees, can proceed with full confidence that the average level of prices will behave in a known way in the future—preferably that it will be highly stable. Under any conceivable institutional arrangements, and certainly under those that now prevail in the United States, there is only a limited amount of flexibility in prices and wages. We need to conserve this flexibility to achieve changes in relative prices and wages that are required to adjust to dynamic changes in tastes and technology. We should not dissipate it simply to achieve changes in the absolute level of prices that serve no economic function.

In an earlier era, the gold standard was relied on to provide confidence in future monetary stability. In its heyday it served that function reasonably well. It clearly no longer does, since there is scarce a country in the world that is prepared to let the gold standard reign unchecked—and there are persuasive reasons why countries should not do so. The monetary authority could operate as a surrogate for the gold standard, if it pegged exchange rates and did so exclusively by altering the quantity of money in response to balance of payment flows without "sterilizing" surpluses or deficits and without resorting to open or concealed exchange control or to changes in tariffs and quotas. But again, though many central bankers talk this way, few are in fact willing to follow this course—and again there are persuasive reasons why they should not do so. Such a policy would submit each country to the vagaries not of an impersonal and automatic gold standard but of the policies—deliberate or accidental—of other monetary authorities.

In today's world, if monetary policy is to provide a stable background for the economy it must do so by deliberately employing its powers to that end. I shall come later to how it can do so.

Finally, monetary policy can contribute to offsetting major disturbances in the economic system arising from other sources. If there is an independent secular exhilaration—as the postwar expansion was described by the proponents of secular stagnation—monetary policy can in principle help to hold it in check by a slower rate of monetary growth than would otherwise be desirable. If, as now, an explosive federal budget threatens unprecedented deficits, monetary policy can hold any inflationary dangers in check by a slower rate of monetary growth than would otherwise be desirable. This will temporarily mean higher interest rates than would otherwise prevail—to enable the government to borrow the sums needed to finance the deficit—but by preventing the speeding up of inflation, it may well mean both lower prices and lower nominal interest rates for the long pull. If the end of a substantial war offers the country an opportunity to shift resources from wartime to peacetime production, monetary policy can ease the transition by a higher rate of monetary growth than would otherwise be desirable—though experience is not very encouraging that it can do so without going too far.

I have put this point last, and stated it in qualified terms—as referring to major disturbances—because I believe that the potentiality of monetary policy in offsetting other forces making for instability is far more limited than is commonly believed. We simply do not know enough to be able to recognize minor disturbances when they occur or to be able to predict either what their effects will be with any precision or what monetary policy is required to offset their effects. We do not know enough to be able to achieve stated objectives by delicate, or even fairly coarse, changes in the mix of monetary and fiscal policy. In this area particularly the best is likely to be the enemy of the good. Experience suggests that the path of wisdom is to use monetary policy explicitly to offset other disturbances only when they offer a "clear and present danger."

III. HOW SHOULD MONETARY POLICY BE CONDUCTED?

How should monetary policy be conducted to make the contribution to our goals that it is capable of making? This is clearly not the occasion for presenting a detailed "Program for Monetary Stability"—to use the title of a book in which I tried to do so [3]. I shall restrict myself here to two major requirements for monetary policy that follow fairly directly from the preceding discussion.

The first requirement is that the monetary authority should guide itself by magnitudes that it can control, not by ones that it cannot control. If, as the authority has often done, it takes interest rates or the current unemployment percentage as the immediate criterion of policy, it will be like a space vehicle that has taken a fix on the wrong star. No matter how sensitive and sophisticated its guiding apparatus, the space vehicle will go astray. And so will the monetary authority.

Of the various alternative magnitudes that it can control, the most appealing guides for policy are exchange rates, the price level as defined by some index, and the quantity of a monetary total—currency plus adjusted demand deposits, or this total plus commercial bank time deposits, or a still broader total.

For the United States in particular, exchange rates are an undesirable guide. It might be worth requiring the bulk of the economy to adjust to the tiny percentage consisting of foreign trade if that would guarantee freedom from monetary irresponsibility—as it might under a real gold standard. But it is hardly worth doing so simply to adapt to the average of whatever policies monetary authorities in the rest of the world adopt. Far better to let the market, through floating exchange rates, adjust to world conditions the 5 percent or so of our resources devoted to international trade while reserving monetary policy to promote the effective use of the 95 percent.

Of the three guides listed, the price level is clearly the most important in its own right. Other things the same, it would be much the best of the alternatives—as so many distinguished economists have urged in the past. But other things are not the same. The link between the policy actions of the monetary authority and the price level, while unquestionably present, is more indirect than the link between the policy actions of the authority and any of the several monetary totals. Moreover, monetary action takes a longer time to affect the price level than to affect the monetary totals and both the time lag and the magnitude of effect vary with circumstances. As a result, we cannot predict at all accurately just what effect a particular monetary action will have on the price level and, equally important, just when it will have that effect. Attempting to control directly the price level is therefore likely to make monetary policy itself a source of economic disturbance because of false stops and starts. Perhaps, as our understanding of monetary phenomena advances, the situation will change. But at the present stage of our understanding, the long way around seems the surer way to our objective. Accordingly, I believe that a monetary total is the best currently available immediate guide or criterion for monetary policy—and I believe that it matters much less which particular total is chosen than that one be chosen.

A second requirement for monetary policy is that the monetary authority avoid sharp swings in policy. In the past, monetary authorities have on occasion moved in the wrong direction—as in the episode of the Great Contraction that I have stressed. More frequently, they have moved in the right direction, albeit often too late, but have erred by moving too far. Too late and too much has been the general practice. For example, in early 1966, it was the right policy for the Federal Reserve to move in a less expansionary direction—though it should have done so at least a year earlier. But when it moved, it went too far, producing the sharpest change in the rate of monetary growth of the post-war era. Again, having gone too far, it was the right policy for the Fed to reverse course at the end of 1966. But again it went too far, not only restoring but exceeding the earlier excessive rate of monetary growth. And this episode is no exception. Time and again this has been the course followed—as in 1919 and 1920, in 1937 and 1938, in 1953 and 1954, in 1959 and 1960.

The reason for the propensity to overreact seems clear: the failure of monetary authorities to allow for the delay between their actions and the subsequent effects on the economy. They tend to determine their actions by today's conditions—but their actions will affect the economy only six or nine or twelve or fifteen months later. Hence they feel impelled to step on the brake, or the accelerator, as the case may be, too hard.

My own prescription is still that the monetary authority go all the way in avoiding such swings by adopting publicly the policy of achieving a steady rate of growth in a specified monetary total. The precise rate of growth, like the precise monetary total, is less important than the adoption of some stated and known rate. I myself have argued for a rate that would on the average achieve rough stability in the level of prices of final products, which I have estimated would call for something like a 3 to 5 percent per year rate of growth in currency plus all commercial bank deposits or a slightly lower rate of growth in currency plus demand deposits only.[6] But it would be better to have a fixed rate that would on the average produce moderate inflation or

moderate deflation, provided it was steady, than to suffer the wide and erratic perturbations we have experienced.

Short of the adoption of such a publicly stated policy of a steady rate of monetary growth, it would constitute a major improvement if the monetary authority followed the self-denying ordinance of avoiding wide swings. It is a matter of record that periods of relative stability in the rate of monetary growth have also been periods of relative stability in economic activity, both in the United States and other countries. Periods of wide swings in the rate of monetary growth have also been periods of wide swings in economic activity.

By setting itself a steady course and keeping to it, the monetary authority could make a major contribution to promoting economic stability. By making that course one of steady but moderate growth in the quantity of money, it would make a major contribution to avoidance of either inflation or deflation of prices. Other forces would still affect the economy, require change and adjustment, and disturb the even tenor of our ways. But steady monetary growth would provide a monetary climate favorable to the effective operation of those basic forces of enterprise, ingenuity, invention, hard work, and thrift that are the true springs of economic growth. That is the most that we can ask from monetary policy at our present stage of knowledge. But that much—and it is a great deal—is clearly within our reach.

---

[6] In an as yet unpublished article on "The Optimum Quantity of Money," I conclude that a still lower rate of growth, something like 2 percent for the broader definition, might be better yet in order to eliminate or reduce the difference between private and total costs of adding to real balances.

REFERENCES

1. Ellis, H. S. ed. *A Survey of Contemporary Economics*. Philadelphia 1948.
2. Friedman, Milton. "The Monetary Theory and Policy of Henry Simons," *Jour. Law and Econ.*, Oct. 1967, *10*, 1–13.
3. ———, *A Program for Monetary Stability*. New York 1959.
4. Goldenweiser, E. A. "Postwar Problems and Policies," *Fed. Res. Bull.*, Feb. 1945, *31*, 112–21.
5. Homan, P. T. and Machlup, Fritz, ed. *Financing American Prosperity*. New York 1945.
6. Lerner, A. P. and Graham, F. D., ed. *Planning and Paying for Full Employment*. Princeton 1946.
7. Mill, J. S. *Principles of Political Economy*, Bk. III, Ashley ed. New York 1929.

GUIDELINES FOR MONETARY POLICY—THE CASE AGAINST SIMPLE RULES*

Lyle E. Gramley†

There are several things that seem worthwhile mentioning by way of a prelude to the substance of my remarks. First, I do not regard it as my function to defend, explain, or otherwise comment on the course of monetary policy during the past several years. My comments will be confined to the more general question of running monetary policy by simple rules, and what the empirical evidence seems to say about the issue. Second, of necessity, I must take the Federal Reserve off the hook for what I have to say. I could scarcely present a Federal Reserve consensus in any brief period without grossly misrepresenting someone's position, since there is at least as much diversity of view within the Federal Reserve as elsewhere on the appropriate guidelines for monetary policy. You might already have guessed that from reading the November 1968 *Review* of a certain Midwestern Reserve Bank, whose brand of monetary policy is known around the Board as Brand X.

Third, I do not intend to present a personal point of view on how a central bank should run its affairs. My function is to present sympathetically the case against simple rules in monetary management—and in particular the case against rules defined in terms of growth rates of the money stock, or related monetary aggregates. In this role, I find myself in something of a quandary. Among my friends outside the Board, I seem to have developed a reputation, such as it is, for being an anti-quantity theory man, perhaps even a violent one. At the Board, on the other hand, I am not infrequently accused of having dangerous leanings in the opposite direction, since I have a habit of insisting that a Yo-Yo is not the appropriate physical analogy for monetary policy.

Fourth, since my subsequent remarks about simple rules and quantity theories will be rather critical, it seems appropriate to emphasize at the

outset that the fields of monetary economics and stabilization policy, in my judgment, owe an enormous debt to Professor Friedman for insisting that the role of money as a determinant of national income be given more careful consideration than it was from the period of roughly 1935 to 1965. Apart from a few lonely souls such as Milton Friedman, monetary economists argued for about three decades that central banking was largely wasted motion and sneered at those with contrary ideas. Professor Friedman fought for more careful attention to monetary variables when the going was the roughest—and he deserves our commendation.

The danger now is that the pendulum has swung too far in the other direction. Recognition of nonmonetary factors as a potential disequilibrating influence in the economy is in grave danger of being overlooked. An increasing proportion of economists, financial writers, and others appears to be reaching the conclusion that nonmonetary factors can be safely disregarded as important potential sources of economic turbulence, and that fiscal policy is the wet noodle among our economic stabilization tools.

The case for discretionary monetary management starts from the premise that money matters, and matters a great deal. But other things can and do matter too—specifically, fiscal policy and changing propensities to spend in the private sector. The case also hinges on the assumption that we have learned enough about the sources and the nature of economic fluctuations to do something useful about them, and that the prospects for learning more remain bright.

Let me begin the defense of this case by discussing a grubby statistical problem. Technical arguments may be a little boring, but this one cannot be avoided if the evidence supporting the case for steady growth of the money stock is to be evaluated properly.

As you are well aware, one of the principal supports for the monetarist position is the empirical evidence of a relatively stable relation between money and income, or between changes in these variables—evidence of the kind represented by Professor Friedman's extensive studies or by the Andersen-Jordan paper in the November 1968 issue of the *Federal Reserve Bank of*

*A paper delivered at the Financial Conference of the National Industrial Conference Board, New York, February 21, 1969. Reprinted by permission of the author. Lyle E. Gramley is Adviser, Division of Research and Statistics, Board of Governors of the Federal Reserve System.

† The views expressed in this paper are the responsibility of the author alone and are not necessarily shared by the Board of Governors or by the author's staff colleagues.

St. Louis Review.[1] In the latter study, changes in GNP from 1952 through mid-1968 are regressed on variables taken as proxies for monetary and fiscal actions, with the monetary variables alternately defined as changes in the money stock or in the monetary base, i.e., currency plus total bank reserves. In the Andersen-Jordan regressions, fiscal variables turn out not to bear a statistically significant relation to changes in nominal income. The results, therefore, cast serious doubts about the role of fiscal policy as a stabilizing instrument and by implication on the significance of *all* nonmonetary factors as determinants of nominal income. Meanwhile, monetary variables come booming through as important determinants of GNP.

The problem with this study, and with others of its kind that I am familiar with, is that they are potentially biased, in a statistical sense, towards overemphasis of monetary factors as determinants of income. I use the word "potentially" advisedly since it is hard to prove one way or another, even though the nature of the argument is straight-forward. The argument runs as follows.

If the central bank sits on its hands and does nothing, a rise in GNP resulting from (say) an expansive fiscal policy tends to increase the money stock, mainly because it induces banks to borrow more from the central bank and to reduce excess reserves, but partly also because the induced rise in interest rates reduces demand for time deposits, and thus permits an increase in demand deposits and the money stock. The money stock is not independent, in a statistical sense, of current changes in GNP. Consequently, a regression of GNP on the money stock combines the effects of GNP on money with those of money on GNP. Regressions of GNP on money would not, therefore, yield statistically unbiased estimates of the effects of monetary policy on the economy. Rather similar arguments hold if the monetary variable used is the monetary base.

On the other hand, if the Federal Reserve has not sat on its hands, but has behaved the way monetarists often claim, the potential bias in the historical data is much larger. Professor Friedman, for example, has argued that the Federal Reserve's inept performance in monetary management (as he sees it) results heavily from the fact that too often it leans against the trend of the credit markets—moderating upward pressure on interest rates during economic expansion,

and cushioning the downward rate adjustments that occur in recessions. As a result, he argues, the money stock tends to accelerate or decelerate at just about the time it should be doing the opposite.

If you believe that story, it follows that regressions of GNP on the money stock, with or without other variables to represent fiscal policy, are biased even more towards overestimating the effects of monetary factors as economic determinants. Indeed, a close correlation between money and GNP could occur in those circumstances even if monetary policy had no effect at all on national income.

This problem of statistical bias is an old and familiar story—and monetarists as well as their critics are quite well aware of it. The question at issue, of course, is whether it is a serious enough problem to really worry about. I suggest that it is.

Consider for a moment the implications of concluding that fiscal policy has no discernible effect on money income, apart from its effects on the money stock. This is the conclusion you would reach, presumably, if you accepted as reliable, and statistically unbiased, the evidence set forth in the St. Louis Bank article mentioned earlier, in which fiscal variables were found not to bear a statistically significant relation to money income. The properties of an economic system in which fiscal policy acts the way it does in the Andersen-Jordan model have been discussed in the economic literature for 100 years or more and are reasonably well understood. It is widely known that fiscal policy would have no effect on money income, apart from induced changes in the money stock, if and only if the demand for money were completely interest inelastic. And if that were true, changes in private spending propensities *also* would have no effect on money income, except through their impact on the demand for, or the supply of, money. Indeed, in such a world, the behavior of the money stock would completely determine the course of money income if the demand function for money were stable.

The demand function for money has probably been estimated statistically as many times as, and perhaps more than, any single behavioral equation commonly used in economics. While the nature of the public's demand for money is not understood to anyone's full satisfaction, the empirical evidence accumulated over the past 10 to 15 years—of which a significant part comes from the monetarist camp itself—points over-

[1] L. C. Andersen and J. L. Jordan, "Monetary and Fiscal Actions: A Test of Their Relative Importance in Economic Stabilization," *Federal Reserve Bank of St. Louis Review*, November 1968, pp. 11–24.

whelmingly to the conclusion that the public's desired holdings of money balances are interest sensitive. And this is true whether money is defined narrowly to exclude time deposits of commercial banks or broadly to include them.

In view of this, it seems to me, Andersen and Jordan should not have concluded that their regressions had satisfactorily sorted out the relative roles of monetary and fiscal policy as determinants of GNP. Rather, they should have concluded that something was rather badly wrong with their method.

As I noted, this bias problem is an old familiar one; nevertheless, precious little has been done about it until just recently. I commend for your reading, in this respect, a "Comment" on the Andersen-Jordan study by two staff members at the Board (Frank de Leeuw and John Kalchbrenner).[2] De Leeuw and Kalchbrenner find that different results emerge from the Andersen-Jordan equations if the monetary and fiscal variables are redefined in such a way as to reduce the degree of statistical influence running from GNP to the policy variables. Most importantly, the monetary policy variable is redefined as the monetary base less the public's holdings of currency and member bank borrowings. With this definition, monetary factors decline in importance, and fiscal variables turn out to have significant effects on GNP after all. Also, the relative potency of monetary and fiscal policies resulting from use of the Andersen-Jordan equations, as modified by de Leeuw and Kalchbrenner, turn out to be in the same ball park as those emerging from the larger and more elaborate FRB-MIT model developed by the Board staff working jointly with Professors Ando and Modigliani. Since the structure of the FRB-MIT model differs markedly from the Andersen-Jordan single-equation models, the coincidence of results would seem to be more than accidental.

Let me move now to the next point, which is that, even taken at face value, regressions relating GNP to the money stock (or relating changes in these variables) over the long sweep of history generally are quite consistent with the view that nonmonetary factors play a significant role in determining national income. In elaborating this contention, it seems appropriate to concentrate particularly on the empirical work of Professor Friedman, the leading advocate of the monetarist view.

An article of his published in *The Journal of Law and Economics* a couple of years ago discussed a simple regression equation relating annual changes in M_2—that is, the money stock defined to include time deposits—and GNP. Friedman defines money this way for pragmatic reasons—M_2 is more closely related to GNP, over the long run, than M_1. What I have to say about the flexibility of the M_2–GNP relation thus applies in spades to the relation between M_1 and GNP.

Friedman's equation, based on data from 1870 to 1963, shows a correlation between annual changes in M_2 and GNP of .70.[3] This means that half of the annual changes in nominal income are explained by contemporaneous changes in M_2, and the other half are not. The significance of that degree of accuracy can be illustrated by considering what Friedman's equation says about changes in nominal income during recent years.

From 1962 onward, the equation predicts better than in earlier years. Given knowledge of the annual percentage change in M_2 and the previous year's income, it predicts levels of nominal income for the years 1962–66 with an accuracy of about 1¼ percent. This is worth about $11 billion in GNP, given the present size of the economy, an error that is not negligible when we are talking about average annual levels. Indeed, I suspect a prediction that GNP in 1969 will hit an annual average of $921 billion (the CEA forecast) plus or minus $11 billion would strike almost everyone in this room as unusually imprecise. But in the preceding 10 years—that is from 1952 to 1961—the predictions from Friedman's equation are far worse. The mean absolute error over the 10-year period is roughly 3¼ percent, or about $28 billion in terms of today's GNP. What would you do with a 1969 GNP forecast of $921 billion, plus or minus $28 billion?

A 3¼ percent average prediction error produces a strange picture of short-term economic developments during the 1950s. Annual percentage changes in current income predicted by Friedman's equation are about equal for the three years 1953–55, though you will remember that income growth turned negative in the recession year 1954 and rose sharply in 1955. His equation also predicts an acceleration of income growth in the recession year 1958 and a slight reduction in the boom year 1959. And if its description

---

[2] Frank de Leeuw and John Kalchbrenner, "Monetary and Fiscal Actions: A Test of Their Relative Importance in Economic Stabilization—Comment," *Federal Reserve Bank of St. Louis Review*, April 1969, pp. 6–11; see also L. C. Andersen and J. L. Jordan, "Reply," same issue of the *Review*, pp. 12–16.

[3] Milton Friedman, "Interest Rates and the Demand for Money," *The Journal of Law and Economics*, Vol. 9, October 1966, p. 78.

of short-term economic changes leaves something to be desired, its longer term predictions are even more astonishing. The predicted growth of nominal income over the ten years 1952–61 as a whole is only a bit over one half as large as the actual growth that took place.

If these results surprise you, they shouldn't, since there has always been a good deal of variability in the M_2–GNP relation. The facts are there to read in Professor Friedman's *Monetary History of the United States*. Annual variations of 3 percent or more in the income velocity of M_2 are the rule, not the exception. They occur in two thirds of the some 90-odd years covered by the study. Even if the first 12 years of this period of history are thrown out on grounds of unreliable data, as Friedman suggests, and if the years of the Great Depression and the two World Wars are also discarded, for reasons that are not so clear, annual velocity changes of 3 percent or more still occur in more than one half of the remaining years.

As I read the historical evidence, therefore, one of the two main pillars on which the monetarist position rests is a bit shaky. The second one strikes me as even less stable. It is the contention that the money stock should grow at a constant rate because, to quote Professor Friedman, ". . . we simply do not know enough, we are not smart enough, we have not analyzed sufficiently and understood sufficiently the operation of the world so [that] we know how to use monetary policy as a balance wheel."[4] Consequently, he argues, we ought to convert monetary policy from a factor that he contends has been positively destabilizing to one that is neutral.

The argument has intuitive appeal, but not much more. If we do not know how to use monetary instruments to offset the disequilibrating effects of nonmonetary factors, then we do not know enough to accentuate these effects either—or to judge whether the central bank has done so.

To strike an analogy, Friedman's argument is that the central bank is like a person lost near the edge of a forest, with insufficient evidence as to the shortest way out.

Friedman advises the wanderer to stay put, since otherwise he may wander deeper into the woods. He may, but then again he also may wander out. Friedman's advice is sound if the wanderer can be reasonably sure that a rescue

party is on the way. But if there is no rescue party, the poor lost soul might just as well start walking—he might just stumble onto some tracks that lead him home.

The point I am making is perhaps obvious, but I did not originate it. The credit goes to Professors Lovell and Prescott, who deal with the question at considerable length, and in a theoretical fashion, in a recent article.[5] They conclude that in the absence of knowledge about the strength and timing of monetary changes, it cannot be demonstrated that a policy rule specifying a constant growth rate of the money stock is superior, in terms of smoothing out income fluctuations, to a rule specifying that interest rates be stabilized. Also, one cannot demonstrate the superiority of either rule over any specific set of policies pursued by the central bank.

Rational conduct of monetary policy—whether by the pursuit of rigid rules or by allowing central banks substantial discretion in deciding the course of monetary affairs—cannot be specified if we assume complete lack of knowledge. Our understanding of how the economic system works is imperfect, and we must recognize that an optimal policy strategy has to take uncertainty into account. But we must begin with what we know, and build on it. The Lovell-Prescott approach is an excellent example of one direction of fruitful inquiry.

Perhaps I am a hopeless optimist on this score, but I think we have learned a great deal in the past 10 years or so about the use of stabilization policy—and particularly monetary instruments. The most hopeful sign, in this regard, is the fact that we are gradually whittling away the wide diversity that once existed as to the effects of monetary policy on the economy. A consensus has developed that monetary policy is vitally important to economic performance, and the estimates of the money multipliers seem to be converging. Our understanding of the paths of transmission has increased greatly, and here, too, people from opposing camps find they have more in common than they thought. Professors Tobin and Friedman speak much the same language when they are talking about the processes of monetary policy. And the Board's staff, working together with Professors Ando and Modigliani, has developed a model in which the wealth effects of monetary policy, working through the

---

[4] "The Federal Reserve System after Fifty Years," House Banking and Currency Committee, 88th Congress, Vol. 2, *Hearings*, 1156.

[5] Michael C. Lovell and Edward Prescott, "Money, Multiplier Accelerator Interaction, and the Business Cycle," *Southern Economic Journal*, Vol. 35, July 1968, pp. 60–72.

markets for equities, bear directly on consumer spending in a way that would warm even Milton Friedman's heart. This is a far cry from the simple-minded Keynesianism of the 1930s and early 1940s or the equally naive quantity theories expounded at that time.

Lags, of course, there are, but they are not hopelessly long. I understand Professor Friedman's current view is that the average lag is something like six months between changes in the growth rate of money and changes in the growth rate of GNP. Our own empirical work at the Board suggests the average lag may be slightly longer, but we, too, find that significant economic effects can be obtained within the space of half a year by manipulating the instruments of monetary policy. We are making progress, also, in understanding why the lags are variable, and how to estimate the lengths of lags in economic systems in which this variation occurs.

Above all, we are learning how immensely complex the economic and financial world really is. Money, however we define it, is not unique, in any meaningful sense of that word. Demand deposits substitute for CD's, for other classes of commercial bank time and savings accounts, for claims on nonbank intermediaries, and for market securities.

This does not mean, of course, that the central bank can ignore the money stock and concentrate on (say) interest rates. The behavior of the money stock contains useful information for measuring and interpreting monetary policy, more information, I think we should acknowledge, than most economists other than the monetarists have recognized. Reducing the growth rate of bank demand deposits, and hence the narrowly defined money stock, *does* reduce the growth rate of GNP. But so also does a reduction in the growth rate of commercial bank time deposits, or a decline in the growth rate of savings and loan shares or mutual savings bank deposits. In fact, there is no reason in theory for regarding a dollar change in the growth rate of claims against nonbank intermediaries as any less significant, in terms of its effects on GNP, than a dollar change in M_2 or in M_1. We ignore fluctuations in commercial bank time deposits or in claims against nonbank intermediaries at our peril in a world in which all sectors of the financial market are be-

coming more closely related, and in which the processes of monetary policy are increasingly extending beyond the boundaries of the narrowly defined money stock.

Surely, Professor Friedman would not deny, in principle, that we ought to try to take into account these more complex aspects of the effects of central bank policies on economic activity in the formulation of monetary policy. What is needed is an analytic framework, a conceptual apparatus, to do this more systematically and with greater success than we have been able to in the past. That is precisely the goal of our research effort at the Board, and I am fully convinced that these efforts are paying off, in the sense that we have been already, are now, and will be in the future, getting informational inputs that are useful for improving monetary policy decisions.

We occasionally hear remarks that belittle the usefulness of large econometric models such as ours, on the grounds that such models are unstable, not robust, poor predictors, and so on. If, by those comments, it is meant that the art of building large mathematical models is still undeveloped and needs improvement, I fully agree. But if it means that such models are in a substantive sense inferior to the one-equation models produced by Professor Friedman or by Andersen and Jordan, I disagree wholeheartedly.

Finally, let me note that models of monetary policy variables and their effects on the economy, whether they be one-equation models or more complex ones, never can be (and I would argue never should be) push-button devices that provide automatic, unqualified answers to policy questions—answers that human judgment cannot then refine further, or discard altogether if it seems appropriate. We send spaceships to the moon with human lives aboard mainly to permit on-the-spot reaction to developments that cannot always be anticipated and allowed for in advance. Changes in plans made in such a context must, obviously, take into account what we know, as well as what we don't know. Spacemen are not allowed to play God in the decision-making process, and central bankers should not have such freedom either. But reducing them to subhumans, grinding out a constant growth rate of money, is not justified by logic or by empirical fact.

SOME ISSUES OF MONETARY POLICY*

Council of Economic Advisers

The record of the past 8 years demonstrates that flexible, discretionary monetary policy can make an effective contribution to economic stabilization. The economy's gradual return to full productive potential in the early 1960's was partly attributable to a monetary policy which kept ample supplies of credit readily available at generally stable interest rates. And in early 1967, the prompt recovery of homebuilding after the 1966 slowdown was the direct result of timely and aggressive easing of credit conditions by the Federal Reserve.

The most dramatic demonstration of the effectiveness of monetary policy came in 1966, however, when a dangerously inflationary situation was curbed primarily by a drastic application of monetary restraint. Credit-financed expenditures at the end of that year appear to have been as much as $8 billion below what they might have been had monetary policy maintained the accommodative posture of the preceding 5 years. And there were substantial further "multiplier" effects on GNP as these initial impacts reduced income and consumption spending.

THE CONDUCT OF MONETARY POLICY

The primary guides for monetary policy are the various broad measures of economic performance, including the growth rate of total output, the relation of actual to potential output, employment and unemployment, the behavior of prices, and the Nation's balance-of-payments position. Extensive research, together with the experience of the last few years, has increased our knowledge of the complex process by which monetary policy influences these measures. While there are still major gaps in our knowledge of the precise chain of causation, some conclusions seem well established.

Like fiscal policy, monetary policy affects economic activity only after some lag. Thus actions by the Federal Reserve must be forward-looking. In considering the prospects ahead, however, an assessment must be made of both the expected behavior of the private sector and of the likely

* From *The Annual Report of the Council of Economic Advisers,* January 1969, pp. 85–93. Reprinted by permission of the Council of Economic Advisers.

future course of fiscal policy. As noted earlier, the inherent flexibility in the administration of monetary policy permits frequent policy adjustments to take account of unexpected developments in either the private or the public sector.

Sectoral Impacts

Monetary policy can affect spending through a number of channels. To some extent it works by changing the terms of lending, including interest rates, maturities of loans, downpayments, and the like, in such a way as to encourage or discourage expenditures on goods financed by credit. There may also be market imperfections or legal constraints and institutional rigidities that change the "availability" of loans as monetary conditions change—that is, make it easier or more difficult for borrowers to obtain credit at given terms of lending. Under some circumstances, purchasers of goods and services may finance their expenditures by liquidating financial assets, and changes in the yields on these assets produced by a change in monetary policy may affect their willingness to engage in such transactions. Changes in monetary policy may also, on occasion, change the expectations of borrowers, lenders, and spenders in ways that affect economic conditions, although these expectational effects are rather complex and dependent upon the conditions existing at the time policy is changed.

Monetary policy affects some types of expenditures more than others. The extent of the impact depends not only on the economic characteristics of the activity being financed but, in many instances, on the channels through which financing is obtained and the legal and institutional arrangements surrounding the financing procedures.

Residential Construction. The sector of the economy most affected by monetary policy is residential construction. Although the demand for housing—and for mortgage credit—does not appear to be especially responsive to mortgage interest rates, the supply of mortgage funds is quite sensitive to several interest rate relationships.

The experience of 1966 clearly demonstrated how rising interest rates can sharply affect flows of deposits to banks and other thrift institutions and thereby severely limit their ability to make new mortgage loans. In the first half of that year, the net deposit gain at savings and loan associations and mutual savings banks was only half as large as in the preceding 6 months. These institutions could not afford to raise the rates paid on savings capital to compete with the higher rates available to savers at banks and elsewhere because of their earnings situation—with their assets concentrated in mortgages that earned only the relatively low rates of return characteristic of several years earlier. Commercial banks experienced a similarly sharp slowing in growth of time deposits in the second half of the year, as the Federal Reserve's Regulation Q prevented them from competing effectively for liquid funds. This forced banks to make across-the-board cuts in lending operations.

In addition, life insurance companies had a large portion of their loanable funds usurped by demands for policy loans, which individuals found attractive because of relatively low cost. High-yielding corporate securities also proved an attractive alternative for some institutional investments that might otherwise have gone into mortgages.

Table 1 provides some indication of the extent of these various influences. As can be seen, savings and loan associations and mutual savings banks together supplied less than 10 percent of total funds borrowed in 1966, well below their 22 percent share in the preceding 5 years. This was the main factor limiting the availability of household mortgage loans. The effect on home-

building was quick and dramatic, as the seasonally adjusted volume of new housing units started fell by nearly half between December 1965 and October 1966.

In 1967, as interest rates in the open market retreated from their 1966 highs, the thrift institutions were able to regain their competitive position in the savings market. A good part of their funds was fairly quickly channeled into the mortgage market. By fall, housing starts had recovered nearly to the level of late 1965.

. . . many factors—including several significant institutional reforms, sharply improved liquidity positions, and the widespread expectation that monetary restraint was only temporary pending passage of the tax bill—helped to moderate the adverse effects of renewed monetary restraint on mortgage lending in 1968. But the thrift institutions again experienced some slowing of deposit inflows when market interest rates rose to new heights, and mutual savings banks switched a good part of their investments away from the mortgage market to high-yielding corporate bonds.

State and Local Governments. State and local governments also felt the effects of monetary restraint in 1966. These governments cut back or postponed more than $2.9 billion, or nearly 25 percent, of their planned bond issues that year.

It is difficult to determine precisely what caused these postponements. In cases involving

TABLE 1   NET FUNDS RAISED BY NONFINANCIAL SECTORS, 1961–68

Nonfinancial Sector	1961–65 Average	1966	1967	1968*
Total funds raised (billions of dollars)	59.2	69.9	83.1	97.1
Percent of total raised by:				
Private domestic nonfinancial sectors	84.5	88.7	79.9	80.4
State and local governments	10.8	9.7	12.6	11.7
Nonfinancial business	34.6	48.1	44.8	37.0
Households	39.0	30.9	22.5	31.7
Mortgages	25.5	18.6	13.7	17.1
Other	13.5	12.3	8.8	14.6
U.S. Government	10.6	9.0	15.3	16.7
Rest of world	5.1	2.1	4.8	2.9
Percent of total supplied by:				
Commercial banks	35.1	24.7	43.6	39.1
Nonbank financial institutions	43.6	32.2	39.0	29.7
Savings and loan associations and mutual savings banks	22.1	9.9	19.5	14.0
Other	21.5	22.3	19.5	15.7
Federal Reserve and U.S. Government	10.1	16.3	11.2	12.9
State and local governments	6.8	8.9	9.4	7.7
Foreign lenders	1.2	−2.0	3.9	− .3
Nonfinancial business	2.7	4.6	.5	5.1
Households, less net security credit	.5	15.3	−7.5	5.8

* Preliminary.
Note: Detail will not necessarily add to totals because of rounding.
Source: Board of Governors of the Federal Reserve System.

more than half the dollar volume, the reasons given related to the prevailing high level of interest rates. In some instances, the interest costs simply exceeded the legal ceiling governments were permitted to pay for borrowed funds. In other cases, finance officers decided to delay bond issues for a few months in the expectation that interest rates would decline.

This sizable cutback in borrowings had a relatively small effect on State and local government expenditures. Larger governments apparently were able to continue most of their projects about as scheduled by drawing down liquid assets or borrowing temporarily at short term. Smaller governmental units, however, cut their contract awards by a total estimated at more than $400 million.

Because of the problems State and local governments often face in raising funds, the Administration is proposing the establishment of an Urban Development Bank, which could borrow economically in the open market and then lend in the amounts needed to individual local governments. The Bank could lend at federally subsidized interest rates, with the Federal Government recovering the cost of the subsidy through taxation of the interest income earned by holders of the Bank's securities.

Business and Consumer Spending. The 1966 credit squeeze undoubtedly also had some effects on business and consumer spending, though the amount of impact is not easily determinable. Most theoretical and empirical studies find that business firms in some way balance the cost of borrowed capital against the expected returns from their capital projects. Some small firms may also simply not be able to obtain funds during tight money periods. In 1966, bank lending to business did slow sharply during the second half of the year. Many of the larger firms shifted their demands to the open market—and paid record high interest rates for their funds—but some of the smaller ones probably were forced to postpone their projects.

Household spending on durable goods—particularly automobiles—has been shown to be affected by changes in the cost and availability of consumer credit, as reflected in the interest rate, maturity, downpayment, and other terms. While it is difficult to sort out cause and effect, households borrowed only two-thirds as much through consumer credit in the second half of 1966 as in the preceding half year. Capital gains or losses on asset holdings accompanying changes in yields may also induce consumers to spend more or less on goods and services.

Active and Passive Elements

Monetary policy, like fiscal policy, has what might be termed active and passive components. Recognition of this distinction played an important role in formulating the accommodative policy of the early 1960s. In the 1950s, economic expansion had generally been accompanied by rising interest rates, which tended to produce an automatic stabilizing effect somewhat similar to the fiscal drag of the Federal tax system discussed earlier. The large amounts of underutilized resources available in the early 1960s made such restraint inappropriate, and credit was expanded sufficiently to prevent it from occurring.

It is especially important to distinguish between these elements in monetary policy at cyclical turning points. If, for example, private demand weakens and causes a decline in economic activity, interest rates will generally fall as credit demands slacken, even without any positive action by the Federal Reserve to push rates down. This induced fall in interest rates can help to check the decline in economic activity but may not, by itself, induce recovery. Similarly, as the economy rises above potential, the induced rise in interest rates may only moderate the expansion but may not bring activity back into line with capacity.

An active monetary policy during such periods requires positive effort by the Federal Reserve to produce further changes in interest rates and in availability of credit beyond those that would occur automatically. Since expectational responses may either accentuate or moderate the effects of the initial action, it is sometimes difficult to know in advance precisely how much of a policy change is needed. But the main point is clear—at such turning points, interest rate movements alone are not likely to provide an accurate reflection of the contribution of monetary policy to economic stabilization. Careful attention must also be paid to credit flows, particularly those to the private sector of the economy.

MONETARY POLICY AND THE MONEY SUPPLY

Examination of the linkages between monetary policy and various categories of expenditures suggests that, in the formulation of monetary policy, careful attention should be paid to interest rates and credit availability as influenced by and associated with the flows of deposits and credit to different types of financial institutions and spending units. Among the financial flows generally considered to be relevant are: the total of funds raised by nonfinancial sectors of the economy, the credit supplied by commercial banks, the net amount of new mortgage credit, the net change in the public's holdings of liquid assets, changes in time deposits at banks and other thrift institutions, and changes in the money supply. Some consideration should be given to all of these financial flows as well as to related interest rates in formulating any comprehensive policy program or analysis of financial conditions.

Much public attention has recently been focused on an alternative view, however, emphasizing the money supply as the most important— sometimes the only—link between monetary policy and economic activity. This emphasis has often been accompanied by the suggestion that the Federal Reserve can best contribute to economic stabilization by maintaining growth in the stock of money at a particular rate—or somewhat less rigidly, by keeping variations in the rate of growth of the money stock within a fairly narrow band.

There are, of course, numerous variants of the money view of monetary policy. The discussion below focuses only on the simple version that has captured most of the public attention.

Money and Interest Rates

In a purely theoretical world, abstracting from institutional rigidities that exist in our financial system and assuming that relationships among financial variables were unvarying and predictable, it would make little difference whether monetary policy was formulated in terms of interest rates or the money supply. The two variables are inversely related, and the alternative approaches would represent nothing more than different paths to precisely the same result. The monetary authorities could seek to control the money stock, with interest rates allowed to take on whatever values happen to result. Or alternatively, they could focus on achieving the interest rates that would facilitate the credit flows needed to finance the desired level of activity, allowing the quantity of money to be whatever it had to be.

But financial rigidities do exist that often distort flows of credit in response to swings in interest rates. And financial relationships have changed steadily and significantly. Just since 1961, several important new financial instruments have been introduced and developed, including negotiable time certificates of deposit and Euro-

dollar deposits. Attitudes of both investors and lenders have also undergone marked shifts, with sharp variations in the public's demand for liquidity superimposed on an underlying trend toward greater sensitivity to interest rates.

There is, to be sure, enough of a link between money and interest rates at any given time to make it impossible for the Federal Reserve to regulate the two independently. But this linkage is hardly simple, and it varies considerably and unpredictably over time. The choice between controlling the stock of money solely and focusing interest rates, credit availability, and a number of credit flows can therefore make a difference. This choice should be based on a judgment—supported insofar as possible by empirical and analytical evidence—as to whether it is money holdings alone that influence the decisions of various categories of spending units.

Money and Asset Portfolios

The Federal Reserve conducts monetary policy primarily by expanding and contracting the supply of cash reserves available to the banking system. Such actions seek to induce an expansion or contraction in loans and investments at financial institutions, with corresponding changes in the public's holdings of currency and deposits of various kinds. The proportions in which the public chooses to hold alternative types of financial assets depend upon a complex set of preferences, which, in turn, depend upon interest rate relationships.

The process of expansion and contraction of money and credit stemming from Federal Reserve actions is fairly complex. But one aspect of it should be clearly understood: The money so created is not something given to the public for nothing as if it fell from heaven—that is, it is not a net addition to the public's wealth or net worth. There can be an immediate change in public wealth, but only to the extent that changes in interest rates generate capital gains or losses on existing assets.

Any change in the money stock is associated with a change in the composition of the public's balance sheet, as people and institutions are induced to exchange—at a price—one asset for another or to increase (or decrease) both their assets and their liabilities by equal amounts. Since all the items in the public's balance sheet might be changed as a result of these compositional shifts, the change in the public's liquidity is not likely to be summarized adequately in terms of any single category of financial assets.

It is, of course, possible that decisions to spend on goods and services are affected more by the presence of one type of financial asset than another in a spending unit's portfolio. But there is only scattered evidence of such behavior in various sectoral studies that have been undertaken to analyze the factors affecting the spending decisions of consumers, businesses, or State and local governments. Indeed, to the extent these studies do find spending decisions systematically affected by financial variables, it is often through changes in interest rates and availability of credit.

Money and Income and a Monetary Rule

One problem with the money supply as a guide to monetary policy is that there is no agreement concerning the appropriate definition of "money." One definition includes the total of currency outside commercial banks plus privately held demand deposits. A second also includes time deposits at commercial banks, and even more inclusive alternatives are sometimes used. On the other hand, there is a more limited definition, sometimes called "high-powered money" or "monetary base," which includes currency in circulation and member-bank reserve balances at the Federal Reserve banks.

These different concepts of money do not always move in parallel with one another—even over fairly extended periods. Thus assertions that the money supply is expanding rapidly or slowly often depend critically on which definition is employed. In the first half of 1968, for example, there was a sharp acceleration in the growth of currency plus demand deposits, but growth of this total plus time deposits slowed considerably.

On the other hand, relationships between movements in GNP and any of the money concepts have been close enough on the average— especially when processed through complex lags and other sophisticated statistical techniques—to be difficult to pass off lightly.

There is, of course, good reason to expect some fairly close relationship between money and income. This would be true even in a completely abstract situation in which it was assumed that the money supply per se had no direct influence on GNP, and that monetary policy worked entirely through interest rates. Since interest rates and the money supply are inversely related, any rise in GNP produced by a reduction in interest rates and increased credit availability would be accompanied by at least some increase in the money supply.

The relationship also exists in a sort of "reverse causation" form—that is, as income goes up so does the demand for money, which the Federal Reserve then accommodates by allowing an increase in the actual money stock. This is precisely what happened during the 1961–65 period of accommodative policy, and it is always present to some extent as the Federal Reserve acts to meet the economy's changing credit needs. The problem of sorting out the extent of causation in the two directions still challenges economic researchers.

A one-sided interpretation of these relationships is sometimes used to support the suggestion that the Federal Reserve conduct policy on the basis of some fixed, predetermined guideline for growth of the money supply (however defined). Given the complex role of interest rates in affecting various demand categories and the likely variations in so many other factors, any such simple policy guide could prove to be quite unreliable.

The experience of the past several years illustrates the kinds of difficulties that might be encountered in using the money supply (defined here as currency plus demand deposits) as the exclusive guide for monetary policy. As described previously, high interest rates in 1966 began affecting the nonbank thrift institutions, the mortgage market, and the homebuilding industry soon after the start of the year. But during the first 4 months of that year, the money supply grew at an annual rate of nearly 6½ percent, well above the long-term trend. Later that year, the financial situation of major mortgage lenders improved somewhat and housing eventually rebounded despite the fact that growth of money supply plus bank time deposits was proceeding at only a snail's pace.

Growth of the money supply in the second quarter of 1968 was at an annual rate of 9 percent. The reasons for this acceleration—to a rate almost double the growth in the preceding quarter—are not fully apparent. The Federal Reserve could have resisted this sizable increase in the demand for money more than it did, but interest rates in the open market would then have risen well above the peaks that were in fact reached in May. Whether still higher rates would have been desirable is another issue, which cannot be settled merely by citing the rapid growth of the money supply.

These illustrations suggest that any simple rigid rule related to the growth of the money supply (however defined) can unduly confine Federal Reserve policy. In formulating monetary policy, the Federal Reserve must be able to take account of all types of financial relationships currently prevailing and in prospect and be able to respond flexibly as changing economic needs arise. In deciding on such responses, especially careful consideration must be given to likely changes in interest rates and credit availability, in view of the effects of these factors on particular sectors of the economy—especially the home-building industry.

THE MATURITY STRUCTURE OF INTEREST RATES*

Warren L. Smith

The interest rate structure at any particular time is determined by a combination of factors, of which the most important are the expectations of borrowers and lenders concerning future interest rates. As the economy moves from prosperity to recession and back again, the rate structure moves in a way which is at least roughly predictable.

Generally, interest rates on debt contracts of all maturities move up and down together.[1] This is simply because demand schedules for credit in all sectors tend to move up and down together as credit conditions change and because both lenders and borrowers commonly have some flexibility with respect to the maturity sector in which they will operate, so that if rates in a particular maturity range get out of line with other rates, corrective forces are set in motion.

Thus, in a boom period interest rates in all maturity sectors ordinarily rise, while in recession periods they fall. However, the changes in interest rates are ordinarily different for different maturities. In particular, as the level of interest rates rises and falls, short-term interest rates usually move over a considerably wider range than do long-term interest rates. These differential movements of rates in different maturity ranges can be explained, at least approximately, by reference to patterns of interest rate expectations.

To illustrate how interest rate expectations influence the interest rate structure, let us consider a situation in which the consensus of expectations on the part of borrowers and lenders is that interest rates are going to rise in the near future. Before these expectations developed, for whatever reason, suppose that short-term and long-term interest rates were approximately equal. As a result of the change in expectations, lenders would have a tendency to eschew long-term securities, because they would expect to suffer capital losses on investments in such securities when interest rates rose and because they would feel that it was preferable to hold back and wait until prices of longer term securities fell before investing in them. Investors with this kind of expectations would tend to shift their flow of funds toward shorter term loans and securities. In fact, some investors might even sell out their existing holdings of long-term securities in advance of the expected price decline and put their funds into short-term securities. Thus, there would be a shift in the supply of funds from the long- to the short-term market. Borrowers, on the other hand, would tend to make a reverse shift. To the extent that they felt that interest rates were going to rise, they would feel that the present was an auspicious time to borrow at long-term in order to take maximum advantage of the existing relatively low rates. As a consequence of the shift of supply from the long- to the short-term market and the shift of demand from the short- to the long-term market, the long-term rate would tend to rise relative to the short-term rate, thus producing an upward-sloping yield curve. Under circumstances in which interest rates were expected to fall, precisely the opposite kinds of shifts would tend to occur. Supply would shift from the short- to the long-term market and demand from the long- to the short-term market, thus producing a rise in the short-term rate relative to the long-term rate and a downward-sloping yield curve.

If investors or speculators are prepared to

---

*From Warren L. Smith, *Debt Management in the United States,* Study Paper No. 19 for the Joint Economic Committee; materials prepared in connection with the study of Employment, Growth, and Price Levels (86th Cong., 2d sess., 1960), pp. 81–88.

[1] This is not always the case—occasionally short-term and long-term interest rates move in opposite directions. However, this is usually a transition phenomenon which lasts only a short time. See footnote 6 below.

move funds between the various maturity sectors on a carefully calculated basis, the determination of the rate structure becomes somewhat more precise than the above discussion suggests. If investors held identical expectations with complete certainty, the long-term rate for any specified period would become equal to the average of the expected short-term rates over that period. That is, neglecting compounding of interest, if the present rate for 6-month loans were 3 percent and this rate were expected to rise continuously to 4 percent, 5 percent, and 6 percent, respectively, for the next three 6-month periods, the current rate for a 2-year loan would be about 4.5 percent, the average of these rates.[2] The reason for this is that the investor would have to be able to get the same return for investing for 2 years as he could obtain for investing now for 6 months and successively reinvesting in similar 6-month contracts over the next 2 years. If this relationship did not hold, shifts of demand and supply similar to those discussed above would occur until it did prevail.

When allowance is made for the fact that the expectations of investors are uncertain and that expectations differ from one investor to another, the precision of the expectational theory is destroyed. Nevertheless, the expectational theory seems to explain, at least in broad outline, the typical pattern of movement of the interest-rate structure. To complete the explanation however, it is necessary to add one further element. It appears that, at least as regards movements of interest rates associated with short-run fluctuations of business conditions, investors' expectations are determined in relation to some level of interest rates which they regard as "normal" or "conventional." Thus, as interest rates rise to "high" (at least by recent standards) levels during a period of inflation, the expectation that they are going to decline in the near future becomes more and more widespread, and as a consequence, short-term rates rise relative to long-term rates. In such circumstances, short-term rates may actually rise above long-term rates. On the other hand, when interest rates fall to "low" levels during recession periods, the expectation becomes increasingly widespread that they are going to rise, and, accordingly, short-term rates fall substantially below long-term rates. At times when rates are not expected to change or when an increase or a decrease seems approximately equally likely, short-term and long-term rates may be approximately equal, although this statement is subject to an important qualification to be pointed out shortly.

It is a commonly observed phenomenon that, as interest rates and security prices move up and down, short-term interest rates ordinarily fluctuate over a wider range than long-term interest rates, while long-term security prices fluctuate over a wider range than short-term security prices. This typical pattern of movement constitutes a fairly impressive piece of indirect evidence in support of the expectational theory as outlined above. It can be shown that if investors' elasticities of interest rate expectations are between zero and unity—that is, if a rise in current interest rates causes investors to revise upward their expectations of future interest rates over their planning horizon but by an amount less than the rise in current interest rates—the expectational theory will produce the patterns of movement in interest rates and security prices that are typically observed.[3]

---

[2] The "expectational" theory of the interest-rate structure is expounded in J. R. Hicks, *Value and Capital* (2d ed.; Oxford: The Clarendon Press, 1946), chap. xi; F. A. Lutz, "The Structure of Interest Rates," *Quarterly Journal of Economics*, Vol. LV (November 1940), 36–63, reprinted in W. Fellner and B. F. Haley (eds.), *Readings in the Theory of Income Distribution* (Homewood, Ill.: Richard D. Irwin, Inc., 1946), pp. 499–529. See also R. A. Musgrave, *The Theory of Public Finance* (New York: McGraw-Hill Book Co., 1959), chap. xxiv.

[3] To illustrate, suppose we have two securities, a $1,000 3 percent "bill" having a maturity of 1 year and a $1,000 3 percent consol. Suppose the typical investor has a planning horizon of 1 year and his elasticity of expectations is 0.5. To begin with, both securities are selling at par, to yield 3 percent. Suppose now that, for whatever reason, the yield on consols rises to 3.1 percent so that the price of consols falls to $967.74. With an elasticity of yield expectations of 0.5, the investor will expect that the yield on consols at the end of his 1-year horizon will have fallen halfway back to its original level, or will be 3.05 percent so that the price of consols will be $983.61. If he invests $967.74 in a consol and holds it for 1 year, his expected return will be $30 interest plus a capital gain of $15.87, or a total of $45.87, giving a yield (for 1 year) of 4.74 percent. In order to equalize the returns for holding consols and "bills," the interest rate on bills will have to rise to 4.74 percent, and the price of outstanding 3 percent bills will have to fall to $983.39. Thus, the yield on bills will rise more than the yield on consols, while the price of consols will fall more than the price of bills. This pattern of behavior will be obtained only if the elasticity of expectations lies between zero and unity—which is a technical translation of the idea that investors' expectations are dominated by convention or the concept of a normal yield level. It may be noted that in this illustration it was assumed that the short-term yields adjust to become consistent with current and expected long-term yields rather than the other way

CHART 1   ILLUSTRATIVE INTEREST-RATE PATTERNS

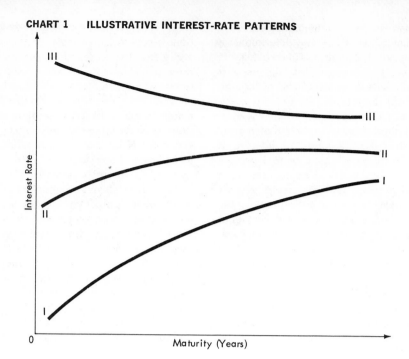

Lenders may have a preference for liquidity—that is, price stability—because of the possibility that an unforeseen contingency may require them to sell securities on short notice. At the same time, borrowers, particularly those who are borrowing for long-term purposes such as investment in fixed plant and equipment, clearly have a distinct preference for long-term debt contracts, since with such contracts they avoid the necessity for frequent renewal of their loans perhaps at inconvenient times. Thus, lenders have an inherent preference for short debt and borrowers for long debt, and this tends to bias the short-term interest rate in a downward direction compared to the long-term rate. For this reason, even when interest rates are not expected to change, the short-term rate is likely to be somewhat below the long-term rate. Also, of course, there are limitations on the mobility of funds from one maturity sector to another, and some lenders and borrowers have conventional preferences for debt of certain maturities, which interfere with the full realization of the rate pattern that would be produced by the free reign of expectations.[4] Nevertheless,

the actual movements of the interest rate structure seem to be broadly consistent with the expectational theory.

Chart 1 presents a somewhat idealized picture of the way in which the term structure of interest rates might be expected to behave according to the expectational theory as outlined above. Yield curve I is the kind of pattern that would tend to prevail in recession periods when interest rates were low and most investors expected them to rise in the future. Curve III is the type that would prevail in boom periods when interest rates were high and most investors expected them to fall. Curve II is the type that would prevail in periods in which most investors expected rates to remain unchanged for some time in the future or when expectations of increases were about as common as expectations of decreases.[5] As business conditions change, the rate structure would move continuously from one position to another—for example, during a period of recovery from recession, the structure would gradually change from type I to type III.[6] Thus interest

around. In fact, however, the two approaches are equivalent. This extension and adaptation of the expectational theory is developed by Tibor Scitovsky in "A Study of Interest and Capital," *Economica*, Vol. VII n.s. (August 1940), pp. 304–6. See also Musgrave, *op. cit.*, p. 596.

[4] These factors are stressed in J. M. Culbertson, "The Term Structure of Interest Rates," *Quarterly Journal of Economics*, Vol. LXXI (November 1957),

pp. 485–517. We shall also make use of them below to explain certain peculiarities that have appeared in the rate structure recently.

[5] Curve II has a gentle upward slope due to the inherent preferences of lenders for short-term debt and of borrowers for long-term debt, referred to above.

[6] There may be times when short- and long-term rates move in opposite directions. For example, during the early stages of a recovery period when interest

rates would tend to rise together, but with short-term rates moving over a considerably wider range than long-term interest rates.

For many years up until rather recently, the term structure of interest rates in the United States was of the type I variety, with short-term interest rates substantially lower than long-term rates. During the depression of the 1930s, interest rates fell to low levels, as is characteristic of such periods, and investors, judging the rate level by the conventional standards established in the 1920s, felt that rates were abnormally low and could be expected to rise. Accordingly, short-term rates fell to very low levels and the yield curve took on a sharply upward-sloping shape. During World War II, the Federal Reserve System, in coordination with the Treasury, decided to peg the interest rate structure in order to assist the Treasury in financing the war. The rate structure selected for pegging was approximately the one then prevailing, which reflected the effects of the prolonged depression. The Treasury bill rate was fixed at ⅜ percent and the certificate rate at ⅞ percent, with rates rising to 2½ percent for long-term Treasury bonds.[7] Although the bill

and certificate rates were freed in July and August 1947, and somewhat greater flexibility was introduced into the short-term end of the rate structure, the fixing of the long-term rate and control over the rate structure was maintained until the accord of March 1951. Even after the accord, flexibility was introduced only gradually. Since the "bills-only" policy was put into effect in 1953 by the Federal Reserve System, the rate structure (as distinct from the rate level) has been determined almost entirely by market forces with very little intervention by the authorities other than the incidental effects caused by the open market operations in bills.

The combined result of the depression, war finance, and the policies of the early postwar period was to produce a situation in which the short-term rate was below the long-term rate—and frequently very much below it—continuously for approximately a quarter of a century. As a result of this experience, the notion came to be widely accepted that a rate curve sloping steeply upward was the normal thing. In accordance with the expectational theory, the existence of this view in itself tended to inhibit movements of the rate structure away from the upward-sloping position. Historically, however, during the period prior to 1930, short-term rates appear to have been above long-term a good deal of the time.[8] And the basic forces of the market appear to be reasserting themselves as the implications of a flexible interest rate policy come to be more widely understood. Thus, we seem to be witnessing a reappearance of the classic pattern in which the short-term rate is above the long-term rate during prosperous times, while the opposite relation holds during recession periods.

In one respect, however, the interest rate structure during recent periods when monetary policy has been restrictive and the level of interest rates has risen has departed from the pattern described above. As interest rates have risen recently, a bulge has appeared in the yield curve in the intermediate maturity range. This is illustrated in Chart 2, which shows the yield curves for Treasury securities in March 1958 and in August 1959. The March 1958 curve is a typical yield curve for a recession period, with the short-term rate very low relative to the long-term rate. By August 1959 the forces of recovery which in-

rates begin to rise and investors expect the rise to continue for some time as the recovery develops, lenders may hold funds back from the long-term market to wait until rates begin to stabilize, putting these funds temporarily into the short-term market, while borrowers may anticipate their needs for long-term funds and accelerate their long-term borrowing in order to meet their requirements before rates rise further. In these circumstances, long-term rates may rise sharply while short-term rates are rising only slightly or perhaps even declining. In terms of our earlier analysis, this is a circumstance in which market participants have elastic expectations rather than the inelastic expectations which normally seem to prevail. This is likely to be a transition phenomenon, however, which accelerates the rise in long-term interest rates to a point where inelastic expectations again prevail and short-term rates rise sharply to produce a type III curve.

[7] For a discussion of the decision to fix the rate structure, see H. C. Murphy, *The National Debt in War and Transition* (New York: McGraw-Hill, 1960), pp. 92–103. The fixing of this rate structure created some problems for the Treasury and the Federal Reserve, because the structure itself contradicted the expectations created in the minds of investors. The upward slope of the yield curve corresponded with expectations of rising rates, while the decision to fix rates created expectations that rates would not change. Under these circumstances, it became increasingly difficult to get investors to hold short-term securities. If the rate structure is to be pegged, the structure selected should be one in which short- and long-term rates are approximately equal—that is, a curve of the type II variety as shown in Chart 1.

[8] See David Durand, *Basic Yields of Corporate Bonds, 1900–1942*, National Bureau of Economic Research Technical Paper 3 (New York: National Bureau of Economic Research, 1942), especially charts showing yield curves for individual years from 1900 to 1942.

CHART 2   TERM STRUCTURE OF INTEREST RATES: MARCH 1958 AND AUGUST 1959

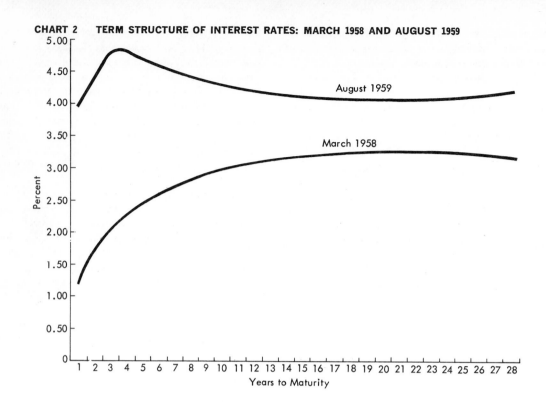

creased credit demands, combined with a rather restrictive Federal Reserve policy, had caused a considerable rise in interest rates generally. Short-term rates had risen sharply from their recession lows. However, the rate structure in August 1959 rose quite sharply from about 3.80 percent for the shortest term securities to about 4.85 percent at a maturity of about 2½ years and declined steadily thereafter to a level of slightly over 4 percent for the longest term securities.[9]

It seems likely that the tendency for the shortest term interest rates to remain below the rates on intermediate-term securities, even when rates rise to relatively high levels, is due to the existence of important groups of investors who are strongly interested in liquidity. For example, nonfinancial corporations have become an important factor in the Government securities market in recent years. Corporate treasurers have become increasingly sophisticated in managing their cash positions so as to economize on cash balances and earn interest by investing in Treasury bills and other short-term Government securities.[10]

These investors seldom invest in anything but quite short-term securities because of their aversion to price variability, since the funds invested are, in effect, transactions balances which may be needed on short notice to make payments.[11] Commercial banks are also interested in short-term Governments, which constitute the bulk of their secondary reserves. Foreign accounts and State and local governments have become increasingly important investors in Governments. Like nonfinancial corporations, these groups of investors, being interested chiefly in liquidity, do not ordinarily speculate on changes in security prices and therefore concentrate their holdings in the short-term sector regardless of interest rate expectations.[12] The fact that all of these investor

---

[9] A similar pattern made its appearance in 1956 when monetary policy became restrictive and persisted through most of 1957 until the trend of monetary policy was reversed to counter the recession late in that year.

[10] Corporations also invest their surplus funds in open market commercial paper and in repurchase

agreements with Government security dealers. However, short-term governments are by far the most important outlet for their funds. See C. E. Silberman, "The Big Corporate Lenders," *Fortune* (August 1956).

[11] On the theoretical aspects of the management of transactions balances, see James Tobin, "The Interest-Elasticity of Transactions Demand for Cash," *Review of Economics and Statistics*, Vol. XXXVIII (August 1956), pp. 241–47, and W. J. Baumol, "The Transactions Demand for Cash: An Inventory Theoretic Approach," *Quarterly Journal of Economics*, Vol. LXVI (November 1952), pp. 545–56.

[12] Of course, commercial banks do shift the composition of their portfolios of Government securities

groups added substantially to their holdings of Government securities between mid-1958 and mid-1959 suggests that their activities may have served to moderate the rise in interest rates in the shortest maturity range and thus have been mainly responsible for the failure of short-term

---

in accordance with changing interest rate expectations. But, as far as their secondary reserves are concerned, they tend to maintain large holdings in the short-term sector under most circumstances.

interest rates to rise more than they did. If a restrictive monetary policy continues to be applied, it may become necessary at a later time for some of these investor groups to liquidate their holdings of short-term Governments in order to finance expenditures or to meet loan demands (in the case of commercial banks). If and when this happens, short-term rates may rise sharply, thus producing the sort of downward-sloping yield curve which characterized prosperous periods in earlier times.

THE CHANGING VIEWS ON DEBT MANAGEMENT*

William E. Laird

In the period before the Great Depression debt management was not a topic of active controversy. There was virtual unanimity regarding the elements of "sound" debt management policy and very little debt to manage. An interesting similarity of opinion was observed among academic economists and between the economists and the Treasury.

The events of the 1930s and 1940s created problems for the Treasury; the prolonged depression and the demands of war finance resulted in a greatly expanded federal debt which led the Treasury to retreat from its older and simpler precepts of debt management. Some observers were concerned about the debt and the possibility that it might permanently lay to rest independent and flexible monetary policy. Economists set about reconsidering their views on the relationships of debt management, monetary policy, and economic stabilization. The revision of Treasury policy did not coincide with the advance of the newer doctrines. Academic economists disagreed among themselves, and usually they disagreed with the Treasury. Conflicting policy positions developed; proponents described them as sound, and they were judged by various standards to contribute to stability.

Currently there is some dispute about every major aspect of debt management. This paper delineates the changing views on debt management, contrasts the older views with the various newer concepts of policy, and points out the cur-

rent, and very significant, divergence of thought on debt policy.

OLDER VIEWS ON DEBT MANAGEMENT

In the pre-Keynesian, pre-fiscal policy era the benchmark of sound finance was to be found in the concept, and practice, of funding the debt. Short-term or floating debt was not looked upon with favor by the Treasury, and sound policy avoided excessive reliance on shorter-term securities. The objectives of debt policy were all related to these fundamental principles of debt management. Important advantages were seen to accrue from funding the debt and minimizing reliance on floating debt. A longer debt was less likely to expose the Treasury to the mercy of the market, since the Treasury would face fewer holders of maturing debt at any one time. The Treasury would not be tied so closely to the market, and shifts in the market would not be so serious from the Treasury's point of view. Refinancings could be smaller with longer debt. Also, a funded debt could more easily be adapted to plans for debt retirement, and debt retirement was considered a worthy endeavor.

Treasury policy was concerned with the interest burden of the debt, but the Treasury contemplated neither a program of inflation to cope with the debt nor extensive reliance on floating debt. Interest costs were to be kept down by retirement and by refinancing at lower rates.

Pre-Keynesian Treasury policy did not relate debt management to the cycle; neither did pre-Keynesian writers on public finance and debt management. One may observe the interesting

* From *Quarterly Review of Economics and Business*, Vol. III (Autumn 1963), pp. 7–17. Reprinted by permission of the publisher and the author. William E. Laird is Professor of Economics, Florida State University.

similarity of academic view and Treasury policy. Shirras writes:

> It is therefore necessary to reduce the floating debt within manageable proportions, so that it can never be a source of great danger. It is better to borrow for a long time and to pay a higher rate of interest than to be perpetually at the mercy of holders of Treasury bills for repayment.[1]

C. F. Bastable's earlier statement is similar.

> As a general principle of finance it is unquestionable that the floating debt should be kept within the narrowest limits possible. . . . A growth of floating charges is at best a mark of weakness in the treatment of the state liabilities. . . . The great evil of a floating debt is its uncertainty.[2]

Others, including Henry C. Adams, had expressed similar views.[3]

Academic opinion favored debt retirement. It was judged to strengthen the national credit, to facilitate further borrowing should the need arise, and to increase the capital available for industrial growth. Debt reduction increased confidence and gave a favorable tone to government finance.

THE GREAT DEPRESSION, WORLD WAR II, AND AFTER

The Great Depression intensified interest in economic stabilization. Full employment and stability became virtually synonymous, and as a policy goal full employment had no peer. While monetary policy, interpreted as interest rate policy, was relegated to a position of insignificance, fiscal policy emerged as the new and respected tool of analysis and policy. As the Depression lengthened, more attention was paid to this newly discovered weapon. Fiscal deficits became more than respectable. In certain groups deficits were considered the principal defense against secular stagnation.

As pump-priming shaded into compensatory finance, with deficits becoming more a rule than an exception, the growth of the debt appeared certain. Active compensatory finance had as its adjunct a growing federal debt, which would almost inevitably become a problem in its own right, as debt must be managed in some fashion. Since it was widely assumed that money was

impotent, monetary policy would increasingly be directed toward "managing the debt." It was assumed that in any monetary policy–debt management conflict, debt would win.

It was World War II rather than the Depression which brought the monetary policy–debt management conflict to the surface, and for a while it appeared that the war debt had completely submerged the final traces of monetary policy. At the end of the war there seemed to be relatively little enthusiasm for ending the Federal Reserve's bond support program. Opinion within the Reserve System gradually solidified against the policy, and the Treasury reluctantly consented to ending the program.

About the time of the Accord, analysis had begun turning to a more sophisticated reinterpretation of classical and neoclassical economics and policy measures tended to reflect this development. Economic stability remained an important objective while discussion and analysis turned to the pressing question of means to attain that end.

It was difficult to ignore the role of liquidity in the postwar inflation and attention was turned to that vast conglomeration of liquid assets, the federal debt. In an era preoccupied with stabilization it is not surprising that any controllable sector in the economy that showed promise as a tool of policy came under consideration. Post-Accord discussion pointed to the possibility of the debt contributing to the goal.

THE DEBT MANAGEMENT CONTROVERSY

The Countercyclical Approach

Post-Accord discussion relating debt management to economic stabilization, although a break with tradition, was not entirely without precedent. One version of stabilization via debt had been forcefully presented some years earlier by Henry Simons, at a time (1944) when few were prepared for such a view of the debt.[4]

STABILIZATION VIA COMPOSITION OF DEBT INCLUDING MONEY

Simons recognized the debt as exerting an influence on economic stability, and he believed the real danger of the debt to be inflation. Understanding the climate of opinion of the postwar

---

[1] G. Findlay Shirras, *Science of Public Finance*, Vol. 2 (3rd ed.; London: Macmillan, 1936), p. 799.

[2] C. F. Bastable, *Public Finance* (3rd ed.; London: Macmillan, 1903), pp. 694–95.

[3] Henry C. Adams, *Public Debts, An Essay in the Science of Finance* (New York: D. Appleton, 1893), p. 148.

[4] Henry C. Simons, "On Debt Policy," *Journal of Political Economy*, Vol. 52, No. 4 (December, 1944).

years, he foresaw the inflation to come and stated quite specifically in 1946 that "we probably shall have, in the near future, no substantial protection against inflation save that which debt policy affords."[5]

In 1944, he had clearly linked debt policy to economic stabilization. Conceiving of debt to be either paper money or consols (having neither call nor maturity features), he prescribed a simple rule of action. "The rule for policy as to consols and currency, that is, the *composition* of the debt including money, is simply stabilization of the value of money."[6] The correct combination depends upon the particular circumstances of the time. "Converting money into consols is an anti-inflation measure; converting consols into money is a reflationary or anti-deflation measure. . . ."[7]

Should inflation be the problem, the appropriate action is to sell consol bonds—convert money into consols—which reduces liquidity in the economy, retards spending, and stabilizes the price level. With the economy under deflationary pressure the contrary action is appropriate. Simons assumed that actions taken to stabilize the price level work automatically toward stabilizing the economy. Thus, price level stability provided a clear and serviceable criterion of performance.

Within his framework it is proper for the Treasury to pursue that policy indicated by the general condition of the economy regardless of interest cost. In fact, *within that framework* it is legitimate to say that the Treasury should pay as much interest as possible. Since transactions would take place in a competitive market and be subject to a price level stabilization rule, maximizing interest payments is equivalent to saying "pay only enough to achieve the goal."

Several comments about Simons' debt policy are in order. First of all, there is some logic to the position that Simons actually had no debt policy in the conventional sense, but rather merely translated his monetary policy into the language of the federal debt. His debt policy is contained in the opening sentence of "On Debt Policy." "I have never seen any sense in an elaborate structure of federal debt."[8] His debt policy

per se consists of transforming all federal debt into pure consol bonds. His program is directed toward assuring that the proper quantity of money will be in circulation. He proposes counter-cyclical monetary policy couched in terms of the federal debt. It may be no more than simple semantic exercise to discuss his concept of countercyclical debt management, as he is actually taking the back door to a flexible monetary policy and merely emphasizing the point that the size of the debt is of secondary importance. A more conventional or "front door" approach would speak explicitly in terms of the money supply and its variations. At the time Simons wrote, fear of the large federal debt was effectively frustrating any real control of the money supply. By approaching the stabilization problem in this unusual fashion, he apparently was attempting to free monetary policy by abating fears of the federal debt. Essentially, he was expressing confidence that the federal debt would not crush the economy while warning that continued fear of the debt would lead to an inflation of the price level. He struck at the debt phobia then existing by posing the alternatives of inflation or interest payments.

STABILIZATION VIA CONVENTIONAL DEBT COMPOSITION (EXCLUDING MONEY)

In 1954 the Committee for Economic Development published a study entitled *Managing the Federal Debt*, which clearly related debt management to economic stabilization, as the following statement shows:

Debt management is important primarily because it affects the economic stability of the country—whether we have high employment and economic growth and price stability, or inflation or depression. The main test of debt management is whether it contributes as much as it can to stability of employment and production at a high and rising level without inflation.[9]

According to the CED approach, the composition of the debt is to be varied in a generally countercyclical manner, with the Treasury operating in long-, intermediate-, and short-term debt. A great variety of debt is to be utilized, excluding money. The CED does not conceive of debt management influencing the *size* of the debt, nor the supply of money; those items are classified as "budget policy" and "monetary policy." Consistent with

[5] Henry C. Simons, "Debt Policy and Banking Policy," *Review of Economic Statistics,* Vol. 28, No. 2 (May 1946), pp. 85–89. Reprinted in his *Economic Policy for a Free Society* (Chicago: University of Chicago Press, 1948), p. 235.

[6] Henry C. Simons, "On Debt Policy," *loc. cit.,* p. 223.

[7] Ibid.

[8] Ibid., p. 220.

[9] Committee for Economic Development, *Managing the Federal Debt* (New York, 1954), pp. 13–14.

the current institutional arrangements, debt policy determines only the composition of the debt.

The Treasury is to sell long-term securities in boom periods in order to reduce liquidity in the economy, thus contributing to stability. Short-term highly liquid securities are to be sold during deflationary periods in order to increase the over-all liquidity of the economy. There is a minor qualification to the general policy. The CED retains some of the classical flavor in that it favors longer debt; lengthening the debt (at least in 1954), or selling long-term, gives a more "desirable debt structure."[10]

Interest costs would not be minimized, as higher-yielding long-term securities would be sold in larger quantities just at the times when these rates would tend to be highest. It is conceded that interest costs are important, "but reducing the interest cost of the debt is only a secondary objective, to be pursued insofar as it is consistent with a debt policy that conforms to the needs of economic stability."[11] The policy obviously breaks with the older views.

Debt policy is viewed as a potentially valuable supplement to conventional monetary and fiscal policies, not as a substitute for them. Ideally monetary, fiscal, and debt management policies would be coordinated. It is argued that debt policy can increase the flexibility and range of influence of fiscal and monetary policy.

It is worth stressing that the CED position is the antithesis of Simons' policy position on the structure of the debt. Unlike Simons the CED pictures the *structure* of the debt changing in a countercyclical fashion but the *size* of the debt not changing so far as debt policy itself is concerned. Simons pictures the *structure* of the debt remaining unchanged during all phases of the cycle, but the absolute *size* of the debt varying in a countercyclical manner, being simply the reflection of flexible monetary policy. Simons carefully avoids the uncertainties associated with Treasury near-moneys, whereas the CED policy proposal is based on a flexible use of near-moneys in order to influence total spending. What Simons eliminates from consideration, the CED converts into a policy instrument. Whereas Simons views short- and intermediate-term government debt as creating intolerable monetary uncertainty and

economic instability, the CED views such debt as an instrument of stabilization policy.

STABILIZATION VIA DEBT SIZE AND COMPOSITION

In 1957 Earl Rolph developed another system of countercyclical debt management.[12] His system in a sense combines the Simons and CED approaches in that it involves the manipulation of the size of the debt *as well as* the composition of the debt. He states:

Our first main proposition is that an increase in the size of the net debt of a national government, given the debt composition, has the effect of *decreasing*, and a decrease in the net debt has the effect of *increasing* GNP expenditures. It is elementary that the sale of government securities by a central bank is a deflationary policy. We simply generalize this observation to sales of government debt by any official agency.

The defense of this proposition is identical with the defense of monetary policy.

. . . . . .

A shift in the composition of an outstanding public debt of a given size that reduces its average maturity increases private expenditures, and vice versa for increases in its average maturity. Like any empirical generalization, this proposition does not hold for all circumstances.[13]

Debt policy is to operate in a countercyclical manner; during recession periods the size of the debt as well as its term may be reduced. Both of these debt operations would tend to increase the over-all liquidity of the economy. With inflationary pressures the size of the debt as well as its term might be increased.[14] Debt management may be viewed as the purchase of illiquidity.

Obviously such a policy is consistent with the

---

[10] The CED thinks that debt can become "too short" and states that "every opportunity to lengthen the debt without seriously affecting economic stability should be taken." This longer debt "would contribute to stability." Ibid., pp. 23–24.

[11] Ibid., p. 14.

[12] Earl Rolph, "Principles of Debt Management," *American Economic Review,* Vol. 47, No. 3 (June, 1957), pp. 302–20.

[13] Ibid., pp. 305–8. A very similar statement of policy is made by Richard A. Musgrave. "A given degree of restriction [stabilization] may be obtained through various combinations of public debt differing in composition and total amount. The problem, then, is to find that combination which secures the desired degree of restriction at least cost." *The Theory of Public Finance* (New York: McGraw-Hill, 1959), p. 601.

[14] As originally presented by Rolph, the scheme involved a unique solution to debt management policy and interest minimization. However, this involved a minor slip in logic and proved untrue. Multiple possibilities are present rather than one single solution. For purposes at hand this is of little significance and will not be pursued.

debt growing either larger or smaller, and either longer or shorter, depending upon secular tendencies in the economy. Unlike the CED, Rolph does not appear to have any particular preference for longer-term debt. There is no single correct composition of the debt. What is correct depends on the circumstances of the economy; thus what is correct now may be mischievous at a later date.

In Rolph's system interest is minimized only in the sense that an efficient stabilization policy is pursued. For a given amount of stabilization the lowest cost combination of debt size and structure is chosen. Interest is minimized relative to the stabilization goal.

While the Rolph system of policy is a hybrid of sorts, it is worthwhile to point out briefly the contrast with the CED and Simons. Rolph would vary the *size* of the debt in the same manner as Simons, but he violates Simon's debt structure rule by using alleged near-moneys.

Thus three variations on the countercyclical debt management theme are found. These positions in part conflict with, and in part reinforce, one another. Yet they are only part of the debt management controversy. Two important positions remain to be discussed.

The Pro-Cyclical Approach to Stabilization

Most prominent among those taking the pro-cyclical approach to stabilization are United States Treasury spokesmen. The Treasury position is of interest for two significant reasons. First, the Treasury is actually in charge of debt management operations. Second, Treasury policy is in sharp contrast with the countercyclical approaches just discussed.

Treasury experts believe that debt management can most effectively contribute to economic stabilization by following policies that will allow those directly charged with stabilization to pursue vigorous and appropriate countercyclical programs. The debt should be managed so as to minimize interference with responsible monetary policy. Treasury spokesmen assert that the difficulties involved in debt management make the debt best considered a problem in itself, capable of generating substantial difficulties for the government and the market if not properly handled. Poor debt management operations are capable of creating instability in the economy. They do not view countercyclical debt management favorably, believing that it would accentuate the stabilization problem through a build-up of short-term debt over time and would greatly increase costs.[15]

Treasury authorities do not contemplate debt management as influencing the money supply, but regard that as the proper power of the Federal Reserve System. This view reflects the contemporary division of existing powers and the Treasury's acceptance of this institutional arrangement.

Treasury policy directly contradicts countercyclical debt management. The Treasury "tailors the debt to the market," which in practice has meant that longer-term issues have been offered during periods of recession and shorter-term issues during prosperous times. Obviously this results in liquidity restriction during periods of recession and liquidity ease during more prosperous times. This considered by itself is obviously pro-cyclical and antagonistic to the previously discussed positions. However, spokesmen argue that this policy is the most practical policy to follow in stabilizing the economy, because this allows the Treasury to maintain a longer debt and thus lessen the danger of debt management interfering with monetary policy. Absence of the Treasury from the market as much as possible gives the Federal Reserve more latitude in executing its policies. Treasury policy contributes "to the amount of free time which the Federal Reserve has to take effective monetary action without always having to be concerned with a new issue of securities which is still in the process of being lodged with the eventual holders of the securities."[16] The Treasury's continued presence in the market might bias the Federal Reserve toward an easier monetary policy than it would otherwise follow.

The policy of tailoring new securities to the particular needs of the market enables the Treasury to secure necessary funds at lower cost than would otherwise be possible. The Treasury has a practical political interest in lowering the interest burden of the debt, and officials believe that countercyclical debt management would greatly

---

[15] A reasonably good statement of Treasury policy in recent years can be found in U.S. Congress, Joint Economic Committee, *Employment, Growth, and Price Levels*, Part 6C, *The Government's Management of Its Monetary, Fiscal, and Debt Operations* (86th Cong., 1st sess., 1959).

[16] Remarks by Secretary of the Treasury Anderson, April 7, 1958, at the opening of the "Share in America" savings bonds campaign, New York City, New York. Reprinted in the *Annual Report of the Secretary of the Treasury for the Fiscal Year Ended June 30, 1958* (Washington, D.C.: U.S. Government Printing Office, 1959), p. 263.

increase interest costs. "Economical borrowing is an important goal of Treasury debt management."[17] This is not doctrinaire interest minimization. "The goal of holding down interest cost on the public debt, although important, does not take precedence over other major goals of debt management."[18] On the other hand, Treasury authorities assert that such policies as the CED recommends would significantly increase interest costs.

Thus, lengthening the debt and minimizing interest costs are both important goals of Treasury policy. These goals are reconciled in the Treasury's tailoring procedures. This tailoring is, in principle, destabilizing in its impact on the economy. Yet officials insist that this policy aids in stabilizing the economy because it lessens the danger of debt management disrupting monetary policy. They conclude that Treasury policy is in practice a program for economic stability and that the opposite policies in practice would be destabilizing, costly, and impractical.

It is apparent that on the policy level the Treasury spokesmen are in direct conflict with the proponents of countercyclical debt management, although both relate debt management to the cycle and to problems of economic stabilization. The policies border on being black and white contrasts, yet their proponents declare them both practical and stabilizing.

The Treasury has retreated somewhat from the simpler precepts of classical debt management. Policies have changed, but much of the old lies beneath the surface of the new. Older precepts did not relate debt operations to the cycle, and they laid greater stress on funding than does present Treasury policy. On the other hand, the current policy definitely retains a bias in favor of longer-term debt. Treasury policy has not departed entirely from the older views, but there has been a change in emphasis and mood. Some believe expediency has come to play a larger role.

Warren Smith develops a debt policy along unmistakably pro-cyclical lines,[19] thus, in effect,

defending the essential aspects of Treasury policy: Long-term securities would be sold during recession periods to take maximum advantage of low interest rates. As interest rates rose during periods of expansion, the Treasury would gradually shift to the short-term market. The advantage is to minimize the interference of the Treasury's debt management operations with freedom of action by the Federal Reserve during periods of inflation and/or tight credit. Debt lengthening during recessions would reduce the frequency of the Treasury's presence in the market. Smith states that this approach would require a concomitant flexible monetary policy. If debt managers overshoot the mark in raising long-term funds during a recession, with the result that recovery is impeded, the Federal Reserve should be prepared for offsetting action.

Smith attacks countercyclical debt policy as "mystical." He argues that shifts in debt length do not significantly affect the liquidity of the debt and that "neither the interest rate nor the liquidity effects of marginal changes in the debt structure appear to be very important."[20] Treasury spokesmen often imply that such shifts are important. Smith opposes using liquidity shifts for stabilization and states that "to the extent that such changes do have a net effect on the public's aggregate spending, it would appear that similar effects could be produced by the use of monetary policy. For this reason, it is difficult to see what can be accomplished by contracyclical debt management policy that cannot be accomplished more efficiently by Federal Reserve monetary policy."[21] Further, such a policy would tend to maximize interest costs.

Smith explicitly recognizes the existing debt as an automatic stabilizer, whereas this is largely implicit in the Treasury position. He also clearly states that the benefits of maintaining the debt (rather than inflating it away) must be weighed against the cost of the debt. Treasury officials have said little about this.

Thus the Treasury is not alone in defending pro-cyclical debt management. However, the Treasury's theorists and academic supporters appear subject to the criticism that there is no questioning of the Federal Reserve's ability (or willingness) to adapt monetary policy quickly and accurately to unmeasurable liquidity shifts within the debt. This is of particular interest

[17] U.S. Congress, Joint Economic Committee, *Employment, Growth, and Price Levels*, Part 6C, p. 1723.

[18] Ibid., pp. 1723–24.

[19] Warren L. Smith, *Debt Management in the United States*, Study Paper No. 19 for The Joint Economic Committee; materials prepared in connection with the Study of Employment, Growth, and Price Levels (86th Cong., 2d sess., 1960). Herbert Stein also defends pro-cyclical policy. In doing so he clearly distinguishes between debt length and temporal structure and calls for careful control of the

amount of debt coming due in any year. "Managing the Federal Debt," *Journal of Law and Economics*, Vol. 1 (October, 1958).

[20] Smith, *op. cit.*, p. 8.

[21] Ibid.

in light of the apparently divergent assumptions regarding the importance of such shifts.

The advocates of pro-cyclical management in the Treasury and their academic supporters constitute another major division of the debt management controversy. They disagree with the proponents of countercyclical debt management, and the final faction in the controversy disagrees with both groups.

The third and most recent major group taking part in the debt management controversy sets forth a debt policy which is neither countercyclical nor pro-cyclical, but rather aims at "neutrality" and tends to stress the simplification of debt operations. This position divorces debt management policy from the cycle.

The Neutrality Doctrine

Milton Friedman, representative of the neutrality position, in 1959 published *A Program for Monetary Stability*. He set forth the view that our main need regarding debt management is "to simplify and streamline, in such a manner as to keep debt operations from themselves being a source of instability, and to ease the task of coordinating Treasury debt operations and [Federal] Reserve open market operations."[22] Debt operations should be "regular in timing, reasonably stable in amount, and predictable in form."[23] Friedman would reduce the variety of debt instruments, retaining the tap issues (savings bonds) plus two standard debt forms, a short-term (possibly 90-day) bill and a moderately long-term security (8 to 10 years). Both of these securities would be sold at regular and frequent intervals, and amounts would be kept reasonably stable as a policy goal.

Friedman is critical of the Treasury's tailoring, which he states has resulted in

a bewildering maze of securities of different maturities and terms, and lumpiness and discontinuity in debt operations, with refunding of major magnitude occurring on a few dates in the year. Instead of proceeding at a regular pace and in a standard way to which the market could adjust, debt management operations have been jerky, full of expedients and surprises, and unpredictable in their impact and outcome. As a result they have been a continuing source of monetary uncertainty and instability.[24]

Tailoring is also criticized on the grounds that in reality it does not lower costs and that it implies that the government is more efficient than the market in the conduct of a particular class of financial operations. Friedman rejects this notion.

He also points out that interest minimization is more complex than the Treasury assumes because "it is necessary to take into account not only interest-bearing debt but also non-interest-bearing debt—Treasury currency and Federal Reserve notes and Federal Reserve deposits."[25] If the debt is made longer and thereby less liquid, it can be reduced in size without inflationary pressures appearing.

It is difficult if not impossible in the present state of knowledge to predict whether one or another pattern of securities will involve or did involve lower costs, correctly interpreted; hence there is no real basis for judging or improving performance.[26]

Friedman takes the position that minor changes in the length of the debt have only slight influence on the demand for money; hence, changes in the length of the debt are not viewed as a promising tool of stabilization policy. He points out that "shifts in maturity add nothing to open market operations." Furthermore, open market operations seem "likely to be more consistent and predictable in . . . impact."[27] Thus debt management operations, in the strict sense, are not technically good instruments for economic stabilization activity. Countercyclical debt management is rejected.

Tilford C. Gaines develops a position similar in some respects to Friedman's, stating that neutrality should be the object of policy and that Treasury operations should be put on a more orderly basis. Debt operations should be on a routine basis, and the amount of securities offered at any time carefully controlled relative to the market's absorptive capacity. This policy would tend to stabilize the liquidity of the debt and introduce greater certainty into the market. Gaines argues that lengthening the debt "whenever possible" (tailoring) creates a great deal of uncertainty about Treasury operations and tends to disturb the market. Tailoring is a "massive source of instability in the capital market,"[28] and has probably involved added costs because

---

[22] Milton Friedman, *A Program for Monetary Stability* (New York: Fordham University Press, 1959), p. 60.

[23] Ibid., p. 65.

[24] Ibid., p. 60.

[25] Ibid., p. 62.

[26] Ibid.

[27] Ibid., p. 61.

[28] T. C. Gaines, *Techniques of Treasury Debt Management* (New York: The Free Press of Glencoe, 1962), p. 266. See especially Chapter 8.

of higher interest rates associated with uncertainty. Further, it tends to make debt operations work counter to monetary policy. Countercyclical debt policy is also rejected because of the inadequate present state of technical knowledge. It is not deemed feasible.

This analysis divorces debt management from the cycle and advocates leaving stabilization to monetary policy, which is judged technically better and more appropriate for that purpose. It argues that debt policy should be based upon simplicity, regularity, and predictability. Both pro-cyclical and countercyclical policies are rejected as inappropriate. The neutrality approach conflicts with the other positions and differs from the classical precepts which stressed funding and interest minimization. It is reminiscent of the classical attitude, however, as debt management is not related to the cycle, and it has a tone of simplicity and certainty. Still, neutrality remains a distinct policy differing from the older and conflicting with the newer views.

CONCLUDING REMARKS

Before the Great Depression and World War II there was virtual unanimity regarding the elements of "sound" debt policy, and there could be observed a striking similarity of opinion among academic economists and between the economists and the Treasury. Events since that time have shattered this picture, and there is now much disagreement over what constitutes sound policy.

At the present time three general positions are recognizable, and there is some divergence of thought within each of the basic categories. These can be termed *countercyclical* (Simons, the CED, and Rolph), *pro-cyclical* (the Treasury and Smith), and *neutral* (Friedman and Gaines). All of these positions diverge in some degree from, or conflict with, the older views.

The newer positions are clearly in basic conflict with one another and tend to rest on con-

tradictory assumptions regarding the nature of the stabilization problem and the technical impact of debt operations. They reflect basic disagreement about (1) the importance of interest minimization, (2) the best way to secure lowest cost on debt operations, (3) the relevant sense in which interest is to be minimized, (4) what constitutes a desirable or sound temporal structure for the debt, (5) how frequently debt operations should be carried on, (6) how long the debt should be, and (7) the technical impact of changes in debt length.

There is even more disagreement than indicated here, because the topic of institutional reorganization has not been considered. There is disagreement regarding the necessity and/or desirability of changing our institutional framework, and of course a number of plans are suggested. Hence, there is even disagreement as to *who* should manage the debt.

It is obvious that the debt management controversy has many sides, and there seems to be some dispute regarding every major aspect of debt management at the present time. This controversy is one facet of the more general stabilization debate that arose in the 1930s and the 1940s. That debate continues today in a somewhat abated form, although the area of disagreement seems to have narrowed, and emphasis has again drifted toward classical and neoclassical interpretations. The debt controversy may yet follow the same pattern and work toward a more sophisticated reinterpretation of older doctrines. If that is the case, it is likely to mean the eventual triumph of the neutrality school of debt management. For that pattern of thought stressing simplicity and predictability and divorcing debt management from the cycle has much in common with earlier views, though it is more clearly and explicitly formulated and differs somewhat in emphasis. Its eventual impact may well be to bring the old views up to date on such topics as debt length, interest minimization, and debt structure.

chapter 6

INTERNATIONAL FINANCE

The selections included in this book up to this point have been concerned with the theoretical aspects and policy issues involved in the use of monetary and fiscal policy in an environment from which problems of foreign trade and the balance of international payments have been excluded. In other words, in the jargon of the economist, we have been discussing a "closed economy."

In reality, of course, the U.S. economy is closely linked to that of the rest of the world. In 1972, for example, our exports of goods and services amounted to $74 billion, while our imports came to $78 billion. Although each of these totals amounted to less than 7 percent of U.S. GNP, imported consumer goods are a significant element in our high standard of living, while both imported raw materials and export markets for our products are of major importance to some of our industries. Moreover, since most of our trading partners are less self-sufficient and more dependent on foreign trade than we are, our trade is more important to the rest of the world than it is to us. In addition to our trade relations, our financial markets are closely linked to the financial markets of other countries through a complex network of international borrowing and lending activities.

As a result of these trade and financial ties, our prosperity is affected by economic developments occurring in other countries and by policies followed by other governments. And the converse is true, perhaps in even greater degree: since trade with the United States is of major importance to many other countries, economic developments here and the policies we follow will often have a major impact on the prosperity of the rest of the world.

The way in which economic impulses are transmitted from one country to another and the nature of the resulting interdependence that exists among countries depends to a considerable extent on the structure of the international monetary system—that is, the complex web of rules and arrangements governing financial relations among countries. From early 1947 until the beginning of 1973, world trade was based on a financial system which had its origins in the Bretton

Woods Conference of 1944, at which the International Monetary Fund (IMF) was established. This system bore some resemblance to the so-called gold exchange standard that was developed in the 1920s, under which participating countries held their reserves partly in gold and partly in national currencies— such as the dollar and sterling—which were themselves freely convertible into gold. The gold exchange standard proved to be unstable, and under pressures of the Great Depression in the early 1930s, it broke down completely as a result of speculative movements of funds induced by fears of currency devaluation. The result was nearly a decade of international monetary chaos which helped to spread depression throughout the world and brought a drastic decline in world trade. The Bretton Woods system contained features designed to prevent a repetition of the international financial disaster of the 1930s, and the strength of the system is most clearly reflected in the vigorous growth and prosperity of the world economy and the rapid expansion of international trade that occurred during the quarter century following its establishment. But with the passage of time certain problems with the system became increasingly apparent, and its future is in doubt as of this writing since the convertibility of dollars into gold which was a fundamental part of the system was suspended by the United States in 1971 in response to massive short-term capital outflows; and in February, 1973, eight of the European participants decided to let their currencies float jointly against the dollar, while maintaining fixed rates among themselves. Such an arrangement is, of course, inconsistent with the Bretton Woods system, which was based on fixed exchange rates among all currencies. However, work is beginning on the construction of a new system which seems likely to evolve along the lines of the Bretton Woods plan. While this work is only in its preliminary stages, so that it is impossible to say precisely how the new system will differ from the old, there is a good deal of opinion that it will be basically a fixed-rate system, although there undoubtedly will be somewhat more scope for exchange-rate flexibility than there was under the former plan.

The first selection in this chapter, which is taken from the 1969 *Annual Report of the Council of Economic Advisers,* analyzes the working of the Bretton Woods system, points out its strengths and weaknesses, and discusses various proposals for reforming the system to make it serve the world's needs more effectively. This article was written before the currency crises of the early 1970s resulted in the abandonment of fixed rates between all currencies in favor of the arrangement mentioned above in which a bloc of European currencies (plus some others) float against the dollar. In view of the fact that preliminary work is beginning on a new system which seems likely to be based on fixed rates, however, the problems of the Bretton Woods system, and possible solutions to those problems, are still of considerable interest. The selection by the Council of Economic Advisers classifies these problems under three headings:

1. The *liquidity problem* arises because in a growing world economy with essentially fixed exchange parities among national currencies, there is need for a growing stock of international monetary reserves to enable countries to finance balance-of-payments deficits during the period while underlying corrective forces are working to eliminate the deficits in an orderly way. At the present time monetary reserves are held in the form of gold and so-called reserve currencies, supplemented by rights to borrow from the IMF. For various reasons, there is no way to control the creation of reserves in these forms to ensure that reserves will grow in pace with the world's needs for them.

2. The *confidence problem* arises primarily because of fear that a country experiencing a persistent balance-of-payments deficit will exhaust its supply of international monetary reserves and will be forced to devalue its currency in order to eliminate its deficit. Devaluation (a reduction of the exchange parity of one national currency relative to other currencies) is permitted in some circumstances under the IMF rules. Countries are, however, very reluctant to devalue; at the same time, if a devaluation should occur, holders of the currency that is devalued may make large profits if they are foresighted enough to anticipate the devaluation and transfer their funds into another currency before it occurs. Waves of such speculative activity are the objective manifestation of the confidence problem.

3. The *adjustment problem* arises because there are only a limited number of actions that a country experiencing a balance-of-payments deficit can take to eliminate the deficit, and all of these actions may under some circumstances be either unpleasant for the country involved or undesirable from the standpoint of world economic efficiency. A similar statement can be made, with some qualifications, with respect to the actions required to eliminate a balance-of-payments surplus. In a sense, the inherent logic of a system of essentially fixed exchange rates calls for a country experiencing a deficit to adopt restrictive fiscal and monetary policies to moderate the growth of income and put downward pressure on prices. Such policies will retard imports and encourage exports, thereby working to correct the deficit. Conversely, a country experiencing a balance-of-payments surplus should adopt expansionary fiscal and monetary policies. The trouble with this kind of prescription is that it often puts pressure on countries to accept either more unemployment or more inflation than they judge to be desirable for domestic reasons. As a consequence, serious conflicts sometimes arise between the policies needed to achieve domestic objectives and those called for by the balance of payments.

As a means of dealing with the liquidity problem, steps have been taken to create a new form of international reserve asset, the so-called Special Drawing Right (SDR). The SDR plan, which is discussed in the selection from the 1969 Council Report, was formulated as an amendment to the IMF Articles of Agreement. The plan provides machinery for the creation of additional reserves in the form of SDR's (to supplement gold and reserve currencies) in the amounts deemed necessary to meet the requirements of a growing world economy.

In his paper, "The Bretton Woods System, Key Currencies, and the Recent Dollar Crises," Harry G. Johnson examines the evolution of the international monetary system in the postwar period in terms of both the political economy of its genesis and development, and the more technical aspects of its operation. While he uses the same problem categories that appeared in the article by the Council of Economic Advisers—the confidence problem, the liquidity problem, and the adjustment problem, plus one more, the possible bias toward deflation in the system—he provides new and provocative insights into their nature and relevance. Johnson takes a somewhat different point of view than the Council of Economic Advisers, arguing essentially that it is not a set of problems inherent in the system which led to its current difficulties, but rather the willingness of the other participants to let the dollar become the "key currency" in a system set up on the basis of presumed equality among members, and the subsequent decision of the United States to inflate at an unacceptable rate in the latter 1960s, which is the crux of the matter.

The paper by Warren L. Smith contends that the basic dilemma created by the Bretton Woods system is that the participating countries do not possess sufficient policy instruments to achieve simultaneously all of the goals that are implicit in the system, including domestic stability in each country, a viable balance-of-payments situation, maximum freedom of international trade, and fixed exchange parities among national currencies. The paper also attempts to indicate the directions that fundamental reform of the system might take. The discussion in this paper should, incidentally, help the student to answer a question that may have troubled him: Why is it that under an international monetary system with fixed exchange parities balance-of-payments problems are constantly arising, whereas within a country—such as the United States—exchange rates between regions are absolutely and permanently fixed (i.e., the same money is used throughout the country so that all exchange rates are equal to unity), but, far from worrying about regional balances of payments, we do not ordinarily even bother to calculate them?

The selection from the 1969 *Annual Report of the Council of Economic Advisers* and the Smith paper point up the basic dilemma that the international monetary system often poses for the authorities responsible for the formulation of monetary and fiscal policy: the policies needed to achieve domestic employment/price-stability objectives (i.e., to attain the desired point on the Phillips curve) may be different from those needed to maintain or restore equilibrium in the balance of payments.

In the course of history, this dilemma has often confronted the policy makers of most countries. In Britain, the authorities have almost always had to pay close attention to the balance of payments and the nation's gold reserves in formulating monetary and fiscal policies, and not infrequently balance-of-payments considerations have prevented the adoption of policies judged to be desirable from the standpoint of the domestic economy. For most other countries, the balance of payments has similarly constituted a constraint that has had to be taken into account in the formulation of monetary and fiscal policies. However, largely as a result of a series of lucky historical accidents, for many years prior to about 1958 the United States experienced either balance-of-payments surpluses and gold inflows or conditions in which other countries were eager to accept dollars in settlement of U.S. deficits. As a consequence, the United States was almost continuously in the favorable position of being able to use monetary and fiscal policies to achieve domestic goals without the necessity of worrying about its balance-of-payments position.

The United States has had a balance-of-payments deficit almost continuously since World War II. In the early and middle 1950s—the period of the so-called dollar shortage—other countries were eager to obtain dollars both to pay for desperately needed imports and to restore their war-depleted foreign exchange reserves, and, as a result, the U.S. deficits created no problems for us and no significant drains on our gold reserves. By 1958, however, the leading industrial countries had, partly as a result of U.S. aid, overcome the decline in their competitive positions caused by the war and were able to compete effectively in world markets. As a result of the improvement in their competitive strength, together with the restoration of their foreign exchange reserves, they were able to reestablish currency convertibility and dismantle most of their exchange controls.

After the restoration of currency convertibility, the United States continued to have balance-of-payments deficits—indeed, the deficits increased in size. At the same time, other countries, having restored their holdings of dollars to desired levels, became less willing to hold dollars and more inclined to convert portions of the added dollars resulting from continuing U.S. deficits into gold, thus reducing our gold stock. The continuing growth of foreign liquid dollar claims against the United States combined with the decline in the U.S. gold stock generated periodic fears that the United States would be forced to devalue the dollar, fears that finally became a reality in 1971. On several occasions this led to speculative shifts of funds from dollars into other currencies, thereby increasing our deficit still further.

Our problems were considerably complicated by the fact that from 1958 to 1965, and again in 1969, we were suffering from unemployment and inadequate aggregate demand. Normally, this would have called for expansionary fiscal and monetary policies. However, because of legislative delays, administrative inflexibility, and fear of budget deficits on the part of Congress and the public, it was difficult to implement a sufficiently expansionary fiscal policy—indeed, in the earlier episode, vigorous expansionary fiscal action was not taken until early 1964, when the tax cut discussed in Chapter 4 was enacted. Expansionary monetary policies—which might normally have been put into effect—were impeded by fear of their effects on the balance of payments. After the restoration of currency convertibility, international movements of capital—especially short-term funds—became increasingly sensitive to differentials in interest rates between countries. As a consequence, the United States was reluctant to adopt the vigorously expansionary monetary policy that our domestic unemployment situation called for, because the resulting decline in U.S. short-term rates would lead to a flow of short-term funds abroad, substantially increasing our deficit and indirectly accentuating the drain on our gold stock. In fact, this was precisely what happened in the 1969–70 period. Monetary policy was eased here in response to increasing stagnation of domestic activity, while in Europe monetary restraint continued to be applied. Thus, there developed a substantial spread between European and U.S. short-term rates in favor of Europe, and the result was a massive movement of short-term capital.

Of course, the United States has taken many measures other than adjustment of its monetary policies to reduce its balance-of-payments deficit. One of the sections of the selection from the 1969 *Annual Report of the Council of Economic Advisers* discusses the overall strategy employed in dealing with the balance-of-payments problem and outlines the specific measures that were taken to reduce the adverse balance-of-payments impact of our overseas military and foreign aid programs and to cut down capital outflows.

The sharp increase in U.S. defense spending which occurred in connection with the escalation of the Vietnam conflict in late 1965 had a number of direct and indirect effects on the U.S. balance of payments. The increase in military expenditures overseas added directly to the deficit. Moreover, the rapid expansion of aggregate internal demand caused by increased defense spending brought a sharp rise in incomes and prices. Rising incomes caused a sharp expansion of imports, while price increases weakened our competitive position in export markets. Accordingly, the U.S. merchandise trade surplus, which had risen to a peak of $6.8 billion in 1964 after a period of several years in which U.S. prices rose less than those in most other countries, began to dwindle as U.S. imports rose much more rapidly than exports. By 1968 the trade surplus had fallen to $0.6 billion. Income from growing U.S. investments abroad continued to increase, offsetting a portion of the deterioration of the trade surplus. Moreover, by 1968 the high profits in U.S. industry resulting from booming business activity, together with the high interest rates caused by heavy credit demands combined with a generally restrictive monetary policy, were sufficient to attract a large flow of foreign funds into the U.S. stock market and into interest-bearing U.S. debt obligations. In addition, restrictions on U.S. capital outflows through banks and business firms operating overseas were tightened up. As a result of these developments, the net capital outflow of earlier years was reversed; and, despite the deterioration of the trade balance, the overall U.S. balance of payments showed a modest surplus in 1968 and again in 1969, when almost $9 billion of short-term private capital flowed into the United States—both sharp reversals from the deficits of the preceding years. However, the situation changed drastically beginning in 1970. As the economy expanded in response to fiscal and monetary stimulus, merchandise imports rose from $36 billion in 1969 to about $54 billion in 1972, while exports changed from $36 billion in 1969 to only $47 billion in 1972. While income from private investments abroad rose by about $3.5 billion annually over the period, private long-term and (especially) short-term capital flowed out in massive amounts, leading to balance-of-payments deficits of almost $10 billion in 1970, almost $30 billion in 1971, and about $12 billion in 1972.

It may be noted that in most recent years—in marked contrast to the situation of 1961–65—there has been no serious conflict between the fiscal and monetary measures called for to achieve domestic targets for aggregate demand and those needed to achieve equilibrium in the U.S. balance of payments. In times of high levels of domestic activity, measures that succeed in restraining demand and the inflation rate will also slow down the growth of imports, and, by helping to improve our competitive position in foreign markets, lead to a better performance of U.S. exports. Whether the actual policies followed have been adequate is another question. Price inflation continues at a high level, and, as indicated, our trade balance has deteriorated dangerously.

It is possible to classify the situations in which conflicts do and do not exist between the monetary and fiscal policies called for by the domestic economic situation and those called for by the nation's balance-of-payments position. Such a classification is presented in the following table:

	Domestic Economic Situation	Balance-of-Payments Position	Type of Monetary and Fiscal Policies Called for by:		Overall Situation
			Domestic Economy	Balance of Payments	
Case I.........	Excessive unemployment	Deficit	Expansive	Restrictive	Conflict
Case II........	Excessive inflation	Deficit	Restrictive	Restrictive	No conflict
Case III........	Excessive unemployment	Surplus	Expansive	Expansive	No conflict
Case IV........	Excessive inflation	Surplus	Restrictive	Expansive	Conflict

Case I is the situation of the U.S. economy during the period 1961–65. Following 1965 we moved into a Case II situation, and have remained there in most recent years. There is another type of conflict situation (Case IV) that may arise: a country may experience domestic inflation, calling for restrictive monetary and fiscal measures, combined with a balance-of-payments surplus, correction of which requires expansionary measures. The German economy has often been in this position in recent years. The conclusion to be drawn is that while the policies required for internal and external stability are not always in conflict, such conflicts occur with sufficient frequency to make it impossible to depend on monetary and fiscal policies alone to maintain both internal and external stability.

One possibility that has sometimes been suggested is that countries that encounter conflicts between the requirements of internal and external stability attempt to accommodate these conflicts by making adjustments in the "mix" of monetary and fiscal policies employed. For example, a country faced simultaneously with domestic unemployment and a balance-of-payments deficit might take sufficiently expansionary fiscal action (by increasing government expenditures and/or reducing tax rates) to restore full employment, while at the same time taking restrictive monetary measures to raise domestic interest rates to high enough levels to attract a sufficient inflow of capital to cover the excess of imports over exports that would occur under full-employment conditions. This approach to the reconciliation of conflicts is discussed in Smith's paper and in the selection taken from the 1969 *Annual Report of the Council of Economic Advisers;* it is also analyzed in a somewhat more formal way in a paper by Robert A. Mundell which is reprinted in Chapter 7. While there is undoubtedly some limited possibility of using changes in the policy mix to deal with conflict situations, there are difficulties with this approach, several of which are discussed briefly in the selection from the 1969 Council Report. As a consequence, this approach can be relied upon only to a very limited extent.

Recent discussions of further reform of the international monetary system have generally focused primarily on the possibility of allowing somewhat greater flexibility of exchange rates. The extreme solution, which has a considerable number of advocates among economists, would be to allow exchange rates to fluctuate freely in response to changes in private demand and supply with no intervention by governments. In principle, this would completely eliminate the balance-of-payments problem, since exchange rates would automatically adjust in such a way as to keep payments in continuous equilibrium. For a variety of reasons, many students of international financial problems doubt the wisdom of such an extreme solution. As a consequence, a number of proposals have been advanced which would allow more flexibility of exchange rates than now exists without going all the way to completely flexible rates. The paper by Lawrence B. Krause contains an analysis of exchange rate adjustments and a catalog of various proposals that have been advanced. Some of the proposals are also appraised in the selection from the 1969 *Annual Report of the Council of Economic Advisers.* The Krause paper contains a discussion of one type of proposal, often referred to as the "gliding peg," which has a number of adherents. It may be noted that traditionally bankers and government officials have generally been strongly opposed to greater flexibility of exchange rates, arguing that generally fixed rates with only very infrequent adjustments create an atmosphere of certainty which is conducive to the expansion of internal trade. However, their unalterable opposition to increased exchange rate flexibility seems to have moderated somewhat recently as evidence of the instability of the present system has accumulated.

A development which is very likely to be of considerable importance for the international monetary system in the future is the formation of the European Economic Community and the intent of its members to develop a single currency system by the beginning of 1981. While the Community has declared itself to be committed to this goal, there are substantial obstacles and problems involved in achieving it. Richard N. Cooper examines these transitional problems in his paper "European Monetary Unification and the International Monetary System," and concludes with a discussion of the possible implications of such a development for the international monetary system.

PROBLEMS OF THE INTERNATIONAL MONETARY SYSTEM*

Council of Economic Advisers

THE BRETTON WOODS SYSTEM

The rapid growth in the world economy in the postwar period has been built on a greatly improved financial base. At the 1944 Bretton Woods Conference, the major industrial countries created through the IMF an international monetary system based on pegged exchange rates. The system has been strengthened by the great strides in cooperation in the IMF and in other institutions such as the Organization for Economic Cooperation and Development (OECD) and the Bank for International Settlements (BIS).

This cooperation has paid handsome dividends in times of crisis. International understanding, carefully nurtured during periods of calm, has permitted the multilateral assessment of problems and the determination of mutually acceptable solutions. This was well illustrated in March 1968, when decisions taken with respect to the private gold market ended the immediate threat to stability and basically strengthened the system. At times of severe strain, such as the British devaluation in 1967, international cooperation has contained crises and prevented chain reactions.

To be sure, the international monetary system has had its problems. Crises have occurred all too frequently. Yet the system has consistently been able to meet the needs of the day, it has evolved and adapted, and it can be strengthened further to meet the remaining strains. While conserving proven arrangements, governments seem increasingly ready to consider additional improvements. Proposed evolutionary changes require careful study and deliberation, based on widespread official and public discussions. It is particularly important that these involve the bankers

* From *The Annual Report of the Council of Economic Advisers,* January 1969, pp. 128–50. Reprinted by permission of the Council of Economic Advisers.

and traders who would be directly affected. The following discussion is intended to contribute to such a dialogue, rather than to make specific recommendations.

International monetary disturbances have centered around three interrelated problems: adjustment, confidence, and liquidity.

"Adjustment" is the process of reestablishing balance-of-payments equilibrium when a country is substantially out of balance. An adjustment problem exists when the relevant forces and policies are either too weak to reestablish equilibrium within a reasonable period or involve domestic or international effects that are inordinately costly.

"Confidence" refers to the willingness to hold monetary assets. A problem arises when holders either become dissatisfied with the safety of some of these assets or see the possibility of profit in switching them abruptly into a different form. This problem is related to adjustment: dissatisfaction with a currency often reflects a lack of faith in the ability of the issuing country to eliminate its balance-of-payments difficulty without resort to a change in its exchange parity.

"Liquidity" relates to international monetary reserves which are held by countries to finance temporary balance-of-payments deficits. If world reserves are too low or too high, or if their rate of growth is inadequate or excessive, a liquidity problem exists. Liquidity needs are closely related to adjustment: the less rapidly and effectively the adjustment process works, the higher the level of reserves needed to finance temporary balance-of-payments deficits, and the less likely it is that any given level of reserves will be adequate.

THE LIQUIDITY PROBLEM

A country incurs a balance-of-payments deficit when its payments to other countries exceed its receipts from them, apart from "settlement items" required to square accounts. The immediate consequence of a deficit is that the foreign exchange market becomes unbalanced. More of the deficit country's currency is supplied than demanded at the existing price of the currency, and this will depress the price—the exchange rate. Because of their commitment to a fixed exchange rate, however, central banks intervene to limit the fall in the rate. The floor on the exchange rate is within 1 percent of the official parity established by the country in agreement with the IMF.

In order to prevent the exchange rate from dropping below this floor, a country in deficit must use its foreign exchange reserves to buy the excess supply of its own currency. If the country has ample reserves, it will have sufficient breathing space to restore equilibrium—without resort to policies of excessive domestic restraint or direct intervention in external transactions. If reserves are scanty, however, pressures will develop to deal immediately with the deficit, even through undesirable means. If a general shortage of reserves should occur, economic growth could be retarded by widespread deflationary policies, and international trade and investment could be burdened by restrictions. On the other hand, excessive amounts of reserves could unduly weaken the incentives of deficit countries to adjust, thereby encouraging worldwide inflation.

Types of Reserves

Existing stocks of world reserves include gold, foreign exchange, and IMF reserve positions.

Gold is the largest component of reserves, but gold holdings have expanded very little for many years; most recently, they have declined. As was discussed in the Council's 1968 Annual Report, nonmonetary demand for gold seems to be absorbing a substantial and increasing share of current new production at existing prices.

The value of official gold reserves would be increased if the official price of gold were raised. This action is explicitly rejected for compelling reasons. Although it would immediately increase world reserves, it could not provide the orderly growth of reserves needed by the world economy. It would grant unearned windfall gains to private speculators, to gold producers, and to countries holding their reserves mainly in gold; it would encourage speculation; and it would divert scarce resources into the production of a metal already adequately supplied for nonmonetary uses.

The foreign exchange component of reserves grows only if the major reserve currency countries, the United States and the United Kingdom, incur balance-of-payments deficits, and if surplus countries are willing to hold more dollars and sterling. Thus, as the foreign exchange component of world reserves is expanded, the liquidity position of the reserve currency countries may be undermined. It is generally recognized that the United States should not run large deficits, and policies have been formulated and implemented for reaching an acceptable payments position. The United Kingdom also is determined not to run deficits and has in fact designed its economic policy to yield balance-of-payments surpluses in order to retire external debt. To some extent, such debt repayments will actually contract world reserves.

Thus world reserves cannot be expected to grow substantially through expansion of official holdings of either gold or foreign exchange. Some limited expansion through normal IMF lending is to be expected. Reserve positions in the Fund are expanded, however, only when countries draw on the Fund beyond their "gold tranche" or automatic drawing rights. In so doing, they accept obligations to repay. The natural reluctance of countries to become over-committed to the Fund or to other countries through borrowings sharply limits the probable expansion of reserves in this form.

Special Drawing Rights

In order to deal with the liquidity problem, steps have been taken to create a new international reserve asset, the Special Drawing Right (SDR), as discussed in the Council's 1968 Annual Report. SDR's will be allocated by the IMF to member countries. They will be a form of owned reserves, usable for balance-of-payments needs without an obligation of repayment. Their use is subject only to the reconstitution provision, which requires that during the initial 5-year period a country's average holdings of SDR's should be at least 30 percent of its average net cumulative allocation over this period.

A draft outline of the proposed arrangements for issuing SDR's was approved at the 1967 meetings of the IMF in Rio de Janeiro and subsequently translated into legal form by the Executive Directors of the Fund. In March 1968, at a meeting in Stockholm of Ministers and Central Bank Governors of the major industrial countries, a consensus was reached on an amendment to the IMF Articles of Agreement. The amendment was subsequently approved by an overwhelming majority of the Board of Governors of the Fund.

The amendment was then submitted to member countries for ratification, which requires acceptance by 67 member countries (total membership is 111) having 80 percent of the voting power in the IMF. By January 1, 1969, the amendment had been accepted by 27 countries representing 47 percent of the voting power. Seven countries have taken the further required step of depositing with the IMF instruments of participation indicating that they are prepared to carry out their obligations under the proposed amendment. The United States, acting with overwhelming bipartisan support in the Congress, was the first country to complete both of these steps. When participation has been certified by member countries having 75 percent of total IMF quotas, the new facility will be established in the Fund.

Resolving the world liquidity problem requires actual creation of SDR's—a major step beyond legal establishment of the facility. The basic decisions lie ahead—namely when to activate the facility and in what amounts. These decisions will require collective judgment concerning the desired growth of world reserves and the portion of that growth which should take the form of Special Drawing Rights.

The Need for Reserve Growth

The problem of estimating reserve needs has attracted much interest among economists and government officials in the last few years. The needed volume of reserves depends in part on the probable size of temporary balance-of-payments deficits which must be financed, because this affects the judgment of monetary authorities as to the amounts of reserves they need to hold. According to findings by the staff of the IMF, the magnitude of deficits requiring financing has tended to increase at the same rate as the volume of world transactions. This suggests that the prospective growth of world transactions might be a helpful guide to the required growth in reserves. Since trade in commodities makes up the largest portion of international transactions and is the one most reliably reported in statistics, it is useful as an indicator of trends.

The historical relation between the growth of reserves and the growth of trade (measured by imports) is depicted in Chart 1. Between 1950 and 1968 imports increased 7.6 percent a year, while reserves grew at only 2.5 percent a year. Thus, in the aggregate, reserves declined quite substantially in relation to imports, and probably in relation to the average size of deficits. These over-all results are, however, heavily influenced by the large net decline in reserves of the United States, the world's largest holder. The United States was able to give up these reserves because of its excess holdings at the beginning of the period. But this loss cannot continue. No other country now appears to have excess reserves sufficient to replace the United States as a willing and able net loser of reserves.

The relationship between growth of reserves and growth of imports is significantly altered

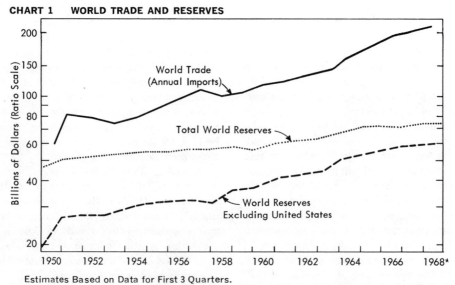

CHART 1   WORLD TRADE AND RESERVES

Billions of Dollars (Ratio Scale)

World Trade (Annual Imports)

Total World Reserves

World Reserves Excluding United States

Estimates Based on Data for First 3 Quarters.
Note: Trade during Year, Reserves at End of Year. Data Include Yugoslavia, but Exclude U.S.S.R., Other East-European Countries, Mainland China, and Cuba.
Source: International Monetary Fund.

when the United States is excluded from world totals. Between 1950 and 1968, reserves of countries other than the United States grew 5.6 percent a year, on the average, while their imports grew at 7.8 percent.

Some have suggested that reserves in the future should grow at essentially the same rate as world transactions—about 8 percent a year—to avoid any further decline in the ratio of average reserves to potential deficits. However, the world economy has been able to adapt to reductions in this ratio in the past. And a moderate further decline may be appropriate, both because countries should have increasing access to borrowed reserves and because possible improvements in the adjustment process may reduce the need for reserves.

Some guidance might be derived from the 5.6 percent growth rate of reserves experienced between 1950 and 1968 by countries other than the United States. In any case, a major increase from the very slow growth of the past 2 years is needed. Whatever the desired rate of growth of reserves, its achievement will depend mainly on the creation of Special Drawing Rights, since other components of total reserves, as noted above, are unlikely to expand significantly.

While it is still too early to make a decision about the proper size of the initial issue of SDR's, amounts of $1 billion or $2 billion a year—which have been used as illustrative examples of SDR creation—appear to be inadequate. These amounts imply a rate of reserve growth of only about 1.4 to 2.8 percent. With such slow growth, the SDR facility might fail to achieve its objective of avoiding a destructive competition for reserves.

THE CONFIDENCE PROBLEM

Shifts in confidence can be reflected in two ways: through actions initiated in the private economy and through actions by governments. Private holders of liquid assets constantly adjust the composition of their holdings. When they decide to shift from the financial assets of one country to those of another—a process described for simplicity as shifting from one currency to another—either exchange rates or official reserve holdings or both are affected. In addition, shifts by private holders between currencies and gold can have an impact on monetary stability, although the significance of such shifts has been substantially altered by the gold accord reached in Washington in March 1968.

Private Shifting among Currencies

Some shifts by private holders out of one currency into another are merely responses to differentials in short term interest rates. Other shifts among currencies may be induced by the expectation of, or anxiety about, a change in exchange rates—and thus can be viewed as reflecting changes in confidence. Such speculative movements occur when the payments and reserve positions of some countries create significant uncertainties that exchange parities will remain fixed. Speculative capital flows can result from direct sales of the suspect currency for stronger ones, or through the operation of the so-called "leads and lags" mechanism, under which normal commercial disbursements denominated in foreign currency are accelerated while receipts denominated in domestic currency are delayed. (This was an important element in the 1968 French crisis.) A crisis of confidence can severely deplete the monetary reserves of a nation. Flows of this kind can be very large—up to $1 billion in a single day.

Crises resulting from shifts of confidence have occurred from time to time. At different times in 1968, the Canadian dollar, the British pound, and the French franc were under downward pressures, and the German mark was subjected to upward pressures. As international businesses and financial institutions have matured, additional currencies have been brought into wide international use. Thus the number of currencies potentially subject to such crises has increased.

It is quite appropriate that countries should borrow reserves, if necessary, to deal with temporary emergencies of this kind. The "swap network" has traditionally provided lines of credit among central banks for this purpose; it was expanded and enlarged during 1968. Further improvements could be made in central bank borrowing procedures through a proposal whereby speculative funds would be immediately "recycled"—returned to countries suffering losses from countries experiencing gains.

Even if generous lines of short term credit are available, they leave countries vulnerable, because crises may be long lasting. Lenders or borrowers may be reluctant to renew loans, fearing overcommitment. Fortunately, in recent years, improvements in cooperation among the central banks and in the procedures of the IMF have reduced such fears.

However generous borrowing facilities may be, they cannot deal fully with a crisis of private confidence that arises from a major disequilibrium in the underlying balance-of-payments position of a country. In such circumstances, prompt and decisive measures to achieve a basic adjustment are the key to the restoration of confidence. But the requirements for adequate adjustment are aggravated when a loss of confidence imposes a heavy drain on reserves.

Private Demand for Gold

Private asset holders may respond to a loss of confidence in a currency by buying gold rather than other currencies, particularly when the choice of a "safe" foreign currency is not obvious. Gold speculation is rather common in many countries, although not in the United States where it is illegal. Private imports of gold can be an important channel for currency flight and thus become a claim on a country's reserves. Furthermore, because the price of gold in the private market is sometimes used by speculators as a barometer of confidence in currencies, increases in that price can intensify currency runs.

While governments still retain some concern over private demands for gold, they are now much less directly involved than prior to March 1968. For the preceding 7 years, countries participating actively in the "gold pool" had stabilized the price of gold in the private market in London by buying and selling near the official price of $35 an ounce. In March 1968, these countries agreed to discontinue their activities.

Prior to 1966, the pool was a net purchaser of gold, and the resulting additions of gold to monetary reserves strengthened the international monetary system. Subsequently, however, the pool became a substantial net seller, parting with gold out of monetary stocks to keep the price from rising. Following British devaluation in late 1967, and in the early months of 1968, the volume of net gold sales became a serious drain on international monetary reserves. Moreover, the market took on a highly speculative tone. Several large and irregular waves of gold purchases had destabilizing domestic monetary effects in certain countries and transmitted speculative fever to foreign exchange markets.

In March, the active gold pool countries agreed to cease selling gold in the private market, and agreed that purchases of gold from the private market were no longer necessary. They obtained the cooperation of other central banks in this decision. As a result, the international monetary system has been substantially insulated from the destabilizing effects of changes in the private demand for gold, and gold can no longer be drained from monetary stocks into private uses.

Shifts among Official Reserve Assets

Problems may arise if monetary authorities decide to shift their holdings abruptly among the various reserve assets. They may shift for political or other reasons, but they are often motivated by changes in the relative degrees of confidence attaching to the future values of these assets. For example, if official holders, fearing a sterling devaluation, were to shift into dollars, the United Kingdom would be forced to give up some of its international reserves. Likewise, if official holders of dollars decided to convert them into gold, the United States would lose some of its reserves. Crises of confidence may feed on themselves; for example, a significant decline in U.K. reserves could further weaken the confidence of both official and private holders of sterling.

Shifts out of officially held sterling by sterling area countries became a serious problem following the British devaluation of November 1967. The great majority of the sterling area countries did not devalue along with the British; thus the purchasing power of the reserves of sterling holders was reduced in terms of their own currencies as well as in dollars. This loss led to a movement toward reserve diversification which became particularly pronounced in the spring of 1968.

In recognition that the burden of such reserve diversification should not be borne by the British alone, 12 industrial countries, including the United States, together with the Bank for International Settlements, set up a new $2 billion loan facility in September 1968. It was designed to provide finance to Britain to replace reserves lost as a result of the decline of sterling balances within the sterling area. The BIS will act as an intermediary and will obtain the required funds by borrowing in international markets, by accepting reserve deposits from central banks of the sterling area, and by calling upon standby lines of credit provided by the cooperating countries. The United Kingdom has given a dollar-value guarantee to the sterling area on eligible official sterling reserves, and the sterling-area countries in return have undertaken to maintain an agreed proportion of their reserves in sterling. The new facility should go far toward moderating the sterling diversification problem.

Some observers have pointed to the possibility of large-scale conversions of dollars into gold by central banks. The likelihood of such an abrupt shift of preferences must, however, be viewed in perspective. There are several reasons why countries choose to hold dollars. Dollars are useful because they can be readily employed in exchange markets and are more easily put to use in emergencies than gold. Countries recognize that they can convert dollars to gold as they see fit, although they may at times refrain from gold conversions through a cooperative desire not to weaken the international monetary system by reducing total world reserves. Dollars—unlike gold—earn interest, and the efficient American money and capital markets make investment easy. Thus there is and should continue to be a strong demand for dollars by central banks.

Some central banks have a preference—arising mainly from tradition—in favor of gold as a reserve asset. They often appear unconcerned about earning interest on reserves, perhaps because their income is usually turned over to their national treasuries.

When dollars are acquired by countries with a preference for gold from countries with a preference for currencies as reserves, conversions into gold may occur. This could happen even with no increase in total dollars held abroad and no shift in general sentiment toward gold or away from the dollar. Furthermore, as world reserves grow, there would be a demand for added gold if countries attempted to maintain their "traditional" ratios of gold to total reserves. However, countries recognize that gold will decline as a proportion of total world reserves. And as the SDR agreement indicated, they seem prepared collectively to adjust the composition of their reserve holdings.

Preferences that now exist among sterling, dollars, and gold could become more complicated as SDR's are added, thereby creating further possibilities for shifts in the composition of reserves. Certain safeguards, however, were provided in the plan: the power given the IMF to direct SDR's to various holders was designed to prevent inadvertent destabilizing shifts from SDR's into other types of reserves. Furthermore, additional SDR's could be created to offset world reserve losses arising from shifts among reserve assets.

Proposals for Improving Reserve Management

It has been suggested that agreement on mutually acceptable rules of reserve management might help to avoid destabilizing changes in reserve composition. If deficit countries used each of their reserve assets in proportion to its share in their total holdings, and if surplus countries were willing to accept and hold different types of reserves in the exact proportions made available, the system would be internally consistent. Before such rules could be endorsed, their workings would need to be examined and agreed upon in detail.

A more sweeping suggested reform would be to eliminate the differences among reserve assets. Countries could combine all their reserves by depositing them in a joint account, which would be drawn upon when reserves were used. Such a scheme was discussed in the September 1968 Report of the Subcommittee on International Exchange and Payments, of the Joint Economic Committee (JEC) of the Congress. In an examination of proposals of this kind, many questions arise which would require careful study: What would be the role of the United States? Would participation be voluntary or compulsory? Would countries be permitted to withdraw from the pool? In view of the progress already made in dealing with world liquidity and in strengthening international cooperation, how urgent is such a major reform?

THE ADJUSTMENT PROBLEM

The Bretton Woods system was designed to correct the weaknesses in the international monetary system that were apparent in the interwar years. Faced with domestic economic collapse during the 1930s, some countries attempted, by deliberately undervaluing their currencies, to stimulate exports, retard imports, and thus add to employment. But one country's gain was another country's loss. Competitive devaluations, and restrictions on exchange and trade, imposed a heavy toll on international commerce.

The postwar economy was built upon the general understanding that full employment would be the target of national economic policies, and that this goal would be sought primarily through domestic monetary and fiscal policies. It was also expected that excessive price increases would normally be avoided. In the absence of both chronic deflation and chronic inflation, continuous balance-of-payments problems were viewed as unlikely. The IMF was to help in the adjustment process by granting credit to allow countries time to adjust without parity changes.

Provisions were included to put pressure on surplus countries to take an appropriate part in the adjustment process—for example, the "scarce currency" clause, which permits discrimination in trade against persistent surplus countries whose currencies are formally declared to be scarce.

Under these conditions, a system of stable exchange rates was expected to operate successfully and to stimulate international trade and capital movements, while removing the temptation for governments to solve domestic problems by external means.

Although pegged parities were made the normal operating rule of the system, provision was also made for changing parities to correct fundamental disequilibria. The meaning of "fundamental disequilibrium" was not fully clarified, but the expectation at the time was that changes in parities would not be unusual. Actually, parity changes for developed countries have been rare. In part, this is because major countries have been reasonably successful in avoiding excesses of inflation and deflation; but it also reflects concern about the serious economic and political consequences of changes in the parities of major currencies, including the possibility of a worldwide chain reaction. Furthermore, greater freedom for international capital transactions has complicated the process of changing parities.

Causes of Disturbances

Despite the real accomplishments of stabilization policies, the international economy has been subject to disturbances. Some have been caused by the relatively mild cyclical fluctuations that have occurred, and others by differences among countries in long term trends of prices, economic growth, technological advance, and import demand. Countries differ with respect to the maximum rate of price increase—or the maximum volume of idle resources—that they view as tolerable. In general, a country incurring price increases greater than the average of other countries will find its exports becoming less competitive and its domestic market more accessible to imports. Countries which grow particularly rapidly tend to experience stronger increases in imports (although they may simultaneously improve the competitive position of their exports). Or a country may experience long term deterioration in its external position if its demand for imports is more responsive to income growth than is the demand for its exports. These factors, singly and in combination, have led to some serious imbalances.

Adjustment problems may also reflect, in part, an insufficient growth of global reserves. When over-all reserves are growing only slowly, there can be acute pressures on deficit countries to adjust. At the same time, surplus countries may find that their reserves are not accumulating too rapidly; hence they may have little incentive to correct their imbalances. A world shortage of reserves could particularly complicate the adjustment problem of the United States, subjecting it to intense pressures from other countries in weak payments positions or from countries not satisfied with their reserve holdings. The United States might literally be prevented from correcting its balance-of-payments deficit, because every improvement in the U.S. position would cause some other countries to take protective actions to counter any weakening of their own positions.

There are a number of means open to a country for correcting balance-of-payments disequilibria without altering its exchange rate. These means differ in speed, in effectiveness, and in their side effects. They include internal measures such as fiscal and monetary policies, together with supporting incomes, manpower, and regional policies; and direct measures affecting international movements of goods, services, or capital.

Internal Adjustments

Often the domestic policies which would contribute to balance-of-payments adjustments are also desirable for domestic reasons. Thus if a country faces a balance-of-payments deficit and rapidly rising prices, it should follow tighter monetary and fiscal measures, supported by incomes policy to help restrain wages and prices, both to improve its trade balance and to curb inflation. Indeed, one argument sometimes made in favor of a system of fixed exchange rates is that balance-of-payments deficits stiffen the resolve of governments to achieve price stability. Conversely, if high levels of unemployment are accompanied by payments surpluses, expansionary domestic policies are clearly indicated.

However, a country may face a balance-of-payments deficit at a time when domestic demand is not excessive. It will then be understandably reluctant to attack its payments problem by restrictive monetary and fiscal policies. The opposite problem may arise if a payments surplus occurs when the domestic situation calls for anti-inflationary policies.

While the situations of surplus and deficit countries are symmetrical, incentives to adjust may not be equally strong in the two cases. There is no definite limit on the accumulation of reserves, so surplus countries often are under little pressure to restore equilibrium. But for deficit countries whose freedom of action is constrained by a limited supply of reserves, pressures to take corrective action may become inexorable. If real progress is to be made in achieving a better balance of world payments, it is crucial that surplus countries participate in the adjustment process, as was indicated in the 1966 Report on the Balance of Payments Adjustment Process by Working Party No. 3 of OECD.

Changes in the Policy Mix. There are some opportunities to mitigate conflicts between international and domestic goals by altering the mix of monetary and fiscal policies. By influencing interest rates, monetary policies have direct effects on capital flows as well as on domestic demand. If a country has a balance-of-payments deficit and a satisfactory or inadequate level of domestic demand, fiscal policy may be eased and monetary policy simultaneously tightened. This combination can, in principle, avoid any reduction of internal demand, and capture the benefits of tighter money in reducing capital outflows or attracting foreign capital. Thus it may be possible to improve the balance of payments without adding to unemployment. The reverse combination of policies may be used by countries facing the surplus-inflation dilemma.

While changes in the mix of monetary and fiscal policy have significant possibilities, and they can be reinforced by appropriate incomes and manpower policies, such adjustments cannot always be relied upon as an escape from major conflicts in objectives.

Some of the balance-of-payments gains resulting from interest rate adjustments may be temporary. A change in interest rates may initially cause investors to make large adjustments in the composition of their existing portfolios of financial assets. Once this initial stock adjustment is completed, however, further gains from this source may be quite small.

There are limits on the willingness of countries to alter the mix of monetary and fiscal policies. A deficit country may hesitate to raise interest rates, fearing that such a move would deter capital formation and thereby curtail the improvement in productivity that may be a basic solution to its balance-of-payments difficulties. Or high interest rates may be objectionable because of their uneven impact on the domestic economy. Or a growing level of foreign indebtedness may be undesirable because it will increase the burden of service payments.

Finally, increases in domestic interest rates may lead to higher interest rates abroad. In that event, the differentials between foreign and domestic rates may diminish, weakening the impact on capital flows. In the absence of international coordination of monetary policies, efforts by deficit countries to tighten credit may lead to a worldwide escalation of interest rates. This may not only impede the immediate objectives of the deficit countries but may also dampen world economic growth. Clearly, the adjustment mechanism could benefit from a continued strengthening of international cooperation in this area of policy.

Thus there are often important limitations on the practical scope for adjustments in the monetary-fiscal mix as a means of reconciling domestic and international objectives. One important principle stands out. In a country with a serious balance-of-payments problem, the use of monetary policy for expansionary domestic purposes may be severely constrained; and primary reliance may therefore have to be placed on fiscal policy to pursue stabilization objectives. In the United States and in many other countries, this implies the need for greater speed and flexibility in the implementation of fiscal measures.

Measures Directly Affecting International Transactions

In the OECD Adjustment Process report, it was recognized that fiscal and monetary policies, no matter how skillfully combined, cannot always be relied upon as the exclusive means of balance-of-payments adjustment. Given the many goals of economic policy, numerous instruments are needed. Under some circumstances, the report suggests the use of measures directly affecting international transactions.

Most countries do make use of specific measures affecting trade or capital movements as part of their adjustment. These policies may help to reconcile domestic and international objectives. Such measures as import duties or quotas, export subsidies, changes in border taxes, and taxes and prohibitions on international capital movements offer opportunities for improving the payments balance while avoiding major effects on the domestic economy. Some of these measures, such as special tariffs and export subsidies, are prohibited by the GATT, but their use has at times been sanctioned, implicitly or explicitly, so long as they were considered temporary. Likewise, exchange controls on current transactions are generally discouraged for countries accepting the full obligations of convertibility in the IMF, but specific authorizations have been granted under emergency conditions.

Trade Measures. The only trade measure explicitly condoned by the GATT for safeguarding the balance of payments is the use of temporary quantitative restrictions. Quotas on imports can be a very powerful instrument. But they can be very disruptive of normal commercial arrangements, troublesome to impose and administer, and difficult to abandon. Over the last few years, developed countries have shown a growing preference for the use of import surcharges, export subsidies, or combinations of the two.

At times, countries change their normal pattern of tax adjustments at the border in an attempt to promote balance-of-payments equilibrium. When a deficit country is taking only partial advantage of its opportunity under the GATT to make border adjustments for domestic indirect taxes, it can help itself by moving to full compensation. However, such action by a surplus country conflicts with the policies that should be followed for balance-of-payments adjustment. For example, on January 1 and July 1, 1968, in conjunction with an internal tax reform, the German government raised its rate of border adjustment. This tended to increase the German merchandise surplus—much as a small devaluation of the mark would have done—and at a time when Germany's balance-of-payments position was very strong indeed.

Another example of a change in a domestic tax which permitted an increase in border adjustments was the action taken by the French government in November 1968. A rise in value-added taxes, which are eligible under the GATT for border adjustments, was substituted for the existing payroll tax, which was not eligible. In this case, the aim of the increase in border adjustments was to help restore over-all payments equilibrium.

Also in November, the German government reduced by 4 percentage points its border charge on most imports and its tax rebate on most exports, without any corresponding domestic tax changes. This measure was taken deliberately to reduce the large German trade surplus and had effects somewhat similar to an upward valuation of the mark.

When countries resort to trade measures to affect their balance-of-payments positions, efforts should be made to minimize distortions. General import charges imposed by themselves favor production for the domestic market, thus shrinking the volume of international trade, while general export grants alone unduly favor production for export. When general import charges are combined with general export grants at the same rate, these two tendencies offset each other, with no more distortion of merchandise trade than would result from a devaluation.

Even such a uniform and general combination of import charges and export grants would distort the choice between merchandise transactions and other international flows, such as tourism. Furthermore, serious misallocations could occur if exemptions were given individual industries or classes of products. Finally, even under the best of circumstances, temporary trade measures may in practice become embedded and thus should be used with great caution. Nevertheless, this approach may be useful under some conditions. It should be explored further to determine whether proper safeguards can be established to ensure that equal use is made by surplus and deficit countries, and that the goals of liberal commercial policy are maintained.

Capital Account Measures. All major countries take actions at times to influence international capital flows. The techniques employed range from special incentives for domestic investment to exchange controls and capital issues committees. There is some rationale for concentrating on the capital account, since fewer basic adjustments in the allocation of real resources are required by shifts in financial flows than by changes in trade. And measures to influence the capital account are generally more easily reversed in response to shifting balance-of-payments fortunes.

Sometimes, however, restraints on capital movements develop into a patchwork of controls that involve major administrative difficulties, bear down unevenly and inefficiently on different types of capital flows, and create a search for loopholes. The distortions can be reduced to the extent that restraints can be applied more equally among categories of capital flows and interference can be minimized within any particular category.

There may be opportunities to make greater use of the price system by applying variable taxes to capital flows or by auctioning permits to export capital. While the allocation of capital might be improved and administrative burdens eased by innovations in the techniques of controlling capital flows, any system of major restraints is bound to be far from ideal. The possible need for temporary direct measures on the capital account must be recognized, but so should the long term benefits of greater freedom in capital flows among nations.

The Adjustment Problem of the United States

The difficulties of balance-of-payments adjustment for deficit countries are evident from the recent experience of the United States. In the early 1960s, the United States was faced with a payments deficit at a time when its economy was operating far below capacity.

The causes of the deficit were numerous. The United States was shouldering an extraordinarily large share of the burden of providing for the security of the Free World and of supplying aid to less developed countries. The United States possessed the only large and sophisticated capital market in which foreigners could borrow freely, and the European countries had advanced to the point where they desired capital and could attract it. Moreover, because of Europe's general economic progress and the formation of the EEC and the European Free Trade Association, American companies had developed an intense interest in making direct investments there. Finally, the U.S. competitive position had deteriorated during the 1950s.

The Over-All Strategy. In the early 1960s, U.S. domestic needs called for expansionary policies, while traditional balance-of-payments remedies would have required greater restraint on demand. To reconcile this conflict, a mixed strategy was followed. It emphasized those elements in the domestic expansion which tended to improve international competitiveness, together with specific measures of a temporary nature to influence the external position. The selection of balance-of-payments measures reflected several concerns: the determination to maintain, as far as possible, liberal policies with respect to international trade and capital flows; the desire not to shift problems to countries in a weak balance-of-payments positions; and the need to maintain the stability of the international monetary system, which was so crucially dependent on the dollar. Further difficulties in designing appropriate balance-of-payments measures arose from uncertainty over how much correction was needed, from the unpredictability of the immediate quantitative impact of particular actions, and from the large and uncertain "feedback" effects inherent in the large size of the United States.

Some policies were clearly desirable on all counts, such as improving knowledge with respect to export prospects, trimming unnecessary government expenditures abroad, encouraging other industrial countries to give larger amounts of aid to less developed countries, pressing for a more equitable sharing of military burdens, and removing a tax penalty on foreigners trading in American securities.

Reducing the Impact of Government Activities. A further group of measures to reduce the foreign exchange costs of U.S. military and foreign aid required more difficult decisions. In principle, savings of foreign exchange in the military area could have been pursued through three alternative strategies: (1) reducing the level of security, (2) obtaining increased contributions of military forces from other countries, or (3) reducing, offsetting, or neutralizing the foreign exchange costs of a maintained level of U.S. military effort. The first alternative was ruled out. The second was pursued but with little immediate prospect of success. Thus the third became the approach emphasized in the short run. Domestic producers were given a preference over foreigners in supplying defense needs, at some added cost to the Federal budget. Foreign governments were urged to purchase more of their military equipment in the United States. In recent years, special U.S. Treasury bonds have been sold to countries to neutralize their balance-of-payments inflows from U.S. military expenditures.

Reducing the foreign exchange costs of U.S. aid presented an equally difficult choice. Either the amount of foreign aid had to be reduced, or a method had to be found to ensure that more of the money provided by the United States was spent in this country. The second alternative—aid-tying—was chosen. This tended to reduce the effectiveness of a given dollar amount of aid, but the alternative of slashing the volume of aid would have been even more costly to recipient countries.

Restraining Capital Outflows. While gains were obtained through these measures in the early sixties, the over-all payments problem was intensified by a major increase in private capital outflows. Faced with an apparently insatiable demand for capital abroad, the United States had the choice of raising domestic interest rates enough to price foreigners out of our market, of taxing foreign loans specifically, or of using direct controls to stop capital outflows. The first alternative was inconsistent with domestic needs for economic expansion. The second alternative was chosen when the Interest Equalization Tax (IET) was proposed in 1963. It substantially reduced foreign portfolio investments by Americans, except new security issues from Canada and investments in less developed countries, which were exempted. But demand for capital shifted to American banks, so the IET was extended to longer term loans of banks. Other types of bank loans and direct investment were not covered by the tax, and these forms of capital outflow kept expanding.

In response to a large outflow of capital at the end of 1964, voluntary programs were initiated in February 1965 to cover the major remaining capital flows. The American corporations which were large direct investors were asked to help by reducing their capital expenditures, abroad, by relying on foreign financing for a greater share of their investments, or by expanding reflows of dividends to the United States. Banks and other financial institutions were meanwhile asked to follow guidelines established by the Federal Reserve Board which suggested quantitative limits on foreign lending.

Most, if not all, of these measures have been successful in achieving the objectives for which they were designed. The basic balance-of-payments position improved through 1964 and 1965, and the liquidity deficit was sharply reduced. Further progress was interrupted in 1966 by the mounting foreign exchange costs associated with the war in Vietnam and by the reduced trade surplus resulting from overly rapid domestic expansion.

Because the U.S. external position deteriorated sharply late in 1967 and the stability of the international monetary system seemed in serious danger, a new set of measures was proposed by the President on January 1, 1968. This program included mandatory restrictions on foreign direct investment, further tightening of the guidelines on lending by banks and other financial institutions, and various other steps to reduce the deficit. The program was successful. . . . the balance of payments has improved. In particular, American direct investors have managed to finance a much greater proportion of their investments abroad by foreign borrowing, and there has been a net reduction in U.S. bank credit to the rest of the world.

With the exception of more timely action to assure adequate domestic restraint in recent years, it is hard to see, even in retrospect, any preferable strategies in U.S. policies to correct the deficit. The eclectic, ad hoc measures that were taken involved certain costs. But they maintained the strength of the dollar and the health of the world economy. More basic improvements lie ahead—pending peace and the restoration of price stability.

EXCHANGE RATE ADJUSTMENTS

An efficient international adjustment mechanism should permit countries to choose their own domestic economic targets for growth, employment, and price-cost performance. Policies that restore balance at home should not lead to pressures on the international accounts—in the form of either excessive accumulation or rapid depletion of reserves.

Suggestions have been put forward for amending the adjustment mechanism to lessen the conflict between domestic and balance-of-payments objectives. It is claimed by some that greater reliance on changes in exchange rates would work in this direction.

Present System

Present IMF rules provide for adjustments of exchange parities as a means of correcting a fundamental disequilibrium. In practice, however, the process of exchange rate adjustment may involve major difficulties; and in consequence, there is often extreme reluctance to change exchange rates even when balance-of-payments difficulties are severe.

To illustrate, the currency of a country with a large and persistent deficit will become widely recognized as a candidate for devaluation and this may touch off a crisis in private confidence, as discussed above. Speculation based on the prospect of devaluation will aggravate the initial balance-of-payments difficulties and increase the outflow of reserves. To discourage such speculation, governments tend to make categorical assertions that devaluation is not being considered; once such assertions have been made, it becomes a matter of national pride and political reputation to maintain the parity.

Furthermore, an actual adjustment in an exchange rate may generate the expectation of a further change; once an exchange parity has been adjusted, a second adjustment seems less unthinkable. Fear of such a perverse reaction may cause a country to depreciate by an excessive amount in the first instance. This may lead other countries to devalue also, thus reducing the potential balance-of-payments gain of the initiating country. Such a chain reaction can severely disrupt foreign exchange markets. Thus the difficulties associated with parity adjustments have at times driven countries to commit themselves to existing parities in all but the most extreme situations.

Proposals for Exchange Rate Flexibility

A number of suggestions—ranging from minor adjustments to far-reaching changes—have been made for altering the current exchange rate arrangements of the IMF.

The most sweeping change, advocated primarily by some academic economists, would be to abandon the pegged exchange system in favor of "floating rates," completely free to fluctuate in response to market forces.

In contrast, other proposals call for a modest widening of the existing 1 percent limit on fluctuations of rates on either side of parity. Still another type of proposal would provide for small but frequent changes in parities.

Each of the proposals is intended to make adjustments in exchange rates a more acceptable and effective means of correcting payments imbalances, and to reduce the speculative disturbances that sometimes develop under the present system. Opinions differ widely over the probable effects of the various proposals; intensive study would be required before serious consideration could be given to the adoption of any of them. The dramatic advances in world trade and prosperity achieved under the present system provide a strong case for conservatism in considering innovations; at the same time, the recurrence of financial strains has aroused widespread interest in possible amendments to the system.

In general, the wider the latitude for changes in exchange rates, the greater would be the amount of adjustment provided; but also the greater would be the uncertainty of those engaged in international commerce and the possibility of a disturbance to trade and investment relationships.

Floating Rates. While a system of floating exchange rates would ensure essentially automatic adjustment to balance-of-payments disturbances, serious questions arise about its operation.

Advocates of flexible exchange rates are divided on whether official intervention in exchange markets should be permitted. A complete ban on official intervention would be a very radical change, obviating any need for central banks to hold international reserves. Exchange rates might fluctuate quite widely, causing substantial uncertainty. If, on the other hand, official intervention were permitted under a system of floating rates, it might smooth out transitory fluctuations in exchange rates, but it would open up the danger of exchange rate manipulation. For example, a government might wish to drive down the price of its currency in order to strengthen the competitive position of its exports. It is difficult to devise rules which would permit desirable smoothing and yet ban manipulation.

In general, fluctuating exchange rates would require shifts of resources among industries that export, those that compete with imports, and others, as relative prices in world markets reflected changes in exchange rates. Moreover, un-

certainty about future exchange rates would concern international traders and investors. They could obtain some insurance by entering forward exchange markets, buying or selling foreign currencies at definite prices for delivery at some specified future date. But such forward transactions might be quite expensive and thus add to the costs of world trade. Furthermore, international investors might not be able to satisfy their needs for protection in forward exchange markets, given the long time horizon of many capital transactions.

Advocates of floating exchange rates believe that the benefits outweigh the costs of these uncertainties. They point out that uncertainty about exchange rates is not unique to a system of floating rates. Indeed, no feasible international system can guarantee against exchange rate adjustments. Moreover, they emphasize that international businessmen live with many uncertainties, both political and commercial. Finally, it is their contention—not universally accepted—that under floating rates, there would be an easing of pressures for exchange controls and trade barriers.

The adoption of floating exchange rates would constitute a drastic change in the international monetary system. If the present system were functioning very badly and if no other possibility of reform were available, there might be a compelling argument for adopting this one; but such is not the case.

Wider Bands. Under present arrangements, day-to-day market pressures can be reflected in small fluctuations of each exchange rate within a narrow band. Central banks of countries other than the United States intervene in the market by buying and selling foreign exchange to keep the dollar prices of their currencies within 1 percent or less of established parities. The United States rounds out the system by selling and buying gold in dealings with central banks at $35 an ounce. Proposals have been made by the JEC Subcommittee on International Payments and by others to introduce greater flexibility of rates by widening the permissible band of fluctuation around the par value. With a band of 2 percent on either side of parity, the exchange rate between two nondollar currencies could change by as much as 8 percent. Suggestions for a wider band, like other proposals for greater flexibility in exchange rates, are *not* directed at the official price of gold. The latter is not an exchange rate. There is no need whatsoever for it to be altered to accommodate greater flexibility of exchange rates.

A widening of exchange rate bands could contribute to the adjustment process. The currency of a country with an incipient deficit would fall in price, thus making imports more expensive and lowering the cost of exports to buyers in world markets. Imports would be discouraged and exports stimulated, strengthening the balance of payments. If the exchange rate approached the floor with its future course expected to be upward, the stimulus might be particularly strong; there would be an incentive to take advantage of the temporary low price of the country's exports.

Advocates of a wider band believe that it might deter speculative runs in two ways. First, the additional adjustment permitted by the wider band might make discrete changes in parities appear less likely, thus reducing uncertainty. Second, a wider band would increase the potential loss on a "wrong bet" against a currency. Under the present narrow band, the speculator has relatively little to lose if he bets against a currency and it is not in fact devalued. With a wider band, the risk of loss would be increased, because a currency that was initially under pressure could experience a larger rebound in price. There is, however, no concrete basis for estimating the extent to which these features would be speculation.

The wider the band is made, the greater the potential uncertainty about the course of exchange rates, but also the greater the amount of balance-of-payments adjustment which may take place within the band. In an evaluation of a wider band, these conflicting considerations would have to be weighed in determining its optimum width. A very wide band comes close to a floating exchange rate and thus shares the shortcomings of this drastic reform. A small widening of the band, on the other hand, might not markedly reduce the need for, and the expectation of, discrete changes in parity.

Gradual Adjustment of Parities. The evolution toward greater exchange rate flexibility could involve a gradual, limited adjustment of exchange parities. Two forms of the so-called "crawling peg" have been proposed, one discretionary and one automatic.

Under the discretionary variant, a country in disequilibrium would no longer make one substantial change in its parity, but rather would announce a rate of increase (or decrease) in its parity of some specified small percentage per month, until further notice. Once the desired effect had been attained, the country would halt the process. This might make the transition to an equilibrium parity easier, and perhaps curb

speculation. Its effect on the political obstacles to changes in parities is not entirely clear; governments might find it just as painful to announce a parity change in a series of small steps as in a single abrupt one. The discretionary crawling peg might therefore be used no more frequently than the present "adjustable peg."

The automatic form of gradual adjustment would remove parities from the direct control of individual countries. Under one variant, the parity on any business day would be the average of the actual exchange rates over the preceding 12 months (or some other suitable period). The actual exchange rate would be within a band around the parity prevailing on that day, with official intervention permitted only at the floor or ceiling. For a period of 1 year and a band of 1 percent, the largest possible change in the parity—attained only if a currency were continuously at its floor or ceiling—would be 2 percent a year. Larger or smaller potential changes could be permitted by adopting a different period for calculating the moving average, or by altering the width of the band. Again an optimum choice would depend upon the importance of certainty about future exchange rates, on the one hand, and on the speed of balance-of-payments adjustment to be permitted through the crawling peg, on the other.

Unlike fully flexible rates, the crawling peg would not be intended to offset all cyclical and random fluctuations in international transactions; but, unlike a widening of the band, it would permit sizable changes in exchange rates over the long run. Thus, is could cope with the problem of modest trends in the equilibrium values of currencies resulting from divergent national trends of prices, economic growth, export supply, import demand, or investment flows.

It might seem that, if a currency showed fundamental weakness and was therefore expected to move downward for an extended period, speculation would become a problem because of the predictability of the exchange rate movement. This kind of speculation could, in principle, be avoided by raising interest rates above the otherwise prevailing level by an amount equal to the anticipated rate of downward crawl of the currency. The exchange gain from moving out of the currency would then be offset by the loss of interest. Such changes in interest rates might, however, necessitate offsetting adjustments in fiscal policy and, as discussed earlier, marked changes in the policy mix are sometimes difficult to achieve. Limits on tolerable interest rate changes would thus be one constraint on the speed of parity adjustment which could be permitted in such a system.

The various proposed modifications in the exchange rate system raise many difficult technical issues, and clearly a proper evaluation of these proposals must be preceded by a great deal of careful study.

CONCLUSION

By far the most important attribute of the postwar international economy has been steady and rapid growth. The spectacular nature of recent international monetary disturbances should not obscure the mighty contribution that the international economic system has made to world prosperity. Worldwide flows of goods and investments have been the cornerstones on which the prosperity of many nations has rested; at the same time, the growth of national economies has made possible the tremendous increases in world trade and international investment.

Trade is the center of the international economic system, and it cannot prosper in the face of highly restrictive national policies. Only a continuous chipping away at tariffs and other trade barriers can provide assurance against backsliding. Pressures for protection must be successfully resisted.

The fruits of unprecedented prosperity are still not being fully shared by many nations in Africa, Asia, the Middle East, and Latin America. The future growth of these nations must be built primarily on the skills, intelligence, and labor of their citizens. But the developed countries must facilitate the process by providing technical assistance, capital resources, and access to markets.

The international monetary system established at Bretton Woods and developed through the years has made a major contribution to international economic growth. This system has served the world well, but it has increasingly been subject to serious strains.

To ensure the continuing smooth operation of the monetary system, work must go forward on the problems of liquidity, confidence, and adjustment. Great progress has been made in recent years as exemplified by the agreement creating Special Drawing Rights. This achievement required careful study and long negotiations. Similar extensive efforts will be needed in the future if progress is to be maintained, but the prospects for eventual success are bright.

THE BRETTON WOODS SYSTEM, KEY CURRENCIES, AND THE RECENT DOLLAR CRISES*

Harry G. Johnson

During the past several years, the international monetary system has experienced a series of crises, in most cases related to the value of the dollar relative to other currencies and/or the dollar's role as a reserve currency in the system. The "dollar crisis" of 1971 was the first international monetary crisis since the establishment of the International Monetary Fund to shake the foundations of the international monetary system established by the Bretton Woods Conference of 1944. (The "gold crisis" of 1968 in an important sense strengthened those foundations by

* This is a revised version of the paper entitled, "The Bretton Woods System, Key Currencies, and the 'Dollar Crisis' of 1971," *The Three Banks Review* (June 1972), pp. 3–22. Reprinted by permission of the publisher and the author. Harry G. Johnson is Professor of Economics, University of Chicago, and Professor of Economics, London School of Economics and Political Science.

eliminating private convertibility of paper money to gold as a threat to control of the system by the central banks involved.) The result of the 1971 crisis was to reestablish the preexisting international monetary system of fixed exchange rates, albeit with a realignment of their relative values intended to secure international equilibrium for a reasonable period ahead—though it should be noted that the complete inconvertibility of the American dollar into gold for the foreseeable future meant technically that the International Monetary Fund system ceased to exist, since it rested formally on gold as the base of the international monetary system. However, the stability which was the goal of the 1971 Smithsonian agreement never came close to being really achieved, as first the pound and then the dollar were subjected to heavy downward pressures in 1972–73. The British were forced to suspend their participation in the Smithsonian agreement in mid-1972, and in early 1973 the U.S. balance-of-payments situation, concern abroad over prospects for continued inflation in the United States, and other developments led finally to a 10 percent devaluation of the dollar in mid-February. This change, which was coupled with a floating yen, only resulted in new speculative attacks on the dollar and, through the stable exchange-rate system, its relationships with other currencies. One month later, six of the Common Market countries (later joined by two outsiders, Sweden and Norway), announced that each of their currencies would be kept in close alignment with the others, none being allowed to vary more than 2.25 percent with respect to another (the range accepted under the Smithsonian agreement); at the same time, the currencies as a group were to float against the dollar.

While currencies are floating in the manner described above at the time of this writing, it seems likely that a system of stable currency values will be reintroduced in the near future—or at least that an attempt will be made to reintroduce such a system. Therefore, the purpose of this article is to set and discuss the recent crises in the context of the Bretton Woods system rather than to discuss the results of the crises in short-term near perspective. To begin with, however, some remarks on the broader implications of the crises and their resolution for the character and evaluation of world economic organisation are appropriate.

First, and most important, contrary to many popular predictions, a major breakdown in international monetary arrangements was *not* accompanied by any significant consequential recession, let alone collapse, in world trade, production and employment. Whatever view one takes of the interplay of real and monetary factors in the 1930s collapse of the international economic system, by analogy with which these dire predictions were derived, it seems a safe generalisation that the world can ride out international monetary storms without great loss of economic life provided that governments are unprepared to allow a consequential collapse of production and employment and that they do not resort to drastic trade and payments interventions to meet passing squalls.

Second, the fact the the Americans were able in 1971 to use the import surcharge and investment tax credit and the consequential European fear of a trade war as a bargaining weapon, successfully, is a hopeful sign of general understanding that the purpose of international monetary arrangements is to facilitate international trade

and investment; and not *vice versa*, as individual national actions in the past have frequently suggested. The crises laid the basis for a further movement towards the goal of a liberal international trade and payments system through international trade negotiations.

Third, and not a matter of optimism, the fact that a system of floating exchange rates, however "dirty" the floating was, proved not only possible, but the only feasible immediate reaction to the American crisis initiative is likely—as occurred with earlier experiences of floating rates in the 1920s and 1930s—to be confused in the official and political mind with the nastiness of the crises itself, and to be absorbed into the conventional wisdom and imitative magic of the standard official arguments against exchange rate flexibility.

Finally, on the educational hypothesis that man learns only slowly from experience but does learn, these crises should make a significant long-run contribution to progress in the international monetary field. There is an ancient legend of a giant who was condemned to run around the world backwards, seeing nothing of what lay ahead but seeing fairly clearly what lay behind. One imagines that the more he tripped backwards over obstacles, the more glimpses he caught of what lay ahead and the more careful attention he paid to what lay behind. The management of the international monetary system has resembled that giant very closely, with two exceptions: the monetary giant was forcibly stopped from running during the Second World War, and therefore was forced to contemplate the terrain he had passed through and devise a better running strategy for the territory ahead; but precisely because he had a better running strategy, he stumbled fewer times and so paid less attention to the experience once he got up and resumed running. To drop the analogy, postwar international monetary experience has amply shown the need for greater exchange rate flexibility, but every exercise in this direction has been regarded as an unfortunate aberration; in the longer run, the crises of 1971–73 seem likely to force recognition of the general need for greater flexibility, even though their shorter-run effect has been and is likely to be to restore the conventional rigidity.

The Bretton Woods system had and has two aspects: the technical economic and the political economy aspects. Technically, the International Monetary Fund was (as will be detailed later) designed to cope with and overcome certain problems that the experts involved could agree had constituted the major defects of the interwar monetary system and caused its collapse in the 1930s. However, the institutional arrangements for doing so were worked out primarily between the Americans and the British, with the Canadians playing the role of honest brokers and the Europeans having no real say. Moreover, due to the actual and even more the prospective disparity between the two major negotiators, the new arrangements were cast in the fictional form beloved by the United States of equality of nations and therefore of currencies, though, in the International Monetary Fund as in the United Nations, the United States took care to represent the then actual structure of political power in the structure of management and voting power in the institution created on this fictional basis.

The result was a mixture of fictional equality of currencies and actual inequality of countries in the decision-taking processes of the system. The fictional equality of currencies has given rise to many problems in the details of IMF management, most notably the necessity of inventing the General Arrangements to Borrow so as to guarantee supplies of currencies actually internationally usable, and also the need for complex manœuvres in the treatment of gold on the occasion of increases in IMF quotas. Fictional equality combined with actual inequality in management has also provided a fertile source of grievance for the less developed country lobby, expressed most recently and persistently in the demand that the provision of additional liquidity in the form of Special Drawing Rights should be taxed with the obligation to serve as development assistance. And the inequality of management rights among the countries specially privileged in this respect has given rise to tensions in the system as it has had to be adjusted to the increasing importance in the world economy of the recovered European powers and Japan and the relative decline of the United States.

From the point of view of both political economy and economics proper, it has been one of the major defects of the Bretton Woods system, in contrast at least to the theoretical if not the actual gold standard system of the nineteenth century, that it has forced international monetary issues that are in principle capable of rational solution either by private bargaining among the nations directly affected or by dispassionate arbitration with reference to some concept of cosmopolitan good, into this ambiguous framework of fictional equality of nations and actual inequality defined by a constitution rather than by the free play of politics.

In this connection, it is worth recalling that

at the time of Bretton Woods there was an alternative conception of the problem and its solution, based on a view of the political realities of what had happened in the 1930s rather than a theoretical analysis of the economic problems, which was disregarded and overruled in the enthusiasm for reestablishing an international rule of law. This conception, which grew out of the efforts to reestablish a viable international exchange rate system after the suspension of the gold convertibility of the pound in 1931, the revaluation of the U.S. price of gold in 1934, and the abandonment of their original gold parities by the gold bloc in 1936, and culminated in the Tripartite Agreement, was expressed most powerfully and forcefully in the "key currencies" theory of John H. Williams of Harvard University and the Federal Reserve Bank of New York. According to this, in very broad terms, only a few currencies (then the pound, the dollar, the franc, and the mark) really matter in international trade and payments, and the essential problem is to get political agreement among their managers to behave themselves responsibly. (This view has also been consistently maintained by Lionel Robbins.) But it gained no significant hearing in the climate of opinion of the immediate postwar II period; and it has been more or less swamped ever since as an intellectual position by the tendency of both academic economists and practitioners to accept as a framework for argument the fictitious assumption of a large number of equal countries and currencies on which the formal structure of the IMF system is built, and the corresponding assumption that it is useful to discuss the problems of the system in terms of anonymous deficit and surplus countries and their responsibilities towards the system.

Nevertheless, if one looks at the realities of what has been happening in the evolution of the system, the key currency approach helps one to understand a great deal. Notably there is the long-sustained special position of the pound sterling, inherited from the turn-of-the-century position of sterling as the unique key currency, salvaged in part by the formulation of the sterling area in the 1930s and its strengthening by wartime financial exigencies, and increasingly supported by the Americans until immediately before the devaluation of 1967 in the belief that if sterling went under so would the dollar. There is also the postwar II emergence of the dollar as the key currency par excellence, a position which in the early 1960s led the European countries reluctantly to accept the view that, so long as the American authorities behaved reasonably responsibly, they would have to wait on the slow operation of natural adjustment processes for correction of the dollar deficit and associated international disequilibrium. All that changed with the escalation of the war in Vietnam and the U.S. failure to finance it by appropriate tax increases, which meant that the United States became an inflationary and not a stabilising force in the system, while the major continental European countries became aware that their currencies had the economic backing but not the domestic and international political strength to play the key currency game. Hence the two major developments of the late 1960s: the agreement to establish Special Drawing Rights, envisaged as the means of gradually terminating the key currency role of the dollar in the system in favour of an internationally-controlled monetary system; and the proposal to establish a common European currency as a means of establishing a European money that would rival the dollar as a key currency.

The key currency approach also helps one to understand what has been happening in the evolution of the international monetary system itself. The emergence of the Group of Ten as the effective decision-centre of the system reflects Williams' basic point (to paraphrase Orwell's *Animal Farm*) that all currencies are equal but some are more equal than others. The hostility of the less developed countries to the Group of Ten and its "monopoly power" reflects at once their awareness and their intense resentment of this fact. On the other hand the Group of Ten—which itself includes some currencies in a minor key—has not been all that effective in arriving at the kind of collective responsibility for the system that Montagu Norman and Benjamin Strong thought they had achieved in the 1920s, or that the "key currency" school thought was achievable on the basis of latter-1930s experience.

The fundamental reason, in my view, has been that the overwhelming dominance of the dollar through most of the postwar II period has enabled the other currencies to coast intellectually on the basis of carping about the behavior of the United States, while concerning themselves less about the system as a whole than about their own position in it. When the U.S. Administration finally tired of the burden of holding the umbrella for the rest, and challenged them to display some genuine leadership out of the *impasse* that resulted, it was the United States that by good poker-playing exercised all the leadership that was displayed. But whether skill in winning at poker redistributes the stakes in an economically

desirable fashion is not a question to which economists have ever been willing to return an affirmative answer.

I have put these observations in the rather novel context of the "key currency" versus "Bretton Woods" approaches to postwar II international monetary reconstruction partly to recall that the establishment of the IMF was not merely a compromise on detail among men of different (but not very different) nationalities each representing a national interpretation of universal truth, but a compromise among men like-minded in their belief in the efficacy of international institutions to contain and control international power politics; and partly to emphasize that institutions serve often to civilise the barbarian's manners without transforming his motives into cosmopolitan ones. But the implications are really no different than one can arrive at—and many have arrived at— by more conventional analysis. These are that, while the "impersonal" gold standard of the nineteenth century, painfully resurrected in the twentieth-century interwar period, and fossilised into the structure of the Bretton Woods agreements, has been disposed of—the 18th December 1971 agreement to raise the dollar price of gold by a derisory 8½ percent reduces gold to a mere numéraire with no real monetary role—there still remains a choice between a Special Drawing Rights standard, a dollar standard, and a dollar-Europa standard. In the terminology employed so far, there is a choice between no key currency, one key currency, and two key currencies. And since one key currency now exists by virtue of postwar II history and both the other alternatives will have to be created by deliberate agreement among sovereign national states at a considerable cost to themselves in terms of economic policy autonomy, there is a strong historically-based probability that the one-key-currency system (i.e., the dollar standard) will prevail. An alternative outcome depends either on the mismanagement of the dollar continuing and being sufficiently offensive and disruptive to the other major countries to prompt them to a defensive establishment of a rival European currency; or on the responsibilities of the key currency role becoming sufficiently onerous to the U.S. Administration to prompt it to force the pace of evolution of the SDR system. "Benign neglect" of the U.S. balance of payments by a President anxious for re-election points in the former direction; the current U.S. desire for exchange rate freedom points in the other. But inertia in the absence of crisis may carry the day.

Turning from political economy to economics more narrowly conceived and specifically to the framework of analysis of the international monetary system that has been gradually built up by the efforts of a host of scholars (in interaction with the responsible officials) over the past fifteen years or so, one can visualise the Bretton Woods system as having been devised to deal with four aspects of the breakdown of the gold exchange standard that was restored in the middle 1920s, only to crash disastrously in the early 1930s. Further—a matter of extreme historical irony—one can view the deficiencies of the IMF system as it has developed since as consisting precisely in the recrudescence of three of these problems and the appearance of the obverse of the fourth.

The four problems of the pre-existing system with which the Bretton Woods plans were intended to deal can be described as the confidence problem, the liquidity problem, the adjustment problem, and the problem of deflationary bias.

The confidence problem in a fixed exchange rate system in which reserve assets are partly gold and partly currencies convertible into gold has two aspects: the possibility of loss of confidence in the ability of a particular country to maintain its existing exchange rate—which may be speculation on either devaluation or revaluation; and the possibility of loss of confidence in the ability of the reserve currency country to maintain its exchange rate, which is inevitably speculation on a devaluation relative to gold or the other currencies in general. The IMF system attempted to insure against the first possibility both by affording additional credit (drawing rights) and by allowing quantitative control of short-term capital movements (the "hot money" of the 1930s). The former has proved inadequate and the latter effectively impossible in a world of liberal capital movements and integrated capital markets. The second possibility—loss of confidence in the reserve currency—was not foreseen or dealt with by the "equality of currencies" philosophy, except as under insurance against the first problem.

The second problem, liquidity, stemmed from the inadequacy of new supplies of monetary gold to meet reserve demands, reflected in the growth of the gold exchange standard itself and resulting in the vulnerability of the system to confidence crises. The IMF system attempted to meet this problem by the provision of drawing rights that could be used to supplement gold reserves, though it also provided for an internationally agreed increase in the price of gold in case of a general shortage of liquidity.

The third problem was adjustment, which under the gold standard of classical theory involved inflation or deflation of domestic prices and wages. The IMF system provided the alternative of devaluation or revaluation, reached by international agreement in cases of "fundamental disequilibrium." One purpose was to avoid the alleged problem of "competitive devaluations" cancelling one another out, which was thought to have occurred in the 1930s (in reality, "competitive devaluations" in that period are most accurately conceived of as an internationally painful process of raising the price of gold).

The fourth problem, which does not appear on most lists but which has recurred in the discussions of the past few years, is that of "deflationary bias," derived from the idea that deficit countries under the gold standard must sooner or later deflate but surplus countries are under no pressure to inflate. For the deficit countries the availability of devaluation in fundamental disequilibrium was intended to provide the remedy. Surplus countries that chronically sucked reserves from the rest and obliged them to deflate or devalue were to be discriminated against under the "scarce currency" clause; but this has never been activated.

These four problems are of course facets of a single whole. More rapid adjustment of exchange rates would forestall the confidence problem for individual countries, remove the pressures for deflationary domestic policies, and reduce the liquidity needs of the system as a whole; on the other hand more ample liquidity and more rapid liquidity growth would both reduce the need for adjustment by domestic deflation and modify any general "deflationary bias." The Bretton Woods system attempted to deal with them as such; and, as mentioned, the major irony of postwar II international monetary history has been that all the problems have reappeared, with the exception that deflationary bias has been replaced by inflationary bias—though, as one might expect, the name of the villain is still the United States.

The problems have, however, reappeared as successive separate problems, and never (at least until possibly in the wake of the 1971 crisis) as an interconnected package of problems. The result has been a series of painfully taken *ad hoc* measures which one could argue with some plausibility have made the system function worse rather than better than the original Bretton Woods scheme would have done. The main reason would be that because the Bretton Woods agreements represented a compromise between the Keynes and the White Plans and were therefore regarded by the dominant Keynesian view as an undue concession to deflationary orthodoxy, the assumption of the academic experts, and also of many of the national and international monetary officials, has been that the system must be deflationary and require reform in the direction of expansionary changes. In fact, though this has only been realised gradually and recently, the problem of the system is that it is inflationary and not deflationary, and the solution is to reform it in a less inflationary direction. The words "inflationary" and "deflationary" are however rather slippery, and will require further discussion below.

Let us consider the various problems or alleged problems of the system in turn. The "confidence problem" was the one that most concerned Robert Triffin in his pioneering work on the international monetary system in the late 1950s, based on the dangers of an international monetary collapse of the 1930s variety. But this problem, at least as regards other countries than the United States, has proved very easy to solve. Nothing is easier than for central banks to grant each other credits, *unless* they have a motivation to bring down a government either because they dislike its political complexion or because they consider its economic policies unsustainable. This was the case in the 1931 *débâcle* of the schilling and the pound. But in the early 1960s the European countries felt more solidarity towards one another, the pound had the support of the United States, and the United States could not be brought down without predictable disaster for others greater than for the United States itself. So inflationary Britain was supported by European and American credit, and the American deficit covered by European credit. In the latter 1960s and 1970–73, it was not lack of foreign central bank willingness, albeit grudgingly, to hold a mounting flood of dollars but U.S. concern about the effect of dollar overvaluation on its current and capital accounts that precipitated the crisis. In short, the confidence problem in the 1960s, in contrast to the 1930s analogy, has been either a question of a country's own self-confidence or a matter of very tactful and prolonged exploration of methods of mutual reconciliation.

Take next the liquidity problem. Much of the work that led to general belief in the existence of an actual or prospective shortage of international reserves requiring action to increase international liquidity rested either on extremely crude transactions-demand-for-money theory or on war and dollar-shortage-period concepts of the need for hard foreign exchange reserves to pay for imports in case of an export embargo. No one until recently has looked at the question in terms of the effects of the actual growth of international liquidity on the world economy and especially on world inflation. Admittedly the issues are difficult, and do not readily permit us to apply the simple quantity theory view that too much money relative to demand for it spells price inflation and too little spells price deflation—though that principle is a good starting point. One can conceive a contrary case in which a shortage of international liquidity leads to a proliferation of controls on international trade and payments, a consequential rise in domestic price levels relative to a residual free world market price level, and so a combination of observed inflation with observed liquidity shortage. This may well have been the case in the early postwar II dollar shortage period. But given the progressive reduction of barriers to trade and payments that has occurred since, it is plausible to attribute chronic world inflation to an excess and not to a shortage of international liquidity.

Thirdly, there are the questions of adjustment and of deflationary bias in the system. It is true that until the realignments of 1971 most of the exchange rate adjustments were devaluations and not revaluations; and in terms of the Keynesian views of the 1930s and after this could be interpreted as evidence of liquidity shortage and deflationary bias. But the observed facts are equally consistent with the hypothesis of an inflationary bias. Consider the following Keynesian argument, set in the context of a generally inflationary world economy. The governments of countries that want to pursue high employment at the cost of inflation will take the risk that their domestic inflation will be offset by the world inflationary trend, leaving their balance of payments in reasonable order. If they overdo it, they will have to devalue, and if they do their domestic prices will inflate by more than the world average; but they may be able to adjust without devaluing, by temporarily restraining their inflation until inflation elsewhere catches up with them. The governments of countries that do not want to import world inflation via fixed exchange rates will find political opposition to the necessary appreciation, because it will hit the fortunes of prospering export and import-competing sectors, and they will find it easier to keep the exchange rate where it is and allow the inward seepage of inflation; hence their domestic prices too will inflate more than they would have done with revaluation or upward currency flotation. Hence, for reasons that are essentially political, we arrive at a system that has a *devaluation bias*, but not a *deflation bias*; on the contrary it combines a *devaluation bias* with an *inflation bias*. One can arrive at the same conclusion by noticing that devaluation increases and revaluation decreases the purchasing power of gold, and of dollars whose price is fixed in terms of gold, the base reserves of the system.

This conclusion is clearly reinforced if we assume a more realistic system in which one country both bulks large in world trade and investment, and issues a national currency that is accepted as an international monetary reserve asset by the others. So long as its currency is acceptable, however grudgingly, this country will not be subject to a balance-of-payments constraint on domestic inflation like the others; it can inflate and by so doing both satisfy the domestic full employment objective and attract real resources from the rest of the world by imposing an "inflation tax" on holders of its currency. Moreover, the others will be willing within wide limits to accept the inflation and the related tax for either of the two reasons mentioned—political need for the support of world inflation, or political inability to counter it by exchange appreciation. For those motivated by the first reason, acquisitions of the reserve currency will be welcome, for their own inflationary policies make foreign exchange chronically scarce. For those motivated by the second reason, acquisitions of the reserve currency will not be welcome, and will be resisted by the various means available to the authorities, but will in the end be accepted as a lesser evil or the price of keeping exporters and import-competing sectors happy.

In the model of the international economy just described, inflation can and will go on quite happily, at a moderate pace, so long as the reserve currency country itself inflates at a reasonably modest pace. Adjustment problems will not occur too frequently or be too difficult, and can be handled by changes in the exchange values of particular national currencies against the key currency. However, such adjustments are politically difficult for the governments concerned and typically have to be forced by some sort of international monetary crisis; hence there will be generated concern about improving the adjustment mechanism by making it more automatic, more frequent, and less disturbing. This was the position reached by the autumn of 1969, when academic prescriptions of wider bands, crawling pegs, etcetera suddenly became popular among international monetary officials.

The situation changes, however, if the reserve currency country begins to inflate at an immodest pace; and this was true of the United States from 1965 on, and formed the background to the recent crises, beginning in 1971. The reserve currency country then becomes an active source of inflation within the system, through the direct influence of its own prices on world prices, through the demand-injecting influence of a deterioration in its current account, and through the monetary implications for others of a vastly enlarged outflow of its currency. The fixed rate system, instead of enabling the non-reserve-currency countries to go their own pace with inflation, becomes an engine for forcing unwanted inflation on them all.

Their logical defence against this—which I wrongly predicted in 1969 that the European countries would resort to—would be to revalue or float their currencies against the key currency. But there were resistances to that solution, both because each country's exchange rate affects mainly its trade with its neighbours, so that it is difficult for each independently to work out the adjustment it should make and predict the reactions of its neighbours, and because for the first time the European countries were obliged to think of themselves collectively rather than individually in relation to the U.S. dollar, and they were unaccustomed to doing so. Instead, though Canada and Germany individually adopted the logical solution, they collectively concentrated on berating the United States for the excess liquidity and the inflation, and exploring schemes for bringing the U.S. power to create international money under control—though it must be admitted that some of the proponents of a common European currency have seen it as a way of achieving collective flexibility against the dollar and protection from U.S. inflation. In the event, it was the United States, alarmed for both internal and external reasons by the sharp deterioration of its current account, and panicked by a vast outflow of dollars on capital account (and specifically by a British claim for conversion of a substantial sum of dollars into gold), that floated the dollar against the other currencies and forced them to make the exchange rate adjustments that the United States considered necessary.

We then went back, at least temporarily, on the Bretton Woods system, with a token change in the price of gold that kept its average accounting value in terms of currencies more or less unchanged, and a widening of the margins of market exchange rate variations about par values to 2¼ percent each way. In view of the well-known points that the "wider band" proposal was intended to put some of the burden of stabilising speculation on private as contrasted with official asset-holders, and also allow the central banks to penalise private operators more severely for unjustified speculation against maintenance of the par value, while the "crawling peg" proposal is intended to provide for automatic adjustment of parities and hence exchange rates among countries experiencing different trend rates of price change, adoption of the former but not the latter scheme in the new arrangements implied that the new parities were expected to last and that the extra flexibility of wider bands was intended to ensure this. In other words, the new arrangements both restored and strengthened the Bretton Woods system.

The new arrangements, however, lasted hardly long enough for the ink to dry on the Smithsonian agreement—or, more cynically, for President Nixon to win the American elections partly on the strength of "the greatest international monetary agreement in the history of the world." The British decision to float the pound in June 1972 was the first break in the agreement, though tolerance of that decision and contemporary minimization of its significance is explainable by the decline in Britain's importance in the international monetary system since the 1967 devaluation (which disposed of the American belief that if the pound went, the dollar would have to go too) and especially following the independent 1971 devaluation of the dollar, as well as by sympathy with Britain's natural reluctance to peg a rapidly-inflating domestic economy to the European Community currencies. The decision to devalue the dollar in February 1973 was in part predictable, since there was some reason to think that Secretary Connally's desire to resolve the 1971 crisis by the Smithsonian agreement led him to settle for a smaller devaluation of the dollar than was in fact necessary. Immediately after the 1973 devaluation, there was some tendency in informed American circles to fear that that devaluation was too large, and portended a recurrence of dollar scarcity in another year or two; but renewed speculation against the dollar and the decision of the majority of the enlarged European Community to float in common against the dollar make this opinion look very much like wishful thinking. At the time of writing, the international economy is on a *de facto* regime of floating exchange rates; but the prospects are still unclear, both because the European Community has still a long way to go in establishing a common currency capable of being allowed to float freely against the dollar, and because official U.S. opinion still seems wedded to a fairly speedy return to a fixed rate system and continues to concentrate on proposals for more orderly exchange rate adjustment within such a system.

How the system will evolve in the longer-term future remains problematical: on the liquidity side, there remains the choice between an SDR-based system, internationally controlled, a dollar standard, and a dollar-Europa standard; on the adjustment side, there is the need for more regular and automatic flexibility of exchange rates. At the present time, there is much talk of the so-called "overhang" of U.S. dollars and the need to fund them, though on this issue American enthusiasm for getting the dollars out of the way to permit the United States more freedom of exchange rate adjustment meets deep European suspicion of the possibility of being obliged to absorb a new tidal wave of inflation-created surplus dollars. Actually, the "overhang" has two quite different dimensions. The first is the approximately twenty billion dollars increase in foreign holdings of dollars created in 1971; it is arguable—and the argument is strengthened by the failure of the alleged "gold overhang" after the 1968 gold rush to materialise—that these dollars are not an overhang but a desired substitute for the roughly forty billion dollars of gold that has now become at once too valuable and too speculative an asset to be usable as a means of international settlement. The second is the continuing large-scale outflow of dollars associated with the continuing U.S. deficit; this is not an overhang but a symptom of continuing disequilibrium portending the need for further exchange rate adjustments. Whether that threat can be countered either by funding existing dollars into some sort of extended SDR system and then obliging the United States to submit to the discipline of international control of the total and the rate of growth of the pool of SDRs, or by establishing the Europa as a common European currency that could be revalued or would float against the U.S. dollar, is an open question on which the answer must be rendered by international political judgment rather than by economic science. Monetary history, only a small part of which has been reviewed in this article, suggests very strongly the pessimistic conclusion that, except when men are forcibly detached from preoccupation with current affairs and forced to think about basic principles, as happened in the circumstances that led up to Bretton Woods, human intelligence and ingenuity are unlikely to be able to counteract and improve on the blind forces of natural evolution. Concretely, the world-wide use of the dollar has been a natural development, a reflection of commercial advantage rather than a result of deliberate planning; and while both the SDRs and the Europa proposal represent a flowering of the human intellect under the pressure of crisis, it is problematical to say the least whether the intellectual force behind them will be sufficiently strong to overcome the natural inertial tendency to live with the dollar and put up with the crises that result. Whether this pessimism is justified or not (and perhaps it is optimism given the ironical failure of the Bretton Woods system to solve the problems that it was intended to solve),

the best course for those in charge of the international monetary system at the present time would seem to be to concentrate on the development of better devices for exchange rate flexibility, as a cushion against the consequence of errors and failures of international monetary control, rather than on attempts to preserve and strengthen a system in which policy errors have serious consequences, while at the same time seeking to devise more error-free controls over the management of the system that require sacrifices of national sovereignty which the member nations are very unlikely to concede, and more importantly, to abide by when a real crunch comes.

ARE THERE ENOUGH POLICY TOOLS?*

Warren L. Smith

I. INTRODUCTION

If I were asked to sketch the main features of the world economy as it exists today, with particular reference to the advanced industrial countries, I would describe the situation in the following way:

1. Each country insists on the free exercise of its sovereign authority to regulate its level of internal demand for the purpose of maintaining suitable economic conditions at home in terms of employment and the behavior of its internal price level. In addition, the idea of governmental responsibility for the attainment of a satisfactory rate of long-term economic growth is widely accepted, and some efforts are made to influence the composition of demand in favor of investment-type activities as a means of accelerating growth.

2. In many countries, fiscal policy is, as a practical matter, a relatively inflexible instrument, partly because of unsatisfactory administrative arrangements and in some cases also because of outmoded and unenlightened views about budget deficits. Monetary policy is administratively more flexible, but, in practice, freedom to use it for domestic purposes has become increasingly limited by balance-of-payments considerations.

3. Free international movement of goods and of capital as a means of achieving efficient use of resources is generally accepted as a goal, and substantial progress has been made in achieving

* From *American Economic Review*, Vol. LV (May 1965), pp. 208–20. Reprinted by permission of the publisher.

it. In particular, since the advent of general currency convertibility in 1958, controls over the international flow of capital have been relaxed and investors have become increasingly inclined to shift funds internationally in response to differential changes in expected rates of return.

4. Subject to some important qualifications to be discussed below, trade is conducted under a system of fixed exchange parities, with actual exchange rates fluctuating only within very narrow limits around these parities.

5. Countries hold limited supplies of monetary reserves in the form of gold, foreign exchange, and lines of credit at the IMF. The reserves available and potentially obtainable set a limit—albeit a somewhat elastic one—on the cumulative size of a country's balance-of-payments deficit. For this reason, each country operates subject to a balance-of-payments constraint—not in the sense that the balance of payments must always be in equilibrium but in the sense that there is some limit on the size and duration of deficits that can be tolerated. There is no corresponding limit for surpluses.

Some of the features in the above list need to be spelled out a little more fully. First, with regard to the goal of internal stability (item 1 above), countries are often said to seek the twin goals of "full employment" and "price stability." For some time, however, it has been getting increasingly clear that this way of describing the situation is quite out of touch with reality. Indeed, the concept of full employment, while perhaps useful as a slogan, is without precise meaning. A more accurate way to describe the situation is as follows: There is in each country a "trade-off" between employment (or unemployment) and price stability; that is, over a considerable range the more unemployment is reduced by policies to expand aggregate demand the higher is the price that must be paid in terms of inflation. This relation holds primarily because of the tendency of money-wage increases to outstrip increases in productivity even under conditions of substantial unemployment. The trade-off varies from country to country, depending on the organization, traditions, and aggressiveness of the labor movement, the price policies followed by industry, and so on, and from time to time depending on the attendant circumstances. The trade-off may be influenced by policy measures—wage-price guideposts, incomes policies, etc.—but I am not aware of any cases in which efforts to change it have been notably successful. Not only does the trade-off itself vary from country to country but so also do the relative weights attached to price stability and employment in the implicit social welfare functions that govern the behavior of the authorities responsible for economic policy in the various countries. As a consequence, to the extent that each country is left free to decide what combination of price inflation and employment to select from the many choices open to it, price trends may vary considerably from country to country.[1]

The other feature that calls for further comment is exchange rate arrangements (item 4 above). Although, as indicated above, fixed exchange rates appear to be one of the generally accepted goals of economic policy, we do not now have a system of really fixed rates. Indeed, the most serious difficulty with the present international monetary system seems to lie in the area of exchange rate policy. The present arrangements, under which exchange rates are fixed within very narrow limits at any particular time but are subject to readjustment from time to time to correct "fundamental" disequilibria in national balances of payments, seem ideally calculated to encourage speculation. Since opportunities for the investment of capital, viewed broadly, do not ordinarily vary widely as between major countries, even a mild suspicion that a country may

devalue its currency can cause a speculative outflow of capital from that country. And, as more and more investors become familiar with the possibilities of transferring capital internationally, it seems likely that the potential size of speculative capital flows will become even larger. The result is that most countries will entertain the possibility of devaluation only in the most dire emergency, but the threat is nevertheless sufficient to induce speculation. And there is always the possibility that speculation will exhaust a country's reserves and force the devaluation that the speculators are hoping for.

It does not strain reality very much to describe the world economy we seek to achieve as one in which (1) there is complete freedom in the international movement of goods and capital, (2) exchange rates are fixed, and (3) individual countries are free to use monetary and fiscal policy—primarily the former—to attain their domestic price and employment goals. And the system is subject to the constraint that each country possesses a limited supply of reserves with which to cover deficits in its balance of payments.

The trouble with this system is that it is basically inconsistent. There are three possible ways of correcting a deficit or surplus through adjustment of the current account: through the use of trade or exchange controls, through an adjustment of exchange rates, and through internal price and income changes. Since all of these violate the principles of the system, they are ruled out. Consequently, when a country experiences a deficit, there is no assurance that the deficit will be eliminated before its limited supply of reserves is used up. And the difficulty is further compounded by the nature of the prevailing exchange rate system under which a persistent deficit creates a fear of devaluation, possibly leading to a speculative outflow of capital and an unlimited self-generating expansion of the deficit.

Thus, if the underlying principles are adhered to, there is no mechanism that can be depended upon to eliminate a balance-of-payments disequilibrium brought about by such disruptive forces as changes in tastes or technology. Beyond that, even if the system is in equilibrium to begin with, the diverse price trends inherent in the independent economic policies of the member countries may themselves in due course produce disequilibrium.

Of course, the system has worked after a fashion—although the road has been pretty rocky, especially in view of the fact that only six years have elapsed since the restoration of convertibility in 1958. And it has survived only because its

[1] Much lip service is paid to price stability as a goal of national economic policy but in reality it is an extremely unrealistic objective, since no one is in fact willing to pay the price in terms of unemployment required to achieve it. And since it is a practically unattainable goal for individual countries, it is obviously an unrealistic objective for the world as a whole.

fundamental principles have been violated in various ways.

1. The underlying principle of free movement of goods and capital has been compromised through the imposition of trade restrictions for balance-of-payments reasons by Canada in 1962 and the United Kingdom in recent weeks. The United States has also persistently violated the principle by tying foreign aid, by discriminating in favor of American suppliers in its defense procurement policies, and by the recent enactment of the so-called "Interest Equalization Tax."

2. Minor use has been made of exchange rate adjustments in the Dutch and German revaluations of March, 1961. Such adjustments, however, probably do more harm than good by weakening confidence in the overall stability of exchange rates and encouraging speculation.

3. In practice, domestic monetary and fiscal policies have not been entirely unaffected by the balance-of-payments situation. In part, this is because, due to the less than perfect effectiveness of domestic monetary and fiscal tools, it has not always been feasible to offset completely the automatic corrective effects of deficits and surpluses on internal demand. But beyond that, deficit countries have found it necessary to adapt their domestic policies to the exigencies of the balance-of-payments—albeit reluctantly—when their international reserves have been seriously threatened. The leading example here is the United States, which has suffered from an unnecessarily high rate of unemployment and a resultant irrecoverable loss of output amounting perhaps to $150 billion in the last 5 years, partly as a result of its balance-of-payments deficit. This has not been due, in my opinion, however, to the fact that policies to expand aggregate demand have been held back by fear that they would worsen the trade balance. Rather it has been a result of the administrative inflexibility of fiscal policy (as a consequence, in part, of unenlightened views about budget deficits and growth of the public debt) combined with the fact that the need to avoid an accentuation of short-term capital outflows has acted as a significant constraint on monetary policy, the one flexible and acceptable instrument that might in the absence of the balance-of-payments constraint have been used to expand aggregate demand. No doubt similar considerations have to some extent operated in European countries to limit the use of restrictive monetary policies to check excessive inflation in the face of balance-of-payments surpluses. But it is quite clear that the system has an inherent deflationary bias. The limited supply of reserves sets some upper bound on the size of a nation's cumulative deficit, whereas there is no equivalent upper bound to the size of a cumulative surplus and the associated expansion of monetary reserves.

Techniques of central bank cooperation through the use of currency "swaps" and intervention in foreign exchange markets to deal with minor speculative crises have been progressively developed and refined. To deal with more serious crises, massive supplies of foreign exchange have been mobilized to support threatened currencies and combat the activities of speculators. Up to now, these efforts have been successful in fending off disaster, but the world lives in dread of a forced devaluation of sterling or the dollar, which would in all probability create a state of international financial chaos from which recovery would be extremely difficult. Moreover, the present situation gives the opinions of international currency speculators an entirely disproportionate weight in the determination of economic policy.

It seems clear that the present international economic arrangements are seriously defective. It is doubtful whether they can survive in their present form for very long. The question is: What changes should be made? In the extensive discussions of the international economy that have taken place in the last few years, much energy has been expended on the formulation of proposals for reform of the world's monetary institutions, and many ingenious schemes have been proposed. However, it is difficult for me to see how the mere establishment of an improved international banking arrangement for providing liquidity can be depended upon to yield a satisfactory solution to our problems as long as private international transactions are conducted by the use of national currencies whose exchange parities are felt to be subject to change. Even if gold were completely demonetized and official settlements between countries were carried out by the transfer of credits on the books of a reformed IMF, the problem would remain. Suppose, for example, that under such an arrangement the United States were to run a substantial balance-of-payments deficit. The dollar would decline in foreign exchange markets, and foreign central banks would have to buy dollars to prevent the exchange rate from moving outside the prescribed limits. The dollars would be deposited with the IMF for credit to the other country's account, and they would be debited to the U.S. account. If the latter account were to become exhausted, the United States would presumably have to arrange a loan from the IMF which would replenish its balance. As long as there was felt to be an effective limit to the credit line available, so that eventually devaluation (or direct controls) might have to be employed to correct the deficit, private investors would have essentially the same motive to speculate against the dollar as they have under the present system, and the speculation itself would help to exhaust the credit line. Since claims against the IMF would presumably be subject to an exchange guarantee, countries might be willing to extend sufficiently large credits through the IMF to make the effective supply of reserves available for meeting speculative runs larger than it is at present. But there is no assurance that the fundamental problem of speculation would be eliminated.

Schemes to reform the financial system and increase the supply of monetary reserves can undoubtedly be of some help. But the more fundamental need is to introduce some workable mechanism for restoring and maintaining balance-of-payments equilibrium. Can this be done more or less within the confines of the present system by making more flexible use of traditional policy instruments? Or are some fundamental reforms of the system required, and if so, what reforms would be appropriate? These are the questions to which I shall devote the remainder of my paper.

II. MORE FLEXIBLE USE OF MONETARY AND FISCAL MEASURES

I believe a considerable improvement in economic performance could be achieved within the framework of the present international monetary system if fiscal policy could be rendered substantially more flexible than it now is. For example, in the United States some arrangement, such as that proposed by the Commission on Money and Credit in its 1961 report or that recommended in the January, 1962, *Annual Report of the Council of Economic Advisers,* giving the President discretionary authority to change personal income tax rates for countercyclical purposes would be very helpful.

The idea would be to develop a policy arrangement under which the Western industrial countries would agree to rely on flexible fiscal policy, implemented primarily through tax adjustments, to regulate internal demand to achieve domestic goals. Monetary policy would then be assigned the task of maintaining balance-of-payments equilibrium by establishing interest rates at levels which would induce a sufficient inflow

or outflow of private capital to cover the deficit or surplus on current account (including government military and foreign aid transactions) that would occur at target levels of income and employment. To be workable, such an arrangement would require that tax policy be rendered much more flexible than at present not only in the United States, but in other countries as well.

Machinery would need to be set up to provide careful international coordination of the monetary policies of participating countries. The objective would be to establish a matrix of interest rate differentials among countries which would be sufficient to achieve approximate overall equilibrium in the balance of payments of each country. Marginal adjustments would need to be made in interest rates from time to time to preserve equilibrium in the face of changes in underlying conditions. Strong efforts would be needed in order to avoid competitive increases in interest rates which would raise the general level of rates without contributing to the maintenance of payments equilibrium. It would be highly desirable that steps be taken to increase the freedom of capital movements—especially of long-term funds—in order to make capital flows adjust more sensitively to interest rate changes.

Under such a system, the mix of monetary and fiscal policies would be used to achieve internal and external equilibrium simultaneously. If, for example, it was necessary to raise interest rates for balance-of-payments reasons, any undesired restrictive effects on internal demand would be offset by a reduction in taxes. Fairly frequent adjustments in both monetary and fiscal policies would presumably be necessary. Since, at best, only an imperfect adjustment could be achieved, monetary reserves would, of course, continue to be needed to deal with temporary balance-of-payment deficits. But, hopefully, persistent large deficits resulting in heavy drains on reserves could be avoided more and more effectively as accumulating experience led to increased skill in the use of the available policy instruments and in the coordination of monetary policies.

One of the objections to such an arrangement is that the use of the monetary-fiscal mix as a means of dealing with the balance of payments precludes its use to regulate capital formation for economic growth. To enable the country to regulate capital formation and thereby influence growth in the face of the adjustments in interest rates that would be needed to maintain balance-of-payments equilibrium, a second flexible fiscal instrument could be introduced. The best possibility for this purpose would probably be an investment tax credit, along the lines of the 7 percent credit introduced in the United States in the Revenue Act of 1962. Provision could be made for flexible adjustments of the rate of tax credit when such adjustments were deemed desirable—as, for example, to offset the restrictive effect on investment of a rise in domestic interest rates called for by balance-of-payments considerations. It is in principle possible to have—within limits at least—any desired level of investment in combination with any desired level of interest rates through appropriate use of fiscal incentives to shift the marginal efficiency of investment schedule.

Would such an arrangement be feasible as a means of eliminating the contradictions in the present system? This I find difficult to judge. If price trends among participating countries diverged persistently leading to progressively larger current account deficits and surpluses to be covered by interest-induced capital flows, the arrangement would in due time prove to be unworkable. Some supplementary efforts to coordinate other policies to prevent this would therefore be necessary. The possibilities of success seem sufficient to warrant consideration. Of course, the political difficulties of obtaining greater flexibility of fiscal policy are undoubtedly substantial in some countries. But this problem will almost certainly have to be tackled anyway, because monetary policy is already sufficiently hamstrung by the balance-of-payments problem to make it an ineffective instrument of domestic policy in many countries. More use will have to be made of fiscal policy to achieve domestic goals even if no effort is made to achieve such far-reaching international coordination of policies as that described above.

This means of achieving balance-of-payments equilibrium would not, of course, be entirely optimal, because the equilibrating adjustments would occur entirely in the capital account. It should be remembered, however, that a balance-of-payments surplus is a form of national investment, and a deficit is a form of disinvestment. If a country ran a persistent surplus, it could, in principle at least, use tax adjustments to trim its rate of domestic investment so as to achieve the desired overall division of national resources between consumption and capital formation. Similarly, a country having a persistent deficit could offset its adverse growth effects by employing a policy mix that would encourage domestic investment. Some inefficiency would nevertheless be present, because if domestic investment was viewed as more conducive to growth than an

equal amount of accumulation of foreign claims, there would be no way to shift resources between the two. The current account surplus or deficit would be primarily determined by the level of overall domestic demand and there would be no policy instrument available to change it.

III. APPROACHES TO FUNDAMENTAL REFORM OF THE SYSTEM

The arrangements outlined above would be a possible way of making the present system work more effectively by means of a much more flexible and sophisticated use of monetary and fiscal policies. If such an arrangement is unacceptable—or, after a trial, proved to be unworkable—there are as far as I can see only two approaches to fundamental reform: currency unification or the adoption of flexible exchange rates. Experience gives us strong reasons for believing that the first of these is definitely workable; however, it would involve a substantial cost that countries might well not be willing to pay. The second might involve a less serious cost but is less certain to work effectively. The two solutions could be combined in various ways.

A. Currency Unification

One solution to the problem of lack of sufficient tools to achieve the desired goals would be through the establishment of a unified currency system with absolutely and permanently fixed exchange rates. In this way, the balance-of-payments problem could be eliminated entirely, but I shall argue that the price that would have to be paid to make such an arrangement acceptable and viable would be the surrender of sovereignty over monetary and fiscal policies by the nations involved to a central body.

Under a fixed exchange rate system, individual countries would from time to time experience structural balance-of-payments deficits resulting from changes in tastes, technology, and so on, and some corrective mechanism would be necessary to restore external equilibrium in these cases. Since prices in industrial countries are characteristically rigid in a downward direction, deflation, which would serve primarily to create unemployment of labor and capital, is both an economically inappropriate and politically unacceptable means of dealing with a balance-of-payments deficit. Under modern conditions, the maintenance of high levels of employment and capacity utilization requires that such changes in relative prices as are needed to correct chronic balance-of-payments disequilibria be accomplished primarily through price increases in surplus countries rather than price declines in deficit countries. In addition, as indicated earlier in this paper, the procedures of wage determination are such in most countries as to produce some inflationary tendencies at acceptable levels of unemployment. Thus, with fixed exchange rates it is necessary that the international monetary system have a moderate inflationary bias built into it. However, under fixed exchange rate systems in the past the pressure on deficit countries to eliminate deficits has been much stronger than the pressure on surplus countries to eliminate surpluses, so that such arrangements have characteristically had a substantial deflationary bias. Unless some means could be found to eliminate this bias, it is doubtful whether a fixed exchange rate system would be able to survive in the modern world.

By means of a thoroughgoing currency unification, however, it would be possible, in principle, to devise a fixed exchange rate system which would not have the deflationary bias that has characterized past arrangements of this kind. The banks in each country might agree to accept for deposit at par checks drawn on banks in all of the other countries. Thus, exchange rates would be absolutely fixed (with no margin of fluctuation). To simplify the bookkeeping, it would be desirable to redefine the national units of account so as to permit all exchange rates to be set equal to unity. The banks of each country would give credit in that country's currency for all checks deposited, no matter where the checks originated or in what currency they were denominated. Each bank would send all checks denominated in other currencies to its central bank for collection. Settlements between central banks would be handled by reciprocal accounts, or, better yet, through an international clearing agency along the lines of our Federal Reserve Interdistrict Settlement Fund. All barriers impeding the free flow of capital among countries would be removed.

The key characteristic of such an arrangement is that the central bank of each country would have an unlimited credit line with the central banks of the other participating countries. The availability of unlimited credit would eliminate the deflationary bias that has ordinarily characterized fixed exchange rate systems. However, if each country was left free to pursue an independent monetary and fiscal policy, serious difficulties might arise as a result of differences in economic structure or policies among the various participating countries. Suppose, for example, that an important country chose to follow an

inflationary domestic policy—perhaps because cost-push pressures on its price level made such a policy necessary for the achievement of the desired level of employment. The inflationary policy would tend to generate a balance-of-payments deficit, through which the inflationary pressure would be transmitted to other countries. These countries could take domestic action to offset the inflationary pressures, but this would mean an enlargement of the inflating country's balance-of-payments deficit, the counterpart of which would be a surplus in the consolidated balance of payments of the other countries. If the other countries did not wish to run surpluses in their balances of payments and thereby provide a flow of goods and services to meet the rapacious demands of the inflating country, their only recourse would be to inflate their own economies in pace. In other words, by following an inflationary policy, a single major country might be able to force the rest to choose between balance-of-payments surpluses in its favor and domestic inflation. Thus, a fixed exchange rate system which provided unlimited automatic credits to deficit countries while leaving participants free to pursue independent national monetary and fiscal policies would probably have an immoderate inflationary bias and would certainly be unacceptable.

The necessary condition for currency unification to be workable is that the participating countries give up their sovereign authority to conduct independent monetary and fiscal policies directed at internal price and employment goals. Such policies would have to be conducted by a centralized monetary and fiscal authority charged with responsibility for internal stability for the group of countries as a whole. This centralized authority, in order to carry out its responsibilities effectively, would need to have sole power to regulate the supply of money and credit and to levy certain taxes and control certain categories of government expenditures. Under such an arrangement, internal price and income changes and interest rate adjustments would take care of the balance-of-payments problems of the individual countries. The arrangement would be very similar to the internal monetary system of the United States, and balance-of-payments problems would presumably no longer be a matter of concern.

The price that would have to be paid for this arrangement would be the loss of sovereignty over economic policy by the individual participating countries; in this respect, their position would become similar to that of individual states or Federal Reserve districts in the United States.

Thus, individual countries would no longer be able to choose their optimal levels of internal demand but would have to accept the levels that were associated with the overall policies judged by the central authorities to be appropriate for the group as a whole. In other words, some countries might find themselves in the position of depressed areas—a position very similar to that of a state like West Virginia in the U.S. Federal system. The central government could, of course, alleviate localized distress by programs of expenditures and tax incentives aimed at the stimulation of production and employment in depressed areas, just as the Federal government is able to do in the United States.

The above argument needs to be qualified a little. Actually, it would be possible for participating countries to engage to a limited extent in fiscal policy to stimulate or retard aggregate demand to influence their internal employment and price levels. However, monetary policy would have to be centralized, and countries would have to finance their deficits by selling their securities at interest rates that would make them acceptable to investors in the financial environment generated by the central monetary authorities. And, since they would not possess the power to create money, their securities would not be free of default risk; indeed, like the securities of our state governments, their rating would presumably depend on their financial condition. As a result, persistent deficit financing might be prohibitively difficult and expensive, especially for those countries in a depressed economic condition, for which it would be particularly important. In practice, it would no doubt be desirable for fiscal action to regulate demand to be conducted almost entirely by the central government, both because such action by the constituent members would prove to be difficult and costly and because there might otherwise be troublesome competition in economic policy and serious difficulties in the proper coordination of fiscal and monetary policy.

Since the power to create money is perhaps the fundamental element of national sovereignty, it would be difficult—although perhaps possible—for the participating countries to carry out independent military and foreign policies, especially those involving heavy expenditures overseas for national security and economic aid to underdeveloped countries. With monetary sovereignty eliminated, the other elements of national sovereignty would probably wither away, with the corresponding powers being shifted to the central government.

While currency unification might provide a satisfactory solution to the problems of economic policy, it would require, directly and indirectly, such a sweeping surrender of the accepted and widely revered prerogatives of national sovereignty that it is hard to believe that it would be acceptable at the present time to many countries. The United States would be especially unlikely to be willing to accept it, given our sense of responsibility as the political and economic leader of the free world.

B.   A System of Flexible Exchange Rates

A second fundamental reform that would eliminate the inconsistencies of the present system would be the adoption of a system of flexible exchange rates. This would, in principle, permit the participating countries to carry out independent monetary and fiscal policies directed at the maintenance of adequate levels of internal demand, with exchange rates adjusting in such a way as to maintain balance-of-payments equilibrium.

This is not the place for an extended discussion of the already hotly debated question of the merits of a system of flexible exchange rates. While I tend to be sympathetic to such an arrangement, I realize that it would be impossible to tell for sure how it would work until it had been tried. Moreover, the prevailing views of important officials and men of affairs are generally so hostile to the idea that I judge its general adoption to be impracticable.

C.   A Mixed System

The two solutions described above—currency unification and centralization of responsibility for monetary and fiscal policy on the one hand, and flexible exchange rates on the other—can be combined. According to the recent work on optimum currency areas, countries having close trading relations might properly be combined into blocs within which currencies would be unified.[2] It should be clearly recognized, in my opinion, that to be workable this would require the acceptance by the members of each bloc of a common centralized monetary and fiscal policy. Then flexible exchange rates could be employed between the blocs—which would constitute areas between which trading relations were more limited. As an example, the countries of Western Europe

---

[2] See especially R. I. McKinnon, "Optimum World Monetary Arrangements and the Dual Currency System," *Banca Nazionale del Lavoro Quarterly Review*, Vol. XVI (December 1963), pp. 366–96.

might constitute one bloc and the United States and the United Kingdom another, with a flexible exchange rate between the bloc currencies. A solution somewhat along these lines was suggested in the Brookings Report on the U.S. balance of payments.[3]

On the face of it, this sounds like a reasonable solution. However, I find it difficult to believe that, even in such an economically interrelated area as Western Europe, individual countries would be willing to give up their historic sovereign power to control money, as would, in my judgment, be absolutely vital to the success of monetary unification. In many ways, monetary sovereignty lies at the very heart of national sovereignty in all fields, including foreign and military affairs. Moreover, in strictly economic affairs, the countries may differ very substantially in their trade-offs between price stability and employment, as well as in the weights they attach to these two competitive goals. This, too, might make them very cool toward accepting a group consensus with regard to monetary and fiscal policy.

IV. CONCLUDING COMMENTS

It seems to me that the present adjustable-peg exchange rate system is unworkable and has to be abandoned in favor of either firmly fixed rates or continuously flexible rates. I do not believe any of the proposed purely financial schemes for providing more reserves can be depended upon to shore up the present system and make it workable. The trouble is that with adjustable parities, the possible size of speculative runs is so vast—remember that the entire stock of private financial

claims denominated in a particular currency is potentially available to finance a run on that currency—that unlimited, or virtually unlimited, supplies of reserves are needed to provide firm assurance that a speculative run could not succeed in forcing a devaluation.

What is vitally necessary is to introduce into the system some means of maintaining or restoring balance-of-payments equilibrium. Possibly this could be done by using monetary and fiscal policies in a flexible way to provide for a systematic off-set of deficits and surpluses on current account with surpluses and deficits on private capital account—with some limited interim reliance on monetary reserves while the necessary adjustments were being brought about. This would have to be done, of course, without any use of exchange-parity adjustments so that over a period of time the system would become one of reliable *de facto* exchange rate stability.[4]

As I have indicated, the only other alternatives I can see are (1) currency unification combined with full unification of monetary and fiscal policies, (2) flexible exchange rates, or (3) some combination of the two. Of course, with suitable financial tinkering and *ad hoc* adjustments, the present system may survive for many years, even without a basic reorientation of monetary and fiscal policy. But its deflationary bias and its basic instability seem inherent and likely to constitute a continuing element of weakness in the world economy that may be especially dangerous in times of crisis.

---

[4] I suppose there are other possible ways of making the present system work, such as the introduction of exchange or trade controls to be employed under accepted rules to deal with balance-of-payments problems. However, I am convinced that such arrangements would prove in practice to be so cumbersome, unworkable, and subject to evasion and abuse that they would ultimately collapse under their own weight.

---

[3] W. S. Salant *et al.*, *The United States Balance of Payments in 1968* (Washington, D.C.: The Brookings Institution, 1963), pp. 258–62.

FIXED, FLEXIBLE, AND GLIDING EXCHANGE RATES*

Lawrence B. Krause†

"Should we have an international monetary system based on fixed or flexible exchange rates?"

is a question that will hardly attract attention on grounds of originality. Yet it is being posed

---

* "Fixed, Flexible, and Gliding Exchange Rates," by Lawrence B. Krause, is reprinted from the *Journal of Money, Credit, and Banking*, Vol. 3 (May 1971, Part II), pp. 321–38. Copyright © 1971 by the Ohio State University Press. All Rights Reserved. Reprinted by permission of the publisher and the author. Law-

rence B. Krause is a Senior Fellow, Brookings Institution.

† The views expressed in this paper are those of the author and do not purport to represent the views of the staff members, officers, or trustees of the Brookings Institution.

more frequently today than at any time since the end of World War II. The questioners of today tend to be practical men who once scorned such deliberations as a sport worthy only for economists or philosophers. No doubt the frequent and disturbing international financial crises that have occurred since the devaluation of the British pound sterling in November, 1967, have been most instrumental in changing the atmosphere. During recent years, real calm has seldom been present in currency markets, thereby undermining support for the status quo among all participants in the market. Thus I can say unequivocally that my subject has relevance.

In order to try to balance the discussion, certain arguments will be disallowed. It is not legitimate to argue that flexible exchange rates necessarily imply unstable rates by postulating an economic situation so basically disorganized that no exchange rate system could work well. The unhappy history of the 1930s does not provide evidence that flexible exchange rates are bad—indeed the contrary may be true. International trade and investment contracted when the world was still pledged to fixed exchange rates and it was only when they were abandoned that some revival took place. Similarly, it is not legitimate to argue implicitly that fixed rates always mean disequilibrium rates. Proponents of pegged exchange rates—the best terminology to describe the present Bretton Woods' system—advocate a different mechanism for re-establishing equilibrium which on the face of it would be untenable.

Also the consequences of fixed or flexible exchange rates on the need for international liquidity will not be considered a relevant argument in this discussion. It is assumed that Special Drawing Rights will be issued by the International Monetary Fund (IMF) in sufficient amounts to adequately satisfy the world's need for official liquidity. It is further recognized that whatever system is in existence, individual countries or groups of countries might well choose to operate by different rules. Less developed countries, for instance, might operate with a flexible rate while the rest of the world remains fixed, or might peg their rates to large countries while the rest of the world was flexible. However, most advanced countries must adhere to the rules if the system is to be meaningful.

To make sure that the argument is joined, agreement must be reached at the outset on what the objectives of an international monetary system should be. Without such an agreement it would be impossible to find criteria for judging which did it better. The technical discussion of fixed and flexible rates will be followed by an evaluation of both systems under the condition and institutions existing today. The final section will explore the possibilities of compromise solutions of limited flexibility.

OBJECTIVES OF THE INTERNATIONAL MONETARY SYSTEM

The main objective of the international monetary system must surely be to provide an institutional arrangement whereby individual countries can obtain maximum economic growth with full employment. To maximize growth, economic efficiency has to be promoted which includes encouraging international trade and capital movements up to the limits determined by comparative advantage. Next in line to growth and full employment is the promotion of price stability. While price stability in one sense is only a means to achieve other economic objectives, in another sense it is a worthy objective in itself because of what it portends for social and political stability. The growth rate, employment level, and degree of price stability need not be identical for all countries. The appropriate targets for a country are those selected by the country itself.

Another objective of the international monetary system is the promotion of international cooperation. This objective transcends the realm of economics. A situation in which cooperative and harmonious economic relationships are maintained among countries is one in which political cooperation is likely to be present and the cause of peace in the world advanced. While one would not create economic crises merely to promote the good-fellowship that comes from reaching a cooperative solution, the system that finds its optimum solutions to economic difficulties through multinational rather than national actions has much to recommend it.

CRITERIA FOR EVALUATION

In measuring one system against the other, it is useful to have some specific criteria in mind to help assess how the international monetary system is affecting the objectives noted above. First, the system which requires or leads to the fewest restrictions on international trade and capital movements or, in general, interferes the least with private decisions is likely to be the one that maximizes economic efficiency. Second, the system that indirectly promotes the most responsive monetary and fiscal policy to the needs of the domestic economy will be most desirable. Third, the system that interferes least with national decisions concerning current consumption versus investment, public versus private use of resources and the appropriate distribution of income is the one that is likely to promote harmonious relationships among countries and minimize irritating conflicts. Finally, the system that most rewards countries for taking action which helps other countries is likely to be the one that promotes basic international cooperation.

THE VIRTUES OF THE PEGGED EXCHANGE RATE SYSTEM

The technical literature on the virtues of both the fixed and flexible system is so extensive that only a bare outline of the arguments is required for present purposes.[1]

The main argument used by the proponents of the pegged rate system is that it exists and it has served the world quite well. World economic growth since the end of World War II has been truly remarkable. Economic expansion has proceeded at rates never previously achieved and the expansion has not been interrupted by even a single significant depression. Progress has been made by developed and less developed countries alike, although real income growth on a per capita basis has generally been greater for the developed countries. At least some of this progress can be traced directly to the improvement in international commerce which was made possible by the fixed exchange rate system. The international trade of goods has expanded almost twice as fast as incomes, suggesting that economic efficiency has been promoted by the greater involvement in international trade. The thrust of this argument suggests that while the present system may not be perfect, it has worked remarkably well and the burden of the argument must be borne by those who would want to change it.

The theoretical basis for expecting a fixed exchange rate system to promote world economic progress comes from viewing the benefits of a single currency in a national economy and arguing that some of these same benefits will accrue to the international economy with fixed exchange rates since they are almost the equivalent of a single currency. The international trade of goods and services is made easier and more profitable in the absence of exchange rate uncertainty. The advantages of certainty in exchange rates are even greater in connection with business invest-

ment decisions since a long time horizon is involved. Economic efficiency is promoted as more rational decisions can be made for domestic investments in export- and import-competing industries as well as for productive foreign investment. The net result is the encouragement of closer economic integration among all countries.

When the single currency thesis is pushed to its logical conclusion, the argument requires completely rigid exchange rates thus rejecting even the small amount of flexibility within the bands now permitted by IMF rules. Such rigidity was in fact established between the Italian lira and the dollar for many years and has been advocated by the Commission of the European Community as proper for the EC currencies amongst themselves.

A rigorous application of the single currency thesis requires three conditions to be fulfilled. First, goods, services, and all factors of production must be free to move without hindrance throughout the entire currency area. Second, there must either be political indifference to sharply unequal regional distribution of economic gains, or a political mechanism for redistributing gains within the currency area. Third, a reasonable degree of stability must be maintained in the real value of the currency so that financial and real markets can function properly. It is the nonfulfillment of these conditions which leads Harry Johnson to reject fixed exchange rates [8].

The proponents of the pegged-rate system have recognized that the ideal conditions of a single currency do not exist and are unlikely to exist in the near future. However, they do contend that the necessary conditions are approached closely enough to capture many of the benefits. In particular, if countries are able to maintain a sufficient degree of viability in their balance of payments, then parity changes will be rarely necessary. Certainty of exchange rates will be created and will provide the expected benefits. Furthermore, having a fixed exchange rate system will itself reduce the need for parity changes because discipline is exerted on governments to keep inflation within reasonable bounds. If excessive internal demand develops, large increases in imports of goods and services will occur and exports will be discouraged. The worsening of the current account balance will rapidly be felt in currency markets requiring the central banks to intervene by supplying dollars to the market in order to keep the exchange rate from piercing the lower support point. The loss of reserves serves as a signal to the central bank that more restrictive demand managing policies are re-

[1] For a recent and an excellent presentation see Harry G. Johnson [8].

quired, and monetary policy will be adjusted accordingly. Armed with the leverage of the reserve loss, central banks can often convince their own governments to take restrictive actions in the fiscal field which they might otherwise be hesitant to take. Since central bank reserve holdings are finite, borrowings from the IMF or other countries may become necessary. At such times, additional leverage can be used on governments to get them to adopt restrictive actions by making conditions on granting loans. Thus an institutional mechanism is provided for countries to participate in economic policy decisions of national governments, which is only proper since other countries are affected by the actions taken. The discipline thus exerted should reduce the need for parity changes to those rare cases when fundamental disequilibrium would develop.

Fundamental disequilibria might occur if, for instance, inflation was allowed to proceed for an extensive period of time so that a country's cost structure got seriously out of line with its competitors. Under such circumstance, it would clearly be unwise to attempt to make the necessary adjustment through internal means and a discrete parity adjustment would be called for. IMF rules permit such adjustments and the Fund's resources are made available to assist countries in meeting transition problems that may accompany the parity change. But fundamental disequilibria should seldom occur, and must not be frequent if the benefits are to be gained from fixed exchange rates.

The Bretton Woods' system was designed with international political as well as economic relations in mind [7]. The competitive devaluations of the 1930s plus the other attributes of a beggar-thy-neighbor world added to political difficulties and led to World War II. The IMF rules thus provide strong penalties for devaluing in the absence of fundamental disequilibria, and also provide rewards for international cooperation. The basic premise underlying this philosophy is that countries should be made to recognize that they are in the same economic boat and that cooperative behavior is expected of them. The furthering of economic integration that results will carry over into more harmonious political relations among countries [2].

WILL THE PEGGED RATE SYSTEM CONTINUE TO WORK?

The critics of the present system are not against exchange rate stability or international cooperation, and many of them favor anti-inflation discipline on governments. The main concern of the critics is based on the belief that the system can no longer function as well as it has during the last two decades, which was admittedly already less than perfect. They foresee increasing difficulty resulting from three interrelated weaknesses of the system; the inadequacy of the balance-of-payments adjustment mechanism, the unintended stimulation of speculation, and the asymmetry of pressures on deficit and surplus countries.

If there were few divergencies in the evolution of the economies of major countries, then a fixed exchange rate could exist without being fundamentally tested. But divergencies have occurred for a number of reasons and the adjustment mechanism has not been adequate to correct the situation. The divergencies can be traced to different rates of growth of resources, different import elasticities and propensities, different public attitudes and governmental policies towards inflation and unemployment, and different economic structures [6]. While some of these differences are offsetting, balance-of-payments difficulties have still developed.

Although documentation of each of these differences seems unnecessary, some evidence on the question of relative inflation is worthwhile in view of the crucial role domestic prices play in the theory of fixed exchange rates. Because all advanced countries have important domestic interests that are hurt by inflation, opposition by these forces plus the discipline of the balance of payments is expected to prevent run-away inflation, and to restrain creeping inflation to modest proportions. As seen in Table 1, this expectation has been reasonably well achieved. The average increase in the cost of living of the ten industrial countries listed in Table 1 between 1954 and 1968 was only 2.8% per year. It should be noted that the cost-of-living index is utilized only as an indicator of general price movements. No single price index is perfectly suitable for international price comparison, particularly if countries are at different levels of industrialization—Japan is excluded because of this consideration. The advantage of the CPI is that it is well developed in these countries and easily available. There was remarkably little divergent behavior among the countries as measured by this price index as the average deviation from the mean increase was only 1.3 percentage points. But despite this, major maladjustments did occur because deviations above and below the mean were not random among countries. Some countries consistently had less inflation than the average while others consistently had more. For instance, over

TABLE 1   COST OF LIVING CHANGES, SELECTED COUNTRIES 1955–1968*
(percent change from previous year)†

	1954–1955	1955–1956	1956–1957	1957–1958	1958–1959	1959–1960	1960–1961	1961–1962	1962–1963
United States.............	0	+2	+4	+2	+1	+2	+1	+1	+1
United Kingdom..........	−1	+5	+5	+2	+1	+2	+3	+5	+1
Canada...................	+1	0	+3	+2	+1	+1	+1	+1	+2
Belgium.................	−1	+4	+3	+1	+2	0	+2	+3	+1
France...................	+1	+2	+2	+17‡	+5	+4	+2	+6	+5
Germany................	+1	+4	+2	+4	0	+3	+2	+4	+2
Italy.....................	+4	+5	+2	+1	+1	+4	+2	+5	+7
Netherlands.............	+1	+2	+7	+2	+2	+2	+2	+5	+2
Sweden..................	+2	+6	+5	+4	0	+4	+3	+5	+3
Switzerland.............	+1	+2	+4	+1	0	+2	+1	+5	+4
Mean change.............	+.9	+3.0	+3.2	+3.6	+1.3	+2.1	+1.9	+4.0	+2.8
Average deviation........	1.0	1.6	1.3	2.8	1.0	0.9	1.0	1.9	1.6

* Mid-year calculations.   † Source: IMF, International Financial Statistics, various years.   ‡ Year of devaluation.

the whole period a difference of 25 percentage points developed between more-than-average France and less-than-average Germany. Thus even with very similar experience, problems still arose which required adjustment.

Since divergencies were slow to develop, it might seem possible to make the required adjustment through internal policy changes. Indeed some observers believe that most governments can do a better job at controlling inflation. This view appears overly optimistic. Persistent differences in inflation rates appear to stem from deep-seated economic factors. As an example, for France to achieve the same degree of price inflation that in Germany is consistent with rapid growth and full employment would seem to require France to maintain a growing margin of unused capacity because of structural differences in the two economies. With the German public showing little tolerance for inflation and the French public unwilling to accept growing unemployment, it is clear why policies are not adopted which would equalize price movements in the two countries. Thus occasional external adjustments via exchange rates would seem to be required. But discrete parity changes are becoming increasingly difficult to accomplish. Governments are unwilling to publicize the failure of their economic policies by devaluing—until they have no other choice—and market speculation has made discrete changes very expensive.

The second weakness of the system has become apparent with the increased speculative activity that has occurred in currency and gold markets during recent years. Speculation on a large scale has been made possible by the easing of restrictions on capital movements, the growth

of liquid assets in private hands and the growing internalization of business horizons. Speculation has been made extremely profitable by a weakness in the pegged system itself. Since currencies must be supported within a narrow band of 0.75% on either side of par according to the European Monetary Agreement (IMF rules permit 1%), speculators face little chance for a capital loss even if their expectation of a parity change is not fulfilled. Since the cost of speculation for even a lengthy period of time is minimal (only a minor transaction fee plus possible interest rate differential) and the risk is almost non-existent, large amounts of speculation can be generated even with a small probability of a large gain. This technical characteristic of the market would be a major source of instability and uncertainty even if speculative runs were a random event, since the magnitude of speculation has proven to be a multiple of any country's international reserves (Germany is a possible exception). But speculation is not random as basic international disequilibria do occur.[2]

Since a country is required to wait to alter its exchange rate until a difficulty develops into a fundamental disequilibrium, it is quite certain that market traders will be well aware of the prospects for a speculative gain. A change in exchange rates requires a major political decision. It is a major decision because it reflects badly on the economic policies previously followed with all the political implications that it holds, and it requires other policy adjustments in the fiscal

---

[2] Some of the arguments made in the following section and in the discussion of limited flexibility were taken from my recent article on a related subject [9].

1963–1964	1964–1965	1965–1966	1966–1967	1967–1968	Total change 1954–1968
+1	+2	+3	+3	+4	+25
+3	+5	+4	+2	+5‡	+42
+2	+3	+3	+3	+4	+27
+5	+4	+5	+2	+3	+34
+3	+4	+1	+3	+4	+59
+2	+4	+3	+2	+1	+34
+6	+4	+2	+4	+1	+48
+5	+6	+4	+4	+1	+45
+3	+4	+8	+4	+2	+53
+3	+3	+5	+4	+2	+37
+3.3	+3.9	+3.8	+3.1	+2.7	+2.8
1.2	0.5	1.3	0.7	1.2	1.3

and monetary area to support it because large parity changes themselves cause severe pressures in the economy. No government can make such a decision lightly. While governments examine the situation, speculators look for a signal that a decision on a parity change is near at hand and sometimes they position themselves even without a signal, making a difficult situation even worse. Most democratic governments find it extremely difficult to hide the decision-making process from the public; others find it impossible. Thus speculators align themselves against the government in the market and must be rewarded if the desired change is to be made. Even the French devaluation in 1969, which, unlike the British, was extremely well handled from a technical point of view, led to substantial speculative gains. Because of all this, governments tend to delay the change long after it is necessary. Stop-gap measures such as exchange controls, border taxes, trade restrictions and the like are instituted to preserve the fixed exchange rate despite the fact that these measures undermine the very goals the fixed exchange rates are supposed to further. Delays in making parity changes not only lead to economic inefficiency, but ultimately to greater political and speculative costs as well.

There is a growing tendency among defenders of the present system to look more favorably upon some so-called "efficient" forms of market interference such as uniform border taxes and subsidies on exports and imports such as employed by Germany in November, 1968. Also many short-term capital movements are thought to be useless and it has been suggested that some direct investments may serve no useful economic function and may even be perverse [4]. Thus it is believed that certain interferences on capital

movements to defend a fixed rate may not inhibit real economic welfare. The correctness of this argument is moot and the efficacy of controls in limiting only unproductive investments is even more uncertain.

The third weakness of the present system, the asymmetry of pressures on deficit and surplus countries, is of special concern to the United States. While both deficit and surplus countries delay making required adjustments in their exchange rates, surplus countries can more easily resist the discipline of the system and thus perpetuate their disequilibrium. Deficit countries must either use their own reserves to support their currencies in the market or borrow reserves for this purpose. In either case an obvious limit will be reached, and devaluations must ultimately follow. In contrast surplus countries have no limit on the amount of reserves they can accumulate. Surplus countries can counter the pressure put on them through monetary policy, the result of which may be some unintended foreign lending and possibly greater domestic inflation, but revaluation can be successfully avoided indefinitely. The consequence of the asymmetric pressure is that the international monetary system as a whole has a devaluation bias. Since the United States cannot itself devalue vis-á-vis other currencies because the dollar is the numeraire in the system, the United States must either have better domestic price performance than the average of other countries or the dollar will become gradually overvalued. In the decade of the 1950s the problem of the dollar was solved by other countries liberalizing their discriminatory restrictions previously maintained against U.S. exports, and in the early 1960s by improved U.S. price competitiveness, but neither factor has been working during the last few years. Without some revaluations, it may well be impossible for the system as a whole to maintain a sustainable position.

VIRTUES OF A FLEXIBLE EXCHANGE RATE SYSTEM

The most severe critics of the present system believe that the defects can best be cured by adopting flexible exchange rates [3]. An exchange rate is only a price of one currency for another, and if the price is free to respond to changes in supply and demand, balance-of-payments equilibrium will always be maintained. Without having to concern themselves about their foreign balance, governments would be able to design their monetary and fiscal policies to the needs of the domestic economy. The exchange rate would thus be another instrument of adjustment making all economic goals more easily attainable.

Flexible exchange rates provide no guarantee of good economic policy, for countries would still be dependent upon their own political process. But flexible exchange rates will make well-designed economic policies more effective. Recent U.S. experience suggests that monetary and fiscal policy must work in tandem if stabilization objectives are to be achieved in reasonable time. If one of these instruments has to be targeted for balance-of-payments needs, then the domestic economy will suffer. If poorly designed economic policies are instituted under flexible rates, the consequences will be easily observed in exchange rate changes and might conceivably lead to political pressures to correct the policy errors. Under the present system, however, the external consequences of policy mistakes can be concealed for some time through disguised variations in the reserves of central banks. Furthermore, disturbances originating abroad need not dominate the economies of countries under flexible rates since the exchange rate itself can take up most of the adjustment.

Advocates of flexible exchange rates argue that the benefits of international specialization will also be more fully attained under their system than under present arrangements. In the absence of balance-of-payments worries, countries will not institute trade restrictions and capital controls. These restrictions cause substantial economic inefficiencies because they are selective, unpredictable or arbitrary, and no market mechanism exists for spreading the risks of loss that result to the private economy. Even diplomatic relations among countries might improve with the removal of some of these irritants.

Flexible exchange rates should reflect the same degree of stability as found in the economies of the major countries in the system. If countries evolve reasonably similar to one another as in the recent past, then exchange rates will evidence basic stability. Small fluctuations from whatever source should bring forth stabilizing speculation from the private sector. Central banks could be permitted to operate in exchange markets for smoothing purposes if private stabilizing speculation was not adequate. As long as central banks do not accumulate or dissipate reserves on balance over a reasonable period of time, the principle of a free market in currencies is not undermined [10]. If a basic change should occur in competitive positions among countries, then flexible rates will speed the adjustment to a new equilibrium and this would be accomplished without the financial crises that mark the present system.

WILL A FLEXIBLE EXCHANGE RATE SYSTEM WORK?

Critics of flexible exchange rates seldom deny the benefits of a free market, but they seriously question the feasibility of freedom when applied to exchange rates. Frequently no distinction is made between transitional and fundamental problems, although such a distinction is clearly required. If flexible rates cannot work only because financial institutions have no experience with them, then attention must be directed toward gaining the experience and encouraging the required institutional development. However, unsolved transition problems may be enough to dissuade governments from ever risking a revolutionary change. The critics concentrate their arguments under three headings: exchange rate uncertainty, inflationary bias, combined with destabilizing domestic economic consequences and the promotion of nationalism.

When exchange rates are free to change without limit, there is some probability that they will move a great deal, and the uncertainty that this creates is thought to be extremely destructive to normal business behavior [14]. Under some circumstances, exchange markets might degenerate into chaos if they are set adrift without guidance. What is feared is destabilizing speculation: a massive buying or selling wave fed by capital movements which could force exchange rates to extreme movements and wild fluctuations. The counter argument to this fear is that if speculation is truly destabilizing (not in response to basic economic factors), then speculators on balance must lose money and it is self-destroying. This reply is not completely satisfying since professional speculators who lead the market may well make profits at the expense of amateur speculators who are the herd-like followers. As long as new groups of amateur speculators can be attracted to the market, the instability can be perpetuated.

Even if exchange rate fluctuations are rather mild, the uncertainty adds to the risk of doing international business. Exporters and importers could not assume risks of even moderate amounts since profit margins (as a percent of sales value) are seldom very high in competitive international markets. Traders will, therefore, try to insure against exchange loss by dealing in the forward market. Even assuming that forward cover is available, the added cost of buying it will reduce the volume of international trade similar to an increase in transport cost. Furthermore, forward cover will be very difficult to obtain for transactions with long lead times such as custom designed machinery, jet planes or ships. Also certain services like insurance involve assuming liabilities well into the future and the absence of forward cover for exchange risks could easily seriously inhibit the supplying of this service on an international basis. Thus some degree of international specialization might have to be sacrificed. Some productive capital movements like bond flotations would also be seriously inhibited.

The availability of forward cover at reasonable costs is a major determinant of how well a flexible exchange rate system would work and this would depend on the expansion and development of financial institutions. Experience has shown that the theorist is correct in believing that when the profitability of providing a financial service is increased, resources are attracted and the service is provided. But there is a crucial time dimension required to achieve this result. Thus the providing of adequate forward cover is a major problem for flexible rates, even if it is only a transitional one.[3]

Most forward cover is now provided by commercial banks. The constraints on providing expanded service grow out of the technical nature of the business. Banks act as principals in each forward transaction they make—as distinct from a broker who would merely bring buyers and sellers together. Thus banks have to worry about the credit standing of their customers as well as the exposure of the banks in different currencies at different maturities. If the demand for cover expands tremendously with flexible rates as most experts think it would, then banks would have to provide greatly expanded credit lines for their foreign departments. They would have to develop better technical devices for calculating their currency exposure and many more foreign exchange traders would have to be trained. All of this is certainly possible, but time is required to get this done and in the interim, the market for forward cover, particularly for long-term contracts, would be much less than perfect.

The second major criticism of fluctuating rates is that such a system would have an inflationary bias and would cause domestic price instability for many countries. If governments are relieved of balance-of-payments discipline, then more in-

flationary economic policies are believed to be the likely result. Central banks would lose their leverage on governments concerning fiscal matters now provided by reserve losses and this leverage is of great importance in some countries. Also fluctuations in exchange rates themselves may give an upward lift to prices. When a currency depreciates, prices of imports rise in terms of domestic currency and these are usually quickly passed on to consumers both directly and indirectly as imported raw materials and other imports create cost pressures for domestic production. These price increases in turn add to pressures for larger wage settlements and still higher costs and prices. When a currency appreciates, however, not all cost reductions get translated into price reductions. Wage rates are notoriously sticky downward and thus part of the appreciation gain will be absorbed in higher real wages. Also producers will be tempted to raise profit margins if import costs decline, particularly if the decline is thought to be temporary. The asymmetric adjustment to exchange rate changes—depreciation leading to higher prices and appreciation to higher real factor returns—will on balance leave the price level higher than it would be in the absence of exchange rate fluctuations.

A more serious concern of some governments is the domestic price instability that they believe might result from fluctuating rates. Countries with high ratios of imports and exports to domestic production—the Netherlands provides a rather extreme illustration of the point—find that price impulses emanating from the foreign sector can dominate their entire domestic economy. If short-term capital flows should cause a depreciation in the exchange rate—possibly triggered by a political event at home or abroad—then the inflationary forces engendered thereby would lead to higher wage demands and a general inflationary situation. If the domestic reaction was extreme, then a dynamically unstable situation could develop in which a depreciation could lead to domestic inflation requiring even further depreciation, etc. For this reason, many governments feel that they could not leave the exchange rate to market forces without giving up almost all control over their domestic economy. Such governments would be very reluctant indeed to give up their responsibility for their exchange rate.

The third criticism of flexible rates is based on the belief that they would inhibit the development of economic and political integration and instead would foster nationalism. The belief relates to the analogy of a single currency previ-

[3] I am indebted to the participants of the Burgenstock Conference in June, 1969 for the following discussion.

ously discussed. It is often pointed out that a common-market arrangement would be unworkable if the members had independently fluctuating exchange rates without limits. To a lesser extent, the same argument applies to all the major countries in the western world. Visions are raised of currency manipulations to solve domestic economic problems regardless of the consequences for other countries, as in the 1930s. The possibility also exists of currency runs encouraged for political purposes. Such a world could hardly evidence the cooperate diplomatic spirit needed to sustain prosperity and peace.

COMPROMISE SOLUTIONS— LIMITED FLEXIBILITY

Within the last few years, a great deal of interest has been generated in proposals that fall somewhere between maintaining the status quo and fully flexible exchange rates [1, 5, 11, 12, 13]. The new proposals seek limited flexibility and usually involve widening the band of permitted flexibility around the par value of currencies, more frequent and smaller adjustment of par values, or some combination of the two. The purpose of the suggested reforms are to improve the balance-of-payments adjustment mechanism, to reduce the profit potentials in currency speculation, and to mitigate the devaluation bias of the present system without running the risks inherent in jumping into a fully flexible system. These proposals are also given a better chance of being seriously considered by governments and are, therefore, more likely to be adopted than flexible rates.

WIDER BANDS

The consequences expected from widening the band depends on the size of the authorized spread and on the intervention policies of central banks within it. The larger the spread becomes, the closer the system approaches fully flexible rates. The largest spread being proposed which would maintain the essence of a fixed exchange rate system is 10%—5% on either side of par. Such a spread would permit a substantial amount of balance-of-payments adjustment—indeed between two non-dollar currencies, a 20% change is theoretically possible. If all central banks limited their intervention within the band to smoothing operations, then the devaluation bias of the present system would be significantly eased. Also the prospects for speculation would be altered. Since the market rates could move substantially

within the band, the risk of speculating against a weak currency or in favor of a strong currency would be increased manifold. If losses become a possibility, then speculation will likely be reduced and more stabilizing in character.

The difficulties foreseen with a 10% spread is that it might provide too much flexibility in the short run and too little adjustment in the long run. A possible 20% change in cross rates would raise most of the uncertainty problems that were noted in the discussion of flexible rates. Many European countries would feel that their economies were too closely integrated to permit that degree of flexibility. They would not permit their exchange rate to move in the band, but instead, would maintain the current narrow margins and frustrate the system. In the long run, however, the 10% spread would provide too little room for balance-of-payments adjustment. If the economic trends in major countries continue to diverge in the future as they have in the past, then in time fundamental disequilibria will occur even with wider margins and a parity change will be required. At that point, the weaknesses of the present system would reappear.

A more modest widening of the band to a spread of 3% or a bit more might be a feasible alternative. Such a change would not cause serious technical difficulties for foreign exchange markets, nor hard institutional problems for the IMF. It would add a useful amount of uncertainty to the market as speculation would become riskier as penalties for guessing wrong would increase, but not so much uncertainty as to make governments uncomfortable. One might also try to ease the asymmetry in the system by introducing a compensating asymmetry in the opposite direction, i.e., a larger margin above par than below it. However, asymmetric bands of modest width could not greatly affect the situation, nor could any modest widening help the adjustment problem very much.

GLIDING PEG

The adjustment problem requires a mechanism for changing parities with less delay, by smaller amount and through a more automatic process. The most feasible suggestion along these lines is the gliding peg (or crawling peg) plan. A variety of alternative formulations of the plan is possible depending on the degree of automaticity desired. The possibilities run from a fully automatic scheme based on a rigid formula to one totally discretionary with pre-announced changes as part of a country's general economic policy. A great deal of automaticity would seem to have much to recommend it. One of the great difficulties with the present system is the inability of countries to make significant decisions on exchange rates within a political setting and, therefore, a fully discretionary system would seem to offer little improvement. Also a fully discretionary system would perpetuate the depreciation bias of the present system.

The most automatic plan would be the self-adjusting peg which would gear parity changes to actual movements in spot exchange rates. The exchange parity at the beginning of any trading day would be made equal to the simple average of spot rates experienced during the previous year. Thus exchange parities would be determined by a moving average of spot prices. The determination of spot prices would have to be left to market forces if the system is to be self-adjusting, thus eliminating smoothing-out operations by central banks. Central banks would still have to intervene at the edges of the (moving) band and, therefore, changes in international reserves would still play an important role in the system.

Since spot prices would determine exchange parities, it is of some importance whether parities are defined in terms of dollars, gold, or some other numeraire. There must be active private trading between the numeraire and currencies for a price to be established which would rule out gold—if the two-tier gold market is continued—and SDR's. While there may be problems involved in using the dollar as the numeraire, they are minor compared to the alternatives. With the dollar as numeraire, the United States itself can only be in equilibrium when all other countries are in equilibrium or when there are exactly offsetting disequilibria of deficits and surpluses in other countries. Also U.S. monetary policy would have to be geared more closely to the needs of the world as a whole as well as to the domestic situation.

Some operating characteristics of a self-adjusting peg system can be anticipated. There would be little need to widen exchange margins and they could be maintained at the 1% on either side of par now permitted by the IMF. If a country's price performance, for instance, deviated from the behavior of other countries, then exchange parities would slowly reflect this in a corrective fashion. With continued deviations over an extended period of time, a change of 2% per year in a parity is possible. This amount of adjustment would appear to have been adequate to correct the maladjustment among indus-

trial countries during the last 15 years. A situation might develop in which the market could anticipate the direction of change of a parity over a lengthy period of time—perhaps because of a spurt of inflation. To prevent the speculative flows that would be generated, an interest rate differential would have to be established in favor of the weak currency equal to the maximum possible depreciation (2%). While this would constrain monetary policy, the burden should not be great since higher interest rates would in any event be required in an inflating economy. Under this system, speculation based on expected changes in parities would soon atrophy for lack of profitability.

There are also some difficulties with the self-adjusting peg that have to be recognized. First, parities would adjust only to those transactions which actually go through the exchange market. But some major transactions such as government-to-government payments for maintaining troops abroad are done outside the market. Recognition of these transactions could be taken by adding changes in official reserves as a variable within the parity-determining formula: but the required conversion factor translating reserves into price equivalents would be difficult to estimate and unstable over time. Second, central banks can influence spot exchange rates by dealing in the forward market and by monetary policy which they could substitute for direct intervention. In order to ensure purely market-determined spot prices, stringent rules would have to be agreed upon for central bank actions which could well be too binding for the proper exercise of monetary policy. Third, a fully automatic system would force governments to relinquish their responsibility for determining their own exchange rate. For some real and some imaginary reasons, governments are very reluctant to do this, making the pure system almost impossible to negotiate.

Most of the benefits of a fully automatic system could be obtained by some modifications of the plan yielding what has been called a presumptive system. Threshold changes in the crucial variables which would be directly or indirectly involved in an automatic formula, such as spot prices, future prices, reserve changes and interest rate differentials, would provide the signal for a presumptive change in exchange rates. The decision to make the change, however, would be left to governments. The changes could be frequent and small such as 1% every half year or 0.5% every quarter. However, the larger any discrete change may be, the wider must be the band to avoid upsetting the spot exchange market. International cooperation and multilateral surveillance would be required to ensure that changes would be made and in an equilibrating direction. Failure to make a change would call for a complete explanation by the country involved. The IMF might play a very active role in such confrontation. Small changes might not be too difficult for governments to initiate, even with present political machinery, particularly since international embarassment could be avoided by making an appropriate change. Some international sanctions might be considered, but would likely be unnecessary. A presumptive gliding peg plus a widening of bands might well be sufficient to solve both the speculation and adjustment problems. If special pressure was exerted on surplus countries to appreciate, then the asymmetry problem could also be alleviated. The advocates of this plan suggest that it permits the maintenance of fixed rates, if it is possible, but gives the option of some useful flexibility, if it should be necessary.

Two important criticisms of the gliding peg have been raised and need be faced. The first relates to possible erosion of discipline if governments could relieve themselves of some of the external consequences of inflation through regular depreciations of exchange rates. How significant the erosion may be depends on two factors: the actual role of external constraints in the formation of domestic economic policy and the difference in political reaction to a loss of international reserves as compared to a depreciating exchange rate. The domestic problems that inflation causes for governments of industrial countries would appear to be sufficient to preclude them from adopting economic policies which were known to be inflationary unless the provocations were very great. At such times, external constraints have never been an effective barrier. A gliding peg system would merely make more efficient the adjustment process to "unavoidable" disturbances. As was implied earlier, it would seem that a depreciating exchange rate would bring greater political penalties than would a loss of reserves. If a government had to face its electorate with a record of frequent devaluations during its stewardship, then the opposition could make much of its mismanagement of the economy. A loss of official reserves is neither visible nor understandable to the electorate and is less of a political liability. Thus the erosion of discipline should not be a serious problem.

The second criticism of the gliding peg is that it would not equalize the willingness of countries to appreciate their currencies as compared with depreciating them, and the devaluation bias of the present system would be perpetuated unless a fully automatic system were adopted. Surplus countries gain political power through leverage over deficit countries (and the United States) and conceivably some economic benefits which they might be hesitant to relinquish. Thus they may be unwilling to accept the automaticity of a self-adjusting peg. While this is a serious problem for a discretionary system, it can be overdone. Surplus countries could utilize currency depreciations as an effective tool to help control inflation and for anti-inflation minded countries like Germany, the attraction may be considerable. However, the risk is still substantial that a discretionary system would maintain the present bias toward devaluation, suggesting that some compulsion toward appreciation should be seriously considered.

CONCLUSION

After having enumerated theoretical criteria for choosing and reviewing the characteristics of fixed, flexible, and gliding exchange rates, some conclusion is required. But a choice among the different systems is difficult to make because it can not be authoritatively determined from economic criteria alone. There may simply be no theoretical answer to the question of which is the better—as among fixed, flexible or gliding exchange rates. Under a set of ideal conditions with existing political and economic institutions, a fixed exchange rate system could work admirably. Alternatively, under a set of less ideal conditions, but with somewhat altered institutions, flexible rates would be superior. Likewise, a set of circumstances can be conjured in which neither of these will work well.

One is tempted to search for theories which explain and could predict the conditions and institutions which seem to be determining for the choice. Historically we know that fixed exchange rates have been fully satisfactory only during periods of economic hegemony of a single country. Is it possible to create the same result through cooperative actions of many countries since hegemony does not exist today? Until satisfactory answers to such questions can be found, the choice between fixed and flexible rates will be difficult to make. But definitive answers to this type of question are even harder to come by than answers to purely economic questions.

The political world of today is based on a system of sovereign nation states and the international monetary system must reflect the political reality. National governments are constrained in their choice of economic policies by the degree of economic integration already in existence, but they still retain much scope for independence. The divergence of economic trends which results from this independence requires an effective adjustment mechanism. It is my opinion that the gliding exchange rate system provides the required adjustment mechanism without sacrificing the real benefits of economic integration.

LITERATURE CITED

1. Black, J. "A Proposal for the Reform of Exchange Rates," *Economic Journal*, (June, 1966).

2. Cooper, Richard N. *The Economics of Interdependence.* Council on Foreign Relations. New York, 1968.

3. Friedman, M. "The Case for Flexible Exchange Rates," *Essays in Positive Economics.* Chicago, 1953.

4. Furth, J. Herbert. "International Monetary Reform and the 'Crawling Peg'—Comment," *Review,* Federal Reserve Bank of St. Louis (July, 1969).

5. Halm, G. N. *The "Band" Proposal: The Limits of Permissible Exchange Rate Variations* (Special Papers in International Economics No. 6, International Finance Section), Princeton, 1965.

6. Houthakker, H. S. and Magee, S. "Income and Price Elasticities in World Trade," *Review of Economics and Statistics* (May, 1969).

7. International Monetary Fund, *Annual Report, 1951,* pp. 36–41.

8. Johnson, Harry. "The Case for Flexible Exchange Rates 1969," *Review,* Federal Reserve Bank of St. Louis (June, 1969).

9. Krause, L. B. "Recent International Monetary Crises: Causes and Cures," in W. Smith and R. Teigen (eds.), *Readings in Money, National Income and Stabilization Policy,* Rev. Edition. 1970.

10. Marsh, D. "Canada's Experience with a Floating Exchange Rate," paper presented at Conference on the Foreign Exchange Market, Ditchley, England, March 1967.

11. McKenzie, G. W. "International Monetary Reform and the 'Crawling Peg,'" *Review,* Federal Reserve Bank of St. Louis (February, 1969).

12. Meade, J. E. "The International Monetary Mechanism," *The Three Banks Review* (September, 1964).

13. Murphy, J. C. "Moderated Exchange Rate Variability," *National Banking Review* (December, 1965).

14. Roosa, R. V. *Monetary Reform for the World Economy,* Council on Foreign Relations (New York, 1965).

EUROPEAN MONETARY UNIFICATION AND THE INTERNATIONAL MONETARY SYSTEM*

Richard N. Cooper

I. MONETARY UNIFICATION IN EUROPE

The members of the European Community have expressed "their political will to introduce, in the course of the next 10 years, an economic and monetary union" which *inter alia* will involve the formation of "an individual monetary unit within the international system, characterized by the total and irreversible convertibility of currencies, the elimination of fluctuation margins of rates of exchange and the irrevocable fixing of parity rates"—in short, a single currency in every-thing except possibly name.[1] Irrevocably fixed exchange rates combined with total and irreversible convertibility imply that balance-of-payments adjustment *within* the Community will be of the same type that prevailed during the gold standard, *viz.,* any net outflow of funds from a region (country) within the Community will automatically result in monetary deflation in that region sufficient to bring the outflow to a halt.

These two conditions also imply a common monetary policy, even if only a passive one, for the Community as a whole, since any attempt by member countries to pursue divergent monetary policies will automatically result in payments imbalances that will, in turn, force countries back

* From Richard N. Cooper, *Sterling, European Monetary Unification, and the International Monetary System* (Washington, D.C.: National Planning Association, British-North American Committee, 1972), pp. 18–28. Reprinted by permission of the British-North American Committee and the author. Richard N. Cooper is Provost and Professor of Economics, Yale University.

[1] EC Resolution of February 9, 1971, reprinted as Annex I in *Economic and Monetary Union* (Werner Report), Supplement to *Bulletin of the European Communities* (1970), No. 11.

into monetary harmony. Thus, national governments will be sharply limited in their ability to finance budget deficits through domestic credit creation; they will have to rely instead on their capacity to raise funds in private markets. The pursuit of a common monetary policy for the Community as a whole raises questions both about the mechanism for accomplishing this and about the political responsibility of those who are entrusted with determining that policy.

Monetary union in Europe does not, however, imply fixity of exchange rates and reliance on gold-standard type monetary adjustment concerning Community-wide payments imbalances with the outside world; these could be handled with the variety of techniques currently available to national governments, such as exchange controls or changes in exchange rates.

1. Three Approaches to Monetary Unification

If monetary union is the objective, what are the means for achieving it? Three ways to begin have been proposed:

—The official Werner Report on European monetary union at the operational level lays heavy emphasis on narrowing the range of permissible fluctuation in exchange rates among the European currencies, which, because the dollar is used as the intervention currency, can now fluctuate more against one another than they can against the dollar.
—European, and especially German, critics of the Werner Report have argued that monetary union cannot be achieved and exchange rates successfully narrowed without first coordinating economic policies, and especially budgetary policies, among the members of the Community. They therefore urge a concerted effort to coordinate policies, with increasing authority for determining policy guidelines to be centered with the Community in Brussels.
—Third, Robert Triffin has proposed that the first steps toward monetary union should consist of a limited pooling of reserves with joint management, followed by extension of conditional credit among members of the Community, to help finance payments deficits.[2]

These approaches are not, of course, mutually exclusive, and by being cast as alternatives have generated much needless controversy over their relative merits. Triffin's conditional credits, for example, can be linked to some harmonization of policies, and so can the narrowing of exchange-rate movements. Some conscious parallelism in all three approaches is no doubt desirable. Several observations on these current controversies can be made.

First, the strong emphasis placed on the need to coordinate policies, especially by Germany and the European Commission, reflects the dominant European view that government policies are the principal source of disturbance to the balance of payments, and that if only they can be brought into line everything will be all right. It is true that excessively expansionist policies often have been a source of payments difficulty. There are other sources as well, however, and full harmonization of government policies will by no means assure equilibrium in international payments. Cost movements in different national economies may diverge over time for a variety of reasons, including differential strengths and tactics of labor unions, different rates of adoption of new technology, and the like; and demand for foreign products may grow at differential rates as a consequence of the growth in incomes. For all these reasons, and others, a country's balance-of-payments position may gradually slip out of equilibrium under a regime of fixed exchange rates, even when monetary and fiscal policies have been "harmonized" in some conventional sense of the term, e.g., common rates of growth of money stocks. Pointing to the fundamentally monetary character of all payments difficulties is not sufficient to establish that inappropriate monetary policy is the source of the difficulty, except in the trivial, and to policy makers totally uninteresting, sense that sufficiently stringent monetary action can always eliminate a payments deficit. For it may generate a major depression in the process. An implication of monetary union, as noted above, is that monetary adjustments will be relied upon to assure balance among its constituent parts; but, monetary adjustment may require substantial deflation or expansion in some regions relative to the union as a whole, and, in particular, may cause serious regional unemployment problems in the absence of Community-financed regional policies to mitigate them.

Second, harmonization of national policies within the Community should not be carried too far prematurely. In particular, precisely because of the regional pressures that may be created by a monetary adjustment mechanism, it would be desirable to allow governments considerable latitude to adjust their budgets to their national requirements. The important point is that governments would cease to be able to finance government deficits, beyond specified limits, through domestic credit creation, i.e., at their central

---

[2] Robert Triffin, "On the Creation of a European Reserve Fund," Banca Nazionale del Lavoro, *Quarterly Review* (December 1969), pp. 327-46.

banks. Instead, they would have to issue their securities in a Community-wide capital market when they needed to finance a budget deficit, and this would tend to draw funds into the area in question, thus compensating, at least temporarily, for the deflationary pressures of a regional payments deficit. Hence, governments would retain, through the flexible use of fiscal policy, some influence on the level of total demand within each national market. Such flexible use of fiscal policy can be reconciled with tight Community-wide control on monetary policy by the development of an effective and efficient capital market within the Community, so that each region (national member) could, in effect, achieve monetary expansion by selling securities (in the form of government bonds or bills) to residents of other regions, using the proceeds for expansionary policies. Such a program for regional stabilization is not, of course, sufficient for offsetting persistent differences in regional costs; it will work only if the regional imbalance is a temporary one, or if it is one that can be corrected through sufficient capital investment. There are limits to which borrowers, even national governments, can raise funds for nonproductive expenditures.

Third, therefore, exchange rates between members of the Community cannot be fixed irrevocably until the underlying trends of the national economies, not merely the government policies, come into close harmony, or until the Community develops a mechanism for effecting sufficiently large transfers among the regions of the Community to compensate for the depressive effects on some regions of a gold-standard type adjustment mechanism that relies on monetary movements alone. The transfers that take place under the common agricultural policy represent the beginnings of a large intra-Community transfer mechanism, although that particular one may occasionally be perverse from the point of view of cushioning depressed regions by giving rise to transfers from regions of low income and employment to regions of high income and employment (e.g., from Belgium and Italy to France). Movement toward Community-financed unemployment compensation would represent a much more direct and effective step in this direction.

Fourth, the creation of a European Reserve Fund will not in itself help to solve any of the functional problems that will confront national economies during the process of integration. At best, it would permit the conservation of some international reserves, which members of the Community now use (via multilateral clearing through the exchange market) to settle imbalances among members as well as between members and the rest of the world. But, conservation of reserves has hardly been one of the most pressing needs of the Community in recent years, in contrast to the position of some less-developed countries. Creation of a reserve fund would, however, institutionalize concern for the monetary integration of the Community, encourage and accustom national officials to discussion of monetary policies *before* monetary actions are taken, and provide the institutional basis for joint action when other conditions were ripe for it, e.g., for intervention in exchange markets on behalf of the Community as a whole, *vis-à-vis* the dollar or other outside currencies.

Finally, however, the controversy over transitional tactics really conceals divergent objectives. At least one member of the Community, France, does not accept in principle the desirability of supranational control of monetary policy; but, it is very much interested, for foreign policy reasons, in achieving a concerted position of the Community on alterations in the international monetary system, and, in particular, on the role of the dollar and on the creation of SDRs. After President Nixon's announcement in August 1971, other members of the Community have come increasingly to share this desire, but as much out of concern for the continuing viability of the system as for foreign policy reasons. The Commission, in addition, has an institutional interest in maintaining momentum toward a supranational community and sees the monetary realm as the most promising one for this purpose at present.

2. Monetary Unification without a Single Currency

The EC Resolution of February 1971 speaks of "an individual monetary unit" but is otherwise vague on the question of a European money. As far as their monetary autonomy is concerned, the position in which member countries will find themselves after monetary union is similar with or without a common currency, but important differences remain between a single currency and several currencies with irrevocably fixed exchange rates. In particular, with several currencies, a mechanism is required to preserve fixity of rates between them, while still maintaining some flexibility, or at least the possibility of movement, with respect to nonmember currencies. A subsidiary problem involves clearing the accounts among the various currency units within the Community.

Broadly speaking, there are three ways in which fixity of exchange rates among a group of currencies can be maintained while preserving flexibility against other currencies. The first involves a direct commitment by each central bank or its agents (e.g., the commercial banks) to buy and sell the currencies of the other member countries at announced buying and selling rates. Net balances accumulated by these transactions would be settled periodically by transfers of some reserve asset directly between the central banks. Central banks would in effect "make the market," and the present practice of relying on a relatively free private market for foreign exchange would be abandoned.

If the advantages of a vigorous, competitive market in foreign exchange are judged too great to abandon, even among member currencies, then fixity of exchange rates must be maintained through official intervention in the private market to prevent exchange rates from straying outside the permitted range. Past practice has been to do this through the intermediary of the U.S. dollar, leaving to private arbitrage the task of keeping exchange rates between any two currencies other than the dollar in line. This practice has the well-known disadvantage, from the viewpoint of the Community, of permitting twice the fluctuation in exchange rates between any two Community currencies that can take place between any one currency and the dollar. Yet, the objective is, if anything, to *widen* the possible fluctuations against the dollar, while *narrowing* the fluctuations between member currencies. This practice has the further consequence, increasingly resented, of reinforcing the position of the dollar as a reserve currency, for countries routinely deal in dollars and therefore must hold at least working balances in dollars.

External margins can be widened while internal margins are narrowed in two ways consistent with continued reliance on private markets: (1) close coordination of the points of intervention in dollars by all member countries, with a view to assuring that no two member currencies find themselves at sharply different points in the permissible band of variation with respect to the dollar; and (2) substitution of some member currency for the dollar as the intervention currency for all but one of the member countries, calling on the final member to intervene in its markets with respect to the dollar, and leaving it to private arbitrage to take care of the rest. The Werner Report adopted the first of these possibilities, giving rise to the "snake in the tunnel" metaphor under which coordinated intervention would

hold exchange rates between members' currencies to a narrower band of variation than would be permitted for all member currencies, moving together, with respect to the dollar.[3]

The alternative of a European intervention currency would permit greater institutional autonomy but would also require a sharper break in prevailing practices. Because of the technical facilities available, sterling would be a natural choice for the new intervention currency within the enlarged Community, but any member currency would do. All members would, in practice, define permissible ceilings and floors for the rates of exchange between their currencies and sterling, just as they do now in dollars, and would intervene by buying or selling their currency against sterling to assure that those limits were not exceeded. Britain, in contrast, would continue to deal in dollars. This arrangement would break the fixed relationship between exchange margins for the dollar and exchange margins between any pair of member currencies, and would permit wider exchange-rate variation for the former and narrower variation for the latter. The choice of sterling need not involve extension of credit to Britain beyond the minimum working balances which other member countries would have to maintain for daily intervention and which, indeed, several of them maintain already; and even this credit could be avoided if the Bank of England would agree to provide sterling whenever needed for such intervention, or to be the sole intervenor in the market. The choice of sterling would have the disadvantage, from Britain's point of view, of denying sterling the slightly enlarged flexibility against the dollar that the other currencies would enjoy. From this point of view, it would be preferable to choose a currency that is not likely to be either very strong or very

---

[3] After the currency disruptions of late 1971, the European Commission in Brussels recommended in early 1972 that each member of the community accomplish this objective, not by coordinating their market intervention in dollars as under the Werner Plan, but by intervening in the currencies of *all* other member countries simultaneously. Intervention in dollars would be confined to the vicinity of the borders of the new 4½ percent band of flexibility, whereas exchange variations among member currencies would be held to about half that range by direct intervention. This proposal greatly underestimates the technical difficulties involved in intervening simultaneously in eight currencies at consistent rates in a changing market, of coordinating that intervention with other member countries who may also be intervening in the market in all member currencies, *and* of coordinating intervention in dollars, all of which would be necessary.

weak among currencies of the Community, such as the Dutch guilder, which would also have the attraction of being less controversial politically within Europe than would the choice of sterling or the German mark. But, Dutch financial markets are too small relative to the potential size of the reserve movements required, so special provision would have to be made to insulate the Dutch domestic market from reserve flows of other countries.

3. Creation of a European Currency

The idea of a genuinely new European currency—call it the Europa—is being increasingly bruited about, and, once in place, the separate identities of existing national currencies would presumably disappear over a period of time, thus eliminating the technical problem of maintaining fixed rates among them. A single currency would be necessary, moreover, to make "irrevocability" of parities really credible.

It is not technically difficult to design a new currency and its relationship to existing currencies, although it should be noted that the IMF's SDR is not a precedent in this case because it is a claim held by central banks alone, whereas the Europa would circulate with the public. The problem rather would be to gain public acceptance. The efficient financial services of the City of London would be available for the Europa, provided the basis could be established for its use. To make it work, it would be necessary to create both an adequate supply of Europa-denominated claims and a demand for them. Community governments would almost certainly have to issue debt denominated in Europas (to provide the basis for a secondary market in claims) and to accept it in payment for taxes (to create a demand for Europas). Even then, the Europa would face stiff competition from respected national currencies in domestic use, especially under arrangements, such as those described above, that facilitated the easy exchange of one member currency for another at a virtually fixed price. To launch the Europa successfully, it would be necessary not only to solve the problem of basic adjustment within the Community—that would be a political precondition for a common monetary policy—but also to denigrate existing national currencies. Thus, public debt denominated in national currencies would gradually have to be retired and, even then, somewhat higher interest rates might have to be offered on Europa securities to encourage the banks and the public to hold them, although the necessary premium

would, of course, diminish as Europas became more widely accepted.

In addition to facing stiff competition in domestic economies from national currencies, the Europa would also face stiff competition on the international plane from the U.S. dollar. Unless it is brought under a persistent cloud by prolonged disequilibrium in the U.S. payments position (which is not the same as a recorded deficit on definitions currently employed by the U.S. government), the dollar is likely to retain and indeed to strengthen its position as an international currency for private transactions and short-term investment. There are substantial economies of scale in any financial market, arising from the greater chance of being able to match supplies of and demands for funds on any given maturity without a sharp change in price—in a phrase, the greater the market, the greater the liquidity of the assets that are traded in the market. It will be difficult for a new and untried currency, even when backed by the world's largest trading area, to overcome the leading advantages of the dollar for many years to come.

A new European currency would have a greater chance of success on the international scene—and even possibly within Europe—if it represented an evolution from some existing currency. If one could abstract from political considerations, and from the balance-of-payments difficulties that are likely to attend Britain's entry into the Community, the logical candidate for this enlarged role is sterling. Important technical facilities already exist for dealing in sterling, not the least of which is the large outstanding public debt, which provides the basis for a sizable secondary market in interest-bearing claims, and this is essential if a currency is to be widely held outside its country of issue. The transformation of sterling into this European role would, of course, require placing its management in European hands, on the one side, and having other EC members issue their public debt in Euro-sterling, on the other. The Bank of England would become a Bank of Europe, and under European management would determine the amount of issue of Euro-sterling. There would be no special credit to Britain arising from this role. All governments, including the British government, would be limited in their capacity to finance budget deficits by resort to the central bank. Even the outstanding sterling liabilities would remain fully Britain's liabilities, although, of course, the external reserves of the entire Community would be available to "cover" them against a run.

The only feasible alternative to the pound in this new "European" role would be the German mark, for which the absence of the technical advantages available to sterling might be more than outweighed by the large external savings (attested by the large German current account surplus) of the German public, making the DM an attractive currency in which to borrow. Even after taking this into account, however, sterling is likely to have the edge.

There is, of course, some relationship between the arrangements under which national currencies are linked at fixed and unchanging parities and the possible evolution of a national currency into a supranational one. A currency that is adopted as an intervention currency for purposes of limiting movements in exchange rates is more likely to evolve naturally into a supranational currency than is another, and this may be a consideration that led the Community to reject the use of one European currency by all member countries in favor of the more cumbersome "snake in the tunnel" or "intervention in all currencies" approaches. Indeed, political considerations of national prestige, as well as longstanding suspicion of sterling in European official circles, is likely to militate against what might otherwise be the easiest, the fastest and the most efficient route to the creation of a European currency.

II. IMPLICATIONS FOR THE INTERNATIONAL MONETARY SYSTEM

Suppose now that the practical difficulties have been overcome and a new European currency has been successfully brought into existence, with the corresponding adjustments in European monetary management. What are the possible implications for the monetary system as a whole? Seven can be mentioned briefly, to conclude this survey of the issues.

First, by internalizing much "foreign" trade into a single monetary area, the demand of the EC members for international reserves would presumably drop substantially because European countries today use international reserves to settle imbalances among themselves, whereas within a monetary union they would not.[4] Unless the European Community willingly held these newly "excess" reserves, its actions could result in world inflationary pressures or could disrupt the international payments system, depending on the compo-

[4] Under certain patterns of intra- and extra-European transactions, the demand for external reserves following unification could conceivably increase; but these are not likely to prevail in practice.

sition of its reserve assets, how it chooses to run them down, and how the rest of the world responds.

Second, sterling balances, if not handled by then in some other way, would become Europa balances by virtue of the conversion of British public debt from sterling to Europas and, while they would remain British liabilities, they would clearly and automatically be covered against conversion into other currencies by the reserve assets of the enlarged Community.

Third, the Community would have to agree on a common set of exchange controls, or on their removal, since distinctions between national monetary systems would have been eliminated. Thus, either the Germans will have to abandon their predilection for relatively free capital movements or Britain and France will have to relax substantially their present controls and, as a result, might once again become substantial net lenders to the world.

Fourth, the Europa would willy-nilly become a new reserve currency, at least to a modest degree, because of the overwhelming importance of the enlarged European Community as a trading area, the fact that a large fraction of world trade would be denominated in Europas, and the large market in Europa claims that would have developed for internal use. Stringent steps would have to be taken to prevent the emergence of the Europa as an international currency, if that should be desired (as some Europeans claim), requiring the virtual exclusion of non-member governments from Europa financial markets.

Fifth, the emergence of a single European currency would create the possibility for easier movement of exchange rates between the United States and Europe as a whole, movements that are now inhibited by a structural situation involving a number of European countries that cannot revalue or devalue without also considering moves of other European countries, but who find it exceedingly difficult to coordinate effectively among themselves a matter as sensitive as parity changes. During the prolonged transition and breaking-in period, however, the formation of a European currency is likely to involve greater rather than less rigidity in exchange rates *vis-à-vis* the dollar, because interests of the various members of the Community in exchange-rate movements are likely to diverge sharply much of the time; the result will be immobilism.

Sixth, Europe would regain its monetary independence from the United States in the sense that it could more successfully pursue monetary policies at greater variance from those in the United States than is now possible, both because concerted monetary action in Europe would have great influence on world monetary conditions even under a regime of fixed exchange rates, and because greater exchange-rate flexibility would permit somewhat greater monetary autonomy.

Seventh, under a regime of fixed exchange rates, the emergence of a new, major currency with correspondingly strong financial institutions (probably centered in London) will aggravate the problem of large shifts of financial capital between two centers in response to slight interest differentials or slight changes in sentiment regarding exchange rates. These massive shifts of funds will, in turn, complicate greatly the task of monetary management and will occasionally disrupt foreign exchange and money markets. On the other hand, this problem is not unfamiliar even today; and the existence of two strong financial markets both creates the incentive for and holds out the possibility of close and even-sided collaboration between Europe and America in monetary management.

chapter 7

COORDINATION OF ECONOMIC POLICY

Various aspects of macroeconomic policy have been dealt with in the last three chapters. Chapter 4 contains a collection of readings relating to fiscal policy, while Chapter 5 provides a corresponding treatment of monetary policy. The readings on the balance of payments and the international monetary system in Chapter 6 contain some references to problems of the conduct of fiscal and monetary policy in an open economy—that is, an economy having trade relations with other economies.

Fiscal policy affects the flow of purchasing power and aggregate demand by altering the relation between government spending and tax collections. Monetary policy also affects aggregate demand by altering the terms on which credit can be obtained to finance certain types of spending and by changing the relationships among the yields available on financial and real assets. Thus aggregate demand can be influenced through the use of either fiscal or monetary policy. Indeed, it may be possible to achieve the same level of aggregate demand with a variety of combinations of fiscal and monetary policy. But these different combinations may have quite different effects on other aspects of the economy's performance—on its rate of long-run growth, on its balance-of-payments position, and so on.

Those responsible for formulating economic policy commonly have a number of goals. In particular, they will usually want to achieve a low level of unemployment, reasonable stability of the general price level, a suitable rate of long-term growth, a viable balance-of-payments position, and an acceptable allocation of resources between the public and private sectors of the economy.

RELATIONS BETWEEN POLICY GOALS AND POLICY INSTRUMENTS

In some cases, if there are several instruments of policy and several goals to be achieved, it may be possible to make a combination of changes in the instruments such that all of the goals are attained. Perhaps the best way to demonstrate this possibility is by means of a relatively simple illustration.

Illustrative Example

Suppose that the economy is described by the following model:

$$C = C_o + cY_d \tag{7.1}$$
$$Y_d = Y - T \tag{7.2}$$
$$T = T^* + xY \tag{7.3}$$
$$I = I_o + iY_d - vr \tag{7.4}$$
$$G = G^* \tag{7.5}$$
$$Y = C + I + G \tag{7.6}$$
$$M_d = M_o + kY - mr \tag{7.7}$$
$$M_s = M^* \tag{7.8}$$
$$M_s = M_d \tag{7.9}$$

Here C is consumption expenditure by households, Y_d is disposable income (i.e., income after taxes), Y is gross national product, T is total tax collections (net of transfer payments, which may be regarded as negative taxes), I is investment expenditure, r is the interest rate, G is government purchases of goods and services, M_d is the quantity of money demanded, and M_s is the money supply. The government is assumed to have three instruments, the values of which it can adjust to regulate the economy: the level of taxes (designated by T^*), the level of government purchases of goods and services (G^*), and the size of the money supply (M^*).

This model is very similar to Model III employed in the introduction to Chapter 1 (pages 7–14). Indeed the only significant difference is that in that model investment was assumed to depend only on the interest rate, whereas in the present model investment depends not only on the interest rate but on disposable income. The coefficients used here are accordingly designated in the same way as in the earlier model, except that we now have one additional coefficient, i, the marginal propensity to invest out of disposable income.

Let us suppose that those responsible for economic policy in this economy have three objectives. First, they want to achieve a level of GNP that is consistent with full employment. Second, they want to achieve a target level of investment that will increase the stock of capital at a rate consistent with the desired long-run growth of productive capacity. Third, they want to achieve a target level of government expenditures that will provide the appropriate allocation of resources between the private and public sectors of the economy. That is, they have three goals which can, for our present purposes, be expressed as target values of Y, I, and G. Let us consider how they might proceed—on the assumption that they had complete knowledge of the structure of the economy—to achieve their three goals.

First, we can solve equations (7.1) through (7.9) for Y as a function of the policy instruments G^*, T^*, and M^*. We begin by substituting (7.2) and (7.3) into (7.1), obtaining

$$C = C_o - cT^* + c(1 - x)Y. \tag{7.10}$$

Substituting (7.2) and (7.3) into (7.4) yields

$$I = I_o - iT^* + i(1 - x)Y - vr. \tag{7.11}$$

Now substituting (7.5), (7.10), and (7.11) into (7.6), we obtain

$$Y = C_o + I_o - (c + i)T^* + (c + i)(1 - x)Y - vr + G^*. \qquad (7.12)$$

This equation, which contains only two variables, Y and r, is the IS curve for this economy.

Next we substitute (7.8) and (7.9) into (7.7) and solve for r, a process which yields the equation

$$r = \frac{1}{m}(M_o - M^*) + \frac{k}{m}Y. \qquad (7.13)$$

This is the equation of the LM curve of the economy. Substituting (7.13) for r in (7.12) and solving for Y, we obtain

$$\dot{Y} = \frac{1}{1 - (c + i)(1 - x) + \dfrac{vk}{m}}\left[C_o + I_o - \frac{v}{m}M_o - (c + i)T^* + \frac{v}{m}M^* + G^*\right].$$

$$(7.14)$$

The reader will note that this is the same as equation (3.15) in the introduction to Chapter 1, except for the presence of the coefficient i, the marginal propensity to invest out of disposable income.

If C_o, I_o, and M_o are held constant while incremental changes are made in T^*, M^*, and G^*, the change in Y is given by

$$\Delta Y = \frac{1}{1 - (c + i)(1 - x) + \dfrac{vk}{m}}\left[-(c + i)\Delta T^* + \frac{v}{m}\Delta M^* + \Delta G^*\right]. \quad (7.15)$$

This equation tells us how changes in the level of taxes (ΔT^*), changes in the stock of money (ΔM^*), and changes in government purchases of goods and services (ΔG^*) will affect income.

Next we want to find out how changes in the policy instruments $(T^*, M^*,$ and $G^*)$ will affect investment, since one of the objectives of policy is assumed to be the achievement of a target level of investment. Substituting (7.14) for Y and (7.13) for r in (7.11), we obtain (after considerable algebraic manipulation)

$$\Delta I = \frac{1}{1 - c(1 - x) + \dfrac{vk}{m}}\left[\left(\frac{vkc}{m} - i\right)\Delta T^* + \left(\frac{v}{m}[1 - c(1 - x)]\right)\Delta M^*\right.$$

$$\left. + \left[i(1 - x) - \frac{vk}{m}\right]\Delta G^*\right]. \quad (7.16)$$

This equation tells us how changes in taxes (ΔT^*), changes in the stock of money (ΔM^*), and changes in government purchases of goods and services (ΔG^*) affect investment.

The third objective of policy, as indicated above, is the achievement of a target level of government purchases of goods and services (G). Since government purchases is itself an exogenous variable, we have the relation derived from (7.5),

$$\Delta G = \Delta G^*. \qquad (7.17)$$

TABLE I EFFECTS OF INSTRUMENTS ON THE SELECTED TARGETS

| Targets | Effects Produced by Instruments | | |
	ΔT^*	ΔM^*	ΔG^*
ΔY	$\dfrac{-(c+i)}{1-(c+i)(1-x)+\dfrac{vk}{m}}$	$\dfrac{v/m}{1-(c+i)(1-x)+\dfrac{vk}{m}}$	$\dfrac{1}{1-(c+i)(1-x)+\dfrac{vk}{m}}$
ΔI	$\dfrac{vkc/m - i}{1-(c+i)(1-x)+\dfrac{vk}{m}}$	$\dfrac{(v/m)[1-c(1-x)]}{1-(c+i)(1-x)+\dfrac{vk}{m}}$	$\dfrac{i(1-x)-vk/m}{1-(c+i)(1-x)+\dfrac{vk}{m}}$
ΔG	0	0	1

That is, the level of government purchases is not affected by changes in the level of taxes (T^*) or changes in the stock of money (M^*). Thus the relation between government purchases as a target (G) and government purchases as a policy instrument (G^*) is the simple one indicated by (7.17).

At this point it will be useful to summarize our results. The effects of changes in the three instruments, T^*, M^*, and G^*, on the three targets, Y, I, and G, are brought together in Table I. The entries in this table are taken from equations (7.15), (7.16), and (7.17).

The best way to proceed from here is to use a numerical example. Suppose that the equations are as follows:

$$C = 70 + .75Y_d$$
$$Y_d = Y - T$$
$$T = -40 + .20Y$$
$$I = 81 + .10Y_d - 4r$$
$$G = 155$$
$$Y = C + I + G$$
$$M_d = 20 + .25Y - 10r$$
$$M_s = 220$$
$$M_s = M_d$$

This is the model used above with the following parameters: $c = .75$, $x = .20$, $i = .10$, $v = 4$, $k = .25$, $m = 10$, $C_o = 70$, $I_o = 81$, and $M_o = 20$. The values of the policy instruments are $T^* = -40$, $M^* = 220$, and $G^* = 155$. The student can verify for himself that if these values are substituted into equation (7.14), they yield a value of 1,000 for equilibrium income. The corresponding values of all of the variables are given in the "Original Equilibrium" column of Table II.

Suppose now that those responsible for economic policy are not satisfied with the situation. After careful study, they conclude that GNP should be increased by 100 in order to achieve full employment, investment should be increased by 14 in the interest of achieving the desired rate of long-term growth, and government purchases of goods and services should be increased by 20 in order to arrive at a suitable allocation of resources between the private and public sectors. That is, the policy targets, expressed as increments from present levels, are: $\Delta Y = 100$, $\Delta I = 14$, and $\Delta G = 20$. The problem is to find the combination of incremental adjustments, ΔT^*, ΔM^*, and ΔG^*, in the policy instruments that will achieve the three targets.

As a first step, let us find the values of the expressions given in Table I. Substituting the numerical values of the parameters into these expressions, we obtain the following results:

| | Effects Produced by Instruments | | |
Targets	ΔT^*	ΔM^*	ΔG^*
ΔY	$-\dfrac{85}{42}$	$\dfrac{20}{21}$	$\dfrac{50}{21}$
ΔI	$-\dfrac{5}{84}$	$\dfrac{8}{21}$	$-\dfrac{1}{21}$
ΔG	0	0	1

Using this table of coefficients, we can write down the following set of equations:

$$\Delta Y = -\frac{85}{42}\Delta T^* + \frac{20}{21}\Delta M^* + \frac{50}{21}\Delta G^*$$

$$\Delta I = -\frac{5}{84}\Delta T^* + \frac{8}{21}\Delta M^* - \frac{1}{21}\Delta G^*$$

$$\Delta G = \Delta G^*$$

We are given the values of the targets—that is, we know that $\Delta Y = 100$, $\Delta I = 14$, and $\Delta G = 20$. We can therefore write:

$$100 = -\frac{85}{42}\Delta T^* + \frac{20}{21}\Delta M^* + \frac{50}{21}\Delta G^*$$

$$14 = -\frac{5}{84}\Delta T^* + \frac{8}{21}\Delta M^* - \frac{1}{21}\Delta G^*$$

$$20 = \Delta G^*$$

Substituting the value $\Delta G^* = 20$ from the third equation into the first two equations, and multiplying the first equation through by 42 and the second equation through by 84 to get rid of the fractions, we obtain the two equations:

$$-85\Delta T^* + 40\Delta M^* = 2{,}200$$
$$-5\Delta T^* + 32\Delta M^* = 1{,}256.$$

Solving these two equations simultaneously, we obtain the values $\Delta T^* = -8$ and $\Delta M^* = 38$. Thus we find that in order to increase GNP (Y) by 100, increase investment (I) by 14, and increase the portion of GNP allocated to the public sector (G) by 20, it is necessary to make the following three adjustments in the policy instruments: increase the stock of money (M^*) by 38, lower the level of the tax function (T^*) by 8, and increase government purchases of goods and services (G^*) by 20. The position of the economy after these adjustments have been made is shown in the "New Equilibrium" column of Table II. The student should verify the entries in this column by calculating GNP using equation (7.14) with the new values for T^*, M^*, and G^* and then computing the new values of the remaining variables through the use of the other equations.

	Original Equilibrium	New Equilibrium	Change
Gross national product (Y)...............	1,000	1,100	+100
Consumption (C).......................	700	766	+ 66
Investment (I).........................	145	159	+ 14
Government purchases (G^*)...........	155	175	+ 20
Taxes (T).............................	160	172	+ 12
Disposable income ($Y - T$)...............	840	928	+ 88
Saving ($Y_d - C$).......................	140	162	+ 22
Government deficit ($G - T$)...............	−5	3	+ 8
Money stock (M^*)......................	220	258	+ 38
Tax intercept (T^*)......................	−40	−48	− 8
Interest rate (r)........................	5%	3.7%	− 1.3%

For the most part, in the discussions of monetary and fiscal policy in the earlier chapters of this book, we have started with the policy instruments and attempted to discuss their impact on income, employment, and other relevant economic variables. That is, the policy instruments were viewed as the independent variables and the various measures of performance of the economy were viewed as the dependent variables whose values were changed as a result of alterations in the policy instruments. It should be noted that in the above exercise this relationship was reversed. We started with the changes in the performance variables (in this case Y, I, and G) that we desired to see take place and calculated the changes in the policy instruments (T^*, M^*, and G^*) that would be required to produce these results. That is, in this exercise the targets (performance variables) were treated as the independent variables and the policy instruments as the dependent variables.

Need for Independence of Instruments

In the above illustration we had three policy instruments, and this enabled us to hit three policy targets at the same time. This suggests the general rule that if we have n policy instruments, we will be able to achieve n policy goals simultaneously. This generalization is, in principle, correct with one major qualification: the policy instruments must be *independent* in their effects on the target variables. The problem that arises if the instruments are not independent may be illustrated by means of a simple example.

Suppose our two instruments are open market operations—i.e., the change (ΔR^*) in the central bank's holdings of government securities—and changes (Δr_d^*) in the central bank's discount rate. Assume that the two targets are a desired change in GNP (ΔY) and a desired change in investment expenditures (ΔI). Finally, assume that the following relationships hold: an open market purchase of $1 billion will increase GNP by $4 billion and will increase investment by $2 billion, while an increase of 1 percentage point in the discount rate will reduce GNP by $2 billion and reduce investment by $1 billion. Thus we may write the following two equations to show the effects on Y and I of making simultaneous adjustments in R^* and r_d^*:

$$\Delta Y = 4\Delta R^* - 2\Delta r_d^*$$
$$\Delta I = 2\Delta R^* - \Delta r_d^*$$

Suppose now that we decide we would like to increase GNP by $10 billion and increase investment by $2 billion. This would require the solution for ΔR^* and Δr_d^* of the two equations:

$$10 = 4\Delta R^* - 2\Delta r_d^*$$
$$2 = 2\Delta R^* - \Delta r_d^*$$

On a moment's reflection, it is apparent that this is an insoluble problem. If we multiply the second equation by 2 we obtain $4 = 4\Delta R^* - 2\Delta r_d^*$; obviously $4\Delta R^* - 2\Delta r_d^*$ cannot simultaneously be equal to 10 and equal to 4. The two equations are inconsistent, and no solution exists. There is an infinite number of combinations of open market operations and discount rate adjustments that will satisfy the first equation. For example, income can be increased by $10 billion by either (a) open market purchases of $2 billion combined with a discount rate reduction of 1 percentage point, or (b) open market purchases of $4 billion combined with a discount rate increase of 3 percentage points. But by reference to the equation $\Delta I = 2\Delta R^* - \Delta r_d^*$, it is apparent that either of these policy adjustments will increase investment by $5 billion. Indeed, any policy adjustment that raises income by $10 billion will also increase investment by $5 billion. In this case the two policy instruments are perfect substitutes for each other, at least insofar as these two goals are concerned. That is, an open market purchase of $1 billion has exactly the same effects as a reduction of 2 percentage points in the discount rate. Thus, the GNP and investment goals referred to about cannot be achieved simultaneously by using these two instruments. Indeed, for all practical purposes, there is only one policy instrument rather than two.

The need for policy instruments to be independent is especially important to bear in mind in connection with monetary policy. It is often said that the Federal Reserve has three instruments of general monetary control: open market operations, changes in the discount rate, and changes in reserve requirements. This might seem to suggest that the Federal Reserve alone could select three goals—for example, full employment, price stability, and a suitable rate of long-term growth—and achieve all three simultaneously by appropriate adjustments in its three instruments. The fact is, however, that the three instruments—at least given the present state of knowledge—are not independent insofar as their effects on the major goals of economic policy are concerned.[1] Their effects are not identical, but we do not yet understand the differences very well, and, in any case, their differential effects on the major goals of policy are probably not great enough to be very significant. By sophisticated adjustments of *both* monetary and fiscal policy instruments, it may be possible to achieve several goals simultaneously; however, such results can hardly be achieved by monetary policy alone.

A special problem relating to the independence of the instruments of monetary and fiscal policy appears to exist with respect to the goals of high employment and price stability. It appears that the causal relationships can be described approximately as follows: (1) The level of aggregate demand in relation to productive capacity determines the level of employment (and unemployment), and (2) the level of unemployment determines the rates of change of wages and prices through a Phillips curve type of relationship, as discussed in the

---

[1] See W. L. Smith, "The Instruments of General Monetary Control," *National Banking Review*, Vol. I (September 1963), pp. 47–76, reprinted in Chapter 3 of this book, pp. 236–258 above.

articles by Tobin and by Hymans reprinted in Chapter 1. Thus, monetary and fiscal policy, both of which operate on aggregate demand, are not capable of exerting independent effects on the rate of unemployment and the rate of inflation. That is, we cannot achieve the two goals of full employment and price stability by using fiscal and monetary policy instruments only.

It is true, of course, that the chain of causation is not quite as simple as that suggested in the previous paragraph and that monetary and fiscal policy may in fact be able to exert some independent effects on employment and prices. A policy mix involving relatively easy money may stimulate capital accumulation, thereby accelerating the growth of labor productivity. If the faster growth of productivity does not cause wages to rise more rapidly, the rate of increase in unit labor costs at a given rate of unemployment may be slowed down, reducing the upward pressure on prices. Offsetting adjustments in monetary and fiscal policy may also, under some conditions, be able to mitigate the effects of changes in the composition of private demand, thereby preventing inflation of the "demand shift" variety.[2] But the possibilities in these respects must realistically be regarded as quite limited. Other kinds of policy measures capable of exerting direct effects on wage and price decisions and on the functioning of labor and product markets are likely to be necessary if the relation between inflation and unemployment is to be changed.

Social Welfare Functions

In the illustrative example given above, we simply assumed that the goals of policy were given—that the authorities wanted to increase Y by 100, G by 20, and I by 14—and calculated the adjustments in the policy instruments that would be required to produce these results. Nothing was said about how the goals themselves were chosen. In principle, the choice of goals requires the use of some explicit or implicit social welfare function by which the authorities balance against each other the benefits that they feel will accrue to the nation from the various alternative outcomes of economic policy.

To illustrate, consider a closed economy (i.e., one without foreign trade), in which the authorities believe that economic welfare depends on the rate of unemployment, the rate of change of the price level, the volume of current private consumption, the amount of resources devoted to capital accumulation, and the amount of resources allocated to government activities. The social welfare function for such an economy might be as follows:

$$ W = f(u, \frac{\Delta p}{p}, C, I, G), $$

where W is welfare, u is the unemployment rate, $\Delta p/p$ is the percentage change in the price level, C is private consumption, I is private investment, and G is government purchases of goods and services. We may suppose that welfare is increased as u is reduced, as $\Delta p/p$ is reduced from a positive number toward zero, as C is increased, as I is increased, and as G is increased.

The social welfare function by itself is of no use in policy formulation. It must be considered in conjunction with some kind of model of the structure of the economy. The scientific procedure would be to maximize welfare subject

---

[2] For an explanation of "demand shift" inflation, see C. L. Schultze, *Recent Inflation in the United States* (Study Paper No. 1, *Study of Employment, Growth, and Price Levels,* Joint Economic Committee, 86th Cong., 1st sess., 1959).

to the "constraints" imposed by the economic structure. While a formal analysis of this approach is beyond the scope of this book, it is possible to get an idea of its meaning.[3] Suppose that a relation between unemployment and inflation of the Phillips curve type exists. Then an expansion of aggregate demand will yield two types of benefits: it will reduce unemployment (u) directly and it will also increase the total amount of output available to be divided up among the three desiderata, consumption (C), investment (I), and government purchases (G). On the other hand, an expansion of aggregate demand will involve a cost: the rate of price increase ($\Delta p/p$) will rise. The maximization of welfare will involve expanding aggregate demand to the point at which the marginal increase in welfare from expanded employment and output will just equal the marginal loss of welfare from accelerated inflation. Having determined on this basis how much total demand is appropriate, the relations among government purchases, tax rates, and monetary expansion should be determined in such a way as to equate the marginal benefits of the last unit of consumption, the last unit of investment, and the last unit of government purchases.

While this is an enlightening way to look at the formal process of establishing economic policy, its practical applicability has, up to now, been very limited. To solve policy problems in this way the authorities need to have (a) an explicit form of the welfare function to be maximized and (b) a detailed and accepted model describing the structure of the economy and its responses to changes in various policy instruments. Neither of these requirements has been met, with the result that, while attempts are often made to formulate policy in ways that are somewhat in the spirit of this approach, its scientific application is not yet possible.

COMMENTS ON THE READINGS

It is apparent from the above discussion that fiscal, monetary, and other economic policies must be coordinated and must work in harmony if a satisfactory performance of the economy is to be achieved. In the United States, a variety of federal government agencies and instrumentalities have powers and responsibilities bearing on economic policy, with the result that the coordination of policy involves some complex problems. The President receives advice on economic policy from the Chairman of the Council of Economic Advisers, the Director of the Office of Management and Budget, and the Secretary of the Treasury, as well as, on occasion, from other federal officials. The President makes recommendations concerning federal expenditures and taxes in his annual budget message, which is prepared in January of each year and which covers the fiscal year beginning six months later. However, many of his proposals require congressional action; as a consequence, the Congress often has a major hand in shaping the budget. Monetary policy is the prerogative of the Federal Reserve, which has the power to act independently, although in practice in recent years there has generally been close liaison between the Federal Reserve and the President's chief economic advisers, as well as, on many occasions, the President himself.

The Employment Act of 1946 sets forth the basic responsibilities of the federal

---

[3] For relatively simple expositions of this approach to policy making, see C. C. Holt, "Linear Decision Rules for Economic Stabilization and Growth," *Quarterly Journal of Economics,* Vol. LXXVI (February 1962), pp. 20–45; and Henri Theil, "Linear Decision Rules for Macrodynamic Policy Problems," in B. G. Hickman (ed.), *Quantitative Planning of Economic Policy* (Washington, D.C.: The Brookings Institution, 1965), pp. 18–37.

government in the field of overall economic policy. That act also established the three-member Council of Economic Advisers to provide advice to the President and the Joint Economic Committee of the Congress, which has become an important focus of congressional interest in economic policy. One notable feature of the federal government, however, is the absence of any formalized procedure for coordinating policy in the executive branch. The way in which the Council of Economic Advisers, the Bureau of Management and Budget, the Treasury Department, the Federal Reserve, and other executive agencies are geared into the process of policy determination is left up to the President and depends upon his style and way of doing things. The problems and procedures of policy coordination as they appeared during the Kennedy and Johnson administrations are discussed in the paper by W. H. Locke Anderson, who speaks from a background of practical experience as a staff economist of the Council during a portion of the Kennedy-Johnson period.

The paper by Robert A. Mundell illustrates the use of two policy instruments to achieve two goals. It deals with the differential impacts of monetary policy as compared with fiscal policy on domestic employment and on the balance of payments. The basic point of the paper is relatively simple: It is possible to achieve full employment with many different combinations of fiscal and monetary policy; a "mix" of the two which achieves full employment with a relatively easy fiscal policy—high government expenditures or low tax rates—combined with a tight monetary policy and high interest rates will result in a more favorable balance-of-payments position than the opposite kind of "mix" involving tight fiscal and easy monetary policy. The reason is that the balance of trade in goods and services will be determined primarily by the level of income, which will be the same in either case, while high interest rates will attract more capital from abroad and lead to a more favorable balance on capital account. While the principle set forth in the Mundell paper is subject to several qualifications, it has been a rather important element in some recent discussions of optimal fiscal-monetary strategy in countries experiencing balance-of-payments problems.[4]

The paper by Warren L. Smith discusses ways in which monetary and fiscal policies can be adjusted both to keep aggregate demand growing in pace with productive capacity at high employment and to increase the growth of productive capacity itself. Growth of productive capacity can be accelerated by policy adjustments which reduce current consumption and channel the resources thereby released into uses that add to capacity. These uses include (a) private investment which accelerates the growth of the stock of private physical capital, (b) research and development activity which speeds up the pace of technological development, and (c) increased public investment in the development of human and physical resources. The paper discusses various ways in which such adjustments may be brought about while at the same time keeping the economy operating at high employment.

The concluding paper by Arthur M. Okun reviews and integrates much that has been dealt with earlier in this book with regard to monetary and fiscal policy. He argues that both instruments of stabilization policy are capable of stimulating or restraining aggregate demand and reaching the socially acceptable employment-inflation tradeoff. Therefore, it is the side effects of each kind of

---

[4] Some of the qualifications applicable to the principle expounded by Mundell, together with some of the practical difficulties involved, are briefly discussed in Chapter 6 above (pages 452–465) in the selection entitled "Problems of the International Monetary System," reprinted from the January 1969 *Annual Report of th Council of Economic Advisers.*

policy—the impact of monetary restraint on homebuilding and on asset values, the implications of monetary policy decisions for growth and for the balance of payments, and the effects of budget decisions on the composition of output—which should govern choices between them. Based on these and other considerations, Okun offers a set of working rules for the conduct and coordination of stabilization policy.

ECONOMIC COUNSELLING AND STABILIZATION POLICY IN THE UNITED STATES*

W. H. Locke Anderson

INTRODUCTION

In order to understand the problems of stabilization policy in the United States and the role of counselling in the determination of policy, it is necessary to remember several of the broad features of the structure of the government. To an extent which is perhaps unmatched among the other industrial countries of the world, policy making power in the U.S. is widely dispersed among many governmental organizations which have responsibility to many different constituencies. This makes it extremely difficult to arrive at or to implement common policies. Indeed, in a sense there is no such thing as stabilization policy in the singular; there are stabilization policies, and the various policies are often in direct, though usually tacit, conflict.

This fragmentation of power has been a potent force for political stability and conservatism in the United States. Only rarely in our history has the vast majority of political forces been aligned behind a program of change. The usual situation is one in which legislation and administrative actions are the products of shifting alliances among strange bedfellows. This makes it difficult for policy to be consistent as to its goals, for programs of action to be arrived at quickly, and for agreed-upon programs to be implemented in a manner consistent with their intent.

PROBLEMS CREATED BY FEDERALISM

To begin with, it is important to note the extent of fiscal power exerted by the fifty state

* From *Grundsatzprobleme wirtschaftspolitischer Beratung: Das Beispiel der Stabilisierungspolitik*, in *Schriften des Vereins für Socialpolitik*, Neue Folge, Band 49 (1968), pp. 233–45. Reprinted by permission of the publisher and the author. W. H. Locke Anderson is Professor of Economics, University of Michigan.

governments and the thousands of county, municipal, and school district governments throughout the country. Nearly forty percent of total governmental expenditure is under the control of these sub-national governmental units. Until the past year, state and local expenditure had been growing much more rapidly than federal, and the long-term expectation is for the locus of fiscal power to be shifted away from the central government toward the smaller governmental units.

In many respects, state and local governments may be expected to behave like private firms and individuals, curtailing expenditures in bad times and expanding them in good. Furthermore, their tax structures tend to draw heavily on sources which make them regressive over time. Therefore, a large portion of governmental activity in the United States is neutral, or even antithetical, to the goals of stabilization policy. No matter how skillful and effective counselling is on the national level, its overall effectiveness is limited by the importance of sub-national governments.

PROBLEMS CREATED BY THE INSTITUTIONAL STRUCTURE OF THE NATIONAL GOVERNMENT

The distrust of centralized power which was so dominant in shaping the decisions of the framers of the Constitution has continued to exert a powerful influence over the evolution of political institutions even in the present century. The presumption that power leads inevitably to tyranny is responsible for the parcelling out of policy responsibility to several loci of power. To a certain extent the development of national political parties has made more cohesive a system which is structurally divisive, but it is not an easy matter to maintain even a semblance of party discipline when much of the legislature has nothing to lose by frustrating the policies of its own party's executive.

The separation of powers within the national government makes it possible for the legislature to block the stabilization policies of the executive. The President submits in January a budget which has implicit in it his resource allocation and stabilization program, reflecting the expert advice and political considerations which he and his advisers have taken into account. The Congress considers the budget and modifies it according to its views of the economic and political situation. The budget which is finally passed may be very different from that which the President proposed, with regard both to resource allocation and to stabilization impact.

In a parliamentary, cabinet government, the budget proposed would usually be assured of the support of at least the majority party. In a congressional, presidential government, the executive and the legislative majority need not be of the same party. Even when they are, party discipline is so weak that the President cannot be certain of support for his program. This structural cleavage has frequently been responsible for the frustration of stabilization programs. The tax reduction of 1964 was delayed for more than a year by a recalcitrant Congress, and it seems probable that this year's proposed increase will not be enacted.

The stabilization problem is further complicated by the independence of the central bank. In its regular operation, the Federal Reserve is independent of both the legislature and the executive. It must, of course, act in such a manner as to avoid provoking the kind of political wrath which would produce legislation restricting its independence. This is not often a binding constraint, however, and the bank has plenty of opportunity to act in a manner which runs counter to the policies of the President and Congress.

GOVERNMENTAL STRUCTURE AND THE ROLE OF COUNSELLING

This decentralization of economic power built into the structure of the United States government makes it quite difficult for expert counselling to be effective in guiding stabilization policy. The President may be reluctant to follow the advice of his experts when his sense of the political realities leads him to doubt that Congress will accept a given stabilization program. Moreover, even when the President is persuaded of

the wisdom of some line of action, his program may be delayed or blocked in Congress. Finally, even when the President and Congress are in accord, the monetary authorities or the state and local governments may act in such a way as to undermine the effectiveness of the budgetary program.

THE INSTITUTIONALIZATION OF COUNSELLING IN THE EXECUTIVE BRANCH—THE COUNCIL OF ECONOMIC ADVISERS

In order to convey accurately the role of expert counselling in the planning of United States stabilization policy, it is necessary to consider the Council of Economic Advisers to be essentially a counselling board rather than a part of the government to be counselled. Although the scope of the Council's activity extends way beyond that of a narrowly scientific board, it is none the less the principal (although not the only) institution through which the advice of professional economists is brought to bear on stabilization problems.

Through the Council of Economic Advisers, the President receives directly professional advice on economic policy problems. Under some administrations this has been the President's only formal contact with an economist, although this has not been the case in recent years. The last three Directors of the Bureau of the Budget have all been professional economists with academic as well as governmental experience. This has not been true of Secretaries of the Treasury. However, both the Bureau of the Budget and the Treasury are amply staffed with economists, and their views are often transmitted to the President through the heads of their agencies. Nonetheless, the Council of Economic Advisers provides the only institutional arrangement which guarantees that a professional economist will have the direct ear of the President.

The Chairman of the Council and the two Members have in most cases been drawn from the academic community. They are chosen by the President on criteria of professional status, familiarity with governmental procedures and problems, and sympathy with the economic goals of the party in power. The Council, in turn, applies similar criteria in its selection of staff.

This staff has a few key members who have seen service under several administrations and who provide continuity of contact with the civil service. It also draws on the civil service for personnel on a temporary basis. However, it draws chiefly on the academic community for members who work at the Council for a year or two and who then return to their academic posts. There is thus a continual transfusion of academic talent into the counselling agency. This makes it possible not only to bring in new views and enthusiasms, but also to provide a higher level of average staff expertness than would be possible if the Council had to rely entirely on a permanent staff or on personnel loaned by other agencies. Under the Kennedy administration, the Council had such eminent economists as Kenneth Arrow, Robert Solow, and Warren Smith on its full-time staff.

In addition, the Council calls from time to time on the academic profession for consultation on particular policy problems and for assistance in preparing its Economic Report. The roster of the Council's consultants contains the names of many of the nation's leading economists.

There are no representatives of business, labor, agricultural, or other economic pressure groups on the Council or its staff. The presence of such persons would be wholly inconsistent with the Council's character. It functions primarily as a source of professional advice to the President on economic problems. Although its members must share general political, social, and economic predispositions of the President in order to be at all effective in advising him, they are first and foremost scientific advisers. The presence of pressure-group representatives in such an institution would be not only inappropriate to its role but disruptive to its operation. Pressure groups have ample opportunity to make their views known to the President. Indeed, one of the duties of the Council is to maintain contact with such groups and present to the President the pros and cons of their positions on policy problems. However, if the Council itself contained representatives of these groups, it would cease to be a useful source of expert advice for the President.

THE TREASURY CONSULTANTS

Within the executive branch, the principal counselling group other than the Council of Economic Advisers is the Treasury Consultants. This is a group of two dozen or so academic, government, and other professional economists (not all of whom are strong supporters of the party in power) who meet periodically with the Secretary of the Treasury and the Under and Assistant Secretaries to discuss stabilization and other policy problems and to answer questions which the Treasury poses. Representatives of the Bureau of the Budget and the Council of Economic Advisers are usually present and also question the consultants.

In some respects this body provides the Secretary of the Treasury with a counterweight to the expert advice coming from the Council. It not only provides the Secretary with advice which is intrinsically valuable to him but also enables him to buttress his position in occasional disputes with the Council over the proper course of policy action.

Since the Treasury Consultants meet infrequently, they have little influence on the details of program development. Their main function is to provide the Secretary with a general picture of how academic economists view the business cycle situation and what they think the broad outlines of policy ought to be. Since they have no institutionalized access to the President, their influence on policy making depends entirely on their impact on the Secretary's thinking and thence indirectly on his influence with the President.

COUNSELLING IN THE LEGISLATURE

The Senate and House Appropriations Committees, the Senate Finance Committee, and the Ways and Means Committee of the House all play a key role in the development of stabilization policy, for it is through these committees that all fiscal legislation must pass in order to be considered by the Congress at large.

These committees all possess expert staffs, to be certain, but it is important to note that there is little attention given by the staff experts to stabilization questions. The principal way in which these committees receive advice on stabilization questions is through hearings, in which academic economists, representatives of pressure groups, and officers of the Administration are called upon to comment on stabilization and other aspects of the budget. One of the principal shortcomings of the institutionalization of counselling in the United States is the lack of a permanent commission of experts to provide the Congressional committees which report out fiscal legislation with an independent source of opinion on the overall fiscal impact of the President's budget. The preparation of the budget by the executive involves a searching overall appraisal of its stabilization impact by a staff of policy experts, but the consideration and modification of the budget by the legislature is not subject to such overall control.

The Joint Economic Committee, established by the same legislation which established the Council of Economic Advisers, is the principal formal locus within the Congress of consideration of the stabilization impact of the budget. The Joint Committee has an expert staff of its own, holds hearings on the President's program, and commissions special studies of stabilization policies. The study of Employment, Growth, and the Price Level commissioned by the Joint Economic Committee during the 1950s contained many distinguished analyses of stabilization problems. However, the role of the Joint Economic Committee is purely educational. Its published hearings and special analyses have an important impact on the economic understanding of the Congress, but since the Committee has no control over the course of legislation, its direct influence on policy making is not very substantial. It is the one part of Congress which is the most receptive to expert advice on stabilization policy, but because of its place in the structure of Congress, much of the expert opinion which it receives is wasted.

The overall quality and consistency of stabilization policy making could be considerably strengthened in the United States without reducing the independence of the executive and legislature if the Congress were to establish a procedure whereby some committee—such as the Joint Economic Committee—would consider the stabilization impact of the President's budget with the assistance of expert counselling and lay down recommendations which would guide the legislative committees in their consideration of the details of the budget. This would strengthen the role of Congress in the guidance of fiscal policy and would provide a welcome alternative to the piecemeal, meat-axe approach to budgeting which the legislative committees now apply.

THE LEGISLATIVE MANDATE FOR STABILIZATION POLICY

The machinery and general mandate for stabilization policy in the United States were established by the Employment Act of 1946. The version of this bill which was originally introduced into the Senate in January, 1945, specifically required the federal government to take such policy actions as were necessary to maintain full employment. This bill came under heavy fire from conservative pressure groups, and the version which finally became law contained the following much weaker and vaguer mandate:

SEC. 2. The Congress hereby declares that it is the continuing policy and responsibility of the Federal Government to use all practicable means consistent with its needs and obligations and other essential considerations of national policy with the assistance and cooperation of industry, agriculture, labor, and State and local governments, to coordinate and utilize all its plans, functions, and resources for the purpose of creating and maintaining, in a manner calculated to foster and promote free competitive enterprise and the general welfare, conditions under which there will be afforded useful employment for those able, willing, and seeking to work, and to promote maximum employment, production, and purchasing power.

The law required the President to submit to the Congress each year an Economic Report which was to characterize the current situation and developing trends in the economy and to present a program for carrying out the policy outlined in the above-quoted Section 2. It provided for a Council of Economic Advisers to assist the President in preparing his report and the program embodied in it. It also established the Joint Economic Committee, which was to study the President's report and to make recommendations to the Senate and House.

The general mandate expressed in Section 2 of the Employment Act placed the government squarely on record in the realm of economic matters as favoring good rather than evil, but it was not much more specific than that as to policy goals. The law left it up to the President and his advisers to translate the general mandate into concrete goals. The interpretation of the mandate has therefore varied from one administration to another, reflecting in large part the social philosophy of the party in power. Republican administrations have tended to emphasize heavily the "foster(ing of) free competitive enterprise"; Democratic administrations have placed heavier emphasis on "maximum employment, production, and purchasing power."

THE GOALS OF STABILIZATION POLICY

It would be mistaken to suppose that the concrete goals of stabilization policy as developed within the executive are determined by the Council of Economic Advisers. It would also be mistaken to suppose that they are provided to the Council by the President, the Cabinet, and the other political leaders. Rather, the goals have been developed through the discussion and interaction of politicians and experts, considering what is economically, socially, and politically desirable and achievable.

Four goals of stabilization policy have been enunciated many times by the present administration in its Economic Report and other statements:

1. Full employment.
2. Rapid growth.
3. Price stability.
4. International balance.

These goals are not usually spelled out in more concrete form, but the following seems to be what the President and Council have in mind when discussing these goals:

1. Full employment under existing labor market conditions involves an unemployment rate of about four percent.
2. An acceptably rapid rate of growth at full employment is thought to be about four percent per annum.
3. A rise in the wholesale price index of about one percent per annum and in the consumer price index of about two percent per annum is thought to constitute reasonable stability at full employment.
4. Although balance of payments goals are rarely spelled out specifically, an annual deficit of about one-half billion on a liquidity basis (without resort to extensive special transactions) would seem to constitute acceptable balance.

These are the present stabilization goals of the present [1968] administration, it should be stressed. They represent what now seems to be the best set of circumstances which could be achieved under favorable conditions. If the administration were to change, or if conditions were to permit the achievement of a more ambitious target, the goals would surely change.

HIERARCHY OF GOALS

Of the four announced goals of stabilization policy, full employment receives the most lip service, and it is probably in fact considered to be the most important. However, when it became apparent in 1962 that the recovery from the 1960–61 recession was slowing down, there was little strong sentiment within the government for a crash program to restore full employment immediately. It was recognized that an increase in the rate of demand expansion sufficient to achieve four percent unemployment within a year would create severe inflationary strains and exacerbate

already severe balance of payments difficulties. The administration was willing to put up with a more gradual restoration of full employment in return for greater price stability and better international balance.

Most Americans have a strong antipathy to inflation and many are also strongly opposed to large budget deficits, which they regard as intrinsically inflationary. Moreover, those who are aware of the international payments situation are concerned about the continuing payments deficit.

No administration can politically afford to ignore those concerns, even in those cases in which the concerns are ill-founded. The recent Democratic administrations and their advisers have waged a vigorous public education campaign on behalf of a functional approach to federal government finance. They have also stressed the real benefits of full employment and more rapid growth. Nonetheless, policy makers must remain sensitive to the particular aversions of the people, and the advisers know this. The substance of their policy advice is therefore tempered somewhat by their knowledge of the sorts of advice which the political leaders will be able to heed.

In pursuing its price stability and international balance goals, the present administration has tried to avoid deflationary policies which would impair the achievement of full employment and suitably rapid growth. Thus the emphasis has been on wage and price guideposts, the Interest Equalization Tax, and "voluntary" restraints on direct foreign investment. The Council has been active in devising and supporting such means of developing greater consistency among goals.

The American approach to tradeoffs and goal reconciliation, like its approach to so many problems, is one of continual testing through experience. Cut and fit. Try to achieve something a little better than the present situation. American economists and policy advisers are quite modest about the accuracy of extrapolations made by econometric methods. They prefer to move gradually in the direction of what seems to be the best among the attainable alternatives, to hope for good luck, and to invent stopgaps or revise goals when their hopes and expectations are not fulfilled. This accounts for the vagueness of the specification of goals and the lack of much formal apparatus for judging tradeoffs.

THE OBTAINING OF INFORMATION

The Council does no direct gathering of data, but relies on other branches of the government to supply it with information. In addition to the routine *ex post* data on national income, industrial production, prices, employment, etc., it also receives *ex ante* data from the Census Bureau on consumer intentions and from the Office of Business Economics on investment plans. The other agencies are extremely cooperative with the Council, providing data as soon as possible after it is gathered. In addition, several private information gathering institutions have been kind enough to provide their data from time to time.

The Council has an extensive library of data sources and several statistical clerks to provide information and to prepare tables. It does not have a statistical computation staff, however. When Council members require econometric information, it is generally necessary either to rely on the professional literature, or for one of the staff economists to do the work.

On occasion, it has been necessary for the Council to commission a large scale study which exceeds the capability of its own small staff. On these occasions it has sometimes relied on the services of the Brookings Institution, a nonprofit social science research organization having a close affiliation with the government.

In most cases, it seems desirable that the Council relegate data gathering and large scale studies to other agencies. Its flexibility and hence its usefulness to the President are enhanced by its remaining small. If the Council were to subsume the functions of the various data-gathering agencies throughout the government, it would become an enormous bureaucracy and lose completely the *esprit de corps* which makes it such a hard-working and dependable organization. There is much to be said for keeping the advisory board small enough to have a sense of identity as a group. In emergency situations, such as during a major national strike, and in seasonal peaks in government activity, such as just before the submission of the budget, it is very important that the President have an advisory group which is sufficiently cohesive that its staff will work around the clock if necessary. Only from a small organization with a pride in its own eliteness can this be expected.

INFORMAL SOURCES OF INFORMATION

In addition to formal sources of information— *ex post* data, anticipations surveys, and the like—the Council uses the opinions and insights of business and labor leaders gathered through informal and semiformal contacts. Whenever it is invited to do so, the Council sends representatives to meetings held by business groups to discuss the current economic situation. It has several standing arrangements of this sort. Council members also have occasional luncheons with business and labor leaders to discuss economic developments. These informal, off-the-record contacts are likely to produce discussions which are more frank than those which would develop in formal hearings.

INTERAGENCY CONSULTATIONS

The Council not only relies on other agencies for data, it also draws on them for opinions on the business cycle situation and the likely consequences for various stabilization measures. The Treasury and the Budget Bureau have personnel with considerable experience concerning the revenue and expenditure sides of the budget. At the staff level, Council, Treasury, and Budget Bureau economists meet regularly to pool their expertise for purposes of arriving at sounder scientific analyses than would be possible if they worked separately. The heads of these agencies meet regularly also, usually with the President, to discuss policy planning. On some of these occasions, the Chairman of the Federal Reserve Board joins in the discussions.

PUBLICATION OF REPORTS

The principal report of the Council is the *Report of the Council of Economic Advisers* which is transmitted to the Congress each January along with the *Economic Report of the President*. It contains an amplification of the major problems and policies discussed in the President's message and should therefore be considered as a supporting appendix to the President's program. Although the Report treats many matters other than stabilization, this is its principal concern, and the first few chapters are nearly always devoted to macroeconomic developments and policies.

Ostensibly, the addressee of the President's report is the Congress, and although the Council's report is addressed to the President, it is forwarded to the Congress by the President. However, the readership of these documents is much broader than the Congress. Over 70,000 copies were distributed last year, and wide coverage of their contents was given in newspapers (such as the *New York Times*) which are read by those who are interested in public affairs. The *Report* is deliberately designed to provide a broad segment of the public with an understanding of the administration's views and policies and to enlist public support for them.

Each winter the Council is called upon to testify before the Joint Economic Committee in public hearings held shortly after the publication of the *Report*. This provides the opposition party with an opportunity to challenge the Council's views and to make public its own views on policy problems. It also enables the Council to expand upon those aspects of its report which are of special interest to the Committee.

As befits its role as an advisory group to the President, the Council makes many additional reports to him. Several times a week the latest key statistics are transmitted with interpretive comments. When a Presidential press conference is scheduled, briefing material is usually prepared on economic matters. Whenever particularly significant economic events transpire or seem imminent, extensive reports are prepared for the President's information. These are not usually made public, although the President often refers to their contents in his public statements.

These *ad hoc* reports are a key element in the executive's continual attention to stabilization and other economic matters. Since their contents are confined primarily to the economic aspects of various situations and the possible responses to them, they represent only part of the information which the President must weigh in reaching decisions. It is therefore necessary that they be confidential until a plan of action is decided upon. Once a decision has been reached, the economic evidence used in reaching the decision may be used in defending it.

POLICY ADVICE AND POLICY FORMULATION

The Council's contribution to the formulation of stabilization policy consists to a great extent of providing information of the sort, "If A is done, then B will follow, but if C is done then D will follow." That is, it attempts to set out the consequences of alternative courses of action. Whenever the state of economic knowledge permits, the action-consequence relations are set out in quantitative form. The advisers may stress that certain courses of action seem to them more economically desirable than others, but they recognize the range of noneconomic considerations which must enter into policy formulation, and so they try to provide estimates of the consequences of a range of alternative actions.

Once a policy program has been decided upon, the Council prepares a formal statement of the economic events which are likely to transpire if it is adopted. In doing so, it must take into account the likely actions of the independent central bank. Its statement takes the form of the forecast of the gross national product for the calendar year which follows the publication of the *Report*. This forecast is published in the *Report*.

The forecast, which in its published form is seldom more than a page or two in length, indicates which of the major components of the gross national product are likely to expand strongly and which weakly, what seems likely to happen to unemployment, and how much of the expansion is expected to be accounted for by price increases.

The forecast is always made conditional on the acceptance by the Congress of the President's economic program. Because of all the complications in policy formation discussed at the beginning of this paper, any forecast must necessarily be conditional. To a limited extent, the *Report* spells out the consequences of a failure to adopt key features of the program. This is done both to stress the conditionality of the forecast and to indicate the importance of the program.

VERIFICATION OF ADVICE

Because of the enormous slippage between the recommendations of the Council and the economic programs actually adopted by Congress, and because of the complications introduced by the independence of the Federal Reserve and the state and local governments, it is impossible to assess the quality of advice by scientific analysis. Since much of the advice has not been followed in detail or timing, the requisite evidence for assessing its quality has simply not materialized.

It is true, of course, that the American economy has been in excellent health in the past few years. Growth has been rapid, unemployment has fallen to acceptable levels, the balance of payments has at least not worsened, and the price level has only recently been rising at an unacceptable rate. There is a strong tendency to infer that a government which has been in power during a period of such success has been a well-advised government. Although this position cannot be defended by a strict scientific argument, it is at least consistent with events.

The success of the American economy over the past six years has enhanced enormously the prestige of economists both within and outside the administration. Whether the success should be attributed to good counselling or not, it has raised the influence of expert advice in stabilization policy making to an unprecedented level.

THE APPROPRIATE USE OF MONETARY AND FISCAL POLICY FOR INTERNAL AND EXTERNAL STABILITY*

Robert A. Mundell

Fixed exchange rates

This paper deals with the problem of achieving internal stability and balance of payments equilibrium in a country which considers it inadvisable to alter the exchange rate or to impose trade controls. It is assumed that monetary and fiscal policy can be used as independent instruments to attain the two objectives if capital flows are responsive to interest rate differentials, but it is concluded that it is a matter of extreme importance how the policies are paired with the objectives. Specifically, it is argued that monetary policy ought to be aimed at external objectives and fiscal policy at internal objectives, and that failure to follow this prescription can make the disequilibrium situation worse than before the policy changes were introduced.

The practical implication of the theory, when stabilization measures are limited to monetary policy and fiscal policy, is that a surplus country experiencing inflationary pressure should ease monetary conditions and raise taxes (or reduce government spending), and that a deficit country suffering from unemployment should tighten interest rates and lower taxes (or increase government spending).[1]

THE CONDITIONS OF EQUILIBRIUM

Internal balance requires that aggregate demand for domestic output be equal to aggregate supply of domestic output at full employment. If this condition is not fulfilled, there will be inflationary pressure or recessionary potential according to whether aggregate demand exceeds or falls short of, respectively, full employment output. It will be assumed here that, during transitory periods of disequilibrium, inventories are running down, or accumulating, in excess of desired changes, according to whether the disequilibrium reflects a state of inflationary or recessionary potential.

External balance implies that the balance of trade equals (net) capital exports at the fixed exchange parity. If the balance of trade exceeds capital exports, there will be a balance of payments surplus and a tendency for the exchange rate to appreciate, which the central bank restrains by accumulating stocks of foreign exchange. And likewise, if the balance of trade falls short of capital exports, there will be a balance of payments deficit and a tendency for the exchange rate to depreciate, which the central bank prevents by dispensing with stocks of foreign exchange.

In what follows it is assumed that all foreign policies and export demand are given, that the balance of trade worsens as the level of domestic expenditure increases, and that capital flows are responsive to interest rate differentials. Then domestic expenditure can be assumed to depend only on fiscal policy (the budget surplus) and monetary policy (the interest rate) at the full employment level of output. The complete system can thus be given a geometric interpretation in the two policy variables, the interest rate and the budget surplus[2] (Diagram 1).

In the diagram, the *FF* line, which will be referred to as the "foreign-balance schedule," traces the locus of pairs of interest rates and budget surpluses (at the level of income compatible with full employment) along which the balance of payments is in equilibrium. This

* From *International Monetary Fund Staff Papers*, Vol. IX (March 1962), pp. 70–79. Reprinted by permission of the publisher and the author. Robert A. Mundell is Professor of Economics, University of Waterloo, and Professor of International Economics, Graduate Institute of International Studies, Geneva.

[1] This possibility has been suggested, and to a limited extent implemented, elsewhere. See, for example, De Nederlandsche Bank N.V., *Report for the Year 1960* (Amsterdam, 1961).

[2] The assumptions could be made less restrictive without detracting from the generality of the conclusions. Thus, an assumption that capital imports directly affect domestic expenditure, as in theoretical transfer analysis, would tend to reinforce the conclusions. Even the (plausible) assumption that, in addition to capital flows, capital indebtedness is responsive to the rate of interest (to take account of the "stock" nature of much of international floating capital) would not change the conclusions, although it may affect the quantitative extent of the policy changes required.

Notice, however, that I have implicitly assumed away strong "Pigou" effects, speculation on international markets that is related to the size of the (positive or negative) budget surplus, forward rate movements that more than offset interest-rate-differential changes (an unlikely occurrence), and concern about the precise composition of the balance of payments; the last assumption may mean that the method of achieving equilibrium suggested below is desirable only in the short run.

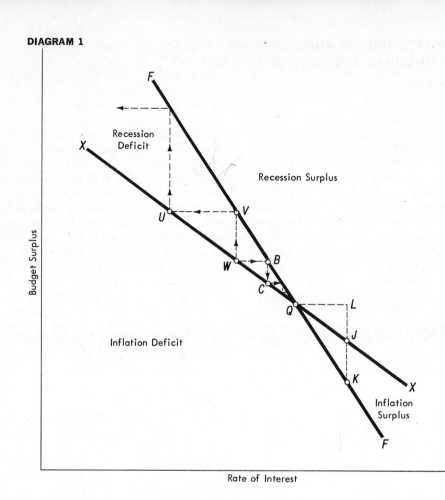

DIAGRAM 1

Recession Deficit

Recession Surplus

Budget Surplus

Inflation Deficit

Inflation Surplus

Rate of Interest

schedule has a negative slope because an increase in the interest rate, by reducing capital exports and lowering domestic expenditure and hence imports, improves the balance of payments; while a decrease in the budget surplus, by raising domestic expenditure and hence imports, worsens the balance of payments. Thus, from any point on the schedule an increase in the rate of interest would cause an external surplus, which would have to be compensated by a reduction in the budget surplus in order to restore equilibrium. Points above and to the right of the foreign-balance schedule refer to balance of payments surpluses, while points below and to the left of the schedule represent balance of payments deficits.

A similar construction can be applied to the conditions representing internal balance. The XX line, or "internal-balance schedule," is the locus of pairs of interest rates and budget surpluses which permits continuing full employment equilibrium in the market for goods and services. Along this schedule, full employment output is equal to aggregate demand for output, or, what

amounts to the same condition, home demand for domestic goods is equal to full employment output less exports. There is, therefore, only one level of home demand for domestic goods consistent with full employment and the given level of exports, and this implies that expenditure must be constant along XX. The internal-balance line must therefore have a negative slope, since increases in the interest rate are associated with decreases in the budget surplus, in order to maintain domestic expenditure constant.

Both the internal-balance and the foreign-balance schedules thus have negative slopes. But it is necessary also to compare the steepness of the slopes. Which of the schedules is steeper?

It can be demonstrated that FF must be steeper than XX if capital is even slightly mobile, and by an amount which depends both on the responsiveness of international capital flows to the rate of interest and on the marginal propensity to import. The absolute slope of the internal-balance schedule XX is the ratio between the responsiveness of domestic expenditure to the rate of interest and the responsiveness of domestic expenditure to the budget surplus. Now, if it is assumed for a moment that capital exports are constant, the balance of payments depends only on expenditure, since exports are assumed constant and imports depend only on expenditure. In other words, if capital exports are constant, the slope of *FF* also is the ratio between the responsiveness of domestic expenditure to the rate of interest and the responsiveness of such expenditure to the budget surplus. Therefore, apart from the effects of changes in capital exports, the two slopes are the same. It is then possible to see that the responsiveness of capital exports to the rate of interest makes the slope of *FF* greater in absolute value than the slope of *XX*.[3]

Consider, for example, what happens to an initial situation of over-all equilibrium at *Q* as this equilibrium is disturbed by an increase in the rate of interest equal to *QL*. Because of the higher rate of interest, there would be deflationary pressure and a balance of payments surplus at the point *L*. If the budget surplus is now lowered, the deflationary pressure can be eliminated at a point like *J* on the internal-balance schedule. But at *J*, expenditure is the same as it was at *Q*, and this means that imports, and hence the balance of *trade*, must be the same as at *Q*. The balance of *payments* is therefore in surplus at *J* because of capital imports attracted by the higher rate of interest; this makes necessary a further reduction in the budget surplus in order to bring the balance of payments again into equilibrium. It follows, then, that the point *K* on the foreign-balance schedule is below the point *J* on the internal-balance schedule, and that *FF* is steeper than *XX*. It can then also be concluded that the absolute difference in slopes is greater, the more mobile is capital (because this causes a larger external surplus at *J*) and the lower is the marginal propensity to import (because this necessitates a larger budget deficit to correct any given external surplus).[4]

In Diagram 1, the two schedules separate four quadrants, distinguished from one another by the conditions of internal imbalance and external disequilibrium. Only at the point where the schedules intersect are the policy variables in equilibrium.

TWO SYSTEMS OF POLICY RESPONSE

Consider now two possible policy systems determining the behavior of fiscal policy and monetary policy when internal and external balance have not been simultaneously achieved. The government can adjust monetary policy to the requirements of internal stability and fiscal policy to the needs of external balance, or it can use fiscal policy for purposes of internal stability and monetary policy for purposes of external balance.

It will be demonstrated first that the policy system in which the interest rate is used for internal stability and fiscal policy is used for external equilibrium, is an unstable system. Consider, for example, a situation of full employment combined with a balance of payments deficit, represented by the point *W*. To correct the deficit by fiscal policy, the budget surplus must be raised from that indicated by *W* to that given by *V*. At *V* there will be equilibrium in the balance of payments, but the increased budget surplus will have caused recessionary pressure. If now the threatening unemployment is to be prevented by monetary policy, the rate of interest must be lowered from that indicated by *V* to that described by *U*. But at *U* there is again a balance of payments deficit; which in turn necessitates a further increase in the budget surplus. The process continues with the interest rate and the budget surplus moving ever further from equilibrium.[5]

---

[3] Both the absolute and relative values of the slopes depend on the particular fiscal policy in question. The discussion in the text applies to income tax reductions because that instrument tends to be neutral as between home and foreign spending. The conclusions would be strengthened or weakened, respectively, as the particular fiscal policy was biased toward or against home goods; the more the change in the budget surplus results from a change in spending on home goods, the greater is the difference between the slopes of *XX* and *FF*.

[4] The assumption that imports depend only on expenditure, while the latter depends partly on the rate of interest, means that imports are affected by

the rate of interest, although the *share* of imports in expenditure is not. This assumption could be relaxed without fundamentally altering the results, although an exception—remote in practice but possible in theory—does arise, if import goods are highly responsive to the rate of interest while home goods are not, capital flows are only slightly responsive to the rate of interest, and the marginal propensity to buy imports is high relative to the marginal propensity to buy home goods. Under these conditions, it is possible that *XX* may be steeper than *FF*. More formally, then, it is necessary to limit the present conclusions to countries in which the ratio of the effect of budget policy on the balance of payments to its effect on domestic excess demand is less than the ratio of the effect of the interest rate on the balance of payments to its effect on excess demand.

[5] It need hardly be mentioned that the demonstration of instability in this instance (or of stability in the subsequent analysis) is not dependent upon the particular assumption that the government corrects imbalance first in one sector and then in the

To show formally that the system is unstable, it is sufficient to note that the payments deficit at U, after the first round of policy changes, exceeds the deficit at W. This is evident since it is known that the balance of *trade* at U and W is the same but, because of the lower rate of interest, the balance of *payments* at U is worse. It follows that this type of policy reaction is unstable.

On the other hand, the opposite type of policy response is stable. Suppose that the authorities adjust the interest rate to correspond to the needs of external equilibrium and adjust fiscal policy to maintain internal stability. Then from the same disequilibrium point W, the rate of interest would be raised to B, thereby correcting the external deficit. But the tendency toward unemployment generated by the restrictive credit policy must now be corrected by a reduction in the budget surplus or increase in the budget deficit. At C there is again internal balance and a balance of payments deficit, as at W. But it is now possible to see that the deficit at C is *less* than the deficit at W. This follows, as before, because the balance of *trade* at C is identical with that at W but, since the rate of interest is higher at C, the balance of *payments* deficit must be less. The system is therefore stable.

The diagrammatic argument can be absorbed at once when it is realized that at W—or anywhere in the quadrant representing a deficit and recession—the interest rate is lower, and the budget surplus is higher, than is appropriate to the overall equilibrium at Q. The use of fiscal policy for external balance, and monetary policy for internal balance, drives the interest rate and budget surplus further away from equilibrium, while the alternative system moves the instruments closer to equilibrium.

The same argument applies to an initial disequilibrium in the opposite quadrant, representing inflationary pressure and external surplus. To restore equilibrium, the interest rate must be reduced, and fiscal policy must be made more restrictive. Only if monetary policy is used for the external purpose, and fiscal policy for the internal purpose, will correction of the disequilibrium automatically ensue.[6]

In the other two quadrants, monetary and fiscal policies will be moving in the same direction under either system of policy response, because both tighter monetary policy and an increased budget surplus correct inflationary pressure and external deficit, and both easier monetary policy and a reduced budget surplus tend to alleviate recession and external surplus. The distinction between the two policy systems appears less important in these phases of the international trade cycle; it nevertheless remains, since inaccurate information about the exact location of the point Q could propel the situation into one of the quadrants involving either recession and deficit or inflation and surplus.[7]

CONCLUSIONS

It has been demonstrated that, in countries where employment and balance of payments policies are restricted to monetary and fiscal instruments, monetary policy should be reserved for attaining the desired level of the balance of payments, and fiscal policy for preserving internal stability under the conditions assumed here. The opposite system would lead to a progressively worsening unemployment and balance of payments situation.

The explanation can be related to what I have elsewhere called the Principle of Effective Market Classification: policies should be paired with the objectives on which they have the most influence.[8] If this principle is not followed, there will develop a tendency either for a cyclical approach to equilibrium or for instability.

The use of fiscal policy for external purposes and monetary policy for internal stability violates the principle of effective market classification,

---

other, an assumption which is made only for expositional convenience. The conclusions follow, for example, even if the authorities simultaneously adjust fiscal and monetary policies.

[6] Even if the authorities do not wish to pair instruments and targets, they can use the information provided by the analysis to determine the relation between *actual* policies and *equilibrium* policies. Thus,

situations of deficit and recession imply that the budget surplus is too high and the interest rate is too low, while situations of surplus and inflation imply the opposite. In this manner, appropriate policies can be determined by observable situations of target disequilibria.

[7] The system can be generalized for a two country world by assuming that the other country adjusts fiscal policy to maintain internal stability. The only difference in the conclusion is that the conditions of dynamic stability of the adjustment process are slightly more restrictive, requiring that the marginal propensities to import be, *on the average*, no greater than one half; this is the usual assumption necessary to rule out any "reverse transfer" that is due to policies affecting expenditure.

[8] "The Monetary Dynamics of International Adjustment under Fixed and Flexible Exchange Rates," *Quarterly Journal of Economics*, Vol. LXXIV (1960), pp. 249–50.

because the ratio of the effect of the rate of interest on internal stability to its effect on the balance of payments is less than the ratio of the effect of fiscal policy on internal stability to its effect on the balance of payments. And for precisely this reason the opposite set of policy responses is consistent with the principle.

On a still more general level, we have the principle that Tinbergen has made famous: that to attain a given number of independent targets there must be at least an equal number of instruments. Tinbergen's Principle is concerned with the *existence* and location of a solution to the system. It does not assert that any given set of policy responses will in fact lead to that solution. To assert this, it is necessary to investigate the stability properties of a dynamic system. In this respect, the Principle of Effective Market Classification is a necessary companion to Tinbergen's Principle.

MONETARY AND FISCAL POLICIES FOR ECONOMIC GROWTH*

Warren L. Smith

INTRODUCTION

In a modern, predominantly free-enterprise nation such as the United States, the central government must accept responsibility for the stability of the economy—that is, for the prevention of excessive unemployment on the one hand and excessive price inflation on the other. There is agreement on this matter not only among political liberals but among most conservatives as well, although, of course, there are still differences of opinion as to the extent of the responsibility, the precise methods to be employed to fulfill it, and, in particular, the selection of the appropriate balance between the goals of price stability and high employment in given circumstances. Still, the area of agreement is far more important than the specific points of disagreement. Indeed, the responsibility of the Federal Government in this regard has been recognized by both major political parties and was formalized in the Employment Act of 1946.[1]

The maintenance of economic stability is pri-

marily a matter of regulating aggregate demand for goods and services. The accepted instruments for controlling demand are primarily the monetary policies of the Federal Reserve System, which exert their influence by altering the supply of money and the cost and availability of credit, and the fiscal policies of the Federal Government, which affect the aggregate flow of purchasing power and spending by altering the relation between Federal tax collections and expenditures.[2]

In the last few years, an additional dimension has been added to the discussion and analysis of economic stabilization: It has come to be recognized that the capacity of the economy to produce goods and services grows month by month and year by year. Full employment and reasonable price stability can be maintained only if aggregate demand grows in pace with productive capacity. We no longer feel, as we used to, that we can indulge in self-congratulation merely because the national income in the current year exceeds that of the previous year, thereby "breaking all records." We now recognize that income and product need to expand each year by as

* From *Perspectives on Economic Growth*, edited by Walter W. Heller. Copyright © 1968 by Walter W. Heller. Reprinted by permission of Random House, Inc.

[1] The intellectual foundation for this view of governmental responsibility was laid in the 1930s by Lord Keynes when he demonstrated that while the free market is an institution of great social utility in organizing production and allocating resources in an efficient manner without detailed central planning, the modern free-enterprise economy does not contain adequate built-in mechanisms for maintaining overall economic stability. See J. M. Keynes, *The General Theory of Employment, Interest, and Money* (New York: Harcourt, Brace and Co., 1936).

[2] Even in the 1920s, of course, the Federal Reserve System, established in 1914 to correct structural defects in the banking system which had led to repeated and sometimes disastrous banking crises in the late nineteenth and early twentieth centuries, came to accept some responsibility for regulating the supply of money and credit in the interest of economic stabilization. Then, in the 1940s and 1950s, a number of economists, following up the work of Lord Keynes, developed the economic theory underlying fiscal policy—that is, the deliberate use of the Federal budget as an instrument of overall economic regulation.

much as the growth of productive capacity if we are to maintain a healthy economy and avoid rising unemployment. On the other hand, if we permit aggregate demand to expand more rapidly than productive capacity, inflationary pressures will result. That is, we must run hard—but not too hard—merely to avoid falling behind.

Thus, recognition that monetary and fiscal policies to maintain full employment and stable prices must be formulated in a framework which makes allowance for the growth of productive capacity is now reasonably well established. Beyond this, it is now accepted by many economists, both in and out of the Federal Government, that by skillful use of monetary and fiscal policies we may be able not only to keep aggregate demand growing in pace with capacity but also to influence the growth of capacity itself.

FULL EMPLOYMENT AND ECONOMIC GROWTH

For purposes of our discussion, the productive capacity of the economy is the output of goods and services that can be produced under conditions of full employment. However, full employment is not an easy concept to define satisfactorily. It can scarcely mean the complete absence of unemployment, since, under almost any conceivable circumstances, there will be a certain amount of so-called "frictional unemployment," resulting from the fact that some workers are always in the process of moving from one job to another.

The best way to arrive at a workable definition of full employment is in terms of the behavior of the price level. Beyond some point, further reduction of unemployment through an expansion of demand will lead to progressively stronger inflationary tendencies for three reasons. First, as production expands, plant capacity bottlenecks are likely to develop in some industries, leading to a rise in the prices of the products of these industries while there is still excess plant capacity available in other parts of the economy. Second, shortages of certain types of labor may be encountered, leading to sharply rising wages which push up prices at a time when the general level of employment is still substantial. Third, as expansion of demand reduces the general level of unemployment and at the same time leads to rising business sales and profits, the strategic position of labor unions in collective bargaining negotiations becomes stronger relative to that of employers, causing wages to rise more rapidly than labor productivity is increasing, thereby raising

labor costs and pushing up prices.[3] Full employment may be defined as the lowest level of unemployment that can be achieved without encountering significant inflationary pressures—or, somewhat more generally, as the level of unemployment beyond which, in the opinion of the responsible public officials (whose decisions presumably reflect the views of the general public), the social benefits of a further reduction in unemployment are not worth the social costs of the inflation associated therewith.

The Kennedy Administration selected a 4 percent unemployment rate as its tentative definition of full employment—its so-called "interim" unemployment target—in 1961. That is, the Administration presumably believed that it would be possible to reduce unemployment to 4 percent of the labor force without encountering a serious problem of inflation.[4] Although one might quarrel with the selection of this particular percentage as a definition of full employment, the specific definition is not important for our present purposes, and I shall accordingly accept it as a working assumption.

On this basis, we may regard the Gross National Product (GNP) that can be produced when unemployment is 4 percent as a measure of the aggregate productive capacity of the economy. The smoooth curve in Figure 1 depicts, at least crudely, the growth of productive capacity in this sense. Capacity GNP, represented by

---

[3] The first two conditions referred to—plant capacity bottlenecks and shortages of certain types of labor—can presumably be corrected by a once-and-for-all adjustment of prices which would adapt patterns of demand and supply to coincide with available resources. Since prices are, in general, more flexible upward than downward, this price adjustment would probably require some rise in the general level of prices. Strictly speaking, such a "one-shot" upward price adjustment does not constitute inflation, since inflation means a *continuing* rise in the price level. In practice, however, the distinction is a difficult one to apply, especially because the "one-shot" adjustment would take some time to work its way through the price structure and while this process was going on would be practically indistinguishable from "genuine" inflation.

[4] During the current expansion, which began in the first quarter of 1961, wholesale prices did not rise appreciably during the first four years while the unemployment rate was falling from 6.8 percent to 4.8 percent. Beginning early in 1965, however, prices began to rise rather sharply; from the first quarter of 1965 to the first quarter of 1966, wholesale prices rose by 4.2 percent as the unemployment rate declined quite rapidly to 3.8 percent. However, during the ensuing year, price pressures moderated considerably while the unemployment rate held steady at just under 4 percent.

FIGURE 1   GROSS NATIONAL PRODUCT: ACTUAL AND POTENTIAL

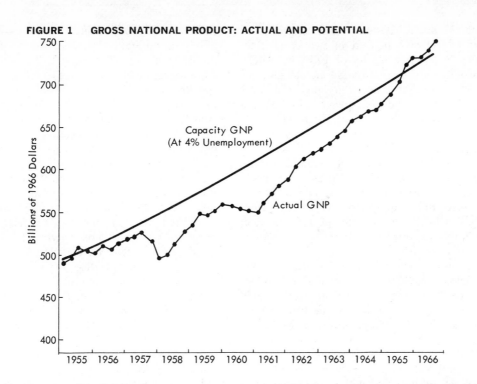

the smooth curve in Figure 1, is valued at 1966 prices, and the assumption is that it was equal to actual GNP in mid-1955 when the unemployment rate was approximately 4 percent. The growth rate of capacity GNP is assumed to be 3.5 percent from mid-1955 to the end of 1962, 3.75 percent from then until the end of 1965, and 4 percent thereafter.[5] The broken line in Figure 1 traces the movement of actual GNP, also valued at 1966 prices.

Capacity GNP cannot be measured or observed directly except when the economy is operating close to the 4 percent target unemployment rate. But there is enough indirect evidence based on levels of GNP achieved when unemployment has been 4 percent in the past, on productivity trends, and so on, to justify the use of the smooth curve in Figure 1 as a crude working approxima-

[5] The calculations used here are similar to those made by the Council of Economic Advisers. See the *Annual Reports of the Council of Economic Advisers,* January 1962 (pp. 49–53), January 1965 (p. 81), and January 1967 (p. 44). There are many problems, both conceptual and statistical, in measuring the economy's productive capacity. The intellectual basis for the Council's estimates was provided by Arthur M. Okun in his paper, "Potential GNP: Its Measurement and Significance," 1962 *Proceedings of the Business and Economic Statistics Section of the American Statistical Association,* reprinted as *Cowles Foundation Paper* No. 190 (Cowles Foundation for Research in Economics, Yale University, 1963).

tion of the recent trend of productive capacity. Moreover, the validity of the estimates for earlier years is borne out to some degree by the fact that when unemployment declined to the neighborhood of 4 percent in late 1965, actual output turned out to be very close to the estimate of productive capacity. The reader is cautioned, however, not to attach much significance to the precise values indicated by the capacity output curve but to regard them as the center of a range of perhaps $5 billion within which the true value lies. Furthermore, the curve cannot safely be projected very far into the future, since the growth of productive capacity may change both because of essentially adventitious factors, such as alterations in the rate of growth of the labor force or in the rate of capital accumulation, and because the choice of economic policies, such as those discussed in this paper, may significantly change the growth of capacity.

What can we say about economic growth and the means of achieving it on the basis of Figure 1? To begin with, it is apparent that, starting from a situation such as existed in early 1961 when unemployment was in the neighborhood of 7 percent of the labor force and the gap between actual GNP and capacity GNP was in excess of $50 billion, significant amount of growth in actual GNP can be achieved merely by reducing unemployment to 4 percent and bringing actual GNP up to the level of capacity GNP. To illustrate, in order to reduce unemployment to the target level of 4 percent in two years' time beginning in the first quarter of 1961, we would have had to raise GNP from its actual level of $550 billion at that time to its potential level of $652 billion in the first quarter of 1963 (as shown on the smooth curve in Figure 1). This would have been an increase of about 18 percent in two years, or roughly 9 percent per year. Actually, unemployment was not reduced to the 4 percent level until the first quarter of 1966, but even with this relatively slow rate of expansion toward full employment, GNP rose from $550 billion in the first quarter of 1961 to $735 billion in the first quarter of 1966, for an average increase of about 6 percent per year.

Thus, substantial growth is possible in the short run through the elimination of unemployment when the economy is operating substantially below capacity, as was the case in 1961. Under such conditions, if unemployment is to be reduced to 4 percent of the labor force and the associated growth achieved, aggregate demand must expand sufficiently to absorb the quantity of goods and services that will be produced when 96 percent of the labor force is employed—or, to put it another way, aggregate demand must become equal to productive capacity as defined above. As long as demand continues to fall short of this level, producers will not find it profitable to turn out sufficient quantities of goods and services to employ 96 percent of the labor force, and unemployment will remain above 4 percent.

Eliminating transactions in materials and components to be used in further production, the total output of the economy (GNP) must necessarily be absorbed by demands which can be classified into four categories: consumer demand; business demand for new plants and equipment and additions to inventories; net export demand of foreign buyers; and government demand, Federal, state, and local. When aggregate demand is growing less rapidly than capacity, the following measures can be taken to speed up the growth of some or all of these components of demand:

1. Taxes may be reduced, as was done in the Revenue Act of 1964, by cutting the tax rates applicable to various categories of income. The effects will depend to some extent on the exact nature of the tax-reduction measures adopted, but, in general, tax reduction will leave consumers and businesses with larger incomes after tax than previously and thereby lead directly to increases in "consumer demand" and "investment demand." These increases in demand will generate additional production of consumer goods

and capital goods, thereby creating additional jobs. The additional wage incomes and business profits resulting from expanded production and employment will lead to still further consumer spending and generate additional production, employment, and income. Thus, through repeated "rounds" of additional production, income generation, and consumption spending—a process which economists call the "multiplier"—GNP will be raised by an amount in excess of the initial reduction in taxes. The available evidence suggests that a reduction of $1 billion in individual income taxes might lead, in the course of time, to an associated rise in consumption and GNP of roughly $2 billion, thereby giving rise to a "multiplier" of about two. Beyond this, if the expansion of consumption spending produced by the cut in taxes is sufficiently rapid to narrow the gap between actual GNP and productive capacity, it will lead to a more intensive utilization of existing plant capacity and create a stimulus for businessmen to increase their spending on new plants and equipment, thus raising the "investment demand" component of GNP. This will, of course, generate additional income and employment and lead to a further increase in consumption. Although the investment effects are more difficult to estimate than the direct consumption effects referred to above, they may under some circumstances be substantial.

2. Federal expenditures on such projects as highways, dams, and school construction may be increased. Such expenditures will directly raise GNP by adding to the "government demand" component. The added construction activity will put people to work, not only directly on the construction sites but also in factories producing materials needed in construction. As workers receive additional income in wages and salaries, and as businessmen earn additional profits from expanded production, they will increase their spending on goods and services, adding to the "consumer demand" component of GNP and stimulating additional production, employment, and income in industries producing consumer goods. Thus, through repeated "rounds" of additional production, income generation, and consumption spending similar to those set off by tax reduction, GNP will be raised by an amount in excess of the initial increase in government spending. An increase of $1 billion in government spending might lead, in the course of time, to an associated rise in consumption of roughly $1 billion, thereby producing a total rise in GNP of around $2 billion, taking account of consumption effects only, giving rise to a "multiplier" of approximately

two.[6] Moreover, as in the case of tax reduction, the rise in government spending and the associated increase in consumption may, by leading to more intensive utilization of existing productive capacity, induce businessmen to increase their expenditures on additional plant, equipment, and inventories, thus generating a still further rise in GNP.

3. The Federal Reserve authorities may adopt a more expansionary monetary policy by, for example, expanded purchases of U.S. Government securities in the open market. Such purchases increase the cash reserves available to the commercial banks and enable the banks to expand their loans and investments and the amount of money held by the public in the form of bank deposits and currency by an amount equal to several times the additional reserves through the familiar process of bank credit expansion. Thus, bank loans will become easier to obtain, and the interest rates charged will probably be reduced. Furthermore, the expansion of credit will indirectly lower interest rates on bonds issued by private corporations to finance plant expansion as well as on bonds issued by state and local government units to finance highways and schools. Mortgage credit for the financing of new homes and installment loans for the purchase of automobiles and other consumer durable goods will become easier to obtain and less costly. As a result of these developments, some expansion can be expected to take place in those components of demand that are frequently credit-financed, including housing demand, business investment demand, and the demand for consumer durable goods. The increased demand will stimulate production, income, and employment directly, and set off the same "multiplier" effects produced by an increase in government expenditures or a reduction in taxes. While it is generally agreed that measures to increase the supply of money and credit will have a stimulative effect on the economy, in the present state of knowledge it is difficult to estimate the magnitude of these effects.

---

[6] Actually, both *a priori* reasoning and empirical evidence derived from statistical models of the U.S. economy suggest that the multiplier applicable to an increase in government expenditures on goods and services is a little larger than that applicable to a reduction in taxes. The reason for this is that, in the first instance, the entire increase in government expenditures constitutes, by definition, an increase in demand for goods and services, whereas some portion of a reduction in taxes is likely to be saved so that the resulting direct increase in consumer or business demand will be somewhat smaller than the tax reduction.

Thus, when the economy is operating substantially below full employment, fiscal and monetary measures which expand aggregate demand may, by pushing the economy up to full employment, be able to produce a rather high rate of growth in the short run. Once capacity operations have been achieved, however, the growth of aggregate demand must be slowed down and brought into line with the growth of capacity if an unacceptable degree of inflation is to be avoided. That is, once full employment has been reached, the limit on economic growth is set not by the rate of expansion of aggregate demand but by the rate of growth of capacity. Of course, if full employment is to be sustained on a continuing basis, demand must grow in line with capacity—that is, along the smooth curve in Figure 1. But, under these conditions, if any further increase in the rate of growth is to be achieved without undue inflation, an acceleration in the growth of capacity itself is required.

The achievement of full employment is likely, however, to have a favorable effect on the growth of productive capacity. The productive capacity of the economy at any particular time depends upon the size of the labor force; the skill, experience, and education of the workers; the nature of the technology available and in use; the quantity and quality of social overhead capital, including communication and transportation facilities and facilities for the maintenance of the health of the population; and the size, quality, and age distribution of the stock of private capital. Thus, the rate of growth of capacity depends upon the rate of growth of the labor force; the rate at which its skill, experience, and education are improving; the rate of technological advance; and the rate of accumulation of social overhead and private capital. The achievement of full employment is itself likely to have a favorable effect on some of these forces determining the rate of growth of capacity. In this connection, two factors are likely to be particularly important.

First, the improvement in rates of utilization of existing productive facilities associated with the achievement of full employment is very likely to provide a stimulus to private investment in new plant and equipment, thereby leading to faster growth of the stock of capital. And, since the installation of equipment is often the vehicle by which new technology is introduced into productive processes, the allocation of more resources to investment should also lead to more rapid introduction of new techniques. Between 1947 and 1955, both years in which unemployment was in the neighborhood of 4 percent of the labor force, real GNP grew at a rate of 4.4 percent per year. This rate is substantially greater than the rate of growth of capacity of about 3.5 percent per annum recorded during the period 1955 to 1962. Probably one of the reasons for the more rapid growth of capacity during the early postwar period is that a substantially greater proportion of the total GNP was allocated to private capital formation in the earlier period. Between 1947 and 1955, business outlays on fixed capital ranged from 10 to 12 percent of GNP, whereas between 1958 and 1963 the ratio was consistently less than 10 percent.[7] No doubt many factors contributed to the decline of the share of national output devoted to capital accumulation, but probably one of the important reasons was that for several years after 1957 markets for goods and services were consistently so weak that most firms were unable to sell at profitable prices the full output that could be produced efficiently with their existing plant capacity. As a consequence, the inducement to invest in further productive facilities was severely weakened. In 1965 and 1966, as markets strengthened, as rates of utilization of existing plant facilities rose, and as the economy moved strongly back toward full employment, investment spending took on renewed vigor, rising to 10.7 percent of GNP in 1965 and 11.2 percent in 1966. At the same time, as noted above, the rate of growth of capacity appears to have moved back up to 4 percent per year.

Second, unemployment and underutilization of productive facilities increase incentives to seek job security and the protection of limited markets through the adoption of restrictive practices which cut down the effective productive capacity of the economy and reduce its rate of growth. Labor unions seek to protect their members by engaging in "featherbedding" and resisting the introduction of improved production techniques which may eliminate jobs. Businessmen are motivated to adopt pricing policies designed to protect

their existing markets and to avoid risky new ventures which might seem attractive in a period of strong and expanding markets.

Undoubtedly, the particular kinds of measures that are used to expand aggregate demand may have some effect on the fraction of national resources devoted to investment during the course of an expansion to full employment. For example, if the expansion is powered by an easy monetary policy which reduces interest rates, expanded investment may play a more important role in the expansion than will be the case if the recovery is caused by a reduction in personal income taxes to stimulate consumption or by an increase in government expenditures. Measures such as the liberalized regulations governing the tax-treatment of depreciation which were put into effect in 1962 and the 7 percent tax credit for investment enacted in the Revenue Act of 1962 may have effects somewhat similar to an easy monetary policy. But when the economy has operated below full employment for a number of years, the most important factor in strengthening the inducement to invest in new plant and equipment is an expansion of aggregate demand which will increase utilization rates of existing facilities. That is, in such circumstances, the generation of additional aggregated demand is much more important than the precise nature of the measures adopted to achieve this objective, even though these specific measures may have a second-order influence on the size of the investment component of the expansion.

POLICIES TO INCREASE PRIVATE INVESTMENT

As indicated above, when the economy is operating below full employment, we may be able to achieve rapid growth in the short run merely by adopting policies to expand aggregate demand, thereby putting existing resources more fully to use. Moreover, the very process of demand expansion which drives the economy to full employment will set up forces conducive to higher rates of investment and more rapid introduction of technological improvements, thus accelerating the growth of productive capacity and creating an atmosphere generally more favorable to long-run growth. Suppose, however, we find that growth is not rapid enough to satisfy our tastes at a time when the economy is already operating at full employment. Under these conditions, mere expansion of aggregate demand will not be able to increase the rate of growth without generating inflation. If we are to accelerate growth in these circumstances, we can only do

---

[7] Actually, the rate of growth of capacity presumably depends (among other things) on the fraction of *capacity* output used for capital formation. In the earlier postwar period unemployment was 4 percent or lower much of the time, so that actual output was more or less equal to productive capacity. From 1958 to 1963, on the other hand, unemployment consistently exceeded 4 percent and output remained well below capacity, as is indicated by the gap between the smooth curve and the broken line in Figure 1. As a result, the ratio of investment to *capacity* output declined even more relative to the earlier period than did the ratio of investment to *actual* output.

so by reallocating resources from uses that do not contribute to growth of capacity to uses that do so contribute.

One way to increase the rate of growth of capacity under full-employment conditions would be to shift resources from the production of goods and services for current consumption to the production of capital equipment. Two steps would be needed to bring about such a shift of resources from consumption to private investment. First, it would be necessary to increase the overall rate of saving in the economy—to reduce current consumption—in order to release resources for the production of more capital goods. Second, measures would have to be taken to increase expenditures by businesses for plant and equipment in order to absorb the resources released by the increased saving. If we succeeded in accomplishing the first step—the increase in saving—but failed to achieve the second—the increase in spending on plant and equipment— the result would be not an increase in the rate of growth of productive capacity but instead the appearance of unemployment and underutilization of existing productive facilities.

There are a number of methods by which the overall saving rate might be increased, all of which would involve revisions in the tax structure. Private saving might be increased by a shift toward a less progressive tax system—that is, a reduction in taxes on high-income individuals who save a large portion of their incomes, combined with an increase in taxes on low-income persons who ordinarily save relatively little. However, there is evidence that the response of saving to *changes* in income at the margin does not vary greatly among income-size brackets, except perhaps as between the very highest and the very lowest income individuals. Thus, it would probably take a very large redistribution of income to change the aggregate amount of saving significantly. Such a massive redistribution from low-income to high-income individuals would violate accepted principles of equity in the distribution of income.

An alternative means of increasing personal saving would be the enactment of a Federal sales or expenditure tax as a partial substitute for the individual income tax. Since the sales or expenditure tax would not be levied on the portion of income that was saved, it might cause an increase in personal saving. Once again, however, such a substitution of a sales or expenditure tax for the income tax would be objectionable to many people, because it would reduce the progressivity of the overall Federal tax structure.

Various other tax devices for stimulating personal or business saving could be devised, but in most cases they would probably be found objectionable on the grounds that they would either be inequitable in their effect on the distribution of income after taxes or would distort private decisions concerning the use of resources. Furthermore, in the present state of economic knowledge, it would be difficult to predict the magnitude of the increase in personal or business saving that would be caused by such measures.

Probably the best means of increasing total saving in the economy would be a general increase in taxes or a reduction of the Federal Government's non-investment expenditures for the purpose of creating a Federal budget surplus. Such a surplus would mean that the Federal Government was contributing to total saving in the economy by withdrawing more dollars from the spending stream through taxation than it was injecting through expenditures.[8] A Federal budget surplus would release resources for private investment in the same way as would an increase in private saving. Whether the surplus should be created by raising taxes or by reducing government non-investment expenditures would depend upon whether it was felt to be socially more desirable to reduce private consumption or public consumption.[9]

If taxes were increased to create a budget surplus, equity could be maintained by distributing the increase in taxation among income brackets in an appropriate way.[10] Since consump-

---

[8] If the Federal Government was running a budget deficit at the time and reduced the size of its deficit either by increasing taxes or by cutting expenditures, the effect would be the same as would be produced if an equal increase in taxes or reduction in expenditures created a surplus or increased the size of an existing surplus. Reduction of an existing deficit would mean that the Federal Government was absorbing less private saving than before, thereby leaving more available for private investment.

[9] A reduction of Federal investment expenditures—on such activities as education, highways, and so on—would, of course, also increase public saving through the Federal budget. Whether an increase in public saving produced in this way would serve to increase the rate of growth would depend upon whether the productivity of the additional private investment made possible by the increased saving was greater or smaller than the productivity of the Federal Government investment projects which were eliminated.

[10] In a growing economy, it may be possible to achieve the budget surpluses needed for a still further acceleration of growth without actually raising tax *rates* (or reducing expenditures). Assuming a 4 percent growth of real GNP and a 2 percent annual

tion has generally been within the range of 93 to 95 percent of personal disposable income in recent years, a tax increase that was reasonably evenly distributed among income brackets could be expected to reduce personal saving by 5 to 7 percent of the tax increase, thus leading to an overall increase in saving, at the then existing level of income, of about 93 to 95 percent of the increase. A cut in Federal non-investment expenditures on goods and services, on the other hand, would increase the Federal budget surplus dollar for dollar without directly depressing private saving, thereby increasing total saving in the economy by the full amount of the cut. Thus, adjustments in the overall level of taxation or in Federal expenditures would have the advantage over tax devices designed to increase private saving of being both more equitable and more predictable in terms of effects on total saving.

As indicated above, measures designed to increase saving—that is, to release resources from the production of goods and services for current consumption—would need to be accompanied by measures to stimulate an equal amount of additional investment spending. Otherwise, the result would be reduced employment rather than accelerated growth.[11]

One measure that might be taken to stimulate private investment would be to use the budget surplus resulting from the increase in taxes or the reduction in Federal expenditures to retire a portion of the outstanding public debt. By retiring debt, the Federal Government would be putting the funds collected through the budget sur-

plus into the capital market, thereby bringing down interest rates and making the funds available for the financing of private investment.

While the use of surplus funds collected through the Federal budget for debt retirement would be desirable in itself and would help to a limited extent to spur private investment, debt retirement alone would not generate sufficient investment to absorb the full amount of resources released by the initial reduction in consumption spending. That is, one dollar of debt retirement will not generate a full dollar of additional private investment. The reason is that a decline in interest rates will cause individuals and business concerns to increase their holdings of money balances. That is, a portion of the additional dollars injected into the capital market by debt retirement will be "hoarded" in the form of additional money holdings rather than being spent for private investment. In fact, it appears that the demand for money holdings is sufficiently responsive to a decline in interest rates to cancel out a substantial portion of the effect of debt retirement. In other words, an increase in taxes or a reduction in Federal expenditures, combined with the use of the resulting budget surplus to retire an equivalent amount of public debt, would, in all probability, have a net deflationary effect on the economy, thereby causing a reduction in income and employment.

One way to supplement the expansionary effects of using the budget surplus to retire debt would be for the Federal Reserve System to shift simultaneously toward an easier monetary policy. For example, the Federal Reserve could, in effect, retire *additional* publicly held debt through open-market purchases of U.S. Government securities, thereby lowering interest rates directly and also adding to the supply of cash reserves of the commercial banks and permitting them to engage in a further expansion of money and credit.

Under some circumstances, a shift toward an easier monetary policy by the Federal Reserve would be the logical means of supplementing the use of the budget surplus to retire debt as a means of stimulating private investment. However, since the available evidence suggests that private investment is only moderately sensitive to declining interest rates and increased availability of credit, the Federal Reserve System should be prepared to use its full powers to bring about the needed increase in private investment. To the extent that the Federal Reserve failed to act with sufficient vigor, the result would be defla-

---

rise in the average prices of the goods and services included in GNP, capacity GNP at current prices would rise by about 6 percent per year. Thus, under full-employment conditions, starting from present levels, GNP would rise by about $45 billion a year, and with our present tax system, taxes would increase by about 25 percent of this amount, or about $11 billion a year. Unless Federal expenditures were to rise by this amount or unless tax rates were periodically reduced, the budget would show a steadily increasing surplus at full employment. Thus, one possible strategy for accelerating growth would be to limit the secular rise of Federal expenditures while taking monetary or fiscal measures to increase private investment to match the budget surpluses automatically generated by the secular growth of tax revenues.

[11] Paradoxically, if appropriate measures were not taken to stimulate investment, the measures designed to increase saving would reduce income, and this would *depress* saving. When all the adjustments had been completed, therefore, total saving might differ very little from its initial level, but income and employment would be lower.

tionary, leading to reduced income and employment rather than the desired increase in investment and productive capacity.

Under the conditions that have existed in the
last few years—and probably will continue for
some time to come—a sharp reduction in interest
rates for the purpose of stimulating private investment might seriously increase the U.S. balance-of-payments deficit and lead to a loss of
gold. This is because a decline in U.S. interest
rates relative to those prevailing in foreign markets would be very likely to cause an outflow
of private capital.

What we have described above is what has
come to be an almost standard post-Keynesian
prescription for increasing the rate of economic
growth: a shift toward a tighter fiscal policy to
generate a budget surplus through increased taxation or reduced government expenditures, combined with a shift toward an easier monetary
policy to spur private investment. However, if
monetary policy is constrained by the balance-of-
payments situation, as has been the case in the
last few years, the second half of the prescription
may prove to be impossible to put into effect.
If this is the case, a policy of stimulating economic growth will require the use of some measures other than easy money to produce the
needed increase in private investment.

If easy money and reduced interest rates
should in fact prove to be either inadequate or
impossible, there are various tax-incentive devices
that might be employed to increase private investment. The most straightforward of these would
be a reduction in corporate income tax rates,
which would stimulate investment in plant and
equipment by leaving corporations with larger
after-tax incomes for the internal financing of
investment, and also by increasing the prospective
after-tax returns on newly installed facilities, and
thereby strengthening incentives to invest. An
alternative device would be a liberalization of
the regulations governing the treatment of depreciation for tax purposes. By allowing faster write-
offs of plants, machinery, and equipment, liberalized depreciation would increase the so-called
"cash flow" of internal funds for financing investment and would also strengthen investment incentives by increasing the prospective rate of
return on new investment. Still a third possibility
would be an increase in the investment tax credit
enacted in the Revenue Act of 1962 and liberalized in the Revenue Act of 1964. Such a tax
credit has somewhat the same effect as would
be produced by a reduction in the initial cost

of eligible productive facilities and hence makes
investment more attractive to business.[12] In addition, to the extent that it reduces taxes, the credit
provides firms with additional internal funds to
finance investment. Of the three devices, the last
one—an increase in the investment credit—has
the advantage of being pinpointed most sharply
toward the stimulation of investment, and it
therefore seems preferable to the others.

By appropriate adjustments in fiscal policy—
and, to the extent that the balance-of-payments
situation permits, in monetary policy—it should
be possible in the course of time to increase the
proportion of national resources employed in private capital formation and thereby to raise to
some extent the rate of economic growth. But
such a policy adjustment is delicate and risky
and should be pursued cautiously. If the fiscal
and monetary measures that are designed to increase investment do not have the desired effects,
the result will be unemployment and underutilization of existing productive capacity—and probably reduced investment—rather than increased
growth of capacity.

The relation of budget deficits and surpluses
to economic growth is generally rather poorly
understood. It is often said that exponents of
the vigorous use of fiscal policy for the maintenance of economic stability believe that continuing budget deficits year after year serve to stimulate growth. This is simply not the position held
by the more sophisticated exponents of an active
fiscal policy. It is true that when the economy
is suffering from unemployment, a reduction in
taxes or an increase in Federal expenditures, leading to a budget deficit, may be desirable as a
means of increasing aggregate demand and raising economic activity to the full employment
level. But, as explained above, if the objective
being sought is long-run economic growth—that

---

[12] The Revenue Act of 1962 allowed the investor
a credit against income tax amounting to 7 percent
of investment in eligible assets (including, in general,
machinery and equipment but not buildings) having
a life of eight years or more (with smaller percentage
credits for investments with lives of between four
and eight years). Originally, the tax credit had to
be deducted from the base on which depreciation
was calculated; as a result, the effect on investment
was exactly the same as that of a reduction in the
price of the asset by the tax-credit percentage. The
Revenue Act of 1964 liberalized the credit by eliminating the provision requiring that the credit be deducted from the depreciation base. Thus, at present
the tax credit has a stronger stimulating effect on
investment than would be produced by an equal
percentage reduction in the price of the asset.

is, growth of productive capacity—budget surpluses, not budget deficits, will, by increasing aggregate national saving, contribute to that end, provided the surpluses are accompanied by monetary or fiscal action which increases private investment sufficiently to employ all the saving, including the surplus, that will be forthcoming at full employment. That is, if effective stimuli to investment can be put into effect, a policy of surplus financing rather than deficit financing is generally recognized by economists as being favorable to long-run economic growth.

OTHER POLICIES FOR GROWTH

In addition to the policy adjustments discussed above to increase private investment, there are other measures involving the use of fiscal policy which might be taken to speed economic growth. Most of these measures would involve either increased spending on government programs which would increase the future productive capacity of the economy or the use of tax incentives to encourage private activities—other than investment in plant and equipment—directed at that end.

Policies to make the labor market work more efficiently should be placed high on the agenda of programs aimed at increasing the effective productive capacity of the economy. Increased appropriations to enable the United States Employment Service to expand its activities in disseminating job information for the benefit of workers seeking employment, the use of Federal subsidies or perhaps credits under the individual income tax to reduce the cost to workers of moving from one locality to another to accept employment, and greatly increased Federal expenditures on programs for the training and retraining of the unemployed would be helpful. Combined with efforts—through such devices as the so-called "wage-price guideposts" of the Council of Economic Advisers—to prevent inflationary excesses in collective bargaining, measures of this kind might permit the unemployment rate to be reduced below 4 percent without creating excessive inflationary pressure. While not necessarily increasing the *percentage rate of growth* of productive capacity, such policies would, if effective, produce a "once-and-for-all" increment to capacity, thereby permitting the growth curve of capacity to be redrawn at a higher level, corresponding perhaps to a 3 percent rather than a 4 percent unemployment rate. Since they would enable the economy to produce larger quantities of goods and services not only currently but in the future,

these measures, should be classified as growth policies. And, since they would reduce the economic distress and disillusionment created by unemployment, they would be valuable measures from the standpoint of social policy as well.

Expenditures on research and development which increase both the size and quality of the available stock of technical knowledge—that is, which expand the scope of the "book of recipes" for combining resources to produce goods and services—are of critical importance for growth. The benefits to society from private expenditures on research and development often cannot be fully captured by those who put up the money to finance the required research activities. This is especially true of basic research of potentially wide applicability, but which may not lead to an immediately marketable product. That is to say, the social benefits of research and development expenditures often exceed the benefits accruing to the private sponsors of such activities. Under these conditions, if the full costs of research and development programs are borne by their private sponsors, the activities of these sponsors will be carried only to the point where private benefits and private costs are brought to equality at the margin, and the resources devoted to research and development will be smaller than would be desirable from the standpoint of society as a whole. This is a classic example of a situation where the free market does not perform its allocative function with optimal efficiency, and some form of government intervention is therefore in order.

The Federal Government's expenditures in support of research and development quadrupled—from $3.1 billion to $12.4 billion—between 1954 and 1964. However, a large portion of its research and development effort is related to the improvement of defense technology and the development of the space program and has limited direct applicability in the private economy.[13] Indeed, Federal support of basic research—the area into which private market incentives are least likely to channel an adequate volume of resources—amounted to only about $1.5 billion in 1964. In view of the probably wide disparity between the social benefits of expenditures on

[13] Knowledge accumulated as a result of defense and space activities does have some private applications. This knowledge is certainly not being disseminated and used to the greatest possible extent at the present time. Expanded efforts by the Federal Government to make available to private users some of the technical knowledge accumulated as a result of defense-and-space-connected research would contribute to economic growth.

research and development and their costs to private sponsors, increased Federal expenditures in support of such activities—especially basic research—would be desirable and would contribute to economic growth.

Another method of increasing expenditures on research and development would be to provide tax incentives to business firms for such expenditures. For example, a tax credit similar to the 7 percent credit for investment in machinery and equipment enacted in the Revenue Act of 1962, could be given for research and development spending.[14] By reducing the effective cost to business of research activities, such a tax credit should be capable of providing a strong stimulus to private research. Any tax credit proposal should disallow credits for such activities as market research and sales promotion, because their contribution to economic growth is likely to be minimal and because, in any case, private market incentives are likely to call them forth in adequate amounts.

Public investment in such fields as health, education, highway construction, the conservation and development of natural resources, and urban planning and development have a vital role to play in spurring economic growth. Accordingly, within limits at least, increased Federal expenditures in these areas—or perhaps grants to state and local government units to permit them to increase such expenditures—should be an important part of any program aimed at increasing the rate of growth. In defining public investment, it is important to avoid emphasizing the accumulation of "bricks and mortar"—public buildings, highways, dams, and so on—and in the process neglect those areas of public investment which do not take this form. Most students of growth believe that outlays for the improvement of human resources are capable of yielding spectacularly high returns. Programs for improving health and for education and training are of special importance. Investment in the improvement of

human resources includes not only outlays for the construction of physical facilities, such as hospitals and schools, but also expenditures required for the current operation of medical and educational institutions, such as the payment of teachers' salaries. The criterion for defining investment should be not the acquisition of physical assets such as buildings and equipment, but rather the existence of a future payoff in terms of increased productivity. Moreover, expenditures for health and education yield benefits in the form of greater happiness and increased personal fulfillment, benefits which are by no means fully reflected in the GNP that is used as a material index of economic growth.

Increased government spending on research and development and on public investment, as well as tax credits which succeed in stimulating private outlays on research and development, will, if introduced at a time when the economy is already at full employment, need to be accompanied by measures designed to depress some other kinds of expenditures if inflation is to be avoided. That is, under conditions of full employment, policies designed to stimulate growth-generating expenditures—whether these expenditures be private or public and whether they be for investment in physical facilities, for research and development to improve technology, or for the improvement of human resources—should be accompanied by measures designed to increase saving (i.e., reduce consumption) in order to release resources to be used for their fulfillment. Thus, the measures designed to increase saving—private or public—discussed earlier in this paper are a necessary accompaniment of policies to stimulate growth-oriented expenditures, whether such expenditures be in the private or in the public sector.

Those who favor an expanded program of public investment aimed at the development of the economy and the improvement of human resources often advocate the adoption of a so-called "capital budget" by the Federal Government. In a full-fledged capital budget, government expenditures would be classified between capital outlays (which should be defined to include all expenditures yielding future benefits) on the one hand, and expenditures yielding only current benefits on the other. According to the capital-budget principle, taxes should cover expenditures yielding current benefits together with debt interest and amortization, while capital outlays should be financed by borrowing. This procedure is supposed to have the advantage of spreading the cost of financing capital expenditures, in the form

---

[14] Taxpayers are permitted to deduct outlays for research as current expenses in computing their income tax liabilities. This favorable tax treatment may not, however, be applied to long-lived equipment used for research; the cost of such equipment must be recovered by depreciation allowances spread over its life. As a means of stimulating research and development in the interest of economic growth, the tax reform program proposed by President Kennedy in 1963 contained a provision that would have permitted the taxpayer to deduct the cost of research equipment as an expense for tax purposes in the year in which the equipment was acquired. However, this provision was rejected by the Congress and was not included in the tax reform program as finally enacted in the Revenue Act of 1964.

of interest and amortization, over the life of the facilities acquired so that the persons who, as a group, benefit from the added productivity of the facilities are required to bear the costs. In addition, a parallel is sometimes drawn between the principles underlying a public capital budget and the tenets often accepted as sound for private finance. The argument runs that just as it is regarded as proper for a business firm or a family to borrow money for the purpose of acquiring long-lasting assets such as an automobile, a house, a store, or a plant, 'so should it be viewed as appropriate for the government to borrow to finance the construction of a dam, a highway, or outlays for the education of its citizens. Conversely, it would be improper for the government to borrow to finance outlays yielding only current benefits just as it would be improper for a family to borrow to buy food or clothing. Unfortunately, even if this somewhat Puritanical theory of private finance is accepted—note that it is an ethical rather than an economic theory—there is no reason why the same principles should be applied to governments, especially the Federal Government. Indeed, there are two extremely serious objections to the theory as applied to the Federal budget.

First, acceptance of the theory of the capital budget as outlined above might at times interfere seriously with the maintenance of full employment. When the forces of private demand are particularly weak, the needs of economic stabilization may require the Federal Government to reduce taxes or increase expenditure to such an extent that tax revenues would be inadequate to cover even that portion of Federal expenditures yielding only current benefits. On the other hand, at times when private demand is exceptionally buoyant and the economy is therefore threatened by inflation, the maintenance of economic stability may require such a large increase in taxes or reduction in expenditures that tax revenues will be more than sufficient to cover all Federal expenditures including capital outlays. Indeed, it will only happen by accident—if ever—that the Federal budget deficit that would occur when tax revenues were just sufficient to cover expenditures yielding current benefits would be the appropriate budgetary situation from the standpoint of economic stabilization. In other words, the capital budget is almost certain to come into serious conflict with the overriding principles of countercyclical fiscal policy.

Second, the principle underlying the capital budget is not even acceptable in terms of its effects on the allocation of resources, at least

to one who, like myself, accepts the idea that the government has an important role to play in influencing the rate of economic growth. If the government wishes to accelerate growth, it may be quite inappropriate to finance public investment by borrowing, since such borrowing may drive up interest rates and reduce private investment which also contributes to growth; rather, from the standpoint of optimal growth policy, it may be desirable to finance government capital outlays by an increase in personal taxes designed to release from private consumption the resources needed for the government's investment program. Indeed, an effective program aimed at the twin objectives of stability and growth requires that the whole complex of monetary and fiscal policies be the subject of flexible adjustments and be kept continuously under review. Dogmatic rules which connect certain kinds of expenditures with certain means of finance are likely to prove unsatisfactory because they prevent appropriate policy adjustments.

Arguments that justify Federal deficits to the extent that they result from borrowing to finance public capital outlays by analogy to so-called "sound" tenets of private finance are generally fallacious. The soundness of the Federal Government's credit rests not on the value of its assets but on the strength of the economy, its taxable capacity, and, ultimately, on the Government's power to create money. If needed to maintain high employment and optimal resource allocation, borrowing and deficit spending to finance *current* government expenditures are perfectly appropriate—indeed, if the alternative is widespread unemployment, failure to accept the necessary borrowing and deficit financing should be roundly condemned as a failure of the Government to live up to its responsibility for the maintenance of a sound economy. Nor should the capital budget be favored, as it certainly has been by some people and at some times, as a device for justifying deficits that are required to keep the economy operating at full employment. It is better to make the case for deficit financing when needed for economic stabilization on the basis of correct fiscal-policy reasoning rather than to use expedient arguments to justify it by means of false analogies to private finance.[15]

---

[15] Although a capital budget procedure of the kind outlined seems unwise, it is perfectly appropriate—indeed desirable—for the Federal budget to present a breakdown of expenditures between those yielding benefits primarily in the future and those yielding benefits primarily in the current year. This breakdown is in fact provided in Special Analysis D of the Fed-

CONCLUDING REMARKS

I have discussed a number of ways in which changes in the level and structure of taxation, changes in the level and composition of Federal expenditures, and changes in monetary policy might be capable of expediting growth of real output in the United States. Apart from the possibility of accelerating growth in the short run by putting to work resources that are currently idle, nearly all of the measures discussed require significant reallocations of resources—the application of measures to reduce the use of resources for current consumption combined with measures to absorb these released resources into uses that increase the total productive power of the economy, such as private investment in plant and equipment, increased activity in the field of research and development, increased public investment in physical facilities such as highways and development of natural resources, and increased investment in human resources. All of these policies for promoting economic growth require us to make choices: We must decide the extent to which we are willing to give up the current enjoyment of the fruits of the economy in the form of consumption for the purpose of accumulating additional capital of one kind or another which will increase the capacity of the economy to produce goods and services in the future. Moreover, it should be understood that the policy adjustments needed to produce a deliberate speed-up of growth are rather sophisticated, uncertain as to effects, and difficult to put into operation. On the basis of the evidence currently available, it is extremely difficult to predict the magnitude of the effects likely to be produced on the growth of the productive capacity of the economy by any particular measure, such as increased private investment, or by any combination of measures. As a consequence, it is vitally important that we have in our arsenal of fiscal policies instruments that can be employed quickly and flexibly to adjust aggregate demand to whatever the growth rate of capacity turns out to be, if we are to be able to maintain full employment on a continuing basis.

It is almost certain that the optimal way to increase economic growth is by the use of some combination of the proposals discussed above: to allocate some additional resources to private investment, some to the expansion of research and development activities, some to increased public investment in physical facilities, and some to the improvement of human resources. The general principle that should underlie selection of the optimal mix of policies for achieving a given growth objective is to carry each of the various growth-generating activities to the point where the marginal social productivities of all of them are equated. Then, having decided the optimal combination of these activities for each given increment to the growth rate, the total amount of resources withdrawn from current consumption for use in promoting growth-oriented activities should be decided on the basis of our willingness as a nation—as reflected in the decisions of our policy makers chosen through democratic political processes—to give up current consumption in exchange for future consumption.

Unfortunately, while it is a relatively simple matter to state, at least crudely, the principles that should underlie the selection of an optimal growth policy, it is, as a practical matter, impossible to make such a rational calculation in the present state of knowledge. Opinions differ substantially concerning the relative. magnitudes of the contributions to economic growth that have been made by private investment, technological change, education, and so on; and it is possible to marshal the evidence in such a way as to support a fairly wide range of estimates with respect to these contributions. Of course, further empirical work on the sources of economic growth may in time enable us to make better judgments concerning the contributions of different kinds of growth-promoting activities. For the present, however, about the best that can be said is that a combination of measures aimed at all of the main sources of economic growth simultaneously is probably better than single-minded concentration on one source such as private investment. But, with respect to the relative emphasis to be placed on different kinds of activities, the judgments of qualified students of growth differ, and no clear choice seems possible. In other words, in the present state of knowledge, the choice of an appropriate combination of policies for promoting economic growth is an art rather than a science.

---

eral budget. (See *The Budget of the United States Government for the Fiscal Year Ending June 30, 1967,* pp. 406–25).

RULES AND ROLES FOR FISCAL AND MONETARY POLICY*

Arthur M. Okun†

When economists write text books or teach introductory students or lecture to laymen, they happily extol the virtues of two lovely hand-maidens of aggregate economic stabilization—fiscal policy and monetary policy. But when they write for learned journals or assemble for professional meetings, they often insist on staging a beauty contest between the two. And each judge feels somehow obliged to decide that one of the two entries is just an ugly beast. My remarks tonight are in the spirit of bigamous devotion rather than invidious comparison. Fiscal policy and monetary policy are both beautiful; we need them both and we should treat them both lovingly.

THE GENERAL ECLECTIC CASE

In particular, both fiscal and monetary policy are capable of providing some extra push upward or downward on GNP. In fact, if aggregate stimulus or restraint were all that mattered, either one of the two tools could generally do the job, and the second—whichever one chose to be second—would be redundant. The basic general eclectic principle that ought to guide us, as a first approximation, is that either fiscal or monetary policy can administer a required sedative or stimulus to economic activity. As every introductory student knows, however, fiscal and monetary tools operate in very different ways. Monetary policy initially makes people more liquid without adding directly to their incomes or wealth; fiscal policy enhances their incomes and wealth without increasing their liquidity.

In a stimulative monetary action, the people who initially acquire money are not simply given the money; they must part with government securities to get it. But once their portfolios become more liquid, they presumably use the cash proceeds to acquire alternative earning assets, and in so doing they bid up the prices of those assets, or equivalently, reduce the yields. Thus prospective borrowers find it easier and less expensive to issue securities and to get loans; and investors

who would otherwise be acquiring securities may be induced instead to purchase real assets such as capital goods. Also, because market values of securities are raised, people become wealthier, if in an indirect way, and may hence increase their purchases of goods and services. Thus many channels run from the easing of financial markets to the quickening of real economic activity.[1]

A stimulative fiscal action is appropriately undertaken when resources are unemployed; in that situation, an action such as expanded government purchases, whether for good things like hospitals or less good things like military weapons, puts resources to work and rewards them with income. The additional cash received by some people is matched by reduced cash holdings of those who bought government securities to finance the outlay. But the securities buyers have no income loss to make them tighten their belts; they voluntarily traded money for near money. In contrast, the income recipients become willing to spend more, and thus trigger a multiplier process on production and income. So, while fiscal and monetary routes differ, the ultimate destination—the effect on national product—is the same, in principle.

Indeed, the conditions under which either fiscal tools or monetary tools, taken separately, have zero effect on GNP are merely textbook curiosities rather than meaningful possibilities in the modern U.S. economic environment. For stimulative monetary policy to be nothing more than a push on a string, either interest rates would have to be just as low as they could possibly go, or investment and consumption would have to show zero response to any further reduction in interest rates. The former possibility is the famous Keynesian liquidity trap, which made lots of sense in describing 1936, but has no relevance to 1971. With prime corporations paying 8 percent on long-term bonds, interest rates are still higher than at any time in my lifetime prior to 1969.[2]

* From James J. Diamond (ed.), Issues in *Fiscal and Monetary Policy: The Eclectic Economist Views the Controversy* (Chicago: De Paul University, 1971), pp. 51–74. Reprinted by permission of the publisher and author. Arthur M. Okun is a Senior Fellow, Brookings Institution.

† The views expressed are my own and are not necessarily those of the officers, trustees, or other staff members of the Brookings Institution.

[1] There is general agreement between Keynesians and monetarists regarding the mechanism for transmitting monetary changes. See Milton Friedman and Anna J. Schwartz, "Money and Business Cycles," in Milton Friedman, *The Optimum Quantity of Money and Other Essays* (Aldine, 1969), pp. 229–34. Reprinted from *Review of Economics and Statistics,* Vol. 45 supplement (February 1963), pp. 59–63.

[2] Even when any reasonable allowance is made for inflation, it is hard to view today's *real* rates as low by historical standards.

There is plenty of room for them to decline, and, in turn, for states and localities, homebuyers and consumer installment credit users, as well as business investors, to be encouraged to spend more by lower costs of credit.

The opposite extreme, impotent fiscal policy, is equally remote. Fiscal policy must exert some stimulative effect on economic activity (even when the monetary policy makers do not accommodate the fiscal action at all) unless the velocity of money is completely inflexible so that no economizing on cash balances occurs. Though the money supply does not rise in a pure fiscal action, spending will tend to rise unless people are totally unable or unwilling to speed up the turnover of cash. And money holders do economize on cash to a varying degree—they do so seasonally and cyclically, and they do so dependably in response to changes in the opportunity cost of holding money. The holder of zero-yielding cash is sacrificing the opportunity to receive the going interest rates of earning assets. The higher interest rates are, the more he sacrifices; and hence, economic theory tells us, the more he will economize on his holdings of cash.

And the facts confirm the theory. The negative relationship between the demand for money and the rate of interest is one of the most firmly established empirical propositions in macroeconomics.[3] So a pure fiscal stimulus produces a speedup in the turnover of money and higher interest rates, and more GNP.

The fact that people do economize on cash balances in response to rises in interest rates demonstrates the efficacy of fiscal policy. Anybody who reports that he can't find a trace of fiscal impact in the aggregate data is unreasonably claiming an absolutely inflexible velocity—a vertical liquidity preference function[4]—or else he is revealing the limitations of his research techniques rather than those of fiscal policy.

A few other artful dodges, I submit, make even less sense. Try to defend fiscal impotence on grounds of a horizontal marginal efficiency schedule—that means investment is so sensitive to return that even the slightest interest variation will unleash unlimited changes in investment demand. Or make the case that people subjectively assume the public debt as personal debt and feel commensurately worse off whenever the budget is in deficit. Or contend that businessmen are so frightened by fiscal stimulation that their increased demand for cash and reduced investment spoils its influence.[5] Or use the argument that Say's law operates even when the unemployment rate is 6 percent.[6] It's a battle between ingenuity and credulity!

The eclectic principle is terribly important, not because it answers any questions, but because it rules out nonsense questions and points to sensible ones. It warns us not to get bogged down in such metaphysical issues as whether it is really the Fed that creates inflation during wartime. Every wartime period has been marked by enormous fiscal stimulus, and yet that fiscal fuel-injection could have been neutralized by some huge amount of pressure on the monetary brakes. In that sense, the Fed could have been sufficiently restrictive to offset the stimulus of military expenditures. Anyone who chooses to blame the resulting inflation on not slamming on the monetary brakes, rather than on pumping the fiscal accelerator, can feel free to exercise that curious preference. Take another example: Did the expansion following the tax cut in 1964–65 result from monetary policy? Of course it did, the eclectic principle tells us. If the Fed had wished to nullify the expansionary influence of the tax cut, surely some monetary policy would have been sufficiently restrictive to do so. There is no unique way of allocating credit or blame in a world where both tools can do the stabilization job.

SIDE EFFECTS AS THE CENTRAL ISSUE

So long as both tools are capable of speeding up or slowing down demand, the decisions on how to use them and how to combine them must be made on the basis of criteria other than their simple ability to stimulate or restrain. Nor do we typically get any help by considering *how much* work monetary or fiscal tools do, because usually the right answer is, "as much as needed,"

---

[3] See Arthur M. Okun, *The Political Economy of Prosperity* (Brookings Institution, 1970), p. 58, and the bibliography on pp. 146–47 for a list of articles reporting empirical results confirming this relationship.

[4] For discussion of a model implying the existence of a vertical liquidity preference function, see Leonall C. Andersen and Jerry L. Jordan, "Monetary and Fiscal Actions: A Test of Their Relative Importance in Economic Stabilization," Federal Reserve Bank of St. Louis, *Monthly Review* (November 1968).

[5] See Roger W. Spencer and William P. Yohe, "The 'Crowding Out' of Private Expenditures by Fiscal Policy Actions," in Federal Reserve Bank of St. Louis, *Monthly Review*, Vol. 52, No. 10 (October 1970), pp. 17–24.

[6] See "Interest Rates and the Demand for Money," Chapter 7 in Milton Friedman, *The Optimum Quantity of Money*. Reprinted from *The Journal of Law and Economics*, Vol. 9 (October 1966), pp. 71–85. So far as I can see, Friedman is invoking Say's Law.

providing the shift in policy is large enough. In more formal terms, two instruments and one target produce an indeterminate system.

Of course, there are two basic targets of stabilization policy: price stability and maximum production. But the two tools will not serve to implement those two goals simultaneously. A pen and a pencil are one more tool than is needed to write a letter, but the second tool can't be used to mow the lawn. In the same way, fiscal and monetary policy can both push up aggregate demand or push down aggregate demand, but neither can solve the Phillips curve problem. Subject to minor qualifications,[7] the fiscal route to a given unemployment rate is neither less nor more inflationary than the monetary route to that same unemployment rate.

We can have the GNP path we want equally well with a tight fiscal policy and an easier monetary policy, or the reverse, within fairly broad limits. The real basis for choice lies in the many subsidiary economic targets, beside real GNP and inflation, that are differentially affected by fiscal and monetary policies. Sometimes these are labeled "side effects." I submit that they are the main issue in determining the fiscal-monetary mix, and they belong in the center ring.

Composition of Output. One of the subsidiary targets involves the composition of output among sectors. General monetary policy tools, as they are actually employed, bear down very unevenly on the various sectors of the economy. Homebuilding and state and local capital projects are principal victims of monetary restraint. Although the evidence isn't entirely conclusive, it suggests that monetary restraint discriminates particularly against small business. In the field of taxation, we agonize about incidence and equity. The same intense concern is appropriate in the case of monetary restraint and, in fact, increasing concern is being registered in the political arena. In the 1969–70 period of tight money, many efforts (such as Home Loan Bank and Fannie Mae operations) were made to insulate housing from the brunt of the attack. But the impact on homebuilding was still heavy. Moreover, there is considerable basis for suspicion that these actions defused—as well as diffused—the impact of monetary restraint. A more restrictive monetary policy,

as measured in terms of either monetary aggregates or interest rates, is required to accomplish the same dampening effect on GNP if the sectors most vulnerable to credit restraint are shielded from its blows.

The concern about uneven impact may be accentuated because, in 1966 and again in 1969–70, monetary restraint hit sectors that rated particularly high social priorities. But that is not the whole story. Any unusual departure of monetary policy from a "middle-of-the-road" position may lead to allocations that do not accord with the nation's sense of equity and efficiency. For example, in the early sixties, it was feared that a very easy monetary policy might encourage speculative excesses in building because some financial institutions would be pressured to find mortgage loans in order to earn a return on their assets.

In the last few years, some economists—most notably, Franco Modigliani—have argued that monetary policy may have a significant impact on consumption through its influence on the market value of equity securities and bonds[8] in addition to its more direct impact through the cost and availability of installment credit. In my view, the jury is still out on this issue. On the one hand, it's easy to believe that a huge change, say, $100 billion, in the net worth of the American public, such as stock market fluctuations can generate, could alter consumer spending in relation to income by a significant amount like $3 billion, even though that change in wealth is concentrated in a small group at the very top of the income and wealth distribution. On the

---

[7] An unbalanced composition of demand among regions and industries means more inflationary pressure at a given overall utilization rate. Thus, particularly concentrated excess demands (e.g. for defense goods or for new homes) may harm the cause of price stability. But the degree of balance cannot be uniquely linked to fiscal-monetary choices.

[8] See Franco Modigliani, "Monetary Policy and Consumption—The Linkages Via Interest Rate and Wealth Effects in the Federal Reserve-MIT-Penn Model" (paper prepared for the Federal Reserve Bank of Boston Conference at Nantucket, Massachusetts, June 1971; offset), esp. part I.3. For earlier discussions of the effects of monetary policy as it operates in the Federal Reserve-MIT-Penn Model, see the following: Robert H. Rasche and Harold L. Shapiro, "The FRB-MIT Econometric Model: Its Special Features," in American Economic Association, *Papers and Proceedings of the Eightieth Annual Meeting, 1967* (*American Economic Review*, Vol. 58, May 1968), pp. 123–49; Albert Ando and Franco Modigliani, "Econometric Analysis of Stabilization Policies," in American Economic Association, *Papers and Proceedings of the Eighty-first Annual Meeting, 1968* (*American Economic Review*, Vol. 59, May 1969), pp. 296–314; Frank de Leeuw and Edward Gramlich, "The Federal Reserve-MIT Econometric Model," *Federal Reserve Bulletin*, Vol. 54 (January 1968), pp. 11–40; de Leeuw and Gramlich, "The Channels of Monetary Policy," *Federal Reserve Bulletin*, Vol. 55 (June 1969), pp. 472–91.

other hand, previous empirical work on this issue came up with a nearly unanimous negative verdict.[9] In 1966 and 1969, however, the timing of stock market declines and the sluggishness in consumer demand seemed to fit fairly well with the hypothesis. One would like to believe the wealth hypothesis because it would suggest that monetary policy has broad and sizable effects on consumption, especially on that of high-income consumers; monetary restraint would then be revealed as less uneven and less inequitable. But before embracing that judgment, one should wait for more decisive evidence.

Interest Rates and Asset Values. Another major consideration in monetary policy is its effects on interest rates and balance sheets. Some economists may argue that the only function of interest rates is to clear the market and the only sense in which rates can be too high or too low is in failing to establish that equilibrium. Every Congressman knows better! Interest rates are a social target. That is the revealed preference of the American public, reflected in the letters it writes to Washington and the answers it gives to opinion polls. And this is no optical illusion on the part of the citizenry. They have the same good reasons to dislike rising interest rates that apply to rising prices—the haphazard, redistributive effects. And they are concerned about *nominal* interest rates just as they are concerned about prices. It is not clear that such major groups as businessmen or workers are particularly hurt or particularly helped by tight money (or by inflation), but the impacts are quite haphazard in both cases. The resulting lottery in real incomes strikes most Americans as unjust.

The largest redistributive effect of tight money, like that of inflation, falls on balance sheets rather than income statements. People care about their paper wealth and feel worse off when bond and equity prices nose dive. Even though society is not deprived of real resources when security prices drop, it is hard to find gainers to match the losers. Although Alvin Hansen stressed the social costs of distorted, fluctuating balance sheets in the 1950s,[10] this issue gets little

attention from economists. But it never escapes the broader and keener vision of the American public.

Financial Dislocation. A restrictive monetary policy may also have important, dislocating effects on the financial system. The key function of a financial system is to offer people opportunities to invest without saving and to save without investing. If people want risky assets, they can acquire them beyond the extent of their net worth; if they wish to avoid risk, they can earn a moderate return and stay liquid. The trade of funds between lovers of liquidity and lovers of real assets produces gains to all. "Crunch" and "liquidity crisis" are names for a breakdown in the functioning of the financial system. Such a breakdown deprives people of important options and may permanently impair their willingness to take risks and to hold certain types of assets. To the extent that very tight money curbs an inflationary boom by putting boulders in the financial stream, a considerable price is paid. And to the extent that extremely easy money stimulates a weak economy by opening the flood gates of speculation, that too may be costly.

Balance of Payments. The pursuit of a monetary policy focused single-mindedly on stabilization goals would have further "side effects" on the balance of payments, to the extent that it changes international interest rate differentials and hence influences capital flows. There are strong arguments for fundamental reforms of the international monetary system—especially more flexible exchange rates—that would greatly reduce this concern. But those reforms are not on the immediate horizon; nor is the United States prepared to be consistently passive about international payments.[11] Meanwhile, the external deficit casts a shadow that cannot be ignored in the formulation of fiscal-monetary policies.

Growth. A final consideration in the mix of stabilization tools is the long-run influence of monetary policy on the rate of growth of our supply capabilities. An average posture of relatively easy money (and low interest rates) combined with tight fiscal policy (designed especially to put a damper on private consumption) is most likely to produce high investment and rapid growth of potential. That becomes relevant in

---

[9] See John J. Arena, "The Wealth Effect and Consumption: A Statistical Inquiry," *Yale Economic Essays*, Vol. 3 (Fall 1963), esp. pp. 273–84 and "Postwar Stock Market Changes and Consumer Spending," *Review of Economics and Statistics*, Vol. 47 (November 1965), pp. 379–91; Saul H. Hymans, "Consumption: New Data and Old Puzzles," *Brookings Papers on Economic Activity* (1:1970), pp. 121–26.

[10] See, for example, *The American Economy* (McGraw-Hill, 1957), pp. 53–55.

[11] On the question of a passive stance, see Lawrence B. Krause, "A Passive Balance-of-Payments Strategy for the United States," *Brookings Papers on Economic Activity* (3:1970), pp. 339–60; and Gottfried Haberler and Thomas D. Willett, *A Strategy for U.S. Balance of Payments Policy* (American Enterprise Institute, February 1971).

the short-run because the long-run posture of monetary policy is an average of its short-run swings. If, for example, the nation relies most heavily on monetary policy for restraint and on fiscal policy for stimulus, it will unintentionally slip to a lower growth path. The contribution of extra investment to growth and the value of the extra growth to a society that is already affluent in the aggregate are further vital issues. Recently, enthusiasm for growth-oriented policies has been dampened by the concern about the social fallout of rapid growth and by the shame of poverty, which calls for higher current consumption at the low end of the income scale. Nonetheless, the growth implications of decisions about the fiscal-monetary mix should be recognized.

In the light of these considerations, there are good reasons to avoid extreme tightness or extreme ease in monetary policy—even if it produces an ideal path of real output. Tight money can be bad medicine for a boom even if it cures the disease, just as amputation of the hand is a bad remedy for eczema. The experience of 1966 provides an object lesson. Judged by its performance in getting GNP on track, the Federal Reserve in 1966 put on *the* virtuoso performance in the history of stabilization policy. It was the greatest tight-rope walking and balancing act ever performed by either fiscal or monetary policy. Single-handedly the Fed curbed a boom generated by a vastly stimulative fiscal policy that was paralyzed by politics and distorted by war. And, in stopping the boom, it avoided a recession. To be sure, real GNP dipped for a single quarter, but the unemployment rate did not rise significantly above 4 percent; the 1967 pause was as different from the five postwar recessions, including 1970, as a cold is different from pneumonia. Moreover, inflation slowed markedly in the closing months of 1966 and the first half of 1967. What more could anyone want? Yet, you won't find the 1966 Fed team in the hall of fame for stabilization policy. In the view of most Americans, the collapse of homebuilding, the disruption of financial markets, and the escalation of interest rates were evils that outweighed the benefits of the nonrecessionary halting of inflation. The Fed itself reacted by refusing to give an encore in 1967–68, accepting renewed inflation as a lesser evil than renewed tight money.

All of this leads up to my first rule for stabilization policy: *Keep monetary conditions close to the middle of the road.* Let me explain that, no matter how monetary policy affects GNP, the rule must be interpreted in terms of interest rates and credit conditions, and not in terms of monetary aggregates. Suppose, for a moment, that the monetary impact on GNP is so powerful and the growth rate of the money supply is so critical that a growth rate of money only a little bit below normal will offset the aggregate demand impact of a huge fiscal stimulus (just for example, a $25 billion Vietnam expenditure add-on). The results would still be very tight money in terms of credit conditions, interest rates, and the impact on the composition of output. The shift in financial conditions required to "crowd out" $25 billion of private expenditures can hardly be trivial—even if the needed shift in monetary growth were trivial.

The "middle of the road" is deliberately a vague concept, relying on the existence of some general long-run notion of appropriate and normal interest rates and liquidity ratios. To be sure, it is hard to tell when we are in the middle of the road, but it is easy to tell when we are far away from it.

THE IMPLICATIONS FOR FISCAL POLICY

My second rule follows immediately from the first: *Operate fiscal policy to avoid forcing monetary policy off the middle of the road.* If fiscal policy is inappropriately stimulative or restrictive, a conscientious and (at least somewhat) independent monetary authority will be obliged to shoulder most of the burden for stabilizing the economy. In historical perspective, it is important to recognize that this sense of responsibility has not always prevailed. In World War II and again in the initial stages of the Korean War, the Federal Reserve reacted to an inflationary fiscal policy simply by pegging interest rates and creating all the liquidity demanded in an inflationary boom. Through these actions, the Federal Reserve not only passed the buck right back to fiscal policy but became an active accomplice in the inflation, intensifying excess demand by holding nominal interest rates constant as prices accelerated. It was technically feasible for the Federal Reserve to behave similarly during the Vietnam war. The fact that it picked up the ball after the fiscal fumble of 1966 demonstrated a new and greater sense of responsibility by the central bank for overall stabilization. So long as both fiscal and monetary policy makers feel that responsibility, as they appropriately should, an inappropriate fiscal policy is bound to push monetary policy off the middle of the road. Obviously, fiscal buck passing can also occur in a situation when stimulus is in order. In 1971, a rather neutral fiscal program accompanied by ambitious targets for recovery threatens to overburden the Federal Reserve with the responsibility for stimulus.

FISCAL TOOLS AND COMPOSITION

To avoid pushing monetary policy off the middle of the road, fiscal policy must itself depart from the middle of the road—turning markedly more stimulative or more restrictive than its normal long-run posture—when private demand is especially weak or especially strong. But such swings in fiscal policy must also be made in light of compositional constraints that apply to federal expenditures, and especially to federal purchases of goods and services. Our preferences about the composition of output imply some notion of appropriate levels of civilian public programs. No one would wish to double or halve the size of the Census Bureau or the Forest Service in order to accord with the cyclical position of the economy. Moreover, these limitations based on principle are reinforced by limitations of a practical character. First, federal civilian expenditures on goods and services involve a mere 2½ percent of GNP and thus afford very little leverage for stabilization. Second, most federal programs involving purchases of goods and services have long start-up and shut-off periods that make it extremely difficult to vary timing greatly without impairing efficiency.

Popular discussions of fiscal stabilization tend to stress expenditure variation despite these clear constraints. Why are the lessons ignored? Could any informed person have seriously regarded a curb on civilian public programs during the Vietnam build-up period as a meaningful antidote to the stimulus of increasing military expenditures? Could anybody familiar with the history of the lags in public spending support a public works program as a way to create jobs and strengthen recovery in 1971 or 1972?[12] The evidence suggests that people with strong views on the desirable size of the public sector tend to invoke the cause of stabilization as a rationalization for their social preferences. To an advocate of additional government spending, a recession provides a useful additional talking point; to a crusader for cutbacks in government

spending, excess demand inflation offers an excellent excuse.

Federal "transfer" programs, such as social security, unemployment compensation, and veterans' benefits, are not subject to serious implementation lags, but their room for maneuver is limited by the principle of intertemporal equity. The aged, the poor, or the unemployed cannot justifiably be treated better in a recession than in prosperity or in a boom. The unfortunate people who are jobless when the unemployment rate is low deserve no less generous benefits than those who are unemployed when the rate is high; indeed, if misery loves company, those unemployed in prosperity may suffer psychically because they have less of it.

Some significant elbow room nevertheless appears for varying such transfer programs. Society's agenda always contains some new initiative or additional step to strengthen transfer programs in a growing economy with growing overall income; and the next step can be timed to come a little sooner or a little later, depending on the economy's cyclical position. In the present context, the administration's family assistance program provides a good example. The proposed initial date for benefits is July 1, 1972, but the program could be made effective six months earlier. Similarly, there is some opportunity for varying the timing of benefit liberalization and of payroll tax increases with respect to the social security program. Congress displayed wisdom early in 1971 by deferring for a year the proposed increase in the maximum earnings base of the payroll tax.

While this pure timing flexibility is important, it may not provide enough leeway for a flexible fiscal policy to respond to the needs of a very slack or very taut economy. Beyond it, the most attractive fiscal tool is variation in personal income tax rates. In principle, significant and indeed frequent changes in these rates are acceptable. Because they affect the huge consumption sector most directly and because their impact is spread over Americans throughout the middle- and upper-income groups, personal taxes are an ideal instrument for flexibility. While the income tax is specifically aimed to redistribute income in a more egalitarian way, the basic function of taxation is simply to restrain demand, given the socially desired level of public expenditures. A prima facie case exists for suspending or repealing any tax (or tax rate) that is not essential for the purpose of restraining demand sufficiently to avoid both inflation and monetary restraint. Moreover, according to compelling historical evi-

---

[12] For a brief documentation of the disappointing results of the 1962 public works program, see Nancy H. Teeters, "The 1972 Budget: Where It Stands and Where It Might Go," *Brookings Papers on Economic Activity* (1:1971), pp. 232–33.

dence, changes in personal tax rates—upward or downward, permanent or temporary—have reasonably reliable effects on consumer spending and hence on GNP.[13]

Political implementation is the one troublesome problem with changes in personal tax rates. Obviously, unlike shifts in monetary policy, any change in tax rates requires legislative action. And the record of congressional response to presidential requests for such changes has left much to be desired. Many constructive proposals have been made to improve that story. In 1961, the Commission on Money and Credit asked Congress to delegate authority for tax changes to the President subject to congressional veto; others have urged Congress to enact rules that would commit it to fast action—favorable or unfavorable—in response to a presidential request. Presidents Kennedy and Johnson made proposals for speeding the legislative process in their Economic Reports of 1962 and 1969, respectively. Herbert Stein presented a constructive proposal along similar lines in 1968. Even the Joint Economic Committee of the Congress expressed its concern in its 1966 report, "Tax Changes for Shortrun Stabilization."[14] But the Congress has generally ignored these proposals, jealously guarding its prerogatives over taxation, and refusing to bind its own hands with respect to procedures.

Under the present rules of the game, the President must ask Congress to do what seems best for the country and must count on presenting the case persuasively. The discussion and debates of recent years have put Congress on its mettle to respond promptly and pragmatically to any presidential request for tax changes designed for short-run stabilization purposes. Moreover, the 1963 and 1967 stalemates reflected special factors that seem obsolete—budget orthodoxy in the earlier case and Vietnam strategy in the later one. Our traditional procedures deserve another try.

These thoughts on the uses of alternative fiscal tools can be summarized as my third rule: *When additional fiscal stimulus or restraint is needed, opportunities for varying the timing of new initiatives in federal spending or tax programs should be the first line of attack: if these are inadequate to achieve the desired swing in fiscal policy, a change in personal tax rates should be sought.* We must keep urging and prodding the Congress to respond more promptly when tax changes are proposed. And we must not give up, for it will heed this message eventually.

FULL EMPLOYMENT SURPLUS

The problems of executive-legislative coordination apply to expenditures as well as taxes. The fractionated process by which appropriations are made on Capitol Hill leads to frightful difficulties in the overall control of federal spending. As I have suggested elsewhere, one path to improvement might involve the following procedures: The President would make explicit the fiscal decision underlying his budget; and the Congress would then focus on that decision, approving or modifying it; and it would then commit itself to undertake an iterative review of appropriations and tax legislation during the course of the year to assure that the budget stayed within the bounds.[15]

I believe that the concept of the full employment surplus can be extremely useful as the focus of the fiscal plan and review. It is a simple enough summary number of the budget's impact on the economy to be understood by the participants, and it is a good enough summary to serve the purpose. It permits the stimulus or restraint in the budget to be compared with that of the previous year and other relevant previous periods.[16] While administration officials cannot hope to provide a scientific demonstration that the budget has the proper amount of stimulus or restraint, they can generate an informed discussion and enlightened decision process by explaining their forecast of the strength of private demand, the proper role for monetary policy, and the likely

---

[13] See my papers, "Measuring the Impact of the 1964 Tax Reduction," in Walter W. Heller (ed.), *Perspectives on Economic Growth* (Random House, 1968); and "The Personal Tax Surcharge and Consumer Demand, 1968–70," *Brookings Papers on Economic Activity* (1:1971), pp. 167–204.

[14] Report of the Commission on Money and Credit, *Money and Credit—Their Influence on Jobs, Prices, and Growth* (Prentice-Hall, 1961), pp. 133–37; *Economic Report of the President together with the Annual Report of the Council of Economic Advisers, January 1962*, pp. 17–19, and *Economic Report*, January 1969, pp. 12–13; Herbert Stein, "Unemployment, Inflation, and Economic Stability," in Kermit Gordon (ed.), *Agenda for the Nation*, (Brookings Institution, 1968), pp. 292–93; *Tax Changes for Shortrun Stabilization*, A Report of the Subcommittee on Fiscal Policy of the Joint Economic Committee, 89 Cong. 2 sess. (1966), p. 16.

[15] See Okun, *The Political Economy of Prosperity*, pp. 121–22.

[16] Arthur M. Okun and Nancy H. Teeters, "The Full Employment Surplus Revisited," *Brookings Papers on Economic Activity* (1:1970), pp. 77–81.

response of the economy to proposed fiscal changes.

The main function of the full employment surplus in policy discussion is to correct the misleading impression generated by the actual budget surplus or deficit when the economy is off course. In a weak economy, revenues automatically fall far below their full employment level and the budget is hence pushed into deficit. That automatic or passive deficit may be misread as evidence that the budget is strongly stimulating the economy and hence that further expansionary action is inappropriate. By the same token, a boom resulting from a surge in private demand or an easing of monetary policy would automatically swell federal revenues, thereby tending to produce a surplus in the budget. These automatic shifts in federal revenues are important and significant; such built-in stabilizers help to cushion cumulative declines and dampen cumulative upsurges, but they should be properly recognized as shock absorbers rather than either accelerators or brakes.

I believe the focus on the full employment budget by the administration this year has helped to raise the level of fiscal debate. It reveals that the big deficits of fiscal years 1971 and 1972 are symptoms of a weak economy, rather than of a strong budget.

Guide vs. Rule. The full employment budget shows where the fiscal dials are set; but it cannot say where the dials *ought* to be set. It is an aid to safe driving much like a speedometer, but it cannot prescribe the optimum speed. That depends on road conditions. A maintained target for the full employment surplus represents a decision to drive by the dashboard and to stop watching the road. Road conditions do change significantly from time to time in our dynamic economy. The evidence of the postwar era suggests that zero is too low a full employment surplus for a period of prosperity and too high a full employment surplus for a period of slack and slump. From long-term saving-investment patterns, one might guess that a full employment surplus of one-half of one percent of GNP would be about right on the average to accompany a middle-of-the-road monetary policy. But even that judgment would be highly speculative; and it would not tell us how to identify the rare case of an average year or how to quantify the departure of any particular year from the average. Economists have no right to be presumptuous about their ability to forecast in either the short-run or the long-run; and it is far more presump-

tuous to claim that the proper size of the full employment surplus can be determined for the long-run than to believe that it can be nudged in the correct direction in any particular year on the basis of the evidence then at hand.

Adoption of a fixed full employment surplus implies a firm determination by fiscal policy makers to counteract any major surprises that arise *within* the federal budget. If Congress rejects the President's proposals for major expenditure programs such as revenue sharing or family assistance, the advocate of a fixed full employment surplus is committed to propose alternatives for those stimulative actions. Similarly, if uncontrollable expenditures spurt, some compensatory action is required to keep the overall full employment budget close to its original position.

At the same time, however, the advocate of the fixed full employment surplus is determined *not* to act in response to surprises in private demand or monetary policy, no matter how large or how definite these may be. The resulting decision rule is illogical and indefensible. Once it is recognized that some surprises within the federal budget are large enough to call for offsetting fiscal action, it must be conceded that some surprises in consumer spending, plant and equipment outlays, or Federal Reserve decisions might also point to shifts in the fiscal course.

In fact, the Nixon administration has not adopted a fixed full employment surplus, but rather a rule that the full employment budget shall be *at least* in balance on the unified basis of budget accounting. The doctrine of balancing the full employment budget has obvious antecedents in the less sophisticated orthodoxy of balancing the actual budget. The new rule is far less harmful than its predecessor, but it is equally arbitrary. Its arbitrariness is perhaps illustrated by the fact that zero on the unified basis for the 1972 fiscal year turns out to be $7 billion on the national income accounts basis, which is the way Herbert Stein[17] first unveiled the concept and the way every economics student has learned full employment budgeting for a generation.

Statics vs. Dynamics. The rule really reflects the administration's concern about overdoing fiscal stimulus, and that concern has a valid basis. There is genuine danger that stimulative fiscal

---

[17] Committee for Economic Development, *Taxes and the Budget: A Program for Prosperity in a Free Economy* (CED, November 1947), pp. 22–25; and Herbert Stein, *The Fiscal Revolution in America* (University of Chicago Press, 1969), esp. pp. 220–232.

action appropriate to today's slack and sluggish economy could commit the nation to stimulative budgets in future years when they would be markedly inappropriate. We might then be obliged to offset that stimulus by relying on monetary restraint or by seeking tax increases or cutbacks in expenditure programs once the economy approached full employment. Reliance on monetary restraint as an antidote to excessive budgetary stimulus violates rules one and two above. And to count on subsequent neutralizing measures of fiscal restraint is to ignore the serious doubts about the political feasibility of such legislative action. Congress is particularly unlikely to raise tax rates for the purpose of bailing out an overly enthusiastic antislump program that added mightily to federal spending. It would see such action as an open invitation to continued upward ratcheting of federal expenditures through time—with major expenditure initiatives in slumps and offsetting tax increases in booms. Whatever one's views on the appropriate size of the public sector, a cyclical ratchet is not a proper tool for decision making in the democratic process.

All of this argues for making stimulative fiscal policy with one eye on preserving our fiscal fitness for the next period of full employment. And that does require a rule, or at least some form of discipline that guards against excessive long-term commitments of revenue or expenditure. Hence, my fourth rule: *Stimulative fiscal programs should be temporary and self-terminating so that they don't jeopardize our future budgetary position.* The rule reminds us that the key issue is not whether full employment balance is maintained when the economy needs fiscal stimulus, but whether the budget remains in a flexible position from which it can be moved back readily into full employment surplus when restraint once again becomes appropriate.[18] It cautions against permanent changes in the levels of taxation or expenditure programs for stabilization purposes; it puts a time-dimension on the third rule, which identifies the types of fiscal variation consistent with compositional objectives. Both rules argue against public works as a tool for stabilization. They also cast doubt on the recent liberalization of depreciation allowances as a stabilization device; that measure sacrificed $4 billion of revenue annually on a permanent basis in order to get $2 billion into the economy in 1971.

THE DEPENDENCE ON FORECASTING

The rule for relying on quick-starting and self-terminating fiscal measures is designed to ensure flexibility and thus to limit the time horizon over which the forecasting of aggregate demand is essential to policy decisions. But that time period remains substantial and the success of policy remains dependent on the accuracy of economic forecasting. Tax cuts, for example, add cumulatively to aggregate demand for a considerable period after enactment. Thus, while they deliver some prompt stimulus to aggregate demand, they also involve a package of future add-ons to demand. The only way to lift the economy this quarter is through a tie-in sale that lifts the economy further for several subsequent quarters.

If any fiscal or monetary tool exerted its full impact instantaneously, stabilization policy making would be a different ball game. Indeed, this difference has been highlighted by the Laffer model, which finds that the effects of a shift in the money supply on aggregate demand are concentrated in the very quarter of the policy action.[19] While GNP is determined by the money supply in the Laffer model, the implication for policy strategy is diametrically opposite to that of previous monetarist views. Because of its instantaneous total effects, the Laffer model issues an unequivocal mandate in favor of monetary fine tuning. Monetary policy makers are encouraged to take all the action appropriate to hit their economic targets today; and they should then wait for tomorrow and correct any errors by twisting the dials again. Unlike more traditional views about the timing impact of economic policies, the Laffer model finds no tie-in sale or longer-term commitment that would caution against large and abrupt changes in policy.

Because Keynesians and most monetarists agree that the time stream of economic impact following a policy action begins virtually at once but continues into the more distant future, they seat the forecaster at the right hand of the policy maker. When policy decisions necessarily affect the future, they must be made in light of uncertain forecasts of the future and not solely on the basis of the facts of the present. To act otherwise is to adopt implicitly the naive forecast that the future is going to be merely a continuation of the present. The historical record of economic forecasting in the past two decades demon-

---

[18] See Frank Schiff's development of this point in "Control of Inflation and Recession" (speech delivered before the Seventy-fifth Annual Meeting of The American Academy of Political and Social Science, Philadelphia, April 1971; processed), pp. 12–16.

[19] Arthur B. Laffer and R. David Ranson, "A Formal Model of the Economy" (paper prepared for the Office of Management and Budget, 1971; offset), pp. 25–27.

strates that professional forecasting, despite its limitations, is more accurate than such naive models.[20] Moreover, even the naive model that tomorrow will be like today is far more accurate than the super-naive or agnostic model that tomorrow's aggregate demand is just as likely to be below the social target as above it regardless of where today's aggregate demand stands. That agnostic model is the extreme point in the decision analysis set forth by Milton Friedman and William Brainard.[21] If forecasts could not beat the agnostic model, it would be important to do nothing. The stabilization policy maker should simply stay home, for action by him would be just as likely to push the economy in the wrong direction as in the right direction and it could push the economy off the proper course when it would otherwise be there.

In fact, the professional forecaster can beat the agnostic model by a wide margin. I can think of only two years in the past twenty—1955 and 1965—when the January consensus prediction of economic forecasters would have led policy makers to administer stimulants when they were inappropriate and no cases when the consensus forecast would have pointed toward sedatives when stimulants were really appropriate.

A PROPENSITY TO OVERREACT?

Nonetheless, the fact that forecasters can guide policy makers to the right choice as between sedatives and stimulants is not necessarily decisive. Even if some sedative medicine would help a patient, he may be better off with nothing than with a massive overdose of sedation. And it is sometimes claimed that policy makers tend

to prescribe overdoses.[22] According to this claim, because their medicines operate only with a lag and because neither the time shape of that lag nor the total impact of the policy is readily determined in advance, the policy makers become impatient; hence they continue to take more and more action until they have done too much of a good thing, which may be worse than nothing.

This intuitive argument has a certain appeal as a description of a human foible. We have probably all behaved in much this way in taking a shower. When the water is too cold, we turn up the hot faucet; and, if we are still cold ten seconds later, we may turn up the faucet some more, assuming that the first twist was inadequate. As a result of our first impatience, we may find ourselves scalded. And even after one or two experiences of this sort, we repeat that behavior and indeed find it difficult to discipline ourselves completely. If, indeed, fiscal-monetary policy makers have the same proclivities as the man in the shower, rules or discipline may help them to resist their impulses to overreact. But whether the Federal Reserve Open Market Committee or the Troika overtwist the faucets in their respective showers is an empirical issue, a proposition about their behavior that ought to be supportable or refutable by evidence. And I have yet to see evidence to support the proposition.

In the case of fiscal policy, I believe the record shows that policy makers generally have not behaved like the man in the shower. Below is a list of the major changes in fiscal policy during the past fifteen years, as defined by shifts in the full employment surplus,[23] and a capsule evaluation based on hindsight.

1. During 1958, the full employment surplus was reduced from more than 1 percent of GNP to near zero.
   Stimulative direction proper; inadequate size, and timing delayed.

2. In 1959–60, fiscal policy was sharply reversed toward restraint with the full employment surplus reaching 2½ percent of GNP in 1960. *Inappropriate restraint.*

[20] See Victor Zarnowitz, *An Appraisal of Short-term Economic Forecasts* (National Bureau of Economic Research, 1967), esp. pp. 6, 14–19, and 83–120; Geoffrey H. Moore, "Forecasting Short-Term Economic Change," *Journal of the American Statistical Association*, Vol. 64 (March 1969), esp. pp. 3–4 and 15; and Victor Zarnowitz, "Forecasting Economic Conditions: The Record and the Prospect" (paper prepared for the National Bureau of Economic Research's Colloquium on Business Cycles, September 24, 1970; offset).

[21] "The Effects of a Full-Employment Policy on Economic Stability: A Formal Analysis," in Milton Friedman, *Essays in Positive Economics* (University of Chicago Press, 1953), pp. 117–132; and William Brainard, "Uncertainty and the Effectiveness of Policy," in American Economic Association, *Papers and Proceedings of the Seventy-ninth Annual Meeting, 1966* (*American Economic Review*, Vol. 57, May 1967), pp. 411–25.

[22] See "The Role of Monetary Policy," Chapter 5 (esp. p. 109), in Milton Friedman, *The Optimum Quantity of Money*. Reprinted from *American Economic Review*, Vol. 58 (March 1968), pp. 1–17.

[23] Okun and Teeters, "The Full-Employment Surplus Revisited," pp. 102–103; Teeters, "Budgetary Outlook at Mid-Year 1970," *Brookings Papers on Economic Activity* (2:1970), p. 304; and Teeters, "The 1972 Budget: Where It Stands and Where It Might Go," p. 228.

3. During 1961–62, that surplus was gradually trimmed.
   Stimulative direction proper; inadequate size and timing delayed.

4. After backsliding during 1963, fiscal policy became considerably more stimulative with the enactment of the tax cut at the beginning of 1964.
   Appropriate stimulus.

5. From the second half of 1965 to the end of 1968, the full employment budget was in deficit, reflecting the build-up of Vietnam expenditures.
   Inappropriate stimulus.

6. In 1969, as the result of the tax surcharge and expenditure cutbacks, a full employment surplus of 1 percent of GNP was restored.
   Appropriate restraint; much delayed timing.

7. In 1970 and the first half of 1971, fiscal policy was relaxed a bit with the full employment surplus roughly cut in half.
   Relaxation proper; inadequate size.

Items 1, 3, 6, and 7 all depart from the ideal in the direction of too little and too late rather than too much and too soon. In each of these cases moves that were larger or earlier or both would have produced better stabilization results. Item 5—the inappropriate fiscal stimulus of the Vietnam period—was not the overreaction of the man in the shower. The hot water was turned up, but not because anyone believed that the economy needed warming.

Item 2—the shift to restraint in 1959—can be viewed, in a sense, as a premature and excessive cooling of economic expansion. But that policy simply was not keyed to the general economic diagnosis or forecast, which saw the temperature as remaining extremely mild, but rather to a non-economic budgetary orthodoxy. The full employment surplus was jacked up enough to balance the actual budget, as an end in itself rather than as a means to curb any present or prospective boom.

By any standard, the preponderant balance of mistakes in fiscal policy is revealed as errors of omission rather than commission—errors of doing too little too late, rather than too much too soon. Our fiscal man in the shower, in fact, tends to wait too long to ascertain that the water is really staying cold before he decides to turn it up. When he finally does turn the faucet, he acts timidly and hesitantly. When the water is hot, he also hesitates too long and moves indecisively. To shift metaphors, he is not trigger

happy, but, rather, slow on the draw. And so I come to my fifth rule: *Face the fact that policies must be made on the basis of a forecast, and don't be slow on the draw!*

My rules for fiscal discretionary judgment will work well only if stabilization policy is guided by the professional expertise of economists. Obviously, that has not always been the case; and when politics vetoed economics, serious fiscal destabilization resulted. Indeed, in the past generation, the economy has been more severely disrupted by government actions obviously inconsistent with the objective of economic stabilization than by autonomous shifts in private demand. The 1950–51 Korean inflation, the 1953–54 post-Korean recession, the 1960–61 recession, and the Vietnam inflation were all government-induced fluctuations, in which the budget departed from any and all professional prescriptions for stabilization. In three of the four cases, swings in military expenditures created the problem; in the remaining case, it was caused by attachment to a taboo of budgetary balance. In light of these instances, one might well find that a fixed, moderate full employment surplus in peace and war, even years and odd years, would have yielded better overall results than those obtained from the actual fiscal process. But this is no argument for fixed parameters! The proposal to control political officials with a nondiscretionary rule reminds me of the suggestion to catch birds by pouring salt on their tails. Neither the political officials nor the birds will cooperate. If every economist in the nation had sworn (falsely) to Lyndon Johnson and Wilbur Mills that any deviation of the full employment surplus from 0.5 percent of GNP was a mortal sin, that wouldn't have changed fiscal policy in 1965–68. Why not tell our statesmen the truth and try to convince them to heed professional advice on fiscal policy? As unpalatable as that message might be, it has more chance of convincing elected public officials than the rule of maintaining a fixed and rigid full employment surplus for all time. And so I offer my sixth rule: *Presidents should listen to the advice of their economists on fiscal policy and so should the Congress.*

SIGNALS FOR THE MONETARY AUTHORITIES

Under the circumstances I envision, the tasks of the Federal Reserve would depend upon how well the fiscal rules operate. If the budget no longer generates disruptive shifts in aggregate demand and if it offsets, to some degree, any major autonomous shift in private demand, then the monetary policy makers may be able to hold money and credit conditions close to the middle of the road without much difficulty. Under those best of all possible circumstances, economists might begin to wonder what all the shouting was about in the debate on the relative importance of aggregate quantities and interest rates as guides to monetary policy. In 1962–65, a monetary policy that was oriented toward interest rate targets did not produce large or abrupt shifts in the growth of the money stock, simply because the demand for money did not undergo enormous fluctuation. Presumably, if monetary policy had been pursued with respect to quantity rather than rate targets, those quantity guides would have left interest rates reasonably stable. If the demand for goods and the demand for money stay on course, then it makes little difference whether the directives to the trading desk are couched in terms of maintaining a given set of interest rates in the money markets or a given growth of the money supply.

It is not safe, however, to count on the world becoming that tranquil. Surprises will occur, and the policy makers will be forced to decide on the emphasis they wish to give to interest rates and aggregate quantities relative to one another. And it is a matter of degree—of relative emphasis. Anyone interested in diagnosing or influencing financial markets would obviously pay attention to both prices and quantities, just as he would in looking at any other market. Nobody has ever improved on Paul Samuelson's summary that Federal Reserve governors were given two eyes so that they could watch both yields and quantities.[24] In a more serious vein, James Duesenberry has recently sketched how the monetary authorities might appropriately be guided by both quantities and interest rates.[25] At a theoretical level, William Poole has shown the conditions for preferring rate-oriented, quantity-oriented, or mixed monetary strategies.[26]

[24] "Money, Interest Rates and Economic Activity: Their Interrelationship in a Market Economy," in American Bankers Association, *Proceedings of a Symposium on Money, Interest Rates and Economic Activity* (ABA, 1967), p. 44.

[25] "Tactics and Targets of Monetary Policy," in Federal Reserve Bank of Boston, *Controlling Monetary Aggregates*, Proceedings of the Monetary Conference, Nantucket Island, June 8–10, 1969 (FRB of Boston, 1969).

[26] "Optimal Choice of Monetary Instruments in a Simple Stochastic Macro Model," *Quarterly Journal of Economics*, Vol. 84 (May 1970), pp. 197–216.

Quite apart from the issue of appropriate guides, the chief problem facing the monetary authority is likely to be when and how much to depart from a "normal" or average posture in order to provide additional stimulus or restraint to economic activity. Monetary policy can and should find some elbow room without major deviations from the middle of the road. For one thing, monetary policy is light on its feet; the short implementation lag in Federal Reserve decisions provides an enviable contrast with the long lags in the legislative process for altering fiscal policy. In nudging economic activity to offset modest surprises, the speed of implementation makes monetary policy particularly useful.

Second, there is a case for a belt and suspenders strategy of making fiscal and monetary changes in the same direction when stimulus or restraint is desired. The quantitative effect of specific fiscal and monetary changes on GNP is uncertain. Errors in the estimates of these effects are likely to be negatively related or at worst unrelated—if the economy's response to monetary changes is larger than expected, the response to fiscal swings seems likely to be less than our estimates. How extensive the monetary swings should be and at what point the benefits in aggregate stabilization are outweighed by the costs of the side effects discussed above, are issues that require careful judgment and the best use of discretion.

Any recommendation for discretionary monetary policy runs into the contention that the Federal Reserve also shares a propensity to overreact; I find it more difficult to interpret that contention than the one regarding fiscal policy; but, as I read the evidence, it is also untrue. Whether judged in terms of interest rates or of aggregate quantities, I cannot see that the Federal Reserve has behaved like the man in the shower. It was not overly expansionary during most recessions and early recoveries. If the monetary policies of 1957–58, 1960–62, or 1970 could be replayed with the aid of perfect hindsight, monetary policy would surely be more expansionary than it was in fact. The only example of such a period that might stand on the opposite side is late 1954, when in retrospect the Fed seems to have been excessively generous.

Nor in periods of strong economic advance has the Fed generally applied the brakes too strongly or too soon. It may have done so in the case of 1959, but it clearly stayed off the brakes too long in 1965 and probably in 1955. Most clearly, the Federal Reserve has revealed the propensity to underreact to economic chill in late expansions and early stages of recession: with perfect hindsight, it is clear restriction was maintained too long in 1953 and again in 1957. In my judgment, the error in the 1969 performance should also be interpreted as unduly prolonged restraint—staying on the brakes too long and too hard late in the year—although others might argue, that the restraint was applied too vigorously early in the year. There have been other mistakes in monetary policy, like the misdiagnosis of 1968, but they have little to do with either overreaction or underreaction, so far as I can see. Nor does the basic decision of 1967, which gave side effects priority over aggregate stabilization targets, reveal a propensity to overreact.

Thus I come to my final rule: *The makers of monetary policy should be guided by both aggregate quantities and interest rates and by the present and prospective state of aggregate demand; they will serve the nation best by using fully their capability to make small and prompt adjustments in light of the best current evidence and analysis.*

THE LESSONS OF 1969–71

My rules aren't nearly so elegant nor so definitive nor as capable of making a high school boy a qualified CEA or Federal Reserve Chairman as the rules for maintaining fixed growth of the money supply and fixed full employment surpluses. The only thing in favor of the rules I am offering is that they happen to be better rules. We can do far better by using our intelligence in diagnosing, forecasting, and prescribing than by adopting rigid formulas that ignore the state of economic activity, the outlook for private demand, and the "side effects" of policies.

My kind of rules calls for an activist economic policy. Events since early 1969 strengthen my conviction that the optimum amount of activism is a lot of it. This debate easily degenerates into a semantic game. The opposition scoffs at "fine tuning"; I call it "sensible steering." Some people warn against going overboard; I worry about napping at the wheel. Trying diligently to avoid loaded words, I state as fact that, for better or for worse, the Nixon administration has been much more reluctant than its predecessors to alter fiscal-monetary policies on the basis of discretionary judgment. Apart from the issue of wage-price or "incomes" policy, this has been the biggest difference in economic policy since early 1969. (And the incomes policy difference may also be related to the preference for less activism.)

Along with a messy economic situation, the Nixon administration inherited a reasonably appropriate fiscal policy and an appropriate target of achieving disinflation without recession. The fiscal policy was not altered much within the course of 1969 and it was not controversial. While opinion differed about the extension of the tax surcharge, the repeal of the investment credit, and the desirability of the revenue-losing "tax reforms" of 1969, the controversies reflected primarily preferences for more or less public expenditure rather than for more or less fiscal restraint. Nor did the fiscal 1971 budget program presented in January 1970 seem surprising or unreasonable. What was highly questionable, as I saw it then and see it now, was the emphasis on achieving an *actual* surplus in fiscal 1971 with no explicit contingency for the obvious risk of an economic slump that would make the surplus inappropriate. Although the father of the full employment surplus concept was a member of the Council of Economic Advisers, and one of the most ardent and effective exponents of the concept was the CEA Chairman, the lesson of the full employment surplus was essentially ignored in the initial Nixon budget. Instead, it unveiled a new, very short-lived budget concept known as the "credible surplus."

By May 1970, actual economic developments were clearly far more recessionary than had been predicted by the administration (and by me!) at the beginning of the year. Nonetheless, when the administration re-estimated the budget on May 19, it stuck to a tight fiscal program which called for a $10 billion full employment surplus (on the national accounts basis) in the face of a recession. And it advanced two new proposals to increase tax revenues—a speedup of estate and gift taxes and a tax on leaded gasoline. The economic situation had changed enormously between January and May 1970, but the fiscal posture was not changed. After fifteen months during which fiscal policy had been basically bipartisan, it became strongly controversial at that point.

On July 18, 1970, the President adopted the principle of full employment budgeting, but he did not alter the posture of the fiscal 1971 program. Indeed in August, he vetoed appropriations for education and for housing, endorsing those programs on social grounds but insisting that additional expenditures on them would be excessively stimulative.

After the economy sank far below the target path, the administration set an ambitious goal for rapid economic recovery in 1971, but the fiscal program continued to propose a full employment surplus on a national income accounts basis of about $7 billion, virtually unchanged from the level of 1970. The cautious fiscal program has failed to achieve the bold targets for output and employment growth, but the fiscal program has been reaffirmed. It is hard to understand the midyear decision to stand pat. Does the jack-in-the-box view of private demand linger on? Has the rule of full employment balance on the unified budget paralyzed fiscal policy? Does the rapid monetary growth of the first half of 1971 convince some administration economists that rapid expansion is just around the corner? Perhaps all of these contribute, but I would emphasize still another factor—the propensity to underreact.

Monetary policy in 1969–71 has also differed from the prescriptions that were being offered by outside observers of the Keynesian "new economics" school. Unlike the monetarists, most of us applauded extreme monetary restraint through the spring and summer of 1969 as necessary medicine to halt the investment boom and curb excess demand. In the fall, however, the Keynesians joined the monetarists in calling for less restraint. We heard the economy yelling "Uncle," but the Federal Reserve did not. Thus, extreme monetary restraint was maintained until 1970 began; again the error was in underreacting.

During the first half of 1970, attachment to consistency and a desire for a steady pace of monetary growth inhibited the Federal Reserve from making a full contribution to the end of recession and the start of the recovery. Since the fall of 1970, the Federal Reserve has had a difficult problem of interpreting divergent signals coming from money growth, on the one hand, and interest rates, on the other. From September 1970 to January 1971, credit conditions eased dramatically and interest rates fell sharply, but demands for active cash balances were weak and the money supply grew very slowly despite a high rate of growth of overall bank reserves. For reasons that are not clear, the demand for active balances rose sharply between January and June 1971—more than enough to provide a catch-up for the period of sluggish growth. Meanwhile, interest rates turned up spectacularly. Balance-of-payments problems added further compli-

cations. The Federal Reserve has seemed to compromise on these goals: it wishes to strengthen an evidently sluggish recovery, but it wants to avoid a massive outflow of short-term funds and big numbers on money growth. The Federal Reserve official directives focus on money supply targets, while the actions have been much more eclectic and pragmatic. The seeming inconsistency of word and deed had confused the Fed watchers in the financial markets and thereby added to the instability of interest rates and to the demand for liquidity. I strongly suspect that a policy of holding the Treasury bill rate close to some moderate level—like 4 percent—through the first half of 1971 would have produced much lower long-term interest rates *and* slower monetary growth.

At times during the early months of 1971, spokesmen for the administration and the Federal Reserve made no secret of their preference for a more stimulative stabilization policy than was in fact being pursued. The administration's fiscal policy makers emphasized the possibility for additional monetary stimulus while Federal Reserve spokesmen pointed toward additional fiscal stimulus. Anyone familiar with the problems of the bureaucratic division of labor in Washington can understand, sympathize with, and agonize about the tendency to "let George do it." It is only natural that the Federal Reserve would prefer to "let George [Schultz] do it" while the administration would wish the Board to do it. The picture has been disturbing, nonetheless, in raising doubts about the effectiveness of monetary-fiscal coordination between the independent Federal Reserve and the administration. Proper coordination ought to guarantee that the fiscal-monetary mix has approximately the overall degree of stimulus or restraint that seems appropriate to both fiscal and monetary policy makers. Disagreements on the appropriate amount of stimulus may be inevitable, but when both sides agree that more stimulus is necessary, that should be forthcoming. It is much less important how much George does and how much the Board does, than that somebody act with determination to promote the solid recovery the administration wants and the nation needs. The eclectic principle reminds us that both can and should contribute.